Literature Criticism from 1400 to 1800

Guide to Gale Literary Criticism Series

For criticism on	Consult these Gale series
Authors now living or who died after December 31, 1999	*CONTEMPORARY LITERARY CRITICISM (CLC)*
Authors who died between 1900 and 1999	*TWENTIETH-CENTURY LITERARY CRITICISM (TCLC)*
Authors who died between 1800 and 1899	*NINETEENTH-CENTURY LITERATURE CRITICISM (NCLC)*
Authors who died between 1400 and 1799	*LITERATURE CRITICISM FROM 1400 TO 1800 (LC)* *SHAKESPEAREAN CRITICISM (SC)*
Authors who died before 1400	*CLASSICAL AND MEDIEVAL LITERATURE CRITICISM (CMLC)*
Authors of books for children and young adults	*CHILDREN'S LITERATURE REVIEW (CLR)*
Dramatists	*DRAMA CRITICISM (DC)*
Poets	*POETRY CRITICISM (PC)*
Short story writers	*SHORT STORY CRITICISM (SSC)*
Literary topics and movements	*HARLEM RENAISSANCE: A GALE CRITICAL COMPANION (HR)* *THE BEAT GENERATION: A GALE CRITICAL COMPANION (BG)*
Asian American writers of the last two hundred years	*ASIAN AMERICAN LITERATURE (AAL)*
Black writers of the past two hundred years	*BLACK LITERATURE CRITICISM (BLC)* *BLACK LITERATURE CRITICISM SUPPLEMENT (BLCS)*
Hispanic writers of the late nineteenth and twentieth centuries	*HISPANIC LITERATURE CRITICISM (HLC)* *HISPANIC LITERATURE CRITICISM SUPPLEMENT (HLCS)*
Native North American writers and orators of the eighteenth, nineteenth, and twentieth centuries	*NATIVE NORTH AMERICAN LITERATURE (NNAL)*
Major authors from the Renaissance to the present	*WORLD LITERATURE CRITICISM, 1500 TO THE PRESENT (WLC)* *WORLD LITERATURE CRITICISM SUPPLEMENT (WLCS)*

ISSN 0740-2880

Volume 107

Literature Criticism from 1400 to 1800

Critical Discussion of the Works of Fifteenth-, Sixteenth-, Seventeenth-, and Eighteenth-Century Novelists, Poets, Playwrights, Philosophers, and Other Creative Writers

Thomas J. Schoenberg
Project Editor

THOMSON
*
GALE

Detroit • New York • San Francisco • San Diego • New Haven, Conn. • Waterville, Maine • London • Munich

THOMSON

GALE

Literature Criticism from 1400 to 1800, Vol. 107

Project Editor
Thomas J. Schoenberg

Editorial
Jessica Bomarito, Kathy D. Darrow, Jeffrey W. Hunter, Jelena O. Krstović, Michelle Lee, Ellen McGeagh, Linda Pavlovski, Joseph Palmisano, Lawrence J. Trudeau, Russel Whitaker

Data Capture
Francis Monroe, Gwen Tucker

Indexing Services
Synapse, the Knowledge Link Corporation

Rights and Acquisitions
Margie Abendroth, Peg Ashlevitz, Lori Hines

Imaging and Multimedia
Dean Dauphinais, Leitha Etheridge-Sims, Lezlie Light, Mike Logusz, Dan Newell, Christine O'Bryan, Kelly A. Quin, Denay Wilding, Robyn Young

Composition and Electronic Capture
Kathy Sauer

Manufacturing
Rhonda Williams

Product Manager
Janet Witalec

LIBRARY OF CONGRESS CATALOG CARD NUMBER 94-29718

ISBN 0-7876-8724-3
ISSN 0740-2880

Printed in the United States of America
10 9 8 7 6 5 4 3 2 1

Contents

Preface vii

Acknowledgments xi

Literary Criticism Series Advisory Board xiii

Preface

*L*iterature *Criticism from 1400 to 1800* (*LC*) presents critical discussion of world literature from the fifteenth through the eighteenth centuries. The literature of this period is especially vital: the years 1400 to 1800 saw the rise of modern European drama, the birth of the novel and personal essay forms, the emergence of newspapers and periodicals, and major achievements in poetry and philosophy. *LC* provides valuable insight into the art, life, thought, and cultural transformations that took place during these centuries.

Scope of the Series

LC provides an introduction to the great poets, dramatists, novelists, essayists, and philosophers of the fifteenth through eighteenth centuries, and to the most significant interpretations of these authors' works. Because criticism of this literature spans nearly six hundred years, an overwhelming amount of scholarship confronts the student. *LC* organizes this material concisely and logically. Every attempt is made to reprint the most noteworthy, relevant, and educationally valuable essays available.

A separate Thomson Gale reference series, *Shakespearean Criticism,* is devoted exclusively to Shakespearean studies. Although properly belonging to the period covered in *LC,* William Shakespeare has inspired such a tremendous and ever-growing body of secondary material that a separate series was deemed essential.

Each entry in *LC* presents a representative selection of critical response to an author, a literary topic, or to a single important work of literature. Early commentary is offered to indicate initial responses, later selections document changes in literary reputations, and retrospective analyses provide the reader with modern views. The size of each author entry is a relative reflection of the scope of the criticism available in English. Every attempt has been made to identify and include the seminal essays on each author's work and to include recent commentary providing modern perspectives.

Volumes 1 through 12 of the series feature author entries arranged alphabetically by author. Volumes 13-47 of the series feature a thematic arrangement. Each volume includes an entry devoted to the general study of a specific literary or philosophical movement, writings surrounding important political and historical events, the philosophy and art associated with eras of cultural transformation, or the literature of specific social or ethnic groups. Each of these volumes also includes several author entries devoted to major representatives of the featured period, genre, or national literature. With volume 48, the series returns to a standard author approach, with some entries devoted to a single important work of world literature and others devoted to literary topics.

Organization of the Book

An *LC* entry consists of the following elements:

- The **Author Heading** cites the name under which the author most commonly wrote, followed by birth and death dates. Also located here are any name variations under which an author wrote, including transliterated forms for authors whose native languages use nonroman alphabets. If the author wrote consistently under a pseudonym, the pseudonym will be listed in the author heading and the author's actual name given in parenthesis on the first line of the biographical and critical information. Uncertain birth or death dates are indicated by question marks. Topic entries are preceded by a **Thematic Heading,** which simply states the subject of the entry. Single-work entries are preceded by the title of the work and its date of publication.

- The **Introduction** contains background information that introduces the reader to the author, work, or topic that is the subject of the entry.

- A **Portrait of the Author** is included, when available.

- The list of **Principal Works** is ordered chronologically by date of first publication and lists the most important works by the author. The genre and publication date of each work is given. In the case of foreign authors whose works have been translated into English, the title and date (if available) of the first English-language edition is given in brackets following the original title. Unless otherwise indicated, dramas are dated by first performance, not first publication. Lists of **Representative Works** by different authors appear with topic entries.

- Reprinted **Criticism** is arranged chronologically in each entry to provide a useful perspective on changes in critical evaluation over time. The critic's name and the date of composition or publication of the critical work are given at the beginning of each piece of criticism. Unsigned criticism is preceded by the title of the source in which it appeared. All titles by the author featured in the text are printed in boldface type. Footnotes are reprinted at the end of each essay or excerpt. In the case of excerpted criticism, only those footnotes that pertain to the excerpted texts are included. Criticism in topic entries is arranged chronologically under a variety of subheadings to facilitate the study of different aspects of the topic.

- Critical essays are prefaced by brief **Annotations** explicating each piece.

- A complete **Bibliographical Citation** of the original essay or book precedes each piece of criticism. Source citations in the Literary Criticism Series follow University of Chicago Press style, as outlined in *The Chicago Manual of Style,* 14th ed. (Chicago: The University of Chicago Press, 1993).

- An annotated bibliography of **Further Reading** appears at the end of each entry and suggests resources for additional study. In some cases, significant essays for which the editors could not obtain reprint rights are included here. Boxed material following the further reading list provides references to other biographical and critical sources on the author in series published by Thomson Gale.

Indexes

A **Cumulative Author Index** lists all of the authors that appear in a wide variety of reference sources published by Thomson Gale, including *LC*. A complete list of these sources is found facing the first page of the Author Index. The index also includes birth and death dates and cross references between pseudonyms and actual names.

A **Cumulative Nationality Index** lists all authors featured in *LC* by nationality, followed by the number of the *LC* volume in which their entry appears.

A **Cumulative Topic Index** lists the literary themes and topics treated in the series as well as in *Nineteenth-Century Literature Criticism, Twentieth-Century Literary Criticism,* and the *Contemporary Literature Criticism* Yearbook, which was discontinued in 1998.

An alphabetical **Title Index** accompanies each volume of *LC*. Listings of titles by authors covered in the given volume are followed by the author's name and the corresponding page numbers on which the titles are discussed. English translations of foreign titles and variations of titles are cross-referenced to the title under which a work was originally published. Titles of novels, dramas, nonfiction books, and poetry, short story, or essay collections are printed in italics, while individual poems, short stories, and essays are printed in roman type within quotation marks.

In response to numerous suggestions from librarians, Thomson Gale also produces an annual paperbound edition of the LC cumulative title index. This annual cumulation, which alphabetically lists all titles reviewed in the series, is available to all customers. Additional copies of this index are available upon request. Librarians and patrons will welcome this separate index; it saves shelf space, is easy to use, and is recyclable upon receipt of the next edition.

Citing *Literature Criticism from 1400 to 1800*

When citing criticism reprinted in the Literary Criticism Series, students should provide complete bibliographic information so that the cited essay can be located in the original print or electronic source. Students who quote directly from reprinted criticism may use any accepted bibliographic format, such as University of Chicago Press style or Modern Language Association (MLA) style. Both the MLA and the University of Chicago formats are acceptable and recognized as being the current standards for citations. It is important, however, to choose one format for all citations; do not mix the two formats within a list of citations.

The examples below follow recommendations for preparing a bibliography set forth in *The Chicago Manual of Style,* 14th ed. (Chicago: The University of Chicago Press, 1993); the first example pertains to material drawn from periodicals, the second to material reprinted from books:

Morrison, Jago. "Narration and Unease in Ian McEwan's Later Fiction." *Critique* 42, no. 3 (spring 2001): 253-68. Reprinted in *Literary Criticism from 1400-1800.* Vol. 76, edited by Michael L. LaBlanc, 212-20. Detroit: Gale, 2003.

Brossard, Nicole. "Poetic Politics." In *The Politics of Poetic Form: Poetry and Public Policy,* edited by Charles Bernstein, 73-82. New York: Roof Books, 1990. Reprinted in *Literary Criticism from 1400-1800.* Vol. 82, edited by Michael L. La-Blanc, 3-8. Detroit: Gale, 2003.

The examples below follow recommendations for preparing a works cited list set forth in the *MLA Handbook for Writers of Research Papers,* 5th ed. (New York: The Modern Language Association of America, 1999); the first example pertains to material drawn from periodicals, the second to material reprinted from books:

Morrison, Jago. "Narration and Unease in Ian McEwan's Later Fiction." *Critique* 42. 3 (spring 2001): 253-68. Reprinted in *Literary Criticism from 1400-1800.* Ed. Michael L. LaBlanc. Vol. 76. Detroit: Gale, 2003. 212-20.

Brossard, Nicole. "Poetic Politics." *The Politics of Poetic Form: Poetry and Public Policy.* Ed. Charles Bernstein. New York: Roof Books, 1990. 73-82. Reprinted in *Contemporary Literary Criticism.* Ed. Michael L. LaBlanc. Vol. 82. Detroit: Gale, 2003. 3-8.

Suggestions are Welcome

Readers who wish to suggest new features, topics, or authors to appear in future volumes, or who have other suggestions or comments are cordially invited to call, write, or fax the Product Manager:

Product Manager, Literary Criticism Series
Thomson Gale
27500 Drake Road
Farmington Hills, MI 48331-3535
1-800-347-4253 (GALE)
Fax: 248-699-8054

Acknowledgments

The editors wish to thank the copyright holders of the excerpted criticism included in this volume and the permissions managers of many book and magazine publishing companies for assisting us in securing reproduction rights. We are also grateful to the staffs of the Detroit Public Library, the Library of Congress, the University of Detroit Mercy Library, Wayne State University Purdy/Kresge Library Complex, and the University of Michigan Libraries for making their resources available to us. Following is a list of the copyright holders who have granted us permission to reproduce material in this volume of *LC*. Every effort has been made to trace copyright, but if omissions have been made, please let us know.

Thomson Gale Literature Product Advisory Board

The members of the Thomson Gale Literary Criticism Series Advisory Board—reference librarians and subject specialists from public, academic, and school library systems—represent a cross-section of our customer base and offer a variety of informed perspectives on both the presentation and content of our literature criticism products. Advisory board members assess and define such quality issues as the relevance, currency, and usefulness of the author coverage, critical content, and literary topics included in our series; evaluate the layout, presentation, and general quality of our printed volumes; provide feedback on the criteria used for selecting authors and topics covered in our series; provide suggestions for potential enhancements to our series; identify any gaps in our coverage of authors or literary topics, recommending authors or topics for inclusion; analyze the appropriateness of our content and presentation for various user audiences, such as high school students, undergraduates, graduate students, librarians, and educators; and offer feedback on any proposed changes/ enhancements to our series. We wish to thank the following advisors for their advice throughout the year.

Cavalier Poetry and Drama

INTRODUCTION

The term "Cavalier" denotes a literary movement that flourished from 1625 to 1649, characterized by its practitioners' use of lighthearted wit, elegant mannerisms, amorous and sometimes erotic themes, and adherence to upper-class values.

The chief Cavalier writers were Thomas Carew (1594-1640), Sir John Suckling (1609-1642), Robert Herrick (1591-1674), and Richard Lovelace (1618-1657). Critic Thomas Clayton notes that Cavalier literature "is *precisely* the corpus of poems by these four 'Cavalier Lyrists,' and by that measure it is a composite of the qualities abstracted from their collected works." Characteristically, the Cavaliers were cultured, carefree, behaved as courtly gentlemen, and avoided the overserious. Their works typically celebrate the commonplace and even trivial aspects of daily life.

Sometimes referred to as the "Sons of Ben" or the "Tribe of Ben" in recognition of their debt to Ben Jonson, the writings of the Cavaliers were also significantly impacted by John Donne. Lovelace and Carew were clearly informed by Petrarch. Politically the Cavaliers were Royalists, supporting Charles I against Parliament and the Roundheads in the Civil Wars. Three of the authors—Carew, Suckling, and Lovelace—fought for Charles I. Herrick was not a courtier at all, but an Anglican clergyman. His works show a strong influence by Jonson's adaptations of classical Latin forms.

The light poetry and drama of the Cavaliers has not fared well in general with modern critics preferring more serious material. To many current critics, Alexander Pope's description of the Cavaliers as a "mob of gentlemen who wrote with ease" is justification for a lack of scrutiny. Clayton, however, in his discussion of the lives and works of the major Cavaliers, points out that their purpose in writing was to please the king, not future critics. Manfred Weidhorn discusses Lovelace's reputation and achievements, noting that critical respect for him has fallen over the centuries but also pointing out that, of his poems, "some fifteen to twenty are effective and readable; repay study; change our view of life ever so little; leave us wiser, amused, or moved." Lynn Sadler examines Carew's life and influences, and asserts that he is at his best when he takes elements from Jonson, Donne, the Elizabethans, and the other Cavaliers and makes something new from the combina-

tion. Warren W. Wooden concentrates on Suckling's love letters, in which, according to Wooden, the poet "is both playing and subverting the courtly love game." Wooden calls for a critical reassessment, contending that the epistles are "more complex, sophisticated, and unconventional than generally assumed." Geoffrey D. Aggeler provides context for the Cavaliers in his analysis of the plays of the period 1642 through 1660, when theaters were closed by ordinance. Aggeler notes that plays continued to be written, read, and also performed, although typically to small, private audiences. He finds the Cavalier plays of this period full of topical references to politics and religion. Michael H. Markel explores Andrew Marvell's Cavalier poetry, which employs standard Cavalier themes but with the injection of skepticism. Markel explains that Marvell felt the themes addressed by the Cavaliers were more complex than they seemed to realize and that they deserved fuller treatment. Marjorie Swann and Joseph Scodel examine the treatment of women by the Cavaliers. Swann considers how Herrick made objects of women and then either fragmented these objects into constituent anatomical parts or concentrated on adornments such as lace and jewelry in substitution for intimacy. Scodel explains that the ideal woman to the Cavaliers would maintain a delicate balance in her sexual attitude and behavior, neither totally frustrating nor satiating her lover.

REPRESENTATIVE WORKS

Thomas Carew
The Poems of Thomas Carew with His Masque Coelum Britannicum [edited by Rhodes Dunlap] (poetry and drama) 1970

Robert Herrick
The Complete Poetry of Robert Herrick [edited by J. Max Patrick] (poetry) 1963

Richard Lovelace
The Poems of Richard Lovelace [edited by C. H. Wilkinson] (poetry) 1953

John Suckling
*The Works of Sir John Suckling 2 vols. (collected works) 1971

*Includes *The Non-Dramatic Works* [edited by Thomas Clayton] (poetry) and *The Plays* [edited by L. A. Beaurline].

OVERVIEWS

Felix E. Schelling (essay date 1913)

SOURCE: Schelling, Felix E. "The Lyric in the Reigns of the First Two Stuart Monarchs." In *The English Lyric*, pp. 73-111. Port Washington, N.Y.: Kennikat Press, Inc., 1967.

[*In the following excerpt, first published in 1913, Schelling classifies the poetry of Carew, Herrick, and the other Cavalier poets as secular, and stresses its relation to the social life of the period.*]

Analogies frequently mislead and disprove what they are invoked to illustrate; and yet the often-repeated comparison of the reign of Elizabeth to the spring, the period of peculiar and rapid quickening, the time of bloom and promise, is as useful as it is obvious and hackneyed. In such an age poetry is careless in form and subject as we have seen, more intent on saying many things than cautious in selection; and the moral significance of art with questions of its mission are things little thought on, and, even if considered, carelessly neglected. There was vice and sin in these old days, and there were serious-minded men who deplored it; but, although the forces of disintegration were already at work, there was as yet no open break between the cult of beauty and the spirit of holiness. With the accession of King James a change came over the English world. First, the national spirit fell slack, with a foreigner come to the throne. As a consequence Puritanism, with its dangerous political aspirations, began to kindle, fanned by the fitful unwisdom of the king and his preoccupations pedantic and unkingly. The frivolous became more frivolous with their masques, revels, and costly entertainments, and royalty led the rout of folly; while the prudent, grave, and God-fearing felt themselves gradually alienated from much which they had hitherto been able to accept without question or cavil. The arts, and particularly the stage, suffered in this cleavage between the pursuits of pleasure and the dictates of morals. But to speak of Puritanism in its more inclusive sense, as wholly inimical to poetry, is totally to misrepresent the truth. The history of the sacred lyric alone, in the reign of James and Charles, with its splendid dedication to the worship and glory of God, whether the devotee were Anglican, Puritan, or Roman, is enough to disprove so gross a misrepresentation. This however must be confessed, the poets now chose between earthly and divine love or lived in later regret for their celebration of the former. Amor, Venus, and the rest were now felt verily to be gods of the heathen, to be sung with apologies if not with shame; and song, like other good gifts of the world, was enlisted in the services of virtue and godliness.

As a result of this split between the sacred and the secular world in poetry as elsewhere, the age of King Charles I produced the purest of our poetical worshippers of beauty as it produced the most saintly and rhapsodic of English devotional poets. Among the former Carew and Herrick stand preëminent, alike in their general characteristics and in the delicacy and perfection of their workmanship, but contrasted in many other things. Thomas Carew is described as an indolent student while at Oxford, a diplomat of modest success, later promoted to a close attendance on King Charles as the royal cupbearer. He wrote, like a gentleman, for his pleasure and that of his immediate friends, and his poetry came into print only after his death and after the passing of the immediate experiences that occasioned it. Carew was devoid of Jonson's scholarship as he was devoid of Jonson's show of it; but his learning was adequate and, if worn negligently, was always in the height of the contemporary mode. But neither the form nor the thought of Carew's lyrics is ever negligent. Here he is strict as Jonson himself, and far more easy. Carew seldom trespasses on serious or important subjects, dwelling preferably in the world of compliment, polite love-making, pointed repartee, and sentiment only half serious. And yet Carew is a very genuine poet, full of fancy, unerring in his correctness of phrase, happy in his choice and management of stanza, and admirably in command of himself and his art. His taste for the most part preserved him from the conceit, whether of Sidney or of Donne. Carew, in a word, is the ideal poet of Waller's imagination, an ideal that Waller in his narrower, poetically desiccated, and less well-bred age, never approached.

Our other English poetical hedonist, Robert Herrick, is a very different type of man. Born in 1591, several years before Carew, Herrick probably began writing not long after the death of Shakespeare. He was one of the authentic sons of Ben and has left more than one poetical memorial of the brave old days at "the Dog, the Sun, the Triple Tun," where Jonson sat enthroned, the august potentate of literary Bohemia:

> Where we such clusters had,
> As made us nobly wild, not mad;
>   And yet each verse of thine
> Out-did the meat, out-did the frolic wine.

Herrick somewhat unfittingly entered the Church and remained long years Vicar of Dean Prior in Devonshire, of which he was deprived during the Commonwealth, to be restored on the accession of King Charles. The publication of Herrick's poetry in a volume called the *Hesperides* was delayed until 1648, when his spirit of joy was peculiarly out of touch with the turbulent days of the trial and execution of King Charles. Herrick's volume seems to have fallen dead from the press despite a minor part of it on more serious subjects, designated *Noble Numbers*; and his reputation remained obscured to a time almost within the recollection of the scholarship of to-day. The lyrical poetry of Herrick—and save for his epigrams, which in comparison are negligible, he wrote no other—is of a range far contracted within the ample bounds of the Elizabethan muse at large. Ever remembering the minor number of his religious poems, many of them very beautiful, no English poet is so sensuous, so all but wholly erotic, and so frank and whole-souled a follower of hedonism in his philosophy of life, and of Anacreon, Sappho, and Catullus for his art of poetry. Herrick is a lover of all the joyful things of the world: the spring with its blossoms and country mirth, fair women, their youth, and the charming details of their beauty, its fragility and imperishable charm. He finds uncommon joy in common, often in trivial, things: the tie of a ribbon, the flutter of his mistress's dress, the small pleasures and superstitions of his country parish, his dog, his maid, the simple provender of his larder—better furnished, one may surmise, than the humility of some of his poems confesses; and he shudders at death as the negation of all that he adores, lamenting the approach of years with unfeigned regret for the joys that are past and irrecoverable. Yet Herrick's success lies less in all these things—which he shares with a dozen other poets—than in the vividness and simple directness with which he has realized them in an art as sure as it is delicate, as apparently unsophisticated as it is metrically and stylistically impeccable. Happiness of imagery rarely lapsing into actual conceit, sly humor, witchery of phrase, all are Herrick's. In a score of delightful poems—"Corinna Going a-Maying," "To Primroses," "Meadows," "Daffodils," "His Grange," and "Thanksgiving"—Herrick has equalled the best of the Elizabethan lyrists; and, in general, his technique is more perfect than theirs. As much cannot be said on this score either of William Cartwright, of whom Jonson said that he wrote "like a man," or Richard Lovelace, admirable gentleman that he was in the halls of Oxford, at court, and in the field. Both are lyrists of great inequality, Lovelace especially, varying between some two or three perfect little songs (such as the immortal "To Lucasta, going to the Wars," and "To Althea, from Prison"), sure of a place in any anthology including his time, and poems that fall into mere slovenliness and unintelligibility.

In the poetry of Herrick, and more particularly in that of Carew and Lovelace, to which we may add poems of Sir Robert Ayton, Cartwright, Brome, King, Hoskins and many more, we meet with the earliest considerable body of verse that comes under the category of *vers de société*. This variety of the lyric recognizes in the highly complex conditions of modern society fitting themes for poetry, and makes out of the conventions of social life a subject for art. Only the poet who knows this phase of life from within can truly depict it; not because it is superior to other life, but because it is broken up into a

greater number of facets, each reflecting its own little picture. *Vers de société* makes demand not only on the poet's breeding and intimate acquaintance with the usages and varieties of conduct and carriage which distinguish his time, it demands also control, ease, elegance of manner, delicacy of touch, with an entire absence of pedantry, perfection of technique and finish. As to the result, exacting criticism has found its cavil and its sneer. *Vers de société* has been found wanting in seriousness as occupied purely with trifles; and in part this is true. Yet neither of poetry nor of life is it fair to demand that it be concerned wholly with

Thrones, dominations, princedoms, virtues, powers.

The hyperbole of emotion would fare ill if judged by the standards of the hyperbole of compliment; and those who find nothing but shallowness and insincerity in the lyrics of Carew, are judging these delicately cut little cameos by standards better applicable to the portraiture of heroes hewn of granite or cast in bronze. "Breadth of design," "sustained effort," "artistic seriousness," all have their place in the jargon of the critic as measures to apply to the larger dimensions of heroic and romantic art; but such standards belong not to the distinguishing of the scents and colors of roses nor to the appraisement of the gossamer delicacy of many a lyric which is no less sincere because it happens to be founded on the superficialities of social intercourse that conceal very little after all the mainsprings of true human feeling.

Thomas Clayton (essay date 1978)

SOURCE: Clayton, Thomas. Introduction to *Cavalier Poets: Selected Poems*, edited by Thomas Clayton, pp. xiii-xxii. Oxford: Oxford University Press, 1978.

[*In this essay, Clayton presents an overview of the four major Cavalier poets: Robert Herrick, Thomas Carew, John Suckling, and Richard Lovelace.*]

Herrick, Carew, Suckling, and Lovelace share a continuing appeal that continues also to change as the times change. They are 'for all time', as Ben Jonson wrote of Shakespeare, but they are also much more 'of an age'; hence their varying critical fortunes with ages and audiences like and unlike theirs. They have always found most favour with those who prefer their poetry first to be poetry ('creation through words of orders of meaning and sound', as the late Reuben Brower once put it), and who recognize 'high seriousness' as not necessarily to be demanded everywhere in the same measure, kind, and character. Not that these poets don't speak to the human condition. They do. But heirs of the opposing puritans have difficulties with the Cavalier perspective, for reasons suggested by Hume in his assessment of re-lations between art and society: 'in a republic, the can-didates for office must look downwards, to gain the suf-frages of the people; in a monarchy, they must turn their attention upwards, to court the good graces and favour of the great. To be successful in the former way, it is necessary for a man to make himself *useful,* by his industry, capacity, or knowledge; to be prosperous in the latter way, it is requisite for him to render himself *agreeable,* by his wit, complaisance, and civility. A strong genius succeeds best in republics, a refined taste in monarchies. And consequently the sciences are the more natural growth of the one, the polite arts of the other' ('Of the Rise and Progress of the Arts and Sciences', 1742).

For better as well as for worse 'the protestant ethic and the spirit of capitalism' have given us much of the modern West, but it is still not for nothing that the puri-tans have also given their name to stern-faced repres-sion in the parsimonious interests of a theocratic mil-lennium. And it was the puritans who closed the theatres, restricted sports and pastimes, took the land by force and violence, and beheaded the Archbishop of Canterbury and the King—a course of national and in-ternational events that brought about Suckling's death in 1641 and possibly Carew's in 1640, and that Lovelace and Herrick saw most feelingly, Lovelace on occasion as a political prisoner and Herrick by expul-sion from his parish living in Devon. Herrick expresses a keen sense of the times' universal upheaval in 'Fare-well Frost, or Welcome the Spring': rejoicing over the turn of the greening season, he hopes that,

> . . . when this war (which tempest-like doth spoil
> Our salt, our corn, our honey, wine, and oil)
> Falls to a temper, and doth mildly cast
> His inconsiderate frenzy off at last,
> The gentle dove may, when these turmoils cease,
> Bring in her bill, once more, *the Branch of Peace.*

Here Herrick speaks plaintively and forcefully for the free-from-party-coloured heart, although the cast of his allegiance is clearly in evidence when 'the palms put forth their gems, and every tree / Now swaggers in her leafy gallantry.'

Carew and Suckling were close friends, and they were certainly acquainted with their younger contemporary, Lovelace. All three served in the first Bishops' War in 1639, and Suckling and Lovelace served in the second, in 1640. And all three were closely associated with a Court in which the King was as much a connoisseur of the arts as he was a perennial innocent in matters of politics and society at large. Their Cavalier commit-ment may be said to have been total, as it was also for Herrick, though in different ways, as one would expect of an Anglican clergyman—but not so different as all that. Herrick was educated at Cambridge, as Suckling

was (Carew and Lovelace were Oxford men); he clearly had his years in London, too, if a lesser day in Court, and he fondly recollects the good old days in apostro-phes to Ben Jonson.

Jonson himself has helped a suggestible posterity to see the so-called 'Sons of Ben' as a sort of masonic lodge of classically inclined Court poets. Holding lordly court in such congenial quarters as the Devil Tavern's 'Apollo Room' (which Jonson named), remarking that 'my son Cartwright writes all like a man', and writing 'An Epistle to One That Asked to be Sealed of the Tribe of Ben', with its ringing allusion to Revelation 7: 8 ('Of the tribe of Benjamin were sealed twelve thousand'), Jonson lent lofty countenance and even conviction to those who have sought a tribe or family that is the clas-sical, secular, social, mannerly, and lucid counterpart of the strongly vernacular, divine, private, self-assertive, and often obscure Metaphysical 'school' of Donne and others, itself accredited by convenience more than by credentials. There is something to be said for the Sons of Ben as a historical grouping of well educated and convivial tavern wits bowing to Jonson's poetical ma-jority and commanding presence, but Herrick is almost the only certain as well as No. 1 Son, and even he found his own way, though he walked in his poetical father's footsteps to get there. Suckling's dislike of Jonson is abundantly apparent in 'The Wits', which lampoons him; Lovelace was too young to have known him well, if at all; and Carew seems to have been an ambivalent and occasional 'cousin' in the indeterminate sense. In short, there is no real Tribe of Ben, so far as these Cavalier poets are concerned. Many poets of the period have varied orders of poetical expression, and Carew, for example, can sound very like Jonson in his epitaphs and like Donne in his great elegy on the Dean of Paul's. This is not surprising, for an age eminently conscious of decorum as a principle of total integration—some-thing quite beyond what 'decorous' implies.

What, then, is 'Cavalier poetry'? By tradition it is *pre-cisely* the corpus of poems by these four 'Cavalier Lyrists',[1] and by that measure it is a composite of the qualities abstracted from their collected works. The other way of defining the poetry is by attending to the senses and applications of the term 'Cavalier', which derives ultimately from late Latin *caballarius* 'horseman', and yields in the seventeenth century such pertinent senses as (*OED*): 'a horseman; esp. a horse-soldier; a knight'; 'a gentleman trained to arms, "a gay sprightly military man"', in Dr. Johnson's phrase, or 'a courtly gentleman, a gallant'; and 'a name given to those who fought on the side of Charles I in the war between him and Parliament: a 17th c. Royalist'. In at-tributive or adjectival use, 'gallant' (citing Suckling: 'The people are naturally [i.e. by nature] not valiant, and not much cavalier'); 'careless in manner, off-hand, free and easy'; and 'Royalist'. The word was also incorporated in 'Cavalierism' (1642) for 'the practice or principles of . . . the adherents of Charles I; an expression characteristic of the Cavalier party.'

It is thus hardly surprising that Charles delighted to be portrayed by Van Dyck as 'just dismounted from his horse on a hunting expedition', and it is in fact to Van Dyck 'that we owe an artistic record of this society with its defiantly aristocratic bearing and its cult of courtly refinement'; he 'showed the Stuart monarch as he would have wished to live in history: a figure of matchless elegance, of unquestioned authority and high culture, the patron of the arts, and the upholder of the divine right of kings, a man who needs no outward trappings of power to enhance his natural dignity'—in short, a Cavalier King.[2] With reference to such qualities as these, which were inherently aesthetic as well as 'social', it used to be customary to speak of 'the Cavalier spirit', and once, indeed, there seems to have been one, which, lost to history, found its archetypal way readily into the fictions of gallantry of Dumas and Rostand, for example.

In 'The Line of Wit' F. R. Leavis did much to prepare for more recent thinking about the poets of the Caroline period by arguing that, in 'the idiomatic quality of the Caroline lyric, its close relation to the spoken language, we do not find it easy to separate Donne's influence from Jonson's'; the line 'runs from Ben Jonson (and Donne) through Carew and Marvell to Pope'; and the Cavalier manifestation, 'which is sufficiently realized in a considerable body of poems, may be described as consciously urbane, mature, and civilized.'[3] More recently Josephine Miles has studied the poetry of the period in relation to 'a part of literary style more clearly limitable than tone or theme or genre or even manner', namely 'mode: the selective use of the elements and structures of language'.[4] Her studies have led to the conclusion that in some vital respects 'the so-called "sons of Ben" turn out to be even more strongly sons of Donne'.[5] For, in connection with a stylistic factor 'in which Donne's uses are clearly dominant', of thirty poets those with the nearest affinities are Carew, Suckling, Shirley, and Herrick. Another factor places Lovelace as a member of smaller mid-century groups including, in proximate order, Cowley, Marvell, Crashaw, and Quarles. The study reveals for the first group a poetical vocabulary 'remarkably packed with verbs of action, and with a world-time-love-death-reciprocal-action complex which we may recognize as part of what has been called "metaphysical". These terms together bear a very high proportion of the whole burden of metaphysical vocabulary'. The practice of the mid-century group, in its 'more domesticated metaphysics', was also a 'carrying on and modifying of the Donne tradition'. Finally, in a strictly grammatical perspective (the ratio of verbs to adjectives, nouns, and verbs together), one finds Milton, Sylvester, and Spenser at one extreme, and at

the other Carew, Herrick, Jonson, Donne, and Suckling, in order of increasing difference. In short, the 'idiolects' of the Cavalier poets are manifestly non-Spenserian. Theirs are Strong Lines, by turns more like Jonson's (especially Carew and Herrick), but quite as often like Donne's (Lovelace and Suckling). Ultimately, their poetical ethos is their own.

These Cavalier poets are the most prominent and significant of the royalist poets of the reign of Charles I. It is not so often, nowadays, that one meets with an overgeneralized notion of literary Cavalierism, but such a notion persists, in some quarters: viewed as interchangeable, Carrick and Herew, Sucklace and Loveling, materialize in this presbyopic vision as a four-way poetical Janus that their trochaic surnames seem to suggest. But for all they have in common they clearly had their differences: Herrick died a priest at 83, Carew a debauchee at 45 or 46, Lovelace a bankrupt gentleman at 39, and Suckling a rash royalist conspirator at 32. Juxtaposed in contrast here are Herrick's scholarly squinting, widely smiling, city-country curiosity; Carew's shaded vein of witty but felt-in-the-blood-and-felt-along-the-heart sense of transiency; Suckling's often surprisingly modest and almost always playful but not unreflective *sprezzatura*; and Lovelace's soldier's-courtier's-philosopher's brightly interwoven thought, charm, and keen bravura.

Herrick had the best chance of major poetical achievement, and *Hesperides* and *Noble Numbers* in a measure reflect the fifty-six years that preceded their publication in 1648. Crashaw attained a generally granted poetical majority in fewer years (36 or 37) than Carew or Lovelace lived, and in an earlier generation Marlowe at 29 left a corpus of work far more substantial than Suckling did in his thirty-two years. The achievement of each and all of these poets is not insubstantial, nevertheless, and what Dr. Johnson wrote of the Earl of Rochester (who died at 33) applies in some degree to Carew and Lovelace and in a pronounced degree to Suckling: 'in all his works there is sprightliness and vigour, and everywhere may be found tokens of a mind which study might have carried to excellence. What more can be expected from a life spent in ostentatious contempt of regularity, and ended before the abilities of many other men began to be displayed?' ('Life of Rochester'). A brief descriptive survey will help to convey a sense of the character of the respective canons of these Cavalier poets.

Herrick's first datable poem, 'A Country Life' (32), was probably written *c.* 1610, when the poet was nineteen.[6] He wrote virtually all the rest of his poems before 1648, when the 1,130 poems of *Hesperides* (with the 272 of *Noble Numbers*) were published. Only eight of his poems are known to have been published before *Hesperides,* and only thirty-nine (and one of the *Noble*

Numbers) circulated in manuscript, so Herrick evidently shared the time's and gentleman's preference for private to public circulation, at least for most works short of an authorized collection. As Mark L. Reed asserts, in arguing that many of Herrick's poems could have been written before Herrick moved to Dean Prior in 1630, 'if these poems do not grow from and sing of Devonshire', as some of them certainly did, however, 'they do, in a manner unparalleled by any other group of lyrics of the time, grow from and sing of England . . . , more exactly of the beauties and meaning of the countryside, the inhabitants, and popular activity of England itself.' They are, in fact, manifestations of a wholly new consciousness: 'the growing awareness in the English artistic sensibility of natural scenery and folk and rural life other than that of Arcadia or classical verse.'[7]

If one examines and loosely classifies the first and last twenty poems in *Hesperides*, an interesting fact emerges that tends to be true of most of the collection: Herrick's world is prominently one of apostrophic address, in which he enacts the 'social life' of a person who finds much of his companionship in his imagination.[8] The following kinds of poem make up the forty: thirteen epigrams, fifteen apostrophes (including five to his 'mistresses' named or collective, and ten to other persons and things), five soliloquies and epigrammatic meditations, three poems to and on himself, two 'other' dramatic monologues, a narrative witch-poem in lyric stanzas ('The Hag'), and a *carmen figuratum*. As for the longer poems that are customarily taken to measure poetical reach, Herrick's fifteen include three wedding poems, three 'fairy' poems, and nine 'miscellaneous' poems: 'Corinna's Going a Maying', two 'Country Life' poems, a 'Farewell' and a 'Welcome to Sack', 'His Age', 'A Panegyric', 'The Parting Verse', and 'The Apparition of His Mistress Calling Him to Elysium'. These range from 54 to 170 lines; twelve of them are included in the present collection. The shorter masterpieces, which are not easily categorized, are such poems as 'Delight in Disorder', 'To the Virgins, to Make Much of Time', and 'Upon Julia's Clothes', and Herrick is no doubt most widely known for these shorter poems, which are indeed among his best.

In a creative life of at least two decades' duration (*c.* 1619-40), Carew wrote *Coelum Brittanicum* (a masque, 1634), 121 poems, and translations of nine Psalms. His first datable poem, 'A Fly That Flew into My Mistress' Eye' (24), was written when he was twenty-five or thereabouts, but it is difficult to imagine that he didn't write similar lyrics before that age. Thirty-five of his poems are more or less 'occasional' in the strict sense, and many of these are datable at least within a year or so. Ten of the poems were printed during his lifetime, and his poems circulated widely in manuscript, as was usual with the members of his circle; at least two manuscript collections contain a substantial number (42

and 65, respectively). Just over half of his poems are conveniently characterized as amatory poems, complaints, and compliments. Of his twelve longer poems (56-166 lines, five in the present collection), his longest and one of his two most famous is the erotic body-topographical poem, 'A Rapture' (28). The categories of the remaining poems do not contain many members, and the social connection looms large, from the two bountiful Country-House Poems (19, 39), the seven elegies and consolatory poems of which the elegy on Donne is generally thought to be his best poem (34), the two poems on sickness, the four celebratory and congratulatory marriage-poems (48), the three New Year's greetings (40), the five epitaphs (29-32), the two miscellaneous occasional-poems (35, 38), to the two verse epistles (one the Country-House Poem, 39). This group of social genres suggests that some claim could be made for Carew as the master of Cavalier greeting-card verse, but virtually all such poems at Carew's hand transcend their genres, and few fall short of considerable accomplishment. Carew also has a poem to a painter, three pastoral and amatory dialogues (26), a dramatic monologue (21), a remonstration to Ben Jonson (33), four choric songs, six commendatory poems (41, 42), and a poem for a picture (36). His magnitude as a poet is established rather less by the canon as a whole, perhaps, than by the brilliance of his performance in a wide variety of individual poems both short and long. In Carew's short and profligate life a real poetic and intellectual gift was largely dissipated.

The scope of Suckling's work is represented in part by a group of religious and Christmas-seasonal poems written in or before 1626, when the poet was seventeen; his four plays, *The Sad One* (c. 1632, unfinished), *Aglaura* (1637), *The Goblins* (1638-41), and *Brennoralt* (1639-41); his *Account of Religion by Reason*; several political tracts; and over fifty letters, some of literary character and many of literary quality. Of his seventy-eight poems, written between 1626 and 1641, the two 'major' ones introduced minor genres into English verse, 'The Wits' as a 'trial for the bays' of poetry (26, 1637), and 'A Ballad upon a Wedding' as a burlesque, rusticated epithalamion (27, 1639). Suckling was the arch-Cavalier in prizing 'black eyes, or a lucky hit / At bowls, above all the trophies of wit', as he claimed to do, and it is doubtful whether he would have gone on to truly disciplined and serious work even if he had not died a suicide at thirty-two; but he managed to get rather a lot done for all his apparent insouciance, and he is the most often neglected, underrated, and misrepresented of the Cavalier poets. The canon consists in only 2,010 lines, and only the poems already mentioned are of any length (118 and 132 lines). The rest average about twenty-three lines.

Of the prominently quasi-dramatic poems in the secular-metaphysical manner, there are two dialogues (7, 28);

eighteen answers, arguments, and dramatic monologues (10-15, 22, 23); three *carpe diem* poems (13); four compliments and protestations (4, 8); two valedictions (25); eleven exclamations, expostulations, and 'soliloquies' (3, 16-20); and three 'impersonations' (2). A second group is made up of descriptive, narrative, or explicitly 'written' poems: three imprecations (9), five narratives and retrospectives, a 'trial for the bays' (26), a dramatic-narrative burlesque epithalamion (27), two 'songs' (6), four occasional-commendatory poems, a prologue, a verse epistle, four extended conceits and definitions (1, 21, 24), an 'amatory cosmology' poem, and a poem in the 'praise of ugliness' genre. Finally, the eleven (juvenile) religious poems. Suckling's verse is emphatically an art of stance, poise, and the medium, and his single most famous poem, probably, is a pungent avowal of constant inconstancy that concludes,

> Had it any been but she,
> And that very very face,
> There had been at least ere this
> A dozen dozen in her place.

If it is taken as 'male-chauvinistic' psycho-sociology, it may displease (or elate); if it is taken as lyric fiction, it can sing for itself.

Lucasta's sixty-one poems (1-25 here) were published in 1649, when Lovelace was thirty-one, and most of the forty-three in *Lucasta*. *Posthume Poems* (1659, 26-47 here) were probably written 1649-57. Like Carew and Suckling, Lovelace turned his hand to drama, with his comedy *The Scholars,* written during his first year at Oxford when he was 16-17 (1634-5), and *The Soldier* (1640). He is best known for his war-connected (1, 2) and prison poems (9, 10, 17), but well known also for his poems of compliment and amatory lyrics, of which there are forty-four in all (28 in *Lucasta,* 16 in *Posthume Poems*) and fifteen in this collection. What Lovelace is less well known for (except through 'The Grasshopper'), but which are very characteristic as well as unique for his time, are his nine meditative 'creature poems' (most included here), and his 'painting poems' (13, 45). His occasional verse is scant and most of it is late, except for the prologue and epilogue to *The Scholars*. The four funeral-elegiac poems were written 1638-49, and the anniversary (44) and wedding poems after 1649. Lovelace's longest, and in several other ways also 'major', poems conclude each volume: *Aramantha: A Pastoral* (384 lines) complements but far exceeds 'Amyntor's Grove' in accomplishment as well as length, in *Lucasta*; and 'On Sanazar's Being Honoured' (267 lines), in *Posthume Poems,* is his only formal satire. Also typical of Lovelace are his meditation and advice poems (15, 43), and a mixed bag of ten ironical meditations and anti-love songs (e.g. 22, 23). The remaining poems are four mythological conceits and paradoxes (6, 7), four dialogues (42, which is also a political satire), a

political 'Mock-Song' (39), and a translation (a number of other translations are appended at the end of *Posthume Poems*).

The character and direction of Lovelace's poetical career is similar to the movement of poetry in general during the mid-seventeenth century, from the private and personal, through the social, to the public, or at any rate impersonal, including the detached and philosophical (lyrics continue to be written, but most are depersonalized songs). If, as seems likely, some of the compliments and amatory lyrics in *Posthume Poems* were in fact written before 1649 but not included in *Lucasta,* then the poems written after 1649, the year Charles was beheaded, are characterized by an increasingly meditative strain and a gathering gloom. There is not a simple transformation of gallant courtier into hounded and pessimistic royalist fugitive, but a general movement of the kind seems indicated: from a witty amatory lyrist to a poet personally and poetically *engagé* to one whose main hope of stability and deliverance is found in personal stoicism and friendship. Lovelace's gifts did develop in his known twenty-two years as poet, and interesting and larger accomplishment might have been expected of him had he lived beyond thirty-nine.

It is fair to say that of these four Cavalier poets only Herrick outlived his poetical gifts, but he had the good fortune within his lifetime to bring them to their relative perfection in full in a book of his own making, *Hesperides* well named.

Notes

1. The title of ch. i of the *Cavalier and Puritan* volume (vii) of the old *Cambridge History of English Literature,* ed. Sir A. W. Ward and A. R. Waller (1911).

2. E. H. Gombrich, *The Story of Art,* 12th edn. (1972), pp. 316-17.

3. *Revaluation: Tradition and Development in English Poetry* (1947), pp. 18, 19, 29.

4. *Eras and Modes in English Poetry,* 2nd edn. (1964), p. viii.

5. Josephine Miles and Hanan C. Selvin, 'Factor Analysis of Seventeenth Century Poetry', *The Computer and Literary Style,* ed. Jacob Leed (1966), p. 122.

6. The poem-numbers given here and below in parentheses are those of the poems in this edition.

7. 'Herrick Among the Maypoles: Dean Prior and the *Hesperides*', *SEL* [*Studies in English Literature*] v (1965), 133-50 (quotations from pp. 148-50).

8. The poems are classified for convenience by salient characteristics; there are obviously alternative ways of classifying many poems.

Joshua Scodel (essay date spring 1996)

SOURCE: Scodel, Joshua. "The Pleasures of Restraint: The Mean of Coyness in Cavalier Poetry." *Criticism* 38, no. 2 (spring 1996): 239-79.

[*In the essay below, Scodel argues that Cavalier poets "playfully and sometimes outrageously" replaced temperance with "a mistress's tantalizing coyness or a man's tantalized desire" as the appropriate middle ground between abstinence and lust.*]

Up through the middle ages, Christian attitudes toward sexuality combined an ascetic repugnance toward sinful carnality with a Christianized version of the pagan ethical focus on moderating bodily pleasures. The former celebrated celibacy as the purest state; the latter fostered restrained, temperate sexuality between married couples. With the Protestant Reformation, celibacy was unseated as an ideal and the promotion of moderate conjugal love intensified.[1] Like the medieval Scholastics, late sixteenth-century English Protestants often invoked Aristotle's conception of temperance, the mean with respect to bodily appetites, to define proper conjugal sexuality. Temperate sexual relations between married partners were the mean between a sin-producing abstinence and sinful fornication. In his *Domesticall Duties,* for example, William Gouge argues that proper sexual relations between husband and wife—what he and his fellow clergymen, following Saint Paul, call "due benevolence"—prevent spouses from falling into the "defect" of abstinence, which increases desire and promotes sinful onanism, and lustful "excess," which debilitates body and soul.[2] While celebrating conjugal affection, ministers warned against excessive desires and feelings. They distinguished between temperate love and lust, which the Jacobean minister Alexander Niccholes notes had "no meane, no bound." Lust could not provide a solid basis for a lifelong conjugal relationship, for it was not only excessive but also transient: the fire of intense passion soon turned cold.[3]

Yet while Protestant didactic writings sought to control conjugal sexuality and affect, some contemporaneous Cavalier poets sought, playfully and sometimes outrageously, to expand the boundaries of permissible sexual and emotional practice. Adapting and greatly expanding upon motifs in Roman erotic poetry, these poets wittily identify an erotic mean not with temperance but rather with a mistress's tantalizing coyness or a man's tantalized desire. By means of this subversive application of the mean, love poets transform the ethical regulation of

pleasure into a hedonistic technique for the increase of pleasure.[4] They celebrate as a mean the exquisite blending of the contrary extremes of pleasure and pain, hope and fear. While moralists advised spouses to discipline desires and emotions within the marriage bond, some seventeenth-century love poets promoted intense and oscillating emotions between lovers lest boredom cut all affective ties.

Imagining illicit pleasures, these poets take pleasure in twisting normative discourse against itself. By manipulating the traditional moral restrictions associated with the mean to maximize pleasure, poets explore the role of inhibitions in *producing* as well as regulating pleasure. Such love poetry thus reveals the emergence of a subject defined by his sense of freedom vis-à-vis traditional cultural codes, his conception of sexual norms as conventions to be playfully transformed for the intensification rather than containment of pleasure. This "libertine" revolt has a strong aesthetic dimension, furthermore, for poets emphasize the *pleasures* of the act of writing and reading at the expense of literature's didactic functions.

The freedom and pleasure of such poetry was, of course, the preserve of men. Poets imagined the female objects of their desire as means to increase their own joys as desiring, heterosexual males. They played with, but ultimately supported, the early modern gender hierarchy. Early modern marriage was an unequal partnership: the man was expected to rule his wife.[5] The ideal of conjugal moderation sustained this gender hierarchy. It was a commonplace of classical and Renaissance thought that women, the less rational and more emotional of the two genders, had a dangerous tendency to run to emotional extremes. It was therefore up to men, by "moderate" exercise of authority, to ensure that moderation prevailed.[6] The Elizabethan Homily on Matrimony, read in every church in the land, calls upon each husband to be "the leader and author of love, in cherishing and increasing concord with moderation, and not tyranny. . . . For the woman is a weak creature."[7] The Elizabethan prelate Edwin Sandys notes that because virtue inheres in golden "mediocrity," a husband should forgive "many faults" of his mate to maintain marital concord but must not be so doting as to "nourish foolishness." An early seventeenth-century minister, Samuel Hieron, argues similarly that the husband should keep a "meane" by loving his wife without "too much uxoriousness."[8] Some "libertine" poets, by contrast, decline the role of authoritative male moderation. Instead, they celebrate subversive female agency, reveling in titillating behavior that in fact conforms to negative stereotypes of the "extreme" female but which they positively value for posing an exciting *challenge* to the male. The freedom of the women imagined in such poems is, however, carefully and continually circumscribed as an enticement to the reassertion of male mastery.

The hedonistic mean, with its subversions of early modern conjugal ideals, can neither be reduced to a symptom of, nor be dissociated from, sociopolitical developments. Early modern sexual attitudes and practices develop in complicated interaction with other ideological formations. A brief survey of the poets I examine suggests the complex relations between erotic compositions and general ideological positions. Ben Jonson treats the hedonistic mean as the ideology of outsiders, those who flout society's moral codes and thus fail to fulfill the poet's social responsibilities and to earn the gratitude of society's rulers. Erotic license is associated with social irresponsibility in general. Yet Jonson also indulges in poetry's subversive potential, displaying his mastery of the illicit form of poetry that he ostensibly rejects. By contrast, Sons of Ben such as Thomas Randolph and William Cartwright unequivocally embrace the hedonistic mean as a pagan flight from the strictures of Protestant ethics and as an assertion of the poet's freedom from dominant moral postures. For them the mean articulates primarily a fantasy of escape from prevailing social norms.

Writing during the 1630s, Sir John Suckling wittily adapts the new form of mean to praise foreplay without consummation. He identifies his position not with individual fantasy but rather with courtly refinement and insouciance. He invokes the mean of coyness to assert the courtier's superiority to common people and to benighted, mainstream Protestant marriage ideology. Yet while his use of the mean participates in the cultural conflict between the court and its enemies, Suckling wages a battle on two fronts by also mocking the cult of "Platonic love" associated with Henrietta Maria at the Caroline court. In the late 1640s, a poet at the court-in-exile of Henrietta Maria, Abraham Cowley, follows Suckling in associating non-fruition with the mean of coyness but uses the mean nostalgically, to celebrate a court culture defeated in civil war.

Robert Herrick's *Hesperides* (1648) is also a nostalgic work, depicting a world of pleasure, part fantasy and part rural retreat, apart from—and in contestation with—the victorious Puritans' world. But Herrick provides a more comprehensive alternative to contemporary norms by applying the mean of coyness to new domains. He suggests a broad continuity between the pleasures offered by a coy mistress and a chaste wife by essentially reducing all female modesty to a strategy for enhancing her worth as an object of male desire. A professed Jonsonian, but endowed with a moral temper very different from his master's, Herrick applies the hedonistic mean indifferently to mistresses, brides, and wives, suggesting that laws of desire are more powerful than the distinctions central to early modern moral discourse concerning women. By use of the rhetoric of the mean, he collapses the distinction between Protestant calls for conjugal temperance and classical calls for

strategic coyness. Herrick further valorizes the mean of coyness by foregrounding its aesthetic dimension, associating the ideal woman's sexual tactics with the accomplished poet's textual strategies, both of whom use coyness to satisfy but not satiate.

Yet the mean of coyness does not go wholly unchallenged within Cavalier poetic tradition. Writing during the 1650s, Katherine Philips self-consciously transforms the rhetoric of the Cavaliers in order to idealize a virgin whose decorous moderation is *not* subservient to men's pleasures. Philips, whose husband worked for the Interregnum government but whose social circle was largely composed of Royalist sympathizers, celebrates a female subject whose "equall mind" remains steadfast whatever the vagaries of both historical change and male desire.

1

Jonson's *Poetaster* (1601), which contains the first major English articulation of what I call the mean of coyness, contrasts the poet's mouthpiece, the ethical satirist Horace, with licentious erotic poets, their beloveds, and their hangers-on.[9] Jonson presents a party of Roman elegiac love poets, their lady loves, and groupies at which the pseudo-poet Crispinus and the musician Hermogenes each sing a stanza of Hermogenes' song describing the perfect mistress:

> If I freely may discover,
> What would please me in my lover:
> 　I would have her fair, and witty,
> 　Savouring more of court, than city;
> 　A little proud, but full of pity:
> 　Light, and humorous in her toying.
> 　Oft building hopes, and soone destroying,
> 　Long, but sweet in the enjoying,
> Neither too easy, nor too hard:
> All extremes I would have barred.
> She should be allowed her passions,
> So they were but used as fashions;
> 　Sometimes froward, and then frowning,
> 　Sometimes sickish, and then swooning,
> 　Every fit, with change, still crowning.
> 　Purely jealous, I would have her,
> 　Then only constant when I crave her.
> 　'Tis a virtue should not save her.
> Thus, nor her delicates would cloy me,
> Neither her peevishness annoy me.[10]

The final couplet of each stanza underscores the ideal of the mean: Hermogenes' beloved avoids the "extremes" of too "easy" granting or too "hard" refusal of favors. Her virtuous "mediocrity" is tailored, however, to her lover's desires. The ideal wife of much early modern moralizing is associated with an even tenor that avoids the supposedly all-too-feminine penchant for "toying" in its most general sense of trifling as well as in its specifically erotic sense of flirting (s.v. "toy," *OED* 1, 2): thus an early seventeenth-century poem describes the ideal wife as "Not toying, fond, nor yet unkinde."[11] Hermogenes, by contrast, defines the mean in terms of a constantly changing "toying." Many of the features of the traditional misogynist depiction of female extremism—peevishness, deceitfulness, moodiness, triviality—are reconceived as spurs to the male lover. Hermogenes begins by emphasizing his freedom, which he states as a conditional ("If I freely may discover . . .") but treats as a fact, and the song as a whole expresses his freedom to reject the traditional male function of controlling female weakness. He emphasizes, however, his ultimate control over the titillating freedom of the woman, who will be "allowed" a circumscribed liberty but cannot in the end be "save[d]" from his embrace.

As is appropriate in a play set in ancient Rome, Hermogenes bases his songs on Roman models. He revives for England a Latin tradition of licentious adaptations of the mean. The final couplets of each stanza echo Martial's two-couplet epigram 1.57, which invokes the mean to authorize the poet's sexual preferences: "Do you ask, Flaccus, what sort of girl I would want or not want? / I dislike one who's too easy, and one who's too hard. / The mean [*medium*] between the two we approve: / I don't want what torments me, nor do I seek what cloys."[12] Jonson's classically-trained readers would have recognized the debt not only to Martial, who expresses similar preferences for a coy love partner in various epigrams (4.38, 4.42, 4.71, 4.81), but also to Ovidian love poetry, one of Martial's major models in his erotic epigrams. Hermogenes' wish that his mistress be "Sometimes froward, and then frowning, / Sometimes sickish, and then swooning" recalls Ovid's desire for a beloved who will "sometimes speak blandishments, sometimes quarrel" (*Amores,* 9b.45). Hermogenes' celebration of a woman's "toying"—"Oft building hopes, and soon destroying"—recalls Ovid's advice to women for attaining, retaining, and increasing a lover's sexual desire in *Ars amatoria*: Ovid notes that "an occasional repulse should be mixed with your merry sports" (3.583) and that a woman should first let her lover hope he is her sole partner and then cause him to doubt (3.595-96). Like Martial after him, Ovid associates such sexual tactics with the mean by recommending that a mistress who wishes to incite her pursuer's desires must avoid the extremes of being too yielding or too obstinate: "Neither promise yourself easily to him who entreats you, nor yet deny what he asks too stubbornly, / Cause him to hope and fear together" (3.475-76).

Ovid's and Martial's adoptions of the venerable concept of the mean to erotic sport are playful and self-consciously naughty. Martial's rhetorical shift between verbs in the plural and singular plays with the conceptual gap between the mean as a norm "we" all "approve" ("probamus," line 3) and its more dubious appli-

cation to his own personal erotic preferences, signaled by four verbs in the first-person (lines 1-2, 4). Both Ovid and Martial parody the Roman tendency to apply the mean mechanically as a guideline for every aspect of human behavior. Such uses of the mean attenuated its specifically ethical significance and rendered more plausible its application to an *ars erotica*—to sexual activity conceived of as a hedonistic practice with its own precise rules and protocols. Aristotle himself authorized the tendency to invoke the mean as a general principle of behavioral decorum when he applied it to the proper conduct of relaxing conversation (*Nicomachean Ethics* 4.8). Arguing that we must avoid not only moral turpitude but also minor breaches of decorum, Cicero's *De officiis* goes far beyond Aristotle in invoking the mean ("mediocritas") to describe—in bathetic detail—the qualities and manners of the supposed pinnacle of humanity, the Roman gentleman. Cicero argues that a man's physical appearance, deportment, and dress must be neither too "soft" ("molle") nor too "hard" ("durum"), neither "effeminate" ("effeminatum") nor "boorish" ("rusticum"), and that one must walk neither too fast nor too slow (1.35-36, 1.40). Thus when Martial applies the mean to describe a beloved's ideal appearance—a boy neither too sleek nor too slovenly, neither too masculine nor too effeminate (2.36), a mistress neither too fat nor too thin (11.100)—he is wittily extending the Ciceronian vision to a new, erotic context. Similarly, in their celebrations of coy mistresses, both Ovid and Martial cheekily extend the mean, applied by Cicero to paragons of Roman manliness, to erotically enticing women. Such women must have a decorum all their own, the erotic poets imply, one consonant with women's stereotypical character—emotional moodiness and willfulness.

Just as Ovid and Martial play with contemporaneous Roman norms, so Jonson has his Hermogenes twist and parody the early modern tendency to apply the mean to all aspects of everyday life. Cicero's applications of the mean to manners was very much alive among the educated elite of early modern England, for whom *De officiis* was a central text. Frequently reprinted both in Latin and in English translation, taught in humanist grammar schools and at the universities, *De officiis* was often treated by English humanists as the most authoritative classical guide to proper behavior, surpassing even the *Nicomachean Ethics* because of its philosophical accessibility and practicality as a rules-oriented handbook.[13] Both the Italian and native English courtesy books popular in early modern England, which testify to a massive attempt to define and regulate proper behavior, follow Cicero in using the mean to codify "gentle" manners.[14] Baldesar Castiglione's influential *Book of the Courtier,* translated into English in 1561, invokes the mean as a norm applicable to all aspects of courtly deportment, including appropriate clothes, jokes, and dance movements.[15] Giovanni della Casa's *Galateo,* translated in 1576, warns against walking or talking too quickly or slowly, discoursing too much or little, and smelling too "sweete" or "sowre"; Stefano Guazzo's *The Civile Conversation,* translated in 1581-86, cautions against overly stiff or "too busie" gestures and against speaking too much or little, too quickly or slowly, too loudly or softly, too carefully or carelessly.[16] Among English works, Sir Thomas Elyot's *Book named the Governor* (1534) claims gentlemen should "do neither too much nor too little, too soon nor too late, too swiftly nor slowly, but in due . . . measure"; the anonymous *Institucion of a Gentleman* (1568) cites Cicero against clothes too elegant or too "rude"; and John Ferne's *The Blazon of Gentrie* (1586) advises "measure" in the gentleman's appetites and attire.[17]

Unlike Ovid and Martial, however, Jonson does not himself espouse a parodic travesty of contemporary mores. He undercuts the Ovidian-Martialesque feminine ideal by ascribing it to Hermogenes. Jonson's musician is based on the Tigellius Hermogenes described in Horace's *Satire* 1.3, a poem which advocates the mean and presents this figure as a negative example of foolish oscillation from one extreme to another, now singing with a loud, now with a low voice, now running, now moving deathly slow, now talking of grand things, now of trivial (1-19).[18] Jonson's Hermogenes wishes for a narcissistic phantasm to mirror his own inconstancy: the mistress who is "Sometimes froward, and then frowning, / Sometimes sickish, and then swooning, / Every fit, with change, still crowning" is a feminine version of the extreme Hermogenes himself.

Thus Jonson suggests that Hermogenes, who cannot conceive of a true mean because of his own extremism, travesties the ideal. Yet in one sense his desired mistress is ironically Hermogenes' superior. The imagined mistress's ability to change quickly and thus avoid cloying or frustrating is precisely what Hermogenes lacks in his relations with others. While the mistress would be a master of the opportune, Hermogenes is inept. Horace introduces his portrait of Tigellius Hermogenes by noting that he is like all singers: "if asked to sing . . . they are never so inclined; / if unasked they never leave off" (*Satire* 1.3.2-3). True to character, Jonson's Hermogenes first refuses to sing his love ditty and then refuses to stop. One of the partygoers, Julia, the daughter of Augustus whom Jonson follows tradition in portraying as Ovid's dissolute lover, echoes Horace's judgment. She puns on "mean" as both way and proper middle way in order to underscore the singer's socially inept deviation from the very mean he proposes to cherish: "'Tis the common disease of all your musicians, that they know no mean, to be entreated, either to begin or end."[19] Hermogenes is presumably as inept a lover as he is a singer, and his imagined affair with an ideal mistress would presumably be dashed on the principle that any such interaction must be a duet.

Poetaster dramatizes contrasting poetic world-views and their aesthetic, ethical, and political implications. Jonson's contrast between the frivolous elegiac poets and the serious, didactic poets Horace and Virgil adapts the commonplace Renaissance contrast between heterosexual love and male friendship; while the love poets and their hangers-on pursue the favors of mistresses real and imagined, the true Augustan poets earn the respect and support of their patron and friend Augustus. Just as Hermogenes' ideal mistress mirrors his false understanding of the mean, so Horace's and Virgil's ideal patron Augustus reflects their true appreciation of the ideal. Augustus embodies the mean by avoiding the extremes of bad rulers, who "by their excess / Of cold in virtue, and cross heat in vice / Thunder, and tempest, on . . . learned heads." Instead of coyly building and destroying hopes like Hermogenes' desired mistress, Caesar embraces the true mean of liberality, rewarding a writer such as Horace on his merits and condemning those who provide gifts either in a profligate or stingy fashion: "Hands that part with gifts, / Or will restrain their use, without desert; / Or with a misery [i.e., a miserliness] . . . / Work as they had no soul to govern them."[20]

Caesar's beneficent treatment of Jonson's mouthpiece Horace embodies the generous patronage that Jonson desired from Queen Elizabeth and her court. Jonson presents himself in his "Prologue" (17-24) as one worthy of such beneficence because of his adherence to the mean. He avoids both "arrogance" and "base dejection," finding "a mean 'twixt both. / Which with a constant firmness he pursues, / As one, that knows the strength of his own *muse*."[21] Unlike the "toying" Hermogenes, Jonson associates his mean with a manly "firmness" and "strength." The properly bestowed gifts of a monarch and her courtiers, not the passing fancies of a coy wench, are the reward sought by a serious poet like Jonson.

Jonson also clearly prides himself, however, on mastering Ovid's and Martial's erotic poetry, bringing their works up-to-date and adding a lyric lilt to their epigrammatic wit. Jonson hints, furthermore, that there is really no absolute opposition between the moral Horatian tradition, on the one hand, and the licentious Ovidian tradition, on the other. Jonson's inclusion of Hermogenes Tigellius in his play would remind his classically-educated audience of Horace's notoriously obscene *Satire* 1.2, which begins with an attack on Tigellius as an extremist but then adapts the mean in a risqué fashion to advise would-be philanderers to have sex with freedwomen rather than with the "extremes" of common whores or Roman matrons. Horace adapts the mean to Epicurean/Cynic notions that one should seek pleasure and avoid pain: freedwomen cause less pain than whores or matrons (47-48). Horace mocks the "sorrow, passion, and the burden of care" of those who pursue "fleeing" objects of desire instead of finding sexual satisfaction the easy way—with women who embody the mean by being accessible but not too common (105-11). While in his satire Horace disagrees with poets like Ovid and Martial on whether an easy object is desirable or not, the poets agree in using the mean to celebrate a sensuality shorn of highminded moralizing. Jonson's oblique allusion to *Satire* 2 suggests that a Horatian poet need not wholly eschew a playful, erotic poetics.

Jonson's implicit depreciation of Hermogenes' Martialesque song is complicated, furthermore, by Jonson's identification of his own poetic stance in *Poetaster* not only with Horace but also with Martial. Jonson frames his play with an epigraph and a final line from the Roman epigrammatist.[22] Martial himself combines Horatian moralizing and Ovidian eroticism; many of his epigrams are stylistically and tonally indebted to the Horatian *sermo* while others are, as we have seen, in an Ovidian erotic vein.[23] Jonson's identification with Martial thus underscores the instability of his own moral-aesthetic allegiances. Jonson simultaneously revives, expands, and denigrates the Roman erotic tradition's mean of coyness.

2

Various Sons of Ben espouse the hedonistic mean without framing it with Jonson's moral disclaimers. At the time of his death in 1635, Randolph was considered Jonson's major heir. Randolph was thoroughly imbued with the Aristotelianism of the social elite: his comedy *The Muses' Looking Glass,* first performed in 1630, dramatizes the virtuous means and their respective vicious extremes as expounded by "great Aristotle."[24] Yet Randolph's erotic verse rejects Aristotelian ethics for Ovidian poetics. In one love lyric Randolph notes that he has "not *Aristotle* read alone" but is "in *Ovid* a proficient too"; he proceeds to request a mistress who is "coy, / Not easily wonne, though to be wonne in time; / That from her nicenesse I may store my rhime."[25] Coyness sparks not only erotic but also poetic interest; the male poetic subject finds himself and his self-expression in temporarily thwarted desire.

Randolph translated an epigram by Ausonius, a late Latin, early Christian poet popular in the Renaissance, which follows Ovid and Martial in adapting the ethical tradition's praise of the mean to a wish for erotic stimulation. Published posthumously in 1638, Randolph's epigram renders each of the Latin poet's elegiac couplets with two iambic tetrameter couplets:

> Shee which would not I would choose:
> Shee which would I would refuse.
> *Venus* could my mind but tame;
> But not satisfie the same.
> Inticements offer'd I despise,

> And deny'd I slightly prize.
> I would neither glut my mind,
> Nor yet too much torment find.
> Twice girt *Diana* doth not take mee,
> Nor *Venus* naked joyfull make mee.
> The first no pleasure hath to joy mee,
> And the last enough to cloy mee.
> But a crafty wench I'de have
> That can sell the art I crave.
> And joyne at once in me these two,
> I will, and yet I will not doe.[26]

The speaker moves rather awkwardly from the simple paradox of seeking a mistress who will deny him and thus whet his appetite all the more (1-4) to seeking a mistress who will avoid the extremes of naked availability and overdressed inaccessibility—what the original Latin calls "moderate sex" ("mediae veneris")—and thus provide him with a mean of pleasure between the glut of satisfaction and the torment of deprivation. Randolph was probably attracted to Ausonius' poem because, besides the Martial epigram imitated by his master Jonson, it was the only extant classical epigram to adapt the mean to increasing erotic pleasure. The Ausonius epigram provided rare classical authority for flouting traditional cultural norms.

Ausonius' epigram no doubt especially appealed to Randolph for the way it uses but subverts a conventional method of categorizing women. In early Christian through early modern writings, the notion that women were by nature subject to extremes infected even "encomia" of women, so that their virtues were often paradoxically seen as proofs of their extremism: women could be either saints or sinners, goddesses or devils; what they could never or only rarely attain, according to their critics, was the middle ground of normal, rational (i.e., male) humanity.[27] Ausonius asks for a woman who avoids two extremes that dominate early modern binary categorizing of women: the extremes of male-disdaining virgin and shameless whore. The protagonist of Robert Greene's *Never too Late* (1590) complains that women are "either too scrupulous with Daphne to contemne all, or too voluptuous with Venus to desire all"; an Elizabethan lyric complains that woman are either "so imperious no man may endure them, / Or so kind-hearted any may procure them."[28] Ausonius imagines a mistress who escapes this supposedly general feminine condition.

The ideal mistress "sells" her "art" both literally and figuratively: she is a courtesan or prostitute—as Randolph's translation of Ausonius's "femina" by "wench" suggests—but she is also a "crafty" woman who knows how to make the male "pay" in the sense of struggle to attain her. Ausonius here follows Ovid's economic understanding of female value and male desire. In a poem arguing that forbidden things bring greater pleasure, Ovid claims that a woman's "price" ("pretium") is increased by difficulties in attaining her (*Amores* 3.4.29-31). Randolph's translation intensifies the Ausonian epigram's focus on the male as desirer and the female as desired object. In his final couplet Ausonius wishes for a clever mistress who "delights because she joins, (as they say) I wish to and I don't." Ausonius's phrase "I wish to and I don't" could refer either to the mistress's or to the speaker's desires (or both); Randolph restricts its effect to the male speaker: "And joyne at once in me these two / I will, and yet I will not do." Randolph imagines a woman who will preserve the poet's erotic interest by making him simultaneously wish to attain and defer consummation. The mistress's "art" of coyness thus will arouse in him an arousing combination of opposed sensations.

By associating the woman's avoidance of the "extremes" of acceptance and rejection with the male's contradictory sensations, Ausonius plays with the notion, common in both ancient and Renaissance thought, that the mean simultaneously avoids and combines opposite extremes.[29] In another epigram, entitled in Joseph Scaliger's Renaissance edition of Ausonius "An Exhortation to Moderation" ("Exortatio ad modestiam"), the Latin poet celebrates the moderation of King Agathocles of Sicily as a combination of extremes. In order to remind himself of his humble origins amidst his regal prosperity, Agathocles dined with ornate cups and rustic dishes, thus "mixing wealth and poverty together."[30] The seventeenth-century writer Owen Feltham, who translated the poem in one of his essays, reveals the perceived connection between combining and avoiding extremes by linking Ausonius's epigram with a Roman emperor's moderation in "neither too much . . . remember[ing], nor altogether . . . forget[ing] high position."[31] While in the Agathocles epigram Ausonius exploits the ethical resonances of the mean as a mixing of opposites, in the erotic epigram translated by Randolph he deploys the same notion as a formal pattern susceptible to witty manipulation.

Despite the epigram's male point of view, the emphasis on the woman's intelligence and its effects on the speaker reveals a (circumscribed) appreciation of the female's independent agency. Indeed elsewhere Randolph imagines a woman's coyness as a genuine though perforce temporary exercise of *her* freedom. His play *Amyntas* (1638) dramatizes a woman's attempt to both avoid and combine extremes as a response to the unsatisfactory nature of marital relations. Though courted by two men, Damon and Alexis, Laurinda avoids choice until the end of the play by claiming to love "neither" and "either." To her servant's puzzled exclamation—"Either, and yet not both, both best, yet neither; / Why doe you torture those with equall Racks / That both vow service to you?"—Laurinda responds that she has perceived the "feares, / Jarres, discontents, suspicions, jealousies" that scar marriage and has con-

sequently decided to "temper" her affection and bear herself "equall" to both suitors. Within the fiction of the play, the disharmonies of marriage stem from a magical curse, and the drama concludes with the curse lifted, Laurinda's acceptance of Alexis as her husband, and Damon happily wedded to another. Yet despite the necromantic romance plot, the play hints that Laurinda's "temperate" strategy of deferring choice is a legitimate response to the realistic situation of a woman's being unhappy with—and in—an early modern marriage. Laurinda at one point exclaims, "See what 'tis to live a maid! / Now two at once doe serve us and adore, / Shee that weds one, serves him, serv'd her before."[32] Woman's power resides solely in this liminal period, the moment when she can say both yes and no and thus have "two at once." Once she is wed she must serve her husband. Randolph's play presents eventual submission as inevitable: he does not—cannot—reconcile the woman's desire for freedom with a patriarchal marriage system. Instead his play represents a woman's temporary freedom from constraint.

The Ausonian translation similarly presents an alternative to contemporaneous marriage practices, albeit one that treats female freedom solely as an instrument of male pleasure. A "crafty wench" is more erotically appealing than a wife precisely because the former's titillating form of freedom kindles and preserves the male's desire for conquest.

3

Other writers assign to the mean of coyness that Randolph posits as a liberating alternative to early modern marriage relations a role in the "official" libidinal economy: they treat it as a necessary *stage* in a maiden's journey to the altar. Alan Macfarlane notes the protracted nature of English courtship and the relative freedom of the participants: various kinds of physical intimacy were permitted in order that the partners get to know each other (since a happy marriage depended upon mutual consent and physical compatibility), but ideally consummation was delayed until the wedding night. Thus, as Macfarlane puts it, "the difficulty was to have sufficient nearness without over-exposure."[33] A woman being courted was expected to protect her chastity without wholly alienating her suitor(s): while "nearness" depended upon (active) male persistence, avoidance of over-exposure was up to the (passive) female. A song in William Corkine's *The Second Book of Ayres* (1612) provides a poetic epitome of this cultural paradigm: a lover declares that he can accept a "little coynesse" from his beloved, which "doth but blow mens fires," as long as she does not refuse to marry him in the end.[34]

Yet however necessary coyness was for pleasure, poets sometimes treated a maiden's behavior as a potentially dangerous threat to male prerogative. They gave advice concerning a maiden's proper attitude toward lovers designed to constrict the freedom of the woman who, like Laurinda in Randolph's play, is pursued by, but not yet subservient to, men. Poets sought to reassert the gender hierarchy by outlining the proper mean of coyness for a maid, a mode of behavior designed simultaneously to preserve females from sinful fornication and make them fully responsive to male needs and desires. While in marriage the husband has the authority to control his wife for her own well-being, the maid must be controlled by being made to feel responsible for her suitors—despite the fact that she does not have any true, socially sanctioned power over them.

Such guidelines for maidens adapt and moralize both the exciting coyness of the erotic tradition's ideal mistress and the etiquette prescribed for Italian Renaissance court ladies, who were supposed to be simultaneously affable, thus endearing themselves to men, and modest, thus keeping men at bay. Castiglione, who did so much to popularize the mean as a norm for courtly deportment, offered guidance to court ladies as well as male courtiers. Ladies are warned (to quote Thomas Hoby's Elizabethan translation) that they should be "esteemed no less chaste . . . than pleasant . . . and therefore must keepe a certeine meane verie hard, and (in a maner) dirived of contrary matters."[35] Ann Rosalind Jones, who treats this passage as an epitome of the Italian courtly ethics, contrasts that tradition's focus on the proper behavior of courtly, public women with the English Protestant focus on the behavior of wives in bourgeois households.[36] Yet English writers express such "Italian" preoccupations when they focus on maidens, who have not yet been domesticated as wives and thus have some of the independence of the court lady. In Francis Quarles's popular verse adaptation of a tale in Philip Sidney's *Arcadia, Argalus and Parthenia* (1629), the maiden Parthenia's virtuously balanced behavior toward men provides a model for all virgins who would preserve both their virtue and potential suitors' affections:

> Merry, yet modest; witty, and yet wise;
> Not apt to toy, and yet not too too nice;
> Quick, but not rash; Courteous, and yet not common;
> Not too familiar, and yet scorning no man.[37]

In *Fair Virtue* (1622), George Wither explicitly judges the maiden responsible for the well-being of her suitors as well as her own: he praises the "Coy one" who will prove "true . . . being won," but he also advises the virtuous maid to avoid being either "too precise" or "o'erkind" to suitors, for she must keep her suitors from both presumptuous audacity and suicidal despair. Wye Saltonstall's poem "A Maide" (1633) similarly argues that maids must "avoyd each rash extreame" and "draw forth the golden meane" by being neither "coy to quench all Lovers fires" nor "so kind" as to enflame

"mens unchast desires." They must "cherish chast hopes, make unchast despaire." A maiden should not "surrender" that which "doth so sweeten expectation," i.e., her virginity, until her marriage, at which time she must with "blushes . . . unwilling yeeld, / And weakely striving lose at last the field."[38]

Some male writers recognized—at least intermittently—the unjust difficulties they imposed upon women who were supposed to enact a perfect mean by being both chaste and "kind." Fulke Greville, for example, has his beloved Caelica complain that men want a blend of contradictory behavior from women and are prone to damn women whatever they do precisely because men are themselves riven by paradoxes:

> Men are false . . .
> Humble, and yet full of pride;
> Earnest, not to be denied;
> Now us, for not loving, blaming,
> Now us, for too much, defaming.[39]

Greville suggests that what might be praised as a female's virtuous moderation could easily be redescribed from a captious perspective as the extremes of coldness or doting fondness. Following Aristotle's *Nicomachean Ethics* (2.8.1-3), classical and Renaissance moralists often lament that the proximity of virtuous means like courage to vicious extremes like rashness makes it difficult to discern the difference between a virtue and its neighboring vices; following Aristotle's *Rhetoric* (1.9.28-29), classical and Renaissance rhetoricians often celebrate a sophisticated speaker's consequent ability to denigrate virtues as vices and exalt vices as virtues for tactical advantage.[40] Ovid exhibits the power of such male rhetoric to idealize or debase woman: in *Ars amatoria,* he recommends that the lover misidentify his beloved's physical shortcomings as attractions by "conceal[ing] a flaw with its nearness to a virtue" (2:662, Loeb translation modified); in *Remedia amoris,* he reverses his advice, counselling the lover who would free himself of passion to convert his mistress's physical and behavioral charms into shortcomings, calling a mistress "pert" for not being "simple" or calling her "simple" for being "honest" (323-30).

By both attacking and celebrating a woman's coyness, Jonson's poetic disciple Cartwright reveals—and delights in—how much the evaluation of a woman's behavior as virtuously moderate or viciously extreme depends upon male whim and rhetoric. The first verse paragraph of his "On a Gentlewomans Silk-hood" condemns as vicious extremism a woman's covering her face with an enticing veil (9-12, 15-22):

> Tell me who taught you to give so much light
> As may entice, not satisfie the Sight,
> Betraying what may cause us to admire,
> And kindle only, but not quench desire?
> . . . . .

> . . . O then
> May we not think there's Treason against Men?
> Whiles thus you only do expose the Lips,
> 'Tis but a fair and wantonner Eclipse.
> Mean't how you will, At once to shew, and hide,
> At best is but the Modesty of Pride;
> Either Unveil you then, or veil quite o'r,
> Beauty deserves not so much; Foulness more.[41]

Cartwright attacks the woman's veil as a wily device that is either excessive (as a half-covering of beauty) or deficient (as a half-covering of ugliness). The initial depiction of the veiled lady recalls not the Roman erotic tradition's playful celebration of female coyness but rather Renaissance moralists' didactic condemnations of coy temptresses. In Torquato Tasso's *Jerusalem Delivered,* evil Armida's coy mixture of exhibitionism and concealment—"Her breasts half hid, and half . . . laid to show," to quote Edward Fairfax's 1600 translation—inspires the soldiers' lust for what is "unseen." In Spenser's *Faerie Queene,* the wanton women in the Bower of Bliss similarly hide enough flesh to make the male gaze more "desirous" (II.xii.66.9).[42]

Far from conceding the sinful power of the veiled *femme fatale,* however, Cartwright blithely affirms the overriding power of male fantasy and desire by explicitly denying that the woman's motives are relevant ("Mean't how you will"). Since male fancy renders the woman a coy temptress, fancy can equally well declare the woman a modest maiden. In the second verse paragraph, the poet announces his change of viewpoint by announcing "My Fancy's now all hallow'd, and I find / Pure Vestals in my Thoughts, Priests in my Mind / (27-28)." While the first paragraph condemned the woman's veil as extreme, the third and final paragraph exalts the veil as the "Blest Mean" of a virtuous virgin (51-60):

> Methinks the first Age comes again, and we
> See a Retrivall of Simplicity;
> Thus looks the Country Virgin, whose brown hue
> Hoods her, and makes her shew even veil'd as you.
> Blest Mean, that Checks our Hopes, and spurs our
>   Fear,
> Whiles all doth not lye hid, nor all appear:
> O fear ye no Assaults from Bolder men;
> When they assaile be this your Armour then.
> A Silken Helmet may defend those Parts,
> Where softer Kisses are the only Darts.[43]

The final paragraph is as much a male fantasy—a "Methinks"—as the first. The poem self-consciously testifies not to any truth about the lady but rather to the poet's rhetorical power either to debase or exalt, to declare the lady viciously extreme or decorously moderate as male mood dictates. It thus foregrounds the judging male as the (whimsical) arbiter of female behavior. The ending indeed half-reveals the poet's praise as itself a coy maneuver: while the poet claims that the veil prevents "Bolder men" from brutalizing a beautiful but

decorously covered maiden, the concluding image of "softer Kisses" as the "only Darts" of love underscores eros's tender attractions and allows the poet to court the enticingly chaste woman.

4

Suckling invokes the mean of coyness not only to assert men's freedom and power at the expense of women but also to assert courtiers' superiority to common people. In his most distinctive poems, Suckling mocks both mainstream Protestant marriage ideology and the cult of "Platonic love" popular at the Caroline court. Caroline Neoplatonism, associated with Henrietta Maria and largely derived from the salon culture of Henrietta's youth in Paris, celebrated both the non-physical love between courtly friends of opposite sexes and the chaste love of married partners like Henrietta and Charles. Dissociating itself in both cases from "mere" bodily pleasures, it idealized court ladies as the ethereal embodiments of spiritual ideals.[44] While Suckling borrows from the Platonic cult its pretensions to aristocratic superiority, he rebels against the "effeminizing" values of the court, substituting a cynical, manly hedonism that debases rather than idealizes women.

Suckling writes several poems in praise of coyness. Using the economic model of Ovid and Ausonius, Suckling's "To his Rival" (II) recommends that a mistress deny what lovers "crave," and "such a rate / Set on each trifle, that a kisse / Shall come to be the utmost blisse" (14-16); thus she can preserve, in a provocative mean state, men's amorous fires, which would die if they "either flame too high" or "cannot flame" at all (7-8). Switching to a military model that suggests his desire to find male glory in the erotic realm, Suckling recommends in "Upon A.M." that the addressee be coy because "The Fort resign'd with ease, men Cowards prove / And lazie grow" / (3-4).[45]

His play *Aglaura* (1638) mocks courtly "Platonism" and its idealization of noble women. Attacking a "Platonic" lady's contempt for bodily gratification, a cynical courtier argues that the true erotic feast is "there, where the wise people of the world / Did place the vertues, i'th'middle—Madam." The analogy between the genitalia and the Aristotelian mean crudely suggests that "Platonic" asceticism is excessive in its attempt to escape the body. The play further suggests that courtly Platonism is motivated by the same concerns as the mean of coyness expounded by Suckling and other Sons of Ben: the need to avoid satiety and boredom in venereal sport. A "Platonic" lady argues against consummation of love on the hedonistic ground that "feares, and joyes, / Hopes, and desires, mixt with despaires, and doubts, / Doe make the sport in love." One of the play's cynical courtiers reduces this "new religion in love" to a mere "tricke to inhance the price of kisses." The "Platonic" ladies differ from the cynics only in one respect, that the former believe that only by extending coyness *indefinitely* can desire be maintained. In short they fear, the same cynic suggests, that "they should not satisfie" the desires they have coyly nurtured.[46] Just as Cartwright guesses that the veiled woman might be hiding her ugliness, so this courtier treats Platonism as a female trick to make men imagine women more desirable than they are.

Suckling's two most distinctive poems, both entitled "Against fruition," similarly insist upon the common hedonistic basis of the mean of coyness and fashionable, courtly "Platonic" love by playfully using the rhetoric of moderation to advise against consummating a relationship with a woman. Here are the two opening and closing stanzas of "Against Fruition" (I) (1-12, 19-30):

> Stay here fond youth and ask no more, be wise,
> Knowing too much long since lost Paradise;
> The vertuous joyes thou hast, thou would'st should
>   still
> Last in their pride; and would'st not take it ill
> If rudely from sweet dreams (and for a toy)
> Th'wert wak't? he wakes himself that does enjoy.
>
> Fruition adds no new wealth, but destroys,
> And while it pleases much the palate, cloyes;
> Who thinks he shall be happyer for that,
> As reasonably might hope he should grow fat
> By eating to a Surfet: this once past,
> What relishes? even kisses loose their tast.
>
>   . . . . .
>
> Women enjoy'd (what s'ere before th'ave been)
> Are like Romances read, or sights once seen:
> Fruition's dull, and spoils the Play much more
> Than if one read or knew the plot before;
> 'Tis expectation makes a blessing dear:
> It were not heaven, if we knew what it were.
>
> And as in Prospects we are there pleas'd most
> Where something keeps the eye from being lost,
> And leaves us room to guesse, so here restraint
> Holds up delight, that with excesse would faint.
> They who know all the wealth they have, are poor,
> Hee's onely rich that cannot tell his store.[47]

Suckling was not the first English poet to advise against erotic consummation. Jonson's translation of a fragment ascribed to Petronius, published posthumously in *Underwoods* in 1640, glorifies perpetual foreplay rather than consummation, which is rejected with disgust as the filthy pleasure of lustful beasts.[48] As early as 1600, a Jacobean song identifies erotic fulfillment with excess: "Disdaine me still, that I may ever love / . . . Love surfets with reward."[49] Suckling's poem expands upon this theme, identifying non-consummation with the mean by choosing the resonant words "too much," a "Surfet," and "excesse." He argues that the wise lover will refrain from an excess of carnal knowledge that

paradoxically will only render erotic life deficient by delimiting it. In *Romeo and Juliet,* Juliet proclaims "They are but beggars that can count their worth, / But my true love is grown to such excess / I cannot sum the sum of half my wealth" (II.vi.32-34); in *Antony and Cleopatra,* Antony proclaims that "There's beggary in the love that can be reckoned" (I.i.15). Suckling wittily turns Shakespearean lovers' hyperbolic declarations of excess into recommendations for "moderate" anti-fruition. Identifying carnal knowledge with the knowledge of good and evil that caused the fall, Suckling supports his case by drawing upon the Renaissance cult of *docta ignorantia* or learned ignorance, suggesting that it is the wise lover who stifles his desire for carnal knowledge out of an enlightened respect for true erotic delight. By comparing non-fruition to unread romances, unknown plays, and artful landscapes, he further undergirds his claims with a hedonistic aesthetic.

Given the physiological and psychological unpleasantness of perpetually unfulfilled arousal as well as other poems by Suckling declaring sexual satisfaction the only reasonable goal of heterosexual relations,[50] one cannot of course take this celebration of erotic frustration at face value. Playing with his fellow Cavaliers' rediscovery of the hedonistic mean, Suckling delights in taking their arguments one sophistic step further, praising as the true mean what his contemporaries and predecessors in erotic literature normally treated as a painful extreme. There is a psychologically authentic aspect of the poem, however: the contempt for women and their bodies as the disappointing embodiment of tedious "excess" and the concomitant sense that male fantasy is always superior to female reality. Suckling's diction suggests a male anxiety that in making love to a woman he will lose himself ("the eye [I?] . . . being lost") and his manhood as embodied in his erect phallus ("restraint / Holds up delight, that with excesse would faint"). Thus he reveals the strong misogynistic impulse behind his demystification of "Platonic" love as hedonistic strategy.

While providing a hedonistic reduction of what he considers the posturing of courtly "Platonism," Suckling associates his technique of anti-fruition with aristocratic superiority. In *Aglaura,* female advocates of "Platonic love" contrast their sophistication with the crudity of lower-class lovers:

> Will you then place the happinesse, but there,
> Where the dull plow-man and the plow-mans horse
> Can finde it out? Shall soules refin'd, not know
> How to preserve alive a noble flame?[51]

In the middle stanza of "Against Fruition" (I), the poet adapts this argument to his own purposes:

> Urge not 'tis necessary, alas! we know
> The homeliest thing which mankind does is so;

The World is of a vast extent we see,
And must be peopled; Children then must be;
So must bread too; but since there are enough
Born to the drudgery, what need we plough?

(13-18)

Classical authors use the agricultural metaphor for sex to evoke contempt for sexual love: in Sophocles's *Antigone,* Creon mocks his son Haemon's love for Antigone by noting that if she dies Haemon can still plough other fields (569); in his depiction of sex as a disgusting madness in *De rerum natura,* Lucretius describes love making as "sowing the woman's field" (4.1107). Instilling a particular class resonance to the metaphor, Suckling plays with the commonplace Platonic hierarchy of body and soul and the identification of the lower classes with brutes in order to argue for a new form of aristocratic superiority.[52] The recognition of limits becomes their willful creation, as bored gentlemen seek ways of enlivening the chase. Sophistication replaces the tempering of desire as the ideal.

Suckling died in exile at the opening of the Civil Wars after having attempted to rally troops against Parliament; his anti-fruition poems were published posthumously in 1646. Cowley, another Royalist, published his collection of love poems *The Mistresse* in 1647, while he served the court-in-exile of Henrietta Maria as a diplomat and spy. Following Suckling, in his own poem "Against Fruition" Cowley identifies moderation with a hedonistic refusal of consummation. "Too much riches"—fruition—will destroy love; even amorous "Hopes" will create a "surfeit" unless they are tempered by "Fears."[53] Instead of linking anti-fruition to aristocratic superiority like Suckling, however, Cowley associates anti-fruition more specifically with the royal cause that had been routed in the first English civil war of 1642-46. Representing his mistress as a queen who must rule him properly, Cowley links sexual dalliance short of consummation to the royal mean between tyranny and indulgence that many self-consciously moderate royalists celebrated as the ideal regime (7-10):

> Thou'rt *Queen* of all that sees thee; and as such
> Must neither *Tyrannize,* nor *yield* too much;
> Such *freedoms* give as may admit *Command,*
> But keep the *Forts* and *Magazines* in thine hand.

Cowley's notion that a queen should confer "freedoms" that do not abrogate her "Command" resembles the political message in his friend William Davenant's poetic epistle "To the Queen." Written sometime late in 1640 or early in 1641 with the alienation between Parliament and the King growing, Davenant obliquely criticizes Charles's exercise of the prerogative by complimenting his wife's supposed moderation. He suggests that queens can moderate kings' "extreme obdurateness" and praises Henrietta for realizing that moderation in the exercise of monarchical prerogative actually supports rather than undermines royal power:

> When you have wrought it [the prerogative] to a
>   yieldingness
> That shews it fine but makes it not weigh less.
> Accurst are those Court-Sophisters who say
> When Princes yield, Subjects no more obey.[54]

Some ten years later, Cowley encodes his own continuing allegiance to this moderate royalist position in his anti-fruition poem. Yet in the light of recent history, Cowley shifts the emphasis from the commendation of a monarch's gracious yielding to a ruefully realistic admonition concerning a monarch's prudent preservation of military force. Giving newly topical resonance to Suckling's military analogy of the "Fort resign'd," Cowley reveals how royalist moderation perforce changes its nature with the stresses and polarizations of war.

Cowley's poem is ostensibly much more respectful of female power than Suckling's anti-fruition poems. Yet Cowley's comparison of mistress and monarch perforce demeans the actual queen he serves by diminution, and Cowley implicitly denigrates his true female sovereign by suggesting that his erotic queen should be a more skillful tactician than Henrietta Maria. Celebrating the mean of non-fruition, Cowley simultaneously laments and demeans through trivialization the monarchical cause.

5

With the military defeat of Charles I, praise of the hedonistic mean often represented a Cavalier (and cavalier) rejection of the Parliamentary-Puritan regime. Alexander Brome, for example, wrote many Cavalier poems celebrating wine, women, and song as a response to the Puritan victory. His "Advice to Caelia" modified the traditional carpe diem argument against refusal with a complementary argument against giving in too easily, urging a decorous avoidance of extremes:

> Then while thou'rt fair and young, be kind but wise,
> Doat not, nor proudly use denying;
>
> . . . . .
> There is a knack to find loves treasures;
> Too young, too old, too nice, too free, too slow, destroys your pleasures.[55]

In his *Hesperides* (1648), Herrick challenges the victorious Puritans' world by invoking the mean of coyness in a manner more comprehensive than other Cavalier poets could imagine.[56] Treating the pleasures offered by a coy mistress and by a chaste wife as the same, Herrick obscures the distinction between Protestant celebrations of conjugal temperance and Ovidian and Cavalier calls for a mean of strategic coyness. Herrick further extends the mean of coyness by exploring the links between the erotic pleasure derived from female reserve and other pleasures dependent on restraint, ranging from eating and drinking to the experience of poetry itself.

In a poem entitled "What kind of Mistresse he would have," Herrick suggests his disdain for distinctions among different sorts of women by imagining a mistress who provocatively combines the licit devotion of a wife and the illicit sexuality of a whore:

> Be the Mistresse of my choice,
> Cleane in manners, cleere in voice:
> Be she witty, more then wise;
> Pure enough, though not Precise:
> Be she shewing in her dresse,
> Like a civil Wildernesse;
> That the curious may detect
> Order in a sweet neglect:
> Be she rowling in her eye,
> Tempting all the passers by:
> And each Ringlet of her haire,
> An Enchantment, or a Snare,
> For to catch the Lookers on;
> But her self held fast by none.
> Let her *Lucrece* all day be,
> *Thais* in the night, to me.
> Be she such, as neither will
> *Famish me, nor over-fill.*

(H-665)[57]

Herrick's last four lines offer two formulations concerning the mixture of order and disorder embodied in the perfect erotic partner. Lucretia, the wife who committed suicide after being violated, is the extreme example of the chaste wife; Thais, a Greek courtesan famous for her many lovers,[58] the extreme version of the refined prostitute. The combination of a daytime Lucretia and nightime Thais imagines the mistress's alternating between two extremes, the daylight, public role and the nighttime, private one. Herrick borrows his penultimate couplet from the final couplet of a Martial epigram, in which the Roman poet, attacking his mistress for her cold behavior, wishes for her at least to be a pleasing whore for him at night: "If austerity please you, you may be Lucretia all through the day: Lais I wish for at night" (11.104.21-22). There is a significant difference in attitude, however, between Herrick's and Martial's poems: rather than simply conceding that his mistress may be a daytime Lucretia, as does Martial, Herrick *desires* it. While Martial wishes for a sexually responsive woman without worrying about her relations to others, Herrick desires an oxymoron, a prostitute who is yet, like an early modern wife, his exclusive property. Herrick thus celebrates the target of so much Renaissance misogynistic abuse, female inconsistency—on the condition that he alone can control it.

Female inconsistency provokes—and licenses—the poet's own shifting moods. Herrick's emphasis upon his mistress's seductive frustration of daytime observers suggests his desire not only for personal property but also to experience the daytime observer's frustration as a tantalizing prelude to consummation. Herrick often describes women as spectacle, himself as spectator: in his most famous celebration of female beauty, "Delight in Disorder," Herrick praises a woman wholly in terms of her effect on him as a spectator: he "see[s] a wilde civility" that "bewitch[es]" him more than "Art / . . . too precise in every part" (H-83, 12-14). In his fantasy of the perfect mistress, the opposition between other observers of the daytime woman and the poet of nightly enjoyments partially breaks down, for if she is held fast by none daily, the none includes the poet himself—at least for half the time.

Herrick's title "What kind of Mistresse he would have" recalls the title given in the Renaissance to Ausonius's epigram on the ideal mistress, "Qualem velit amicam," and Herrick follows Ausonius in associating the erotic mean with a provocative combination of opposite extremes of sensation. Herrick's oscillation between the extremes of frustrated voyeur and exclusive possessor motivates the appearance of the mean in the final couplet. Though the connection between the two final couplets is not explicit, their juxtaposition suggests that the woman's combination of the extremes of courtesan and chaste wife, of licentiousness and provocative reserve, allows the poet to experience the contradictory emotions that produce a mean of sexual pleasure between satiety and frustration.

Throughout his poetry Herrick recommends an erotic mean that sharpens pleasure by means of frustration.[59] Love—which Herrick characteristically reduces to sexual relations—is an "extreame" (H-1120, 5) that tends toward a sickening excess:

> Love is a sirrup; and who er'e we see
> Sick and surcharg'd with this sa[t]ietie:
> Shall by this pleasing trespasse quickly prove,
> *Ther's loathsomnesse e'en in the sweeets of love*

(H-949).

Erotic pleasures must therefore be tempered by pains to preclude satiety, as the distich "Another on Love" suggests: "Love's of it self, too sweet; the best of all / Is, when loves hony has a dash of gall" (H-1084). In both Scriptural and classical proverbial lore, honey symbolizes the moral dangers of unrestraint (Proverbs 25:16, 25:27, 27:7; *Greek Anthology* 16:16), and Herrick's "The Hony-combe" (H-909) echoes Scripture to warn against "excess" (3). Herrick's gnomic distich on love, by contrast, uses the common Renaissance figure of honey as sexual pleasure in order to support a hedonistic dictum about erotic joys.[60]

Herrick's marriage poems further erode the boundary between the licit and illicit. Classical and Renaissance epithalamia traditionally describe the bride's combination of desire, which testifies to her virtuous love and consent, and bashfulness, which reveals her chastity.[61] Epithalamia also conventionally depict the bride's virtuous resistance as the (unintended) spur to the husband's increased pleasure, which makes the consummation of marriage sound uncomfortably close to a rape.[62] Herrick, however, collapses these topoi—the one concerned with the bride's morality, the other concerned with the bridegroom's pleasure—by imagining a bride who adheres to a decorous measure *because* it will stimulate the bridegroom's pleasure. Like Ovid, Martial, and Ausonius to their mistresses, he urges that a bride be strategically coy but not too coy. In one poem he commends a bride's "bashfull willingnesse," which combines a "heart consenting" and a "will repenting," because "a measure / Of that Passion sweetens Pleasure" ("An Epithalamie," H-149A, 74-80); in another he warns a bride that "Coyness takes us to a measure; / But o'racted deads the pleasure" ("The delaying Bride," H-850, 5-6); in yet another he uses the Ovidian economic model of sexual pleasure by praising the bride for the "bashfull jealousies" whereby she sets a "price" on herself but warning that "though you slow- / ly go, yet, howsoever, go" ("A Nuptiall Song," H-283, 51-60).

Herrick's reference to the bride's "price" reveals the problem with this understanding of the "economics" of marriage: if the bride sets a "price" on herself by being coy, how can she maintain her value once she is an obedient wife? Epithalamia celebrate a unique, unrepeatable event, the loss of the woman's virginity. (Like many epithalamia writers, Herrick does not assume the man's virginity.) Though epithalamia often express the hope that the couple will long maintain their conjugal pleasures, the male pleasure in overcoming the virgin bride's resistance raises a problem: will not the bride's submission to her husband and her loss of the fear that causes her to resist lead to his becoming bored? Alone among major epithalamia writers, Herrick explicitly addresses this problem. In "Connubii Flores" (H-633), a chorus of old men advises moderation during the connubial rites:

> Go to your banquet then, but use delight,
> So as to rise still with an appetite.
> Love is a thing most nice; and must be fed
> To such a height; but never surfeited.
> What is beyond the mean is ever ill:
> *'Tis best to feed Love; but not over-fill*;
> Go then discreetly to the Bed of pleasure;
> And this remember, *Vertue keepes the measure.*
>
> (18-25)

Herrick once more disburdens the traditional call for conjugal temperance of ethical weight by collapsing it with purely hedonistic imperatives. The old men advise the couple to adhere to the ethical mean with appropriately sententious maxims, but moderation is here advised to avoid precluding future sensual pleasures. The old men's joint address to husband and wife masks a characteristic asymmetry: the puns on the male erection ("rise still," "fed / To such a height") reveal Herrick's

focus on the preservation of the *male's* pleasure, with the bride figured as the (strategically coy) provider of enduring pleasure.

Herrick's use of a chorus of old men to advise the couple regarding the preservation of sexual delight through moderation seems intentionally comic. It certainly underscores the poet's subversive blurring of traditional ethical considerations with hedonistic motives. In Elizabethan literature, old men's advice to young men traditionally combine calls for moderation with stern warnings against sexual pleasure. In John Lyly's *Euphues* (1578), for example, the old man Euboulos who advises the young Euphues to be "merrye . . . with modestie" warns against "luste" and lascivious "Syrens."[63] In Thomas Lodge's *Rosalynde* (1590), a dying father advises his sons to keep the "most safe, middle way" ("medium tutissimum") and "above all" to "beware of love, for it is far more perilous than pleasant."[64] Herrick's old men, by contrast, wish youth to prolong—rather than avoid—erotic pleasure. In several lyrics, Herrick portrays himself as the elderly would-be lover of the Anacreonic tradition, comically or pathetically seeking erotic "sport" despite his loss of physical vitality (H-43, H-527, H-852). The epithalamium's avuncular counselors issue the poet's own wistful advice that youth preserve as long as possible love's fleeting pleasures, and expressions of wise moderation become a vicarious means of reimagining a young man's joys.

Herrick's most startling move in his marriage poetry is to imagine the male's truest conjugal pleasure as the continuing deflowering of the bride. In "Julia's Churching, or Purification," the poet claims that

> She who keeps chastly to her husbands side
> Is not for one, but every night his Bride:
> And stealing still with love, and feare to Bed,
> Brings him not one, but many a Maiden-head
>
> (H-898, 13-16)

Heather Dubrow has discussed passages like this one in terms of Herrick's fears and ambivalence concerning the loss of virginity, which he associates with transience and mutability.[65] The ambivalence regarding virginity is undeniable, and it is no accident that Herrick described himself as a virginal "Maid" (H-235). Dubrow does not take into account, however, Herrick's evident pleasure in imagining himself in the virile husband's role. Like all of Herrick's other strategic deployments of moderation, the fantasy of continually being able to deflower one's wife takes the sting, the boredom, out of fulfillment. According to a classical and Renaissance misogynist commonplace, a wife provided but two pleasant moments, the night she is deflowered and the day she dies: on the wedding night alone, to quote a sixteenth-century text, "The Bride is fresh and new, and all new things are pleasaunt."[66] Herrick imagines the wife as an ever-renewable bride, so that the husband has the satisfaction of being ever to receive "many" rather than merely "one" "Maidenhead."

Once more the increase of pleasure is not mutual, for it is the man's pleasure that is at stake. Indeed the woman's *fear* is itself a spur to the man's pleasure. Herrick has transformed a standard feature of Protestant marriage ideology: the call for obedient wives not only to love but also to fear in the sense of revere their authoritative husbands.[67] By localizing the wife's fear within the couple's nightly lovemaking, Herrick reductively equates the wife's fear-as-reverence to a virgin's sexual fear of penetration. The chaste wife's enduring fear allows the husband to feel some of the transgressive charm of an illicit act within the most licit form of sexuality.

In "A Country life: To his Brother, Master Thomas Herrick" (H-106), Herrick similarly celebrates the joys of restrained conjugal sexuality. Praising his brother's retired moderation in various aspects of daily life, the poet commends his brother for "cool[ing]" his appetites (26) and adhering to the mean of liberality, knowing how much to "spend" and "spare" and thus avoid "extreame[s]" (129-132). Near the end of the poem Herrick connects virtuous moderation to erotic satisfaction when he advises that his brother's conjugal pleasures also be regulated by the mean:

> Thus let thy Rurall Sanctuary be
> *Elizium* to thy wife and thee;
> There to disport your selves with golden measure:
> *For seldome use commends the pleasure.*

> (137-140)

Moderation or the "golden measure" (139) is not only more virtuous but also more pleasurable than excess because sexual restraint increases the pleasure of erotic fulfillment. The final line applies to sex the same hedonistic argument for temperance that Herrick applies earlier in the poem to eating when praising his brother's moderation with respect to food: "Hunger makes coarse meats, delicates" (110).

Herrick's two gnomic utterances concerning moderation—"Hunger makes coarse meats delicates" and "For seldome use commends the pleasure"—diverge from Aristotelian understandings of the mean but derive from a strong hedonistic current within classical and Renaissance thought. Xenophon claims that Socrates "ate just sufficient food to make eating a pleasure, and he was so ready for his food that he found appetite the best sauce; and any kind of drink he found pleasant, because he drank only when he was thirsty" (*Memorabilia,* 1.3.5).[68] Socrates's understanding of temperance as providing the most pleasure is central to the two major, competing

Hellenistic schools of ethics, Epicureanism and Stoicism. Epicurus claims that bread and water "confer the highest possible pleasure when they are brought to hungry lips" (Diogenes Laertius 10.130-31); in Cicero's *De finibus,* a Stoic approvingly cites Socrates's claim that "the best sauce for food is hunger and the best flavouring for drink thirst" (2.28.90); and Seneca claims hunger will make even bad bread "delicate" (*Epistuale ad Lucilium* 123.2). Erasmus popularized this form of temperate hedonism in the Renaissance. In the *Adagia,* Erasmus associates the Socratic dictum that "hunger is the best sauce" with the Juvenalian claim (here given in Richard Taverner's translation) that "seldom use of pleasures maketh the same the more pleasaunt" (*Satire* 11.208). In his colloquy *Epicureus,* Erasmus cites these two classical dicta in support of his own brand of Christian hedonism.[69] Quoting the same two classical maxims as Erasmus, Herrick provides a similarly hedonistic understanding of moderation.

Herrick's recommendation that his brother practice "seldome use" in his conjugal sexual relations contradicts, however, his earlier celebration of his sister-in-law's chaste but nightly yielding of herself to her husband: "But still thy wife, by chast intentions led, / Gives thee each night a Maidenhead" (41-42). As in "Julia's Churching," Herrick suggests that a wife's chastity provides the husband, over and over again, with the excitement of the wedding night's deflowering of a reluctant maiden. The contradictory celebration of the wife's chaste but nightly offering of herself and of "seldome use" suggests their equivalence in terms of the poet's hedonic calculus; both are conceived of simply as strategies for increasing the husband's pleasure.

Herrick's poems on the ideal mistress and wife intertwine sexual and aesthetic values, and Herrick's recommended strategies for increasing and prolonging erotic pleasure parallel his poetic strategies for increasing and prolonging the reader's aesthetic pleasure by avoiding both frustration and satiety. Critics have discussed generic variety as a structural principle in Herrick's *Hesperides,*[70] but they have not explored the way this variety reflects Herrick's conception of both sexual and textual pleasure as a hedonistic mean. Renaissance writers categorized epigrams into "mel" ("honey"), on the one hand, and various contrasting qualities of "fel" ("gall"), "acetum" ("vinegar"), and "sal" ("salt").[71] When Herrick claims "loves hony" should have "a dash of gall" (H-1084), his use of traditional literary terms hints that his book's mixing of sweet lyrics and bitter or salty satiric and comic epigrams parallels the necessary mixture of indulgence and restraint in love.[72]

Just as Herrick's conception of a mean of erotic pleasure derives from ancient love poetry, so his conception of a mean of aesthetic pleasure based on variety derives from ancient rhetorical and symposiastic lore, discourses more open to the valorization of pleasure than was ethical theory. In his *Rhetoric,* which often propounds popular Greek views more amenable to a hedonistic ethics than the *Nicomachean Ethics,* Aristotle notes that change is pleasant because perpetual sameness is an unpleasant "excess" (*hyperbole*) (1.11.20). Plutarch (to quote Philemon Holland's Jacobean translation) similarly notes that "varietie" is itself "very pleasing" and argues that the competent symposiarch (the leader of a drinking party) mixes the playful and the serious "with measure" in order to prevent the excess of one quality or the other.[73] Such associations of variety and moderation informed both literary theory and practice. In *De oratore* 3.98-102, Cicero notes that excessive pleasure causes satiety and that poems and speeches must therefore not be sweet without "relief or check or variety." While in *Poetaster* Jonson sharply distinguished the decorous relations between poets and rulers from the relations between lovers and coy mistresses, Martial treats such relations as similar. Martial's preface to Book 8 of his epigrams notes that he will "diversify" his book, mixing serious praise of Domitian with "pleasantry" in order to avoid "wearying" the emperor with unmodulated celebration. Thus the poet will avoid satiating the emperor just as he asks a mistress, through coyness, to avoid wearying him. Martial's contemporary Pliny the Younger, notes in his letters his (lost) poetry's variety of subject matter and style and associates such variety with the avoidance of unpleasant extremes: "In literature, as in life, I think it a becoming sign of humanity to mingle grave and gay, lest the one becomes too austere and the other indelicate" (*Epistulae,* 8.21.1). Like these classical writers, Herrick seeks to follow nature and avoid excess by mingling the grave and gay—in epigrammatic literature as in erotic life.

6

While Herrick provides the most wide-ranging version of the Cavalier mean of coyness, one of his female contemporaries provides the most trenchant rejection of Cavalier sexual values. Using Cavalier motifs against the Cavaliers, Katherine Philips invokes the mean to proclaim the validity of a woman's life independent of men's desires. Her poem "The Virgin," published posthumously in 1667 but probably written in the 1650s, idealizes a virgin whose moderation is not subservient to men:

> The things that make a Virgin please,
> She that seeks, will find them these;
> A Beauty, not to Art in debt,
> Rather agreeable than great;
> An Eye, wherein at once do meet,
> The beams of kindness, and of wit;
> An undissembled Innocence,
> Apt nor to give, nor take offense:
> A Conversation, at once, free
> From Passion, and from Subtlety;

> A Face that's modest, yet serene,
> A sober, and yet lively Meen,
> The vertue which does her adorn,
> By honour guarded, not by scorn;
> With such wise lowliness indu'd,
> As never can be mean, or rude;
> That prudent negligence enrich [sic],
> And Time's her silence and her speech;
> Whose equal mind, does alwaies move,
> Neither a foe, nor a slave to Love;
> And whose Religion's strong and plain,
> Not superstitious, nor prophane.[74]

Philips' description of the qualities that "make a Virgin please" recalls the tradition that begins with the Jonsonian Hermogenes' Martial-inspired description of "What would please me in my lover." Yet Philips sharply deviates from her masculine predecessors by neglecting to identify precisely to whom the ideal virgin is pleasing. Philips thus suggests that the ideal virgin is pleasing to all people—including herself. Though the focus on the virgin's moderation regarding love ("Neither a foe, nor slave to Love") recalls earlier poetic celebrations of the virgin's temperate behavior toward potential male suitors, Philips declares her own love for other women so often in her poems that the gender of the ideal virgin's audience is indeterminate.[75] Such indeterminacy frees the virgin from her normal status in seventeenth-century English male poetry as a mere bride-to-be. Ideal virginity is a perfect, complete state in itself, rather than a way station to union with and dependence upon a man.

Philips further emphasizes the virgin's freedom as a moral agent by applying to her attitudes towards love a Stoic language of self-sufficiency normally used of men. Her "equall mind" in matters of love recalls the Stoic ideal of the man who preserves his inner freedom and equanimity whatever his external circumstances. Horace claims that one can find contentment in any situation if one has an "equal mind" ("animus . . . aequus," *Epistle* 1.11.30; cf. *Epistle* 1.18.112); Seneca frequently praises the wise man's "aequus animus" in the face of adverse fortune;[76] echoing these Roman authors, Jonson praises the "equal mind" of Robert Carr, earl of Salisbury, who supposedly contents himself with his own good deeds rather than depending upon the often erroneous "public voice" of fame (*Epigram* 63. 6-8).[77]

Philips gives her ideal virgin not only a Stoic but also a deeply Christian subjectivity that preserves her ultimate independence of body and soul. The final couplet's praise of the virgin's "Religion," which is neither "superstitious" nor "prophane," evokes the traditional conception of true religion, first expounded by Plutarch and widely accepted in early modern England, as a mean between superstition and atheism or unbelief.[78] The concluding couplet raises the virgin's concern for moderation from the merely social realm of manners to a transcendent realm of devotion in order to suggest that the virgin's ultimate approbative audience is neither male nor female human beings but God. One might compare an early, unpublished poem by Philips that praises the virgin's life for allowing women spiritual access to God unhindered by earthly duties to men: "No Blustering husbands to create yr fears. . . . / Few worldly crosses to distract yr prayers."[79] Philips, herself married to a husband working for the Interregnum government but with a social circle that was heavily Royalist, uses a formulation of the mean of true religion vague enough to be accepted by English Protestants across the spectrum and thus effectively removes the ideal virgin's views from the raging conflict amongst the various religious factions in Interregnum England. The virgin is thus "protected" from the vagaries of both seventeenth-century socioreligious conflict and male desire.

Philips further distances her views from Cavalier celebrations of coy women by echoing a very different kind of poem equally beloved by the Cavaliers, Martial's famous epigram celebrating the happy, contented life of the man of retirement (10.47), which was translated and imitated in the seventeenth century by Jonson and several of the Sons of Ben (including Randolph, Cowley, Mildmay Fane, and Charles Cotton). Philips's first couplet—"The things that make a Virgin please, / She that seeks, will find them these"—signals her debt by recalling the opening couplet of Martial's poem ("Vitam quae faciant beatiorem . . . / haec sunt"), especially as rendered in the first line of Jonson's translation ("The things that make the happier life, are these"). Both the accretive structure and emphasis upon moderation in Philips's poem further recall Martial's epigram, as this extract from Jonson's translation suggests (2-10):

> Substance got with ease,
> Not laboured for, but left thee by thy sire;
>
> . . . . .
>
> A quiet mind; free powers; and body sound;
> A wise simplicity [prudens simplicitas]; friends alike-
>   stated;
> Thy table without art, and easy-rated;
> Thy night not drunken, but from cares laid waste;
> No sour, or sullen bed-mate, yet a chaste.[80]

The "wise lowliness" and moderation of Philips's virgin recall the "wise simplicity" and moderation of Martial's happy man. By evoking Martial's portrait of an independent and morally responsible male rather than his sketches of coyly seductive objects of male desire, Philips combats the gender hierarchy assumed by Martial and his Cavalier imitators. Philips's modifications of Martial's vision of true happiness further combats the patriarchal values of the Roman poet and his English imitators. While Martial's epigram celebrates patrilineal descent, the material estate passed from father to son, Philips's poem celebrates a moral estate

that the virgin obtains in and for herself. While Martial includes as one of the contented man's possessions a wife who pleases him with a moderation that reduces her to a "bedmate" neither too cold nor wanton, Philips's virgin pleases all with a moderation that preserves her integrity as a moral agent.

Late seventeenth-century male "libertine" poets closely follow the Cavaliers' celebration of the mean of female coyness—with a stale repetitiveness, indeed, that belies the poets' alleged desire to escape satiety.[81] Philips's poem, by contrast, provides an original and defiant counter-statement, all the stronger for its Roman classicism, to the Cavalier erotic tradition inspired by Roman poetry and inaugurated by the Jonsonian Hermogenes' song.

Notes

1. On early Christian views regarding sexuality, see Peter Brown, *The Body and Society: Men, Women and Sexual Renunciation in Early Christianity* (New York: Columbia University Press, 1988). For the development of the ideal of temperance within marriage from the Greeks to the Reformation, see James A. Brundage, *Law, Sex, and Christian Society in Medieval Europe* (Chicago: University of Chicago Press, 1987). On the early modern English ideal of moderate sexual activity within marriage, see Richard L. Greaves, *Society and Religion in Elizabethan England* (Minneapolis: University of Minnesota Press, 1981), 223-28; Ralph A. Houlbrooke, *The English Family, 1450-1700* (London: Longman, 1984), 103; and Lawrence Stone, *The Family, Sex, and Marriage in England, 1500-1800* (New York: Harper, 1977), 498-501.

2. *The Workes of William Gouge* (London, 1627), 130. Cf. Robert Cleaver, *A Godlie form of Householde Government* (1598), 158, 163-64.

3. Alexander Niccholes, *A Discourse of Marriage and Wiving* (London, 1620), 7. Roland M. Frye cites many such warnings against transient lust in "The Teachings of Classical Puritanism on Conjugal Love," *Studies in the Renaissance* 2 (1955): 156-58. An Elizabethan ballad enunciates the widely-held view that love's endurance depended on moderation: "Love that is too hot and strong / Burneth soon to waste: / Still, I would not have thee cold, / Not too backward, nor too bold. / . . . / Constant love is moderate ever, / And it will through life persèver" ("Love me Little, Love me long," in Norman Ault, ed., *Elizabethan Lyrics* [New York: Capricorn Books, 1949], 61).

4. In Michel Foucault's terms, the poets transfer the concept of the mean from the domain of *scientia sexualis* to that of *ars erotica*; see *The History of*

Sexuality, vol. 1: An Introduction, trans. Robert Hurley (New York: Random House, 1978), 53-73. Foucault himself notes that the two domains are complexly interrelated in Western culture despite their evident opposition (70-73). Recent critics have explored the interest of seventeenth-century poets in coyness as a stimulus to male desire and pleasure; see Gerald Hammond, *Fleeting Things: English Poets and Poems, 1616-1660* (Cambridge, Mass.: Harvard University Press, 1990), 302-305; William Kerrigan and Gordon Braden, *The Idea of the Renaissance* (Baltimore: Johns Hopkins Univ. Press, 1989), especially 183-89 and 200-206. These studies do not explore, however, poetic applications of the mean to the psychology of desire.

5. Houlbrooke, 96-102.

6. Publius Syrus's proverbs, studied in Elizabethan grammar schools, contain the famous adage, "A woman either loves, or hates, there is no third thing" ("Aut amat aut odit mulier: nihil est tertium"). Thomas Nashe cites the proverb in *The Anatomie of Absurditie* (1589); see *The Works of Thomas Nashe,* ed. Ronald B. McKerrow, rev. F. P. Wilson, 5 vols. (Oxford: Basil Blackwell, 1958), 1:15; for Shakespearean variants, see Hamlet III.ii. 162-3, and Charles G. Smith, *Shakespeare's Proverb Lore* (Cambridge, Ma.: Harvard University Press, 1963), 131. For other Renaissance assertions of women's emotional extremism, see Baldesar Castiglione, *The Book of the Courtier,* trans. Sir Thomas Hoby (1561; reprint, New York: AMS Press, 1967), 239; George Pettie, *A Petite Pallace of Pettie His Pleasure* (1576), ed. Herbert Hartman (London: Oxford University Press, 1938), 37-38; John Lyly, *Euphues: The Anatomy of Wit* (1578) in *The Complete Works of John Lyly,* ed. R. Warwick Bond, 3 vols. (Oxford; Clarendon, 1902), 1:253; and Joseph Swetnam, *The Araignment of . . . Women* (London, 1622), 18. Leonard Wright explicitly associates women's extremism with their dangerous disobedience: "Most women by nature are saide to be . . . all in extreames without meane, either loving dearely or hating deadly: desirous rather to rule than to be ruled" (*A Display of Dutie . . .* [London, 1589], 36). The male's authoritative moderation was thus essential.

7. Cited and discussed in Lisa Jardine, *Still Harping on Daughters: Women and Drama in the Age of Shakespeare* (Sussex: Harvester Press, 1983), 43-44. In a seventeenth-century manuscript poem, a man resolves to curb his future wife's emotional extremes: "If shee sleepe I'le raise her upp, / if proude I'le take her downe, / for womans humors they are such, / they either want or have to[o] muche" ("I cannot call my mistress fayre," in *Sev-*

enteenth Century Songs and Lyrics, ed. John P. Cutts [Columbia, Mo.: University of Missouri Press, 1959], 167).

8. *The Sermons of Edwin Sandys,* ed. John Ayre, The Parker Society (Cambridge; Cambridge University Press, 1842), 318; Samuel Hieron, "Marriage-Blessing," in *The Sermons of Master Samuell Hieron* (London, 1635), 470.

9. For an excellent discussion of Jonson's self-presentation in *Poetaster,* see Richard Helgerson, *Self-Crowned Laureates: Spenser, Jonson, Milton, and the Literary System* (Berkeley: University of California Press, 1983), 111-16.

10. Jonson, *Poetaster,* II.ii.163-72, 179-88 in *The Complete Plays of Ben Jonson,* 4 vols., ed. G. A. Wilkes (Oxford: Clarendon, 1981), 2:148-49.

11. Patrick Hannay, "A Happy Husband . . . Together with a Wives Behaviour after Marriage," 2d ed. (1622) in *The Poetical Works of Patrick Hannay* (1622; reprint, New York: Benjamin Blom, 1968), 168.

12. Martial, *Epigrams,* 1.57, Loeb trans. modified. All translations of classical works are, unless otherwise specified, from the Loeb Classical Library.

13. On the popularity of *De officiis* among English humanists and its place in the English educational curriculum, see the editor's introduction to Nicholas Grimald, trans., *Marcus Tullius Ciceroes Thre Bokes of Duties* (1556), ed. Gerald O'Gorman (Washington: Folger Shakespeare Library, 1990), 13-15. Thomas Elyot recommends that a student first read the first two books of the *Nicomachean Ethics* and then proceed to *De officiis* (*The Book named the Governor,* ed. S. E. Lehmberg [London: Dent, 1962], 39). Nicholas Grimald claims that Cicero's treatise surpasses Aristotle's *Nicomachean Ethics* because of its "lightsomnesse, and eloquent handeling" (Grimald, 45-46). Philip Sidney informs his brother that *Nicomachean Ethics* is philosophically supreme but "dark," while *De officiis* is perhaps "not equal" to Aristotle but is (presumably in terms of applicability) "for you and myself, beyond any" (*Sir Philip Sidney: Oxford Authors,* ed. Katherine Duncan-Jones [Oxford: Oxford University Press, 1989], 288).

14. On courtesy books and the early modern regulation of behavior, see Norbert Elias, *The Civilizing Process: The Development of Manners,* trans. Edmund Jephcott (New York: Urizen Books, 1978); on the courtesy book in Renaissance England, see Frank Whigham, *Ambition and Privilege: The Social Tropes of Elizabethan Courtesy Theory* (Berkeley: University of California Press, 1984). Neither study examines the pervasive Ciceronian influence upon these works.

15. On Castiglione's diverse applications of the mean, see Albert D. Menut, "Castiglione and the *Nicomachean Ethics*," *PMLA* 58 (1943): 320-321, and J. R. Woodhouse, *Baldesar Castiglione: A Reassessment of the Courtier* (Edinburgh: Edinburgh University Press, 1978), 44-45, 72-73, 98-102. Neither of these studies notes that the primary source for Castiglione's understanding of the mean is Cicero rather than Aristotle.

16. Giovanni della Casa, *Galataeo,* trans. Robert Peterson (London, 1576), 89-90, 94, 108; Stefano Guazzo, *The Civile Conversation,* trans. George Pettie and Batholomew Young, 2 vols. (1581-86; reprint, London: Constable, 1925), 1:101, 130, 133, 135, 151, 214, 231.

17. Elyot, 80-8; *The Institucion of a Gentleman* (London, 1568; reprint, London, 1839), 90; John Ferne, *The Blazon of Gentrie* (London, 1586), 113. For later examples, see *The Political Works of James I,* intro. Charles Howard McIlwain (New York: Russell & Russell, 1965), 45-47; Richard Brathwaite, *The English Gentleman* (London, 1630), 356.

18. Modern scholars generally believe that the butt of Horace's *Satire* 3 is Tigellius the elder rather than the younger musician, Tigellius Hermogenes, satirized elsewhere in Horace's *Satires*; see Alain Baudot, *Musiciens romains de l'antiquité* (Montréal: Les presses de l'université de Montréal, 1973), 73-77. The ancient scholiasts and their Renaissance heirs, however, conflated the two figures, so Jonson undoubtedly did the same; see Porphyrion's note in F. Plessis et P. Lejay, ed., *Oeuvres d'Horace: Satires* (Paris: Librairie Hachette, 1911), 38, n. 3.

19. Jonson, *Poetaster,* II.ii.201-202 in *Complete Plays,* 1:149. The extremism of musicians might have been an early modern stereotype. An Elizabethan writer compares women's extremism to that of musicians "who being intreated, will scant sing . . . but undesired, straine to sing" (Wright, 36). Hermogenes the musician is as "womanish" in his extremism as the woman he desires.

20. Jonson, *Poetaster,* V.i.50-52, V.i. 61-64 in *Complete Plays,* 2:199. While Jonson recalls Horace's depiction of Augustus as a ruler who showed good judgment in bestowing gifts upon worthy poets (*Epistle* 2.1.245-8), the Jonsonian emphasis upon avoiding the two extremes of not giving to the meritorious or giving to the undeserving recalls classical philosophic discussions of liberality as a mean: see Aristotle, *Nicomachean Ethics* IV.i; Cicero, *De officiis* 2.15.54-2.16.64; and Seneca, *De beneficiis* 1.15.3, 2. 15.3-2.16.2.

21. Jonson, *Complete Plays,* 1:127.

22. Ibid., 121.

23. On the links Jonson would have recognized between Horatian poetry and Martial's epigrams, see Wesley Trimpi, *Ben Jonson's Poems: A Study of the Plain Style* (Palo Alto, Calif.: Stanford University Press, 1962), 16-19.

24. *The Poetical and Dramatic Works of Thomas Randolph,* ed. W. Carew Hazlitt (London, 1875), 194.

25. Randolph, "*A Complaint against* Cupid . . . ," 132-33, 150-52 in *The Poems and Amyntas of Thomas Randolph,* ed. John Jay Parry (New Haven: Yale University Press, 1917), 82.

26. Randolph, "Ausonii Epigram 38," in Randolph, ed. Parry, 144. In line 14 I have emended "act," the reading of the posthumous 1638 edition of Randolph's poems retained by all subsequent editions, to "art." Randolph's translation is very faithful to Ausonius's poem, which has "art" ("artem") in the equivalent line, "art" makes far better poetic sense, and the misprint is easy. Randolph's numbering of the poem follows Joseph Scaliger's edition, which renders the epigram thus: "Hanc volo, quae non vult. Illam, quae vult, ego nolo. / Vincere vult animos, non satiare Venus. / Oblatas sperno illecebras, detrecto negatas: / Nec satiare animum, nec cruciare volo. / Nec bis cincta Diana placet, nec nuda Cythere. / Illa voluptatis nil habet, haec nimium. / Callida sed mediae Veneris mihi venditet artem / Femina: quae iugat, quod volo nolo vocet" (Ausonius, *Opera,* ed. Joseph Scaliger and Elia Vineto [Geneva, 1588], 11).

27. On the paradoxically extreme nature of female virtue in Renaissance thought, which can be traced back to the Church fathers, see Ian Maclean, *The Renaissance Notion of Woman* (Cambridge: Cambridge University Press, 1980), 7, 16, 97 n. 7 and 100 n. 66; and Howard Bloch's discussion of the Christian treatment of woman as "perpetual overdetermination—either too rich or too poor, too beautiful or not beautiful enough, too rational or out of her senses" in *Medieval Misogyny and the Invention of Western Romantic Love* (Chicago: University of Chicago, 1991), 65-95 (citation on p. 90). Claiming that all women deviate from the "golden mean" into "extremes," the late Cavalier poet Charles Cotton's "The Joys of a Marriage" alleges that every woman is "either Saint or Devil" (*Poems of Charles Cotton, 1630-1687,* ed. John Bereford [London: Richard Cobden-Sanderson, 1923], 319). Wives who die for their husbands can be simultaneously praised for their devotion and condemned for their extremism: see, e.g., Castiglione, 239, and Pettie, 38. Edmund Tilney has a female defender of women stoutly defend

their having "no meane in love" in his dialogue *A Brief and Pleasant Discourse* (London, 1568), D7r; the author himself seems to view women's "extreme" devotion to men with patronizing approval.

28. Robert Greene, *The Life and Complete Works,* ed. A. B. Grosart, 15 vols. (London: Huth Library, 1881-6), 8:127; "Are women fair and are they sweet?" in *More Lyrics from the Song-Books of the Elizabethan Age,* ed. A. H. Bullen (London, 1888), 5.

29. See Brendan O'Hehir, "Balanced Opposites in the Poetry of Pope, and the Historical Evolution of the Concept" (Ph.D. dissertation, Johns Hopkins University, 1959); and Joshua Scodel, "'Mediocrities' and 'Extremities': Francis Bacon and the Aristotelian Mean," in *Creative Imitation: New Essays on Renaissance Literature,* ed. David Quint et al. (Binghamton, N.Y.: SUNY Binghamton Press, 1992), 104-105.

30. Ausonius, *Opera,* 3, trans. mine.

31. Owen Fel[l]tham, *Resolves, Divine, Moral, and Political,* ed. James Cumming (London, 1820), 155.

32. Randolph, ed. Parry, 240-41, 285 (*Amyntas* I.i.44-80, III.i.58-60).

33. Alan Macfarlane, *Marriage and Love in England: Modes of Reproduction, 1300-1840* (Oxford: Basil Blackwell, 1986), 294-98 (quotation on p. 298); cf. John R. Gillis, *For Better, For Worse: British Marriages, 1600 to the Present* (New York and Oxford: Oxford University Press, 1985), 30-31.

34. *Lyrics from English Airs, 1596-1622,* ed. Edward Doughtie (Cambridge, Mass.: Harvard University Press, 1970), 396.

35. Castiglione, 217.

36. Ann Rosalind Jones, "Nets and Bridles: Early Modern Conduct Books and Sixteenth-Century Women's Lyrics," in *The Ideology of Conduct: Essays in Literature and the History of Sexuality,* ed. Nancy Armstrong and Leonard Tenenhouse (New York and London: Methuen, 1987), 44-46 and 52-63.

37. Francis Quarles, *Argalus and Parthenia,* ed. David Freeman (Washington: Folger Shakespeare Library, 1986), 53.

38. George Wither, *Fair Virtue, or The Mistresse of Philarete,* 2467-68, 3601-3652, in *The Poetry of George Wither,* ed. Frank Sidgwick, 2 vols. (London: A. H. Bullen, 1902), 2:94, 132-34; Wye Saltonstall, "A Maide," in *Picturae Loquentes*

(1631, 1635; reprint, Oxford: Basil Blackwell, 1946), 9, 15. For later advice along the same lines, see Cotton's "Old Tityrus to Eugenia," in Cotton, 144-46.

39. Fulke Greville, "Caelica: Sonnet LXXV," ll. 154-58 in *Poems and Dramas of Fulke Greville, First Lord Brooke,* ed. Geoffrey Bullough, 2 vols. (London: Oliver and Boyd, 1939), 1:125.

40. For a careful discussion of Roman and English Renaissance writers' treatment of the proximity of virtuous means and vicious extremes, see Quentin Skinner, "Moral Ambiguity and the Renaissance Art of Eloquence," *Essays in Criticism* 44 (1994): 267-92. Skinner notes that moralists decried but rhetoricians neutrally described or celebrated the possibilities of confusion; he does not note that both attitudes are traceable back to Aristotle.

41. *The Plays and Poems of William Cartwright,* ed. G. Blakemore Evans (Madison: University of Wisconsin Press, 1951), 483.

42. Torquato Tasso, *Jerusalem Delivered,* trans. Edward Fairfax, intro. John Charles Nelson (1600; reprint, New York: Putnam, 1963), 69 (canto 4, stanzas 31-32); Edmund Spenser, *The Faerie Queene,* ed. A. C. Hamilton (London: Longmans, 1977), 293.

43. Cartwright, 483-84.

44. Erica Veevers provides the most detailed discussion of Caroline Neoplatonism in *Images of Love and Religion: Queen Henrietta Maria and Court Entertainments* (Cambridge: Cambridge University Press, 1989). Cf. Kevin Sharpe, *Criticism and Compliment: The Politics of Literature in the England of Charles I* (Cambridge: Cambridge University Press, 1987), 64-68; and Lawrence Venuti, *Our Halcyon Dayes: English Prerevolutionary Texts and Postmodern Culture* (Madison, Wisc.: University of Wisconsin Press, 1989), 220-60.

45. *The Works of Sir John Suckling, vol. 1: The Non-Dramatic Works,* ed. Thomas Clayton (Oxford: Clarendon, 1971), 42, 27.

46. *The Works of Sir John Suckling, vol. 2: The Plays,* ed. L. A. Beaurline (Oxford: Clarendon Press, 1971), 47, 56 (*Aglaura* I.v.8-10, 49-50, II.ii.24-29, 35).

47. Suckling, 1:37-38.

48. Jonson, "Fragmentum Petron. Arbitr. The Same Translated," in Ben Jonson, *The Complete Poems,* ed. George Parfitt (New Haven: Yale University Press, 1975), 251.

49. "Disdaine me still, that I may ever love," in John Dowland, *A Pilgrimes Solace* (London, 1603), I, in Doughtie, 402.

50. See, for example, "I pray thee spare me, gentle boy . . . ," in Suckling, 51-52.

51. Suckling, 2:47 (_Aglaura_ I.v.16-19).

52. Cf. the Platonic Theander of Davenant's _The Platonic Lovers,_ who describes consummation as "coarse and homely drudgeries" necessary only to generate those who "fill up armies, villages, / And city shops" (II.i, in _The Dramatic Works of Sir William D'Avenant,_ ed. J. Maidment and W. H. Logan, 5 vols. [Edinburgh, 1872-4], 2:43).

53. Abraham Cowley, "Against Fruition," 16, 29-30, in _The Collected Works of Abraham Cowley,_ volume 2, part 1 (_The Mistress_), ed. Thomas O. Calhoun et al. (Newark: University of Delaware Press), 58-59.

54. Sir William Davenant, "To the Queen," 19, 39-42 in Davenant, _The Shorter Poems, and Songs from the Plays and Masques_ (Oxford: Clarendon, 1972), 139-40; cf. Sharpe, 98-100.

55. Alexander Brome, "Advice to Caelia," 35-36, in his _Poems,_ ed. Roman R. Dubinski, 2 vols. (Toronto: Univ. of Toronto Press, 1982), 1:109.

56. Paul R. Jenkins provides an excellent close reading of Herrick's treatment of moderation and the mean in "Rethinking what Moderation Means to Robert Herrick," _ELH_ 39 (1972): 49-65. Jenkins is misleading, however, regarding literary and cultural history: his contrast between Herrick's "modern" concern with a "sensational psychology" (63) and ancient ethical views of moderation neglects Herrick's Roman models, and Jenkins does not sufficiently contextualize Herrick's "modern" position within seventeenth-century erotic discourses.

57. All citations and the numbering of the poems are from _The Complete Poetry of Robert Herrick,_ ed. J. Max Patrick (Garden City, N.Y.: Doubleday, 1963).

58. See Propertius, _Elegy_ 2.6.4.

59. See Jenkins, 59.

60. Eric Partridge provides several examples of Shakespeare's use of "honey" as the "sweets of sexual pleasure" in _Shakespeare's Bawdy_ (New York: Dutton, 1960), 100, 128 (s.v., "delight," s.v., "honey").

61. The fifteenth-century poet Giovanni Pontano describes the bride as one who simultaneously both "fears and desires" in _Carmen nuptiale tibicinem alloquitur_ (cited in Forster, _The Icy Fire: Five Studies in European Petrarchism_ [Cambridge: Cambridge University Press, 1969], 109). Forster ascribes the taste for antitheses concerning the bride's emotion to the combination of two different cultural tropes—the Petrarchan lady, chaste and hardhearted, and the necessity of surrender in a marriage poem (114-15). Classical epithalamia traditionally dwell, however, on female modesty as well as the necessary surrender of virginal bride; see, e.g., Claudian's description of the bride's "pudor" in _Fescennina_ 4.3.

62. See, e.g., Claudian's address to the bridegroom concerning the bride's refusals: "The difficult struggle increases the joy; the desire for that which flies us is the most inflamed" (_Fescennina_ 4, 11-12, Loeb trans. modified).

63. Lyly, 1:189-90.

64. Thomas Lodge, _Rosalynde, or Euphues' Golden Legacy,_ ed. Edward Chauncey Baldwin (Boston: Ginn and Company, 1910), 3-4.

65. Heather Dubrow, _A Happier Eden: The Politics of Marriage in the Stuart Epithalamion_ (Ithaca: Cornell University Press, 1990), 239-42.

66. Pierre Bouaistuau, _Theatrum Mundi,_ trans. J. Alday (London, 1566?), 136, cited in Chilton Latham Powell, _English Domestic Relations, 1487-1653_ (New York: Columbia University Press, 1917), 153. Cf. Cartwright's epigram "Women," based on _Greek Anthology_ 11.381, which claims women offer only two "good Houres," when they are in their "Nuptiall or . . . Winding Sheet" (Cartwright, 471).

67. For citations of the recommendations by the Protestant ministers William Ames, William Gouge, and Nathaniel Hardy that wives show what Ames calls "conjugall feare," see John Halkett, _Milton and the Idea of Matrimony: A Study of the Divorce Tracts and Paradise Lost_ (New Haven: Yale Univ. Press, 1970), 86-87.

68. On the "moderate hedonism" of Xenophon's Socrates, see J. C. B. Gosling and C. C. W. Taylor, _The Greeks on Pleasure_ (Oxford: Clarendon, 1982), 37-40.

69. Desiderius Erasmus, _Opera Omnia,_ ed. Jean Le Clerc, 11 vols. (Leiden, 1703-1706), 2:634; _Proverbs or Adages,_ trans. Richard Taverner (1569; reprint, Gainesville, Florida: Scholars' Facsimiles & Reprints, 1956), 23r; _Colloquia,_ ed. L-E. Halkin, F. Bierlaire, and R. Hoven (Amsterdam: North-Holland Publishing Company, 1972), 731.

70. Ann Baynes Coiro, _Robert Herrick's Hesperides and the Epigram Book Tradition_ (Baltimore: Johns Hopkins University Press, 1988), 2-113; and Alastair Fowler, _Kinds of Literature: An Introduction to the Theory of Genres and Modes_ (Cambridge, Mass.: Harvard University Press, 1982), 197-98, 229-30.

71. Rosalie Colie, *Shakespeare's Living Art* (Princeton: Princeton University Press, 1974), 80-96.

72. Coiro notes but does not pursue the implications of this sexual-textual parallel (46-47).

73. Plutarch, *The Philosophie, commonlie called, The Morals,* trans. Philemon Holland (London, 1603), 650-51.

74. Catherine Cole Mambretti, ed., *A Critical Edition of the Poetry of Katherine Philips* (Ph.D. dissertation, Univ. of Chicago, 1979), 297-98.

75. For recent discussions of Philips's poetry of same-sex love, see Celia A. Easton, "Excusing the Breach of Nature's Laws: The Discourse of Denial and Disguise in Katherine Philips' Friendship Poetry," *Restoration* 14 (1990): 1-14; Dorothy Mermin, "Women Becoming Poets: Katherine Philips, Aphra Behn, Anne Finch," *ELH* 57 (1990): 342-44; and Arlene Stiebel, "Subversive Sexuality: Masking the Erotic in Poems by Katherine Philips and Aphra Behn," in *Renaissance Discourses of Desire*, ed. Claude J. Summers and Ted-Larry Pebworth (Columbia and London: University of Missouri Press, 1993), 223-36.

76. See, e.g., Seneca, *Epistulae morales* 9.5, 55.10, 66.36, 71.12, 73.14, 76.4, 23, 98.10, 99.22.

77. Jonson, *Complete Poems,* 53.

78. On the conception of true religion as a mean, see Scodel, "'Mediocrities' and 'Extremities,'" 120-21. Phillips's terms for the opposed extremes may be compared to Joseph Hall's character sketches of "The Superstitious" and "The Profane man" in *Characters of Virtues and Vices* (1608); see *The Works of Joseph Hall,* vol. 6, ed. Peter Hall (Oxford, 1837), 107-108.

79. Katherine Philips, "A marryd state affords but little Ease," in *Kissing the Rod: An Anthology of Seventeenth- Century Verse,* ed. Germaine Greer et al. (London: Virago, 1988), 189.

80. Jonson, *Complete Poems,* 254. On seventeenth-century English translations and imitations of this poem, see Maren Sofie-Røstvig, *The Happy Man: Studies in the Metamorphoses of a Classical Ideal, 1600-1700,* 2 vols. (Oxford: Basil Blackwell, 1954), 1:82-83.

81. For examples, see *The Book of Restoration Verse,* ed. William Stanley Braithwaite (New York, 1910), 638-39, 648. One late seventeenth-century poet does manage to adapt the Cavalier mean in original fashion: in *Paradise Lost,* John Milton's portrait of unfallen Eve gives a new moral seriousness to the mean of coyness by placing it within the context of Scriptural and Protestant marriage ideology; see Joshua Scodel, "*Paradise Lost* and Classical Ideals of Pleasurable Restraint," *Comparative Literature* (forthcoming).

Marjorie Swann (essay date 1996)

SOURCE: Swann, Marjorie. "Cavalier Love: Fetishism and Its Discontents." *Literature and Psychology* 42, no. 3 (1996): 15-35.

[*In the following essay, Swann examines how Cavalier poets fetishized women in their works and discusses what this reveals about masculine anxiety.*]

Stephen Greenblatt has argued that the critic who examines Renaissance literature through the lens of psychoanalysis has gone badly astray. Greenblatt maintains that the mode of subjectivity, the "continuous selfhood" of the individual assumed by psychoanalysis was unavailable to men during the Renaissance. In Greenblatt's early modern world of hegemonic power, the community acts as subject, shaping and controlling the individual as object. Identity originates not in the "unique biology" of the individual, but in "the community's determination that this particular body possesses by right a particular identity and hence a particular set of possessions." Rather than perceiving himself as subject, then, Greenblatt's Renaissance man would consider himself first and foremost as an object, "the placeholder in a complex system of possessions, kinship bonds, contractual relationships, customary rights, and ethical obligations."[1] In this paper, I shall suggest that while our concept of "continuous selfhood" may have been denied to the Renaissance woman, we find a recognizably "modern" male subjectivity assumed and explored in the literature of this period. Moreover, I shall argue, only through a reading informed by psychoanalytic, feminist and historical analysis may we discern and understand the distinctive presentations of masculine anxiety we find throughout the amatory verse written by the seventeenth-century English "Cavalier" poets.

In his magisterial survey of English literature of the Tudor era, C. S. Lewis identified two distinct stages in sixteenth-century literary history, the "Drab Age" and the "Golden Age." According to Lewis, Sir Philip Sidney and his contemporaries climbed triumphantly up the artistic evolutionary ladder, escaping from the primordial slime of late medieval "drabness" into the literary brilliance of the Elizabethan era:

> Men have at last learned how to write; for a few years nothing more is needed than to play out again and again the strong, simple music of the uncontorted line and to load one's poem with all that is naturally delightful—

with flowers and swans, with ladies' hair, hands, lips, breasts, and eyes, with silver and gold, woods and waters, the stars, the moon and the sun.[2]

Learning how to write, it seems, entails learning how to dismember women, how to "load" a poem with fragments of female anatomy, "ladies' hair, hands, lips, breasts, and eyes." Lewis allies himself unquestioningly with the erotic imagination of his "Golden" poets: it is "naturally delightful" to perceive a female figure as anatomical bits, and to write poems in praise of these isolated bodily fragments. Lewis implicitly establishes vision and description as universal givens, and thus preempts any consideration of the constructed quality of visual perception and its representation in literature. However, as the art historian Michael Baxandall asserts, "Some of the mental equipment a man orders his visual experience with is variable, and much of this variable equipment is culturally relative."[3] And, I would emphasize, the viewer's "variable equipment" is also necessarily gendered. We do not see things "naturally," we do not share one mode of visualization which has also been the common property of both C. S. Lewis and Sir Philip Sidney.

As Lewis observes, however, fragmented female bodies are strewn throughout Renaissance amatory verse. We may trace the lineage of these dismembered women back to Laura, the unattainable beloved who inspired Petrarch to write his *Rime sparse*. Within Petrarch's work, praise of Laura entails the fragmentation and reification of her body. The poet frequently depicts Laura as a collection of beautiful, dissociated objects, transforming her into jewels and precious metals which he scatters across his mental landscape:

> Non fur giamai veduti si begli
> occhi o ne la nostra etade o ne' prim' anni
> che mi struggon cosi come 'l sol neve,
> onde procede lagrimosa riva
> ch'Amor conduce a pie'del duro lauro
> ch'a i rami di diamante et d'or le chiome.
>   . . . . .
> L'auro e i topacii al sol sopra la neve
> vincon le bionde chiome presso a gli occhi
> che menan gli anni miei si tosto a riva.

(There never have been seen such lovely eyes, either in our age or in the first years; they melt me as the sun does the snow: whence there comes forth a river of tears that Love leads to the foot of the harsh laurel that has branches of diamond and golden locks. . . .

Gold and topaz in the sun above the snow are vanquished by the golden locks next to those eyes that lead my years so quickly to shore.)[4]

Significantly, Petrarch often casts himself as the mythical hunter Actaeon. In Ovid's *Metamorphoses,* Actaeon inadvertently sees the naked goddess Diana, who punishes the man for his transgression by turning him into a stag; Actaeon's pack of hunting dogs subsequently tears him to bits. Thus in Ovid's account of Actaeon's death, male sight and bodily disintegration are inextricably related. In a brilliant analysis of Petrarch's descriptions of Laura, Nancy J. Vickers has argued that the poet deliberately refashions this story of a male encounter with a forbidden, naked, female body. According to Vickers, "Petrarch's Actaeon . . . realizes what will ensue: his response to the threat of imminent dismemberment is the neutralization, through descriptive dismemberment, of the threat."[5] The female form, if uncontrolled by the male imagination, threatens to destroy masculine identity. For Petrarch, the fragmentation of women's bodies becomes a male survival skill.

From a psychoanalytic perspective, Petrarch counters the myth of Actaeon with the practice of fetishism. According to Freud, fetishism occurs when "the normal sexual object is replaced by another which bears some relation to it, but is entirely unsuited to serve the normal sexual aim."[6] Fetishism is essentially an act of metonymy, a substitution of a part or adjunct for the whole. As Freud notes, "What is substituted for the sexual object is some part of the body (such as the foot or hair) . . . or some inanimate object which bears an assignable relation to the person whom it replaces and preferably to that person's sexuality" (Freud 66). Like Petrarch's Actaeon, the fetishist adopts such a tactic to preserve his self-identity, which would be threatened by the sight of a naked woman. In Freud's narrative, the fetishist's castration anxiety, his fear that he will lose his masculine identity, can be traced to a specific childhood experience:

> The fetish is a substitute for the woman's (the mother's) penis that the little boy once believed in. . . . The boy refused to take cognizance of the fact of his having perceived that a woman does not possess a penis. No, that could not be true: for if a woman had been castrated, then his own possession of a penis was in danger.
>
> (66)

The fetishist needs to distract his attention from the reality of the "castrated," hence threatening female body, and so he creates a substitute for the worrisome "lack" he has discerned there: he simultaneously acknowledges and feigns ignorance of female anatomy. In Freud's words, the fetish acts as "a token of triumph over the threat of castration and a protection against it" (Freud 352). This appropriation and restructuring of a woman's body is fundamentally self-referential. The fetishist recreates the female body in his own image, fashioning an object of fantasy by which he may affirm his own identity. As Berkeley Kaite notes, what the fetishist "sees, and finds seductive, is a simulated rendition of his own masculine possessions."[7] Stephen Greenblatt, we will recall, finds central to an understanding of Renaissance subjectivity the relationship between identity and the communally sanctioned right to own "a particular set of possessions." Psychoanalysis, by contrast, allows us to examine how Renaissance men could fashion themselves through the "ownership" and imaginative distribution of specific, very personal "possessions."

During the Renaissance, English poets avidly pursued Petrarch's course of erotic self-defense. Anatomical fragments, jewelry, and items of female clothing regularly fill poets' fields of vision and inspire their praise. As Ben Jonson remarked of his contemporaries' fascination with small, personal objects, "There is not worn that lace, purl, knot or pin, / But is the poet's matter."[8] The Petrarchan motif of the disembodied hand, for example, reappears in the English cult of glove-worship. Henry Constable relishes a moment of love amidst the haberdashery in his sonnet "To his Ladies hand vpon occasion of her gloue which in her absence he kissed." With his "Lady" safely out of sight, Constable's lover can allow himself to make physical contact with the true object of his affections: "And I thy gloue kisse as a thinge devine / Thy arrowes quiver and thy reliques shrine."[9] Barnabe Barnes similarly fantasizes about gaining limited access to a woman's body:

> Would I were chang'd but to my mistress gloues,
> That those white louely fingers I might hide,
> That I might kisse those hands, which mine hart loues,
> Or else that cheane of pearle, her neckes vaine pride,
> Made proude with her neckes vaines, that I might folde
> About that louely necke. . . .[10]

Here, the glove serves to mediate Barnes' contact with his mistress' person. Like the hand in the margin of a Renaissance book which points to a maxim, the glove directs the lover's attention to the woman's pearl necklace: as fetishes, the glove and "cheane of pearle" embody the "meaning" the lover ascribes to the woman's form, a sign of his male wholeness imaginatively imposed upon a female bodily text.

English poetry of the Renaissance abounds with such examples of fetishism. What particularly interests me, however, is the increasing self-consciousness and unease which tranform such depictions of the female body. Previous critics have remarked upon the psychological emphasis, the fascination with interiority which distinguishes seventeenth-century amatory verse. As William Kerrigan and Gordon Braden have observed recently, the seventeenth-century love lyric displays a "pronounced tendency to replace the woman with her image."[11] The relativity of "Beauty" and the role of the male imagination in love become explicitly acknowledged by poets like Henry King:

> Why slightest thou what I approve?
> Thou are no Peere to try my Love.

Nor canst discerne where her forme lyes,
Unless thou sawest her with my Eyes.
  Say shee were foule, and blacker than
The Night, or Sun-burnt African,
  If lik't by mee, tis I alone
  Can make a beauty where was none.
  For rated in my Phant'sy, shee
  Is so, as shee appeares to mee.[12]

When seventeenth-century poets examine the conventions of Petrarchan love, they often rewrite the amatory scenario as the indulgence of male narcissism. In a poem ascribed to John Hoskins, we find Petrarch's "love" for the unattainable Laura revealed as a mind-game for one player:

> By absence this good means I gaine
>   That I can catch her
>   Where none can watch her
> In some close corner of my braine:
>   There I embrace and kiss her,
>   And so enjoye her, and so misse her.[13]

However, the verse of the mid-century royalist ("Cavalier") poets nervously inhabits a middle ground between this radical solipsism and the blissfully unknowing Petrarchism of Lewis' "Golden" poets.

As he announces in the programmatic "Argument" of his collection *Hesperides,* Robert Herrick regularly "sing[s] of cleanly-*Wantonnesse,*" an aesthetic of purified sensuality.[14] The hybrid term "cleanly-*Wantonnesse,*" in its yoking of two apparently contradictory words, captures precisely the paradoxical quality of Herrick's amatory vision. Just as the meaning of the noun "*Wantonnesse*" is subject to and thus circumscribed by the adjective "cleanly," so too Herrick carefully delimits the potentially threatening sight of the female body. In the amatory verse of *Hesperides,* we find fetishism central to Herrick's program of evasive perceptual manoeuvres.[15] Herrick regularly celebrates his bevy of mistresses in terms of their jewelry and clothing, and he poetically ogles selected anatomical fragments of his favourite, Julia, devoting separate poems to her legs, hair, breasts, nipples, and lips. An examination of one of his poems to Julia reveals Herrick's procedures for neutralizing the sensory threat posed by the female body:

> How rich and pleasing thou my *Julia* art
> In each thy dainty, and peculiar part!
> First, for thy *Queen-ship* on thy head is set
> Of flowers a sweet commingled Coronet:
> About thy neck a Carkanet is bound,
> Made of the *Rubie, Pearle* and *Diamond*:
> A golden ring, that shines upon thy thumb:
> About thy wrist, the rich *Dardanium.*
> Between thy Breasts (then Doune of Swans more white)
> There playes the *Saphire* with the *Chrysolite.*

No part besides must of thy selfe be known,
But by the *Topaz, Opal, Calcedon.*[16]

Much of the jewellery decorating the woman encircles various parts of her body, and thus visually fragments her. Rings, crowns, necklaces—these items reappear time and time again in Herrick's amatory poems. Such adornment helps Herrick to focus upon individual, framed portions of a woman's body, small areas of detail isolated from the larger vista. In this poem, Herrick presents a vast expanse of beauty—Julia's body—which he warily explores as separate "parts."

In light of seventeenth-century gem-lore, Herrick's fetishistic preoccupation with the gems adorning Julia's body suggests a concerted effort to frustrate eroticism. As Thomas Nicols wrote in 1653, it was believed that gems "have vegetative souls, or lapidisick spirits infused into them from above, by which they live and draw the likenesse of their substance, their lapidisick juyce, their proper nourishment, for their sustenation, for the preservation of their being, and for their further growth."[17] The precious stones adorning Julia, once absorbing nourishment in the earth, are thus literally dead. Moreover, many of the jewels which Herrick scatters over the woman's body were held to counteract passion or truncate awareness. Nicols reports that a sapphire is "good against feverish distempers," and that "the wearing of it, doth hinder the erections that are caused by Venus."[18] Reputedly the opal "cloudeth the eyes of [spectators], so that they can either not see, or not mind what is done before them," while chrysolite "freeth men from passions, and from sadnesse of the mind," and moreover "doth drive away nocturnall fears; and . . . is a very effectuall Amulet against cholerick distempers o[f] the brain"; similarly, calcedon "driveth away evil spirits . . . [and] is good against melancholy and sadnesse."[19]

By converting Julia into a gem collection, Herrick invests her body with the capacity to regulate emotions and diminish consciousness. This simultaneously erotic yet prophylactic inertia captivates Herrick's imagination, and he takes pains to underscore Julia's intriguing stasis. Only the jewels, the dead entities in Herrick's field of vision, are granted active verbs by the poet: a golden ring "shines," as does a bracelet of "rich *Dardanium,*" while a sapphire "playes" with chrysolite in Julia's cleavage. The ostensible motion of the jewels is produced by passivity, for their "shining" and "playing" occur as light glances off them. Through Herrick's use of syntax, Julia becomes a kind of human Christmas tree, a motionless entity decorated by unseen hands. She plays no role in the process of her adornment: the coronet of flowers "is set" on her head, a necklace "is bound" around her neck. As a conglomeration of jewelled sections, Julia is beautifully dead. Herrick's closing injunction to the woman demands our careful attention:

"No part besides must of thy selfe be known, / But by the *Topaz, Opal, Calcedon*" (30.1.11-12). The speaker decrees that no other part of Julia should be described— "be known"—except in terms of precious stones; but the phrase "of thy selfe" also suggests that Julia herself must not "know"—that is, be aware of—her own body except as a collection of jewels. The imperative force of "must" suggests the speaker's urgency as he summons Julia to perceptual orthodoxy. Julia, in her mind's eye, must adopt the fetishistic gaze which Herrick imposes upon her: the woman *must* be dismembered, *must* be reified as a collection of jewels, or she will escape from the imaginative control of the poet.

Elsewhere in *Hesperides,* Herrick's poetry seems to confirm Freud's suggestion that the fetishist will exhibit "an aversion . . . to the real female genitals [which] remains a *stigma indelebile* of the repression that has taken place" (Freud 353). In Herrick's poem "The Vine" we may observe this phenomenon as Herrick creates a strategic gap in his text, a gap designed to conceal the uniquely female—and thus uniquely threatening—portion of Lucia's body. In a dream, Herrick is "Metamorphoz'd to a Vine," and he wraps his "*Tendrils*" and "*Nerv'lits*" around various sections of Lucia's anatomy until she cannot move, "All parts there made one prisoner" (16.2). The most significant aspect of the dream, its abrupt conclusion, is occasioned by a feature of Lucia's body:

> But when I crept with leaves to hide
> Those parts, which maids keep unespy'd,
> Such fleeting pleasures there I took,
> That with the fancie I awook.
>
> (16.2.18-21)

Herrick uses the term "parts" to refer euphemistically to Lucia's genitals, which the vine, an obliging seventeenth-century fig leaf, intends to cover. On the verge of contact with the site of sexual difference, Herrick finds it increasingly difficult to protect his careful ignorance, so he wakes himself up. Herrick thus evades an unmitigated, traumatic vision of the female form. His unease about Lucia's "parts" further reveals the fetishistic motive behind Herrick's odd instructions that Julia be regarded strictly as gem-stones. No "part" of Julia—her genitals, her sexual difference—can be "known" unless simultaneously denied by the presence of a fetish, "the *Topaz, Opal, Calcedon.*"

Elsewhere, however, Herrick cannot maintain his comforting perspective on the amatory world. Whereas Lucia, in Herrick's dream of vegetable love, seems oblivious to the phallic vine demarcating her body, Julia, it seems, will not internalize the poet's vision of her, and refuses to play scenery to Herrick's fetish:

> For sport my *Julia* threw a Lace
> Of silke and silver at my face:

Watchet the silke was; and did make
A shew, as if't'ad been a snake:
The suddenness did me affright;
But though it scar'd, it did not bite.

(116.1)

This apparently innocuous account of playfulness actually explores the fear and hostility which underlie fetishism. With one gesture, Julia destroys Herrick's carefully constructed image of her—and thus his image of himself. As with Lucia in "The Vine," Herrick had appropriated Julia's body as background for the presentation of a sign of his masculine identity—the phallic "Lace." Julia, however, refuses to endure this exploitation of her body as passive scenery, and her actions demonstrate her cognizance of the structure of Herrick's eroticism. Julia demystifies Herrick's supposed "love" for her by restoring the true object of Herrick's affections—his surrogate phallus—to its place of imaginative origin, Herrick's own body. Moreover, Herrick specifies that Julia throws the fetish at his face: Julia exposes the structure of Herrick's amatory vision by forcibly juxtaposing the "Lace" with Herrick's eyes, emblematizing the perceptual closed loop of the phallic image and the male gaze. As Julia rebels, the hostility which informs the objectification of women is turned back upon the fetishist, and in Herrick's anticipation of bodily harm we find his renewed fear of castration, a fear which can no longer be allayed by the reassuringly immutable sight of a fetishized woman.

Lest we think Herrick's concerns atypical of this period, we should also examine Waller's verse "To a Fair Lady, Playing With a Snake." In this poem, a man contemplates the nubile Chloris, who conceals a snake in her clothing. (One of Waller's editors has suggested that "'Twas formerly not unusual among our English ladies for coolness in the hot weather to carry a snake in their sleeve."[20]) In the Petrarchan schema, as we have noted, male love is predicated upon female absence: it is Laura's unattainability which allows Petrarch to refashion her image and scatter her body in poem after poem. Julia's rebellion against fetishism, however, suggests that female obduracy can take undesirable forms. Whereas Julia flings the serpentine lace, the sign of her objectification, back at its maker, Chloris seems disinclined to relinquish the snake which adorns her person. Indeed, the creature becomes the focus of eroticism for Chloris herself: "'Tis innocence, and youth, which makes / In Chloris' fancy such mistakes, / To start at love, and play with snakes."[21] Chloris, in other words, will adopt the stance of the fetishist: because she "starts at" or avoids love, she will employ her "fancy" and fix her attention upon phallic substitutes. The poet complains that the snake has contributed to Chloris' lack of interest in men: "By this and by her coldness barred, / Her servants have a task too hard; / The tyrant has a double guard." In the next stanza, however, Waller con-

firms the fetishistic identity of Chloris' play-thing and reveals the true nature of his love: "Thrice happy snake! that in her sleeve / May boldly creep; we dare not give / Our thoughts so unconfined a leave." Waller's snake is Herrick's vine relieved of its inhibitions.

Waller's poem has been recently interpreted as a narrative of female sexual cruelty: "Chloris is well aware of what she is doing, allowing the snake all the scope which her rejected lover is denied. Hers is a flaunted self-sufficiency aimed at humiliating the man with a living symbol of his impotence."[22] Chloris certainly exhibits a kind of erotic autonomy, but Waller himself suggests that the men who watch her snake-charming routine all have their psycho-sexual blinkers firmly in place: "we dare not give / Our thoughts so unconfined a leave." Is Chloris really "flaunting" her self-reliance for the sake of "humiliating" the male audience which gazes at her? Or, like Herrick's Julia, does Chloris merely "start" from her traditional role as amatory object by recognizing the structures of the male erotic imagination, and appropriating them for her own use? When you begin to look for her, the sexually self-sufficient woman appears with surprising frequency in later seventeenth-century literature. Milton's Eve, of course, initially fell in love with her own reflection and fled from Adam when she first laid eyes on him. Only through the intervention of God, the Divine Sexual Therapist, was Eve persuaded to abandon the error of her narcissistic ways.[23] Cavalier amatory verse, by contrast, often records the poets' failures to justify the ways of men to women. As we have seen, the unkind mistress assumes a new form in this period when women reject their role as passive backdrops for fetishistic displays.

I would like to compare two poems to demonstrate further how the structure of "Golden Age" eroticism disintegrates within Cavalier verse. In the forty-fifth poem of the *Amoretti,* Spenser exhorts a daughter of Eve to accept for her self-image the product of a male imagination:

Leave lady in your glasse of christall clene,
Your goodly selfe for evermore to vew:
and in my selfe, my inward selfe I meane,
most lively lyke behold your semblant trew.[24]

The dangerous narcissism of the woman gazing into the mirror becomes the healthful recognition of "trew" female identity which originates from the male "inward self." Rather than create an autonomous female identity, the "lady" must perceive herself as the product of a male mind. In "Lucasta's Fan, With a Looking-Glass in It," written by Richard Lovelace, Spenser's self-regarding mistress again takes up her mirror. Rather than swerving from her mirror to internalize a male viewpoint, however, Lucasta seems determined to gaze forever in her "glasse of christall clene." Near the poem's conclusion, Lucasta looks into the mirror and addresses her fan:

> My lively shade thou ever shalt retain
>   In thy enclosed feather-framed glass,
> And but unto our selves to all remain
>   Invisible thou feature of this face.[25]

It would seem that Lucasta, unlike Milton's Eve or Spenser's mistress, will not "know" herself properly. For Lovelace, only violence can disrupt such female self-absorption:

> So said, her sad swain overheard, and cried
>   Ye gods! for faith unstain'd this a reward!
> Feathers and glass t'outweigh my virtue tried?
>   Ah show their empty strength! The gods accord.
> Now fall'n the brittle favourite lies, and burst!
>   Amazed Lucasta weeps, repents, and flies
> To her Alexis, vows herself accursed
>   If hence she dress herself, but in his eyes.

The male lover Alexis destroys Lucasta's erotic self-sufficiency. By shattering the mirror and fan with which the woman had structured her subjectivity, Alexis procures Lucasta's renewed passivity as the object of his gaze: she will no longer "dress herself, but in his eyes." I imagine that Alexis would advise Waller to strangle Chloris' pet snake without delay.

In Lovelace's account of the rise and fall of Lucasta's fan, we find the dynamics of the perceptual coercion by which, Susanne Kappeler argues, a patriarchal society objectifies women:

> The fact that women, as individual subjects, have inserted themselves into the cultural audience . . . , have apprenticed to the male viewpoint which surveys women as objects and as products of fine art, is itself one of the most fundamental sources of female alienation: women have integrated in themselves, have internalized, a permanent outpost of the other gender—the male surveyor.[26]

But some women in Cavalier poetry leave their seats in the "cultural audience" to watch the performance of their very own one-woman shows. In Freud's analysis, we might recall, the fetishist simultaneously acknowledges and disavows sexual reality: he manages to gaze at a "castrated" woman but see a reassuringly intact self-portrait at the same time. The Cavalier poets try but often fail to achieve this stance of knowing ignorance. As we have seen, one intriguing cause of their failure is uncooperative women. Poetic female characters like Julia and Chloris refuse to assume the role of object, and Herrick and his contemporaries cast their refusal as the seizure of the fetish. Long before Sarah Kofman or Naomi Schor tried to theorize a female fetishism,[27] the Cavalier poets explored the issue through their poetry. From Freud's analysis, it would seem logi-

cally impossible for women to become fetishists. As Laura Mulvey's description indicates, the gendered polarity of subject and object appears fixed:

> The message of fetishism concerns not woman, but the narcissistic wound she represents for man. . . . [Women] are being turned all the time into objects of display, to be looked at and gazed at and stared at by men. Yet, in a real sense, women are not there at all. . . . The true exhibit is always the phallus. Women are simply the scenery on to which men project their narcissistic fantasies.[28]

The Cavalier poets, however, pose an interesting question: what happens if the scenery appropriates the exhibit for her own purposes?

Arthur F. Marotti has drawn attention to the political freight borne by amatory discourses in Renaissance poetry. For John Donne and his Elizabethan contemporaries, Marotti argues, the language of Petrarchan love served as a polite code for political aspirations, providing "an amorous vocabulary" through which courtiers could express their "ambition and its vicissitudes."[29] In this context, the Ovidian poetry of Donne and his peers functioned as a kind of wish-fulfillment, as idealizing "courtship" was replaced by libertine sexual conquest: "Socially, economically, and politically vulnerable Inns gentleman . . . found it pleasant to turn the tables imaginatively by composing, circulating, and collecting love poetry of another sort, literature that celebrated male social, economic, and sexual power."[30] The verse of the Cavalier poets charts a similar attempt to retreat into a compensatory utopia of eroticized male dominance; however, as their failures of fetishism indicate, the mid-century writers sometimes encounter obdurately self-sufficient women whom, try as they will, the poets cannot imagine as submissive. In an analysis of pornography, Susan Gubar has argued that feminist critics need to pay greater attention to "male literary traditions in terms of their production of images of male and female sexuality." Gubar advocates combining insights from psychoanalysis with an historical framework to examine the "aesthetic interactions between the sexes in literary history as an index of the relationship between the sexes in history."[31] To conclude this discussion, then, I would like to suggest one way in which we might historicize the portrayals of failed fetishism which distinguish Cavalier amatory verse.

In Sir John Suckling's poem "Upon my Lady Carliles walking in Hampton-Court garden," we find another depiction of frustrated Cavalier eroticism. Ostensibly a dialogue between Suckling and Thomas Carew, the poem presents what seem to be contradictory perspectives on the same woman. To Carew, Lady Carlisle is "A thing so near a Deity" that she seems a miraculous, disembodied essence:

> Didst thou not find the place inspir'd,
>   And flow'rs, as if they had desir'd

No other Sun, start from their beds,
And for a sight steal out their heads?
Heardst thou not musick when she talk't?
And didst not find that as she walkt
She threw rare perfumes all about
Such as bean-blossoms newly out,
Or chafed spices give?————[32]

Suckling the libertine reacts differently to the sight of Lady Carlisle strolling in the garden:

Alas! *Tom,* I am flesh and blood,
And was consulting how I could
In spite of masks and hoods descry
The parts deni'd unto the eye;
I was undoing all she wore,
And had she walkt but one turn more,
Eve in her first state had not been
More naked, or more plainly seen.

(ll. 24-31)

We find in Suckling's retort the paradigm of erotic ignorance so familiar in *Hesperides*: like Herrick, Suckling seems to pursue a frank sensuality which he does not achieve. As in Herrick's interrupted vine-dream, Suckling's interest in Lady Carlisle's "parts" remains unfulfilled, although he implies that other, lesser men are better informed on the subject than he:

'Troth in her face I could descry
No danger, no divinity.
But since the pillars were so good
On which the lovely fountain stood,
Being once come so near, I think
I should have ventur'd hard to drink.
What ever fool like me had been
If I'd not done as well as seen?
There to be lost why should I doubt,
Where fools with ease go in and out?

(ll. 40-49)

According to Carew, however, Suckling should be thankful that he could not complete his imaginative strip-tease:

'T was well for thee she left the place,
For there's great danger in that face;
But had'st thou view'd her legg and thigh,
And upon that discovery
Search't after parts that are more dear,
(As Fancy seldom stops so near)
No time or age had ever seen
So lost a thing as thou hadst been.

(ll. 32-9)

If we find in Carew's words of commiseration a brief survival guide for fetishists—knowledge of a woman's "dear parts" must be avoided, or phallic identity will become a "lost thing"—the poem also evokes a specific historical context which produced such a concept of female "danger."

Lucy Hay, Countess of Carlisle, was the center of a Neoplatonic coterie, an aristocratic salon in which men and women followed an idealistic code of amatory social behavior. Although her standing at court fluctuated, the Countess became increasingly influential in the 1630s, and the hyperbolic compliment mocked by Suckling was regularly offered by her admirers.[33] In 1632, Carew himself wrote "A New-yeares Sacrifice. To Lucinda," in which he abjectly worships Lady Carlisle as his "Goddesse":

. . . it were Apostasie in me,
To send a prayer to any Deitie
But your divine selfe, who have power to give
Those blessings unto others, such as live
Like me, by the sole influence of your eyes,
Whose faire aspects governe our destinies.[34]

Platonic love was promoted at court by Henrietta Maria, and the queen's fashionable cult of love not only codified decorous, respectful relationships between men and women, but also enshrined female independence and influence at court. Henrietta Maria's Neoplatonism thus entailed what Erica Veevers has recently termed "conservative feminism": women were to exercise their beauty and virtue to improve male behavior and foster social harmony, at the same time enjoying a new measure of independence, free from aspersions cast upon their sexual propriety.[35] The conclusion of Suckling's poem counters Lady Carlisle's political power, figured in Carew's real and ventriloquized Neoplatonic discourse, with the innuendo of the sexual double standard. If, unlike Lovelace's repentant Lucasta, Lady Carlisle will not "dress herself" (or *un*dress herself) in the male poet's eyes, Suckling will at least insinuate that others have successfully braved the "great danger in that face." Suckling, however, cannot imagine himself as the sexual conqueror of a powerful woman. Suckling's stance of simultaneous sexual ignorance and knowledge replicates the paradoxical mind-set of the fetishist. Yet the attenuated nature of Suckling's eroticism—his truncated X-ray vision of the woman's body, followed by the blustering, optative claim of vicarious sexual mastery—underlines the creative difficulty Suckling encounters when he tries to objectify the Countess. Although he scoffs at Carew's Neoplatonic praise, it seems that the new ideology of female "danger" constrains Suckling's imagination.

In a recent discussion of seventeenth-century literature and politics, Lawrence Venuti argues that poets like Suckling, by undermining Neoplatonic ideals, demystify courtly culture and "subvert the Caroline ideology of absolutism and thereby question the court's hegemony."[36] I would suggest, however, that the Cavalier poets found their poetic strategies for objectifying women demystified, subverted, and questioned by specific aspects of Caroline gender ideology. The gender-roles established by Henrietta Maria's Neoplatonic love-fashions subverted male hegemony over women, and contemporary poets found this new sexual politics threatening. The dialogic principle of Suckling's poem on the Countess cuts both ways, and throughout Cavalier verse, the female "danger," the female power and autonomy espoused by the worshipful Carew, impairs traditional structures of male amatory vision. While Ben Jonson could, in 1629, satirize the précieuse Lady Frampul as a woman "runne mad with pride, wild with selfe-loue,"[37] Lady Frampul's daughters Julia, Charis, Lucasta, and Lady Carlisle evoke unease, rather than laughter. The Cavalier failures of fetishism indicate the presence of an ideological prophylactic, a new conception of gender which played imaginative havoc with time-honored poetic strategies of eroticized male self-gratification.

Henrietta Maria's challenge to the existing sex-gender system was one variation on a seventeenth-century theme, the questioning of traditional hierarchies. By the 1640s, Cavalier anxiety about emasculation moved from the margins of the cultural psyche to the political mainstream, as civil war engulfed England. The structures of both church and state were transmuted by force, and Charles I was beheaded. Freud himself, I think, would not have been surprised that fetishes and their frailty should have preoccupied writers who faced such political and cultural upheaval. A little boy experiences anxiety when he first becomes cognizant of his mother's lack of a certain bodily possession; "in later life," writes Freud in his essay on fetishism, "a grown man may perhaps experience a similar panic when the cry goes up that Throne and Altar are in danger, and similar illogical consequences will ensue" (Freud 352). The Cavalier poets wrote their love lyrics with this cry crescendoing around them; their complex, fascinating poetry embodies the "illogical consequences" of their increasing sense of panic.

Notes

1. Stephen Greenblatt, "Psychoanalysis and Renaissance Culture," in Patricia Parker and David Quint, eds., *Literary Theory/Renaissance* Texts (Baltimore and London: Johns Hopkins UP, 1986) 216. For a trenchant, non-feminist critique of Greenblatt, see William Kerrigan, "Individualism, Historicism, and New Styles of Overreaching," *Philosophy and Literature* 13 (1989): 115-126. Kerrigan recognizes the theoretical stakes in Greenblatt's dismissal of psychoanalysis: "Another way of looking at the Renaissance, through the lens of Freud, has been finding individuals there, and this activity threatens the foundation of new historicism" (117).

2. C. S. Lewis, *English Literature of the Sixteenth Century Excluding Drama* (Oxford: Oxford UP, 1954) 65.

3. Michael Baxandall, *Painting and Experience in Fifteenth-Century Italy* (Oxford: Clarendon Press, 1972) 40.

4. *Petrarch's Lyric Poems: The "Rime sparse" and Other Lyrics,* trans. and ed. Robert M. Durling (Cambridge, Mass.: Harvard UP, 1976) 86-88, Poem 30, ll. 19-24, 37-39.

5. Nancy J. Vickers, "Diana Described: Scattered Women and Scattered Rhyme," in Elizabeth Abel, ed., *Writing and Sexual Difference* (Brighton: Harvester Press, 1982) 103-104. Poem 23 in the Rime exemplifies Petrarch's response to the myth of Actaeon.

6. Sigmund Freud, *On Sexuality: Three Essays on the Theory of Sexuality and Other Works,* trans. James Strachey, The Pelican Freud Library, Vol. 7, ed. Angela Richards (London: Penguin Books, 1977 [1953]) 65. All future references to Freud are to this edition and volume of his works.

7. Berkeley Kaite, "Reading the Body Textual: The Shoe and Fetish Relations in Soft- and Hard-Core," *American Journal of Semiotics* 6 (1989): 84.

8. Ben Jonson, "An Elegy," ll. 16-17, from *The Underwood,* in *Ben Jonson: Poems,* ed. Ian Donaldson (London and New York: Oxford UP, 1975) 191.

9. *The Poems of Henry Constable,* ed. Joan Grundy (Liverpool: Liverpool UP, 1960) 131. For a discussion of the *bella mano* motif in Constable and his contemporaries, see James Mirollo, *Mannerism and Renaissance Poetry* (New Haven: Yale UP, 1984) 125-159.

10. Barnabe Barnes, Sonnet 63, ll. 5-10, in his *Parthenophil and Parthenope,* ed. Victor A. Doyno (Carbondale and Edwardsville: Southern Illinois UP, 1971) 39.

11. William Kerrigan and Gordon Braden, *The Idea of the Renaissance* (Baltimore and London: Johns Hopkins UP, 1989) 182. Other helpful, although untheorized assessments of the interiority of seventeenth-century amatory verse include Earl Miner, *The Cavalier Mode from Jonson to Cotton* (Princeton: Princeton UP, 1971) and H. M. Richmond, *The School of Love: The Evolution of the Stuart Love Lyric* (Princeton: Princeton UP, 1964).

12. "The Defence," ll. 1-10, in *The Poems of Henry King,* ed. Margaret Crum (Oxford: Clarendon Press, 1965) 145-146.

13. John Hoskins, "Absence," ll. 17-24, in Herbert J. C. Grierson, ed., *Metaphysical Lyrics and Poems of the Seventeenth Century* (Oxford: Clarendon Press, 1921) 24.

14. For a discussion of "cleanly-*Wantonnesse*" as refined sensuality, see Thomas R. Whitaker, "Herrick and the Fruits of the Garden," *ELH* 22 (1955): 16-33.

15. Few critics have explored the implications of J. B. Broadbent's remarks that "fetichistic [sic] superficies" fill Herrick's love poetry (*Poetic Love* [London: Chatto and Windus, 1964] 246). Gordon Braden, in a subtle and perceptive reading of Herrick, argues that in the amatory poems, "The emphasis on foreplay and nongenital, especially oral gratification, . . . and the generally voyeuristic preference of perception to action . . . are all intelligible as a wide diffusion of erotic energy denied specifically orgastic focus and release" (*The Classics and English Renaissance Poetry*, Yale Studies in English 187 [New Haven and London: Yale UP, 1978] 223). William Kerrigan elaborates upon Braden's interpretation in "Kiss Fancies in Robert Herrick," *George Herbert Journal* 14 (1990-91): 155-71; see also Lillian Schanfield, "'Tickled with Desire': A View of Eroticism in Herrick's Poetry," *Literature and Psychology* 39 (1993): 63-83.

Recent examinations of the "politics" of *Hesperides* have ignored the specifically gendered nature of Herrick's amatory verse. In *Robert Herrick's "Hesperides" and the Epigram Book Tradition* (Baltimore and London: Johns Hopkins UP, 1988), Ann Baynes Coiro argues that *Hesperides* chronicles the poet's growing disillusionment with Stuart ideals and policy; from this perspective, Herrick's poems about women participate in the "dreaming fantasy" of pastoral beauty which Herrick steadily subverts (11). Coiro elsewhere analyzes Julia as a progressively transformed "metaphor for language" ("Herrick's 'Julia' Poems," *John Donne Journal* 6 [1987]: 67-89).

16. Robert Herrick, "To *Julia*," in *The Poetical Works of Robert Herrick*, ed. L. C. Martin (Oxford: Oxford UP, 1956) 30. All future references to Herrick's poetry are to this edition. I have followed Martin's format for citing Herrick's poems: i.e., page number. number of poem on page. line number(s).

17. Thomas Nicols, *Arcula Gemmea: Or, A Cabinet of Jewels* (London, 1653) 2. Nicols relies upon authorities such as Boethius and Cardanus.

18. Nicols 84.

19. Nicols 90, 105-106, 129.

20. Cited Gerald Hammond, *Fleeting Things: English Poets and Poems 1616-1660* (Cambridge, Mass.: Harvard UP, 1990) 313.

21. *The Poems of Edmund Waller*, ed. G. Thorn-Drury, The Muses' Library (London: Lawrence and Bullen, 1893) 334.

22. Hammond 314.

23. For a provocative reading of Eve's role as "doomed narcissist" whose loss of autonomy underwrites patriarchy, see Christine Froula, "When Eve Reads Milton: Undoing the Canonical Economy," *Critical Inquiry* 10 (1983): 321-347.

24. Sonnet XLV, ll. 1-4, from *Amoretti*, in *The Yale Edition of the Shorter Poems of Edmund Spenser*, ed. William A. Oram et al. (New Haven and London: Yale UP, 1989) 627.

25. *The Poems of Richard Lovelace*, ed. C. H. Wilkinson (Oxford: Clarendon Press, 1930) 51.

26. Susanne Kappeler, *The Pornography of Representation* (Minneapolis: Univ. of Minnesota Press, 1986) 57-58.

27. Sarah Kofman, *The Enigma of Woman: Women in Freud's Writing*, trans. Catherine Porter (Ithaca and London: Cornell UP, 1985); Naomi Schor, "Female Fetishism: The Case of George Sand," in Susan Rubin Suleiman, ed., *The Female Body in Western Culture* (Cambridge, Mass.: Harvard UP, 1985) 363-372. For a critique of recent feminist theories of fetishism, see Emily Apter, "Splitting Hairs: Female Fetishism and Postpartum Sentimentality in Maupassant's Fiction," in her book *Feminizing the Fetish: Psychoanalysis and Narrative Obsession in Turn-of-the-Century France* (Ithaca and London: Cornell UP, 1991) 99-123.

28. Laura Mulvey, "You Don't Know What is Happening Do You, Mr. Jones?," *Spare Rib* 8 (Feb. 1973): 30.

29. Arthur F. Marotti, "'Love Is Not Love': Elizabethan Sonnet Sequences and the Social Order," *ELH* 49 (1982): 398.

30. Marotti, *John Donne, Coterie Poet* (Madison: Univ. of Wisconsin Press, 1986) 73.

31. Susan Gubar, "Representing Pornography: Feminism, Criticism, and Depictions of Female Violation," *Critical Inquiry* 13 (1987): 739.

32. *The Works of Sir John Suckling*, ed. Thomas Clayton, Vol. 1, *The Non-Dramatic Works* (Oxford: Clarendon Press, 1971) 30.

33. For an assessment of the Countess' role in Caroline politics and poetry, see Raymond A. Anselment, "The Countess of Carlisle and Caroline Praise: Convention and Reality," *Studies in Philology* 82 (1985): 212-233.

34. *The Poems of Thomas Carew*, ed. Rhodes Dunlap (Oxford: Clarendon Press, 1949) 33.

35. Erica Veevers, *Images of Love and Religion: Queen Henrietta Maria and Court Entertainments* (Cambridge: Cambridge UP, 1989) 15. Veevers argues that Lady Carlisle's Platonism was rooted in French salon *préciosité,* whereas Henrietta Maria's practice reflected the devout humanism of St. François de Sales. The distinction was often lost on contemporaries, however (Veevers 37-39).

36. Lawrence Venuti, *Our Halcyon Dayes: English Prerevolutionary Texts and Postmodern Culture* (Madison: Univ. of Wisconsin Press, 1989) 259.

37. Ben Jonson, *The New Inne* 5.2.30, cited Veevers 38.

CAVALIER DRAMA

Geoffrey D. Aggeler (essay date winter 1978)

SOURCE: Aggeler, Geoffrey D. "The Rebellion in Cavalier Drama."[1] *Western Humanities Review* 32, no. 1 (winter 1978): 53-75.

[*In this essay, Aggeler discusses Cavalier drama of the interregnum and notes that it is rich in political and religious content.*]

In spite of the great contributions by Hyder Rollins, Leslie Hotson and Alfred Harbage, the history of the drama between 1642 and 1660 remains "perhaps the obscurest chapter in the history of English literature."[2] Students still commonly assume that the ordinance of September 2, 1642, ordaining that "publike Stage-playes shall cease, and bee forborne," succeeded in halting the activities of playwrights and players for nearly two decades.[3] In fact, as Professor Rollins demonstrated long ago, "theatrical productions never ceased, in spite of the active and relentless hostility of the government," throughout the period of the Great Rebellion. Several London playhouses, including the Red Bull, Salisbury Court, and the Cockpit, presented surreptitious performances regularly during the entire interregnum, and there are records indicating that it was necessary for the authorities in the provinces to exercise considerable severity to enforce the laws against playing.[4]

Professor Rollins's conclusions were based largely on his examination of newsbooks, pamphlets and broadsides in the Thomason Collection of Tracts in the British Museum. He was concerned primarily with presenting "facts connected with the stage" rather than discussing any of the plays themselves. Stimulated by the Rollins essay, Leslie Hotson continued the study, combining some of Rollins's discoveries with some of his own based upon further examination of newsbooks, pamphlets and other sources. But the early chapters of his *Commonwealth and Restoration Stage* are primarily concerned with performances and conditions affecting them rather than Commonwealth plays.[5] It remained for Alfred Harbage to produce the first major study of the drama itself, a work which has yet to be superseded.[6] Harbage's *Cavalier Drama* examines the continuity of literary tradition in the English drama during the Caroline and Commonwealth periods and the early years of the Restoration. It includes the only critical discussions of a number of Commonwealth plays that are still available only in manuscript or early printed editions. Since the purpose of Harbage's survey was to reveal trends in English drama over an extensive period, he tended to confine his discussions to aspects of the plays that illustrate the trends and the nature of the development of the "Cavalier mode" which culminated in Restoration heroic drama. He also chose not to discuss some plays which are among the more distinguished achievements of an age which, overall one must admit, produced little in the way of distinguished drama. But again, Harbage was justified in these omissions by the limitations of his critical focus.

The focus of the present study is the drama of the interregnum, not as it reveals trends and transitions, but as it reveals an interesting variety of political and religious responses to historical events. I will not however confine my discussion to the ways in which the plays reveal social history. I will suggest, at least in passing, that some of these plays are worthy of serious critical attention, which they are not likely to receive until they are made more accessible, perhaps in facsimile editions or modern critical reprints.

The ordinance of 1642 prohibited the staging of "publike Stage-playes." It did not prohibit the writing or publication of plays, and even if it had, the ill success of the authorities in suppressing performances suggests how effective such a prohibition would have been. In fact, one gathers that the prohibition may have stimulated some individuals to try their hands at play writing for the first time, possibly as an act of rebellion against the triumphant rebels who had overthrown the King. It is significant that many of the satiric pamphlets of the 1640's are dramatic in form, playlets divided into five acts and running to about a dozen or twenty pages in quarto.[7] Most of these are ferociously anti-Roundhead, and one infers that their dramatic form was chosen partly to increase the sting of their satire, a reminder that the English appetite for theatre was not to be dampened by Puritanical restrictions.

A number of the longer plays written in the same period and later during the Commonwealth, plays which cannot be classified as dramatic pamphlets, appear to have been similarly inspired in their composition, literary rebellions against a Puritan establishment brought into being by the Great Rebellion. But it would be a mistake to assume that all of the plays of this period were written by disgruntled Royalists. Indeed, "Cavalier drama," as it has been applied to virtually all of the drama of the interregnum is in many ways a misnomer. According to Harbage, "After 1642 plays became an avowed instrument of partisanship and propaganda. Naturally they were on the Cavalier side, the Roundheads disdaining to use a devilish instrument even in a righteous cause."[8] The only exception to this rule he acknowledges is the translation of George Buchanan's *Baptistes sive Calumnia,* a political allegory which the House of Commons itself ordered published in 1643, and which may have been the work of John Milton.[9] In fact, if we compare the dramatic treatments of a subject that is an obsessive concern of a number of dramatists, the Great Rebellion itself, it becomes apparent that the drama of the interregnum represents virtually every current political stance, from Royalism to ardent Republicanism.

Perhaps the most indisputably Royalist extant dramatic treatment of the Rebellion is *The Famous Tragedie of King Charles I* (1649). Written and published in the year of the regicide, this raging dramatic attack on the Roundheads supports Harbage's generalizations fully and reveals how extensively even very recent history can be distorted to support a political viewpoint. It is, however, by its very one-sidedness, not representative of the majority of Commonwealth dramatic treatments of the Rebellion. The analysis I offer here is intended primarily to illuminate the ways in which it is representative of a minority of the extant plays in which partisanship is so intense that every dramatic element and history itself are made to serve narrowly propagandist ends.

King Charles himself never appears in *The Famous Tragedie.* The protagonists are the Roundheads, and, like Shakespeare's Richard III or the French in his *1 Henry VI,* they are comic villains. The Royalists were especially fond of pointing out that while the Roundheads had shut down the theatres they were themselves in the process of acting out a prolonged comedy at Westminster.[10] Clearly intending to reveal this same tragicomic "irony," the author of the *Famous Tragedie* opens his play with a ludicrous exchange between two of the principal comedians, Oliver Cromwell and Hugh Peters. Oliver asks the chaplain if he is ready to preach to the Parliament ("all my *Myrmidons*") "against the *essence* and *the power of KINGS.*" The chaplain prefaces his reply with an hilarious hyperbolic tribute to Oliver's might that gorgeously parodies the rhetoric of *Tamburlaine.* Like other Cavalier dramatists, the author of this play is steeped in the works of the Elizabethan masters, several of whom he mentions in

his prologue.[11] That he intends to parody Marlovian hyperbole is clearly indicated by his specific reference to Tamburlaine's caging of Bajazeth, to which he parallels Cromwell's imprisonment of Charles I. Like Tamburlaine, Cromwell is defined and magnified by mythic parallel, a Herculean figure with death in his countenance. But whereas Tamburlaine is not diminished until he is mocked by the satiric commentary of Calyphas,[12] Oliver is made ridiculous from the outset:

> . . . thy
> Nose, like a bright Beacon, sparkling still (the *Aetna,*
> that doth fame our English world) hangs like a Comet o're
> thy dreadfull face, denouncing death & vengeance; the
> Ancients fam'd *Alcides* for his Acts, thou hast not slaine,
> but tane the Kingly *Lyon,* and like great *Tamberlaine* with
> his *Bajazet,* canst render him within an Iron-Cage a spectacle of mirth, when e're thou pleasest.[13]

Peters goes on to assure Cromwell that he is prepared to speak against kingship in general and the reign of Charles in particular. In fact, the sermon is no invention by the playwright. Shortly before the execution of the King, Peters was commanded to preach before the two Houses, and, as G. P. Gooch observes, "took advantage" of the occasion to urge the abolition of monarchy "both here and in all other places." Only in this way could the nation be freed from its Egyptian bondage. In the same sermon, Peters compared Charles to Barabbas, whom it had been folly to release.[14]

Beyond this point, the plot becomes more fanciful, as does the characterization of both Cromwell and the chaplain. As in other Royalist propaganda, Peters is revealed as a gluttonous, loose living lecher, and in this play he serves Cromwell's appetites as well by functioning as his pander in an invented affair with the wife of General Lambert, who had, by his campaign in the early summer of 1648, been largely responsible for the final Parliamentarian victory.[15] A loosely related subplot dramatizes the siege of Colchester and a much publicized atrocity that followed the surrender of the Royalists. Following the surrender, on 28 August 1648, two of the Royalist leaders, Sir Charles Lucas and Sir George Lisle, had been executed by a firing squad to serve as examples to other would-be insurgents against the Parliamentarian regime. According to contemporary accounts, the Parliamentarian officer mainly responsible was General Ireton. In the words of Clarendon:

> The manner of taking the lives of these worthy men was new, and without example, and concluded by most men to be very barbarous; and was generally imputed to Ireton, who swayed the general, and was upon all occasions of an unmerciful and bloody nature.[16]

In *The Famous Tragedie,* however, Ireton merely seconds the urging of Colonel Rainsborough, the great champion of the Levellers. It would appear that the dramatist measured and assigned the villainy of the various Roundheads according to the intensity of their opposition to monarchy itself. Ireton, like Rainsborough, was an Independent and a convinced republican, but he was not opposed to a monarchy that would exercise its power within clearly defined "limitations."[17] Rainsborough, on the other hand, was regarded as being wholly in sympathy with the Levellers.[18] At the meeting of the Council of the Army at Putney Church on 16 September 1647, he had led the minority which opposed further negotiation with the King, and during the subsequent debates in the House of Commons concerning relations with the King, had been one of the leaders of the Independent faction which aimed at the abolition of monarchy.[19]

Rainsborough's political stance may also explain why the dramatist alters the facts concerning his death. The colonel was actually killed by a party of Cavaliers from the besieged Pontefract Castle who were trying to kidnap him. Their intention was to exchange him for Sir Marmaduke Langdale, then held prisoner by the Parliamentarians.[20] When he resisted these Cavalier commandos, Rainsborough was run through by their swords.[21] The author of *The Famous Tragedie* makes Rainsborough's death a direct result of the atrocity at Colchester. One of the soldiers who serves on the firing squad, thrilled with remorse and resolved to expiate his crime by avenging Lucas and Lisle, follows Rainsborough toward Pontefract and challenges him. In the ensuing duel, Rainsborough is disadvantaged by the guilt that "hangs heavie" on his arm and slain. This brief triumph of virtue is, however, followed by a scene in which Cromwell, in bed with Mistress Lambert, receives the news of the Regicide, and the tragedy concludes with a doleful chorus assigning blame to various Royalist leaders, especially the Duke of Hamilton, "sole Causer of the strife . . . Betwixt the King and Parliament."

The Famous Tragedie is one of the very few plays concerned with the Rebellion that deals explicitly with current events and personages. Others, such as T. B.'s *The Rebellion of Naples* (1649), *The Disloyall Favorite* (165?), *The Tragedy of Marcus Tullius Cicero* (1651), Tatham's *The Distracted State* (1651), Manuche's *The Just General* (1652), and *The Banish'd Shepheardess* (1660?), Baron's *Mirza* (1655), and Kirkham's *Alfrede or Right Reinthroned* (1659), provide commentary by implicit parallels with either dramatized history in remote settings or invented plots. In most of these plays, partisanship is a good deal less obvious than it is in *The Famous Tragedie,* but this is not to say that they are lacking in the expression of political and religious points of view. These points of view are not, however, readily identifiable or capable of being labelled as either unreservedly "Cavalier" or "Roundhead." Most of them were, in fact, probably written by individuals who leaned toward Royalism, but few could, like *The Famous Tragedie of King Charles I,* be accurately described as instruments of partisanship and propaganda. Most of them appear to be serious attempts to illuminate dramatically various aspects of the Great Rebellion, its causes, and its consequences. With such material, total objectivity may not be possible, even for the historians. (S. R. Gardiner is clearly as supportive of the Roundheads as Clarendon is of the Royalists.) But most of the dramatists, like the historians, appear to be at least attempting to reveal more than their biases in assessing the responsibility, and irresponsibility, of participants in the conflict.

T. B.'s *The Rebellion of Naples, or the Tragedy of Massenello,* another tragedy published in the year of the Regicide, is introduced as a dramatization of recent events abroad, "Written By a Gentleman who was an eyewitness where this was really acted upon that bloody Stage, the streets of NAPLES Anno Domini MDCXLVII."[22] In the address to the reader, T. B. denies that the play is a commentary on recent English history: ". . . if there be any thing in my booke which points at the present condition of our affairs, I assure you the times are busie with me, and not I with the times." However, the prologue contradicts this:

> If wonders do delight ye: on this Stage
> Acted's the greatest wonder of our age
> Or if you'r pleas'd with seasonable things,
> Here's fightings 'twixt the people and their Kings.

And it seems fairly obvious that the play is an attempt to dramatize events in England by implicit parallels with recent Neapolitan history.[23] The dramatist apparently intended to reveal some of the underlying causes of the Rebellion, the nature of the Rebellion itself, and consequences he foresaw. In effect, he telescoped a period of English history extending from about 1634 until the Restoration, which he dimly foresaw, into the brief and "bloudy" span of Neapolitan history that mirrored it.

In the first act of *The Rebellion of Naples,* Di Arcas, the Vice-Roy, is overthrown and seized by the citizens of Naples under the leadership of Tomaso Massenello, a Neapolitan general. The main reason for the Vice-Roy's overthrow is that he has yielded to the advice of evil counselors in matters involving revenue. Moments before the rebellion actually begins, a counselor who has been dismissed for protesting against unjust taxation prophesies the downfall of the politicians surrounding the Vice-Roy who "think the Sacred Unction not sufficient to anoynt [their] King, except it mingled with the peoples tears." His view of these counselors is verified in the next scene, when the Vice-Roy's Lord-Treasurer is heard urging him to lay an excise on fruit in order to raise money for supplies demanded by Spain. The Vice-

Roy indulges in a bit of guilty hand-wringing at "having laid Excise on all things upon earth, on fire, in water," but the Lord-Controller soothes him with assurances that the nobility's current prosperity is all that matters. When they are interrupted by news of the rebellion, the desperate Vice-Roy is willing to promise any redress but is told that the people will not believe someone who has broken his word so often. A mob led by Massenello rushes in and seizes the Vice-Roy, but he escapes, and the enraged general lays down martial law.

It is not difficult to see in this rather crowded first act a dark reflection of English affairs. Di Arcas is a far from flattering image of Charles—weak, vacillating, treacherous, capable of exercising a feeble cunning,[24] as when he escapes by scattering handfuls of coins among the rabble, but mostly controlled by self-serving counselors. The Lord-Controller could be modelled on practically any one of the powerful favorites of either Charles or his father. The Neapolitan Lord Treasurer seems clearly to be modelled on Weston, the Lord Treasurer who encouraged the King to raise his revenues by fines, the enforcement of forest laws, the issue of ship-money writs and other measures that effectively alienated many subjects of every class.[25] The fact that the Lord Treasurer in the play is urging an excise in order to pay for military supplies for Spain would also support the identification, for Weston was a strong proponent of an English alliance with Spain that would threaten the Dutch commercial supremacy, and shortly before his death in 1635 an agreement was negotiated whereby Spain would meet part of the expenses of vindicating Charles' claim to Dunkirk in return for England's entrance into an alliance with Spain against the Dutch and the French. Money for a fleet was raised by the issue of ship-money writs in 1634 and again in 1635, but these measures met with tremendous resistance since they effectively reduced the right of parliamentary taxation and indeed the need for Parliament itself.[26]

The remainder of *The Rebellion of Naples* is taken up with the ultimately successful struggles of the Vice-Roy to regain power and the degeneration of Massenello from a champion of liberty into a raving tyrant. Again it requires little effort of imagination to see the essential similarity of the schemes of the Vice-Roy and his advisors to the schemes of Charles and his supporters in 1647 and '48. Like Charles delivering England up to Scottish Presbyterianism, in the secret treaty of Newport, the Vice-Roy is willing to deliver his city into the hands of practically anyone as long as he himself is restored to the throne. He is delighted with a plan proposed by one advisor to arrange for a takeover of the city by bandits. The project fails, even as the Scottish invasion under Hamilton failed, and the Vice-Roy's advisors are forced to "tack about again." Their new plan involves the circulation of false rumors of a French invasion that will cause the citizens to be armed against

Massenello and then a secret Austrian invasion that will restore the Vice-Roy. The role planned for Don John and the Austrians corresponds to the one Queen Henrietta Maria and her advisors apparently had in mind for the Marquis of Ormond and the Irish Royalists, to accomplish in 1649 what the Scots had failed to accomplish in 1648.[27] Like Henrietta Maria, the Vice-Roy's Queen plays an important part in affairs of state. While the Vice-Roy deludes Massenello with promises that he will subscribe to "articles of agreement" between himself and the general as representative of the people, the Queen lulls his suspicions by arranging a marriage between her son and his daughter.

As it turns out, none of these Royalist machinations is necessary, for Massenello, who may be a crude caricature of Cromwell, degenerates with astonishing and rather unconvincing rapidity into a tyrannical maniac who alienates the people and brings about his own downfall. After carrying out numerous atrocities in the name of "justice," he finally undoes himself by tearing down the marble monument upon which the "articles of agreement" are inscribed and which would restrain his own tyranny as well as the Vice-Roy's. Ironically, the monument is counterfeit and meaningless anyway. The dramatist may intend here some reference to *The Agreement of the People* and Cromwell's opposition to it,[28] but no real parallel is worked out.

T. B. was no doubt more of a Cavalier than a Roundhead in his sympathies, but his dramatic handling of the Rebellion reveals no belief in the essential righteousness of either cause. Unlike other Cavalier dramatists who base their prophecies of a restoration on optimistic faith in the benevolence of Divine Providence,[29] he expresses no hope for the future. His belief in the likelihood of a restoration appears to be based wholly upon a cynical appraisal of human nature. Power corrupts, and a new-made tyrant will inevitably render himself even more obnoxious than an established predecessor. T. B. may even be suggesting further, in his picture of the weak Vice-Roy and his court, that a restoration is more than likely to be followed by yet another revolution, since kings cannot be trusted to rule justly without some constitutional restraints, which they will seek to avoid by any means including deceit and treachery. Although T. B. does not give any positive expression of his political philosophy, beyond depicting the horrors of two different types of tyranny, we may reasonably infer that he was, like Clarendon, a moderate Royalist who was capable of sympathizing with some of the Parliamentarian aims. His pessimism may be explained by the fact that in 1649 there seemed to be so little likelihood of a compromise between extremes of tyranny. Charles had been sentenced to death by a tribunal nominated for the occasion by the army leaders, who had come to accept the necessity of sailing without legal ballast. Triumphant Independents, who had been champions of toleration, legal and political reform, advocates of democratic change, they had been driven by the reluctance of the people themselves to rely increasingly on the army as an instrument of government.[30] Massenello's progress from a champion of liberty and constitutional reform into an arbitrary and corrupt dispenser of "justice" is obviously a crude parody of this ironical development, and the play as a whole dramatizes T. B.'s sense of the utter futility of all revolutionary endeavor.

The Famous Tragedie and *The Rebellion of Naples* dramatize and interpret from two rather differing Royalist points of view the Rebellion as a *fait accompli.* Other Royalist plays dramatize what in effect might have been if the rebels had been dealt with differently. One of these, *The Disloyall Favorite or the Tragedy of Metellus,* survives in a single tattered manuscript in the Bodleian.[31] It is impossible to date with any precision, but references to the horrors of civil war and a scene in which quarreling citizens argue about who contributes most to the "commonwealthe" suggest sometime after 1649. It is a crudely wrought play, knit together by little besides typical Cavalier sentiments regarding the virtue of loyalty and the dangers of rebellion and treachery in a royal court, but it is illuminating in connection with this discussion as a dramatic expression of a Royalist point of view that is intensely anti-democratic yet enlightened by a recognition of a monarch's need for policy and a willingness to concede in dealings with rebellious subjects.

As the title indicates, the main plot concerns the treachery of Metellus, favorite of the king of Egypt. When it is revealed to the king that Metellus has had an affair with his queen and has murdered a fellow courtier to maintain their secrecy, the king orders her banishment and the execution of Metellus by burning. The ordinary citizens ("Rable"), who regard Metellus as their "champion," are put into a rebellious mood by the king's action. They believe it is their right to be consulted:

2 Rab:

> Why I tell you . . . a word with you neighbour (calls him from the rest). It is perfect arbitrary government. I know noe reason why we should be imposed upon. The Queen he has banisht her, executed Metellus, and we never acquainted with it (comes to the rest) Think you neighbours is the king guilty or not guilty?

Omnes ira:

> Guilty (!)

Having been advised of the disorder by one of the citizens, the king appears, accompanied by his nobles. With remarkable ease, he succeeds in pacifying the "rable," and preventing an uprising. Significantly, he accomplishes this by promising to yield to them in whatever has been the cause of their grievance. Unlike the Vice-Roy in *The Rebellion of Naples,* he does not give us any reason to suspect his sincerity, and he is willing to make any concession that will avert civil war:

> I am beholden to you countrymen, & I will be a father
> to you all &
> to my country & pray unite your selves.
> Love one another & be free from jare
> Noe pestilence so bad as civil ware.

We may reasonably infer that the author of this play was one of those Royalists who saw the possibility of compromise between the demands of King Charles and those of the Commons and earnestly wished that the King had been capable of yielding more. The turbulent scene with the "rable" may also have been intended as a commentary on the King's trial, both reflecting the lawless nature of the arrival at a guilty verdict and suggesting how the fatal outcome might have been avoided by an exercise of regal policy.

What is puzzling about *The Disloyall Favorite* and in some ways atypical of Cavalier drama is the handling of religious themes. It's clear that the author has a puritanical horror of idolatry. The Egypt of his play is much given over to idolatrous worship that is condemned by various characters, including even the adulterous queen, who maintains a proud loyalty to an unnamed religion. A barely connected subplot is introduced for no other apparent purpose than to contrast true spiritual devotion with idolatry. The protagonist, Doriman, has been thrown into prison to starve by order of the king for ridiculing the Egyptian gods. While the prison guards are attending an idolatrous devotion with the king and his court, Doriman manages to escape with the help of a woman named Maria. Her loyalty to him has prevented his dying for his loyalty to his religion.

On the basis of the play's religious elements, as well as the main plot's implication that kings must render an account to their people and justify themselves, I would suggest that the author may have been a Presbyterian, perhaps one of those who turned Royalist during the second civil war and who, as a result of this war, were more than ever hostile to the champions of toleration, the Independents.[32]

The three plays I have discussed so far are not among the more distinguished extant dramas of the Commonwealth, and it is highly unlikely that we will ever know who wrote them. All three appear to be closet dramas, though it is not difficult to imagine private performances of *The Famous Tragedie of King Charles I* in the homes of ardent Royalists. The surviving plays of Major Cosmo Manuche, on the other hand, which boldly proclaim his authorship on their title pages, seem clearly to have been written for performance.[33] The fact that there is no record of their having been acted does not warrant the assumption that they were not, perhaps surreptitiously or privately, and as the prologue and epilogue to *The Just General* (1652) indicate, it at least was "intended for the stage." Lacking records of performances, I would argue the likelihood of their having been acted mainly on the basis of the quality of the dramatic craftsmanship and their obvious stageability.[34] While hardly in the same class with the great dramatists of the previous age, Manuche is a competent builder of complex tragi-comic plots involving a wide variety of characters, some of whom are clearly recognizable as types drawn from Elizabethan tragi-comedy while others are obviously modelled on the contemporary London citizenry. They reveal themselves naturally in speech that is suited both to character and setting, whether it be the court, an idealized pastoral scene, or the streets of a city resembling London. In comic dialogue especially Manuche is at his best. Clearly he was schooled in the plays of Beaumont and Fletcher, Jonson, and Massinger, among others, and was gifted with a knack for exploiting comic situations.

That Manuche's plays reflect his Royalism has been noticed by the few critics who have bothered to discuss them.[35] *The Loyal Lovers* combines romantic tragi-comedy with savagely funny satire involving Puritan caricatures. The scene is "Amsterdam," but Gripe-man, a "Committee-man," Sodome, "One of the Synod," and the hypocritical divine Phanaticus obviously represent the powers in control of Commonwealth England, even as Adrastus, Albinus, and Symphronio, "Loyall Comrades," represent pleasure-loving, alienated Cavaliers. Though he satirizes the triumphant rebels, Manuche does not deal with the Rebellion in this play. In *The Just General,* however, it appears to be one of his central concerns. As my previous discussion may suggest, Cavalier dramatists generally tended to share the Roundheads' opinion that the King's evil, self-serving counselors were ultimately to blame for the Rebellion. The culpability of the kings in the drama who are threatened with rebellion may vary, but almost invariably they are shown to be misled by treacherous advisors. In *The Just General* Manuche dramatizes the saving of a kingdom for its rightful ruler by the wise actions of a loyal counselor. Like *The Disloyall Favorite,* it seems to suggest what might have been.

The central conflict in *The Just General* arises from the fact that the young king of Sicily, Amasius, is in love with Aurelia, a woman of surpassing beauty and virtue but lowly birth. His most trusted counselor, the great general Bellicosus, attempts unsuccessfully to dissuade him from marrying her because he fears the possibility of rebellion by subjects who will regard the match as unsuitable. That Manuche intended here a parallel with Charles's persistence in his decision to marry a Roman Catholic princess, a course of action inevitably condu-

cive to widespread discontent, seems likely. But Bellicosus is no Buckingham. In fact, one gathers that Manuche in drawing his ideal courtier-advisor, may have intended to reveal the virtues Charles's advisors conspicuously lacked and a freedom from the weaknesses common among courtiers generally. Bellicosus "hath to much honesty, mixt with knowledg" to act against the interests of either the king or his country. While the other courtiers urge the king to gratify his desires and not concern himself with "that many headed beast (the commonwealth)" the general is steadfast in his opposition to a match "the subject may make his pretence of quarrel."[36]

Beyond this there would seem to be implicit parallels with events in England on the very eve of the Rebellion. When Aurelia disappears, led into hiding in the country by a friend who would save her from the murderous plots of a jealous woman named Artesia, the king is convinced that she has either been spirited away or murdered by Bellicosus. Resolving to abandon the court and search for her himself, he leaves behind a letter to the general bitterly accusing him of murder and treason. Bellicosus, who prides himself on his loyal service, on having saved for the young ruler an "unhappy Kingdome with fear and conquest almost spent," is understandably bitter. But his loyalty remains unshaken. When the king's absence causes "the factious People (mutable by nature)" to threaten an uprising, Bellicosus yields to pressure to take the crown himself rather than allow the kingdom to be led by either Sicilian Levellers who "would have no King" or those who "Would have they knew not what." When the young king returns with his beloved Aurelia, Bellicosus immediately restores the crown to him. The trials of loyalty have been severe. Bellicosus has had to endure not only the king's ingratitude and distrust but the pain of sentencing his own son, Delirus, to death for his involvement in Artesia's plot to murder Aurelia. Loyalty, however, is abundantly rewarded with the pardoning of all offenders by the restored king.

The specific historical reference of *The Just General* to the Rebellion emerges, I believe, if we compare it briefly with an earlier Royalist drama, John Denham's *The Sophy,* published in August 1642. *The Sophy,* like Baron's *Mirza* (1655), deals with a tragic event in recent Persian history, the destruction of the good prince Mirza by the machinations of the evil courtiers surrounding his father, the emperor of Persia.[37] The prince, having achieved a tremendous victory over the Turks, returns in triumph to his father's court but only remains a short time before departing again. During the prince's absence, an evil courtier arouses in the emperor's mind fears and jealousy against his son. When the prince returns, he is blinded and killed, and soon after, the remorseful emperor dies. In a recent article, John M. Wallace argues persuasively that *The Sophy,* as a dramatization of the destructive effects of fears and jealousies on a state, was a timely fable constructed around morals King Charles might well have heeded. Had a contemporary of Denham's read this closet drama closely, says Wallace, "he would have observed that both the arbitrary ruler and the good prince were largely to blame for their misfortunes, one by letting too much power fall into the hands of evil counselors, the other by absenting himself from the capital at the crucial moment. Charles was guilty of both errors, as his friends lamented."[38] Wallace goes on to note that "Parliament repeatedly requested that Charles return to London after he left the city on January 10, 1642."[39] After it began to appear that the king could not raise an army, Parliament began to assume an uncompromising attitude. Some of his most trusted advisors, having given up all hope of his being able to raise an army, urged him to surprise the houses by a sudden appearance at Westminster which might startle them into granting favorable terms.[40] I would argue that Manuche too, in *The Just General,* consciously dramatized the dangers of an untimely departure by a ruler from his kingdom, and, like Denham, appears to be suggesting that Charles was at least partially responsible for his misfortunes.

In a later play, *The Banish'd Shepheardess,* Manuche celebrates the Restoration and pays a graceful tribute to the Queen Dowager. The play, a courtly pastoral comedy rather in the tradition of Lyly and Peele, has been tentatively dated 1665,[41] and the references to General Monck clearly indicate a date no earlier than 1660.[42] In it the story of the rebellion is told by a character named Lysander, a loyal subject to Charilaus, son of the Banish'd Shepheardess. Neither in his account nor anywhere else in the play is there criticism explicit or implicit of the late king:

> The Arcadians: surfeiting, with Ease, and plenty
> . . . . .
> Under, a neuer to be forgotten, vertuous prince.
> (An unfortunate shepheard: to such a woolvish
> And ungratefull flock) began, under that
> Common cloake for Rebellion (Religion) To pretend
> Earnist desyers, to a Conformitie therein.
> finding fault with what had no fault in it, but decency.[43]

The fact that this play reveals a far narrower Royalist point of view than *The Just General* is not difficult to explain. For one thing, this play was written to be presented to Henrietta Maria herself. In the dedicatory address, he beseeches her to accept "(by the hands of my perishing Children) The Endeavors of a poore suffering subiect Whose Loyallty (the cause of his many crewell imprisonments) May iustly hope your Gracious pardon for his weakness, When the head still suffers for the bodies distemper." It would appear that Manuche's primary intention was to ingratiate himself with the Court and perhaps to put to rest all doubts that may have arisen concerning his loyalty. It could hardly have been

a secret that he had been in the service of the Protectorate.[44] If in fact he truly suffered for his "Loyallty," it may have been the result of his having served as a double agent. The fact that several prominent noblemen were willing in 1661 to sign a certificate attesting his loyal service suggests that he was able to explain his apparent defection.[45]

With the exception of *King Charles I* and *The Banish'd Shepheardess,* all of the plays I have discussed might be regarded as representing a kind of return to the tradition of the *Mirror for Magistrates.* And even in *The Banish'd Shepheardess* we may see, along with the obvious intention of flattery, a didactic burden intended to profit princes and magistrates. As in Lyly's *Endymion,* a pastoral setting is used to project an idealized image of the Court and to criticize all the forces that inhibit the realization of that ideal in the world outside it. In another Cavalier drama in manuscript, written on the eve of the Restoration, *Alfrede or Right Reinthroned* (1659) drama in the *Mirror* tradition and pastoral tragi-comedy are fully fused. The play is dedicated to Lady Blounte by R. K. ("your most affectionate Brother"). The author has been identified as R. Kirkham, though there appears to be some question about this.[46] Whoever the author was, and I will assume for now that it was Kirkham, he appears to have been a member of that most threatened of Royalist minorities, the Roman Catholics. I find this abundantly reflected throughout the play itself but especially in the dolorous epilogue spoken by St. Cuthbert:

> O wretched England! would thou still did's't know
> that ancient happy state; thou wouldst not now
> As from ye world thou separated art,
> So from ye worlds true faith be kept apart:
> Thou wouldst not then be cald an Isle ingrate
> ffrom Heau'n rebelliously degenerate;
> Nor wouldst thou consecrated Temples spoile,
> Nor them with sacrilegious Hands defyle;
> Nor let unparent-like thy Children bee
> Shipwrackt upon ye Rockes of Heirsy
>   But England's now a Stepmother, alas
>   which once of Saints a fertile Parent was.[47]

One could argue, I suppose, that the dramatist was an Episcopalian lamenting Puritan domination, or even a Presbyterian lamenting toleration. Indeed the accusation of "Heirsy" (heresy) was one levelled by virtually every sect in England against all rivals. But the reference in this speech to an "ancient happy state" in which England had been one with the rest of the Christian world in religion seems strongly to suggest a time prior to the Reformation. And while the shattering of stained glass windows and the stabling of horses in cathedrals certainly outraged Episcopalians as well as Catholics, the lamentation of this writer for the widespread desecration and sacrilege of the time seems to come from one whose spiritual ancestors "consecrated" the "Temples" appropriated by the Protestants.

Whether Catholic or Episcopalian, Kirkham dramatically recreates an England in which there was no government "of saints" on the Genevan pattern, but the possibility of assistance from saints such as St. Cuthbert, who might be looked to in times of crisis. The crisis dramatized in *Alfrede* is an invasion by the Danes under the bloodthirsty King Gothurnus. As the play begins, King Alfred, his generals, and all the members of his family are fleeing the invaders and lamenting their misfortunes in speeches that reveal Kirkham's fondness for Senecan rhetoric. The longer speeches are classic set speeches of lamentation, complete with all the expected *topoi,* apostrophes, imprecations, rhetorical questions, epic similes and longing for annihilation. Not surprisingly, much of the dialogue takes the form of stichomythia. Clearly, Seneca's tragedies were among Kirkham's models, but they were not his only ones. The titanic self-definition of Gothurnus raging over his brother's supposed death inevitably recalls Tamburlaine:

> Call downe ye Gods with an imperious voice.
> and Marshall that treasonous, impious Band
> against me; like Atlas Ile encounter all.
> Doe's the supernall Crew then envy me?
> perhaps they were affraid least after earth
> their Heaven should next become due to my
> uncontroled triumphs. So 'twas. Ile climbe
> Heav'ns lucide spheare and dislocate the stars;
> Nor shall the Sun afford ye world his light;
> Nor ye Moone lend any brightnesse to th' earth:
> Jove shall not find within the Orbs a seat
> secure, till Osbern's death be expiate.

And the progress of King Alfred from grief and self-pity toward Christian Stoic acceptance recalls the similar progress of the defeated Duke Andrugio in Marston's *Antonio and Mellida,* even as the fusion of materials for a revenge play with a comedy of forgiveness recalls *The Malcontent.*[48] Kirkham's use of a pastoral setting as a regenerative force suggests Shakespearean models as well, though the radical transformations of his characters are far less convincing than anything in Shakespeare. A number of comic interludes involve a *miles gloriosus* and a clever *servus,* not unlike Armado and Moth, and a family of English rustics. Obviously, Kirkham was a perceptive student of Elizabethan as well as Roman drama who sought to imitate in the language, structure and characterization of his play the techniques of the masters. If he did not succeed in creating a "tragical-comical-historical-pastoral" drama comparable to the Elizabethan masterpieces, he succeeded nonetheless in creating a lively piece of reading entertainment which probably could, unlike so many other Commonwealth closet dramas, be staged successfully.

Like *The Disloyall Favorite* and *The Just General,* *Alfrede* seems to suggest what might have been if King Charles had been wiser and his counselors more just. Alfred's generals are good counselors who assist him in shaking off the paralysis of self-pity. But even more helpful in this regard is the spiritual advisor he encounters in the wilderness. Neothus, a holy hermit, recognizes the King beneath his disguise but refuses to comfort him. Instead he urges him to regard his downfall as a just punishment for his failures as a king. The King acknowledges the justice of the indictments and repents. The hermit then comforts him with the assurance that he will be given even greater kingdoms than he has lost. Meanwhile, the King's mother, who is repeatedly tempted to suicide, is being consoled by a simple swineherd. Significantly, as a result of their misfortunes, the royal family has come to know the people, who, as Neothus's speech suggests, have been neglected. The Danish invasion, which appeared to be nothing but disastrous, has been a kind of grace.

The play moves toward a joyously triumphant conclusion as everyone, including even the Danes, undergoes some form of spiritual regeneration. Alfred's forces are victorious, and he is reconciled with Gothurnus to the extent even that he is willing to share the rule of England with him. Again, it is possible to see here a dramatic expression of the wish of many Royalists that the King had been capable of compromise, as well as a Catholic yearning for England's return to the True Faith which would, presumably, protect her against future civil wars.

One of the most distinguished and interesting plays of this period, the anonymous *Tragedy of Marcus Tullius Cicero* (1651), cannot, at least in terms of its political sentiments, be properly termed "Cavalier drama." Rather surprisingly, it has not received any critical attention at all beyond Harbage's brief comment that it was one of the plays making 1651 "a banner year for rimed plays."[49] In fact, it deserves a good deal more attention as a very competently written closet drama which could, with very little revision, be acted. A director might wish to cut some of the longer speeches, though few lines are superfluous.

Unlike other Commonwealth writers of history plays who used the genre to comment on their own times, the author of *Cicero* did not find it necessary to alter history drastically to suit his didactic purposes. He knew his Roman history and chose an episode, the fall of Cicero, which clearly mirrored the destruction of the Republican dream in Commonwealth England. Like "T. B." and other Royalist playwrights, he suggests that England has leaped from the frying pan of one tyranny into the fire of another, but unlike the Royalists, he seems to imply that England's folly has been the acceptance of a faulty dilemma and the rejection of a scheme involving neither king nor dictator. The Republican alternative appears in the play as an ideal that Rome has not really known since her Golden Age. Cicero's man Laureas sings of it:

> How happy was the Roman State
> when her chiefest Magistrate
> was rais'd to the fasces from the plow,
> When such as Cincinnatus sway'd
> The helme of th' Common-wealth, and made
> Her proudest Adversaries humbly bow[50]

It is this ideal that had inspired Brutus and the other conspirators against Julius Caesar, and it is in Brutus that Cicero places his hopes for Rome's deliverance from tyranny under Antony:

> 'Tis *Brutus* whom *Antonius* copes with, *Brutus*
> The Omen of whose very name, and blood
> Fatall to State usurpers were sufficient
> To fortifie our drooping souls, and raise them
> From thought of servitude.

Brutus never appears in the play, but Cicero frequently refers to him, always with unreserved admiration and affection.

Cicero himself is a sympathetically drawn tragic figure, a great Roman patriot whose commitment to Republican principles is unshakable. One of the few unhistorical aspects of the play is the character's utter freedom from the vanity, conceit, changefulness and other faults reflected so clearly in the letters of the historical Cicero. Also omitted is the fact that Brutus had reproached him for his enthusiasm about Octavius.[51] In the play, it is Cicero who reproaches himself for having thrown his support so unreservedly to Octavius in order to counter the threat of Antony. Significantly, Octavius, whose alliance with Antony brings about Cicero's downfall and who appears in the play as an embodiment of ruthless ambition, shares the Republicans' admiration for Cicero. Pondering the necessity of letting Antony destroy the great orator, Octavius is severely exercised in conscience:

> And shall *Octavius* ruine so great worth?
> Be still my melting passions: He must die,
> And therefore 'cause he is his Countreys parent,
> He that is *Caesars* friend must be a foe
> Unto his countreys freedome, which he prizes
> Above his life, and for this cause must lose it.
> Shall he then die—? Ambition sayes he must.

Indeed, only Antony and his supporters refuse to share in the general reverence for Cicero as a great patriot. In the play, Antony is willing to spare Cicero, provided that he will burn his Philippic orations. Thus the dramatist gives his Cicero the opportunity, not available to the historical Cicero in 43 B.C., to choose between life under the Triumvirate and death with the rest of the proscribed. Cicero chooses to reject both alternatives, as well as a third, Stoic suicide, and his death while in flight, betrayed by the servant Philologus, occurs as Plutarch describes it.[52]

The author of *Cicero* had a goodly share of both talent and learning. Politically, he (or she) obviously shared his protagonist's ideals. Monarchy is unequivocally condemned, not merely in the speeches of Cicero and his friends, but in speeches not limited in point of view by political prejudices. One of these, a choric speech coming at the end of Act IV, recalls Rome's historic resistance to monarchy, manifested in the expulsion of Tarquin and the condemnation of Manlius, among other actions, but continues dolefully:

> Boast this, and more, doe, but withall
>   With horrour say,
> You did it only to install
>   Worse plagues then they,
> That you one viper of the State
>   Have chang'd for three;
> And for a worse Triumvirate
>   A Monarchy.

Earlier in the same act, Cicero and the Senators solicit the prophecies of soothsayers, one of whom falls dead immediately after uttering the following:

> Then fathers, hear your dismall fate,
> Your freedome shall be lost, your state
> Converted to a Monarchy,
> And all be slaves but only I (stops his breath and falls
>   down dead)

In 1651, the year this play was published, the progress of England toward a dictatorship was already apparent. Cromwell and his generals, along with Sir Henry Vane and other leaders in Parliament, were still committed to the ideal of a free state governed according to the resolutions of elected representatives and guaranteeing individual liberties, but it was evident that most Englishmen did not revere this ideal and were, in fact, quite willing to return to monarchy. Gardiner conjectures that at this time Cromwell's "thoughts were beginning to crystallise round the notion of reconciling monarchy and commonwealth by entrusting some undefined measure of executive power to a 'single person' not of Stuart blood."[53] 1651, it will be recalled, was also the year in which Hobbes's *Leviathan* appeared, a work which argues in favor of monarchy based on reason and which asserts, among other things, that the State is omnipotent over human action so long as it is able to put to death those who violate its laws.[54] The great Leveller John Lilburne and Cromwell were on good terms at this time, but within a year Lilburne would be banished by the Rump for his pamphlet attacking Hazlerigg.[55] The author of *The Tragedy of Marcus Tullius Cicero,* who was clearly a Republican, perhaps even a Leveller, could see the imminent betrayal of the ideals which had inspired the Great Rebellion, and his play is a tragic lament.

Cicero was by no means the only dramatic commentary on the current political situation to appear in 1651. The title sheet of John Tatham's *The Distracted State* indicates that it was "Written in the Yeer, 1641," but as Professor Wallace observes, the play is filled with clear references to England's progress toward dictatorship in 1651, which only a man of extraordinary perception could have prophesied ten years earlier.[56] It is a much less polished play than *Cicero.* Like *The Rebellion of Naples,* it begins with the downfall of a ruler who is "not without his faults," and most of the subsequent action involves the struggles of various successors to gain and maintain power. Not surprisingly, Agathocles, one of the protagonists who is an outspoken anti-monarchist, is one of those who aspires to the kingship. The play concludes with the restoration of the lawful king and his forgiveness of the churchmen and others who had assisted in overthrowing him. With heavy irony, Tatham represents the ambitious anti-monarchists in his play as being inspired by ancient Roman republican ideals. To his fellow conspirators Agathocles exclaims:

> How sweet and freely *Rome* enjoy'd her self
> 'Till she submitted to the Power and pride
> Of one mans Rule?[57]

It would appear that quite a few citizens of the Commonwealth were aware of parallels between England's post-civil war progress toward a new tyranny and Rome's post-civil war progress toward dictatorship under Augustus. Another work that appeared in 1651 was Part III of Clement Walker's *Historie of Independencie,* in which Cromwell is shown to be following in the footsteps of Sulla and Augustus, as well as the Duke D'Alva in his suppression of the Netherlands. The parallel with Augustus is the most fully developed because, in Walker's view, the rise of Augustus had involved essentially the same hypocrisy and betrayal of professed ideals as had Cromwell's rise:

> Augustus usurped the Title of *Tribune of the People,* whereby his Person became sacred and inviolable; and (humouring the irrational Animals) tooke upon him the especial Protection of that Brutish heard, the Rascall multitude, The Tribunes of the People having bin originally instituted to protect the People. His next step was to make himself *Perpetual Dictator,* whereby he arrogated to himself a vaste, unlimited power above all Laws. The Tribuneship was his Buckler, The Dictatorship was his Sword. And last of all (for Ornament only, *He having already the full power of an absolute Monarch (although he forbore the Title of (King) because it was hateful to the People* and against the Laws ever since the Regifugium) he took upon him the Title of *Princeps Senatus,* or *President of the Senate;* to keep a corresponding power over that great Counsell or Parliament: And finally usurped the Title and Office of *Imperator or Generalisimo* of all forces by Land and Sea, Garisons, &c.[58]

That the author of *Cicero* was also thinking of similarities between Augustus and Cromwell in 1651 seems likely.

It is apparent, then, that the extant drama of the interregnum provides a faithful mirror of virtually the whole spectrum of contemporary political and religious attitudes toward the Great Rebellion. Raging Royalists, thoughtful moderates, disappointed Republicans, alienated Catholics, Episcopalians and Presbyterians all turned to a genre whose *raison d'etre,* performance, was suppressed by a Puritan government, which would itself in the course of the interregnum manifest a variety of governing styles. The few plays I have discussed are merely a representative sampling. There is certainly plenty of room for another book length study to extend the investigations of Rollins, Hotson and Harbage. Like their studies, it should focus initially on the conditions affecting playing, but mainly it should include extensive discussion of the plays themselves and their numerous topical references. There is room as well for studies of individual playwrights, Manuche for instance, who have been underservedly neglected. Obviously such studies would be greatly stimulated if the plays were made more accessible. Admittedly, some of them are hardly worth editing for publication, but this is not the case with Manuche's plays, with *Alfrede, Marcus Tullius Cicero,* Fane's *De Pugna Animi,*[59] Baron's *Mirza,* the anonymous comedy *The Hectors,* or with *A Comedy* by "R. M." This last named play, which can, I believe, be identified as the work of the economic writer Ralph Maddison, has almost totally escaped notice and is not even listed in the *C.B.E.L.*[60] Perhaps new studies and individual editions would in turn encourage the publication of an anthology of these plays, which are of considerable interest to the historian of the English drama as well as revealing reflections of England under the Puritans.

Notes

1. From a book-in-progress, *English Drama Under the Puritans.*

2. Hyder E. Rollins, "A Contribution to the History of the English Commonwealth Drama," *Studies in Philology* XVIII (July, 1921) p. 267.

3. The ordinance has recently been reprinted in *Commonwealth Tracts 1625-1650* ed. Arthur Freeman (New York & London: Garland Publishing, Inc., 1974).

4. Rollins, *op. cit.* pp. 304-305.

5. Leslie Hotson, *The Commonwealth and Restoration Stage* (Cambridge: Harvard, 1928).

6. Alfred Harbage, *Cavalier Drama an historical and critical supplement to the study of the Elizabethan and Restoration Stage* (New York: Modern Language Association, 1936).

7. E.g. *The Committee Man Curried* by S. Sheppard, Parts I & II (1647); Scottish *Politic Presbyter* (1647); M. Nedham, *The Levellers Levell'd* (1647); *Crafty Cromwell, or Oliver Ordering Our New State,* Parts I & II (1648); *Mistress Parlia-*

ment Presented In Her Bed (1648); *Mistress Parliament Brought to Bed* (1648); *Mistress Parliament Her Gossiping* (1648); *Newmarket Fair,* Parts I & II (1649); *The Disease of the House* (1649). Professor Rollins conjectures plausibly: "Perhaps some of these brief plays were performed (what better could the noblemen who hired actors at their private homes want?") *op. cit.* p. 299.

8. Harbage, *op. cit.,* p. 178.

9. *Ibid.* The translation, entitled *Tyrannicall-Government Anatomized, or a Discourse concerning Evil-Councellors, being the Life and Death of John the Baptist* and "Presented to the King's most Excellent Majesty by the Author. *Die Martis, 30. Januarii, 1642."* was "Ordered by the Committee of the House of Commons concerning Printing, That this Book be forthwith printed and published." It was reprinted in *George Buchanan Glasgow Quatercentenary Studies 1906* (Glasgow: Maclehose, 1907) pp. 92-173. It is prefaced with an essay by the editor, J. T. T. Brown, arguing the likelihood that Milton is the translator. Harbage was impressed by Brown's arguments (*op. cit.,* p. 178). William Riley Parker, on the other hand, simply lists the translation among works attributed to Milton which "may safely be ignored as not his work." (*Milton A Biography* Vol. II Oxford, 1968, p. 836).

10. This idea becomes virtually a cliché of Royalist propaganda. E.g. *Mercurius Pragmaticus* (October 26-November 2) 1650: "Unlesse the *houses* take some speciall Order, *Stage-playes* will never downe while the heavenly *Buffones* of the Presbyterie are in Action, all whose *Sermons* want nothing but *Sence* and *Wit,* to passe for perfect *Comedies.*" And *Mercurius Elencticus* (October 29-November 5): "They of Westminster have Acted their parts now seaven years upon the stage of this Kingdome; insomuch that they have even tyred and wearyed out the Spectators, and are themselves ready to be hissed off the Stage, and yet they cannot endure that their Elder brethren of the *Cock-pit* should live by them . . ." Quoted by Rollins, *op. cit.,* p. 285.

11.   "Though *Johnson, Shakespeare, Gosse,* and *Devenant,*
     Brave *Sucklin, Beaumont, Fletcher, Shurley* want
     The life of action, and their learned lines
     Are loathed, by the Monsters of the times;
     Yet your refined Soules, can penetrate
     Their depth of merit, and excuse their Fate . . ."

12. See my article "Marlowe and the Development of Tragical Satire," *English Studies* LVIII (June 1977) 209-220.

13. All quotations are from the copy in the Worcester College Library, Oxford.

14. G. P. Gooch, *English Democratic Ideas in the 17th Century* (New York: Harper & Row, 1959) p. 149. Cf. the entry in John Evelyn's *Diary* for Jan. 17, 1649: "I heard the rebell *Peters* incite the Rebell powers met in the Painted Chamber, to destroy his Majestie & saw that Arch Traytor *Bradshaw,* who not long after condemn'd him." ed. E. S. DeBeer (London: Oxford, 1959) p. 275. See also Godfrey Davies, *The Early Stuarts 1603-1660* (Oxford: Clarendon, 1967) p. 157 for discussion of the chaplain's role in persuading the members of the court to sign the King's death-warrant.

15. See Maurice Ashley, *Cromwell's Generals* (London: Jonathan Cape, 1954) pp. 102-103.

16. Clarendon, *History* Bk XI, p. 2306. Cf. Evelyn, *Diary* February 6, 1652: ". . . this day I saw the Magnificent Funeral of that arch-Rebell *Ireton,* carried in pomp from Somerset house to *Westminster . . .* This *Ireton* was a stout rebell, & had ben very bloudy to the Kings party, witnesse his severity at Colchester, when in cold blood he put those gallant gent: Sir *Charles* Lucas & G. *Lisle* to death:" See also July 8, 1656. Rainsborough was one of those appointed to witness the execution. (Gardiner, *Civil War* IV, p. 203).

17. Gooch, *op. cit.,* pp. 134-140. Ireton was the principal author of the *Heads of Proposals* issued in August, 1647, which includes the following: "That (the things here before being provided, for settling and securing the rights, liberties, peace and safety of the kingdom) His Majesty's person, his Queen, and royal issue, may be restored to a condition of safety, honour and freedom in this nation, without diminution to their personal rights, or further limitation to the exercise of the regal power than according to the particulars foregoing." (S. R. Gardiner, *The Constitutional Documents of the Puritan Revolution 1625-1660* Oxford: Clarendon, 1899, p. 321-322.).

18. Gooch, *op. cit.* p. 129.

19. Gardiner, *Civil War* III, p. 366.

20. Clarendon, *History* XI, pp. 2318-2319.

21. Gardiner suggests that these men were motivated by a desire for vengeance since Rainsborough was known to have been one of the first to advocate a trial of the King. (*Civil War* IV, p. 232).

22. British Museum, E. 1358 (one of the plays collected by Thomason). All quotations are from this copy.

23. Harbage remarks: "Although an address to the reader cautions that the play is not to be mistaken as English allegory, some of its preachments leave no other alternative." *op. cit.,* p. 224.

24. Phrase borrowed from S. R. Gardiner, *The First Two Stuarts and The Puritan Revolution* (New York: Scribners, 1891) p. 155. Used to describe Charles attempting to play off the Army against the Parliament in November 1647.

25. *Ibid.,* p. 77.

26. *Ibid.,* p. 96.

27. Gardiner, *Civil War* IV, p. 224.

28. *Ibid.,* Vol. III, p. 383.

29. E.g. Sir Gilbert Talbot's Epistle Dedicatory prefacing his translation of Bonarelli's *Filli di Sciro* "To his sacred Majesty Charles 2d—prophetically written at Paris an: 1657": "I must confess, I was desirous to represent to your Majesty the providence which herein appeareth soe highly miraculous, although but in the fictitious redemption of two captive Lovers, and the unexpected restitution of theyre country to its ancient freedome, that I might take occasion, from hence, to give the world this sad (yet cheerefull) account of my fayth: That, as Heaven hath been pleased to punish the sinnes of yr. kingdomes upon the most innocent of Kings, in the martyrdome of your royall father, and exile of your selfe; soe its justice will never suffer such horrid, and unparallel'd villany to prosper into generations, either through the open defection, or (which little differs) the tame temporising of your Subjects under a tyrannical Imposter: but that all yr. persecutions, and sufferings hitherto have bin onely to render you more glorious, and magnify the day of your redemption; which is ye firme hope and humble assurance of . . . Your Maiestyes Most dutifully, and faythfully devoted Subject, and servant." (Bodleian MS. Rawlinson, poet. 130).

30. See Davies, *op. cit.* Chapt. VII; Gardiner, *Civil War* IV, pp. 327-28.

31. Bodleian MS. Rawlinson D. 1361, ff. 285-306.

32. See Davies, *op. cit.* Chapt. VIII.

33. Manuche's extant printed plays include *The Just General* (1652), *The Loyal Lovers* (1652), and possibly *The Bastard* (1652) though its attribution to Manuche has never been supported. Surviving plays in manuscript include *The Feast* (MS Worcester College, Oxford) and *The Banish'd Shepheardess* (MS Huntington Lib. EL 8395).

34. Harbage apparently assumes that the printed plays were not acted. He conjectures that the plays in manuscript may have been privately acted. *op. cit.,* p. 274.

35. Harbage, *op. cit.,* pp. 226-227. Frank H. Ristine, *English Tragicomedy Its Origin and History* (New York: Russell & Russell, 1963) pp. 154-155. See also Thornton S. Graves, "Notes on Puritanism and the Stage," *Studies in Philology* XVIII (1921) p. 163.

36. All quotations are from the Bodleian Library copy.

37. Robert Baron's *Mirza* (British Museum, E. 1449. 360) is one of the plays collected by Thomason. *The Sophy* is reprinted in Sir John Denham, *The Poetical Works,* ed. Theodore H. Banks, 2nd. ed. (Hamden, Conn., 1969).

38. John M. Wallace, "'Examples Are Best Precepts': Readers and Meanings in Seventeenth-Century Poetry," *Critical Inquiry* I (Dec. 1974) p. 274.

39. *Ibid.*

40. Davies, *op. cit.,* pp. 129-130.

41. Alfred Harbage, *Annals of English Drama 975-1700* (Philadelphia: Univ. of Penn. Press, 1940) p. 130. The brief note "(Past.?)" suggests that he did not have the opportunity to view the manuscript.

42. In the last act, a gentleman kneels before Prince Charilaus and informs him that he has been restored to the throne of Arcadia:

> The Common people: hight'ned, by the Noble Actions:
> Of Their (late come) General:
> (Who, still, receives his orders, from the Godds)
> speaking, no other language,
> But the restoring, Their: lawful & long suffering
> prince: To His just rights. Seem'd All on fyre
> (With impacience) for that blest houre.
> Whils't the braue General: (with swift motion)
> Brought, Their desyers, to that mature Effect,
> Hee: (through the Citty) streight, proclaimes you: king:
> With such a generall aclamation, of a reall joye.
> Roomes: Conquests: ne'er brought home.

43. All quotations are from the Huntington Library MS EL 8395.

44. On June 4, 1656, he sent to Cromwell, through Secretary Thurloe, the following:

> Petition of Cosmo Manuche to the Protector. I have long laboured to serve you and this late distracted State, and acknowledge your bountiful relief to enable my endeavors. But in making discoveries of the disturbers of our present happy Government, I have spent 20 £ more than I have received, which, if not speedily paid, will deprive me of liberty, and be my undoing, my former livelihood, by boarding scholars, being taken away. I have more knowledge now, and a better will to increase your store than exhaust it.

> (*Calendar of State Papers,* Domestic Series, 1655-56, p. 348.)

45. *Dictionary of National Biography* Vol. XXII Supplement p. 1010.

46. Harbage, *op. cit.,* p. 277. Also attributed to Kirkham with a parenthetical question mark in *Research Opportunities in Renaissance Drama* VIII (1965) p. 21.

47. All quotations are from Bodleian MS. Rawlinson, poet. 80.

48. See my article "Stoicism and Revenge in Marston," *English Studies* LI (Dec. 1970) 507-517.

49. Harbage, *op. cit.,* p. 64.

50. All quotations are from the copy in the Worcester Library, Oxford. (Checked against British Museum 643. d. 11.)

51. See Brutus's letter from Macedonia to Atticus, at Rome, (middle of June, 43 B.C.) Included in *Letters of Cicero* ed. L. P. Wilkinson (London: Arrow Books, 1959) pp. 234-236, and Cicero's reply, pp. 236-239.

52. Plutarch, *Lives of the Noble Grecians and Romans,* "Cicero."

53. S. R. Gardiner, *History of the Commonwealth and Protectorate 1649-1656* in 4 volumes (London: Longmans, Green & Co., 1903) Vol. II, p. 77.

54. See Gardiner's discussion of the relevance of *Leviathan* to the situation in England at this time. *Commonwealth and Protectorate* II, pp. 77-78.

55. *Ibid.,* pp. 79-80. See also Gooch, *op. cit.,* pp. 214-216.

56. John M. Wallace, "The Date of John Tatham's *Distracted State,*" *Bulletin of the New York Public Library* LXIV (Jan. 1960) pp. 29-40.

57. All quotations are from John Tatham, *The Distracted State* (1651) Huntington Library 128944.

58. Clement Walker, *The High Court of Justice or Cromwell's New Slaughter-house in England* With the Authoritie that constituted and ordained it, Arraigned, Convicted, and Condemned; for Usurpation, Treason, Tyrannie, Theft, and Murder. Being the III. *Part of the Historie of Independencie* Printed Anno Dom. 1651. (Huntington Library 347116).

59. Fane's *Raguaillo D'Oceano* and *Candy Restored* have been edited by Clifford Leech (Louvain, 1938).

60. Bodleian MS. Rawlinson C.923 is listed with the untitled plays and fragments in the rough checklist included in *Research Opportunities in Renaissance Drama* VIII (1965), p. 33. In fact, its title is "A Comedy."

MAJOR FIGURES

Manfred Weidhorn (essay date 1970)

SOURCE: Weidhorn, Manfred. "Reputation and Achievement." In *Richard Lovelace,* pp. 160-71. New York: Twayne Publishers, Inc., 1970.

[*In the essay that folllows, Weidhorn discusses Richard Lovelace's critical reputation and considers his body of work as a whole.*]

I. REPUTATION

Lovelace's reputation as a poet begins early indeed—in his twenty-first year. Though he had left Oxford two years earlier, his lines on the Princess Katherine were inserted into copies of a volume of elegies by Oxford students. Similarly, when Fletcher's *Wild Goose Chase* appeared in 1652, Lovelace's prefatory verses were printed in larger type than the others' and given the place of honor among them. He was evidently prominent in his time.

Another interesting sidelight is the recent discovery, amid sober entries for 1643-44 in an ordnance notebook, of doodles of the first stanza of "The Scrutiny." It is amusing to think of an ordnance officer or clerk passing the tedious hours by attempting to jot down the stanzas of a brash new poem by a fashionable young poet. Judging from the numerous reprintings this poem underwent in various collections during the rest of the century, "The Scrutiny" became one of Lovelace's most popular. But the best known of his poems was, of course, "To Althea," referred to as early as 1644-45 and continually reprinted.[1]

Before *Lucasta* came out in 1649, Marvell wrote introductory lines which, after decrying the decline in culture, spoke of "insects" who rose against Lovelace, partly because of his role in the Kentish Petition. The implication is that the volume had not yet been licensed but was being scrutinized in accordance with the Printing Ordinance. Politically innocuous as the poems seem to us, their publication may well have been delayed for a while.

The rest of Marvell's poem sketches a different sort of Lovelace fame—as a ladies' man. John Tatham makes similar remarks in his prefatory lines, which suggest that Lovelace also enjoyed repute as poet: the lasses, he says, in Lovelace's absence "do only sigh thy Airs," and the swains "deny to write a line / And do only talk of thine"; he urges Lovelace "by sweet Athea's voice" to return. This passage indicates that Lovelace was known around 1644 as the poet of Althea rather than of Lucasta and that the prison poem, the only one to

Althea, was popular before the 1649 confinement and publication of the book. Praised by friends, Lovelace's poetry was set to music by such eminent composers of the day as Henry Lawes and John Wilson. In Cotgrave's *Wit's Interpreter* (1655), the leading mid-seventeenth-century anthology, one and a half of his poems appeared.

Though Lovelace received brief honorific mention in Joshua Poole's 1657 *English Parnassus,* in Edward Phillips's 1675 *Theatrum Poetarum,* and in William Winstanley's 1687 *Lives of the Most Famous English Poets,* his popularity during the next century and a half was not equal to that of Suckling, Randolph, Cartwright, Habington, Cleveland. Indeed his friend Suckling, in presenting a critique of major and minor contemporary poets, including himself, in "A Session of Poets," makes no mention of Lovelace.

A curious indication that Lovelace had, nevertheless, become the archetypal Cavalier very early was brought to light not too long ago. In his edition of Lovelace, C. H. Wilkinson, at the suggestion of G. Thorn-Drury, pointed out that in Sir Charles Sedley's Restoration play, *The Mulberry Garden,* there are—besides paraphrases of and allusions to famous Lovelace lyrics like "Wars," "Althea," "To Lucasta. From Prison"—numerous parallels with the poet's putative life: his loss of property to the wars and of his beloved to another man; his part in Royalist activities; his being arrested over an incriminating paper and as a by-product of the search for someone else; the unusual name Althea. The ending is happy in the play, as not in life; but, even so, a character's gallant surrender of the lady may perhaps be a picture of some similar action on Lovelace's part and thus give renewed life to Wood's story of Lucasta. If the identification is correct, Sedley's play is an interesting sign of how Lovelace's career and poetry captured the imagination of his age.

In the first half of the eighteenth century, the Neo-Classical Augustan period, Lovelace was not referred to anywhere. He seemed not to have existed at all. He reappeared on the poetic scene in 1765, or just a little over a hundred years after his death, with the publication of Thomas Percy's *Reliques of Ancient English Poetry,* which contained "Wars" and "Althea." The first attempt at a critical appreciation was made in *The Gentleman's Magazine* of 1791-92, over the pseudonym of Cliffordiensis, generally presumed to have been Sir Samuel Egerton Brydges. The period 1817-18 saw the publication, by S. W. Singer, of all of Lovelace's poems, but with expurgations and deletions. Both *Lucastas* came out in 1864 in one volume edited by W. Carew Hazlitt, who segregated the poems by topic. Thus in Part I (1649) all verses addressed to Lucasta (and Aramantha) were gathered, followed by the ones to Ellinda, and rounded off by miscellaneous works and

commendatory poems. Hazlitt's notes were good, but his biographical material was superseded by A. E. Waite, who in 1884 brought new documents to light.

The many twentieth-century students of Donne's influence, emphasizing Lovelace's greater proximity to the Metaphysicals than to the "Sons of Ben," found him, vis-à-vis the master, sorely wanting. Amateur and gentleman, he seemed, though modeling his work on Donne's, to be working in a style uncongenial to him. Some of his best things, like "To . . . Sea," are most memorable when most Metaphysical, yet Lovelace remained on the fringes of the Donne tradition. A piece like "La Bella Bona Roba" is static next to Donne's not because of a lack of "wit" or ingenuity but because to Donne "wit" was a means of expressing complex states of mind and achieving intellectual self-mastery; to the Cavalier, "wit" was exercised and enjoyed for its own sake. The "Grasshopper" shows that he should have followed the simplicity and clarity of Horace rather than the abstruseness of Donne, but he was unable to approach Herrick's grace and too indifferent, too "witty" to move from Metaphysical to the rising Neo-Classical vein. His effort in preserving the courtly stance of polished detachment nevertheless foreshadowed the elegant social wit of the Augustans.[2]

The greatest year in Lovelace's posthumous fame, 1925, saw the publication of the definitive edition of his poems and of the only book-length study of his work. In a lavishly annotated and illustrated edition, bringing together all the biographical material, C. H. Wilkinson furnished the best account yet of the poet's life. Issued in a limited printing, the edition reappeared in one volume, shorn of its illustrations, in 1930; and it is not likely to be superseded for some time.

As a scholar who lived with Lovelace's work more than any other person, Wilkinson also provided the lengthiest, most detailed and considered evaluation of it. Two or three of the poems, he notes, are everywhere anthologized and given a "high place among the lyrics of an age supreme in the art of song"; but they have overshadowed his other lyrics. Wilkinson is aware that this neglect is partly justified: one of the "mob of gentlemen who wrote with ease," Lovelace, following the Cavalier imitation of devices made fashionable by Donne, wrought "slender conceits and labored particularities." His many obvious faults—obscurity, discontinuity, frigidity, slovenliness, striving after effect, lack of the light touch—add up to a case of (as Douglas Bush later put it) "the pernicious anemia of the secular Metaphysical muse, with its dwindling from cosmic audacities into labored and eccentric artifice." Lovelace writes reams of dull verse, minor poems of a minor poet; and, despite incidental attractions, his superlative achievements remain a handful of poems. On the other hand, these successes are the product of an informed sense of art, not mere luck; and a considerable portion of his work is better than is generally believed. Though he sometimes carries a conceit off with the best of them, he does not, when most effective, depend on Metaphysical effects; he is not sufficiently profound or clever to take naturally to this mode of writing. At his best, he exhibits a grace and ease, spontaneity and elegance in the manner of Wyatt. Lovelace is, in short, a worthy representative of the Cavalier class of amateur poets; "he writes very well for a gentleman," but, as a reviewer put it, "he can write worse than any other poet in England who can write as well."[3]

The other event of 1925, C. H. Hartmann's book on Lovelace, proved disappointing. Utilizing a faded nineteenth-century approach, it assumed that every lyric is a "sincere" autobiographical expression and therefore usable as a document. Neither did this study, being limited in its survey of the culture of the age, have much new to say about the "Cavalier spirit." Hartmann's conclusions are predictable: Lovelace writes much that is fashionable, complimentary, occasional, trivial, and only when inspired by love (Lucasta) and honor (Charles I) is he a real Cavalier and a fine poet.

Various reviews greeted the Wilkinson edition but none by a major critic or poet. The most stimulating, in the *Times Literary Supplement,* forwarded the thesis that Lovelace is, in such works as "Aramantha," not at all Cavalier but Elizabethan; that he has more in common with Wyatt, Surrey, Raleigh, and the "miniature grace" of Campion than with Suckling, Carew, and Stanley. So too, a generation later, David Daiches, relating the chivalric and Royalist ideal to Sidney, Raleigh, and the older Renaissance tradition of courtesy, associated Lovelace's poems, at their best, with the strengths of Wyatt. The anachronistic Neo-Platonic Sidneyan and Spenserian values of ideal love, beauty, honor were given one last expression by Lovelace. Mario Praz, on the other hand, found Lovelace, despite his slender contribution and derivativeness, not only of his time but the most picturesque and striking Caroline poet—an important index of seventeenth-century customs and predilections, of the complexity of the age's poetic development.[4]

Though we speak nowadays of Lovelace, Suckling, Carew in one breath, the earlier centuries did not. Often ignoring Lovelace, they lumped Carew with Suckling. The two indeed share a libertine strain, but it is found in Lovelace also. Moreover, neither Suckling nor Lovelace approaches Carew at his best; they share his urbanity, not his artistic devotion and consistency. To F. R. Leavis, Carew, as the bearer, with Marvell, of the line of wit from Jonson and Donne to Pope, deserves better than to be bracketed with Suckling and Lovelace.

The consensus of modern criticism regards Lovelace more unequal as an artist but also more serious at his best than Suckling. As craftsman, Lovelace is closer to Carew; but his art is not so rewarding because his grotesque ingenuity, beyond Carew's, defeats him. Of the three poets, Lovelace is sometimes the least naturally, at other times the most naturally, a Metaphysical poet. Possessed of a curious mind, he has a wider range of interests, themes, and images. But lacking Donne's erudition and insight, he points the way to the dead end of John Cleveland's artificial, contorted style in wandering beyond the limits set by his subject and by the capacity of words. He could sing as sweetly as Carew or Suckling, yet not be as polished as the one or as natural as the other. In an age of dilettantism, he was more uneven than they.

Some find Lovelace quite unlike Suckling or Carew. He uniquely has a rare strain of sensuousness and tenderness. He seems more of a dreamer than the other two, but he also observes nature more closely—whether recording the ubiquity of conflict in it or (in the pastoral) its repose and beauty. Above all, Lovelace expresses a sense of honor and chivalry that is alien to the others. Suckling and Carew dramatize the Cavalier's worldliness; Lovelace presents the Cavalier ideal. His gentility was so strong as to make his attempts at Sucklingesque cynicism seem to some unconvincing, as though he were trying to prove he was no prig. To Albert Baugh, he belongs rather with Godolphin and Montrose as the "noblest and most hapless of the Cavaliers," poets of slender performance but fragrant memory. In the two famous exalted lyrics, Lovelace, expressing the "sense of honor in manly alliance with his love," is, therefore, *the* exemplary Cavalier spirit.[5]

The postwar years produced several essays with fresh insights. In *Velvet Studies,* C. V. Wedgwood speaks (like an earlier reviewer) of the anachronistic, escapist aspect of Lovelace. She stresses a certain self-mockery; many a conceit of his is a piece of bravura, of deliberate showing off, as though the poet were to turn to us admiringly and say, "Now isn't that a quaint conceit I've got!" Lovelace deliberately marries the sublime to the ridiculous in order to raise a smile. Geoffrey Walton in "The Cavalier Poets," finds Lovelace a courtier and soldier of European culture expressing with clarity and sophistication "the surviving code of chivalry and the public values of the seventeenth-century country gentleman" and, in the insect poems, the "private interests of the Kentish squire and the rural roots of the Cavalier." Not a "Son of Ben," Lovelace lacked the discipline that would have controlled somewhat "the suns and flowers that burst forth a little too brightly in this poetry."

Robin Skelton notes, in his *Cavalier Poets,* a contrast in Lovelace's work between the polite, social, formal poetry and the celebration of food, wine, music, women; between the pretentious, ornate compliments and the insect fables, the charming drink and prison poems. Even the latter kind, though vigorous, passionate, and conversational, do not put us into familiar relationship with the speaker, do not convey a presence. Without emotional involvement, the poet seems to be playing with words and ideas, enjoying his virtuosity and providing "well-mannered and graceful diversion for the cultured reader." His wit has an impersonal withdrawn air that is unlike the animal spirits of Carew and Suckling in pursuit of women. Not a questioning soul, Lovelace accepts at face value fashionable compliment, cosmic similitude, pastoral language. He presents moral sentiments in lucid lines of restrained rhythm reinforced with parallelism, antithesis, paradox. This "poetry of ceremony rather than spontaneity" furnishes, adds Skelton, a "sense of inner dignity of humanity . . . lacking in Carew and Suckling." Lovelace's lines have a sweetness, even his humor has more gentleness than raillery; without genius, he has his own radiance. His Cavalier poems are, however, his least typical; the strength, control, gaiety, courage, personal touch of "To Althea" are rare.

The latest essay, one of the best, is by Bruce King. Stimulating, even if wrong-headed, it logically extends random suggestions of earlier writers and constructs a portrait of Lovelace as a modern *Angst*-ridden Existentialist. King begins with the assertion, first made by Empson and Holland, that Lovelace's famous two "Cavalier" poems really are about the flight from the demands of love and the beloved—an analysis resting on the assumption that what the poems say literally is not what they mean. King's approach was anticipated as well by Walton's remark that Lovelace, though not often vulgar like Suckling, exhibits a surprising vein of deeper cynicism; by Skelton's contrast between the animal spirits of Carew and Suckling and the withdrawn air of Lovelace; by Alvarez' complaint at Lovelace's posturing.[6]

King finds the image of Lovelace as a gay, debonair Cavalier spirit mainly Restoration and Victorian propaganda. Most readers, who have missed the deep streak of skepticism and cynicism in Lovelace, accept the affirmative poems at face value instead of seeing them for what they are: examples of a disillusioned mind desperately trying to hang on to anything in the world. Exploiting venerable ideals, the poems are not affirmations of the chivalric code but a turning inwards. The ideals celebrated are mere postures, defensive masks—psychological necessities to ward off reality. Lovelace's confidence continually falters, for demoralization lies behind the affirmation.

The cynicism is not merely political but affects his whole sensibility, as is seen from the way references to prison appear in all sorts of unlikely places. Not only defeat in war but a complete spiritual and physical insecurity is intimated by "Advice"; all activity, on land as well as on sea, leads to disaster, as do even inactivity and the "golden mean." "The Grasshopper" gives a medieval picture of mutability in all things and dismisses conviviality as an external crutch that is doomed like the insect.

Without the values arbitrarily and blindly imposed on a disintegrating society, Lovelace's sentiments turn coarse. The lesser poems are more completely disillusioned and offer only the crudest sort of protection or none at all. In the "Loose Saraband [1659]" the carefree Cavalier attitude suddenly appears a desperate reaction to brutal reality, and the withdrawal into drink and gross sensuality is made in a manner more aggressive than that found in other libertine poets. Lovelace's libertinism, lacking the balance of Carew's, suggests a total disillusionment with experience; it stems from hatred of life rather than love of the senses. The 1659 volume, especially, seems to King distrustful, violent, paranoiac in its reaction to society. It fills the natural world with emblems of distasteful reality—ant, fly, snail. The law of animal life is the law of man; life itself is insecure and empty. With such an interpretation, Lovelace may be truly said to have been made currently relevant.

II. Achievement

In arriving at a final evaluation of Lovelace's poetry, we cannot ignore his limitations. His tastes are simple; his mind bare of complex ideas. His unquestioning commitments to lady and king are childlike and, though intensely asserted, of but passing interest. He has no theory of politics, love, or indeed anything. Unless it be the epicurean flourish in the face of a lowering night, he has no central vision, no abiding emotion. The Cavalier posture for which he is so well known is but a glimmer in a few poems. The courtly amatory, like the drinking and cynical seduction poems, are sometimes amusing but heavily derivative. The insect and creature poems are peculiar to him and affecting in a limited way. He is not haunted by time, death, or history; by loss of prosperity or rise of Cromwell; by *carpe diem* thoughts. Nor is he moved to towering rejection or acceptance of love or regicide. Except for the problems of liberty and confinement and of the conflict in nature, which are at the heart of his best things, many great themes and issues pass by him—despite his living through a dramatic epoch.

It is undeniable that Lovelace wrote numerous poems which remain, after all explication, bad; that even his good poems are often static and two-dimensional; that his style is marred by all the things earlier critics listed; that he is, in short, a minor poet. Yet, in spite of all, Lovelace's successes, as this study has attempted to show, have *not* been limited to the two well-known poems. His work contains a substantial number of beautiful lines and images, most of which we have examined.

He evinces virtuosity in several kinds of poetry. We saw that in the Carolingian period octosyllabic verse became the vogue. While Lovelace offers no poem of quality comparable to Marvell's "Coy Mistress" or Milton's twin poems, he manages quite a few successful couplets. Many of the good, limpid octosyllabics are in his pastoral. Some of them have satiric thrust to them; and indeed, the satiric pentameter couplet, is also an area of the poet's proficiency too little noticed. Another forte of Lovelace's is his conclusion. Though incapable of the Miltonic resolution—for lack of supreme mastery in the body of the poem—he yet can achieve fine lines at the end of stanza or lyric.

Besides the stereotyped image of Lovelace the Cavalier, we have seen the cynical seducer as well as the wailing, unrequited lover; the biting satirist of the social scene, alongside the bemused observer of insects; the celebrator of the arts no less than the man haunted by conflict and prison; the recorder of small incidents and of a great dilemma. The important Lovelace themes are: in the microcosmic life of insects and small beasts, combat and entrapment; in the dissolving social structure, imprisonment; in amatory matters, separation. These adversities can be overcome by a renewed dedication to transcendent lover and honor, or by Epicurean conviviality and retirement, or by hedonistic abandonment to drink and sex.

In the insect poems, confinement, unrelieved by spiritual self-mastery, means ignominious, painful death. For man, on the other hand, blessed or cursed with consciousness, incarceration can be redoubled because, "grief too can manacle the mind" and physical constraint may not be so severe as the emotional subjection to the lady. But that same human consciousness provides liberation: in one poem, through wine, song, and self-abandonment; in another, through honor, by renewal of allegiance to the king amidst general dissolution. In "To Althea" and "The Guiltless Lady," physical confinement is transcended by love, wine, the certainty of one's own integrity, or by one's personal magnetism. In "The Scrutiny" and in "Wars," the confinement is entirely spiritual, stemming from possession by woman, love; freedom is found by turning to other sexual liaisons, or by renewed devotion to the ideal of honor.

In the last analysis, the haunting sense of universal conflict and entrapment, and the problem of liberty and confinement, are part of his one recurring motif or major theme—"Honor." He is of two minds about honor: giving himself with equal zest to deriding it in drink or erotic lyric or to lauding it, with reference to king or lady, in poems on prison, camp, or court. Whether writing of mute insect or Renaissance gentleman, Lovelace has sketched the range of responses to the universal predicament of confinement—from passive death to active choice of pleasure or something "higher." His basic contribution to English literature, therefore, is his dramatization of the two ways of acting in the face of disaster—by self-abandonment or by self-discipline; or, as a moral relativist might describe it, by two different modes of self-abandonment.

Evaluating his total output, we can say that Lovelace is least inspired in his occasional and Petrarchan love poetry, better in his jaunty erotica and sociopolitical stuff, best at the juncture of courtly, amatory, and political which he made peculiarly his own area. His insect poems likewise constitute a contribution to the age. Hardly anything of his poetry is original; but the same can be said of Shakespeare, and not originality but aptness in expressing what oft was thought is the criterion. Lovelace manages to give genre pieces like "The Grasshopper" or "The Fair Beggar" a touch of his own. The existence of twin poems on the same subjects—on the snail, the fly caught, the patch on the lady's face, Lucasta at the bath, himself in prison, Lely's painting—suggests a tentativeness on the part of the poet or, more likely, a certain open-mindedness: a willingness to experiment, to re-examine appearances from varying perspectives.

But—besides individual lines, images, octosyllabics, conclusions, satiric couplets; besides beautiful fragments from flawed poems like "Aramantha" and "On Sannazar"; besides a recurring theme or two—does Lovelace present more substantial, complete achievement; any self-contained, finished works of art, however brief, any "well-wrought sonnets"?

From his collection of a hundred and three poems we can salvage about forty, or two-fifths. While this may not be a high percentage compared with Donne, Herbert, Marvell, it is substantial. Of these forty, some fifteen to twenty are effective and readable; repay study; change our view of life ever so little; leave us wiser, amused, or moved. Each has its flaws, to be sure, but none is incapacitated by them. This list of poems certainly would include "A Paradox," "Gratiana singing and dancing," "To Ellinda . . . written," "The Vintage to the Dungeon," "A Guiltless Lady," "The Apostacy," "La Bella Bona Roba," "In Allusion," "The Duel," "Dialogue. Lute and Voice," "An Anniversary," "Painture," "Valiant Love," "A Fly . . . Cobweb," "To Lucasta. From Prison," "You Are Deceived," "The Advice."

There are, moreover, a dozen poems which are very good; in these the flaws are nearly effaced by striking images or lines, by effective rhetoric, or by a sense of humor. This group, containing no masterpieces, is typical of that great age of lyric poetry when so many men were able to write beautiful poems with little apparent effort. It includes "To . . . Hair," "Depose," "The Rose," "The Scrutiny," "Loose Saraband [1659]," "Cupid Far Gone," "The Ant," "On Sannazar," "The Snail,"

"A Fly . . . Claret," "Love . . . First Age," "Strive Not." And there are the half-dozen perfect poems, the masterpieces from Lovelace's pen which take their place with the finer lyrics of the age and which are in all the anthologies: "To . . . Sea," "To . . . Wars," "The Grasshopper," "Ellinda's Glove," "To Althea," "The Fair Beggar." Of these, "Ellinda's Glove" and "The Fair Beggar" have hardly been noticed until lately; "To . . . Sea" and "The Grasshopper" have been coming into prominence in the twentieth century; and, of course, "To . . . Wars" and "To Althea" have been acknowledged for the last two hundred years as supreme utterances of the heroic temperament in duress; as the swan song of the old order seen in its noblest moment; as, in Grierson's famous words, the "only poems which suggest what 'Cavalier' came to mean when glorified by defeat."[7]

What is Lovelace's place in seventeenth-century English literature? If we put Shakespeare and Milton in the first rank, the peers of other world geniuses; Donne, Jonson, Herbert, Marvell, Dryden in the second rank of consistently very fine to excellent poets; Vaughan, Crashaw, Carew, Herrick in the third rank, of good to very good talents; then Lovelace no doubt belongs with Suckling, Lord Herbert, Cowley, Waller in a fourth category of sporadically good poets who are certainly superior to Stanley, Denham, Habington, Traherne. Fourth class does not sound very exalted, but it is no mean achievement to be accounted among the leading dozen poets in a century of very great poetry.

Notes

1. C. H. Wilkinson, ed. *The Poems of Lovelace* (Oxford, 1930), pp. lxii ff., 260; Herbert Berry and E. K. Timmings, "Lovelace at Court," *Modern Language Notes,* LXIX (1954), 396-98.

2. George Williamson, *The Donne Tradition* (Cambridge, Mass., 1930), pp. 208-9; R. C. Bald, *Donne's Influence in English Literature* (Gloucester, Mass., 1932), p. 20; R. L. Sharp, *From Donne to Dryden* (Chapel Hill, 1940), pp. 106-8; Alvarez, p. 73.

3. Wilkinson, pp. lxvi-lxxi; Douglas Bush, *English Literature in the Earlier Seventeenth Century* (Oxford, 2nd ed., 1962), p. 123; *Times Literary Supplement,* January 21, 1926, p. 41.

4. Cyril H. Hartmann, *The Cavalier Spirit and Its Influence on the Life and Works of Richard Lovelace* (London, 1925), pp. 116-19; David Daiches, *A Critical History of English Literature* (New York, 1960), I, 382; Mario Praz, Review of Wilinson's 1925 edition, *Modern Language Review,* XXI (1926), 319-22.

5. The last few paragraphs are an amalgam of observations by the following: R. A. Blansard, "Carew and the Cavaliers," *Transactions of the Wisconsin Academy of Sciences, Arts, and Letters,* XLIII (1954), 97-101; Thomas Seccomb in *Dictionary of National Biography* (1937-38), XII, 171; Bush, pp. 122-23; A. C. Baugh, *A Literary History of England* (New York, 1948), pp. 660-61; Legouis and Cazamian, *A History of English Literature* (New York, rev. ed., 1935), p. 563; F. R. Leavis, *Revaluations* (New York, 1947), pp. 15, 37; Hugh Kenner, ed., *Seventeenth Century Poetry* (New York, 1964), p. 371; Philip Lindsay, *For King or Parliament* (London, 1949), p. 178.

6. C. V. Wedgwood, *Velvet Studies* (London, 1946), pp. 23, 27-28; *Seventeenth-Century Literature,* p. 72; Geoffrey Walton, "The Cavalier Poets," in *From Donne to Marvell,* ed. Boris Ford (London, 1956), pp. 169-72; Robin Skelton, *The Cavalier Poets* (London, 1960), pp. 26-34; Bruce King, "Green Ice and a Breast of Proof," *College English,* XXVI (1964), 511-15; William Empson, *Seven Types of Ambiguity* (New York, 2nd ed., 1947), p. 210; Norman Holland, "Literary Value: A Psychoanalytic Approach," *Literature and Psychology,* XIV (1964), 43-55; Alvarez, pp. 72-73.

7. Grierson and Bullough, *The Oxford Book of Seventeenth-Century Verse* (Oxford, 1934), p. viii.

Selected Bibliography

PRIMARY SOURCES

LOVELACE, RICHARD. *Lucasta.* London: Thomas Harper, 1649.

———. *Lucasta: Posthume Poems.* Ed. Dudley Posthumus Lovelace and Eldred Revett. London: William Godbid, 1659.

———. *Works* in *Minor Poets of the Seventeenth Century.* Ed. R. G. Howarth. New York: E. P. Dutton & Co., 1931.

SECONDARY SOURCES

ALLEN, DON CAMERON. "Lovelace: The Grasshopper." *Seventeenth Century English Poetry.* Ed. W. R. Keast. New York: Oxford University Press, 1962. Learned analysis of the Classical and medieval background of the grasshopper, poem and symbol.

EVANS, WILLA M. "Lawes' and Lovelace's 'Loose Saraband.'" *Publications of the Modern Language Association,* LIV (1939), 764-67.

———. "To Amathea." *Philological Quarterly,* XXIII (1944), 129-34.

———. "Lovelace's 'Mock Song.'" *Philological Quarterly,* XXIV (1945), 317-28.

———. "An Early Lovelace Text." *Publications of the Modern Language Association,* LX (1945), 382-85.

————. "'The Rose': A Song by Wilson and Lovelace." *Modern Language Quarterly,* VII (1946), 269-78.

————. "Lovelace's Concept of Prison Life in 'The Vintage to the Dungeon.'" *Philological Quarterly,* XXVI (1947), 62-68.

————. "Tormenting Fires." *Modern Language Quarterly,* IX (1948), 11-16.

A series of brief studies by an expert on the manuscripts of the period. Despite a propensity for assigning anonymous lyrics to Lovelace on tenuous grounds, Evans is good on the "Loose Saraband," "Mock Song," "Rose," "Vintage."

FLETCHER, J. B. *Précieuses* at the Court of Charles I." *Journal of Comparative Literature,* I (1903), 120-53. Background material for the genteel aspect of Lovelace's poetry.

HARTMANN, CYRIL H. *The Cavalier Spirit and Its Influence on the Life and Work of Richard Lovelace.* London: G. Routledge & Sons, 1925. Adds nothing to the documentation of Waite and Wilkinson and only a little to the understanding of the "Cavalier Spirit" or of the poetry.

HENDERSON, F. O. "Traditions of *Précieux* and *Libertin* in Suckling's Poetry." *English Literary History,* IV (1937), 274-96. Background material for the libertine and French aspects of Lovelace's poetry.

HOLLAND, NORMAN. "Literary Value: A Psychoanalytic Approach." *Literature and Psychology,* XIV (1964), 43-55, 116-27. Excellent analysis of "The Scrutiny" and "To . . . Wars."

JONES, G. F. "Lov'd I Not Honour More: The Durability of a Literary Motif." *Comparative Literature,* XI (1959), 131-43. Thorough examination of the meaning of "honor" in earlier Western literature, as background material to "To . . . Wars."

KING, BRUCE. "Green Ice and a Breast of Proof." *College English,* XXVI (1964), 511-15. Stimulating if somewhat wrong-headed survey of Lovelace's *Weltanschauung* which turns him into a despairing, *Angst*-ridden modern.

O'REGAN, M. J. "The Fair Beggar—Decline of a Baroque Theme." *Modern Language Review,* IV (1960), 186-99. Scholarly and critical tracing of the various earlier, continental versions of the poem.

PEARSON, N. H. "Lovelace's 'To Lucasta . . . Wars.'" *Explicator,* VII (1949), 8, item 58. Fine brief explication of the poem.

PRAZ, MARIO. Review of Wilkinson's 1925 edition. *Modern Language Review,* XXI (1926), 319-22. Evaluation by a scholar acquainted with the continental background to seventeenth-century currents.

Review of Wilkinson's edition. *Times Literary Supplement,* January 21, 1926, p. 41. Presents Lovelace as a belated, misplaced Elizabethan in a time out of joint.

SKELTON, ROBIN. *The Cavalier Poets.* "Writers and their Work," No. 117. London: Longmans, Green, 1960. Sympathetic appreciation of Lovelace's strengths.

VAN DOREN, MARK. *Introduction to Poetry.* New York: Sloane, 1951. Brilliant brief analysis of "To . . . Wars."

WALL, L. N. "Some Notes on Marvell's Sources." *Notes and Queries,* CCII (1957), 70-73. Discusses Lovelace's influence on Marvell and lists parallels.

WALTON, GEOFFREY. "The Cavalier Poets." *From Donne to Marvell.* Ed. Boris Ford. London: Penguin Books, 1956. Good appraisal of Lovelace's sensibility.

WEDGWOOD, C. V. "Cavalier Poetry and Cavalier Politics." *Velvet Studies.* London: J. Cape, 1946. Fine evocation of Cavalier and court milieux.

Warren W. Wooden (essay date November 1977)

SOURCE: Wooden, Warren W. "The Cavalier Art of Love: The Amatory Epistles of Sir John Suckling." *West Virginia University Philological Papers* 24, no. 5-1 (November 1977): 30-36.

[*In the following essay, Wooden examines John Suckling's love letters and contends that they demonstrate control, awareness, sophistication, and unconventionality.*]

To our era as to his own, Sir John Suckling seems the quintessential Cavalier, "the greatest gallant of his time, and the greatest Gamester," in John Aubrey's phrase.[1] Today, however, his reputation rests almost exclusively on the body of lyrical verse—witty, masculine, playfully irreverent—which was collected posthumously in *Fragmenta Aurea* (1646) and *The Last Remains of Sir John Suckling* (1659). But both of these volumes contained, in addition to the poetry, separate collections of Suckling's letters set off from the poems and provided with their own titlepage within each volume ("LETTERS To divers Eminent PERSONAGES: Written on several Occasions" in *Fragmenta Aurea*; "LETTERS TO SEVERAL PERSONS OF HONOR" in *The Last Remains*). While little read or esteemed today, these letters were very popular in their time (the volumes containing the letters went through seven editions in the seventeenth century, several more in the eighteenth) and combined with the poetry to establish the public perception of the author as Millamant's "natural, easy Suckling." For despite the popularity of such letter-writing formularies as those of Angel Day or Henry Peacham or such miscellaneous collections of letters as Nicholas Breton's *A Poste with a Packet of Madde Letters* (1602), the appearance of Suckling's "Letters Fragrant and Sparking," as Gerald Langbaine characterized them in 1691,[2] marked in 1646 the first collection by an eminent and titled literary figure to see print in the seventeenth century. Buoyed by Suckling's reputation as a wit and gallant, the letters rapidly became the model for epistolary style for the succeeding age.

The twenty-nine letters in *Fragmenta Aurea,* in addition to twelve first published in the *Last Remains,* are properly classified as familiar letters, that paradoxical Renaissance genre which like the sonnet sequence straddled precariously the public and the private modes, the literary and the intimate. The familiar letter, writes one authority on the subject, "was literary, and though it was in most cases written for and sent to the person whose name appears on the superscription, it was written with a larger audience in view and . . . found its way to that larger audience."[3] The familiar letter often used stock themes, such as persuading a friend to marry or dissuading him from it, admonishing and advising a son, daughter, or friend on life at court or in the city. These themes were popularized by writers such as Breton and his imitators and followed strategies laid down in popular epistolary guidebooks like Angel Day's *The English Secretorie* (1586), the best known and most influential of the group. For all the casual *sprezzatura* which informs Suckling's letters, they afford ample evidence of mere art and of Suckling's knowledge, and occasional direct use, of these earlier middle-brow formularies.[4] The letters are not, then, intimate and confessional; while the sentiments they express may well be genuine, both the language and attitudes adopted in them depend primarily upon the familiar tradition within which Suckling wrote and the larger audience which it presupposes. Thus in the letters as in the poetry, the affectation of nonchalance is belied by evidence of careful craftsmanship, awareness of literary tradition and decorum, and even occasional indebtedness to specific sources. The creative tension in these letters, which arises from the combination of negligence and care, defines the Cavalier style and justifies the assertion of Dryden's Eugenius in the *Essay of Dramatick Poesie* that the era prior to the Restoration could "produce nothing so courtly writ, or which expresses so much the Conversation of a Gentlemen, as Sir John Suckling."[5]

I would like to concentrate on the most notable group in the seventeenth-century collections of Suckling's letters: the amatory correspondence. It was this group which was chiefly imitated, for example in Edward Phillips' *The Mysteries of Love and Eloquence* (1658), and accounted for the primary popularity of Suckling's letters. The modern critical appreciation of his amatory letters is slight, as witness W. H. Irving's description of

Sir John Suckling (1609-1642).

them as filled "with compliments to women of the most vapid kind," remarkable chiefly for their "phenomenal emptiness."[6] A closer study, however, suggests a careful control and an awareness of both social and literary decorum in conjunction with a more sophisticated underlying design than anything found in the merely formulary amatory epistles of the age. Thus while the view of women and love in Suckling's letters ranges across the full spectrum from the rapt adoration recommended by Angel Day and the other authors of letter-writing handbooks to the obligatory view of woman as sex object in witty letters to his fellow Cavaliers, in the letters to Mary Cranfield a more complex and mature view of women and the courtship procedure emerges. I believe these letters in particular provide the key to a proper reading of Suckling's amatory epistles and, perhaps, to their popularity and influence during the Restoration.

The amatory epistles in *Fragmenta Aurea* are found in three groups, all lacking a superscription by which the addressee might be identified. Modern scholarship, however, assigns them to two ladies: seven letters to Mary Cranfield, Suckling's cousin, and ten to a lady addressed as "Dear Princesse" or "Aglaura," tentatively identified by Suckling's most recent editor, Thomas Clayton, as Mary Bulkeley. The ten "Aglaura" letters occur in the midst of the collection as a group in apparently chronological order, except for a pair of witty formulary letters modeled on Breton, arguing pro and con the consequences of marrying a widow ("chewed meat," as Suckling calls her in the dissuasion letter). On the other hand, the letters to Mary Cranfield are treated in a different fashion. Although they all date from approximately the same period (1629-32), three stand at the beginning of the collection, with a formulary dissuasion from love separating the first two, but the remaining four are printed at the conclusion of the volume, as Nos. 24-27 of the thirty in the collection. The letters to Mary Cranfield have thus been separated so as to form a frame for the group of amatory epistles in the center of the collection. This order may have been the printer's or it may have been prescribed by the procurer of the letters, as seems to have been the case with those in the *Last Remains*. In this latter volume, the correspondence is arranged in chronological order apparently, as Thomas Clayton suggests, at the direction of Suckling's sister, Lady Southcot, who supplied them to the printer. Given the careful ordering of the letters in the *Last Remains* and the odd separation of the Mary Cranfield letters in *Fragmenta Aurea,* it seems possible that the order in *Fragmenta Aurea* was a deliberate and even dramatic attempt to frame one set of letters, the Aglaura ones, with another significantly different type, the Mary Cranfield letters. An examination of the letters in these groups suggests an explanation for this ordering.

The initial letters to Mary Cranfield which introduce us to Suckling as correspondent are essential to an appreciation of his attitude toward love and the courtship ritual of his day. In these early letters Suckling appears as a modern lover, capable of the standard effusions while yet aware of the limitations and artifices of convention in the relationship of suitor and beloved. In the Mary Cranfield letters, he broaches the view of courtship as a social game, in a larger society itself obsessed with games, and invites the lady to join him in both playing and mocking the love game.

The initial letter of *Fragmenta Aurea* catches the reader's attention with a clever opening: "Fortune and Love have ever been so incompatible, that it is no wonder (Madam) if having had so much of the one for you, I have ever found so little of the other for my self."[7] Suckling continues to elaborate the occasion of his letter (he has arrived in London only to find Mary removed to the country), assuring her that, although surrounded by the lovely ladies of the city, "the use that I shall make of that Sex now, will be no other then that which the wiser sort of Catholiques do of Pictures; at the highest, they but serve to raise my devotion to you: Should a great Beauty now resolve to take me in (as that is all they think belongs to it) with the Artillery of her eyes, it would be as vain, as for a Thief to set upon a new robb'd passenger" (p. 108). Although fulsome-

ness and ingenuity are the rule rather than the exception in seventeenth-century amatory epistles, the reader who perceives a facetious playfulness in both Suckling's language and protestations receives confirmation of his suspicions in Suckling's closing remarks, where, as so often in his poetry, he simultaneously reminds his mistress that there are others who would not spurn and have not spurned his suit and takes a swipe at fashionable Platonic love: "You (Madam) have my heart already, nor can you use it unkindly but with some injustice, since (besides that it left a good service to wait on you) it was never known to stay so long, or so willingly before with any; After all, the wages will not be high; for it hath been brought up under Platonicks, and knows no other way of being paid for service, then by being commanded more" (p. 108). Here Suckling has both flattered the lady and, by exaggerating slightly the form of the compliment and facetiously mocking the Platonic-Petrarchan tradition on which it draws, wittily directed attention to the artificiality of the courtship game where X number of compliments are rewarded by wages in the amount of Y.

The next amatory letter in *Fragmenta Aurea* moves beyond facetious playfulness to consider, in the polite tone decreed by decorum, the conflict between individual sensibility and intuition and the social code. It is a fruitful theme which inspired some of Suckling's finest poems such as "Why So Pale and Wan, Fond Lover" and "Love's Siege." The apparent background to the epistle is that Mary Canfield has laid down the rules by which their courtship will be conducted, the approved Platonic-Petrarchan forms, and Suckling replies, recognizing the limitations and absurdities of the courtship ritual while nevertheless agreeing to play the game as directed. Suckling begins thus: "Though (Madam) I have ever hitherto beleeved play to be a thing in it self as meerly indifferent as Religion to a States-man, or love made in a privie-chamber; yet hearing you have resolved it otherwise for me, my faith shall alter without beccomming more learned upon it, or once knowing why it should do so" (p. 108). The natural man will bend to social conventions, then, not because they are correct or morally fit but only because his lady would have it so. While all this may sound conventionally Petrarchan, it is not, for the natural man's doubts are not allayed; he will play the game, at his lady's request, without believing in its tenets, such as, he continues, "The losse of a Mistris (which kills men onely in Romances, and is still digested with the first meat we eat after it)" (p. 108). This attitude of skepticism toward the value and poses of the love game even while one plays it Suckling attributes to his mistress as well as to himself in the final paragraph of this letter: "And now, since I know your Ladyship is too wise to suppose to your self impossibilities, and therefore cannot think of such a thing, as of making me absolutely good; it will not be without some impatience that I shall attend to know what sin you will be pleased to assign me in the room of this: something that has lesse danger about it (I conceive it would be) and therefore if you please (Madam) let it not be Women: for to say truth, it is a dyet I cannot yet rellish, otherwise then men do that on which they surfetted last" (p. 109).

These initial amatory epistles establish the tone and condition the reader's response to those which follow. Here both suitor and mistress recognize the limitations and absurdities of the courtship ritual while yet agreeing to utilize it as the channel for their wooing. Such an attitude is relatively complex and presupposes a respect for the intelligence, tact, and good humor of the beloved. In the final group of letters to Mary Cranfield (Nos. 24-27 in *Fragmenta Aurea*), those placed at the conclusion of the volume, Suckling delivers the praises due her in the Petrarchan ritual while again gently mocking the social attitudes of Petrarchism. Thus in the final amatory letter in *Fragmenta Aurea,* Suckling returns to notice the discrepancy between his recent behavior and that called for by the courtship game. In noting his refusal to abase himself to the role of worshipper and acolyte, he writes: "But that I know your goodness is not merciary, and that you receive thanks, either with as much trouble as men ill news, or with as much wonder as Virgins unexpected Love, this letter should be full of them. A strange proud return you may think I make you (Madam) when I tell you, it is not from every body I would be thus obliged; and if I thought you did me not these favours because you love me, I should not love you because you do me these favours. This is not language for one in Affliction, I confesse, and upon whom it may be at this present, a cloud is breaking; but finding not within my self I have deserv'd that storm, I will not make it greater by apprehending it" (p. 112).

In contrast to the Mary Cranfield letters, witty, masculine, complex, which open and close the *Fragmenta Aurea,* there is the large group of ten letters to "Aglaura" or "Dear Princesse" in the center of the volume. These letters are stuffed with vehement protestations and lavish compliments. Individual passages remind one that they are the work of a poet ("Abruptness is an eloquence in parting, when Spinning out of time, is but the weaving of new sorrow" [p. 139]), but for most of these letters such passages are too rare. Rather, the best consist of patterned and graceful compliments or old formulas reworked (e.g., to apologize for his delay in answering a letter, Suckling begins "My Dear Dear / Think I have kist your letter to nothing, and now know not what to answer. Or that now I am answering, I am kissing you to nothing, and know not how to go on!" [p. 138]). Although some are excessively given to rhetorical personification and needless amplification, these letters are generally competent, although there is little in this group one could not find just as readily in, for instance, the model amatory epistles of Angel Day's *English Secretorie*. This group, by and large quite conventional in both language and sentiment, seems unlikely in itself to have provoked the popularity of Suckling's letters.

Thus there are apparently two distinct and qualitatively different groups of amatory epistles in *Fragmenta Aurea,* one complex and individualistic, the other relatively simplistic and conventional. To lump them together indiscriminately as "vapid" (or under any other rubric) seems critically suspect. What is more, the order of the letters in the volume does not seem accidental. The Mary Cranfield letters are unchronologically divided to frame the conventional Aglaura letters. Thus the seventeenth-century reader of the *Fragmenta Aurea* collection first encounters the letters in which Suckling plays the modern lover, skeptical, masculine, witty. The courtship ritual here appears as an elaborate social game with set rules; but the two players, Suckling and his mistress, intend to use these love conventions, perhaps to explore and reinvigorate some of the more fossilized, without being bound to or by them.

The Aglaura letters, then, the reader views from this early perspective on the courtship game. While recognizing the limitations of convention, the lover nevertheless praises the mistress to the heavens. "For," in the words of another Cavalier to his coy mistress, "lady, you deserve this state, / Nor would I love at lower rate." The image of the Cavalier lover which arises from a reading of Suckling's amatory epistles is of a man who can accommodate his wooing to the sensibilities of his lady, be they conventional or extraordinary. Despite the greater number of the conventional letters, however, I believe their ordering reflects a desire to emphasize the more sophisticated and complex view of love, one calculated to appeal to the tastes of a new age. If this emphasis is intended, then the order in the *Fragmenta Aurea* volume is designed to set off the conventional letters as but one movement in a very sophisticated larger social ritual. Whether or not this conclusion is accepted, the recognition that through polished compliment and familiar poses Suckling is both playing and subverting the courtly love game requires that the style and content of these amatory letters be reassessed from a new perspective. Far from being a homogeneous or monotonous series, they are more complex, sophisticated, and unconventional than generally assumed, and these elements may well account for both their popularity and imitation in subsequent collections and anthologies and for Suckling's stature as "the prototype and model of the Court Wits of the Restoration."[8]

Notes

1. *Brief Lives,* ed. Oliver L. Dick (Ann Arbor: Univ. of Michigan Press, 1957), p. 287.

2. Cited in *The Works of Sir John Suckling: The Non-Dramatic Works,* ed. Thomas Clayton (Oxford: Clarendon Press, 1971), p. lxxii.

3. William H. Irving, *The Providence of Wit in the English Letter Writers* (Durham: Duke Univ. Press, 1955), p. 14. Additional useful background information on the familiar letter during the Renaissance may be found in K. G. Hornbeak, *The Complete Letter-Writer in English 1568-1800* (Northampton: Smith College, 1934) and Jean Robertson, *The Art of Letter Writing: An Essay on the Handbooks Published in England during the Sixteenth and Seventeenth Centuries* (Liverpool: Liverpool Univ. Press, 1942).

4. Both E. N. S. Thompson in *Literary Bypaths of the Renaissance* (New Haven: Yale Univ. Press, 1914) and Thomas Clayton in *The Works of Sir John Suckling: The Non-Dramatic Works* have demonstrated direct borrowings by Suckling from earlier formularies.

5. *The Works of John Dryden,* ed. H. T. Swedenberg, Jr., XVII, *Prose 1668-1691* (Berkeley: Univ. of California Press, 1971), 14.

6. Irving, pp. 103-04.

7. *The Works of Sir John Suckling,* ed. Thomas Clayton, p. 107. All subsequent quotations from the letters refer to this edition with page reference cited in the text.

8. Thomas Clayton's judgment in *The Works of Sir John Suckling,* p. xxvii.

Lynn Sadler (essay date 1979)

SOURCE: Sadler, Lynn. "Carew's Life and 'School' of Poetry." In *Thomas Carew,* pp. 11-23. Boston: Twayne Publishers, 1979.

[*In the essay below, Sadler offers a biography of Thomas Carew, considers his reputation, and praises him for showing variety and care in his work.*]

As one can see from the Chronology, facts about the life of Thomas Carew are rare. The would-be biographer is further hampered by the confusion and ambiguities that lace such "facts" as do exist. Was he born in 1594 or 1595? Where was he born? Which of the three contemporaries, Thomas Carew/Carey, is the poet? Was his college Merton or Corpus Christi? Did he die in 1638 or 1639 at age forty-four, in 1640 at age forty-five, in 1645 at age fifty, or when he was much older? Did he die of syphilis? Did he receive the Manor of Sunninghill from King James or King Charles, and was it recalled for lack of payment before or at his death?

Did he marry a rich widow? Did he marry at all? Did he become Ben Jonson's "research assistant" for a history of Henry V? Which is his authentic portrait? Is there a portrait of Carew? The problems indicated here persist into *current* criticism, not to mention the disorder among older treatments of Carew.

Only ten poems were published during Carew's life, and some of those lacked his name and his authorization. His masque, *Coelum Britannicum,* was also published without his name. His signature in the Oxford subscription register and three letters survive. For the remainder of his works and life story, modern critics have been obliged to seek manuscripts, random records, anthologies, and miscellanies. Even the advent of the standard edition in 1949 has not entirely settled the inconsistencies among this mishmash of materials.

I. Generally Accepted Information about Carew

Thomas Carew was born, perhaps in the family county of Kent, though he is not listed in its baptismal records, in 1594 or 1595. His clan was well connected; and his father, Matthew, hailed by one critic as his "son's worst enemy,"[1] was a Master in Chancery. He eventually practiced law in London and was knighted about 1603. Sir Matthew would have liked for his son to become a lawyer, too.

The family, according to its antiquarian, Richard Carew, Thomas's cousin, "came over" with William the Conqueror and took its name from *carru,* "plow." However, Professor Rhodes Dunlap derives the surname from Carew (Caer Yw) Castle, County Carmarthen.[2] Whatever its etymology, its pronunciation is also in doubt: "Ca-*rew*" versus "*Car*-ey." The latter seems the more promising[3] and perhaps accounts for at least part of the confusion of Thomas Carew, the poet, with the two contemporaries who spelled their names "Thomas Carey."

The first Thomas Carey (1597-1634), the son of the Earl of Monmouth, was a favorite of James I and served as Groom of the Bed-Chamber to the King. He married one Margaret Smith, received Sunninghill Manor from King James, and died on April 9, 1634. To make matters more confusing, he, like Thomas Carew, the poet under discussion, had poems (two) set to music by Henry Lawes. The second Thomas Carey was a member of Gray's Inn and Gentleman-Porter of the Tower. He translated Puget de la Serre's *Mirrour which flatters not.*

While the information about his early education is also scant, it is known that Carew entered Merton College, Oxford, in June 1608, at age thirteen. He received his B.A. on January 31, 1610/11, somewhat early, and, by

February, was a reader in the Bodleian Library, being incorporated a B.A. of Cambridge in 1612. He was apparently meant to follow his father in the pursuit of law and was admitted to the Middle Temple on August 6, 1612. The events forestalling his projected legal career remain undetermined.

II. CAREW AND THE CARLETONS

Perhaps the financial reverses that plagued Sir Matthew Carew during his last years brought about Thomas's change of mind about the profession of lawyer. At any rate—no doubt with the urging of his father, who recorded that his son "studied the law very little"—he entered the service of Sir Dudley Carleton, probably in the position of secretary. Lady Carleton was Sir Matthew Carew's niece. Thus Thomas was exposed to the culture of Italy, where Carleton was ambassador to Venice in 1613. Italian influence is marked in his poetry, and a letter by him, dated 1616, speaks of the languages he was able to acquire in Carleton's service. He remained in this position during Sir Dudley's embassy to The Hague. Sometime, however, in the course of this second tour of duty, a disruption in relations occurred. Carleton somehow discovered Carew's written slanders ("to set his head aworke without any meaneng either to shew it to anye, or to make any other use therof then to hym selfe"[4]) of Lady Carleton and himself. Carew was not told of the discovery; rather, Lord Carleton urged his return to England to find other employment that would more readily advance his career.

Once back home, about the middle of August 1616, Thomas acted upon Sir Dudley's advice. He first approached, unsuccessfully, his kinsman Lord Carew, who had recently become a member of the Privy Council. Next he turned to Thomas Howard, the Earl of Arundel, whom he had apparently met in Italy and who favored Thomas's suit but had already promised the place being sought to another. While engaged in this search for a position, Thomas plied Lord Carleton with letters citing his failures to secure other employment and requested that he be allowed to return to his "primum mobile,"[5] the director of his course. He also begged for a letter of recommendation to the Earl of Arundel. His father, too, baffled by his son's unannounced arrival in England, wrote to his kinsman in letters proclaiming his dismay at the turn of Thomas's fortunes. Sir Matthew's own financial troubles were deepening, and the loan which Carleton had promised to help him meet the mortgage on his London home was not forthcoming. Ultimately, Lord Carleton had his agent, Edward Sherburne, inform the old man (and the Earl of Arundel) of the reasons for Thomas's dismissal. In Sherburne's presence, Sir Matthew called his unrepentant son to account, thereby launching the quarrel that persisted between them.

Thomas seems to have spent this difficult period (1616-18) in visiting those whose connections might help him, in cutting a fine figure, and in continuing his tendency to make ill-chosen comments. He accompanied his brother Matthew to Woodstock, where the court was. He certainly saw Lady Carleton's stepfather, Sir Henry Savile, a kinsman by marriage and Warden of Merton College during Thomas's tenure there. He proceeded to incense his onetime benefactor further with Savile's subsequent report that Thomas had spoken lightly of Sir Dudley Carleton's horses. Carew was obviously not very tactful; but whether, as his father indicated by letter to Sir Dudley (September 1, 1616), he "thought too highly of himself" and suffered from "self-pride," cannot be surely known. His demand for a letter of apology to Carleton being of no avail, the ailing father gave his son up for lost and complained bitterly of him in a letter to Carleton dated October 4, 1617. Sir Matthew recorded, not without some sense of God's justice, that Thomas now suffered from the "new disease" (presumably syphilis)[6] and that all of his plans for his son had come to naught. Sir Matthew died on August 2, 1618, at age eighty-five. Of his three children, he was pleased only with his daughter.

III. DUTIES IN FRANCE AND ENGLAND

Perhaps as a result of some of his visiting patterns during the period of his rift with Carleton and his father, Carew was making his way at court. He is recorded as being among the most elegant in attendance when Charles was installed as Prince of Wales on November 4, 1616. He may also have begun his wooing of the lady celebrated in so many of his poems as "Celia." Finally, in May of 1619, he accompanied Sir Edward Herbert (later Lord Herbert of Cherbury, also a poet) in his embassy to Paris and became the fast friend of John Crofts, whose family home of Saxham was to assume an important place in his life and poetry. A number of his poems seem to have been written during his stay in France. He may also have met, in Paris, the Italian, Giambattista Marino, who influenced his poetic style.

Much later, during the period from 1630-33, he cemented his ties with the English court, being named, first, Gentleman of the Privy Chamber Extraordinary and then Sewer in Ordinary to the King.[7] The latter appointment was made despite the fact that the Scots were promoting another candidate. A life of some ease was thus achieved, and Carew became known as one of the wittiest poets and courtiers of Charles I.

IV. ANECDOTES ABOUT CAREW

Carew's contemporary reputation as a witty courtier is borne out by a series of anecdotes told of him. For example, George Clarke, once Lord of the Admiralty, reported to Sir John Percival this confirmation of Carew's "quickness." Lighting King Charles to Henrietta Maria's chamber, Carew saw Jermyn Lord St. Albans with his arm around the Queen's neck. He feigned a stumble, put out the light, and thus helped to secure the gentleman's escape. While the King never knew of the episode, the Queen naturally became one of Carew's great patrons.

In the winter of 1624-25, Carew was rumored to be on the verge of marrying the rich widow of Sir George Smith. His friend, fellow poet, and fellow Gentleman of the Privy Chamber, Sir John Suckling, chided him for such a rash proposal and received Carew's clever reply. Both letters were printed in parallel columns, paragraph for paragraph, with Carew forcefully surmounting each charge (e.g., ". . . I'le marry a *Widow,* who is rather the *chewer,* then *thing chewed*"[8]). So far as is known, Carew was never married.

One report, in a letter from James Howell to Sir Thomas Hawke on April 5, 1636, provides a glimpse of Carew the man: "I was invited yesternight to a solemn supper by B. J. [Ben Jonson], where you were deeply remembered; there was good company, excellent cheer, choice wines, and jovial welcome: one thing intervened, which almost spoiled the relish of the rest, that B. began to engross all the discourse, to vapour extremely of himself and by vilifying others to magnify his own muse. T. Ca. [Thomas Carew] buzzed me in the ear, that though Ben had barrelled up a great deal of knowledge, yet it seems he had not read the *Ethics,* which, among other Precepts of Morality, forbid Self-commendation."[9] As will be seen, Carew was no submissive "Son of Ben," but could see faults wherever they were to be found.

Finally, there is the story of the supposed deathbed recantation, though variations of this anecdote are so characteristically applied to famous men as to be immediately suspect. Like many of his peers at Charles I's court, Carew was reputed to be a profligate and a libertine. During one of his illnesses (another bout of syphilis?), when he thought he was dying, he sent for John Hales, who had been a fellow of Merton College in 1606, and who had become connected with Thomas by marriage. At the poet's promise to amend his life, Hales gave him absolution. However, upon recovering, Carew resumed his "life scandalous." Then, according to information gathered by Izaak Walton for a life of Hales, in the poet's last illness when he again called upon Hales for spiritual aid, he was refused both the sacrament and absolution. The account of this double repentance is also provided by Joseph Hunter in the *Chorus Vatum Anglicanorum* from the narration of Lady Salter, to whose son Hales was tutor.

The truth of this tale of contrition cannot be known, but Carew had a reputation for licentiousness such that his poems were blasted in Parliament as part of the traffic of pornography afoot in London. And Lord Clarendon, Carew's friend, records (thereby adding more confusion as to the length of Thomas's life): ". . . his Glory was that after fifty Years of his Life, spent with less Severity or Exactness than it ought to have been, He died with the greatest Remorse for that Licence, and with the greatest Manifestation of Christianity, that his best Friends could desire."[10]

Others cite Carew's choice of Psalms for translation and adaptation, as well as his self-"laceration" in "To My worthy friend Master Geo. Sand[y]s, on his translation of the Psalmes," as evidence of his intended correction of his life. The Psalms he paraphrased, however, were probably early efforts written during his first siege of syphilis while he was under his father's care. They show no particular personal revelations. Of the nine Psalms he elected to deal with, only Numbers 51 and 119 have any special penitential cast. The commendation of Sandys[11] seems little more than the homage of one poet to another upon such an occasion:

> I Presse not to the Quire, nor dare I greet
> The holy place with my unhallowed feet;
> My unwasht Muse, polutes not things Divine,
> Nor mingles her prophaner notes with thine;
> Here, humbly at the porch she listning stayes,
> And with glad eares sucks in thy sacred layes.
>
> Perhaps my restlesse soule, tyr'de with persuit
> Of mortall beauty, seeking without fruit
> Contentment there, which hath not, when enjoy'd,
> Quencht all her thirst, nor satisfi'd, though cloy'd;
> Weary of her vaine search below, Above
> In the first Faire may find th' immortall Love.
>
> (ll. 1-6, 23-28)[12]

V. THE ABSENCE OF A PORTRAIT OF CAREW

Another bit of gossip introduces the problems concerning the authenticity of the portraits of the poet. Carew's friend Thomas Killigrew quarreled with Cecilia Crofts (later his wife) and asked Carew to intervene. To oblige, Carew wrote the poem "Jealousie," used in a masque at Whitehall Palace in 1633 and included in Killigrew's play, *Cicilia and Clorinda, or Love in Arms* (written 1649-50). Horace Walpole subsequently reported, quoting other sources, that Anthony Van Dyck's 1638 portrait of Killigrew and Carew commemorated this argument of the lovers and Carew's service as intermediary. However, Professor Dunlap has conclusively shown that this is an impossible interpretation of the origin of the portrait.[13]

Van Dyke's painting, in the Royal Collection of Windsor Castle, shows Killigrew on the left holding a paper with two female figures drawn on pedestals. On the right, Carew holds a paper, too. Following the lead of Ernest Law's study of the Van Dyck pictures at Windsor, Dunlap suggests that the two women were intended for a sepulchral monument to Cecilia Crofts

Killigrew and to the Countess of Cleveland, who died in 1637/38; both were sisters of John Crofts. Carew's paper may represent his avocation of poet. While Law has discounted the authenticity of the likeness of Carew, Professor Dunlap accepts this half of the Van Dyck portrait as the only genuine one of the poet. However, since the standard edition of Carew's works was published, further research has been done on the Van Dyck portrait. The figure once thought to be Carew is almost certainly Thomas Killigrew's brother-in-law, William, Lord Crofts.[14]

Many of Carew's editors and critics, including one publishing as recently as 1960, have used for Carew's picture one from a medal produced by Jean Warin/Varin of Thomas Carey, the Gentleman of the Bedchamber. William Carew Hazlitt went so far as to alter the medal's inscription in order to use a copy of it for his edition of Carew in 1870.

VI. Carew's Death

Carew's "To my friend G. N. [Gilbert North?] from Wrest" (86-89), probably his last poem, sheds some light on the actual facts of his death. It contrasts the munificence of Wrest Park Manor in Bedfordshire, which belonged to the De Greys, with the deprivation of the expedition led by King Charles against Scotland in 1639:

> I Breathe (sweet *Ghib*:) the temperate ayre of *Wrest*
> Where I no more with raging stormes opprest,
> Weare the cold nights out by the bankes of Tweed,
> On the bleake Mountains, where fierce tempests breed,
> And everlasting Winter dwells; where milde
> *Favonius,* and the Vernall windes exilde,
> Did never spread their wings: but the wilde North
> Brings sterill Fearne, Thistles, and Brambles forth.
>
> (ll. 1-8)

Carew apparently was with Charles in this First Bishops' War, and the rigors they encountered, it is conjectured, hastened his death, which occurred about March 21, 1639/40. At any rate, after a rather costly funeral, he was buried in St. Anne's Chapel, the Church of St. Dunstan's-in-the-West. The church was remodeled in the early nineteenth century, and no trace of the tomb of Thomas Carew is now to be found.

Despite their estrangement, Thomas was interred beside Sir Matthew Carew, a fact all the more unexpected in view of the distance between Thomas and the rest of the family. After Matthew Carew's death, his London house was sold, and his widow went to live with her older son, Matthew, in the country. Her highly detailed will, dispensing properties and goods down to her grandchildren, servants, and tenants, failed to mention Thomas. It seems likely that no reconciliation was ever effected.

VII. Carew's "School" of Poetry

Thomas Carew continues to be presented principally in anthologies, which label him, without very careful qualification, a "Cavalier" poet along with Sir John Suckling and Richard Lovelace. The tag derives from their association with King Charles, from their use of military imagery, and particularly from their supposed lack of high seriousness. The two greatest influences upon his poetry are John Donne[15] and Ben Jonson.[16] He owes much directly to the Classical tradition: specifically to the Latin poets, as Ovid (Publius Ovidius Naso), Gaius Valerius Catullus, and Sextus Propertius;[17] and more generally to the Greeks, as Anacreon and other lyric poets and the *Greek Anthology.* Constant echoes of the Elizabethan "Petrarchan"[18] sonneteers are also to be found in Carew's poems. Strongly marked are the effects of the Continental poets: from France, Pontus de Tyard, Pierre de Ronsard, Philippe Desportes, and the whole *libertin* (libertine) tradition;[19] from Italy, Torquato Tasso, Giovanni Battista Guarini, and especially the great leader of the Baroque, Giambattista Marino, whom Carew probably met in Paris.[20]

Carew assimilates all of these forces and influences and yet stamps his poetry with his own witty mark. As a lyricist and a court poet, mildly cynical and skeptical, he combines the accents of pure worship of the lady from the Petrarchan tradition with a prosaic, rather detached, worldliness. Commendatory and occasional verse fill most of his pages; but he is best known as a writer of amorous, not infrequently erotic, poetry. Typically, he polishes his gemlike poems with care, revising and improving.[21] He may nonetheless occasionally lapse into inexact syntax, not so excessively, however, as his fellow Cavalier, Richard Lovelace. If Sir John Suckling's description in "A Sessions of the Poets" (c. 1638) can be taken as any indication, Carew seems to have had a reputation among his contemporaries similar to that of his mentor, Ben Jonson—his Muse was "hardbound," delivering her offspring only with hard work and concentration. Carew learned this craftsmanship from Jonson[22] and his attitude toward it from the Elizabethans; for, generally, the reader is hardly aware of effort in his poems. He has imbibed the *sprezzatura* tradition of Edmund Spenser and Sir Philip Sidney and so hides his labor under a smooth demeanor that earned him the dubious later reputation of writing effortlessly and sometimes carelessly.

This reputation for lack of care was aided by the slender content of the majority of his poems. The court poetry of his day did not moralize or philosophize. Writing poetry was still an avocation of the courtier, who used it to demonstrate his own and the court's urbanity. The reader must accept that view of poetry before accusing Carew of a failure of depth and high purpose as a poet.

Carew does avoid the large-scale allegories of the Elizabethans but occasionally adopts such Petrarchan analogies as the "ship of love" or the "besieged fort." Similarly, he may fleetingly dip into Neo-Platonic lore but could never be labeled a "Neo-Platonist" in the manner of Spenser. At the same time, he borrows from Italian and French poets who were interested in both Petrarchanism and Neo-Platonism.[23]

From Donne (and his own short-lived legal training), he derives his use of logic; his conversational, often colloquial tone in the midst of the most "hallowed" service at his lady's shrine; perhaps his occasional obscurity; some of his conceits, especially those he uses to show their limitations and obsolescence; much of his wit; and his use of well-developed, emphatic, and bold metaphors and occasional juxtapositions of disparate materials. In contrast to the poetry of Donne, Carew's poetry remains almost totally secular, with no flights of mysticism. He is also more conscious of regularity of meter than is Donne, to the extent that Pope ultimately included him in the School of Waller and that modern critics find in his works a tone of civility and a precision of form (both from Jonson and the Classical writers) that anticipated Pope and other Neoclassical and Augustan poets.

Perhaps an examination of two poems, the second better than the first, will help to point out the difficulties of classifying Carew even at his least original.

The first, "To her in absence. A Ship" (23), is thoroughly derivative:

> Tost in a troubled sea of griefes, I floate
> Farre from the shore, in a storme-beaten boat,
> Where my sad thoughts doe (like the compasse) show
> The severall points from which crosse winds doe blow.
> My heart doth like the needle toucht with love
> Still fixt on you, point which way I would move.
> You are the bright Pole-starre, which in the darke
> Of this long absence, guides my wandring barke.
> Love is the Pilot, but o're-come with feare
> Of your displeasure, dares not homewards steare;
> My fearefull hope hangs on my trembling sayle;
> Nothing is wanting but a gentle gale,
> Which pleasant breath must blow from your sweet lip:
> Bid it but move, and quick as thought this Ship
> Into your armes, which are my port, will flye
> Where it for ever shall at Anchor lye.

Among its most positive attributes, aside from the smooth, pentameter couplets, is the concentration upon developing the Petrarchan conceit of the unrequited lover adrift on a "sea of griefes" (also adumbrated by Classical writers like Catullus and Virgil). Though a different kind of compass, the compass image may suggest Donne as well as Carew's own "An Excuse of absence" (131) and "To *Celia,* upon Love's Ubiquity" (123-24); but it remains Elizabethan here rather than

Metaphysical or Donnean. This claim is further supported by the fact that the companion image ("You are the bright Pole-starre") evokes comparison with Shakespeare's Sonnet 116, ll. 5-8.[24] Carew's poem, however, achieves a simplicity of statement that makes the reader entirely forget the combined influences. Sounded at the last is a hope of amendment that sets itself in opposition to the "head-banging," forlorn lover of sonnet lore. The natural, instinctive sweetness in the lady herself belies the "disdainful one" of the same school.

The second poem, "The Comparison" (98-99), proves that Carew knows the ways of Elizabethan compliment and commendation, yet immediately indicates that he is going to adopt the skeptical tone of Shakespeare's or Donne's deflation of Petrarchan conceits (e.g., Sonnet 130 or "The Canonization," respectively):

> Dearest thy tresses are not threads of gold,
> Thy eyes of Diamonds, nor doe I hold
> Thy lips for Rubies: Thy fair cheekes to be
> Fresh Roses; or thy teeth of Ivorie:
> Thy skin that doth thy daintie bodie sheath
> Not Alablaster [sic] is, nor dost thou breath
> *Arabian* odours, those the earth brings forth
> Compar'd with which would but impaire thy worth.
> Such may be others Mistresses, but mine
> Holds nothing earthly, but is all divine.
> Thy tresses are those rayes that doe arise
> Not from one Sunne, but two; Such are thy eyes:
> Thy lips congealed Nectar are, and such
> As but a Deitie, there's none dare touch.
> The perfect crimson that thy cheeke doth cloath
> (But onely that it farre exceeds them both)
> *Aurora's* blush resembles, or that redd
> That *Iris* struts in when her mantl's spred.
> Thy teeth in white doe *Leda's* Swan exceede,
> Thy skin's a heavenly and immortall weede,
> And when thou breath'st, the winds are readie strait
> To filch it from thee, and doe therefore wait
> Close at thy lips, and snatching it from thence
> Beare it to Heaven, where 'tis *Joves* frankincense.
> Faire Goddesse, since thy feature makes thee one,
> Yet be not such for these respects alone;
> But as you are divine in outward view
> So be within as faire, as good, as true.

Carew is not so crass as Shakespeare, avoiding such excesses as "in some perfumes is there more delight / Than in the breath that from my mistress reeks." Yet he takes the Shakespearean route of rebuking the inanities of the traditional Petrarchan and Elizabethan blazon (ll. 1-8). Then he shocks the reader by dropping the realism of Shakespeare's final compliment to trumpet forth extravagances more extravagant than those he has rejected (ll. 9-24). These lines also, however, employ a characteristic Carew touch of logic, as they build to the obvious conclusion. Since the poet's mistress lacks the attributes of mortal mistresses, he can only accept that she is divine. Having drawn parallel after parallel with

Classical figures, the poet must address her in the new identity he has provided for her: "Faire Goddesse, since thy feature makes thee one."

Then comes an additional witty twist, strangely reinstating at least part of the Petrarchan tradition he has banished—the emphasis on spiritual as well as physical beauty. Yet this reinstatement is tempered by realism and stated as directly, gracefully, and simply as are the last lines of "To her in absence. A Ship." (Carew is almost without exception excellent in his endings.) The final couplet is worth repeating: "But as you are divine in outward view / So be within as faire, as good, as true." Many women can look like goddesses. The trick is to be better-than-mortal internally. Neither does there seem to be any shrinking of the meaning of these lines to the libertine view that "being 'good' means being my mistress."

Carew is neither totally Jonsonian, Donnean, Elizabethan, nor Cavalier. When he is at his best, synergism occurs.

The two poems above are in Carew's favorite form, iambic pentameter couplets. The striving for regularity is emphasized by the use of elision or telescoping of syllables (as l. 4 of "To her in absence. A Ship" and ll. 7, 20, and 24 of "The Comparison").

The regularity one so often finds in Carew's poetry has been partially responsible for his being known as a facile, largely negligible poet. Yet his verse forms show a great variety and care,[25] and he experiments rather frequently with catalexis or lines terminating in imperfect feet, and with truncation or omission of syllables at the beginning of lines. Some of his best-known poems in fact contain truncated lines (e.g., "Disdaine returned," 18), catalectic lines (e.g., "An Excuse of absence," 131), or both (e.g., "The Complement," 99-101). At his most successful, Carew seems aware of form as meaning.

Of the 130 canonical poems, which include nine translations from the Psalms, some eighty employ rhyming couplets. Approximately thirty-eight of those are in pentameter and thirty-seven in tetrameter (octosyllabic couplets). Classical influence shows itself especially in Carew's tetrameter lines (as in "A New-yeares gift. To the King," 89). The tetrameter poems may use various stanzaic patterns and may display shifts to pentameter by catalexis or in the final couplet. For the poems, the iambic foot is Carew's overwhelming choice, with trochaic variations worth noting in "To my Cousin (C.R.) marrying my Lady (A.)" (47) and "The tinder" (104). Both in couplets and in stanza forms, Carew is fond of alternating line length and sometimes uses such combinations as trimeter and dimeter, tetrameter and dimeter, tetrameter and trimeter, or pentameter and

dimeter. Several (e.g., "Upon some alterations in my Mistresse, after my departure into France," 24) present pentameter, dimeter, trimeter, and tetrameter lines.

After rhyming couplets, Carew prefers six-line stanzas (used in sixteen poems). Most of these rhyme ababcc, but there are variations. He provides a refrain for one ("Song. To a Lady not yet enjoy'd by her Husband," 36) and occasionally adds an extra couplet to the last stanza or uses a final couplet, set off from the poem, as a coda for the whole.

Couplet stanzas are used in one ("Psalme 119," 144-49) of the translations of the Psalms (which, despite being early projects, show much experimentation). The eight poems in tercets are all regular (aaa) except for the unusual handling of the rhyme scheme in "An Hymeneall Song on the Nuptials of the Lady *Ann Wentworth,* and the Lord *Lovelace*" (114). Six poems are in quatrains, ten in five-line stanzas, two in seven-line stanzas, two in eight-line stanzas, and one in eleven-line stanzas. Carew has four "sonnets," so-called only from the fourteen lines in each, for they are highly experimental.

Carew does not always or often in fact succeed in making the form of the verse inherently functional. He is best at creating the illusion that each stanza or unit (often a verse paragraph) moves deftly to the point of the whole poem. His method is frequently the use of graceful, easy caesuras within the line and connective words at the beginning of lines. This illusion of logical movement, culminating in a terse, sometimes gnomic final couplet or statement, is one of his principal characteristics and prevents him from being cloyingly sweet. The sensation of movement also derives from his free-flowing couplets, almost never end-stopped but spilling over to form whole units (as "paragraphs") of thought.

Notes

1. Arthur Vincent, ed., *Poems of Thomas Carew* (London, 1899), p. xix.

2. *The Poems of Thomas Carew with His Masque Coelum Britannicum* (Oxford, 1949), p. xiv. The link between the name and a plow persists, appearing, for example, in William Styron's *The Confessions of Nat Turner* (New York, 1966), p. 125.

3. See Jack Dalglish, ed., *Eight Metaphysical Poets* (London, 1961), p. 147; Vincent, p. xxviii. Sir Arthur Quiller-Couch, *Adventures in Criticism* (Cambridge, 1926), p. 14, points out that Carew's editor, Ebsworth, in his dedicatory prelude, is mistaken in pronouncing the name "Carew;" he also scans verses from seventeenth-century poems to show that the pronunciation is "Carey." Cf. Dunlap, p. xiv, n.

4. So Sir Matthew describes his son's revelation of his purposes. The letter quoted in the text was written to Carleton on October 4, 1617. See Dunlap, pp. xxii-xxviii, for this and Matthew Carew's other letters to Sir Dudley.

5. Dunlap gives Carew's three letters in Appendix C, pp. 201-206. This compliment occurs in the one dated September 2, 1616.

6. In "Upon T. C. having the P.," given in Dunlap, p. 209, Sir John Suckling twits Carew for suffering from the "French disease."

7. Both offices were largely ceremonial by Carew's day. Members of the Privy Chamber attended the King in his private quarters. The Sewer in Ordinary originally helped with the arrangements of the royal table.

8. Both are given in Dunlap, pp. 211-12.

9. *Epistolae Ho-Elianae.* Cited in Vincent, pp. xxiv-xxv.

10. *The Life of Edward Earl of Clarendon . . . Written by Himself.* Cited in Dunlap, p. xxxix.

11. George Sandys (1578-1644) was also a Gentleman of the Privy Chamber. He is best known for his translation of the Psalms and of Ovid's *Metamorphoses.*

12. Dunlap, pp. 93-94. All references for the works of Carew are to this edition, and page numbers are given in the text in parentheses.

13. Pp. xliv-xlv, 244-45.

14. According to a letter to the writer from the Lord Chamberlain's Office, St. James's Palace, dated October 1, 1974.

15. Among the poems offering suggestions of Donne's influence are "Secresie protested" (11), "To my Mistresse in absence" (22), "Eternitie of love protested" (23-24), "To T. H. a Lady resembling my Mistress" (26-27), "Upon a Ribband" (29), "Upon the sickness of E. S." (31-32), "To one that desired to know my Mistris" (39-40), "A Rapture" (49-53), "Maria Wentworth" (56), "Incommunicabilitie of Love" (62), the elegy on Donne (71-74), "To my friend G. N. from Wrest" (86-89), "The Comparison" (98-99), "The tinder" (104), "The tooth-ach cured by a kisse" (109-10), "Upon a Mole in Celias bosome" (113-14), "To *Celia,* upon Love's Ubiquity" (123-24), "An Excuse of absence" (131), "On the Duke of Buckingham" (57), "An Hymeneall Dialogue" (66), "Obsequies to the Lady Anne Hay" (67-68), "Loves Courtship" (107-108), and "An Hymeneall Song on the Nuptials of the Lady *Ann Wentworth,* and the Lord

Lovelace" (114-15). Carew shows Donne's fondness for alchemical images and calentures. See also Chapter 4. (In this and the following footnotes on Carew's sources, the writer acknowledges help from Dunlap and other critics.)

16. Jonson's influence is shown less in individual poems, but see especially "To the Reader of Master William Davenant's Play" (97), "To Ben. Johnson" (64-65), "To Saxham" (27-29), "To my friend G. N. from Wrest" (86-89), "Mediocritie in love rejected" (12-13), "To my worthy Friend, M. D'avenant, Upon his Excellent Play, *The Just Italian*" (95-96), and "To the King at his entrance into Saxham" (30-31). All of the elegies and country-house poems and Carew's masque should be compared to Jonson's efforts in those genres. See Chapters 4-6.

17. For Ovid, see, for example, "A flye that flew into my Mistris her eye" (37-38), "Celia singing" (38), "Truce in Love entreated" (41), "A Rapture" (49-53), "Incommunicabilitie of Love" (62), "Upon Master W. Mountague his returne from travell" (77-78), "Upon my Lord Chiefe Justice" (83-84), and "To my friend G. N. from Wrest" (87-89); for Catullus, see "Secresie protested" (11), "A Rapture" (49-53), "A New-yeares gift. To the King" (89-90), "To his mistresse retiring in affection" (129-30), "To my inconstant Mistris" (15-16), "To her in absence. A Ship" (23), and "Good Counsell to a young Maid" (25); for Propertius, see "To my inconstant Mistris" (15-16), "Ingratefull beauty threatned" (17-18), "The willing Prisoner to his Mistris" (37), "On the Marriage of T. K. and C. C. the morning stormie" (79-80), and "The Complement" (99-101). Minor Latin influences are Lucretius and Horace (especially in the Jonsonian poems).

18. For the probable influence of Francesco Petrarch himself, see "The Spring" (3), "My mistris commanding me to return her letters" (9-11), "A prayer to the Wind" (11-12), "Mediocritie in love rejected" (12-13), "A flye that flew into my Mistris her eye" (37-38), "Truce in Love entreated" (41), and "A Rapture" (49-53). A good discussion of the Petrarchan tradition as it is applicable to Carew is to be found in Francis G. Schoff, "Thomas Carew: Son of Ben or Son of Spenser?" *Discourse,* 1 (1958), 8-24.

19. Primarily, the French poets of the Pléiade, who had influenced such sixteenth-century English poets as Edmund Spenser and Samuel Daniel. For probable influence of Pierre de Ronsard, see "Perswasions to enjoy" (16), "The Spring" (3), and the epitaph on Mary Villiers ("This little Vault . . . ," 54); for Desportes, see "My mistris commanding me to return her letters" (9-11), "Truce

in Love entreated" (41), and "To the Painter" (106-107); for Pontus de Tyard, see "The willing Prisoner to his Mistris" (37).

20. For Tasso, see "A cruell Mistris" (8), "Mediocritie in love rejected" (12-13), "In the person of a Lady to her inconstant servant" (40), "A Rapture" (49-53), and "Upon a Mole in Celias bosome" (113-14); for Guarini, see "A flye that flew into my Mistris her eye" (37-38), "Upon a Mole in Celias bosome" (113-14), "A Ladies prayer to Cupid" (131), and "An Excuse of absence" (131); for Marino, see "To A. L. Perswasions to love" (4-6), "A beautifull Mistris" (7), "Lips and Eyes" (6), "A Looking-Glasse" (19), "Upon the sicknesse of (E. S.)" (31-32), "Red, and white Roses" (46-47), "For a Picture where a Queen Laments over the Tombe of a slaine Knight" (81), "The Complement" (99-101), and "The tinder" (104).

21. For Carew's revisions of his poems, see Dunlap, pp. lvii-lix.

22. Cf. John Erskine, *The Elizabethan Lyric, A Study* (New York, 1903), pp. 233-34, who traces Carew's standard form to Thomas Campion.

23. Carew's "Neo-Platonism" may be only generalized borrowings. For ideas suggesting comparison with the doctrines of Giovanni Pico Della Mirandola, however, see these poems: "A divine Mistris" (6-7), "Ingratefull beauty threatned" (17-18), "Celia singing" (39), "Epitaph on the Lady S." (55), "To A. D. unreasonable distrustfull of her owne beauty" (84-86), and "An Hymeneall Song on the Nuptials of the Lady *Ann Wentworth,* and the Lord *Lovelace*" (114-15).

24. See Alan J. Biggs, "Carew and Shakespeare," *Notes & Queries,* N.S., 3 (1956), 225.

25. The verse has been studied by Charles J. Sembower, "A Note on the Verse Structure of Carew," *Studies in Language and Literature in Celebration of the Seventieth Birthday of James Morgan Hart* (New York, 1910), pp. 456-66, and Rufus A. Blanshard, "Thomas Carew's Master Figures," *Boston University Studies in English,* 3 (1957), 214-27.

Selected Bibliography

Primary Sources

Dunlap, Rhodes, ed. *The Poems of Thomas Carew with His Masque Coelum Britannicum.* London: Oxford University Press, 1949; rpt. 1970.

Vincent, Arthur, ed. *The Poems of Thomas Carew.* London: Lawrence & Bullen, Ltd.; New York: Charles Scribner's Sons, 1899.

Secondary Sources

Biggs, Alan J. "Carew and Shakespeare." *Notes and Queries,* 3 (1956), 225. On "To her in absence. A Ship."

Blanshard, Rufus A. "Thomas Carew's Master Figures." *Boston University Studies in English,* 3 (1957), 214-27. Carew's use of four figures from George Puttenham's *The Arte of English Poesie.*

Dalglish, Jack. *Eight Metaphysical Poets.* London: Heinemann, 1961. Brief but good account of Carew, the leading representative of the Caroline school.

Quiller-Couch, Sir Arthur. *Adventures in Criticism.* Cambridge: Cambridge University Press, 1926 [1896]. An amusing discourse on the pronunciation of Carew's name.

Schoff, Francis G. "Thomas Carew: Son of Ben or Son of Spenser?" *Discourse,* 1 (1958), 8-24. Invaluable article pressing for recognition of Elizabethan influences on Carew.

Sembower, Charles J. "A Note on the Verse Structure of Carew," *Studies in Language and Literature in Celebration of the Seventieth Birthday of James Morgan Hart.* New York: Henry Holt and Co., 1910, pp. 456-66. Carew's variety seldom organic. Best at the "arch pretense of logic."

Michael H. Markel (essay date 1982)

SOURCE: Markel, Michael H. "Perception and Expression in Marvell's Cavalier Poetry." In *Classic and Cavalier: Essays on Jonson and the Sons of Ben,* edited by Claude J. Summers and Ted-Larry Pebworth, pp. 243-253. Pittsburgh, Pa.: University of Pittsburgh Press, 1982.

[*In the following essay, Markel discusses poetry by Andrew Marvell that engages the Cavalier mode while at the same time exploring its conventions and limitations.*]

As Marvell's major lyrics have become better understood, commentators have turned their attention to his later, satirical poetry, in search of the balance and paradox that characterize his more famous works.[1] In his curious evolution from encomiast of Lovelace to Restoration satirist, Marvell is the greatest enigma of all English poets. Finding a private man who makes sense as Marvell the poet is likely to pose the ultimate scholarly riddle; his bloodless newsletters from Parliament to his constituents in Hull are as bizarre, in their own way, as the unbridled invective of the satires. In response to the current tendency to categorize the poet, Elizabeth Story Donno argues that he was not a Cavalier, a Puritan, or a satirist, but "the ultimate Renaissance poet," that is, a poet interested in literary traditions and uninterested in justifying his work on any but aesthetic grounds.[2] In a more Marvellian statement that makes essentially the same point, William Empson writes that, around 1650, Marvell "immediately stopped being in love with dead Cavalier heroes; he fell in love with Nature and mixed farming."[3]

In discussing his Cavalier poetry I take for granted that Marvell was familiar with his contemporaries. Margoliouth's edition makes clear that he was an avid reader who freely incorporated echoes of lines and ideas he admired.[4] And J. B. Leishman comprehensively traces Marvell's literary antecedents.[5] It is time now to analyze not whether, but in what ways and to what end, he read such contemporaries as Suckling, Waller, Cowley, Lovelace, and Carew.

Modern readers have rightly suggested that Marvell's interest in the Cavaliers was not simple and enthusiastic. Leah Sinanoglou Marcus, for example, writes that "The Unfortunate Lover" is a "mocking answer to the flocks of dilute Petrarchanists of his day who strained hard to express the torments of their passion."[6] To John Dixon Hunt, the conclusion of Marvell's commendatory poem to Lovelace's *Lucasta* demonstrates the poet's "not entire identification with the Cavalier mode in either costume or verse."[7] Most readers would probably agree about the difficulty of finding any mode of verse with which Marvell entirely identifies. Indeed, one of the poet's chief characteristics is his ability to freeze a moment in time and then casually stroll through his fictional world, pointing out inherent paradoxes, conflicts, and ambiguities, without ever denying its beauty. Louis L. Martz writes accurately that Marvell "looks back upon the remains of courtly culture with attraction and regret."[8] Barbara Everett, discussing pastorals such as "Daphnis and Chloe," comments that the poet makes the conventions "seem dated beyond belief . . . yet these same conventions still exert power over the mind."[9]

Four of Marvell's poems about love—"The Gallery," "Mourning," "Daphnis and Chloe," and "The Fair Singer"—analyze Cavalier poetic conventions by focusing on the twin issues of perception and expression. In the four poems, Marvell investigates the extent to which a poet's awareness of multiple perspectives affects his ability to define his subject accurately. These Cavalier exercises constitute Marvell's playful definition of the limitations inherent in contemporary social poetry.

A favorite Cavalier topic—the relationship between natural beauty and artifice in women—is the subject of "The Gallery," a poem based on the conceit of a lover's envisioning his beloved in various pictures that make up a gallery in his mind. The lover depicts Clora in alternately benign and malignant poses, as "an Inhumane

Murtheress," "Aurora in the Dawn," a cannibalistic "Enchantress," and "Venus in her pearly Boat." The final stanza describes the favorite pose:

> Where the same Posture, and the Look
> Remains, with which I first was took.
> A tender Shepherdess, whose Hair
> Hangs loosely playing in the Air,
> Transplanting Flow'rs from the green Hill,
> To crown her Head, and Bosome fill.

Critical attention given this poem has focused on the relationship between the woman and the pictures, especially the one described in the last stanza. Bradbrook and Thomas, for example, refer to the "last and natural picture of the 'tender Shepherdess' which she was at first."[10] Such readers as Rosalie L. Colie see even this last picture as only another affected pose: "She is artificial, and she is his artifice."[11] Both explanations are plausible, but Clora's essence remains enigmatic. As A. J. Smith points out, the poem does not allow us to decide what she is.[12] In fact, the reader cannot tell even if Clora "exists" within the fictional confines of the poem. Colie writes that "The Gallery" has about it "a curiously aseptic quality . . . , as if the situation were in fact only mental, as if there were no real lady, no real love affair."[13] Nothing in the poem rules out this list of "as if's." On the contrary, Marvell's extraordinary subtlety makes the idea of an imaginary Clora just as persuasive as any other reading of the poem. But this equivocation is merely the beginning; the performance culminates when the reader realizes that the speaker too remains unknowable. The wit of "The Gallery" is that Marvell invites us to ask one question as we read the poem—What is Clora?—and then quietly suggests that we might reexamine whether we are inquiring about the right character.

In one deft stroke, Marvell has raised an interesting and troubling point about a common Cavalier strategy. Carew's excellent poem "Ingratefull Beauty Threatned," about a poet whose verse has turned the common beauty Celia into something of a celebrity, offers a characteristic instance. In threatening to destroy her fame if she does not remain faithful, the speaker reminds her that "Wise Poets that wrap't Truth in tales, / Knew her themselves, through all her vailes."[14] Marvell's "The Gallery" poses two simple questions: What is the truth? How do we know? Carew's truth might be that he created her through his artistry; Celia's truth might be that she created the poet.

In "Mourning," Marvell complicates the issue of nature and artifice by adding an uninvolved speaker, a poet whose task is to evaluate the relationship between the lamenting woman and those with whom she interacts. His poem about Chlora and her response to the death of her lover, Strephon, is probably based on Cowley's "Weeping." Cowley's four-stanza poem elaborates the idea he introduces in his first thought: "See where she sits, and in what comely wise, / Drops *Tears* more fair then others *Eyes!*"[15] In the first three stanzas of the poem, he elaborates the idea of her beauty. In the last stanza, we see what Cowley has been leading up to: her tears are so cold "that I admire they fall not *Hail.*" We suspect that the highly embellished praise in the first three-quarters of the poem has been mere scaffolding for his final witticism. Clearly, the poem conveys no emotion beyond the speaker's admiration of her beauty, and it completely ignores the question of context. Why is the woman weeping? We do not know; the speaker apparently does not know. He certainly does not care.

The first stanza of Marvell's poem immediately demonstrates what interests him about the kind of situation developed by Cowley:

> You, that decipher out the Fate
> Of humane Off-springs from the Skies,
> What mean these Infants which of late
> Spring from the Starrs of *Chlora's* Eyes?

Asking what Chlora's tears mean, Marvell asks several questions at once: What caused the tears? What are the speculations of the observers? What, if anything, can we know by watching the interplay between Chlora's behavior and public reaction to it? Adding a speaker who is completely uninvolved with the situation he is viewing enables Marvell to isolate and portray that situation effectively. Each of the poet's character groups is assigned a different mode of communication. The woman does not speak; she merely acts. The onlookers self-confidently interpret her actions. The speaker, through his use of ambivalent phrases and metaphors, only suggests possible meanings.

The woman weeps over the death of Strephon; her role is simple. One group of onlookers is sure that she is weeping "Only to soften near her Heart / A place to fix another Wound." Another group has a more cynical explanation for her tears: "That whatsoever does but seem / Like Grief, is from her Windows thrown." The last two stanzas of the poem are the speaker's:

> How wide they dream! The *Indian* Slaves
> That sink for Pearl through Seas profound,
> Would find her Tears yet deeper Waves
> And not of one the bottom sound.

> I yet my silent Judgment keep,
> Disputing not what they believe
> But sure as oft as Women weep,
> It is to be suppos'd they grieve.

The first of these two stanzas contains one of Marvell's finest word plays. If "sound" is a verb, her behavior reflects a profound grief; if it is a predicate adjective, she is an actress. In an excellent essay about "Mourning," Paul Delany points to the ambiguity of the final couplet

of the poem: it can mean either that gentlemen respect women's tears, or that women's grief is artful dissimulation.[16]

What do Chlora's tears mean? We cannot know, and that, again, is Marvell's whole point. One group of onlookers might be correct; perhaps neither is correct. It is logically possible, as well, that Chlora genuinely grieves at the loss of Strephon. The closest we can come to the ultimate meaning of Chlora's tears is a careful articulation of the possible meanings, and, beyond that, we must preserve a wise reticence. As A. J. Smith describes the poet's tactic at the end of the poem, Marvell "will coolly leave the conflicting possibilities unresolved in the interest of a more wisely perceived equivocalness."[17] Marvell's "Mourning" is thus a brief epistemological essay.[18]

By raising these simple but fundamental questions about the nature of perception, Marvell suggests the limitations of the Cavalier compliment poem and, by implication, of any work which assumes that perceptions are necessarily accurate. In "Daphnis and Chloe" and "The Fair Singer," he goes one step further in his analysis of the complexity of artistic expression by investigating the dangers inherent in trying to describe what we think we see.

In "Daphnis and Chloe," Marvell's mode—and subject—is the seduction poem typified by "Love turn'd to Hatred," a comic sonnet attributed to Suckling.[19] That poem comprises thirteen and a half lines of exquisite raillery against women, men who love women, even the minuscule element of goodness that—not to their credit, of course—women possess. The remaining half-line— "what, wilt thou love me yet?"—economically demonstrates the Cavalier mating dance. The lady's ritualistic surrender must be delayed until the gentleman has wooed her long and well. The words are a prerequisite to the action. In "Daphnis and Chloe," Marvell orchestrates a similar encounter between two dull-witted sophisticates.

Chloe "neither knew t'enjoy, / Nor yet let her Lover go." And Daphnis

> came so full possest
> With the Grief of Parting thence,
> That he had not so much Sence
> As to see he might be blest.

This is Marvell's beautiful irony: Daphnis does not realize that he is only supposed to *threaten* to leave Chloe, that a skillfully delivered threat will prevent his having to leave. But he has worked himself into such a frenzy that he cannot deal with her acquiescence. Instead of enjoying her favors, Daphnis runs on for thirteen stanzas filled with frantic and sometimes incoherent references to executions, cannibalism, necrophilia, the wandering Hebrew tribes, and the magical properties of ferns.

The last two stanzas, by contrast, are the speaker's:

> But hence Virgins all beware.
> Last night he with *Phlogis* slept;
> This night for *Dorinda* kept;
> And but rid to take the Air.
>
> Yet he does himself excuse;
> Nor indeed without a Cause.
> For, according to the Lawes,
> Why did *Chloe* once refuse?

Like the poet-persona in "Mourning," the speaker here simply repeats Daphnis's understanding—or, rather, misunderstanding—of "the Lawes." It is illogical for Chloe's cavalier to leave *now.* Daphnis's real confusion is suggested by his hectic promiscuity after the debacle with Chloe. For any self-respecting cavalier, such behavior would be infra dig. And the speaker's warning to "Virgins all" is of course ironic, for it is unlikely that the clumsy Daphnis could pose a threat to any real fort. Phlogis and Dorinda are not innocent victims; they just capitulate quickly.

The irony of the poem is reinforced by its title. Marvell chose not to call the female character Chlora only because he wanted to allude to Longus's Greek romance *Daphnis and Chloe.* In the original, Daphnis receives instruction in the art of love from a libidinous woman who takes an interest in him; he then goes on happily to consummate his marriage to Chloe. Marvell's allusion to the romance reinforces his witty comment on the relationship between words and action. The poem does not stretch the pastoral "quite out of shape," as Rosalie L. Colie suggests; instead, it simply parodies big talkers. To assert that "Daphnis and Chloe" is "emotionally anti-pastoral and anti-love"[20] is to overburden the poem with excess philosophical baggage. Games shouldn't be taken so seriously.

Suckling would have enjoyed this poem, for he knew that the game whose rules he codified requires a good deal of native intelligence and verbal dexterity. An unintelligent cavalier confuses the thing and its expression and, consequently, cannot achieve the goal for which he has been preparing so earnestly.

Perhaps Marvell's most interesting examination of the relationship between perception and expression is "The Fair Singer," which demonstrates that, in the process of describing something, one can learn that it is in fact quite different from what he had thought it to be. Whereas in "Daphnis and Chloe" Marvell explores the idea that words can forestall action, in "The Fair Singer" he suggests that words can actually engender action, for they lead his speaker to a new and disquieting understanding of his situation.

The speaker seems initially to seek a rather innocent goal: he wants to join the large group of poets who have immortalized their ladies through hyperbolic and ingenious verse. Rather than settle for the most tired metaphor of all—the man ensnared by the woman's physical beauty—he decides to fuse to it a second idea—the man captivated by her beautiful voice. One close parallel to this strategy of combined metaphor is Waller's "Of Mrs. Arden":

> Behold, and listen, while the fair
> Breaks in sweet sounds the willing air,
> And with her own breath fans the fire
> Which her bright eyes do first inspire.
> What reason can that love control,
> Which more than one way courts the soul?
>
> So when a flash of lightning falls
> On our abodes, the danger calls
> For human aid, which hopes the flame
> To conquer, though from Heaven it came;
> But, if the winds with that conspire,
> Men strive not, but deplore the fire.[21]

Another close parallel is Carew's "Song. Celia Singing":

> You that thinke Love can convey,
>   No other way,
> But through the eyes, into the heart,
>   His fatall Dart:
> Close up those casements, and but heare
>   This Syren sing;
>   And on the wing
> Of her sweet voyce, it shall appeare
> That Love can enter at the eare:
>   Then unvaile your eyes, behold
>   The curious mould
> Where that voyce dwels, and as we know,
>   When the Cocks crow,
>   We freely may
>   Gaze on the day;
> So may you, when the Musique's done
> Awake and see the rising Sun.

Despite their superficial differences, these two poems share the same graceful artificiality. Waller's conceit of the wind conspiring with heavenly lightning is decorously imaginative: it praises the lady by assigning her divine powers. Carew's version, with Cupid's darts entering the lady's ear, is less felicitous; still, it directs its praises toward the lady, especially in the final image of the rising sun.

"The Fair Singer" is by far the best of the three poems:

> To make a final conquest of all me,
> Love did compose so sweet an Enemy,
> In whom both Beauties to my death agree,
> Joyning themselves in fatal Harmony;
> That while she with her Eyes my Heart does bind,
> She with her Voice might captivate my Mind.
>
> I could have fled from One but singly fair:
> My dis-intangled Soul it self might save,
> Breaking the curled trammels of her hair.

But how should I avoid to be her Slave,
Whose subtile Art invisibly can wreath
My Fetters of the very Air I breath?

It had been easie fighting in some plain,
Where Victory might hang in equal choice,
But all resistance against her is vain,
Who has th' advantage both of Eyes and Voice,
And all my Forces needs must be undone,
She having gained both the Wind and Sun.

The traditional reading holds that the poem is "a well calculated mixture of gallantry and wit."[22] Certainly, it has an intellectual unity that Waller's and Carew's similar poems lack; the sea battle logically extends the traditional idea of the battle between the sexes. Compared to this conception, the ideas of heavenly lightning and Cupid tie for a weak second place.

Marvell's strategy in "The Fair Singer" exploits his metaphor-referent cluster to suggest the possibility that love is in fact a battle, that the figure of speech tells literal truth. Whereas the metaphors in the first stanza are used in a traditional way, as hyperbolic expressions of the lady's ability to keep the speaker enthralled, the imagery in the second stanza establishes a distinctly different mood. Gone are the musical terms that gave balance to such phrases as "fatal Harmony." In their place are such terms as "subtile Art," whose ambivalent connotations suggest the woman's contrived, even covert tactics. When we finish reading the second stanza's relentless images of entrapment—"dis-intangled," "trammels," "fetters"—we share the speaker's feelings of claustrophobia; the first stanza's "bind" and "captivate" begin to take on their more ominous connotations. This in turn contributes to the almost realistic tone of the second stanza, which now clearly opposes the more hyperbolic first stanza.

The speaker's tired resignation in the final stanza further reinforces our impression of his uncertainty. When he finally admits that "all resistance against her is vain," he seems to surrender not to a lovely lady with beautiful eyes and voice but to a deliberate and calculating military force. The speaker's concluding the poem with references to the military metaphor rather than to the lady herself implies that, on one level at least, he has begun to understand the ironic aspect—or at least the possibility of an ironic aspect—of his relationship with the woman: despite her great beauties, she might not be fair. The poem concludes without a definite statement. Marvell will not say that love is sweet surrender, or that it is literally a kind of warfare. What he has demonstrated, however, is the process by which his speaker has grown to realize the complexities of poetry and the integral relationship between an idea and its articulation.

The phenomenon traced in "The Fair Singer" relates to what William Empson has called a self-inwoven simile or a short-circuited comparison. Using Empson's terminology, Christopher Ricks has written of Marvell's characteristic use of the figure of speech "which goes beyond saying of something that it *finds* its own resemblance, and says instead, more wittily and mysteriously, that something *is* its own resemblance."[23] Ricks concludes his essay by demonstrating Lovelace's successful use of this figure of speech in his snail poems, and by implying that Marvell, who admired him, might have learned this technique from him.

Whether this is so cannot, of course, be determined. Balachandra Rajan writes that "The Garden" is "another one of those poems which must be resignedly described as 'elusive'. That word in Marvell criticism has come to connote exasperation as well as admiration."[24] But Rajan argues convincingly that, in Marvell, "controlled uncertainty is the objective of the poem rather than its enmeshment."[25] The Cavalier world that Marvell explored in some of his early lyrics was rife with simple truths that he saw as neither simple nor true: that lovers act consciously and meaningfully, that they send clear signals which are received and interpreted accurately, that in describing these lovers poets say what they mean and are never entrapped by their own words. The Cavalier social ritual was a perfect subject for Marvell's exercises because it enabled him to explore the behavior of art while chronicling the art of behavior. The phrase "controlled uncertainty" might be revised to "controlled, limited certainty." In his Cavalier poems, Marvell was absolutely precise in defining the limits of human perception and expression. Unlike the Cavaliers, he frequently insisted on the right to keep his silent judgment.

Notes

1. See, for example, Warren L. Chernaik's "Marvell's Satires: The Artist as Puritan," in *Tercentenary Essays in Honor of Andrew Marvell,* ed. Kenneth Friedenreich (Hamden, Conn.: Archon Books, 1977); Barbara Everett's "The Shooting of the Bears: Poetry and Politics in Andrew Marvell," in *Andrew Marvell: Essays on the Tercentenary of His Death,* ed. R. L. Brett (Oxford: Oxford University Press, 1979); and Annabel M. Patterson's *Marvell and the Civic Crown* (Princeton: Princeton University Press, 1978).

2. "The Unhoopable Marvell," in *Tercentenary Essays,* ed. Friedenreich, p. 44.

3. "Natural Magic and Populism in Marvell's Poetry," in *Andrew Marvell: Essays,* ed. Brett, p. 40.

4. *The Poems and Letters of Andrew Marvell,* ed. H. M. Margoliouth, 3rd ed., comp. Pierre Legouis and E. E. Duncan-Jones, (Oxford: The Clarendon Press, 1971), vol. 1. All quotations follow this edition.

5. *The Art of Marvell's Poetry* (London: Hutchinson, 1966).

6. *Childhood and Cultural Despair: A Theme and Variations in Seventeenth-Century Literature* (Pittsburgh: University of Pittsburgh Press, 1978), p. 214.

7. *Andrew Marvell: His Life and Writings* (Ithaca: Cornell University Press, 1978), p. 57.

8. *The Wit of Love* (Notre Dame: University of Notre Dame Press, 1969), p. 153.

9. "The Shooting of the Bears," in *Andrew Marvell: Essays,* ed. Brett, p. 97.

10. M. C. Bradbrook and M. G. Lloyd Thomas, *Andrew Marvell,* 2nd ed. (Cambridge: Cambridge University Press, 1961), p. 30.

11. *"My Ecchoing Song": Andrew Marvell's Poetry of Criticism* (Princeton: Princeton University Press, 1970), p. 109.

12. "Marvell's Metaphysical Wit," in *Approaches to Marvell: The York Tercentenary Essays,* ed. C. A. Patrides (London: Routledge and Kegan Paul, 1978), p. 58.

13. *"My Ecchoing Song,"* p. 108.

14. *The Poems of Thomas Carew with His Masque "Coelum Britannicum,"* ed. Rhodes Dunlap (Oxford: The Clarendon Press, 1949; rpt. 1970), p. 18. All other quotations in the text derive from this edition.

15. *Poems,* ed. A. R. Waller (Cambridge: Cambridge University Press, 1905), p. 136.

16. "Marvell's 'Mourning,'" *Modern Language Quarterly* 33 (1971), 35.

17. "Marvell's Metaphysical Wit," p. 58.

18. Thomas Clayton, in "'It is Marvel He Outdwells His Hour': Some Perspectives on Marvell's Medium," in *Tercentenary Essays,* ed. Friedenreich, p. 68, calls "Mourning" "an anamorphic study in poetical epistemology."

19. In his edition of *The Works of Sir John Suckling: The Non-Dramatic Works* (Oxford: The Clarendon Press, 1971), Thomas Clayton writes that the poem is "probably not by Suckling" (p. lxxxix).

20. *"My Ecchoing Song,"* p. 48.

21. *The Poems of Edmund Waller,* ed. G. Thorn Drury (London: George Routledge and Sons, 1905), vol. 1, p. 91.

22. Michael Craze, *The Life and Lyrics of Andrew Marvell* (New York: Barnes and Noble, 1979), p. 51.

23. Ricks, "'Its own Resemblance,'" in *Approaches to Marvell,* ed. Patrides, p. 108. Empson created the phrase in *Seven Types of Ambiguity* (London: Chatto and Windus, 1930; 2nd rev. ed., 1947), pp. 160-61.

24. "Andrew Marvell: The Aesthetics of Inconclusiveness," in *Approaches to Marvell,* ed. Patrides, p. 168.

25. Ibid., pp. 160-61.

FURTHER READING

Criticism

Bush, Douglas. "Jonson, Donne, and Their Successors." In *English Literature in the Earlier Seventeenth Century 1600-1660,* pp. 104-69. Oxford: Oxford University Press, 1945.
> Traces the currents of Cavalier and metaphysical poetry in the seventeenth century.

Butler, Martin. "Lovers and Tyrants: Courtier Plays 1637-42." In *Theatre and Crisis 1632-1642,* pp. 55-83. Cambridge: Cambridge University Press, 1984.
> Rejects popular notions about English drama in the decade before the closure of the theaters.

Deneef, A. Leigh. "The Courtly Ceremonial." In *"This Poetick Liturgie": Robert Herrick's Ceremonial Mode,* pp. 69-108. Durham, N.C.: Duke University Press, 1974.
> Analyzes the ceremonial mode in Herrick's courtly lyrics, focusing on either their 'Cavalier' or 'functionary' voice.

Hammond, Gerald. "Richard Lovelace and the Uses of Obscurity." *Proceedings of the British Academy* 71 (1985): 203-34.
> Attempts to remove Lovelace's poetry from the "Cavalier" classification by arguing that Lovelace's work embodies the major concerns of mid-seventeenth-century lyric poetry in England.

Harbage, Alfred. "The Cavalier Mode." In *Cavalier Drama: An Historical and Critical Supplement to the Study of the Elizabethan and Restoration Stage,* pp. 28-47. New York: Russell & Russell, Inc., 1964.
> Delineates the distinctive themes, characterization, and language of Cavalier plays.

Hartmann, Cyril Hughes. *The Cavalier Spirit and Its Influence on the Life and Work of Richard Lovelace (1618-1658).* New York: Haskell House Publishers Ltd., 1973, 158 p.
> Explores the character and philosophy of the Cavaliers and pronounces Lovelace the "ideal Cavalier."

Judkins, David C. "Recent Studies in the Cavalier Poets: Thomas Carew, Richard Lovelace, John Suckling, and Edmund Waller." *English Literary Renaissance* 7, no. 2 (spring 1977): 243-58.

Bibliography focusing on, but not limited to, research published in the 1960s and 1970s.

Maclean, Hugh. *Ben Jonson and the Cavalier Poets: Authoritative Texts, Criticism,* edited by Hugh Maclean, New York: W. W. Norton & Company, Inc., 1974, 591 p.

Includes poems of eighteen different poets and extensive criticism.

Malcolmson, Cristina. "The Garden Enclosed/The Woman Enclosed: Marvell and the Cavalier Poets." In *Enclosure Acts: Sexuality, Property, and Culture in Early Modern England,* edited by Richard Burt and John Michael Archer, pp. 251-69. Ithaca, N.Y.: Cornell University Press, 1994.

Considers Marvell's criticism of the Cavalier poets, which contends that they attempted to justify the pursuit of their desires as part of the natural order.

Miner, Earl. "The Good Life." In *The Cavalier Mode from Jonson to Cotton,* pp. 43-99. Princeton, N.J.: Princeton University Press, 1971.

Examines Cavalier poetry in the context of seventeenth-century ideas about the pursuit of pleasure and morality.

Rando, Sharon Sanders. "'On My First Sonne': The Aesthetic Radical of Cavalier Poetry." *Concerning Poetry* 9, no. 1 (spring 1976): 27-30.

Regards Ben Jonson's funeral tribute to his son as "representative of the finest in Cavalier poetry."

Skelton, Robin. Introduction to *The Cavalier Poets,* edited by Robin Skelton, pp. 21-30. New York: Oxford University Press, 1970.

Discusses the prevailing themes of the Cavaliers and why their importance and influence has generally been undervalued by critics.

Summers, Joseph H. "Gentlemen of the Court and of Art: Suckling, Herrick, and Carew." In *The Heirs of Donne and Johnson,* pp. 41-75. New York: Oxford University Press, 1970.

Explains how the Cavaliers advanced the new ideal of gentlemanly behavior.

Anthony Ashley Cooper, Earl of Shaftesbury
1671-1713

English philosopher, editor and essayist.

INTRODUCTION

Shaftesbury was one of the leading thinkers of the Enlightenment and his associations with such figures as John Locke, Pierre Bayle, and John Toland placed him among Europe's intellectual elite. Today he is chiefly remembered as the founder of the "moral sense" school of ethics and as one of the first philosophers to write about aesthetics. His ideas regarding the importance of emotion in relation to morality were taken up later by Adam Smith and David Hume. Shaftesbury also significantly influenced European writers and philosophers from Jean-Jacques Rousseau to Friederich Schiller to Emmanuel Kant. Although he was known as a Deist because of the emphasis he placed on reason and his criticism of conventional religious teachings, Shaftesbury also stressed the importance of religious feeling, which he termed "enthusiasm." A Neoplatonist, Shaftesbury maintained that the purpose of religion, goodness, beauty, and philosophy is to identify completely with the universal system of which one is a part. Although he was plagued with ill health throughout his life, Shaftesbury produced an impressive number of philosophical essays, the most important of which were published in his collection *Characteristics of Men, Manners, Opinions, Times* (1711). Shaftesbury was a prominent figure during his day, but his significance as a philosopher has diminished, in large part because his ideas were more rigorously examined and more fully expressed by later thinkers. Many scholars also argue that Shaftesbury was a greater stylist than a thinker, so his philosophical views were quickly overshadowed by those of other philosophers. His engaging style, humor, biting satire, and frequent use of a literary persona in his writings, have interested literary critics and rhetoricians in Shaftesbury's works.

BIOGRAPHICAL INFORMATION

Shaftesbury was born Anthony Ashley Cooper in February 1671, in London. He grew up in the home of his grandfather, the first Earl of Shaftesbury, who was one of the most prominent political figures of his day. The first Earl appointed the philosopher John Locke, his close friend and secretary, to supervise his grandson's

education. Young Shaftesbury would eventually disagree with Locke on many important philosophical issues, but Locke was an important influence on his philosophical development and the two men remained friends until Locke's death. Shaftesbury was tutored at home in Latin and Greek before being sent to a private school. At the age of fifteen he set out on a three-year tour of Europe. On his return to England he devoted himself to the study of philosophy. In 1695 he entered the House of Commons but was forced to leave in 1698 because of ill health. He traveled to Holland, where among others, he met the eminent thinker Pierre Bayle.

In 1698 Shaftesbury brought out his first work, an edition of the sermons of the Platonist Benjamin Whichcote, to which he wrote the introduction. The following year Shaftesbury's *An Inquiry Concerning Virtue* (1699) was published without his permission by the Deist John Toland. That year Shaftesbury's father, the second Earl, died, and Shaftesbury inherited the title of third Earl. He entered the House of Lords in 1700, but ill health made it necessary that he leave politics once again. In the first decade of the 1700s he traveled occasionally to Holland and also produced his most important writings—a revised version of *An Inquiry Concerning Virtue* and completed versions of *A Letter Concerning Enthusiasm* (1708), *Sensus Communis: An Essay on the Freedom of Wit and Humour* (1709), *The Moralists* (1709), and *Soliloquy; or, Advice to an Author* (1710). In 1709 Shaftesbury married, and his son was born the following year. In 1710 the family traveled to Italy because of Shaftesbury's bad health. Despite his physical ailments, he continued to write. In 1711 he published *Characteristics of Men, Manners, Opinions, Times,* a collection of his writings with extensive notes and commentary. He worked on revisions to the *Characteristics* over the course of the next two years, until his death in Naples in 1713.

MAJOR WORKS

Today Shaftesbury is best known for inventing the "moral sense" concept in ethics. He is regarded as a Deist because of his stress on the importance of rational thought, but unlike other Deists he also pointed out the importance of religious feeling. He was a committed Platonist, although he differed from most other Neoplatonists of his day in emphasizing the role of emotion in questions of ethics, as well as because of his concept of religious feeling, or "enthusiasm." Shaftesbury's philosophy was in large part a reaction against the ethical positions of Thomas Hobbes and Locke, particularly their notions of egoism. In his first published work, the preface to the collection of sermons by Whichcote that he edited, Shaftesbury praises Whichcote's belief in the goodness of human beings and presents Whichcote's idea of "good nature" as an antidote to the Hobbesian tenet of self-interestedness. Shaftesbury's second work, *An Inquiry Concerning Virtue,* attacks Locke's egoism and proposes a set of practical rules for living, derived from the natural dispositions of all human beings. According to Shaftesbury, these dispositions are not merely self-regarding but also directed to the good of others; thus human beings have a "moral sense"—a sense of right and wrong that apprehends beauty or deformity in actions and affections.

The Sociable Enthusiast (1704), written in the form of a dialogue among three men, reiterates many of the ideas found in the *Inquiry.* It also introduces the idea, important in many of Shaftesbury's later works, of "enthusiasm," or creative imagination that is necessary in order for an individual to attain higher levels of understanding and to glimpse the ideal. *The Sociable Enthusiast* was printed without Shaftesbury's permission and he revised and published the work as *The Moralists* five years after its initial publication. In his next work, *A*

Letter Concerning Enthusiasm, an attack on religious fanaticism, Shaftesbury argues that humans have a natural inclination to enthusiasm and urges readers to distinguish ordinary enthusiasm from divine enthusiasm, which is true inspiration. Shaftesbury answered the attacks on his *Letter Concerning Enthusiasm* with *Sensus Communis: An Essay on the Freedom of Wit and Humour,* in which he also talks about the problem of writing in the face of censorship and religious intolerance. *Soliloquy; or, Advice to an Author,* the last of Shaftesbury's essays to be published individually, discusses the necessity of self-knowledge and self-criticism as a precursor to authorship. In it he argues that not only is soliloquy the means by which self-enlightenment can be achieved, it is also the attitude befitting enlightened humanity. Shaftesbury recommends that soliloquy should become a habit for authors in order that they inspire in their readers a free, critical view of themselves and the world.

Although Shaftesbury's 1711 *Characteristics* is a collection of the philosopher's previously published works, it is more than the sum of its parts. In addition to extensive notes, the volume includes Shaftesbury's "Miscellaneous Reflections," a running commentary on the other texts. In these reflections Shaftesbury, in the guise of a detached critic, expands upon some of his central themes and discusses his own role as author in a satirical vein.

A number of Shaftesbury's works were published posthumously. The most important of these are two works on aesthetics—the essay "Letter Concerning Design" and the fragment "The Judgement of Hercules"—and "The Adept Ladys," a reaction to the Rosicrucian movement active in England at the time. Shaftesbury's philosophical notebooks, or "Exercises," were also published after his death.

CRITICAL RECEPTION

While Shaftesbury was highly respected during his own time and continued to exert considerable influence into the nineteenth century, he is no longer considered a major philosopher. His enduring contribution has been his influence on some of the greatest thinkers of the eighteenth and nineteenth centuries: the publication of Shaftesbury's works gave rise to discussions in Britain among such notable philosophers as Bernard Mandeville, George Berkeley, Frances Hutcheson, Smith, and Hume. In France he was admired by Voltaire, Rousseau, and Denis Diderot, and in Germany his ideas were taken up by Gottfried Leibniz, Gotthold Lessing, Johann Wolfgang von Goethe, Kant, and Schiller. Recent criticism on Shaftesbury has focused on his moral theory, especially the important concepts of enthusiasm and religious feeling. Many scholars have commented on his interest in religion despite his stance as a Deist and his advocacy of feeling and subjectivity even while he espouses rationalism and objective understanding. Some critics have also examined his use of satire, humor, and literary persona in his writing, comparing his work with that of Jonathan Swift. His writings on aesthetics are regarded as important because of their focus on the centrality of art to human life and because his aesthetic theory is linked intimately with his moral theory. Shaftesbury's ideas about aesthetics are considered original and innovative because he was the first philosopher to elevate the role of the creator of artistic works over the works themselves. Some contemporary critics have championed him as the father of modern aesthetic theory and his reputation continues to grow in this area.

PRINCIPAL WORKS

Select Sermons of Dr. Whichcote [editor] (sermons) 1698

An Inquiry Concerning Virtue, in Two Discourses (essay) 1699

Paradoxes of State, Relating to the Present Juncture of Affairs in England and the Rest of Europe [with John Toland] (essay) 1702

The Sociable Enthusiast (essay) 1704

*A Letter Concerning Enthusiasm, To My Lord ******* (essay) 1708

*The Moralists: A Philosophical Rhapsody. Being a recital of certain conversations upon natural and moral subjects (essay) 1709

Sensus Communis: An Essay on the Freedom of Wit and Humour. In a letter to a friend (essay) 1709

Soliloquy; or, Advice to an Author (essay) 1710

Characteristics of Men, Manners, Opinions, Times [*Characteristics*] (essays) 1711

The Life, Unpublished Letters, and Philosophical Regimen of Anthony Earl of Shaftesbury (essays, letters, notebooks) 1914

*This work is a revised version of *The Sociable Enthusiast.*

CRITICISM

Stanley Grean (essay date 1967)

SOURCE: Grean, Stanley. "Enthusiasm" and "Concluding Remarks." In *Shaftesbury's Philosophy of Religion and Ethics: A Study in Enthusiasm*, pp. 19-36; 258-63. Athens, Ohio: Ohio University Press, 1967.

[*In the first of the following essays, Grean explores the background and significance of Shaftesbury's central doctrine of enthusiasm and discusses how it is related to his religious concepts; in the second, he offers an overview of Shaftesbury's thought, viewing him as a poet rather than a philosopher because of his belief that reason ought to be transcended to reach higher truths.*]

ENTHUSIASM

In a letter to a friend, Shaftesbury once wrote, "You know me for a great enthusiast. . . ."[1] Despite this self-admission, and despite the frequent discussions of enthusiasm in his writings, one finds that Anglo-American scholars have on the whole failed to recognize the central place of love and enthusiasm in Shaftesbury's thought. This is true even of such reputable scholars as Leslie Stephen, Thomas Fowler, Basil Willey, and R. L. Brett. Basil Willey, for example, sees the importance of Shaftesbury's "enthusiasm" only as an attribute of man's response to Nature's beauties.[2] An important recent exception is Marjorie Nicolson's study of "the aesthetics of the infinite," in which she explores the concept of enthusiasm in relation to Shaftesbury's aesthetics.[3] What there has been in the standpoint of Anglo-American critics that has made them uninterested in or unaware of the importance of this concept is an interesting question. In contrast, German scholars like Cassirer and Wilhelm Windelband have recognized the centrality of enthusiasm in the English philosopher's world-view. Perhaps one reason is that a more vital tradition of philosophic idealism has survived into the twentieth century in Germany. Windelband wrote of Shaftesbury that "the centre of his doctrine and of his own nature is formed by what he himself called *enthusiasm*,—enthusiasm for all that is true, good, and beautiful, the elevation of the soul above itself to more universal values, the living out of the whole peculiar power of the individual by the devotion to something higher."[4] This is the motif that is repeated throughout Shaftesbury's writings and that gives them their characteristic tone: by giving himself to that which is greater than self, man *makes* himself and *is made*. To understand this doctrine in all its ramifications is a main goal of this study. In this chapter we will explore its background and try to define its essential significance in Shaftesbury's philosophy, with special reference to his religious concepts. . . .

Significantly, the first version of **The Moralists,** as privately circulated in 1705, was entitled by Shaftesbury **The Sociable Enthusiast: a Philosophical Adventure.**[5] He reports having changed this "much" before its public printing in 1709 under the final title, **The Moralists, A Philosophical Rhapsody.**[6] Shaftesbury first addressed the public at length on the subject of enthusiasm in the **Letter Concerning Enthusiasm** published in 1708, though written the previous year.[7] The immediate stimulus to the writing of the **Letter** was the behavior of the Camisards, a religious group popularly known as the

"French prophets," who had sought refuge in England from religious persecution in France. The Camisard movement, which first appeared in France in the Cévennes shortly after the revocation of the Edict of Nantes in 1685, proved to be short-lived, for it rapidly declined after 1715.[8] Brutally repressed in France, the Camisards fought back with all the fury they could muster, committing massacres of Catholic priests and laymen in the name of religious truth and under the guidance of prophets who claimed supernatural inspiration. Though they had emerged from the ranks of the Huguenots, they were looked upon with dismay and disapproval by the more conservative members of that group. When some of the "prophets" arrived in London in the early years of the eighteenth century,[9] the established Huguenot community there quickly disowned them, and eventually excommunicated them.

The Camisards followed the usual pattern of evangelical pneumatism, emphasizing the necessity for direct contact with God and claiming to be "possessed" at times by the Holy Spirit. Such possession was consciously cultivated, and it manifested itself in certain extraordinary ways. An English clergyman, Nathaniel Spinckes, describes

> . . . The Shakings of their Heads; Crawling on the Knees; Quakings and Tremblings; their Whistlings, Drummings, Trumpettings; their Thundrings; their Snuffling; Blowing as with a Horn; Panting, and Difficulty of Breathing, Sighing and Groaning; Hissing; Smiling; Laughing . . . Striking . . . Howling in their Assemblies like a Dog, and being in all manner of Disorder.[10]

As with other "enthusiastic" sects, the members of this one are also reported as falling into trancelike catatonic states for minutes or hours, or becoming ecstatic and speaking with tongues, or doing "violence" to themselves, though without injury. There were claims of clairvoyance and prophecy, in some cases by children. And there were the familiar predictions of the end of the world, or more modestly, of the destruction of London. In one of their most publicized pronouncements, toward the end of 1707, they predicted that a certain man, then dying, would be raised from the dead five months after his burial. A huge crowd of Londoners, waiting at the cemetery on the appointed day, were disappointed, while the prophets themselves were wisely absent. Little wonder that on some occasions the prophets were attacked by angry mobs.

Three of the prophets had been placed on trial in July, 1707, for their predictions of disaster for England, and sentenced to the pillory in November.[11] In that same year, when the literary propaganda and popular renown of this sect reached a peak, Shaftesbury wrote the **Letter Concerning Enthusiasm.** The prophets had succeeded in converting "two English Gentlemen of Quality and Estates," John Lacy and Sir Richard Bulkeley, the former of whom wrote a "defence of revived prophecy" in 1707 under the title, *A Cry from the Desart: or Testimonials of the Miraculous Things lately come to pass in the Cévennes.* Shaftesbury quotes from this and reports that he saw Lacy "lately under an agitation" prophesying in a Latin style of which he was ordinarily incapable. (I, 32) Apparently the philosopher was not satisfied with second-hand reports but wanted the opportunity to observe the behavior of the prophets at first-hand; to do this, he "probably attended one of the prophet's meetings in a private bench-filled parlor."[12]

It would be a mistake to suppose that Shaftesbury's knowledge of evangelical sectarianism of this sort was restricted to the French prophets or that his doctrine of enthusiasm was shaped solely or even largely by their behavior. Shaftesbury had had ample opportunity to observe other such "enthusiastic" sects, of which England had her plentiful share.[13] Though the Camisards provided the immediate occasion for the writing of the **Letter,** Shaftesbury's attitude toward "enthusiasm" had already taken shape in the first draft of **The Moralists** (1705). Marjorie Nicolson writes that in the **Letter** Shaftesbury's "mood of wit against false enthusiasms reflected Swift,"[14] whose attack on religious fanaticism, *A Tale of a Tub,* appeared in 1704. Indeed, the **Letter,** which appeared anonymously like most of the treatises in the **Characteristics,** was attributed by some to Swift. Yet Shaftesbury mentions Swift disparagingly in a letter accompanying **The Sociable Enthusiast** to Lord Somers, to whom Swift had also dedicated his book. At a later time Shaftesbury attacked the *Tale* in the strongest terms as "that detestable writing of that most detestable author."[15] It is more likely that the *Tale* was a stimulus to the writing of **The Moralists** than of the **Letter.** The latter concentrates on the criticism of false enthusiasm, though it gives due recognition to the nature of true enthusiasm. But **The Moralists** represents Shaftesbury's major attempt to describe the character of true enthusiasm. It is his answer to the charge, implied in the common use of the term "enthusiast" in his time, that a religious enthusiast must and could only be a fanatic.

The distinction between true and false enthusiasm is not original to Shaftesbury, for it can be found in such writers as Meric Casaubon,[16] Ralph Cudworth, Henry More, and John Dennis, though J. M. Robertson is probably right in asserting that Shaftesbury's was the main influence leading to the modern positive use of the term. In contrast, Locke and Whichcote had stressed the dangers of enthusiasm. Shaftesbury was particularly influenced by Henry More's *Enthusiasmus Triumphatus; or a Brief Discourse of the Nature, Causes, Kinds, and Cure of Enthusiasm* (1656).[17] Though More paved the way for a new understanding of the significance of enthusiasm, the emphasis in his discourse also still lay on the *triumphatus*—the conquest of false enthusiasm—and it was only at the end of it that he gave some attention to true enthusiasm, insisting that he had no intention of criticizing it. While Shaftesbury drew heavily from this work and the *Enchiridion Ethicum,* he comments that in other writings More "was perhaps as great an Enthusiast, as any of those, whom he wrote against."[18]

Enthusiasm is described by Shaftesbury as a "powerful and extensive" phenomenon of which we all have had some experience. It is the state of mind which occurs when the mind envisages the "prodigious," the "more than human," and receives or creates ideas or images too big for it to contain.[19] Enthusiasm is characterized by intense emotions, either delightful or fearful, that are felt "when the mind is taken up in vision, and fixes its view either on any real object, or mere spectre of divinity." (I, 37) It can occur when the mind is transported by some apparition, and it is associated by Shaftesbury with the apprehension of the great and awesome. "We can admire nothing profoundly without a certain religious veneration." (II, 177) The fact that such emotions border on fear has led some to regard them as products solely of that emotion, but Shaftesbury rejects this explanation, finding the real basis of enthusiasm not in fear but in man's natural passion for the sublime and the beautiful.

Whether Shaftesbury was familiar with John Dennis's early critical writings I do not know, but there are some interesting parallels in their views.[20] According to Dennis, "enthusiasms" in contrast with ordinary emotions are strong passions such as "Admiration, Terror or Joy" whose cause is "not clearly comprehended by him who feels them,"[21] though "Poetical Enthusiasm is a Passion guided by Judgment . . . ,"[22] for otherwise it would be madness. The greatest enthusiasms are stimulated by religious subjects, "for all which is great in Religion is most exalted and amazing, all that is joyful is transporting, all that is sad is dismal, and all that is terrible is astonishing."[23]

Dennis distinguished between beauty and the sublime, finding the true source of the latter "in God and in the manifestations of His greatness and power in Nature."[24] Marjorie Nicolson further interprets Dennis as believing that beauty and sublimity were antithetical, and Shaftesbury as considering the sublime a "higher beauty." This seems correct of Shaftesbury, but I think Professor Nicolson errs in stating that "the word *sublime* was so seldom on Shaftesbury's lips that it surprises. When he used it at all, it was usually with disparagement."[25] The word "sublime" is not that rare in Shaftesbury, and by my tabulation it is used considerably more often in an approving than in a disapproving sense. A breakdown of the way in which he uses the term reveals two basic usages: first, as a stylistic concept referring to various of the arts; and second, as

characterizing the higher types of human behavior, thought, or character. He rarely uses the term to refer directly to Nature's grandeur.[26] In the stylistic context it is true that Shaftesbury is often critical of the "false sublime." (I, 157 ff.) For just as there are true and false forms of enthusiasm, so there are of the sublime, in both art and life. The sublime, on the one hand, may be linked with the truly lofty, noble, and inspired, and on the other, with the pompous, bombastic, and vulgarly sensational. Shaftesbury understood that the enthusiastic and the sublime by only a slight transformation can be falsified and perverted. The true sublime is not mere rhetoric but grounded on a true idea of Nature and of God. We experience the sublime when the mind is taken hold of by that which is infinitely greater than itself, by that which can only be grasped by intuitive vision in an act of enthusiasm.

Shaftesbury writes in the **Letter** that "inspiration is a real feeling of the Divine Presence, and enthusiasm a false one." (I, 37) But he means to say that true inspiration or enthusiasm is based upon the actual apprehension of the Divine, while false enthusiasm is produced by a mistaken sense of the Deity's presence. Henry More agreed, and both writers considered false enthusiasm to be a product of an unregulated imagination. True enthusiasm, in contrast, employs the powers of the imagination as controlled by reason in order to attain a higher, intuitive grasp of truth. But More's language in describing true inspiration differs significantly from Shaftesbury's, for More writes that "to be inspired is to be moved in an extraordinary manner by the power or Spirit of God to act, speak, or think what is holy, just and true."[27] The Cambridge Platonist is still using the language of traditional religion which implies a God who is personal and transcendent, though immanent in certain respects. But in Shaftesbury's philosophy God is largely impersonal, and His immanence is given greater stress. More still believes in the effectiveness of supernatural grace, while for Shaftesbury this doctrine has in large part been either eliminated or naturalized. For More, a special divine act of revelation is still possible; for Shaftesbury, revelation is general in the sense that the individual makes himself capable of receiving what is always given or being given to all men. This is one of the points at which we can see rather clearly how Shaftesbury contributed to the growing process of secularizing and "demythologizing" the religion of his time.

Ronald Knox interprets Shaftesbury to mean that those who are taken with false enthusiasm are really conscious frauds.[28] Actually, Shaftesbury's position was that they may be entirely sincere though deceiving themselves as well as others. Shaftesbury's attitude seems a good deal more judicious than that of some of his contemporaries—the so-called "men of wit"—who regarded all religion as the product of conscious fraud. The third Earl points out that the Bible itself discriminates between a good and evil spirit of prophecy. But he notes ironically the difficulty in distinguishing the two since their outward symptoms are so much the same in all religions. His description of their characteristic "ecstasies . . . quakings, tremblings, . . . convulsions" (I, 35) sounds much like the reports of the behavior of the French prophets. Shaftesbury's approach to this problem was more complex than that taken by some of his contemporaries who denied that any higher, divine power could affect the human mind. In examining the symptoms of enthusiasm, Shaftesbury reports that some thinkers "endeavour to solve the appearances of this kind by the natural operation of our passions and the common course of outward things." (II, 173) While attempting on the one hand to deny a crude supernaturalism, Shaftesbury sought to formulate a genuine doctrine of inspiration. Thus, he suggests that there is "a kind of enchantment or magic" in enthusiasm. The harmonious and the beautiful grasp us, "inspires us with something more than ordinary, and raises us above ourselves." (II, 174) Yet this is an ecstasy of reason, not an abandonment of it. Shaftesbury characterizes his ***Philosophical Rhapsody, The Moralists,*** as comprising a "variety of styles . . . even the poetic or sublime, such as is the aptest to run into enthusiasm and extravagance." (II, 334) Yet, significantly, he insists that it is at bottom just as "systematical" and rational as the more formal ***Inquiry.*** Indeed, he goes even further, contending that ***The Moralists*** is his "principal performance" because it stirs the imagination and excites the mind as the more "scholastic manner" cannot do. (II, 334)[29]

To discriminate between true and false enthusiasm required careful and objective reasoning, according to Shaftesbury. The claims of religious enthusiasts must be assessed and checked by impartial observers. He agreed with Henry More that enthusiasm could be tested by whether or not it issued in moral behavior and reasonable beliefs. However, Shaftesbury would not have agreed to More's third condition for true enthusiasms— that it be based on belief in the Bible, rightly interpreted, and in Jesus Christ, Son of God and Saviour. But both men warned that if we were to avoid the contagion of powerful delusions we had to have self-understanding as well as self-control.

Since the doctrine of enthusiasm provides an important link between Shaftesbury's religious, moral, and aesthetic doctrines, it is not surprising that he considered poetry to be characterized by enthusiasm. To be great, a poet must imagine a "divine presence" and be inspired by a vision of that which is greater than himself and greater than mankind. "Poets are fanatics too," though "poetic madness" must be subject to the control of the mind if it is to be genuinely creative. (I, 36) Shaftesbury approvingly quotes More's statement that "a poet is an enthusiast in jest, and an enthusiast is a poet in good earnest," (II, 197)[30] though he adapts More's thought to a more positive conception of poetic inspiration.

Shaftesbury follows More and Cudworth in finding an affinity between atheism and enthusiasm also. He recognizes that the atheist, like other men, has his ultimate concerns for which he may even sacrifice his life. Shaftesbury quotes Cudworth's delightful explanation:

> All atheists being that blind Goddess Nature's fanatics . . . are possessed with a certain kind of Madness, that may be called Pneumatophobia, that makes them have an irrational but desperate Abhorrence from Spirits or Incorporeal Substances, they being acted also, at the same time, with an Hylomania, whereby they madly dote upon Matter, and devoutly worship it, as the only Numen.
>
> (II, 196 f.)[31]

Even the "cold Lucretius," disciple of "this unpolite philosophy," is forced despite himself to give way "to admiration and rapturous views of Nature" while at the same time he "arraigns the order of it. . . ." (II, 175) In Shaftesbury's model of human nature this capacity for enthusiasm or ultimate commitment is a necessary trait of man. Yet it is a paradox of Shaftesbury's dialectic that the same psychological phenomenon can in one context lead to the highest forms of creativity and self-affirmation, and in another to the greatest delusion and self-deception. It is in part explained by Shaftesbury's belief that extremes tend to generate their opposites, as "the extreme passion for religious objects" can turn into an extreme aversion for them.

Unless it is properly regulated and directed toward the appropriate objects, enthusiasm is likely to be perverted either into fanaticism through excess of love or into superstition through excess of fear. Shaftesbury notes a similarity between the emotions of lovers and the ecstasies of "quietists" and "pietists." This "amorous" type of enthusiasm he finds cultivated particularly by female saints. (II, 179) Superstition, on the other hand, results when the religious objects on which we focus are terrifying to us. However, religious zeal is seldom without a mixture of both these tendencies, as love and fear alternate with the changes in an individual's mood. Shaftesbury writes that "in religions, therefore, which hold most of love, there is generally room left for terrors of the deepest kind," (II, 180) and the converse is also true. But in Shaftesbury's own religious philosophy fear is transmuted into awe, and terror into love. Despite the similarities between his and John Dennis's concept of enthusiasm, Dennis's God is a God of infinite power who arouses "Enthusiastic Terrour"; Shaftesbury's is a God of infinite benevolence who inspires love.[32]

Like Henry More, Shaftesbury considers melancholy or "ill-humour" to be a basic source of false enthusiasm, and, in fact, he even wonders "whether anything beside ill-humour can be the cause of atheism." (I, 17) This makes more sense when we remember that for Shaftesbury atheism means the denial of all natural order. Shaftesbury quotes More to the effect that the religious fanatic who thinks he is moved by the Spirit of God is actually subject to "the power of Melancholy, . . . a kind of natural inebriation," which works in a way deceptively similar to divine grace. (II, 198)[33] It can produce "ecstatic" states which are completely convincing to the individual in its grasp, since all power of free judgment has been temporarily destroyed. Shaftesbury had observed how easily such ecstatic states are communicated to others by a kind of mass hysteria, or in his terms, "panic." Any emotion, he comments, is stronger when it is "social and communicative." (I, 13) Melancholy and ill-humor distort our vision of God, for we project our own ill-temper upon Him, which prevents us from approaching Him freely and joyfully. In a state of dread or anxiety we cannot have a true conception of God: "We can never be fit to contemplate anything above us, when we are in no condition to look into ourselves, and calmly examine the temper of our own mind and passions." (I, 24) If Shaftesbury's analysis here seems superficial in the light of modern Crisis Theology, there is, nevertheless, an important element of truth in it. Religion, like all fundamental human institutions, is subject to the distortions of neurosis and mental derangement.

Actually, Shaftesbury's philosophy is part of a broad movement—not always connected—which manifested itself in seventeenth- and eighteenth-century Europe in such diverse quarters as Spinozism, Hasidism, and Cambridge Platonism, a movement to recover the joy in religion. Shaftesbury himself was, of course, primarily influenced by the Cambridge men as well as by the English Latitudinarian divines. Good humor, he writes, is "not only the best security against enthusiasm, but the best foundation of piety and true religion." (I, 17) And Christianity itself, "notwithstanding the dark complexion and sour humour of religious teachers . . . [is] in the main a witty and good-humoured religion." (II, 217) Shaftesbury believed that there was a close correlation between one's emotional mood and one's beliefs, and he thought, moreover, that a good-humored and joyful state of mind made possible a more objective and better-rounded conception of God.

We have seen then that for Shaftesbury true enthusiasm was a state of being in which man was inspired by the Divine and raised beyond his ordinary capacities. Henry More eloquently described it as "the triumph of the Soul of man inebriated, as it were, with the delicious sense of the divine life. . . ."[34] All true greatness, according to Shaftesbury, whether in "heroes, statesmen, poets, . . . even philosophers," is the product of some "noble enthusiasm." (I, 38 f.) Yet enthusiasm is not restricted to great men or to special occasions; it belongs

to common experience. It is whatever makes men seek something beyond mere animal satisfactions. The joys of "the lover, [and] the ambitious man," would be much less if in that "which they admire and passionately pursue there were no reference or regard to any higher majesty or grandeur than what simply results from the particular objects of their pursuit." (II, 175)

> All sound love and admiration is enthusiasm: "The transports of poets, the sublime of orators, the rapture of musicians, the high strains of the virtuosi—all mere enthusiasm! Even learning itself, the love of arts and curiosities, the spirit of travellers and adventurers, gallantry, war, heroism—all, all enthusiasm!"
>
> (II, 129)

But if enthusiasm has its roots in the common pursuits of man, it has its flower in "whatever is sublime in human passions." (I, 38)

Yet Shaftesbury sharply differentiates his concept of enthusiasm from supernatural revelation. Enthusiasm has a natural basis in the structure of the human mind: "There is a power in numbers, harmony, proportion, and beauty of every kind, which naturally captivates the heart, and raises the imagination to an opinion or conceit of something majestic and divine." (II, 174) Shaftesbury draws an analogy between our grasping of a particular harmonious whole, as in a work of art, and our apprehension of Deity.

> For is there a fair and plausible enthusiasm, a reasonable ecstasy and transport allowed to other subjects, such as architecture, painting, music; and shall it be exploded here? Are there senses by which all those other graces and perfections are perceived, and none by which this higher perfection and grace is comprehended?
>
> (II, 129)

But just as in aesthetic experience man must develop and train his taste, so in the sphere of religious experience the affections must be ordered and the capacities of the mind exercised.

The concepts of enthusiasm and of love are inextricably connected in Shaftesbury's thought. The Platonic doctrine of *eros,* as developed by Plotinus and reformulated by the Renaissance and Cambridge Platonists, is given new life in his philosophy.[35] In Plotinus, *eros* was the bond between the highest and the lowest forms of being, as the lower reaches for the higher, and the higher for the lower. The Cambridge men, fusing Neoplatonic and Christian doctrine, made a fundamental part of their philosophy what Pope was to describe as

> . . . *the chain of Love*
> *Combining all below and all above.*[36]

For Shaftesbury too, love is the energy that unites all things.

Just as enthusiasm has its highest object in God, so does love; and just as enthusiasm appears at different levels of human experience, so does love. There is a hierarchy of love—similar to that found in other idealistic philosophies—extending from self-love to familial love, to love of friends, of country, of mankind, and finally of the cosmos itself. Each level involves higher and wider spheres of affection; each entails a further possibility of self-transcendence.[37] Though man has an obligation to expand the objects of his affection, Shaftesbury does not place emphasis on that but rather on the point that only by so doing can man realize his own true being. There is a natural movement, he contends, from the more restricted to the more comprehensive loves. One notes the ease with which Shaftesbury can use the same term, "natural affection," to mean either love within the family, or the social affections in general, or finally the love of Nature as a whole. He is aware though that there are counterforces and that the lesser loves can be an obstacle to the higher. But man alone of all creatures is capable of grasping his relationship to the Whole of Being; and man alone is under an obligation to strive for the good of the Whole, which takes priority over all partial goods. Shaftesbury was convinced, as we will see in the following chapters, that all things in the universe worked for the good of the Whole. In his notebook he wrote that, if this be true, "it follows that I must in a certain manner be reconciled to all things, love all things, and absolutely hate or abhor nothing whatsoever that has being in the world."[38] Only when this supreme affection is dominant can we properly regulate our lesser affections.

In *The Moralists* Theocles seeks to convince the skeptical Philocles of the importance of the love of humanity and of Nature. But Philocles finds it hard to grasp such "universal friendship," or "mystical love." While he can understand love of the individual, affection for humanity is "too mysterious, too metaphysical"; affection ordinarily requires a "sensible, material image." (II, 39) Theocles (who is Shaftesbury's spokesman) responds that a mental image may be an object of affection. One may, for example, become fond of an individual even before meeting him in person, or may love a particular nation before having any direct contact with it. Philocles concedes this possibility but he wonders if he could love a mental image of mankind or Nature very deeply unless "it could be sensible of my love and capable of a return." (*Ibid.*) Theocles dares to meet even this challenge, saying: "I will endeavor to show you that beauty which I count the perfectest, and most deserving of love, and which will not fail of a return." However, Philocles must first attain "at least some faint and distant view of the sovereign genius and first beauty." (II, 40) Nowhere is it clearer that Shaftesbury conceived the relationship of God and man as being dialectical and dynamic in character. While he sought to preserve the nonpersonal character of Deity, he also had a suffi-

ciently deep understanding of religious experience to know that when man loves God, he is in turn "loved."

In developing his philosophy of love, Shaftesbury, like the Cambridge Platonists, tried to steer a path between the extremes of the mystics and the Deists. The mystics' "high-raised love" went beyond reason (II, 55); the Deists, on the other hand, had stripped their "rational religion" of all genuine religious feeling and imaginative vision.[39] Henry More had remarked that they "ill deserve the name of Christians, who so indulge a sort of dry and hungry Reason, as wholly to exclude all manner of Enthusiasm."[40] Shaftesbury further charges the advocates of rational religion with grounding religion on the fear of punishment and the hope of reward, rather than on disinterested love of God for His own sake. By so doing, they debase religion, "for how shall one deny that to serve God by compulsion, or for interest merely, is servile and mercenary?" (II, 55) True affection for Deity is distinct "from everything worldly, sensual, or meanly interested. [It is] a love which is simple, pure, and unmixed, which has no other object than merely the excellency of that being itself, nor admits of any other thought of happiness than in its single fruition." (II, 54)

Shaftesbury admits that he is propounding a "paradox of faith," (II, 56) for in his system God is the symbol of man's true good or true interest. To love God is to love one's own true good; yet at the same time it must be a disinterested love. Only in relation to the dialectic of enthusiasm can this be understood. In religious, moral, and aesthetic experience, Shaftesbury pictures man as involved in a continual process of self-transcendence. By giving himself to that which is more than self, man both *makes* himself and *is made*. Self-giving is a necessary condition of self-discovery and self-realization; without it we cannot comprehend either Nature or God. The process itself is not only the means *to* Deity, but *is* Deity. Love is the energy that impels man beyond himself to seek the good, to seek that which has intrinsic value. Love of others—the giving of self to others—means participation in wider and deeper communities of meaning. Enthusiasm is the rapturous state in which the mind is "taken up in vision," and possessed by the highest—the state in which man experiences his own true fullness of being.

In Shaftesbury's system, the highest point of man's inner development is the "free and voluntary love" of God, in which all enthusiasms have their consummation:

> Shall I be ashamed of this diviner love and of an object of love so far excelling all those objects in dignity, majesty, grace, beauty, and amiableness? Is this enthusiasm? Be it: and so may I be ever an enthusiast. Happy me, if I can grow on this enthusiasm, so as to lose all

those enthusiasms of every other kind and be whole towards this. . . . Is the beatific vision enthusiasm? Or
suppose it enthusiasm, is it not justifiable and of a right
kind? What can be more highly reasonable?[41]

. . . . .

CONCLUDING REMARKS

Montesquieu described Shaftesbury as one of *"les
quatres grands poètes,"* along with Plato, Malebranche,
and Montaigne,[42] and it is as a "poet" that he must finally be judged. Shaftesbury understood the philosopher's need for inspiration in the highest reaches of
thought. Philocles, the skeptic, can only become a convinced theist when he is able to share Theocles's vision
of Nature and man—when he can share his enthusiasm.
Enthusiasm . . . is not only the culmination of
Shaftesbury's philosophy, but is the dynamic element
that gives it life and sets his thought apart from that of
the Deists and rationalists of the Augustan age. Not that
he was any less devoted to reason than they, but he understood (more, perhaps, than he was fully aware of)
that reason must continually seek to transcend itself,
that the processes of discursive reason are not and never
can be complete in themselves. They are completed
only in intuitive vision—in those moments when man is
"lifted out of himself" and catches sight of the higher
beauty and truth. This is not for Shaftesbury an irrational or antirational act. His entire philosophy may be
viewed as an attempt to refute the claim that, in Hocking's words, "no rational enthusiasms are possible."[43]
Enthusiasm is the fulfillment of our highest potentialities as rational beings—the extension of the powers of
reason to their highest limits. However, "reason" is understood here in its broadest sense: it includes but is
more than the processes of the discursive intellect. It
comprehends that whole realm of common concepts
that arise out of the shared life and experience of the
human community. The symbol-making, form-creating
capacity of man, which is the basis of language and art,
is also part of the rational nature of man. Enthusiasm,
like Tillich's description of "faith," is "reason in ecstasy," but it is ecstasy that is "fulfilled, not denied, rationality."[44] Shaftesbury carefully distinguished between
his idea of religious commitment and what he regarded
as the false enthusiasm of the evangelical sects. Denying supernatural revelation, he proposed rational tests
for claims of inspiration; religious zeal unchecked by
reason and by "common sense" not only subjects men
to mental delusions but produces social disorder.
Shaftesbury was not unaware of the dangers in his own
type of enthusiasm though. In one place he warned that
since we know more clearly what is evil than what is
good,

> we are to work rather by the weaning than the engag-
> ing passions; since if we give way chiefly to inclina-
> tion, by loving, applauding, and admiring what is great
> and good, we may possibly, it seems, in some high ob-

jects of that kind, be so amused and ecstasied as to lose
ourselves and miss our proper mark for want of a steady
and settled aim.

(II, 280 f.)

It may seem strange to have linked Shaftesbury, an advocate of rational theology, with a modern theologian
like Tillich, who is identified with the critical reaction
against liberal theology, for which Shaftesbury's philosophy is one of the basic historical sources. But besides the connection already established between their
respective concepts of enthusiasm and faith, there is an
even deeper link in their common emphasis on the necessity of commitment. Tillich defines faith as "the
state of being ultimately concerned";[45] similarly,
Shaftesbury's concept of enthusiasm calls for a total
commitment to those higher values which define the
character of human life—which make it what it is and
what it ought to be. (I, 87) The giving of self to that
which is more than self is the only true mode of self-
realization. This stress on commitment anticipates the
central concern of modern religious thought, and in particular of existentialism, which seems at first sight so
distant in tone and approach from the Augustan philosopher.

Actually, theologians like Tillich, Reinhold Niebuhr,
and others have a greater debt to the Enlightenment than
is commonly acknowledged in theological circles
today. So-called "post-liberal theology" owes much to
the very tradition of liberalism that it has sought to re-
examine and in part to replace. These theologians take
for granted a body of biblical criticism that has taken
them far beyond the simple biblical literalism that was
still rife in the seventeenth century. It must not be forgotten that Shaftesbury and the Deists played an important role in stimulating and in some respects even forcing the critical study of religious scriptures. Their
impetus contributed to the growing body of studies in
the following centuries, historical, psychological, an-
thropological, and sociological, which have in turn vi-
tally affected the methods and content of contemporary
theology. We owe to the Enlightenment such basic pre-
suppositions as the rights of freedom of thought and of
freely examining religious beliefs. The seventeenth century, for all its seminal vitality, still clung to much of
the furniture of medieval religious doctrine, as for example, the belief in an actual hell of eternal torment for
the wicked, and the argument for God based on
miracles. . . . Shaftesbury delivered a powerful blow
to the whole theology of retribution and contributed to
the important shift in man's conception of God, stressing His love rather than His justice or power. The abandonment of the argument based on miracles was paralleled by attacks on the other classical proofs of Deity.
Shaftesbury's own favorite argument—the teleological—which Hume was to attack so strongly, still survives, though generally it dons the garb of evolution, as

in Teilhard de Chardin. But the primary criticisms of the arguments for God generated by the Enlightenment lead directly to Tillich's abandonment of the attempt to prove the "existence" of God by rational argument, and instead to demonstrate the dynamic significance of faith in human experience.

All this is not to deny the many differences that lie between Shaftesbury's thought and modern existential theology; they are so obvious that they need not be spelled out here. One, however, that is particularly interesting is the absence of any concept of symbolism in Shaftesbury. His understanding of poetic truth, his doctrines of creative imagination and enthusiasm, all would suggest that a genuine theory of symbols would not only have been consistent with his thought but would have provided a valuable means for the development of the implications of his ideas. However, like the Deists, he tended to dismiss religious myths as mere legends or products of unregulated fancy. No doubt the abuses of the allegorical method in the Middle Ages militated against the positive use of symbolic interpretation, but the lack of such a method made it impossible for Shaftesbury and the Deists really to grasp the significance of much of traditional theology.[46]

John Brown criticized Shaftesbury's conception of disinterested love for God as "not calculated for Use," and fit only for "a Mind taken up in Vision."[47] Yet Shaftesbury wrote precisely in order to make it possible for other minds to share his vision of Nature and God, to see Reality as an aesthetic Whole—the harmonious product of a Supreme Artist. Thus, he does not rest his case on logical argument alone, and his appeal to experience is not to a mere accumulation of sense-data; Shaftesbury seeks to develop our aesthetic capacity as a means of arriving at higher truths—the ability to see things in their connections as parts of organic unities. His approach to Nature and to God is finally aesthetic and intuitive rather than analytical or logical—"a mere dream; but . . . truly rational, and divine. . . ."[48] It is the poetry of thought and aspiration that gives his work its final form.

The universe no longer seems as orderly as it did to those who lived in the age of Newton, and yet we still seek order and believe that it is there to be found. The type of optimism that Shaftesbury preached has been seriously challenged, and yet many who reject it accept some modified form of it, though sometimes without being fully conscious of the fact. . . . Shaftesbury was not a simple optimist; he was well aware of the depths of potential evil in man, and that he did not seek to deny the reality of proximate evil. Yet his "solution" to the problem of evil is acceptable only as an enthusiastic *faith,* not as a logical argument. Shaftesbury's formulation of the basic faith of the Enlightenment is neither as naïve as its critics have sometimes regarded it, nor as

convincingly reasonable as its proponents thought. It is a faith that still underlies in large part the liberal, democratic culture of the Western world, despite the intensive re-examination of it that has been going on for over a hundred years. Which of its axioms are we prepared to abandon? and what will the consequences be? These are the questions that modern man must ask. But in asking them we must still hope, as Shaftesbury did 250 years ago, for a new birth of freedom which will

> bring not Europe only but Asia (which is now concerned), and in a manner the whole world, under one community; or at least to such a correspondence and intercourse of good offices and mutual succour as may render it a more humane world than it was ever known, and carry the interest of human kind to a greater height than ever.[49]

In the last analysis, Shaftesbury's philosophic faith has to be assessed by what it means for the making and re-making of man. According to Shaftesbury, man is truly himself only when he acts creatively, as a co-creator with Deity. And the creative life is supremely the life of love in which man finds his true freedom and true being. In Shaftesbury's words:

> We are made to contemplate and love God intirely, and with a free and voluntary Love.[50]

> The highest principle, which is the Love of God, is best attained not by dark Speculations and Monkish Philosophy, but by moral Practice, and Love of Mankind, and a Study of their Interests.[51]

Notes

1. *Life, Letters,* p. 399.

2. *The Eighteenth Century Background* (London: Chatto and Windus, 1953), pp. 62-64.

3. See the chapter on "The Aesthetics of the Infinite" in *Mountain Gloom and Mountain Glory* (Ithaca, N. Y.: Cornell Univ. Press, 1959).

4. *A History of Philosophy,* trans. by J. H. Tufts (New York: The Macmillan Company, 1901), p. 488.

5. *Life, Letters,* p. 336.

6. *Ibid.,* p. 394. Letter dated Dec. 10, 1708. Rand describes a printed copy of "The Sociable Enthusiast" in the London Record Office that is "full of corrections and additions in the handwriting of the third Earl . . . nearly as printed in the *Characteristics*" (*Life, Letters,* p. 336, n. 2). I interpret this corrected version to be the one printed in 1709 and 1711. Some small revisions were presumably then made by Shaftesbury for the 1714 edition.

7. It bears the date Sept., 1707.

8. For a fuller account see Ronald A. Knox, *Enthusiasm* (Oxford: The Clarendon Press, 1951), ch. xv, though there are some curious lapses in the book.

(See below, note 28.) The Wesleys encountered some of the survivors of the movement twenty years later (Knox, p. 361; also p. 371).

9. Three of the prophets arrived in London in September, 1706, according to Aldridge (*Shaftesbury and the Deist Manifesto*, p. 315). D. P. Walker writes that "quite a number" were in England by 1706. See *The Decline of Hell: Seventeenth-Century Discussions of Eternal Torment* (Chicago: Univ. of Chicago Press, 1964), p. 254.

10. *The New Pretenders to Prophecy Examined* in George Hickes *et al.*, *The Spirit of Enthusiasm Exorcised* (London, 1709), pp. 499 f. It should be added that the prophets were also accused of advocating antinomianism.

11. One of them was Nicholas Fatio, "an eminent mathematician" and "member of the Royal Society" (D. P. Walker, *op. cit.*, pp. 254 f.).

12. Aldridge, *Shaftesbury and the Deist Manifesto*, p. 316.

13. See the Introduction to Robertson's 1900 edition (I, xxiv).

14. *Op. cit.*, p. 297. Its date of composition is mistakenly given as 1708.

15. *Life, Letters*, p. 504.

16. *A Treatise Concerning Enthusiasm As It is an Effect of Nature . . .* , 2nd ed. (London, 1656) (1st ed., 1655).

17. My references are to the edition published in *A Collection of Several Philosophical Writings of Dr. Henry More* (London, 1712).

18. *Letters to a Young Man*, p. 43. Shaftesbury was no doubt thinking of More's belief in miracles performed by supernatural spiritual agencies.

19. Cf. Joseph Addison, *The Spectator,* No. 412.

20. E.g., *The Advancement and Reformation of Modern Poetry* (London, 1701). In later years, Dennis praised Shaftesbury's "good sense," and described him as "most ingenious and most judicious." *The Critical Works of John Dennis,* ed. Edward N. Hooker, 2 vols. (Baltimore: The Johns Hopkins Press, 1939), II, 255 and 257.

21. *The Advancement and Reformation of Modern Poetry*, p. 26.

22. *Ibid.*, p. 29.

23. *Ibid.*, p. 33; also p. 46.

24. Marjorie Nicolson, *op. cit.*, p. 282.

25. *Ibid.*, p. 294. For references to "sublime" see the new Index in the 1964 reprinting of *Characteristics* (New York: The Bobbs-Merrill Co., Inc.).

26. See *Second Characters*, p. 163. But such references as *Char.* II, 124, may be taken to imply this association.

27. *Enthusiamus Triumphatus*, p. 2.

28. *Enthusiasm*, p. 8. Knox not only shows little comprehension of Shaftesbury's views but also misdates and mistitles the "Letter Concerning Enthusiasm." He is apparently not familiar with "The Moralist" or Shaftesbury's other writings. He is unaware of the earlier studies of enthusiasm by Meric Casaubon and Henry More, and he thinks that Bishop Hickes started the vogue of the word in his sermon of 1680, "The Spirit of Enthusiasm Exorcised."

29. Also *Life, Letters*, p. 449.

30. *Enthusiasmus Triumphatus*, p. 14. One is reminded of Santayana's famous definition: "Poetry is called religion when it intervenes in life, and religion, when it merely supervenes upon life, is seen to be nothing but poetry."

31. *The True Intellectual System of the Universe* (London, 1678), Bk. I, Ch. iii, Sect. xix, pp. 134 f.

32. See Marjorie Nicolson, *op. cit.*, p. 299.

33. *Enthusiasmus Triumphatus*, p. 12.

34. *Ibid.*, p. 45.

35. There are some interesting similarities between Shaftesbury's philosophy of love and that of Marsilio Ficino, though there are no direct references to the Italian thinker in Shaftesbury. The Cambridge Platonists may have transmitted some of his doctrines. On the other hand, if Shaftesbury was familiar with Ficino's Latin translations of and commentaries on Plato and Plotinus, he would have found some of the ideas expressed there. The *De Amore*, which contains Ficino's theory of love, was included in all editions of the translation of Plato. However, when the English philosopher quotes from Plato it is from the Greek text.

36. *Essays on Man*, Ep. III, ll. 7-8.

37. Since the types of love belong to the "social affections," they will be discussed further in Ch. IX.

38. *Life, Letters*, p. 5 (PR).

39. *Infra*, Ch. IV.

40. *Enthusiasmus Triumphatus*, p. 54.

41. *Life, Letters*, p. 33 (PR).

42. *Pensées Diverses*, in *Oeuvres Complètes*, 7 vols. (Paris: Garnier Frères, 1879), VII, 171.

43. W. E. Hocking, quoted in *The Journal of Philosophy*, XLVIII (May 10, 1951), 325.

44. Paul Tillich, *Dynamics of Faith* (New York: Harper and Brothers, 1957), pp. 76 f.

45. *Op. cit.*, p. 1.

46. When Shaftesbury does refer to allegorical interpretation, it is likely to be in the course of an attempt to discredit the Scriptures, as, for example, in *Char.* II, 231, where he refers to Thomas Burnet's *Archeologicae philosophicae* in which an "allegorical" interpretation of the Fall was presented. Its publication in 1692 caused Burnet to lose his post as Clerk to the King. Ernest Tuveson writes that "although Burnet calls his interpretation 'allegorical,' he actually abandons the great allegorical tradition. . . . The story is a parable, and nothing more. . . . Burnet, unlike most writers of generations before him, found allegory in general unsatisfactory and uninteresting except historically." (*Millennium and Utopia*, pp. 175 f.)

47. *Essays on the Characteristics*, p. 211.

48. *Second Characters*, p. 52.

49. *Life, Letters*, p. 417 (1709).

50. *Letters to a Young Man*, p. 12.

51. *Ibid.*, p. 8.

Selected Bibliography

Writings of Shaftesbury

Characteristics . . . Ed. John M. Robertson. 2 vols. London: Grant Richards, 1900.

Characteristics . . . Ed. John M. Robertson. 2 vols. in one. New York: The Bobbs-Merrill Co., Inc., 1964. With a new Introduction by Stanley Green and an expanded Index.

The *Characteristics* includes the following treatises listed here with their date of first publication:

I. "A Letter Concerning Enthusiasm," 1708.

II. "Sensus Communis; An Essay on the Freedom of Wit and Humour," 1709.

III. "Soliloquy, or Advice to an Author," 1710.

IV. "An Inquiry Concerning Virtue or Merit," 1699; revised, 1711.

V. "The Moralists, A Philosophical Rhapsody," 1709.

VI. "Miscellaneous Reflections on the Preceding Treatises, etc.," 1711.

The following are printed in some editions of the *Characteristics* although Shaftesbury originally intended them to be part of another work which he did not complete. The latter has been partially reconstructed and published as *Second Characters* (see below).

"A Notion of the Historical Draught or Tablature of the Judgement of Hercules," 1712 (French), 1713 (English). Included in the 1714 edition of *Characteristics*.

"A Letter Concerning the Art, or Science of Design." First published in the 1732 edition of *Characteristics*.

Several Letters Written by a Noble Lord to a Young Man at the University. London, 1716.

The Life, Unpublished Letters, and Philosophical Regimen of Anthony, Earl of Shaftesbury. Ed. Benjamin Rand. London: Swan Sonnenschein & Co., Ltd., 1900.

Second Characters, or the Language of Forms. Ed. Benjamin Rand. Cambridge: Cambridge University Press, 1914.

Second Characters includes:

I. "A Letter Concerning Design" (see above).

II. "The Judgment of Hercules" (see above).

III. "The Picture of Cebes" (translated from the Greek).

IV. "Plastics" (uncompleted notes).

Writings Related to or about Shaftesbury

Brown, John. *Essays on the Characteristics*. 3rd ed. London, 1752.

More, Henry. *Enthusiasmus Triumphatus; or, a Brief Discourse of the Nature, Causes, Kinds, and Cure of Enthusiasm*. London, 1712. Published in *A Collection of Several Philosophical Writings of Dr. Henry More*. London, 1712.

Aldridge, Alfred O. *Shaftesbury and the Deist Manifesto. Transactions of the American Philosophical Society*, Vol. XLI, Part II. Philadelphia: The American Philosophical Society, 1951.

Knox, Ronald A. *Enthusiasm: A Chapter in the History of Religion with Special Reference to the Seventeenth and Eighteenth Centuries*. Oxford: The Clarendon Press, 1951.

Nicolson, Marjorie. *Mountain Gloom and Mountain Glory: The Development of the Aesthetics of the Infinite*. Ithaca, N. Y.: Cornell University Press, 1959.

Tuveson, Ernest. *Millennium and Utopia: a Study in the Background of the Idea of Progress*. Berkeley: University of California Press, 1949.

John G. Hayman (essay date spring 1970)

SOURCE: Hayman, John G. "Shaftesbury and the Search for a Persona." *SEL: Studies in English Literature 1500-1900* 10, no. 2 (spring 1970): 491-504.

[*In the following essay, Hayman examines Shaftesbury's use of a literary persona that embodies flexibility, composure, grace, and penetration, which the critic says marks the author as a deliberate artist.*]

The preoccupation of Swift and Pope with the creation of *personae* has naturally received a good deal of attention, but the extent to which this preoccupation was also shared by other writers of the period has perhaps been insufficiently recognized. In discussions of Shaftesbury, for example, commentators have usually paid merely token respects to the gentlemanly air of his discourses and have then concentrated on the ideas that they advance.[1] Yet Shaftesbury was a highly conscious, if not altogether successful, literary artist, as much concerned with embodying and describing intellectual dispositions as with advancing a systematic body of thought. Indeed, there is a special sense in which—to use a current phrase—his medium is his message. An adequate understanding of his achievement has, as a result, to take account of his concern with literary expression. And since a major part of this concern relates to the problem of a literary *persona,* a consideration of this particular concern is, I believe, valuable for an appreciation of Shaftesbury's own works and the general preoccupation with *personae* at this time.

In part, it is the background to Shaftesbury's concern that makes this consideration valuable, for Shaftesbury was also concerned with the formulation of a "character" in everyday life. "All turns upon the nature of a Character," he commented in a notebook, "and according to what the fancy make of this, so in general the conduct will prove."[2] This problem of a social character was especially acute for Shaftesbury, moreover, since he maintained that "the end or design of nature in man is society" (**PR,** [**The Life, Unpublished Letters, and Philosophical Regimen of Anthony, Earl of Shaftesbury**] p. 4), and yet he was at the same time highly critical of the actual society of his day. Furthermore, he consistently stressed the importance of an individual's "inward economy" (that is, the correct ordering of his different faculties), and this stress seems on occasion to have been independent of his concern with man's end as a social being. His solution of the problem of a "character" had, therefore, to take account of both the constant effort to maintain a deeply personal coherence and the need to appear sociable. A mode of "dissimulation" thus became almost inevitable:

> Remember that sort of dissimulation which is consistent with true simplicity: and besides the innocent and excellent dissimulation which Socrates used, remember that other sort (not less his) which hides what passes within, and accommodates our manners to those of our friends and of people around us, as far as this with safety can be allowed.
>
> (*PR,* p. 182)[3]

The mention of Socrates is significant here, for the "socratic character" is the essence of Shaftesbury's subsequently more detailed description of a correct *persona,* and it is also, as we shall notice, an important influence on his writings:

> Remember, therefore, in manner and degree, the same involution, shadow, curtain, the same soft irony; and strive to find a character in this kind according to proportion both in respect of self and times. Seek to find such a tenour as this, such a key, tone voice, consistent with true gravity and simplicity, though accompanied with humour and a kind raillery, agreeable with a divine pleasantry.
>
> (*PR,* p. 193)

It was obviously a tall order, and the complexity of its paradoxes is even more apparent as Shaftesbury continues: "neither solemnity nor drollery, neither seriousness nor jest. . . . Earnestness but not in earnest. Jest, but not really jest. . . . A mirth not out of the reach of what is gravest, a gravity not abhorrent to the use of . . . [socratic] mirth. In this balance seek a character, a personage, manner, genius, style, voice, action" (*PR,* pp. 194-195). But one is not, as one might suppose, listening simply to one private, isolated voice here. A somewhat diluted form of this model could, I believe, be pieced together from the comments of Addison and Steele. Much later in the century, in fact, we find the young Boswell attempting to formulate a "character" akin to that recommended by Shaftesbury and in the process associating it with the actual characters of Addison and Steele. Conscious that he had in the past been too much a "comical being," delighting in the buffoonery and type of ridicule that Shaftesbury also despised, Boswell records:

> I was now upon a plan of studying polite reserved behaviour, which is the only way to keep up dignity of character. . . . Indeed, I had accustomed myself so much to laugh at everything that it required time to render my imagination solid and give me just notions of real life and religion. But I hoped by degrees to attain to some degree of propriety. Mr. Addison's character in sentiment, mixed with a little of the gaiety of Richard Steele . . . were the ideas I aimed to realise.[4]

But Boswell's notebooks and journals disclose a succession of such "models"—Addison and Steele, Lord Chesterfield ("Study to be like Lord Chesterfield, manly"), Gray, and many others. Shaftesbury held to the socratic character. Consistent with this, Shaftesbury maintained, too, the value of irony—an evaluation that led naturally enough to the cultivation of *personae* in his writings.

In the opening treatises of the **Characteristics** (1711), the **Letter concerning Enthusiasm** (1708) and **Sensus Communis: An Essay on the Freedom of Wit and Humor** (1709), Shaftesbury partially evaded the difficulty of an address to the general public, together with the problem of a *persona,* by using the form of a letter addressed to a particular person. That this was merely a literary device is of course obvious; Shaftesbury was immensely interested in the public reaction to the works. But he also maintained—and with good reason—that a reader should recognize the letter form. Thus, in a response to some critics of the ***Letter concerning Enthusiasm,*** he declared that they had failed to recognize that "there was *a real* GREAT MAN characterized [Lord Somers] and suitable Measures of Address and Style preserved."[5] Similarly, in ***Sensus Communis,*** even though the character of the "friend" to whom the work is ostensibly addressed is not indicated very clearly, Shaftesbury commented at one stage in a footnote: "Our Author, it seems, writes at present, as to a young Gentleman chiefly of a Court-Breeding" (III, iv). More generally, the use of a letter-form permitted in both instances an apparent informality of organization, a free range among topics, and a use of raillery.

But while these features are particularly relevant to a letter addressed to Lord Somers and to the "Liberty of the Club" that is appealed to in ***Sensus Communis,*** Shaftesbury's manner in these works also has a kinship with that outlined in his private notebooks. In particular, it embodies both the urbanity of tone and the underlying seriousness of concern that are recommended there.

The use of private address for public ends is apparent, for example, from the opening section of the ***Letter concerning Enthusiasm.*** The section, as a whole, establishes the letter-form in that it renders a graceful compliment to Lord Somers on account of his inspiring the writer in the way that earlier writers had been inspired by their notion of a muse. But it does not merely demonstrate an urbanely indirect approach to a compliment. The initial remarks, which appear at first to be rather inconsequential, actually have a thematic relevance to the work's central concern. Thus, Shaftesbury's comment on the awkwardness with which a modern writer invokes a muse in whose existence he cannot really believe leads to the pertinent conclusion: *"Truth is the most powerful thing in the World,* since even Fiction itself must be governed by it, and can only please by its resemblance." Similarly, the suggestion that ancient writers may actually have had faith in their invocations introduces the notion of self-deception that is subsequently shown to accompany certain forms of "enthusiasm." Indeed, their situation is explicitly compared to that of a "good Christian . . . [who] thinks he can never believe enough . . . [and who] may, by a small Inclination well improved, extend his Faith so largely, as to comprehend in it not only all Scriptural and Traditional Miracles, but a solid System of Old-Wives Stories." In this way, then, the section illustrates both the focus of an address to a particular person and also the blend of urbanity and seriousness that is of general validity in the cultivation of a "correct" character.

The relevance of Shaftesbury's concern with a social character to these works is illustrated further by his use of raillery.[6] This may be appreciated by noticing just a few instances of the form of raillery that emerges, I believe, as Shaftesbury's most important strategy: namely, his quiet ridicule of some attitude or belief by turning back upon it its unfortunate or self-contradictory implications. Thus, when contrasting the tolerance of free inquiry in ancient days with the intolerance of his contemporaries, Shaftesbury remarks in the ***Letter concerning Enthusiasm***:

> Reason had fair Play; Learning and Science flourished. Wonderful was the Harmony and Temper which arose from all these Contrarities. . . . But a new sort of Policy, which extends it self to another World, and considers the future Lives and Happiness of Men rather than the present, has made us leap the Bounds of natural Humanity; and out of a supernatural Charity, has taught us the way of plaguing one another the most devoutly.
>
> (II)

The raillery that is directed here against religious zealots is similarly apparent when Shaftesbury touches on their attitude towards virtue: "They have made *Virtue* so mercenary a thing, and have talked so much of its *Rewards,* that one can hardly tell what there is in it, after all, which can be worth rewarding" (***Sensus Communis***: II, iii). Other attitudes are also subjected to such raillery. Shaftesbury notices, for example, that Hobbes was "a good sociable Man, as savage and unsociable as he would make himself appear by his Philosophy" (***Sensus Communis,*** II, i). He suggests, too, that those who maintain that man consistently acts from motives of "self-interest" have misconstrued man's "true *Interest*" (***Sensus Communis,*** III, iii). Such turns of raillery fit Shaftesbury's notion of a correct character for a number of reasons. They reflect, in a general way, the "sober kind of Cheerfulness . . . and easy pleasant way of Thought" that he wished both to recommend and embody. They direct a gentle ridicule at those religious zealots and Hobbesists who deny the value or existence of a primary value Shaftesbury wished to advance: "good nature." And, perhaps most important of all, they register a particular aspect of that controlled state of mind which reveals itself in the movement between scepticism and affirmation. Thus, there is in the instances noticed the sceptical withholding of assent from some attitude or opinion—and the throwing of new light upon it by a use of ridicule. But in the complete procedure there is the final affirmation of an alternative attitude that is implicit in the raillery. The raillery is in this way part of a larger rhetorical device by which Shaftesbury sought to render the composure of a philosophical gentleman.[7]

But it seems that Shaftesbury also wanted to indicate explicitly what lay behind this gentlemanly air. There is a hint of this in the ***Letter concerning Enthusiasm,*** when he speaks of the importance of inward scrutiny. "We can never be fit to contemplate anything above us," he declares, "when we are in no condition to look into ourselves, and calmly examine the Temper of our own Mind and Passions" (IV, iv). Shaftesbury does not, however, engage in self-examination in this work; the **Letter** is intended to appear the civilized result of such scrutiny. It is in **Soliloquy: or Advice to an Author** (1710) that he stressed the importance of "inward colloquy" and indicated a way of conducting this both in an individual's private life and in a literary form.

From the present point of view, the especial interest of this work is that it comments explicitly on the difficulty of writing *in propria persona* and reflects an attempt to resolve the difficulty by the use of an artificial *persona*. The difficulty itself seemed perhaps especially acute to Shaftesbury because of the acknowledged oddity of the intellectual discipline that he wished to recommend (I, i). But he also recognized more generally the difficulty confronting authors who wished to write sociably about deeply personal matters. "If their Meditation and Revery be obstructed by fear of a nonconforming Mein in Conversation," he remarked, "they may happen to be so much the worse *Authors* for being finer *Gentlemen*" (I, i). For this reason, then, Shaftesbury adopted—with a deliberately self-conscious air—a *persona*. It was his intention, he declared, "not so much *to give Advice*, as to consider *the Way and Manner of advising*" (I, i). "My Science, if it be any, is no better than that of a Language-Master, or a Logician." And yet by this guise he also hoped to express more than his notions concerning literary expression, as his comment in **Miscellaneous Reflections** reveals: "His pretence has been to *advise Authors*, and polish styles, but his Aim has been to correct *Manners* and regulate *Lives*" (III, ii). The guise is, in fact, a form of socratic depreciation, and it aims at the advantages that Shaftesbury associated in this particular work with the hero of the ancient dialogue:

> The Philosophical *Hero* . . . was in himself *a perfect Character*; yet, in some respects, so veiled, and in a Cloud, that to the unattentive Surveyer he seemed often to be very different from what he really was: and this chiefly by reason of a certain exquisite and refined Raillery which belonged to his Manner, and by virtue of which he could treat the highest Subjects, and those of the commonest Capacity both together, and render 'em explanatory of each other.
>
> (i, iii)

Shaftesbury's own success in achieving these ends is quite considerable. There is a range of considerations in the work—from the dramatic convention of the soliloquy to the developed procedure of self-analysis. Moreover, an actual demonstration of self-analysis both indicates its general value and serves as a means by which Shaftesbury advances some of his most crucial notions. But one may also feel that the guise is somewhat self-regarding in its mock modesty. Contrasting the coquetry

of a modern writer who "purchases his Reader's Favor by all imaginable Compliances and Condescensions" (I, iii) with the ancient writer's cultivation of objectivity by means of a dialogue, Shaftesbury remarks of the latter procedure: "Here *the Author* is annihilated; and *the Reader* being by no way applied to, stands for Nobody" (I, iii). Shaftesbury himself makes a show of "annihilating" the common reader; his publisher, he declares, is his amanuensis, and he writes only for fellow-writers. But one can scarcely feel that he has abstracted himself from the work.[8]

It was in his **Miscellaneous Reflections,** a work first published in the final volume of **Characteristics** (1711), that Shaftesbury came closer to achieving this end by adopting the *persona* of a "miscellany writer." This strategy and its implications constitute, in fact, Shaftesbury's most fascinating solution to the problem of addressing a reader, even while the pose is not fully sustained and there remains some vacillation between direct statement, a rather transparent irony, and a fully characterized *persona*.

The essence of these varying effects is apparent from the first chapter alone. It opens with an obviously ironic celebration of "the ingenious way of MISCELLANEOUS *Writing*," but the adoption of a *persona* very soon becomes apparent as the writer outlines his intention "to descant cursorily upon some late Pieces of a *British* author." The satirical gibe at miscellany writing that is by this stage already implicit in this guise is advanced, too, by the arrogance that the writer displays: "According to this Method, whilst I serve as *Critic* or *Interpreter* to this new Writer, I may the better correct his Flegm, and give him more of the fashionable Air and Manner of the World." By the end of the chapter the characterization of a vain and obtrusive author is, indeed, fairly complete:

> Nor ought the Title of a MISCELLANEOUS *Writer* to be denied me on the account that I have grounded my *Miscellanies* upon a certain Set of Treatises already published. *Grounds* and *Foundations* are of no moment in a kind of work which, according to modern establishment, has properly neither Top nor Bottom, Beginning nor End. Besides that, I shall no way confine myself to the precise contents of these treatises, but, like my Fellow-Miscellanarians shall take occasion to vary often from my proposed subject, and make what *Deviations* or *Excursions* I shall think fit, as I proceed in my *random* ESSAYS.

After such an overture, it would not even be surprising to encounter "A Digression in Praise of Digressions!" By the use of a *persona* at such points, Shaftesbury has, then, reversed his earlier procedures. No longer simply intent on embodying a "correct" intellectual disposition and a "correct" mode of writing, he is instead embodying the "faulty"—and in the process he exposes it to satirical effect. But, as in the *Soliloquy,* the *persona* serves more than one end. For Shaftesbury not only exposes something of the "Froth and Scum" of the miscellanarian; he also makes use of such a writer's digressive bent to effect the movement between different tones and different topics that he had himself attempted in his other works. After a serious consideration of the *Letter concerning Enthusiasm,* for example, the miscellany writer re-emerges and "lightens" the tone by an extended comparison of his procedure with the "variableness of the English climate" (I, iii). The passage is itself perhaps a little heavy-handed, but it is justifiable in dramatic terms—and it also effects a transition. Indeed, the guise may again be associated with that "involution, shadow, curtain . . . [and] soft irony" that we earlier noticed Shaftesbury associating with Socrates.

It is, however, the relationship of the work to Swift—and most especially to *A Tale of a Tub*—that is especially worth developing. It is even possible that *Miscellaneous Reflections* was influenced by the "Apology" that Swift added to the fifth edition of his work in 1710. There is certainly a similarity in the way the writers remark on themselves in the third person and defend their works. And they also display the kinship of attitude that had earlier resulted in Swift's being credited with the *Letter concerning Enthusiasm,* for they both maintain the permissibility of a ridicule directed against corruptions in religious belief. More specifically, too, they direct such ridicule against faulty forms of religious enthusiasm—and they even concur in viewing such enthusiasm as a form of "sexual sublimation."

But one must also recall that Shaftesbury was highly critical of *A Tale of a Tub* (**PR,** p. 504), for the points of similarity between the works are offset by obvious differences. And this is revealed perhaps most vividly by their substantially different use of a *persona.* A convenient illustration of this is supplied by two passages which compare a writer's progress in his work with a journey. In *A Tale of a Tub,* we are clearly aware of Swift's digressive dupe at this point, as the "author" turns back to the "Tale" after two "Sections" of "Digressions":

> After so wide a Compass as I have wandred, I do now gladly overtake, and close it with my Subject, and shall henceforth hold on with it an even Pace to the End of my Journey, except some beautiful Prospect appear within the sight of my Way; whereof, tho' at present I have neither Warning nor Expectation, yet upon such an Accident, come when it will, I shall beg my Readers Favour and Company, allowing me to conduct him thro' it along with my self. For in *Writing,* it is as in *Travelling*: If a Man is in haste to be at home, (which I acknowledge to be none of my Case, having never so little Business, as when I am there) if his *Horse* be tired with long Riding, and ill Ways, or be naturally a Jade, I advise him clearly to make the straitest and the commonest Road, be it ever so dirty; But, then surely,

> we must own such a Man to be a scurvy Companion at best; he *spatters* himself and his Fellow-Travellers at every Step: All their Thoughts, and Wishes, and Conversation turn entirely upon the Subject of their Journey's End; and at every Splash, and Plunge, and Stumble, they heartily wish one another at the Devil.[9]

The image is pursued in a subsequent paragraph as the "author" demonstrates further the way he does indeed tend to digress when tempted by such delights as an extendable analogy. In contrast, Shaftesbury does not give his *persona* his head in this fly-away fashion, even though one may feel that something of a miscellanarian's luxuriant fancy is present in his use of the analogy—and that it is this backing that "justifies" the style of the passage:

> The just Composure of a legitimate Piece is like an abler Traveller, who exactly measures his Journey, considers his Ground, premeditates his Stages and intervals of Relaxation and Intention to the very Conclusion of his Undertaking, that he happily arrives where he first proposed when he set out. He is not presently *upon the Spur,* or in his full *Career,* but walks his *Steed leisurely* out of his stable and settles himself in his Stirrups, and when fair road and season offer, puts on perhaps to a *round Trot,* thence into *a Gallop,* and after a while takes up. As Down or Meadow or shady Lane present themselves, he accordingly suits his Pace, favours his Palfrey; and is sure not to bring him puffing, and in a heat, into his last Inn.

> (I, iii)

Here, as elsewhere, Shaftesbury's use of some touches of a miscellanarian's manner is not allowed to cloud his basic concern with coherence. Moreover, his specific concern throughout his works is with the coherence of character that an individual must cultivate, and this basic concern may well have checked the free development of a confused *persona.* It is fitting, then, that the aristocratic image of horsemanship should finally represent an ease of control and an artistry. The passage from *A Tale of a Tub,* on the other hand, illustrates the way Swift's predominantly satirical intention permits the more sustained use of a *persona* who embodies mental incoherence. Swift's ironical recommendation of chaotic movement stands in pointed contrast to Shaftesbury's positive image of an orderly journey.

Consistent with this difference, there is also Shaftesbury's pervasive uncertainty about the value of a mode of writing that consisted of "raillery and irony." This uncertainty is apparent, for example, in *Miscellaneous Reflections* when the "author" turns from his sober consideration of *An Inquiry concerning Virtue* to *The Moralists,* and in doing so returns to his "original miscellaneous manner and capacity":

> 'Tis here . . . that *Raillery* and *Humour* are permitted; and Flights, Sallies, and Excursions of every kind are found agreeable and requisite. Without this, there might

be less Safety found, perhaps, in thinking. Every light Reflection might run us up to the dangerous state of Meditation. And in reality profound Thinking is many times the cause of *shallow Thought*. To prevent this contemplative *Habit* and *Character,* of which we see so little good effect in the World, we have reason perhaps to be fond of the *Diverting Manner* in *Writing* and *Discourse,* especially if the Subject be of a *solemn* kind. There is more need, in this case, to interrupt the long-spun thread of Reasoning, and bring into the Mind, by many different Glances and Broken Views, what cannot so easily be introduced by one steady bent or continued Stretch of Sight.

(IV, ii)

The argument is persuasive, and it is also consistent with the attitude which Shaftesbury had earlier outlined. But the "perhaps" that is included several times in the passage is by no means an empty gesture. Shaftesbury's doubts are more clearly expressed in his remarks on Leibnitz's criticism of his apparent recommendation of raillery. Writing of himself in the third person, Shaftesbury comments to Pierre Coste:

> does he not seem to despise himself in his third and last volume of Miscellanies at the very entrance when, after having passed his principal and main philosophical work in the middle volume, he returns again to his mixed satirical ways of raillery and irony, so fashionable in our nation, which can be hardly brought to attend to any writing, or consider anything as witty, able, or ingenious which has not strongly this turn?

(*PR,* p. 504)

Even this comment, however, does not reflect a finally considered position, for Shaftesbury subsequently contemplated taking up the manner of ***Miscellaneous Reflections*** in his projected ***Second Characters***.[10] Essentially, one is left aware of the conflict between Shaftesbury's different attitudes towards the "satirical ways of raillery and irony" and more direct statement.

Against this uncertainty, however, there remains the clearly defined "character" that Shaftesbury described in his notebooks, and it is possible to relate his experiments with *personae* to this larger concern with the formulation of a sociable character that is consistent with an inward economy. No doubt the impetus behind this concern is closely connected with the social situation of the time—or, at least, to Shaftesbury's understanding of it. In particular, it appears to reflect Shaftesbury's contempt for the "men of pleasure" who are more usually associated with the Restoration era. But one may also see it, I believe, as a response to the philosophical questioning of personal identity that was very much in the air at this time. Certainly, this was a topic that Shaftesbury touched upon throughout his works, and he invariably appealed to the individual's consciousness of his own being and the possibility of developing a coherent character from this consciousness.[11] Moreover,

this concern was by no means peculiar to Shaftesbury and the "speculators" of his time. It is reflected in Pope's *Epistles I* and *II,* where the search for a principle of order within man's being culminates in the discovery of a "new hypothesis"—the ancient and highly dubious theory of a "ruling passion." And it might even be related to Swift's display in *A Tale of a Tub* of that uncontrolled sensation and thought which can find coherence only in megalomania—and perhaps also to the disintegration of character that gives to Part IV of *Gulliver's Travels* some of its compelling power. It is also against this background that some aspects of the narrower concern with literary *personae* are finally of most interest. For while a *persona* most commonly served as a satirical strategy and while the final volume of ***Characteristics*** displays the movement towards this use, Shaftesbury was again not alone in his quest for a positive stance that embodied flexibility and composure and reflected a poise with a distinctly social value. There is, for example, that section of Pope's literary career when the poet attempted both to carry good-breeding one step higher into gentlemanly philosophizing and to keep open at the same time the possibility of engaging in ridicule. A considerable part of Shaftesbury's value for us lies in his providing an explicit background to such endeavors. But as this consideration of his use of *personae* has intended to suggest, Shaftesbury's own artistry is also worthy of attention.

Notes

1. A notable exception to this is Martin Price's section, "The Method of Dialogue," in *To the Palace of Wisdom* (Anchor Books, 1965), pp. 85-93. The importance of recognizing Shaftesbury's artistry has also been noticed by Ernest Tuveson ("The Importance of Shaftesbury," *ELH*, XX (1953), 267-299: especially Footnotes 29 and 39), but the topic was not developed in this account.

2. *The Life, Unpublished Letters, and Philosophical Regimen of Anthony, Earl of Shaftesbury,* ed. Benjamin Rand (1900), p. 189. Hereafter cited in the text as "*PR.*"

3. The first type of dissimulation noticed here presumably refers to Socrates's pose of humility and ignorance.

4. *London Journal,* ed. F. Pottle (1950), pp. 61-62.

5. *Miscellaneous Reflections,* I, iii. Quotations throughout are taken from the 1714 edition of the *Characteristics,* but modern spellings have been introduced. Shaftesbury's own divisions are used in indicating the location of quotations.

6. Some agreement seems to have been reached among those concerned with explicating Shaftesbury's comments on "raillery" and "ridicule." A. O. Aldridge has maintained that

Shaftesbury "did not advance the theory of ridicule as a test of truth," and he has further argued that "the chief value of ridicule to Shaftesbury was its use as a test of demeanour or attitude, as a weapon against imposture" ("Shaftesbury and the Test of Truth," *PMLA,* LX [1945], 155). With this, Stuart Tave has concurred, though he has stressed, too, that a use of ridicule constituted a part of that free and good humored inquiry among equals that Shaftesbury was essentially intent on recommending (*The Amiable Humorist* [Chicago, 1960], pp. 36-39). In relating this use to the socratic procedure, his account agrees with that of Norman Knox, *The Word IRONY and its Context* (Durham, N. C., 1961), pp. 51-54. These analyses have removed a good deal of the confusion caused by Shaftesbury's free use of terminology. But it is of course only by examining Shaftesbury's actual use of raillery that the value of the practice can be recognized—and this examination has never, I believe, been undertaken by a modern commentator.

7. It can also be claimed that such raillery is not simply concerned with "demeanour or attitude"; ideas themselves are involved. Indeed, an argumentative procedure is involved in such raillery, and for this reason those critics who associated ridicule with "eloquence" and "Imagination, Passion, Prejudice, and preconceived Opinion" did not quite hit their target when attacking Shaftesbury on this issue (John Brown, *Essays on the Characteristics* [1750], pp. 43 and 54).

8. In adopting a dialogue-form, Shaftesbury ostensibly achieved this anonymity in *The Moralists.* In this work he also gave an objective form to an inward soliloquy; Philocles (a "sceptic") and Theocles (a "sociable enthusiast") represent two aspects of a mind engaged in such soliloquy. A kinship between Theocles and Shaftesbury is indicated by the relationship between several of Theocles's speeches and passages in the *Philosophical Regimen.*

9. *A Tale of a Tub,* ed. A. C. Guthkelch and D. Nicoll Smith (Oxford, 1920), p. 188.

10. Ed. B. Rand (1914), pp. 6-8.

11. In the concluding section of *An Inquiry concerning Virtue,* Shaftesbury writes: "let us doubt, if we can, of everything about us; we cannot doubt of what passes *within* ourselves. Our Passions and Affections are known to us" (II, ii). Similarly, in *The Moralists,* a more distinctly metaphysical form of this notion is the climax to Theocles's "argument": "In fine, continued Theocles (raising his Voice and Action), being thus, even by *Scepticism* itself, convinced the more still of my own being and this *Self* of mine 'that 'tis a *real Self* drawn out and copied from another principal and *original SELF* (the Great One of the world),' I endeavour to be really *one* with It and conformable to It, as far as I am able" (III, i).

Pat Rogers (essay date summer 1972)

SOURCE: Rogers, Pat. "Shaftesbury and the Aesthetics of Rhapsody." *British Journal of Aesthetics* 12, no. 3 (summer 1972): 244-57.

[*In this essay, Rogers explores the reasons for Shaftesbury's use of the word "rhapsody" in the subtitle of his treatise* The Moralists, *arguing that the philosopher was responsible for the positive association of the term in relation to aesthetics.*]

One of the cheats of time is to rob us of surprise. History acts as a buffer against that sense of shock which contemporaries, lacking such insulation, must often have felt. For the literary student this attenuation of the unexpected affects—and distorts—judgement in several ways. Among the more serious results there is our failure to recognize linguistic shock tactics whenever they appear in literature of the past. Some verbal collocations which must once have produced a violent jolt in the reader's mind slip unnoticed through our consciousness. Fielding's 'comic epic in prose' is a good example. The constituent parts of the phrase arrive from such different directions (so far as the eighteenth-century view of things went) that it must have possessed a startling air of innovation, of paradox, of daring. We find it hard today to realize that this planned oxymoron carries with it the absurdity that would go with, say, farce *larmoyante* or bedroom tragedy or dark soap-opera. When Gay invented his 'Tragi-comi-pastoral Farce', *The What d'ye call it,* and solemnly set about justifying this categorization, he was embarking on a lighter undertaking than Fielding's. Yet the phrase used by Gay is scarcely more a case of literary miscegenation than the formula Fielding employed, from an Augustan viewpoint. In each case the imaginative impact derives from semantic misalliance: that is from verbal surprise.

I wish to suggest that there is a similar, though not quite identical, trick played by the Earl of Shaftesbury in the title of his treatise ***The Moralists, A Philosophical Rhapsody*** (1711).[1] Briefly, my argument is that Shaftesbury calculates on the same unexpected effect in words as had Gay and Fielding. However, instead of a comic or critical-taxonomic point, Shaftesbury was bent on a realignment of taste. His linguistic jolt is intended to force a reappraisal of attitudes in the reader: to be more specific, he is trying to convert a pejorative or, at best, neutral term into one with highly favourable overtones. The technique is rather like planting landmines. The context forces an innocent-looking word to come up against a foreign body (here the word 'philosophical'), which detonates it into violent activity. Really, that is to simplify the process; for Shaftesbury's achievement is to make of his entire treatise a kind of matrix in which this activating energy can come into play. By the end of the essay we have accustomed ourselves to the description 'rhapsody'. But that is to justify the boldness, and not to negate it.

Few of Shaftesbury's critics, in my knowledge, have given much attention to this issue.[2] Perhaps they have felt that the label which the author conferred on his work was accurate and evocative. Now the truth is that in terms of eighteenth-century lexis it was anything but an obvious choice. To later commentators the word may have the air of a *mot juste* plucked neatly out of the air. That is because—it is barely hyperbole to say— Shaftesbury gave 'rhapsody' its modern acceptation, therefore its *justesse*. A large claim, but I do not believe a rash one. If proof is desired, look around the great lexical edifices, Bailey, Johnson and others: look, too, at the occurrence of this word in the writings of the age.

It is important to distinguish between the root noun and its derivatives. Leaving aside for the moment the original 'rhapsode' figure, we have on the one hand 'rhapsody' itself and against this a series of back-formations: *rhapsodic, rhapsodical, rhapsodist, rhapsodize,* and so on. From an early date these have acquired in English and American usage a somewhat tight lipped, unenthusiastic ring, even though they may not be downright condemnatory. They bear with them a certain impression of gushing; uncontrolled fervour; ecstatic but not very sensible admiration. The plain noun 'rhapsody' can on occasion preserve this connotation to some degree. But the tone is generally one of lesser asperity. Moreover there are different occasions, more numerous in all probability, where no sense of disfavour is connoted. These include the use of the word in music or, more rarely, in the visual arts; a limited but persistent usage in literary terminology (Eliot's 'Rhapsody on a Windy Night', and the like); and a fitful appearance in transferred senses. In these contexts the idea of rhapsody is essentially neutral and descriptive: the word has an admittedly vague range of reference, but it is without any normative element in the bulk of its appearances.

What we forget, then, is that this disjunction between the root noun and its derivatives grew up comparatively recently. When this family of words first entered English no such separation was visible. 'Rhapsody' originally had two narrow technical senses; as soon as the modern overtones came to predominate (the sense, that is, from which words like 'rhapsodic' spun off), there

was a markedly hostile aura round the noun. It was this process which Shaftesbury, by main literary force, did so much to arrest. His emphatic and influential use of 'Rhapsody', set conspicuously at the head of his most personal work, diverted the flow of semantic currency.

The *New English Dictionary* provides five subheadings for 'Rhapsody'. The first and last of these are comparatively marginal. Sense 1 is the original meaning of an epic poem or part of one 'suitable for recitation at one time'. Here the only point of interest concerns an alleged transferred use, exemplified by Scott's phrase 'my rhapsodies' in a letter quoted by Lockhart. It is arguable that this might more properly and more obviously be entered under senses 3 or 4, considered presently. Against this sense 5 is the musical application of the word. *NED* quotes nothing earlier than Grove's *Dictionary* in its 1880 edition. Certainly the term had become common, in the French and German forms of *r[h]apsodie,* well before this date. Liszt's *Hungarian Rhapsodies* are prominent examples, though Brahms too used the title more than once (*e.g.* the *Alto Rhapsody,* Opus 53 (1869), his own favourite among his compositions). Subsequently the label grew a highly popular one. As one writer has it, 'some of [the so-called] rhapsodies are by analogy appropriately so called, but the title has become loosely used for a composition of imaginative and melodious character of no specific form'.[3] For my immediate ends it is enough to observe that this vogue presupposed an underlying meaning of *favourable* intent. Composers only call their pieces 'rhapsodies', meaning loosely structured, when it is an approved thing to seek an apparently spontaneous organization or freedom from restraint. Naturally we find Romantic or post-Romantic composers, among them Chabrier, Delius, Ravel and Gershwin, the most fond of this word. On occasion it seems to be virtually synonymous with 'fantasia'. The musical fortunes of 'rhapsody' constitute an independent issue, but they do serve to emphasize the admiring tone which the word picked up in the wake of Romanticism.

NED's second sense, though obsolete, brings us nearer to the situation as it was in Shaftesbury's day. This is 'the stringing together of poems'. Examples are cited from the seventeenth century. Under 2 (b), 'the recitation of epic poetry', a quotation from Shelley is supplied. It is no long step from 2 (a) to sense 3 (a): 'A miscellaneous collection; a medly or confused mass . . . a "string" (of words, sentences, tales, etc.). Likewise obsolete, this shade of meaning dominated all others for a long period of time. Of the instances quoted, Hamlet's 'A rhapsody of words' [III. iv. 48] is the best known. We are also given Bentley's phrase for Boyle's unlucky book, a 'Rhapsody of Errors and Calumnies'; Addison's phrase 'Rhapsody of Nonsense' (*Spectator* No. 46); the expression 'rhapsody of impertinence' from *The Castle of Otranto*; and one example as late as

Hallam. Then comes sense 3 (b), 'a literary work consisting of miscellaneous or disconnected pieces; a written composition having no fixed form or plan. *Obs.*' This definition appears to straddle two rather different uses. Most of the citations from 1602-3, 1685, 1710 and 1764 seem to mean a literary medley, an *omnium gatherum,* with no suggestion of evaluative intent. On the other hand certain examples come nearer the idea of 'a (culpably) formless work', which would move the usage into the fourth class. A minor sense 3 (c) is interesting chiefly on account of a case in point represented by Defoe's *True-Born Englishman*:

> Which Medley canton'd in a Heptarchy,
> A Rhapsody of Nations to supply . . .

Defoe has been itemizing the strange and heterogeneous compound which went to make the Anglo-Saxons—'a Mongrel half-bred Race.' *NED* glosses this sub-meaning: 'A collection of persons, nations. *Obs.*' It is clear that Defoe has a strong ironic tinge in his use: 'a strange random collection of which one can't make head or tail'.

This leaves us with sense 4, the ordinary modern 'rhapsody':

> An exalted or exaggeratedly enthusiastic expression of sentiment or feeling; an effusion (e.g. a speech, letter, poem) marked by extravagance of idea and expression, but without connected thought or sound argument.

Citations are made from 1639 onwards, including *Spectator* 30, by Steele; Junius; Cowper's *Task*; and Gladstone. This corresponds to the dictionary's entry for 'rhapsodical', second sense: 'exaggeratedly enthusiastic or ecstatic in language, manner, etc.' My own impression is that in modern usage the idea of excessively effusive speech or manner is stronger in the adjective than in the noun. Thus one can use 'rhapsody' as a quasi-technical term in the arts, whereas 'rhapsodic' inevitably brings with it pejorative overtones. The noun may, as the definition allows, convey an idea of justified exaltation; the epithet rarely does so.

The broad lines of the history of this word-group are therefore clear. There are three main semantic layers, more or less chronologically divisible. First, the classical meaning of epic recitation—this is *NED*'s sense 1 for 'rhapsody', sense 2 for 'rhapsodic' and 'rhapsodize'. Next, the idea of a miscellany, something pieced together without close or integral connexion. This is 'rhapsody', senses 2-3; 'rhapsodist' and 'rhapsodize', sense 1. It is also sense 1 for 'rhapsodical', where there is a nice instance from *Tristram Shandy*. Lastly, the idea of effusive outpouring of sentiment. *NED*'s entry 'rhapsody', sense 4, is matched by 'rhapsodical', sense 2; 'rhapsodist' and 'rhapsodize', sense 3; and 'rhapsodic'. The last entry appositely quotes Vicesimus

Knox: 'that rhapsodic style, which wearies by its constant efforts to elevate the mind to ecstasy'. Further examples are given from Fanny Burney and George Eliot.

However, the picture thus afforded is neither complete nor wholly accurate. A clue is provided by *NED*'s gloss for 'rhapsodist', sense 3: 'one rhapsodizes or uses rhapsodical language; in early usage, with implication of want of argument or fact'. This is the only recognition which the lexicographers betray that certain members of this word-family have gone up in the world. Something has happened since the shift from the second to the third phase of those outlined above. After 'rhapsody' ceased to connote principally a medley and came to mean an effusion of doubtful value (a transference in which one can easily read the Neo-Classical mind at work), its headlong descent has been to some extent arrested. As the use in various art forms, including literature, makes plain, the term can be a respectable and indeed honorific one.

How intimately this semantic process is linked with the history of taste Johnson's *Dictionary* helps to show. The entry for 'rhapsody' looks at first sight neutral enough—'any number of parts joined together, without necessary dependence or natural connection'. However, the examples supplied—the *Hamlet* case, from the divine Hammond, from Locke and his disciple Isaac Watts—make it clear that disapproval is bedded deeply into that definition: to an Augustan it was too obvious to need explicit comment. The only derivative given a separate entry by Johnson is 'rhapsodist', which is 'one who writes without *regular* dependence of one part upon another' [my italics]. A rhapsody is then the direct antithesis of 'a frame', defined as a fabric made up of 'various parts or members' which support one another.[4] The very notion is one in breach of 'the basic principle of classicism in design', defined by Sir John Summerson as 'that the design shall be an indivisible unity, so that nothing can be altered or subtracted without destroying the whole, every part being dependent on every other part'.[5] By Johnson's definition a rhapsody was that unAugustan thing, a casual assemblage of a random number of parts.

The full depth of the obloquy implied by this term around 1700 can easily be guessed. Nor do the facts of linguistic life disappoint this expectation. In 1714 Defoe wrote to Robert Harley of a new book by John Dunton, a man whom he greatly despised. His comments are instructive: 'The whole book is Such a Continued Rhapsody of Scandal and Raillery That it Seems Enough to Name it, and to Collect from it would be to Transcribe it from One End to the Other . . .'[6] One might note how the old idea of an *omnium gatherum* hovers behind the detraction: yet the fundamental sense is 'a huge tissue of nonsense'. Similarly when John Dennis can think of nothing else abusive to say of *The Dunciad* (which is all too often), he calls the poem a 'rhapsody'. The word occurs at least six times in his fairly brief *Remarks,* either nakedly or suitably qualified. 'Wonderful Rhapsody' is found twice; 'his whimsical Rhapsody' in another place.[7] The year before, Thomas Hearne had written of the compendium entitled *The Chronological Historian* that it was a 'strange Rhapsody from Pamphlets'.[8] Along with such instances as that from Locke which Johnson was to quote in the *Dictionary,* these give a fair indication of the standing of the term in the high Augustan period. Dennis, incidentally, had written some *Reflections upon a late Rhapsody, called An Essay on Criticism* in 1711.

Yet matters were soon on the turn. When Swift gave the title 'On Poetry: A Rhapsody' to a work of 1733, his aim cannot have been very flattering: at best, an ironic and give-little-away kind of usage. By 1783 things were sufficiently different to allow Thomas Tyers to put on a semantic quick-change act behind the convenient folds of ambiguity. A new ambiguity, that is, touching not merely the meaning of the word but its whole moral identity. During the course of the year Tyers brought out two laudatory volumes, *An Historical Essay on Mr. Addison* along with *An Historical Rhapsody on Mr. Pope.* With regard to the latter Tyers makes a great show of studied inconsequence. 'Protected by the title of this Essay, which disdains method, the writer has said something of every thing that has the most distant relation to the Life and Writings of Mr. Pope.' He does not quite say that irrelevance is a merit; but that it is good to disdain method, we can hardly doubt. Tyers draws a contrast with Joseph Warton's *Essay* on Pope, an avowed critique—'*This* is a historical Rhapsody, the *other* a critical one' (*touché*).[9] Tyers is of course somewhat defensive about his choice of title. Yet he *did* feel bold enough to enlist the concept in the service of his undertaking. Well before the high tide of Romanticism, then, we find 'rhapsody' shaking off its more disreputable associations and achieving some literary standing. Partly this is the result of critical realignments, that *renversement des alliances* which took place in the third quarter of the eighteenth century. But the lexical displacement, like the critical shift, had begun much earlier—with Shaftesbury.

The central juncture of *The Moralists* occurs in the third section. Indeed it was this part of the *Characteristicks* which was to affect later generations most powerfully. Theocles moves abruptly into what the side-note calls 'meditation', that is passages of emotive utterance. The style is compounded of familiar 'rhetorical' motifs: its note is exclamatory, its sentence-structure tends towards a staccato pattern. Direct invocation is common ('Ye Fields and Woods . . .'). Allied to the use of the archaic second-person forms, a measure of inversion and a conscious rhythmic emphasis give the writing a biblical air: 'Thee I invoke, and Thee

alone adore.' Repetition is frequent: parallelism and listing devices abound: 'Thy Being is boundless, unsearchable, impenetrable.' The vocabulary is at times highly wrought; phrases such as 'supremely Fair, and sovreignly Good!' or 'Thou impowering DEITY, Supreme Creator!' illustrate a fondness for a kind of unobtrusive neologism. At its best the language achieves a thoroughgoing poetic quality, to which the elevated diction and sharply cut-off syntax contribute: 'Prodigious Orb! Bright source of vital Heat, and Spring of Day! . . . Supreme of the Corporeal World! Unperishing in Grace, and of undecaying Youth!' At other times we encounter a simpler note, set off by deliberate paradox: 'In vain we try to fathom the Abyss of SPACE, the Seat of thy extensive Being; of which no Place is empty, no Void which is not full.'[10]

Plainly, it was this mode of writing—impassioned, urgent, unconstrained—which struck contemporaries as the stable element in Shaftesbury's 'Rhapsody'. It was passages such as these which Pope had in mind when he gave to the deistical 'gloomy Clerk' of *The Dunciad* these lines:

> Or that bright Image to our fancy draw,
> Which Theocles in raptur'd vision saw,
> While thro' Poetic scenes the Genius roves,
> Or wanders wild in Academic Groves . . .

> [B, IV, 487-490]

Pope indeed set out as blank verse in his note some of the sections I have quoted. Rapture is often linked closely with rhapsody, perhaps through false etymology: epithets such as 'poetic' regularly accompany the discussion of *The Moralists.* Thus a modern critic, Professor R. L. Brett, observes: 'The style in which Shaftesbury wrote *The Moralists,* as the title would suggest, is a rhapsodical one. In prose which comes near to being poetry, Theocles (who represents Shaftesbury) apostrophizes nature in a series of hymns of a most romantic sort.' Professor Brett goes on to invoke such words as 'visionary', 'lyrical' and 'Wordsworthian'. He further quotes an apposite section of Horace Walpole's *Catalogue of Royal and Noble Authors.*[11] Similarly, Professor A. D. McKillop discusses Shaftesbury's influence on the enthusiasm of James Thomson and his readers. He cites a writer of 1738, heavily indebted to Thomson, who 'rhapsodizes on rural philosophy'.[12] Because of the great currency of these interpolated hymns, and their observable impact on other writers, we have come to see them as the 'rhapsodic' portions of *The Moralists*—as the parts which justify Shaftesbury's subtitle.

But this is unhistorical. As we have seen, the term was primarily a derogatory one around 1700. If 'rhapsody' were to be invoked in a non-opprobious sense, then the meaning of 'literary medley' or 'string, loose assemblage' would be the likeliest.[13] The point is that Shaftesbury, when he chose the word, was not hiding behind its implications in quite the same way as Tyers was to do. He was not simply creating a chance for himself to indulge in 'rhapsodic' (modern sense) writing. He was in fact carrying over the associations of miscellaneity, lack of connexion—but at the same time he was suggesting that a looser, more disjunctive mode of composition was fitted to some branches of literature. *The Moralists* is rhapsodic, in the only approbatory sense available to Shaftesbury, by reason of its loose-knit manner of proceeding and by its far from rigorous layout. (Another hidden oxymoron: philosophy connoted science, method, logic: a 'philosophical rhapsody' was pretty well a contradiction in terms.) In short, *The Moralist* does not suddenly become rhapsodic when the apostrophes occur: that is its vein throughout.

Consequently, in order to understand the structural and stylistic properties fitting to literature in this vein, we need to examine the content of Shaftesbury's thought. We have to see *why* he wished to adopt a different method of presentation from that approved by the age for philosophical writing. An answer to this question is bound to be speculative. But I think that an intelligible account can be given, which makes aesthetic, as well as historical and lexical, sense.

Shaftesbury is among the first important upholders of an organicist approach to the world. When he wants an emblem of unity, in an effort to comprehend by analogy the oneness of the universe, he lights on a significant example:

> For to instance in what we see before us; I know you look upon the *Trees* of this vast Wood to be different from one another: And this tall *Oak,* the noblest of the Company, as it is by itself a different thing from all its Fellows of the Wood, so with its own Wood of numerous spreading Branches (which seem *so many different TREES*) 'tis still, I suppose, *one* and *the self-same TREE.* . . . If you question'd me fairly, and desir'd I shou'd satisfy you what I thought it was which made this Oneness or Sameness in the Tree or any other Plant; or by what it differ'd from [a] waxen Figure [of the same size and shape], or from any such Figure accidentally made, either in the Clouds, or on the Sand by the Sea-shore; I shou'd tell you, that neither the *Wax,* nor *Sand,* nor *Cloud* thus piec'd together by our Hand or Fancy, had any real relation within themselves, or had any Nature by which they corresponded any more in that near Situation of Parts, than if scatter'd ever so far asunder. But this I shou'd affirm, 'That wherever there was such a *Sympathizing of Parts,* as we saw here, in our *real TREE*; Wherever there was such a plain Concurrence in one common End, and to the Support, Nourishment, and Propagation of so fair a Form; we cou'd not be mistaken in saying there was a peculiar Nature belonging to this Form, and common to it with others of the same kind.' By virtue of this, our Tree is a real *Tree*; lives, flourishes, and is still *One and the same*; even when by Vegetation and Change of Substance, not one Particle of it remains *the same.*[14]

No more representative analogy could have been chosen. The 'model of reality', as we might say nowadays, is a living organism, set moreover against a contrivance 'pieced together . . . by our Hand'. The great archetype of Augustan thinking had been the interlocking frame, which appeared to fit the cosmos as revealed by Newton so exquisitely. The definition offered by Johnson in the *Dictionary* for the word 'mechanism' is to the point: sense 2 is that of a 'construction of parts depending on each other in any complicated fabrick'. This metaphysical or ontological notion could be translated into aesthetic terms. We then find what Paul Fussell has described as 'the rhetorical and Horatian concept of art', which assumes 'a purposeful procedure, in which the end is foreseen from the beginning, part is fitted to part, and the whole is adapted to the anticipated effect on the reader'.[15] Against this we have here the Shaftesburian version of reality, which might be broadly described as Platonic or organicist.

The phraseology of Theocles's contribution to the dialogue is highly indicative of this bias of mind. We hear of 'particular Forms, who share this simple Principle, by which they are really *One,* live, act, and have *a Nature* or *Genius* peculiar to themselves. . . .' Or again 'a uniting Principle in NATURE'. And 'every *particular* NATURE certainly and constantly produces what is good to itself; unless something *foreign* disturbs or hinders it . . .' And: 'If . . . every *particular Nature* be thus constantly and unerringly *true* to itself, and conducting to its own right State. . . .'[16] Typically the first-person interlocutor, Philocles, had used the image of machines, 'their Order, Management and Motions', to point up his own metaphysical speculations. He had used terms such as 'Breach of Laws, Variation and Unsteddiness of Order . . . no Controul . . . tumultuous System . . . *Chaos* and *Atoms*' to depict the errors of atheists, atomists, materialists and other unregenerate men. His positives were '*Order, Uniformity,* and *Constancy*'. Theocles, on the other hand, seeks a different principle:

> And when you, reply'd he, with your newly-espous'd System, have brought All things to be as *uniform, plain, regular* and *simple,* as you cou'd wish; I suppose you will send your Disciple to seek for DEITY in Mechanism; that is to say, in some exquisite System of *self-govern'd* Matter. For what else is it you Naturalists make of the World, than a mere Machine?

Theocles's insinuating, gently ironic manner undoubtedly has Shaftesbury behind it.[17]

One aim of the *Characteristicks* is to promote imaginative liberty at the same time as enthusiasm is discountenanced. In the *Inquiry concerning Virtue and Merit* the writer had stressed the consequences of sensitivity to the grandeur of the world: 'For 'tis impossible that such *a Divine Order* shou'd be contemplated without Extasy and Rapture; since in the common Subjects of

Science, and the liberal Arts, whatever is according to just Harmony and Proportion, is so transporting to those who have any Knowledge or Practice in the kind.'[18] The submerged musical metaphor here is taken up in **The Moralists,** where Theocles speaks of 'rising in [his] Transports', and needing the assistance of a lyre to sustain his flights. However, Theocles rejects in the second part of the same treatise a view uttered by Philocles: namely, that it was profane to reason calmly and unconcernedly about religion. Earlier still in **The Moralists** we find Philocles using the defensive word '*Rant*' in connexion with one passage, a speech attributed to his friend Palemon. At this point Philocles finds himself required to 'ask Succour of the *Muses,* as Poetical as I am oblig'd to shew my-self in this Enterprize'.[19]

Now all these concerns fit together. Theocles's use of an organic model and the sustained organicist imagery which goes with that: the adumbration of poetic and even musical concepts to explain the undertaking; the cultivation of a tone that avoids the extremes of 'rant' and overly prosaic, unimaginative literalism: all these call for a flexible literary medium. The work needs to be organized along less analytic and systematic lines than those of the conventional philosophical treatise; the idiom needs to be more poetic, that is more varied, intense and emotive in its use of language; and the overall rhetorical character of the discourse must be one of heightened (though not exorbitant) feeling that overrides the categories of literary decorum to prescribe its own formal and stylistic bounds. There was no such vehicle ready to hand. Shaftesbury evolved his own, and he called it a philosophical rhapsody.

To surprise by a fine excess was, of course, the ambition of many writers who remained content with the Augustan forms as given. Recent studies have shown that the grace beyond the reach of art[20] was an element fully covered in the Neo-Classical theory of art. However, it should not be supposed that Shaftesbury's undertaking was of its nature quite unique. In fact certain historical analogues can be discerned. The point is that other attempts were less successfully mounted, less clear-minded, less influential. Moreover the effort to forge a new set of artistic principles was often carried out on unsuitable occasions, in an unsuitable literary venue. Notably, the ambition was evident in the development of the pindaric form; and the process was in all likelihood retarded by this historical accident.

The misunderstanding which surrounded the pindaric are too numerous to examine here. When the revival of the form was being mounted in 1656, Abraham Cowley wrote in the preface to his *Poems*:

> They [pindarics] are, or at least were meant to be, of that kinde of *Style* which *Dion* [*yssius*] *Halicarnasseus* . . . attributes to *Alcaeus*—the digressions are many,

and sudden, and sometimes long, according to the fashion of all *Lyriques,* and of *Pindar* above all men living. The *Figures* are unusual and *bold* even to *Temeritie,* and such as I dare not have to do withal in any other kind of *Poetry:* the *Numbers* are various and irregular, and sometimes (especially some of the long ones) seem harsh and uncouth, if the just measures and cadencies be not observed in the *Pronunciation.* So that almost all their *Sweetness* and *Numerosity* (which is to be found, if I mistake not, in the roughest, if rightly repeated) lies in a manner wholly at the *Mercy* of the *Reader.*[21]

The confusion rife here can be traced in a large volume of unreadable pindarics written in the last quarter of the seventeenth century. Among the writers involved was Swift, whose reaction to his early, rather awful attempts in the kind was marked by his 'familiar' low ode to Congreve. And it was Congreve who in his *Discourse on the Pindarique Ode* (1706) did most to dispel the fog.

> The Character of these late Pindariques, is, a Bundle of rambling incoherent Thoughts, express'd in a like Parcel of irregular Stanza's, which also consist of such another Compliment of disproportion'd, uncertain and perplex'd Verse and Rhimes.[22]

True pindaric, Congreve argued, was regular and highly disciplined. However, the view that 'Nonsense is the essence of an ode'[23] died hard. Fifty years later Gray with his learning was very uncertain of the reaction likely to be accorded his own odes; 'The Progress of Poesy', he wrote to Horace Walpole, was 'a high Pindaric upon stilts'—Dodsley accordingly would be sure not to understand it.[24]

Inevitably the debate about the pindaric form was bedevilled by pseudo-archeological considerations. Not everyone agreed about the terms of debate; the historical facts were in dispute; and much of the energy expended had more to do with Pindar's reputation than the immediate cultural situation.[25] So with other attempts to subvert the hierarchy of Augustan forms. Shaftesbury's departure from orthodoxy, though as radical as any, was better calculated. He did more than pitch his style a degree or two higher; he did more than lard his text with 'many and sudden Digressions' (a digression, after all, honours systematic narrative in the breach); he did more than violate decorum with 'unusual' and 'irregular' locutions. His strategy was a positive one. Seeking a vehicle for a whole new regime of taste, he evolved a new rhetoric. The artist, and specifically the poet, was to be the model figure—the Promethean creator who most nearly approximated to the Great Maker, and who responded most directly to the universe in its concrete, plastic, palpable forms. The philosopher was to learn this true Promethean fire from '*Lovers* either of the Muses or the Graces'. It follows that the mechanical operation of the philosophic spirit, as exemplified in the level prose and consecutive argument of a Locke or a Spinoza, was ill-fitted to the new task. The last part of *The Moralists* considers the search for beauty 'as it relates to us, and makes our highest *Good,* in its sincere and natural Enjoyment'. The quest for wisdom and self-knowledge is paraphrased in the formula, 'O PHILOCLES! may we improve and become Artists in the kind.' Philocles recognizes that this way of reasoning could hardly be more 'odd, or dissonant from the common Voice of the World', and Theocles accepts this. Likewise Shaftesbury did not blench at the necessity of restructuring aesthetic norms duly.[26]

His great stroke was to couch what he had to say in the guise of 'a philosophical rhapsody'. The phrase is arresting, as holding within its own semantic compass that very breaking-down of categories, that precise style of rhetorical innovation, which his undertaking involved. The oxymoron implies the nature of the breakthrough. In addition 'rhapsody' was happily invoked because of its associations. It meant, respectably, a literary medley: *NED*'s sense 3 (b). More idiomatically, and therefore more prominently, it meant a farrago or gallimaufry. Shaftesbury dignifies this shop-soiled word with the prestigious epithet 'philosophic'; he means to imply that a discontinuous series of scenes or reflections may be imaginatively potent—philosophy is capable of being written in ways other than the point-by-point demonstration. Even more important, the modern sense (No. 4 in *NED*) had already developed. Shaftesbury shows in the course of his treatise that 'an exalted . . . expression . . . of feeling' need not be 'exaggeratedly enthusiastic'. He developed an idiom which would permit the inclusion of such intense 'rhapsodic' sections as the apostrophes in Part III of *The Moralists,* without damage to its argument or artistic fabric.

It was not an overnight revolution which he initiated. The history of ideas rarely allows so sudden a *coup*. Yet his influence gradually permeated English culture. In 1738 Thomas Cooke, a dunce best known for his classical translations, brought out *A Rhapsody on Virtue and Pleasure*—an amalgam of leading terms from the *Characteristicks*. Fitly in a work so titled, the personages invoked at the start are Virgil, Horace, Cicero and—Shaftesbury.[27] The triad who went so far to form Augustanism, supplemented by the man who went far to herald its dislodgement. When we consider Shaftesbury's total achievement, it seems a tiny thing to have helped to rescue for future aesthetic use the word 'rhapsody'. Yet the two are not wholly unconnected.

Notes

1. Published in vol. II of *Characteristicks of Men, Manner, Opinions, Times* (2nd ed. 1714). All references are to this edition, using the cue-title *Char.*

2. Valuable recent commentaries are those of Ernest Tuveson, 'The Importance of Shaftesbury', *ELH,* XX (1953), pp. 267-99; R. L. Brett, *The Third Earl of Shaftesbury* (1951); and Robert W. Uphaus, 'Shaftesbury on Art: the Rhapsodic Aesthetic', *The Journal of Aesthetics and Art Criticism,* XXVII (1968), pp. 341-48.

3. Robert Illing, *A Dictionary of Music* (1950), p. 231.

4. *Cf.* Martin Kallich, *Heav'n's First Law: Rhetoric and Order in Pope's Essay on Man* (De Kalb, Ill., 1967), p. 47.

5. John Summerson, *Sir Christopher Wren* (1965), p. 106.

6. *The Letters of Daniel Defoe,* ed. G. H. Healey (1955), p. 438. In Mist's *Weekly Journal* for 21st June 1718, an attack on George Ridpath, very possibly the work of Defoe, includes the phrase 'a villainous Rapsody of Scandal against the Person of Mr. *Mist . . .*'

7. John Dennis, *Remarks upon several Passages in the Dunciad* (1729), pp. 6-50. The most interesting of these passages is the comment, 'There is no such Thing as Action in his whimsical Rhapsody' (p. 17). According to Dennis's neoclassic principles, or indeed to those of Aristotelians in any age, the putative lack of a continuous narrative in *The Dunciad* means the loss of any principle of intellectual order—hence 'rhapsodic' qualities. Dennis called *The Rape of the Lock* 'a Rhapsody written for the Amusement of Boys . . .' and *Windsor Forest* 'a mere Rhapsody' without beginning or end. Pope used the same term in a counterattack on Dennis: see his *Prose Works,* ed. N. Ault (1936), I, 9, 17.

8. Quoted by G. V. Bennett, *White Kennett 1660-1728 Bishop of Peterborough* (1957), p. 177.

9. [Thomas Tyers], *An Historical Rhapsody on Mr. Pope* (1783), pp. vi-xi.

10. *Char.,* II, 344-6, 366-74.

11. Brett, p. 63.

12. A. D. McKillop, *The Background of Thomson's Seasons* (Minneapolis, 1942), p. 26.

13. Shaftesbury speaks elsewhere of a nation's '*Poets, Rhapsoders, Historiographers, Antiquarys . . .*' (*Char.,* I, 224). Here the word means a literary collector, a miscellanist—the sense it bears in Donne and Thomas Browne also.

14. *Char.,* II, 347-9.

15. Paul Fussell, *The Rhetorical World of Augustan Humanism* (1965), pp. 192-4. Fussell's phrase, 'Augustan accumulative or aggregative methods of organisation' (p. 194), summarizes what might be called anti-rhapsodic principles of *ordonnance*.

16. *Char.,* II, 352, 359-60.

17. *Char.,* II, 355-7.

18. *Char.,* II, 75-6.

19. *Char.,* II, 192-3, 375.

20. For the implications of this phrase, see S. H. Monk's article in *Journal of the History of Ideas,* V (1944), pp. 131-50.

21. Abraham Cowley, *Poems,* ed. A. R. Waller (1906), p. 11. *Cf.* the views of Christopher Smart in 1746: 'There is in them both [St. Cecilia odes by Dryden and Pope] an exact unity of design, which though in compositions of another nature a beauty, is an impropriety in the *Pindaric,* which should consist in the vehemence of sudden and unlook'd for transitions: hence chiefly it derives that enthusiastic fire and wildness, which greatly distinguish it from other species of Poesy.' Quoted by Arthur Sherbo, *Christopher Smart Scholar of the University* (East Lansing, 1967), p. 49.

22. *William Congreve: Letters and Documents,* ed. J. C. Hodges (1964), p. 214.

23. Joseph Spence, *Anecdotes,* ed. J. M. Osborn (1966), I, 359.

24. Quoted by Morris Golden, *Thomas Gray* (1964), p. 28.

25. I have discussed some of the implications of this situation in 'Swift's Anti-Rhetoric', *Cambridge Review,* LXXXXIX[A] (1968), 336-8.

26. *Char.,* II, 394, 426-8. Irving Babbitt wrote that Shaftesbury 'undermines insidiously decorum, the central doctrine of the classicist, at the very time that he seems to be defending it'—*Rousseau and Romanticism* (1919), p. 45. I believe that in many ways Shaftesbury's technique was more daring and frontal than Babbitt seems to allow.

27. Thomas Cooke, *Original Poems* (1742), pp. 49-61. Some other later uses of the word were satirical, as in *The Inspector's Rhapsody on the Loss of his Wig* (1752), an attack on Dr. John Hill; theatrical, as in the Haymarket show of 1760, *A Rhapsody on the Death of a late Noble Commander*; or unclassifiable, if not indescribable, such as Colley Cibber's, *A Rhapsody upon the Marvellous* (1751), and 'A Bachanalian Rhapsody', which appeared in Dodsley's *Museum* (1746).

James W. Davidson (essay date summer 1974)

SOURCE: Davidson, James W. "Criticism and Self-Knowledge in Shaftesbury's *Soliloquy.*" *Enlightenment Essays* 5, no. 2 (summer 1974): 50-61.

[In the essay below, Davidson examines Shaftesbury's ideas about self-examination, criticism of society, and the control of the irrational.]

In the second treatise of the *Characteristics, An Essay on the Freedom of Wit and Humour,* Shaftesbury proposes that criticism of self and society, regulated by the standard of taste—"common sense"—be initiated through literature. If poets are "to ridicule folly, and recommend wisdom and virtue (if possibly they can) in a way of pleasantry and mirth," then they must acquire "knowledge of our passions in their very seeds, the measuring well the growth and progress of enthusiasm, and the judging rightly of its natural force, and what command it has over our very senses" (*Characteristics of Men, Manners, Opinions, Times,* ed John M. Robertson with an introduction by Stanley Grean, 2 Vols. in one (New York, 1964), I, 89; I, 31. All references to the *Characteristics* are to this edition). They must acquire self-knowledge. And following his own advice in the Essay to utilize whatever part of the past is valuable (I, 59-61) Shaftesbury recommends that the model for self-examination be dramatic soliloquy.

The language in which the recommendation is introduced suggests an absence of seriousness. But the wit is a sign of anxiety because it is a reply to several relevant criticisms of Collier in *A Defence of the Short View of the Profaneness and Immorality of the English Stage.* When Shaftesbury writes,

> For whether the practice (of soliloquy) be natural or no, in respect of common custom and usage, I take upon me to assert, that it is an honest and laudable practice; and that if already it be not natural to us, we ought however to make it so, by study and application
>
> (I, 106),

he is replying to Collier's criticism of Congreve's use of the word "Inspiration." (*A Defence* in *A Short View of the Profaneness and Immorality of the English Stage with the Several Defences of the Same,* 5th Ed. (1730), p. 227. All references to Collier and Congreve in this passage are to p. 227 of *A Defence.*) Congreve had replied to Collier's charge of profanity by making a distinction between religious and non-religious senses of "inspiration." But Collier denied the distinction: "all people," he wrote, "that talk English know that *inspiration,* when it stands without epithets and addition, is always taken in a religious signification." He rejects etymology and insists upon the criterion of common usage:

> Thus when words are made inclosure, when they are restrain'd by common usage, and ty'd up to a particular sense: in this case to run up to etymology, and construe them by dictionary and preposition, is wretchedly ridiculous and pedantick.

Now Congreve had argued that when "inspiration" is not prefixed by "Divine," "to inspire, is no more than to breath (sic) into; and a trumpet, etc. may be said, without profaneness, to deliver a musical sound by the help of inspiration." Shaftesbury's reference to soliloquy as "bestowing a little breath and clear voice purely upon ourselves" (I, 106) is a defense of the etymological meaning of "inspiration" (=enthusiasm) and a rejection of Collier's position that "custom . . . gives law to language."

Shaftesbury's ridicule of Collier is an instance of his comparative procedure in the *Characteristics* whereby use is distinguished from abuse; here, Shaftesbury's language provides a model for the language of advice, to be contrasted with the language of controversial writing. But the criticism of Collier is also integral to the argument of *Soliloquy,* for the purpose of soliloquy is to control "inspiration" or "enthusiams"—to ensure that inspiration is "rational" because "when the party is struck by the apparition, there follows always an itch of imparting it, and kindling the same fire in other breasts. For thus poets are fanatics too" (I, 36). Soliloquy is a necessary method of self-criticism whereby the irrational is controlled.

When *Soliloquy* was written contemporary drama had been recently defended as a means of social reform. Richard Flecknoe, for example, had argued in *A Short Discourse of the English Stage* (1664) that "its chieftest end is to render folly ridiculous, vice odious, and vertue and noblesse so amiable and lovely, as every one shu'd be delighted and enamoured with it . . ." (In *Critical essays of the Seventeenth Century,* ed. Joel E. Spingarn, 3 vols. (1908; rpt. Bloomington, Indiana, 1957), II, 96). Temple had pointed out on *Of Poetry* (1690) its usefulness as a social control (Spingarn, III, 109); Farquhar in "A Discourse Upon Comedy, in Reference to the English Stage" (1702) had defined comedy as "no more at present than a well-framed tale handsomely told as an agreeable vehicle for counsel or reproff . . ." (In *Eighteenth Century Critical Essays,* ed. Scott Elledge, 2 vols. (Ithaca, New York, 1961), I, 91). And critics, also, had pointed to the need for self criticism. Roscommon, for example, had recommended in *An Essay on Translated Verse* (1684) that

> The first great work (a Task perform'd by few)
> Is that your self may to your be True:
> No Masque, no Tricks, no Favour, no Reserve;
> Dissect your Mind, examine ev'ry Nerve.
>
> (Spingarn, II, 299)

What Shaftesbury does in *Soliloquy* is to suggest a specific way in which literature can initiate a habit of self-criticism. Literature is to serve as a means to thinking of the world as a stage (I, 109) on which everyone wishes to become, like Shaftesbury,

> a worthy spectator of things so goodly to contemplate: and not only a spectator, but an actor, such as Thou wouldst have me to be in this Thy theatre. Let my en-

tire applause accompany whatever is there produced; as knowing *whence* it comes, and to *what perfection* it contributes.

> (This passage occurs in a prayer published in F. H. Heinemann, "The Philosopher of Enthusiasm, with material hitherto unpublished, "*Revue Internationale de Philosophie,* 6 (1952), 317.

Drama is to become the model of interior dialogue by means of which the spectator understands his relation to the whole and, therefore, pursues pleasure of a "rational" kind.

The pursuit of pleasure of the right kind is Shaftesbury's anxious concern because he believes, following Locke, that the pursuit of pleasure and avoidance of pain motivates action. The problem has been explained by Jean Starobinski as follows:

> (For the eighteenth century) nothing is more variable than our consciousness of existing, and nothing is more necessary than to try to vary our sensations and thereby to multiply our ideas. An unoccupied mind is in a sense annihilated. Fortunately, natural human impatience and uneasiness never leave us in peace: we are forever urged to escape from the anxiety of emptiness and to seek, through outside sensations and fleeting thoughts, a fullness and intensity that must be continually renewed.
>
> . . . . .
>
> . . . from the very beginning (of the eighteenth century) the work of art was given the psychological function of exciting the emotions through surprise and intensity . . . aesthetic emotion was merely one of the resources which men used excessively in order to intensify and stimulate the momentary joy of sensing their own vital existence.
>
> (*The Invention of Liberty: 1700-1789,* trans. Bernard Swift [Geneva, 1964], pp. 10-11.)

Following Locke and DuBos this interpretation of the psychological function of eighteenth century art identifies precisely that kind of pleasure from which Shaftesbury wishes to free his contemporaries: "the abhorrence of an insensible state makes mere vitality and animal sensation highly cherished." (I, 203)

That people seek pleasure does not, in itself, explain Shaftesbury's anxiety. That they live in growing cities, have leisure time, and interact in groups begins to explain it. Soliloquy, Shaftesbury argues, will prevent embarrassment in company; but this is by no means his main concern. The social problem which Shaftesbury confronts is stated by Addison in his second essay on the "Pleasures of the Imagination" (*Spectator,*No. 411):

> There are, indeed, but very few who know how to be idle and innocent, or have a relish of any pleasures that are not criminal; every diversion they take is at the expense of some one virtue or another, and their very first step out of business is into vice or folly.

On Shaftesbury's view of the connatural idea of sympathy, company will be sought. If, as a result of pedantry and bigotry (I, 50-51) conversation is found unpleasant, pleasure will be pursued elsewhere—in "sensual delights." This behavior is for Shaftesbury socially dangerous:

> In reality has not every fancy a like privilege of passing, if any single one be admitted upon its own authority? And what must be the issue of such an economy if the whole fantastic crew be introduced, and the door refused to none? What else is it than this management which leads to the most dissolute and profligate of characters?
>
> (I, 201-202)

Soliloquy controls the passions so that the right company will be sought at the right time. It also prevents loss of identity: disgust with a succession of "irrational" pleasures (I, 200) can cause repression and repression, as Locke pointed out in *An Essay Concerning Human Understanding,* a fragmenting of self:

> But if it be possible for the same man to have distinct incommunicable consciousness at different times, it is past doubt the same man would at different times make different persons . . .
>
> (2.27.20)

If a person has no fixed self but turns "on a sudden" from pursuing one pleasure to pursuing another he cannot "'be depended on in friendship, society, and the commerce of life.'"

Shaftesbury's advice to authors rests on his belief that men must be reading (I, 173). To what does he attribute this necessity? He provides two different explanations of the motivation to action—anxiety and "common sense." The first, argued in his notebooks, is Locke's; the second, argued in *Soliloquy,* is his own (*contra* Locke). In the *Regimen* Shaftesbury warns himself against "false sociableness," "*familiarity,* and that sympathy of a wrong kind" (*The Life, Unpublished Letters and Philosophical Regimen of Anthony, Earl of Shaftesbury,* ed. Benjamin Rand [London, 1900], p. 144. References to the *Philosophical Regiman* are followed by the abbreviation **PR.** References to letters in Rand are followed by **L,L**). Such behavior, he argues, stems from not being able to "rest out of company," that is, from what Locke describes as the "uneasiness of desire" (see **PR,** p. 144). As long as a person is a "disordered false self" his desire to read is motivated not by the desire for self-knowledge but by the desire to rid himself of self-consciousness. This kind of desire is satisfied by any object of ("false") pleasure, e.g., the eager "hunt after conversations, parties, engagements, secrecies, confidences, and friendships of this wrong kind" (I, 144). Such desire undoubtedly accounts for the appeal of the puppet show at Bartholomew's Fair, "the diversion of seeing Bedlam," and "the extraordinary inclination we have for amphitheatrical spectacles" (I, 176). And it accounts for indiscriminate reading, reading for excitement:

> We go to plays or to other shows, and frequent the theatre as the booth. We read epics and dramatics as we do satires and lampoons; for we must of necessity know what wit as well as what scandal is stirring. Read we must; let writers be ever so indifferent.
>
> (I, 173)

Shaftesbury attributes such reading to curiosity. But curiosity is a description of the desire for "irrational" pleasure.

Now Shaftesbury is concerned about this kind of reading because it develops a character of a certain kind. He sees the same disposition in seeking diversion by observing madmen as he does in reading "scurrilous, buffooning" satire: Malevolence. This is the "passion" which is to be purged by tragedy (see II, 319) and which, no doubt, accounts for the people's admiration of contemptuous representations of great men (I, 147). And he fears the indulgence of this passion because it will lead to the uncontrollability of all passions. If malevolence is not expressed in the reading of traveller's tales, the passion which it reinforces, wonder, is dangerous, for it is a false enthusiasm which can readily lead to atheism (I, 222) and to "enthusiasm of second hand." The author, therefore, who accommodates his writing to his readers' false taste is sowing the seeds for social disorder.

In *Soliloquy,* however, Shaftesbury argues that the desire to read stems from innate admiration of beauty and that curiosity is a corruption of "common sense." Action is not motivated by desire for stimulation but by desire for beauty:

> Every one is a virtuoso of a higher or lower degree. Every one pursues a Grace and courts a Venus of one kind or another. The *venustum,* the *honestum,* the *decorum* of things will force its way. They who refuse to give it scope in the nobler subjects of a rational and moral kind will find its prevalency elsewhere in an inferior order of things.
>
> (I, 92)

Curiosity about particulars—e.g., scandals disclosed in scurrilous satires, references to "inns and ordinaries, passage-boats and ferries, foul and fair weather, with all the particulars of the author's diet, habit of body, his personal dangers and mischances on land and sea" (I, 223)—is a result of not having developed the ability to find pleasure in the general:

> They who overlook the main springs of action, and despise the thought of numbers and proportion in a life at large, will, in the mean particulars of it, by no less

taken up and engaged, as either in the study of common arts, or in the care and culture of mere mechanic beauties.

(I, 92)

Finding pleasure in literature that deals with particulars, then, is analogous to finding pleasure in "cantonising" (I, 76). These pleasures imply the absence of the direction of the "conspiring virtue" by "right reason" (I, 75). But there is no contradiction in holding the position implied in the **Regimen** and the position argued in **Soliloquy**: because Shaftesbury is arguing for the connatural idea of common sense he suppresses the first view in **Soliloquy.**

The direction of the "conspiring virtue" by "right reason" is the function of dialogue. The interiorization of the Socratic dialogues creates in the reader a speculative habit; he learns to apply the dialogical method to himself, seeing himself in his "natural capacity" as one of the second characters and his best self as Socrates:

> Whatever we employed in, whatever we set about, if once we had acquired the habit of this mirror we should, by virtue of the double reflection, distinguish ourselves into two different parties. And in this dramatic method, the work of self-inspection would proceed with admirable success.

(I, 128-29)

An objection to this part of the theory is that Shaftesbury gives no evidence of support the claim that one does, in fact, read the dialogues as allegories. But the objection can be met on two grounds:

(1) Shaftesbury is arguing that the ancient poets, following Horace's prescription to study the dialogues, read them in this way. That they did so is plausible given Shaftesbury's interpretation of their opinion that each person is born with and committed to his "genius" (I, 112);

(2) Shaftesbury is not arguing that his contemporaries do, in fact, read dialogues allegorically, but that they ought to. His urging the reader to practice soliloquy applies as well to the method of reading dialogue: "it is an honest and laudable practice; and . . . if already it be not natural to us, we ought however to make it so, by study and application. (I, 106).

Everyone in his "natural capacity" ought to see himself reflected in dialogue as both what he is and what he ought to be. The "second character" ought to function as a foil by means of which one discerns "the beauty of honesty, and the reality of those charms which before we understood not to be either natural or powerful" (I, 93). That it can do so follows from the doctrine of connatural goodness. The foil should jolt the mind out of moral complacency (I, 93) or self-deception (I, 115).

But if miseducation and custom alienate a person from his best self, why, one might object, should Shaftesbury suppose that the corrupt man would see *himself* reflected in a second character? A direct confrontation by a philosopher using dialogue may "draw sound out of our breast, and instruct us to personate ourselves in the plainest manner" (I, 114); but in direct confrontation there can be no escaping the identification of self with the second character.

Shaftesbury is aware of the difficulties involved in applying the practice to the self for he recognizes the power both of self-deception (I,6) and of the association of ideas (I, 199). Custom and education are responsible for a partial scepticism (I, 56, 221) that not only exempts the "false jest" from criticism but the "false earnest" as well. Furthermore, self-criticism requires not only a powerful understanding, the possession of few (see I, 50), but patience, which is also wanting: "men love to take party instantly. They cannot bear being kept in suspense. The examination torments them." (II, 7). Now Shaftesbury believes that all these difficulties can be overcome in and through the practice of soliloquy. However, his explanation of why dialogue is no longer a dominant form seems to suggest that there is a degree of corruption beyond which there can be no recovery of the best self: the "thorough profligate knave" seems to be too self-alienated to soliloquize.

But even though these objections to the possibility of developing the speculative habit can be met, the theory raises a major difficulty: the explanation of appropriating a work by sympathy is inconsistent with the function of soliloquy. Since the "passions" (=emotions, desire, will, beliefs) are continuously present they must be continuously controlled (I, 207-208):

> Either I work upon my fancies, or they on me. If I give quarter, they will not. There can be no truce, no suspension of arms between us . . . For if the fancies are left to themselves, the government must of course be theirs. And then, what difference between such a state and madness?

(I, 208)

Now for Shaftesbury meaning is communicated by sympathy. But since the combat of the fancies by reason is never to be suspended, control must be interrupted. That sympathy ought to be interrupted by soliloquy while experiencing a work of art is suggested in **Soliloquy**:

> Every pretty fancy is disturbed by it; every pleasure interrupted by it. The course of good-humour will hardly allow it, and the pleasantry of wit almost absolutely rejects it.

(I, 122)

In the **Regimen** the necessity for the interruption is explicitly prescribed, the response to a play serving as the model for the response to events in the world outside the theatre:

How is it, therefore, as to other fancies?—A king appears—and what then? So in a play a king appear, also guards, courtiers, lords, attendants.—But this is but a play. And what is this other? When the tragedy chances to be overmoving, and the action strikes us, do not we say to ourselves instantly, "This is but a play?" Is not this the correcting, redressing, rectifying part? And how does this part carry itself in that other play—the serious one of life?

(**PR,** p. 175)

This advice is inconsistent with Shaftesbury's analysis of tragic catharsis:

And the misfortunes naturally attending such excesses being justly applied, our passions, whilst in the strongest manner engaged and moved, are in the wholesomest and most effectual manner corrected and purged.

(II, 319)

The remainder of the passage from the **Regimen** (p. 175) calls into question drama as a source of knowledge; for control of one's response to the sight of a real king is not dependent upon having seen a tragedy and learned that the great are beset with "disorders and misery" (I, 143) and that therefore one ought to be content with one's position. The understanding of kingship is independent of viewing the play. What Shaftesbury is arguing in the passage is that there ought to be an analogous use of reason in both art and life. Now he does regard the theatre as the most important contemporary source of moral instruction (II, 314). And he does believe that the observed relation between virtue and vice is socially useful (I, 93). But he seems to find the primary significance of drama in it habituating the spectator to soliloquy (I, 128).

Soliloquy is a method of controlling the irrational: "our thoughts have generally such an obscure implicit language, that 'tis hardest thing in the world to make them speak out distinctly" (I, 113). "By this practice they conceal half their meaning . . ." (I, 123. Cf. I, 202). Through the discovery and control of meaning, soliloquy produces a rational self, governed by common sense, the expression of which is an ordered whole, the opposite of "the monstrous product of . . . a jumbled brain" (I, 48), and by means of soliloquy the spectator, contemplating the accurate and consistent representation of character, "the sublime of sentiments and action, [the contrast between] the beautiful [and] the deformed, the amiable [and] the odious" (I, 136), begins to recover his best self.

What holds the reader's attention? What is the "principle" upon which men ought to ground their "highest pleasure"? Shaftesbury describes it as "that consummate grace, that beauty of Nature, and that perfection of numbers" (I, 214): order, symmetry, proportion, harmony, honesty, goodness, truth, beauty, virtue, mind. "Poetical truth" is an expression of moral truth (I, 216). Although the reader's attention is held by "interior numbers" he does not necessarily know the cause of his pleasure:

the rest of mankind, feeling [the perfection of inward numbers] only by the effect whilst ignorant of the cause, term [it] the *je ne scay quoy,* the unintelligible or the I know not what, and suppose [it] to be a kind of charm or enchantment of which the artist himself can give not account.

(I, 214)

The charm is the "force of Nature," "moral magic" (I, 90). What the reader does is suggested by the explanation of what the "admirers of beauty in the fair sex" admire:

were the subject to be well criticised we should find, perhaps, that what we most admired, even in the turn of outward feature, was only a mysterious expression, and a kind of shadow of something inward in the temper . . . our imagination being busied in forming beauteous shapes and images of this rational kind, which entertained the mind and held it in admiration, whilst other passions of a lower species were employed another way.

(I, 91)

The reader is sympathetically attracted to interior numbers. The attendant pleasure, if the cause is know, is the true joy of enthusiasm.

Now attention is of degrees. What, then, for Shaftesbury, is the relation between different degrees of attention and the unity of a work? In a letter to Pierre Coste he states that in dramatic performances music ought to accompany only the soliloquies and the chorus—"the more sedately passionate parts." (**L,L,** p. 398) Now since he believes that music is an expression of "the passions," ("the proportions and features of a human mind," [I, 90] the morals of men [cf. I, 90-91]); and since he believes that men necessarily admire "that which is purely from itself, and of its own nature" (I, 90) it would seem to follow that to maintain optimum interest music should not be restricted to certain parts of the drama but should be continuous throughout the work. But since Shaftesbury follows Longinus in holding that "to be able to move others we must first be moved ourselves, or at least seem to be so, upon some probable grounds" (I, 6), music expressing intense passion at dispassionate moments of the drama (the recitative) will not sustain interest. The recitative, therefore, ought to "go on peaceably on a plainer foot, just next to common speach." (**L,L,** p. 398). But why not make the recitative as intensely passionate as the arias?

The letter to Coste concludes with Shaftesbury quoting with approval a full paragraph from French author he is criticizing, because he "can't help applying [it] to higher subjects than those he treats of":

"Quelqefois vous entendez une tenue contre laquelle les premiers tons de la basse continue font une dissonance qui irrite l'oreille; mais la basse continuant de jouer, revient à cette tenue par de si beaux accords, qu'on voit bien que le musicien n'a fait ces premiers dissonances, que pour faire sentir, avec plus de plaisir, ses belles cordes où il ramène aussitot l'harmonie."

(*L,L,* p. 399)

Shaftesbury sees the same relation between dissonance and harmony in works of art as he does in the "art" they imitate:

> You know me for a great enthusiast, at least as the world goes. For to talk of the world as harmony, or of a master of the music, is on every side a mystery. The men of wit believe no such hand at all, and the bigots know not what to do with the dissonances: *c'est le diable . . .*

(*L,L,* p. 399)

The understanding of the relation between dissonances and harmony in the universe can be a product of the contemplation of tragedy. This principle is learned by abstracting from particular contrasts in the work. Knowledge of this principle is accompanied by the joy of enthusiasm. The final goal of contemplating tragedy, then, is an acceptance of private and public misfortune. One comes to understand all events as parts of the universal harmony conducted by a master of the music. Such understanding obviously serves the purpose of social control.

If soliloquy does not precede and accompany *poesis* the work, Shaftesbury argues, cannot serve its didactic purpose. Work free of self-criticism is characterized by authorial presence in "epistles dedicatory, prefaces, and addresses to the reader" (I, 131), and by incoherence—the first being a prudent attempt to disguise the second. For in the same way as soliloquy is obstructed in the lover, mystic, and conjuror (I, 116), flattery prevents rigorous criticism. Not only does flattery prevent the appropriation of whatever, if anything, is valuable in a work; in indulges the reader's pride (I, 213) and thus reinforces it. Criticism, of the self or of art, requires disinterestedness, what Shaftesbury refers to in the **Regimen** (following the Stoics) as a fixity of "attention."

"Interestedness" is for Shaftesbury a moral concept. When he writes that

> An author who writes in his own person has the advantage of being who or what he pleases. he is no certain man, nor has any certain or genuine character; but suits himself on every occasion to the fancy of his reader, whom, as the fashion is nowadays, he constantly caresses and cajoles.

(I, 131)

he is criticizing the authorial practice of accommodation (see, e.g., **PR,** p. 193). "Genuine" and "certain" do not refer to roles but to what Shaftesbury terms a

"mixed character," the "state of mind" of Socratic detachment. What Shaftesbury is criticizing is "false sociableness"—unexamined, direct discourse (**PR,** p. 192). It is this moral criticism of false simplicity which he levels against the practice of "winding-up" a work, in which "[the author] ends pathetically by endeavouring in the softest manner to reconcile his reader to those faults which he chooses rather to excuse than to amend." (I, 212-213. Cf. **PR,** p. 183). The model of the "mixed character" is Socrates who

> could treat the highest subjects and those of the commonest capacity both together, and render them explanatory of each other. So that in this genius of writing there appeared both the heroic and the simple, the tragic and the common vein.

(I, 128)

His language, motivated by "common sense," is a product of studying "men, manners, opinions, times."

Excuses by contemporary authors and their apologists for rejecting this knowledge are criticized in Part II of **Soliloquy.** Shaftesbury's argument that modern authors ought to reform their audience, not accommodate to their taste (I, 172), for example, is a reply to Granville's defense of Dryden in his "Essay Upon Unnatural Flights in Poetry" (1701). Granville had written:

> Our King return'd, and banisht Peace restor'd,
> The Muse ran Mad to see her exil'd Lord;
> On the crackt Stage the Bedlam Heroes roar'd,
> And scarce cou'd speak one reasonable word;
> Dryden himself, to please a frantick Age,
> Was forc'd to let his jedgment stoop to Rage;
> To wild Audience he conform'd his voice,
> Comply'd to Custom, but not err'd thro' Choice.
> Deem then the Peoples, not the Writer's Sin,
> Almanzor's Rage, and Rants of Maximin;

(Spingarn, III, 294.)

In his annotations to the last three couplets Granville defended Dryden, arguing that (1) Dryden's characters were accurate representations of contemporary types; (2) reform of drama can be expected only when the dramatist is not entirely dependent on the receipts of the third night; and (3) Dryden apologized for his characters in the dedication to the *Spanish-Fryar.* Now in Part II of **Soliloquy** Shaftesbury rejects all three excuses, his argument being that poets ought to rise above financial pressures and by submitting themselves to a regimen of self-criticism reform test. And his justification of this use of the theatre is historical—the "natural" progress of drama (I, 162-63) is that comedy follows and criticizes the "false sublime" of tragedy, and that in time, comedy "naturally" refines itself (I, 163). It is on historical grounds that Shaftesbury recommends comic criticism (I, 169), permissible differences among which are to be explained in terms of individual "character [=taste, genius] and circumstances" (I, 175-76, n. 1; See I, 166-68).

In recommending the "manner" of ancient comedy Shaftesbury is arguing for a language "to explode the false sublime" of heroic drama into which poets "on every occasion [are] ready to relapse." (I, 160). The false sublime is characterized by "what we call sophistry in argument or bombast in style, [as having something] . . . of the effeminate kind or of the false tender, the pointed witticism, the disjointed thought, the crowded simile, or the mixed metaphor . . ." (I, 156-157):

> In poetry and studied prose the astonishing part, or what commonly passes for sublime, is formed by the variety of figures, the multiplicity of metaphors, and by quitting as much as possible the natural and easy way of expression for the which is most unlike to humanity or ordinary use.
>
> (I, 157-168)

The product of false enthusiasm, the effect of the false sublime is momentary "horror and consternation" (I, 157). This effect Shaftesbury finds socially dangerous.

Underlying his urging dramatic poets to follow Horace's advice to "look to the pattern which life presents, and there learn the language of reality" (II, 318, n. 1) is his belief that unnatural language—"metaphorical speech, multiplicity of figures and high-sounding words" (II, 243)—and improbable characters distance the spectator. John Sheffield, whose *An Essay Upon Poetry* (1682) Shaftesbury urges writers to read (II, 331), had criticized the "perfect character":

> Reject the vulgar error which appears
> So fair, of making perfect characters;
> There's no such thing in Nature, and you'l draw
> A faultless Monster which the world ne're saw;
> Some faults must be, that his misfortunes drew,
> But such as may deserve compassion too.
>
> (Spingarn, II, 293.)

Shaftesbury urges a plain language and probable characters because he regards the theater, like a national church (I, 14), as a means of social control. If the language of the theater is too remote to be understood, if action and character seem improbable, then sympathy is precluded. Pleasure will then be sought elsewhere:

> 'Tis not the possible but the probable and likely which must be the poet's guide in manners. By this he wins attention and moves the conscious reader or spectator, who judges best from within, by what he naturally feels and experiences in his own heart. The perfection of virtue is from long art and management, self-control, and, as it were, force on nature. But the common auditor or spectator, who seeks pleasure only, and loves to engage his passion by view of other passion and emotion, comprehends little of the restraints, allays, and corrections which form this new and artificial creature . . . And thus the completely virtuous and perfect character is unpoetical and false. Effects must not appear where causes must necessarily remain unknown and incomprehensible.
>
> (II, 318)

It is to prevent social disorder that Shaftesbury explains that tragedy functioned as an effective method of social control in Rome when it was written in the plain style of the Greeks. It became ineffective when, as Horace explained in his epistle to Augustus, *"Migravit ab aure voluptas / Omnis ad incertos oculos et gaudia vana"* (II, 187-88). The Romans, Shaftesbury argues, had a genius for tragedy because they loved liberty and tragedy imitated the misfortunes and miseries of tyrants. But instead of cultivating this genius, they destroyed it by letting their tragedies run "into the marvellous, the outrageous, the extreme of things." (*L,L,* p. 397). "The marvelous, the outrageous, the extreme of things" of the letter becomes "the miraculous, the pompous, or what we generally call the sublime" (I, 157) of *Soliloquy.* And the false sublime corresponds to the pleasure of the eye.

Since the social function of tragedy is achieved when the spectator understands the misfortunes and miseries of the great; and since the passions and morals of the great are expressed in speech—in the "places (if I may so call them) of reflection, such as soliloquies and the real parts of the chorus" (*L,L,* p. 398) and in the recitative—attention must not be distracted by sight:

> If that be beauty which is pointed to, which every finger can show, and every eye see, why this inward search of things invisible?—Man! use thy legs. Travel up and down, run the balls, run the playhouses, the churches, parks; run whole countries and over seas, and to see sights.—*See! See!*—this is all. And in a child, what else? Is it not the same passion? Novelty, surprise, colours, squares, rounds, triangles, the bustle of children and the business about these things, their architecture, their models, and buildings, and their pleasure of showing this to others.—See! See!
>
> (*PR,* p. 250)

The pleasures of the eye cannot reform morals and manners (I, 135). Hence, Shaftesbury urges the replacement of the "Adventitious ornaments" (II, 259) of spectacle, machinery, and rhyme (II, 320) by the true ornament of moral instruction (see II, 330; cf. II, 259-60), the product of soliloquy.

The arguments and, indeed, the language of *Soliloquy* should be interpreted in relation to social conflict. When Shaftesbury refers to the Glorious Revolution as

> having firmly secured our hitherto precarious liberties, and removed from us the fear of civil commotions, wars and violence, wither on account of religion and worship, the prosperity of the subject, or the contending titles of the Crown
>
> (I, 141),

he implies that the fear of civil commotions, wars and violence has not been removed on all accounts. W. A. Speck has argued that "it was about 1709 that the conflict in society reached critical proportions," the landed interest (mostly Tory) accusing monied interest (Whigs) of protracting the war for monetary gain. ("Conflict in Society," in *Britain After the Glorious Revolution: 1689-1714,* ed. Geoffrey Holmes [London, 1969], p. 148). Quoting from a letter written by Bolingbroke that reveals his program "to smash the Whigs' hold on the City completely," Speck concludes:

> St. John never got the chance to put this programme completely into action. Had he done so he might well have turned the conflict in society into civil war. The political sparks produced by the friction between the landed and monied interests, therefore, were no mere flashes in the pan. On the contrary, their rivalry generated heat so fierce that it threatened to melt the foundations of the political nation.
>
> (Speck, p. 152.)

Shaftesbury's argument for patronage and soliloquy should be seen within this context. A disaffected group of writers supporting the Tories could inflame the public to disorder, especially during time of war; and an unstable self could easily be excited to participate in a "panic"—of the kind, say, that occurred in 1708 when the Jacobites attempted to invade the country. (See Speck, p. 151). But the "mixed self" poses no threat to public order. The meaning of this "real" self, "the judgment we are to make of interest, and the opinion we should have of advantage and good, which is what must necessarily determine us in our conduct and prove the leading principle of our lives" (I, 199) are unfolded in the fourth treatise of the *Characteristics, An Inquiry Concerning Virtue or Merit.*

Raymond A. Anselment (essay date April-June 1978)

SOURCE: Anselment, Raymond A. "Socrates and *The Clouds*: Shaftesbury and a Socratic Tradition." *Journal of the History of Ideas* 39, no. 2 (April-June 1978): 171-82.

[*In the following essay, Anselment discusses Shaftesbury's views on the impact of Aristophanes'* The Clouds *on the trial, imprisonment, and execution of Socrates.*]

Among the many eighteenth-century reactions to Shaftesbury's *Characteristics* the issue of Aristophanes' role in the condemnation of Socrates provoked considerable controversy. Shaftesbury had cited Aristophanes' attack against the philosopher to argue that Socrates' reputation and philosophy were enhanced rather than diminished after he had been "most abominably ridiculed, in a whole comedy writ and acted on purpose."[1] Critics of the *Characteristics,* however, were not al-

ways willing to agree that truth and virtue can "stand the test of ridicule" unscathed. Though many believed "The Comedy inscribed the CLOUDS is an execrable attempt to expose one of the wisest and best of Men to the Fury and Contempt of a lewd Multitude," they also conceded that "it had but too much success."[2] Their contention that Aristophanes' satiric comedy led directly to the charges brought against Socrates had considerable support by the mid-eighteenth century; indeed Shaftesbury's apologists were hard pressed to minimize the damaging influence of *The Clouds.*[3] But in the process of establishing the relationship between Aristophanes' comedy and Socrates' trial both sides considered Shaftesbury's statement out of its original context. The perplexing allusion to Socrates in *A Letter Concerning Enthusiasm* originates in the complex, even contradictory views concerning the philosopher's fate current in the early eighteenth century. Shaftesbury's understanding and use of a tradition important to the history of ideas are valuable guides to the essay's controversial interpretation of the lore surrounding Socrates and *The Clouds.*

The traditional source for Shaftesbury's position is apparent in the text of his essay. When he proposes that Socrates benefited from Aristophanes' ridicule, Shaftesbury does not allude to Plato's *Apology* and its ambiguous attitude towards *The Clouds.* Instead *A Letter Concerning Enthusiasm* relies upon a later, less reliable account in Claudius Aelian's *Varia Historia* (ca. 200 A.D.) and concludes, "He was not only contented to be ridiculed; but, that he might help the poet as much as possible, he presented himself openly in the theatre; that his real figure (which was no advantageous one) might be compared with that which the witty poet had brought as his representative on the stage. Such was his good humour! Nor could there be in the world a greater testimony of the invincible goodness of the man, or a greater demonstration, that there was no imposture either in his character or opinions" (I, 23-24). According to Aelian's version of events, Anytus and Meletus hired the "trifling fellow" Aristophanes to impugn the reputation of Socrates. The play was performed, and its success was immediate: Aristophanes received great popular acclaim while Socrates was made the source of much derision. But the object of this ridicule was not daunted. "To abolish and blot out all dubitations, and wauering opinions out of the mindes of the straungers," Socrates appeared publicly at the theater and stood throughout the performance of *The Clouds* "so that there coulde be no choyse but the eyes of the people must of necessitie passe and perce unto him, standing in the ful face of the multitude. So little did Socrates set by the canckred natures of the Atheniens, and the spightfull practises of Aristophanes."[4] Although Aelian does not specifically state that Socrates triumphed, later *Varia Historia* reintroduces the issue of the philosopher's presence at the theater as proof that verbal attacks against just men "vanishe lyke smoke in the ayre."[5]

Other classical sources further support Shaftesbury's idea of Socrates' good-humored response to Aristophanes' ridicule. Plutarch's often translated *The Education of Children* introduces the philosopher's demeanor as a paradigm of the wise man. To a questioner who asked whether he felt indignation about the abusive treatment in *The Clouds,* Socrates supposedly replied, "No indeed; . . . when they break a jest upon me in the theatre I feel as if I were at a big party of good friends."[6] Another anecdote recorded in Diogenes Laertius' *Lives of Eminent Philosophers* demonstrates even more emphatically Socrates' affability. "We ought not to object, he used to say, to be subjects for the Comic poets, for if they satirize our faults they will do us good, and if not they do not touch us."[7] While neither of these accounts suggests to the same extent Shaftesbury's image of Socrates' triumph, Laertius' life quotes passages from *The Clouds* to show that the comic writers "in the act of ridiculing him give him high praise."[8] Even if Shaftesbury were not already familiar with this or the other classical traditions, he would have found them along with a translation of Aelian's account in Thomas Stanley's influential *The History of Philosophy* (1655).

Indeed the extent of this tradition is further apparent in a contemporary eighteenth-century commentary on Socrates' attitude towards comic writers. Joseph Addison's essay on ridicule in the March 27, 1711 edition of the *Spectator* might well have had Shaftesbury in mind when it remarks upon a passing reference to comic poets in the *Phaedo.* Socrates' assurance that at this moment of his death even these detractors will forego criticism prompts Addison's comment, "This Passage, I think, evidently glances upon *Aristophanes,* who writ a Comedy on purpose to ridicule the Discourses of that Divine Philosopher: It has been observed by many Writers, that *Socrates* was so little moved at this piece of Buffoonery, that he was several times present at its being acted upon the Stage, and never expressed the least Resentment of it."[9] The essay mentions no sources perhaps because Addison assumes the knowledge is commonplace and perhaps because the generalization is intended to emphasize the departure from tradition in the next sentence. "But with Submission," Addison continues, "I think the Remark I have here made shows us that this unworthy Treatment made an Impression upon his Mind, though he had been too wise to discover it."[10] Addison's belief that he offers new insight into the matter may explain the subsequent eighteenth-century reactions to Shaftesbury's statements. Quite simply, *A Letter Concerning Enthusiasm* depends upon an established understanding of a Socrates impervious to jest while Addison's essay heralds a reas-

sessment of Aristophanes' play that would bolster the positions of later critics who had misgivings about ridicule.

The tradition based largely upon Aelian's account, however, is more complex than Addison implies. Although *Varia Historia* limits its narrative to the origin and initial impact of *The Clouds,* by the seventeenth century many commentators agreed with Thomas Stanley that in the ridicule of Socrates recounted by Aelian lay "the occasion of his death, but begun many years before."[11] The connection between Aristophanes' satiric attack and the trial of Socrates depends upon the central figures of Anytus and Meletus. By making them the instigators of the accusations in *The Clouds,* Aelian overlooks alternative motives for Aristophanes' ridicule and tacitly agrees with Plato's *Apology* that these men were Socrates' primary enemies. Several centuries later Eunapius explicitly links *The Clouds* with the trial of Socrates: "When they saw that the audience in the theatre was inclined to such indulgence, certain men set up an accusation and ventured on that impious indictment against him; and so the death of one man brought misfortune on the whole state."[12] Thomas Magistros' medieval *argumentum* to the text then gives additional weight to the two accusers and thereby adds to the legacy inherited by later ages. In the seventeenth century Palmerius could look back upon these commentators and conclude that the "claque" led by Aelian "seem to signal that this comedy came forth a bit before the accusation and condemnation of Socrates. For if it were the preparation, the prologue of the accusation, they reasoned that that which aroused that drama could be reestablished with fresh objects of hatred."[13]

Their deduction, however, does not trouble Palmerius. He and the other prominent scholars later included in Ludolph Kuster's 1710 edition of Aristophanes' plays express important reservations about Aelian's reliability. Evidence from the play and its scholia indicate to them that at least twenty years elapsed between the production of *The Clouds* and the public condemnation of Socrates. Men bent on prejudicing the Athenians would not, in their opinion, postpone the opportunity to capitalize upon the play's success; therefore many of these influential authorities discount Aelian's version of the play's inception.[14] Besides suggesting that Aristophanes actually wrote the comedy as part of a long-standing general dispute between philosophers and comic poets, they and others point to passages in the play that appear to praise the character of Socrates. In addition, Plato would not have included Aristophanes favorably in *The Symposium* if the playwright were any sort of threat to Socrates. Indeed Aristophanes' failure to win the prize suggests to some that Aelian greatly exaggerates the play's initial success.[15]

Shaftesbury's familiarity with these arguments remains, of course, conjectural. While Kuster's edition appeared after the publication of *A Letter Concerning Enthusiasm,* the modifications of Aelian were readily available in earlier editions of Aristophanes and in various seventeenth-century commentaries. Shaftesbury would also have had the opportunity to read François Charpentier's *La vie de Socrate* in one of the three editions issued before the English translation of 1712. Charpentier includes many of the criticisms raised by the supporters of Aristophanes against the authority of Aelian and, more important, anticipates Shaftesbury's position. For when all of the objections have been considered, Charpentier concludes, "This is a Truth which all the Authors confirm; he regarded this dangerous Invention of *Aristophanes* with contempt, and was no more mov'd at it." He then further adds, "Thus too *Aristophanes* and his Party found themselves mistaken, thro' the constancy of *Socrates,* and only furnish'd him with an occasion to render himself more illustrious, by the very Design which they had concerted to ruin his Reputation."[16]

Shaftesbury could not, however, disregard the growing belief that Aristophanes' ridicule ultimately destroyed Socrates. Even before Voltaire and the eighteenth century popularized this notion, the harmful effect of Aristophanes' comedy was commonly established. By the last decades of the seventeenth century the fate of Socrates illustrated to many the ease with which truth can be obscured. Earlier in the century Robert Burton in *The Anatomy of Melancholy* assures readers that Socrates laughed and remained unconcerned when ridiculed: "Socrates still kept the same countenance. Even so should a Christian soldier do, as Hierom describes him, march on through good and bad reports to immortality, not to be moved: for honesty is a sufficient reward; . . . naughtiness will punish itself at last."[17] When Richard Allestree, however, turns to the example of Socrates in *The Government of the Tongue* (1674), the optimism is noticeably missing. Allestree contends that "bare honesty" cannot sustain itself when stripped of its adornments. "Thus the enemies of *Socrates,* when they could no otherwaies suppress his reputation, hired *Aristophanes* a Comic Poet to personate him on the stage, and by the insinuations of those interludes, insensibly conveied first a contemt, then a hatred of him into the hearts of the people."[18] Walter Charleton also agrees that the example of Socrates illustrates the consequences of malignant wit. In *Two Discourses* (1675) Aristophanes' "most inhuman persecution of the Divine *Socrates*" is described by Charleton as a malicious attempt "to render that best and wisest of Mortals odious to the base Vulgar." The instigators Anytus and Meletus "not long after by false accusations robb'd the innocent Philosopher [*sic*] of his life, and the world of its richest Treasure."[19]

Despite evidence disputing both Aelian and the harmful influence of *The Clouds,* many commentaries on drama increasingly contribute to the growing belief that Aristophanes was responsible for the death of Socrates. Plutarch had established in general terms the abusive quality of Aristophanes' plays, and Renaissance classicists such as Daniel Heinsius and Ben Jonson point to the ridicule of Socrates as an instance of dramatic wit "invented for scorne and laughter";[20] but the late seventeenth century finds even greater significance in Boileau's recognition that "A Socrates himself, in that loose age / Was made the pastime of a scoffing stage."[21] For the first time discussions of drama assert with conviction "that *Aristophanes's* Plays did not a little contribute to the death of the famous *Socrates* by exciting the People against him" and maintain that "the credit that *Aristophanes* had among the *Athenians,* which was powerful enough to ruine *Socrates,* is singly sure sufficient."[22] To many Aristophanes was destructive, not merely abusive, and the persecution of Socrates at the hands of the satirist offers a commonplace example of ridicule's destructive power.[23]

An exception, such as Thomas Rymer's *A Short View of Tragedy* (1692), finds itself with the unenviable task of criticizing the venerable philosopher. Rymer's suggestion that Socrates may have been injudicious in his criticism of the old religion and his characterization of Aristophanes as a moderate reformer reveal the unorthodoxy of the survey's famous pronouncements on *Othello.* His additional argument that Socrates was not arraigned until some twenty years after the comedy's performance might appeal to some but not all of the "Many . . . offended with *Aristophanes* as accessory to the death of *Socrates.*"[24] A 1701 translation of André Dacier's *The Works of Plato Abridg'd* expresses so strongly the damaging effects of Aristophanes' calumny that its author finds distinctions based on time irrelevant. "His Comedy of the Clouds had such an absolute influence upon the People, that it mov'd them to receive the Accusation brought against this Philosopher more than twenty Years after, branding him for a profligate Wretch that introduc'd new Deities."[25] Dacier's pronouncement carries more than the usual weight accorded a man of his stature, because it emphasizes Socrates' own admission. When Socrates alludes in the *Apology* to Aristophanes' caricature of the philosopher swinging in a basket, Dacier adds in a footnote, "*Socrates* treats the Calumnies of *Aristophanes* and his first Enemies, as if it were a just Charge formally presented upon Oath."[26] By focusing on the philosopher's statement, Dacier avoids issues involving the credibility of later accounts such as Aelian's. The motive and dates associated with *The Clouds* do not concern him, since its devastating effects are so demonstrable.

They are also apparent to writers involved in a late seventeenth-century controversy that anticipates *A Letter Concerning Enthusiasm.* Shaftesbury's interest in the limits of religious toleration and the effectiveness of ridicule also forms a central concern of a dispute involving the future bishop of Oxford, Samuel Parker. One of the divine's critics, John Owen, objects to Parker's endorsement of dialogue and ridicule against enthusiasts unwilling to conform to his Erastian vision of religious polity, and he supports his misgivings with the example of Socrates. Relying heavily upon Aelian, he recalls the events familiar to many of his contemporaries and warns, "By these means, and through these advantages, they ceased not until they had destroyed the best and wisest person, that ever that City bred in its Heathen condition, and whereof they quickly repented themselves."[27] His fear that all religion could be made to appear similarly ridiculous—an objection later shared by many who reacted to Shaftesbury—is not easily dismissed in Parker's response. Although he tries to minimize the criticism, Parker does not dispute the harm Aristophanes inflicted on Socrates. In a response later followed by Shaftesbury's eighteenth-century supporters, he first argues that the single defamation of an honest individual should not prevent all ridicule of obvious wrongs. Another argument proposes that Aristophanes never "design'd any appearance of Truth"; his audience was meant to laugh at the discrepancy between the grave philosopher they actually knew and the buffoon they saw suspended in the basket.[28] Before he turns the tables on Owen, rejecting the parallel between Socrates and the Nonconformists and suggesting the philosopher fell "A Sacrifice to the Zeal and Fury" of the Nonconformists' Athenian counterparts, Parker comes close to Shaftesbury's apparent position. Despite his admission at one point that an unscrupulous wit can make any individual appear ridiculous, he refuses to relinquish the belief, "if Men Publish Sense, all the World can never make them ridiculous; if Nonsense, they make themselves so. And no Gaggs, nor Lime-twigs can disable them from defending their Books against any Adversary, but either a bad Cause, or an ill Management; . . . so if they are lime-twigged with Ink and Paper, 'tis with Rods of their own laying; and if they are exposed in a Fools Coat, 'tis with one of their own making."[29]

The conflict in Parker's position represents the tension in early eighteenth-century attitudes towards Aristophanes' ridicule of Socrates. When Shaftesbury wrote *A Letter Concerning Enthusiasm* he could rely upon a long tradition to support his assertion that *The Clouds* actually enhanced Socrates' reputation. But the arguments against his optimistic view of Socrates' fate were also strong. In fact the objections raised later in the eighteenth century are not original. By the Restoration the growing emphasis on the philosopher's mistreatment results, at least in part, from a reassessment of ridicule. While many contemporaries of these decades note the increasing popularity of wit, considerable misgivings are voiced about its misuse. The more "amiable humor" of the next century has growing sup-

port, and a reaction against intemperate and misguided ridicule is apparent. Shaftesbury surely recognized the concerns of his age expressed in the greater attention given to Aristophanes, yet he sweeps them aside in his faith in Socrates' ability to withstand attack.

The reference to Socrates at the end of a section dealing with "right" or "good" humor confirms Shaftesbury's contention that this manner affords the fullest protection against enthusiasm and is the "best foundation of piety and true religion." Socrates' invulnerability to Aristophanes' mockery illustrates that wit separates the "truly serious" from the merely ridiculous, and his reaction to ridicule demonstrates the proper attitude. Both points are implicit in the next paragraph, and in the essay's immediate concern, the freedom to ridicule religion. Socrates' "invincible goodness" proves by analogy "true" religion's similar unassailability, and his genial nature represents the only way to deal with criticism. Each of these principles is underscored in the conditional statement, "provided we treat religion with good manners, we can never use too much good-humour, or examine it with too much freedom and familiarity" (I, 24). The freedom to ridicule religion, however, assumes secondary importance. Although *A Letter Concerning Enthusiasm* never mentions Socrates again, he remains a model for Shaftesbury's primary interest, the good-humored manner that ensures truth. The rest of the essay explores the way to avoid undesirable enthusiasm.

Here Shaftesbury relies upon an undisputed tradition. His ideal of conduct presupposes the widely admired Socratic injunction, *nosce teipsum. A Letter Concerning Enthusiasm* insists that criticism of others begins with one's self. "For to judge the spirits whether they are of God, we must antecedently judge our own spirit, whether it be of reason and sound sense; whether it be fit to judge at all, by being sedate, cool, and impartial, free of every biassing passion, every giddy vapour, or melancholy fume" (I, 39). Shaftesbury's contemporaries recognized that the man who professed his own ignorance therein actually displayed the "great Sense and Probity" necessary to challenge the "Fabulous" nature of Athenian faith and return it to a "Standard of Natural Religion."[30] Indeed the man Shaftesbury acknowledges elsewhere as the world's greatest philosopher had been long considered a very religious, even Christian teacher. Appropriately an essay that defines divinity as the love of the public and the promotion of universal goodness turns to Socrates as the model of behavior best suited against the modern enthusiasts who threaten disruption. One of Benjamin Whichcote's *Moral and Religious Aphorisms* aptly describes Shaftesbury's rationale: "It is a pregnant argument, that Wisdom hath not governed the world: that many have more readily received pretending *Enthusiasm* and Prescience, with sacred regard; than wisest Laws and best Reasons. *Socrates* overthrew

Enthusiasm and Superstition; when he taught men to receive *no* Doctrine, against or without Reason."[31]

The characteristic expression of conduct founded upon reason and self-knowledge is good-humored raillery. Although Shaftesbury does not fully discuss its nature until *An Essay on the Freedom of Wit and Humour,* the figure of Socrates represents the ideal. As an acknowledged originator of both ridicule and philosophy, Socrates typifies the unpretentious, easy pleasantness that for Shaftesbury is good humor. Cicero believes "Socrates far surpassed all others for accomplished wit in this train of irony or assumed simplicity," and he recommends this blend of humor and seriousness for both public statements and "the conversation of gentlemen."[32] Later satirists pressed to defend their ridicule commonly cite the example of Socrates, and by the early eighteenth century "the Droll" offered a well-established precedent for banter suited to grave matters.[33] When Shaftesbury lauds the philosopher's attitude and then recommends a genial outlook characterized by wit as well as self-awareness, he advocates a conduct many recognized. René Rapin summarizes it in the description of Socrates found in *Reflections upon Philosophy*: "he preserv'd an Air of Pleasantry in treating of the gravest Subjects; and his most serious Meditations never rob'd him of his good Humour. As 'twas his constant Intention not to speak like a Wit, but like an honest Man, so there was always somewhat just and noble in his very Trifling, and his Raillery. He pretended to no Accomplishment, and was capable of All."[34]

Rhetorically two different traditions influence Shaftesbury's emphasis on Socrates' genial reaction to criticism and his discussion of good humor in criticism. But since the first tradition involves disagreement about the harmful influence of *The Clouds,* its questionable nature obscures the essay's stronger focus on Socrates' admirable behavior. Perhaps Shaftesbury intentionally runs this risk, even though he must have been familiar with the objections raised about Aristophanes' comedy, because he wants to exploit with maximum rhetorical effect the precedent Socrates provides for the essay's ideal of behavior. Shaftesbury finds, after all, considerable support for his suggestion that the philosopher benefited from the ridicule; and, in any case, he is not reluctant to interpret tradition for his own ends. This is apparent in his later, though similar use of the parallel figure of Christ as an illustration of ideal religious conduct.

In contrast to the morose, angry attacks of some religious leaders, *Miscellaneous Reflections* lauds the "festivity, alacrity, and good humour" apparent in the "pleasant manner" of Christ's teaching: "'tis not more vehement and majestic in his gravest animadversions or declamatory discourses than it is sharp, humorous, and witty in his repartees, reflections, fabulous narrations,

or parables, similes, comparisons, and other methods of milder censure and reproof" (II, 231). Some justification for this characterization may be found among the Cambridge Platonists Shaftesbury admired, but the description is by no means conventional. The traditional view, generally attributed to Chrysostom, is very explicit: "Yea, for He also wept, both over Lazarus, and over the city; and touching Judas He was greatly troubled. And this indeed one may often see Him do, but no where laugh, nay, nor smile but a little; no one at least of the Evangelists hath mentioned this."[35] When controversialists in the seventeenth and early eighteenth centuries rely upon Christ's example as a sanction for their religious satire, they commonly invoke illustrations of this harsh, uncompromising disposition. Their image of Christ whipping the money lenders from the temple justifies a ridicule quite unlike the good-humored with Shaftesbury envisions.[36]

Like the earlier impression of Socrates, the essay's view of Christ entertains a provocative position which enables Shaftesbury to find the ideal embodiment of humor in one of the two greatest individuals of his civilization. Later critics who attack his use of Socrates but not his impression of Christ ignore both the general direction of *A Letter Concerning Enthusiasm* and the insistence upon "good manners" or interpret its allusion to the ancient philosopher in terms of Shaftesbury's later *An Essay on the Freedom of Wit and Humor.* When John Brown, for example, criticizes the latter essay's statement "One may defy the world to turn real bravery or generosity into ridicule" with the example of Socrates, he overlooks the contexts of the essays as well as their careful qualifications. From his understanding of the role Aristophanes plays in the death of Socrates and from his own sense of experience, Brown sees entirely different results from conflicts between ridicule and truth.[37] Others who share his views argue that the ridicule of Socrates confirms only the great precariousness of truth. Shaftesbury, in their opinion, uses tradition selectively, and he oversimplifies the degree of dangerous distortion actually inherent in ridicule.

These criticisms, which do not take into account the conditions Shaftesbury imposes upon the freedom to ridicule, are not entirely to the point. Near the beginning of *A Letter Concerning Enthusiasm* Shaftesbury recognizes that not all people equally appreciate ridicule: "The vulgar, indeed, may swallow any sordid jest, any mere drollery or buffoonery; but it must be a finer and truer wit which takes with the men of sense and breeding" (I, 10). Like Swift who appeals in *A Tale of a Tub* to "Men of Wit and Tast," Shaftesbury suggests he addresses a similarly select audience. Rhetorically the essay flatters its readers and then appeals to their judgments to confirm its characterization of them. The strategy admits only one response to the essay's fundamental questions, "For what ridicule can lie against reason?

or how can any one of the least justness of thought endure a ridicule wrong placed" (I, 10)? With an ironic turn befitting an admirer of Socrates, Shaftesbury challenges his audience to act as reasonable individuals. Although the essay may seem to advocate the ideal rather than the practical, Shaftesbury is not unaware of reality. Rather he encourages his readers to examine the values of their civilization and to act accordingly. He offers them a pattern of reason and good humor that conforms to the actions of Christ and Socrates.

The historical accuracy of his models remains secondary. Prior to the introduction of the controversial example of Socrates, the essay describes a mythic, golden age of "natural humanity" in which both reason and wit are freely balanced against enthusiasm and superstition. This Athens of Socrates might well fulfill the essay's opening promise to entertain its readers "with a sort of idle thoughts, such as pretend only to amusement," but the ambiguous seriousness does not obscure Shaftesbury's ironic treatment of those who have lost sight of this ideal in their obsession with eternal life and the "saving of souls." Contemporaries consumed with their own religion and unwilling to tolerate other beliefs only drive civilization further from the era of Socrates. Towards the revival of this desirable, even mythical world Shaftesbury offers his vision of good humor. The ideal of Socrates may well be based upon disputed tradition, and the present, fallen world may well frustrate the imitation of this model, but similar difficulties also challenge the established religion. As the carefully defined and qualified manner of his essays indicate, Shaftesbury has no illusions about the obstacles confronting his ideal. Contemporaries who considered Socrates and Christ divine martyrs, however, would agree with him that even death is not defeat. The quest for truth, the means and not merely the end, motivates Shaftesbury's advocacy of good humor. For him Socrates embodies an ideal which, like its Christian counterpart, requires its own act of faith.

Notes

1. Anthony Ashley Cooper [Third Earl of Shaftesbury, 1671-1713], *A Letter Concerning Enthusiasm* in *Characteristics of Men, Manners, Opinions, Times* (1711), ed. John M. Robertson (New York, 1964), I, 23. Hereafter cited in the text.

2. Thomas Blackwell, *Letters Concerning Mythology* (London, 1748), 262.

3. Thomas B. Gilmore, Jr., who surveys the later, eighteenth-century reactions to Shaftesbury's allusion to Socrates, concludes, "Every argument intended to disprove the disastrous effect of Aristophanes' ridicule on Socrates was weak or inconclusive"—see *The Eighteenth-Century Controversy Over Ridicule As A Test of Truth: A Reconsideration,* Number 25 of Georgia State Research Papers (Atlanta, Georgia, 1970), 24.

4. Claudius Aelianus, *A Registre Of Hystories,* trans. Abraham Fleming (London, 1576), The second Booke, 17 v.

5. *Ibid.,* The fifth Booke, 63 v.

6. Plutarch, *The Education of Children in Moralia,* trans. Frank C. Babbitt (Cambridge, Mass., 1949), I, 10.

7. Diogenes Laertius, *Lives of Eminent Philosophers,* trans. R. D. Hicks (Cambridge, Mass., 1942), I, 167.

8. *Laertius,* I, 157.

9. *The Spectator,* ed. Donald F. Bond (Oxford, 1965), I, 98.

10. *Ibid.*

11. Thomas Stanley, *The History of Philosophy* (London, 1665), III, 30.

12. Eunapius, *Lives of the Philosophers,* trans. Wilmer Cave Wright (New York, 1921), 381, 383.

13. Jacobus Palmerius [Jacques Le Paulmier de Grentemesnil], *Exercitationes in Optimos Fere Auctores Graecos* (1668), 729. Translated by Reuben R. Lee.

14. Palmerius remains the most influential proponent of this position.

15. See, for example, the commentary by Kuster and the selections he includes from Frischlin, Petit. Palmerius, and Spahn in *Aristophanis Comoediae undecim, Graece et Latine* (1710).

16. François Charpentier's *The Life of Socrates* (1668) is included in the edition of Xenophon's *The Memorable Things of Socrates* (London, 1712). The passages quoted are from page 28.

17. Robert Burton, *The Anatomy of Melancholy,* ed. Floyd Dell and Paul Jordan-Smith (New York, 1927), 551.

18. Richard Allestree, *The Government of the Tongue* (London, 1674), 131.

19. Walter Charleton, *Two Discourses* (London, 1675), 130.

20. Ben Jonson, *Timber, or Discoveries* in *Critical Essays of the Seventeenth Century,* ed. J. E. Spingarn (Oxford, 1957), I, 59. Jonson relies upon Heinsius; Plutarch's judgment is made in his comparison of Aristophanes and Menander.

21. Nicolas Boileau, *Art of Poetry,* trans. William Soame (1683) in *The Art of Poetry,* ed. Albert S. Cook (New York, 1926), 204.

22. François D'Aubignac, *The Whole Art of the Stage* (London, 1684), 47; James Drake, *The Antient and Modern Stages survey'd* (London, 1699), 60.

23. See, for example, Gerard Langbaine, *An Account of the English Dramatick Poets* (London, 1691), I, 444; George Farquhar, *A Discourse upon Comedy* (1702) in *Critical Essays of the Eighteenth Century,* ed. Willard Durham (New York, 1961), 271.

24. Thomas Rymer, *A Short View of Tragedy* in *The Critical Works of Thomas Rymer,* ed. Curt Zimansky (New Haven, 1956), 173.

25. André Dacier, *The Works of Plato Abridg'd* (London, 1701), II, 3.

26. *Ibid.,* II, 12.

27. John Owen, *Truth and Innocence Vindicated* (London, 1669), 50.

28. Dryden earlier makes this distinction in the *Essay of Dramatic Poesy*; it is also developed by eighteenth-century supporters of Shaftesbury.

29. Samuel Parker, *A Defence and Continuation of the Ecclesiastical Politie* (London, 1671), 176.

30. Jeremy Collier, *A Short View of the Immorality and Profaneness of the English Stage* (London, 1698), 37.

31. Benjamin Whichcote, *Moral and Religious Aphorisms. Collected from the Manuscript Papers of The Reverend and Learned Doctor Whichcote* (London, 1753), #1085.

32. Cicero, *De Oratore,* trans. E. W. Sutton and H. Rackham (Cambridge, Mass., 1967), III, 403.

33. Among the most famous of the many satirists who cite Socrates are Erasmus in his *Letter to Martin Dorp,* defending the *Praise of Folly,* and Milton in his response to Alexander More, *Pro Se Defensio.* For a significant statement by a writer not directly involved in satire see Isaac Barrow's sermon on Ephesians 5:4 in *Several Sermons Against Evil-Speaking* (London, 1678).

34. René Rapin, *Reflections upon Philosophy* in *The Whole Critical Works of Monsieur Rapin* (London, 1706), II, 353. This Socratic ideal is central to Shaftesbury's works; see, for example, John G. Hayman, "Shaftesbury and the Search for a Persona," *Studies in English Literature,* 10 (1970), 491-504.

35. Chrysostom, *Homily VI. Matt. II. 1, 2* in *The Homilies of S. John Chrysostom on the Gospel of Matthew* in *A Library of Fathers* (Oxford, 1843), 88.

36. See, for example, Thomas Edwards, *Gangraena* (London, 1646), 210; Samuel Parker, *A Discourse of Ecclesiastical Politie* (London, 1670), vii; John Edwards, *Some New Discoveries* (London, 1714), 186.

37. John Brown, *Essays on the Characteristics* (London, 1751), 56ff. Eighteenth-century criticisms of the Socratic allusion are relevant if Socrates represents for Shaftesbury proof that ridicule is a test of truth. But modern critics now generally agree that Shaftesbury never explicitly makes this famous statement in any of his essays; *A Letter Concerning Enthusiasm,* in any case, is not as narrowly focused as its eighteenth-century critics suggest.

Garland P. Brooks (essay date autumn 1982)

SOURCE: Brooks, Garland P. "Shaftesbury and the Psychological School of Ethics." *Dalhousie Review* 62, no. 3 (autumn 1982): 431-40.

[*In the essay below, Brooks examines the theory of morality propounded by Shaftesbury, which the critic views as essentially subjective despite the philosopher's search for an objective system of ethics.*]

British eighteenth-century psychology: the most typical association is probably to the *Nihil est in intellectu, quod non prius fuerit in sensu* epistemology of the empiricists. The view that the psychology of the period was synonymous with *tabula rasa,* sensation and association has long been widespread. Such a perception stems in part from the tendency of certain historians to stress the over-riding importance of the nineteenth-century German experimentalists in the development of psychology and hence, by extension, of the empirical tradition which had nurtured them. Yet modern psychology had roots other than these, and the eighteenth-century had additional, and at times apparently more pressing, intellectual concerns than the epistemological. Among these, problems of ethics and aesthetics—or in Neo-Platonic fashion, some fusion of the two—loomed large.

Predominant among British ethical theories of the first half of the eighteenth-century was the Moral Sense School whose founder was Anthony Ashley Cooper, third Earl of Shaftesbury (1671-1713). John Locke, as medical attendant to the Ashley household, was present at the birth of its heir, whose education he was also to superintend. "Mr. Locke having the absolute direction of my education, and to whom, next my immediate parents, as I must own the greatest obligation, so I have ever preserved the greatest gratitude and duty" (quoted by Fowler, 1882, p. 5). The 'polite arts' and the classics played a prominent role in this education, and the young Cooper later broadened his knowledge of those fields through the requisite Continental travel. Returning to Britain, he was briefly involved in politics—the family motto was "Love, Serve"—but ill health forced him to adopt a more retiring life. During his final decade the moralist was primarily involved in writing and revising the essays which were eventually included in his *Characteristics of Men, Manners, Opinions, Times* (1711).

Shaftesbury's first published work—in 1698—was a Preface to the *Sermons* of Benjamin Whichcote, a Cambridge Platonist. The following year a rough version of the *Inquiry Concerning Virtue, or Merit* was published—without permission—by John Toland: the author, when apprised of the fact, bought and apparently destroyed the unsold copies. This treatise had apparently been outlined as early as 1691 and is a "self-sufficient work which seems to have been intended to stand alone" (Voitle, 1955, p. 25). It was, however, later included—in substantially revised form—among the essays comprising the *Characteristics.* It was again corrected and revised by the author for what was to be a posthumous edition of that work (1714). Although Shaftesbury constantly returned to the same themes throughout the two volumes of the *Characteristics,* it is in the *Inquiry* that the most important statement of his moral theory is to be found. This treatise, in its final form, was his last official statement on the topic and was also the most formal and systematic presentation of that theory. His other papers, which add little to the moral theory described in the *Inquiry,* are more discursive in style, in keeping with his intention of bringing philosophy into 'polite society': the goal of philosophic discourse, he claimed, should be to improve mankind and not merely to describe and analyse.

As Fowler (1882, p. 63) has stated, Shaftesbury was "emphatically a Moral Philosopher." A true son of the Enlightenment, he believed that to understand morality—like so many other subjects—one must begin with a study of human nature. It is, furthermore, by motives that men are "esteem'd good or ill" (p. 35).[1] An examination of actions or their consequences alone is not of much value to the moralist since these may be influenced by external constraints or "a fear of some impending Punishment, or thro the allurement of some exteriour Reward" (p. 33). One must turn instead to the "inward Anatomy" (p. 138) of the mind, for only a study of the "Temper" can reveal the "Springs and Sources of all Actions" (p. 100) and the "Motive" or "sufficient Cause" of morality.

The "Fabrick of the Mind" (p. 140) is composed of various motives. Among these are such private or "self-affections" as love of life, resentment of injury, the appetites for nourishment and procreation, and love of praise and honour. Shaftesbury agreed with Hobbes that self-love is natural and necessary, but argued that the complexity of behaviour is too great to be explained by any one motive—such as egoism—or by one class of motives with varying forms. There are, he argued, two other major categories of affections, the "natural" and the "unnatural." The former are the social motives and are "suited to the publick Good, or Good of the Species" (p. 44). Included among them are love, compassion, kindness, gratitude, equity, sociableness, goodwill and sympathy. The motives of the third category, the unnatural affections, benefit neither the self nor others; these include "*INHUMAN DELIGHT in beholding Torments,* and in viewing Distress, Calamity, Blood, Massacre and Destruction, with a peculiar Joy and Pleasure" (p. 254). Such inclinations are particularly strong among "Tyrants, and barbarous Nations" (p. 254). Other unnatural affections include "WANTON MISCHIEVIOUSNESS"(P. 255), and "MALICE, MALIGNITY, or ILL-WILL" (p. 256). Shaftesbury's disciple, Francis Hutcheson, was to doubt the very existence of such unnatural motives in pure form.

It is to the class of natural affections that we must look for the basis of morality. In Shaftesbury's view virtue is primarily a matter of one's relationship with others. It is a "social Passion" (p. 94) and the various motives which lead to virtuous behaviour are, therefore, those which involve relationships with others of one's kind—generosity, compassion, love, kindness, succour or "whatever else is of a social or friendly sort" (p. 167). Everyone, he claimed, "discerns and owns a publick Interest" and is aware of "what affects his Fellowship or Community" (p. 73). Being aware of the public good, we naturally seek "Advantage to Society" (p. 55). Yet behaviour which benefits others but is motivated by some hoped for gain cannot be considered moral or virtuous. Only when the affections are "suited to the publick Good . . . is the *natural Temper* intirely good" (p. 44).

Animals as well as men are capable of acting in a 'prosocial' fashion, since they too have an innate disposition to respond in ways which benefit their fellow-creatures; but they cannot, in Shaftesbury's opinion, be allowed "VIRTUE or MERIT" (p. 46). This requires not only the natural affections but also the capacity to observe and reflect upon these motives and upon actions and their consequences. Men, being capable of forming concepts, can develop a "Notion of publick Interest, and can attain the Speculation or Science of what is morally good or ill, admirable or blameable, right or wrong" (p. 53). Once we have such an idea, "the Heart cannot possibly remain neutral" (p. 51) and feelings of approval and disapproval will inevitably result. We will "be taken with any shew or representation of the social Passion" (p. 94). There arises, therefore, a new rational affection "towards those very Affections the social, themselves" (p. 47); this disposition, like the others, is original and natural—an inevitable consequence of man's original nature. It is the "*Sense of Right or*

Wrong," the moral sense, and it provides an evaluation or "Judgement of what is done" (p. 54). Man has, therefore, both an inclination to goodness stemming from the natural affections and a moral sense by which he makes moral judgements.

Since to have a rational notion of moral worth is also to have an inclination towards it, it is essential to have correct ideas of right and wrong. Whatever, therefore, "causes a Misconception or Misapprehension of the Worth or Value of any Object, so as to diminish a due, or raise any undue, irregular, or unsocial Affection, must necessarily be the occasion of Wrong" (p. 58). Such virtue-destroying errors are the product either of "Superstition or ill Custom" (p. 60). Shaftesbury believed that fashion, political institutions, laws and religion are all major contributors to the development of mistaken ideas; such errors appear whenever "certain Actions naturally foul and odious are repeatedly view'd with Applause, and Honour ascrib'd to them" (p. 81). Religion is particularly culpable in this respect, although 'right' religion is the firmest support of true morality. Reason is absolutely necessary to "secure a right application of the Affections" (p. 61) and to produce that "uniform and steedy *Will* and Resolution" (p. 65) which enables us to resist those passions or affections which prompt us to behave in immoral ways. It alone can ensure a correct knowledge of right and wrong. Luckily the natural temper is typically strong, and it is only through "long Practice and Meditation" (p. 76) that it is overcome and erroneous conceptions of morality creep in and a "second Nature"—an immoral one—is created by "Habit or Custom" (p. 77).

What led Shaftesbury to develop this particular theory of morality? Most obviously the doctrine of the social affections was proposed as an alternative to the Hobbesian view of human nature. Shaftesbury claimed, as we have seen, that behaviour is too complex to be explained by any single motive: Hobbes had forgotten to "mention Kindness, Friendship, Sociableness, Love of Company and Converse, Natural Affection, or anything of this kind" (quoted by Willey, 1940, p. 59, from Shaftesbury's Preface to Whichcote's *Sermons*). However, opposition to Hobbes' one-sided and pessimistic view of human nature cannot alone account for the distinctive features of Shaftesbury's moral theory. For this one must look to the intellectual problems which certain of the theories of his old mentor, John Locke, had created for him.

Despite Shaftesbury's life-long friendship with Locke, he was not constrained from criticizing, particularly after Locke's death, certain of the principles of his philosophy. First of all Shaftesbury was not impressed by the emphasis which Locke had placed on epistemology. Distinctions between simple and complex ideas and analyses of space and time were, for Shaftesbury, of

little use, for as a consequence of them man "is neither better, nor happier, nor . . . of a more . . . enlarged mind or generous heart" (quoted in Rand, 1900, p. 269). Such theories did not help philosophy to fulfill its prescriptive function. More importantly, Locke's attack on innate ideas raised serious difficulties for Shaftesbury, the moralist. In the eighth of the "Several Letters written by a Noble Lord to a Young Man at the University," he wrote:

> Mr. *Locke,* as much as I honour him on account of other writings . . . and as well as I knew him, and can answer for his sincerity as a most zealous *Christian* and believer, did however go in the self-same track as Hobbes. . . .
>
> It was Mr. Locke that struck the home blow: for Mr. *Hobbes's* character and base slavish principles in government took off the poison of his philosophy. It was Mr. *Locke* that struck at all fundamentals, threw all *order* and *virtue* out of the world, and made the very ideas of these . . . *unnatural,* and without foundation in our minds.
>
> (Shaftesbury, 1757, Vol. 1, pp. 309f)

Shaftesbury became progressively more concerned by this implication that moral principles are "unnatural." If there are no innate moral ideas, must one accept that there is no objective basis for ethical principles, that virtue "has no other measure, law, or rule, than *fashion* and *custom*" (p. 311)? Are moral ideas purely a product of individual experience and therefore totally relative and subjective?

Like Shaftesbury, Locke had felt a need to find some firmer foundation for moral behaviour. His solution had been to root morality in the "Will of God," but this did not satisfy Shaftesbury who believed that such a theory implied the possibility of capricious behaviour on the part of the Deity who is "free to will, *any thing, that is however ill*" (Shaftesbury, 1757, Vol. 1, p. 311). Further, it suggested that men are moral merely because of a desire to obtain heavenly rewards and avoid eternal punishment. Such a utilitarian theory was as egoistic as that of Hobbes. And as we have seen, to perform right acts and eschew wrong merely because of external constraints or a desire for personal gain—even when meted out by God—cannot be considered moral. Other views about the religious foundation of morality Shaftesbury found—on several counts—to be just as unacceptable. Clergymen had too often adopted a view of human nature as black as Hobbes': in attempting to demonstrate the necessity of revealed religion, they argued "as if Goodness and religion were enemies." Shaftesbury, as the "friend of man" (Thomson, 1790, p. 100), found the view of human nature propounded by Hobbes and the typical divine disturbingly similar and equally wrong. Furthermore, historical criticism had led to doubts about the accuracy of the Bible. Shaftesbury was quick to expose any such inconsistencies and improbabilities. Again, he was disturbed by the prevalence of factional religious strife and noted the frequency with which the various sects each justified their opposing beliefs by reference to 'the Word of God.' Clearly Revelation was at best open to a variety of interpretations. Concerns such as these account for Shaftesbury's statement at the beginning of the ***Inquiry*** that it would be his goal to establish independent bases for morality and religion.

If any notion of innate ideas must be discarded, the existing alternative accounts of the foundation of morality—Hobbesian egoism, Divine Revelation or some doctrine of the "Will of God"—were all unacceptable, in Shaftesbury's opinion. Yet having been steeped in classical thought, he could not accept that morality was relative; he felt compelled, instead, to defend the principle that morality has an objective existence. The possibility occurred to Shaftesbury of rooting morality in what was then called the "nature of things." As a self-proclaimed Deist, he believed that the universe has been so created and designed by a benevolent God that "every thing is govern'd, order'd, or regulated *for the best*" (p. 12). It is a single system comprised of many levels of interconnecting subsystems, the parts of which interact lawfully. There are no chance events.

The concept of a system was to play a key role in Shaftesbury's thinking. Everything in the universe is composed of interacting parts which, since each has its own "End" or role to play in the grand "Oeconomy," must be in proportion, harmony and balance. In the animal kingdom, each creature—to fulfill its purpose in this scheme—is compelled by nature to seek its own "private Good and Interest" and its constitution is so created that all its "Appetites, Passions, or Affections" (p. 21) propel it in that direction. But no animal is complete in itself; each is "discouver'd to have relation to some other Being or Nature besides his own" (p. 24). Each species, in turn, is "a *Part*" of some other System" (p. 25) to whose well-being it contributes.

> For instance; To the Existence of the Spider, that of the Fly is absolutely necessary. The heedless Flight, weak Frame, and tender Body of this latter Insect, fits and determines him as a Prey, as the rough Make, Watchfulness, and Cunning of the former, fits him for Rapine, and the ensnaring part. The Web and Wing are suited to each other. . . . In the same manner are Flys also necessary to the Existence of other Creatures, both Fowls, and Fish.
>
> (pp. 26, 27)

There is, then, an harmonious "System of all Animals; an *Animal-Order* or *Oeconomy,* according to which the Animal Affairs are regulated and dispos'd" (p. 27). Animals in turn, existing in a balanced relationship with plants and inanimate things, form a part of the earthly

system or "Globe," which is itself dependent on the sun and the other planets. There is "in like manner a SYSTEM of *all Things, and a Universal Nature*" (p. 29). The human species is one of the earthly parts of this "Universal Nature." Each of its parts, individual men, has been created by God with his own self-interest, but 'no man is an island.' Each is a part of the whole of humanity and as such has roles to play and responsibilities to fulfill towards others. Just as the body is a whole, constructed of inter-related parts, yet with connections outside itself, so too is the mind. Its parts are the affections or passions.

The affections, like other 'parts,' do not operate singly: there is a "mutual Relation and Dependency" (p. 138) among them. And again, the ideal is harmonious balance. "*Timourousness,* and an habitual strong Passion of Fear," for example, "may be according to the *Oeconomy* of a particular Creature . . . while, *Courage* may be contrary to his *Oeconomy*; and therefore vitious" (p. 155). Even within one species there may be a different balance of the affections for the "different Sexes, Ages, and Growths" (p. 155) depending on the function and capacity of each. In Shaftesbury's words, "the inside work is fitted to the outward Action and Performance" (p. 214). Living creatures are not mere machines but are distinctive organic unities whose natural form is determined by their functions, roles or purposes in nature. In animals there is typically an exact balance among the affections. In man, however, the original motives—each of which has a "natural degree" in keeping with its appointed role—are capable of being strengthened by exercise and weakened by disuse. But for proper functioning in both man and animals there must always be "Order and Symmetry" (p. 138) among the parts. "Whoever is the least vers'd in this moral kind of Architecture, will find the inward *Fabrick* so adjusted, and the *whole* so nicely built; that the barely extending of a single Passion a little too far, or the continuance of it too long, is able to bring irrecoverable Ruin and Misery" (p. 214). Even with the most admirable of the social motives, if one is "over-great, it must be injurious to the rest" (p. 147), since too little attention will be paid to others equally natural and useful. Too intense a love of one's children, for example, will destroy the "effect of love" (p. 45). Since each affection has a useful role to play, there is no necessary conflict between the self and the social affections as long as each is in its proper degree and a proper balance exists among them. Indeed it is "impossible that the public Good, or Good of the System, can be preserv'd without . . . the Affections towards private Good" (p. 150). In further support of this argument is the contention that

> [a] part of an organism cannot be said to be in a healthy or 'natural' condition if it is working against the good of the whole of which it is a part. Since Shaftesbury assumes an organic relationship, between the individual

and the species, the man who acts against the good of the species is unhealthy or 'unnatural.' Since man's 'natural end is society,' to work for the public welfare is to work for one's own good, and vice versa. Self-interest is 'not only consistent with, but inseparable' from public interest."

(Crean, 1964, p. 43)

Mind is a microcosm of the external macrocosm. In its operation one sees the same principles of proportion, balance and harmony which govern all systems in the universe. An animal is good when its affections predispose it to fulfill its functions towards others of its type and man is moral when he has, through reflection, developed a "Notion of the Publick Interest."

> We have found, that to deserve the name of Good or Virtuous, a Creature must have all his Inclinations and Affections, his Disposition of Mind and Temper, suitable, and agreeing with the Good of his Kind, or of that System in which he is included, and of which he constitutes a PART.

(p. 129)

There is, therefore, a *natural* and objective basis for morality even if there may not be an innate idea of right and wrong. Morality is founded on those principles of human nature which an all-seeing and benevolent Deity has created.

Although morality always remained one of Shaftesbury's primary concerns, the significant differences between the 1699 and 1711 editions of the *Inquiry* attest to his increasing interest in aesthetics. Indeed, the content of several of the essays included in the *Characteristics* is primarily aesthetic. Concurrent with the emergence of beauty as a major focus of Shaftesbury's writing was an increase in his concern with the wider implications of Locke's dismissal of innate ideas. He realised that if there are no innate ideas, there is a problem in providing an objective basis for beauty as well as for morality. The classical conception of beauty, he noted, had avoided subjectivity and relativity without necessarily positing the existence of an innate idea of the beautiful. Adopting a version of this classical view, Shaftesbury argued that the beauty of "ordinary *Bodys,* or common Subjects of *Sense*" (p. 48) is dependent upon perception. When there is, in objects, a balance and harmony among the parts, the observer inevitably has an impression of beauty. "The Shapes, Motions, Colours, and Proportions of *the subjects of sense,* being presented to our Eye; there necessarily results a Beauty or Deformity, according to the different Measure, Arrangement and Disposition of their several Parts" (p. 48). There is a "natural Joy in the Contemplation of . . . *Harmony, Proportion and Concord"* (p. 171).

It is apparent that Shaftesbury's conceptions of beauty and morality were essentially identical; the one is a per-ception of external harmony, balance and proportion, the other of inward.

> The MIND, which is spectator or Auditor of other *Minds,* cannot be without its *Eye* and *Ear*; so as to discern Proportion, distinguish Sound, and scan each Sentiment or Thought which comes before it. It can let nothing escape its Censure. It feels the Soft and Harsh, the Agreeable and Disagreeable, in the Affections; and finds a *Foul* and *Fair,* a *Harmonious* and a *Dissonant,* as really and truly here, as in any musical Numbers, or in the outward Forms or Representations of sensible Things. Nor can it with-hold its *Admiration* and *Extasy,* its *Aversion* and *Scorn,* any more what relates to one than to the others of these Subjects.

(p. 49)

Virtue, then, is "no other than the Love of Order and Beauty in Society," and the pleasure to be derived from observing harmoniously balanced affections and their resultant actions is even greater than that from observing the physical world. Our sense of physical beauty is firmly rooted in the nature of things and so too, by analogy, is our sense of right and wrong. Although there may be no innate ideas, it is still possible to argue that there is an objective basis for ethical judgement and beauty.

It is ironic that Shaftesbury's elucidation of a moral sense should so soon have led to the very thing against which he was reacting—a thoroughly subjectivist theory of morality and aesthetics. His successor Francis Hutcheson adopted his idea of original senses of morality and beauty. But in the writings of that Hibernian Scot, the notion of the "inward Anatomy" as a microcosm of the universal macrocosm was de-emphasized, while the analysis of the psychological bases of the two innate senses—or rather three, for Hutcheson proposed both a benevolent sense and a moral sense which makes ethical judgement—are innate, and so formed as to respond naturally to specific features of the world, each also has a *learned,* and therefore idiosyncratic, component. As an inevitable product of experience, each of us acquires certain new and 'unnatural' ideas of what is beautiful or moral; these are then akin to the errors in our notions of right and wrong which Shaftesbury had attributed to custom and habit. Hutcheson, carrying the argument one step further, claimed that they are the result of associations of ideas. John Gay, in responding to Hutcheson, argued that if association could account for the individual differences in perceptions of beauty and morality, there is no logical reason why the innate faculties of beauty and morality could not be dispensed with entirely. Beauty and morality could be explained completely by this associational process. David Hartley and a host of other successors accepted Gay's argument and for the moment subjectivity had won the day.

Note

1. This and following numbered references are to the paragraphs of the *Inquiry*. The edition used, which is based on the final version included in the 1714 edition of the *Characteristics,* is that of David Walford.

Works Cited

Crean, S. Self-interest and Public Interest in Shaftesbury's Philosophy. *Journal of the History of Philosophy,* 2 (1964), 34-35.

Fowler, T. *Shaftesbury and Hutcheson.* London: Sampson Low, Marston, Searle & Rivington, 1882.

Rand, B. (ed.) *The Life, Unpublished Letters, and Philosophical Regimen of Anthony, Earl of Shaftesbury.* London: Swan Sonnenschein, 1900.

Shaftesbury, Anthony Ashley Cooper, Third Earl of. *Characteristics of Men, Manners, Opinions, Times. With a Collection of Letters.* (Vol. 1), 1757.

Shaftesbury, Anthony Ashley Cooper, Third Earl of. *An Inquiry Concerning Virtue, or Merit.* Edited by David Walford. Manchester: Manchester University Press, 1977.

Thomson, J. *The Seasons.* (18th ed.). London: 1790.

Voitle, R. B. Shaftesbury as a Moral Philosopher. *Westminster Review,* 63 (1955), 71-97.

Willey, B. *The Eighteenth Century Background.* London: Chatto & Windus, 1940.

Chester Chapin (essay date August 1983)

SOURCE: Chapin, Chester. "Shaftesbury and the Man of Feeling." *Modern Philology* 81, no. 1 (August 1983): 47-50.

[*In the following essay, Chapin explores the influence of Shaftesbury's ideas about benevolence on other eighteenth-century philosophers.*]

Referring to what he calls "the mid-eighteenth-century cult of the 'man of feeling,'" R. S. Crane argued that this cult owed much to "the propaganda of benevolence and tender feeling carried on with increasing intensity by the anti-Puritan, anti-stoic, and anti-Hobbesian divines of the Latitudinarian school."[1] Donald Greene has challenged this argument in the pages of this journal,[2] but neither Crane nor Greene has paid much attention to writers who might be said to exemplify this cult. Who were these men of feeling? Henry Mackenzie's *The Man of Feeling* was published in 1771, and while proponents of Crane's thesis might argue that "divines of the Latitudinarian school" had prepared the public for the appreciative reception of Mackenzie's novel, Gerard A. Barker has shown that the Harleyan mode of sensibility is more adequately explained by reference to the doctrine of sympathy (or empathy) as expounded in Adam Smith's *Theory of Moral Sentiments* (1759) than it is by reference to the writings or sermons of divines.[3] Smith's theory owes little to such writings or sermons but something to Francis Hutcheson,[4] whose own ethical thought owes much to the *Characteristics* of the third Earl of Shaftesbury, a deist whose ethical theory owes more to Plato and the ancient stoics than it does to the teachings of Christian divines.

As long ago as 1916, Cecil A. Moore had argued that Shaftesbury and his disciples were chiefly responsible for the rise of the ethic of benevolence and tender feeling during the period 1700-1760.[5] But Crane, taking note of Moore's article, argued that the influence of Shaftesbury began too late to have been an important factor in "the popular triumph of 'sentimentalism' toward 1750." Yet toward the conclusion of his essay, Crane admits that the influence of Shaftesbury in this "popular triumph" was very real and very important "especially after 1725 when it was reinforced by that of his disciple Hutcheson."[6]

Leaving the reader to make what he can of this, I would emphasize that Crane's essay blurs the distinction between the man of feeling and the benevolent man. The former was recognized as exceptional, however admirable. Mackenzie and his readers understood that Harley was unfit for this world. His extreme sensibility set him apart from other men of benevolent temper, an Allworthy in fiction or a Ralph Allen in real life. And while everyone approved of the benevolent man, not everyone approved of the man of feeling. Here I am concerned only with the latter. It seems safe to say that there were no eighteenth-century Harleys in real life, but some writers *did* impress contemporaries as especially distinguished for tender or sentimental feeling.

In one such writer the Shaftesburian influence appears to have replaced the "Latitudinarian" influence. Known to a wide circle of friends as a man possessed "of a most *tender* and *benevolent heart,*" the poet James Thomson everywhere praises what he calls "humanity" or "social love" as the highest virtue.[7] In the 1727 edition of *Summer,* Thomson praises Barrow and Tillotson, two of the "Latitudinarian" divines cited by Crane, as expressing "the Strength, and Elegance of Truth." But in the 1730 edition these divines are replaced by "the generous ASHLEY," the "Friend of Man." And Thomson's conception of social love as a divinely implanted emotion seems closer to Shaftesbury's moral sense theory than to the ethical teaching of Barrow or

Tillotson. In the opinion of James Sambrook, Thomson's latest editor, "Thomson's ethics are Shaftesburian; so is his rhapsodic tone, so at times, it seems, is his theology."[8]

Thomas Percy praised William Shenstone as "one of the most elegant and aimiable of men," whose "tender writings were but the counterparts of his heart, which was one of the best that ever animated a human body." According to Robert Dodsley, "tenderness" was Shenstone's "peculiar characteristic; his friends, his domestics, his poor neighbours, all daily experienced his benevolent turn of mind. Indeed, this virtue in him was often carried to such excess, that it sometimes bordered upon weakness."[9] Shenstone's twentieth-century biographer, Marjorie Williams, finds "echoes of Shaftesbury's philosophy on almost every page of Shenstone's *Works*."[10] Indeed, Shenstone writes as though certain Shaftesburian ideas were hardly a matter of controversy: "LORD Shaftesbury, in the genteel management of some familiar ideas, seems to have no equal. He discovers an eloignment from vulgar phrases much becoming a person of quality. His sketches should be studied, like those of Raphael. His Enquiry is one of the shortest and clearest systems of morality."[11] Shenstone was a man of leisure who devoted a major portion of his time and energy to the improvement of his *ferme ornée* at Leasowes. Hence it was important for Shenstone's self-esteem that taste be regarded as a faculty worth cultivating. Not only did Shaftesbury emphasize the importance of good taste; he argued that taste and virtue are near allied, an opinion Shenstone was happy to embrace. "Surely it is altogether unquestionable," he writes, "that taste *naturally* leads to virtue."[12] Shenstone may have regarded himself as a Christian, but in ethics he follows Shaftesbury and the ancients rather than Christian divines: "An obvious connexion may be traced betwixt moral and physical beauty; the love of symmetry and the love of virtue; an elegant taste and perfect honesty. We may, we must, rise from the love of natural to that of moral beauty: such is the conclusion of Plato, and of my Lord Shaftesbury."[13]

But perhaps the best example of the writer as man of feeling at mid-century is the minor poet and essayist, John Gilbert Cooper. If Dodsley believed that Shenstone's tenderness of feeling was sometimes carried to an excess, others believed this to be deplorably true of Cooper. A deist and an ardent admirer of Shaftesbury and Hutcheson, Cooper goes further than Shaftesbury in rejecting "the authority of analytical reason both in the arts and in the sphere of morals."[14] If for Shaftesbury our natural love for truth, beauty, and virtue "must mature in cognition and must be controlled by reason," for Cooper "whatever is true, just, and harmonious, whether in nature or morals, gives an instantaneous pleasure to the mind, *exclusive of reflection*"

(my italics).[15] Feeling is not all for Cooper, but it is much, and this valuation evidently impelled him on occasion toward an expression of sentimental feeling which some contemporaries found ridiculous.

According to Edmond Malone, Cooper "was the last of the *benevolists*, or sentimentalists, who were much in vogue between 1750 and 1760, and dealt *in general* admiration of virtue. They were all tenderness in *words*; their finer feelings evaporated in the moment of expression, for they had no connection with their practice. [Cooper] was the person whom, when lamenting most piteously that his son then absent might be ill or even dead, Mr. Fitzherbert so grievously disconcerted by saying, in a growling tone, 'Can't you take a post chaise, and go and see him?'"[16] This story, recorded also by Boswell and Mrs. Thrale, is included by Alexander Chalmers in his life of Cooper as an instance "of that romantic feeling which is apart from truth and nature."[17] As another instance of this, Chalmers cites Cooper's Latin epitaph upon the death of his first son, an infant who expired the day after he was born. What contemporaries thought of this effusion is sufficiently apparent from a burlesque translation which Chalmers included in his edition of Cooper's poetry because he believed it was precisely what so "ridiculous an original" deserved. A few lines will indicate its tenor: "Beneath doth lie / OF HENRY GILBERT COOPER / All that could die: / The prettiest, sweetest, dearest babe / That ever dropt into a grave. / This lovely boy, / His dad's first joy, / Was son of 'Squire JOHN, / And SUE his wife, who led their life, / At town call'd Thurgaton." And so on for seventeen more lines.[18]

The Fitzherbert story is biased testimony, reported by friends of Johnson, and Johnson entertained a hearty dislike for Cooper.[19] The Latin epitaph, on the other hand, is, as Chalmers says, "a curious specimen of *sentimental* grief." But Chalmers, unlike Malone, is not a biased critic. He has some complimentary things to say about Cooper's poetry and remarks that "if the general tenour of his works may be credited," Cooper "possessed an amiable and affectionate heart."[20]

I do not contend that writers especially known for tender or sentimental feeling are invariably admirers of Shaftesbury, but I hope enough has been said to show that Crane's is not the *only* genealogy of the man of feeling. One is not surprised to find that Cooper was deist. After all, the belief that man's innate goodness is such that he has no need of redemption through faith in Christ is more likely to encourage tender or sentimental feeling than the belief that man is a fallen creature. And, as Greene has shown, Barrow, Tillotson, and the other divines cited by Crane, however they might praise benevolence, never denied the Fall.[21]

Notes

1. R. S. Crane, "Suggestions toward a Genealogy of the 'Man of Feeling'" (1934), in *Studies in the Literature of the Augustan Age,* ed. Richard C. Boys (New York, 1966), pp. 206, 230.

2. Donald Greene, "Latitudinarianism and Sensibility: The Genealogy of the 'Man of Feeling' Reconsidered," *Modern Philology* 75 (1977): 159-83.

3. Gerard A. Barker, *Henry Mackenzie* (Boston, 1975), pp. 28-34.

4. Smith's theory differs in important respects from Hutcheson's, but Smith builds upon Hutcheson's conclusion that "the first perceptions of right and wrong" cannot be the "object of reason." These perceptions derive from "immediate sense and feeling," and so far as Smith is concerned, Hutcheson had explained this point "fully" and "unanswerably" in his "illustrations upon the moral sense." See Adam Smith, *Theory of Moral Sentiments* (New York, 1966), pp. 470-71 (pt. 7, sec. 3, chap. 2).

5. Cecil A. Moore, "Shaftesbury and the Ethical Poets in England," in *Backgrounds of English Literature, 1700-1760* (New York, 1969), pp. 3-52.

6. Crane, pp. 207, 229-30.

7. George Lyttleton, *Works,* ed. George Edward Ayscough, 3d ed. (London, 1777), 2:203 ("Dialogue 14" of Lyttleton's *Dialogues of the Dead* [1760]). According to Ralph Cohen, it became a commonplace of Thomson's biographers that the poet lived a life of "indolence and benevolence" (*The Art of Discrimination: Thomson's "The Seasons" and the Language of Criticism* [Berkeley, 1964], p. 111). For Thomson's praise of humanity and social love, see James Sambrook's commentary on *Spring* 878-903 in his edition of *The Seasons* (Oxford, 1981), p. 336.

8. Thomson, *The Seasons,* ed. Sambrook, p. xx. For the substitution of Shaftesbury for Barrow and Tillotson, see *Summer* 1551-55 and apparatus (pp. 130-31), and Sambrook's note to *Summer* 1551 (p. 361).

9. University Microfilms facsimile (Ann Arbor, Mich., 1977) of *The Correspondence of Thomas Percy and Richard Farmer,* ed. Cleanth Brooks (Baton Rouge, La., 1946), p. 37; William Shenstone, *Works,* ed. Robert Dodsley, 5th ed. (London, 1777), 1:8.

10. Marjorie Williams, *William Shenstone: A Chapter in Eighteenth Century Taste* (Birmingham, Warwickshire, 1935), p. 133.

11. Shenstone, *Works,* 2:174-75.

12. *Letters of William Shenstone,* ed. Marjorie Williams (Oxford, 1939), p. 529 (Shenstone to Richard Graves, October 26, 1759).

13. Shenstone, *Works,* 2:273. Dodsley tells us (*Works,* 1:8) that in his private opinions Shenstone "adhered to no particular sect, and hated all religious disputes. But whatever were his own sentiments, he always shewed great tenderness to those who differed from him."

14. Hoxie Neale Fairchild, *Religious Trends in English Poetry* (New York, 1942), 2:323. Fairchild's work is dated, but his account of Cooper's religion (pp. 320-24) seems to me accurate in almost every respect. In his chief poem *The Power of Harmony* (1745), and in his *Letters Concerning Taste* (1754), Cooper attacks "superstition," but it is immediately apparent that "superstition" is a code word for "Christianity."

15. Stanley Grean, *Shaftesbury's Philosophy of Religion and Ethics: A Study in Enthusiasm* (Athens, Ohio, 1967), p. 245; Cooper's prefatory "design" to *The Power of Harmony* in *The Works of the English Poets,* ed. Alexander Chalmers (London, 1810), 15:519.

16. Sir James Prior, *Life of Edmond Malone* (London, 1860), p. 427.

17. James Boswell, *Life of Johnson,* ed. G. B. Hill and L. F. Powell (Oxford, 1934-50), 3:149; *Thraliana,* ed. Katharine C. Balderston, 2d ed. (Oxford, 1951), p. 62; *Works of the English Poets,* 15:504.

18. *Works of the English Poets,* 15:504, 538.

19. Prior, p. 428.

20. *Works of the English Poets,* 15:504-6.

21. Greene (n. 2 above), pp. 169-73.

Robert Voitle (essay date 1984)

SOURCE: Voitle, Robert. "The Patterns of Shaftesbury's Later Thought 1704-1713." In *The Third Earl of Shaftesbury, 1671-1713,* pp. 313-66. Baton Rouge, La.: Louisiana State University Press, 1984.

[*In this excerpt, Voitle discusses Shaftesbury's philosophical works after 1700, which he argues are heavily influenced by Platonic idealism but also stress the importance of the creative imagination.*]

Before considering Shaftesbury's ***Philosophical Rhapsody*** it would be well to see where it lies among his more serious studies. His earliest printed philosophical work is his preface to the *Select Sermons* of Benjamin Whichcote published in 1698. He must have begun this after Thomas Firmin's death the previous year. In 1699 *An Inquiry Concerning Virtue or Merit* was published by Toland, but as we have seen there is evidence that Shaftesbury began working on it and probably completed it long before he wrote the preface to Whichcote. Still another reason for assuming that the *Inquiry* is early is that by the time *The Sociable Enthusiast* [SE] was printed his fundamental attitude toward humanity seems to have changed markedly. The same bitter judgments of humanity we find in *Inquiry I* are typical of his letters from the early 1690s—those on Carolina, for example. But a decade later, the edge has gone from his bitterness, even though he may have no better practical hopes for the human race. He has grown up, he has gone through a period of self-examination in Holland, and, despite his illness and his complaints, these are better times for him. We must also, I suppose, give some credit to the idealism of Plato, whose influence is obvious by 1700.

He began to write his **"Exercises"** between the time of his arrival in Holland and his return in April or May of 1699. Surely the next "philosophical" work was *The Adept Ladys,* which is dated January 19, 1702. It is not yet published. Following this is *The Sociable Enthusiast,* which was printed privately in 1703 or 1704, for a very limited distribution. S. F. Whitaker in a fine article, perhaps too modest in its conclusions, established that Arent Furly had found an imperfect copy of the *Enthusiast* in Rotterdam and then described it in a letter of September 6, 1704 NS.[1] This contradicts Shaftesbury's own statement about the book to Lord Somers in a letter dated October 20, 1705, that "No body has sett Eyes on it, nor shall, besides yourself."[2] Whitaker also remarks that the book appears to be of English rather than the finer Dutch workmanship, which could push the date of its printing back to 1703. The two copies in the Record Office are, so far as I know, all that survive, Arent's having disappeared and that of Lord Somers probably burned up in that infamous fire that destroyed his library.

The Sociable Enthusiast is in the form of a dialogue, which oddly enough is stripped of much of its drama by being recited in the past tense. There are three major figures: Palemon, a young man of high rank and character, who knows all about the nature of plants and animals but has little fondness for mankind. He is an engaged person and a rationalist, yet scrupulous in matters of religion. Then there is Philocles the quondam skeptic, who carries the burden of the argumentation. He knows nothing, believes all. Finally, there is Theocles, the mild enthusiast with no trace of bigotry, all understanding and forbearance. He loves the muses and they love him. Theocles bears Shaftesbury's message, but we must heed his prefatory note, that "as for the Characters, & Incidents; they are neither wholly feign'd nor wholly true."

Palemon begs Philocles to recount what they had talked about the day before, which he does and then looks back earlier to two days spent in discussion with Theocles. The sequence of tenses becomes mixed up—even Shaftesbury shows some confusion in his emendations—so that it is difficult to tell whether he recounts all three days to Palemon in one day or two. Palemon, already a convert, must in the twice-told dialogue, first appear a skeptic, only revealing the full extent of his own change in attitude at the end of the essay. Obviously, I am not the first to note how muddled the book is; in his *Miscellaneous Reflections* Shaftesbury admits its weaknesses as a dialogue and yet defends them. First, in a very long paragraph he proves, by recasting it, that he could have told the story straightforwardly, but he related the story as a philosophical adventure or rhapsody to avoid giving the impression that a dialogue was involved. After all a writer must create some impression of verisimilitude and he was "put to a hard shift, to contrive how or with what probability he might introduce Men of any Note or Fashion, reasoning expressly and purposely . . . for two or three hours together, on mere PHILOSOPHY and MORALS" (*Char.,* III, 287). These subjects are now relegated to the school, the university, and pulpit. In any case the mode is now altogether unfashionable. In the *Miscellaneous Reflections* he also speaks of "the direct way of DIALOGUE; which at present lies so low, and is us'd only now and then, in our Party-Pamphlets, or new-fashion'd *theological Essays,*" which is a glance at the replies in dialogue to his *Letter Concerning Enthusiasm.* It is hard to know how to take all of this, for, as the preliminary notes to Shaftesbury's *Second Characters* prove, his miscellaneous style involves one of the most complex personas of the day. He laughs at others continually, loud and very softly, but often he is the butt of his own humor.

Days one and two of *The Sociable Enthusiast: A Philosophical Adventure, Written to Palemon* are largely concerned with repeating, adding to, and rarely, modifying what has already been said in *Inquiry I.* Indeed, the book is cited and Theocles, especially, defends "our friend" against his opponents. Only one printed response to *Inquiry I.* has been found so far, but enough copies of the treatise must have been distributed to cause a good deal of comment, if Shaftesbury's defense is any measure.[3]

Some of the differences between the *Inquiry* and the *Enthusiast* are due to a sagacious change in the nature of the persona he offers us. Consider the attitude toward a future state. In the *Enthusiast* a strong conviction of reward and punishment is necessary until man can be led up to affection and a disinterested love of God. The existence of a future state he proves quite traditionally by the imperfections of this world, which seldom rewards virtue. And he asks in a Miltonic vein, how would there be merit in the world without the sort of trial which an imperfect world provides? Philocles is even willing to accept miracles so long as they happened in olden times and are received from the best authorities. Neither Catholic saints nor those other saints of the seventeenth century need apply, though. Any reader of the **"Exercises"** knows that Shaftesbury's personal belief in these propositions is weak. But the therapeutic **"Exercises"** should also teach us that how a man acts is far more important than the real truth of what he believes. Contemporary Americans are especially suspicious of this theory of truth; Shaftesbury as a moralist never had any hesitations, which is one of many reasons why he is opposed to systems. Shaftesbury's moral comments, indeed his very attitudes, when he talks to servants, to farmers, or when he writes to Wilkinson, Ainsworth, or even Arent Furly are irreproachably pious in the most conventional sense.

When his ultimate purposes are metaphysical rather than moral, Shaftesbury usually speaks with a different sort of conviction:

> For as the Branch is united, and is all one with the Tree, so is the Tree with the Earth, Air, and Water, which feed it, and as much as the fertile Mold is fitted to the Tree, as much as the strong and upright Trunk of the Oak or Elm is fitted to the twining and clinging Branches of the Vine or Ivy; so much are the Leaves, the Seeds, and Fruits of these Trees fitted to the various Animals; and they again to one another, and to the Elements in which they live, and to which they are in a manner join'd, as either by Wings for the Air, Fins for the Waters, Feet for the Earth, and other things of a like nature.
>
> (*SE,* 91-92)[4]

Theocles is speaking, but all of the three speakers are what now would be called ecologically sound. Philocles asks Palemon, who knows much about natural history, whether the unity of visible nature does not imply a continuous design. When Palemon admits this truth, Philocles then asks whether this does not imply a universal mind which alone can view the whole universal system at once and see it reconciled of inconsistencies.

It is because Palemon sees nature as a whole that he is distressed by natural evil when it occurs. Philocles has an explanation for him new to Shaftesbury's published work. Natural evil is caused by conflict of systems. One system is "o'erpowr'd by a superior Rival, and by another Nature's justly conquering Force" (*SE,* 29). Prodigies are merely another reflection of the order persisting in the great chain of being, which is universally recognized as just in its workings. "Every corruptible and mortal Nature by its Mortality and Corruption yields only to some better, and all in common to that best and highest Nature, which is incorruptible and immortal" (*SE,* 29-30).

In addition to loving nature, Palemon loves individuals, but he hates mankind for their corruption. This is perhaps the weakest phase of *The Sociable Enthusiast,* for the treatise is in a sense too cosmic in its point of view to devote much time to the problem. Perhaps the best exchange takes place between Philocles and Theocles on the subject of friendship, private and public. Philocles admits that he never found it unpleasing to serve a friend. He also admits that gratitude and bounty are among the chief acts of friendship. Theocles then asks him whether weaknesses discovered in the giver should diminish gratitude in the receiver. No, Philocles replies, it makes it more satisfying because the weaknesses can be borne as failings in a friend. Theocles gets him to concede that bounty is owed to relations whether or not they are deserving. And with this he asks:

> Consider then what it was you said, when you objected against the Love of *Mankind* because of Human Frailty; and seem'd to scorn the *Publick,* because of its Misfortunes. Where can we with Pleasure exert Friendship, if not here? To what shou'd we be true and grateful in the World, if not to Mankind and that Society to which we owe so much? What are the Faults or Blemishes that can excuse such an Omission or that in a grateful Mind can ever lessen the Satisfaction of making a grateful kind Return?
>
> (*SE,* 45)

The appeal becomes even stronger when we recognize the strength the bonds of natural affection have for Shaftesbury, and his conviction that weak man is safe only in a strong society.

Most of what is new in *The Sociable Enthusiast* is focused in the third book where Philocles is by the rhapsodic utterances of Theocles solidly convinced of the truth of what he says. During the last thirty years or so a considerable disagreement has arisen over what Shaftesbury intended, especially when the *Enthusiast* in its successive forms is contrasted with the *Inquiry.* No two interpreters of Shaftesbury are ever likely to agree in full—he has too many roots in the past and augured too much for the future. Yet a good many of these disagreements are resolved when Shaftesbury is looked at broadly, and readers admit, as his critics sometimes fail to, that he shares the eclecticism of his day. In a world where the whole intellectual milieu was in upheaval, Shaftesbury chose a novel means to preserve his inheritance. Those who followed him, however, Continental aestheticians or English moralists or still others, picked and chose as they wished. Of course, they chose differently. Most disastrously for an understanding of what Shaftesbury attempted to do, certain phases of his thought were generally ignored by all who borrowed from him.

For the first time in **The Sociable Enthusiast** he publicly revealed how strong the appeal of the past was for him. In later editions this was toned down, so that the truth that he would have preferred to have been born a pagan was somewhat obscured. Publicly he admired Roman republicanism; philosophically he is a follower of Marcus Aurelius, Epictetus, and Xenophon; in art, the choice of Hercules was his ideal subject. Study of the Ancients is the privilege of the few but they are brothers in this regardless of rank. One of Shaftesbury's most meticulously revised letters is the one that he wrote to Pierre Coste, Locke's amanuensis, on the subject of Horace. His classical correspondents range from General Stanhope and the great Dutch scholar Gronovius, whose *Epictetus* he had hoped to have dedicated to him, to Stanhope's man of business, Arent Furly, and his own librarian Paul Crell. As Theocles remarks to Philocles in a passage on retirement, which was tactfully altered before the work was reprinted as **The Moralists,** Horace and Virgil, however different, "both join'd, to love Retirement; and for the sake of such a Life as you call contemplative, they were willing to sacrifice the highest Advantages, Pleasures, and Favour of a Court, more agreeable and polite than any that has since been known" (**SE,** 38).

Nor is there any question about the Platonic influence in **The Sociable Enthusiast** and elsewhere among Shaftesbury's works. Take his attitude toward science, for instance. Shaftesbury is quite willing to use the discoveries of contemporary science, but only to the point where one grasps the variety and splendor of the world and at the same time understands its underlying coherence and harmony: "But 'tis in vain for us to search the Mass it self of *Matter*: seeking to know its Nature. . . . If knowing only some of the Rules of *Motion,* we seek to trace it further, 'tis in vain we follow it into the Bodys it has reach'd. . . . In vain we try to fathom the Abyss of *Space*" (**SE,** 159-60). And with a glance at Locke: "In vain we labour to understand that Principle of *Sence* and *Thought,* which seeming in us to depend so much on Motion, yet differs so much from it, and from Matter it self. . . . And thus are we made sensible that the Nature of all the Beings in this Universe is *Incomprehensible* . . . attended nevertheless with such Assurance of their Existence, as is beyond the Report of these our Senses. . . . By which we may learn that the Assurance we have of the Existence of these Beings . . . comes from Thee, the God of Truth" (**SE,** 160-61). Nature has a greater lesson to teach.

More specifically it is clear that much of the Platonism in **The Sociable Enthusiast** follows the general pattern of the Cambridge School. Ernst Cassirer long ago cited direct parallels between John Smith's *Select Discourses* and the thought in **The Moralists.** The Cambridge men represent what was an extreme case of a growing tendency among broad churchmen, a tendency which can only be understood in relation to the growth of atomism and the stress among some writers on the sanctions of reward and punishment. Shaftesbury and the Platonists look on the Deity in an optimistic, Arminian way as a God who consults his own goodness in giving laws, a God who is served best by disinterested love, rather than slavishly by men who see God reflected in their own cramped and peevish minds, a God whose mind is paralleled by the best qualities which an ideal human mind could achieve in theory.

As we noted before, he is distinguished from the Platonists by the absence of references to Christ, and he is also much less dogmatic than these churchmen in his attitude toward innatism. He moved from a precisely Lockean definition of moral sense in the **Inquiry** to something more broadly based, what is best defined as a temper—"all that flows from your good Understanding, Sense, Knowledg and Will; all that is engender'd in your Heart . . . and all that derives it self from your Parent-*Mind*" (**SE,** 210). "If you dislike the word *Innate,* let us change it, if you will, for INSTINCT; and call Instinct, that which Nature teaches, exclusive of Art, Culture or Discipline" (**SE,** 212).

Obviously it is a reasonable approach for a Platonist to focus on the central role of an inward colloquy, involving a tension between actuality and the ideal. We know how poorly Shaftesbury thinks of his own conduct from the **"Exercises,"** and the same book illustrates one phase of the dialectic in action. Does this mean that, as some suggest, we must then abandon the notion that the moral sense was first defined by Shaftesbury in purely Lockean terms? Are the Platonic dialectic and the Lockean epistemology compatible for Shaftesbury? Both Robert Marsh in his excellent *Four Dialectical Theories of Poetry* and Stanley Gean in *Shaftesbury's Philosophy of Religion and Ethics* attack E. L. Tuveson's *Imagination as a Means of Grace* for its description of the Lockean origins of moral sense, and presumably they would also object to my similar description in "Shaftesbury's Moral Sense," were they aware of it.[5] All we can conclude is that Shaftesbury did not see any incompatibility, since in 1711 he described the moral sense in terms which will seem Lockean enough to anyone well acquainted with Locke's works and with Locke's arguments in letters to Lord Ashley in the 1690s. And the Earl coupled it with an analogy which is dialectic in impulse and Platonic in spirit.

In regard to his Platonic impulses, Shaftesbury did not sit down one sunny afternoon and begin **Characteristicks.** It is instead a pastiche, the product of over twenty years of thought by a mind which was agile, receptive, and very fruitful. Ideally, had not illness, his family and personal affairs, his changing tastes and a very short life been involved, he might have made it more of a piece. Yet one does not know whether it would ever have become more than a miscellany. Shaftesbury when young was a systematizer; when older, he said the final word on systems.

Shaftesburian "enthusiasm," which is fed by the imagination, also reflects his Platonism. The ultimate purposes of the rhapsodic meditation on nature seem to be moral, though it signalizes a revolution in aesthetic thought. Book Three of the dialogue tells the story of the conversion of Philocles to the belief of Theocles by alternating rational and rhapsodic and imaginative utterances. In the rational sections Philocles provides a counterpoint; in the rhapsodic section he largely listens to Theocles. Both reason and rhapsody are necessary to convince him. Obviously the protracted raptures of Theocles are in a sense cognitive. From these utterances Philocles may learn nothing more than he has already learned rationally, but the inspired meditations fix in his mind permanently that the cosmos is unified and is presided over by a benevolent spirit.

What Susie I. Tucker describes in her book which she calls an extended footnote to the *O.E.D.* definition of *enthusiasm* tends to confirm this. The word, which had been a technical religious term in the seventeenth century, either negative or positive or both, expanded broadly and rapidly as the seventeenth became the eighteenth century, and by 1750 it involves philosophy, writing and the various arts, and even love.[6] When Philocles is satisfied to be called a *new enthusiast* Theocles replies,

> [I] am content you shou'd call this Love of ours *Enthusiasm*; allowing it the Privilege of its Fellow Passions. For is there a fair and plausible Enthusiasm, a reasonable Extasy and Transport allow'd to other Subjects, such as Architecture, Painting, Musick; and shall it be exploded *here*? Are there Senses by which all those other Graces and Perfections are perceiv'd? and none by which to comprehend this higher Perfection and Grace? Is it so preposterous to bring that Enthusiasm hither, and transfer it from those *secondary* Objects, to this *Original* and *Comprehensive One*? . . . But it is not instantly we acquire this Sense by which these Beautys are discoverable. Labour and Pains are requir'd, and Time to cultivate a natural Genius, ever so apt or forward. . . . Is Study, Science, and Learning necessary to understand all Beautys else? and for *the Sovereign Beauty* is there no Skill or Science requir'd?

> (*SE,* 199-201)

Thus it is only by hard training, by strict reasoning, and by enraptured fancy—creative imagination—that there is any hope of the individual glimpsing the ideal. Shaftesbury turns to the very old tradition of inspiration

in art to resolve his metaphysical problems. Ultimately his suggestions were to have far more impact on art than on metaphysics.

For England, these changes by which mankind gets back some of the qualities stripped from reason by English empiricism are well discussed by Professor Tuveson in his *Imagination as a Means of Grace*. There is of course no way of precisely determining where these ideas began. As R. L. Brett remarks, before beginning a chapter on Shaftesbury's effect on later thought, "The tracing of so-called literary influences is a dangerous and generally a profitless pursuit. The influence of one writer upon another is rarely a direct and simple matter, for writers, like other men, live amid a complicated field of forces, personal, social and intellectual, and their work is generally the product of all of these."[7] The roots of Shaftesbury's thought are old, as are those of Locke, but it is ironic that only fourteen years after the publication of the *Essay* Locke's own disciple should be laying the basis for the refutation of the book's main presumption.

A number of ideas which appear later in Shaftesbury's works are adumbrated in *The Sociable Enthusiast* and most of these can be passed over until they are developed more fully. One, however, is stated so clearly that it will pay to look at it now: "Therefore the Beautifying, not the Beautify'd, is really Beautiful" (*SE,* 204). It is statements such as this that really explain why so many more books on Shaftesbury have been written by Continentals than by Englishmen. And the full explanation still eludes those who think in moral terms. Even so shrewd an observer of broad currents of thought as Charles Verecker may know but seems unwilling to venture: "During the last two and a half centuries, Shaftesbury, not unlike Byron, has enjoyed a more exalted reputation on the Continent than at home. It is not easy to explain this addition, but at the time no doubt his championing of universalist optimism met with approval wherever Leibnizian influences penetrated."[8] Verecker shortly turns, quite properly, to Hutcheson, a more systematic moralist. It may well be that empiricism is to blame for the fact that a century later, notions such as these had to be imported back to England from Continental writers who had first learned them from Shaftesbury's *Characteristicks.*

This particular passage from the *Enthusiast* comes when Theocles, borrowing from Plotinus, is using an artistic analogy to explain the nature of the first order of beauty, forming forms, the minds of men themselves. Divine inspiration had always been an element in aesthetic theory, but the theory usually focused, as in Aristotle, either on the artifact or on the effect upon the audience. The ultimate result of statements such as this was to turn attention to the artist and thus supply a basis for Romantic critical theory. For Shaftesbury's own purposes, he had found what seemed to him a far more effective way of bridging the gap between the actual and the ideal than the concept he had once based on Lockean epistemology, yet he remained until the end a moralist.

Although Shaftesbury's notebooks show that he was busy during the interval, it is at least four years after the printing of *The Sociable Enthusiast* that another philosophical work of his appears. Happily, the mysteries which surround the original publications of *An Inquiry* and *The Moralists* are absent in the case of his *Letter Concerning Enthusiasm* (1708). He sent Lord Somers a holograph copy in another's hand in September 1707. The following March, Shaftesbury discovered that a friend of Somers to whom it had been lent had given it to a "worthy Character of good Estate, great Reading & wonderfull Curiosity in the search of Books & Authors." This reader had passed it around to various members of his club, one of whom made a copy and intended to have it published as by the author of *A Tale of a Tub,* to whom all ascribed it. Shaftesbury then wrote to Somers begging him to burn or conceal his copy of the *Letter,* and his letter gives us a candid glance at the motives behind his writing the essay. In the first place, though he may not have intended it to be published, he does not fear acknowledging it or dedicating it to Somers. His own reputation, as he said the following July, "he values not: For be it treated as it will; It can neither hurt nor benefitt the Publick, whose service he is so unfitt for." He made only one change for publication: in the manuscript he said that if an old prelate can believe in fairies, a heathen poet should be able to believe in the muses. It seems very likely that the old prelate, referred to in correspondence as a bishop now active in the Whig cause, is Edward Fowler (1632-1714). Later in the year when Shaftesbury's edition was published to forestall the one to be published by the club member, the old prelate was apparently protected by changing "you know" into "you once knew" in the printed version.[9] Despite the uproar caused by the publication, only stylistic changes were made in two later editions. He was willing to expand and explain his theory elsewhere, but Shaftesbury had made his statement and he was willing to stick by it.

The clamor over the French Prophets which gave Shaftesbury the opportunity to write his *Letter* has been well described.[10] The Camisards were a group of Huguenots that grew up in the Cevennes after the revocation of the Edict of Nantes in 1685. They were ruthlessly repressed, but instead of fleeing fought back vigorously in an exceedingly bloody campaign. According to Ronald Knox, they had English support; this must have been nominal, however. What the English may have welcomed in France was soon found to be unwelcome at home, when several Prophets emigrated to England in the winter of 1706. Their prophecies delivered in every possible antic manner—from trances, in languages unknown to the speaker, with all sorts of bodily contortions, even walking on hands—soon found them converts and sympathizers. The Huguenots disowned the Prophets and three preachers were pilloried, but naturally they thrived on repression. At the same time a rather astonishingly large literary effort was mounted against them and it succeeded very rapidly only because the Prophets themselves made its success inevitable. As one essayist remarked, they had to be fools rather than knaves, because no knave would ever date his prophecies so exactly. April 29, 1708, was the date when London would be destroyed by divine fire. This was not critical, however, since other dates had also been chosen. However, May 25 of the same year did prove fatal. The Prophets agreed that then, six months after his burial, Dr. Thomas Emes would arise from the grave. The Train Bands were called out to control any mass hysteria which might arise. This all too precise timing explains why the publisher of the *Letter* says in the original preface of 1708 that he would have published the essay the summer before, had he been able to find a copy. Tardy pens and tardy publishers account for what came out later; such wellings forth are not stopped off all at once. After May of 1708 only the diehards among the Prophets remained and they were no longer infectious.

In his *Letter* Shaftesbury argues that the melancholy Prophets and other fanatics should be laughed at, not punished. Only ridicule will provide the test whether their gravity is true or false. False gravity is contagious and if we rely on the magistrate to counter it, it may well grow worse. "It was the Wisdom of some wise Nations, to let people be Fools as much as they pleas'd, and never to punish seriously what deserv'd only to be laugh'd at." Nor need we fear mixing raillery and religion. Indeed, good religion requires good humor, which is the best preventative of enthusiasm and atheism. So long as we use good manners we never fear good humor. Too often we look to God only when we are in trouble and the God we envision is often the reflection of our own emotional turbulence. God is either good or he does not exist; this presumption is prior to both revelation and reason. First we must find out according to the cool principles of reason what is the life of a good man, and then live it. One may become a fair judge of music without being a musician, but only a good man can know the good God. Man, of course, has a natural inclination to enthusiasm, and it is our task to distinguish the ordinary species from divine enthusiasm or inspiration. The latter moves the right sort of heroes, statesmen, poets, orators, musicians, and, even, philosophers. An irrational impulse is just only when a good man can examine its roots in a rational manner and find them sound. As if to emphasize the point, Shaftesbury refers to himself in the final paragraph as "your Enthusiastick Friend." What began as an attack on false enthusiasm ends up as a treatise on telling the false from the true species.

Ronald Knox calls the *Letter Concerning Enthusiasm* "the only considerable literary work to which the Camisard agitation gave rise," and I suppose he is correct. Writers were, at least, debating its merits for decades after the rest of the anti-Camisard literature was forgotten and the French Prophets themselves had slipped from human memory. No doubt almost all of what Shaftesbury said in the *Letter* was coffeehouse conversation in certain groups in London, yet one is reminded of a story which has become attached to the first Earl of Shaftesbury. When asked by a lady about his religious persuasion, he replied, "the religion of all wise men." And asked further what that was, he responded, "wise men never tell." By speaking out in deistic tones, Shaftesbury joined the Enlightenment, described by Peter Gay in his brilliant essay as "a single army with a single banner, with a large central corps, a right and left wing, daring scouts, and lame stragglers." It was a philosophic family, drawn together by, among other things, "the demands of political strategy" and "the hostility of church and state."[11]

Although it was not ascribed to him immediately, the *Letter* is the first of Shaftesbury's works to attract much attention. The preface to Whichcote was done in a very arch manner, in a place where most would expect broad churchmanship, and the underlying cynicism must have been missed. Although it has been pointed out that the early version of the *Inquiry* was responded to, it does not seem to have made much of a splash. Whether or not we believe Shaftesbury destroyed copies, the 1699 *Inquiry* is a very scarce book, and, as I have pointed out, we have records of only three or four copies of *The Sociable Enthusiast,* which was printed but not published in 1703 or 1704.

Shaftesbury certainly knew what to expect when he published his *Letter Concerning Enthusiasm.* The Church realized it was under attack not merely from the traditional forces of innovation but also by Deists and those whose doctrines smacked of absolute infidelity. If the Deists and atheists felt freer after 1688, there was also a vast army of defenders on the other side ready to rush hastily into print.[12] I have read three of the immediate replies to the *Letter Concerning Enthusiasm.* Edward Fowler, the Latitudinarian bishop of Gloucester, is the most brilliant, though his shotgun response lacks definition.[13]

The issues are better defined in *Remarks upon the Letter Concerning Enthusiasm. In a Letter to a Gentleman* (1708). In the first place the author objects bitterly to the mixing of ridicule and religion. Some bounds are necessary on religious speculation or perfect infidelity will result. Secondly he protests that Shaftesbury's defi-

nition of God, partly from the Cambridge Platonists, partly Stoic, does not go far enough. To goodness must be added wisdom, righteousness, and purity. He must legislate against immorality, else how pure? He must enforce penalties, how else wise? He must discriminate, how else righteous? God is not the supreme manager but the supreme governor. Similarly he objects to Shaftesbury's definition of goodness as love of the public, study of the good, and promoting the interest of the world—is there no mention of righteousness and holiness here? Finally, all through his *Letter* Shaftesbury, ever the philosophe, had made slyly disparaging comparisons, and some not so sly, of the Ancients with the Moderns. According to his cyclic concept of history the world began to decline in the first centuries after Christ and is now rising slightly, a concept which puts most Christian history in the dark and superstitious ages. Thus the author of the *Remarks* fails to believe the story of the old prelate believing in fairies, which Shaftesbury had told to make the classical poets' faith in the muses more acceptable, and he bitterly rejected the identification of the fathers of the Church with the enthusiastic French Prophets.

Despite Shaftesbury's disclaimer about his reputation, he was sensitive on one point: he wanted to establish a reputation for personal integrity to counterbalance that acquired by his grandfather, whose ideas for England were as completely embraced as his character was deplored. It does seem likely from the evidence that the superficially optimistic, and more trivial, phase of his thought did, by forty or fifty years after his death, triumph over what he said in the *Letter,* but why did he expose his ideas on Christ and the Church in a public controversy when he could have implied these things elsewhere, politely, with a fraction of the risk to his reputation for piety? Granted, he did not expect it to be published at first; on the other hand, his only compunctions involved the comment on Fowler. I think that the answer is that, though the essay seems slight, it definitely exposes fresh ideas which are important to the development of Shaftesbury's thought as a whole.

Although ridicule had always been used in the way he used it, who in the modern world had spelled out so clearly its function in distinguishing false from true gravity? Although scholars have not found them, no doubt Shaftesbury has predecessors. But Shaftesbury got the credit. Ridicule and raillery are entirely too perjorative to convey his meaning, as he soon realized, and afterward he stresses the state of mind, good humor, which he also had clearly defined in the *Letter,* though too far on to do him much good, even if most of his audience had been disposed to understand him.

This brings me to the second major idea he brings forth: the distinction between false and true enthusiasm. Within a year or so *The Moralists* is to be actually published for the first time and dedicated to Lord Somers. Unless his readers clearly have this distinction in mind they will not be able to understand what he will be saying in that book. In his time the word *enthusiasm* had a universally negative ring to it in philosophy or religion. Only in aesthetics was it acceptable and there in a very limited sense.[14] What better occasion for him to distinguish between the two meanings than during the furor over the French Prophets?

Shaftesbury's success always depended on finding an adequate reply to Locke's epistemology and his first version of the "moral sense" was cast in Lockean terms. From the **"Exercises"** we find that his own thinking on enthusiasm was shifting over in the period from 1698 to 1700. He defines very precisely what it means to be in this sense rational, what the mind must be stripped of. On his second journey to Holland in 1698 he says, "If the Writer of *the Table* describ'd, after such a manner, *Imposture* & her Cup; if the Draught was such in those days; what is it now? and how deeply have *We* drunk?" "Consider the Age: vulgar Religion: how thou hast been bred: and what impressions yet remaining of that sordid, shamefull, Nauseouse Idea of Deity." But when these impressions are purged, "then it is that thou mayst soundly, un-affected, & safely sing those Hymns to God which the Divine Man mentions" (**"Ex.,"** 102, 100).[15]

Two years later, January 20, 1700, though not yet pure, he is willing to proclaim himself an enthusiast in a way which renders all other sorts of enthusiasm analogous but far subordinate. After describing love of the artificer as enthusiasm, he writes,

> Happy Me, if I can grow in this sort of Enthusiasme, so as to loose all those Enthusiasms of every other kind, and be whole towards *this*. Shall others willingly be accounted Enthusiastick, & even affect this sort of Passion as Virtuoso's, Men of Witt, Pleasure, Politeness, each in their severall ways, & for their severall Objects (a Song, a Picture, a Pile of Stones, a Human Body, a Shape, a Face:) and shall thou be concern'd at being found Enthusiastick upon another Subject, so far excelling in itself, & which is Originall to all the rest?"
>
> (**"Ex.,"** 153)

Only a rational man contemplating a rational God can be genuinely enthusiastic. He feels that he has found the answer already to what Locke had to say about enthusiasm in the fourth edition of the *Essay*: "And what readier way can there be to run ourselves into the most extravagant errors and miscarriages, than thus to set up fancy for our supreme and sole guide, and to believe any proposition to be true, any action to be right, only because we believe it to be so."[16] The *Letter* prepares the way for *The Moralists*.

Sensus Communis: An Essay on the Freedom of Wit and Humour

Sensus Communis: An Essay on the Freedom of Wit and Humour (1709) defends Shaftesbury's *Letter Concerning Enthusiasm*, while at the same time more cau-

tiously restates what he said in that essay, and it also gives a definition of what he means by *common sense*, which is almost but not quite another subject.[17] The trouble with his defending the *Letter* was that he was not willing to admit that the also anonymous *Sensus Communis* was by the same author. Yet he took no real pains to conceal the fact. For instance, he says, "I have known some of those grave Gentlemen [to?] undertake to correct an Author for defending the Use of Raillery, who at the same time have upon every turn made use of that Weapon, tho they were naturally so very aukard at it" (**Char.,** I, 65). The three immediate responses to the *Letter* which I have seen all used raillery to attack the railer, though only Bishop Fowler really is awkward, largely because he uses too much of it. Even the subtitle of *Sensus Communis* seems to be a response to the critics of the *Letter Concerning Enthusiasm.*

More important than Shaftesbury's defense of his *Letter* is his clarification of what he meant by *ridicule* in that essay. Considering the circumstances of its publication, there was plentiful opportunity for misunderstanding; Lord Somers is hardly typical of its eventual audience. Shaftesbury sent a copy of *Sensus Communis* to Somers but, as he explained in the very bitter letter which accompanied it, he did not dedicate it to him, because he did not want him to be publicly linked with a supposed enemy of the Church. The book is directed to a friend who with Shaftesbury has recently spent an evening with a group of skeptical gentlemen. The conversation ranges widely and by the time it is finished, every issue, large and small, has been reduced to stuff and nonsense. The friend is puzzled by this and *Sensus Communis* is Shaftesbury's explanation.

First he rejects the punning, metaphysical humor of an earlier day in favor of the easy, light, yet functional humor of his own time, a humor which is consistent with the free dialectic now preferred over the heavy rhetoric of the past. Of course, with regard to this sort of wit, he is speaking of private discussion among friends. Those met accidentally should not be forced to listen to what is unpleasant to them, and only those of slavish principles would attempt to impose their principles on the vulgar. In contrast to this sort of open discussion, it is partial skepticism which is to be feared. The real knave attacks nothing overtly; these men laugh at themselves as heartily as at others: "Let the *solemn* Reprovers of Vice proceed in the manner most sutable to their Genius and Character. I am ready to congratulate with 'em on the Success of their Labours, in that authoritative way which is allow'd 'em. I know not, in the mean while, why others may not be allow'd to *ridicule* Folly, and recommend Wisdom and Virtue (if possibly they can) in a way of Pleasantry and Mirth" (**Char.,** I, 134). The others are "those to whom a natural good Genius, or the Force of a good Education, has given a *Sense* of what is *naturally graceful and becoming*." Ridicule is not so significant as the good-humored mood from which it must spring if it is to be functional. As A. O. Aldridge pointed out in one of his earliest articles, it is the demeanor of the discussion which will determine whether ridicule is allied with reason.[18] And it is clear from these quotations that the ridiculers must be balanced and well disposed; in short, they must be essentially moral men.

Shaftesbury's conversationalists so ridicule almost everything that they are unable even to agree on a meaning for *common sense,* to which they constantly appeal in positive tones. He himself follows the most ingenious commentators on the Latin satirical poets who define the term "by a *Greek* Derivation, to signify *Sense* of the *Publick Weal,* and of the *Common Interest*; Love of the *Community* or *Society,* Natural Affection, Humanity, Obligingness, or that sort of *Civility* which rises from a just *Sense* of the *common Rights* of Mankind, and the *natural Equality* there is amongst those of same Species" (*Char.,* I, 104). These "social feelings or *Sense of Partnership* with Human Kind" are the final version of Shaftesbury's moral sense and in this popular context are preferred to *koinonia* in the footnotes.[19]

How different is this from the Lockean definition which he framed, probably a decade and half before? In the first place, *sense* is everywhere equated to *passion* or *affection* in the text, so that there is no difference in this aspect of moral sense.[20] Secondly, in the final pages of *Sensus Communis,* Shaftesbury proceeds up the ladder from the commoner pleasures to the highest: "Nothing affects the Heart like that which is purely from *it-self,* and of its *own nature*; such as the *Beauty of Sentiments; the Grace* of Actions; *the Turn of Characters* and *the Proportions and Features of a human* Mind" (*Char.,* I, 135-36). The artists who portray these "carry a double Portion of this charm about 'em." In other words, they reveal the highest truth and they do so altruistically. "For Who of them composes for *himself?*" Underneath all this verbiage the moral sense remains essentially the same, an affection towards an affection.

In no other work of Shaftesbury's are there more references to Hobbes than in *Sensus Communis.* How is it possible, he asks, to agree to a contract in a state of nature where there are no norms to enforce it? If indeed mankind did come to an agreement, moral standards must have preceded the agreement. Again, he feels that the modern Epicurean has misread his master, for Epicurus by the very fact of banishing concern for relatives and countrymen acknowledged the force of social affections, whereas the Hobbist acts as if such affections are nonexistent. This leads to discussion of the herding instinct, which is true self-interest. "A Life without *natural Affection, Friendship, or Sociableness,* wou'd be found a wretched one, were it to be try'd. 'Tis as these Feelings and Affections are intrinsically

valuable and worthy, that Self-Interest is to be rated and esteem'd" (*Char.,* I, 121). Faction is merely a perversion of the confederate faculty, yet confederation can only go so far, which is a chief reason for the establishment of colonies.

The whole discussion must be seen in terms of the audience of these three popular essays, and Shaftesbury's concept of them. Most of them would be as unlikely to respond to an argument based on the larger community of mankind and the universal good as they would to his abstract description of the moral sense in the *Inquiry.* These are matters which in *Characteristicks* he will confine to the more serious second volume. Here he reduces the social organism to a scale which will have meaning for his prospective readers.

* * *

Soliloquy, or Advice to an Author (1710) is in many ways Shaftesbury's most engaging work. His miscellaneous and familiar style is fully developed in it. According to a copy of the 1711 edition revised by Shaftesbury as copy for the 1714 edition of ***Characteristicks,*** most of the essays must have been read aloud, or he simply has a good ear, because he is much concerned with the sound of his phrases—jingling words and strings of monosyllabic words are expunged, for example. Almost every page of the third and final edition of ***Soliloquy*** involves some change. Most of them, however, are merely mechanical or involve altering sounds. The sentence units remain the same, though much shorter than in the earlier writings, and there are fewer antitheses. They flow together well yet can be very pointed when he wishes. Many of the things one would have liked to have said are said here in this essay. The relaxed miscellaneous style is a help with this, because some of his best sentences are what a comedian would now call "throwaways"—as, for instance, "the most ingenious way of becoming foolish, is *by a System.*"

Nowhere in Shaftesbury's works does he refer so often to the superiority of the Ancients over the Moderns. In one respect he is simply more confident and outspoken. At the same time he took precautions; the response to his ***Letter Concerning Enthusiasm*** had taught him how dangerous it is to mix philosophy and religion together. At one point he defends Christianity against tellers of traveler's tales, such as Locke: "Tho *Christian* Miracles may not so well satisfy em; they dwell with the highest contentment on the Prodigys of *Moorish* and *Pagan* Countrys" (*Char.* I, 456).[21] Most of the time he insists that his topic is generically separate from the divine, and that it would be presumptuous for him even to speak of religious matters. "It becomes not those who are un-inspir'd from Heaven, and uncommission'd from Earth, to search with Curiosity into the Original of those

Holy Rites and Records, *by Law establish'd.*" As to drawing from the Bible, Milton was an exception because of the mythological flexibility of his characters; normally "the Manners, Actions and Characters of *Sacred Writ, are in no-wise the proper Subject of other* authors than Divines themselves." However, "tho the Explanations of such deep Mysterys, and religious Dutys, be allotted as the peculiar Province of *the Sacred Order*; 'tis presum'd, nevertheless, that it may be lawful for other *Authors* to retain their antient Privilege of instructing Mankind, in a way of Pleasure, and Entertainment. *Poets* may be allow'd their Fictions, and *Philosophers* their Systems" (**Char.,** I, 358, 361).[22]

Most of what Shaftesbury has to say in **Soliloquy** on the Ancients and Moderns is based directly on a cyclic but rather supple theory of history best developed in the **Miscellaneous Reflections.** The most powerful stimulus to achievement in human affairs and in the arts is freedom. The word does not refer to a specific political system, though some are certainly preferable to others. Its real measure is the diversity of opinion on all subjects and the degree to which that diversity is tolerated. Life under a benevolent despot may be free, and so may life in a nation where slaves are held, though Shaftesbury disapproves of the practice. Looking back, then, Greece "that sole polite, most civiliz'd, and accomplish'd Nation" stood first among free nations.

> For tho compos'd of different Nations, distinct in Laws and Government, divided by Seas and Continents, dispers'd in distant Islands: yet being originally of the same Extract, united by one single Language, and animated by that social, publick and *free* Spirit. . . . Thus *Greece,* tho she *exported* Arts to other Nations, had properly for her own share no *Import* of the kind. The utmost which could be nam'd, wou'd amount to no more than raw *Materials,* of a rude and barborous form. And thus the Nation was evidently *Original* in Art; and with them every noble Study and Science was . . . *self-form'd.*
>
> (**Char.,** III, 138-40)

Next came Rome, borrowing from Greece and gradually polishing her own arts and sciences until they reach a high degree of finish in the final days of the Republic. The Empire put the fate of the nation too much in the hands of a single man. As the reigns of the Antonines proved, freedom could exist, but almost inevitably the Roman state descended into tyranny.

With the coming of Christianity, the Empire went on, and political tyranny, too. A new impediment to freedom was the insistence on intellectual conformity, and gradually all of western Europe descended into the Gothic age. Liberty began to revive during the Renaissance, and, speaking of England, Shaftesbury says, "We are now in an Age when *Liberty* is once again in its Ascendant. And we are our-selves the happy Nation, who

not only enjoy it at home, but by our Greatness and Power give Life and Vigour to it abroad. . . . 'Tis with us at present, as with the *Roman* People in those early Days, when they wanted only repose from Arms to apply themselves to the Improvement of Arts and Studys" (**Char.,** I, 222-23). Shaftesbury is optimistic about England's progress, but there is no certainty that it will continue. The Glorious Revolution assured for the time freedom from political tyranny, and he is well aware of the state of intellectual freedom in his time. He expects to acknowledge formally his authorship of the **Letter Concerning Enthusiasm,** with no fears of the magistrate enforcing conformity. He is sure, too, that literature is moving toward the simple after all the quibbles and puns of the past age, and the poets of the seventeenth century are to be congratulated for throwing off rhyme. Even in Greece the degree of freedom varied. On the other hand, England is still at war with an absolutist monarch and the continual growth of ceremony runs counter to simplicity.

One characteristic which separates the ancient author from the modern is the natural tendency of the ancient to colloquize. After citing the desire of Persius to carry into the temple "a mind pure in its inner depths," Shaftesbury remarks, "This was, among the Antients, that celebrated *Delphick* Inscription, RECOGNIZE YOUR-SELF: which was as much as to say, *Divide your-self,* or *Be* Two. For if the Division were rightly made, all *within* wou'd of course, they thought, be rightly understood, and prudently manag'd. Such Confidence they had in this Home-*Dialect* of SOLILOQUY" (**Char.,** I, 170). Later on he is more specific:

> When by a certain powerful Figure of inward Rhetorick, the Mind *apostrophizes* its own FANCYS, raises 'em to their proper *Shapes* and *Personages,* and addresses 'em familiarly, without the least Ceremony or Respect. By this means it will soon happen, that Two form'd *Partys* will erect themselves *within.* For the Imaginations or Fancys being thus roundly treated, are forc'd to declare themselves, and take Party. Those on the side of the elder Brother APPETITE, are strangely subtle and insinuating . . . till being confronted with their Fellows of a plainer Language and Expression, they are forc'd to quit their mysterious Manner, and discover themselves *Sophisters* and *Imposters,* who have not the least to do with the Party of REASON and *good Sense.*
>
> (**Char.,** I, 188)

This is, of course, precisely the method which Shaftesbury himself had been using in his private **"Exercises."** As he says, the idea is ancient, but why, if it worked for him, did he wait twelve years to refer to it in one of his final essays? The reason is, I suspect, that he identifies the method of inner colloquy with his own intensely Stoic discipline, which he was so successful in concealing from his contemporaries. After his usual fashion he thinks in terms of personae, and the Stoic persona is almost the furthest removed from those he is addressing in his relaxed and miscellaneous manner. At least four different moral personae are addressed by Shaftesbury; first the average man with whom he deals in his court book, from servant to small landholder, and sometimes his protégés, Wilkinson and Ainsworth. This person, the unphilosophical man, strongly needs the discipline of religion "by law established," and Shaftesbury is quite honest in recommending that its habits must be instilled at an early age for him to be effective as a moral person and good citizen. Secondly, there is the more fashionable person to whom he gradually turned his attention in the first and third volumes of *Characteristicks.* Deception is the key to Shaftesbury's method with him; he must be tricked into thinking about serious matters. He may well be conventionally pious, and his faith should not be affronted; nonetheless, he must be weaned away from the belief that God can ever act without full benevolence. Shaftesbury seems to have felt that the more pious this person was, the less sensitive he would be to the protective sarcastic tone he adopted in these essays. The third persona is made up of thoroughgoing classicists, true disciples of the Ancients, those who have learned the lesson of *The Moralists*—Crell and General Stanhope, for example. These are the philosophers, and to them Deity becomes the more remote figure of Shaftesbury's Platonic-Stoic universe. Fourth comes the well-concealed Shaftesbury in his **"Exercises."** Whereas the third persona is exposed to dialectic truth, truth for this persona is therapeutic truth of the colloquy. A statement may be equally true and equally formative but for the third it is stressed because it is true, for the fourth because it is formative. Of course, the Stoic sage can never really exist. By striving earnestly to be one, by continual exposure to formative truth, the disciple reaches a point where he can let *ataraxia* take care of itself and turn his attention to *koinonia.* The closest analogy I can think of is the meditative mode of religious experience common in the earlier seventeenth century; the parallel is not exact, though.

Obviously certain truths may hold for all these personae. Just as obviously, one must work from one level to another with great care, which is all the more reason for admiring the fine general essays which have been written on Shaftesbury, such as Martin Price's chapter in *To the Palace of Wisdom.*[23] It did not occur to Shaftesbury immediately, then, that the method which he had used in his secret meditations had a broader application. This he developed in *Soliloquy.*

By far the best essay on the inward colloquy is that of Robert Marsh in *Four Dialectical Theories of Poetry.* He tends to use the term more broadly than I do. Some of my reasons for not doing this have already been stated. Too, if colloquy is absolutely central to Shaftesbury's thought, the rapture of *The Moralists* is

devalued, and, more important, making the inward colloquy so important, though it was published last, distorts the situation historically. None of the tremendous epistemological pressures to which Shaftesbury was reacting become evident. The difference is simply a matter of approach. An amusing example of this is Marsh's denial of Tuveson's thesis that Locke's notions of sensation and reflection affected Shaftesbury. Both sides are right. Marsh is a synthesizer and his unhistorical approach is symbolized by his use of the Robertson edition of *Characteristicks,* which eliminates all the emphases which Shaftesbury felt were so important; Tuveson is basically a historian, though I do not agree with all his theses. It may sound heretical, but in the case of someone so complex as Shaftesbury both conflicting writers make valuable contributions to the subject.

* * *

The second volume of *Characteristicks* contains Shaftesbury's revision of *An Inquiry* and *The Moralists*; the third volume, his *Miscellaneous Reflections* and in some copies the English version of his *Judgment of Hercules.* The *Miscellaneous Reflections* provide a commentary on the first two volumes, intended to draw the various tracts together. In this they succeed to a great extent—not that Shaftesbury exceeds the norms of his day in deception regarding the true facts of publication. He was forced to admit that the *Inquiry* was published without authorization in 1699. *The Moralists* is listed as being first published in 1709; on the other hand, *The Sociable Enthusiast* never was published in the ordinary sense of the term.

How Shaftesbury felt about his editions is in part explained by the fact that he calls John Darby, his printer and publisher, his amanuensis. It is true that his best statement of this was written when he was piqued by the response to his *Letter,* but he went on using the term until his death. All of Shaftesbury's books starting with the *Inquiry* were circulated in manuscript, as was common then. How is an author to protect himself from the errors inevitable in this process? The answer is quite simple. Have the book printed, supervise the process, and then all of your friends can enjoy accurate copies. If still others want copies, the publisher can provide them. *Soliloquy* was printed for John Morphew, but Darby, publisher of *Characteristicks,* was also its printer. So voluminous were Shaftesbury's instructions to him for every detail including all features of layout and ornamentation for the 1711 and 1714 editions that having separate printers would have introduced many errors. This explains why *Characteristicks* is such a beautiful book at a time when English books were about the ugliest produced anywhere. More important, the arrangements for publication reflect Shaftesbury's notion that the publisher is merely an amanuensis of the author, however much self-deception the idea may involve.

As one might expect, the first miscellanies which comment on Volume I of **Characteristicks** deal with a wide variety of topics. This is in line with the loose and apparently disorganized structure by which Shaftesbury hopes to recommend to fashionable people "Morals on the same foot, with what in a lower sense is call'd *Manners*; and to advance Philosophy (as harsh a Subject as it may appear) on the very Foundation of what is call'd *agreeable* and *polite*" (**Char.,** III, 163). Some of the topics, such as his theory of history, we have already considered; others are best passed over because they are not significant enough for the development of his thought. However, the third miscellany deals with *taste* and gives us a chance to see how far Shaftesbury has progressed from the man who in his early twenties wrote *An Inquiry Concerning Virtue.*

Shaftesbury calls the various attributes of mind "faculties," but all his life he was aware that Locke had convincingly reduced them to agencies and had again banished innatism. Although Shaftesbury believed moral ideas connate in man—he may not be born with them but their development, in potential at least, is inevitable—he constantly strove to shore up his epistemology with analogies. As we have seen, the first version of the moral sense, though he did not call it that, was an affection toward an affection, which he sought to validate by paralleling it to the affection one member of a family feels toward another, *natural affection.* It was an attempt to evade Locke in his own terms. Later he added another analogy, that of our reaction to beautiful objects. This made more sense then than it does in the present state of aesthetic theory, because then it was assumed that all beauty arose from numbers and harmony. Shaftesbury was in a sense providing a mathematical assurance of correspondence between individual moral judgments and the good. By 1710, he seems confident that the battle has been won: "Nature will not be mock'd. The Prepossession against her can never be very lasting. Her *Decrees* and *Instincts* are powerful; and her Sentiments *in-bred.* She has a strong Party *abroad*; and as strong a one *within our-selves*" (**Char.,** I, 354).

Though the predisposition toward it is connate, taste itself can only be attained by contact with the world outside. The English, "the latest Barbarous, the last *Civiliz'd* or *Polish'd* People of Europe," have a special need of it. As Robert Marsh has remarked, it is very easy to be led into confusion by Shaftesbury's use of abstract terms, but here at least he is as precise as he can be. *Relish, good taste,* and aesthetic *judgment* are all equated, depending on whether he is stressing their

affective or evaluative functions. A man can be said to possess good taste when he reacts positively in a more or less automatic fashion to what is good in the arts or in morals, though, of course, developing taste to this level is a laborious process. Taste is in turn based on enthusiasm, which as we have seen is easily led astray. One must continually reexamine the roots of enthusiasm, an affection, to make sure that they are rationally sound. Their rationality depends on how much they are inspired by the order and symmetry to be found both in the arts and, as Shaftesbury believes, in the spectacle of good actions.

His use of the virtuoso as the model of the man of taste is useful both analogically and in pointing to the pitfalls one may fall into. For one thing, Shaftesbury takes an acknowledged relationship between the viewer and the art object and presses it into service morally. There results a hierarchy of virtuosos ranging from the simplest collector of ingenious objects, through the accomplished patron of the arts, to the moral virtuoso: "To *philosophize,* in a just Signification, is but to carry *Good-Breeding* a step higher. For the Accomplishment of Breeding is, To learn whatever is *decent* in Company or *beautiful* in Arts: and the Sum of Philosophy is, To learn what is *just* in Society, and *beautiful* in Nature, and the Order of the World" (**Char.,** III, 161).

With regard to pitfalls, the collector of cockleshells and the vain devisor of useless systems, Shaftesbury remarks, mockingly, are akin: "*Creation* it-self can, upon occasion, be exhibited; *Transmutations, Projections,* and other *Philosophical* Arcana, such as in the *corporeal* World can accomplish all things: whilst in the *intellectual,* a set Frame of metaphysical Phrases and Distinctions can serve to solve whatever Difficultys may be propounded either in *Logick, Ethicks,* or any *real Science,* of whatever kind" (**Char.,** III, 160). As with Milton, it is the moral function of an activity which determines its value. The collector whose chief impulse is to collect is as vain as the philosopher who delights only in systematizing.

It must be clear that Shaftesbury's moral theories could be stated in purely rational terms. Why did he not do so? Why so much stress on an affectively based quality such as enthusiasm, no matter how securely he thinks it rooted in reason? The answer is, I think, tied up with the restrictions which Locke had put upon reason. Even if Shaftesbury did not believe that the only function of reason was ratiocination—that reason had become an agent rather than an intuitive faculty—he needed mental properties which would reach up to apprehend the Platonic-Stoic cosmos, a vertical, rather than horizontal, Lockean concept of mind:

> Something there will be of Extravagance and Fury, when the Ideas or Images receiv'd are too big for the narrow human Vessel to contain. So that *Inspiration*

may be justly call'd *Divine* ENTHUSIASM: For the Word it-self signifies *Divine Presence,* and was made use of by the Philosopher whom the earliest Christian Fathers call'd *Divine,* to express whatever was sublime in human Passions. This was the Spirit he allotted to *Heroes, Statesmen, Poets, Orators, Musicians,* and even *Philosophers* themselves.

(Char., I, 53-54)

Without this element, Shaftesbury's philosophy would have remained a more or less forgotten species of seventeenth-century Platonism. As it was, the English missed the element of challenge and reduced much of his thought to its least common denominator, until by mid-century most of that had become accepted and boring. Only the Germans seized upon this fruitful notion of the creative imagination, so that it returned to England almost a century later. . . .

Notes

1. S. F. Whitaker, "The First Edition of Shaftesbury's *Moralists," The Library,* 5th series, VII (1952), 235-41.

2. The Earl of Shaftesbury to Lord Somers, October 20, 1705, in PRO [Public Record Office] 30/45/ 22/4/ p. 13.

3. See A. O. Aldridge, "Shaftesbury's Earliest Critic," *Modern Philology,* XXIV (1946), 10-22.

4. The last five words are explained in the 1709 edition, "inward Parts of a more curiouse nature."

5. Robert Marsh, *Four Dialectical Theories of Poetry: An Aspect of English Neo-classical Criticism* (Chicago, 1965); Stanley Grean, *Shaftesbury's Philosophy of Religion and Ethics: A Study in Enthusiasm* (Athens, Ohio, 1967); Ernest L. Tuveson, *The Imagination as a Means of Grace: Locke and the Aesthetics of Romanticism* (Berkeley, 1960); Robert Voitle, "Shaftesbury's Moral Sense," *Studies in Philology,* LII (1955), 17-38.

Some of the problems in accepting Professor Tuveson's thesis may arise from the eccentricity of his footnotes. As I have pointed out, Ashley first defined the "moral sense" in his 1699 edition of the *Inquiry* and later he added the aesthetic analogy when he hastily revised the work for the first edition of *Characteristicks* in 1711. On page 53 Tuveson cites the passage defining the moral sense using the words of page 27 of the 1699 edition, but he says he found them in *Characteristicks* (1711), where they are phrased differently—see II, 28 of this edition. He then cites the passage on the aesthetic analogy from the 1732 edition. This edition is identical here to the final edition of 1714, but there is a very similar passage on II, 28 of the 1711 edition which he does not tell us

about. Despite the fact that he cites from it twice, there is no mention of the 1699 edition in Tuveson's book, so that one is left to infer that Shaftesbury made all these changes between 1711 and 1714. There is no doubt of the authenticity of the date of the first edition—which is held by the British Library and elsewhere—because we have a letter from Stringer in 1699 specifically referring to it. Professor Caroline Robbins has provided me with a poem which William Popple wrote on the occasion of its publication. The poem is dated 1699 in a contemporary hand.

6. Susie I. Tucker, *Enthusiasm: A Study in Semantic Change* (Cambridge, 1972).

7. R. L. Brett, *The Third Earl of Shaftesbury: A Study in Eighteenth-Century Literary Theory* (1951), 186.

8. Charles Verecker, *Eighteenth-Century Optimism: A Study of the Interrelations of Moral and Social Theory in English and French Thought Between 1689 and 1785* (Liverpool, 1967), 57. See especially the last chapter of Ernst Cassirer's *The Platonic Renaissance in England,* trans. James P. Pettegrove (Austin, Tex., 1953).

9. The Earl of Shaftesbury to Lord Somers, March, 1708, in PRO 30/24/22/4/pp. 67-70; to the same, July 12, 1708, in PRO 30/24/22/4/pp. 86-87; *Lettre sur l'enthousiasme* appeared in the same year at The Hague.

10. James Sutherland, *Background for Queen Anne* (1937); Ronald A. Knox, *Enthusiasm: A Chapter in the History of Religion with Specific Reference to the XVII and XVIII Centuries* (1950), Chap. 15; and, better balanced, Grean, *Shaftesbury's Philosophy,* Chap. 2.

11. Knox, *Enthusiasm,* 368; Peter Gay, *The Enlightenment: An Interpretation* (2 vols.; New York, 1966-69), I, 7-8.

12. John Redwood's *Reason, Ridicule and Religion: The Age of Enlightenment in England, 1660-1750* (1976) gives some idea of the number of issues involved and the ferocity of the struggle.

13. Bishop Edward Fowler, *Reflections upon a Letter Concerning Enthusiasm, To my Lord XXXX. In another Letter to a Lord* (1709). See also *Bart'lemy Fair: Or An Enquiry After Wit* (1709) by Mary Astell. And also *Remarks upon the Letter Concerning Enthusiasm. In a Letter to a Gentleman* (1708).

14. See again Tucker's admirable *Enthusiasm.*

15. The *Tabula Cebetis* is referred to and the divine man is Epictetus.

16. Locke, *Essay,* II, 437.

17. *Essai sur l'usage de la raillerie et l'enjouement dans les conversations qui roulent sur les matieres les plus importantes,* signed S.C.S.V., appeared in The Hague in 1710, translated by J. van Effen. The next year Shaftesbury used illustrative citations from it in the second English edition of *Sensus Communis.*

18. A. O. Aldridge, "Shaftesbury and the Test of Truth," *PMLA,* LX (1945), 129-56.

19. *Final* because this was his last full definition.

20. For a discussion of the meaning of the term in the two versions of the *Inquiry,* see my "Shaftesbury's Moral Sense." *Studies in Philology,* LII (1955), 17-38.

21. See also I, 350-53.

22. The passage is bitterly satirical, but he means what he says about laws governing religion; this is the justification for the religious system which he feels that men most need.

23. Martin Price, *To the Palace of Wisdom: Studies in Order and Energy from Dryden to Blake* (Garden City, N.Y., 1964).

Abbreviations

Manuscripts

PRO Public Record Office

Works by Shaftesbury

Char. *Characteristicks of Men, Manners, Opinions, Times.* The second edition, corrected. (1714)

Ex. "Exercises." PRO 30/24/27/10.

SE *The Sociable Enthusiast: A Philosophical Adventure, Written to Palemon.* (1704?)

Bibliography

Principal Works of Shaftesbury Consulted

An Inquiry Concerning Virtue, in Two Discourses. London, 1699.

The Sociable Enthusiast. A Philosophical Adventure Written to Palemon. [1704?]

*A Letter Concerning Enthusiasm, To My Lord *****.* London, 1708.

The Moralists, a Philosophical Rhapsody. Being a recital of certain conversations upon natural and moral subjects. London, 1709.

"ΑΣΚΗΜΑΤΑ" ["Exercises"]. PRO 30/24/27/10. Written from 1698 to 1712. Edited by Benjamin Rand in 1900 in *The Life, Unpublished Letters, and Philosophical Regimen of Anthony, Earl of Shaftesbury.*

Characteristicks of Men, Manners, Opinions, Times. 3 vols. The second edition corrected. London, 1714.

Letters of the Earl of Shaftesbury. Collected into one volume. London, 1750.

Secondary Sources

Locke, John. *An Essay Concerning Human Understanding.* 2 vols. Oxford, 1894.

Robert Markley (essay date 1987)

SOURCE: Markley, Robert. "Style as Philosophical Structure: The Contexts of Shaftesbury's *Characteristicks.*" In *The Philosopher as Writer: The Eighteenth Century,* edited by Robert Ginsberg, pp. 140-54. Selinsgrove, Pa: Susquehanna University Press, 1987.

[*In the following essay, Markley argues that Shaftesbury's work is important not only for its ideas but because it shows the interaction of philosophical and stylistic concerns.*]

Shaftesbury has traditionally proved a difficult writer for both literary critics and philosophers. Most of his commentators have taken his self-proclaimed status as a "philosopher" as both the beginning and logical conclusion of their attempts to interpret his work: Shaftesbury is located within the historical traditions of philosophic thought and his "ideas" examined and explicated as disinterested contributions to the history of knowledge. These efforts, however, have led most of his critics to neglect a good portion of his writing, concentrating (albeit understandably) on the *Inquiry Concerning Virtue* and the *Letter Concerning Enthusiasm.* They ignore or dismiss the stylistic and literary traditions which influenced Shaftesbury, and, by emphasizing the timeless, "philosophical" aspects of his work, neglect its social, political, and ideological assumptions and values.[1] Their concerns, in this regard, pay homage to the success of one important aspect of Shaftesbury's program as a writer: the championing of a disinterested philosophic language that is both morally instructive and aesthetically pleasing.

There are however, problems with this traditional, ahistorical perception of Shaftesbury's thought—and, as John Richetti has argued, with the ways in which we approach much late seventeenth- and early eighteenth-century philosophy.[2] Shaftesbury's concern with the realm of ideas cannot—by his own account—legitimately be divorced from the stylistic and historical contexts of his work. Repeatedly in *The Characteristicks,* Shaftesbury calls attention to the historical situation of his writing: he satirizes his detractors, develops elaborate defenses of his previous work, footnotes his classical authorities, offers his opinions on contemporary developments in art, politics, and religion, and does what he can to advance his aristocratic social, aesthetic, and philosophical judgments. Seen in this light, his very "disinterestedness," his appeals to—and for—the ahistorical realms of beauty and truth are themselves ideological constructs, the products of a complex interaction of social, philosophical, and stylistic traditions. Shaftesbury often seems as concerned with his literary strategies, his "style," as he is with his "ideas." Unlike many of his critics, he sees "philosophy" as a strategic and polemical discourse designed to inculcate in his readers a decidedly aristocratic sense of virtue. In this respect, the pretext that his language follows "*The Simple* Manner . . . endeavouring only to express the effect of Art, under the appearance of the greatest Ease and Negligence" (1:257)[3] is crucial to his self-perception as both a writer and philosopher. The "natural," disinterested mode of philosophical discourse that Shaftesbury advocates, then, is an end as well as a means. For our purposes, a study of the relationships between Shaftesbury's style and his thought becomes an examination of the interests—historical, social, literary, and critical—that the author uses to promote philosophic disinterest.

I

Underlying the diverse literary forms of Shaftesbury's *Characteristicks* are two major seventeenth-century stylistic traditions: Jonsonian "humour" and Fletcherian "wit" or, as other critics have termed them, the "self-consuming" and the "self-satisfying," the Senecan and the "scientific," or the two plain styles.[4] The Jonsonian tradition (derived from the example of Ben Jonson's poems and prose comedies)[5] is essentially Horatian and satiric; it emphasizes the moral utility of language, taking as its model the classical ideal of instruction and delight. It acknowledges the ideal possibility of an objective language which embodies moral truth, but concentrates most of its energy on anatomizing the seemingly irrevocable corruptions of human speech, or probing, through the author's often tortuous progress toward self-knowledge, the moral complexities of the individual consciousness. In contrast, the Fletcherian tradition (an outgrowth of the Cavalier aesthetic of the 1620s and 1630s) reifies aristocratic speech—what Dryden calls "the language of gentlemen"[6]—into both a stylistic and social ideal. Language embodies a code of gentlemanly behavior and values that makes the creation of an "objective" or "natural" discourse both a means and an end. Style, in short, becomes a measure of social worth, a badge of aristocratic self-definition.

Theoretically, then, Jonsonian humour and Fletcherian wit offers writers of the late seventeenth century two seemingly distinct stylistic opinions, two different philosophical traditions on which to draw. In practice, however, these traditions interact dialectically to produce a Cavalier, or Royalist, or aristocratic, prose style that conflates moral virtue and the external manifestations of "good breeding"—a key phrase for writers from Fletcher and James Shirley in the seventeenth century to Shaftesbury and Pope in the eighteenth. The result, for writers of the Restoration period, is a nearly fanatic concern with stylistic propriety, with making one's writing conform to aristocratic standards of verbal decorum.[7] As Brian Corman has shown, even a self-professed Jonsonian like the playwright Thomas Shadwell subordinates his satiric concerns to the stylistic prerogatives of Fletcherian wit comedy.[8] In trying to reconcile the often contradictory demands of "wit" and "humour," late seventeenth-century writers frequently blur the distinctions between them; in Shaftesbury's writings, for example, the terms often become interchangeable. William Congreve (to take only one example from among Shaftesbury's contemporaries) in the "Prologue" to his comedy *Love for Love* (1695) asserts his claims as both a satirist and a gentleman:

> Since *The Plain Dealer's* scenes of manly rage,
> Not one has dared to lash this crying age.
> This time the poet owns the bold essay,
> Yet hopes there's no ill-manners in his play:[9]

The falling off in these lines from the satiric "rage" of William Wycherley's play to Congreve's worries about "ill-manners" suggests something of the dilemma that confronts late seventeenth-century writers who must try to reconcile morality and stylistic decorum. As Jonson's prose comedies had demonstrated early in the century, the language of satire is inherently unstable; it inevitably participates in the corruption it condemns.[10] Or, to define the problem in Augustinian terms, the language of moral reflection must always be inadequate to the celebration of a deity who, by definition, cannot be understood or encompassed linguistically: this is the dilemma that confronts the anti-Ciceronian writers of the sixteenth and seventeenth centuries, from Montaigne and Bacon to Robert Boyle and Isaac Newton.[11] Almost by definition, the languages of satire and moral reflection work against the linguistic stability sought by an aristocratic discourse that prides itself on what Shaftesbury, Congreve, and Dryden refer to—unabashedly—as its own "perfection."

In one respect, Shaftesbury's *Characteristicks* may be read as an eighteenth-century attempt to resolve the crises of seventeenth-century prose style, to unite the languages of satiric morality and aristocratic manners. In practice, however, Shaftesbury's championing of "*The Simple* Manner" as "the strictest Imitation of Nature"

(1:257) assumes stylistic values that emphasize aristocratic authority and verbal grace rather than the kind of epistemological inquiry which characterizes the writings of his seventeenth-century predecessors, notably Bacon. In the *Letter Concerning Enthusiasm,* Shaftesbury insists, "Justness of Thought and Stile, Refinement in Manners, good Breeding, and Politeness of every kind" (1:10) are "naturally" and irrevocably related; and he reiterates this point throughout his writings. This assumption prevents him from acknowledging the instability of classical or Jonsonian satire, its tendency to call into question even those values it seeks to affirm. In Shaftesbury's writings, the "self-consuming artifacts" of epistemological questioning give way to the reification of moral values—virtue, truth, and even aesthetic beauty—as idealized, ahistorical absolutes.[12] This process, the appropriation of traditional moral categories by a language of aristocratic authority, defines the stylistic construction of Shaftesbury's thought.

II

Throughout the *Characteristicks* Shaftesbury describes his prose style as "simple," straightforward, and unambiguous. This description suggests an almost Lockean conception of language as a transparent, utilitarian medium; and, to be sure, language, for Shaftesbury, always reflects what he sees as stable social values and timeless moral and aesthetic truths. Yet, at the same time, the act of writing—the dramatic presentation of self—fascinates Shaftesbury in a way that puzzled Locke. Style in *The Characteristicks* is part revelation, part complex game. It does not simply convey or passively reflect objective ideas but demonstrates, even embodies, the values it upholds.

Shaftesbury's prose style usually assumes one of three basic forms: the satiric, the self-consciously philosophical or analytic, and, in *The Moralists,* the rhapsodic. In defending his "variety of STILE," Shaftesbury calls these modes the "*Comick, Rhetorical,* and . . . the *Poetick* or *Sublime*; such as is the aptest to run into Enthusiasm and Extravagance" (3:285). Although diction and syntax vary widely among these styles, they are different strategies to the same or similar ends—demonstrating that good writing and "Good Breeding" are inseparable. Part of this demonstration is the idealizing of gentlemanly discourse as it appears in his texts. For Shaftesbury, "the appearance of the greatest Ease and Negligence" (1:257) defines a conscious stylistic program that attempts to bring philosophic discourse within the realm of polite conversation. Shaftesbury refers casually to his *Letter Concerning Enthusiasm* as "a sort of idle Thoughts, such as pretend only to Amusement, and have no relation to Business or Affairs" (1:3); but, in the first of his *Miscellanies,* he takes pains to defend his "*Concealment of Order*": "the *Art* was to destroy every . . . Token or Appearance [of order], give an *ex-*

temporary Air to what was writ, and make the *Effect* of Art be felt, without discovering the *Artifice*" (3:21-22). Style, realized as its own ideal, becomes ironically self-effacing. In defending himself against charges that his writing is unsystematic, Shaftesbury claims that he has been "sufficiently *grave* and *serious,* in defense of what is directly contrary to Seriousness and Gravity. I have very *solemnly* pleaded for *Gaiety* and GOOD-HUMOUR: I have declaim'd against *Pedantry* in learned Language, and oppos'd *Formality* in Form" (3:129). This kind of irony, a deliberate dissociation of content from form, emphasizes that language can be manipulated in various ways to produce different kinds of self-presentation. In this respect, Shaftesbury sees style (to borrow Dryden's metaphor) not as the man but as his clothing.

The studied artlessness of Shaftesbury's prose, though, is consciously crafted, drawing on diverse stylistic traditions and assuming diverse syntactical forms. In much of his writing, his stylistic models are the Roman satirists, Horace, Juvenal, and Persius. All three are quoted throughout his work; Horace is cited more than twice as often as all other writers—ancient and modern—combined. Shaftesbury frequently strives for a Horatian ideal of conversational ease and pointed wit. His language often tries to create its own sense of satiric authority:

> We may defend Villany, or cry up Folly, before the World: But to appear Fools, Mad-men, or Varlets, to *our-selves*; and prove it to our own faces, that we are really *such,* is insupportable. For so true a Reverence has every-one for himself, when he comes clearly to appear before his close Companion, that he had rather profess the vilest things of himself in open Company, then hear his Character privately from his own Mouth. So that we may readily from hence conclude, That the chief Interest of *Ambition, Avarice, Corruption,* and every sly insinuating *Vice,* is to prevent this Interview and Familiarity of Discourse which is consequent upon close Retirement and inward Recess.
>
> (1:173-74)

Shaftesbury's target in this passage is a staple of much seventeenth- and eighteenth-century satire: the kind of monstrous hypocrisy that deludes the individual even as he or she tries to dupe "the World." Stylistically, his prose is closer to, say, Jonson's than to Swift's in its subtle but significant disruptions of balanced rhetorical structures. The syntax of this passage is deliberately fragmented; what could be read as one leisurely sentence breaks into three. The emphasis is less on the logical development of the author's thought than on the cumulative rhetorical force of a series of aphoristic clauses structured around strong, unambiguous verbs. The intransitive verbs—"is"—in the first and third sentences carry the weight of universal decrees. In essence, Shaftesbury creates an authoritative satiric voice by his refusal to particularize. The generalizing tendency of his imagination transforms personal observation into what he calls elsewhere "a simple, clear, and *united View*," unbroken "by the Expression of any thing peculiar, or distinct" (1:143). In this respect, then, Shaftesbury presses the idiosyncratic language of satire into the service of promoting universal "truths." Its assertions about human "Villany" and "Folly" describe a satiric world distinct from the author's ideal realm of philosophical self-examination and self-knowledge.

Elsewhere, however, Shaftesbury assumes different stylistic strategies. In the *Inquiry Concerning Virtue,* his language becomes more self-consciously "philosophical," his syntax more complex and periodic, than in his other writings. The satiric, Horatian mode of Jonson and the English satirists is replaced by the stylistic model of Locke's philosophical writings. Citations of classical authorities largely disappear; atypically, Shaftesbury becomes less ironic than descriptive:

> Thus the several Motions, Inclinations, Passions, Dispositions, and consequent Carriage and Behaviour of Creatures in the various Parts of Life, being several Views or Perspectives represented to the Mind, which readily discerns the Good and Ill towards the Species or Publick; there arises a new Trial or Exercise of the Heart: which must either rightly and soundly affect what is just and right, and disaffect what is contrary; or, corruptly affect what is ill, and disaffect what is worthy and good.
>
> (2:30)

This sentence is carefully constructed around a central antithesis: "Good" versus "Ill." Clauses and phrases precisely balance or oppose each other; the verbs "affect" and "disaffect" are contrasted to achieve a logical as well as rhetorical closure. The syntax is relaxed, almost leisurely; Shaftesbury avoids the terse, epigrammatic statements that characterize his prose in other essays. In this passage, as throughout the *Inquiry,* he is rhetorically persuasive rather than satirically assertive.

In *The Moralists,* Shaftesbury attempts to articulate straightforwardly a coherent, idealistic philosophy in the person of Theocles. The dialogue form in which this essay is cast allows the author the opportunity to juxtapose the languages of wit and analytic philosophy. In turn, these modes are set against the "enthusiastic" language of Theocles' "Meditations," set pieces best described as deliberately rhapsodic excursions into Vergilian hyperbole. Theocles' first "Fit" (his own term) is a cross between what he calls "a sensible kind of Madness, like those Transports . . . permitted to our *Poets*" and "downright Raving" (2:346-47):

> Ye Fields and Woods, my Refuge from the toilsom World of Business, receive me in your quiet Sanctuarys, and favour my Retreat and thoughtful Solitude.—Ye verdant Plains, how gladly I salute ye!—Hail ye bliss-ful Mansions! Known Seats! Delightful Prospects!! Majestick Beautys of this Earth, and all ye Rural Powers and Grace!—Bless'd be ye chaste Abodes of happiest Mortals, who here in peaceful Innocence enjoy a Life unenvy'd, tho Divine; whilst with its bless'd Tranquility it affords a happy Leisure and Retreat for Man; who, made for Contemplation, and to search his own and other Natures, may here best meditate the Cause of Things; and plac'd amidst the various Scenes of Nature, may nearer view her Works.
>
> (2:344)

As Theocles' comments suggest, this passage verges on self-parody; it both takes itself seriously and draws our attention to its excessive rhetoric. Its diction, tone, and subject set it apart from the language that Shaftesbury employs to characterize his more rational (and imaginatively limited) "dialogist," Philocles. It is, in short, very much a set speech or, to borrow one of Shaftesbury's favorite terms, a "Performance."

This passage marks itself, then, as the stylistic equivalent of Shaftesbury's "Enthusiasm," the dialectical opposite of the author's satire. Near the end of *The Moralists,* after several more rhapsodies, Theocles reaches the climax of this hyperbolic mode: "all sound *Love* and *Admiration* is ENTHUSIASM: the Transports of *Poets,* the Sublime of *Orators,* the Rapture of *Musicians,* the high Strains of the *Virtuosi;* all mere ENTHUSIASM! Even *Learning* it-self, the Love of *Arts* and *Curiositys,* the Spirit of *Travellers* and *Adventurers; Gallantry, War, Heroism;* All, all ENTHUSIASM!" (2:400). "ENTHUSIASM" here, as Stanley Grean notes,[13] exemplifies the joy and idealism of Shaftesbury's philosophy. His style in this case reaches an extreme of authorial assertion. The range of eighteenth-century arts and sciences are comprehended by a single word: the capitalized abstraction—part cry of joy, part expression of awe, part command—becomes the linguistic representation of what Shaftesbury calls "the Good and Perfection of *the* UNIVERSE, [the deity's] *all-good* and *perfect Work*" (2:374). Language here yearns to transcend itself, to transcend the social conditions of its mundane existence and ascend to the realm of a mystical perfection.

III

Throughout his writings, Shaftesbury insists on the power of forms to affect the reader, viewer, or beholder, whether for good or ill: "beautiful forms beautify; polite polish. On the contrary, gothic gothicize, barbarous barbarize."[14] Style, then, is an affective process as well as a reflection of a writer's values; it polishes the reader's manners as it incites the reader to virtuous actions. In his defense of *Advice to an Author,* Shaftesbury maintains that although "his pretence has been to *advise Authors,* and polish *Stiles* . . . his Aim has been to correct *Manners,* and regulate *Lives*" (3:187). This "pretence" is less a deception than an unambiguous strategy. Shaftesbury's "literary" advice becomes a means of correction and regulation; the plural "*Lives*" suggests that he has more in mind than self-improvement. Language, in other words, embodies and deploys a system of values; it does not passively reflect a moral or aesthetic order but attempts to define and shape what "order" itself may be.

Shaftesbury appropriates the languages of satire, analytical philosophy, and rhapsodic praise as part of a larger, and at times explicit, effort to make the language of philosophy an active social force rather than merely a vehicle of scholastic definition and debate. His stylistic practice is often frankly polemical. He has, as he says, little interest in the "Magnificent Pretension" of trying to define "*material* and *immaterial Substances*" and distinguish "their *Propertys* and *Modes*" (1:289); in an important passage, he describes the purpose of his efforts as an appeal to "the grown *Youth* of our polite World . . . whose *Relish* is retrievable, and whose *Taste* may yet be form'd in *Morals*; as it seems to be, already, *in exteriour Manners* and *Behaviour*" (3:179). The significance that Shaftesbury places on this ideological aspect of his writing is implicit in his general definition of philosophy: "To *philosophize,* in a just Signification, is but To carry *Good-Breeding* a step higher. For the Accomplishment of Breeding is, To learn whatever is *decent* in Company, or *beautiful* in Arts: and the Sum of Philosophy is, To learn what is *just* in Society, and *beautiful* in Nature, and the Order of the World" (3:161). Polished language, "*Good Breeding,*" "*Manners,*" social grace, aesthetic perfection, natural harmony, and universal order form a natural progression in Shaftesbury's mind. Stylistically, the transition from one to the next is as smooth as the unfolding of his syntax.

The ease with which Shaftesbury equates stylistic decorum and aristocratic virtue reflects the insistent idealism which characterizes his perception of writing. Again and again in **The Characteristicks,** Shaftesbury emphasizes that the true artist, "tho his Intention be to please the World . . . must nevertheless be, in a manner, *above it*; and fix his Eye upon that consummate *Grace,* that Beauty of *Nature,* and that *Perfection* of *Numbers*" which allows him to maintain "at least the *Idea of* PERFECTION" (2:332) in his work. This ideal perfection, if unattainable, still guides "those Artists who . . . study the Graces and Perfections of *Minds*" and become "real Masters" who are "themselves improv'd, and amended in their *better Part*" (2:206) by their own endeavors. The "Moral Artist" who "can describe both *Men* and *Manners* . . . is indeed a second *Maker*: a just PROMETHEUS, under JOVE"; his art demonstrates "the Harmony of a Mind" (2:207). This kind of idealistic outburst goes beyond the often defensive rhetoric that characterizes many conventional Restoration apologies for "modern" literature. Shaftesbury's concern with

"the *Idea* of PERFECTION," his idealizing of the poet as "a second *Maker,*" translates historical literary opinion into a system of absolute aesthetic and moral values that finds its ultimate expression in the bold statement that "all *Beauty is* TRUTH" (1:142).

This equation, however, is more problematic than it first seems. Shaftesbury's idealization of the artist, his celebration of the "study of the Graces and Perfections of *Minds,*" reflects an ideological bias against writers who do not fit his conception of what art and literary style should be. His comments on two significant figures in his literary past, Shakespeare and Seneca, are suggestive of both his indebtedness to the conventional critical prejudices of his era and his more radical attempts to define language as an ideological construct.

IV

In general, Shaftesbury's criticism of English poets reveals his resistance to much of his literary heritage. His tastes are often narrowly conservative, if not downright derivative; he tends to repeat familiar charges rather than analyze specific texts or writers. The "stammering Tongues" of his forerunners, he says, "have hitherto spoken in wretched Pun and Quibble. Our *Dramatick* SHAKESPEAR, our FLETCHER, JOHNSON, and our *Epick* MILTON preserve this Stile. And even a latter Race, scarce free of this Infirmity, and aiming at a false *Sublime,* with crouded *Simile,* and *mix'd Metaphor,* (The Hobby-Horse, and Rattle of the MUSES) entertain our raw Fancy, and unpractis'd Ear" (1:217). This criticism, if extreme, is nonetheless characteristic of much seventeenth-century literary thought; William Cartwright, Dryden, and Thomas Rymer, among others, had earlier made similar arguments.[15] Like these critics, Shaftesbury sees Shakespeare's achievement as a triumph of natural wit over the primitive, nearly barbaric nature of his dramatic language: "Notwithstanding his natural Rudeness, his unpolish'd Stile, his antiquated Phrase and Wit, his want of Method and Coherence, and his Deficiency in almost all the Graces and Ornaments of [dramatic] Writing; yet by the justness of his MORAL, the Aptness of many of his *Descriptions,* and the plain and natural Turn of several of his *Characters,* he pleases his Audience, and often gains their Ear; without a single Bribe from Luxury or Vice" (1:275). Shaftesbury's criticism of Shakespeare's "natural Rudeness" and "antiquated" language reveals both social and aesthetic prejudices that turn the dramatist into an intuitively virtuous country bumpkin. Shaftesbury's easy dismissal of his predecessor's dramatic language is largely a function of his own rhetoric of aristocratic exclusion. This is criticism by snob appeal. Yet, at the same time, Shaftesbury's praise of Shakespeare's moral authority suggests that the example of natural virtue can be instructive for eighteenth-century readers and audiences. Shakespeare and his contemporaries have "broken the Ice for those who are to follow 'em"; their eighteenth-century successors will "polish our Language, lead our Ear to finer Pleasure, and find out the true *Rhythms,* and harmonious Numbers, which alone can satisfy a just Judgment, and *Muse-like* Apprehension" (1:218). The implication in Shaftesbury's criticism of Shakespeare is that although morality and virtue remain the same in every era, the languages in which they are cast can be consciously and deliberately improved.

Language, for Shaftesbury, is therefore a social and political as well as a cultural artifact; it necessarily reflects the ideological conditions under which it is produced. At several points in his writings, he contrasts the literary products of "English liberty" (post-1688) with those of French, Italian, or ancient Roman "tyranny." He is particularly severe on Seneca. He prefaces his attack on "the random way of *Miscellaneous* Writing" (3:24) with an account of Seneca's influence as a writer: "We own *the Patriot,* and *good Minister:* But we reject *the Writer.* He was the first of any Note or Worth who gave credit to that *false* Stile and Manner [of miscellaneous writing]. He might, on this account, be call'd in reality *The Corrupter* of ROMAN *Eloquence*" (3:22). Yet given the "horrid Luxury and Effeminacy of the *Roman* Court . . . there was no more possibility of making a Stand for Language, than for Liberty" (3:23). Seneca, the honest statesman, is corrupted by the court in style rather than in personal morality. Though noble and patriotic, he writes "with infinite Wit, but with little or no Coherence; without a Shape or Body to his Work; without a real *Beginning,* a *Middle,* or an *End*" (3:24-25). Seneca, then, becomes both the victim of an artistically stifling and morally repressive society and the perpetrator of a kind of linguistic corruption that reaches down to modern times. In this manner, his "*false* Stile" reflects the tyranny of the Roman Empire's aggression; "by their unjust Attempts upon the Liberty of the World," says Shaftesbury, the Romans "justly lost their own. With their Liberty they lost not only their Force of Eloquence, but even their Stile and Language it-self" (1:219). Literary style in this passage is perceived as historically determined, the product not of an individual consciousness but of a politically corrupt ideology. The aesthetic shortcomings of Seneca's miscellaneous writing, in short, reflect the disorder and irrationality which Shaftesbury sees as the inevitable result of tyranny.

As his remarks on Shakespeare and Seneca indicate, Shaftesbury, as critic, combines an acute sensitivity to the ideological nature of writing with an almost naïve belief in idealistic, ahistorical standards of literary value. His discussions of the history of language and style, whether Roman, British, or Greek (see 3:138-41), are, even by early eighteenth-century standards, fanciful, less attempts at historical reconstruction than assertions of his faith in the near-sanctity of classical tradition. If Shaftesbury is less hostile to received knowledge than Locke, he is also inclined to judge historical figures solely by the standards of contemporary aristocratic "breeding." He praises Menander, for example, by observing that "he join'd what was deepest and most solid in Philosophy, with what was easiest and most refin'd in Breeding, and in the Character and Manner of a Gentleman" (1:255). The vocabulary Shaftesbury employs to describe a comic playwright of the fourth century B.C. is reminiscent of the language that he uses throughout the ***Characteristicks*** to discuss his aesthetic and social ideals of writing and behavior. Menander is, in effect, imaginatively re-created as an English gentleman of the eighteenth century, an historical embodiment of values that Shaftesbury finds congenial. The implication is that the standards of art and breeding—like virtue itself—remain unchanged from era to era; what differ are merely the forms of corruption or barbarism that lead Seneca and Shakespeare to fall short of the stylistic ideals of polished wit, verbal grace, and aesthetic unity.

Shaftesbury's remarks on Shakespeare and Seneca, then, are less significant as original evaluations of his literary past than as demonstrations of the moral and aesthetic bases of his thought. Criticism, in his mind, is no mere parasitic commentary on primary texts but a dialectical attempt to distinguish between true and false standards of language, art, and morality. As a form of original discourse it mediates between the languages of poetry and philosophy; it complements—even rivals—creative art. Shaftesbury defends the critic's prerogatives to judge and improve the language—and manners—of his age. He "condemn[s] the fashionable and prevailing Custom of inveighing against CRITICKS, as the common Enemys, the Pests, and Incendiarys of the Commonwealth of Wit and Letters . . . on the contrary, they are the *Props* and *Pillars* of this Building; and without the Encouragement and Propagation of such a Race, we shou'd remain as GOTHICK *Architects* as ever" (1:235-36). For Shaftesbury, critics as well as poets must be the legislators of any civilized race; they are the guardians of a classical learning which prevents one from falling prey to the trap of cultural relativism. In distinguishing between "*Criticks by Fashion*" and "just *Naturalist[s]* or *Humanist[s],*" Shaftesbury offers his own attack on literary fashion-mongering: "They who have no Help from Learning to observe the wider Periods or Revolutions of Human Kind, the Alterations which happen in Manners, and the Flux and Reflux of Politeness, Wit, and Art; are apt at every turn to make the present Age their standard, and imagine nothing barbarous or savage, but what is contrary to the Manners of their own Time" (1:271-72). Criticism offers a defense against novelty by promoting a cyclical view of literary history as the ongoing struggle of "Learning" against mere fashion. In this respect, Shaftesbury's praise of the ancients, like Ben Jonson's a century earlier, is an attempt to return to—and revitalize—what he sees as broadly Horatian standards of instruction and delight.

V

Shaftesbury's defense of criticism and the role of the critic is, at heart, a justification of his ambitions to perfect the English language as a medium for an aristocratic discourse of liberty and culture. The number of pages he devotes to a metacritical commentary on his previous work indicates how crucial the designation "critic" is to his self-perception as a writer. He sees the critic's task as an almost heroic undertaking, distinct from the kind of carping that, in his mind, characterizes his detractors: "To *censure* merely what another Person writes; to *twitch, snap, snub up,* or *banter*; to torture *Sentences* and *Phrases,* turn a few Expressions into Ridicule, or write what is now-a-days call'd an *Answer* to any Piece, is not sufficient to constitute what is properly esteem'd a WRITER, or AUTHOR in due form. For this reason, tho there are many ANSWERERS seen abroad, there are few or no CRITICKS or SATIRISTS" (3:271). Shaftesbury's linking of "CRITICKS" and "SATIRISTS" virtually erases traditional generic distinctions between critical and creative writing, between secondary and primary forms of discourse. Like satire, criticism participates in the radical, creative activity of trying to generate its own linguistic authority. The critical act, in this sense, becomes an attempt to establish one's authority and to reassert the "authority" of aristocratic and neoclassical values. For Shaftesbury, then, to write is to create an authoritative discourse, to redefine the traditional "authority" of language itself.

Like John Wilkins a generation earlier, Shaftesbury is intent on creating an authoritative, "natural" discourse that remains distinct from biblical tradition. Language, in his mind, imitates nature itself; it is not, as it is for Boyle, an imperfect refraction of a perfect biblical Logos.[16] Throughout the *Characteristicks,* Shaftesbury argues implicitly and explicitly that literary language is always historically mediated; it has no metaphysical existence beyond the limits of the printed page. His theistic enthusiasm—the direct contemplation of nature—therefore takes precedence over the written authority of the Bible. "The best Christian in the World," he states, "who being destitute of the means of *Certainty,* depends only on History and Tradition for his Belief in these Particulars [i.e., miracles], is at best but *a Sceptick-Christian.* He has no more than a nicely critical *Historical Faith,* subject to various Speculations, and a thousand different *Criticisms* of Languages and Literatures" (3:72). Biblical language, in this respect, cannot be distinguished from the "Criticisms" it inspires. It is a literary, and therefore historical, work; it can lay no real claim to being the mystical origin of language, the divine Logos. By inserting the Bible into the tradition of "a thousand different *Criticisms* of Languages and Lit-

eratures," Shaftesbury effectively rejects the logocentric assumptions that underlie Western linguistic theory from Augustine through the anti-Ciceronian prose stylists of the seventeenth century. One task Shaftesbury sets for himself is to relocate the origins—the authority—of critical or philosophical language.

In an important passage in the *Advice to an Author,* Shaftesbury contemplates what he perceives as the similarities between the origins of poetry and philosophy.

> 'Tis pleasant enough to consider how exact the resemblance was between the Lineage of *Philosophy* and that of *Poetry*; as deriv'd from their *two* chief Founders, or Patriarchs; in whose Loins the several Races lay as it were inclos'd. For as *the grand poetick* SIRE was . . . allow'd to have furnish'd Subject both to the *Tragick,* the *Comick,* and every other kind of genuine Poetry; so *the Philosophical* PATRIARCH, in the same manner, containing within himself the several Genius's of Philosophy, gave rise to all those several Manners in which that Science was deliver'd.
>
> (1:253-54)

The imagery in this passage—patriarchal and deliberately sexual—parodies the biblical rhetoric of both creation and procreation. Homer and Aristotle become nearly mythic, rather than merely historical, figures, containing "inclos'd" within themselves all of their subsequent poetic and philosophical progeny. These "Patriarchs" are truly originary; they stand at the beginning—or before—literary-historical time. The "several Manners" of poetic and philosophical discourse are similarly original. They are not redefined or invented by subsequent generations of writers but exist embryonically within the works of Homer and Aristotle. For Shaftesbury, then, the role of the poet or philosopher is to develop, explicate, or (as Pope said of poets who must follow in the footsteps of Homer) paraphrase an authoritative discourse which already exists.

Philosophy, criticism, and poetry are, for Shaftesbury, languages of regeneration. They assert the timeless truths of order and harmony that structure both the natural and social worlds. To write is to enter into a dialectical relationship with literary or philosophical tradition, to revitalize classical authority, even as that authority justifies one's own writing. Shaftesbury's *Characteristicks,* in this respect, is less the articulation of a self-consciously original system than a celebration of what the author sees as his position within the classical tradition of his "Patriarchs." The literary dimensions of Shaftesbury's work are ultimately defined by the goals of his "performance" as an author—to demonstrate the values of an aristocratic culture that, in itself, remains essentially unchanged by the stylistic forms in which it is described.

Notes

1. One important exception has appeared since this chapter was written, Lawrence Klein, "The Third Earl of Shaftesbury and the Progress of Politeness," *Eighteenth-Century Studies* 18 (1984-85): 186-214. Klein demonstrates that in *The Characteristicks,* "Shaftesbury was self-consciously engaged in 'polite' literary performance, a phenomenon he construed in many" ideologically determined ways (p. 208). Klein's reading of Shaftesbury might be set against John Andrew Bernstein in *Shaftesbury, Rousseau, and Kant: An Introduction to the Conflict between Aesthetic and Moral Values in Modern Thought* (Rutherford, N.J.: Fairleigh Dickinson University Press, 1980). Robert Voitle's recent biography, *The Third Earl of Shaftesbury, 1671-1713* (Baton Rouge: Louisiana State University Press, 1984), though generally disappointing in its treatment of Shaftesbury's thought, raises valuable points about the relationship between his published work and his private philosophical "exercises" (see especially pp. 160-62). For representative views of Shaftesbury's aesthetic theories see Ernest Tuveson, "The Significance of Shaftesbury," *ELH* 20 (1953): 267-99; A. Owen Aldridge, "Lord Shaftesbury's Literary Theories," *Philological Quarterly* 24 (1945): 45-64; Robert Marsh, *Four Dialectical Theories of Poetry: An Aspect of English Neoclassical Criticism* (Chicago: University of Chicago Press, 1965), pp. 18-47; R. L. Brett, *The Third Earl of Shaftesbury: A Study in Eighteenth-Century Literary Theory* (London: Hutchinson, 1951); Stanley Grean, *Shaftesbury's Philosophy of Religion and Ethics: A Study in Enthusiasm* (Athens: Ohio University Press, 1967); Robert W. Uphaus, "Shaftesbury on Art: The Rhapsodic Aesthetic," *Journal of Aesthetics and Art Criticism* 27 (1969): 341-48; Pat Rogers, "Shaftesbury and the Aesthetics of Rhapsody," *British Journal of Aesthetics* 12 (1972): 244-57; Jerome Stolnitz, "On the Origins of 'Aesthetic Disinterestedness,'" *Journal of Aesthetics and Art Criticism* 20 (1961): 131-43; Dabney Townsend, "Shaftesbury's Aesthetic Theory," *Journal of Aesthetics and Art Criticism* 41 (1982): 206-13.

2. John Richetti, *Philosophical Writing: Locke, Berkeley, Hume* (Cambridge: Harvard University Press, 1983).

3. All quotations, cited parenthetically in the text by volume and page, are from the sixth edition of *Characteristicks of Men, Manners, Opinions, Times,* 3 vol. (London, 1737-38). This edition, which follows the authoritative second edition closely, includes the late, but significant, "Letter Concerning Design."

4. On seventeenth-century literary style see especially Stanley Fish, *Self-Consuming Artifacts: The Experience of Seventeenth-Century Literature* (Berkeley: University of California Press, 1972); *"Attic" and Baroque Prose: Essays by Morris W. Croll,* ed. J. Max Patrick et al. (Princeton: Princeton University Press, 1966); and, for a critique of traditional categories of stylistic description, Paul Arakelian, "The Myth of a Restoration Style Shift," *Eighteenth Century: Theory and Interpretation* 20 (1979): 227-45.

5. On the structure and historical significance of Jonson's prose see Jonas Barish, *Ben Jonson and the Language of Prose Comedy* (Cambridge: Harvard University Press, 1960).

6. The phrase occurs repeatedly throughout his work; see, for example, his reference to the comic style of Beaumont and Fletcher in W. P. Ker, ed., *The Essays of John Dryden* (Rpt., New York: Russell and Russell, 1962), 1:80-81.

7. See, for example, Dryden's remark in "Defense of the Epilogue," *Essays* 1:167-73. On Shaftesbury's aristocratic ideology, see Bernstein, *Shaftesbury, Rousseau, and Kant,* pp. 13, 55.

8. Brian Corman, "Thomas Shadwell and Jonsonian Comedy," in Robert Markley and Laurie Finke, eds., *From Renaissance to Restoration: Metamorphoses of the Drama* (Cleveland, Ohio: Bellflower Press, Case Western Reserve University, 1984), pp. 126-52.

9. Herbert Davis, ed., *The Complete Plays of William Congreve* (Chicago: University of Chicago Press, 1967), p. 214.

10. See Barish, *Jonson and the Language of Prose Comedy,* passim.

11. On Boyle and Newton, see Robert Markley, "Objectivity as Ideology: Boyle, Newton, and the Language of Science," *Genre* 16 (1983): 335-72.

12. On Shaftesbury's aesthetic theory, see Rogers, "Shaftesbury and the Aesthetics of Rhapsody," pp. 244-57; Uphaus, "Shaftesbury on Art," pp. 341-48; Townsend, "Shaftesbury's Aesthetic Theory," pp. 206-13.

13. See Grean, *Shaftesbury's Philosophy,* especially pp. 19-36.

14. Benjamin Rand, ed., *Second Characters, or the Language of Forms* (Cambridge: Cambridge University Press, 1914), p. 123.

15. See Cartwright's commendatory verses in John Fletcher and Francis Beaumont, *Comedies and Tragedies* (London, 1647), Sig. d4r-d4v; Dryden,

Essays 1:79-83; and Rymer, "Tragedies of the Last Age," in Curt Zimansky, ed., *The Critical Works of Thomas Rymer* (New Haven: Yale University Press, 1956), especially pp. 38-39.

16. See Boyle's *Some Considerations Touching the Style of the Holy Scriptures* (London, 1661). On the significance of Boyle's influence on the language theories of Locke and other philosophers, see Hans Aarsleff, "Leibniz on Locke on Language," rpt. in *From Locke to Saussure: Essays on the Study of Language and Intellectual History* (Minneapolis: University of Minnesota Press, 1982), pp. 42-83.

Richard B. Wolf (essay date August 1988)

SOURCE: Wolf, Richard B. "Shaftesbury's Wit in *A Letter Concerning Enthusiasm.*" *Modern Philology* 86, no. 1 (August 1988): 46-53.

[*In the essay below, Wolf discusses Shaftesbury's ironic wit, focusing particularly on his use of paradox and the conceit, which he says are used to attack dogmatists.*]

Comparing his reaction to *Characteristics* with his earlier response to the French translation of *A Letter Concerning Enthusiasm,* Leibnitz observed that the third earl of Shaftesbury "s'etoit merveilleusement corrigé dans le progrès de ses meditations, et que d'un Lucien il etoit devenu un Platon."[1] Leibnitz's observation has also turned out to be descriptive of the development of Shaftesbury's critical reputation. The philosopher has come almost wholly to eclipse the satirist.

Apart from lamenting his affected prose, most students of Shaftesbury have ignored his art to concentrate on his thought. Although a few critics have examined his handling of the dialogue form in *The Moralists,* only Erwin Wolff and John G. Hayman have commented at any length on his literary performance in the "mix'd Satyrical Way of Rallery and Irony" employed in *A Letter Concerning Enthusiasm, Sensus Communis, Soliloquy,* and *Miscellaneous Reflections.*[2] My intention is to add to Wolff's and Hayman's efforts by examining two prominent features of Shaftesbury's ironic mode: the paradox and the conceit. In doing so, I will focus on *A Letter Concerning Enthusiasm* to show how Shaftesbury adapts these devices to a specific writing occasion.[3]

Shaftesbury places his wit at the service of truth in the *Letter,* but the work does not so much offer truths as argue for the outer and inner freedom needed for their pursuit. Ostensibly addressing the controversy provoked by the Camisards, or French Prophets, Shaftesbury playfully weds reflections on religious enthusiasm to a plea

for "good humoured" introspection and toleration. Unlike Henry More in *Enthusiasmus Triumphatus* (from which he appears to borrow) or most of the writers responding to the episode of the French Prophets, Shaftesbury does not attempt to provide a definitive account of religious enthusiasm or specific criteria for distinguishing enthusiasm or imposture from true inspiration. The effect of his playing with the concept of enthusiasm seems, indeed, antithetical to these purposes. The *Letter* expands the label "enthusiast" to include religious fanatics, poets, lovers, atheists, and, ultimately, those great men who are animated by "whatever [is] sublime in human Passions."[4] It links the French Prophets to both bacchants and Christian martyrs. It associates melancholy (the cause of enthusiasm in humors pathology) with the formalism and dogmatism often found in "unenthusiastic" orthodoxy. Shaftesbury does not argue for a total skepticism in the *Letter.* However, his treatment of enthusiasts and enthusiasm supports his call for a tolerant, but critical, examination of these phenomena by suggesting that "*Enthusiasm* is wonderfully powerful and extensive; that it is a matter of nice Judgment, and the hardest thing in the world to know fully and distinctly" (pp. 80-81).

Shaftesbury's wit in the *Letter* is well suited to the task of freeing the reader's mind from prejudices and of inducing the questioning approach that the work advocates. Its essential principle is paradox, the artful posing of real or apparent contradictions. Its effect is the usual one of delight produced by a surprising but just linking of ideas, but the surprise takes the extreme form of shock produced by a connection that appears wholly illogical but undeniable. Shaftesbury develops a number of central general paradoxes in the *Letter*: repression stimulates the growth of enthusiasm; ridicule serves as an aid to reverence; uncritical praise dishonors its object. But the most arresting form of paradox in the work is the verbally pointed, aphoristic, sometimes oxymoronic form that he frequently uses to intensify his arguments.

One of Shaftesbury's wittiest paradoxes appears in his account of men's "Faculty of deceiving themselves," by means of which "a very small Foundation of any Passion will serve us, not only to act it well, but even to work our selves into it beyond our own reach" (pp. 8-9). An ingenious oxymoron points the first illustration of this phenomenon: "Thus by a little Affectation in Love-Matters, and with the help of Romance or Novel, a Boy of Fifteen, or a grave Man of Fifty, may be sure to grow a very natural Coxcomb, and feel the *Belle Passion* in good earnest" (p. 9). Exposing the lover's folly, the phrase "natural Coxcomb" puns on the association of both words with idiocy. But by Shaftesbury's time "Coxcomb" had become applicable to fops as well as to pure and simple fools, creating the paradoxical linking here of nature and affectation.

Shaftesbury's "natural Coxcomb" points to a true paradox or mystery—one designed to shock the reader into reassessing conventional assumptions or prejudices. The lover's metamorphosis is a psychological mystery. Despite his inappropriate age and the artificial stimulus to his passion, the lover cannot be accused of dissembling. Nor can he simply be dismissed as deluded, however ridiculous he may appear. He has become the thing he pretended to be; he "feel[s] the *Belle Passion* in good earnest." But Shaftesbury's paradoxes are usually more apparent than real, a satiric device employed in what Hayman calls "Shaftesbury's most important strategy: namely, his quiet ridicule of some attitude or belief by turning back upon it its unfortunate or self-contradictory implications."[5]

To do justice to Shaftesbury's handling of the paradox as a satiric device, I wish to examine two examples in some detail. The first is quoted in part by Hayman to illustrate the author's mode of "quiet ridicule." It is the passage in which Shaftesbury contrasts heathen tolerance with Christian intolerance:

> NOT only the Visionarys and Enthusiasts of all kinds were tolerated, your Lordship knows, by the Antients: but on the other side, Philosophy had as free a course, and was permitted as a Ballance against Superstition. And whilst some Sects, such as the *Pythagorean* and latter *Platonick,* join'd in with the Superstition and Enthusiasm of the Times; the *Epicurean,* the *Academick,* and others, were allow'd to use all the Force of Wit and Raillery against it. And thus matters were ballanc'd; Reason had fair Play; Learning and Science flourish'd. Wonderful was the Harmony and Temper that arose from all these Contrarietys. Thus Superstition and Enthusiasm were mildly treated; and being let alone, they never rag'd to that degree as to occasion Bloodshed, Wars, Persecutions and Devastations in the World. But a new sort of Policy, which extends it self to another World, and considers the future Lives and Happiness of Men rather than the present, has made us leap the Bounds of natural Humanity; and out of a supernatural Charity, has taught us the way of plaguing one another most devoutly. It has rais'd an Antipathy which no temporal Interest cou'd ever do; and entail'd upon us a mutual Hatred to all Eternity.
>
> [Pp. 28-29]

The Christian/heathen contrast is a commonplace in the toleration literature of the period. Shaftesbury introduces an element of novelty by adapting it to his argument for freedom of raillery, and it is also well suited to his practice elsewhere in the *Letter* of using classical antiquity for a perspective on contemporary issues.[6] But the primary claim to literary merit here rests on Shaftesbury's witty development of the paradox of Christian persecution, a fact that becomes clear when the passage is compared with a similar one in Matthew Tindal's *Essay Concerning the Power of the Magistrate, and the Rights of Mankind, in Matters of Religion* (1697):

> The Heathens, who had more and wider Differences about Matters of Religion than the Christians, yet because they tolerated one another, had not those irreconcilable Animosities, fierce Contentions and unnatural Wars, which have frequently happened since the Propagation of the Christian Religion; which yet without Impiety cannot be imputed to its Genius, which is pure, peaceable, and inoffensive, and requires a universal Love and Charity for all Men of what Profession soever. No, it's the Antichristian Doctrine of Persecution that has transformed the mild and sociable Nature of Man into greater Ferocity than that of Wolves and Tigers. . . . So by degrees Men arrive to the height of Fury, Rage, and Madness, and break thro not only all the Ties of Christianity, but even Humanity; tho whilst they thus furnish such powerful Provocations to endless Discords, Hatreds, Factions, Wars, Massacres, *&c.* they have nothing in their Mouths but the Good of the Church and Salvation of Souls, not considering that without Love they cannot be Christ's Disciples, (John 13.) and that all other Duties without Charity profit nothing.[7]

Tindal's treatment of Christian intolerance also emphasizes the ironic discrepancy between tenets and practice but not in the form of paradox. By making an overt distinction between the true "Genius" of Christianity and "the Antichristian Doctrine of Persecution," Tindal precludes the apparent linking of irreconcilable ideas that is the basis for Shaftesbury's technique. In Tindal the charge of hypocrisy is explicit; in Shaftesbury it is implicit, conveyed with satiric indirection. Against the *concordia discors* of the ancients, Shaftesbury poses the modern Christian paradox of salvation through destruction. Pointed by a series of antitheses ("future Lives and Happiness" vs. "present"; "natural Humanity" vs. "supernatural Charity"; "temporal Interest" vs. "Hatred to all Eternity"), his paradox is epitomized in the phrase "plaguing one another most devoutly," an oxymoron sharpened by the pun on "devout." In Shaftesbury's satiric context this phrase produces a further shock as an ironic echo of the most repeated injunction to charity in the New Testament: Christ's admonition to his disciples "That ye love one another." Lacking such a context, Tindal's phrase "they tolerated one another" fails to evoke this association. His overt reference to the Gospel of John at the end of the passage effectively caps his argument, but it does not deliver the full ironic jolt of Shaftesbury's allusion.

Shaftesbury's introduction of the French Prophets provides another instructive illustration of his use of paradox:

> THERE are some, it seems, of our good Brethren, the *French* Protestants, lately come amongst us, who are mightily taken with this Primitive way ["of affronting the publick Worship"]. They have set a-foot the Spirit of Martyrdom to a wonder in their own Country; and they long to be trying it here, if we will give 'em leave: that is to say, if we will do 'em the favor to hang or imprison 'em; if we will be so kind as to break their

Bones for 'em, after their Country fashion, blow up their Zeal, and stir a-fresh the Coals of Persecution. But no such Grace can they yet obtain of us. So hard-hearted we are, that tho their own Mob are willing to bestow kind Blows upon 'em, and stone 'em now and then in the Street; tho the Priests of their own Nation wou'd gladly give 'em their desir'd Discipline, and are earnest to light their probationary Fires for 'em: We *English* Men, who are Masters in our own Country, will not suffer the Enthusiasts to be thus us'd.

[Pp. 41-42]

Behind the Prophets' apparently paradoxical desire to be abused, Shaftesbury implies, is not disinterested love of religious truth but a calculated design. The Prophets seek persecution in order to stimulate their enthusiasm, acquire glory, and enlarge their following. Shaftesbury playfully emphasizes the point with a pun on "blow up" (set up by the preceding phrase "break their Bones"): the Prophets court their opponents' attempts to "explode" their zeal as a means of inflating it. Evoking the etymology of "inspiration," moreover, "blow up" further debunks the Prophets' pretensions by suggesting that they are artificially "inspired" rather than truly infused with the spirit of God. Shaftesbury also sharpens the paradox epitomized in "kind Blows" with a device akin to biblical allusion, the ironic use of technical religious terms such as "Grace" and "Discipline."

Shaftesbury is less interested here in exposing the hypocrisy of the French Prophets, however, than in exposing the folly of those favoring their suppression. By revealing the Prophets' ulterior motives, he presents their would-be persecutors as gulls, whose intolerance only furthers the Prophets' cause. Despite their inhuman— not to mention unchristian—delight in persecution, they are ultimately fools manipulated by knaves. In contrast to their folly, Shaftesbury proposes the wise virtue of tolerance, paradoxically and patriotically embodied in the "hard-hearted" lenience of "we *English* Men." Shaftesbury's later, more sympathetic portrait of the Prophets as pitiful, if contemptible, victims of delusion (pp. 68-73) appears to result from a shift in satiric objectives rather than from an inconsistent explanation of their zeal. In the later instance, the Prophets themselves—not their intolerant opponents—are the primary object of attack.

A second prominent device of Shaftesbury's ironic art is the ingenious (and often extended) analogy or conceit. Although it unites merely disparate rather than antithetical elements, the conceit too can produce a powerful shock of delight, especially if the elements come from radically different associative contexts. The satiric potential of this device is succinctly illustrated by the treatment accorded proponents of Pascal's wager (as advanced by Archbishop Tillotson). Shaftesbury compares them to "crafty Beggars" who prudently award a title to every stranger they approach: "For if there

shou'd be really a *Lord,* in the case; we shou'd be undone (say they) for want of giving the Title: But if the Party shou'd be no *Lord,* there wou'd be no harm; it wou'd not be ill taken" (p. 55). The meanness of the second term of Shaftesbury's comparison forcefully deflates the first, suggesting that the position of Pascal and Tillotson results from spiritual cowardice and venality.

As with paradox, a proper appreciation of Shaftesbury's use of the conceit requires more extensive examples. The first I have chosen develops the standard toleration argument that persecution inflames rather than extinguishes the zeal of its victims:

I CAN hardly forbear fancying, that if we had but an Inquisition, or some formal Court of Judicature, with grave Officers, and Judges, erected to restrain Poetical Licence, and in general to suppress that Fancy and Humour of Versification; but in particular that most extravagant Passion of Love, as it is set out by Poets, in its Heathenish Dress of *Venus*'s and *Cupid*'s; if the Poets, as Ringleaders and Teachers of this Heresy, were under grievous Penaltys forbid to enchant the People by their vein of Rhyming; and if the People, on the other side, were under proportionable Penaltys forbid to hearken to any such Charm, or lend their Attention to any Love-Tale, so much as a Play, a Novel, or a Ballad; we might perhaps see a new *Arcadia* arising out of this heavy Persecution: Old People and Young wou'd be seiz'd with a versifying Spirit; we shou'd have Field-Coventicles of Lovers and Poets; Forests wou'd be fill'd with romantick Shepherds and Shepherdesses; and rocks resound with Ecchoes of Hymns and Praises offer'd to the Powers of Love. We might have a fair Chance by this means to bring back the whole Train of Heathen Gods, and set our cold Northern Island burning with as many Altars to *Venus* and *Apollo,* as formerly either *Cyprus, Delos,* or any of those warmer *Grecian* Climates.

[Pp. 32-33]

Shaftesbury's coupling of religious with poetic persecution is unexpected but apt, drawing on both the traditional Christian linking of religious with amatory experience and the "theological" trappings of love poetry in the classical mode. Shaftesbury's development of the conceit, moreover, illustrates one of the device's distinctive effects—the pleasure produced by the author's ingenuity in working out an elaborate series of similarities. To this delight is added one deriving from context. The conceit pulls together earlier strands of the ***Letter,*** linking its opening remarks on belief in the Muses with its passing references to enthusiasm in love (pp. 9, 21, 27-28, 31). Shaftesbury's references to males of fifteen and fifty who turn "natural Coxcomb" with the aid of a romance and to "Modifications of Spleen" such as "Love, or Gallantry, or Knight-Errantry" fittingly culminate in the ludicrous vision of English lovers of all ages wandering the countryside as crack-brained shepherds and shepherdesses hymning the pagan gods.

Shaftesbury's satiric assault on romantic love and the pastoral, however, is only incidental. His primary targets in the passage are the proponents of persecution and, to a lesser extent, opportunistic enthusiasts such as the French Prophets. Absurdly overreacting to a patently harmless deviation from orthodoxy, Shaftesbury's grave suppressors provoke a major outbreak of heresy. Their actions are linked explicitly to the Roman Catholic excesses of the Inquisition and perhaps implicitly to the excesses of English Puritanism, which sanctioned its own form of literary repression during the Interregnum. Shaftesbury's enthusiasts, on the other hand—their zeal and ranks swollen by persecution—become the ridiculous inhabitants of a pastoral cloud-cuckoo-land, with their religious fervor linked ironically to the pagan and profane. Shaftesbury's diction accentuates the ironies generated by the conceit. The preposterous seriousness with which his persecutors undertake their attempt "to restrain Poetical License" is underscored by the formality of quasi-legal phrases such as "formal Court of Judicature" and "proportionable Penaltys." The vocabulary of religious enthusiasm, on the other hand, is applied with devastating effect to the new Arcadians in phrases such as "seiz'd with a versifying Spirit" and "Field Conventicles of Lovers and Poets"—the latter linking Shaftesbury's pagan revival to the clandestine open-air meetings of the French Prophets in the Cévennes.

A second conceit worth examining in detail follows the "kind Blows" passage discussed earlier. Its comparison of the Prophets to puppets provides a memorable transition from the argument that persecution enflames enthusiasm to the argument that toleration and raillery most effectively extinguish it:

> But how barbarous and more than heathenishly cruel are we tolerating *English* Men! For not contented to deny these Prophesying Enthusiasts the Honor of a Persecution, we have deliver'd 'em over to the cruellest Contempt in the World. I am told they are at this time the Subject of a choice Droll or Puppet-Shew at *Bart'lemy*-Fair. There doubtless their strange Voices and involuntary Agitations are admirably well acted, by the Motion of Wires, and Inspiration of Pipes. For the Bodys of the Prophets, in their state of Prophecy, being not in their own power, but (as they say themselves) mere passive Organs, actuated by an exterior Force, have nothing natural or resembling real Life in any of their Sounds or Motions: so that how aukardly soever a Puppet-Shew may imitate other Actions, it must needs represent this Passion to the life. And whilst *Bart'lemy*-Fair is in possession of this Privilege, I dare stand Security to our National Church, that no Sect of Enthusiasts, no new Venders of Prophecy or Miracles, shall ever get the start, or put her to the trouble of trying her Strength with 'em, in any Case.

[Pp. 42-44]

The puppet show conceit may shed little light on the nature of the Prophets' enthusiasm, but it forcefully illustrates Shaftesbury's point about the effectiveness of raillery (as opposed to persecution) as a means of countering the sect's appeal. Detailing the correspondence between the grotesque, unnatural sounds and motions of the Prophets in their ecstasies and the imperfect, mechanical mimicry of marionettes, Shaftesbury ridicules the bizarre behavior that scandalized the sect's opponents. With the first of several ironic allusions in the *Letter* to John Lacy's defense of the Prophets in Lacy's preface to the second edition of *A Cry from the Desart* (1707), Shaftesbury denigrates the group's pretensions to divine inspiration by comparing the Prophets' account of possession by the Holy Spirit to puppets' manipulation by a puppeteer.

The Bartholomew Fair setting itself contributes to Shaftesbury's attack. In the first place, it links the Prophets to an institution with a distinctly unsavory reputation (a fact illustrated by the attempt mounted in 1708 to reduce the fair from two weeks to three days). Shaftesbury enhances this damaging association when he dismisses the sect as "new Venders of Prophecy or Miracles," identifying them with the fair's mountebanks and sellers of gimcracks. In the second place, the setting links the Prophets with Rabbi Zeal-of-the-land Busy in Ben Jonson's *Bartholomew Fair* (performed around fair time in 1702, 1704, and 1707). Busy, whose greed and gluttony provide an ironic contrast to his censorious Puritanism, attempts to shut down a puppet show in the final act of the play, only to be bested in argument by one of the puppets, who asserts against him: "Nay I'le proue, against eer a *Rabbin* of 'hem all, that my standing is as lawfull as his; that I speak by inspiration, as well as he; that I haue as little to doe with learning as he; and doe scorne her helps as much as he."[8]

While the "new *Arcadia*" conceit ties together earlier strands of the *Letter,* the puppet show conceit—extended to the stage in general—unites the pages immediately following it. The triumph of Protestantism in England, Shaftesbury suggests, was greatly helped by the Papists' treating their opponents (burned as heretics at Smithfield, the site of Bartholomew Fair) "in a more tragical way" than that of a puppet show (p. 44). The Romans would have posed a greater threat to Christianity "if they had chose to bring our primitive Founders upon the Stage in a pleasanter way than that of Bear-Skins and Pitch-Barrels" (pp. 44-45). The Jews might have countered the teachings of Jesus more successfully if they had "but taken the Fancy to act such Puppet-Shews in his Contempt, as at this hour the Papists are acting in his Honor" (p. 46). Arguing that raillery is a foe to falsehood but a friend to truth, Shaftesbury asserts that Socrates' good-humored response to Aristophanes' puppet show tactics in *The Clouds* enhanced the philosopher's reputation and confirmed the truth of his teachings (pp. 47-49). Finally, in preparing to move on to discuss misconceptions of God, he observes that "the melancholy way of treating Religion is that which, according to my Apprehension, renders it so tragical, and is the occasion of its acting in reality such dismal Tragedys' in the world" (p. 49). By the time that Shaftesbury rings his last change on it, the puppet show conceit has encompassed a whole history of religious enthusiasm and persecution.

Hayman's description of Shaftesbury's ironic procedure as "quiet ridicule" seems accurate if the style of raillery in the **Letter** is compared with the strident invective found in most attacks on religious enthusiasts or their opponents in the period. The distinction is one that Shaftesbury himself hinted at in a marginal query in the hand-corrected set of 1711 **Characteristics** now housed in the British Library. Nettled by attacks on his advocacy of ridicule in questions of religion, he asked "whether *Raillery* wch signifys back biting & that wch means Banter be writ ye same way."[9] If Shaftesbury's ridicule in the **Letter** is "quiet" in this sense, however, it is certainly not timid or easily ignored. And the grudging praise of early answerers speaks less to this fact than their heated condemnation of a work that does not restrict its ironic wit solely to targets on the fringes of orthodoxy.

Shaftesbury may have claimed to deplore the standards of taste that obliged him to turn to satire in order to court "the airy Reader" who would find the formal **Inquiry Concerning Virtue or Merit** "oppressive."[10] But his compunction about his ironic works in no way undermines their achievement. Shaftesbury's witty use of devices such as the paradox and the conceit to question the assumptions and deflate the pretensions of dogmatists of all persuasions reveals a distinctive literary talent.

Notes

1. "Leibniz an Remond," no. 11, February 11, 1715 N.S., *Die philosophischen Schriften von Gottfried Wilhelm Leibniz,* ed. C. I. Gerhardt (1875-90; reprint, Hildesheim, 1960), 3:637.

2. Erwin Wolff, *Shaftesbury und seine Bedeutung für die englische Literatur des 18.Jhs.: Der Moralist und die literarische Form,* Buchreihe der Anglia, Zeitschrift für englische Philologie, vol. 8 (Tübingen, 1960); John G. Hayman, "Shaftesbury and the Search for a Persona," *Studies in English Literature, 1500-1900* 10 (1970): 491-504. Wolff describes Shaftesbury's experimentation with the various genres represented in *Characteristics,* while Hayman discusses the evolution of the author's persona in his ironic works. Shaftesbury employed the phrase "mix'd Satyrical Way of Raillery and Irony" in a letter commenting on

Leibnitz's remarks on *Characteristics* (Shaftesbury to Pierre Coste, July 25, 1712 N.S., Public Record Office, Shaftesbury Papers, PRO 30/24/23/9, p. 249).

3. One reason for the relative neglect of Shaftesbury's ironic works may be that we rarely read them in the form that suits them best. When contemporaries prefaced their attacks on *A Letter Concerning Enthusiasm* (hereafter referred to as *Letter*) by acknowledging its sparkling style and wit, they were responding to a version of the piece that few people have read since the publication of *Characteristics* in 1711. Shaftesbury made numerous minor changes in the *Letter, Sensus Communis,* and *Soliloquy* in preparing these previously published works for the first and second editions of *Characteristics.* His stylistic revisions aimed at courting the style-conscious British gentleman, "the age running so much into the politeness of this sort" (Shaftesbury to Thomas Micklethwayte, January 19, 1711 N.S., PRO 30/24/23/8, p. 114). But editors and textual critics since John M. Robertson have noted the unfortunate effect of much of Shaftesbury's tinkering with style. His crusade against ten or more consecutive monosyllabic words, for instance, produced some sixty-five changes in the fifty-three pages of *Letter* text in the first edition of *Characteristics:* "fit" became "capacitated"; "first" became "antecedently"; a "dark" hour became a "heavy and dark" one. Such changes helped bloat a prose already inclined to fullness. Various other changes associated with the incorporation of the *Letter* into *Characteristics* have also tended to obscure Shaftesbury's satiric art. The "treatise" label, the numbering of sections, and the footnotes (eleven in 1711; thirty-two in 1714) added the foreign trappings of more formal and methodical writing without exploiting the ironic potential that results. Unlike Swift's *Tale of a Tub,* the *Letter* makes no grandiose claims for system and comprehensiveness; unlike the *Mechanical Operation of the Spirit,* it makes no attempt to play with the contradiction between methodic and epistolary form. Shaftesbury's footnotes do not parody the machinery of pedantry in the manner of the Scriblerians, and his cross-references—fully half of the notes to the *Letter*—repeatedly interrupt the play of wit to direct the reader outside the passage at hand. If we are to appreciate the literary properties of works such as the *Letter,* we might do better to read them in their original printed form.

4. Shaftesbury, *A Letter Concerning Enthusiasm* (London, 1708), p. 82; hereafter cited in the text.

5. Hayman, p. 495.

6. For Shaftesbury's use of classical literature and history in attacking Christianity, see A. O. Aldridge, "Shaftesbury and the Classics," in *Gesellschaft. Kulture. Literatur: Rezeption un Originalität im Wachsen einer europäischen Literatur un Geistigkeit: Beiträge Luitpold Wallach gewidmet,* ed. Karl Bosl, Monographien zur Geschichte des Mittelalters, vol. 11 (Stuttgart, 1975), pp. 248-53.

7. Matthew Tindal, *An Essay Concerning the Power of the Magistrate, and the Rights of Mankind, in Matters of Religion* (London, 1697), pp. 34-36.

8. C. H. Herford and Percy Simpson, eds., *Ben Jonson* (Oxford, 1925-52), 6:136.

9. *Characteristicks* (London, 1711), 1:65 (British Library, C.28g.16).

10. *Characteristicks,* 2d ed. (London, 1714), 3:8. In commenting on Leibnitz's remarks about *Characteristics,* Shaftesbury asserted even more forcefully that ironic works such as the *Letter* were for him a distasteful concession to the corrupt taste of the audience that he courted (see n. 2 above).

Robert Voitle (essay date 1989)

SOURCE: Voitle, Robert. "Lord Shaftesbury and Sentimental Morality." *Studies on Voltaire and the Eighteenth Century* 263 (1989): 489-91.

[*In this essay, Voitle considers the factors that contributed to the rationally inclined Shaftesbury becoming an early leader in the movement towards sentimental morality.*]

How did Lord Shaftesbury, who was not at all pious in the ordinary sense of the word, who was remote and austere in his dealings with mankind, who strove all of his life to achieve a purely rational mode of behaviour, come to be regarded as one of the founders of sentimental morality?

Some modern critics have difficulty interpreting Shaftesbury because they do not realise that the whole nature of his moral statements changes as the audience he is addressing changes. By examining these audiences we can learn something about his real place in intellectual history.

One audience, which comprises most of mankind, is addressed chiefly in his correspondence. To it belong servants, members of his extended family, politicians, noblemen—just about anyone. Shaftesbury is certain that for this large group of people, the best guarantee of moral behaviour lies in the fear of God. This may seem strange for a moment, coming from someone whose piety is, to say the least, unorthodox, and who conceives the afterlife in terms just as strange. But it is not odd if we reflect on the speaker's background: he was an aristocrat, a member of a group of a few hundred persons who actually ran England at the time. He is the last person in the world to wish to disturb the patterns of religious thought which he must have considered the basis of the society of his day, the basis upon which his own rank ultimately depended.

Another audience Shaftesbury addresses is much smaller than this first group, but ultimately far more influential, because it is their thought which tends to mould the ideas of others. These he addresses in his printed works, especially in the later ones. This group he hopes will learn to follow the moral sense, but achieving the status of moral virtuosos will not be easy. Only by intense effort will they succeed in that task, which he finally paralleled to that of becoming a virtuoso in art.

Shaftesbury knew very few, alas, who sought virtue for its own sake, so that the final group addressed only in his letters is by far the smallest. From their study of the Ancients, these persons had become truly benevolent. And if we include Shaftesbury among these lovers of virtue for its own sake, we can see how they learn to act well: by the study of Marcus Aurelius and Epictetus, his lifelong guides. These are strange leaders for the proponent of a morality supposedly based on emotion.

You will note that two of these groups are addressed only in his letters, which means that most readers are not familiar with the concept of various audiences, since the majority of the letters have not yet been published. Combine this fact with the peculiar history of his publications—the Platonic element, not evident until *The Moralists* was published in 1709; the aesthetic element, which evolved from the Platonic, briefly treated during his own day but not wholly appreciated until manuscripts were printed about eighty years ago; finally the Stoic element, only evident at all during the present century from the publication of a manuscript—and it becomes quite clear where some of the confusion arises. Were you to ask a contemporary scholar what interested him most he would be likely to point to the Platonic, the aesthetic or the Stoic, not the moral sense, which was subsumed into English thought by the middle of the eighteenth century.

There were other factors which contributed to Shaftesbury's becoming an early leader of the movement towards sentimental morality. The timing of the publication of *Characteristicks* (1711) was very significant. Using hindsight, most contemporary scholars agree that the shift from the traditional system of morality, based on the badly eroded concept of Reason, to emotional bases was by this date already under way. Furthermore the optimistic view of human nature advocated by the Cambridge Platonists was increasingly accepted. All that was needed was to find a spokesman for these views.

To convert the shapers of opinion during his time, Shaftesbury worked very hard to cultivate an easy offhand manner, which contrasted strongly with the stiff, formal style of earlier essays such as ***Inquiry concerning virtue*** (1699). This style must have done much to make him seem the spokesman. The moral sense also had a unique advantage in being introduced by someone who had decided to appear as a populariser rather than as a theoretician. The theory, then, came later, in contrast to the way most intellectual developments take place.

Another matter also helped him into the role of spokesman. All his life, Shaftesbury had struggled to develop an appearance of impeccable morality, which he thought would counteract the bad reputation which he felt that his grandfather, the first Earl, had unjustly acquired. He succeeded so well that he was able even to make people forget how much some of the clergy mistrusted him. He became the 'good' Earl of Shaftesbury. Whatever accomplishments the noble classes achieved, very few of them were thought of as moral exemplars.

Circumstance also made a further contribution, in the form of the man who first chose to imitate Shaftesbury's pattern of thought, Francis Hutcheson. If many of the clergy doubted Shaftesbury's piety, none could doubt Hutcheson's. As most scholars know, Shaftesbury eventually came to hate a 'system'. Hutcheson was overwhelmingly systematic, so much so that he came to postulate the existence of a whole family of senses parallel to the moral sense. From this point on, the role of emotion became more or less unbounded.

Shaftesbury could not have known what effect the forces of history were going to have on his notion of the moral sense. Sentimental morality ultimately involved a broad dependence on the emotions. Emotions suggest ease of access, in complete contrast to the discipline he was proposing. Granted his psychology has emotional roots, granted he was optimistic with regard to human nature, but certainly this austere, deliberate man, who sought all of his days to follow reason, could not have dreamt that historians would one day point to his idea of the moral sense as a significant step in the growth of emotional values in life and art, replacing the rational ones he himself had learned from the Ancients. His ghost cannot be happy with the results, and we have reason to examine, however necessary they may seem, our methods of tracing the pattern of development of ideas from one philosopher to another, in a sort of intellectual daisy chain.

Susan Griffin (essay date fall 1990)

SOURCE: Griffin, Susan. "Shaftesbury's *Soliloquy*: The Development of Rhetorical Authority." *Rhetoric Review* 9, no. 1 (fall 1990): 94-106.

[*In the following essay, Griffin analyzes Shaftesbury's* Soliloquy, *examining its ideas about the role of the author and arguing that the work shows how eighteenth-century notions about rhetoric differ from contemporary rhetorical thought.*]

> Vous savez que je suis habitué de longue main à l'art du soliloque. Si je quitte la societé et que je rentre chez moi triste and chagrin, je me retire dans mon cabinet, and là je me questionne et je me demande: Qu'avez vous? de l'humeur? . . . Oui . . . Est-ce que vous vous portez mal? . . . Non . . . Je me presse, j'arrache de moi la vérité. Alors il me semble que j'ai une ame gaie, tranquille, honnête and sereine, qui en interroge une autre qui est honteuse de quelque sottise qu'elle craint d'avouer. . . .
>
> Je conseillerai cet examen secret a tous ceux qui voudront ecrire; ils en deviendront a coup súr plus honnétes gens et meilleurs Auteurs.
>
> Diderot 2:2 89-90[1]

The "art of soliloquy" that Diderot describes here is not his own invention—his source is an essay by Anthony Ashley Cooper, the 3rd Earl of Shaftesbury, ***Soliloquy, or Advice to an Author*** (1711), in which the practice of self-examination is recommended as the essential prerequisite to authorship. In this essay I would like to take both a practical and theoretical look at this eighteenth-century practice. As a writing teacher, I have discovered that the soliloquy encourages students to develop what I'll call "authority," a voice or *ethos* that is not only individual but commands respect. Practice, however, is never independent of theory; as Berlin cautions, "to teach writing is to argue for a version of reality . . ." ("Contemporary Criticism" 766). The version of reality that underlies Shaftesbury's soliloquy is a rich mix of Platonic epistemology and classical rhetorical notions—a complex theory that the practice of soliloquy doesn't necessarily imply, since specific practices can result from a number of different theories. However, Shaftesbury's ideas are in themselves useful counterpoints to some modern assumptions about rhetoric. The "art of soliloquy" is thus worth our reconsideration, both pragmatically and theoretically.

The soliloquy that Diderot adopted from Shaftesbury is an imitation of Platonic dialogue, a strict exchange of question-and-answer designed to effect an internal division, and thus allow the thinker to distinguish better ideas from worse. It is a process of judgment, a way of defining one's own values. Shaftesbury argues that this internal search for values must take place *before* the author addresses his public, for two reasons. First, authorship is an assumption of authority; to publish one's thoughts to the world is to presume to give advice. So "all authors are, in a manner, professed masters of understanding to the age" (*Sol.* 1:104), who must be sure of their own ideas before they try to persuade others. Shaftesbury's second, and related, concern is the influence of the audience on the author. A premature consciousness of an audience's desires can influence thought itself—the anxious writer may think whatever his audience would most like to hear. Shaftesbury's example is the cleric who pens "private" meditations with an eye to eventual publication, who becomes for his public an "author-character . . . always considering how this or that thought would serve to complete some set of contemplations, or furnish out the commonplace book from whence these treasured riches are to flow in plenty on the necessitous world" (*Sol.* 1:109). Shaftesbury's eighteenth-century authors might seem at first to have little in common with student writers, who are in most cases not writing for publication, and whose work is not intended to instruct but to demonstrate that they have absorbed instruction. And writing teachers are more apt to complain that students ignore audience than that they are unduly influenced by it. If we look more closely at the nature of student writing, however, we see that in fact student writers are expected to develop authority in their writing, and that they are as vulnerable as Shaftesbury's cleric to the desires of their audiences.

Most writing assignments students are given demand a rhetorical response. We introduce them to genres that are both public and persuasive, e.g., opinion essays, analysis and criticism of texts. Even purely expository works, like research reports, are arguably persuasive in an implicit way. Finally, we ask students to imagine readers beyond their immediate classrooms, to write *as if* for the public. And that means we are asking that they write *as if* they had authority, an ability to command attention and respect for their views. Composition pedagogy, then, should offer them some means of developing authority—something beyond the mere imitation of the authoritative forms of the genre. Students know that format, footnotes, and academic jargon don't truly entitle them to take positions or make claims. To speak with true authority, they must have some inner sense of the value of what they're going to say.

I would also argue that students are uncomfortably aware of the desires of their audiences, especially since academic success frequently hinges on pleasing professors. When student writing is ineffective, it can be seen as lacking audience awareness, a conclusion that modern research tends to validate. But researchers have also recognized the problems of audience awareness. Ede and Lunsford point out that an exclusive focus on what the audience wants "in its extreme form becomes pandering to the crowd" (159) and undermines the writer's

responsibility to determine the meaning of her own work. Elbow has recently noted the inhibiting effect of audience awareness; he suggests preliminary writing that closes out audience altogether, as a way of overcoming writer's block. Students in particular "often feel 'they don't have anything to say' until they have succeeded in engaging themselves in private desert island writing for themselves alone" (Elbow, "Closing" 65).

Both objections echo Shaftesbury's warning against the "author-character," who has lost all identity in his preoccupation with pleasing his audience. Student writers are particularly vulnerable to such a loss. They are not only asked to take on a public voice, which may feel unfamiliar to them, but are then evaluated on their performance by their instructors. They thus begin with a sharp anxiety about pleasing this immediate audience, and become, for their instructors, a particular type of "author-character"—the good student. They produce prose that has the qualities they assume college professors admire, e.g., inflated diction, formal tone, that meticulous attention to "rules," whether appropriate or not, that Rose has observed. They also become entangled in the "character" that the genre seems to demand, whether research scientist or literary critic, and are understandably awkward in its imitation. They are, finally, almost anyone but themselves.

Self-discovery, according to Berlin, is itself the end of many current "expressionistic" rhetorical theories (*Rhetoric* 145-55). In Shaftesbury's rhetoric, it is only the beginning—but an absolutely essential beginning. Escape from the "author-character" can be achieved by turning within, by substituting the self for the external audience, by listening for self-approval. Once internal conflicts are resolved, however, the author takes up her proper role, i.e., influencing public opinion. Self-discovery is not, however, easily achieved. Shutting out audience isn't sufficient; the author is left to confront her own mysterious subterfuges. "One would think," Shaftesbury notes, "there was nothing easier for us than to know our own minds, and understand what our main scope was; what we plainly drove at, and what we proposed to ourselves, as our end, in every occurrence of our lives. But our thoughts have generally such an obscure implicit language, that 'tis the hardest thing in the world to make them speak out distinctly" (*Sol.* 1:113). Shaftesbury's warning here, that the mind can mask thoughts from the thinker, is not often echoed in current composition texts, most of which assume that the mind's ideas are relatively accessible and can be accepted at face value. Frequently, the emphasis is on the collection of ideas, as if overcoming a lack of content were usually the writer's problem. Too often, there is no suggestion that the ideas students have gathered may be suspect. Yet we all know that not all the thoughts that occur to us during a session of brainstorming are equally good—some are irrelevant, others vague, others illogical. These we may eliminate quickly. What we are not likely to notice are those ideas that are suspiciously self-serving, that arise from assumptions so deeply held as to go unquestioned.

The soliloquy questions those assumptions; like Platonic dialogue, its motive is to shake faiths that are unwarranted, to unmask the true nature of ideas. The dialogue exercises of current composition textbooks have rather different motives. True, modern pedagogy has never lost a sense of the efficacy of dialectical thinking. In *The Practical Stylist,* for example, Baker reminds us that "our minds naturally swing from side to side as we think" (16), and then recommends using the swing to construct proleptic argument, by favoring one side of the swing: "The basic organizing principle here is to get rid of the opposition first, and to end on your own side" (17). The dialogue exercises recommended in textbooks reflect this approach to dialectical thinking; internal opposition is useful as a representation of possible external opposition. These exercises thus differ from the soliloquy in a subtle yet significant way. The structure is the same, an exchange of relatively brief questions and answers. But the exchange is not seen as essentially internal, even when the writer is playing both roles. When the "other" of the conversation is not a real person—friend, fellow student, or teacher—it is the writer's imaginative construct of another person. Instructions frequently specify this: "Imagine that you are discussing the subject you have to write on with another person, but you do the talking for both . . ." (Cowan 19); "Imagine one reader, someone who would question your assessment of the problem or your tentative solution" (Axelrod 189). Such dialogues, however solitary, have a different dynamic than the soliloquy. They carry the writer to the outside, encouraging anticipation of audience objections, helping the writer prepare possible responses.

In a few cases, the existence of internal "voices" is suggested; then the direction of the dialogue begins to reverse, to turn inwards, and become the self-examination of soliloquy. One set of instructions characterizes the voice of the other as "a tough stranger in your head who keeps pestering you with questions" (Duke 86). A brief pamphlet of 1971, Herum and Cummings' *Writing: Plans, Drafts and Revisions,* specifically notes the unmasking power of the exercise; "the clash of minds in a dialogue can force hidden ideas and feelings to the surface" (70). The switch from dialogue to monologue, they argue, involves choosing the best voice, a voice in part created from the dialogue itself:

> Because it has been listening to the other voices, that voice can now anticipate their questions and objections in monologue form. Not only that, but the voice you choose might find that it has learned something from the others and that its original stance is no longer what it used to be. . . .

> (74)

Shaftesbury's soliloquy operates in much the same way—from the inner debate of voices, the wiser one emerges. It is important, however, that the soliloquy *not* involve an imagined audience; writers must know that they are speaking only to themselves, must identify as their own the ideas and feelings, certainty and doubt, that the exercise reveals. To illustrate the process more concretely, I'd like to present two student soliloquies, one written by a relatively unsophisticated freshman, the other by an advanced student. In both cases the instructions given were to ask a question, answer it, and alternate question and answer, keeping both fairly brief, until the conversation seemed to end. Since most of us have had at least casual conversations with ourselves, it's not difficult to model soliloquy for the students. Nor do most students have trouble producing these exchanges. Occasionally, a writer is so unused to any kind of self-criticism that she will ask only questions to which she has prefabricated answers. More often, students involve themselves in a thicket of doubts, as this freshman does in response to George Orwell's "Politics and the English Language."

Q: How do you react to the statement "Political language . . . is designed to make lies sound truthful and murder respectable"?

A: I guess my first reaction would be that it is scary.

Q: What do you mean scary?

A: Well, in a way you are brought up to trust politicians in three piece suits, and to think that they lie is scary. Politicians have a big responsibility on their hands.

Q: You just trust politicians who wear three piece suits?

A: I didn't mean it that way, but I guess if a bag lady went out on a stage to make a serious political speech I wouldn't take her very seriously.

Q: What if she were telling the truth, and had some good ideas?

A: I still don't think I would take her very seriously.

Q: Isn't that a form of discrimination?

A: Sure it is.

Q: Then why would you react that way?

A: I'm not sure. I recognize it's discrimination, but I still feel that way. Maybe it isn't acceptable because it is out of what we consider proper.

Q: So are you saying appearance makes the politician?

A: A good appearance doesn't hurt. Maybe appearance is another shield politicians hide behind.

This writer faithfully followed the instruction to begin with something that disturbed her, an assertion of Orwell's that she finds "scary." In a move typical of soliloquy, she stops to ask herself what she means by the term. Her answer is tentative, and leads to a contrast between two icons, so to speak, the three-piece suit and the bag lady. The strictness of the dialogue form allows this writer to pursue the meaning of these symbolic types, and label her own distrust of the bag lady "discrimination." "Sure it is," she agrees, reaching the soliloquy's point of certainty. An assumption she would like to hold about the relative trustworthiness of politicians in three-piece suits has been shaken—not by an outside critic, but by the critic inside her own head.

For some freshmen, the soliloquy is their first exercise in self-questioning. Most advanced students have already experimented with methods of testing their own ideas and tend to use the soliloquy in more varied and complex ways. Students in a pre-law writing course, for example, did use it to construct proleptic argument, by proposing possible objections to their own positions and then answering them. The reflexive nature of the soliloquy, however, involves the writer simultaneously in *both* roles, proponent and opponent, prosecution and defense. In this student's soliloquy on the insanity defense, the result is a playful nagging voice that keeps the problems of the argument constantly before the thinker. The soliloquy begins with the problem of defining insanity for legal purposes. The writer is drawn to motivation as the crucial difference, and speculates that the insane motivation comes in a different way:

Q: So what you want to look for is a problem with the killer's wiring.

A: In a way, yes. We can trace the behavior of a "normal" killer to some sort of logic based on desire, greed, passion, anger, etc. We can say he was angry because of A or he was desperate because of B, where A and B are things we can accept as part of the real world.

Q: Whatever that is.

A: Hush. I'm on a roll. Okay. But the insane killer's motives may also be traced to A or B, but there's a problem in the way the stimulus we recognized as reality is processed. The insane killer adds an element of his own to the cause/effect decision to kill somebody. And if that element depends upon something outside what we consider the real world, we can recognize that as insane.

Q: This is all a complicated way of saying it depends, right?

A: It depends.

The description of insane motivation that the writer is working out is sophisticated, and one that legal experts have developed in greater detail, as she found when she began to research the subject. The other voice here seems merely to interfere with the construction of the theory, and at one point, the writer tells it to be quiet— "Hush. I'm on a roll." But its presence can't be ignored; its objections are valid. And immediately after her attempt to quiet it, she picks up its objection to the indefinite nature of the term *real world* and begins to work that into her theory, by qualifying its use, i.e., "what we consider the real world."

Of course, one might object that students asked to write soliloquies merely imitate forms of cross-examination that are available to them in their social context, from "L. A. Law" to the marginal comments of instructors. Even if the exercise begins as imitation, however, it can end in serious self-examination. Students are not always enthusiastic about the possibilities they discover in their soliloquies. For every student delighted with the prospect of becoming her own critic there is another who complains that the exercise has undermined her ideas, and now she doesn't know what to think—and the essay is *due*. Certainly invention techniques that merely generate lists of usable ideas are more efficient. But do they produce more thoughtful essays? Soliloquy may lead to an essay without a clear thesis, to an almost heretical expression of doubt. If the teaching of rhetoric should include critical thinking, perhaps the clear expression of doubt is itself a legitimate pedagogical goal. In practice the soliloquy adds to the arsenal of invention techniques with self-discovery as their end, a collection that begins with Rohman and Wlecke's journal-keeping, meditation, and metaphor exercises,[2] and now includes various forms of freewriting, brainstorming, and of course dialogue. Shaftesbury, however, does not propose the soliloquy as merely one more invention exercise—he claims that it is the essential prerequisite to authorship. "'Tis the hardest thing in the world to be a good thinker without being a strong self-examiner and thorough-paced dialogist in this solitary way" (*Sol.* 1:112). The soliloquy is crucial for Shaftesbury because of his underlying epistemological and rhetorical convictions. Those are worth a closer examination, both for what they imply about the practice of soliloquy itself and as they represent a strand of rhetorical theory bypassed in the eighteenth-century rush to empiricism.

According to Shaftesbury, soliloquy is necessary because the mind is self-deceptive, because "our thoughts have generally such an obscure implicit language, that 'tis the hardest thing in the world to make them speak out distinctly" (*Sol.* 1:113). Shaftesbury attributes the mind's self-deceptiveness to its double nature, "two persons in one individual self" (*Sol.* 1:121). The only way to distinguish these two "persons," to make them speak out distinctly, is to divide in a self-conscious way. The process begins, Shaftesbury explains, "when by a certain powerful figure of inward rhetoric the mind apostrophises its own fancies, raises them in their proper shapes and personages, and addresses them familiarly, without the least ceremony or respect" (*Sol.* 1:123). In the ensuing dialogue, the mind's ideas, or "fancies," will divide into two parties, those of Appetite and those of Reason:

> Those on the side of the elder brother Appetite are strangely subtle and insinuating. They have always the faculty to speak by nods and winks. By this practice they conceal half their meaning, and, like modern politicians, pass for deeply wise, and adorn themselves with the finest pretexts and most specious glosses imaginable; till, being confronted with their fellows of a plainer language and expression, they are forced to quit their mysterious manner, and discover themselves mere sophisters and impostors who have not the least to do with the party of reason and good sense.
>
> (*Sol.* 1:123-24)

This description invokes two classical notions, one freely acknowledged and the other merely implied. The description of the mind as a duality of better and worse is clearly Platonic, and the soliloquy, Shaftesbury owns, is modeled on Platonic dialogue (*Sol.* 1:128). The other assumption here is that effective rhetoric is linked to good character. The voice of Reason triumphs in the internal debate not by virtue of the ideas it proposes—the whole purpose of the soliloquy is to judge those ideas—but through its straightforward rhetoric, the "plainer language and expression." Appetite also announces itself rhetorically, with the worst kind of sophistry, "subtle," "insinuating," "specious," remarkable more for what it omits than what it says. Shaftesbury is here echoing a classical doctrine, most fully developed by Quintilian, that the good orator is necessarily the good man.[3] His innovation is to apply this doctrine to an internal rhetorical contest. The inner orator who argues most effectively is also the more virtuous part of the self.[4]

Once the author has identified his own better ideas, he can address the public with authority. And his authority will be effective, because his audience has that same double nature of better and worse, Reason and Appetite. The final point, and most basic assumption, of the *Soliloquy* is that all humans share basic notions of value. It is evident, Shaftesbury claims, "that in the very nature of things there must of necessity be the foundation of a right and wrong taste, as well as in respect of inward characters and features as of outward person, behaviour, and action" (*Sol.* 1:216-17).[5] Shaftesbury's assumption of a common sense of right and wrong allows him to assume that those arguments that the self approves will be rhetorically effective for the public, a

correspondence that Isocrates also assumes, in his claim that "the same arguments which we use in persuading others when we speak in public, we employ when we deliberate in our thoughts" (327).

As all audiences have ideas of Reason, they also have those of Appetite—and in his essay, Shaftesbury sadly concludes that the audiences of his day may be ruled by this baser part. But the audience's poor taste can never excuse the author's poor performance. Authors are responsible for correcting taste, not catering to it: "One would expect it of our writers that if they had real ability they should draw the world to them, and not meanly suit themselves to the world in its weak state" (*Sol.* 1:171) Authors, finally, can serve as agents of moral change; like the ancient poets, they can be "authentic sages for dictating rules of life, and teaching manners and good sense" (*Sol.,* 1:104). They cannot take on this role, however, until they have resolved their own inner conflicts, through soliloquy. Only then can they be sure that their rhetoric appeals to the higher nature of their audience, rather than its baser one.

Although Shaftesbury's advice is coherent in its own terms, there are three major points here that are problematic in the context of current composition theory: the nature of the self, the evaluative function of common sense, and the ethical obligation of the rhetor. A thorough discussion of each point is beyond the scope of this paper, but I would like to suggest some ways in which Shaftesbury's ideas offer useful perspectives on some current issues.

Modern theory has taken issue with the very concept of *self,* as an autonomous entity. In the field of composition theory, this scepticism about the self has found its strongest expression in the work of the "social constructionists." However, their notion that the ideas of the individual are determined by social structures is still controversial; as Patricia Bizzell noted recently, her own work "seems to arouse the most violently negative reactions in its implications that people as intellectual agents are totally constituted by the discourse communities to which they belong" (229). Those negative reactions have several possible sources. Bizzell mentions the "American ambivalence about belonging to any community" (229). Jim Corder hit a different note, and a very personal one, in his lament for the poststructuralist death of the author: ". . . if the author is not autonomous, I'm afraid that I've lost my chance not just for survival hereafter . . . , but also for identity now" (301).

Shaftesbury's "author-character" suggests a third sort of objection, that is, if authors are in fact "constituted" by their communities, the distinction between author and audience blurs. Shaftesbury's "author-character" is an example of a writer almost totally identified with his potential readers. He is not a deceptive rhetor, who holds one opinion, but offers his audience another, for his own purposes. In the "author-character," the desire to please is so strong that he never *has* an idea of which his readers might disapprove. His flattery is thus ingenuous and entirely sincere. Of course, we might see such a writer in a positive light, as one in harmony with his community, expressing shared values. A more negative interpretation is one that Stewart borrows from Fromm, describing the self that merely reflects a social role as "a pathological phenomenon, the result of which is deep insecurity and anxiety and a compulsion to conform" (50; Stewart 79). However we regard such a character, the problem is that such deep agreement of the individual with her community erases the need for rhetoric in anything but a superficial sense, since there will be no disagreement on basic values, at least within specific social groups or discourse communities.

Individuals do think within the social and cultural constraints of particular communities, yet I doubt that any community exists in which disagreement about basic values never occurs. Burke points out that even the rhetoric used to affirm community values is evidence of the potential for discord: "Identification is affirmed with earnestness precisely because there is division. Identification is compensatory to division. If men were not apart from one another, there would be no need for the rhetorician to proclaim their unity" (22). Rhetoric exists because individuals disagree.

And where individuals disagree, the question of authority arises. The rhetor is not always a spokesperson for community values—frequently she is trying to persuade a community to *change* its values. In that case, her authority, her sense of having something important to say, cannot come from the community—it must come from herself. Yet we distrust the self as a judge, for a complex of reasons that have philosophical, political and cultural roots. Shaftesbury's self, however, is not a simple reference point that operates in an immediate, intuitive way. It is an internal parliament of discordant voices, a microcosm of the divided community, that must persuade itself, effect some sort of internal agreement, before it can persuade others.

The notion of the divided self has been lost to composition pedagogy, largely because the Scottish empirical rhetoricians rejected it.[6] Current composition theory, however, seems to have rediscovered the double self. Murray, for example, describes a "first reader" who engages in a kind of dialectical activity with the writing self: "The self speaks, the other self listens and responds, the self proposes, the other self considers. The self makes, the other self evaluates" (140). Elbow moves toward the Platonic duality by explicitly positing a "second reader" as "a kind of 'best self'" (*Writing* 179) that makes judgments on the writing process as it

occurs. Finally, in a classroom-based study, Roth found empirical evidence of the split self in students' approach to the unanalyzable general audience. They "geared themselves to the public at large—at times, paradoxically enough, by addressing their own best selves" (51).

One objection that Berlin raises to these "expressionistic" approaches to rhetoric is that truth, here, is accessible only to the individual who discovers it: "Truth can thus be known but not shared, not communicated" (*Rhetoric* 12). Murray, Elbow, and Roth all envision the discoveries of the other or "best" self as communicable; the real sticking point seems to be the source of the discovery, the positing of truth as an inner reality. The "transactional" rhetoric that Berlin favors sees truth as the product of a rhetorical transaction, "an interaction of subject and object or of subject and audience or even of all the elements—subject, object, audience, and language—operating simultaneously" (*Rhetoric* 15). Transactional rhetoric seems to avoid the dangers of both idiosyncratic visions and dictatorial audiences. Truth, for each community, is finally negotiated.

The notion that truths, or values, are thus cooperatively determined is attractive, but it too suggests difficulties. What happens, for example, if one of the interacting elements is absolutely corrupt? In *The New Rhetoric*, Perelman and Olbrechts-Tyteca face the problem squarely in their discussion of the adaptation of the speaker to the audience. The orator must fit his behavior to the audience, they argue, yet some audiences are morally corrupt. In such cases, the authors remind us, "the orator is nearly always at liberty to give up persuading an audience when he cannot persuade it effectively except by the use of methods that are repugnant to him" (25).

Shaftesbury's "common sense" is a different kind of solution to both the problems of idiosyncratic values and morally corrupt audiences. Rather than advising an honorable retreat, he charges authors with the moral obligation to effect a change, to "draw the world to them" (*Sol.* 1:171). No audience is so absolutely corrupt as to be beyond the reforming power of rhetoric, because all audiences share with their authors this natural evaluative capacity, "Reason" or "common sense," as Shaftesbury alternatively calls it. As Shaftesbury discusses more fully in an earlier essay, *Sensus Communis; An Essay on the Freedom of Wit and Humour* [*SC*] (1709), "common sense" is what finally ties the individual to his community, since it not only discovers common values but simultaneously creates in the individual a concern for the common welfare (*SC* 1:69-72).

The most ethical motivation for writing is this concern for one's community. And here Shaftesbury's theory falls into line with the most recent opinion. Research in composition is unlike that in many other fields, in that it never seems to leave behind the pragmatic concerns of pedagogy, the question of what to do in class on Monday morning. Researchers seem particularly aware of the ethical implications of writing instruction, of its power to effect social change. Bizzell justifies her "cultural criticism" approach with the hope that "the activity of cultural criticism will foster social justice by making people aware of politically motivated ideological concealments" (225). Robert J. Connors refers to the ethical motivation of composition scholars more simply as the "open and almost ingenuous desire to do some good in the world with our study and our teaching" (327). Bizzell and Connors want to give students not only the power to persuade but also the power to resist persuasion. But to do that, students must understand more than the principles of good writing or the effect of rhetorical strategies. They must be able to determine ethical values. No composition pedagogy can foster "social justice" unless it teaches students to distinguish the just from the unjust; no writing teacher can do good in the world unless she gives her students some means of deciding what the good is.

Shaftesbury's advice to authors brings into focus this central problem for any writer, the necessity of determining first the nature of the good. Composition pedagogy too often presents writing as an ethically neutral activity. And students too often think of rhetoric, the art of persuasion, as ethically negative. "Rhetoric," they volunteer, "is what sleazy politicians use to convince you that something they want for themselves will be good for everyone." The move from neutral to negative is not surprising. If we present rhetoric as the art of persuasion without discussing the art of deciding what the end of persuasion should be, our students will of course sense that rhetoric can be used for evil as well as good ends. Yet we are not teachers of ethics; most of us are reluctant to impose any particular set of values on our students, and frown even at attempts to create a common culture that might eventually produce a shared set of values, as the troubled response to Hirsch's work indicates.[7]

Our pedagogical goal, however, should be to provide the impetus for thinking about values, and the means for developing them. Shaftesbury never advises his authors to think in a certain way—he emphasizes instead the social importance of the author's role, his potential for influencing his community. Authors inevitably have authority; people will be affected by their words. Our students need to recognize *their* authority as writers, take seriously their potential influence. They must begin, then, with a serious search for their own values—or their rhetoric will be merely manipulative. The soliloquy gives writers an opportunity to develop values,

without positing such values for them. It demonstrates a rhetoric that is more than manipulation, one that begins with a rigorous examination of one's own ideas.

Notes

1. Diderot had translated the *Soliloquy* into French in 1771.

2. Rohman and Wlecke mention the colloquy as part of the classic meditation, but do not give explicit instructions for it (26-32); it may have certain similarities to Shaftesbury's soliloquy, which has also been called a colloquy (Marsh, "Shaftesbury and the Inward Colloquy," 18-47).

3. For a fuller discussion of the *vir bonus* doctrine in Quintilian, see Alan Brinton, "Quintilian, Plato, and the *Vir Bonus*."

4. The fact that rhetoric is an essential component of internal judgments of value makes Shaftesbury's theory "epistemic" in Berlin's terms, i.e., that rhetoric is involved in the discovery of truth. See *Rhetoric and Reality* 165.

5. In a later essay of the *Characteristics, The Moralists, a Philosophical Rhapsody,* Shaftesbury calls the ideas of value "pre-conceptions," and argues that they are divine in origin (2:135-36).

6. Smith, Campbell, and Blair all objected specifically to Shaftesbury's doctrine of the divided self.

7. *Profession 89* gives a fair sampling of such responses.

Works Cited

Axelrod, Rise B., and Charles R. Cooper. *The St. Martin's Guide to Writing.* New York: St. Martin's, 1985.

Baker, Sheridan. *The Practical Stylist.* 5th ed. New York: Harper and Row, 1981.

Berlin, James A. "Contemporary Composition: The Major Pedagogical Theories." *College English* 44 (1982): 765-77.

———. *Rhetoric and Reality: Writing Instruction in American Colleges, 1900-1985.* Carbondale: Southern Illinois UP, 1987.

Bizzell, Patricia. "'Cultural Criticism': A Social Approach to Studying Writing." 1988 CCCC Research Network Symposium: What Are We Doing as a Research Community? *Rhetoric Review* 7 (1989): 224-30.

Brinton, Alan. "Quintilian, Plato, and the *Vir Bonus*." *Philosophy and Rhetoric* 16 (1983): 167-84.

Burke, Kenneth. *A Rhetoric of Motives.* New York: George Brazillier, 1955.

Cooper, Anthony Ashley. 3rd Earl of Shaftesbury. *Soliloquy, or Advice to an Author. Characteristics of Men, Manners, Opinions, Times, etc.* Ed. John M. Robertson, 2 vols. Gloucester, Mass.: Peter Smith, 1963. 1:101-34.

———. *The Moralists, a Philosophical Rhapsody.* Characteristics 2:1-153.

———. *Sensus Communis; An Essay on the Freedom of Wit and Humor. Characteristics* 1:43-99.

Corder, Jim W. "Hunting for *Ethos* Where They Say It Can't Be Found." *Rhetoric Review* 7 (1989): 299-316.

Cowan, Gregory, and Elizabeth. *Writing.* N.p.: Scott Foresman, 1980.

Diderot, Denis. "De La Poésie Dramatique." Afterword. *La Pere de Famille. Oeuvres de Theatre avec un discours sur la Poésie Dramatique.* 2 vols. Amsterdam. 1771. 2:263-438.

Duke, Charles R. *Writing Through Sequence: a Process Approach.* Boston: Little Brown, 1983.

Ede, Lisa, and Andrea Lunsford. "Audience Addressed/Audience Invoked: The Role of Audience in Composition Theory and Pedagogy." *College Composition and Communication* 35 (1984): 155-71.

Elbow, Peter. "Closing My Eyes As I Speak: An Argument for Ignoring Audience." *College English* 49 (1987): 50-69.

———. *Writing With Power.* New York: Oxford UP, 1981.

Fromm, Erich. "The Creative Attitude." *Creativity and Its Cultivation.* Ed. Harold H. Anderson. New York: Harper, 1959. 44-54.

Herum, John, and D. W. Cummings. *Writing: Plans, Drafts and Revisions.* New York: Random, 1971.

Isocrates. *Isocrates.* Trans. George Norlin. Cambridge, MA: Harvard UP; London: William Heinemann, 1966.

Marsh, Robert Harrison. *Four Dialectical Theories of Poetry: An Aspect of English Neoclassical Criticism.* Chicago: U of Chicago P, 1965.

Murray, Donald M. "Teaching the Other Self: The Writer's First Reader." *College Composition and Communication* 33 (1982): 140-47.

Perelman, Chaim, and L. Olbrechts-Tyteca. *The New Rhetoric.* Notre Dame: Notre Dame UP, 1969.

Rohman, D. Gordon, and Albert O. Wlecke. *PreWriting: The Construction and Application of Models for Concept Formation in Writing.* East Lansing, MI: Michigan State UP, 1964.

Rose, Mike. "Rigid Rules, Inflexible Plans, and the Stifling of Language: A Cognitivist Analysis of Writer's Block." *College Composition and Communication* 31 (1980): 389-400.

Roth, Robert G. "The Evolving Audience: Alternatives to Audience Accommodation." *College Composition and Communication* 38 (1987): 47-55.

Stewart, Donald C. "Collaborative Learning and Composition: Boon or Bane?" *Rhetoric Review* 7 (1988): 58-83.

Richard B. Wolf (essay date summer 1993)

SOURCE: Wolf, Richard B. "Shaftesbury's Just Measure of Irony." *SEL: Studies in English Literature 1500-1900* 33, no. 3 (summer 1993): 565-85.

[*In this essay, Wolf examines Shaftesbury's use of satiric wit and discusses how his distinctive use of raillery is influenced by his philosophical beliefs and classical background.*]

John Hayman has justly linked the third earl of Shaftesbury to Augustan satiric reformers such as Addison and Steele, who were intent on curbing the malice of contemporary raillery and providing a proper model of good humored mental disposition.[1] These writers reacted against the cynical and predatory image of humankind associated with Hobbes and the Restoration wits, as well as against the kind of vitriolic satire written by contemporaries such as Jonathan Swift. They sought to promote both a more optimistic vision of individual and social potential, and a more refined ironic mode. But Shaftesbury's satiric practice was strikingly different from that found in the *Spectator*. While Addison and Steele's guiding principle of Christian charity resulted in a genial corrective banter that reaffirmed traditional values, Shaftesbury's loyalty to Stoic thought—despite creating strong misgivings on his part about the satirist's enterprise—ultimately produced satire with a sharper edge, designed to unsettle rather than to affirm conventional perspectives. Shaftesbury's attempt at satiric reform sought to refine and redirect—rather than wholly to subvert—the destructive impulses of the genre.

A Letter Concerning Enthusiasm (1708) and *Sensus Communis: An Essay on the Freedom of Wit and Humour* (1709) brought Shaftesbury notoriety as a champion of raillery in the discussion of serious subjects such as religion. At the same time, these works brought him considerable praise as a witty practitioner of the railler's art. Even the hostile author of *Reflections upon "A Letter Concerning Enthusiasm,"* who found its wit "full of Wind, and much Froth," conceded the *Letter* its "sparkling Air, nice Turns, and clever sorts of Fancy, or lively Allusions." Yet, as Hayman has noted, Shaftesbury had strong reservations about his advocacy and use of satiric wit.[2] These reservations are seen clearly in his reply to Leibnitz's critique of *Char-*

acteristics (1711), a work in which Shaftesbury coupled previously published pieces with a volume of *Miscellaneous Reflections.* Early in his reply, Shaftesbury voiced agreement with Leibnitz's complaints about "the too great Concessions . . . in favour of *Raillery* and the way of *Humor*" in his book. "Does not the Author himself secretly confess as much, in his Work?" Shaftesbury wrote:

> And does he not seem to despise himself in his Third and last Volume of Miscellanys, at the very entrance, when after having pass'd his principal and main philosophical Work of the Middle Volume [*An Inquiry Concerning Virtue* and *The Moralists*], he returns again to his mix'd Satyrical Way of Raillery and Irony, so fashionable in our Nation, which can be hardly brought to attend to any writing, or consider any thing as witty, able or ingenious which has not strongly this Turn?[3]

Hayman usefully connects Shaftesbury's reservations about raillery to the concern with coherence in personal identity that the author shared with his contemporaries. But to appreciate Shaftesbury's satiric achievement fully and to distinguish his approach from that of writers such as Addison and Steele, it is also important to understand the role of his individual values and inclinations in shaping the mode of raillery that the author first employed in *A Letter Concerning Enthusiasm.* Shaftesbury's distinctive satiric style emerged from a conflict between deeply held philosophic beliefs and contrary natural talents and inclinations. Characteristically both Shaftesbury's reservations about raillery and his ultimate manner of harnessing wit and humor to the service of philosophy were strongly influenced by his devotion to certain strands of classical thought and to classical models.

Three of Shaftesbury's primary objections to raillery were rooted in his allegiance to Stoicism. One of these is suggested by his extraordinary reluctance to be identified with his early literary works. According to Horst Meyer, Shaftesbury's refusal to acknowledge his authorship of *The Sociable Enthusiast* (an early form of *The Moralists*) and *A Letter Concerning Enthusiasm,* even in private letters of dedication to his friend Lord John Somers, was due not only to misgivings about his abilities but also to his embarrassment in failing to maintain a proper philosophical attitude toward writing. The aspiring Stoic should value writing as a means of acquiring self-knowledge and self-mastery, not as a performance to impress others. In a passage cited by Meyer from the author's Stoic Exercises (the so-called *Philosophical Notebooks* or *Regimen*), Shaftesbury advocated writing "Not for Shew: but for Exercise, Practice, Improvement."[4] Such a view demanded that he condemn the railler's employment of wit and humor as pointless, distracting verbal display.

A second reason for Shaftesbury's rejection of raillery was even more fundamental to his philosophical beliefs. As a student of Stoicism, Shaftesbury necessarily ob-

jected to the mental disruption produced by those passions that the railler indulged in himself and raised in his audience. Robert Voitle quotes a passage from the Exercises in which Shaftesbury condemned, among other passions, "extravagant Mirth, Airy-ness, Humour, Fantasticallness, Buffoonery, [and] Drollery": "when once any of these are let loose, when once they have broke their Boundaryes & forc'd a passage, what ravage & destruction is sure to follow? and what must it cost ere all be calm agin within?"[5] Once raised, Shaftesbury believed, such passions hurry the mind away from reason and the pursuit of truth; the individual loses control of his thoughts. Thus in the "Maxims" section in his Exercises, Shaftesbury decried the "Itching" of wit and humor: "New Fancyes starting bubbling. . . . Froth, Vapour, Scum, Witt, Story . . . a laugh raisd. . . . One Foolery drawing on another: one Levity making way for another."[6] At its worst, such an inclination could become habitual, permanently precluding rational thought. The disciplined Stoic should be able to direct any idea, using his highly developed faculty of reason, to the service of truth and virtue. But, noted Shaftesbury,

> This is just the Revers of what happens to those who are grown into the thorow-buffooning Habit. Every thing y^t they see, be it ever so grave or seriouse, has a ridiculouse appearance, & whether they will or no, becomes Burlesque. every thing is travested so as to make Diversion out of it: and, whatever be the Face y^t offers, there are Glasses ready, y^t make it to be seen after a thousand rediculouse ways, & y^t instead of that one reall Face, present a thousand Masks of a Grotesque & Fantastick kind.

> (pp. 128-29)

Finally, Shaftesbury as aspiring Stoic was troubled by the nature of the distorting medium of laughter. Quoting Epictetus's injunction "Let not your laughter be excessive" in his Maxims, he asserted: "Consider the Thing itself: in the Bottom, what? . . . Ἐπιχαιρεκάκι [malevolence]. Nothing else. . . . Gall, Venom; but of a different kind, more hid." Such laughter he associated with the malicious and sadistic, with bloody tyrants and common criminals. Where is the laugh heartier, he asked, than among soldiers engaged in acts of brutality (pp. 372-73)? Urging himself to avoid "all that wch in any degree borders upon Mimickry, Buffoonery [and] Drollery," he declared elsewhere in his Exercises:

> Consider what a mean & contemptible state, ye mind is in, at that instant when it gos about any thing of this kind: what it aims at: what its End & Scope is . . . and what sort of Minds those are wch partake with it in this way, & are the ablest in this Art: what Morralls, Manners, Life this brings along with it.

> (pp. 68-69)

The vigor of his denunciation of wit and humor in these and other passages in the Exercises verifies Voitle's observation that in Shaftesbury the Stoic's "longing to be free from the despotism of passion" was coupled with "a very powerful sense of sin which seems to have carried over from his early religious training" (p. 152). But at the same time, the strength of Shaftesbury's abhorrence suggests the tremendous power of this particular temptation. His repeated exhortations to himself in the Exercises to renounce the jester's role illustrate a point that Voitle makes in discussing the discrepancy between Shaftesbury's renunciation of politics in the Exercises and his actual political involvement: "the intensity of his distaste for an action is often directly proportional to the ability of an action to preoccupy him and all of his energies. As a result, frequently the meditations better reflect what he does well or naturally rather than what he dislikes doing" (p. 205). Shaftesbury's inclination to play the role of a wit and humorist was to him embarrassingly strong.

The tension resulting from this inclination and his philosophical objections to it is illustrated by a letter that Shaftesbury penned less than six months before his death. Writing from Naples on 1 September 1712 N.S., he instructed his protégé Thomas Micklethwayte to insist that their mutual friend Sir John Cropley take proper measures to protect a painting that the author had commissioned for Cropley in Italy. Shaftesbury not only urged that Cropley enclose the work with a frame and glass but also strongly suggested that such pictures should be displayed as "Cabinet-pieces," not hung in "the Dining-Room or Parlour; to be left to a House-Maid to dust out, and clean, with the Stools, Stands, and other light Furniture." The danger of failing to take such precautions he demonstrated with his own example, "having had a tight Maid who with a Sponge and Soap wip'd me out the best Features of half a dozen Family-faces in one morning: the Pictures having been of the little Size, fit for handling and rattling about."[7]

At this point Shaftesbury had probably said all that he needed to say to persuade Cropley to take proper care of the picture. But he was not done. The itch of wit and humor carried him into a delightfully cranky, comic account of the indignities to which a small, unprotected painting is exposed in a philistine world:

> Great Pieces are indeed more out of Danger. They can't be made *Toys* or *Play-things*. They are hung at least chair-high (I mean above the top of the Chairs) and by the Frame-Work too, they are defended from the Beau's Perukes and Lady's Fanns. A little Picture is indeed a mere *Play-Thing*. Be it in the Drawing-Room, or in the Closet 'tis seldom plac'd above Chin-high. It must be as often handled as it is look'd upon and admir'd. Seldom it fails of being taken down, and dandled. 'Tis set hastily on the Table, or in the Window; or taken in Lapp. 'Tis forgot, or set aside in hast. It gets a Knock, or a Fall or two. The Tea is spilt upon it, or any other Slop—"*There's no harm!*"—Nobody minds it. 'Tis taken up again, wip'd, and hung up, in its place. Nurse

comes in, and drumms upon it with her fingers. Young Master or Miss must have their turn with it: and the Picture must begin a new Dance; else a Blubber is set up; Nurse pouts; and the Company is disturb'd. Now a most soverain Security against all these ill adventures and Mischances, is, a good stout Glass, which is not only *defensive* but *offensive*; and makes the Picture an Edge-tool, too dangerous for young Master, and as much respected as a Piece of China or costly Ware; which if broken is thought to be of some moment. And a Christal-Glass every one knows is worth something. But for the Picture, 'tis a *Virtuoso Crochet*.

> (pp. 280-81)

Shaftesbury returned to a more sober vein in discussing the frame proper in the next paragraph. But in closing he felt compelled to comment on his act of comic indulgence: "I find I have dictated a very comical Letter to You. I wish it may, as well as the Picture, be entertaining to S[r]. John and You" (p. 281). This self-conscious, almost apologetic assessment of his instructions as a humorous performance suggests Shaftesbury's embarrassment in the face of a momentary aberration in the direction of laughter.

An earlier and fuller testament to Shaftesbury's inclination to indulge his itch of wit and humor is provided by *The Adept Ladys or The Angelick Sect. Being the Matters of fact of certain Adventures Spiritual, Philosophical, Political, and Gallant. In a letter to a Brother* (1702).[8] The 10,000 word "letter" is an account of its narrator's encounters with old acquaintances and their new mentor, a Quaker lady who claims to hobnob with angels and to be able to make gold from excrement. Not published during Shaftesbury's lifetime, *The Adept Ladys* is described by A. O. Aldridge as a satire on pantheistic materialism, specifically the doctrines of the Rosicrucians.[9] Voitle's speculations concerning the identities of the "Brother" and others mentioned in the piece suggest that Shaftesbury's audience for this performance was probably at most a few intimate friends (p. 198).

Voitle labels *The Adept Ladys* "a hasty jeu d'esprit and not a very witty one" (p. 199)—a generally accurate assessment. Among other defects, the work suffers from an inconsistent narrative voice. Shaftesbury's narrator not only repeatedly abandons his ironic tone for straightforward diatribes against the folly of the superstition that he encounters, but he also inexplicably shifts from the deferential host in the body of the work to the bantering gallant of the lengthy Post-Script. Despite its considerable shortcomings, however, the *Ladys* offers clear indications of Shaftesbury's satiric abilities as well as his predilection for wit and humor.

The most successful part of Shaftesbury's performance is his opening account of the visit of old Chrysogenes, his wife, and the Quaker lady. Despite tone lapses and prolixity, Shaftesbury reveals a talent for farce. He presents his narrator, the host, as a rational, sensitive soul whose dilemma results from his unwillingness to offend his guests and his revulsion at their religious enthusiasm. Upon the arrival of his guests, the host receives Chrysogenes and the two ladies "with all Possible Civility" (p. 380). Later, having lapsed into a morose silence in response to their ravings, he notes their discomposure and immediately forces himself to return to a cheerful manner. But his efforts to be polite and gracious only encourage his guests' increasingly annoying spiritual confidences. And his repeated attempts to steer the conversation away from their occult obsessions inevitably backfire.

When the host responds to Chrysogenes' prophetic cant at the beginning of the visit by "understanding it in the Best Sence I could; and accomodating it, all that I was able, to Piety & sound Religion" (p. 382), his pious words only lead Chrysogenes to claim that the Quaker lady is miraculously privy to what passes in the host's own soul. When, with "no other Refuge" from the supernatural tales of his guests, the host directs the conversation "with might and main towards Publick affairs" (p. 398), he is treated to an elaborate account of the Quaker lady's communication with generals and statesmen through intermediary spirits. When he cites his ill health in an attempt to cut short prophecies of his future political greatness, he discovers that he has merely returned the conversation to the excremental mysteries previously broached by the enthusiasts. The contents of his chamber pot, he is assured by the Quaker lady, can repair his constitution as well as his fortune. Overwhelmed at one point by "such Discours and Entertainment of down-right Filth, and such a Mess of villanouse Imposture and Enthousiastick Cant as was wors to me than all the Naturall Ordure in the World" (pp. 394-96), the host calls for wine to revive his spirits. Naturally it restores him less than it inspires his guests to even more fulsome displays of zeal.

The humor produced by the host's mental suffering in *The Adept Ladys* is enhanced by his comic physical suffering. His intellectual fastidiousness—so grossly offended at every turn by his guests' credulous fanaticism—has its counterpart in his revulsion at the bodily dross that the Quaker woman repeatedly celebrates. Here again, the host is comically forced to endure his aversion, unwilling to offend his guests and unable to find a way to stop or divert the torrent of their enthusiasm. The high point of this element of the farce comes near the beginning, when the Quaker lady first reveals her grand secret:

> The Q:Woman having open'd the Bundle in which there were Papers that seem'd to contain certain Druggs, which they call'd (as I perceiv'd) *the Subjects,* presented one of them to me ready open'd, & bid me *ob-*

> *serve that well*: which I did with great Gravity, holding the Paper in my hand: and after I had remain'd a little in this Pause, looking still on what was in the Paper; one of them ask'd me Smilingly, & in a very familiar way, *what I thought of it?* I told them with great Submission (as to Persons deeper sighted than my self.) that I thought I saw a Powder of an Earthy Colour. What Tast it had, I did not care truly to try: nor as yet had I offer'd to Smell to it, or so much as feell it with my fingers. The Q:Woman at last applying to me; asked me if I knew a certain Thing which was so vile that we gave money to have it rid out of our houses? This being a pretty odd Question; I sate mute for a while, till she had ask'd this over again two or three severall ways, and began, as I thought, to reproach me for being a little Dull. On this I offer'd to smell to it; making (I Believe) at the Same time some kind of Face not very agreable: and finding, that this had Spread a sort of grum Smile over my Assembly; I ventur'd to Smile a little aukardly my Self too, and told them, I now thought I had gott the Matter right: this being perhaps the Thing which we were glad to get our Bodyes rid of, in the first place, and then our Houses: and from this time I kept the Paper a little further from my Nose; till I had conveniently shifted it from me.

(pp. 388-90)

Tormented but unable to escape from his guests without giving offense, the host vents his frustrations in intermittent sardonic remarks that read like a farceur's asides. One instance occurs when the Quaker lady tells him that her great discovery of the powers of bodily waste came when she made an inspired connection between biblical verses advising her to look into herself and the fact that the newborn Christ was laid in a manger: "It came into her Mind, that *She ought to take up with what was under the Manger.*" Disgusted, the host parenthetically notes that therein she displaid "a greater Humility it should seem than Hers who sought only for what was *under the Table*" (p. 394). Later he remarks in passing that the "dull and heavy" prose of the prophetic letters which the Quaker lady boasts of sending to various men of affairs by angels "ill-answer'd the Sprightlyness of their Sublime Aeriall Messengers" (p. 398). Finally, at the close of the visit, when the prophetess attributes his weak lungs to the quantity of sulfur in his constitution and assures him that the sulfur is "*a Token of my being to become a great Philosopher,*" the host explodes to his correspondent: "truly (I thought with my Self) I was become allready in a proper Sence; having Philosophy enough courageously to endure this Assault of the most raging *Enthousiasme* that ever yet surely broke out into the World" (p. 404).

Shaftesbury's Post-Script to *The Adept Ladys* is awkwardly disjointed and incongruous with the body of the work, but its presentation of the narrator as aggressive railer and rake introduces another comic element in its recurring bawdiness. Characteristic is its final lewd sally, in which the narrator recalls the Quaker lady's account of the solar fire as "it was first Discover'd to her and experimented on her Self by one of her first Masters, a Grand Adept." Her account leads the narrator to speculate about how the Quaker lady might have "melted" (along with the windows of the room where the experiment took place) and about what became of her clothes, since, in the case of her body, "thither (she confess'd) the Fire had penetrated, and made Impression on the Parts." The story, he coyly concludes, "had like to have caus'd a Digression, by the odd Fancyes it occasion'd in me" (p. 428).

More than any other surviving writing by Shaftesbury, *The Adept Ladys* illustrates the sort of jester's performance for which he castigated himself in his Stoic Exercises. As such, it helps clarify significant differences in the satiric approach that Shaftesbury was to employ in the works composing volume 1 of *Characteristics*; for, despite his endorsement of Leibnitz's censure, his satiric performance in this volume does not represent a similar departure from Stoic principles. When Shaftesbury justified his practice to Leibnitz on the basis of a corrupt public taste, he was acknowledging the regrettable gulf between men like himself and the German philosopher, and the typical "airy" English gentleman who was averse to serious thought—a gulf that he sought to bridge by means of a refined and redirected form of raillery quite unlike that displayed in the *Ladys*. Shaftesbury's famous defense of the use of wit and humor in opposing grave imposture derived from his acceptance of their value as a correcting device for preparing the unthinking reader for a philosophical disposition. Although there is "nothing more unsafe, or more difficult of management" than laughter, Shaftesbury observed in his Exercises, he judged that it could serve as a valuable counter to the pleasures and diversions of the world and to "the Pomp & rediculouse solemnity of human affaires" for one who "was yet unfix'd, & only in a way towards improvement" (p. 82). The challenge which Shaftesbury set for himself for the first time in *A Letter Concerning Enthusiasm* was that of managing his dangerous talents as a railler in order to improve rather than impede the growth of reason and virtue in his reader.

As his response to Leibnitz also suggests, Shaftesbury found this challenge all the more compelling in light of the abuses of wit and humor that he found rampant in English writing at the time. In *Soliloquy, or Advice to an Author* (1710), he characterized contemporary satire as "scurrilous, buffooning, and without Morals or Instruction; which is the Majesty and Life of this kind of writing."[10] For him the epitome of such writing was Swift's *Tale of a Tub,* which he cited to Leibnitz as proof of the undiscriminating taste of his countrymen for "the mix'd Satyrical Way of Raillery and Irony": "Witness the prevalency and first Success of that detestable Writing of that most detestable Author of the *Tale of a Tub*; whose Manners, Life and prostitute Pen and

Tongue are indeed exactly answerable to the Irregularity, Obscenity, Profaneness and fulsomeness of his false Wit and scurrilouse Style and Humor."[11] Thus Shaftesbury's aim in *A Letter Concerning Enthusiasm* and the satiric pieces that followed was to harness wit and humor to the service of reason and virtue, and in doing so to offer an alternative to the degraded practice of Swift and other satirists of the period. In this attempt he sought to shape his approach both by avoiding the abuses that he discerned in works such as the *Tale* and by looking to classical models—especially those of Socrates, Xenophon, and Horace—for a form of humor more akin to that "very different kind . . . suitable with one who understands himself" (Exercises, p. 82).[12]

The Socratic model most admired by Shaftesbury was that presented by Xenophon. Both in his accounts of the teaching of Socrates and elsewhere in his writings, Shaftesbury found in Xenophon an author who "was as distant, on the one hand, from the sonorous, high, and pompous Strain; as, on the other hand, from the ludicrous, mimical, or satirick."[13] To the "Gall" or "Venom" of common laughter, Shaftesbury opposed the type produced by Socrates and Xenophon: "that more reservd, gentle kind, wch hardly is to be calld Laughter, or wch at least is of another Species" (Exercises, pp. 372-74). Shaftesbury conveys something of this concept of benevolent laughter in the term *Good Humour.*

Essential to Shaftesbury's approach in the *Letter* is a Socratic persona that is on the whole very different from the exasperated, humorously victimized host of *The Adept Ladys,* the rake of the Post-Script, or the comically indignant crank of the letter to Micklethwayte. Aside from the opening and closing of the work, he offers his exploration of enthusiasm with very little apology. He elicits his reader's assent as he raises and conducts a kind of internal dialogue, signaling his control of the situation by addressing questions likely to arise in the mind of his reader. For example, after presenting his witty "new Arcadia" conceit comparing the folly of attempting to repress religious enthusiasm to that of attempting to repress love poetry in the classical mode, Shaftesbury's speaker forestalls an obvious objection with the following prelude to his explanation: "BUT, my Lord, you may perhaps wonder, that having been drawn into such a serious Subject as Religion, I shou'd forget my self so far as to give way to Raillery and Humour. I must own to you, my Lord, it is not thro Chance merely, that it has thus happen'd."[14] Shaftesbury's persona establishes his moral authority both through the appearance of good-humored objectivity and through the element of unassuming modesty characteristic of Socrates. Deferentially he acknowledges his "ordinary Humanity" (p. 13), not only in relation to his noble correspondent but also in relation to others who may find his reasoning "odd" (p. 61) or his philosophy "home-spun" (p. 66). After exploring the topic of religious enthusiasm, he modestly submits that "THE only thing I wou'd infer from all this is, that *Enthusiasm* is wonderfully powerful and extensive; that it is a matter of nice Judgment, and the hardest thing in the world to know fully and distinctly" (pp. 80-81). Shaftesbury's modest persona provides an appropriate contrast to those dogmatists whose pretensions to truth are humorously exposed in the *Letter.*

To gain the ear of an audience addicted to the "mix'd Satyrical Way of Raillery and Irony," however, Shaftesbury is careful to establish his authority as wit as well as moralist. In doing so, he appears especially to follow the lead of Horace (the most frequently cited author in *Characteristics*). In Horace, Shaftesbury saw a fellow aspirant to Stoic wisdom who had succeeded in adapting his comic gifts to the service of philosophy while addressing an audience predisposed to wit and humor rather than severe virtue. In the second of two letters that Shaftesbury wrote to Pierre Coste in 1706 on the subject of Horace, he argued that, in writing for men such as the corrupt Maecenas, the Roman poet was forced to cover his Stoicism "artfully" with "an Air of Rallery." Shaftesbury noted, however, that Horace at his best employed a refined form of humor, observing a "just Measure" of irony that could be distinguished from the scurrility of his Epicurean period. Shaftesbury associated this superior form of irony with the Socratic way: not "offensive, Injurouse, Hypocriticall, Bitter, and contrary to all true simplicity, Honesty or good Manners." In *Soliloquy* he was to call Horace "the politest" and "most Gentleman-like of *Roman* Poets."[15]

Shaftesbury sought to establish his authority as a wit in part by exhibiting his mastery of fashionable forms such as the literary letter, attempting that graceful "*Concealment of Order and Method*" that he held to be "the chief Beauty" of Horace.[16] Thus, for example, he subtly introduces the topic of religious enthusiasm in the discussion of poetic inspiration that serves as an opening compliment to his correspondent in the *Letter.*[17] But Shaftesbury also lays claim to the wit and urbanity demanded by his audience through displaying his skill in raillery. And it is perhaps above all else the attempt to attain a just measure of irony in employing his talents as satirist that characterizes Shaftesbury's approach as a wit and humorist in the work. It is the concept of fair, decorous, and proportionally appropriate raillery that makes his approach very different from that found in the *The Adept Ladys* and in works such as Swift's *Tale of a Tub.*

In *A Letter Concerning Enthusiasm* Shaftesbury appears to follow the Socratic model that he discerned in Xenophon: "not to appear positive or deciding (excepting in ye great questions of Vertue ag[ains]t the vitiouse)."[18] Consequently, he both exemplifies and induces a more skeptical, dispassionate assessment of re-

ligious enthusiasm than is seen in *The Adept Ladys* and in Swift. In part he does so by directing his raillery towards both the French Prophets and their zealous orthodox opponents. In part he does so by pointing up paradoxes in the behavior and views of each group, rather than by employing direct censure or overt irony. Shaftesbury's speaker presents real or apparent inconsistencies (the unchristian practices of orthodox churchmen, the enthusiast's pleasure in suffering), but he does not manufacture irony in the manner of the rakish persona of the *Ladys,* who praises the adepts for freeing themselves from "the Burden of fals Shame and modesty, such as attends the Unsanctifyed" (pp. 420-22), or Swift's speaker, who heaps praise on the trivial and venal performances of the moderns or lauds the rogueries of Peter and Jack. When Shaftesbury's speaker celebrates the "hard-hearted" tolerance with which the English baffle the Prophets' attempt to achieve martyrdom (p. 42), it is the Prophets' behavior—not the speaker's inversion of the satiric norm—that generates the irony. The joke is justly in the thing itself, not in the telling. Shaftesbury's technique aims more at stimulating a skeptical appraisal than provoking a scornful dismissal in the manner of Swift. It serves to unsettle prejudices, not confirm them. To describe tolerance as "hard-hearted" and persecution as "kind Blows" is to force a reevaluation of commonly held views, inviting analysis of the real or apparent contradictions embodied in the thought and behavior of both religious enthusiasts and their opponents.

Shaftesbury's general reliance on explicit comparison also produces a less scurrilous treatment of fanaticism than that found in the *Ladys* and in Swift. If, as Aldridge speculates, the *Ladys* is less autobiography than satiric invention, then Shaftesbury's deflating embodiment of his target in the character of the Quaker lady—a vain, deluded, sour-visaged bawd—is analogous to Swift's depiction of various sectarian practices in section 11 of the *Tale* as the "pranks" of the knavish Jack. By contrast, in the *Letter* the French Prophets are exposed by simile or analogy, not metaphor or allegory. Rather than endowing them with garlands or wires, for example, Shaftesbury explicitly presents the Prophets as being *like* ludicrous pastoralists or spasmodic puppets.[19] The difference is slight, but it results in the appearance of a more scrupulously fair treatment of the work's satiric objects.

Nor does Shaftesbury engage in assaults on individuals by name in the manner of Swift, whose explicit depiction of William Wotton and Richard Bentley ("William W-tt-n, B.D." and "Dr. B-tl-y") as arrogant, stupid rogues in *The Battle of the Books* reads like a culmination of similar assaults in the *Tale* itself. A complaint in one of the early replies to the *Letter* merely points up Shaftesbury's comparative delicacy. The author of *Remarks upon the Letter to a Lord Concerning Enthusi-*

asm objected to the *"cruel [Chastisement] in the dark"*[20] provided by Shaftesbury's reference to "an Eminent, Learned, and truly Christian Prelate you once knew, who cou'd have given you a full account of his Belief in *Fairys*" (pp. 9-10). In a postscript to his private letter to Somers accompanying the published work, however, Shaftesbury noted that he had changed the manuscript at this very point for the sake of his victim, Bishop Edward Fowler: "The change of a Tense has put him out of ye way of Reflection & a good Epethite or two bestow'd on him, saves the breach of Charity in one who would willingly say all the Good of him that he cou'd, & conceal the rest." What Shaftesbury apparently meant by "the rest" makes his gentle treatment of Fowler even more remarkable, for he had observed to Somers in a previous letter that the prelate "was once a professd Informer from the Roof & Board (one might say *Service* too) of [the author's] Ancestour."[21] Admittedly, many readers may have had little trouble identifying "A GENTLEMAN who has writ lately in defence of reviv'd Prophecy, and has since fallen himself into the prophetick Extasys" (p. 70) as John Lacy, a prominent English proselyte of the French Prophets. But Shaftesbury's veiled reference at least maintains the appearance of civility.

Equally indicative of Shaftesbury's attempt to eliminate the scurrilous from his satiric treatment of religious enthusiasm in the *Letter* is his handling of potentially prurient material. Compared to the bawdy suggestions of the Post-Script of the *Adept Ladys,* his approach in the *Letter* is extremely oblique. His analogies between enthusiasm and love studiously keep to the Petrarchan or pastoral plane, as when he notes how "by a little Affectation in Love-Matters, and with the help of a Romance or Novel, a Boy of Fifteen, or a grave Man of Fifty, may be sure to grow a very natural Coxcomb, and feel the *Belle Passion* in good earnest" (p. 9) or when he develops his new Arcadia conceit. The closest that Shaftesbury comes to pruriency is his coy refusal to continue his account of Bacchic practices (as detailed by Livy) beyond references to the participants' convulsions: "The detestable Things that follow, I would not willingly transcribe" (p. 73). By raising the issue of these unmentionable practices (including, of course, sexual orgies) while addressing the claims of the unnamed Lacy, Shaftesbury may be alluding to rumors of the Prophets' sexual misconduct that were to surface in print about a month after he composed the *Letter,* in the first part of Richard Kingston's *Enthusiastick Impostors, No Divinely Inspired Prophets.*[22] If such is the case, however, Shaftesbury's approach is extraordinarily delicate—especially when compared with Swift's handling of sex and the Saints in the *Tale* and in the accompanying *Mechanical Operation of the Spirit.*

Scatological humor is also conspicuously absent from the *Letter.* In one of the poems appended to *The Adept*

Ladys, Shaftesbury plays upon the adepts' alchemical claims to produce gold from the contents of the chamber pot by celebrating—as surpassing that of Jove—the "Golden Shower" of one Chrysinda (p. 434). In the couplets of another poem, which satirizes the Quaker lady's account of discovering the key to alchemy, the sleeping Ophiria dreams of "a sprightly youth of heav'nly Meen" who reveals to her the wealth flowing within her own body. As the vision ends,

> By Luck her thought was hitt.
> She wak'd, and found She had herself Be———.
>
> (p. 436)

Shaftesbury's avoidance of scatology in the *Letter.* is especially noteworthy in a work that shares one of the primary sources for Swift's account of the Aeolists and of Louis XIV. Henry More's linking of enthusiasm and flatulence in *Enthusiasmus Triumphatus* finds no echo in Shaftesbury's polite wit in the *Letter.*

Shaftesbury's concept of a just measure of irony is also evident in his pruning of the kind of humorous luxuriance (or buffoonery) found in his letter to Micklethwayte. The speaker of *A Letter Concerning Enthusiasm* never, for example, indulges in the kind of comic extravagance seen in Shaftesbury's account of the abuses to which a small, unprotected picture is subjected or seen in the glorious excesses of *A Tale of a Tub.* His wit is restrained and directed to the point. Swift repeatedly unleashes a richly comic profusion of examples, analogies, or details, whether in his accounts of the "hieroglyphics" employed by ancient writers to comment on True Critics (sec. 3), of the projects, discoveries, and inventions of Peter (sec. 4), of the justification of learning by indexes (sec. 7), or of the tricks of Jack (sec. 11). But three is the limit for Shaftesbury's examples, be they of men's "Faculty of deceiving themselves" (pp. 8-10), of times "when the Spirits of men are low" (p. 25), or of the failures of persecution to suppress Protestantism and primitive Christianity (pp. 44-46).

The author's restraint is equally apparent in his handling of fully developed comparisons. Shaftesbury may expand a conceit to include a range of satiric targets. That of the new Arcadia, for instance, includes gibes at pastoral affectations, at the repressive policies of the Roman Catholic church and of Puritan authorities during the Interregnum, and at the extravagances of enthusiasts such as the French Prophets.[23] But we never lose track of the first term of the comparison; the conceit never becomes a fiction. A glance at Swift's handling of the Aeolists makes this point clear. In Swift's description a wide variety of damaging points of comparison between this imaginary sect and the English dissenters emerges. But Swift's exuberant development of his wind conceit to encompass a complete body of doctrines and rituals extends far beyond bare correspondences. His account of the sect not only achieves the detailed richness of allegorical fiction but also incorporates inventions such as the Aeolists' demons (the chameleon and the windmill) that contemporaries had trouble connecting to his satiric targets. While Swift's mode, to use Edward W. Rosenheim's phrase, is that of a creator of "satiric fictions,"[24] Shaftesbury's is that of a satiric essayist who clearly subordinates his wit to his arguments and observations.

In view of Shaftesbury's apparent efforts to create an alternative to the satiric practice of writers such as Swift, he must have been chagrined to learn that a number of early readers ascribed ***A Letter Concerning Enthusiasm*** to the author of *A Tale of a Tub*. The primary reason for this mortifying mistake seems to have been Shaftesbury's handling of religion in his work. Reporting the dinner-table discussion that first informed him of the false attribution, Shaftesbury recounted to Somers that the *Tale* had been described as written "pretendedly for [religion]: but in so Burlesque a Manner as over threw It more effectually." Similarly, the *Letter* had been described as "a comical Piece . . . concerning *Prophesy,*" which the author treated with marked irreverence, "in a very familiar way of Wit & Rallery."[25] The notoriety of Shaftesbury's work as an attack on religion even secured it a place among books produced at the Sacheverell trial to prove that the defendant's "church in danger" cry was far from a groundless libel.

Voitle notes the author's bitter complaints about the charges of blasphemy that were leveled at the piece, as well as Shaftesbury's greater caution in dealing with religion in later works such as ***Sensus Communis*** and ***Soliloquy.*** But he contends that the writer "certainly knew what to expect" in publishing the ***Letter.*** and he theorizes that Shaftesbury was willing to risk "his reputation for piety" in order to present new ideas in the piece as groundwork for ***The Moralists*** (pp. 327-29). There is evidence in the ***Letter,*** however, to suggest that Shaftesbury, seeking his just measure of irony, had to some extent tried to forestall charges of profaneness by suggesting much more explicitly than Swift had done in the *Tale* that the work's quarrel was with abuses of religion, not religion itself. In several passages he introduces pious disclaimers to qualify his raillery. For example, he notes that the Romans pursued an "ill Purpose" in attempting to suppress Christianity and that ridicule would have proved a more effective weapon "had the Truth of the Gospel been any way surmountable" (p. 45).

That such disclaimers did little to avert charges of blasphemy is hardly surprising. To the extent that Shaftesbury employed his wit to promote a rethinking of received truths, his treatment of religion was bound to offend many readers. And it is this very element of

skepticism that provides one of Shaftesbury's most notable satiric resources. His references—albeit veiled—to specific targets such as John Lacy may partly account for his satire's having a sharper edge than that of such writers as Addison and Steele, whose adherence to tenets of Christian charity precluded attacks on individuals.[26] But Shaftesbury's satiric approach differs from theirs more fundamentally in its tendency to transgress against orthodoxy in religion and other areas by attempting to lead its reader from unthinking faith to philosophical engagement. Shaftesbury's characteristic use of paradox, for example, derives from a freedom and inclination to turn accepted wisdom on its head, as when the ***Letter*** writer suggests that the persecutions of Nero were highly advantageous to the early church or when he presents the inducement to religious faith provided by Pascal's wager as an affront to God.

Freedom from orthodox religious perspectives translates in the ***Letter*** into shifts and reversals of conventional attitudes that offer the witty jolt of the unexpected. Extending the theatrical conceit provided by his puppet-show mockery of the French Prophets, Shaftesbury subverts traditional reverence for early church martyrs by having his speaker flippantly note that the Romans might have succeeded better in opposing Christianity "if they had chose to bring our primative Founders upon the Stage in a pleasanter way than that of Bear-Skins and Pitch-Barrels" (p. 45). Similarly he provides a novel perspective on the Apostle Paul, presenting him wittily defending Christianity to the Athenians and Romans as a courtly gentleman who "accommodates himself to the Apprehensions and Temper of those politer People" (p. 47). Shaftesbury even introduces a saucy Job, who "makes bold enough with God, and takes his Providence roundly to task" (p. 52).

As this last example indicates, Shaftesbury's witty treatment of conventional ideas and attitudes is frequently pointed by freedoms in diction unthinkable in the prose of more orthodox works such as *The Spectator*. Shaftesbury produces numerous tiny shocks of wit by juxtaposing language appropriated by Christianity with that normally restricted to very different contexts. The opening of the ***Letter*** exploits such a discrepancy by linking Christian and pagan, as in the case of the Christian believer who can "extend his Faith so largely, as to comprehend in it not only all Scriptural and Traditional Miracles, but a solid System of old Wives Storys" (p. 9). Similarly the failure of a pagan to believe in the Muses is styled "Profane and Atheistical" (p. 11). Elsewhere Shaftesbury creates witty incongruities from unexpected combinations of the sacred and the wholly secular. Refurbishing Butler's "Errant Saints" (*Hudibras*), Shaftesbury's speaker labels religious persecution "Saint-Errantry" (p. 31). He contends that freedom of raillery will protect the Church of England from false "Venders of Prophecy or Miracles" (p. 44). Wit and humor, he argues, need not be precluded from the discussion of sacred matters "as long as we treat Religion with good Manners" (p. 49).

A final source of unorthodox wit is Shaftesbury's ironic heightening of his paradoxes and conceits by juxtaposing formal religious language and the idiom of informal speech. The freedom of raillery represented by puppet-show presentations of the French Prophets, his speaker says, will spare "our National Church" the task of "trying her Strength with" such sects (p. 44). Nor will we offend "the God of Truth" if we refuse "to put the lye upon our Understandings" by accepting Pascal's wager (p. 53). The "Spirit of Prophecy," says Shaftesbury's speaker, "prov'd so catching amongst the antient Prophets, that even the Profane *Saul* was taken by it" (pp. 69-70). This last example of the author's skeptical wit was a particular bugbear for orthodox critics, who took great offense at the word "catching" in connection with biblical prophecy.[27] For such readers, the irreverence of Shaftesbury's wit—and his arguments for employing it with sacred subjects—tended to overshadow the range of satiric refinements embodied in his performance.

In *A Letter Concerning Enthusiasm* Shaftesbury sought to offer an alternative to contemporary satiric practice—an alternative that obviated his Stoic objections to the display of wit and humor that came naturally to him. Its carefully controlled use of raillery in the service of exposition sought to limit the disruptive potential of wit. Its use of paradox in lieu of more scurrilous ironic techniques sought to further the Stoic ideal of detachment from the passions and to avoid a humor of malice. Finally, to the extent that it encouraged a critical assessment of emotionally charged topics such as religious enthusiasm—unsettling unexamined beliefs and leading the airy reader towards a philosophic disposition—Shaftesbury's just measure of raillery provided an outlet for his talents that could not easily be dismissed as self-indulgence or vain display.

The author's satisfaction with his satiric achievement in the *Letter* appears evident from his use of a similar ironic mode in *Sensus Communis* and *Soliloquy,* the other pieces collected in volume 1 of *Characteristics* The primary difference between these later works and the *Letter* is a marked toning down of the wit directed at religion. In *Miscellaneous Reflections,* however, Shaftesbury's approach underwent a significant change. Although the miscellanist persona's presence there is felt in a relatively small part of the work, his ironic celebration of the modern art of patchwork wit and his other manufactured ironies recall Swift's satiric ploys in *A Tale of a Tub* and the rakish narrator's celebration of the shamelessness of the enthusiasts in *The Adept Ladys.* An equally significant difference is the speaker's more direct and less moderate approach to satiric targets ranging from religious priesthoods in general to

Tory High Churchmen in particular.[28] Whether these changes represent a shift in tactics dictated by the overall structure of *Characteristics* or result from other factors, they mark Shaftesbury's partial abandonment of one of the most interesting satiric experiments of the early eighteenth century.[29]

Unlike his ideas about ridicule, however, the satiric model that Shaftesbury provided in works such as the *Letter* apparently exerted little direct influence, even on admirers such as Antony Collins. The rhapsodic style of *The Moralists* had a much greater impact on later writers. Yet Shaftesbury's attempt to achieve a just measure of irony may in fact have played a significant role in the future of English culture. The author of *Bart'lemy Fair; or, an Enquiry after Wit* showed a prescient anxiety about the skeptical aspects of the *Letter* in complaining that the work was

> industriously spread in the Nation; put, by way of ABC, into the hands of every young Fellow, who begins to speak great swelling Words, against what he Will not Understand, because he is Resolv'd not to Practice: And sent, by way of Mission, into Foreign Parts, upon that *hopeful Project!* which is *now the Heroick Passion of exalted Spirits,* the *saving of Men's Sense,* by the Damning of their Souls![30]

Admired—if often grudgingly—for their wit, and frequently republished during the first half of the eighteenth century as part of *Characteristics,* Shaftesbury's *Letter* and his other satiric works achieved a respectability and sustained hearing rarely granted the literature of free thinking in the period. Their contribution to the spread of Enlightenment thought in England as well as on the Continent should not be underestimated.[31]

Notes

1. John Hayman, "Raillery in Restoration Satire," *Huntington Library Quarterly* 31, 2 (1968): 107-22, 116-22.

2. *Reflections upon "A Letter Concerning Enthusiasm"* (London, 1709), p. 24; John G. Hayman, "Shaftesbury and the Search for a Persona," *Studies in English Literature* 10, 3 (Summer 1970): 491-504, 501-502.

3. Shaftesbury to Pierre Coste, 25 July 1712 N.S., Public Record Office, Shaftesbury Papers, PRO 30/24/23/9/pp. 248-49. The passage in *Characteristics* that Shaftesbury cites is one where his persona (a commentator offering his *Miscellaneous Reflections* on the first two volumes) offers to employ his skills as a miscellany writer to counteract the author's unfashionable seriousness in *An Inquiry Concerning Virtue* and *The Moralists*:

> According to this Method, whilst I serve as *Critick* or *Interpreter* to this new Writer, I may the better correct his Flegm, and give him more of the fash-

ionable Air and Manner of the World, especially in what relates to the Subject and Manner of his two *last* Pieces, which are contain'd in his second Volume. For these being of the more regular and formal kind, may easily be oppressive to the airy Reader; and may therefore with the same assurance as *Tragedy* claim the necessary Relief of the *Little Piece* or *Farce*.

(*Characteristicks*, 2nd edn., 3 vols. [London, 1714], 3:7-8)

4. Horst Meyer, *Limae labor: Untersuchungen zur Textgenese und Druckgeschichte von Shaftesburys "The Moralists,"* European Univ. Papers, Ser. 14, Anglo-Saxon Language and Literature 63 (Frankfurt am Main: Peter Lang, 1978), pp. 37-39.

5. Robert Voitle, *The Third Earl of Shaftesbury, 1671-1713* (Baton Rouge: Louisiana State Univ. Press, 1984), p. 152; hereafter cited in the text.

6. Anthony Ashley Cooper, Third Earl of Shaftesbury, Exercises [ΑΣΚΗΜΑΤΑ], PRO 30/24/27/10/p. 370; hereafter cited in the text.

7. Shaftesbury to Thomas Micklethwayte, 1 September 1712 N.S., PRO 30/24/23/9/pp. 279-80; hereafter cited in the text.

8. Dated 19 January 1701/02, and surviving in two copies in the Public Record Office, this work has been published in full in Anthony Ashley Cooper, Third Earl of Shaftesbury, *Standard Edition: Complete Works, Selected Letters and Posthumous Writings,* ed. and trans. Gerd Hemmerich and Wolfram Benda (Stuttgart: Frommann-Holzbog, 1981), 1:376-443. All citations refer to this edition.

9. A. O. Aldridge, "Shaftesbury's Rosicrucian Ladies," *Anglia* 103, 3/4 (1985): 297-319.

10. Anthony Ashley Cooper, Third Earl of Shaftesbury, *Soliloquy,* in *Characteristicks,* 1:266.

11. PRO 30/24/23/9/p. 249. Shaftesbury had spoken with distaste of *A Tale of a Tub* well before his response to Leibnitz. Explaining his decision to omit his own and his dedicatee's names from an early version of *The Moralists,* Shaftesbury sarcastically observed to Somers: "You have had *a Tale of a Tub* dedicated to you before now: but *a Tale of Philosophy* wou'd be a coarser Present to come publickly upon you, as y^t did" (Shaftesbury to Lord Somers, 20 October 1705, PRO 30/24/22/4/p. 13). In a letter concerning the manuscript of *A Letter Concerning Enthusiasm,* Shaftesbury referred to the author of the *Tale* as Somers's "pretended good Friend" (Shaftesbury to Lord Somers, March 1707/8, PRO 30/24/22/4/p. 69).

12. Shaftesbury's sending Swift's dedicatee his own satiric essay focusing on religious enthusiasm—one of Swift's primary topics—suggests that Shaftesbury may have expected Somers (and anyone to whom Somers chose to show the manuscript) to compare *A Letter Concerning Enthusiasm* with *A Tale of a Tub.* No doubt Shaftesbury would have expected such a comparison to reveal the superiority of his own performance to that of the "coarser" Swift.

13. *Soliloquy,* in *Characteristicks,* 1:255. In his notes for a life of Socrates, Shaftesbury complained that Plato's version of his master was sometimes too buffooning (Design of a Socratick History, PRO 30/24/27/14/p. 53).

14. Anthony Ashley Cooper, Third Earl of Shaftesbury, *A Letter Concerning Enthusiasm* (London, 1708), pp. 33-34; hereafter cited in the text. My choice of editions of Shaftesbury's satiric works predating *Characteristics* for literary analysis is explained in my "Shaftesbury's Wit in *A Letter Concerning Enthusiasm,*" *Modern Philology* 86, 1 (August 1988): 46-53, n. 3.

15. Shaftesbury to Pierre Coste, 1 October 1706, PRO 30/24/45/iii/48v, 44; *Soliloquy,* in *Characteristicks,* 1:258, 328.

16. Anthony Ashley Cooper, Third Earl of Shaftesbury, *Miscellaneous Reflections,* in *Characteristicks,* 3:21.

17. See Hayman, pp. 494-95.

18. Design of a Socratick History, PRO 30/24/27/14/p. 76.

19. Given Shaftesbury's new Arcadia conceit, it is interesting to note Hillel Schwartz's discussion of the pastoral as an element of the French Prophets' appeal to Londoners (*The French Prophets: The History of a Millenarian Group in Eighteenth-Century England* [Berkeley: Univ. of California Press, 1980], pp. 222-29).

20. [Edward Fowler?], *Remarks upon the Letter to a Lord Concerning Enthusiasm* (London, 1708), p. 4.

21. Shaftesbury to Lord Somers, 12 July 1708, PRO 30/24/22/4/p. 87 (the postscript is crossed out in this copybook version); PRO 30/24/22/4/p. 69.

22. Richard Kingston, *Enthusiastick Impostors, No Divinely Inspired Prophets* (London, 1707), p. 33. An advertisement on the verso of Kingston's final page indicates that his book was published on 22 October 1707. On the September 1707 dating of the manuscript *Letter,* see my "The Publication of Shaftesbury's *Letter Concerning Enthusiasm,*" *Studies in Bibliography* 32 (1979): 236-41, 236-37.

23. For a fuller discussion of Shaftesbury's skillful use of conceits (including this one) and paradoxes,

see my "Shaftesbury's Wit in *A Letter Concerning Enthusiasm.*"

24. Edward W. Rosenheim, *Swift and the Satirist's Art* (Chicago: Univ. of Chicago Press, 1963), chap. 3.

25. PRO 30/24/22/4/p. 68.

26. Steele, it is true, presents a case for personal satire in *Tatler* 61, where his speaker justifies its use to combat abuses ignored by the law (e.g., gross ingratitude). But his and Addison's general satiric practice in the *Tatler* and the *Spectator*—as well as the bulk of their commentary on the subject—rejects attacks on individuals.

27. See, for example, *Remarks upon the Letter to a Lord Concerning Enthusiasm,* pp. 62-63; *Reflections upon "A Letter Concerning Enthusiasm,"* pp. 8, 44-47.

28. Jack Prostko uses the example of Shaftesbury's provoked gentleman (who concludes a lengthy diatribe at the end of *Miscellaneous Reflections* without permitting his High Church antagonists to offer a rebuttal) to argue that Shaftesbury employs a form of writing which precludes the free debate that he advocates ("Shaftesbury and Moral Speech," *Eigteenth-Century Studies* 23, 1 [Fall 1989]: 42-61, 59-60). Prostko's generalizations have validity even for the works composing volume 1 of *Characteristics,* but they tend to blur essential distinctions between volumes 1 and 3.

29. For Hayman, the buffoonish miscellanist serves as a negative example, embodying a "faulty" mental disposition and thus serving as a foil to earlier personae in *Characteristics* (pp. 498-99). Shaftesbury's more direct and less moderate form of satiric attack in *Miscellaneous Reflections* can also be explained in terms of the overall design of *Characteristics,* but it may reflect his willingness to sacrifice philosophical propriety for propagandistic power in the face of his alarm at the outcome of the Sacheverell trial and the fall of the Godolphin-Marlborough ministry. In a letter to Somers accompanying *Miscellaneous Reflections,* Shaftesbury expressed the hope, "perhaps too advantageouse and savouring of the Fatherly Love of an Author towards his own offspring," that, should his attack on Tory principles "grow credible, & take either with our growing Youth, or their grown Parents; those endow'd [Tory] Semenarys might chance to make a much worse figure & the October-Club prove less considerable than at present." In lines crossed out in his copy of the letter, he even ventured to suggest that the work's influence might before long be seen in the results of parliamentary elections (Shaftesbury to Lord Somers, 30 March 1711 N.S., PRO 30/24/22/4/pp. 155-56).

30. [Mary Astell], *Bart'lemy Fair; or, an Enquiry after Wit* (London, 1709), p. 23.

31. Although she distorts Shaftesbury's thought in *Characteristics* by reducing his primary intent to an attack on revealed religion, Dorothy B. Schlegel makes a similar point about the importance of Shaftesbury for the French Enlightenment in her *Shaftesbury and the French Deists,* Univ. of North Carolina Studies in Comparative Literature 15 (Chapel Hill: Univ. of North Carolina Press, 1956).

Jorge V. Arregui and Pablo Arnau (essay date October 1994)

SOURCE: Arregui, Jorge V., and Pablo Arnau. "Shaftesbury: Father or Critic of Modern Aesthetics?" *British Journal of Aesthetics* 34, no. 4 (October 1994): 350-62.

[*In the essay below, Arregui and Arnau view Shaftesbury not as the father of modern aesthetics, but as the first great critic of aesthetic modernity.*]

Shaftesbury is usually considered the father of modern aesthetics and, consequently, only those aspects of his thought specially relevant to later aesthetics—the disinterested attitude, the moral and aesthetic sense, and the sublime—are studied.[1] In this sense, Stolnitz has stressed his importance in engendering the central concept of modern aesthetics: the disinterested attitude.[2] For Stolnitz, this notion—which is the corner-stone of the independent status acquired by aesthetics in modernity—is specifically modern and has its origin in Shaftesbury's speculations.[3]

Stolnitz remarks that Shaftesbury is not really in accordance with the concept of aesthetic attitude to which he gave rise; that his aesthetics seems to be 'bound up with his high-level metaphysical principles, generally to its detriment';[4] and that he often denies that there is anything specific in aesthetic phenomena, identifying the aesthetic with other aspects of reality.[5] Therefore, his aesthetics displays a tension between its two central poles. As a classical metaphysician, Shaftesbury had focused his aesthetics on a concept of beauty as a form of harmony which could only be appreciated by the intellect excluding material beauty; as a modern, Shaftesbury was to see aesthetics in terms of the disinterested attitude which established the existence of an aesthetic experience that was different from other experiences, and that deserved study in itself. The author of *The Moralists* would thus find himself in the unfortunate position of the conservative who foresees the revolutionary consequences of his own discovery. By shedding light on the distinctive nature of aesthetic experience, Shaftesbury proved himself to be a great thinker; but his achievement was limited, 'partly because he is not a systematic thinker; partly because he has not been weaned away from the old ways of thinking in aesthetics'.[6]

Townsend has recently objected to some of Stolnitz's views. He admits that the modern concept of aesthetic attitude makes possible the independent status of aesthetics, but he re-examines both Shaftesbury's metaphysics and his concepts of taste and aesthetic attitude. For him, Stolnitz assimilates Shaftesbury to his posteriority; and to interpret him as a pre-romantic and/or pre-Kantian misleads us and conceals what is of greatest value in his thinking. Nevertheless, Townsend does not rehabilitate his metaphysics; he only points out that his neo-platonism is of a very specific kind, and that his metaphysics does not lack empirical content.[7] On the other hand, Shaftesbury's sense of beauty does not admit an empiricist interpretation, because beauty and goodness are both mental, as opposed to being objects of the senses. In contrast with Hutcheson's position, Shaftesbury takes aesthetic taste from the realm of private experience to that of public experience; and in so far as for him immediate taste must be corrected through a rational criticism, Shaftesbury seems not to fall, at least immediately, under Wittgenstein's critique of private language. Besides, in Shaftesbury, disinterestedness does not constitute a special type of perception or of aesthetic experience.[8]

None the less, despite the objections to Stolnitz,[9] the interpretation which considers Shaftesbury as a pre-Kantian or pre-romantic still prevails. Larthomas has recently developed a strongly Kantian reading of Shaftesbury according to which the continuity linking him to modern aesthetics is so strong that he can state that what had been in 1712 the mere germ of a new thought has become imperceptible to us because of its growth. The grain dies in what is born from it. Shaftesbury has vanished in the work of those who followed him.[10] From this point of view, Larthomas presents a Kantian interpretation of Shaftesbury's concepts of moral feeling, *sensus communis,* harmony and natural teleology.

In this line of interpretation, Shaftesbury's interest lies in the concepts he introduces, which—ordered differently—in the following generation came to form modern aesthetics. Shaftesbury would be the 'father' of modernity in the strict sense, because without being modern himself, he engendered modern concepts. Or, in the words of Peter Kivy, 'Shaftesbury is a transitional figure in the history of aesthetics: though he was the nominal founder of a new tradition, he had one foot planted firmly in the past, not only the past as represented by the Italian Renaissance, but that of classical antiquity as well'.[11]

However, this reading of Shaftesbury misunderstands his actual thought and his place in the history of aesthetics: Shaftesbury is not the *father* of modern aesthetics, he is its first great critic. The elements which were later to be interpreted (or misinterpreted) by the Scottish School, and were to make up modern aesthetics, created in Shaftesbury a force field in the opposite direction.[12] In their original sense, they were used against the first characteristically modern views: those of Hobbes and Calvinist orthodoxy.

(A) The Modern Reduction of Aesthetics
to a Decorative Accessory in a
Mechanical World

The independent status of modern aesthetics is a result of the concept of aesthetic attitude, but Shaftesbury's refusal to construct an independent aesthetics is not simply a product of his lack of system, still less that of a naïve classicism. He is openly opposing one of the key characteristics of modernity which was already present in its early stages. For example, in **Miscellaneous Reflections** he complains that 'it has been thought convenient, in these latter Ages, to distinguish the Provinces of Wit and Wisdom, and set apart *the agreeable* from *the useful . . .*'.[13] In **The Moralists** he states that 'Nor can it otherwise happen in the Affairs of Life, whilst that which interests and engages Men as *Good* is thought different from that which they admire and praise as *Honest*—But with us (Philocles!) 'tis better settled: since for our parts, we have already decreed "that *Beauty* and *Good* are still the same".'[14] And, finally, in **Miscellaneous Reflections,** he insists that 'Beauty and Truth are plainly join'd with the notion of Utility and Convenience, even in the apprehension of every ingenious Artist, the Architect, the Statuary or the Painter'.[15] To illustrate the importance of these criticisms against the independence of the aesthetics it is useful to consider in some detail the process by which aesthetics gained in modernity an autonomous status, bringing out some of the negative consequences of this change, especially the appearance of a widening gap between art and life.

Aesthetics can only acquire autonomy if its object becomes distinguished from the other dimensions of reality. Now, for the aesthetic object to appear as a dimension of reality segregated from the others, it is necessary to adopt an aesthetic attitude, that is, a way of viewing reality which consists of paying attention solely to the manner in which an object appears to our senses, isolating this dimension from all the others. The aesthetic attitude is therefore the exclusive attention to an object's mode of appearance, without regard to any of its other dimensions. Thus the object is removed from its normal place in the course of human life, and a break is made in the relationship between that object and what it was made for, so that it can be considered exclusively from the point of view of the way it appears to the senses.

On the other hand, an aesthetic object is just the set of properties which are relevant to the aesthetic attitude; it clearly requires some physical basis, because if it had none it would not appear to the senses, but the aesthetic object is not the physical reality. It is the physical reality seen within a particular perspective or *described in a particular way*. An aesthetic object is a physical reality described from an aesthetic point of view and, therefore, not all true descriptions of the physical reality are descriptions of the aesthetic object. Aesthetic objects are intentional.

The aesthetic attitude also forms the basis of the concept of aesthetic experience and perception. 'Aesthetic experience' is the name given to the characteristic experience which results when one adopts an aesthetic attitude, and which is qualitatively and phenomenologically different from any other experience or perception. Lastly, 'aesthetic pleasure' is the term used to describe the pleasure which is supposed to accompany this experience. Thus the concept of the aesthetic attitude serves as a basis for all the elements (aesthetic experience and perception, aesthetic object and pleasure) needed to build an autonomous aesthetics.

Stolnitz was right when he maintained that the aesthetic attitude is a specifically modern phenomenon, not only because it appears for the first time in modernity, but also because its appearance was conditioned by certain both *philosophical* and *cultural* factors. From the philosophical point of view, aesthetics gained its autonomy in the epistemological turn brought about by modern philosophy.[16] From the sociological one, Woodfield has reflected on some of the cultural conditions which allowed the emergence of the aesthetic attitude.[17] However, it is possible to take a wider view and analyse the arousal of the aesthetic attitude and the consequent autonomy of aesthetics as exemplifying the process of differentiation between the spheres of human life, which we know as the process of modernization.

As Dilthey pointed out, to a very great extent the course of history can be described as a process of increasing differentiation between the spheres of human life. If so-called primitive societies are characterized by what Marcel Mauss described as a *complete social phenomenon,* so that any given phenomenon is at once religious, political, economic, juridical, artistic, and so on, in modern western society these dimensions of human life have become autonomous. The historical tendency is for every area of human life to gain an increasing degree of independence, with the consequence that these areas then interrelate in ever-changing patterns. As far as each of these spheres is defined by its relationship with the others, there is considerable variation in their content.

The process by which economics has become in modernity an independent sphere of human life has been care-fully studied by Dumont,[18] but this process can be seen even more clearly in the emergence of an aesthetic point of view and, consequently, of an autonomous aesthetic realm. It is obvious that in pre-literate societies there exist neither purely artistic objects nor an aesthetic point of view, that is, we find no consideration of reality which deals solely with its aesthetic dimension. The categories 'aesthetic object' and 'artistic point of view' are the product of a particular historical process, they are not phenomena which arise once and for all out of human nature itself.

Gadamer has questioned the legitimacy of the aesthetic consciousness setting out from a study of the limits which beset 'experiential art'. 'Experiential art' means both that art proceeds from an experience of which it is an expression, and that it is ordained towards the evocation of that experience. The concept of art is thus linked to a determinate experience, the aesthetic experience, which is somehow separate and distinct from the experiences which make up the general run of life. This notion of 'aesthetic experience' is characteristic of a specific historical moment, and prior to this period, art was not linked to it. When we look at a Romanesque Christ today, a specific aesthetic experience can be set off; but this was not the original means of relating to such a work. The artist did not purport to create 'a work of art' whose purpose was to prompt an aesthetic experience; on the contrary, he desired to fashion an object for religious veneration. The original attitude towards the Romanesque Christ was not that of aesthetic contemplation, but rather that of prayer, and therefore the experience out of which that work arose and towards which it was directed was not aesthetic but religious or, to be more exact, these two types of experience had not yet undergone a separation. Art and religion did not constitute two different spheres.

The formation of the aesthetic consciousness, and the autonomy of the artistic sphere, imply a break in the ties which bind art and beauty to the other dimensions of reality. 'By disregarding everything in which a work is rooted (its original context of life, and the religious or secular function which gave it its significance), it becomes visible as the "pure work of art".'[19] What remains beyond the reach of the *aesthetic* consideration of the work of art are all the non-aesthetic moments inherent in it, such as its purpose, function, or the meaning of its content. The aesthetic consciousness addresses itself only to the aesthetic essence of that work of art.

Now, the process of differentiation between the spheres of human life entails a redefinition of their content. In this sense, Jacinto Choza has explained that the independence of art must be seen in the context of the development of modern science. The relationship between art, technology, science and philosophy is different in Antiquity and in Modernity. For Aristotle, art and technology flow together, while science is paired off with philosophy; for the former are both areas of technical skill, opposed to prudence on the one hand, and to the habits of theoretical understanding on the other. The development of art and technology is governed by technical interest, and they are directed towards things which could exist otherwise, and which are dependent on us. By contrast, science and philosophy are profoundly disinterested activities which centre on what is necessary, does not depend on us, and cannot be otherwise.

The Aristotelian view contrasts with the modern one: in so far as science is motivated by technical interest and addresses itself to things that can be otherwise, it approaches technology and distances itself from philosophy. Art, however, moves closer towards philosophy, as both are disinterested and concern themselves with what could not exist otherwise.[20] In as much as both reflect our conception of nature, art becomes linked with wisdom. But since philosophy and art are no longer related with science, they become deprived of cognitive value and are reduced to purely 'subjective' experiences. Whereas for Aristotle, *knowing* is seeing, and not transforming, for the first modern thinkers *knowing* is controlling, mastering and transforming. Thus where, for the former, contemplative knowledge was deeply disinterested, knowledge is now essentially interested, and contemplation lacks cognitive value.

In this way, as Gadamer shows, the abstraction performed by the aesthetic consciousness, the emergence of a specific aesthetic experience which is distinct and disconnected from the other experiences whose nexus constitutes human life, means that art, which is now understood as the art of *beautiful appearances,* is placed in opposition to both practical reality and truth, and that it is understood with this conflict in mind. 'Instead of art and nature complementing each other, as has always seemed to be the case, they were contrasted as appearance and reality. Traditionally it is the purpose of "art", which also embraces all the conscious transformation of nature for use by humans, to complete its supplementing and fulfilling activity within the areas given and left free by nature. And "Les beaux arts", as long as they are seen in this framework, are a perfecting of reality and not an external masking, veiling or transfiguration of it. But if the contrast between reality and appearance determines the concept of art, this breaks up the inclusive framework of nature. Art becomes a standpoint of its own and establishes its own autonomous claim to supremacy.'[21]

In this way, the correlative processes of the increasing autonomy of art and of the development of the new science severs the link between art and truth—which is now monopolized by science—and between art and every utilitarian or pragmatic value—which is transferred to technology. In consequence, art is left with the exclu-

sive role of the *disinterested contemplation of beauty.* Beauty can also be produced, and so art never loses its dimension of *poesis,* although beauty is produced with the sole purpose of being contemplated. A 'work of art' in the modern sense, an 'aesthetic object', serves only to be contemplated.

The progressive separation of the spheres of human life, and their reordering, involves a process in which art becomes ever more reflective and abstract, more distanced from ordinary, everyday life which is lived out in the area of what is useful. In mature modernity, art has become something highly intellectual, accessible only to the initiated; something to be explained by recourse to pedagogical techniques, and which no longer has anything to do with human life or truth. This progressive separation of art from life has two extraordinarily negative consequences. In the first place, art's autonomous status is balanced out by the loss of the aesthetic dimension in all the other areas of human life, the confinement of art and artistic creativity within the prison of the aesthetic experience, and the consequent loss of its social validity. Secondly, in the early years of the twentieth century, the separation between art and life set off a general crisis in the identity of art. Thus, the increasing independence of art has implied an anxious questioning of its meaning. This crisis in the identity of art has in turn two paradoxical consequences: on the one hand, modern artists display a gargantuan effort to return art to life. But on the other, in the throes of an identity crisis, art is increasingly its own object, is progressively becoming self-referential and opaque.

In the unfolding of avant-gardes—writes Jiménez—'the denial of art is, on the whole, linked to a proposal of a real universalization of the creative abilities of man, to an attempt to get rid of the gap between creative activity and life, which the spiritualization of art and the idea of the artist as a genius and a demigod had been historically brewing ever since the Renaissance'. Thus behind the war cry of the historical vanguard movements lies the attempt to recover art for life, to make it into a call for a new society, a stimulus to awaken a new culture, by striving to bring it out of the museums and academies in order to turn it back into the everyday exercise of every individual's creative freedom.[22] But as has often been indicated, the attempt to reconcile art to life meets with an obstacle within the avant-garde movements themselves, in the form of their self-referential opacity. 'The bewilderment and uprooting which make art turn in on itself, to the extent of questioning its *raison d'être,* lead avant-garde art along the paths of linguistic experiments and fragmentation, watering down its purpose of sketching new forms of life, of becoming universal as creative experience of all men.'[23] Paradoxically, the modernist movements themselves, which spring from the attempt to bring art closer to life, have succeeded only in recreating the modern inaccessibility of art and facilitating its withdrawal into circles of the initiated. The survival of art in museums, only in museums, is the index of their failure.

Certainly, the autonomization of aesthetics has resulted in a spectacular flowering of art; but this independence of art from life has also led to its relegation to an unreal sphere. It is possible, given these premises, to endeavour to pass judgement on reality; but in the long run, reality always wreaks its revenge in the form of disappointment and disillusionment. If art is only a 'beautiful appearance' which is seen in contrast to a rough, coarse, vulgar reality, its validity is no more lasting than that of a dream. A bitter awakening is inevitable.

Thus we can maintain that the consequences of the autonomous status of aesthetics, as a result of the aesthetic attitude, are ambivalent. It has often been stated that the products of modernity present a certain ambiguity, and that many times the goals which have in fact been reached are the opposite of those which had originally been intended. In this respect, the independence of aesthetics can be said to have brought about its trivialization. Conversion of the aesthetic realm into a sphere which is separate from human life implies that the most real and vital dimensions of existence are stripped of any aesthetic content. There no longer seems to be any place for considerations of an aesthetic nature, or concerning individual creativity in the real existence of men; the latter is governed exclusively along lines other than those of aesthetics, that is, by criteria of technical efficiency.

Again, the loss of the cognitive value of aesthetic contemplation tends to trivialize the latter. To the extent that knowledge is reduced to a positive science, in as much as the truth is identified with scientific objectivity, aesthetics is transferred to the realm of the subjective. What is real consists only of the factual, all that is the case, as Wittgenstein was later to declare. Under these conditions, aesthetics is reduced to a subjective, decorative accessory in a world which is understood in a mechanical fashion. The real world is for the early moderns the world described by Newton's mechanics, a world in black and white made up exclusively of moving atoms, in which there is no place for aesthetic fancies. Early modern thinkers thus established a profound dichotomy. On the one hand, positive science and truth, the objective and the real; on the other, aesthetics and meaning, the subjective and the unreal. What science affirms is genuine and objective, but is devoid of meaning; what aesthetics proclaims has meaning, but lacks truth and objectivity.

Not only the physical world is a mechanical one; the cultural world, that is made up by the socio-cultural institutions which we men have created, is also a me-

chanical universe which allows no scope for individual creativity or aesthetic considerations. The laws which govern human society, the socio-cultural constructs, are as mechanical and as resistant to meaning as those which rule the physical world. Culture is a world governed by a social mechanism which has no place for aesthetics or creativity. And, in a certain sense, as María Antonia Labrada has shown, the situation of the cultural world is worse than that of the natural one.[24] For when Kant, for example, attempts to reconcile the world of nature with that of freedom by teleological postulation (everything occurs *as though* physical nature existed in order for us to know it), he restricts his postulate to physical nature, leaving aside the reality of culture, the sphere of the socio-cultural institutions, which is genuinely the essential *Lebenswelt* in which human existence unfolds.

To sum up, the aesthetic attitude which renders possible the independent existence of aesthetics tends subsequently to turn it into a pure, ornamental complement to a life and a world which are understood in a mechanical sense. If aesthetics has nothing to do with everyday life, or with truth, if it is a sphere which is independent from the other dimensions of reality, if the beautiful or the aesthetic in general has nothing to do with what is true, good, useful or appropriate, aesthetics will ultimately fall prey to triviality and be reduced to a subjective decoration which cannot affect the organization of personal and social life.

(B) SHAFTESBURY AS CRITIC OF THE MODERN IN AESTHETICS

From this point of view, Shaftesbury does not fit the role even of an unwilling *father* to modern aesthetics. He is not an incoherent writer, or a philosophical Janus. Instead, he emerges as the first great critic of aesthetic modernity wholly conscious of the reduction of aesthetics to a subjective ornament in a world and a life which are understood mechanically.

No one has defended the value of art and beauty in human life as sincerely as Shaftesbury. The point is not, as it is usually claimed, that he is a classical thinker because of his inordinate adherence to the rules of artistic creativity. The central issue is his bestowal to art and beauty of an orientative function in personal and social life. 'In early days, *Poets* were look'd upon as authentick *Sages,* for dictating Rules of Life, and teaching Manners and good Sense.'[25] For him, in Cassirer's words, the problems of aesthetics 'were his own personal problems long before they became purely theoretical problems. Shaftesbury does not consider aesthetics exclusively, nor even predominantly, from the viewpoint of the work of art; on the contrary, he seeks and needs theory of beauty in order to answer the question of the true fashioning of character, of the law governing the structure of the inward personal world'.[26]

Naturally, Shaftesbury cannot be said to be defending a kind of aestheticism *à la Wilde,* in which life imitates art; actually, he is a moralist. But he is particularly conscious of the human being as the 'Architect of his own Life and Fortune',[27] and that, therefore, man's own life is thus his first *artificio,* his first and fundamental work of art. Obviously, 'work of art' cannot be taken in the modern sense as meaning *beautiful appearance.* Shaftesbury is not Gide. Beauty and art are neither a mere addition or adjunct to human life, nor are they enclosed within a supposed 'aesthetic experience'; they must have a directive role in man's own existence. 'For—he rhetorically asks—is not a *Workmanship* and *a Truth* in Actions? Or is the *Workmanship* of this kind less becoming, or less worth our notice; that we shou'd not in this Case be as surely at least as the honest *Artizan,* who has no other *Philosophy* than what *Nature* and his *Trade* [have] taught him?'.[28]

Now, Shaftesbury is also especially aware of two further points. If aesthetic considerations, beauty and art, are to have a directive role in human life, then perception of beauty must have cognitive value. If our perception of beauty is cognitively blind, if it does not enable us to know any real property, it cannot have an orientative function in human life. But, in turn, for our perception of beauty to have cognitive value, the world has truly to be beautiful or, in other words, the mechanistic view cannot be true. Shaftesbury is perfectly aware that if we allow a mechanistic approach, if we accept that the world is as Hobbes and Locke propose, then the die is cast as far as the fate of aesthetics is concerned.

His declaration in **The Moralists** that he is a *realist,* his thesis that beauty and goodness are real predicates, cannot be interpreted as a mere survival from classical metaphysics. To defend the role of art in human life, as he aims, means establishing on the one hand a new epistemology which will make the perception of beauty into real knowledge, and on the other hand an ontology which leaves room for beauty and goodness among the real properties of the world. These two issues form the centre from which his main philosophical interests radiate. Seen in this perspective, we cannot concur with Stolnitz in maintaining that 'his metaphysics is the villain of the piece', nor does it suffice to state as Townsend does that his metaphysics has an experiential content. His whole aesthetic approach depends on his metaphysics, on his thesis that physical nature is teleological, not mechanical. Shaftesbury incorporates moral harmony within natural harmony. If we were a little better, he says, we would see in ourselves 'Beauty and Decorum here, as well as elsewhere in Nature; and the Order of the Moral World wou'd be equal that of the Natural. By this the *Beauty of* Virtue wou'd appear; and hence (as has been shewn) *the Supreme* and *Sovereign* Beauty, the Original of all that is Good or Amiable'.[29]

For this reason his first and principal enemy is Hobbes's mechanicism, and he strongly depends on those thinkers who most vigorously maintained the teleology of nature, which cannot be separated from their ethics and aesthetics. In so far as beauty and goodness are not only real properties but can be known by us, Shaftesbury is opposed to all forms of moral theological positivism. The goodness of an action cannot consist exclusively in its conformity with a law, whether human or divine, as if the divine law were arbitrary as Locke had postulated. For Shaftesbury, things are not good because we are commanded to do them, or bad because they have been forbidden, but rather they are prohibited because they are bad and commanded because they are good.

Opposing teleological moral positivism means asserting once again the value of nature. Not only can he speak of the nature of things, but he can also maintain that actions are good or bad by nature. And for him, not only good and evil have their roots in nature and there is a natural capacity to know them, but also *by nature* we possess the ability to act morally well. It must be emphasized that he does not maintain that man is naturally good—in fact he insists repeatedly that virtue is difficult, and that it is hard to acquire good taste—[30] but rather that he is not naturally bad. Affirming the *natural* ability of human beings to act well implies a confrontation not only with Hobbes but also with Calvinist orthodoxy.

Asserting the role of aesthetics in man's life and trying to demonstrate the cognitive value of the perception of beauty also entails a break with early modern thought in its typical identification of positive science, truth, the objective and the real on the one hand, and the aesthetic, the apparent, the subjective and the unreal on the other. It is not simply a question of art and literature, for instance, having a cognitive value in so far as they enable us to get to know others and ourselves better;[31] it means that we cannot admit in any way that all aesthetic questions are up to the individual's taste, or that all taste is subjective, infallible and incorrigible, precisely because it says nothing about reality, but simply expresses our subjective reactions. For him, the modern dichotomy of subjective and objective lacks validity, because he is not committed to a reduction of what is knowable and true to positive scientific knowledge. Precisely because taste tells us something about reality, because in this sense it is *objective,* it can err and require correction. Of course, the assertion that taste is fallible and liable to correction, in other words, that it can be educated, introduces the problem of authority in aesthetics.

On the other hand, the statement that the perception of beauty has cognitive value, the thesis that aesthetic properties are real, serves as ammunition to confront the crisis concerning the foundations of art criticism which had arisen since the *querelle* between classical and modern thinkers. According to Shaftesbury, the *querelle* is above all a crisis caused by a proliferation of those who make 'their Humour alone the Rule of what is *beautiful* and *agreeable,* and having no Account to give of such their Humour or odd Fancy, reject the *criticizing* or *examining* Art, by which alone they are able to discover the *true* Beauty and Worth of every Object'.[32] His thought can in a fair proportion be interpreted as a response to the question as to what are the foundations of art criticism.[33]

Last of all, his criticism of the identification of knowledge and truth with positive science enables him to connect truth to life and thus to set out a concept of philosophy which may sometimes take on shades close to those of vitalism. Philosophy's role is to 'teach us *our-selves,* keep us the *self-same* Persons, and so regulate our governing Fancies, Passions, and Humours, as to make us comprehensible to our-selves, and knowable by other Features than those of a bare Countenance'.[34] Given his vitalistic view, he levels harsh criticism at academic philosophy which is embroiled in derivative scholasticism, that is, the kind of philosophy which has severed its connections with the individual and social life of man. If he refuses to accept the isolation of art in a separate sphere of human life, he equally cannot permit such a status for philosophy.[35] In the last instance, 'To philosophize in a just signification is but To carry *Good-Breeding* a step higher. For the Accomplishment of Breeding is, To learn whatever is *decent* in company, or *beautiful* in arts; and the sum of Philosophy is, To learn what is *just* in Society and *beautiful* in Nature'. 'Tis not Wit merely, but a *Temper* that must form the Well-Bred Man. In the same manner, 'tis a *Head* merely, but a *Heart* and *Resolution* that must complete the real philosopher. Both *Characters* aim at what is *excellent,* aspire to a *just taste,* and carry in view the Model of what is *beautiful* and *becoming*'.[36]

Notes

1. See, for example, M. C. Beardsley, *Aesthetics from classical Greece to the present* (Alabama: The University of Alabama Press, 1966), 173-83.

2. See J. Stolnitz, 'On the Significance of Lord Shaftesbury in Modern Aesthetic Theory' in *The Philosophical Quarterly* 11 (1961), 97-113. The statement to which we refer can be found on p. 78. See also the same author's 'On the Origins of "Aesthetic Disinterestedness"' in *The Journal of Aesthetics and Art Criticism* 10 (1961-2), 131-42; '"Beauty": Some Stages in the History of an Idea' in *The Journal of the History of Ideas* 22 (1961) 185-204; and '"The Aesthetic Attitude" in the Rise of Modern Aesthetics' in *The Journal of Aesthetics and Art Criticism* 36 (1977-78), 409-22.

3. See 'On the Origins of "Aesthetic Attitude"', 131-2.

4. 'On the significance', 98.

5. See Ibid., 101-4.

6. Ibid., 113.

7. See D. Townsend, 'Shaftesbury's Aesthetic Theory' in *The Journal of Aesthetics and Art Criticism* 41 (1982-3) 207; and his 'From Shaftesbury to Kant. The Development of the Concept of Aesthetic Experience' in *The Journal of the History of Ideas* 48 (1987), 289.

8. See D. Townsend, 'Shaftesbury's Aesthetic Theory', 211-3. See also D. A. White, 'The Metaphysics of Disinterestedness: Shaftesbury and Kant' in *Journal of Aesthetics and Art Criticism* 32 (1973-4), 239-48.

9. The most sweeping criticism of Stolnitz's view that the disinterested aesthetic attitude is the corner-stone of the independence of aesthetics in modern thought is that of G. Dickie, 'Taste and Attitude: the Origin of the Aesthetic' in his *Art and the Aesthetic* (Ithaca: Cornell U.P., 1976), 53-77; and his 'Stolnitz's Attitude: Taste and Perception' in *The Journal of Aesthetics and Art Criticism* 43 (1984-5), 195-203. See also R. G. Saisselin, 'Critical Reflections on the Origins of Modern Aesthetics' in *The British Journal of Aesthetics* 4 (1964), 7-21.

10. See J. P. Larthomas, *De Shaftesbury à Kant,* Atélier National de Reproduction des Thèses, Université de Lille III, Lille 1985, VII. The same idea can be found in B. Willey, 'The third Earl of Shaftesbury' in *The British Moralists* (London: Chatto and Windus, 1964), 221.

11. P. Kivy, *The Seventh Sense. A Study of F. Hutcheson's Aesthetics and its Influence in Eighteenth-Century Britain* (New York: Burt Franklin and Co., 1976), 18.

12. The thesis that modernity in aesthetics can be situated within Hutcheson's empiricist interpretation of some of Shaftesbury's principles is explained in more detail in Jorge V. Arregui's introduction to the Spanish edition of Francis Hutcheson's *Investigación sobre el orígen de nuestra idea de belleza* (Madrid: Tecnos, 1992), pp. ix-xxxiii.

13. Anthony Ashley Cooper, third Earl of Shaftesbury, *Miscellaneous Reflections,* Standard edition (Stuttgart: Frommann-Hoolzboog, 1989), I, 1, 26.

14. Shaftesbury, *The Moralists. A Philosophical Rhapsody,* Standard edition (Stuttgart: Frommann-Hoolzboog, 1981), III, 2, 346.

15. *Miscellaneous Reflections,* III, 2, 222.

16. On this point, see, for example, M. A. Labrada, *Belleza y racionalidad: Kant y Hegel* (Pamplona: Eunsa, 1990), 18-20 and the introductory study of Jorge V. Arregui, already cited, to F. Hutcheson, *Una investigación sobre el origen de nuestra idea de belleza,* xxiii-xxvii.

17. See R. Woodfield, 'On the Emergence of Aesthetics' in *The British Journal of Aesthetics* 18 (1978), 217-27.

18. See L. Dumont, *From Mandeville to Marx. The Genesis and Triumph of Economic Ideology* (Chicago and London: The University of Chicago Press, 1977) and *Essays on Individualism* (Chicago and London: The University of Chicago Press, 1986).

19. See H. G. Gadamer, *Truth and Method,* 76.

20. See J. Choza, *Lo satánico como fuente y como tema de la creación artística* in his *La realización del hombre en la cultura* (Madrid: Rialp, 1992), 266-7.

21. H. G. Gadamer, *Truth and Method,* 74.

22. See J. Jiménez, *Imagenes del hombre. Fundamentos de Estética* (Madrid: Tecnos, 1986), 68-9.

23. J. Jiménez, ibid., 70.

24. See M. A. Labrada, *Sobre la razón poética* (Pamplona: Eunsa, 1992), 15-33.

25. Shaftesbury, *Soliloquy: or, Advice to an Author,* I, 1, Standard edition (Stuttgart: Frommann-Hoolzboog, 1981), 42.

26. E. Cassirer, *The Philosophy of the Enlightenment* (Princeton U.P., 1951), 313.

27. Shaftesbury, *The Moralists,* III, 2, 362.

28. Shaftesbury, *Soliloquy,* II, 3, 176.

29. Shaftesbury, *The Moralists,* II, 4, 176. See also *Miscellaneous Reflections,* IV, 2, Standard edition (Stuttgart: Frommann-Hoolzboog, 1981), 256.

30. 'A legitimate and just Taste can be neither be begotten, made, conceiv'd or produc'd, without the antecedent Labour and Pains of Criticism' (*Miscellaneous Reflections,* III, 2, 216). See also for example, *Soliloquy,* III, 2, 224-6.

31. Shaftesbury, *Soliloquy,* I, 3, 94.

32. Shaftesbury, *Miscellaneous Reflections,* III, 2, 202.

33. A summary of the problem of critical authority in Shaftesbury's ideas can be found in *Soliloquy,* II, 2, 140-74; II, 3, 176-8. *Miscellaneous Reflections,* III, 2, 200-8; V, 1, 276-310.

34. *Soliloquy,* III, 1, 202. On Shaftesbury's concept of philosophy as self-knowledge and reflection on one's own life, see the first chapter of the third part of *Soliloquy* and the third section of the third part of *The Moralists.*

35. See, for example, Shaftesbury, *Soliloquy,* III, 1, 208-12; *Miscellaneous Reflections,* III, 1, 190 and following and *Miscellaneous Reflections,* IV, 2, 258-60.

36. Shaftesbury, *Miscellaneous Reflections,* III, 1, 196-8.

Preben Mortensen (essay date October 1994)

SOURCE: Mortensen, Preben. "Shaftesbury and the Morality of Art Appreciation." *Journal of the History of Ideas* 55, no. 4 (October 1994): 631-50.

[*In this essay, Mortensen examines Shaftesbury's notion of aesthetic disinterestedness and his moral defense of art appreciation.*]

It is central to our Western conception of art that art has its value in itself and not just as a vehicle for, say, moral or religious enlightenment. According to this idea of the autonomy of art, when we contemplate art, we adopt a specific "aesthetic attitude" which serves, as it were, to bracket whatever practical, moral, religious, political, or other concerns we may have, and we attend to the object in an aesthetic manner only. This way of attending to works of art (or other objects) is sometimes called disinterested contemplation. Lord Shaftesbury (1671-1713) is often considered the first to call attention to the phenomenon of "disinterested perception" as it relates to aesthetics.

A critical reexamination of Shaftesbury's writings (undertaken below) does not, however, support the view that Shaftesbury separates the contemplation of art from moral concerns in particular.[1] On the contrary Shaftesbury's aim was *to situate the contemplation of art within a morality acceptable to his contemporaries.* To understand why Shaftesbury had to provide a moral defense of the appreciation of art and what this defense amounted to, it is necessary to see it against the background of the attempt to create a new social and moral order in England after the revolution in 1688, particularly as these attempts were expressed in the movement to reform manners. Shaftesbury, and those of his contemporaries who agreed with him, expressed their view of the social order in part in the conception of "politeness." An interest in art and the possession of taste become central ingredients of politeness.

Bringing these historical considerations to bear on Shaftesbury's writings thus provides a new interpretation of his philosophy and a deeper understanding of the philosophical and historical context out of which aesthetics as a philosophical discipline grew.

SHAFTESBURY AND THE MORALITY OF ART

One of the most authoritative recent interpretations of Shaftesbury's philosophy was advanced by Jerome Stolnitz in a series of essays from the 1960s.[2] According to this interpretation, which has to some degree obtained the status of the received view, Shaftesbury's influence in philosophy of art is due mainly to the fact that he introduced the concept of "aesthetic disinterestedness."[3] Historically, "disinterestedness" is essential to the creation of aesthetics as a theoretical discipline and to our conception of art.[4] Shaftesbury's use of this term is not, as Stolnitz also points out, connected to art in particular but is initially part of an argument in ethics directed against the idea that "interest rules the world" (I, 77), an idea which in the early eighteenth century was associated primarily with Hobbes. From its origin in ethics and religion "disinterestedness" becomes a key concept in aesthetics. According to Stolnitz, aesthetics is the most important part of Shaftesbury's thought: "[T]he whole impulse and bent of Shaftesbury's thought, from the very beginning, was toward the aesthetic. . . . He applied his aesthetic insights to ethics, but not to ethics exclusively."[5] It attains this status, according to Stolnitz, by shedding its moral and religious content and letting the aesthetic come "into its own for the first time."[6]

Stolnitz's interpretation of Shaftesbury has not been without its detractors. George Dickie in particular has criticized aspects of Stolnitz's work, especially concerning the historical role of the British theorists (Addison, Shaftesbury, Hutcheson, Burke, Alison, and others).[7] Stolnitz claims that they were the first to advance the idea of disinterestedness and were, therefore, precursors of later theoreticians, such as Kant and Schopenhauer, who refine and develop the work already begun by the British. Since disinterestedness, according to Stolnitz, is a defining concept of aesthetic theory, aesthetics proper can be said to have its origins in Britain in the first half of the eighteenth century.[8] Dickie, on the contrary, thinks that Schopenhauer was the first to advance a developed theory about "aesthetic attitude," which is defined in terms of disinterestedness.[9] Although the issue of the historical role of the British and the character of the development of aesthetics is complicated and lies beyond my immediate topic, I do assume that Stolnitz is correct about the influence of the British. My major disagreement with Stolnitz concerns the character and role of "disinterestedness" and his claim that Shaftesbury liberates the aesthetic from the moral.

Dickie has little to say about Shaftesbury, in part because of Shaftesbury's Platonism, in part because Dickie simply does not think that any conception of aesthetic perception or disinterested contemplation is present in Shaftesbury's writings. I agree with Stolnitz that it is misleadingly one-sided to characterize Shaftesbury as a Platonist and use that as a reason to set him aside in the historical development.[10] Dabney Townsend has argued convincingly that in the historical context sharp distinctions between Platonism and empiricism make little sense.[11] Nor does this distinction make it possible for Dickie to account for the influence Shaftesbury actually had on the theoretical development in the remaining part of the eighteenth century.

What was the meaning of "interest" in the eighteenth century? Today we generally identify that which we have an interest in doing with that which we are inclined to do or desire to do. In the seventeenth and eighteenth centuries following one's interest could be the exact opposite of following one's passions, as illustrated in an incident in Fanny Burney's *Cecilia*. In a conversation with Cecilia, Mrs. Delvile tries, without directly saying so, to make it clear to Cecilia that her son cannot possibly marry her, even though they may all desire it. Mrs. Delvile concludes: "How few are there, how very few, who marry at once upon principles rational and feelings pleasant! Interest and inclination are eternally at strife. . . ."[12]

In this passage interest is something which has to be followed because of one's position in society. It is an imposed obligation. Following one's feelings or inclinations would have destructive consequences; in the situation in *Cecilia,* young Delvile would not be able to carry on the family name. The interests control and counteract desires and passions.

In the early eighteenth century interest was closely connected to the possession of wealth. Shaftesbury defines the term "interest" in this manner:

> Even in *that complicated good of vulgar kind which we commonly call interest, in which we comprehend both pleasure, riches, power and other exterior advantages,* we may discern how a fascinated sight contracts a genius, and by shortening the view even of that very interest which it seeks, betrays the knave, and necessitates the ablest and wittiest proselyte of the kind to expose himself on every emergency and sudden turn [my italics].
>
> (II, 345)

Interest is also defined as "desire of those conveniences by which we are well provided for and maintained" or in more general terms as "self-love" (I, 317). A certain moderate self-love is not necessarily bad, but driven to extremes, it becomes dangerous. Exclusive concern for one's private interest becomes "cowardice, revengefulness, luxury, avarice, vanity, ambition, and sloth" (*ibid.*). Interest in particular leads to avarice.

According to Hirschman, the meaning of "interest," though initially wider, becomes identified in the course of the seventeenth century almost exclusively with the acquisition of material wealth and the pursuit of economic advantages.[13] But paradoxically, the term "interest" gradually develops the function of legitimizing what had hitherto been known under such negative terms as "avarice" or "greed" because it was seen as a control on greater evils, such as ambition, lust for power, or sexual desire.

Shaftesbury argues against a view of good acts that conceives of these as grounded only in the self-interest of individuals, the view that good acts should be done "for the sake of a bargain" (I, 66) or because of a view of "future reward and punishment" (II, 55)—actually a form of bargain, too.[14] As is well known, Shaftesbury was of the opinion that human beings have a "natural moral sense" (I, 262), a sense of "right and wrong," and are naturally inclined to act virtuously. Acting without any regard for the possible personal benefit one might get either in this world or beyond is to act disinterestedly (I, 67-69). In particular one must strive to love God and virtue in a disinterested manner, that is, for "God or virtue's sake" (II, 55).

As already indicated, the core of Stolnitz's interpretation of Shaftesbury's conception of disinterestedness is the claim that the idea from its origin in ethics becomes "properly aesthetic."[15] Stolnitz does not claim that a clear cut case of the use of disinterestedness in the modern, aesthetic sense can be found in the writings of Shaftesbury but only that he is the starting point for this development of the concept, regardless of the intentions which he might have had.[16]

How does the notion of disinterestedness evolve into a concept of a particular manner in which works of art can be perceived? According to Stolnitz, the meaning given to disinterestedness in the passage from *The Moralists* (published 1709) referred to above, in which Shaftesbury discusses the disinterested love of God and virtue, comes close to a meaning which makes it possible also to use the term in connection with aesthetics. In this context Shaftesbury does not use "disinterestedness" in the sense in which the concept is often used in the moral context. It refers not to "benevolence" or acting to further the common good of mankind, but only to *a suspension of any private interest,* to something which is "not motivated by self-seeking."[17] The sense of disinterestedness we are looking for is "opposed, not to benevolence, but to the falling away of self-concern."[18]

In addition to the deliberations about the disinterested love of virtue and God, the aesthetically relevant notion of disinterestedness can also, according to Stolnitz, be seen in another passage from *The Moralists* (a passage central to Stolnitz's interpretation). Here "the aesthetic comes into its own for the first time: aesthetic perception is no longer run together with moral and religious virtue, 'disinterestedness' leaves behind its origins in the Hobbes controversy. . . ."[19]

In *The Moralists* even more than in his other works Shaftesbury discusses a bewildering array of topics, presented in part in the form of a dialogue between Theocles and Philocles as recounted by Philocles to Palemon. Theocles represents the "correct" line of reasoning. In their conversation Theocles and Philocles touch upon the nature of poetry and beauty. Poets and other lovers of the Muses and the Graces copy nature (II, 125). The things in nature we find beautiful, things which can "passionately" strike us, are shadows of a deeper kind of beauty:

> [W]hatever in Nature is beautiful or charming is only the faint shadow of that first beauty. So that every real love depending on the mind, and being only the contemplation of beauty either as it really is in itself or as it appears imperfectly in the objects which strike the sense, how can the rational mind rest here, or be satisfied with the absurd enjoyment which reaches the sense alone?
>
> (II, 126)

In other words the true enjoyment of something excludes mere sensuous enjoyment. Opposed to the sensuous kind of enjoyment there is a higher, rational kind. Theocles further explains the rational kind of enjoyment in a passage quoted by Stolnitz:

[T.:]

> Imagine then, good Philocles, if being taken with the beauty of the ocean, which you see yonder at a distance, it should come into your head to seek to command it, and, like some mighty admiral, ride master of the sea, would not the fancy be a little absurd?

[P.:]

> Absurd enough, in conscience. The next thing I should do, 'tis likely, upon this frenzy, would be to hire some bark and go in nuptial ceremony, Venetian-like, to wed the gulf, which I might call perhaps as properly my own.

[T.:]

> Let who will call it theirs, replied Theocles, you will own the enjoyment of this kind to be very different from that which should naturally follow from the contemplation of the ocean's beauty. . . . But to come nearer home, and make the question still more familiar. Suppose (my Philocles) that, viewing such a tract of country as this delicious vale we see beneath us, you should, for the enjoyment of the prospect, require the property or possession of the land.

[P.:]

> The covetous fancy, replied I, would be as absurd altogether as that other ambitious one.
>
> (II, 126-27)

Shaftesbury wishes to distinguish between admiring something for its beauty and the desire to possess or own it.[20] One objection to this distinction that comes to mind is that there is a kind of beauty, the admiration of which seems naturally to lead to a desire to possess the object (II, 127-28). Shaftesbury's oblique reference is probably to sexual attraction, a type of attraction which is nevertheless natural and so, in Shaftesbury's moral universe, good.[21] It appears, then, that a contradiction arises: what is natural has been praised as good, but according to the passage just quoted, that which is natural now seems to be bad, linked as it is to dangerous desires. To this objection Theocles answers:

[T.:]

> Far be it from us both . . . to condemn a joy which is from Nature. . . . But 'twas not here . . . that we had agreed to place our good, nor consequently our enjoyment. We who were rational, and had minds, methought, should place it rather in those minds which were indeed abused, and cheated of their real good, when drawn to seek absurdly the enjoyment of it in the objects of sense, and not in those objects they might properly call their own, in which kind, as I remember, we comprehended all which was truly fair, generous, or good.

[P.:]

> So that beauty, said I, and good with you, Theocles, I perceive, are still one and the same.

(II, 128)

Speaking for Shaftesbury, Theocles, rather than wishing to carve out an independent realm for the contemplation of beauty, wants to reassert a point frequently made by Shaftesbury: the unity of the good and the beautiful (rational beauty). To know what is true, good, or beautiful requires insight into "inward numbers" (I, 217). Knowledge of truth, beauty, and goodness is insight into an actual, harmonious order in the universe, characterized by given numerical proportions, particularly symmetry:

> [W]hat is beautiful is harmonious and proportionable; what is harmonious and proportionable is true; and what is at once both beautiful and true is, of consequence, agreeable and good (II, 268-69).

> [T]he most natural beauty in the world is honesty and moral truth. For all beauty is truth. True features make the beauty of a face; and true proportions the beauty of architecture; as true measures that of harmony and music. In poetry, which is all fable, truth still is the perfection.

(I, 94)

It is my contention that Shaftesbury, rather than separating the contemplation of beauty from the sphere of morality, wants to place it solidly within the realm of an acceptable morality. He wants to assert that there is a moral way of admiring things, a way which is not to be identified with luxury, covetousness, avarice, ostentation, and similar—to Shaftesbury and most of his contemporaries—immoral qualities.

Taken in its most literal sense, Shaftesbury's argument seeks to separate the desire for possessions and property from the (rational) appreciation of something for its beauty. Why was their separation important to Shaftesbury? As I have shown above, the notion that "interest rules the world" was common in the late seventeenth and early eighteenth centuries, and "interest" was in particular connected with wealth. It was a commonly held opinion that appreciation and desire to possess could be conflated, or that the one (appreciation, admiration) would naturally lead to the other (desire to possess). Shaftesbury was opposing views held by three of the most influential philosophers of his time, Locke, Hobbes, and Descartes. These philosophers all assume that pleasure and enjoyment are entirely sensuous and based on individual self-interest.[22] But Shaftesbury's arguments were not directed solely against the philosophers; they were, at the same time, part of a tangled contemporary controversy which needs examining.

Shaftesbury's argument that we have an ability disinterestedly to observe something beautiful and that this beauty is (or can be) of a non-sensuous, rational kind can now be seen to serve an important function in his general philosophical strategy: it underlines and illustrates his criticism of the view, prevalent in the last half of the seventeenth century and in the eighteenth century, that human beings always act only on the basis of "interest" or "self-love." When we see something beautiful and appreciate it in the proper manner, we have, according to Shaftesbury, an instance where we are beyond any narrow self-interest. Disinterestedness is therefore not a category which takes aesthetic contemplation beyond the sphere of morality but one that places it squarely within the realm of morality. Even when the concept is ostensibly used in its most directly aesthetic sense, it has a clear moral content.

But which moral content? The discussion about pleasure and the possibility of disinterested contemplation had, as mentioned earlier, much more than a narrowly philosophical significance. It was an important part of a cultural struggle about the direction England should take after the revolution of 1688 and about the formation of new ideals of behavior. These changing ideals were apparent, for example, in a shift in the notion of what constitutes a gentleman, a shift from the emphasis on good birth and membership in a family to behavioral criteria.[23] Traditional forms of achievement within the old order had become a threat to the social order. Warfare, horsemanship, swordsmanship, duelling, and other activities related to traditional conceptions of honor were constantly attacked from below. Increasingly, these activities came to be seen as anachronistic, and new, more peaceful, occupations which are proper for a gentleman gradually developed. I will use the German word *Bildungsideal* to designate the new behavioral ideals Shaftesbury and his contemporaries referred to with terms such as "good-breeding," "manners," and "politeness." For Shaftesbury, morality and manners could not be separated, and the content of Shaftesbury's moral-aesthetic view must therefore be understood through an examination of this *Bildungsideal.* Shaftesbury's conception of the virtuoso gentleman becomes part of a new *Bildungsideal,* and an interest in the arts is a central ingredient in this ideal.

In promoting his alternative, Shaftesbury is maneuvering among a number of positions, opposing the vulgar habits of the people as well as the luxurious living identified with the court. He agrees with the need for reform and shares the Puritan disdain for many forms of popular culture, but he does not approve of their total rejection of refinement. Shaftesbury defends his position by showing that their moral suspicions of the arts and refinement are unjustified. Art appreciation is not morally suspect; it does not lead to libertinism.

The Reformation of Manners

Discussion about the arts cannot be separated from that broader political process which was the formation of a new England after 1688. It is in this context that the urgency arises for Shaftesbury to address the relationship between morality, manners, and beauty. The Societies for the Reformation of Manners represented, in the last decade of the seventeenth century and the first decades of the eighteenth century, the most significant attempt at a reformation of behavioral patterns. It is necessary to address Shaftesbury's relationship to these Societies (and attempts to reform manners in general) because his conception of politeness and an alternative *Bildungsideal* emerges out of his theoretical engagement with them.

The political revolution in England in 1688 was accompanied by what has been called a moral revolution, an essential part of which was the reformation of manners.[24] To the extent that they were distinguished at all, manners and morality were seen as two sides of the same issue.[25]

In a larger historical perspective the interest in the reformation of manners is part of the demise of a popular culture in Europe.[26] Throughout the Middle Ages the official ecclesiastical and political culture was paralleled by a less serious undercurrent of folk culture or popular culture. It is important to appreciate this aspect of medieval and renaissance culture in order to understand the Enlightenment's preoccupation with the reform of manners. The popular "laughter culture" or "carnival culture," as Bakhtin calls it, was characterized by total opposition to the serious political, feudal, and ecclesiastical forms and ceremonies. This popular culture was also a culture of the market place, for example Bartholomew Fair in London.[27] Though this was a folk culture, it was not restricted to the lower classes. Both the nobility and the clergy participated widely in popular culture, particularly during festivals.[28] The reformers of the late seventeenth century therefore directed their efforts primarily against the people, but also against the more "backward" elements of the upper classes who retained a connection with popular culture.

Shaftesbury occasionally comments on still existing forms of popular culture. His familiarity with carnivals is evident from his reference to the carnivals at Paris and Venice (I, 57). Shaftesbury considered carnival a ridiculous practice and adds that "he who laughs and is himself ridiculous, bears a double share of ridicule." The carnivalesque laughter has, according to Bakhtin, the exact opposite feature: here there is no difference between being the object and the subject of ridicule. You are laughing at yourself and the world. The carnivalesque laughter is connected with popular culture, and opposition to it is only one part of the changing attitudes to popular culture and the "turn to modernity."

The change in manners was not just left to chance but implemented in a systematic way by the Societies for the Reformation of Manners. The first such society was formed in London in 1690, but the idea rapidly spread to other parts of Britain. In a proclamation from 1689 King William emphasized the significance of the reformation of manners. Another proclamation "For preventing and punishing Immorality and Prophaneness," issued by William in February 1697, had to be read in church at least four times a year.[29] Since many people, if left to their own devices, would prefer to play football or dance rather than go to church, profanation of the Lord's day and popular culture were closely connected in the minds of many Puritans.[30]

A reformation of manners was seen as a necessary prerequisite for social stability. Lewd and vicious persons had a spirit which was conducive not to subordination but to the levelling of social differences.[31] The Puritan divine Richard Baxter (1615-91) found that those participating in the popular festivals are led into "idleness, riotousness and disobedience to their Superiors."[32] The discussion about manners was thus inseparable from political discussions and the struggle to shape the new England after 1688. The societies promoted the Puritan values of industriousness and seriousness. Terms like "frugality," "squandering," and "spendthrift" became widely used for the first time towards the end of the sixteenth century, the first to designate a positive attitude to a certain form of behavior, the latter two to express "a new disapproval of the aristocratic ideal of conspicuous consumption."[33] Though these values were Puritan in origin, they became widely accepted; and they were not limited to dissenters but ultimately accepted by the Church of England, as can be seen in, for example, the Charity School Movement. In the process Puritanism lost whatever revolutionary aspirations it originally had.[34]

In order to understand the role of art in this context, it is important to point out that the arts were not seen only in terms of the fine arts. For most people in the early eighteenth century the arts included gardening, for example; and Francis Hutcheson discusses dress, equipage, and furniture almost on a par with painting and sculpture.[35] The discussion of dress and fashion played a particularly prominent role.[36] Shaftesbury's use of "art" preserves some of the ancient meaning of skill. He classifies as arts not only surgery and horsemanship (I, 105; II, 9) but also most of what we would today include among the fine arts: painting (I, 94, 214, 219; II, 242), music (I, 227), architecture (I, 227; II, 63, 242), sculpture (statuary) (I, 214, 227; II, 242), poetry (*passim*). Rhetoric is also an art (I, 188). Music (I, 104) and painting are also sometimes categorized with the sciences,[37] along with ethics, dialectics, logic (I, 168), and morality (I, 187, 220), revealing that the two terms could be used almost as synonyms, in the broad sense of skill ("is there no skill or science required?" [II, 130]).

An interest in the arts was often seen as directly connected to the life of the idle rich or as a mere display of wealth and therefore morally suspicious. Showing not only that involvement with art was not adverse to virtue but that, on the contrary, it might be part of a virtuous life was a good argument for the appropriateness of the gentleman's occupation with the arts. Shaftesbury could thus hope to deliver a moral justification for the growing interest in the arts in England in the early eighteenth century.[38] The defense he delivered rejected excessive, Puritan sternness and at the same time sought to free the art-lover from the traditional association with the life of the luxurious and debauched aristocracy. Shaftesbury shared the political goals and many of the Puritan values of the middling sort of people (for example their dislike for popular culture and the decadence they detected in aristocratic and courtly circles) but not the religious fanaticism of some of them, and he did not think that use of power was an appropriate way to enforce religious beliefs.

It is often pointed out that Shaftesbury's **Letter Concerning Enthusiasm** (written 1707) is an attack on the excesses of the French Prophets. Shaftesbury was strongly opposed to claims about miracles and religious revelations,[39] but given the charged moral and political atmosphere in England in the first decade of the eighteenth century, his **Letter** was interpreted as a general attack on attempts to reform manners. Ironic statements, such as the remark that "If the knowing well how to expose any infirmity or vice were a sufficient security for the virtue which is contrary, how excellent an age might we be presumed to live in!" (I, 9), could easily be read by contemporaries as a criticism of the efforts of the reforming societies. Part of the motivation of the reformers was to save souls that might otherwise go to hell, a project Shaftesbury also ridiculed:

> [A] new sort of policy, which extends itself to another world and considers the future lives and happiness of men rather than the present, has made us leap the bounds of natural humanity; and out of a supernatural charity has taught us the way of plaguing one another most devoutly. It has raised an antipathy which no temporal interest could ever do; and entailed upon us a mutual hatred to all eternity. And now uniformity in opinion (a hopeful project!) is looked on as the only expedient against this evil. *The saving of souls is now the heroic passion of exalted spirits; and is become the chief care of the magistrate, and the very end of government itself* [my italics].
>
> (I, 15)

Shaftesbury thought the magistrate should keep out of religious controversies and clearly opposes the way in which the royal proclamations and the reforming societies ascribed that role to public officials. He was therefore castigated as an enemy of propriety and morality as such and a defender of aristocratic decadence.

One such attack came from Mary Astell in a pamphlet from 1709.[40] Astell was a Tory but shared the Puritans' pious morality and their suspicion of fashion and empty flattery.[41] Astell read Shaftesbury's letter as an expression of the decay in manners and morals which had happened in the time since the disappearance of the "Ancient *English* Peerage." These ancient peers of England "subdu'd themselves, as well as their Enemies. Their Health was not consum'd in Debauchery, nor were their Estates squander'd in Vanity, Gaming and Luxury."[42] By contrast the present aristocrats are "Covetous, Boasters, Proud, Disobedient, Unthankful, Unholy, without Natural affection . . . lovers of their own selves."[43] The position Shaftesbury defends is repeatedly identified with that of a "libertine," a "great man," or simply a gentleman. The pleasures of a true Christian are of a lasting character, while those of the libertine are of a fleeting and disappearing kind.[44] Christianity is opposed to luxury and sloth. The libertine is enjoying only "Brutal Pleasure," or "Pleasures of Sensation." The libertine is always a "Slave to the Appetites."[45]

Astell was not the only one suspicious of the new rich. A similar attitude is expressed in an early eighteenth-century book on courtesy, *The English Theophrastus,* published in three editions between 1702 and 1708.[46] In it we read that the "generality of Mankind sink in Virtue as they rise in Fortune. How many hopeful young Men by the sudden Accession of a good Estate have deviated into Debauchery, nay turned absolute Rakes."[47] It is different with those who have acquired wealth by their own industry. "It is not for acquiring Wealth, but for misemploying it when he has acquired it, that a Man ought to be blamed."[48] The book is clearly addressed to a middle class audience. The "Middle State both of Body and Fortune" is declared to be the best, and notions of nobility and birthright are dispelled.[49]

Similar sentiments are expressed by Jeremy Collier (1650-1726). To have a high position in society is only deserving of respect if it is a result of one's own achievement. Hereditary nobility is no guarantee for the moral uprightness of the person; on the contrary, if people with a noble title have a certain air about them, it is probably because they have never done an honest day's work and is the result of a "Slothful and Effeminate Life."[50] Differences in social position, Collier repeatedly emphasizes, are necessary for the promotion of industry and the support of government.[51] One should not exhibit one's superior position. For private persons to appear "Pompous in Equipage or Habit, is but a vainglorious Publishing of their own Grandeur." One should conceal rather than make an ostentatious display of wealth. Besides, outward appearance is no reliable guide to people's position in society, since "every one has the liberty to be as Expensive, and Modish as he pleases. . . . [O]rdinary People, when they happen to abound in Money and Vanity, have their Houses and Persons as richly Furnished, as those who are much their superiors."[52] Dressing beyond one's station in life, Collier thought, was not just immoral; it could have the most dangerous political implications. To do so "looks like a Levelling Principle; like an Illegal Aspiring into a forbidden Station. It looks as if they had a Mind to destroy the Order of Government, and to confound the Distinctions of Merit and Degree."[53] For Collier morality, manners, and politics are closely connected—even down to the level of the choice of dress.

The evidence I have offered thus far shows us that the case for refinement and an interest in art needed to be made, and its association with decadence and luxury had to be broken. The historical context sketched provides the reasons why Shaftesbury would present an argument about the morality of art appreciation in the manner suggested by my interpretation. It shows why a moral justification for the involvement with art was a politically and personally urgent task for Shaftesbury.

The type of accusations here exemplified by Astell and others are the kind Shaftesbury tries to keep at a distance in his explanation of disinterested contemplation of art and nature, and they add force to my argument that Shaftesbury's purpose was not to separate the contemplation of art from morality but rather to place it within an acceptable morality, a morality which would free artistically interested gentlemen from accusations of luxury and sloth.

That Shaftesbury saw a need to address these questions can also be inferred from some of the changes made between the publication of *The Sociable Enthusiast* in 1703 or 1704 and the publication of *The Moralists* in 1709. *The Moralists* is essentially an expanded version of *The Sociable Enthusiast.*[54] One of the questions elaborated on in *The Moralists,* as compared to the earlier version, is the distinction between the pleasures of sense and the pleasures of reason. Shaftesbury vehemently attacks those who seek only sensuous pleasures and calls them "our modern Epicures" (*SE,* 92; *RE,* II, 32). Among the "purely mental" satisfactions Shaftesbury mentions the work of the mathematician,[55] the toils of the "bookish man," and "the artist who endures voluntarily the greatest hardships and fatigues." In fact the "satisfactions of the mind" and the "enjoyments of reason and judgement" should not properly be called pleasures at all. These pleasures are not accessible to the Epicureans—they have called them pleasures only to dignify the term pleasure and, by implication, to give themselves a license to practice pleasures of a more vulgar kind (*SE,* 92; *RE,* II, 33).

SHAFTESBURY AND POLITENESS

So far we have seen that Shaftesbury wanted to argue for the moral appropriateness of an interest in art and that in the contemporary context he had good reasons to want to do this. It is now time to look closer at the alternative view of morality and manners provided by Shaftesbury. The positive alternative advanced by Shaftesbury is frequently termed "politeness," but many of his contemporaries saw the connection between manners and morality or virtue as negative. Politeness was all appearance and no soul. Shaftesbury wanted to show that it did not have to be like this—that, rightly understood, politeness and virtue are one.

Politeness is an elusive concept. It is sometimes used in the sense of "civilized" or "cultured," as when Shaftesbury describes ancient Greece as a polite nation. In this sense politeness describes a high degree of development towards some ideal. In Shaftesbury's time, however, terms like "politeness" and "good breeding" were more often expressions for desirable patterns of social behavior. As Klein remarks, "'politeness' was not a form of nostalgia, but a program for modernity."[56] Politeness relates to the behavior of individuals. It expresses an ideal of behavior, a *Bildungsideal.* It is synonymous with good-breeding, manners or gentility, and occasionally with gallantry (Hume). Politeness or breeding is the criterion for membership in the elite.

Manners or politeness show themselves in all areas of behavior, from the taking of snuff (discussed by Steele in *Tatler* No. 35) to the principles of literary criticism (as in Addison's discussion of the critic in *Spectator* No. 291). According to James Forrester, the essence of politeness consists in the right timing and discreet management of "a Thousand little *Civilities, Complacencies, and Endeavours* to give others *Pleasure*."[57]

For Locke, too, the most important accomplishment in politeness or breeding is to please others, to do what is expected of us in social intercourse. Locke emphasizes that the two most important parts of breeding are "a disposition of the mind not to offend others; and secondly, the most acceptable and agreeable way of expressing that disposition." This state is achieved chiefly by emulation of "persons above us," by observation of those "who are allowed to be exactly well-bred."[58] For Forrester it is possible to explain only negatively what politeness is, but its actual mastery must be achieved by emulation, "from Company and Observation," particularly by interacting with "the Ladies."[59]

Locke is sufficiently steeped in the Puritan tradition to modify the emphasis on appearance which gradually became the sole content of the tradition of politeness. For Forrester as for Chesterfield, what you actually think of other people is irrelevant. The rules for politeness Forrester offers "are intended . . . to guide Men in *Company,*" rather than when they are alone. "What we advance tends not so directly to amend People's Hearts, as to regulate their Conduct."[60] Not surprisingly, many writers in the early eighteenth century criticized what they took to be the lack of connection between morality or virtue on the one side and politeness on the other. The lack of connection between virtue and politeness or good manners was a theme for Mandeville: manners and good breeding consist "in a Fashionable Habit, acquired by Precept and Example, of Flattering the Pride and Selfishness of Others, and concealing our own with Judgment and Dexterity. . . . Good Manners have nothing to do with Virtue or Religion; instead of extinguishing, they rather inflame the Passions."[61]

Shaftesbury (as well as Addison and Steele) wanted to reject the widely perceived contradiction between good manners, breeding, and politeness on the one hand and morality and virtue on the other. They set out to show that politeness was compatible with virtue and that a central part of politeness is an interest in the arts and forming a correct taste. The connection holds the other way as well: a proper (disinterested) approach to art reflects back on the moral character of the spectator, as one who is able to overstep the narrow boundaries of self-interest.

One of the stated goals of the ***Characteristics*** is to "recommend morals on the same foot with what in a lower sense is called manners, and to advance philosophy . . . on the very foundation of what is called agreeable and polite" (II, 257). For Shaftesbury philosophy was not an abstract discipline but should be devoted to the question of self-presentation. The purpose of philosophy is to "teach us ourselves" and to teach us self control and a certain consistency in our behavior (I, 184, cf. II, 274-75).[62]

Politeness and virtue are not united in everybody. Poor people may need the threat of a devil and a hell "where a jail and gallows are thought insufficient" (II, 265, cf. I, 84-85), but it is possible for those who are not among "the mere vulgar of mankind" (I, 84) or in other ways corrupted (for example by attending university) to conduct their lives in accordance with the natural order of things and become "gentlemen of fashion":

> By gentlemen of fashion, I understand those to whom a natural good genius, or the force of good education, has given a sense of what is naturally graceful and becoming. Some by mere nature, others by art and practice, are masters of an ear in music, an eye in painting, a fancy in the ordinary things of ornament and grace, a judgement in proportions of all kinds, and a general good taste in most of those subjects which make the amusement and delight of the ingenious people of the world. Let such gentlemen be as extravagant as they please, or as irregular in their morals, they must at the same time discover their inconsistency, live at variance with themselves, and in contradiction to that principle on which they ground their highest pleasure and entertainment.
>
> (I, 89-90)

This is again based on the assumption that nature provides specific measures as to the rightness and wrongness in morality, truth, and beauty. Gentlemen who do not live in accordance with these principles must eventually "discover their inconsistency," for a life in accordance with these principles is also conducive to human happiness, while their violation leads to misery.

The formation of the right taste is not restricted to painting, music etc., but extends to areas such as behavior, countenance, and carriage:

> [I]n the very nature of things there must of necessity be the foundation of a right and wrong taste, as well in respect of inward characters and features as of outward person, behaviour, and action. . . . Even in the Arts, which are mere imitations of that outward grace and beauty, we not only confess a taste, but make it a part of refined breeding to discover amidst the many false manners and ill styles the true and natural one, which represents the real beauty and Venus of the kind.
>
> (I, 216-17)

The "gentleman of fashion" who unites these characteristics may become what Shaftesbury calls a "virtuoso." The task of the virtuoso is, among other things, to inform himself about the true standards in the arts and sciences (II, 252-53) (see also I, 217-18; II, 129). One who goes through this process becomes a "man of breeding and politeness." The purpose of the process is to discover the "foundation of right and wrong taste" (I,

216). Although this is, in principle, a goal attainable by all, it is clear that in practice it is restricted to those with substantial amounts of time and money to spare. To become "a real fine gentleman" is a social privilege. Since the good and the beautiful are the same, a person who has the right taste in arts and manners at the same time has insight into what virtue is and, unless he is a very unnatural person, acts accordingly: "Thus are the Arts and Virtues mutually friends; and thus the science of virtuosi and that of virtue itself become, in a manner, one and the same" (*ibid.*).[63] Only for the person capable of rising above the vulgar and sensuous is a "refined contemplation of beauty" possible (II, 128).

Steele's and Addison's project in some of the *Spectator*-papers must also be seen in the context of the advancement of politeness and manners. Dr. Johnson saw Addison's papers in *The Spectator* as a continuation of Casa's and Castiglione's writings on the conduct of the courtier and the first English contribution to this genre.[64] The ideal gentleman envisioned by Addison and Steele retains elements of the leisured courtier, described for example by Castiglione in *Il Cortegiano* (English translation, 1561). The ideal is, however, strongly modified under influence of what are in effect Puritan values and particularly influenced by what Göricke calls *das Nützlichkeitsideal,* according to which education must be useful for the fulfillment of particular tasks in life.[65] Addison and Steele develop, as does Shaftesbury, a historical compromise between puritan sternness and religious zeal and the traditional leisured life of the aristocracy.[66]

Understandably, this new ideal appealed greatly to the emerging middle class, and Shaftesbury's (and Addison's) new *Bildungsideal* became the victorious one in the course of the eighteenth century. The new *Bildungsideal* offered an alternative to the traditional values of the gentry, though it retained some aristocratic values. It was less harsh than the one proposed by the Puritans. Through the process which led to wide acceptance of this *Bildungsideal,* high- and low-culture became increasingly separated. The upper classes no longer participated in popular culture but came to view it contemptuously. The popular becomes vulgar, and attempts at its systematic oppression increased. The term "polite arts" expressed a social approval of the occupation with certain forms of art. William Aglionby used the term "polite arts" for painting, architecture, sculpture, music, gardening, conversation, and "prudent Behaviour."[67] We find almost the same classification of the "polite arts" in Shaftesbury, though he also expressed some concern that painting is a vulgar art.[68] The "polite arts," which from the mid-eighteenth century simply become the "fine arts," represent in this way a new historical form of the old distinction between the vulgar or mechanical arts and the liberal arts.

Shaftesbury was not interested in showing the existence of a form of aesthetic perception independent of morality. On the contrary he wanted to show that the appreciation of certain kinds of art, those conforming to the true standard of taste, were part of the development of a virtuous character. In his arguments Shaftesbury was waging war on a number of fronts: against the philosophers of "private interest," against the "rustics," people with a "gothic" taste, the entertainments of the people, popular literature, and against the indulgence in luxury identified with the court and parts of the aristocracy.

Shaftesbury did not really think that just anyone would be able to appreciate art in the required manner, but this restriction did not show that it was not universal, only that there is something wrong with certain people. In short, the preferences of a certain group of people, those thought to be "polite," became identified with human nature, and those who did not live up to this standard were consequently regarded as less than fully human. As a matter of historical fact the polite were also the privileged in society. Since the standards of politeness are the standards with which all people must be measured, social privilege was identified with human nature.

Shaftesbury could hope to convince his readers that there was no necessary contradiction between the way a person chooses to present him- or herself and moral virtue, between outward appearance and inward character. By emphasizing that the person who has, among other things, a certain taste in art and a certain etiquette and is a "real fine gentleman," Shaftesbury offers a new set of values for the presentation of the self in social interaction with people of a certain class, for whom birthright is no longer a valid criterion and serves, as he himself put it, ". . . the polite world and the better sort in those pleasures and diversions which they are sometimes at a loss how to defend against the formal censors of the age."[69]

Notes

1. Most of Shaftesbury's writings are in *Characteristics of Men, Manners, Opinions, Times,* ed. J. M. Robertson (2 vols.; London, 1900). Unless otherwise mentioned references in the following are to this edition.

2. "On the Origins of 'Aesthetic Disinterestedness,'" *Journal of Aesthetics and Art Criticism,* 20 (1961), 131-44, and "On the Significance of Lord Shaftesbury in Modern Aesthetic Theory," *The Philosophical Quarterly,* 11 (1961), 97-113.

3. Shaftesbury "sets into motion the idea which, more than any other, marks off modern from traditional aesthetics and around which a great deal of the dialectic of modern thought has revolved, viz.,

the concept of 'aesthetic disinterestedness'" ("On the Significance of Lord Shaftesbury," 98). Aesthetic disinterestedness "describes a certain mode of perceiving" peculiar to a certain kind of experience: aesthetic experience. When perceiving anything in this manner any other concerns, such as practical, moral, political, or religious are suspended (*ibid.,* 98-99). To consider anything, typically a work of art, in a disinterested manner is to value it or perceive it "for its own sake."

4. "On the Origins of 'Aesthetic Disinterestedness,'" 131.

5. *Ibid.,* 133.

6. *Ibid.,* 134.

7. See *Art and the Aesthetic* (Ithaca, 1974), and "Stolnitz's attitude: Taste and Perception," *Journal of Aesthetics and Art Criticism,* 43 (1984), 195-203; also Stolnitz's responses, "'The Aesthetic Attitude' in the Rise of Modern Aesthetics," *Journal of Aesthetics and Art Criticism,* 36 (1978), 409-22, and "'The Aesthetic Attitude' in the rise of Modern Aesthetics—Again," *Ibid.,* 43 (1984), 205-8.

8. "On the Origins of 'Aesthetic Disinterestedness,'" 131.

9. "Stolnitz's Attitude: Taste and Perception," 195.

10. "'The Aesthetic Attitude' in the Rise of Modern Aesthetics," 413.

11. Dabney Townsend, "Shaftesbury's Aesthetic Theory," *Journal of Aesthetics and Art Criticism,* 41 (1982), 206.

12. Fanny Burney, *Cecilia* (London, 1986 [1782]), 488, also 510.

13. A. O. Hirschman, *The Passions and the Interests* (Princeton, 1977), 38ff.

14. Jeremy Collier expresses this view, common at Shaftesbury's time, in his *Essays Upon Several Moral Subjects* (London, 1698): "A good Man is contented with hard Usage at present, that he may take his *Pleasure* in the other World" (Part II, 191). See also Locke, *An Essay Concerning Human Understanding,* I.iii.12 and 13, where he argues that moral principles require rewards and punishments.

15. "On the Significance of Lord Shaftesbury," 105.

16. *Ibid.,* 100-101.

17. *Ibid.,* 106.

18. *Ibid.,* 107: "This passage [about the disinterested love of God] brings us close to the aesthetically relevant meaning of 'disinterestedness.' Perception cannot be disinterested unless the spectator forsakes all self-concern and therefore trains attention upon the object for its own sake." Stolnitz applies the term "aesthetic" in the modern sense, in which it refers to something which is independent of, for example, morality and religion. "Aesthetic perception looks to no consequences ulterior to itself" (108).

19. "On the Origins of 'Aesthetic Disinterestedness,'" 134.

20. A passage by Addison reminds one of this (and other) places in the *Characteristics:* "A man of a Polite Imagination is let into a great many Pleasures, that the Vulgar are not capable of receiving. He can converse with a Picture, and find an agreeable Companion in a Statue. He meets with a secret Refreshment in a Description, and often feels a greater Satisfaction in the Prospect of Fields and Meadows, than another does in the Possession. It gives him, indeed, a kind of Property in every thing he sees, and makes the most rude uncultivated Parts of Nature administer to his Pleasures: So that he looks upon the World, as it were, in another Light, and discovers in it a Multitude of Charms, that conceal themselves from the generality of Mankind" (*Spectator,* No. 411, 21 June 1712; D. F. Bond [ed.], *The Spectator* [Oxford, 1965], III, 538).

21. See also I, 91: "The admirers of beauty in the fair sex would laugh, perhaps, to hear of a moral part in their amours." Cf. I, 324f.

22. See for example Locke, *An Essay Concerning Human Understanding,* II.xx.7; Descartes, "The Passions of the Soul," 2d. part, art. LII, *The Philosophical Works of Descartes,* tr. E. S. Haldane and G. R. T. Ross (Cambridge, 1975), I, 357, and art. XC, 371; Hobbes, *Leviathan,* ed. C. B. Macpherson (Harmondsworth, 1968), 120ff.

23. D. Castronovo, *The English Gentleman* (New York, 1987), 5; also K. Bülbring's introduction to Daniel Defoe, *The Compleat English Gentleman* (Folcroft Library Editions, 1972 [1729]), xxxii ff., and V. B. Heltzel, *Chesterfield and the Tradition of the Ideal Gentleman* (Ph.D. diss., U. of Chicago, 1925).

24. D. W. R. Bahlman, *The Moral Revolution of 1688* (n.p., 1957).

25. "Manners and morals were regulated, because it is through the *minutiae* of conduct that the enemy of mankind finds his way to the soul; the traitors of the Kingdom might be revealed by pointed shoes or golden ear-rings" (R. H. Tawney, *Religion and the Rise of Capitalism* [Harmondsworth, 1984], 124).

26. See Peter Burke, *Popular Culture in Early Modern Europe* (London, 1978), particularly ch. 8, and M. M. Bakhtin, *Rabelais and his World,* tr. H. Iswolsky (Bloomington, 1985).

27. Burke, *Popular Culture,* 112.

28. Burke, *Popular Culture,* 24f.; R. W. Malcolmson, *Popular Recreations in English Society, 1700-1850* (Cambridge, 1973), 13. Regarding festivals in early eighteenth-century England, see Malcolmson ch. 2, and about the participation of the upper classes in popular recreations, ch. 4.

29. Bahlman, *Moral Revolution,* 15. See also J. Woodward, *An Account of the Societies for Reformation of Manners, in London and Westminster, and other Parts of the Kingdom* (London, 1699).

30. Malcolmson, *Popular Recreations,* 9.

31. Bahlman, *Moral Revolution,* 42f. That a reformation of manners "would confirm the present establishment, both in Church and State" was stated directly by John Dennis, *The Person of Quality's Answer to Mr. Collier's Letter,* 29; quoted in Bahlman, *Moral Revolution,* 43.

32. Richard Baxter, *A Christian Directory* (London, 1678²), Book I, 390, quoted from Malcolmson, *Popular Recreations,* 7.

33. Quentin Skinner, "Some problems in the analysis of political thought and action," in J. Tully (ed.), *Meaning and Context* (Princeton, 1988), 114-15.

34. "In both England and New England in the seventeenth and eighteenth centuries puritanism is transformed from a critique of the established order in the name of King Jesus to an endorsement of the new economic activities of the middle classes" (A. MacIntyre, *A Short History of Ethics* [New York, 1966], 150).

35. See for example Francis Hutcheson, *An Inquiry Concerning Beauty, Order, Harmony, Design,* ed. Peter Kivy (The Hague, 1973), 88.

36. See Jeremy Collier, "Upon Clothes," *Essays Upon Several Moral Subjects* (London, 1698), and B. Mandeville, *The Fable of the Bees,* ed. Kaye, (Oxford, 1924 [1714]), *passim*; also N. McKendrick, "The Commercialization of Fashion," in *The Birth of a Consumer Society,* ed. McKendrick (London, 1982), 34-99.

37. Shaftesbury, *Second Characters, or the Language of Forms,* ed. B. Rand (New York, 1969), 20.

38. See I. Pears, *The Discovery of Painting: The Growth of Interest in the Arts in England 1680-1768* (New Haven, 1988).

39. See particularly Shaftesbury's *The Adept Ladies or the Angelic Sect* from 1701-2. Now in A. A. Cooper, Third Earl of Shaftesbury, *Standard Edition* (Stuttgart, 1981), I.1, 376ff (cited as *SE*).

40. *Bart'lemy Fair: Or, An Enquiry after Wit; In Which due Respect is Had to a Letter Concerning Enthusiasm, to my Lord * * *. By Mr. Wotton* (London, 1709).

41. See Ruth Perry, *The Celebrated Mary Astell* (London, 1986).

42. *Bart'lemy Fair,* 83-84.

43. *Ibid.,* 82.

44. *Ibid.,* 89-90.

45. *Ibid.,* 139, 140.

46. Abel Boyer, *The English Theophrastus; or the Manners of the Age. Being the Modern Characters of the Court, the Town, and the City* (2d ed., 1706 [1702]). For evidence of views similar to Boyer's see L. E. Klein, "The Third Earl of Shaftesbury and the Progress of Politeness," *Eighteenth Century Studies,* 18 (1984), 186-214, and, regarding Shaftesbury's possible knowledge of the work, Klein, "The Third Earl of Shaftesbury," 198-99. The work was in any case not original but a compilation of views and statements from other works.

47. *The English Theophrastus,* 71-72.

48. *Ibid.,* 78.

49. *Ibid.,* 75.

50. Collier, *Essays,* Part I, 58.

51. *Ibid.,* Part I, 16, 62, 100.

52. *Ibid.,* 102.

53. *Ibid.,* 111.

54. *The Sociable Enthusiast* is now published in Shaftesbury, *SE,* II.1. The longer version, *The Moralists,* is in Robertson's edition of the *Characteristics* (cited as RE).

55. When doing mathematics it is possible to experience "a pleasure and delight superior to that of sense" (I, 296), but this pleasure has no connection to any advantage we ourselves may derive from it. See also the previously quoted passage by Addison (n. 20).

56. Klein, "The Third Earl of Shaftesbury," 213.

57. James Forrester, *The Polite Philosopher* (3d ed., London, 1745), 10. The popularity of Forrester's little book is suggested by the fact that the *British Library Catalogue* lists 8 different printings between 1734 and 1773. Johnson defined politeness in similar terms. It is "the observance of those little civilities and ceremonious delicacies, which inconsiderable as they may appear to the man of

science, and difficult as they may prove to be detailed with dignity, yet contribute to the regulation of the world, by facilitating the intercourse between one man and another . . ." (_Rambler,_ No. 98, 23 Feb. 1751).

58. John Locke, "Some Thoughts Concerning Education," _The Works of John Locke_ (London, 1823), IX, 134.

59. _Polite Philosopher,_ 40.

60. _Ibid.,_ 20.

61. B. Mandeville, _The Fable of the Bees,_ I, 77, 79.

62. "To philosophise, in a just signification, is but to carry good-breeding a step higher. For the accomplishment of breeding is, to learn whatever is decent in company or beautiful in arts; and the sum of philosophy is, to learn what is just in society and beautiful in Nature and the order of the world" (II, 255) (also II, 3-5).

63. "[H]armony is harmony by nature, let men judge ever so ridiculously of music. So is symmetry and proportion founded still in nature, let men's fancy prove ever so barbarous, or their fashions ever so Gothic in their architecture, sculpture, or whatever other designing art. 'Tis the same case where life and manners are concerned. Virtue has the same fixed standard. The same numbers, harmony, and proportion will have place in morals, and are discoverable in the characters and affections of mankind; in which are laid the just foundations of an art and science superior to every other of human practice and comprehension" (I, 227-28).

64. "Before _The Tatler_ and _Spectator,_ if the writers for the theatre are excepted, England had no masters of common life. No writers had yet undertaken to reform either the savageness of neglect or the impertinence of civility . . ." (Samuel Johnson, _Lives of the English Poets_ [Oxford, 1905], II, 93f).

65. Walter Göricke in "Das Bildungsideal bei Addison und Steele," _Bonner Studien zur Englischen Philologie,_ Heft 14 (1921), 14f.

66. "Das Bildungsideal bei Addison und Steele," 36, and J. H. Plumb, "The Commercialization of Leisure," N. McKendrick (ed.), _The Birth of a Consumer Society_ (London, 1982), 269.

67. Klein, "The Third Earl of Shaftesbury," 201.

68. _Second Characters,_ 18.

69. _Second Characters,_ 4.

Lawrence E. Klein (essay date 1994)

SOURCE: Klein, Lawrence E. "The Culture of Liberty." In _Shaftesbury and the Culture of Politeness:_ _Moral Discourse and Cultural Politics in Early Eighteenth-Century England,_ pp. 195-212. Cambridge: Cambridge University Press, 1994.

[_In the following essay, Klein discusses the concepts of discursive, cultural, and political liberty in Shaftesbury's later essays, arguing that, for Shaftesbury, conditions of freedom were necessary in order for the public to be able to make sound judgments._]

"POLITENESS"

Shaftesbury may have had qualms about the links between Whiggism and the Court after 1688, but polemics in Queen Anne's reign demanded simplicity. Thus, in his published writings, the Whigs were, simply, the party of liberty, the party that made the 1688 Revolution and opposed the French, the Stuart tyrants, and the High Churchmen. While Shaftesbury identified political liberty with post-1688 political arrangements, he was largely concerned with what we can identify, variously, as cultural, intellectual and, especially, discursive liberty. Thus, for Shaftesbury, liberty was the condition for full human development: "Tis Liberty indeed that can only polish & refine the Spirit & Soul as well as Witt of Man." Such liberty operated in the related fields of discourse and politics, "Freedome of Reason in the learnd world, & Good Government & Liberty in the civil world."[1] Since the Church and the Court dominated discourse in unhealthy ways, assuming magisterial or awing postures that promoted their political authority at the expense of individual autonomy, Shaftesbury urgently and repetitively asserted the importance of discursive liberty. Having examined how Shaftesbury mounted a critique of the Church and the Court in psychosocial and discursive terms, we can turn to the positive side of the argument, the promise of Whig political hegemony to initiate a distinctive and flourishing age in British culture.

Shaftesbury sketched his program in a letter of 1706, anticipating that the ultimate victory of Britain over France would lead to a great advance in "Letters and Knowledge." He acknowledged that, like "all good Things," "Liberty of Thought and Writing" had their "Inconveniences," specifically, "a sort of Libertinisme in Philosophy." Nonetheless, the price was worth paying since liberty had the tendency to correct its own excesses. He noted, for example, that, though the early Protestant reformers had been guilty of excess, "Blasphemouse Enthusiasts and reall Phanaticks" no longer posed a danger because excess had diminished naturally. Indeed, he wrote: "I am farr from thinking that the Cause of Theisme will lose any thing by fair Dispute. I can never . . . wish better for it than when I wish the Establishment of an intire Philosophical Liberty."[2] Here, in summary, were Shaftesbury's basic themes: the circumstances were propitious for a great leap forward in British culture; those circumstances centered on liberty, the only felicitous context for cultural and intellectual development; while liberty referred, conventionally, to political arrangements, it also meant specifically discursive liberty, freedom of expression and criticism.

Shaftesbury developed these themes in later essays, especially *A Letter Concerning Enthusiasm* and *Sensus Communis,* first published in 1708 and 1709 respectively.[3] In the *Letter,* Shaftesbury offered the dynamics of discursive liberty as a solution to the topical problem of handling enthusiasm. As a natural and inevitable component of human character and social relations, enthusiasm had to have its vent. Since suppression bred what it sought to eliminate, freedom for enthusiasts was preferable to attempts at magisterial control. Shaftesbury believed society could afford such toleration because discursive liberty meant not only freedom to express but also freedom to examine and criticize. A liberty of reason was the best means to puncture false claims, to reduce imposture, and to drain enthusiasms of their tumescence. Indeed, one form of critical liberty was the liberty to mock and make fun, the freedom of raillery that Shaftesbury investigated further in *Sensus Communis,* subtitled *An Essay on the Freedom of Wit and humour.*

Sensus Communis used the defence of raillery to frame a discussion of the moral principles stated in Shaftesbury's earlier *Inquiry Concerning Virtue.* As a discussion of discursive liberty, *Sensus Communis* elaborated points made in the *Letter* and broadened the range of the discussion beyond the *Letter*'s topical concerns. In particular, *Sensus Communis* proposed rational and sociable conversation as a model for intellectual activity and cultural habits. The critical enterprise, he argued, was essential for moral and cultural health.

Shaftesbury's concern in these two essays with discursive freedom led to explicit and classic formulations of the cultural dimensions of liberty. According to the *Letter*:

> Justness of Thought and Stile, Refinement in Manners, good Breeding, and Politeness of every kind, can come only from the Trial and Experience of what is best. Let but the Search go freely on, and the right Measure of every thing will soon be found. Whatever Humour has got the start, if it be unnatural, it cannot hold; and *the Ridicule,* if ill plac'd at first, will certainly fall at last where it deserves.[4]

Intellectual and discursive freedom had the negative capacity to dissolve unnatural humors (including all pernicious enthusiasms) and, beyond that, to curtail all manner of excess. Hence, truth, civility, and all expressive refinement depended on the freedom of the intellectual and discursive search, what we might call the 'essayistic' ventures of a community of inquiring intellects.

In *Sensus Communis,* the same idea was expressed with greater attention to the specific processes of liberty:

> *Wit* will mend upon our hands, and *Humour* will refine it-self; if we take care not to tamper with it, and bring it under Constraint, by severe Usage and rigorous Prescriptions. All Politeness is owing to Liberty. We polish one another, and rub off our Corners and rough Sides by a sort of *amicable Collision.* To restrain this, is inevitably to bring a Rust upon Mens Understandings. 'Tis a destroying of Civility, Good Breeding, and even Charity itself, under pretence of maintaining it.[5]

The passage brought into direct conjunction the two key terms, politeness and liberty: politeness summed up the proper state of wit, humor, understanding, and manners, in individuals and in society at large, while liberty referred to the condition of unlimited interaction and unlimited criticism. Since the essence of freedom was friendly interaction, the passage lays before us, as the setting for moral and cultural development, a scene of polite conversation, the decorous freedom of discussion among gentlemen. Liberty was thus figured in terms of a healthy interactive situation. At the same time, refined sociability was being constituted as an open-ended and unconstrained ideal, free from authoritarian interference. As we saw in chapter 5, this conversational scene was the paradigmatically apt discursive situation, most likely to eliminate the psychosocial postures that inhibited reason and autonomy. Just as the Church and the Court were associated with interactive models, so too was liberty.

All politeness was owing to liberty because free discussion and interaction tended to eliminate the excessive and the false. However, the relation between liberty and politeness was also based on the fact that the interactions that comprised politeness did themselves constitute a form of liberty. In a sense, conversation itself here became a paradigmatic mode of liberty, and, thus, liberty was assimilated into the notion of culture itself.

In such passages, Shaftesbury gave a significant twist to the notion of liberty. Although he clearly saw his discussion in a Whiggish political light, "liberty" did not refer in these passages to a patently political condition, neither to the establishment of rights nor to independence nor to self-government. Rather, it referred to a social and cultural condition, a condition of unlimited interpersonal interaction. Liberty in the modern world was thus associated with a lively public culture, a public engaged in a culture of examination, criticism, and exchange. This was a significant expansion on the cultural politics of the civic tradition since here the eloquence of senators was transformed into an all-embracing medium for society. The conventional civic point was that cultural achievements had a specifically political foundation: Letters or Arts were based on Liberty, which was a condition of civic existence. Here, however, Shaftesbury was emphasizing liberty's character as a condition of social and cultural life, a condition of discourse and cultural production in society. This was a less civic standpoint. Certainly, the second sense of liberty can be seen as an extension of the first: that is, one can assert—and this no doubt was Shaftesbury's intention—that an aspect of *civic* liberty is *discursive* and *cultural* liberty. At the same time, however, one cannot help but regard Shaftesbury's concern with discursive and cultural liberty as a significant shift of emphasis, one that distanced liberty from its specifically civic setting.

Shaftesbury's advocacy of such a public culture was intended to have a Whiggish force: he was defining what we take as a characteristic feature of eighteenth-century culture as a partisan achievement. However, Shaftesbury's cultural politics also mitigated the stressful relations between virtue and culture in writers of the civic tradition. A truly polite people was no longer in danger of losing its liberty since that liberty was secured in the very fact of the people's being polite. Politeness was so thoroughly enmeshed in discursive and cultural liberty that politeness was not conceivable without such liberty. Shaftesbury had reached a point at which he could dispense with the fear that cultural development in itself threatened liberty or with the conviction that liberty required the utmost cultural simplicity. Thus, he rejected explicitly the nostalgic propensity of the civic tradition, not only in its specifically political respects but in its longing for manners of a by-gone day. Moreover, as we will see, this transvaluation of the cultural put the improvement of taste and the elaboration of criticism at the center of the moral and political endeavor.[6]

GREECE

Abandoning nostalgia did not necessarily mean giving up the search for one's bearings through an examination of the past; and, as Shaftesbury deployed cultural history in his critiques of Church and Court, so he deployed it to elucidate the character and impact of liberty. *A Letter Concerning Enthusiasm* offered a taste of this in its brief evocation of "ancient policy" toward religious and philosophical opinion:

> Not only the Visionarys and Enthusiasts of all kinds were tolerated, your Lordship knows, by the Antients; but on the other side, Philosophy had as free a course, and was permitted as a Ballance against Superstition. And whilst some Sects, such as the *Pythagorean* and latter *Platonick,* join'd in with the Superstition and Enthusiasm of the Times; the *Epicurean,* the *Academick,* and others, were allow'd to use all the Force of Wit and Raillery against it. And thus matters were happily balanc'd; Reason had fair Play; Learning and Science flourish'd. Wonderful was the Harmony and Temper

> which arose from all these Contrarietys. Thus Superstition and Enthusiasm were mildly treated; and being let alone, they never rag'd to that degree as to occasion Bloodshed, Wars, Persecutions, and Devastations in the World.[7]

This passage provided a pedigree to Shaftesbury's faith in the refining power of liberty as a discursive condition. Ancient discursive freedom was contrasted to the policy of modern governments, which interfered forcefully in matters of religious and other belief in order to guard uniformity of opinion.

Elsewhere in his writings, Shaftesbury elaborated the historical picture adumbrated here, fixing on ancient Greece as the classical locus of politeness. That Shaftesbury regarded the ancient Greeks as supremely polite was patent. Jean LeClerc remembered Shaftesbury asserting that "the Grecians were more civilized and more polite than we ourselves, notwithstanding we boasted so much of our improved wit and more refind Manners."[8] In Shaftesbury's own words, ancient Greece was the fountain of all divinity, philosophy, and "polite learning"; it was the "politest of all Nations," the "sole polite, most civiliz'd, and accomplish'd Nation."[9] The politeness of the Greeks was then a cultural condition, signifying both their achievements in society, intellect, expression, and art and also the congruence of all these with (what Shaftesbury designated) natural standards and a just taste. Shaftesbury's Hellenism was aggressive and reductive. His dismissal of alternative claims eliminated complicated and multiple explanations. "The GREEK *Nation,* as it is *Original* to us, in respect to these polite Arts and *Sciences,* so it was in reality *original to it-self.*" Greek accomplishment towered over all innovations of its predecessors. Politeness was an absolutely pure and unitary stream, of which Greece was the spring.[10]

The thrust of Shaftesbury's cultural-historical investigation was significantly non-Roman. Indeed, cultural Hellenism was the complement to Shaftesbury's anti-Augustanism. One reason for this shift of emphasis was the fact that the history of ancient Greece was not yet as predetermined by paradigmatic formulations as the history of ancient Rome. We have already seen how, according to the classical republican version of Roman history, republic and liberty passed into empire and tyranny. Since civic decline was accompanied by the refinement in manners and arts in ancient Rome, republican formulations insisted that liberty was unpolished while politeness was slavish. The model was too thoroughly vested with the presumptions of the Country critique of the Court, leaving no room for Shaftesbury's particular needs to honor both Country and courtly traditions, both civic virtue and politeness.

Of course, the civic humanists had not ignored Greece, but their interest and affection had always fallen on Sparta. For all its cultural achievements, Athens had an unstable political history, which rarely commended it-self to civic writers. However, when Shaftesbury wrote of Greek politeness, he was thinking of Athens. The manner in which polite Athens could serve as a model of liberty and virtue is revealed in the sorts of liberty that Shaftesbury thought were actualized there. Shaftesbury used the Athenian experience to elaborate on the relations of liberty and cultural development. In his discussion, discourse was the exemplary arena in which politics and culture interacted. Moreover, Greek instances put Shaftesbury in a position to specify fur-ther the parameters of polite and impolite forms of ex-pression. At the same time, Shaftesbury's discussion helps us to understand the extent to which he had de-veloped a sophisticated cultural discourse, in which both liberty and culture submitted to the discipline of sociability.

Shaftesbury began with a very general genealogy of hu-man culture. The primitive state of humans was acultural: social life was rudimentary, and language was just sufficient for conferring about wants and necessi-ties. Man's linguistic condition was at zero degree, without self-consciousness, speculation or art. As soci-ety became less rudimentary and more secure, discur-sive opportunities expanded. Discussion of important matters evolved into debate, and speechmaking became common, with a double result. The orators themselves, in order to enhance their powers of persuasion, devel-oped the arts of expression. Meanwhile, the auditors de-veloped a sensitivity to distinctions in the realm of ex-pression, learning what they found agreeable and what not.[11] In short, the exigencies of persuasion and the comparison of oratory were the foundations of linguis-tic self-consciousness and expressive refinement.

From the start, Shaftesbury's natural history adumbrated a politics of eloquence, since the polishing of expres-sion arose in the public arena, in the competition for the assent of something like a primeval public. The exist-ence of this public implied a popular or consensual politics of some sort. Shaftesbury was quick to make this implication explicit. In those of these early societ-ies that gravitated towards the rule of one or of a few and where the power of force, awe or terror replaced that of assent, rhetorical arts atrophied. The very oppo-site occurred where government remained popular, for there persuasion remained important in the public realm and the rhetorical arts had to be elaborated as a basic element in governance.[12] The progress of oratory de-pended on liberty, and the liberty in which oratory flourished was the civic liberty of "*Free Nations.*"

However, another kind of liberty is evident in Shaftesbury's version of the polishing process. The ca-reer of eloquence was launched and propelled by a dia-lectic between rhetorical practice and rhetorical recep-tivity. While a sophisticated audience put pressure on

the orator to be his best, the orator himself had an inter-est in training the audience, promoting "that *Taste* and *Relish* to which they ow'd their personal Distinction and Pre-eminence."[13] The growth of eloquence occurred, in Shaftesbury's account, because of the mutual interac-tions of orator and audience, the orators seeking to please and the audience learning its desires. (It was into this orator-audience relation that Shaftesbury inserted the critics, who "taught the public to discover what was just and excellent in each performance" of oratory.) Thus, the progress of oratory depended on latitude of interaction as well as civic liberty. Even in this most generalized of accounts, Shaftesbury specified two re-lated but non-identical conditions for the refinement of expression: a politics of popular assent and also a con-dition of free interaction.

Since this genealogy of culture was itself of directly Hellenic inspiration, Shaftesbury had put himself in a position to develop these ideas further with specific re-gard to the ancient Greeks, who were, as we have seen, the fundamental datum in the history of politeness. He summarized the polishing of the Greeks in **"Miscella-neous Reflections,"** asserting that it was they who first "brought their beautiful and comprehensive Language to a just *Standard.*" Politeness, having established itself in the domain of their oratory, spread to every aspect of Greek culture. The refinement of the tongue became paradigmatic for all manner of expression in society, "from *Musick, Poetry, Rhetorick,* down to the simple Prose of History, thro all the plastick Arts of *Sculpture, Statuary, Painting, Architecture,* and the rest."[14] Polite-ness operated as a standard for all formal expression. Moreover, the refinement of all the arts was implied in the refinement of the central linguistic one.

In **"Miscellaneous Reflections,"** Shaftesbury traced this development not to specifically political but to more general associative factors. Despite geographical dis-persal and political disunity, the Greeks shared a com-mon "Extract" and a common language. More impor-tant, "animated by that social, publick and *free* Spirit, which notwithstanding the Animosity of their several warring States, induc'd them to erect such Heroick Congresses and Powers as those which constituted the AMPHICTONIAN Councils, the OLYMPICK, ISTHMIAN, and other Games; they cou'd not but naturally polish and refine each other." Politeness here was traced not to po-litical liberty nor to a political condition but rather to sociability, a drive to associate in public, that answered the needs both of cooperation and competition. Greek cultural evolution depended on associating in a public arena devoted to ritual cooperation (the amphictyonies) and to physical agonistics (the games), an arena from which civic politics was absent. On the other hand, a concern with the civic was never far from Shaftesbury's mind, and he appears to have been willing to slide from one sort of liberty to the other. So, shortly after this discussion, he mentioned that the polished Greeks, having attained "SIMPLICITY and NATURE," were able to preserve it "till the Ruin of all things, under a Universal Monarchy," Alexander's.[15]

Shaftesbury's discussion in **Soliloquy** did much to indicate the further specifications of politeness. Generally, the refining process involved moving from showy aspirations, affectation, and falseness to easiness, naturalness, and honesty. The discipline to which cultural artifacts were to submit was a discipline of sociability: modes of cultural expression had to avoid the sorts of postures that were condemned in social life itself.

The labor of the early critics was to banish discursive affectation, by identifying "what was specious and pretending," allowing "no false Wit, or jingling Eloquence," and exposing "the weak Sides, false Ornaments, and affected Graces of mere Pretenders." The aspirations to effect, to which these features corresponded, were found notably in "the *Miraculous,* the *Pompous,* or what we generally call the SUBLIME." That the sublime characterized the earliest writing is fitting, according to Shaftesbury.

> *Astonishment* is of all other Passions the easiest rais'd in raw and unexperienc'd Mankind. Children in their earliest Infancy are entertain'd in this manner: And the known way of pleasing such as these, is to make 'em wonder, and lead the way for 'em in this Passion, by a feign'd Surprise at the miraculous Objects we set before 'em. The best Musick of *Barbarians* is hideous and astonishing Sounds. And the fine Sights of *Indians* are enormous Figures, various odd and glaring Colours, and whatever of that sort is amazingly beheld, with a kind of Horrour and Consternation.[16]

Shaftesbury here set going several devices to signal the complex unpoliteness of the sublime. Developmentally, it was infantile. Culturally, it was primitive. The passage put together a vocabulary of wonderment and wonderfulness ("astonishment," "wonder," "miraculous," "hideous and astonishing," "enormous," "odd and glaring," "amazingly," "horror and consternation") that demarcated the terrain of enthusiasm and superstition. Moreover, sublime writing partook formally of the traits of "Awefulness" and "dazzle," with which our discussion attempted to summarize Shaftesbury's formal sense of the Church and Court. Thus, Shaftesbury could see the sublime as eliciting a sort of responsiveness which was not that of thoroughly morally realized individuals, but rather that of passive and irresponsible subjects. That the sublime constituted, in its way, an unsociable style, Shaftesbury made explicit when he wrote: "In Poetry, and study'd Prose, the *astonishing* Part, or what commonly passes for *Sublime,* is form'd by the variety of Figures, the multiplicity of Metaphors, and by quitting as much as possible the natural and easy way of Expression, for that which is most unlike to Humanity, or ordinary Use."[17]

Shaftesbury assembled this account out of loose and imaginative use of Aristotle. From there, too, he derived the notion that Homer arrived on the scene as a reformer of style who removed the infelicities of the sublime. Homer was described in the vocabulary of discursive preference: the decent, the natural, the simple, beauty of composition, unity of design, truth of characters, imitation of nature.[18] In turn, the Homeric move became paradigmatic for Greek literature generally.

In the rise of politeness, nature was the signature of the polite artifact. When Shaftesbury wrote that "the real *Lineage* and SUCCESSION of *Wit,* is indeed plainly founded in *Nature,*" he referred back to one of his founding premises, that of a designed cosmos in which principles of form and sociability both inhered.[19] Nature was not opposed to the human world, since the normative principles of the human world were already, in Shaftesbury's view, pre-inscribed in the cosmos. Because nature provided the criterion of taste and, one might say, politeness, the lineage of wit—cultural history, we might say—was founded in nature. The vicissitudes of politeness could only be traced using the standard of nature.

In the case of Greece, nothing underlay the formation of culture but nature itself. The first rise of politeness was the Greek self-formation, "wrought out of Nature, and drawn from the necessary Operation and Course of things, working, as it were, of their own accord, and proper inclination."[20] What precisely did this mean for the polite artifact? "In the Days of ATTICK Elegance," Shaftesbury wrote,

> Workmen . . . were glad to insinuate how laboriously, and with what expence of Time, they had brought the smallest Work of theirs (as perhaps a single Ode or *Satir,* an *Oration* or Panegyrick) to its perfection. When they had so polish'd their Piece, and render'd it so natural and easy, that it *seem'd* only a lucky Flight, a Hit of Thought, or flowing Vein of Humour; they were then chiefly concern'd lest it shou'd *in reality* pass for such, and their Artifice remain undiscover'd.[21]

Attic elegance was the art of the natural: at the limit of its perfection, it risked being mistaken for the natural itself; its artifice was at risk of oblivion. We see here how polished cultural artifacts had the qualities of polished social action. Polite expression in the arts submitted to the same standards as polite behavior in society. The standard was striving through real effort to create effects of ease and naturalness. The standard aimed to create pleasure through benign unaffectedness.

This passage suggests the general applicability to cultural artifacts of Shaftesbury's aspirations to sociability and politeness in the creation of the philosophical text (observed in part I). The passage generalized Shaftesbury's laudatory description of the simple style of Xenophon, which "being the strictest Imitation of

Nature, shou'd of right be the compleatest [style], in the Distribution of its Parts, and Symmetry of its Whole, [and] is yet so far from making any ostentation of Method, that it conceals the Artifice as much as possible: endeavouring only to express the effect of Art, under the appearance of the greatest Ease and Negligence."[22] The simple was the ultimately polite style, for it brought into precise focus both nature and art, ease and order, negligence and control. In such a passage, one sees the natural affinity between the classical vocabulary and the vocabulary of politeness. The classical aesthetic criteria approximated those of good fellowship in polite society. The politeness of polite artifacts was a matter of having been polished but also a matter of having been made pleasing in a social way. And as the supposition of the polishing process was a certain sort of liberty, so the result of the process was an artifact understood in terms of the regime of polite sociability in which liberty had a place.

Of the various movements toward refinement in the history of Greek culture, the evolution of comedy, as described by Shaftesbury, was particularly illustrative not only of the dynamics of refinement but of the specific connections between politics and politeness.[23]

To begin with, the Greek Old Comedy, arising out of earlier farce and phallic festivals and assuming some formal coherence at the time of Aristophanes, was the enemy of all affectation and pomposity. Its dialectical operations, directed at "every thing which might be imposing, by a false Gravity or Solemnity," were precisely, according to Shaftesbury, acts of unmasking. The Old Comedy was thus a step toward politeness insofar as politeness eschewed the sorts of pretensions that could not stand up to the Old Comedy's laughter. The Old Comedy exercised the refining power of raillery, and, therefore, like the operations of raillery in modern conversation, depended on freedom of expression.[24]

However, the freedom of the Old Comedy writers was liable to degenerate into license, and their progress toward politeness was limited. Even Aristophanes' achievement was stunted. The progress of politeness could only proceed through a further dialectical move with the appearance of the New Comedy. All that was lacking in the Old Comedy was made up in the New, for Menander represented the perfection of comedy.

Relying on Horace's *Ars poetica*, Shaftesbury proposed that the transition from Old to New Comedy was the product of a legal intervention, new laws that effected the cultural change.[25] However, his understanding of this development was highly significant, since it assumed the coherence of political and cultural sophistication. The new laws arose from a "real Reform of *Taste* and *Humour* in the Commonwealth or Govern-

ment it-self": "Instead of any Abridgment, 'twas in reality an Increase of *Liberty,* an Enlargement of the Security of *Property,* and an Advancement of private Ease and personal *Safety,* to provide against what was injurious to the good Name and Reputation of every Citizen." Thus, the curtailment of the excesses of the Old Comedy expressed not the limiting of freedom but, rather, a new and more sophisticated appreciation of it. A more secure grasp on the nature of liberty, a grasp that itself derived from the experience of political liberty, led to cultural change. Moreover, the laws reforming comedy were reflections of the desires of the Athenian public. Refinement in political sensibility was conjoined to refinement in other areas, so that the legislative reform of drama was merely one expression of the polishing process.

> As this Intelligence in Life and Manners grew greater in that experienc'd People, so the Relish of Wit and Humour wou'd naturally in proportion be more refin'd. Thus GREECE in general grew more and more polite; and as it advanc'd in this respect, was more averse to the obscene buffooning manner. The ATHENIANS still went before the rest, and led the way in Elegance of every kind.[26]

This polishing of the expressive modes was merely the outward manifestation of a profound and inner transformation, the refinement of sensibility.

Shaftesbury's admiration for the ancients did not constitute a rejection of modernity since the ancient had a clarifying, not a disparaging, relation to the modern. Though he ascribed the greatest achievements in art and literature to the Greeks, Shaftesbury was progressive in his views of history. The point of looking back to the Greeks was not to mourn a loss but to celebrate a possibility. While politeness had been realized among the ancients, it also was the end of modern life. To embrace antiquity was to foster a particular sort of modernity.

BRITAIN

Shaftesbury's account of culture and politics in ancient Greece was, obviously, a way of pursuing more immediate and, even, programmatic ends. The Greek past suggested patterns for British cultural history and possibilities for the British cultural future. The Greek model implied an alternative to the Tory interpretation of British cultural history, since it insisted on the relation between politeness and liberty, dissociating politeness from the courtly environment. Shaftesbury's hopes for the present also put him at a distance from the propensities associated with the Country. In the same way that he rejected Country nostalgia for a virtuous polity in the British past, so he had little use for the British cultural past. As British political history was a history of the growth of liberty, so British cultural history was a history of the growth of politeness.

The opportunities for a new British culture were set against the background of the international political conflict between Britain and France in the post-Revolution period. If barbarism was the accompaniment of universal monarchy, the progress of France threatened to replicate that of Rome. Britain was thus allowed to champion liberty against universal monarchy and politeness against ignorance and superstition. Elsewhere, Shaftesbury found it convenient to cast France not as Rome but as another historical incarnation of empire, namely, Persia. This, of course, allowed Britain to retrace the steps of ancient Greece, and most particularly those of Athens, as the champion of liberty. That Britain was also in a position to repeat the Hellenic cultural performance was evident in Shaftesbury's anxiety to exploit, in his own words, "some kind of Comparison between this antient *Growth* of TASTE, and that which we have experienc'd in modern days, and within our own Nation."[27]

In Shaftesbury's view, his own era was an auspicious moment for British cultural improvement, and the opportunity was offered not only by the international situation, but also by the recent rebirth of freedom in Britain itself. The affirmation of British liberty in 1688 had brought new opportunities for British culture: "For in our Nation, upon the foot Things stand, and as they are likely to continue; 'tis not difficult to foresee that Improvements will be made in every Art and Science." The Revolution had set the seal on liberty and law, assuring the progress of politeness. The only impediment remaining, said Shaftesbury, was the preoccupation with the Continental wars.[28]

There were tensions within the view that Shaftesbury was sketching. On the one hand, he was arguing for British cultural superiority on the basis of British genius and British politics. At the same time, however, he recognized the deficiencies of British culture. The British culture that would serve as a counterweight to the force of Continental culture had yet to be created. While "our natural Genius shines above that airy neighbouring Nation," it had to be admitted "that with truer Pains and Industry, they have sought *Politeness*." Nonetheless, he maintained that French politics stunted French culture whereas it was easy to see "what effect [Britain's] establish'd Liberty will produce in every thing which relates to *Art*; when *Peace* returns to us on these happy Conditions."[29] Still, the argument for British cultural superiority was proleptic. Shaftesbury was dissatisfied with much that he found of British culture. His writings, thus, involved a simultaneous effort to remove the locus of politeness from France to Britain and to create a British culture worthy of the ascription "polite."

British impoliteness was patent, and Shaftesbury pointed to several impediments to British cultural growth: Britain was insular, xenophobic, and resistant to positive in-fluences from outside; it was also remote from the breeding grounds both of ancient and modern culture and always came by its culture late.[30] All of this stood in contrast to the associative character of the Greeks who not only interacted among themselves in various athletic and ritual occasions but also (and notwithstanding their originality) traveled widely and tasted cosmopolitanly in their Levantine world. Of course, we have already examined the greatest impediments to British politeness, namely, the domination of politics and culture by courtly and ecclesiastical institutions.

On the other hand, Britain evinced the potential for refinement. Complaint about "the Genius of our People" was commonplace among writers, he said, but "we are not altogether so *Barbarous* or *Gothick* as they pretend." Indeed, "we are naturally no ill Soil; and have musical Parts which might be cultivated with great Advantage, if these Gentlemen wou'd use the Art of Masters in their Composition." Thus, the British were disposed to become more polite: they were ready for cultivation.[31]

In fact, Shaftesbury found reason to believe that the British had already begun to imitate ancient Hellenic experience. The history of the English language paralleled the evolution of the Greek examined earlier. While, to judge by "the *Speeches* of our Ancestors in Parliament," the discourse of the Middle Ages was "very short and plain, but coarse, and what we properly call *home-spun*," the Renaissance brought in a new sophistication, which Shaftesbury characterized, suspiciously, as "scholastic" and "pedantic": "the Fashion of speaking, and the Turn of Wit, was after the *figurative* and *florid* Manner. Nothing was so acceptable as the high-sounding Phrase, the far-fetch'd Comparison, the capricious *Point,* and Play of Words; and nothing so despicable as what was merely of the plain or natural kind." As in the sublime phase of Greek writing, the writers of English in the sixteenth and seventeenth centuries affected artfulness, seeking astonishing effects and dramatizing their creations and themselves. They called attention to themselves, seeking to be admired. By contrast, the improvements that Shaftesbury observed in recent years bespoke a different principle, that "the *natural* and *simple* Manner which *conceals* and *covers* ART, is the most truly *artful,* and of the genteelest, truest, and best study'd Taste."[32] Here again was the ideal of self-effacing self-expression, which we have observed shaping Shaftesbury's estimate of cultural products generally and also his notion of philosophic behavior and writing.

The model of evolution from sublimity and other distortions of form towards politeness informed many of Shaftesbury's judgments about literature. He summed up his view of British literature in these very terms when writing of the infantile state of the British muses:

They have hitherto scarce arriv'd to any-thing of Shapeliness or Person. They lisp as in their Cradles: and their stammering Tongues, which nothing besides their Youth and Rawness can excuse, have hitherto spoken in wretched Pun and Quibble. Our *Dramatick* SHAKESPEARE, our FLETCHER, JONSON, and our *Epick* MILTON preserve this Stile. And even a latter Race, scarce free of this Infirmity, and aiming at a false *Sublime,* with crouded *Simile* and *mix'd Metaphor,* (the Hobby-Horse, and Rattle of the MUSES), entertain our raw Fancy, and unpractis'd Ear; which has not as yet had leisure to form it-self and, become truly *musical.*[33]

This passage offered a complex characterization of literary impoliteness. To begin with, it was a picture of impoliteness because the literature under discussion did not, in Shaftesbury's view, correspond to certain formal criteria. However, impoliteness in the passage was an indication of the unsociability of this literary discourse, an unsociability that was cast on two levels of characterization. In the first place, the writers were cast as infants and children, obviously not thoroughly socialized and not capable of mature expression. However, in addition, the stylistic devices with which Shaftesbury associated them are parts of an unsociable literary equipment. "Pun and Quibble," "crouded Simile and mix'd Metaphor," were devices of literary artifice striving self-consciously for effect, seeking either in the most blatant way for our attention, in the manner of children, or "aiming at a false *Sublime,*" more in the manner of adolescents.

The growth of politeness in Britain meant the maturation of the various modes of expression, what, in keeping with the themes of this study, we can think of as their full socialization. The concept of politeness referred not just to refinement, but to the specific cast of this refinement. Politeness was refinement that had submitted to the disciplines of sociability: the combination of self-confidence and unpretentiousness, the naturalness and ease, the honesty and elegance, of the fully autonomous being.

IN SUM

At the end of his life, retired in Naples, Shaftesbury wrote ***A Letter Concerning the Art, or Science of Design to My Lord*****. Completed by March 1712, it was included in some copies of the second edition of **Characteristicks** in 1714 but only became a standard feature of the eighteenth-century printings of **Characteristicks** in the fifth edition of 1732.[34] The ***Letter Concerning Design*** was originally a cover letter to John Somers, the "Lord" of the title, accompanying Shaftesbury's ***Notion of the Historical Draught or Tablature of the Judgment of Hercules,*** which Shaftesbury also wrote in Naples. The ***Letter Concerning Design*** described the contents of the other essay, but what gave the ***Letter Concerning Design*** enduring

value were the many connections it made between culture and politics: indeed, it was, practically, a broadside encapsulation of the cultural-political themes of ***Characteristicks.***

The central point of the ***Letter Concerning Design*** was that Britain was approaching a new cultural age. Though reiterating several times the excellence of British genius, Shaftesbury focussed on the new circumstances that would allow British genius to flower. Those circumstances were construed in a political and specifically Whiggish way. Shaftesbury congratulated the Whig policy of war with France, assuring the reader, "in a kind of spirit of Prophecy," that victory in war would mean the victory of liberty and the constitution. In turn, this political outcome would have cultural consequences: the development of the national personality in the form of increased knowledge, industry, sense, and, indeed, politeness.[35] Shaftesbury also based his hopes for cultural efflorescence on Britain's domestic political nature: "As her *Constitution* has grown, and been establish'd, she has in proportion fitted her-self for other Improvements."[36] The opposite side of this coin was the criticism of the dire cultural consequences of Stuart rule in passages of the ***Letter Concerning Design.***

Yet, more important than the bald assertion of the connection between liberty and culture was the process by which these two domains were related. In a dense but significant statement, Shaftesbury wrote:

> When the *free* spirit of a Nation turns it-self this way [that is, toward the arts]; Judgments are form'd; Criticks arise; the publick Eye and Ear improves; a right Taste prevails, and in a manner forces its way. Nothing is so improving, nothing so natural, so *con-genial* to the liberal Arts, as that reigning Liberty and high spirit of a People, which from the Habit of judging in the highest Matters for themselves, makes 'em freely judge of other subjects, and enter thorowly into the Characters as well of *Men* and *Manners,* as of the *Products* or *Works* of Men, in Art and Science. So much, my Lord, are we owing to the Excellence of our national Constitution, and legal Monarchy; happily fitted for Us; and which alone cou'd hold together so mighty a People; all sharers (tho' at so far a distance from each other) in the Government of *themselves.*[37]

Explaining why the reign of liberty improved the arts, this passage draws together themes we have been examining throughout this book. Liberty was, in its essence, autonomy, judging for oneself "the Characters . . . of *Men* and *Manners.*" As moral autonomy consisted in having a character, moral judgment consisted in understanding others' characters. However, if moral liberty was ultimately individual in its frame of reference, political liberty was the collective version—each person sharing, though at a distance from others, in the government of himself. Thus, the passage returns us to the problem of part I: how it was possible for humans to attain some autonomy given their status as sociable beings. A free polity was the political form most likely to encourage the autonomy of human beings. Given the extent to which humans were discursive beings, it was the discursive freedom of a free polity that could best nurture the possibility of human autonomy. Unfree polities (and, of course, Shaftesbury was thinking of polities in which Church and Court were domineering entities) created discursive conditions tending to quash the autonomy on which humanity entirely depended.

The next step in the argument was that only the sort of autonomy which was present only in a free polity conduced to autonomous judgment in other matters. Judgment in moral and political characters correlated with judgment in cultural matters. If autonomy was required to grasp character in moral and political forms, then it was required to grasp expressive forms as well. In short, liberty was required for taste.

The beginning of the passage offered another way of putting this. There Shaftesbury suggested that a true public was found only under conditions of liberty. It was impossible for those who were not free to form judgments of any legitimacy since, if they were not free, their judgment had to be a reflection of some authority outside themselves. Moreover, under conditions of unfreedom, it was impossible for judgments to interact in a way that allowed the winnowing of true from false, good from bad, polite from impolite.

Concomitantly, under conditions of freedom, the progress of taste and politeness was irresistible. Once there was a public, people felt a vested interest not only in political matters but in artistic ones. As he said in another passage: "In reality *the People* are no small Partys in this *Cause*. Nothing moves successfully without 'em. There can be no PUBLICK, but where they are included."[38] Thus, the notion of a public only made sense in the context of liberty, and only free polities would have a public. The public was that entity that occupied the cultural zone. The training of the public in morals and taste became a central task. *Characteristicks* and Shaftesbury's other writings were attempts first to define that task and second to carry it out.

Notes

1. P.R.O. 30/24/20/91, Shaftesbury to Arent Furely, February 18, 1705; 30/24/20/143, Shaftesbury to Michael Ainsworth, May 10, 1707.

2. P.R.O. 30/24/22/2, ff.175-176, Shaftesbury to Jean LeClerc, March 6, 1706. The next sentence set the limits of freedom and the conditions for calling in the magistrate: "prophane, mocking, and scurrilouse Language that gives the just offence, makes fatal Impressions on the Vulgar, and corrupts Men in another manner than by their Reason."

3. Another extensive "defence of that freedom of thought" appeared, fittingly, as a conclusion to the "Miscellaneous Reflections" and so to *Characteristicks* itself: "Miscellany" V.iii, III, 297ff. (Robertson, II, 341ff.).

4. "Letter" ii, I, 10 (Robertson, I, 10).

5. "Sensus Communis" I.ii, I, 64-65 (Robertson, I, 46).

6. For criticism's centrality, see "Miscellany" V.i, III, 251-252 (Robertson, II, 312-313).

7. "Letter" ii, I, 18 (Robertson, I, 14-15).

8. P.R.O. 30/24/22/7, ff.487-488, a MS. translation of Jean LeClerc's dedication of his edition of Menander and Philemon (Amsterdam, 1709) to Shaftesbury.

9. P.R.O. 30/24/20/143, Shaftesbury to Michael Ainsworth, December 3, 1709; "Miscellany" III.i and V.i, III, 138, 152, 231 (Robertson, II, 241, 250, 298).

10. "Miscellany" III.i, III, 137 (Robertson, II, 241). Shaftesbury's assertiveness fits with Martin Bernal's account of how the European scholarly tradition denied ancient Near Eastern, especially Egyptian, influences on ancient Greece: see Martin Bernal, *Black Athena: The Afroasiatic Roots of Classical Civilization* (New Brunswick: Rutgers University Press, 1987), I, 1-2, 23-27, 165-167, 174-175. This assertiveness also illustrates the distance between Shaftesbury and John Toland, whose hermetic interests led him to see a positive model of civic religion in ancient Egypt. Viewing Egypt as the model of a priest-ridden society, Shaftesbury was in no position to accept its claims as a source of *prisca sapientia*. For Shaftesbury, *sapientia* was Greek. See Margaret Jacob, *The Radical Enlightenment* (London: George Allen & Unwin, 1981), pp.36, 153.

11. "Soliloquy" II.ii, I, 236-237 (Robertson, I, 153-154).

12. "Soliloquy" II.ii, I, 238-239 (Robertson, I, 155).

13. "Soliloquy" II.ii, I, 239 (Robertson, I, 155).

14. "Miscellany" III.i, III, 138-139 (Robertson, II, 242).

15. "Miscellany" III.i, III, 138, 141 (Robertson, II, 241-242, 243).

16. "Soliloquy" II.ii, I, 241-242 (Robertson, I, 156-157).

17. "Soliloquy" II.ii, I, 242-243 (Robertson, I, 157-158).

18. "Soliloquy" II.ii, I, 243 (Robertson, I, 158). Another version of the transition from sublime to natural appears in "Miscellany" III.i, III, 140-141 (Robertson, II, 243).

19. "Miscellany" III.i, III, 137 (Robertson, II, 241). On cosmic design, see chapter 2, pp.54-55.

20. "Miscellany" III.i, III, 140 (Robertson, II, 242).

21. "Soliloquy" II.ii, I, 233 (Robertson, I, 151-152).

22. "Soliloquy" II.ii, I, 258 (Robertson, I, 168-169).

23. Shaftesbury's discussion of the evolution of Greek tragedy was brief, culminating with Euripides, who recapitulated the Homeric movement from sublimity to nature and simplicity: "Soliloquy" II.ii, I, 244-245 (Robertson, I, 158-159).

24. "Soliloquy" II.ii, I, 245-247 (Robertson, I, 160-161).

25. The relevant lines from Horace are 282-284. There is no evidence that such edicts had any effect. See the comment, s.v. "Comedy (Greek), Old," in *The Oxford Classical Dictionary,* 2nd edn (Oxford: Clarendon Press, 1970), pp.269-270.

26. "Soliloquy" II.ii, I, 250 (Robertson, I, 163).

27. "Soliloquy" II.i, I, 216-217, 222-223 (Robertson, I, 141, 145); "Miscellany" III.i, III, 141 (Robertson, II, 243). Shaftesbury reckoned neither with the imperial career of Athens nor with the Augustan aspect of Periclean Athens, though he once indicated that Pericles' virtue had been compromised, which might attest to some diffidence on the issue: P.R.O. 30/24/27/10, p.192 [f.97v]. On the language of "universal monarchy," see chapter 9, note 39.

28. "Soliloquy" III.i, I, 215-216, 223 (Robertson, I, 141, 145).

29. "Soliloquy" II.i, I, 218-219 (Robertson, I, 142-143).

30. "Miscellany" III.i, III, 151-152, 153-154 (Robertson, II, 249-250, 250-251).

31. "Soliloquy" II.iii, I, 274-275 (Robertson, I, 179). A related passage is found among Shaftesbury's jottings in a 1712 Italian almanac (P.R.O. 30/24/24/14, f.5), in which he noted his belief in design's primacy over color in painting: "Pleasure of Colours, the Debauch-Pleasant Painting!—The Shop. . . . Must be quitted for a true Taste & consequent Enjoymt. English Temper. Hope from It. Affecion of Hardship. Severity in Style, Sense, etc. This may run too far. . . . But easily temper'd. This the right Side. Mark of a good Genius." The passage related the tension between design and color to that between stoicism and Epicureanism and identified the English with the stoic/design pole of the tension. Thus, the English were disposed to actuate Shaftesbury's moral and aesthetic programs.

32. "Miscellany" III.i, III, 141-142 (Robertson, II, 243-244).

33. "Soliloquy" II.i, I, 217 (Robertson, I, 141-142).

34. On the peculiar printing history of *A Letter Concerning Design,* see Kerry Downes, "The Publication of Shaftesbury's 'Letter Concerning Design,'" *Architectural History,* 27 (1984), 519-523.

35. "Letter Concerning Design", p.398 (Rand, pp.19-20).

36. "Letter Concerning Design", p.405 (Rand, p.23).

37. "Letter Concerning Design", p.404 (Rand, pp.22-23).

38. "Letter Concerning Design", p.403 (Rand, p.22).

Works Cited

References to the works comprising Shaftesbury's *Characteristicks* (with the exception of "An Inquiry Concerning Virtue") are to the three-volume 1714 edition, which was published after the third earl's death but included his corrections and revisions of the first edition of 1711. The short title of the work is followed by the part and section and citation of the volume and page. References are also given in parentheses to the widely accessible modern edition, by John Robertson (London: Grant Richards, 1900; reprinted in the Library of the Liberal Arts by Bobbs-Merrill, 1964). Short titles are as follows:

"Letter": "A Letter Concerning Enthusiasm"

"Sensus Communis": "Sensus Communis: An Essay on the Freedom of Wit and Humour"

"Soliloquy": "Soliloquy: Or Advice to an Author"

"The Moralists": "The Moralists, A Philosophical Rhapsody"

"Miscellany": "Miscellaneous Reflections on the Preceding Treatises, Etc."

"A Letter Concerning Design" was included in some copies of the 1714 *Characteristicks,* to which all citations refer, though it only became a standard feature of the text in the fifth edition of 1732. (For the complicated history of its publication, see Kerry Downes, "The Publication of Shaftesbury's 'Letter Concerning Design,'" *Architectural History,* 27 (1984), 519-523.) References to "A Letter Concerning Design" are also given in parentheses to Benjamin Rand's edition of Shaftesbury's writings on art, *Second Characters* (Cambridge: Cambridge University Press, 1914).

The Shaftesbury Papers in the Public Record Office (P.R.O.) include a large correspondence, many notebooks, and other written records of the third earl. In cases where Shaftesbury numbered pages of notebooks, these have been provided in citations as well as folio numbers. Aside from correspondence, the most frequently cited Shaftesbury manuscripts are these:

P.R.O. 30/24/27/10 two notebooks with the head, *Askēmata,* dating primarily from 1698 to 1704, written in England and in Holland

P.R.O. 30/24/27/14 a notebook containing "Design of a Socratick History"

P.R.O. 30/24/27/15 a notebook containing material on the arts and art history and forming part of Shaftesbury's project called "Second Characters"

Joel Weinsheimer (essay date summer 1995)

SOURCE: Weinsheimer, Joel. "Shaftesbury in Our Time: The Politics of Wit and Humor." *Eighteenth Century* 36, no. 2 (summer 1995): 178-88.

[*In the essay below, Weinsheimer compares the criticism of Shaftesbury's satire with prohibitions against certain forms of "offensive" humor in contemporary American culture.*]

"The main problem is we live in a world with no sense of humor or irony." Such was Art Spiegelman's response to the outrage ignited by his *New Yorker* cover depicting a Hasidic Jew kissing an African-American woman. "We are stunned that you approved the use of a painting that is obviously insensitive," wrote the director of the Anti-Defamation League. Likewise Rev. Herbert Daughtry, a black activist, called the artwork "crude and offensive" to both blacks and Jews, saying it "trivializes the problems" between the two communities. "A tasteless publicity stunt," asserted Rabbi Abraham Flint, and so on.[1]

Instances of the humorlessness Spiegelman complains of are not hard to come by. Here is one from Minnesota.

> A T-shirt sold by law students to raise money for a graduation party is being revamped. . . . The shirt compares characteristics of the University of Minnesota Law School and the Minnesota School of Bartending and jokingly suggests students might be better off working behind the bar, rather than before it. One item contrasts a "sexy Scandinavian blonde" on a TV commercial for the bartending school with a "sexy diversity cover girl" pictured on the cover of the law school bulletin. . . . "It's an objectification of women," said Robin Ann Williams, a third year [law] student. "Making fun of diversity is unacceptable."[2]

Further examples of the attempt to curb humor and ridicule are unnecessary, being so common nowadays, and I cite these instances only to indicate the immediate oc-

casion of my return to Shaftesbury, especially to part two of the *Characteristics.* For it must have been something like the present-day climate of prescribed gravity that impelled Shaftesbury to write *Sensus Communis: An Essay on the Freedom of Wit and Humour.* The subjects then and now differ of course, though less than one might expect. In the *Letter concerning Enthusiasm,* Shaftesbury ridicules certain French religious fanatics, with their zealotry and martyr complex. These were Protestant émigrés who had sought relief from French barbarity in the more tolerant climate of England.

> But how barbarous still, and more than heathenishly cruel are we tolerating Englishmen! For, not contented to deny these prophesying enthusiasts the honour of a persecution, we have delivered them over to the cruellest contempt in the world. . . . They are at this very time the subject of a choice droll or puppet-show at Bart'lemy Fair. There, doubtless, their strange voices and involuntary agitations are admirably well acted, by the motion of wires and manipulation of pipes. . . . However awkwardly soever a puppet-show may imitate other actions it must needs represent this passion to the life.
>
> (21)[3]

"Not by wrath does one kill but by laughter," Nietzsche remarks.[4] For Shaftesbury too the truly effectual means of repression is not persecution but ridicule. He goes on to intimate that the Bart'lemy Fair method, so successful with French enthusiasts, might have worked on Germans such as Luther as well: "Many of our first reformers . . . were little better than enthusiasts," and had not Rome preferred blood to ridicule and merriment, the whole Reformation might have dissolved in peals of laughter. Indeed, Shaftesbury concludes, if the Jews had confined themselves to puppet shows instead of crucifixions, "they might possibly have done our religion more harm than by all their other ways of severity" (22).

For John Brown, author of *Essays on the Characteristics,* this was going too far.[5] Here Shaftesbury had overstepped the line. Brown allows that French fanatics, perhaps, are fair game for ridicule, but the great Reformation and indeed the Passion itself—these are no laughing matters. Making fun of Christianity is unacceptable, tasteless, offensive, and insensitive. Admittedly, few today are much concerned to protect the solemnity of Christianity. (I recall a recent cartoon depicting Christ on the cross, with the caption T.G.I.F.) But as Brown indicates, Shaftesbury is raising questions that are nevertheless very current: does the province of humor have its limits? Are there subjects too grave for laughter?

"Perhaps so," Shaftesbury admits (10). Some of his contemporaries and successors subscribed to the universal proscription of laughter that we associate with Chesterfield's remark that there is "nothing so illiberal, and so ill-bred, as audible laughter," or with Fontenelle's reply when asked if he had ever laughed: "No, I have never made ha ha."[6] Shaftesbury was certainly not one of these agelasts, these non-laughers (to borrow Rabelais's term). He does concede, however, that humor is sometimes improper. Some things are not in themselves ridiculous, for the very function of ridicule, on Shaftesbury's account, is to determine what they are. Though his emphasis assuredly lies on the "freedom of wit and humor," by affirming the existence of "true gravity," he acknowledges that this freedom is not unrestricted: laughter at certain things and on certain occasions is out of place; and it is not at all clear that Shaftesbury would have objected in principle to, say, "the University of Connecticut [policy that] forbids not only speech deemed offensive but also 'inappropriately directed laughter.'"[7]

The question is a relative one, as Chinua Achebe writes. "Earnestness and its opposite, levity, may be neither good nor bad in themselves but merely appropriate or inappropriate according to circumstance. I hold, however, and have held from the very moment I began to write, that earnestness *is* appropriate to my situation . . . because I have a deep-seated need to alter things in that situation."[8] To be sure, the reformer's personal zeal almost always metamorphoses into an impersonal political or ethical imperative. As Bergson says, "It is but one step from being agelastic to misogelastic, and the misogelos, the laughter-hating, soon learns to dignify his dislike as an objection in morality."[9] At this point the relative question receives an absolute answer.

The prohibition of laughter has always contained a moral and thus absolutistic element; levity in matters that call for sympathy is never appropriate. As early as the *Poetics,* we find pain specifically excluded from the province of ridicule, and Cicero extends the nonridiculous a step further: "the orator should use ridicule with a care not to let it be . . . aimed at misfortune, lest it be brutal; nor at crime, lest laughter take the place of loathing."[10] This prohibition remained largely unchanged well into the eighteenth century. "What," asks Fielding, "could exceed the absurdity of an author, who should write the comedy of Nero, with the merry incident of ripping up his mother's belly? or what would give a greater shock to humanity, than an attempt to expose the miseries of poverty and distress to ridicule?"[11]

Misery is no fit subject for laughter, we can agree, but such laughter does occur, and it is not limited to banana peel humor. "To mock the heaviest of human afflictions is neither charitable nor wise," Imlac says, and yet the "princess smiled" at the astronomer's lunacy, "and Pekuah convulsed herself with laughter."[12] The impulse to charity or wisdom is no match for the urge to laugh.

Consider the ultimate example. "I do not see how the Holocaust can be comical," Norman Holland avers.[13] However laudable this sentiment, it is unquestionably mistaken. The holocaust can be funny, as the anthropologist Alan Dundes shows in his article "Auschwitz Jokes," which collects dozens of examples: "Nothing is so sacred, so taboo, or so disgusting that it cannot be the subject of humor," Dundes writes. "Quite the contrary—it is precisely those topics culturally defined as sacred, taboo or disgusting which more often than not provide the principal grist for humorous mills."[14] The "anesthesia of the heart"[15] that for Bergson explains humor has no inherent limits.

When the anesthesia wears off, all laughter is suspect of being callous and unfeeling. It is presumably for this reason that the prohibition of sex and gender jokes figures so conspicuously in the Minnesota code which defines sexual harassment in part as "callous insensitivity to the experience of women."[16] Similarly, University of Michigan officials, according to Roger Fisher, "defined as a transgression punishable by expulsion the joke" "How many men does it take to scrub a floor? None; it's women's work."[17] As insensitivity goes, this is pretty tame stuff, of course, compared to Swift's most famous line: "Last week I saw a woman flayed, and you will hardly believe how much it altered her person for the worse."[18] This is not anesthesia but moral coma.

Laughter directed at suffering belongs to a larger category of inappropriate humor, namely jokes that occur in the context of a "power differential," to use the recent phrase, though it is no recent idea. Hobbes seems to have been among the first to call attention to the hierarchy implicit in laughter when he notoriously described it as a "sudden glory arising from some sudden conception of some eminency in ourselves, by comparison with the infirmity of others" (*Human Nature* 9.13). Those infirmities can be of the most various kinds, physical or mental. George Campbell's *Philosophy of Rhetoric* (1776) lists them as "awkwardness, rusticity, ignorance, cowardice, levity, foppery, pedantry, and affectation."[19] But whatever the immediate object, Campbell adds, "contempt always implies a sense of superiority. No wonder then that one likes not to be ridiculed or laughed at."[20]

This contemptuous or top-down humor, directed at the inferior by the superior, clearly has political implications, particularly when it expresses or magnifies existing power differentials. Top-down jokes typically reinforce the status quo. As Virginia Woolf is said to have remarked, "one of the nice things about having settled morals . . . is that at least one knows what to laugh at."[21] So too Christopher Wilson concludes that "reactions to satire, and to ridicule generally, reflect preexisting sentiment. . . . Joking is essentially conservative, and ridicule shows an unattractive face of conservatism, funneling malice and abuse downwards through the social pyramid. People ridicule deviants, subordinates, those with mental or physical abnormalities, members of minority and out-groups."[22] It can come as no surprise that left-wing attempts to sanction humor characteristically focus on the top-down variety and tend to equate politically unacceptable ridicule of inferiority with ethically unacceptable ridicule of pain and suffering.

Yet these sanctions never reach the point of blanket condemnation because the very force of humor that can be marshaled to defend pre-existing power relations can also be deployed to overturn them and create new ones. The politics of this second kind of humor—in low burlesque, for example—are the reverse of the top-down variety we just considered. Here the big is made small, the high is brought low, and the status quo is subverted. "Laughter and jokes," Mary Douglas writes, "attack classification and hierarchy, [and] are obviously apt symbols for expressing community in the sense of unhierarchised, undifferentiated social relations. . . . Whatever the joke, however remote its subject, the telling of it is potentially subversive."[23] Such jokes exist in a political context, a context of power differentials, to be sure; but here the joker is on the bottom, in the position of powerlessness. "Jokes," as Freud says, "are especially favoured in order to make aggressiveness or criticism possible against persons in exalted positions who claim to exercise authority. The joke then represents a rebellion against that authority, a liberation from its pressure."[24] Through such subversive jokes, the mean overcome the mighty. This is what justifies Orwell's quip: "Every joke is a tiny revolution."[25]

The plot of Eco's *The Name of the Rose* memorably hinges on the revolutionary impulse implicit in comedy. The monk Jorge suppresses the second part of the *Poetics,* on comedy, because it tacitly justifies the peasant's laughter and its subversive implications: "When he laughs, as the wine gurgles in his throat, the villein feels he is master, because he has overturned his position with respect to his lord; this book . . . could legitimize the reversal."[26] "The serious aspects of class culture," Bakhtin explains, "are official and authoritarian; they are combined with violence, prohibitions, limitations and always contain an element of fear and of intimidation. . . . Laughter, on the contrary, overcomes fear, for it knows no inhibitions, no limitations."[27] For these reasons, conservative sanctions against laughter typically concentrate on bottom-up, revolutionary humor that threatens to reverse existing power differentials.

This revolutionary laughter is undoubtedly the kind of wit and humor Shaftesbury means to defend, because he identifies laughter above all with freedom, both cognitive and political. Shaftesbury calls for an emancipatory, "skeptical kind of wit" directed at the "systems and schemes imposed by authority" (65). Whatever his disagreements on other matters, John Brown concurs with Shaftesbury that "the very being of knowledge depends on the exercise of freedom. For whatever some may fear from an open and unlimited inquiry, it seems evidently the only means vouchsafed us for the attainment of truth." Brown applauds the "generous spirit of freedom which shines throughout the whole" of the *Characteristics*; and with Shaftesbury he stigmatizes the "unnatural and cruel separation between truth and liberty" as "equally impolitic, irrational, and unchristian."[28] For Shaftesbury unlike Brown, however, all genuine thinking is free-thinking. Laughter is the very manifestation of open inquiry. The cognitive freedom to "question everything" (49) Shaftesbury describes as the freedom to seek "in everything what justly may be laughed at" (85). To circumscribe laughter is to circumscribe thought. "Wit can never have its liberty where freedom of raillery is taken away: for against serious extravagances and splenetic humours there is no other remedy than this" (15). This self-correcting quality of thought is the very cornerstone of the laissez-faire epistemology that Shaftesbury espouses: "Wit is its own remedy. Liberty and commerce bring it to its true standard. . . . Wit will mend upon our hands, and humour will refine itself, if we take care not to tamper with it, and bring it under restraints, by severe usage and rigorous prescriptions" (45-46).[29]

On this view, cognitive is inseparable from political emancipation. Laughter for Shaftesbury is the sound of freedom, the voice of liberty resisting oppression: "If men are forbid to speak their minds seriously on certain subjects, they will do it ironically. . . . 'Tis the persecuting spirit has raised the bantering one" (50). Ridicule is the weapon of the victim against the persecutor, and the freedom of wit and humor is the unerring test, because it is the condition and consequence, of political freedom. "'Tis only in a free nation, such as ours, that imposture has no privilege; and that neither the credit of the court, the power of a nobility, nor the awfulness of a Church can give her protection, or hinder her from being arraigned in every shape and appearance" (9).

Thus, from Shaftesbury's libertarian point of view, joking is not at all "essentially conservative," as Christopher Wilson would have us believe. Consider "the laugh of the Medusa." Despite their reputation for being dour and morose, it is not true, as Nancy Walker has shown, that "feminists never laugh"—though some refuse to laugh at what we have called top-down or condescending humor.[30] But there is also an unsettling, oppositional, antiauthoritarian humor of the kind that Shaftesbury was among the first to describe and defend, and this humor can be employed to emancipatory ends. From a progressive vantage point, then, the question of appropriate ridicule can be answered thus: bottom-up ridicule alone is permissible, while top-down humor is to be avoided or, more radically, prohibited.

This radical solution supposes, of course, that the two categories of humor are as distinguishable in fact as they are in theory, but that is not always the case. One reason is that in our time, when so many groups lay claim to the privileged status of victim, the relative positions of center and margin, powerful and powerless are becoming confused. It is much more difficult to differentiate proper, bottom-up satire from improper, top-down condescension. In parody, for example, the two almost always overlap, because parodists by definition employ the very values they ridicule, even if only to inflate and explode them.

Consider an example from Montesquieu's *Spirit of Laws* (1748): "Were I to vindicate your right to make slaves of the Negroes, these should be my arguments. . . . These creatures are all over black, and with such a flat nose, that they can scarcely be pitied. It is hardly to be believed that God, who is a wise Being, should place a soul, especially a good soul, in such a black ugly body. . . . It is impossible for us to suppose these creatures to be men, because allowing them to be men, a suspicion would follow, that we ourselves are not Christians."[31] Let us allow that this is a parody of common pro-slavery arguments, and a pretty good one (Voltaire described it as written in the spirit of a Molière). Yet, though the author has his heart in the right place, it does not take a "flat nose" to detect a whiff of residual racism here.

Two modern jokes illustrate variant problems in differentiating politically acceptable and unacceptable humor. The first, from Lenny Bruce's autobiography, *How to Talk Dirty and Influence People,* describes his frustration with the obscenity trial: "I was so sure I could reach those judges if they'd just let me tell them what I try to do. It was like I was on trial for rape and there I was crying, 'But, Judge, I can't rape anybody, I haven't got the wherewithal,' but nobody was listening, and my lawyers were saying, 'Don't worry, Lenny, you got a right to rape anyone you please, we'll beat 'em in the appellate court.'"[32] The political complexity of this scene is what interests us here. First, the whole evidently consists of bottom-up satire that attacks puritanical obscenity laws which repress free speech. This is fairly straightforward, ACLU-authorized humor. Second, however, Bruce also satirizes the civil-libertarian lawyers who coerce him into claiming unlimited freedom to "talk dirty." And, third, he couches the latter satire in a rape joke that could easily be construed as offensive and insensitive to the very victims whom obscenity laws are in part designed to protect. Often cited to prove the existence of left-wing humor, Bruce's jokes here at least are politically ambivalent.

For an example of right-wing humor that evidences a similar ambiguity, we can turn to the Republican banquet where Oliver North and others "cracked jokes in after-dinner remarks that made light of President Clinton's order to the military to admit homosexuals. . . . Mr. North's remarks included a line about how he had repeatedly tried to place a telephone call to Mr. Clinton but could not get through until he lisped to the operator, 'Excuse me!'"[33] The charge against North was, of course, that he was belittling homosexuals; the defense, of course, was that he was belittling Clinton. The truth is that he was belittling both, and for us the point is that North's witticism, no less than Lenny Bruce's, illustrates how ridicule of the authorities and ridicule of the disenfranchised can easily coexist in the same joke.

This is why it is so tricky to design proscriptions against one kind of levity without encroaching on the other. The powerful, let us agree, have a moral obligation to enact policies on behalf of the powerless, but it is in precisely this situation that permitted ridicule merges with prohibited: bottom-up ridicule of official policies will simultaneously be top-down ridicule of the powerless. Consequently, privileging certain groups by protecting them from supercilious laughter actually serves to protect the powerful from subversive ridicule as well. The bureaucracy wraps itself in the flag of the victim.

These examples do not represent exceptional or peripheral phenomena, for the political predicament they illustrate is inherent in circumscribing the freedom of wit and humor: somehow encroachments on the liberty of laughter always turn out to protect the interests of the powerful. "'Tis true," Shaftesbury admits, "this liberty may seem to run too far. . . . So every one will say, when he himself is touched, and his opinion freely examined. But who shall be judge of what may be freely examined and what may not?" (9). Whoever assumes the role of judge, prohibiting ridicule for even the best of reasons, creates a sacred cow. They provoke laughter at the very object they want to protect and incite bottom-up ridicule by precisely those whom they would disempower from laughing. "'Tis the persecuting spirit has raised the bantering one," Shaftesbury proclaims. "The greater the weight is, the bitterer will be the satire. The higher the slavery, the more exquisite the buffoonery" (50-51). The very act of stifling laughter arouses it.

If the "freedom of wit and humour" is indivisible from the freedom of thought, we ought to emphasize in conclusion that for Shaftesbury ridicule expresses the "sensus communis" as well. By his definition, common sense is moral, aesthetic, and political in nature. It signifies "a sense of the public weal, and of the common interest; love of the community or society, natural affection, humanity, obligingness, or that sort of civility which rises from a just sense of the common rights of mankind, and the natural equality there is among those of the same species" (70). As a matter of fact, however, Shaftesbury recognizes full well that the sense of community virtually never embraces all members of the species or even extends to the boundaries of the nation state.

> Universal good, or the interest of the world in general, is a kind of remote philosophical object. That greater community falls not easily under the eye. Nor is a national interest, or that of a whole people, or body politic, so readily apprehended. In less parties, men may be intimately conversant and acquainted with one another. They can . . . enjoy the common good and interest of a more contracted public. . . . To cantonize is natural when the society grows vast and bulky. . . . 'Tis in such bodies as these that strong factions are aptest to engender.
>
> (75-76)

Common sense is a sense of a community, to be sure, but it operates only within the limits of a clan, club, or clique small enough to have a sense of fellow-feeling that Shaftesbury does not hesitate to call love. Balkanization, faction, and party, he contends, are due not to a centrifugal, isolationist impulse but, just the opposite, to "that social love and common affection which is natural to mankind" (77), but cannot be indefinitely extended. Neither individualist nor universalist, then, Shaftesbury claims to be writing "in defense only of the liberty of *the club,* and of that sort of freedom which is taken amongst gentlemen and friends who know one another perfectly well" (53). This particular club is limited to powerful white men, of course, but the point is that good humor reigns only within the club, and every club is exclusive.

Among gentlemen and friends, knowing what is rude is a matter as intuitive as knowing what is beautiful—or what is funny. A sense of humor requires no weighing of evidence, no deliberation, no decision. Like all common sense, knowledge of what is ridiculous and false, no less than what is beautiful and true, comes from communal life, not critical reflection. Commonsensical judgments, thus understood, cannot ultimately be distinguished from prejudices, prejudgments. Brown is surely right to describe ridicule as "an engine which tends to fix mankind in their preconceived opinions."[34] It is an expression of group solidarity, shared judgments, and sense of community—but all among a finite group. It certainly makes sense to minimize the provinciality of prejudice by maximizing the club's inclusiveness as far as possible. As we have seen, however, only limited extension is possible before the bonds of "social love" are stretched to their limits and the inevitable process of Balkanization sets in. Ridicule exhibits no "sense of partnership with human kind [as a whole]" (72); it confirms regional or local, not universal, opinion precisely

because it is exclusionary. In large part, fellowship within the club is maintained—indeed, the club is itself brought into existence—by ridiculing those outside it.

"To cantonize is natural." We are in no position to dispute Shaftesbury's assertion. Especially now, when individualism is as much in retreat as universalism—when special interest groups on the national level, and cultural centers on the university level, have become the standard form of political organization—it is once again manifest that ridicule functions both commonsensically and critically, to unite and divide. Unlike invective ("Shut up, you water buffalo!") which merely distances, humor binds together those who are "in on" the joke, as well as segregates them from pariahs who "just don't get it." Laughing-at always involves laughing-with because good humor within the group is achieved in large part by means of outward-directed ridicule.

Attempts to prohibit such ridicule, however understandable, are therefore unlikely to succeed. Hostile laughter performs too much important work; and though ridicule may even be described as war by other means, it is well to remember they are infinitely preferable means. Laughter, however aggressive, is not violence but a substitute for it. In our present cantonized state, there is no reason to believe that we will live together without ridicule, but with Shaftesbury it is perhaps not too much to hope that we can learn to take a joke.

Notes

1. All quotations cited from Toby Axelrod, "Valentine Controversy: Crown Hts. Abuzz over Cover Kiss," *The Jewish Week* (Feb. 12-18, 1993), 39.

2. *Saint Paul Pioneer Press* (April 10, 1993), 2B.

3. Shaftesbury, *Characteristics of Men, Manners, Opinions, Times,* ed. John M. Robinson, 2 vols. in 1 (Indianapolis, 1964). Page references are to volume 1 unless otherwise noted.

4. Friedrich Nietzsche, *Beyond Good and Evil,* trans. Walter Kaufman (New York, 1966), 153.

5. John Brown, *Essays on the Characteristics* (1751; New York, 1970), 80.

6. Both cited in Richard Boston, *An Anatomy of Laughter* (London, 1974), 68.

7. Cited in Gary Saul Morson, "Weeding In," *Academic Questions* 6 (1992): 68.

8. Chinua Achebe, "Colonialist Criticism" (1975), rpt. in Hazard Adams, ed., *Critical Theory Since Plato,* rev. ed., (Fort Worth, 1992), 1196.

9. Henri Bergson, "Laughter," in *Comedy* (Garden City, NY, 1956), 4.

10. Cicero, *Orator* (xxvi.88), trans. H. M. Hubbell, in *Brutus and Orator* (London, 1971), 371.

11. Henry Fielding, *Joseph Andrews and Shamela*, ed. M. C. Battestin (Boston, 1961), 10.

12. Samuel Johnson, *Rasselas*, ed. Warren Fleischauer (Woodbury, NY, 1962), 162.

13. Norman Holland, *Laughing: A Psychology of Humor* (Ithaca, 1982), 22.

14. Alan Dundes and Thomas Hauschild, "Auschwitz Jokes," in *Humour in Society: Resistance and Control*, ed. Chris Powell (New York, 1988), 56.

15. Bergson, "Laughter," 64.

16. *Sexual Harassment* (n.p., n.d.), 3.

17. Roger Fisher, "Salem in Minnesota, II: Northern Exposure," *Minnesota Scholar* 1 (1993): 12.

18. Jonathan Swift, *Tale of a Tub*, ed. A. C. Guthkelch and D. Nichol Smith, 2nd ed. (Oxford, 1958), 173.

19. George Campbell, *Philosophy of Rhetoric* (Carbondale, 1963), 21.

20. *Ibid.*, 29.

21. Cited by Aristides, "Jokes and Their Relation to the Conscious," *American Scholar* 47 (1978): 306.

22. Christopher Wilson, *Jokes: Form, Content, Use and Function* (London, 1979), 230.

23. Mary Douglas, "The Social Control of Cognition: Some Factors in Joke Perception," *Man* 3 (1968): 370.

24. Sigmund Freud, *Jokes and Their Relation to the Unconscious*, trans. James Strachey (New York, 1960), 105.

25. Cited by John Oldani, *Humour in Society*, ed. Powell, 40.

26. Umberto Eco, *The Name of the Rose*, trans. William Weaver (New York, 1984), 577.

27. M. M. Bakhtin, *Rabelais and His World*, trans. Helene Iswolsky (Bloomington, 1984), 90.

28. John Brown, *Essays*, 3-5.

29. I cannot do justice here to the epistemological side of the *Characteristics*. For a fuller exposition, see A. Owen Aldridge's "Shaftesbury and the Test of Truth," *PMLA* 60 (1945):129; and David Marshall, *The Figure of Theater* (New York, 1986), chapter 1.

30. Nancy Walker, "Do Feminists Ever Laugh? Women's Humor and Women's Rights," *International Journal of Women's Studies* 4 (1981):1-9.

31. Montesquieu, *Spirit of Laws*, ed. David Wallace Carrithers (Berkeley, 1977), 262.

32. Lenny Bruce, *How to Talk Dirty and Influence People* (Chicago, 1966), 195.

33. *New York Times* (March 19, 1993), A8.

34. John Brown, *Essays*, 72.

A. Owen Aldridge (essay date June 1996)

SOURCE: Aldridge, A. Owen. "Shaftesbury, Rosicrucianism and Links with Voltaire." *Canadian Review of Comparative Literature* 23, no. 2 (June 1996): 393-401.

[*In the following essay, Aldridge discusses Shaftesbury's critique of religious superstition in* The Adept Ladies.]

Scholars have realized for many years that a close connection exists between Protestantism and Rosicrucianism, but the only major literary figures that have been extensively studied from this perspective are the Renaissance martyr Giordano Bruno (who remained nominally a Catholic) and the political and philosophical propagandist of the early Enlightenment John Toland. Bruno's pantheistic hermetism contributed to the development of Rosicrucian texts of the seventeenth century, and Toland drew upon both Bruno and the Rosicrucians for the construction of his theological system, eventually portrayed under the title *Pantheisticon*. Anthony Ashley Cooper, Third Earl of Shaftesbury, an associate and one-time patron of Toland, approved of the deistical aspects of Toland's system, but ridiculed Rosicrucianism as a particularly invidious type of religious superstition. In so doing, he associated it with the Quakers of his day.

Shaftesbury made this connection between Quakers and Rosicrucians in a prose satire, written ca. 1701-02 but not published during his lifetime: *The Adept Ladys or The Angelick Sect. Being the Matters of Fact of certain Adventures Spiritual, Philosophical, Political, and Gallant. In a Letter to a Brother.* In these adventures, Shaftesbury himself, as protagonist, successfully resists the financial-erotic schemes of a sanctimonious bawd described as a "Woman in a Quaker dress," who operates in association with an "Angelick Sect." The latter is clearly identified as Rosicrucian. The documented historical relations of Shaftesbury with actual Quakers belong to a brief period in 1699-1700 when he lived in Rotterdam.

Although he sought out and established intellectual contacts with Pierre Bayle, Pierre Desmaizeaux, Jean Le Clerc and the Armenian Philip Van Limborch, his most intimate friend was a Quaker, Benjamin Furly, a native Englishman who had taken up residence in Holland as a merchant. Some Quakers at the time were pietistic, given to emotional religious experiences, but others at the opposite extreme were so rational that they were taken for deists. Since Furly completely shared Shaftesbury's religious rationalism, he obviously cannot be associated with the Quaker lady in Shaftesbury's satire. Another prominent resident of the time, however, Francis Mercury Van Helmont, had connections with both Quakers and Rosicrucians. Shaftesbury knew Van Helmont in Holland and describes him in his ***Characteristics*** as a "notable enthusiast," "a successor of Paracelsus, and a master in the occult sciences" (Cooper 1900, 1: 186-87).

While in Rotterdam, Shaftesbury summarized his attitude toward the supernatural in religion.

> Amongst those that are celebrating superstitious rites, what would I have? Why seek Familiarity with these? Can I make my self what they are? Can I reconcile my Opinions to theirs? if not, why do I affect this intimacy? their Principles and mine are opposite as the Antipodes.

> (qtd. in Voitle 90)

This passage has been taken as referring to orthodox Christianity, but the word *rites* suggests Rosicrucian ceremonies as well. Elsewhere, in his private notebook, however, Shaftesbury exhorts himself:

> Remember therefore to respect these rites, whatever they may be, which others have within their own minds erected to the Deity, as well as those other rites which they have publicly erected and in other outward temples. If modern superstition disturb these be thankful it is not Indian and barbarian, that they are not human sacrifices, that they are not Druids.

> (Cooper 1914, 29)

The Quaker woman in Shaftesbury's satire uses a combination of Christian cant, Rosicrucian lore and erotic bait, hoping to lure him into marrying a common prostitute. Shaftesbury was not unique at the time in associating sex and religion with the Quakers. Swift in *A Tale of a Tub,* which was at first attributed to Shaftesbury, describes female priests who convert carnal pruriency into spiritual ecstasy and identifies them with the Quakers, "who suffer their women to preach and pray" (463). In dedicating an early version of his ***The Moralists*** to Lord Somers, Shaftesbury drew a parallel between religious superstition and gallantry, or priests and prostitutes, whores and confessors, in the age of Charles II. In Shaftesbury's words, "Christianity is super-natural Religion: Gallantry is super-natural Love" (qtd. in Voitle 241). This is the pejorative meaning of *Gallant* in his ***Adept Ladys.***

Although Shaftesbury's ***Adept Ladys*** has elements of anti-sectarian satire, it is not a work of deism comparable to the author's widely-known ***Characteristics.*** Indeed it incorporates a notable passage of personal testimony, defending the protestantism of the Church of England against competing forms of religion. Shaftesbury recounts that on the day after his unpleasant encounter with the woman in Quaker dress, he and his brother attended the Anglican Church. The following long passage indicates a strain of piety in Shaftesbury's thought quite at odds with his published works.

> Thither I never went with truer Zeal in a better Disposition, or with wholesomer Reflections. & what Satisfyed me still the more, it was by appointment that we were that Day to receive the Sacrament together; having had no opportunity of a long time; and it being now in a manner our Duty, at least for Examples sake, on the Account of our Stations in Parlement.

> HERE We both of us joyn'd in blessing that good Providence . . . which had given us . . . establish'd Rites of Worship as were so Decent, Chast, innocent, pure, and had plac'd us in a Religion and Church where, in respect of the Moderate Party, and far greater Part; the Principle of Charity was really more extensive than in any Christian or Protestant Church besides in the world.

> (Cooper 1981, 1: 1, 414)

This passage has little in common with the attack on Rosicrucianism that comprises the major part of the ***Adept Ladys.*** The word *adept* in this title ordinarily in Shaftesbury's day referred to those familiar with the scientific and religious mysteries of the Society of the Rosy Cross. Samuel Butler's *Hudibras* also uses the term in delightful reference to four of its most notorious votaries.

> Or Sir Agrippa for profound
> And solid lying much renown'd;
> He Anthroposophus, and Floud
> And Jacob Behemen understood;
> Knew many an amulet and charm,
> That would do neither good nor harm:
> In Rosicrucian love as learned,
> As he that *vere adeptus* earned.

> (Butler 41-42)

These lines refer to Cornelius Agrippa (Agrippa von Nettesheim), Robert Fludd, and Jacob Böhme and to a treatise by Thomas Vaughan *Anthroposophia Theomagica, or a Discourse of the Nature of Man in the State after Death.* Vaughan also translated from the German a major manifesto of the Rosicrucian movement, *The Fame and Confession of the Fraternity of R.C. Commonly of the Rosie Cross* (London, 1652; original German version 1614).

Almost as important in the history of Rosicrucianism is another German work which directly influenced Shaftesbury's ***Adept Ladys*** and which furnishes the basis for interpreting Shaftesbury's satire as being directed in large measure against alchemical religion.

This is a religious and political allegory *Chymische Hochzeit Christiani Rosencreutz* (1616; *The Chemical Wedding of Christian Rosencreutz*) by Johann Valentin Andreae, who is better known in literary history as the author of a religious utopia *Reipublicae Christiano-politanae Descriptio* (1619; English version *Christiana-polis*). The *Chemical Wedding* concerns the activities involved in a week-long marriage ceremony based on Rosicrucian symbolism which culminates in the creation of an alchemical bird. The direct connection between Andreae's allegory and Shaftesbury's **Adept Ladys** is highlighted in one of the verse squibs appended to the latter work entitled "The Golden Lovers, a Ballad. / Being a Dialogue between Mick of the North, and Nan of the Town." The "Golden" in the title refers to both the alchemical metal and human urine. The last stanza of the ballad points directly to the Rosicrucians and Andreae in particular.

> When jolly Lad Mick went to cheer up his Nancy,
> In a Pickle he found her, not much to his Fancy;
> With Gally-Pot, Cruisable, Furnace, and Kettle;
> At the Work of Creation, a making of mettle.
>   What's here, my sweet Rose?
>   Quoth he, holding his Nose,
> Are these the Soft Terms on my Love you impose?
>   I have lov'd Thee for all thour't a Drab and a
> Blouse:
>   But who can Endure a Chemicall Spouse?
>
>   (Cooper 1981, 1: 1, 440)

The reference to Andreae's *Chemical Wedding* is unmistakable.

Another poetic epigram in **Adept Ladys** has the title "To his Adept-Mistress: A Song, by Deisdaemon." As an adept, the lady of the song presumably is a master at the art of alchemy. The poem plays satirically on her two ways of converting base materials to gold—another reference to metal and to urine. In one line "Her single Touch transforms to Gold"; in another, she "Pours from her Urn a Golden Shower!" (Cooper 1981, 1: 1, 434). This subject matter has more in common with Swift's "A Beautiful Young Nymph Going to Bed" than with the elegant prose of the **Characteristics**. The pen name Deisdaemon that Shaftesbury uses for his epigram literally means God-demon and suggests religious superstition and worship of the forces of evil. The term has connections with two other English deists, Sir Robert Howard and John Toland, as well as with Shaftesbury's later **Characteristics**. Howard is known in literary history as Dryden's brother-in-law and collaborator in the heroic play *The Indian Queen* and as a character in *The Rehearsal*. In addition to various dramatic works, he also wrote *The History of Religion* which has been neglected, I might say ignored, in scholarship concerning deism. Yet it is one of the most vigorous and incisive attacks on orthodox Christianity to appear in the Age of the Enlightenment. Through a number of ingenious parallels, Howard suggests that Christianity is a type of superstition, only superficially removed from pagan devil worship. He portrays Christianity as a corruption of natural religion by its deifying of man while acknowledging "a superior Sort of *Daemons,* who never were Men" (11). Quoting Hermes Trismegistus, one of the Rosicrucian hierarchy, he traces the origin of "an Art to make Gods, and to call them Souls of Demons and Angels, and put them into those Images or Gods" (16). He cites the fifteenth satire of the Roman poet Juvenal for authority that men have worshipped "Crocodiles, Serpents, Golden Monkies, Fishes, Dogs, and even Onions and Leeks" (26).

Howard makes the transition to Christianity by affirming that the Romish *Saints*

> and *Angels* answer to the Daemons and Heroes, deified by the Heathen Priests; and their Idol(s) of Bread, Divinity infused into Crosses, Images, *Agnus Dei*'s and Relicks, correspond to the Pillars, Statues and Images consecrated by Pagan Priests.
>
> When St. *Paul* at Athens, preached Jesus Christ risen from the dead; they took, this for a Part of their Doctrine of Daemons; which Word is expressly used in the Original. Our Translation saith, *Others said, He seemeth to be a Setterforth of strange Gods*; but in the Original 'tis, of strange Daemons. For hearing of one, who after his Death had Divine Honours and Worship given to him, they took it presently, according to their own Opinion, that he was proposed as a New Daemon.
>
>   (17-18)

Toland reported that Howard was accused of using his *History of Religion* to whip "the Protestant Clergy on the back of the Heathen and Popish Priests" and that he asked in reply "what they had to do there" (185-86).

In 1697 there appeared in London a pamphlet of 72 pages entitled *A Lady's Religion. In a Letter to the Honourable my Lady Howard. By a Divine of the Church of England.* Its only connection with the *History of Religion* consists in a pseudonym attached to a "prefatory Epistle . . . by a lay-Gentleman." This preface is signed Adeisidaemon, the negative of Deisidaemon. Later in the same year an Irish clergyman Peter Browne in an attack on Toland's deistical *Christianity Not Mysterious,* which had been published in 1696, affirmed that the Adeisidaemon of *A Lady's Religion* was Toland himself (Carabelli 32). The latter in *A Defense of Mr. Toland* printed in the same year, 1696, denied the attribution (Carabelli 32).

In 1699 Toland gave a manuscript copy of Shaftesbury's treatise **An Inquiry concerning Virtue** to a printer for publicaton, perhaps with and perhaps without Shaftesbury's connivance. In his Inquiry Shaftesbury gives an extensive treatment of the significance of daemonism. After defining god as "whatsoever is superior in any degree over the World, or rules in nature with discernment and a Mind," he observes that if there are several gods and if any "are not in their nature necessarily good, they rather take the name of Daemon" (Cooper 1984, 2: 2, 37) To believe in a being who does all things without obligation to good and what is best is "to believe an infinit [sic] Devil, and not an infinit God" (37). Shaftesbury argues that religions incorporate various mixtures of daemonism, polytheism, and theism. "Perfect *Daemonists* there are in Religion; because we know whole Nations that worship a Devil or Fiend, to whom they sacrifice and pray, only to prevent mischief he would do them. And we know that there are those of some Religions, who give no other Idea of their God, but of a Being arbitrary, violent, causing ill, and ordaining to misery, which is a Devil in the place of God." Shaftesbury also defines a vicious god as a "*Daemon* or Idol of the Mind" (103).

In the next year Toland published a work of his own on daemonism, but since he was personally involved with Rosicrucianism and a fallen-away Catholic, he centered his attention upon the Church of Rome. Entitled *Clito: A Poem on the Force of Eloquence,* it consists of a dialogue between Clito and Adeisidaemon, the latter a "Lucretian-Rosicrucian-Miltonic" rhetorician (Carabelli 68). The preface indicates that

> By CLITO is meant a certain eminent Man, who is no more suppos'd to have held this DISCOURSE, *or to be full of these Opinions, than the principal persons* in PLATO's *or* CICERO's *Dialogues to have said whatever we read of 'em there, tho' introduc'd for the dignity of the Subject, and as a mark of the Author's esteem.*

Biographical circumstances suggest that Clito represents Shaftesbury. The preface also affirms that "Mr. TOLAND himself is understood by ADEISIDAEMON, which signifies Unsuperstitious." A later French critic translated the word as "l'Homme sans Superstition" (Carabelli 162). The poem has nothing specific to say about Shaftesbury, but a good deal about the beauty of the natural universe and the horrors of the Catholic religion.

Shaftesbury carried on the crusade against daemonism in his *Advice to an Author,* 1710, by suggesting that the name of Shakespeare's Desdemona is a variant of *Deisdaemon.* He wonders why "amongst his Greek names," Shakespeare "should have chosen one which denoted the lady superstitious" and then concludes that "there is a very great affinity between the passion of superstition and that of tales" (Cooper 1900, 1: 224). So far as I know, Shaftesbury is unique in tracing the etymology of Desdemona to demonism.

In the previous year Toland published two Latin dissertations in a single volume, one of which is entitled in English translation: *Adeisidaemon, or Titus Livius freed from superstition. In which dissertation it is proved that Livy's History on sacred things, portents, and signs of the Romans to be interpreted was by no means unbe-lievable or superstitious; and that Superstition itself is pernicious no less for the Republic (if not more so) than Atheism is pure and bright.* In this work Toland vindicates Livy against the accepted view that the Roman historian was superstitious or a believer in religious absurdities and defends the thesis of the first part of Shaftesbury's *Inquiry concerning Virtue* that atheism is preferable in the state to "false Religion or fantastical Opinion, deriv'd from Superstition and Credulity," (Book 1, Part 3, Sec 2) a concept formerly stated by Pierre Bayle. Toland had prepared his *Adeisidaemon* for publication in the same year as the appearance in print of Shaftesbury's *A Letter concerning Enthusiasm,* which reverses the hard line against superstition of the *Inquiry.* and looks upon religious excesses with amused toleration. Both in tone and reasoning Shaftesbury's *Letter* takes a quite different direction from Toland's *Adeisidaemon* as well as from his own *Inquiry.*

The greatly-needed Standard Edition of Shaftesbury's works now in progress at the University of Erlangen follows a thematic rather than a chronological principle. *Adept Ladys,* therefore, is printed in the same volume as *A Letter concerning Enthusiasm,* presumably because both satires concern religious superstition. It is true that the theme is the same, but the subject matter is quite different. *Adept Ladys* attacks charlatanism, the attempt of unprincipled characters to extract financial benefit through hypocritical religion, pseudo-science, and even political maneuvering. *A Letter concerning Enthusiasm* portrays religious fervor as genuine, although invidious, and argues that it should be resisted by ridicule rather than political force. Shaftesbury's new target is French pietism rather than German Rosicrucianism. A Protestant religious sect known as the Camisards because of its origin in southern France claimed to have the gift of prophecy through the direct inspiration of the Holy Ghost. Late in 1706, three members of the sect fled to London from persecution in their native land and began exhibiting their prophetical gifts in public. In their ecstacies, they rolled their eyes, foamed at the mouth, and frequently fell on the floor in a trance as a preliminary to their inspired utterances. These consisted for the most part of incoherent babble, but some of the English converts to the sect allegedly spoke in Latin even though they had absolutely no prior knowledge of the language. Shaftesbury in his *Letter* refers to "our good Brethren, the *French* Protestants, laterly come among us," who were anxious to turn themselves into martyrs for the sake of propagating their faith (Cooper 1981, 1: 1, 338) This "prophesying Sect," according to Shaftesbury, claimed to have performed an outstanding miracle, "acted premeditately, and with warning, before many hundreds of People, who actually give testimony to the Truth of it" (360). The particular miracle Shaftesbury had in mind is still to be established. The most sensational one to be attempted by the prophets, however, concerned the raising from the dead of a certain Thomas Emes, who had been assured in his dying moments by an English adherent to the prophets, John Lacy, that he would assuredly be brought back to life. A few weeks later the date of the intended miracle was announced in print, and on the appointed day, an enormous crowd appeared at the graveyard, held in check by a detachment of soldiers expressly ordered for the occasion by Queen Anne. Lacy, who was supposed to officiate, stayed away altogether, and poor Emes lost his chance for resurrection. Lacy later explained that he was not able to work his miracle in the presence of a noisy, adverse multitude (Aldridge 315).

Voltaire without reference to Shaftesbury described the same episode in the article "Fanatisme" of his *Dictionnaire philosophique* as well as in his "Dieu et les hommes." Typically, he changed and embroidered details to make the narrative more dramatic and the victims of his satire seem more absurd. Most important, he revealed that one of the prophets who published eyewitness accounts of miracles performed by the group was none other than an eminent mathematician, Nicolas Fatio de Duillier, known in the history of science as an intimate friend of Newton during the final decade of the seventeenth century and the person who initially charged Leibniz with plagiarizing Newton. Voltaire casts Fatio rather than Lacy in the role of mock hero and, completely ignoring the recently defunct Emes, affirms that the subject of the demonstration, the most stinking corpse in the cemetery, was picked at random. Voltaire also affirms that Fatio and the other "pretended resuscitators" were arrested and condemned to the pillory. Historical fact reveals that Voltaire combined two separate events. Fatio and two other scribes were indicted for publishing and for holding illegal assemblies and ordered to the pillory in November 1707. But the scene in the cemetery did not take place until May of the following year, and Fatio had absolutely nothing to do with this fiasco. Also Voltaire maintains that Fatio had come to London from the mountains of the Dauphine; whereas he was actually a Swiss from Geneva. Voltaire sought credibility by asserting that he had derived his information from one of the prophets who had been a witness to the proceedings and had explained that the corpse was not resurrected because one of the prophets at the grave was in a condition of venial sin. Obviously this is another fabrication of Voltaire's since protestant theology makes no distinction between venial and mortal sins.

Shaftesbury does not formally distinguish between superstition and enthusiasm, but it is clear that his **Adept Ladys** concerns the former and his **Letter,** the latter. The distinction could be used to resolve an apparent contradiction between his condemning "false religion or fantastical opinion, derived commonly from superstition and credulity" in his **Inquiry concerning Virtue** and his recommending in his **Letter concerning Enthusiasm** toleration or good humor in regard to vulgar opinions

of the deity. Daemonism is to be condemned and opposed, but enthusiasm is to be tolerated and in some forms accepted. In this way, Shaftesbury combats both Calvinism and Rosicrucianism and balances his interior deism with his external orthodoxy.

Works Cited

Aldridge, A. Owen. *Shaftesbury and the Deist Manifesto*. Philadelphia: American Philosophical Society, 1951.

Butler, Samuel. *Hudibras*. Chandos Classics. Ed. Zachary Grey. London: Frederick Warne, n.d.

Carabelli, Giancarlo. *Tolandia: materiali bibliografici per lo studio dell'opera e della fortuna di John Toland*. Florence: La Nuova Italia Editrice, 1975-78.

Cooper, Anthony Ashley, Third Earl of Shaftesbury. *Characteristics*. Ed. J. M. Robertson. London: Grant Richards, 1900.

Cooper, Anthony Ashley, Third Earl of Shaftesbury. *Life, Unpublished Letters and Philosophical Regimen*. Ed. Benjamin Rand. Cambridge, MA: Harvard UP, 1914.

Cooper, Anthony Ashley, Third Earl of Shaftesbury. *Complete Works*. Vols. 1 and 2. Eds. Gerd Hemmerich & Wolfram Benda. Stuttgart: Fromman-Holzboorg, 1981, 1984.

Howard, Sir Robert. *The History of Religion*. London, 1694.

Swift, Jonathan. *Gulliver's Travels, A Tale of a Tub*. Modern Library Edition. New York, 1931.

Toland, John. *Life of John Milton*. London, 1698-99.

Voitle, Robert. *The Third Earl of Shaftesbury 1671-1713*. Chapel Hill: U of North Carolina P, 1984.

Robert D. Richardson, Jr. (essay date April 1997)

SOURCE: Richardson, Robert D., Jr. "Liberal Platonism and Transcendentalism: Shaftesbury, Schleiermacher, Emerson." *Symbiosis* 1, no. 1 (April 1997): 1-20.

[*In the excerpt below, Richardson briefly summarizes Shaftesbury's major ideas and his influence on writers and philosophers of the eighteenth and nineteenth centuries.*]

It has often been noted that the Cambridge Platonists had a direct impact on American Transcendentalism; what is less often remarked is the even more massive indirect influence exerted by the Cambridge Platonists through Shaftesbury. Indeed, Shaftesbury, whom Herder called 'the beloved Plato of Europe' is probably the main person through whose work Liberal Platonism gets into the mainstream of eighteenth-century thought.[1] Shaftesbury was John Locke's student. He edited a volume of Whichcote's writings, and was, according to his modern editor the 'greatest Stoic of modern times', and together with Epictetus and Marcus Aurelius, one of the three major exponents of Stoic thought. The Stoic element in Shaftesbury was not as evident to his contemporaries as his Platonism, and indeed his real importance is in how he took the Platonic insistence on the adequacy and universality of reason and transformed it into the 'moral sense' of the main line of eighteenth-century thought.[2]

Shaftesbury combined the Stoic focus on nature with the Platonic insistence on the plenitude to be found in nature. He believed that 'the end or design of nature is man in society', and that our end is 'to live according to nature'. In nature, Shaftesbury thought, 'the elements are combined, united, and have a mutual dependence one upon another . . . All things in the world are united, for as the branch is united and is at one with the tree, so is the tree with the earth, air, and water which feed it, and with the flies, worms, and insects which it feeds' (Rand, 49,52,13).

Turning to the individual self, Shaftesbury asks, 'Consider then who am I? What is this self? a part of the general mind, governing a part of this general body, itself and body both governed by the universal governing mind. . . . It is at one with it, partakes of it, and is in the highest sense related to it' (Rand, 39). Shaftesbury's concept of reason is not a narrow, technical, Cartesian ratiocination. It is rather a broad power, which he often calls 'good nature', a quality we all have which is capable of finding truth, which, he good-naturedly observes, 'is the most powerful thing in the world, since even Fiction itself must be govern'd by it and can only please by its resemblance.'[3]

Shaftesbury is at pains to warn against what he calls 'false enthusiasm', which he says is marked by melancholy and by 'pannick' emotionalism, but he comes out carefully in favour of the real thing. 'Inspiration', he writes, 'may be justly call'd Divine Enthusiasm: for the word itself signifies Divine Presence, and was made use of by the philosopher [Plato] whom the earliest Christian fathers call'd Divine, to express whatever was sublime in human passions.' This inspiration, Shaftesbury goes on, 'he allotted to heroes, statesmen, poets, orators, musicians, and even philosophers themselves. Nor can we, of our own accord, forbear ascribing to a noble enthusiasm whatever is greatly performed by any of these. So that almost all of us know something of this principle.'[4]

Shaftesbury's influence has been enormous. In England he is the founder of the 'moral sense school' which includes Francis Hutcheson, Bishop Butler and Adam Smith. He was a friend of the Deists John Toland and Anthony Collins, and he also influenced Addison, Thomson, Akenside, and Fielding. It has been remarked that Shaftesbury's **Characteristics** only ceased to be regularly reprinted when nobody any longer questioned the . . . moral ideas which Englishmen derived from it.'[5] Leibniz said he found in Shaftesbury's **The Moralists** 'almost all of my theodicy before it saw the light of day.'[6] Shaftesbury is represented in more colonial American libraries than Hobbes or Rousseau.[7] Diderot translated Shaftesbury's **Inquiry Concerning Virtue** into French in 1745; a complete translation into French appeared in Geneva in 1769. Rousseau had a copy.[8] The first translation into German appeared in 1738; a complete translation of Shaftesbury appeared in German in 1776-79. His ideas were enthusiastically received by Lessing, Mendelssohn, Kant, Wieland, Goethe, Herder, Schiller, and, most importantly, by Schleiermacher.[9] When the English and American Romantics took up these German writers, they were also taking up the Shaftesbury who lies behind them. Shaftesbury affected the Transcendentalists directly through his own work, semi-directly through Scottish common sense and the moral sense philosophers, and indirectly through the Shaftesburian Germans. These three streams coalesce, with the important addition of Schleiermacher, to create the Liberal Platonism of the Transcendentalists. . . .

Notes

1. For Shaftesbury, see Ernst Cassirer, *The Platonic Renaissance in England* (London: Nelson, 1953) and C. A. Moore 'Shaftesbury and the Ethical Poets in England, 1700-1760,' *PMLA* June 1916.

2. Benjamin Rand, *The Life, Unpublished Letters and Philosophical Regimen of Anthony, Earl of Shaftesbury* (London: Swan Sonnenschein 1900), xii.

3. Shaftesbury, 'Letter Concerning Enthusiasm' in *Characteristics of Men, Manners, Opinions, Times,* 4th edn (np 1727) 1:4.

4. 'Letter Concerning Enthusiasm', 53, 54. Shaftesbury here footnotes the *Phaedo,* the *Meno,* and the *Apology.*

5. R. Voitle, *The Third Earl of Shaftesbury* (Baton Rouge: Louisiana State Univ Press), 414.

6. S. Grean, *Shaftesbury's Philosophy of Religion and Ethics* (Athens: Ohio Univ Press 1967).

7. David Lundberg and Henry F. May, 'The Enlightened Reader in America', *American Quarterly,* 28 (Summer 1976). Shaftesbury is represented in twenty percent of American libraries of the period 1700-1813, and in thirty three percent of the 92 libraries surveyed for the period 1700-1776.

8. See Dorothy B. Schlegel's *Shaftesbury and the French Deists* (University of North Carolina Studies in Comparative Literature, no 15, Chapel Hill, NC, 1956, Johnson Reprint 1969).

9. For Shaftesbury and the Germans see Grean above.

FURTHER READING

Criticism

Alderman, William E. "English Editions of Shaftesbury's *Characteristics.*" *Papers of the Bibliographical Society of America* 61 (1967): 315-34.

> Examines the evidence that suggests there were multiple editions of *Characteristics.*

————. "Pope's *Essay on Man* and Shaftesbury's *The Moralists.*" *Papers of the Bibliographical Society of America* 67 (1973): 131-40.

> Presents evidence to show that Alexander Pope owed a greater debt to Shaftesbury than has previously been established.

Aldridge, A. Owen. "Shaftesbury's Rosicrucian Ladies." *Anglia* 103, no. 3-4 (1985): 297-319.

> Argues that *The Adept Ladies,* commonly seen as antifeminist, was actually an attack against the pantheistic materialism of the Rosicrucians.

————. "Variants in Shaftesbury's *Letter Concerning Enthusiasm.*" *Anglia* 113, no. 1 (1995): 16-25.

> Discusses the claim by an earlier critic that there were two editions of *A Letter Concerning Enthusiasm.*

Bernstein, John A. "Lord Shaftesbury." In *Shaftesbury, Rousseau, and Kant: An Introduction to the Conflict between Aesthetic and Moral Values in Modern Thought,* pp. 21-60. Rutherford, N. J.: Farley Dickenson University Press, 1980.

> Explores the relationship between moral and aesthetic values in Shaftesbury's thought.

Butler, Lance St. John. "Fielding and Shaftesbury Reconsidered: The Case of *Tom Jones.*" In *Henry Fielding: Justice Observed,* edited by K. G. Simpson, pp. 56-74. London, England: Vision Press, 1985.

> Explores the affinity between Shaftesbury and the novelist Henry Fielding, focusing on their views on morality.

Grean, Stanley. *Shaftesbury's Philosophy of Religion and Ethics: A Study in Enthusiasm,* Athens, Ohio: Ohio University Press, 1967, 287 p.

> Detailed analysis of Shaftesbury's works which attempts to examine his philosophy of religion and ethics as a whole.

Inglesfield, Robert. "Shaftesbury's Influence on Thomson's 'Seasons.'" *British Journal for Eighteenth-Century Studies* 9, no. 2 (autumn 1986): 141-56.

> Explores the influence of Shaftesbury on the poet James Thomson, whose poem "The Seasons" stresses an optimistic view of human nature.

Klein, Lawrence E. "Berkeley, Shaftesbury, and the Meaning of Politeness." *Studies in Eighteenth-Century Culture* 16 (1986): 57-68.

> Analyzes George Berkeley's *Alciphron,* a dialogue about politeness, and discusses the relationship between Berkeley and Shaftesbury.

————. *Shaftesbury and the Culture of Politeness: Moral Discourse and Cultural Politics in Early Eighteenth-Century England,* Cambridge: Cambridge University Press, 1994, 220 p.

> Study of Shaftesbury as a political writer, arguing that his moralism, deism, and aesthetic interests were part of a political project.

Rivers, Isabel. Review of *Characteristicks of Men, Manners, Opinions, Times* edited by Philip Ayres. *Review of English Studies* 51, no. 204 (November 2000): 617-21.

> Review of a scholarly, annotated version of *Characteristics* that offers a synopsis and textual history of the work.

Ryan, Robert M. "Keats's 'Hymn to Pan': A Debt to Shaftesbury?" *Keats-Shelley Journal* 26 (1977): 31-34.

> Suggests that some lines in John Keats's poem were inspired by Shaftesbury's *The Moralists.*

Townsend, Dabney. "From Shaftesbury to Kant: The Development of the Concept of Aesthetic Experience." *Journal of the History of Ideas* 48, no. 2 (April-June 1987): 287-305.

> Traces the history of the discussions of taste in the eighteenth century, beginning with Shaftesbury and using him as a reference point for further developments.

Additional coverage of the life and career of Anthony Ashley Cooper, Earl of Shaftesbury, is contained in the following sources published by Thomson Gale: *Dictionary of Literary Biography,* **Vol. 101; and** *Literature Resource Center.*

George Villiers, Second Duke of Buckingham
1628-1687

English essayist, playwright and poet.

INTRODUCTION

During his lifetime Buckingham was considered, as his contemporary Francis Lockier declared, the "most accomplished man of the age," a central figure in the political and literary circles of Restoration England. He was raised with the future king Charles II, and during the Commonwealth period played an active role in the efforts to return the monarchy to power. After the Restoration, Buckingham was the principal member of the Court Wits, a literary circle that included figures such as Charles Sackville and John Denham. Buckingham is principally remembered today for his 1671 play *The Rehearsal,* a satirical attack on theatrical conventions that, as Peter Lewis has asserted, "scattered its progeny throughout the eighteenth and nineteenth centuries and then projected its powerful hereditary strain even into our own comedies, farces, and revues."

BIOGRAPHICAL INFORMATION

Buckingham was born January 30th, 1628, into a wealthy and powerful family. His father, George Villiers, the first Duke of Buckingham, was a favorite of both James I and Charles I. In August 1628 the elder Villiers was assassinated and his son, just seven months old, assumed his title of Duke of Buckingham. Buckingham's mother, Lady Katherine Manners, was pregnant at the time of her husband's death. When she later remarried, Buckingham and his siblings were left in the care of Charles I, who raised them along with his sons, Charles and James, both of whom would later rule England. In 1640 Buckingham and his younger brother, Francis, enrolled in Trinity College, Cambridge, but left two years later to join royalist forces involved in the civil war. Francis was killed in battle in 1648, and Buckingham escaped to the Continent. After Charles I was beheaded in 1649, Buckingham worked to restore the monarchy. In 1657 he returned to England and married Mary Fairfax, whose father had been awarded a significant portion of Buckingham's former estate. Buckingham's close association with the royal family led to his arrest and imprisonment shortly after his marriage, and he was sentenced to death. However, before he could be executed, Oliver Cromwell died and the

monarchy was restored. After the Restoration, Buckingham regained his property and the income it produced, and became an influential member of Charles II's court, serving for a time as the king's first minister. During this time, he began writing plays and poems, and his position at court made Buckingham the most influential of the so-called Court Wits, a circle of courtier artists and intellectuals, among them Abraham Cowley, Christopher Wren, and Samuel Butler. Buckingham's plays were often produced in collaboration with other Court Wits, and several satirical portraits of Buckingham's political and literary enemies achieved great popular acclaim. In 1665 Buckingham began a notorious affair with Anna-Maria, the Countess of Shrewsbury, which provoked her husband to challenge Buckingham to a duel. When Lord Shrewsbury died of wounds he received in the contest, public opinion turned against Buckingham. In 1671 Lady Shrewsbury gave birth to Buckingham's son, but the infant died shortly after birth. Buckingham's very public grief at the loss of his only child—along with the elaborate funeral he staged—caused further scandal. In 1674 Buckingham was ordered by Parliament not to co-habit with Lady Shrewsbury and was removed from office. He lived for a year in retirement in Yorkshire before returning to London to lead the opposition in Parliament. He was briefly jailed in 1677, an event that restored public sympathy for him. He again retired in 1681 and devoted his remaining years to his writing and leisure. Buckingham died on April 16, 1687, two days after catching a chill while fox hunting near his Yorkshire estate.

MAJOR WORKS

Buckingham's literary career began in the early 1660s, when he began composing poems which were circulated among his friends at court. The first of his small handful of plays, a revision of John Fletcher's *The Chances,* was first performed in 1664. His next play was *The Country Gentleman* (1669), written with Robert Howard. In 1671 Buckingham's most famous and enduring work, *The Rehearsal,* was staged in London. The play is believed to be a collaborative effort with other Court Wits, but the extent of each man's contribution has not been determined. A biting satire about the theater, *The Rehearsal* features a play-within-a-play, written by the character Bayes. The play, which unintentionally (by Bayes) burlesques the genre of heroic drama, is observed in rehearsal by two gentlemen, Mr. Smith and Mr. Johnson, who critique and mock it. Bayes is commonly considered to be a caricature of John Dryden, although some critics maintain that the character more closely resembles the Earl of Arlington, Buckingham's political foe. No fewer than seventeen contemporary heroic dramas were directly parodied in *The Rehearsal,* and many more were referenced obliquely. *The Rehearsal* was extremely successful, and was revived over 170 times in the seventeenth and eighteenth centuries. In 1683, after his retirement, Buckingham adapted the tragicomedy *Philaster* by Fletcher and Francis Beaumont and retitled it *The Restauration.* It has never been staged.

CRITICAL RECEPTION

Buckingham's most successful work—and the one that has attracted the most critical attention—is *The Rehearsal.* Several critics, among them Emmett L. Avery and Dane Farnsworth Smith have attested to the play's tremendous popularity in the century following its debut. According to Smith, it was "a burlesque so satirically pungent and so diverting that the public returned to it year after year." Smith has written that the work was a critical as well as a popular success, claiming that *The Rehearsal* was "the criterion of good drama for

more than a century, and still remains the best negative statement on dramatic art." Peter Lewis has cited the play's originality and considerable influence on succeeding satires, noting that Richard Brinsley Sheridan's enormously successful *The Critic* "is closely modeled on Buckingham's exceptionally popular play." G. Jack Gravitt has suggested that the play's appeal for modern audiences lies in the fact that it shares many of the conventions usually associated with a twentieth-century art form. "The modernity of *The Rehearsal* results," according to Gravitt, "from its anticipation of literary techniques and devices present in today's Theatre of the Absurd." Many contemporary critics have also commented on the scope of Buckingham's satire, which targets both political and literary figures as well as the conventions of theater itself, particularly those associated with the heroic drama. Lewis, for example, has described one scene that "simultaneously ridicules the arbitrary inclusion of dramatically irrelevant songs in many Restoration plays, the use of stage machines to obtain sensational effects at the cost of dramatic sense (visual burlesque), and those miraculous reversals in heroic drama accomplished by a *deus ex machina* (situational burlesque)." While most scholars, among them Robert F. Willson, Jr. and Richard Elias, have asserted that the character Bayes represents John Dryden, George McFadden has argued that the true target of Buckingham's satire is the Earl of Arlington. Margarita Stocker has contended that both views are accurate and neither should necessarily be privileged over the other; asserting that "in *The Rehearsal* political and literary satire are analogous, mutually reinforcing, and effectively inseparable. . . . *The Rehearsal* offers a logical political analysis of its time, precisely by diagnosing the ideology implicit in its literary target, the heroic drama."

PRINCIPAL WORKS

The Chances [adapter; from John Fletcher's play] (play) 1664

The Country Gentleman [with Robert Howard] (play) 1669

An Epitaph upon Thomas late lord Fairfax. Written by a person of honour (epitaph) 1671

The Rehearsal [with Martin Clifford, Samuel Butler, and Thomas Sprat] (play) 1671

The Restauration: or, Right will take place [adapter; from Fletcher's and Francis Beaumont's play *Philaster; or, Love Lies a-Bleeding*] (play) 1683

A Short Discourse upon the Reasonableness of Men's Having a Religion, or Worship of God (essay) 1685

The Miscellaneous Works of his Grace, George, late Duke of Buckingham, &c. 2 vols. [edited by Tom Brown] (satire and poetry) 1704-05

Buckingham: Public and Private Man: The Prose, Poems, and Commonplace Book of George Villiers, Second Duke of Buckingham (1628-87) [edited by Christine Phipps] (poetry and prose) 1985

CRITICISM

Arthur Colby Sprague (essay date 1926)

SOURCE: Sprague, Arthur Colby. "The Alterations and Adaptations." In *Beaumont and Fletcher on the Restoration Stage,* pp. 129-262. Cambridge, Mass.: Harvard University Press, 1926.

[*In the following excerpt, Sprague discusses two plays adapted by Buckingham:* The Chances, *originally by Fletcher, and* The Restauration *from* Philaster, or Love Lies a Bleeding, *by Beaumont and Fletcher.*]

BUCKINGHAM (?), THE RESTORATION

In *The Miscellaneous Works of His Grace George, Late Duke of Buckingham,* printed nearly twenty years after his death, appeared two excellent pieces entitled respectively, *A Prologue to Philaster* and *The Epilogue, to be spoken by the Governour in Philaster.*[1] Both, it is expressly stated, were written "by the Duke of Buckingham," and I see no reason to question the attribution.

Our next notice of the play is from the anonymous preface to the octavo Beaumont and Fletcher of 1711—in general a mere scrapbook. Buckingham, we are told, after writing **The Chances,** "bestow'd some time in altering another Play of our Authors, call'd *Philaster,* or *Love lies a Bleeding*; He made very considerable Alterations in it, and took it with him, intending to finish it the last Journey he made to *Yorkshire* in the Year 1686. I cannot learn what is become of the Play with his Grace's Alterations, but am very well inform'd it was since the Revolution in the Hands of Mr. *Nevil Payn,* who was Imprison'd at *Edinburgh* in the Year 1689."[2] Into the career of this personage—a petty writer and political meddler, whose unenviable distinction it was to be the last prisoner who underwent torture in Scotland—it is needless to go.[3] What concerns us is that he seems to have been an acquaintance and supporter of Buckingham's during the Duke's last years, and that as such he might conceivably have got hold of the play.[4]

This at last saw the light in 1714, forming part of another collection of the Duke's **Works.** It was now called **"The Restauration: or, Right will take Place,** A Tragi-comedy. Written by George Villiers, late Duke of Buckingham. From the Original Copy, never before Printed"; and was accompanied by the same prologue and epilogue. Payne, who had died four years before, is nowhere mentioned, nor is any explanation offered how the publisher came by his manuscript.

Finally, in 1719, this brief but emphatic notice appeared in *The Poetical Register* of Giles Jacob: "***The Restauration, or Right will take Place***; a Tragi-Comedy. Injuriously father'd upon the Duke of *Buckingham.* Never acted."[5] And this statement has generally been taken over, with slight variation, in subsequent descriptions of the play.[6]

It remained for Professor Firth to point out that "in the epilogue to his version of Philaster, written evidently in 1683, Buckingham sneers at Shaftesbury as one who claimed infallibility and railed against popery in order to make himself a pope. . . . The prologue and epilogue printed in Buckingham's **'Works'** are clearly his."[7] There can be no reasonable doubt, I think, that Shaftesbury was aimed at in the epilogue, and references to his flight and death, to his having gone wrong for "five years" (that is, since 1678, when the Popish Plot was first broached) are sufficient warrant for dating it early in 1683.[8]

The prologue, furthermore, makes it probable, though by no means certain, that Villiers was author also of the alteration. It runs in part:

> Nothing is harder in the World to do,
> Than to quit that our Nature leads us to.
> As this our Friend[9] here proves, who, having spent
> His Time and Wealth for other Folks Content,
> Tho' he so much as Thanks could never get,
> Can't, for his Life, quite give it over yet;
> But, striving still to please you, hopes he may,
> Without a Grievance, try to mend a Play.
> Perhaps, he wish'd it might have been his Fate
> To lend a helping Hand to mend the State:
> Tho' he conceives, as things have lately run,
> 'Tis somewhat hard at present to be done. . . .
> He, for the Public, needs wou'd play a Game,
> For which, he has been trounc'd by public Fame;
> And, to speak Truth, so he deserv'd to be,
> For his Dull, Clownish Singularity:
> For, when the Fashion is to break ones Trust,
> 'Tis Rudeness then to offer to be Just.

Jacob's statement in 1719 is not in itself of much value.[10] What does throw doubt on the Duke's authorship is the indifferent quality of the alteration itself, and particularly the nerveless mediocrity of the verse. It is hard indeed to believe that the mercurial Villiers, at a time when he was still capable of writing with the vigor which characterizes the two pendant compositions, had anything to do with the lines which follow. Bellario's last speech in iii, 1, had ended:

—let there be
A tear shed from you in my memory,
And I shall rest in peace.

(lines 291 ff.)

This appears in *The Restoration* as:

—let there be
A Tear, at least, shed by you for me; and
I then shall rest in Peace.

(P. 37.)

In the next scene, Philaster had thus addressed Arethusa:

Mistress,
Forget the boy; I'll get thee a far better.

(lines 72, 73.)

And this is changed to

Madam, forget
This Boy; I'll get you one a great deal better.

(P. 39.)

But, not to multiply examples, in the last scene of the fourth act the same personage had pleaded:

Forgive me thou that art the wealth
Of Poor Philaster.[11]

The later hero exclaims:

Oh,
Endymion! Thou that art the Wealth of poor
Philander, and that I have us'd so ill;
Pray let my Crimes be punish'd as they ought,
And don't forgive me, I deserve it not.[12]

Whoever the author was, he had taken cognizance of Dryden's strictures on the tragi-comedy. These were particularly concerned with the behavior of the hero. Fletcher "neither understood correct plotting, nor that which they call 'the decorum of the stage'"; he who would consider the play "will find it much below the applause which is now given it. He will see Philaster wounding his mistress, and afterwards his boy, to save himself; not to mention the Clown, who enters immediately, and not only has the advantage of the combat against the hero, but diverts you from your serious concernment, with his ridiculous and absurd raillery."[13] By the omission of one hemistich ("Oh, do you breathe?")[14] and the addition of a stage direction ("Clown Falls")[15] the victory is now definitely bestowed on Philaster; and a very small but essential change, noted in the analysis, would have satisfied Dryden, in his right mind, on the general subject of the Country Fellow.

The character of the hero has, indeed, been conscientiously reinterpreted. He still wounds both his mistress and the page, but in each case the circumstances are different. Finding Bellario and Arethusa together,[16] he now rushes at them in a frenzy of indignation, and, aiming at the page, wounds his mistress. He is at first ignorant of the accident, and on learning of it is moved to contrition. He still fights with the clown, but afterwards lingers, and when Arethusa bids him flee replies: "D'ye think I'll leave you thus to save my Life."[17] Going at last, he forgives her, though still suspecting that she is guilty. When next we see him he is utterly miserable. He comes upon Bellario asleep and decides to kill him, though "very loth to do so." "Who can trust a woman's word?" he asks himself.

I'm sure I saw him take her in his Arms;
And he deserves to lose his Life for that.[18]

Bellario wakes—and is wounded, pleading that his lord be not angry with him. In other words, Philaster never intends to harm Arethusa, and in wounding Bellario has no thought of saving his own skin, but only of doing an act of justice. Moreover, nearly two pages are added to the later scene[19] in which he begs forgiveness. Arethusa tells him she has a priest ready to marry them, but for her sake, fearing the King's anger, he refuses. She swears to take her own life if he persists; and, finding himself "outdone . . . in all the kindest Proofs of Love," he agrees: "Let's talk no more, but love, love till we die."[20]

One other character has been consistently restudied. The Pharamond of the Jacobean play, though much of a braggart and something of a fool, is still within hailing distance of the conceivable. Thrasomond, his successor, is a complete buffoon throughout, "a pretty forward Boy about four and twenty."[21] In the initial scene, his "Governour" prompts him with "You must be angry, Sir."[22] After the discovery of his *liaison* with Megra (which is now wholly ridiculous) he makes no show of resistance, but is taken sneaking out of the back door "in Drawers, muffled up in a Cloak."[23] And later still he lives up to his new character by swearing, when the Princess bids him, "Why then i' fecks I will."[24] It was, indeed, only in the low comedy scene with the citizens that the reviser felt satisfied to leave him as he was.

The *dramatis personae* have all been rechristened, though, for metrical reasons perhaps, their new names agree with the old in accentuation and number of syllables. Philaster is now Philander; Dion, Cleon; Pharamond, Thrasomond; Thrasilene, Agremont; and Cleremont, Adelard: Arethusa is Araminta; Megra, Alga; Galatea, Melisinda; and Euphrasia-Bellario is Euphrosyne, as Cleon's daughter—Endymion, as Philander's page. Thrasomond's "Governour" is the only added character, and takes little part in the action of the play. In the opening scene, to be sure, we find him talking with the ladies, and later prompting his royal pupil; but thereafter he disappears until we reach the epilogue.

Philander enters a little earlier than Philaster had—in time for an aside, "Thou ugly silly Rogue," following Thrasomond's prolonged blast of self-praise. But Alga (Megra) and Melisinda (Galatea) no longer comment on the two princes—which is a pity—and there is abridgment both at the beginning and end.[25] Some of Arethusa's best lines were sacrificed early in scene 2,[26] and her interview with her lover has been largely re-written. It is a coy princess we have now, and one who no longer speaks out. Philander, too, is a conventional gallant who spares no protestation when once he has been given his cue. On the other hand, the description of Bellario, and the quarrel between Philaster and Pharamond, are taken over with little variation.

This is also the case with the first scene of Act ii. The second scene, in which Pharamond made an assignation with Megra, overheard by Galatea, was dropped, the report of Melisinda to the Princess suffing, in the later playwright's opinion, to prepare his audience for the sensational events to come. Scene 3 of the original is, accordingly, scene 2 in the alteration—and is practically unchanged. It had been followed by the good-nights of the ladies and courtiers, with Pharamond's remarks that he was hunting, next morning, and the notice taken of Bellario by both Megra and Dion.[27] The reviser felt no compunction in reducing this to a line or two, and was wrong in so doing. The original is then taken up again, and is followed, with some cuts and minor changes,[28] to Alga's denunciation of the Princess. This had been imperfectly motivated in the old play, but we knew something, at any rate, about the "lascivious lady" who made it, and that she had taken notice of the new page. In the alteration, Alga is practically a new character, and her accusation is a bolt from the blue.

The third act is retained about as it stood.[29] The fourth, however, is very much changed. The principal divergences have already been described, but there are others not without interest. The hunting scene at the beginning (realistic background again) was cut, and the same fate overtook the jocular talk of the two woodmen.[30] The play is resumed with Philander's soliloquy beginning, "Oh, that I had been nourish'd in these woods,"[31] Endymion, after an added word or two for the audience's sake,[32] breaks in upon his reverie, and the scene then proceeds like its prototype.[33] The Country Fellow enters at the beginning of scene 2, explains his presence by remarking that he wants to see the King, then exit. This transposition serves to avoid the awkwardness, which Dryden had felt, in the succeeding episode. What follows, except for the changes already discussed, is substantially unaltered up to the end of the act,[34] where some lines of an expositional nature—in part from v, 1—are added to the brief remarks of Cleremont and Dion, the latter's successor concluding with: "I can't imagine what all this should mean."

The last act opens with Philaster's contrition (v, 2, of the old play), followed immediately by the added pages concerning the marriage, already mentioned. Then comes, at the beginning of the second scene, a patch of exposition—again in part from v, 1. The rest represents *Philaster*, v, 3, much reduced.[35] The King becomes sententious toward the end, and is no longer merely panicky. But he prepares us for his final act of wickedness:

> I see I must release him now: It goes
> Against my Heart to do a virtuous Act;
> But there's no Remedy. Who's there, Go bring
> *Philander* hither.[36]

The baiting of Pharamond is retained as scene 3, and is followed by the original conclusion (4), as usual somewhat abridged.[37]

. . . . .

BUCKINGHAM, *THE CHANCES*

Swinburne, speaking of *The Knight of the Burning Pestle,* calls it "at least as superior to **The Rehearsal** at all points as the fifth act of *The Chances* substituted by the author of **The Rehearsal** for Fletcher's original fifth act is superior in force, character, and humour to that hasty and headlong scrawl of a sketch."[38] Without going into the comparative merits of the two excellent burlesques first mentioned, I think there can be no doubt that Buckingham left *The Chances* a much better play than he found it. Through the first three acts Fletcher had worked with unusual zest. A romantic Spanish story which must have delighted him[39] was being retold with the swiftness and vigor of an adroit technician. Don John and old Gillian, the landlady, were already among his best portraits. The plot had reached its climax, but there was still, in the disappearance of the First Constantia already motivated, and the foreshadowings[40] of a Second Constantia, abundant material for recomplication. Yet here he faltered. What remained to be done could not have presented much difficulty. The pursuit of Petruchio's sister might always have led to Antonio's mistress, and *vice versa,* with mutual jealousy on the part of the Spanish students, both of whom would be suspected all the while by Petruchio and the Duke. So in Act iv we have the discovery of the First Constantia's disappearance, attended by bickering and heartburning all round, and the running down of one false scent with the impudent Second Constantia at the end. But in the last act the pursuers are separated but momentarily, and the only interest that remains is how, and where, they shall find the lost lady. The hocus-pocus at Peter Vecchio's probably amused a contemporary audience—which is about all that can be said for it.[41] And as we look back, Langbaine's story comes to mind: how he had read or heard tell that Fletcher used to carry three acts to the players, and, if they accepted these, would "huddle up" the other two.[42]

Villiers not only perceived the weakness of these concluding scenes but lighted upon a remedy. By scattering the pursuers, the Second Constantia might be kept at large, and then anything was possible. The result is a rapid succession of episodes, enlivened by a fine (if lawless) wit, and rivalling the best of the earlier incidents for sheer dash. There were gains in characterization as well. Fletcher's Second Constantia is on the stage only a few minutes, and her attendant bawd no longer. In that time they are clearly enough sketched as stock characters, immediately recognizable to the audience and by no means undiverting in themselves. Buckingham chose to individualize both, but particularly the bawd, now called "Mother to the Second Constantia." The incongruity of her affectations of precise good breeding is richly humorous in view of her moral situation. There is in her gabbling something of Mrs. Peacham, something of Mrs. Malaprop—though not the single quality for which either of those estimable ladies is remembered. "As I'm a Christian," she says (it is a favorite expression of hers), "as I'm a Christian, my Position is; That no true Beauty can be lodg'd in that Creature, who is not in some measure buoy'd up with a just sense of what is incumbent to the devoir of a Person of Quality . . . When once a Person fails in Fundamentals she's at a period with me. Besides, with all her wit, *Constantia* is but a Fool, and calls all the Meniarderies of a bonne mine, affectation."[43] And this same Constantia, who finds that "to have always a remorse, and ne'r do anything that should cause it, is intolerable,"[44] must be regarded as no unworthy daughter. "Come, pray unmasque," Don John pleads. "Then turn away your face," she replies, "for I'm resolv'd you shall not see a bit of mine till I have set it in order, and then"—"What?" he asks—"I'll strike you dead."[45]

In short, Fletcher's comedy has been genuinely improved by its Restoration adapter—a somewhat extraordinary thing in itself. And the improvement has been gained by entering fully into the spirit of the original, and applying a simple technical device by which that spirit might be maintained at its best.[46]

Through ii, 3, Villiers follows Fletcher with great fidelity.[47] There are only slight departures in the beginning of the fourth scene—that in which Don John is employed by Petruchio to carry his challenge to the Duke. But in the ensuing dialogue between Don Frederick and Don John,[48] it is worth noting, perhaps, that no mention is made of the mysterious lady's being the same Constantia whom they "were errant two months after." Instead, Don John comments whimsically on what Petruchio has told him, and on the possibility that "in time" the lady might "fall to their shares."

The first scene of Act iii is again substantially Fletcher's, up to Don John's repartee with the landlady,[49] where one regrets to see that the latter is deprived of her caus-

tic reminiscences.[50] The second scene has been curiously treated. The dialogue remains Fletcher's—except for a few cementing phrases of Buckingham's—but is entirely rearranged[51] and reduced to prose.[52] As it stands, Antonio no longer cries for a wench, his song of John Dorrie is not introduced but only alluded to, and his truculent final speech no longer regales us:

> Farewell: and if you find him,
> The mad slave that thus slash'd me, commend me to
> him,
> And bid him keep his skin close.

The third scene—again verse—is a reduction of the corresponding scene in the original; and the same may be said of the fourth. In the fifth,[53] on the contrary, we have prose for verse, and some differences, one or two of them worthy of attention. A man is introduced for Francisco to question, and the impropriety of an overheard soliloquy is thus avoided. Also, the Second Constantia is spoken of as accompanied by a woman—a "grave conductress" who "twattled as they went along." Fletcher had ended his act with the reappearance of the Duke and Petruchio,[54] interrupting the quarrel of the two students. Villiers adds two more scenes.[55] The first (6) comes in the main from iv, 2, of the older comedy. It is once more prose, which continues to the end of the play. The adapter, curiously enough, still has Antonio send for a conjuror, though the Peter Vecchio episode was not to be utilized. Minor changes are determined by the fact that in the revision Constantia's mother is the chief conspirator against Antonio, Francisco's part being reduced almost to nothing.[56] The last scene (7) opens with the discovery of the First Constantia's flight, an episode recounted at the beginning of the fourth act of the original. But now the Duke and Petruchio are not convinced by what the students can say in their defence, and a duel is hinted. The scene, thus developed, closes effectively with the concluding lines of Fletcher's fourth act,[57] as Don John dismisses the subject with a dry jest, the older dramatist's last contribution to the comedy:

FRED.

> If she be not found, we must fight

JO.

> I am glad on 't, I have not fought a great while.

FRED.

> If we die—

JO.

> There 's so much money sav'd in Lechery. . . .

The new fourth act shows us the Second Constantia and her mother, making for the port. We learn that Constantia had been sold by the old woman, and that she had not found the purchaser, Antonio, to her taste. "This sinning without pleasure I cannot endure," she says, and vows henceforth "to live for ever chast, or find out some handsome young fellow I can love."[58] The mother, meanwhile, cannot resist a short halt at a tavern, and Constantia follows her in, determining, however, to seek her freedom. Enter Don John (scene 2), who likes the appearance of the tavern and decides to forego his search for the First Constantia and go in. He meets the Second Constantia coming out. She readily obtains his promise to take her where she may "be secured a while from the sight of any one whatsoever," and they go off together—Don John "in another world" with delight. Frederick is questioning Francisco at the beginning of the next scene (3). Francisco insists that he has seen Don John with Constantia, and Frederick is greatly alarmed. They "step behind this Shop" as Don John and his mistress enter. Don John shows Constantia into a house, and is following when Frederick stops him. A furious quarrel ensues. Francisco, still insisting that John's companion is Constantia, gets a blow for his pains, and runs out. The students fight. A new scene (4) begins as the Duke and Petruchio interrupt them. Frederick declares that he has just seen John "lock Constantia up in that house." John denies it, but will not let them in because of his promise. They threaten a general attack, and old Antonio, now entering, chivalrously takes his part. The newcomer is agreed on as a mediator, and goes in to determine the identity of the lady. A moment or two later, Don John's servant rushes on the stage, crying out that Antonio has "run out o' the back door . . . after the Gentlewoman."

Act v opens with the entrance of Antonio's servant, accompanied by "Constables and Officers" (all drunk, as it happens) in pursuit of the Second Constantia and her mother. That they are on the wrong scent, however, is evinced by the appearance of Petruchio's sister, in the second scene, who tells us that they have just arrested the landlady. Don John enters, looking eagerly for his Constantia, and is too engrossed in that occupation to aid her namesake. The latter, seeing Antonio coming, takes flight, and Antonio follows. In scene 3 an amusing discussion of the Second Constantia takes place between the mother and a kinswoman. This is interrupted by the entrance of Frederick. After much talking at cross purposes he gets an inkling of the truth and hurries off to make amends for the injustice done his friend. The final scene (4) is launched with Don John overtaking his Constantia. She readily accepts his explanations, and they are going off together when "Enter 1. Constantia, and just then Antonio seizes upon her." A stormy altercation ensues. Finally, the Second Constantia threatens to make certain disclosures, and, to avoid the consequent ridicule, Antonio gives her up to Don John. His money is restored with great affability by the mother, who has come on, meanwhile, with Don Frederick.[59] The Duke and Petruchio appear in company

with the landlady, whom they have rescued from the constables. The First Constantia is graciously received by her husband and brother, and Don John then speaks the closing lines.

Notes

1. I, 9-13.

2. I, p. ix.

3. See T. F. Henderson in the *Dictionary of National Biography*, xv, 553.

4. In the *Miscellaneous Works* of 1705-1707, is a "Letter from *Nevill Payne* to a Domestic of the Duke of *Buckingham's*, upon occasion of his Grace's *Discourse Concerning Tolleration*," dated 1686 (i, 71). Payne had defended Buckingham the year before in a pamphlet called *The Persecutor Exposed*; and was honored by having addressed to him the Duke's *Essay upon Reason and Religion* (ii, 58).

5. P. 326.

6. For example, in Baker's *Companion to the Playhouse; Biographia Dramatica* (ed. 1782, ii, 304; ed. 1812, iii, 201); Genest, x, 154; Dyce, i, 203; *Var. Ed.*, i, 120.

7. *Dictionary of National Biography*, xx, 343, 345.

8. Shaftesbury died on January 21 (W. D. Christie, *Life of Anthony Ashley Cooper*, ii, 455).

9. Friend, that is, of the actor who spoke (or was to speak) these lines.

10. It is somewhat singular that the author of *Poetic Reflections on a late Poem, entituled Absalom and Achitophel* (1682), a sufficiently bitter attack on Dryden, should now condescend to borrow a name for Shaftesbury from the very work in which he had himself been ridiculed. Yet our epilogue contains:

    The most egregious of all Scribes could tell
    There never was such an *Architophell*.

11. Lines 123, 124.

12. Pp. 56, 57.

13. *The Defence of the Epilogue*, 1672, Scott-Saintsbury, iv, 229, 230. See also *The Grounds of Criticism in Tragedy*, 1679, vi, 271.

14. IV, 3, 104.

15. P. 50.

16. His jealousy is made more explicable by the omission of Bellario's appeal to him,—"My lord, help, help the princess,"—for which is substituted, "Are you not better yet?" addressed to Arethusa (*Philaster*, iv, 3, 26; *The Restoration*, p. 48).

17. P. 50.

18. P. 53.

19. *Philaster,* v, 2; *The Restoration,* v, 1.

20. P. 62.

21. P. 7.

22. P. 11.

23. II, 4, p. 25.

24. IV, 3, p. 52.

25. Megra has again lost by them. Minor cuts figure in practically every scene.

26. Notably:

> Whilst I
> May live neglected; and do noble things
> As fools in strife throw gold into the sea,
> Drown'd in the doing
>
> (lines 14-17).

MEG[RA].

27. Look you, my lord,
The princess has a Hylas, an Adonis . . .

DION.
Serves he the princess?

THRA[SOLIND].
Yes.

DION.
'T is a sweet boy: how brave she keeps him!

> (iii, 4, 19, 28, 29.)

28. The assignation, for instance, is now at Alga's lodgings instead of Pharamond's. The changed behavior of the Spanish prince has already been noted.

29. One change is worth mentioning. In the second scene, when Philander accuses his mistress of misconduct with her boy, she now asks:

ARA.

Why, did he tell you so?

PHIL.
It may be he did.

ARA.
Alas, then I'm undone

> (p. 40).

Araminta's reproaches to the page, later in the scene, are thus rendered more fully explicable.

30. At the commencement of iv, 2.

31. IV, 2, 33 ff.

32. It grieves me that I'm forc'd to disobey,
His last Commands; but 't is not in my Pow'r
To forbear speaking, when I look on him.
I'll make as if I wanted, tho' Heav'n knows
I can't, because I do not wish to live

> (p. 43).

The last two lines were suggested by iv, 3, 6 ff.

33. There are, of course, minor alterations. The following, for instance, is very plausibly taken from Pharamond and assigned the King:

> There's some treason.
> You, Galatea, rode with her into the wood;
> Why left you her?
>
> (*Philaster,* iv, 2, 138-140; *The Restoration,* p. 46.)

Neither Dyce nor Mr. Daniel chose to record the emendation.

34. One misses Arethusa's reproof:

> What ill-bred man art thou, to intrude thyself
> Upon our private sports, our recreations?
>
> (iv, 3, 94, 95).

35. Particularly the marriage speeches at the beginning.

36. Pp. 66, 67; cf. lines 161-165.

37. The omission of lines 80-85, 150 ff., weakens the episode of Bellario's confession.

38. *Contemporaries of Shakespeare,* 1919, p. 152.

39. *La Señora Cornelia,* one of the *Novelas Exemplares* of Cervantes. From this, however, he could get little help after the third act.

40. The introduction of the Second Constantia motive is not so well handled as it might be. Antonio could easily have mentioned such a person in iii, 2, while Francisco's soliloquy in iii, 5, leaves much to be desired on the score of clarity.

41. Don John is entertaining still, as he discusses the subject of devils, or breaks through all ceremonial restraint at sight of Gillian.

42. *Account of the English Dramatick Poets,* p. 144.

43. V, 3, pp. 56, 57. In the course of alteration, the landlady undeniably suffered, but we receive sufficient compensation in this second old trot. On the other hand, the degeneration of Antonio into amorous impotence can only be excused on the ground that Don John was to get Antonio's mistress at the end of the play.

44. IV, 1, p. 45.

45. IV, 2, p. 47.

46. Buckingham's conclusion lacks, indeed, the romantic flavor which distinguished the earlier acts, but in this respect Fletcher's was little better.

47. A few lines are cut, here and there (for example, in i, 1, and 8), and there are one or two changes of single words. Note that ii, 2, of the Folios and Buckingham is subdivided in modern editions of Beaumont and Fletcher, so that scene 4 above is scene 3 in the alteration.

48. II, 4, 58 ff.

49. III, 1, 74 ff.

50. Perhaps the purpose was to give Gillian a sharper spur to vengeance: she now goes out with "Well *Don John*, the time will come that I shall be even with you." In what is left of the opening dialogue, Anthony replaces Peter. Which servant belonged to which master was something Fletcher left to his noble successor to make clear—by substituting Peter for Anthony in i, 9, Anthony for Peter here and in i, 11, Gillian for Anthony later in iii, 1, and by omitting ii, 2, 10-13.

51. The order of the corresponding lines in Fletcher is as follows: 35, 36, 28-34, 2-19, 36-45, 22, 23.

52. As was also the latter part of ii, 4.

53. Scene 4 is undivided in the old editions.

54. III, 5, 54.

55. Five and six with him.

56. It may be worth nothing that here, and in i, 3, Buckingham has transferred the scene from Bologna to Naples. This is perhaps to be explained as due to a misunderstanding of iv, 2, 16, where Antonio's servant says the fugitives have "taken towards the ports." The alteration reads "port," which would not apply to Bologna: another seacoast of Bohemia could not be tolerated.

57. IV, 3, 142-147.

58. P. 45.

59. Buckingham makes the Second Constantia—not the First—turn out to be the "rare Creature" so long sought by Frederick and John.

Bibliography

I. ALTERATIONS AND ADAPTATIONS

Buckingham's *Chances.*

The Chances, A Comedy: As it was Acted at the Theater Royal. Corrected and Altered by a Person of Honour. London, Printed for A. B. and S. M. and Sold by Langley Curtis on Ludgate Hill. 1682.

Settle's *Philaster.*

Philaster: or, Love lies a bleeding. A Tragi-Comedy. As it is now acted at His Majesty's Theatre Royal. Revised, and the Two last Acts new Written. [Quotation.] London: Printed for R. Bentley, at the Post-House in Russel-Street, in Covent-Garden. 1695.

Buckingham's *Restoration.*

The Restauration: or, Right will take Place. A Tragicomedy. Written by George Villiers, late Duke of Buckingham. From the Original Copy, never before Printed. London: Printed in the Year MDCCXIV. (*The Works of His Grace George Villiers, Late Duke of Buckingham.* 2 vols., London, 1715.)

II. GENERAL

Baker, David Erskine, and others. *Biographia Dramatica; or a Companion to the Playhouse. . . . Originally compiled, to the year 1764, by David Erskine Baker. Continued thence to 1782, by Isaac Read, F.A.S., and brought down to the end of November 1811 . . . by Stephen Jones,* 3 vols., 1812.

Beaumont and Fletcher. *Works. Adorned with Cuts. Revised and Corrected: with some Account of the Life and Writings of the Authors,* London (Tonson), 7 vols., 8vo., 1711.

Beaumont and Fletcher. *Works,* ed. Alexander Dyce, 11 vols., 1843-1846.

Beaumont and Fletcher. *Works, Variorum Edition,* 4 vols., 1904-1912.

Beaumont and Fletcher. *Works,* ed. Arnold Glover and A. R. Waller ("Cambridge English Classics"), Cambridge, 1906-1912.

Buckingham, Duke of. *The Miscellaneous Works of His Grace George, Late Duke of Buckingham,* etc., 2 vols., 1705-1707.

———. *Calendars of the State Papers Relating to Ireland Preserved in the Public Record Office.*

Genest, John. *Some Account of the English Stage from the Restoration in 1660 to 1830,* 10 vols., Bath, 1832.

Langbaine, Gerard. *An Account of the English Dramatick Poets, or, Some Observations and Remarks on the Lives and Writings of all those that have publish'd either Comedies, Tragedies, Tragi-Comedies, Pastorals, Masques, Interludes, Farces, or Operas in the English Tongue,* Oxford, 1691.

Emmett L. Avery (essay date December 1939)

SOURCE: Avery, Emmett L. "The Stage Popularity of *The Rehearsal*, 1671-1777." *Research Studies* 7, no. 4 (December 1939): 201-04.

[*In this essay, Avery lists performances of Buckingham's most famous play, contending that it was far more popular in the century after its debut than was originally believed.*]

In his study of *The Rehearsal* and allied types of drama,[1] Mr. D. F. Smith has given in Appendix D a list of revivals in the eighteenth century of several plays which are discussed in the earlier chapters. Among these is *The Rehearsal,* Buckingham's play, which is treated at considerable length in Chapter II. In his demonstration of the popularity of *The Rehearsal* during the hundred years after its first performance, Mr. Smith has listed a total of 171 performances during the period from 1671 to 1777. In spite of the large number of performances there listed, the table represents a considerable understatement of the popularity of the play. The following list attempts to give all the performances of *The Rehearsal* during that period; in it I have starred the dates which Mr. Smith has overlooked. It will be seen that the performances here noted increase the total number of presentations of the piece during the period from 1671 to 1777 from 171 to 291, an increase of about seventy per cent.[2]

1671: T.R. December 7, 14.

1674: D.L. December 21, 28.

1686: D.L. May 6.

1687: D.L. January 20.

1704: D.L. November 18, 21. December 1.

1705: D.L. January 4. February 2. November 5.

1706: D.L. January 28. December 3.

1707: D.L. March 20. November 18.

1708: D.L. February 12.

1709: D.L. January 18. Queen's: November 18.

1710: D.L. December 18.

1711: D.L. January 29. October 26.

1712: D.L. February 25*.

1717: D.L. February 7, 8, 9, 20, 23. March 21, 28. October 17.

1718: D.L. February 3*. November 17.

1719: D.L. November 25.

1720: D.L. September 27. November 23*.

1721: D.L. January 18*. November 15.

1722: D.L. January 15*.

1723: D.L. January 28. November 29.

1724: D.L. March 7*. November 18. December 1*.

1725: D.L. January 29*. November 9.

1726: D.L. November 14*.

1727: D.L. January 2*, 26. December 1*.

1728: D.L. March 30*. November 1*. December 13.

1729: D.L. September 16*.

1730: D.L. January 23. October 29. November 19*.

1731: D.L. January 18*. October 26. December 15*.

1732: D.L. March 4*. April 25*. September 8. November 8*. December 15*.

1733: D.L. January 17. May 30.

1734: D.L. October 31.

1736: D.L. January 8*. February 6.

1739: C.G. October 10, 11*, 12*, 13*, 15*, 16*, 17*, 18*, 19*, 20*, 27*, 31,*. November 3*, 8*, 14*, 19*, 21*, 23*, 26*. December 1*, 3*, 7*, 14*, 18*, 28*.

1740: C.G. January 5*, 12*, 19*, 26*. February 2*, 4*, 9*. March 13*. April 10*, 15*, 24*. May 1*, 8*, 22*, 30*. June 5, 10, 13. September 19. October 18*. November 3*, 17*. December 3*, 18*.

1741: C.G. February 16*, 21*. March 3*, 14*, 21*, 31*. April 14, 24*, 29*. October 21*, 22*. D.L. November 21, 23, 24, 25, 26, 27*. December 4*, 26*.[3]

1742: D.L. January 25. G.F. February 3, 4, 5. D.L. February 6*. G.F. February 6, 8, 9, 10, 12, 13, 15, 17, 20, 23. March 9. C.G. March 29. G.F. April 28. May 7, 26. D.L. October 7, 8, 20. November 2. L.I.F. December 6*. D.L. December 7. L.I.F. December 8*. D.L. December 16.

1743: D.L. January 7, 17, 29. February 3, 28. March 7. April 4, 30. May 6. December 6, 8, 9, 28*.

1744: D.L. March 15*. April 12*. May 28*. October 19. December 27*.

1745: G.F. January 7*, 8*, 10*, 14*. D.L. January 16*. G.F. February 7*, 8*. March 14*. D.L. December 13. C.G. December 13, 19, 26.

1746: D.L. January 24. C.G. May 2. November 6, 7. December 18.

1747: C.G. January 13. G.F. March 23*. C.G. November 23, 24.

1748: C.G. February 5.

1749: D.L. December 20, 21, 22.

1750: D.L. January 4*. February 14*.[4]

1752: D.L. December 8, 9, 12, 13, 16.

1753: D.L. February 3, 26*. May 21.[5]

1754: C.G. December 30, 31.

1755: C.G. January 1. February 11*, 25*. April 14, 21. Hay. September 11, 15. D.L. October 17, 18. November 5*, 27*. December 19*.

1756: D.L. February 9*. May 15*. November 18.

1757: D.L. September 29. October 22*. November 25.[6]

1759: D.L. May 25. October 30. November 23*.

1760:D.L. March 13*. May 2. October 3. December 12*.

1761: D.L. May 22*. September 14.

1762: D.L. March 2. November 10.[7]

1763: D.L. April 21*. Hay. August 1, 11, 20.

1765: D.L. April 13. May 6. Hay. August 30.

1766: D.L. December 4*.

1767: D.L. April 25. C.G. September 14, 15.

1768: Richmond. July 27*, 30*. Hay. September 19*.

1771: D.L. April 6.

1772: D.L. March 26, 31. Hay. August 10*, 24*, 31*. D.L. October 21. December 7.

1773: Hay. June 18*, 23*. July 19*.

1774: D.L. March 14. April 8. Hay. June 27*. July 11*. C.G. October 11.

1775: Hay. July 31*. August 7.

1776: D.L. May 11. Hay. August 2.

1777: Hay. August 25, 27. D.L. December 13*, 15*.

The following year, 1778, saw **The Rehearsal** condensed to a three-act play and the close of its greatest popularity.

The acting of the play may be most conveniently divided into five periods. Of the first, 1671-87, we know very little, except that there were at least six performances. After 1700 interest centers chiefly in the actor who performed Bayes. From 1700 to 1712 that person was Richard Estcourt, who probably acted in all the seventeen performances during those years, although the advertisements do not always name the actors playing the parts. From 1717 to 1736 Bayes was performed by Colley Cibber, perhaps on every occasion, although the cast was not always advertised; at the most he could have appeared in the part on forty-seven occasions. With the retirement of Cibber **The Rehearsal** was dropped from the repertories of the theaters for a short time, but in 1739 a genuine revival of interest in it began, a revival which lasted a number of years. In the short period from 1739 to 1747 two performers were ri-

vals in acting Bayes: Theophilus Cibber and David Garrick. Once again one cannot be absolutely certain of the cast of all the performances, which totalled 135 in nine seasons, but it seems that Theophilus Cibber acted Bayes 74 times and Garrick 45 times. Six other performers attempted the rôle during the same period, but no one of them was nearly so popular as Cibber or Garrick. Dance, a minor performer, acted Bayes eight times[8]; Chapman acted it on three evenings; Foote played the rôle four times; Catherine Clive attempted it on one occasion; and an unknown actor appeared once. By 1748 the rivalry of Cibber and Garrick had lessened, for Garrick acted the part not at all that year and Cibber played it but once.

From 1748 to 1777 the play declined in popularity, there being only eighty-six performances in nearly thirty years. During this period the part of Bayes was chiefly Garrick's, for he acted it forty-three times. Theophilus Cibber appeared for eight performances before 1756, but Foote acted the part eleven times, chiefly in the Summer Theatre in the Haymarket. The other performers acted Bayes as follows: Shuter, five; Love, five[9]; Henderson, four; King, four; Lee, three; Wilkinson, three. With the retirement of Garrick in 1776, the last great performer of Bayes disappeared from the part, and the play lost a great deal of its popularity.

In the number of performances as well, Garrick leads the group. From 1742 to his retirement he played Bayes on eighty-eight occasions; Theophilus Cibber almost equals Garrick's record with a probable total of eighty-two appearances as Bayes. Colley Cibber is third, with forty-seven performances. Twelve other performers divide the remaining sixty performances in the eighteenth century, with Samuel Foote and Richard Estcourt as the only ones to stand very clearly above the others.

Notes

1. *Plays about the Theatre in England from The Rehearsal in 1671 to the Licensing Act in 1737*, Oxford University Press, 1936.

2. The performances here listed have been taken from the theatrical advertisements in the newspapers and playbills in the British Museum and the playbills in the Huntington Library; it is possible that an occasional projected performance did not actually take place. The abbreviations used are as follows: T. R.—Theatre Royal. D.L.—Drury Lane. Queen's—Queen's Theatre in the Haymarket. C.G.—Covent Garden. G.F.—Goodman's Fields. L.I.F.—Lincoln's Inn Fields. Hay—Little Theatre in the Haymarket (Summer Theatre).

3. The performances which Smith lists for C.G. May 19, 1741, and for D.L. May 26, 1741, apparently were not given; see Ad. Ms. 32,248-32,251. Smith

lists a performance for November 22, 1741, but this date would be Sunday; instead there was a performance on November 27, with the revival totaling six consecutive performances.

4. The performances listed by Smith for April 26 and 27, 1750, and May 3, 1751, were not presentations of Buckingham's play but of Mrs. Clive's *The Rehearsal; or Bayes in Petticoats.*

5. The performance listed for May 4, 1753, was also Mrs. Clive's piece.

6. The performance listed for April 21, 1757, apparently was not given. 1758: C.G. January 24. D.L. May 19*. November 16. The performance on November 16 is misdated November 15 by Smith.

7. The performance listed for March 22, 1762, also was *The Rehearsal; or Bayes in Petticoats.*

8. It is not certain that Dance performed the part eight times, but in Goodman's Fields in the spring of 1741 a "Gentleman" was advertised for the part of Bayes. For the seventh performance the name of Dance appears in the bills; it seems likely that he had been the "Gentleman" earlier advertised. He acted it once more in Covent Garden in 1746.

9. Love is the name assumed by James Dance, who in earlier years had acted Bayes in Goodman's Fields.

Dane Farnsworth Smith (essay date 1953)

SOURCE: Smith, Dane Farnsworth. "Sir William D'Avenant and the Duke of Buckingham." In *The Critics in the Audience of the London Theatres from Buckingham to Sheridan: A Study of Neoclassicism in the Playhouse 1671-1779,* pp. 17-25. Albuquerque, N.M.: University of New Mexico Press, 1953.

[*In the essay below, Smith discusses Buckingham's role as a theater critic and his inclusion of the critic characters Smith and Johnson in* The Rehearsal.]

THE PLAY-HOUSE TO BE LET

Perhaps the first reference to the critic in the drama of the Restoration, like so many other firsts in the history of English drama, is found in the work of Sir William D'Avenant. His *Play-House to be Let* was probably acted in 1663. In this comedy the people of the theatre are discussing expedients for keeping the theatre going during the lean days of vacation. If they are to eat during these scanty days when the lawyers and many other regular patrons are away from London, the players and their retainers back-stage must so far as possible maintain a semblance of prosperity and popularity. Accord-

ingly, the discussion drifts to arrangements for a claque to support the coming performance. They decide to admit a friendly fat man who never fails to clap at every play.

Hous.K[eeper].

> We have some half hearted friends who clap softly
> As if they wore furr'd Mittens.

Play[er].

> We must provide our Party 'gainst tomorrow;
> Watch at the doors before the Play begins,
> And make low congies to the cruel Criticks,
> As they come in; the Poets should do that;
> But they want breeding, which is the chief cause
> That all their Plays miscarry.

Hous.K[eeper].

> There is least malice in the upper Gallery,
> For they continually begin the plaudit.[1]

Since during the off-season when the courts are not in session,

> Most men of judgment are retir'd
> Into the Country, and the remainder that
> Are left behind, come here not to consider
> But to be merry at such obvious things
> As not constrain 'em to the pains of thinking,[2]

noise alone will be sufficient to support their play.

Play[er].

> We'll hire a dozen Laundry-Maids and there
> Disperse 'em, Wenches that use to clap Linen;
> They have tough hands, and will be heard.[3]

The Play-House to be Let is really a *drame à tiroir,* a nest of plays. The portion of the piece to which the title refers serves as a prelude to three other brief but distinct dramatic pieces. Two of these are perhaps the earliest examples of the French variety of dramatic burlesque to be found in English. Though D'Avenant's play says no more about the critic, nevertheless, as a play about the theatre it is a forerunner of Buckingham's masterpiece, ***The Rehearsal,*** the first performance of which was the heyday of Restoration critics. Buckingham, in turn, is to anticipate Thomas Rymer, the trenchant critic of the "School of Rules." In ***The Rehearsal,*** at least, he and his ghost-writers represented the forces of French criticism arrayed against certain native defenders of the English heroic play. Without specifically raising the battle-cry of probability and decorum, or flaunting the colors of French or Italian classicism, his was the first militant attack on the independence of English dramaturgy—inaugurating a trend in criticism which later caused Thomas Rymer to turn against Shakespeare. Perhaps somewhere in the back of his mind the Duke of Buckingham dreamed he was another Richelieu, shaping the literary destinies of his country in the direction of classicism and conformity. The Duke, wishing to see that correctness reached the English theatre, sought to impose on Dryden and his fellows the edicts of French criticism requiring that every play conform to the laws of Nature, Reason, Good Sense. In doing so, Buckingham was to use the then aristocratic weapons of burlesque and ridicule that Sir William D'Avenant had brought over from France and had already made use of in *The Play-House to be Let.*

II *The Rehearsal*

The Rehearsal, that most prolific of all dramatic pieces, which scattered its progeny throughout the eighteenth and nineteenth centuries and then projected its powerful hereditary strain even into our own comedies, farces, and revues, for the first time in English history evidences the complete emergence of the critic in the audience as a prominent figure in the theatre and in the national consciousness of the British people. George Villiers, the Second Duke of Buckingham, its author, who is said to have called in as his collaborators Thomas Sprat, Martin Clifford, Samuel Butler, and probably Edmund Waller and Abraham Cowley, was a critic in the fullest sense of the word, and was typical in everything but his own brilliance, prominence, and influence, of all the amateur and self-appointed critics in the audiences of the seventeenth- and eighteenth-century English theatre. Like his stage counterparts in his own play and in the numerous imitations which followed it, one of his many diversions, in a life dedicated to diversions, was to go to the rehearsals of plays at the two patent houses.[4] He was, moreover, not only a critic but a dramatic author himself, both in writing **The Rehearsal** and in later life when he was the adapter of two pieces of an earlier age, one by Fletcher and one the joint work of Fletcher and his collaborator, Beaumont. Finally, it is noteworthy that Buckingham in 1663, years before **The Rehearsal,** had exercised the last and one of the most feared prerogatives of the amateur critic when he instigated a riot. The occasion was a performance of *The United Kingdoms,* an heroic play by Colonel Henry Howard. Although the disturbers succeeded in breaking up the performance, the Duke of Bucks, as our author was frequently called, extricated himself with difficulty from the melee and barely escaped injury.[5]

The Rehearsal, then, is a play written by a critic who was the epitome of glamour and prestige, "the greatest wit and wealthiest man in England," who a little earlier had served as the King's "foremost minister and policy-maker." If the Duke of Buckingham was a pattern for all who wished to make themselves conspicuous in the theatre by arraigning the author of the evening before the tribunal of wit and good sense, his play was a veritable arsenal of offensive weapons in the form of critical objections that could be vociferated against the av-

erage writer when his play went on trial at a Theatre Royal. Buckingham not only told lesser critics what to say, but also taught them how to say it in the simple and prosaic queries and pronouncements of the characters Smith and Johnson, guests at the rehearsal of Bayes's play.

The first performance of **The Rehearsal** at the Theatre Royal in Drury Lane in December, 1671, was a gala day for the critics. The play itself attacked a critic, for Bayes, the satirical butt of the play, represented John Dryden, not only the author of heroic plays but also their chief critical defender. And in the audience of the first performance there were rival factions of critics, the opponents and supporters of the play.[6] That the Duke was expecting opposition is, as will later be evident, clear from the text of his play. In the Epilogue of *The Conquest of Granada* (1670), the heroic play which was Buckingham's immediate target, John Dryden had given fair warning to all would-be dramatists, in his oft-quoted comparison of his own age with that of the Elizabethans:

> Fame then was cheap, and the first comer sped;
> And they have kept it since, by being dead.
> But were they now to write, when critics weigh
> Each line and every word throughout a play
> None of them no, not Johnson in his height, could pass.

The fashionable public of the Restoration was aware of its own brilliance in conversation, and, as Dryden indicates, was rightly proud of exercising its powers:

> Wit's now arrived to a more high degree;
> Our native language more refined and free;
> Our ladies and our men now speak more wit
> In conversation than those poets writ.

These lines of the previous year perhaps suggest the type of audience that would then be on hand at any first performance. Many of the spectators were Buckingham's supporters; yet at the commencement of the performance

> the friends of the Earl of Orrery, of Sir Robert Howard and his brothers, and other men of rank who had produced heroic plays, were loud and furious in the opposition. But, as usually happens, the party who laughed, got the advantage over that which was angry, and finally drew the audience to their side.[7]

The Duke had won the day.

The Prologue of **The Rehearsal,** though dramatically attributed to the leading actor in the play, announces the purpose of the author in preparing the burlesque. It expresses scorn for the heroic play and indignation over its popularity. A great lord like George Villiers, once a member of the household of James II and also Master of Arts from Oxford, with a background of Italian and French culture acquired in sojourns on the continent, is fairly nauseated at the delight that a stupid form of entertainment gives to English theatre-goers. Personal grievance, boredom, and the principle of *noblesse oblige* all prompt him to do battle with a type of public diversion as monstrous as the heroic play, which is itself doing violence to the highest ideals of the age: Nature, Art, Reason, and Wit. His Prologue tells the audience that this "mock-play of ours" is

> A posy made of weeds instead of flowers;
> Yet such have been presented to your noses,
> And there are such, I fear, who thought 'em roses.
> Would some of 'em were here, to see, this night,
> What stuff it is in which they took delight.

The new dramaturgy is so absurd that gentlemen can endure it no longer:

> Our poets make us laugh at tragedy
> And with their comedies they make us cry.
> Now critics do your worst! . . .
>   . . . . .
> I will both represent the feats they do
> And give you all the reasons for them too.

Finally, to translate Buckingham's thought into the words of Sir William D'Avenant in *The Play-House to be Let,* the author hopes "to introduce such folly as shall make you wise."[8] In fact, Buckingham continues, "If what was once so praised you now despise," *The Rehearsal* "will reform the stage!"

These brief glances at the author and the Prologue prepare the reader for a look at the play itself. This farce, burlesque, or dramatic satire is a piece of dramatic criticism,[9] written by a critic, partly about another critic, and was supported and opposed in its initial performance by two critical factions in the audience. It is not surprising, then, that Johnson and Smith, "the two pillars" on which rests the whole attack upon the poet of the heroic plays and upon the plays themselves, are also critics. And Bayes eventually confesses to them that one of the reasons why the play they have been invited to watch is so difficult to understand is that he has made it so to confuse the critics:

> 'Tis a crust, a lasting crust for your Rogue Critiques. . . . I would fain see the proudest of 'em all but dare to nibble at this; I gad, if they do, this shall rub their gums for 'em.[10]

But Bayes offers critical explanations only to act as a foil and serve as a target. Johnson and Smith, then, are the two most aggressive characters in the outer framework of this play-within-a-play. But they are men of reserve, completely without interest in the welfare of their host, and say just enough to tempt Bayes into foolish explanation and confession.

Critics Johnson and Smith are conservative men of fashion absolutely uncontaminated by the preciosity of the drawing-room where the gallantry of love-making and the coquetry of conversation called for metaphors and similes, or by the aestheticism of the boudoir, where a gentleman or lady might spend long hours reading the society romances of Madeleine de Scudéry and La Calprenède. Smith has just returned from the country, where he has heard rumors of the absurdities now rife on the London stage. He first asks how the business men of the metropolis are faring. Business men and men who profess to be men of business bore Johnson; he regards them as "solemn fops . . . incapable of reason and insensible of wit and pleasure." Like most critics in the Restoration and eighteenth century, Johnson is a gentleman, carrying out the code of a gentleman:

> Eat and drink as well as I can, have a she-friend to be private with in the afternoon, and sometimes see a play.

"But plays," he adds, "have become monstrous things . . . everything but thinking and sense."[11] Even as they are talking, Bayes comes along, and upon being questioned about his last play, invites the two pleasure-seekers to a rehearsal of his new one. They accept the author's invitation and accompany him to the theatre.

Both before and after the trial performance gets under way, these gentlemen ply Bayes with questions, professing incomprehension at various parts of his piece, raising doubts as to its efficacy and correctness, and relieving their own feelings of boredom in ironical praise and sarcastic comment. Bayes, vain, arrogant, and dogmatic by nature, nevertheless, when the occasion demands, shows himself capable of great patience and forbearance. He makes allowance for the incomprehension and lack of appreciation on the part of his guests on the ground that they are not acquainted with the new way of writing. He can, of course, ill afford to be offended by any critics who might otherwise be persuaded to support his play.

When their host is not at hand, Johnson and Smith are even more derisive and become denunciatory. The play is "very fantastical, most abominably dull, and not one word to the purpose."[12]

SMITH.

> What a plague, does this Fop mean by his snip snap, hit for hit, and dash?

JOHNSON.

> Mean? why, he never meant any thing in 's life: what dost talk of meaning for?
>   . . . . .

SMITH.

> Well, I can hold no longer; I must gag this rogue; there's no induring of him.[13]

But these fashionable observers enjoy the sport of baiting an author, and continue to draw him out and lead him on until it is time for dinner, when suddenly Bayes finds to his chagrin and rage that they have slipped away before the last act.

Though the rehearsal ends with Bayes in a state of complete futility, his words at the beginning of the play sum up his views on the character of Smith and Johnson and on that of Buckingham himself:

> There are, now-a-days, a sort of persons, they call Critiques, that I gad, have no more wit in 'em than so many Hobby-horses. A sort of envious persons, that emulate the glories of a person of parts, and think to build their fame, by calumniating.[14]

Buckingham, by including in his piece the very sentiments and feelings of Dryden, his enemy, was, of course, indulging in subtle mockery. He also let Johnson speak out with equal honesty against Mr. Bayes and his faction:

> These critics scorn to imitate nature; but are given altogether to elevate and surprise . . . a phrase they have got among them to express their no-meaning by. I'll tell you, as well as I can, what it is. . . . 'Tis Fighting, Loving, Sleeping, Rhyming, Dying, Dancing, Singing, Crying, and every thing but Thinking and Sence [*sic*].[15]

In the opinion of Buckingham, this is what Dryden himself stood for as a critic. That the hobby-horse passage is an authentic echo of Dryden's estimate of Buckingham as a critic seems to be corroborated twenty years later by John Dryden himself. In his *Essay on Satire* (1693), Dryden asserted that Mr. Smith and Mr. Johnson "were two such languishing gentlemen in their conversation, that I could liken them to nothing but to their own relations, those noble characters of men of wit and pleasure about the town."[16]

The Rehearsal with its mixture of sense and nonsense catered perfectly to the intelligence and the frivolity of the hour. Its parodies, like the strains of a popular song, were reminiscent of many a moment of inflated sentiment in the performances that preceded it, and immediately captured the attention of the amusement-seeking public. No other piece of the theatre in Restoration times created more talk on its first appearance or was referred to so frequently in the literature of its own century and the century which followed. Its continued popularity as a stage play, until it was supplanted by *The Critic* in 1779, was perhaps not entirely without bearing on the coextensive vogue of the critic in the audience. In making fun of D'Avenant, Sir Robert Howard, and Dryden, widely-known figures in the social and literary life of the time, and in burlesquing so popular a form of entertainment as the heroic play, ***The Rehearsal*** returned in spirit and technique to the dramatic cartooning of Aristophanes. It also revived devices of the beginning of the century, when in the stage quarrel between Jonson and two younger rivals in playmaking, theatrical lampooning took the form of the caricature of the rival dramatist, wherein one travesties one's enemy and presents him in the role of a fool.[17] Apart from the effect which ***The Rehearsal*** had on the heroic play, its chief result was to create an atmosphere of skepticism in pit and boxes and, in the average spectator, a distrust of all forms of dramatic illusion and a consequent avidity for realism. As the reverence of the public for the genius of authorship declined, there was a corresponding increase in the number and insolence of critics. Almost immediately, the sixteen-seventies, when the best work of Dryden, Etherege, and Wycherley appeared, became a new era of freedom of expression for the patrons of the theatre.

Notes

1. *The Works of Sr William Davenant K^t* (London: Herringman, 1673), 'Dramas,' p. 77.

2. *Ibid.*, p. 75.

3. *Ibid.*, p. 77.

4. Brian Fairfax, "Memoirs of the Life of George Villiers," quoted in *English Reprints*, edited by Edward Arber, *George Villiers, The Rehearsal* (Westminster: Constable, 1895), p. 9. Charles II granted patents, or charters, to two favorites, and thus created a theatrical monopoly in London, which, with an ever-increasing number of exceptions, extended from 1660 through the eighteenth century to the Theatre Regulation Act of 1843.

5. See George R. Noyes, *Selected Dramas of John Dryden; with The Rehearsal* (Chicago: Scott, Foresman & Co., 1910), pp. xxxi-xxxiii. See also 'The Publisher to the Reader,' *The Rehearsal . . . with a key* (London, 1710), pp. 11, 12.

6. Scott-Saintsbury, ed., *The Works of John Dryden* (Edinburgh: Paterson, 1882), I, 118.

7. *Ibid.*

8. D'Avenant, *Works* (1673), p. 76.

9. For an analysis of the play from the point of view of dramatic criticism and satirical method, see Dane F. Smith, *Plays about the Theatre in England* (New York: Oxford University Press, 1936), pp. 9-37.

10. *The Rehearsal,* II, ii, 26-30.

11. I, i, 21-22, 32-35, 36-37, 60.

12. II, i, 107-110.

13. III, i, 30-32, V, i, 129-131.

14. I, i, 336-349.

15. I, i, 48-50, 55-60.

16. *Works* (1887), XIII, 9.

17. The hostility which the heroic play first aroused in the Duke and his cronies has an English source in their common enthusiasm for Ben Jonson and his classical precepts. See Montague Summers, *The Playhouse of Pepys* (London: Kegan Paul, Trench, Trubner, 1935), p. 280.

Peter Lewis (essay date 1970)

SOURCE: Lewis, Peter. "'The Rehearsal': A Study of Its Satirical Methods." In *Die Englische Satire,* edited by Wolfgang Weiss, pp. 284-314. Darmstadt, Germany: Wissenschaftliche Buchgesellschaft, 1982.

[*In the following essay, originally published in 1970, Lewis explores the methods used by Buckingham in satirizing Dryden, D'Avenant, and others in* The Rehearsal.]

The Rehearsal is the archetype of most later Restoration and Augustan dramatic burlesques. A few pre-Commonwealth plays such as *The Knight of the Burning Pestle* might be regarded as burlesques, and, to judge from Jonson's satirical portraits of his contemporaries in *Every Man out of his Humour* and *Poetaster* and Dekker's equally incisive reply in *Satiromastix,* scurrilous caricature on the stage did not begin with the presentation of Dryden as Bayes in *The Rehearsal*; but in its total organization, the Duke of Buckingham's play was a highly original contribution to English drama.[1] It was also extremely influential, initiating the flow of Augustan dramatic satires and burlesques; the titles of some of these, like Gildon's *A New Rehearsal, or Bays the Younger* (1714) and D'Urfey's *The Two Queens of Brentford: or, Bayes no Poetaster* (1721), proclaim their debt to *The Rehearsal.* Although Sheridan's *The Critic* is sometimes praised as the culmination of the eighteenth century tradition of dramatic burlesque, it is closely modelled on Buckingham's exceptionally popular play, which it refurbishes in order to bring the dramatic and personal satire of *The Rehearsal* up to date. In *The Critic,* pseudo-Shakespearean historical tragedy like Cumberland's *The Battle of Hastings,* and not heroic drama as in *The Rehearsal,* is the dramatic target, and Cumberland in the form of Sir Fretful Plagiary replaces Dryden as the author abused. Nevertheless, Sheridan's methods of burlesquing Georgian drama and many of his satirical jibes are almost identical to Buckingham's. The conversation of the Puff, Sneer, Dangle trio in *The Critic* are obviously derived from those of the Bayes, Smith, Johnson trio in *The Rehearsal,* and Puff's interjections during his mock-play *The Spanish Armada* echo those of Bayes.

Buckingham's example undoubtedly moulded the pattern of much subsequent dramatic burlesque and remained powerful for over a hundred years.

Most commentators on *The Rehearsal* have concerned themselves with the following issues: the problem of the play's multiple authorship (Martin Clifford, Samuel Butler, Thomas Sprat and others are said to have aided Buckingham); the eccentric pre-stage history of the play between its initial conception in 1663 and its eventual stage production at the Theatre Royal on December 7, 1671; the changing identity of the Bayes-figure from Sir Robert Howard (Bilboa) in 1665 to Dryden (Bayes) in 1671; the elucidation of those satirical strokes aimed at D'Avenant, such as the broken nose incident (II, 5), that are incorporated in the main attack on Dryden; the discovery of the passages parodied and the plays alluded to in *The Rehearsal.* Throughout the eighteenth and nineteenth centuries, there was considerable disagreement among critics of the play, such as Dr. Johnson,[2] Edmond Malone,[3] Genest[4] and A. W. Ward,[5] but most of the points of contention were solved by Montague Summers in his useful critical edition of 1914.[6] Since Summers, the most considerable contribution to the study of the play has come from D. F. Smith who has compiled a comprehensive catalogue of forty-four different ways employed to ridicule Bayes and of fifty-nine aspects of heroic drama and Restoration stage presentation burlesqued in *The Rehearsal.*[7] Yet in spite of all the controversy surrounding *The Rehearsal* and all the attention it has received, very little attempt has been made to examine closely the various satirical methods used by Buckingham. Smith's study is a pioneering step in this direction, but although detailed and thorough it is by no means exhaustive. In particular, Smith does not analyse the burlesque techniques employed in the actual mock-play, Bayes's play within the play. Buckingham's professed aim, as stated in the Prologue, was to expose current dramatic trends, notably heroic drama, for the literary and dramatic nonsense they were; it is surprising that the numerous critics of *The Rehearsal* have not concerned themselves more with exactly how Buckingham accomplished his purpose.

The structure of *The Rehearsal,* derived from Molières *L'Impromptu de Versailles* (1663), is ideally adapted to its burlesque function, allowing for ample satire and comment on plot, characterization, style and diction, stage settings, scenic devices and theatrical effects. Apart from the direct parodies of heroic drama and the burlesques of its conventions that constitute Bayes's play, the rehearsal structure permits a commentary on the mock-play by two representatives of practical commonsense and sanity, Johnson and Smith, discussions between them and the author, Bayes, who exposes himself to ridicule with almost every word he utters, occasional mordant asides by the actors, and a satirical display of the theatrical deceptions and tricks which are always in evidence during actual rehearsals. The chief danger in using a rehearsal as the vehicle of satirical comedy is that the commonsense critics might have it all their own way: criticism might be too explicitly stated and not parodically enacted. Buckingham's success in avoiding this danger and achieving an admirable balance between the mock-play and the surrounding commentary is particularly laudable when it is remembered that no tradition of dramatic burlesque existed to guide him when he was writing *The Rehearsal.* Before analysing the burlesque devices used in the mock-play, the satirical methods employed in the surrounding commentary will be examined.

The dialogue of Bayes, Johnson and Smith serves to ridicule the most eminent authors of the genre, especially Dryden, to attack heroic drama directly, and to heighten the passages of parody and burlesque.[8] In spite of Dr. Johnson's refusal to believe that Bayes is a satirical portrait of Dryden[9] and A. W. Ward's ingenuous claim that Buckingham did not intend a crushing attack on Dryden as a dramatist,[10] all the evidence now available is quite unequivocal about the identification of Dryden with Bayes. Edmond Malone's account of the presentation of *The Rehearsal* proves beyond doubt that the name Bayes does indicate, as it obviously appears to, the Poet Laureate of the day, Dryden:[11]

> Much of the success, doubtless, was owing to the mimickry employed. Dryden's dress, and manner, and usual expressions, were all minutely copied, and the Duke of Buckingham took incredible pains in teaching Lacy, the original performer of Bayes, to speak some passages of that part: in these he probably imitated our author's [Dryden] mode of recitation, which was by no means excellent.[12]

Robert Bell's development of Malone's final point is further evidence of Buckingham's determination to make Lacy's Bayes as accurate a depiction of Dryden as possible within the limits of satire:

> Dryden was notoriously a bad reader, and had a hesitating and tedious delivery, which, skilfully imitated in lines of surpassing fury and extravagance, must have produced an irresistible effect upon the audience.[13]

There are also numerous allusions to Dryden in *The Rehearsal* itself, especially in Bayes's speeches:

> If I am to write familiar things, as Sonnets to *Armida,* and the like, I make use of Stew'd Prunes only; but when I have a grand design in hand, I ever take Phisic, and let blood: for, when you would have pure swiftness of thought, and fiery flights of fancy, you must have a care of the pensive part. In fine, you must purge the Belly.
>
> (II, 1)

This might appear to be vulgar caricature, but when Dryden "was about any considerable Work, he used to purge his Body, and clear his Head, by a Dose of

Physick",[14] and his love of stewed prunes was extremely well-known. Unfortunately for Dryden, a number of his personal characteristics made him a sitting-duck for a satirist, and Buckingham did not fail to make the most of them. Because he employs the usual satirical methods of exaggeration and distortion, Buckingham is obviously unfair to Dryden in many ways, but Bayes in nevertheless an extremely effective caricature and a brilliant stage-creation. In *A Discourse concerning the Original and Progress of Satire*[15] and in his conversation,[16] Dryden acknowledged the personal attack made on him in *The Rehearsal*; he obtained his revenge by reserving an honoured place for Buckingham as Zimri in *Absalom and Achitophel.*

Ridicule of Bayes is continuous throughout Buckingham's play, but the first act, which introduces the rehearsal of Bayes's play in the later acts, is a particularly relentless attack on Bayes. At his first appearance, Bayes is revoltingly sycophantic;[17] he is also boastful about his new play, but unable to explain to Johnson the meaning, which he confuses with the plot, of his last play. He can, however, expatiate on his imbecilic rules for play-writing, including his rule of transversion ("changing Verse into Prose, or Prose into Verse") and his view of invention—a mixture of witty aphorisms overheard in coffeehouses and sheer plagiarism:[18]

> Why, Sir, when I have any thing to invent, I never trouble my head about it, as other men do; but presently turn over this Book, and there I have, at one view, all that *Perseus, Montaigne, Seneca's Tragedies, Horace, Juvenal, Claudian, Pliny, Plutarch's lives,* and the rest, have ever thought upon this subject: and so, in a trice, by leaving out a few words, or putting in others of my own, the business is done.
>
> (I, 1)

Bayes reveals himself as stupid, proud, contemptuous and mentally blind in many other ways. He mistakes his own silly paranomasias, such as "I make 'em call her *Armarillis,* because of her Armor", for wit, and confesses that he wrote a part just for his mistress.[19] He comments that his Prologue and Epilogue are interchangeable and just as appropriate for any other play as his own. He plans to ensure applause at the performance of his play by arranging for "two or three dozen of my friends, to be ready in the Pit, who, I'm sure, will clap, and so the rest, you know, must follow". He also launches into a diatribe against critics, which parades his lack of self-awareness until the speech is ironically inverted into a diatribe against himself:

> for let a man write never so well, there are, now-a-days, a sort of persons, they call Critiques, that, I gad, have no more wit in them than so many Hobby-horses; but they'll laugh you, Sir, and find fault, and censure things, that, I gad, I'm sure, they are not able to do

themselves. A sort of envious persons, that emulate the glories of persons of parts, and think to build their fame, by calumniating of persons, that, I gad, to my knowledge, of all persons in the world are, in nature, the persons that do as much despise all that as—a—In fine, I'll say no more of 'em.

(I, 2)

Smith and Johnson do occasionally state directly what they think of Bayes:

SMITH:

What a plague, does this Fop mean by his snip snap, hit for hit, and dash?

JOHNSON:

Mean! why, he never meant any thing in's life: what dost talk of meaning for?

(III, 1)

SMITH:

Well, I can hold no longer, I must gag this rogue; there's no enduring him.

(V, 1)

But the ridicule of Bayes is so successful because most of it comes from his own mouth. In his presentation of Bayes, Buckingham provides the qualities he wishes to mock with dramatic actuality and, like all good satirists, does not rely to any great extent on explicit comments about those qualities.

In the other four acts, during which parody and burlesque assume increasing importance, the ridicule of Bayes is frequently integrated into the satire on heroic drama. By presenting the mock-play within *The Rehearsal* as a serious example of heroic drama written by a typical Restoration dramatist (Bayes), Buckingham intensifies his attack on the genre and at the same time creates many opportunities for abusing Bayes. Several passages in the mock-play exposing the clichés of heroic drama are interrupted by self-congratulatory exclamations from Bayes at what he believes to be instances of his originality and artistic brilliance:

VOLSCIUS:

But thou to love dost *Pretty-man,* incline: Yet love in thy breast is not love in mine?

BAYES:

Antithesis! Thine and mine.

PRETTY-MAN:

Since love it self's the same, why should it be Diff'ring in you from what it is in me?

BAYES:

Reasoning! I gad, I love reasoning in verse.

VOLSCIUS:

Love takes *Cameleon*-like, a various dye From every Plant on which is self does lye.

BAYES:

Simile!

(IV, 2)

Bayes's interjections of spell-bound approval at these trite tropes, which parody a dialogue between Zanger and Achmat in Orrery's *Mustapha* (1665), emphasize the imaginative poverty of heroic drama, as does his similar enthusiasm for the Physician's banal outburst of bewildered sorrow at the news of an unexpected death:

PHYSICIAN:

O ye Gods!

BAYES:

There's a smart expression of a passion; O ye Gods! That's one of my bold strokes, I gad.

(III, 2)

In the context of the mock-play, the commonplace expression, "O ye Gods!", very frequently used as an "expression of passion" by Killigrew, Settle and other Restoration dramatists, is transformed into a satirical lunge at the empty rhetoric of heroic drama.

In Bayes, Buckingham is, in fact, employing a standard Augustan satirical device, later adopted by Swift for his "personae".[20] Buckingham makes Bayes put the case for heroic drama, but in a slightly exaggerated form that reduces the case to absurdity. While expounding on the poetic "merits" and dramatic "subtleties" of heroic drama, Bayes unwittingly reveals all the flaws of the genre as well as his own pompous inanity. Bayes's self-satisfied description of his interminable "conquest", an allusion to *The Conquest of Granada,* is simultaneously Buckingham's condemnation of the unwieldy structure of Dryden's play:

And then, Sir, this contrivance of mine has something of the reason of a Play in it too; for as every one makes you five Acts to one Play, what do me I, but make five Playes to one Plot: by which means the Auditors have every day a new thing.

(IV, 1)

Similar speeches, in which Buckingham projects his satire through the "mask" of Bayes, abound. When Johnson inquires about the identity of Drawcansir, Bayes proudly outlines his hero's characteristics, but in such a way that Buckingham speaks through him to sum up the absurdities of Almanzor and his like:

Why, Sir, a fierce *Hero,* that frights his Mistress, snubs up Kings, baffles Armies, and does what he will, without regard to numbers, good manners, or justice.

(IV, 1)

Some of Bayes's pronouncements, like the above, occur during extended discussions with Johnson and Smith, whereas others are more closely related to actual parodies and burlesques. The scene in which Bayes complacently explains that he contrived the ludicrous meeting between the Gentleman-Usher and the Physician "for the better carrying on of the Plot" exposes both Bayes and the awkward expositions of some heroic plays to ridicule:

PHYSICIAN:

Sir, by your habit, I should ghess you to be the Gentleman-Usher of this sumptuous place.

USHER:

And, by your gait and fashion, I should almost suspect you rule the healths of both our noble Kings, under the notion of Physician.

PHYSICIAN:

You hit my Function right.

USHER:

And you, mine.

PHYSICIAN:

Then let's embrace.

USHER:

Come.

PHYSICIAN:

Come.

JOHNSON:

Pray, Sir, who are those so very civil persons?

BAYES:

Why, Sir, the Gentleman-Usher, and Physician of the two Kings of *Brentford.*

JOHNSON:

But, pray then, how comes it to pass, that they know one another no better?

BAYES:

Phoo! that's for the better carrying on of the Plot.

(II, 1)

The subsequent dialogue between the Physician and the Gentleman-Usher parodies the excessive use of "asides" and the whispering scenes in Orrery's *Mustapha* and Aphra Behn's The *Amorous Prince* (1671) and burlesques all such dramatic chicanery employed to establish mystery, suspense and tension.[21] In his attempt to justify the whispering between the two men, Bayes idiotically fails to distinguish between life and literature:

PHYSICIAN:

But yet some rumours great are stirring; and if *Lorenzo* should prove false (which none but the great Gods can tell) you then perhaps would find that—[*Whispers*]

BAYES:

Now he whispers.

USHER:

Alone, do you say?

PHYSICIAN:

No; attended with the noble—[*Whispers*]

BAYES:

Again.

USHER:

Who, he in gray?

PHYSICIAN:

Yes; and at the head of—[*Whispers*]

BAYES:

Pray mark.

USHER:

Then, Sir, most certain, 'twill in time appear. These are the reasons that have mov'd him to't; First, he—[*Whispers*]

BAYES:

Now the other whispers.

USHER:

Secondly, they—[*Whispers*]

BAYES:

At it still.

USHER:

Thirdly, and lastly, both he, and they—[*Whispers*]

BAYES:

Now they both whisper. [*Exeunt Whispering*]

[. . .]

SMITH:

Well, Sir, but pray why all this whispering?

BAYES:

Why, Sir, (besides that it is new, as *I* told you before) because thay are suppos'd to be Politicians; and matters of State ought not to be divulg'd.

(II, 1)

As is clear from this quotation and the previous one, Johnson and Smith's persistent interrogation of Bayes about the absurdities of his play forces Bayes to make numerous inane defences of his dramatic incompetence and at the same time mediates between the mock-play and the audience to point up the burlesque. In the bustle of a Restoration theatre, the subtle burlesque of *The Rehearsal* cannot have been easy to apprehend without the attendant commentary of Johnson and Smith, whose main dramatic function is therefore to drive home Buckingham's satire:

USHER:

> But what's become of Volscius the great?
>
> His presence has not grac'd our Courts of late.

PHYSICIAN:

> I fear some ill, from emulation sprung,
>
> Has from us that Illustrious *Hero* wrung.

BAYES:

> Is not that Majestical?

SMITH:

> Yes, but who a Devil is that *Volscius*?

BAYES:

> Why, that's a Prince I make in love with *Parthenope*.

SMITH:

> I think you Sir.
>
> *Enter* CORDELIO.

CORDELIO:

> My Lieges, news from *Volscius* the Prince.

USHER:

> His news is welcome, whatso'er it be.

SMITH:

> How, Sir, do you mean whether it be good or bad?

BAYES:

> Nay, pray, Sir, have a little patience: Godsookers you'l spoil all my Play. Why, Sir, 'tis impossible to answer every impertinent question you ask.

> (III, 2)

Smith's questioning about this parody of some lines in Aphra Behn's *The Amorous Prince* elucidates the more general burlesque of those "majestically written" heroic plays that communicate insufficient information about the characters and actions to be intelligible. Johnson and Smith's questions also elicit some of Bayes's finest self-deprecatory speeches, such as his dismissal of

Smith's intelligent curiosity about the totally unexplained meaning of Prince Pretty-man's baffling declamation, "It is resolv'd", as both ignorance of contemporary fashions and failure to appreciate original writing:

BAYES:

> Why, I must confess, that question is well enough ask'd, for one that is not acquainted with this new way of writing. But you must know, Sir, that, to out-do all my fellow-Writers, whereas they keep their *Intrigo* secret, till the very last Scene before the Dance; I now, Sir, (do you mark me)—a—

SMITH:

> Begin the Play, and end it, without ever opening the Plot at all?

BAYES:

> I do so, that's the very plain troth on't; ha, ha, ha; I do, I gad.

> (II, 3)

Smith's severely critical comment is sufficiently two-edged to be regarded as complimentary by Bayes, who is repeatedly duped by Johnson and Smith's irony.[22]

Deceived into believing that Johnson and Smith's ironic astonishment at the actors' refusal to perform his plays is genuine, Bayes rushes into a confession that reflects his own lack of judgment and not that of the actors, as he believes. His self-righteous laughter at the actors' "stupidity" also redounds upon himself:

BAYES:

> It was I, you must know, that have written a whole Play just in this very same stile; but it was never Acted yet.

JOHNSON:

> How so?

BAYES:

> I gad, I can hardly tell you, for laughing (ha, ha, ha) it is so pleasant a story: ha, ha, ha.

SMITH:

> What is't?

BAYES:

> I gad, the Players refus'd to act it, Ha, ha, ha.

SMITH:

> That's impossible.

BAYES:

> I gad they did it, Sir, point blank refus'd it, I gad, Ha, ha, ha.

JOHNSON:

> Fie, that was rude.

BAYES:

> Rude! Ay, I gad, they are the rudest, uncivilest persons, and all that, in the whole world, I gad: I gad, there's no living with 'em, I have written, Mr. *Johnson,* I do verily believe, a whole cart-load of things, every whit as good as this, and yet, I vow to gad, these insolent Raskals have turned 'em all back upon my hands again.

JOHNSON:

> Strange fellows indeed!

> (II, 2)

Johnson and Smith's frequent ironic praise of Bayes's verbal and formal monstrosities is another method of underscoring the satire. In the following passage, the Physician's "Allegory" burlesques all pseudo-poetic claptrap (a web of mixed metaphors in this case) that aspires to the status of true poetry:

PHYSICIAN:

> Sir, to conclude, the place you fill, has more than amply exacted the Talents of a wary Pilot, and all these threatning storms, which, like impregnate Clouds, hover o'er our heads, will (when they once are grasp'd but by the eye of reason) melt into fruitful showers of blessings on the people.

BAYES:

> Pray mark that Allegory. Is not that good?

JOHNSON:

> Yes; that grasping of a storm, with the eye, is admirable.

> (II, 1)

Johnson and Smith usually undermine the pretensions of heroic drama by the oblique method of irony, but when they do express their views overtly, they reveal themselves as upholders of Augustan sanity and reason who invoke the neoclassical yardstick of Nature as a measure of reproof:

JOHNSON:

> . . . and sometimes see a Play: where there are such things *(Frank)* such hideous, monstrous things, that it has almost made me forswear the Stage, and resolve to apply my self to the solid nonsense of your Men of Business, as the more ingenious pastime.

SMITH:

> I have heard, indeed, you have had lately many new Plays; and our Country-wits commend 'em.

JOHNSON:

> I, so do some of our City-wits too; but they are of the new kind of Wits.

SMITH:

> New kind! what kind is that?

JOHNSON:

> Why, your Virtuosi, your civil persons, your Drolls: fellows that scorns to imitate Nature; but are given altogether to elevate and surprise.

SMITH:

> Elevate, and surprise! pr'ythee make me understand the meaning of that.

JOHNSON:

> Nay, by my troth, that's a hard matter: I don't understand that my self. 'Tis a phrase they have got among them, to express their no-meaning by. I'l tell you, as near as I can, what it is. Let me see: 'tis Fighting, Loving, Sleeping, Rhyming, Dying, Dancing, Singing, Crying; and every thing, but thinking and Sence.

> (I, 1)

Johnson, Buckingham's spokesman for the norm of "sence", openly derides the current dramatic pursuit of novelty and specious originality at the expense of art and reason. Bayes, on the other hand, blandly deceives himself about the virtues of "the new way of writing" ("That's a general Rule, you must ever make a *simile,* when you are surpris'd; 'tis the new way of writing"), and unquestioningly equates "new" with "good" when trying to justify the irrationalities of his play:

JOHNSON:

> But why two Kings of the same place?

BAYES:

> Why? because it's new; and that's it I aim at. I despise your *Johnson* and *Beaumont,* that borrow'd all they writ from Nature: I am for fetching it purely out of my own fancy, I.

> (II, 1)

Shortly after this confession, Johnson rightly censures what Bayes calls "good language" as "very fantastical, most abominably dull, and not one word to the purpose", and complains, again in the name of Nature, that no scene in heroic drama is "like any thing thou canst imagine has ever been the practice of the World".[23]

At the opening and again at the end of ***The Rehearsal,*** Buckingham uses the actors of the mock-play to contribute to the cumulative satire of heroic drama and its authors. When discussing the play they have to perform, two of the actors are full of scornful incomprehension while another (the First Player) succeeds in clarifying Buckingham's objections to the indefensible practices of the Restoration stage by ostensibly defending them:

FIRST PLAYER:

> Have you your part perfect?

SECOND PLAYER:

> Yes, I have it without book; but I don't understand how it is to be spoken.

THIRD PLAYER:

> And mine is such a one, as I can't guess for my life what humour I'm to be in: whether angry, melancholy, merry, or in love. I don't know what to make on't.

FIRST PLAYER:

> Phoo! the Author will be here presently, and he'l tell us all. You must know, this is the new way of writing; and these hard things please forty times better than the old plain way. For, look you, Sir, the grand design upon the Stage is to keep the Auditors in suspence; for to guess presently at the plot, and the sence, tires 'em before the end of the first Act: now, here, every line surprises you, and brings in new matter. And, then, for Scenes, Cloaths and Dances we put 'em quiet down, all that ever went before us: and those are the things, you know, that are essential to a Play.

SECOND PLAYER:

> Well, I am not of thy mind; but, so it gets us money, 'tis no great matter.

> (I, 2)

The actors' criticism in the concluding scene is less direct than this but nonetheless valuable. After Johnson and Smith make their final protest against Bayes and his play by leaving the theatre before the rehearsal is over, one of the actors discovers and reads "a foul piece of papyr" outlining the final act of Bayes's play. This *"Argument of the Fifth Act"*, which alludes specifically to Aphra Behn's *The Amorous Prince,* ridicules the sensational dénouements of many heroic plays with their culminating eruptions of love and honour:

THIRD PLAYER:

> *Cloris* at length, being sensible of Prince *Pretty-man's* passion, consents to marry him; but, just as they are going to Church, Prince *Pretty-man* meeting, by chance, with old *Joan* the Chandlers widdow, and remembring it was she that first brought him acquainted with *Cloris*: out of a high point of honour, brake off his match with *Cloris,* and marries old *Joan.* Upon which, *Cloris,* in despair, drowns her self: and Prince *Pretty-man,* discontentedly, walkes by the River side. This will never do: 'tis just like the rest. Come, let's begone.

> (V, 1)

Like Johnson and Smith, the actors cannot endure unlimited nonsense and abandon Bayes's play with unanimous relief. Bayes's response to the departure of Johnson and Smith—"A couple of senceless raskals . . . such dull rogues"—strangely anticipates Dryden's

own view "that Smith and Johnson are two of the coolest and most insignificant fellows I ever met with on the stage".[24] Dryden's peevish comment about these two characters is a clear measure of their satirical effectiveness, as are his even more petulant and Bayes-like remarks in *A Discourse concerning the Original and Progress of Satire*:

> I answered not *The Rehearsal,* because I knew the author sat to himself when he drew the picture, and was the very Bayes of his own farce: because also I knew, that my betters were more concerned than I was in that satire: and, lastly, because Mr. Smith and Mr. Johnson, the main pillars of it, were two such languishing gentlemen in their conversation, that I could liken them to nothing but to their own relations, those noble characters of men of wit and pleasure about the town.[25]

In Dryden's defence, it must be acknowledged that he was virtually the only Restoration dramatist to achieve anything of any lasting interest in the notoriously intractable form of the rhymed heroic play. He himself abandoned the genre only a few years after *The Rehearsal* appeared.

II

The above study of the ways in which the commentary by Bayes, Johnson, Smith and the actors satirizes heroic drama cannot hope to do justice to the comprehensiveness of their criticism; only a reading of *The Rehearsal* can do that. But before considering the mock-play itself closely than has yet been done, it is worth adding that the discussion interwoven with Bayes's play is particularly successful in ridiculing all those ingenious contrivances,[26] improbable events[27] and miraculous discoveries[28] that mar heroic drama. Nevertheless, the true burlesquer like Buckingham cannot depend on barbed strictures and witty denunciations, but must organize his criticism as imaginative enactment as well as explicit statement. Indeed, good burlesque comes primarily from imitations of the poetic style, stock situations and dramatic clichés to be ridiculed that exaggerate the originals just enough to elucidate their absurdities and banalities. If the imitations are overexaggerated, they will depart too far from their targets to be effective as burlesque and will fall to the level of farce even if the burlesque intention is recognizable. In the following analysis of Buckingham's satirical methods, verbal burlesque (parodic, non-parodic and mock-heroic), situational burlesque and visual burlesque are considered separately for the sake of convenience: in *The Rehearsal* they are, of course, closely interwoven.

Despite V. C. Clinton-Baddeley's protestations throughout *The Burlesque Tradition in the English Theatre after 1660* that "unwinking nonsense, which owes nothing to direct parody, is the very marrow of burlesque",[29] direct parody is a vital ingredient of Augustan burlesque drama, particularly of **The Rehearsal.** Several instances have already been cited in connection with the Bayes, Smith and Johnson dialogue, but without comparing the parodies with the originals. By being placed in a context of burlesque, the parodies in **The Rehearsal** ridicule not only particular speeches from heroic plays but also all similar attitudinizing throughout the genre. The specific parody of Almahide's grotesque expression of tender commiseration and loyalty in Dryden's *The Conquest of Granada* is also a general burlesque of all such vapid love-attitudes and precious writing in heroic drama:

ALMAHIDE:

> So, two kind turtles, when a storm is nigh,
> Look up, and see it gathering in the sky:
> Each calls his mate, to shelter in the groves,
> Leaving, in murmur, their unfinished loves:
> Perched on some drooping branch, they sit alone,
> And coo, and hearken to each other's moan.
>
> (Part II, I, 2)

BAYES:

> So Boar and Sow, when any storm is nigh,
> Snuff up, and smell it gath'ring in the sky;
> Boar beckons Sow to trot in Chestnut Groves,
> And there consummate their unfinish'd Loves:
> Pensive in mud they wallow all alone,
> And snore and gruntle to each others moan.
>
> (I, 2)

The replacement of "turtle" by "boar and sow" actually evaluates imaginatively the strained similes and conceits responsible for the feebleness of love poetry in heroic drama. Very similar is Cloris's speech, "As some tall Pine, which we, on *Aetna,* find' (II, 3), which parodies Boabdelin's "delicate" lines to Almahide, "As some fair tulip, by a storm oppressed" (*The Conquest of Granada,* Part I, V, 2), by substituting a tree for a flower and developing the original simile in a consistently magnified way.

Ridicule of the hero is also achieved by means of parody. Many of Drawcansir's lines, which imaginatively define the huffing, puffing boastfulness and self-regard of the typical hero, are very closely modelled on some of Almanzor's most notorious speeches in *The Conquest of Granada*:

ALMANZOR:

> He, who dares love, and for that love must die,
> And, knowing this, dares yet love on, am I.
>
> (Part II, IV, 3)

DRAWCANSIR:

> He that dares drink, and for that drink dares dye,
> And, knowing this, dares yet drink on, am I.
>
> (IV, 1)

and:

ALMANZOR:

> And in that scene,
> Which all thy hopes and wishes should content,
> The thought of me shall make thee impotent.
>
> (Part I, V, 2)

DRAWCANSIR:

> Who e'er to gulp one drop of this dares think
> I'l stare away his very pow'r to drink.
>
> (IV, 1)

The parodic substitution of drink for love in Drawcansir's couplets unveils the petulant pomposity, bullying egomania and self-righteous swagger that pass for "heroism" and "fidelity" in Almanzor's solemn bombast about love and honour. The first of Drawcansir's couplets also ridicules the false rhetoric that expresses simple ideas in unnecessarily complex syntactical forms. For the critic not prepared to accept heroic drama on its own terms, Almanzor's frequent use of "dare" is indicative of puerile foolhardiness rather than proof of heroic stature. Buckingham seizes on heroic "daring" as being particularly vulnerable to mockery in the following magnificent parody:

ALMANZOR:

> Spite of myself I'll stay, fight, love, despair;
> And I can do all this, because I dare.
>
> (Part II, II, 3)

DRAWCANSIR:

> I drink I huff, I strut, look big and stare;
> And all this I can do, because I dare.
>
> (IV, 1)

Very similar to such direct parodies of heroic poetry are Buckingham's non-parodic burlesques of the unendurable dilemmas, stock poses and static debates of heroic drama. Trapped between love and fate, Prince Prettyman soliloquises about his "unendurable dilemma" in lines that expose the incongruity between the rigid unimpassioned couplets of heroic drama and the stupendous emotions they purport to convey:

PRETTY-MAN:

> How strange a captive am I grown of late!
> Shall I accuse my Love, or blame my Fate?
> My Love, I cannot; that is to Divine:
> And, against Fate, what mortal dares repine?
>
> *Enter* CLORIS.
> But here she comes.
> Sure 'tis some blazing Comet is it not? [*Lyes down.*]
> [. . .]
> But I am so surpris'd with sleep, I cannot speak the
>   rest. [*Sleeps.*]
>
> (II, 3)

This speech mocks a conventional heroic argument by deliberate exaggeration so that Pretty-man's dilemma is virtually analysed out of existence. In this context, Pretty-man's description of Cloris as "some blazing Comet" deflates all such far-fetched and hackneyed hyperboles generously scattered throughout Restoration tragedy. Pretty-man's collapse into sleep at the sight of Cloris, whom he has been adulating in his speech, greatly enhances the verbal burlesque of love scenes in heroic drama.

A similar rhetorical device of over-inflating the already inflated yields an even more memorable burlesque of a stereotyped heroic stance in Drawcansir's final speech:

> Others may bost a single man to kill;
> But I, the blood of thousands daily spill,
> Let petty Kings the names of Parties know:
> Where e'er I come, I slay both friend and foe.
> The swiftest Horsmen my swift rage controuls,
> And from their Bodies drives their trembling souls.
> If they had wings, and to the Gods could flie,
> I would pursue and beat 'em through the skie:
> And make proud *Jove,* with all his Thunder, see
> This single Arm more dreadful is, than he.

> (V, 1)

By amplifying the usual boasts of the semi-divine hero about his invulnerability, prowess and capabilities, this speech articulates the absurdities inherent in the braggadocio of the hero, whose "honour" is here implied to be an excuse for disdainful pride and blood-thirsty violence.

Buckingham's non-parodic burlesques ridicule not only the soliloquies of heroes, as in the above examples, but also certain kinds of dialogue that appear fairly frequently in heroic drama. Dryden's penchant for extended argument in verse[30]—Bayes admits, "I love reasoning in verse" (IV, 2)—is burlesqued by the scholastic quibbling and logic-chopping of the Physician and Gentleman-Usher which begins, "The grand question is, whether they heard us whisper? which I divide thus . . . into when they heard, what they heard, and whether they heard or no" (II, 4). Even finer is the following passage, which burlesques both the cut and thrust dialogue of interrogations in heroic drama and the poetic treatment accorded by Restoration tragedians to minds deranged by guilt:

AMARILLIS:

> Villain, what Monster did corrupt thy mind.
> T'attaque the noblest soul of humane kind?
> Tell me who set thee on.

FISHER-MAN:

> Prince *Pretty-man.*

AMARILLIS:

> To kill whom?

AMARILLIS:

> What, did Prince *Pretty-man* hire you to kill Prince *Pretty-man*?

FISHER-MAN:

> No; Prince *Volscius.*

AMARILLIS:

> To kill whom?

FISHER-MAN:

> Prince *Volscius.*

AMARILLIS:

> What did Prince *Volscius* hire you to kill Prince *Volscius*?

FISHER-MAN:

> Prince *Pretty-man.*

FISHER-MAN:

> No: Prince *Pretty-man.*

AMARILLIS:

> So drag him hence,
> Till torture of the Rack produce his Sense.

> (III, 3)

Leo Hughes's remark about the resemblances between burlesque and farce being so great "that it is often difficult to distinguish between the two forms"[31] is applicable to these lines, which appear to be farce but actually burlesque such exchanges as Decio's cross-questioning of Pyramena in Stapylton's *The Slighted Maid* (1663) and Polydamas's examination of Hermogenes in Dryden's *Marriage A-la-Mode* (1671).

Deflation of heroic pretence and pretentiousness is also achieved in ***The Rehearsal*** by the mock-heroic device of introducing into a potentially heroic passage some trivial commonplace or unelevated object:

PRETTY-MAN:

> The blackest Ink of Fate, sure, was my Lot,
> And, when she writ my Name, she made a blot.

> (III, 4)

The incongruous linking of "blot", a product of human clumsiness, with "Fate", an imponderable and ineluctable non-human force, is responsible for the mock-heroic debasement of the typical hero's affected contemplation of his destiny. Buckingham employs the same mock-heroic method, a means of attack to which heroic drama is particularly vulnerable, in the most famous burlesque scene in the play, Volscius's debate between love and honour; this closely resembles many such monologues in heroic drama, especially Palladius's soul-searching disquisition, "I stand between two minds! what's best to do?", from Quarles's *The Virgin Widow* (1649). In this case, the mock-heroic disparity is between the lofty, idealistic debate, usually couched in sonorous abstractions, and the metaphorical terms in which it is conducted here—Volscius compares his mental and spiritual struggles with the putting on and removing of his boots. The injection of these mundane and "low" objects into the otherwise "elevated" and high-pitched poetry ridicules the exquisite and essentially narcissistic self-torturings of heroes by bringing them into contact with concrete reality. In any good metaphor, either serious or mock-heroic, the vehicle and tenor stand in an illuminating relationship with each other; Buckingham makes the vehicle of his metaphor so incompatible with the tenor that it illuminates very clearly the glib, mechanical way in which heroic drama deals with the love-honour dilemma:

> How has my passion made me *Cupid's* scoff!
> This hasty Boot is on, the other off,
> And sullen lies, with amorous design
> To quit loud fame, and make that Beauty mine.
> . . . . .
> My Legs, the Emblem of my various thought,
> Shew to what sad distraction I am brought.
> Sometimes with stubborn Honour, like this Boot,
> My mind is guarded, and resolv'd: to do't:
> Sometimes, again, that very mind, by Love
> Disarmed, like this other Leg does prove.
> Shall I to Honour or to Love give way?
> Go on, cries Honour; tender Love saies, nay:
> Honour, aloud, commands, pluck both Boots on;
> But softer Love does whisper put on none.
> What shall I do? what conduct shall I find
> To lead me through this twy-light of my mind?
> For as bright Day with black approach of Night
> Contending, makes a doubtful puzling light;
> So does my Honour and my Love together
> Puzzle me so, I can resolve for neither.
> [*Goes out hopping with one Boot on, and the other off.*]
>
> (III, 5)

The isolation of certain passages, such as the above speech, from **The Rehearsal** to illustrate the particular satiric device of mock-heroic might seem superfluous considering the mock-heroic nature of the entire play; but although **The Rehearsal** mocks heroic drama, its burlesques only occasionally involve mock-heroic metaphors or substitutions. The parodies and, more conspicuously, the non-parodic burlesques in **The Rehearsal** usually function by exaggeration, although some parodies, such as Bayes's "So Boar and Sow, when any storm is nigh", are truly mock-heroic. Exaggeration is not the hallmark of mock-heroic satire, which substitutes the commonplace and the familiar for the supposedly exotic and the supposedly sublime to dispel the mirage of spurious wonder they evoke. Buckingham's mock-heroic substitution of London place-names for the

remote cities and lands, with their miasma of romantic associations, that are inescapable in heroic drama ridicules the way in which dramatists attempted to create "excitement" and "atmosphere" by incorporating magic-sounding names into otherwise drab and unremarkable poetry:

LIEUTENANT GENERAL:

> Villain, thou lyest.

GENERAL:

> Arm, arm, *Gonsalvo,* arm; what ho?
> The lye no flesh can brook I trow.

LIEUTENANT GENERAL:

> Advance, from *Acton* with the Musquetiers.

GENERAL:

> Draw down the *Chelsey* Curiasiers.

LIEUTENANT GENERAL:

> The Band you boast of, *Chelsey* Curiasiers,
> Shall, in my *Putney* Pikes, now meet their Peers.

GENERAL:

> *Chiswickians,* aged, and renown'd in fight,
> Join with the *Hammersmith* Brigade.

LIEUTENANT GENERAL:

> You'l find my *Mortlake* Boys will do them right,
> Unless by *Fulham* numbers over-laid.

GENERAL:

> Let the left-wing of *Twick'nam* Foot advance,
> And line that Eastern hedge.
>
> (V, 1)

Before turning from verbal burlesque to consider situational burlesque, it is worth mentioning that the General's first two lines above, with their perfunctory rhymes "ho" and "trow", burlesque the silly rhymes and distortions of normal word order that heroic dramatists were often forced into making by their need to find sufficient rhymes for plays of about three thousand lines.[32]

In the satirical texture of **The Rehearsal,** it is hard to separate the various kinds of burlesque. There is certainly no clear dividing line between verbal, situational and visual burlesque, and it should be emphasized that these categories, abstracted from the imaginative actuality of **The Rehearsal,** are critical conveniences. The exchange, quoted above, between the Lieutenant General and the General, contains both verbal and situational burlesque. As already pointed out, its language illustrates mock-heroic ridicule of verbal extravagances, but its action, or lack of it, burlesques the "recitativo" method of representing battles in Restoration drama, especially as exemplified in D'Avenant's *The Siege of Rhodes.*[33] It is nevertheless justifiable to isolate for critical examination the different kinds of burlesque that interlock and overlap in **The Rehearsal** as long as these isolated elements are not presented as existing independently of one another in the play. All the situational burlesque is, in a sense, mock-heroic, but it is usually achieved by satirical exaggeration of particular incidents and stock situations in heroic drama. Buckingham bases his burlesque of the ease with which kings are deposed, governments overthrown and peripeteia effected in Restoration drama on Leonidas's changes of fortune at the end of Dryden's *Marriage A-la-Mode,* but his satire is equally relevant to all similar "topsie-turvy" scenes in heroic drama and tragicomedy:

PHYSICIAN:

Let's then no more our selves in vain bemoan:
We are not safe until we them unthrone.

USHER:

'Tis right:
And, since occasion now seems debonair,
I'l seize on this, and you shall take that chair.

They draw their Swords, and sit down in the two great Chairs upon the Stage

BAYES:

There's now an odd surprise; the whole State's turn'd quite topsie-turvy, without any puther or stir in the whole world, I gad.

JOHNSON:

A very silent change of a Government, truly, as ever I heard of.

(II, 4)

The scene following this usurpation of the Brentford thrones contains a burlesque of "resurrections" in Restauration drama. During a foray concerned with the deposition, a group of soldiers kill one another, but are immediately brought back to life when Bayes sounds a musical note, and shortly afterwards join in a dance.

The final reversal that restores the rightful Kings of Brentford to their thrones and drives out the usurpers is executed with the aplomb and dead-pan humour characteristic of Buckingham's best situational burlesques. This scene satirises the tragicomic method of extricating heroes and heroines from inescapable difficulties and of resolving irresolvable dramatic actions by unexpectedly introducing a *deus ex machina,* who chastises the wicked, rewards the good, reinstates order, and brings happiness to the deserving:

KING USHER:

But stay, what sound is this invades our ears?

KING PHYSICIAN:

Sure 'tis the Musick of the moving Spheres.

PRETTY-MAN:

Behold, with wonder, yonder comes from far
A God-like Cloud, and a triumphant Carr:
In which, our two right Kings sit one by one,
With Virgins Vests, and Laurel Garlands on.

KING USHER:

Then, Brother *Phys* 'tis time we should begon.

The two Usurpers steal out of the Throne, and go away.

BAYES:

Look you now, did not I tell you that this would be as easie a change as the other?

(V, 1)

The funeral scene, the most extended situational burlesque in **The Rehearsal,** is a condensed and slightly heightened rendering of "serious" tragicomic dénouements. At the extremely dramatic crisis when Lardella's two royal lovers, believing her to be dead and unable to live without her, are about to commit suicide, Pallas, a supernatural spirit and a herald of destiny, arrives just in time to announce that Lardella is in fact alive:

KING PHYSICIAN:

Come sword, come sheath thy self within this breast.
Which only in *Lardella's* Tomb can rest.

KING USHER:

Come, dagger, come, and penetrate this heart,
Which cannot from *Lardella's* Love depart.

Enter PALLAS.

PALLAS:

Hold, stop your murd'ring hands
At *Pallases* commands:
For the supposed dead, O Kings,
Forbear to act such deadly things.
Lardella lives; I did but try
If Princes for their Loves could dye.
Such Celestial constancy
Shall, by the Gods, rewarded be:
And from these Funeral Obsequies
A Nuptial Banquet shall arise.

[*The Coffin opens, and a Banquet is discover'd.*]

(IV, 1)

The peremptory authority of spirits and the *deus ex machina,* the sudden, unbelievable revelations, the abrupt changes of fortune from imminent death to expectations of bliss, and the miraculous transformations of things (a funeral into a wedding feast) are features of tragicomedy and heroic drama compendiously burlesqued in this scene.

Although many other excellent examples of situational burlesque exist in **The Rehearsal,**[34] the incidents examined above are sufficient to demonstrate the satirical device. Very closely related to situational burlesque is visual burlesque, which, unlike the other forms of burlesque, can exist only in a theatrical presentation of **The Rehearsal.** The presentation of the entire mock-play is, in a sense, a visual burlesque of dramatic performances during the Restoration, but the term "visual burlesque" as used here has a more limited range of reference. Through the comments made by Johnson, Smith and Bayes about the staging of the mock-play they are witnessing, Buckingham is able to criticize overtly certain aspects of Restoration stage presentation,[35] but he employs visual burlesque to actually recreate, in burlesque terms of course, those scenic devices and theatrical effects he wishes to censure. In the last two acts of **The Rehearsal,** a series of visual burlesques accompanies the situational burlesques. At the end of the funeral scene when Lardella's "restoration" to life is celebrated by a banquet, visual burlesque of ludicrous stage properties is fused with parodic burlesque of the long-winded scene in Porter's *The Villain* (1662) in which the host provides his guests with food stored in various parts of his attire:

PALLAS:

> Lo, from this conquering Lance,
> Does flow the purest Wine of *France*:
>
> [*Fills the Boles out of her Lance.*]
> And to appease your hunger, I
> Have, in my Helmet, brought a Pye:
> Lastly, to bear a part with these,
> Behold a Buckler made of Cheese.

(IV, 1)

An equally fruitful integration of visual burlesque and situational burlesque occurs in the last act. When the genuine Kings of Brentford return to reclaim their thrones, they do not appear at the head of an army. Dressed in white and singing a parody of the Nakar and Damilcar duologue from Dryden's *Tyrannick Love* to an accompaniment by *"three Fidlers sitting before them, in green",* the kings descend from the heavens in a "triumphant Carr". This entrance simultaneously ridicules the arbitrary inclusion of dramatically irrelevant songs in many Restoration plays,[36] the use of stage machines to obtain sensational effects at the cost of dramatic sense (visual burlesque), and those miraculous reversals in heroic drama accomplished by a *deus ex machina* (situational burlesque). In the Thunder and Lightning Prologue (I, 2) and again in the staging of the Eclipse (V, 1), in which the Sun, Moon and Earth perform a

dance symbolizing the movements of celestial bodies, Buckingham visually burlesques the allegorical presentation of natural phenomena, a popular dramatic device in the Restauration theatre, by parodying scenes from Stapylton's *The Slighted Maid*; the Prologue is based on the "Song in Dialogue" between Evening and Jack-with-the-Lantern, and the Eclipse on another "Song in Dialogue", this time between Aurora and Phoebus.

Buckingham's visual burlesques are not always linked with verbal or situational burlesques. The various dances indicated in the mock-play, such as the chaotic dance of the resurrected soldiers (II, 5), the funeral-banquet dance (IV, 1), and the *"grand Dance"* immediately following the miraculous return of the Kings of Brentford (V, 1), are intended as visual burlesques of the many dances incorporated in Restoration plays, very frequently without any dramatic justification. Buckingham introduces these dances in an extremely capricious way; Bayes justifies the funeral-banquet dance by a flimsy argument—"we must first have a Dance, for joy that *Lardella* is not dead"—and the *"grand Dance"* begins even more unexpectedly:

FIRST KING:

> Come, now to serious counsel we'l advance.

SECOND KING:

> I do agree; but first, let's have a Dance.

(V, 1)

In addition to actually ridiculing the dances in contemporary plays, Buckingham's burlesque dances make it clear that dramatic sense and artistic cohesion were being sacrificed for the sake of stupendous stage displays. The stage-direction for the mock-play at the beginning of the last act demands a sumptuous set-piece that is obviously intended to burlesque by exaggeration those scenes in heroic drama in which the stage is crowded with kings, princes, lords, ladies and guards:[37]

> *The Curtain is drawn up, the two usurping Kings appear in State, with the four Cardinals, Prince* Pretty-man, *Prince* Volscius, Amarillis, Cloris, Parthenope, &c. *before them, Heralds and Serjeants at Arms with Maces.*

(V, 1)

Bayes's words about this spectacle, "I'l shew you the greatest Scene that ever *England* saw: I mean not for words, for those I do not value; but for state, shew, and magnificence", show that Buckingham is ridiculing the heroic dramatists' dependence on theatrical sensations rather than on literary art. The stage-direction for the battle sequence near the end of **The Rehearsal** is an invitation for the producer to design a purely visual burlesque of the way in which battles were presented on the Restoration stage:

A battel is fought between foot and great Hobby horses.
At last, Drawcansir *comes in and kills 'em all on both*
sides.

(V, 1)

This study of **The Rehearsal** has concentrated on the satirical devices employed by Buckingham, an aspect of the play that has not been closely examined in the past, but an attempt has also been made to demonstrate the comprehensiveness of Buckingham's satire. Despite its immediate popularity, **The Rehearsal** did not bring to an end the flow of heroic plays or even diminish their success. Even Charles Gildon, who seems to have thought that Buckingham's burlesque did eventually make the rhymed rant of heroic plays unendurable to Restoration audiences,[38] admits (through the mouthpiece of Laudon in Dialogue IV of *The Complete Art of Poetry*) that a widely acclaimed run of **The Rehearsal** could be immediately followed by "Plays not less throng'd, on which that [**The Rehearsal**] was either written, or at least which are guilty of all the Absurdities exploded in that pleasant Criticism".[39] Gildon goes on to draw the conclusion

> that our Audience is extremely stupid, and give their Approbation not by Judgment or their own good Taste, as being on contradictory Foundations, and that therefore to fix the Value of a Piece, we must have recourse to the *better* tho' *fewer* Judges, who understand Nature and Art. For either the **Rehearsal,** or the Authors were in the wrong; chuse which you will, their promiscuous Applause proves that the Audience must be in the wrong.[40]

The failure of **The Rehearsal** to drive heroic drama from the stage does not mean that it is an unsatisfactory satire, as A. W. Ward implies.[41] Literary satire must be judged by aesthetic criteria, as Gildon insists, and not by whether it produces any socially observable effects. Ward's determination to project Dryden's "gorgeous armour" from any "shafts of ridicule" blinds him to the artistic merits of **The Rehearsal** and to Buckingham's shrewed insights into the condition of Restoration drama.

Although the criticism of heroic drama contained in **The Rehearsal** is essentially destructive, Buckingham's ridicule has a vital positive function and is certainly not arbitrary. Buckingham attacked Restoration drama because it departed so far from the neoclassical aesthetic and ethical values of Nature and "Sence" that he wished to keep alive. In the Epilogue to **The Rehearsal,** Buckingham makes a connection between art and life, arguing that a society producing such artistic perversions as heroic drama must itself be in danger of abandoning reason and sanity for their opposites. The plea for an aesthetic revering classical lucidity and simplicity is also a plea for the establishment of social and moral standards based on Reason:

If it be true, that Monstrous births presage
The following mischiefs that afflict the Age,
And sad disasters to the State proclaim;
Plays without head or tail, may do the same.
Wherefore, for ours, and for the Kingdomes peace,
May this prodigious way of writing cease.
Let's have, at least, once in our lives, a time
When we may hear some reason, not all Rhyme:
We have these ten years felt it's Influence;
Pray let this prove a year of Prose and Scence.

Notes

1. George Kitchin argues convincingly that although a number of Elizabethan and Jacobean plays contain burlesque elements, the only play "which may claim to be a real burlesque" is *The Knight of the Burning Pestle*; see *A Survey of Burlesque and Parody in English* (Edinburgh and London, 1931), pp. 38-67.

2. See *Lives of the English Poets,* ed. G. B. Hill (Oxford, 1905), I, 368-370. See also J. Boswell, *Life of Johnson,* ed. G. B. Hill (Oxford, 1934), II, 168 and IV, 320.

3. See "Some Account of the Life and Writings of John Dryden", in *The Critical and Miscellaneous Prose Works of John Dryden,* ed. E. Malone (London, 1800), I (Part I), 94-106.

4. See *Some Account of the English Stage from the Restoration in 1660 to 1830* Bath, 1832), I, 112-119.

5. See *A History of English Dramatic Literature* (London, 1899), III, 362-365.

6. See *The Rehearsal,* ed. M. Summers (Stratford-upon-Avon, 1914). All quotations are taken from this edition, a reprint of the third edition (1675) containing all of Buckingham's revisions and amplifications.

7. See *Plays about the Theatre in England from The Rehearsal in 1671 to the Licensing Act in 1737* (London and New York, 1936), pp. 9-37. (In future this book will be referred to simply as *Plays about the Theatre.*)

8. Matthew Prior and Charles Montague modelled *The Hind and the Panther Transvers'd to the Story of The Country Mouse and the City-Mouse* (1687), their parody of Dryden's poem, on *The Rehearsal.* They apply a similar framework of conversation between Bayes (Dryden), Johnson and Smith to the passages of parody.

9. See J. Boswell, *Life of Johnson,* ed. G. B. Hill (Oxford, 1934), II, 168.

10. See *A History of English Dramatic Literature* (London, 1899), III, 363.

11. Dryden succeeded D'Avenant in the Laureateship in 1669.

12. "Some Account of the Life and Writings of John Dryden", in *The Critical and Miscellaneous Prose Works of John Dryden,* ed. E. Malone (London, 1800), I (Part I), 99-100.

13. "John Dryden", in *Poetical Works of John Dryden,* ed. R. Bell (London, 1854), I, 41.

14. Charles Lamotte, *An Essay upon Poetry and Painting* (London, 1730), p. 103 n.

15. See *Essays of John Dryden,* ed. W. P. Ker (Oxford, 1926), II, 21.

16. See E. Malone, "Some Account of the Life and Writings of John Dryden", in *The Critical and Miscellaneous Prose Works of John Dryden,* ed. E. Malone (London, 1800), I (Part I), 104.

17. Puff's initial entrance in Sheridan's *The Critic* (I, 2) is almost identical to Bayes's in this respect.

18. During his onslaught on Sir Fretful Plagiary in *The Critic,* Sneer accuses the playwright of an identical creative method:

> That as to comedy, you have not one idea of your own . . . even in your commonplace-book— where stray jokes and pilfered witticisms are kept with as much method as the ledger of the lost and stolen office. . . . Nay, that you are so unlucky as not to have the skill even to steal with taste:— but that you glean from the refuse of obscure volumes, where more judicious plagiarists have been before you; so that the body of your work is a composition of dregs and sediments—like a bad tavern's worst wine.
>
> (I, 1)

Buckingham's satire is more effective than Sheridan's because it is voiced through the accused (Bayes) himself.

19. Bayes's words *"bel esperansa de ma vie"* refer to Dryden's mistress, Anne Reeve, who as a member of Killigrew's company played Esperanza in *The Conquest of Granada.*

20. D. F. Smith's study of *The Rehearsal in Plays about the Theatre* contains a list of the specific attacks against Bayes, but makes no attempt to describe the significant role played by Bayes in furthering Buckingham's satire of heroic drama.

21. A close parallel to this scene between the Physician and the Gentleman-Usher, exists in *The Critic* (II, 2). The dialogue between Sir Walter Raleigh and Sir Christopher Hatton, with its unlikely questions and incredible exchanges, burlesques the simple-minded methods used by eighteenth century tragedians to introduce characters and provide information about the action.

22. Very similar and equally telling is Bayes's reply when Smith complains that the plot of the mock-play is static:

BAYES:

> Plot stand still! why, what a Devil is the Plot good for, but to bring in fine things?

SMITH:

> O, I did not know that before.

BAYES:

> No, I think you did not: nor many things more, that I am Master of. Now, Sir, I gad, this is the bane of all us Writers: let us soar but never so little above the common pitch, I gad, all's spoil'd; for the vulgar never understand it, they can never conceive you, Sir, the excellency of these things.
>
> (III, 1)

23. In *The Critic,* Sneer and Dangle perform the function of Smith and Johnson by making ironical comments and asking questions about Puff's *The Spanish Armada.*

24. Quoted by E. Malone, "Some Account of the Life and Writings of John Dryden", in *The Critical and Miscellaneous Prose Works of John Dryden,* ed. E. Malone (London, 1800), I (Part I), 104.

25. *Essays of John Dryden,* ed. W. P. Ker (Oxford, 1926), II, 21-22.

26. See the discussion between Smith and Bayes about Volscius's behaviour (III, 5).

27. See the discussion between Smith and Bayes about the eclipse (V, 1).

28. See the discussion between Johnson and Bayes about Pretty-man's kinship with the Fisherman (III, 4).

29. *The Burlesque Tradition* (London, 1952), p. 31.

30. Good examples can be found in *The Conquest of Granada*: see the discussions between Ozmyn and Benzayda (Part II, III, 2) and between Almanzor and Lyndaraxa (Part II, III, 3).

31. *A Century of English Farce* (London and Princeton, 1956), p. 119.

32. Buckingham's most crushing blow against the poetic impotence resulting from non-sensical rhymes also ridicules the Restoration dramatic practice of giving lines in French to certain high-born characters "to shew their breeding":

FIRST KING.

> I'l lug 'em by the ears

Until I make 'em crack.

SECOND KING:
And so will I, i'fack.

FIRST KING:
You must begin, *Mon foy.*

SECOND KING:
Sweet, Sir, *Pardonnes moy.*

BAYES:
Mark that: I makes 'em both speak *French,* to shew their breed-ing.

(II, 2)

33. Buckingham also ridicules the "battel in *Recitativo*" through Bayes's delighted description of the device to Smith and Johnson: fight a Battle? . . . Can you think it a decent thing, in a Battle before Ladies, to have men run their Swords through one another? . . . I sum up my whole Battle in the representation of two persons only, no more: and yet so lively, that, I vow to gad, you would swear ten thousand men were at it really engag'd. . . . I make 'em both come out in Armor *Cap-a-pea,* with their Swords drawn, and hung, with a scarlet Ribbon at their wrists, (which you know, represents, fighting enough.) . . . And here's the conceipt. Just at the very same instant that one sings, the other, Sir, recovers you his Sword, and puts himself in a warlike posture: so that you have at once your ear entertained with Music and good Language; and your eye satisfied with the garb, and accoutrements of war. (V, 1)

34. The arrival of the disguised army (V, 1) and the stopping of the battle by an eclipse (V, 1) deserve mention.

35. Johnson's ironic remark about fighting on the stage makes fun of the extended duel or battle:

But Mr. *Bayes,* might not we have a little fighting? for I love those playes, where they cut and slash one another upon the Stage, for a whole hour together.

(V, 1)

36. See also the song, "In swords, Pikes, and Bullets, 'tis safer to be", sung to the tune of Dryden's "Farewel, fair Armida", and the ensuing comments:

SMITH:

But Mr. *Bayes,* how comes this song in here? for, methinks, there is no great occasion for it.

BAYES:
Alack, Sir, you know nothing: you must ever interlard your Playes with Songs, Ghosts, and Dances, if you mean to—a—

JOHNSON:
Pit, Box, and Gallery, Mr. *Bayes.*

(III, 1)

Incidentally, Buckingham's parodic song is the most important addition in the revised and expanded third edition of *The Rehearsal*; it parodies Dryden's lament for Captain Digby, killed on 28 May, 1672 during a battle between the English and the Dutch fleets.

37. Roger Boyle, Earl of Orrery was extremely fond of these lavish scenes; his stage-directions are frequently elaborate but some of those for *The Black Prince* are almost unbelievably profuse.

38. See *The Laws of Poetry* (London, 1721), p. 65.

39. *The Complete Art of Poetry* (London, 1718), I, 203.

40. *The Complete Art of Poetry* (London, 1718), I, 203.

41. See *A History of English Dramatic Literature* (London, 1899), III, 362.

Sheridan Baker (essay date spring 1973)

SOURCE: Baker, Sheridan. "Buckingham's Permanent *Rehearsal*." *Michigan Quarterly Review* 12, no. 2 (spring 1973): 160-71.

[*In the essay that follows, Baker contends that* The Rehearsal *still speaks to modern audiences three centuries after its composition.*]

The Rehearsal (1671), the Duke of Buckingham's satire on the heroic play and its chief perpetrator, John Dryden, was a howling success when it appeared at the Theatre Royal in London before an audience that reflected the sophistication of Charles II's court. Everyone knew everything about everyone, and even the slyest hint was not lost. But timely and personal as it was, it nevertheless remained one of London's most popular plays for the next hundred years, a perpetual favorite, until Sheridan's *The Critic* (1779) supplanted it, and the taste for burlesque and satire began to wane. Directors still revive *The Critic* from time to time, but they apparently find ***The Rehearsal*** too remote to risk. Nevertheless, when we open its pages today, we find a life undimmed by time, a hilarious vitality that makes *The Critic* (may my renowned ancestor forgive his namesake) trivial by contrast,[1] setting us laughing even before we discover, through the footnotes, all the fringe benefits.

The Rehearsal is not only a prototype for a kind of farcical burlesque that none of its many imitations has ever quite matched or sustained, but also a work that reaches the necessary orbit of any great literature, where temporary historical particulars become permanent depictions of something permanently true about human nature, so that we can see in a wildly comic play three centuries old some home truths about ourselves and our seemingly very different scene. Though criticism has virtually ignored it, *The Rehearsal* is indeed permanent in this way.

How does this wicked caricature of John Dryden, whom we continue to admire for the virtues the cartoon omits, achieve a meaningful permanence? Boswell's comment to Johnson suggests an answer. The answer resides, as it necessarily must in any mimetic work, in human character, usually, as here, in *a* character: in Mr. Bayes, the Poet Laureate and writer of grandiose plays (named for the bay-leaf crown, the laurels, of laureateship), who is the caricature of John Dryden, the Poet Laureate and writer of grandiose plays. "Bayes, in *The Rehearsal,* is a mighty silly character," says Samuel Johnson, doubting that it was actually aimed at Dryden. "If it was intended for a particular man, it could only be diverting while that man was remembered. . . ." "I maintained [continues Boswell] that it had merit as a general satire on the self-importance of dramatick authors. But even in this light he held it very cheap" (31 March 1772).[2] Boswell is right. Bayes is an energetic display of the universal comedy of human vanity, particularly in that mode of vanity in which literature takes its being. *The Rehearsal,* in its wild abandon, thus deals with a central and dangerous truth about literature itself. Authorship is indeed a mode of vanity, which the good author must refine out of existence as he transfers its energy to the work itself. *The Rehearsal,* a play about producing plays, a mock rehearsal behind the scenes of those literary illusions we take for reality, gets both to the heart of authorship and the heart of literature itself.

The Rehearsal, moreover, goes one step farther, through its irresistible comicality: it takes the permanent dilemma of authorship—to make something ever new from the ever old forms and the ever old stuff of life—as a symbol for the fallacy of modernism, the delusion that the present moment is the only moment, that everything of the past age, or year, or day, is different, dead, and irrelevant, that one's own experience is unique, and that only I, Bayes, the author supreme, can create the ever "new Way of Writing," which somehow the dull age does not yet know how to appreciate.

The play begins as a satire on "the new Things going on," as Smith and Johnson, two young blades, discuss these relatively new heroic plays, by "Fellows who scorn to imitate Nature; but are altogether given to Elevate and Surprise." Then Bayes strolls past, and we almost immediately see the particular satire on heroics transform into a general satire on authorship and modernism. Johnson asks him to explain his latest play:

BAYES.

> Faith, Sir, the Intrigo's now quite out of my head; but I have a new one, in my Pocket, that I may say is a Virgin; 't has never yet been blown upon. . . . 'Tis all new Wit. . . . In fine, it shall Read, and Write, and Act, and Plot, and Show, ay, and Pit, Box and Gallery, I Gad, with any Play in *Europe.*

Indeed, the very idea of a rehearsal emphasizes newness: we, with Smith and Johnson, are getting an advanced peek at this newest of the new. In short, George Villiers, second Duke of Buckingham, gallant soldier, wit, and wastrel, achieved in *The Rehearsal* (with a few collaborators) the very portrait of the Mad Modern that Swift was to create some thirty years later, with a kindred wild brilliance and equally telling permanence, in *The Tale of a Tub* (1704).

Of course, the personal and "temporary" satire at Dryden's expense is devilishly engaging. We respond to it with all our instincts for malice. But the universal satire on vanity and mad modernism saves us from shame as we escape in doubled laughter. Buckingham rehearsed John Lacy, the first Bayes, in Dryden's mannerisms and dressed him in Dryden's customary browns and wig. "Dryden was notoriously a bad reader, and had a hesitating and tedious delivery, which, skillfully imitated in lines of surpassing fury and extravagance, must have produced an irresistible effect upon the audience."[3] Bayes's characteristic *and all that* and *egad* ("I Gad") are evidently characteristic of Dryden too.[4]

But all of these amusing personal Drydenisms immediately become characteristics of mad authorial egotism itself—Mr. Bayes:

> Now! Are the Players gone to Dinner? 'Tis impossible: The Players gone to Dinner! I Gad, if they are, I'll make 'em know what it is to injure a person that does 'em the honour to write for 'em, and all that. A Company of Proud, Conceited, Humorous, Crossgrain'd persons, and all that, I Gad. I'll make them the most Contemptible, Despicable, Inconsiderable persons, and all that, in the whole world for this trick. I Gad I'll be reveng'd on 'em; I'll sell this Play to the other House.

> (V.i, 5th ed., 1687).

The same is true of other facts about Dryden, including, I fear, his mistress. Perhaps nothing is intrinsically comic about taking snuff, or liking stewed prunes. We can even see as an admirable, if misguided, dedication to his craft Dryden's custom, before sitting down to a major piece of work, "to purge his body and clear his head by a dose of physic."[5] But, thrown together for emphasis, each serves as a sign of Bayes's monstrous authorial egotism. Bayes, of course, has his snuff box, once spilling snuff on himself, and any good comedian would make much of it throughout the play. One of the rehearsed play's kings turns it into a ridiculous authorial aid, in an analogy no one could miss, since Bayes is standing, box in hand, looking on: "when a knotty point comes, I lay my head close to it, with a Snuff-Box in my hand, and then I fegue it away i'faith" (III.iv). Sir Walter Scott, a century later, indeed remembers this as coming from Bayes himself, illustrating how comically the snuff box registers as an aid to thought. Scott writes in his journal, "I fegue it away, as Mr. Bayes says."[6] Similarly with Dryden's other habits:

> If I am to write familiar things, as Sonnets to *Armida,* and the like, I make use of Stew'd Prunes only; but, when I have a grand Design in hand, I ever take Physick, and let blood: for when you would have pure swiftness of Thought, and Fiery flights of Fancy, you must have a care of the pensive part. In fine, you must purge the Belly.
>
> (II.i)

Even reference to Dryden's presumed mistress, Anne Reeves, and her actual presence in the play, acting the part of Bayes's mistress, only underlines Bayes's mad conceit, again throwing the light more on Bayes, the mad author, than on Dryden, the errant male, who seems to have almost managed to keep his affair quiet, if indeed it was a fact.[7] Bayes is talking to Mr. Johnson:

BAYES.

> . . . Why, I make 'em call her *Armaryllis,* because of her Armor: Ha, ha, ha.

JOHNS.

> That will be very well, indeed.

BAYES.

> Ay, it's a pretty little Rogue; I knew her Face would set off Armor extreamly: And, to tell you true, I writ that part only for her. You must know she is my Mistress.

JOHNS.

> Then I know another thing, little *Bayes,* that thou hast had her, I Gad.

BAYES.

> No, I Gad, not yet; but I'm sure I shall: for I have talk'd Baudy to her already.
>
> (I.i)

And on Bayes goes, describing his invincible cleverness.

Bayes fluctuates hilariously from a kind of insane laughter at his own irrational new things, to a happy pride, and on to anger and even melancholy at not being taken at his own high rating. Immediately after his pleasure in *Armaryllis,* he falls into the dumps, then immediately turns to boasting "at this time, I am kept by another Woman, in the City." Johnson wonders how he can "make shift to hold out, at this rate."

BAYES.

> O Devil, I can toil like a Horse; only sometimes, it makes me Melancholy: and then I vow to Gad, for a whole day together, I am not able to say one good thing, if it were to save my life. . . .
>
> . . . And that's the only thing, I Gad, that mads me, in my Amours; for I'll tell you, as a Friend, Mr. *Johnson,* my acquaintances, I hear, begin to give it out that I am dull: now I am the farthest from it in the whole World, I Gad; but only forsooth, they think I am so, because I say nothing.
>
> (I.i)

Here, again, Dryden's actual taciturnity has been transmuted into Bayes's mad egotism. His admiration of himself and his defenses on every hand are boundless. No one can properly appreciate his genius; no actor can really do him justice.

This comedy of blind conceit everywhere transcends the personal satire in which it originates, as Buckingham incorporates thrusts at authors other than Dryden (actually remnants from earlier versions), particularly William D'Avenant, whose nose was snubbed and almost nonexistent, presumably from syphilis, and who evidently sometimes wore a false nose to repair the lack.

Soldiers have come in and killed each other, and music begins to play:

BAYES.

> Hold, hold! [*To the Musick.* It ceaseth.] Now here's an odd surprize: All these dead men you shall see rise up presently, at a certain Note that I have made, in *Effaut Flat.* Play on. [*To the Musick.*
>
> Now, now, now, [*The Musick play his Note, and the dead*
>
> O Lord, O Lord! *Men rise; but cannot get in order.*]
>
> Out, out, out! Did ever Men spoil a good thing so! No Figure, No Ear, no Time, no Thing? Udzookers, you dance worse than the Angels in *Harry* the Eight, or the fat Spirits in *The Tempest,* I Gad.

1 SOL.

> Why, Sir, 'tis impossible to do any thing in time, to this Tune.

BAYES.

> O Lord, O Lord! Impossible? Why Gentlemen, if there be any Faith in any person that's a Christian, I sate up two whole nights composing this Air, and apting it for the business: For, if you observe, there are two several Designs in this Tune; it begins swift and ends slow. You talk of time, and time; you shal see me do't. Look you now. Here I am dead [*Lies down flat upon his Face.*]
>
> Now mark my Note Effaut flat. Strike up Musick. Now. [*As he rises up hastily, he falls down again.*] Ah, Gadsookers, I have broke my Nose.

JOHNS.

> By my troth, Mr. Bayes, this is a very unfortunate Note of yours, in *Effaut.*

BAYES.

> A plague of this damn'd Stage, with your Nails, and your Tenterhooks, that a Gentleman cannot come to teach you to Act, but he must break his Nose, and his Face, and the Devil and all. Pray, Sir, can you help me to a wet piece of brown Paper?

Act II closes; and Act III opens with "Bayes *with a Paper on his Nose,"* as bumptious as ever, explaining his ingenuity to his two guests. He evidently wears the paper obliviously throughout the rest of the play, turning D'Avenant's false nose into a symbol of Bayes's ridiculous inability, which he cannot see before his very face.

Here we see him, at the end of Act IV, papered nose undoubtedly still in ridiculous evidence:

BAYES.

> Now the Rant's coming.

PRET.

> Durst any of the Gods be so uncivil, I'll make that God subscribe himself a Devil.

BAYES.

> Ah, Godsookers, that's well writ! [*Scratching his head, his Perruke falls off.*]

Another patch of ranting follows, and Bayes exclaims:

> There's a bold flight for you now! 'Sdeath, I have lost my Perruke. Well Gentlemen, this is that I never yet saw any one could write, but my self. Here's true Spirit and Flame all through, I Gad.

Act IV ends as Bayes walks off for a pot of ale, saying, "I'll make that God subscribe himself a Devil. That single Line, I Gad, is worth all that my Brother Poets ever writ."

Bayes's delight in his powers continues to rebound hilariously from his linguistic and physical ineptitudes, and we delight in him as the comic symbol, a kind of Wigless Victory, of all human pride in one of its most sensitive aspects: that of the writer who presumes to handle language and reality in that most godlike of human activities, authorship, that exposition of reality itself—or so we believe in our enchanted beliefs.

In addition to this essential comedy of blind pride, *The Rehearsal* makes comedy, at our own delighted expense, of literary illusion itself: a play making fun of plays, literature making fun of the most essential literary fact, our joy in these grand illusions of reality. We laugh heartily at Bayes, and through him at our own pretensions. But we are also enchanted into contemplating, comically, this illusion of reality that pulls us in, part way, as we give ourselves knowingly to its power. We enjoy the theater in its very theatricallity, and *The Rehearsal* gives us a kind of comically privileged view into the theatrical mysteries.

In the lines and pageantry of *The Rehearsal,* we also recognize the pleasures of the serious heroic play, in its language and sonorous hauteur, its music and dances, its ingenious mechanisms, as kings descend in clouds, singing. The same companies would play this farce to the "heroic" audiences of the day before and the day after. The heroic play continued to prosper, alongside *The Rehearsal.* Dryden wrote his last heroic play, *Aureng-Zebe,* in 1675, four years after *The Rehearsal* launched out to harry him; and these grand heroic spectacles of his continued to hold the stage for some years to come and to influence the elevated tragedies that were to follow.

Doubtless, *The Rehearsal'*s jovial acid eventually began to bite. Dane F. Smith believes that it undermined the heroic play and created "an atmosphere of skepticism in pit and boxes and, in the average spectator, a distrust of all forms of dramatic illusion and a consequent avidity for realism."[8] He has in mind the unmannerly audiences, who could damn almost anything and everything as they ate their oranges and ogled the ladies, and probably the realistic of manners in comedies. But the serious plays that follow *The Rehearsal* hardly show either a passion for realism or a distrust of illusion, however theatrical. *The Rehearsal* in fact so capitalizes on the essential literary and theatrical delight in illusion that it would seem almost to feed the appetite it teases.

Today, we put *The Rehearsal* down after reading it, in the only theater in which we are likely to see it, that of our minds, with a kind of pleased wonder at the essential fact of literature: that we take these illusions for reality, but with some partial admiration for the illusion itself—the author's style, his evocative powers, and, in the theater, the actor's genius at seeming the role he is only playing. This is the essential literary paradox. We wish to take these unrealities as real, but do not wish them to *be* real, as Samuel Johnson pointed out long ago: they move us because they are life*like,* not life itself but reminders of the possibilities and realities in our own real lives.

The Rehearsal makes constant comedy of this paradox, as we observe the author and two guests observe the absurd illusions he constantly breaks into from his supposed reality. The actor begins to act his mock illusion. Bayes breaks it off, as he corrects the actor, and then sets him to evoking illusion again. The mere breaking off of the pseudo-illusion comes as a comic surprise, as when a film breaks, snapping us back to our own reality. Even the absurd pseudo-illusion has some of the essential literary and theatrical spell-binding effect. We are constantly laughing at our essential propensity for being taken in, for submitting to the grand illusions of the stage. We have a sense that the audience itself must have had: they had recently submitted and would submit again to language and stagecraft almost identical with these. The laughter, as ultimately in all good comedy, turns reflectively on ourselves.

We know that we could respond to one of Dryden's world-shaking heroes, gladly entering the illusion, as he sends even gods to the devil. When Bayes explains that one of his characters is "the Sister of Drawcansir. A Lady that was drown'd at Sea, and had a Wave for her Winding-sheet," we know that we would respond—in fact, we do respond with a touch of pathos glowing through the fun—to the poetry and the idea in its serious context. Dryden's verse-plays actually reach something of the idealized and impassioned resonance that Corneille had achieved, and Racine was achieving, in France.[9] Dryden's Almanzor, in *The Conquest of Granada,* hears the ghost of his mother speak in an elegant passage beginning:

> I am the Ghost of her who gave thee birth:
> The airy shadow of her mouldering earth.
> Love of thy father me through seas did guide;
> On seas I bore thee, and on seas I died.
> I died; and for my winding-sheet a wave
> I had, and all the ocean for my grave.

Buckingham's burlesquing of this passage, with Bayes's little comic sadness at his own created illusion, reminds us, as we laugh, of the language and power of illusion itself, a language and power to which we know we ourselves respond. In all the short passages of parodied poetry—and part of Buckingham's brilliance is in keeping them brief, never letting them grow dull before Bayes breaks them off—we sense the power both of poetry and of the mimetic illusion, even as we laugh at the parodic absurdities.

This comic contrasting of illusory levels is especially evident in the music and dancing. When Bayes leaves to mend his broken nose, he tells his soldiers to remember to "dance like Horsemen." They respond in bewilderment, then try their muddled dance, then give it up. One of the soldiers asks the music to play a dance that Bayes had once found fault with, and we very evidently have a solo dance, by one of the cast's several skillful dancers, to the best music the theater could produce. Then Smith and Johnson cross the stage with a comment on "this Fool" and his nose, and Act II ends, pulled a step back toward the farce from the thorough theatrical illusion of the dance and the music.

The play ends similarly, after Bayes's magnificent comic anger at everybody's having gone off for lunch,

his threat to sell his play to the other theater and turn satirist, "And so farewell to this Stage, I Gad, for ever." After comic Bayes, we move back toward the very level of theatrical illusion at which we have been laughing. A few actors still linger on stage. One says, "But before we go, lets see *Haynes* and *Shirley* practice the last dance," which they can use on some other occasion.

Joseph Haynes, as Samuel Pepys tells us, was "an incomparable dancer," and Shirley (first name unknown) was evidently not far behind.[10] We end, then, with serious music and dance, the best of the day, straight from the heroic realm itself. We enter the illusion at which we laughed. But not quite. We are enjoying the very fact of illusion, with a certain amusement at ourselves as fallibly human and therefore comic creatures, a minor set of Bayeses. For we are seeing not the complete illusion, as in a heroic play, but only its *rehearsal,* by two real men, whose names we know, who themselves are only practicing the illusion they will eventually enter completely, under their assumed roles and pretended names. This double pleasure of having and eating our illusory cake, laughing at ourselves as belonging to the comic kind, comically blinded by our illusions, is certainly the ground-bass of **The Rehearsal,** on which Bayes acts out his hilarious arpeggios and descants.

We are indeed engaged, comically, in an essential dramatic pleasure: that which we enjoy after any final curtain, when the actors and actresses, still in costume, come smiling forth as the real persons we applaud and cheer, and give bouquets, for their illusory powers. The Prologue to **The Rehearsal** sets and illustrates its unique comic version of this basic theatrical fact. John Lacy, Charles II's favorite comic actor, one of the best comedians of the times, comes on stage dressed as John Dryden for his role as Bayes. But he speaks straightforwardly (though breezily):

> We might well call this short Mock-play of ours
> A Poesie made of Weeds, instead of Flowers:
> Yet such have been presented to your Noses,
> And there are such, I fear, who thought 'em Roses.
> Would some of 'em were here, to see, this Night,
> What stuff it is in which they took delight.

And, then, after hoping that audiences will eventually grow wise, and despise the popular heroic play, he concludes:

> Then I'll cry out, swell'd with Poetic rage,
> Tis I, John Lacy, have reform'd your Stage.

Here is real Lacy (whom we know) dressed to look like Dryden (whom we know), ready to step into that full comic personality, Mr. Bayes, yet thinking at the end of swelling with typical heroic rhetoric to declare, with a marvelously pretended Bayesian pomposity that he, John Lacy, the mere actor, has reformed the stage, whereas, in actuality, the reformer will have been Buckingham, the parodist and satirist who has created the role for him to act. This mixing of actuality and theatrical illusion becomes even more intriguing when we contemplate the curious fact I have already mentioned: that Anne Reeves, Dryden's presumed mistress, is playing her own comical counterpart as Bayes's mistress, burlesquing the parts she had played in Dryden's plays. However one can separate these comic layers of theatrics, they highlight the fascinating fact that theatrical illusion works comically upon us throughout *The Rehearsal*—which, of course, is not a real rehearsal at all, but a comic mime of that double layer of actuality and illusion that goes on before the play and behind the scenes.

Lionel Trilling, speaking of Pirandello's *Six Characters in Search of an Author*, has observed that the "essence of the theatre, as everyone is quick to understand, is illusion," and that audiences, beginning with those of Aristophanes, have, again and again, delighted in a playwright's seeming to destroy the illusion.[11] Those modern devastators, Beckett and Ionesco, come to mind as outstanding examples, as we laugh nervously at their shifts of illusion, wondering what we're doing there, and here. But *The Rehearsal*, in its merriment, may be better than the modern illusion-shifters, and more sustained than Aristophanes, in this eternal flirtation between our love of illusion and our need for reality. Certainly, in *The Rehearsal*, more than in any of its lesser descendants, we enjoy a sustained comedy of illusion at our own expense, costing not too much psychic humiliation to join us happily to the general comedy of being fallible and human.

The Rehearsal thus does reach the permanently comic in two supportive ways. Primarily, in the superbly comic Bayes. The quintessential fact of comedy is human ineptitude mistaking itself for omnipotence. Authorship, by nature, assumes an omnipotence it must disguise. And Bayes is authorship laid comically bare, and never more thoroughly and comically so. His Mad Modernity extracts further comedy from the phenomenon of authorship, which must render ever new the unchanging essentials of human existence. The mimicking of John Dryden, which we continue to enjoy as a maliciously augmented seventh in the total comic harmony, is only a means to the basic human comedy that Bayes represents, in his wild prides and pretensions.

Bayes indeed ranks among the best comic characters we have, if we would but blow the dust from the book, and get him back on the stage, which he held for well over a century, lingering in memory for a good bit longer too. *The Rehearsal* reinforces this comedy of Bayes, at a second level of permanence, through its shifts of illusion, which implicate, as Bayes himself does and as all great comedy must, ourselves, the laughers, in the general human comedy, from which we, looking down from the boxes, had thought ourselves immune.

Notes

1. Montague Summers concurs: "Amusing as Sheridan is and full of smartness, even his wit and humor pale before the brilliance of the Restoration Duke"; "The water of *The Critic* is a mean thing to place beside the strong wine of *The Rehearsal*" (*The Rehearsal* [Stratford-Upon-Avon: The Shakespeare Head Press, 1914], pp. xvii, xxv. Dane F. Smith finds *The Critic* "not so great in a literary sense" as *The Rehearsal* (*The Critics in the Audience of the London Theatres from Buckingham to Sheridan* [Albuquerque: The University of New Mexico Press, 1953], p. 141.

2. Twelve years later, Johnson holds it cheaper still: "'It has not wit enough to keep it sweet' [he said]. This was easy;—he therefore caught himself, and pronounced a more rounded sentence; 'It has not vitality enough to preserve it from putrefaction'" (June 1784). *Boswell's Life of Johnson,* ed. George Birkbeck Hill, rev. L. F. Powell (Oxford: The Clarendon Press, 1934), II.168, IV.320.

3. Robert Bell, "Life of Dryden," *Poetical Works* (1854), I.40-42, qtd. Edward Arber, *The Rehearsal* (London: A. Murray & Sons, 1868), p. 17.

4. Pope's *Rape of the Lock* (1714) illustrates both *The Rehearsal*'s enduring popularity, over forty years later, and the way personal peculiarity can become a popular comic touchstone. Pope reinforces his satire on superficiality with this reminder of the prototypically foolish Bayes:

   > *Snuff,* or the *Fan,* supply each Pause of Chat,
   > With singing, laughing, ogling, *and all that.*

5. Charles la Motte, *Essay on Painting and Poetry* (1730), qtd. Summers, p. 95.

6. Summers, p. 100. "Fegue" means to beat or drive.

7. Among other roles in Dryden's plays, Anne Reeves had played Esperanza in his *The Conquest of Granada,* of the preceding year (1670), one of the principal plays parodied, and, as Amaryllis in *The Rehearsal,* she was actually playing herself. See Hester W. Chapman, *Great Villiers* (London: Secker and Warburg, 1949), p. 173. Evidence for and against Dryden's presumed affair remains inconclusive: see Charles E. Ward, *The Life of John Dryden* (Chapel Hill: University of North Carolina Press, 1961), p. 183.

8. *The Critics in the Audience,* p. 25.

9. Dryden emulated Corneille, not only in tight structure but also in versification, as the Prologue to his *The Maiden Queen* suggests:

He who writ this, not without pains and thought
From French and English Theatres has brought
The exactest rules. . . .

                                    . . . and a mingled chime
Of Jonson's humour, with Corneille's rhyme.

Summers, who quotes this, points out that Dryden is pronouncing *Corneille* with the final French *uh* (pp. 79-80), the characteristic mannerism of elevated French dramatic verse.

10. Summers, pp. 152, 102.

11. *The Experience of Literature* (New York: Holt, Rinehart and Winston, 1967), pp. 359-360.

Robert F. Willson, Jr. (essay date 1975)

SOURCE: Willson, Robert F., Jr. "Bayes Versus the Critics: *The Rehearsal* and False Wit." In *'Their Form Confounded': Studies in the Burlesque Play from Udall to Sheridan*, pp. 81-110. The Hague, Netherlands: Mouton, 1975.

[*In this excerpt, Willson discusses the historical context of Buckingham's play.*]

1.

In evaluating Buckingham's inspired farce, we again must turn to historical context, as in the case of *The Knight, Dream,* and *Roister Doister.* The Restoration brought with it a revived interest in the theatre and the arts in general. Escaping from Puritan repression and feeling the influence of Louis XIV's worldly court, the English aristocracy took part in a vital quest for pleasure and entertainment of all kinds. As a reflection of the court's desire to foster some competition yet at the same time retain a degree of control over drama and dramatists, Charles granted patents to Killigrew and Davenant to form new acting companies and to build new theatres. As for repertoire the two men turned in the early years to the stock of Elizabethan and Jacobean plays and proceeded to divide them up for revival and revision. But the reemergent theatre could not continue to depend indefinitely upon just these chestnuts, especially since the age seemed determined to have novelty at all costs. The producers were thus faced with a dilemma: what sorts of plays should make up the staple of their acting repertoires? Should the managers urge poets to write in the vein of Shakespeare, Jonson, and Beaumont and Fletcher, attempting to improve on these accepted formulae? Some of this would obviously work, but clearly Elizabethan taste was less refined than that of the Restoration, and the earlier age's wit was considered by most as either dull or gross. Should Corneille and Racine and other luminaries of the French neoclas-

sical school be translated to the English stage? There were objections and obstacles here as well: the French manner of narration and plotting was, in many critics' views, "too regular"—and dull. Should playwrights return to the classics of the Greek and Roman stage for inspiration and models?

Dryden's *Essay of Dramatic Poesy* (1668) presented a mirror image of the difficult choices facing ambitious and solicitous playwrights and managers. The participants in Dryden's Platonic "quatralogue" debate the various contending positions, as well as stating preferences for particular genres: Eugenius favors the modern English plays, putting special emphasis on wit and comedy; Crites (with his somewhat august and somber manner) favors classical Greek plays, placing his emphasis upon tragedy; Lisidius favors the French school of Corneille, again emphasizing as Crites does, regular and serious plays. Neander, supposedly in the role of arbiter, finds in Ben Jonson a suitable model and compromise for all.[1] He is a classicist but writes witty comedy with engaging humor characters; his model play (*Epicoene, or The Silent Woman*) is regular in that it conforms to the unities; he observes the French technique of *liaison des scènes*; he is an Englishman but from the "last age", and so now something of an ancient; he is a model and not the ultimate poet (as Shakespeare is) whom modern writers could not hope to excel.

Prophetically, then, Dryden's *Essay* points to the form of play which in fact would flourish on the Restoration stage: witty comedy of manners following Jonson's humor scheme, featuring ingenious plots, satire, and sophisticated repartee. But Dryden also infers in the *Essay,* if we are to judge by the cogency of Crites' argument, that the demands of serious drama must be met. Dryden also seems to have felt that this serious form ought to have as its aim some patriotic goal; after all, England was at war with Holland and its victory would surely place the country in a position of world prominence unequalled since the Armada days. The stage ought to be a place where great things as well as mundane affairs take place, where conflicts over duty and honor as well as sex and manners can be debated. So Dryden, Davenant, and others championed an invention which in effect represented the translation of epic poetic form into the idiom of the drama. Just as epic poetry requires its own special kind of hero and grave action, so heroic drama would attempt to discover such figures in new places—Spain, Peru, and Rhodes among them. Just as epic poetry calls for elevated diction and verse, so heroic drama would require the heroic couplet. Blank verse may have been the special province of the Elizabethan age, according to Neander in the *Essay,* but this new age demanded something unique and grander, something both balanced and extravagant, able to convey both vivid description and noble sentiments.

In answer to Crites' objection that heroic verse is both unnatural and awkward (especially for directions like "Open the door!"), Neander responds with a full defense of this manner of writing:

"I answer you, therefore, by distinguishing betwixt what is nearest to the nature of Comedy, which is the imitation of common persons and ordinary speaking, and what is nearest the nature of a serious play: this last is indeed the representation of Nature, but 'tis nature wrought up to a higher pitch. The plot, the characters, the wit, the passions, the descriptions, are all exalted above the level of common converse, as high as the imagination of the poet can carry them, with proportion to verisimility."[2]

Neander's rationality is impressive, but the argument overlooks the fundamental facts of English stage history before the Restoration: no successful play had ever been written entirely in heroic couplets, and the major accomplishments in the form had been in descriptive, narrative, and satiric poetry—not in dialogue. Chaucer, Jonson, and Denham were prime examples of how successfully the heroic couplet could perform in topical and topographical situations; but no one used the form on the stage. Moreover, the greatest epic in the language was to be written not in heroic couplets but in blank verse, a form more ideally suited to Milton's epic purposes and dramatic style of narration. It is probably not surprising to find in Dryden's *Essay* that Crites should take issue with Neander on this score; his claim that rhymed verse sounds unnatural is clearly defensible on classical critical grounds. Aristotle avers that art should imitate nature, but not necessarily "nature wrought up to a higher pitch". As a stanch believer in the rules of the ancients as regards poetry and satire, Dryden seems to have ignored their urgings of restraint and truth to nature in defending his novel dramatic model. In so doing he falls into the pit, so to speak, where his romantic and bombastic scenes were received with loud applause.

It is clear from Dryden's descriptions of his improvements on the heroic formula he had received from Davenant (in *Of Heroic Plays,* prefixed to *The Conquest of Granada* [1672]) that heroic plays constitute an imitation of an imitation (i.e., the heroic poem), and therefore are twice removed from reality or nature. This was, it will be remembered, Plato's reason for banishing the poets from the Republic; in the case of such plays as *The Conquest of Granada* Dryden banishes truth-to-life from our theatrical experience. The Prefatory Essay also draws on the idea that the heroic poem gives the playwright an opportunity, indeed duty, to add variety to the action by including more characters and incidents, raising the work "to a greater height". Such license, of course, emphasizes spectacle above plot, and Buckingham was to lose little time in showing precisely how such multiplicity of event and character destroys

any unity of action. Finally, in defending the improbabilities of epic poetry, especially the presence of spirits and magic, Dryden argues this way in the Essay:

And if any man object to the improbabilities of a spirit appearing or of a palace raised by magic; I boldly answer him, that an heroic poet is not tied to a bare representation of what is true, or exceeding probable; but that he may let himself loose to visionary objects, and to the representation of such things as depending not on sense, and therefore not to be comprehended by knowledge, may give him a freer scope for imagination.[3]

These very lines are almost self-parodic and sound a good deal like Bayes' elaborate arguments for his peculiar type of drama, especially the phrase "not to be comprehended by knowledge". Such an apology, moreover, works best only when the reader has free reign to fly with the poet, when he can employ his imagination to match the one present in the poem. But the stage is limiting and physical, a place where words spoken by the actors must correspond to the setting of the action, which is usually concretely represented. Any effort to reproduce the palace of Boabdelin or mountains of Peru with scenery and other effects must be severely limited by the imagination of the scene-painter and the dimensions of the stage. It is perhaps a sign of Dryden's myopia here that he cites the same reason as evidence for proving the stage a *better* place to portray heroic action than the page, because "it represents to view what the poem only does relate". Dryden also argues, somewhat in the manner of one of the heroes from his extravaganzas, that the poet-playwright is obliged "to endeavor an absolute dominion over the minds of the spectators"—one can easily see how an opponent like Buckingham would extract a statement like the preceding one and travesty it by presenting his hero Bayes as a man "at war" with both spectators and actors, trying to impose his aesthetic will upon them.

This failure on Dryden's part to see the impracticability of translating the imaginary realm of heroic poetry into the idiom of the stage can be seen by tracing the genealogy of Almanzor, hero of *The Conquest of Granada.* Dryden defends his hero's grandiose style by citing characters like Achilles, Rinaldo, and Artaban as models, all of whom were irascible and given to ranting. Their authors, says Dryden, attempted to show us "what men of great spirits would certainly do when they were provoked, not what they were obliged to do by the strict rules of moral virtue" (p. 157). The playwright and not the critic in Dryden is here aiming to rationalize the sensational conduct of these heroes—conduct the epic poet is better able than the playwright to make acceptable through actions described and not necessarily "seen". Moreover, the point of Homer, Tasso, and La Calprenède's treatment of these figures was to demonstrate how such lack of restraint endangered great enterprises; such touches are not present simply to humanize the characters, as Dryden claims. "If the history of the late Duke of Guise be true", he continues, "he hazarded more and performed not less in Naples than Almanzor is feigned to have done in Granada" (p. 158). This defense of his character and method brings Dryden full circle since he argues here from a position of verisimilitude, whereas earlier he claimed his major figure was larger than life. This weakness in argument only serves to underscore the thorny problem of attempting to transfer into the theatrical realm a system and style which clearly belong in the poetic world of imagination. Bayes speaks ironically for Buckingham when, in defense of this very habit of using sources of a poetic or prosaic nature, he declares: "Sir, if you make the least scruple of the efficacy of these my rules, do but come to the play-house and you shall judge of 'em by the effects."

2.

The surprising fact is that many did come to the play-house and apparently judged those effects favorably; heroic drama achieved overnight popularity and continued to be a favorite with audiences throughout the eighteenth century. Clinton-Baddeley believes this is partially due to the continuation of heroic plays in the repertoires of acting companies, as well as the fact that audiences were accustomed to hearing rhymed verse in the poetry of Pope and others.[4] But whatever the reason the most bombastic of these plays were written after and not before the appearance of **The Rehearsal.** Theatre audiences were obviously still moved at the beginning of the Restoration, as they had been in Elizabethan days, to see outlandish adventures and to listen to ranting verse as a way of escaping the mundane events of their own lives. And this escapism existed among both citizens and courtiers. Since such a formula as Dryden's proved to be so popular it deserves some careful scrutiny before we turn to **The Rehearsal** to see how its conventions were lampooned. One of the best ways of doing that is to examine the plot of one of the most successful of these plays, Dryden and Howard's (Sir Robert Howard was another satiric target in **The Rehearsal**) *The Indian Queen.*

The play was first produced by the King's (Killigrew's) Company in January, 1663/4 at the newly-built Theatre Royal.[5] The exotic piece is set in Mexico, a country sufficiently unknown to the London audience and probably evocative of the same mystery attached to such places as the island in Shakespeare's *Tempest.* It is well to remember that distant settings were part of the apprentice-knight plays lampooned by Beaumont, and *Tamburlaine,* another popular success in the Renaissance, was likewise set in far-away and mysterious lands. In doing this the playwright could achieve greater freedom to exploit fantastic feats and events, since the audience knew little and would believe much about the magical influence in these unknown settings. Montezuma, the heroic general of *Queen,* appears at the opening fresh from a victory over the Mexicans, whose prince Acacis he delivers to the Inca (Montezuma is a mercenary) as a prize. The Inca in return offers his general anything his heart desires, but when Montezuma tells him his heart's desire is his daughter, the Inca turns cool. The dilemma or conflict is a typical one in romance: true lovers are frustrated by an older parent who objects to the marriage because the facts about his future son-in-law's birth are obscured. It appears as if Montezuma, though a stanch fighter, is base-born. The frustrated hero then decides to desert the Inca and join the Mexicans, while freeing his new-found friend Acacis, in order to gain revenge. This sudden reversal in the beginning of the play is typical of heroic plays, and it does have its spectacular effect; but the desertion is so rash and contrived that credulity is severely strained. Rather than escaping with his love, the hero instead departs with his friend, thereby providing Dryden with the chance to explore the theme of love versus friendship as well. Immediately we see, as would Buckingham in his parody, that plot is strained for effect, and character and "intrigue" will take precedence over it with a vengeance.

Reminiscent of Coriolanus, Montezuma defects to the army of Zempoalla, the usurping Indian queen and mother of Acacis. In ensuing battles the Inca is defeated and he and his daughter are captured by Montezuma, who now begins to woo Orazia in earnest. But he is challenged in his effort to enjoy the spoils by Traxalla, Zempoalla's general: Montezuma must give up the prisoners and consent to be ruled. Acacis intercedes, but Traxalla reports the revolt to the queen, who then authorizes her general to seize all the participants in her name. Before this can happen, however, Acacis has time to reveal to Montezuma the story of his mother's usurpation of the throne, the murder by Traxalla of the rightful king, and the escape of his queen Amexia, then big with child. No one has seen her child since. At this point in the action the hint is very strong that Montezuma is Amexia's son and that he will somehow help to restore her to the throne and regain his rightful place as heir-apparent. It is also apparent that his friend and he will soon become enemies not only because they are rivals for the throne but also because they will both find themselves in love with Orazia, thus furthering the theme of love versus honor. The weakness in such an intrigue is again one of improbability: rightful heirs rarely emerge out of thin air, only to find themselves at swords' point with their best friends. We can also detect the playwright become wizard, attempting to keep as much information from the viewers as he can for the sake of surprise. And our minds are truly dismayed when, at the close of Act II, Montezuma and Acacis, realizing they are rivals, rush off with swords drawn not to fight each other but to rescue the beautiful Orazia from the clutches of deceiving Traxalla.

Bursting into Zempoalla's court the two men are met by a revenge-mad queen who vows to sacrifice Orazia and Inca to the gods. Acacis then proceeds to plead for his new-found love, arguing that the more honorable thing to do would be to return her to the deserving Montezuma as his lawful prize. Zempoalla responds with a jaundiced definition of honor:

> Honor is but an itch in youthful blood,
> Of doing acts extravagantly good;
> We call that virtue which is only heat
> That reigns in youth, till age finds out the cheat.
>
> (III. i. 96-99)

This kind of philosophizing on the topic of honor becomes tedious in the play, as well as making for long passages of sententious and ranting speech. In this instance the wise queen holds her ground against Acacis' pleas, and Traxalla uses the occasion to urge the killing of Montezuma once again—he is still jealous about losing control of his troops. But Traxalla is refused as it becomes apparent that Zempoalla has now fallen for Montezuma and wants him for her public and private captain. The intrigue has now reached a point of withering complexity: Zempoalla loves the hero and so wishes to rid herself of the rival Orazia; Traxalla wants revenge on Montezuma but he also seems to have fallen in love with Orazia ("lusts for her" is probably a better phrase); Acacis loves Orazia and Montezuma, thus finding himself torn between love and friendship. The demands of both love and lust begin to look ludicrous rather than interesting, and little hope now exists for unravelling such a mess without some kind of divine intervention. A hint of this future appearance of the gods comes when the queen calls on a prophet to interpret a dream she has had about a lion and dove (the dove is Amexia breaking the fetters Zempoalla has used to tie Montezuma, the lion, to her; he will in turn destroy her throne). When the god of dreams' explanation dissatisfies her, Zempoalla vows total destruction—"Victims shall bleed, and feasted altars shine".

Act IV commences simply enough with Traxalla urging Orazia to decide whether Montezuma, asleep before them in his cell, shall live or die. Orazia falters, but in doing so gives the hero time to awake and provoke Traxalla into killing him, since Orazia will not have him and his life is now pain. Just as the general lifts his sword, however, Zempoalla enters, seizes Orazia, and threatens to kill her if Traxalla does not unhand her love. The stalemate is broken by Orazia's sudden and impassioned declaration of love for Montezuma; again, such stylized and artificial outbursts at the propitious moment transform the action into the rankest melodrama. Now both queen and general, their lust frus-

trated, are joined in their determination to sacrifice the young lovers. Acacis also asserts himself by secretly freeing Montezuma and at the same time revealing his love for Orazia, a revelation which again presents the hero with a dilemma related to a conflict of values: "Oh, tyrant love!" declares Montezuma, "how cruel are thy laws! I forfeit friendship or betray thy cause. That person whom I would defend from all the world, that person by my hand must fall." (IV. ii. 37-40)

Orazia prevents the ensuing duel, urging Acacis to accept the truth and live; failing this she vows to return to her father's cell and take her own life. As the two men are about to join her in freeing her father, forgetting for the moment their quarrel, Traxalla and Zempoalla rush in and capture them after a short struggle, during which Acacis is wounded. Now all the central characters are to be sacrificed to the Indian queen's rage—even her own son. But this violent turn of events has wrenched the plot out of all proportion, and the play's action has been transformed into nothing more than a succession of sudden surprises, discoveries, and arrests. The model for such tampering with the plot can be found in Beaumont and Fletcher's *The Maid's Tragedy* and *Philaster,* two plays in which the love versus honorable friendship and displaced heir-to-the-throne themes are central. Buckingham, and others, no doubt saw the obvious resemblance, since Beaumont and Fletcher continued to be popular on the Restoration stage, and decided to expose to ridicule the notion that heroic plays were something entirely new. Obviously Dryden had simply returned to a time-worn, melodramatic technique and altered it to fit the slightly more sophisticated tastes of his Restoration audience.

The sacrificial altar provides the final setting for the denouement of *The Indian Queen*—a scene appropriate to the ensuing slaughter as well as to the expected restoration of Mexico's rightful queen. Conflict returns in this scene between Zempoalla and Traxalla when the general urges that Montezuma die first; but the queen is apparently hoping to save him for herself. She unexpectedly seizes Traxalla and calls him traitor. Acacis, wounded and pale, then bursts in, deplores his mother's selfish acts, declares his lasting love for both Orazia and Montezuma, then stabs himself. As the sentimental favorite, Acacis's death is meant to expose the tragic results of the usurpation and to arouse as much pity as possible for his fate:

> Divine Orazia!
> Can you have so much mercy to forgive?
> I do not ask it with design to live,
> But in my death to have my torments cease.
> Death is not death when it can bring no peace.
>
> (V. i. 132-136)

What looks like the beginning of a mass suicide is interrupted by a succession of messengers announcing the arrival on the scene of Amexia and a popular army declaring their love for a displaced queen and her son, the brave Montezuma. Traxalla urges the quick murder of Montezuma once more, but instead Zempoalla cuts the cords that bound him, freeing the hero to finally silence Traxalla. Zempoalla then stabs herself in a gesture which arouses hope she will join with her son in death just as Montezuma now proceeds to rejoin his mother in their rightful place. The hero now also qualifies for the hand of Orazia, and the two are united in fitting romance fashion with the blessing of the Inca. This even-handed, symmetrical finish is underlined in the hero's final words:

> How equally our joys and sorrows move!
> Death's fatal triumphs, joined with those of love.
> Love crowns him that lives,
> Each gains the conquest which the other gives.
>
> (V. i. 308-311)

From this resumé of *The Indian Queen* it may not be immediately clear what made this play and others like it excellent models for parody. *The Conquest of Granada,* for instance, might have better illustrated the form's inherent violence and bloodiness, piling up as it does many more bodies at the end. Much of the excess in *Queen* is in the verse itself, where frequent hyperbole, involving storm and planetary imagery, keeps the pitch of emotion too high, too long. A good example is Montezuma's speech (II. ii.) in which his rage suddenly turns away from Acacis to Zempoalla after discovering that she intends to kill Orazia:

> That ties my hand, and turns from thee that rage
> Another way, thy blood should else assuage;
> The storm on our proud foes shall higher rise,
> And, changing, gather blackness as it flies;
> So, when winds turn, the wandering waves obey,
> And all the tempest rolls the other way.
>
> (II. iii. 62-67)

This kind of simile, nearly epic in proportion, was intended by Dryden to associate the volatile passions of his hero with tempests in nature; but such a comparison is inevitably difficult to sustain. Montezuma, after all, will say similar things in the course of the play, which sooner or later must come to sound like rant. To keep his protagonist constantly warring with himself and others admits no moments of calm (which are likewise found in nature!) to round out his character and make him seem more real. It is almost as if Dryden has replaced a Hal with a Hotspur for his central figure.

As reflected in Montezuma's simile, another weak point of the play is its excessive change in course. Montezuma, for instance, deserts Inca because his employer will not consent to his marriage with Orazia. He desires revenge until he realizes that as captives of Zempoalla the three must die anyway. His friendship with Acacis is challenged when Acacis vows love for Orazia; but

the two become fast friends in an instant when they must rescue the heroine from death. Zempoalla is truly mercurial. At first she wants to sacrifice all her captives, including the hero; then she falls in love with him and maneuvers to save him. When she realizes he loves Orazia, she attempts to destroy her but is stymied by Traxalla. The solution? She decides again to sacrifice them all, but then relents, cuts Montezuma's ropes, and frees him. This type of oscillation in motive and action, which facilitates the author's efforts to portray conflicts between love and friendship, love and honor, love and lust, etc., inevitably leads to confusion about where a particular character stands at a given moment. The plot is also improbably twisted whenever convenience requires, especially so that noble sentiments might be expressed or a spectacular effect achieved. The usurped kingdom, displaced heir, the rivalry for a mistress' hand, the exotic setting, the numerous threats with swords and daggers drawn—all such touches are part of time-tested tragicomedy and romance, and this is the category into which *The Indian Queen* must ultimately fall.

Recognizing this fact, and at the same time observing the growing taste for plays which reflected in a stylized way the actual social life of the day, Buckingham and his collaborators no doubt felt encouraged to travesty heroic drama. He could be surer than Beaumont about a cosmopolitan and critical audience of gentlemen because the Restoration theatre had become a more cliquish realm than its Jacobean predecessor. He could also be sure of a group of literati whose personal animosities toward Dryden would encourage them to laugh at a cleverly wrought caricature. Most of all he could be confident of finding numerous elements in the plots of heroic drama which could be easily and successfully parodied. He would no doubt agree with the modern critic who so succinctly cites the major flaw in those plots:

> In making fate so obvious, oppressive, and busy an agent, Dryden prevents the action from moving inexorably to its central tragic reversal; instead, we are given a succession of reversals. The solution to any one problem only introduces the next. The fortuitous world makes these characters almost comically impotent.[6]

3.

The phrase "comically impotent" hints at the approach to burlesque taken by Buckingham in his brilliant farce ***The Rehearsal***; he seems to have seized upon the unintentional comic flaws in heroic motivation and exploited them with reference to many characters and situations.[7] Lacy's (the actor who played Bayes) opening reference to the "*strutting Heroes*" who perform in "*King Cambyses vein*" (Prologue, line 10)[8] sets the target of the burlesque clearly in view, just as Shakespeare did in *Dream*, where reference to Preston's ranting play was made as well. (Preston's subtitle was "A Lamentable Tragedie, Mixed Full of Pleasant Mirth . . ."). I think this allusion reflects a conscious attempt to associate the aims of this burlesque play with those of *Dream* and *The Knight,* where the Pyramus and Thisby interlude and Rafe's adventures comically attacked the ranting hero, mixing of genres, excessively sententious and hyperbolic language, and the spectacle of Senecan and chivalric drama. These excesses are also present, it should be noted, in heroic drama; and like his predecessors Buckingham again invokes the ideals of classical criticism (i.e., the unities, plot over spectacle, decorum) in order to make ludicrous the form's flaws. Lacy states this attitude explicitly when he objects, like the Boy in *The Knight,* to the habit among poets of "Changing Rules, of late, as if men writ In spite of *Reason, Nature, Art* and *Wit*" (lines 11-12; the italics are mine). This is a direct slap at Dryden's elaborate defense of his supposedly new form, which in fact only deviates more violently from nature in its attempt to achieve novelty. Lacy goes on to claim that poets today make us laugh at tragedy and cry at comedy—the artistic world of the theatre, in other words, has been turned topsy-turvy by "fresh" effects, which in the end simply derive from sources as old as Preston's play. The Prologue then concludes with a witty reference to the "Critiques" who come to the theatre only to jeer—Lacy says if they do not like the character he is playing he will, in the manner of Bottom, remove his wig and discover to all his real identity. This jab at the fickleness of critics is a new development in the evolution of burlesque dramatic form, and it will be expanded and modified by Fielding and Sheridan in their masterpieces. Here Buckingham chides playwrights for their fear of condemning judges, most of whom were virtuosi attempting to gain status and reputation by damning everything on the stage. Any effort to please them, as the mechanicals tried to please all in "Pyramus and Thisby", is fated to result in chaotic scenes with little coherence.

In establishing his parodic point of view, Buckingham has employed the framing device of an audience-on-stage whose job it is to comment on the action. The method is comparable to that of the verse satirist who invents a persona to express critical opinions and otherwise act as a tool for achieving irony. The two wits who perform a similar task in **The Rehearsal,** Smith and Johnson, are expected to react to the turns and surprises in the performance as well as to Bayes' outbursts about the brilliance of his technique. Unlike George and Nell in *The Knight,* they do not superimpose their own play on the main action, nor do they champion an aesthetic which is being satirized. On the contrary, we see in the exchanges between the two men the emergence of a standard of common sense by which we in the audience can judge the incoherent action of the rehearsed play. They ask the same questions we might ask, which in the context qualifies them as sober judges in contrast

with the bogus playwright. Buckingham adds some touches of characterization to help us differentiate between them—Smith is a country fellow, skeptical yet anxious to see "the strange new things" he has heard about in the city. As the action progresses Bayes becomes more and more alienated by Smith's pointed inquiries, and something of a verbal tug-of-war does take place between them. Johnson, the city friend, knows that all the newfangledness of the stage is "dull" and "fantastical", but he is willing to let his friend see for himself and have some fun in the bargain. In fact at certain points he gleefully urges Bayes on by declaring that Smith's naive questions are only a sign of his country obtuseness: "Phoo! pr'ythee, *Bayes,* don't mind what he says: he is a fellow newly come out of the Country, he knows nothing of what's the relish, here, of the Town" (I. ii.). The two characters' names suggest a kind of typicality, a middle-class reasonableness against which we can easily measure both the excesses of the play and the outrageous remarks of Bayes. Further, I think Buckingham was directing his comic message at just such a reasonable element in the audience, men who paid attention to what takes place in plays and who demanded quality as well as noise. We are urged to hope through Johnson and Smith's remarks that their sense of artistic right and wrong will prevail, as we likewise feel in *The Knight* when the Boy speaks about unities and decorum to George and Nell. As neither "critics" nor courtiers, they do not invade the theatre but seem to belong there, ironically, with better claim than Bayes.

And what of this interloper? Johnson, in an early speech, tells us such fellows "scorns [sic] to imitate Nature; but are given altogether to elevate and surprise", which task he says means depicting "Fighting, Loving, Sleeping, Rhyming, Dying, Dancing, Singing, Crying; and everything but thinking and Sence". The dichotomies here are worth studying in connection with Buckingham's method of satire and caricature. "Elevate and surprise" are Dryden-like terms for heroic drama and point to its larger-than-life aims; but such a purpose is far removed from the classical-critical one, which is, according to Horace and Sidney, to "teach and delight". Dryden's apology in *Of Heroic Plays* was heavily weighted on the side of spectacle, forgetting in the process the instructive aims of dramatic art and the preeminence of plot in achieving those ends. "Thinking and sense" confirm that reading of Buckingham's complaint against excess, and the whole tenor of the argument suggests that the burlesque playwright is often motivated by a belief in ancient "rules" as effective, viable guidelines for the artist. At least these standards are most often appealed to for the sake of criticism. Those who deviate risk chaos, according to this view, because they are then forced to depend solely on their own fancies, something Dryden actually defends in his *Of Heroic Plays.* In shaping Bayes' caricature to fit Dryden and other composers of heroic plays, Buckingham further classes him with the growing class called virtuosi, amateurs who were in Charles' reign beginning to invade all areas of endeavor, including the theatre, claiming special knowledge. These men were to be roundly attacked in *Gulliver's Travels,* but it is increasingly clear that as early as 1671 their antics were arousing the scorn of certain aristocrats and other gentlemen, whose classical training and backgrounds made them suspicious of novelty in general. For this reason Bayes is portrayed as a schemer, a man obsessed with the notion of innovation at all costs.

Though Dryden is probably the central model for Buckingham's mock-playwright,[9] we should more fruitfully think of him as a satiric portrait of the newly-arrived virtuoso; the bad poet brashly pushing himself onto the stage; the popularizer determined to please unlettered taste. He is a Modern open to attack by Ancients, a fellow who scorns to imitate nature and who writes, as he tells us, not for money but "for Reputation". His name may be an intended pun on "base" with the further suggestion that all which drops forth from his pen is "base-born", art struggling to make it among its betters. In short, he is a prototype of the Grub Street hack who turns artist and playwright to get in on a good thing. This view is supported by Johnson in the first scene when he calls upon Bayes to explain the meaning of his last play (probably a reference to *The Conquest of Granada*):

> Faith, Sir, the Intrigo's now quite out of my head; but I have a new one, in my pocket, that I may say is a Virgin; 't has never yet been blown upon. I must tell you one thing. 'Tis all new Wit; and tho I say it, a better than my last: and you know well enough how that took . . . If you and your friend will do it but the honour to see it in its Virgin attire; though perhaps, it may blush, I shall not be asham'd to discover its nakedness unto you . . . [*Puts his hand into his pocket*]
>
> (I. i.)

Buckingham wittily uses this speech to present Bayes as a playwright-panderer—the "piece" is a "Virgin . . . never yet . . . blown upon"; he will "discover its nakedness" to Johnson and Smith at this private showing. The suggestion of pimp is perfectly appropriate to the ridiculing purpose of presenting Bayes as bogus and corrupting—he is an "artist" who ignores the "rules" for the sake of "invention". Paradoxically, his new work turns out to be an old hag, having been handled by earlier playwrights, and the audience is about to be swindled as it has been before by this salesman. Further, Bayes' gesture of reaching into his pocket hints at the "source" of his wit. Such scatological touches are conventional in burlesque and were used by both Shakespeare and Beaumont to ridicule their mock-heroes. In informing us of how he prepares to write, Bayes is even more explicit about his regimen, which suggests that "products" of his "labor" originate somewhere other than the brain: "If I am to write familiar things, as Sonnets to *Armida,* and the like, I make use of Stew'd Prunes only; but when I have a grand design in hand, I ever take Phisic, and let blood: for, when you would have pure swiftness of thought, and fiery flights of fancy, you must have a care of the pensive part. In fine, you must purge the Belly" (II. i.). Bayes, because of his humor-like intensity, might be fittingly called The Knight of the Burning Pen!

The portrait of Bayes as mock-hero has other intriguing dimensions. Besides being a panderer, he is also seen as constantly at war—with sense, the actors, the audience, and himself. He is a kind of general whose purpose is to outmaneuver his audience's awareness of what is happening, hoping to spring surprise attack after surprise attack on them. As the 1st Player tells us: ". . . the grand design upon the Stage is to keep the Auditors in suspense; for to guess presently at the plot, and the sence, tires 'em before the end of the first Act: now, here, every line surprises you, and brings in new matter" (I. ii.). This strategy openly follows the pyrotechnics of heroic drama, where sudden reversals are a crucial part of the effect. But to create his playwright as a bombastic warrior carrying on his own heroic struggle with sense is truly a witty touch by Buckingham. The fellow has done everything to insure success of his enterprise: his prologue will be delivered by a hangman, sword drawn, standing behind the author; if the audience fails to approve the argument, he will lose his head; he has passed out sheets of paper "to insinuate the Plot into the Boxes"; he has planted several friends in the pit to applaud vociferously at the proper times. His attitude toward Johnson and Smith is that they are, like most audiences, dense about this new way of writing; no amount of explanation will ever make his plot clear to them. As for the actors, they too are against him: "Aye, I gad, these fellows are able to spoil the best things in Christendome". He blames them especially for not performing certain things that Bayes himself has neglected to include in the play. In the opening scene, for instance, his two usurpers, the King's Physician and Gentleman-Usher, whisper together without letting the audience hear what they are saying. Then later, when the two lawful kings enter, they seem to know all the details of the imminent overthrow. Bayes is infuriated with Smith's question about how they knew, charging that the actors forgot to pop in their heads to overhear the whispering. He is constantly forcing his way into their midst to demonstrate the right way to sword-fight or dance or deliver one of his brilliant similes. This touch of characterization clearly places Bayes in the tradition of obstreperous managers who try to control every phase of the production: like Bottom he wants to play all the parts and show the other actors how each role is correctly handled; like George and Nell he will impose his taste on everyone and have performed the scenes he admires whenever they suit his fancy. Echoing the greengrocer from *The Knight,* when asked by Smith what has happened to the action at a particular point, since the "Plot stands still", Bayes replies: "Plot stand still! why, what a Devil is the Plot good for, but to bring in fine things?" (III. i.). This incredulous statement of contempt for control by anything beyond his own imagination is a form of comic pride, and Buckingham makes the most of it throughout his caricature of the bogus playwright.

The most devastating touch however is the representation of Bayes as plagiarist, a charge which took precedence over all others among Restoration critics.[10] In this play the direct assault is launched against Dryden, Howard, Davenant, and others for having stolen the incidents, sentiments, and method of characterization of heroic drama from other sources. Bayes proudly displays his book of "*Drama Common places*" to Johnson and Smith in the first act, and defends its use by claiming that all artists need such helps to spur their creative faculties. His rule of "Transversion, or *Regula Duplex*" allows the playwright to change prose to verse or verse to prose according to some high-sounding law, which in effect is self-made. He also "Transverses" witty remarks made at the coffeehouses, taking down any usable gems as they drop from the lips of gentlemen. And if any serious need arises for invention, e.g., finding something quickly, Bayes will

> never trouble my head about it, as other men do; but presently turn over this Book, and there I have, at one view, all that *Perseus, Montaigne, Seneca's Tragedies, Horace, Juvenal, Claudian, Pliny, Plutarch's Lives,* and the rest, have ever thought upon this subject: and so, in a trice, by leaving out a few words, or putting in others of my own, the business is done.
>
> (I. i.)

Buckingham's exaggeration for effect is obvious here: Bayes invents the rules of composition instead of receiving them, a direct attack on the habit of heroic dramatists of borrowing scenes of spectacle from both ancient and English Elizabethan dramatists. Such pilfering from prose sources was accepted practice in the Elizabethan age; we should especially note that Bayes mentions Plutarch's *Lives* among his originals, a source whose words Shakespeare might be said to have transversed. But the habit is out of style, in Buckingham's view, and the clear implication is that playwrights should concern themselves about their own ages and heroes and not the legendary past, glorious and warring though it may be. He also implies that ancient writers should be used as models and not treasure troves which the poet may plunder at will. Of course, Bayes denies the very thing he does without excuse. He is forever contradicting himself over the question of his debt to preceding dramatists, as in II. i., when he declares: "I despise your *Johnson* and *Beaumont,* that borrow'd all they writ from Nature. I am for fetching it purely out of my own fancy, I."

4.

By placing Johnson, Smith, and Bayes in the framework of a rehearsal situation, Buckingham has achieved another ingenious innovation in the burlesque format.[11] Beaumont, we should remember, had his commentators interrupt an actual performance to concoct their own play, while Shakespeare scattered rehearsal scenes by the mechanicals throughout his plot, inserting the actual performance before an audience on stage at the close of the action. Buckingham, however, maintains the rehearsal motif as a continuing device in order to achieve a number of comic effects. First, we notice as audience in the theatre that we are invited to peep through a keyhole to observe the absurdity of a pre-play performance—we are encouraged to laugh even more because no one on stage will notice. Someone has inadvertently left open the curtain and we can look in with no fear of being discovered. Because of the added dimension of an audience on stage, whose remarks lay bare the flaws in the play, we can direct our laughter at both author and work at the same time. Moreover, the actors can feel free to respond freely and naturally to the ridiculous things they are called upon to do, thereby adding another kind of criticism to the proceedings. Speaking as if he were describing the whole action of the piece, instead of a particular dance tune the absurd author has written, one actor complains: "Why, Sir, 'tis impossible to do anything in time, to this Tune." This and other similar comments suggest that the actors are the real heroes of the play, since they show courage and restraint beyond the call in not throttling the bogus playwright. Indeed, the actors, Johnson and Smith, we in the audience, everyone—except Bayes—is aware that if this is the state of the play in dress rehearsal, what can possibly be done to make it stageworthy in the few short hours before performance? (Rehearsals were usually conducted in the morning with performances beginning at three o'clock.) Seeing it at this point in its development is comparable to watching the condemned man before his execution: not even a pardon from the governor (or some new twist in the plot!) will save him from destruction. This strong hint of impending chaos provides the appropriate mood of failure and patchwork. The rehearsal ends with everyone departing the theatre, leaving an empty stage to a Bayes vowing to wreak vengeance on the town:

> I'l be reveng'd on them too; for I'l Lampoon 'em all. And Since they will not admit of my Plays, they shall know what a Satyrist I am. And so farewell to this Stage, I gad, forever.
>
> (V. i.)

This is probably intended as a direct slap at Dryden, who did indeed turn to writing satire; but it also states the critical case against bad poets turned playwrights by simply removing the aesthetic objects and tools they need to function—actors and audience. The true citizens of the theatre, Buckingham seems to hope, will manage to expel the interlopers by ignoring them and their products. By depicting the action in a rehearsal framework, he makes us thankful that the "child" Bayes spoke of earlier has been destroyed before it saw the light of the playhouse.

What then are the flaws in the character of this bastard known as heroic tragedy, and how does the burlesque playwright go about the task of ridiculing them? Bayes' drama, if we can call it that, is an unmanageable catch-all of the elements of heroic drama, romance, and melodrama. The plot, though it really has little, concerns two brothers whose kingdoms are usurped by their gentleman-usher and physician respectively. After the seizure takes place, prince Pretty-man is introduced to laud the beauty of his beloved, Cloris, and to argue about prices of finery with his tailor. Then news comes to the usurping kings that another prince, Volscius, has received word that his beloved, Parthenope, has committed suicide. Amaryllis, another fair maiden, is next discovered walking with a fisherman who is seized by soldiers for supposedly plotting the assassination of Volscius at the instigation of Pretty-man. We suddenly discover in the next scene that the fisherman is really Pretty-man's father, and the son is now forced to pray for his father's life.

Meanwhile, Volscius sees his beloved outside the city's walls (she is not dead after all) and declares his deep passion for her, while Cloris and Amaryllis laugh at his outbursts. Volscius then begins to pull off his boots, thus providing the appropriate setting for a self-debate over love and honor. It is not quite clear what the question of honor is, but for Bayes the occasion is ideal, since he can illustrate the hero's vacillation by having him hip-hop off the stage, one boot on, the other off. A funeral scene follows, the mourners bringing in a casket reportedly containing the remains of Lardella, sister to Drawcansir, the mock-hero of the play, with whom both the usurpers were said to have been in love. As the two men are about to commit suicide, Pallas enters wonderfully to discover a feast instead of funeral, assuring the two that their love is really alive and well. Drawcansir, however, interrupts the festivities, scorns the two usurpers, and drives them from the stage. Volscius and Pretty-man return for a verbal combat as they exchange superlatives in praise of their respective mistresses.

In a final burst of glory, the true monarchs return literally from the skies, wafted down on a magnificent machine meant to look like a cloud, and regain their empty thrones. A general shout and dance follow. But rude messengers barge in to report gathering armies (whose they are no one knows), whose presence constitutes a

threat to their majesties' safety. During the ensuing battle, prepared for by a recitative account of the armies, Drawcansir kills every soldier on both sides, and the play ends with bodies piled high on the stage amid shouts of victory from the winner. As the Epilogue astutely puts it, "The Play is at an end, but where's the Plot?" We might also logically ask: what are other conventions of the form which this mad and absurd piece farcically exaggerates?

I have already mentioned the implied complaint against mixing together comic and tragic elements, stated in the Prologue, or more precisely the habit among playwrights of bringing the action to the brink of disaster, then rescuing it by means of some external force. You will recall that this is what happened in *The Indian Queen* with the sudden, providential appearance of Amexia, the deposed queen, and the discovery that Montezuma was her rightful son and heir. Buckingham parodies this trick of denouement by including a scene in Bayes' play (IV. i.) during which the funeral of the beautiful Lardella is transformed into a banquet by the arrival of Athene, who in her helmet "brought a Pye" and wears a "Buckler made of Cheese".[12] The usurpers, both in love with the dead maiden, were about to commit a double suicide but the sudden appearance of a *deus ex machina* stopped them. The joke here is that these villains should have killed themselves—Pallas has frustrated the event which would have led to restoration of the brother kings. Instead, the deposition is delayed for another two scenes, at which point the rightful rulers drop unexpectedly out of the skies without having to engage in any kind of combat to win back their thrones! The stage direction underlines the drollness of this scene:

> *The two right Kings of Brentford descend in the Clouds, singing, in white garments and three Fidlers sitting before them, in green.*
>
> (V. i.)

Though such a picture seems outrageous and included solely for spectacle's sake, we should not forget that effects just as exaggerated as this were actually a part of Restoration performances, as proven by the following stage direction from Dryden's opera *Albion and Albanius* (1685):

> *The clouds divide and Juno appears in a machine drawn by peacocks; while a symphony is playing, it moves gently forward and as it descends, it opens and discovers the tail of the peacock, which is so large that it almost fills the opening of the stage between scene and scene.*[13]

The hackneyed motif of usurpation is wonderfully lampooned in ***The Rehearsal*** by depicting the usurpers as Gentleman-Usher and Physician, instead of relatives or rivals from other royal families. Moreover, the motives for the act are perfectly obscured in a whispering scene, which effectively hides the details from the audience and actors. A further incongruity, and probably the crucial one of this burlesque segment, is that these two "servants" speak in the same heroic verse as the kings and noble warriors, even though most of what they say is mundane and silly. Even when seizing the throne, which is done in easy fashion, without so much as a quarrel, the Gentleman-Usher announces:

> 'Tis right:
> And, since occasion now seems debonair,
> I'l seize on this, and you shall take that Chair.
>
> (I. iv.)

Since the deposition is accomplished with similar ease and lack of conflict, we can assume that Buckingham is focusing close attention on the weaknesses in plotting and building conflict and tension into the action of heroic plays as well. Here, the battle between soldiers, presumably supporting the opposing sides, takes place *after* the usurpation; in it, *all* the soldiers are killed, after which they arise and begin a dance with Bayes directing the choreography. Though Bayes has already told us the plot exists only to bring in fine things, we might still be expected to blanch at men seizing thrones without any conflict and dead soldiers rising from the ground to do a jig! The habit of interjecting dances and music between scenes in heroic plays is likewise being lampooned.

Extravagant similes are another feature of heroic drama which are fair game for the skilled parodist. Their presence was justified primarily on the basis of their appropriateness to the acting of fine things in epic poetry. But on the stage these similes are likely to flop, possibly because their length, intricateness, and exaggerated tone caused audiences' attention to wander, thus losing the intended impact. Mock-heroic technique is devastatingly employed in Buckingham's parody of a simile from *The Conquest of Granada* (II. ii.) dealing with two turtle doves caught in a storm:

> So Boar and Sow, when any storm is nigh,
> Snuff up, and smell it gath'ring in the sky;
> Boar beckons Sow to trot in Chestnut Groves,
> And there consummate their unfinish'd Loves:
> Pensive in mud they wallow all alone,
> And snore and gruntle to each other's moan.
>
> (I. ii.)

As expected the goal of this mock-epic simile is debasement—the birds become pigs, the branches of trees are reduced to a mud pit, the gentle love-making is transformed into gross breeding. Buckingham's point here is that bad poets unintentionally drag sentiments through the dirt, and this natural bent is particularly noticeable in a play pretending to epic heights. Bayes, like Bottom and Rafe before him, is supremely literal: in addition to this unfortunate simile, he also adds the characters Thunder and Lightning (remember Wall and

Moonshine) to depict a storm (I. ii.). Both "allegorical" characters threaten the audience, critics, gallants, and fine ladies alike, with singing and blasting if they do not applaud the play. The poetaster thus leaves nothing to the imagination, even in the matter of a storm, with the result that all is brought down to a very earthy and earthly level—especially in the expression of sentiments.

At the dead center of all heroic plays is the agonizing debate between love and honor; without it such fare would be nothing more than episodic adventure, lacking both theme and thought. But most of the typical debates with self by heroic protagonists tended to be highly artificial and often tedious to hear. Montezuma's ejaculation on the ambivalence of such situations is a good example in IV. ii. of *The Indian Queen*. Buckingham's parody underlines the hero's feelings of ambivalence by adding a physical dimension to the philosophical debate. Prince Volscius, leader of one of the armies (Bayes is not sure which), is in love with the fair Parthenope, whom he has just met at the town wall where her mother sells ale. Assuming this girl dressed in rags is really a high-born beauty, Volscius cannot resist her charms, even though he knows his army awaits him back at the camp. What is he to do? In an hilarious scene, Bayes has him debate the point while putting on his boots:

> My Legs, the Emblem of my various thought,
> Shew to what sad distraction I am brought.
> Sometimes with stubborn Honour, like this Boot,
> My mind is guarded, and resolv'd: to do't:
> Sometimes, again, that very mind, by Love
> Disarm'd, like this other Leg does prove.
> Shall I to Honour or to Love give way?
> Go on, cries Honour; tender Love saies, nay:
> Honour, aloud, commands, pluck both Boots on;
> But softer Love does whisper put on none.
> What shall I do? what conduct shall I find
> To lead me through this twy-light of my mind?
> For as bright Day with black approach of Night
> Contending, makes a doubtful puzzling light;
> So does my Honour and my Love together
> Puzzle me so, I can resolve for neither. (*Goes out hopping with one Boot on, and the other off*)
>
> [III. v.]

The stage direction undercuts the whole debate skillfully, but it also urges one to look back at the speech to discover more turns of a humorous sort. Love telling Volscius to "Put on none" is clearly a light sexual joke, intended to poke fun at the high-flown view of love in the heroic plays, a view considered very cynically by the morally loose courtiers like Buckingham. Volscius' legs acting as an emblem of the dilemma suggests another incongruous simile about "horns of a dilemma", which further debases this quarrel with principles. The stage directions also tell us that Bayes is mimicking Volscius while he is undergoing his moral struggle with the boots, and this mirror image of absurdity adds even more to an audience's delight with the whole incident. Verbal parody, physical jigging and farce combine to make this one of the most successful scenes in the play; and like many of the others it does not demand from the viewers any previous knowledge about a particular speech or play. Moreover, as the reader later discovers Volscius's problem is never resolved, for as he is about to plead his case to the usurpers the true kings return, and all action is resolved in an anticlimactic battle. This treatment of the love versus honor quarrel suggests the artificiality of such debates as well as their interminable length—the question is completely forgotten when hero and heroine gain permission to be married.

But Buckingham's single boldest stroke is the hatching of Drawcansir, Bayes' ranting protagonist, "a fierce *Hero,* that frights his Mistress, snubs up Kings, baffles Armies, and does what he will, without regard to numbers, good manners, or justice". The ironic truth of the caricature is that most of what is said about Drawcansir applies equally well to Bayes, suggesting that the kind of pugnacity displayed in heroic characters is just as ludicrous when seen in a real person—especially a poetaster at war with the critical world. Since Bayes urges so strongly the originality of his protagonist, he unwittingly identifies himself as the father of a freakish son. To display further ignorance of strategy or plotting, Bayes fails to introduce his hero until the last scene of Act IV, a touch which underscores the habit of suddenly bringing in the hero to display his courage by killing off any problems the complex action might have spawned. Drawcansir simply snatches bowls of wine out of the usurpers' hands, scares them off, and downs the wine with: "I drink, I huff, I strut, look big and stare; And all this I can do, because I dare."

These lines spoken by Drawcansir are parodies of speeches by Dryden's Almanzor in *The Conquest of Granada, Part II* (II. iii.); and Buckingham's mock-hero was no doubt intended as a caricature of Dryden's Spanish adventurer-mercenary. The name Drawcansir is probably suggestive of the hero's habit of drawing his sword at the drop of a crown, since Almanzor is Dryden's most excitable leading man, subject to sudden changes of heart and will. He begins every struggle with pronouncements meant to prove that he is "all man, sir". At the opening of *Conquest* he defends the right of King Boabdelin in battling and defeating the rebellious Duke Arcos, whom he then magnanimously offers to free. When Boabdelin understandably refuses to comply with this gesture, Almanzor leads a revolt of his own, unseats Boabdelin, and puts the friendly Prince Abdalla on the throne. But peace is a fragile thing, especially with passionate young men around. Abdalla denies Almanzor's request to marry the beautiful Almahide, presumably because nothing is known about the warrior's origin or family. As you might guess, Almanzor then turns on Abdalla, deposes him, and returns the crown to the patient Boabdelin; in a final battle, moreover, Almanzor discovers that Duke Arcos is really his father, and his royal blood now gives him license to both the throne and Almahide. (This was only the conclusion of Part I; in Part II a similar ballet goes on, with much more mayhem.) His oscillation of moods and passionate pursuit of Almahide and honor make Almanzor into a proper subject for ridicule. Instead of presenting Drawcansir as the central figure throughout, Buckingham brings him in to scare off the usurpers, then later has him throttle two opposing armies in a final slaughterhouse scene. The satire here is blatant: Drawcansir favors neither side in this grand battle, fought between foot and hobbyhorses, but murders them all! This is Bayes' way of outdoing his predecessors—he simply adds more violence and spectacle, forgetting completely about the plot. In fact, there is no reason for this final battle other than pure entertainment, since the two kings have already secured their thrones.

But as we have seen in preceding burlesque plays, anticlimax is a crucial convention. In *A Midsummer Night's Dream,* the mechanicals' Pyramus and Thisbe play retained the suicides but forgot the reasons for them: and in *The Knight* Rafe enters as a spectre with an arrow through his head simply because George and Nell want to hear a Senecan ghost speech and not because the speech has anything to do with the plot. *Rafe Roister Doister* ended in a battle of pots and pans, representing a parody of the Trojan War (since it is fought over a woman) and the battle of the sexes. Likewise, in heroic plays the stage was required at the end of the action to be filled with corpses, even though the reason for such mass murder might not have been carefully explained. Seven characters are killed on stage in Part II of *The Conquest of Granada,* and others dispatched off. The stage direction in *The Rehearsal* (V. i.) does not specify how many soldiers were supposed to expire in front of the audience, but we can safely assume that Bayes has packed the space between scenes. After Drawcansir has succeeded in dispatching them all, he turns to the audience for his one and only heroic speech:

> Others may bost a single man to kill;
> But I the blood of thousands daily spill.
> Let petty Kings the names of Parties know:
> Where e'er I come, I slay both friend and foe.
> The swiftest Horsmen my swift rage controuls,
> And from their Bodies drives their trembling souls.
> If they had wings, and to the Gods could flie,
> I would pursue, and beat 'em, through the skie:
> And make proud Jove, with all his Thunder, see
> This single Arm more dreadful is, than he.

This hyperbolic declaration places Drawcansir squarely in the tradition of mock-heroes reaching back to Thersites, Roister Doister, and Sir Thopas. All boast about martial prowess and their ability to overkill, thereby qualifying as supreme examples of comic pride run rampant. Drawcansir is a caricature as well of hot-blooded fighters like Hotspur, especially in his ranting vow to pursue his victims into the sky. "I defye all your Histories, and your Romances too", declares Bayes, "to shew me one such Conqueror as this Drawcansir". The point is that Bayes' protagonist is a composite of the heroes from exactly the sources he mentions; his sole distinction is that he is such a perfect copy.

As soon as Drawcansir has strutted off the stage, we assume Bayes' narrative powers have been played out. At this point both actors and audience (Smith and Johnson) take *their* cue and depart before he does have a chance to introduce anything else. And he does plan to spring more nonsense on us. One of the players, while Bayes has gone to fetch the others who tried to escape, discovers a sheet of paper with the argument for Act V scribbled on it. This act develops a subplot involving Prince Pretty-man and Cloris and traces the dissolution of their love. Here again the vignette has nothing to do with the main action, and would if played have constituted yet another anticlimax. Left alone, Bayes' threat to turn satirist and be revenged on them all is as hollow as Malvolio's at the end of *Twelfth Night.* In both these plays, moreover, the appropriate punishment is found for the alien forces—they are ignored, left alone without an audience, to stand on their own merits. Bayes' rejection of the theatre is an ironic bit of rationalization—the theatre in effect has rejected him and his bogus art. To reinforce this point the Epilogue makes a special plea to the remaining viewers:

> Wherefore, for ours, and for the Kingdom's peace,
> May this prodigious way of writing cease.
> Let's have, at least, once in our lives, a time
> When we may hear some reason, not all Rhyme;
> We have these ten years felt its Influence;
> Pray let this prove a year of Prose and Sence.

5.

A final word should be said about the variety of styles presented here in **The Rehearsal.** As in *The Knight* and *A Midsummer Night's Dream,* a good deal of the wit consists in medleys of juxtaposed manners of speech. The rather urbane and conversational type of prose is used by Johnson and Smith, an appropriate form for their function as common sense standards of taste. The mode and tone are conversational, tinged with a few weak oaths and for the most part consisting of questions or simple, devastating observations like Smith's: "I find the Author will be very much obliged to the Players, if they can make any sence out of this." This somewhat normative form is set against the more extravagant and profane idiom of Bayes' speech, filled as it is with hyperbole, oaths, Latin tags, and other signs of his humorous nature. The most consistent tone in Bayes' remarks is exclamatory, thereby indicating his role as mock-heroic jouster-with-sense. Illustrative of this is his attack on the actors, who never seem to do what he requires:

> —Phoo, Pox! you are come out too late, Sir, now you may go out again if you please. I vow to gad, Mr.—

a—I would not give a button for my Play, now you have done this.

PRETTY-MAN.

What Sir?

BAYES.

What Sir! 'Slife, Sir, you should have come out in a choler, rous upon the stage, just as the other went off. Must a man be eternally telling you these things?

(III. iv.)

This oath-filled banter is most effectively contrasted, however, with the heroic verse of the actors as they read the parts while Bayes intersperses his comments, as in IV. ii., where Volscius and Pretty-man are debating the beauty of their two loves:

VOLS.

Let my *Parthenope* at length prevail.

BAYES.

Civil, I gad.

PRET.

I'l sooner have a passion for a Whale:
In whose vast bulk, though store of Oyl doth lye,
We find more shape, more beauty, in a Fly.

SMI.

That's uncivil, I gad.

BAYES.

Yes; but as far a fetch'd fancy tho, I gad, as e're you saw.

VOLS.

Soft, *Pretty-man,* let not thy vain pretence
Of perfect love, defame love's excellence.
Parthenope is sure, as far above
All other loves, as above all is Love.

BAYES.

Ah! I gad, that strikes me.

PRET.

To blame my *Cloris,* Gods would not pretend.

BAYES.

Now mark.

VOLS.

Were all Gods join'd, they could not hope to mend
My better choice; for fair *Parthenope,*
Gods would, themselves, un-god themselves to see.

BAYES.

Now the Rant's acoming.

PRET.

> Durst any of the Gods be so uncivil,
> I'ld make that God suscribe himself a Devil.

BAYES.

> Ah, Godsookers, that's well writ!
> (*Scratching his head, his Peruke falls off*)

Such a long quotation clearly illustrates the effectiveness of the frame device of the rehearsal. Bayes must point out the ingenuity of his writing to the two gentlemen because they obviously cannot see it. His favorite word of praise is "civil", and he even manages to work it into Pretty-man's final speech. Clearly, Bayes' conduct and his verse are both uncivil, or not in keeping with social and aesthetic etiquette: the audience and not the poet should judge the work. When the poetaster warns that the "Rant's acoming" the warning applies both to his speeches in the play and his own prose outside of it. And the loss of his peruke is another farcical touch, comparable to his pratfall in II. v. (actually, we should call it "nosefall") and his attempts to dance, which help to underline the absurdity of this director's actions. His exaggerated physical antics reinforce his outrageous habit of speech.

Other forms of verse include the songs which are interspersed throughout the action, some of which parody Dryden's songs (see III. i.), and the recitative used to elevate the description of battle scenes in heroic plays. This latter technique, similar to operatic recitative, is cleverly parodied in V. i., when the General and Lieutenant list the bands of warriors prepared to do battle. The ironic turn is achieved here through a parody of the epic catalogue of heroes and their home countries ("Phorcys led the Phrygians"); the joke is that these fighters are all from familiar and not exotic places:

LIEUT.-GEN.

> The Band you boast of, *Chelse* Cuirassiers,
> Shall, in my *Putney* Pikes, now meet their Peers.

GEN.

> Chiswickians aged, and renown'd in fight,
> Join with the *Hammersmith* Brigade.

LIEUT.-GEN.

> You'll find my Mortlake Boys will do them right,
> Unless by *Fulham* numbers over-laid.

Here familiarity breeds contempt since by listing these home guard units the grandeur of battle is reduced considerably. Indeed, Bayes undercuts the epic stature of his play from the very beginning by setting it in Brentford, an area close to London, instead of staging the action in some distant and strange-sounding land. And these generals, with their recitation style, lose much of their stature as heroic figures when the scene of their struggle is put so close to the playgoers' everyday world.

A classic stichomythic exchange between Amaryllis and the Fisherman provides yet another type of dialogue to contrast with heroic verse and colloquial prose used in the rest of the play. In fact the method of parody adopted here is frequently associated with the best-known burlesque routines, such as the famous Abbott and Costello "Who's on first?" exchange:

AMA.

> Villain, what Monster did corrupt thy mind
> T'attaque the noblest soul of human kind?
> Tell me who set thee on.

FISH.

> Prince *Pretty-man.*

AMA.

> To kill whom?

FISH.

> Prince *Pretty-man.*

AMA.

> What, did Prince *Pretty-man* hire you to kill Prince *Pretty-man*?

FISH.

> No; Prince *Volscius.*

AMA.

> To kill whom?

FISH.

> Prince *Volscius*

AMA.

> What, did Prince *Volscius* hire you to kill Prince *Volscius*?

FISH.

> No; Prince *Pretty-man.*

AMA.

> So!—drag him hence,
> Till torture of the Rack produce his Sense.[14]

(III. iii.)

One can easily envision Buckingham delighting in the sheer nonsense of this passage, poking fun as he does at the needlessly complex intrigues of heroic plays. The purposely intensified rhythm of the exchanges suggests the kind of pyrotechnics heroic dramatists will use to keep their audiences awake. We remember this patch of dialogue later, when at the end of the rehearsal the witty and polished couplets of the Epilogue stand out as reasonable writing pleading for a return to "Prose and Sense".

Buckingham's stylistic potpourri is a convention of the burlesque play, and we can see such medleys working just as effectively in *The Knight* and especially in *A Midsummer Night's Dream,* where the stately blank verse of Theseus is set against the rhymed verse of the lovers and the prosaic dialogue of the mechanicals. Yet in spite of these and other shared traits it has been claimed that most modern readers miss the fun because they are unacquainted with the heroic language and plots *The Rehearsal* parodies.[15] This may to some degree be true, but such a claim does ignore the tradition of burlesque in which Buckingham is working, a tradition that all but insures success because of certain tested techniques. For instance, the rehearsal device, providing as it does spectators on stage, allows the playwright to establish a standard or norm with which the audience in the theatre can readily identify. They are immediately in on the joke. The creation of a mock-heroic playwright, whose manner and idiom are so obviously ridiculous, presents us with a classic comic type whom we can comfortably feel is inferior to us. Buckingham insures this impression by making Bayes the epitome of literalness, as he brings on the stage all sorts of spectacle and mayhem in an attempt to do something new. For example, his two allegorical scenes, the first involving Thunder and Lightning, his second the Sun and Moon, recall the creation of actual characters to play Wall and Moonshine in *A Midsummer Night's Dream.* The bogus playwright's lack of concern for coherent plot, the unities, and decorum reflects a cultivation of pure fancy, a humor which the satirist attacks by taking a classical-critical point of view. This stance conforms to those taken by preceding burlesque playwrights as well, especially Beaumont. It is most congenial to the audience, moreover, because it appeals to their intellect and sense of proportion, both of which should be at work in a comic situation. Comedy is, we should remember, a form of criticism—it traditionally has seen man as he is and not as he would like to pretend he is. Heroic drama, like chivalric literature and romance epics on which it is founded, was an attempt to elevate human motive and action above the mundane and to see man in god-like garb, defying convention—and often sense—to do great things. It is easy to see why such an aim excited the ridicule of cynical court wits like Buckingham, Butler, Rochester, Sedley, and others. The Restoration liked to see itself on the stage and preferred comedy to tragedy; it tended to be suspicious of both excessive virtue and strained debates over questions of honor, love, and friendship.

Furthermore, in *The Rehearsal* I think we find ample reason to laugh at the antics of Bayes and his play without knowing the main elements of heroic drama. The dramatic flaws Buckingham chooses to attack are recognizably bad theatre in any age, because they depend on twisting the medium out of shape in order to succeed: long debates by the hero with himself or another over moral and philosophical questions, *deus ex machina* endings, spectacle included for its own sake, lack of cogent plot, literalness, and poor taste have consistently been the targets of burlesque. There might even be some envy behind the impulse to ridicule what is popular; Buckingham was not a notably successful dramatist but more a man about town. His satiric treatment of Dryden is particularly rough here, yet we have seen in modern literature (and other media as well) that parody of current and widely-accepted books, poems, and television programs is enjoyed as much by those who have given such trends currency as those who have lampooned them. Vogues in literature, after all, die out when audiences become tired of them and not when a successful travesty has been written. A case in point is the heroic play itself, which did not begin to disappear from the boards until some ten years after *The Rehearsal* appeared. And as we shall see, Fielding too felt the need to burlesque a similar heroic formula when he composed *Tom Thumb* sixty years later. These facts should lead us to enjoy *The Rehearsal* as a unique work of dramatic art whose purpose, though in part to correct, is mainly to give us a memorable play and caricature, and to admire the skill which animates the witty and delightful act of ridicule.

Notes

1. Frank L. Huntley, *On Dryden's Essay of Dramatic Poesy* (Ann Arbor, 1951), 47.

2. W. P. Ker, ed., *Essays of John Dryden* (New York, 1961), I, 100-101.

3. Ker, *Essays of John Dryden,* I, 153. All citations are from this edition.

4. V. C. Clinton-Baddeley, *The Burlesque Tradition in the English Theatre After* 1660 (London, 1952), 36.

5. See Dougald MacMillan and Howard Mumford Jones, eds., *Plays of the Restoration and Eighteenth Century* (New York, 1931), 28. All act and scene references to *The Indian Queen* are from this edition.

6. Martin Price, *To the Palace of Wisdom: Studies in Order and Energy from Dryden to Blake* (Garden City, New York, 1964), 34.

7. Buckingham was the chief of a group of collaborators which included Thomas Spratt, Samuel Butler, and Martin Clifford. They apparently worked over the play for a considerable time before producing it. See MacMillan and Jones, 50-51.

8. All quotes are from Montague Summers, ed., *The Rehearsal* (Stratford-upon-Avon: Shakespeare Head Press, 1914).

9. Legend has it that Buckingham coached Lacy, the actor who first played Bayes, urging him to copy Dryden's mannerisms. Another claim is that

Buckingham brought the poet laureate to the theatre on opening night purposely to watch him squirm. Bayes uses the oath "I gad" or "I gods" numerous times in the play, and these were supposed to be notorious Drydenisms. The suggestion is also made that Bayes (Dryden) wrote the part of Amaryllis into the play for his own mistress. It is well to remember, however, that Dryden was the target of other caricaturists as well, most notably by Arrowsmith in his depiction of the poet laureate as a comic tutor in *The Reformation* (1673). See Dane F. Smith, *Plays About the Theatre in England* (London, 1936), 15.

10. John H. Wilson, *A Preface to Restoration Drama* (Cambridge, Mass., 1968), 47.

11. Dane Smith, 10, holds that Buckingham's source for the rehearsal motif was Molière's *L'Impromptu de Versailles* (1663). Buckingham was in Paris in 1661, and it could be safely assumed he saw a number of Molière plays. I tend to see the motif as evolving from English rehearsal plays, especially *The Knight of the Burning Pestle,* Peele's *Old Wives Tale,* and *A Midsummer Night's Dream.*

12. The poetaster also informs the audience here (IV. i.) that he follows the rule of romance by giving us five plays to one plot. This remark parodies the habit of dividing heroic plays into parts, as was the case with *The Conquest of Granada,* or of writing sequels such as *The Indian Emperor* to follow *The Indian Queen.*

13. Cited in Wilson, *A Preface to Restoration Drama,* 16.

14. This is probably intended to parody a scene in Act I of *Mariage à la Mode,* during which Polydamus questions Hermogenes concerning the fate or whereabouts of his wife and child.

15. Wilson, *A Preface to Restoration Drama,* 137-138.

Richard Elias (essay date March 1978)

SOURCE: Elias, Richard. "'Bayes' in Buckingham's *The Rehearsal.*" *English Language Notes* 15, no. 3 (March 1978): 178-81.

[*In the following essay, Elias discusses similarities between Buckingham's characterization of the playwright Mr. Bayes and John Dryden.*]

Through the figure of Mr. Bayes, the obnoxious playwright in *The Rehearsal* (first acted December 1671), Buckingham and his collaborators extended their satiric attack on heroic drama to include the personal characteristics of the poets who wrote it. Since Dryden was foremost among the new dramatists of the Restoration, he took most of the drubbing, and despite his denials, the name "Bayes" stuck with him throughout his career. "Bayes," of course, helps single out Dryden as *The Rehearsal*'s principal target. As poet laureate since 1670, Dryden wore the official bays of English poetry, and according to the letter from "The Publisher to the Reader" printed with "A Key to *The Rehearsal*" in 1705, it was Dryden's public position that inspired Buckingham's choice of a name for him. After the death of Davenant, so the letter states, "Mr. *Dryden* a new Laureat appear'd on the Stage, much admir'd, and highly Applauded; which mov'd the Duke to change the name of his Poet from *Bilboa* [in an earlier version of *The Rehearsal*], to *Bayes.*"[1] This account, though sound enough, reduces Buckingham's play to the level of a personal attack on Dryden, motivated chiefly by Dryden's new prominence as a dramatist.[2] But as this note will show, the name "Bayes" was also suggested to the authors of *The Rehearsal* by a purple passage in Dryden's *Essay of Dramatic Poesy* (1668), his most important defense of the kind of drama Buckingham brought into ridicule.

In Act I of *The Rehearsal,* Johnson and Smith encounter Mr. Bayes and ask him to explain his last play. Bayes has already forgotten it, but he reaches into his pocket for his new one and invites them to watch a rehearsal of it:

> Faith, Sir, the Intrigo's now quite out of my head; but I have a new one, in my pocket, that I may say is a Virgin; 't has never yet been blown upon. I must tell you one thing, 'tis all new Wit. . . .[3]

With this speech, the central action of the farce—the rehearsal of Bayes's zany play—is set in motion. Buckingham was probably recalling the following passage from Dryden's *Essay,* in which Neander amplifies his argument for dramatic innovation by glancing at the inimitable achievements of Shakespeare and Ben Jonson:

> There is scarce an humour, a character, or any kind of plot, which they have not blown upon: all comes sullied or wasted to us: and were they to entertain this age, they could not make so plenteous treatments out of such decayed fortunes. This therefore will be a good argument to us either not to write at all, or to attempt some other way. There is no bays to be expected in their walks: *tentanda via est, qua me quoque possum tollere humo.*[4]

The quotation from *Georgics,* III, 8-9 effectively sums up Neander's rejection of the English stage tradition: "I must try a way whereby I, too, may rise from the earth." Neander casts himself, and all Restoration dramatists by implication, as the unwilling inheritors of a bankrupt estate, adding the gratuitous suggestion that not even Shakespeare or Jonson would succeed if they wrote in such a refined age as the Restoration. His argument here echoes the related theme expressed in Lisideius' quotation from Velleius Paterculus earlier in the debate. If we cannot surpass our predecessors, the Roman historian wrote, we abandon our attempt, "and leaving aside those things in which we cannot excel, we seek for something in which we can advance."[5]

Despite their polemical modernism, Neander and Lisideius leave themselves open to the charge that innovation is required mainly because the giants of the past have exhausted nearly all the possibilities of the English stage tradition. In their claims, the value of the new drama is less important than the need to innovate. Thus Neander's "other way" becomes Bayes's "new way of writing" in *The Rehearsal.* Where Dryden aspired to supplant the blank verse tragedies of Shakespeare and Jonson with the rhymed heroic play, Buckingham implies that Dryden's new drama has no other basis than his own whimsies. By defiantly rejecting the tradition, moreover, Dryden has willfully cut himself off from whatever possibilities remain to be explored in it. One effect of the thematic parallel between Neander's speech and Bayes's, then, is to undercut Dryden's argument for dramatic innovation.

Verbal similarities undercut Dryden another way as well. Bayes's image of his play as a virgin who has not yet been "blown upon" gives Dryden's phrase a smutty twist. According to Partridge's *Dictionary of Slang and Unconventional English,* "blow upon" meant "to make public" or "to discredit" in colloquial usage between the seventeenth and nineteenth centuries. The *OED* defines it as "to make stale or hackneyed," the sense Dryden uses, but also as "to bring into discredit, defame" ("blow," def. 30). The late seventeenth- and early eighteenth-century examples quoted in the *OED* give the phrase an underlying connotation of sexual defloration which agrees more with Bayes's usage than with Dryden's.[6] Hence, Bayes's use of "blown upon" indirectly deflates Dryden's use of the same phrase to describe the Restoration dramatist's uneasy relationship to the works of his forebears. Again, by extending the virgin image throughout the rest of his speech ("I shall not be asham'd to discover its nakedness to you"), Bayes's attempt at wit brings to mind some of Dryden's equally unsuccessful efforts, as in the dedication of his *Essay*: "Seeing then our theatres shut up, I was engaged in these kind of thoughts with the same delight with which men think on their absent mistresses."[7] Like Mr. Bayes, Dryden manages to sound like an armchair rake.

If Dryden sought his bays in other walks, then, his professed ambition to earn them gave Buckingham yet one more feature to satirize. Contemporaries failed to notice the parallel, but one last piece of evidence suggests that Dryden saw it. His revisions for the 1683 edition of *An Essay* emend Neander's speech to read "used" for the telltale "blown upon."[8] Although most of Dryden's other revisions are stylistic, this one, I suggest, serves mainly to disguise the verbal similarity I have noted. It achieves secrecy at the cost of some force, however, for the original phrase suits the mood and rhythm of Neander's speech far better than the relatively colorless "used." Yet no wise man ever admits he is the target of satire, and Dryden's emendation shows he was clever enough to conceal Mr. Bayes's ironic indebtedness to his prose.

Notes

1. *Miscellaneous Works, Written by George, Late Duke of Buckingham,* ed. Thomas Brown (London, 1705), p. xii.

2. The literature relating Dryden to *The Rehearsal* is too extensive to cite here. George McFadden summarizes much of it in "Political Satire in *The Rehearsal,*" YES, [*Yearbook of English Studies*] 4 (1974), 120-121, which presents evidence that Bayes was partly modeled on Buckingham's political rival, Henry Bennet, Earl of Arlington.

3. *The Rehearsal,* ed. Edward Arber, English Reprints, No. 10 (London, 1868), p. 29.

4. *Of Dramatic Poesy and Other Essays,* ed. George Watson (London, 1962), I, 85.

5. *Of Dramatic Poesy,* I, 56 and note. I quote Watson's translation.

6. For instance, Mrs. Centlivre's *Busie Bodie,* II.ii: "If I can but keep my Daughter from being blown upon 'till Signior Babinetto arrives"; and Addison's *Spectator,* No. 105: "He will . . . whisper an Intrigue that is not yet blown upon by common fame."

7. *Of Dramatic Poesy,* I, 13.

8. The text of *An Essay* in *The Works of John Dryden,* vol. 17, eds. S. H. Monk and A. E. Wallace Maurer (Berkeley, 1971), generally follows the 1683 version. See p. 73 for Neander's speech.

G. Jack Gravitt (essay date winter 1982)

SOURCE: Gravitt, G. Jack. "The Modernity of *The Rehearsal*: Buckingham's Theatre of the Absurd." *College Literature* 9, no. 1 (winter 1982): 30-8.

[*In the following essay, Gravitt suggests that* The Rehearsal *still appeals to modern readers because of its similarity to twentieth-century Theatre of the Absurd.*]

It is hardly a matter for dispute that George Villiers, second Duke of Buckingham, and his collaborators used *The Rehearsal* to satirize the great heroic dramatist John Dryden, and the genre of heroic drama itself.[1] In recent demonstrations of the play's satiric intent and devices, Peter Lewis tells us, "*The Rehearsal* is the archetype of most later Restoration and Augustan dramatic burlesques"; and Robert F. Willson, Jr., concurs, calling it a "witty and delightful act of ridicule." George McFadden has added much new and useful information as to the political satire implicit in *The Rehearsal,* but it is Sheridan Baker who deals with what makes the play continue to fascinate today's readers. The answer, according to Baker, is "this eternal flirtation between our love of illusion and our need for reality."[2]

Despite the importance of all these studies, no one thus far has satisfactorily explained why the play is so attractive to modern readers who know little about the conventions of heroic drama and less about Dryden's biography. There is something modern in the work's appeal, and the foundation for it lies at a level much deeper than the topical satire which inspired much of the play's initial popularity.[3] The modernity of *The Rehearsal* results, I believe, from its anticipation of literary techniques and devices present in today's Theatre of the Absurd.[4] Buckingham's use of the play-within-the-play and his creation of characters who rebel against their maker prefigure not only such twentieth-century plays as Luigi Pirandello's *Six Characters in Search of an Author*[5] and Joseph Heller's *We Bombed in New Haven*[6] but also such contemporary films as François Truffaut's *Day for Night*[7] and Frederico Fellini's *8 1/2.*[8]

When a modern audience first encounters *The Rehearsal,* it is likely to be overwhelmed by the satire that Buckingham marshaled against the conventions of heroic drama; however, satire will not answer all the questions elicited by the play, and it is at this point that the conventions of the Theatre of the Absurd become important. The main elements of absurdist drama present in *The Rehearsal* are structural involution, plotlessness, devalued language, and the equivalent of what is today called "Black Humor."[9]

Alfred Appel in his introduction to *The Annotated Lolita* explains the term *involution*:

> . . . an involuted work turns in upon itself, is self-referential, conscious of its status as fiction [or drama], and . . . [is an] allegory of itself, to use Mallarmé's description of one of his own poems. An ideally involuted sentence would simply read, "I am a sentence. . . ."[10]

The Rehearsal's techniques of involution are the play-within-the-play, or "playness" of the play, and the "interior" playwright-director's loss of artistic control.[11]

Involution begins in *The Rehearsal* with Buckingham's obvious use of an internal dress rehearsal. What is not so obvious is that this play-within-the-play technique not only mocks the historical figure of John Dryden but

subtly assails the traditional playwright's privilege of controlling the ongoings of his plot. The general mode of this attack emphasizes the multi-leveled view of reality present in the play—a view that enables the reader-audience to perceive various layers of reality. The characters of Bayes' play are in the first layer, for they understand nothing. The actors—who are vaguely aware of some of what the inner play is about and who can see some of its deficiencies—reside in the second layer. Bayes, who has created the "drama" and presumably knows more about it than anyone else, appears in the third layer. Johnson and Smith appear here also; and they, after seeing most of the rehearsal, challenge Bayes' knowledge and decide that his play is utter nonsense. There is no doubt that Johnson and Smith are correct in their assessment if we view *The Rehearsal* as being merely satiric, but their challenge to Bayes' artistic integrity indirectly calls attention to the problems of authorship in general.[12] Finally, the audience—which is, of course, outside the play—occupies the fourth level of understanding. This audience should be aware of Buckingham's implicit invitation for them to question the validity of their perceptions as they view *The Rehearsal* in its entirety.[13] Faced with this cross section, we are more likely to be confused than enlightened by this play's reflexivity, its constant calling attention to itself as being a play. The confusion, however, is aesthetically consistent with *The Rehearsal*'s absurdist implications.[14]

Specific references to the reflexivity of Buckingham's play are present throughout the work. In an early conversation with Smith, Bayes brags that he has "made a prologue and an epilogue which may both serve for either . . . [or] for any other play as well as this."[15] Such references remind the audience not only that they are watching Bayes' play but also that there exists a reality outside *The Rehearsal.* At another point Bayes reminds his viewers of the mechanical problems in the play's production. Since he feels a long, obligatory battle scene would be too gory for the ladies and too boring for everyone else, he represents the entire battle with "two persons only" (V.i.185). Here again the usual audience involvement is thwarted because of the absurdly self-referential nature of Bayes' work.

Another method of involution used by Buckingham involves Bayes' lack of aesthetic control of his language, his plot, and his actors. Of the first, Prince Pretty-man's distaste for Parthenope provides an example:

> I'll sooner have a passion for a whale,
> In whose vast bulk, though store of oil doth lie,
> We find more shape, more beauty, in a fly.
>
> (IV.ii.46-48)

Somehow Pretty-man, in his zealous denunciation of Parthenope, is side-tracked by the monetary importance of the "store of oil" (in line forty-seven). Aided more by luck than wit, Pretty-man gets back to his thesis in the last line, though the transition from whale to fly via a whaling voyage is somewhat mind-boggling. Bayes' language, however, appears almost tame in comparison to his runaway plot; for he admits, when accused of making false promises to Johnson, that he no longer holds the reins of his play:

JOHNSON.

> But, Mr. Bayes, did not you promise us, just now, to make Amaryllis speak very well?

BAYES.

> Aye, and so she would have done but that they hindered her.

SMITH.

> How, sir, whether you would or no?

BAYES.

> Aye, sir; the play lay so that, I vow to gad, it was not to be avoided.

SMITH.

> Marry, that was hard.

JOHNSON.

> But, pray, who hindered her?

BAYES.

> Why, the battle, sir, that's just coming in at the door.

> (V.i.155-66)

The actors, who had refused to act an earlier Bayesian fiasco (II.ii.31-38), put an end to Bayes' current play after reading a summary of its fifth act. The absurd "argument" reads:

> Cloris, at length, being sensible of Prince Pretty-man's passion, consents to marry him; but just as they are going to church, Prince Pretty-man meeting, by chance, with old Joan the chandler's widow, and rememb'ring it was she that first brought him acquainted with Cloris, out of a high point of honor breaks off his match with Cloris and marries old Joan. Upon which, Cloris, in despair, drowns herself; and Prince Pretty-man, discontentedly, walks by the river side.

> (V.i.380-89)

Disgusted by such drivel, the rebellious players abandon Bayes' play; and their insurgency provides the real audience with a further involuted look at reality. Like Appel's sentence, "I am a sentence . . . ," *The Rehearsal* forces us to ponder the very basis for existence. Just as in a fun-house gallery of trick mirrors, like that of John Barth's "Lost in the Funhouse," where one is tantalized by the illusion created in his distorted reflec-

tion, so in the play the audience looks at life in entirely new ways.[16] It has seen the creator at work, but his work is fallible and often downright ludicrous.

The preceding techniques of dramatic involution are reinforced by two other absurdist devices, plotlessness and devaluation of language. Martin Esslin in *The Theatre of the Absurd* says that plays of this nature often "have circular structure, ending exactly as they began," and cause audiences to wonder "not so much what is going to happen next but what *is* happening."[17] Buckingham confuses the "world of the play" with the "real world." So it is that the Usher and the Physician in the play-within-the-play cannot openly discuss affairs of state because it would not be proper for the common people in the real audience to know about them.[18] The logic used in the play-within-the-play is not the same as that which Johnson and Smith use; but it makes some sense to the external audience, even though they may laugh at the paradoxes implicit in such logic. This audience disorientation is consistent in that it forces the viewer beyond the traditional interpretations of the play. Thus Bayes describes what might well be called his dark exposition:

> Now, sir, because I'll do nothing here that ever was done before, instead of beginning with a scene that discovers something of the plot, I begin this play with a whisper.

> (II.i.1-4)

What follows is an extended dialogue carried on in whispers by the Usher and the Physician, a conversation which stops any exposition (II.i.26-30, 43-63). So it is that neither the plot of the external play nor that of the internal play progresses, for the only thing of real importance which happens in *The Rehearsal* is that Bayes' play is abandoned.

Along with this plotless chaos, readers will find further evidence of absurdity in the devalued language of Buckingham's drama. Esslin suggests that the "radical devaluation of language" present in absurdist works reflects that "what *happens* on the stage transcends, and often contradicts, the *words* spoken by the characters."[19] Bayes' most famous corruption of the language comes when he gloats over his use of "antithesis" in Act IV: "Reasoning! y' gad, I love reasoning in verse" (IV.ii.19). But here Bayes ignores the fact that reasoning and verse are antithetical themselves. Poetry is suggestive, allusive, figurative—hardly a formula for argumentation. When questioned as to the meaning of his last play, Bayes can only ask, "Do you mean the plot?" (I.i.72-73). In his absurd world, a bloodless *coup d'etat* is enacted when the Physician and the Usher merely slip into the throne room, *"draw their swords, and sit down in two great chairs"* (II.iv. between 76 and 77). From then on they are referred to as "Usurpers." As if this were not enough devalued language, Bayes equates talking "bawdy" with seduction (I.ii.38-71). Bayes also devalues the word *death* by destroying the illusion of it in his play. After Drawcansir has killed all the soldiers on both sides near the end of the play (V.i.335-40), Smith asks, "But, Mr. Bayes, how shall all these dead men go off? for I see none alive to help 'em." Bayes replies, "Go off! why, as they came on—upon their legs. . . . Why, do you think that the people here don't know they are dead? (V.i.354-58).

Bayes' answer also provides an introduction to the final element of absurdist theater found in ***The Rehearsal,*** Black Humor. Esslin explains its relationship to absurd drama by saying that Black Humor mixes "laughter with horror"[20] in order to help man "face reality in all its senselessness."[21] Esslin continues by suggesting that it is "the nature of all gallows humor and *humour noir*" to release "liberating laughter at the fundamental absurdity of the universe."[22] Bayes in some vague, intuitive way grasps this reality and reflects it by his preoccupation with death throughout the play. In his "first prologue" Bayes plans to "come out in a long black veil" and be followed by a great "hangman . . . with a furred cap and his sword drawn" (I.ii.144-49) who will decapitate Bayes if the audience doesn't like the play. In Act II, Scene v, Bayes introduces the dance of the dead soldiers and then begins Act IV by announcing that after so much mirth in the previous act he must "make this [act] to begin with a funeral" (IV.i.3-4). Though the audience has not been apprised of the deceased's identity, the two false kings eulogize her; and Bayes then reads lines which Lardella, the loved one, has composed "just as she is dying, with design to have it pinned upon her coffin, [to be] so read by one of the usurpers, who is her cousin" (IV.i.135-37):

> Since death my earthly part will thus remove,
> I'll come a humble-bee to your chaste love.
> With silent wings I'll follow you, dear couz;
> Or else, before you, in the sun-beams buzz.
>
> (IV.i.163-66)

We may be inclined to share literally Bayes' own assessment of Lardella's verse when he comments, "Yes, I think, for a dead person, it is good enough way of making love . . ." (IV.i.191-92). However, the Black Humor doesn't end there; for just when the false king's grief is verging upon a twin suicide, Bayes has the goddess Pallas intercede and the "*coffin opens, and a banquet is discovered*" (IV.i. stage direction after line 210). Though the fun of the scene is obvious, it is instructive to examine the response of the audience. In its once-removed position from the play-within-the-play, it is treated not only to the enjoyment attendant upon the zany madness of these twists of fortune but also to a glimpse into the alternatives from which Bayes may choose. Lardella does not have to be either reincarnated

(as a bee) or resurrected (as she is). She could just die. Bayes, being both creator and creature, is not satisfied by the latter prospect and chooses to laugh at death rather than cry about it. Once the primacy of this observation about him is established, we can then begin to come to terms with the essentially positive aspects of his nature. Here Bayes' statement about the accidental and incomprehensible nature of individual human destiny is clear. There are no reasons for Lardella's continuing to live; in Bayes' world the causes are just not ascertainable, so why should he try to explain them?[23] To the interior audience, all Bayes' dramatic machinations are pure nonsense, for it can see only snatches of his overall plan. Of course, his play is not the same as Buckingham's, but the two are complementary at this absurdist level of interpretation. Buckingham reveals this human madness under the rather scientifically controlled conditions of a rehearsal. Bayes, in turn, becomes the experimental guinea pig whose human reactions to Buckingham's stimuli may be studied as anthropomorphic projections of what a creator-god's own actions might be. It is an imperfect measuring device to be sure, but given the specific time and place in human history—or perhaps *any* time and place—where would a person find a better one? This is not to say that Bayes is merely the mouthpiece for Villiers. Rather the relationship is much like that which Swift perfects between himself and the Hack in his *Tale of a Tub*. Bayes is an imperfect creation who frequently disagrees with much of what his creator stands for philosophically and aesthetically. Yet in his zest for living, Bayes' attitude seems at one with his creator's.[24] Bayes subconsciously fears death, openly loves life, and defiantly brings what he thinks to be order out of the chaos which surrounds him. Thus his mind can contrive such poetic paradoxes as those Amaryllis speaks:

> Thanks to the powers above, for this deliverance!
> I hope its slow beginning will portend
> A forward exit to all future end.
>
> (III.iii.4-7)

Such an empty yet emphatic oxymoron points up the discrepancy between the reasonable assumptions of man's limited view of the world and the paradoxes arising from these limitations.[25]

The Rehearsal was in its day one of the few overt challenges to a particular world view.[26] Much of the drama of the Restoration era—especially the heroic variety—is compatible with the dramatic and philosophical conventions of Broadway theater.[27] But ***The Rehearsal*** suspends all these conventions of exposition, character development, conflict, and climax in order to have the best of two worlds at the same time. As topical satire, Villiers' play is one of the best in the English language, yet as Theatre of the Absurd it mocks the very basis for its satire, the improvement of human beings and/or their institutions. The hack-playwright is what he is and he is proud of it. There is nothing to be done for his condition. In the absurd world of his play, the only hope for salvation manifests itself in the form of his feckless use of the *deus ex machina*,[28] certainly an unsatisfactory answer for the problems he faces. But he doesn't seem to mind too much, and, undaunted, he has a grudge against the actors to keep him warm. As he departs from the stage for the last time, he bids farewell:

> But I'll be revenged on them [the actors] too; for I'll lampoon 'em all. And since they will not admit of my plays, they shall know what a satirist I am. And so farewell to this stage, 'y gad, forever.
>
> (V.i.425-29)

The Bayesian spirit doesn't die with **The Rehearsal** but lives on through the Restoration and eighteenth century, where we find it not only in Swift's *A Tale of a Tub* but also in the Scriblerus Club's *Memoirs of Martinus Scriblerus,* Henry Fielding's *The Tragedy of Tragedies,* and Laurence Sterne's *Tristram Shandy.* Nor does the tradition die there, for these works anticipate such twentieth-century examples as Flann O'Brien's *At Swim Two Birds* and Vladimir Nabokov's *Invitation to a Beheading.* Given the nature of the human condition, it is likely that these literary anomalies will continue to appear.

Notes

1. George H. Nettleton, "Heroic Drama," in *British Dramatists from Dryden to Sheridan,* eds. George H. Nettleton and Arthur E. Case (Boston: Houghton Mifflin, 1939), p. 5. Nettleton states, "Thomas Sprat, the Duke's chaplain, Martin Clifford, Master of the Charterhouse, and probably 'Hudibras' Butler and others shared variously in the scheme of concerted satire upon serious contemporary dramatists." Since many of the absurdist devices which are used in *Hudibras* may be found in *The Rehearsal,* it seems likely that Samuel Butler had some part in writing Buckingham's play. For a brief account of the origins of Villiers and Dryden's mutual antipathy, see John Harrington Smith, "Dryden and Buckingham: The Beginnings of the Feud," *Modern Language Notes,* 69 (April 1954), 242-45.

2. Lewis, *"The Rehearsal*: A Study of Its Satirical Methods," *Durham University Journal,* NS 31 (March 1970), 96; Willson, *"Their Form Confounded": Studies in the Burlesque Play from Udall to Sheridan* (The Hague: Mouton, 1975), p. 110; McFadden, "Political Satire in *The Rehearsal,*" *The Yearbook of English Studies,* 4 (1974), 120-28; and Baker, "Buckingham's Permanent *Rehearsal,*" *Michigan Quarterly Review,*

12 (Spring 1973), 169. Though Baker here touches upon one of the most important problems in the play, he has already concluded that *The Rehearsal* is a "comedy of blind conceit [which] everywhere transcends the personal satire in which it originates . . ." (p. 164).

3. McFadden, p. 120. Here McFadden argues convincingly that much of the satire in Buckingham's play is aimed at one of Villiers' immediate political enemies, Henry Bennet, Earl of Arlington, who "did wear a black patch on his nose" like the paper one which Bayes wears after breaking his nose.

4. See Martin Esslin, *The Theatre of the Absurd,* Anchor Books ed. (Garden City, N.Y.: Doubleday and Co., 1961), pp. xvii-xxii, 12-13, 48, 220, 229-96, 301-5, 307-11, 313-16.

5. See Philip K. Jason, "A Twentieth-Century Response to *The Critic,*" *Theatre Survey,* 15 (May 1974), 51-58. Jason launches his discussion of the rehearsal format in *The Critic* with a reference to Pirandello's play and then suggests, "Once the artifices of the theatre are laid bare, and the discrepancies between life as it is represented on stage and life as we know it are brought into focus, the relative truths and realities of each may be measured and evaluated" (p. 51). Though Jason seems to overlook the "absurdist" implications of his study, it indirectly supports my arguments for the continuing modernity of Buckingham's play.

6. Though Heller's play doesn't use the rehearsal format, it does break down the barriers between the play and its audience by having the actors speak directly to the audience, acknowledge the fact that they are actors, and refer to their appearances in other real plays.

7. Truffaut's film uses the rehearsal format in that the screenplay is about a director making a film. The device is further complicated by the fact that Truffaut plays the director of the film-within-the-film. Although Truffaut doesn't viciously satirize himself in his film, the situation there is much like that of Dryden's being lampooned in the character of Bayes. Truffaut's preoccupation with the absurdity of death may be seen in the demise of the film-within-the-film's leading actor just before the end of its shooting schedule. Bayes, as I will illustrate later, shares Truffaut's anxiety. See Truffaut, *Day for Night,* trans. by Sam Flores (New York: Grove Press, 1975), pp. 160-61.

8. In *8½* Fellini presents another cinematic version of this creator-within-the-creation technique. Here again the director in the film is making a movie; therefore, the viewer sees the device of a movie-

maker, Fellini, making a movie about a movie-maker making a movie. As in *Day for Night,* the character of the movie director is patterned after the real director, Fellini.

9. Robert Scholes, *The Fabulators* (New York: Oxford Univ. Press, 1967), pp. 35-55. Scholes says that Black Humor "is not concerned with what to do about life but how to take it" (p. 43). Black Humorists see life as being "ridiculous—a joke" and "offer us laughter" (p. 44).

10. Vladimir Nabokov, *The Annotated Lolita,* ed. Alfred Appel, Jr., (New York: McGraw-Hill, 1970), p. xxi.

11. Probably the best-known example of the play-within-the-play occurs in Act III, Scene ii of *Hamlet.* For a discussion of the "playness" of the play, see Norman Holland, *The First Modern Comedies: The Significance of Etherege, Wycherley and Congreve* (Bloomington: Indiana Univ. Press, 1959), p. 100. Holland discusses the technique as it is used in Wycherley's *The Plain Dealer.* The "interior" playwright is, of course, Bayes. It is convenient to refer to his play as the interior or "internal" play while referring to Buckingham's play and the audience watching it as being "external." In similar fashion, Valerie C. Rudolph notes the various levels of reality in Fielding's *The Author's Farce.* See her "People and Puppets: Fielding's Burlesque of the 'Recognition Scene' in *The Author's Farce," Papers on Language and Literature,* 11 (1975), 31-38.

12. Baker, p. 161. Baker says that the play "deals with a central and dangerous truth about literature itself." As he sees it, Bayes' problem is the "dilemma of authorship—to make something ever new from the ever old forms and the ever old stuff of life. . . ." On this point I am in agreement with Baker, though I arrive at a different conclusion about the thematic effect which this dilemma has upon the play.

13. See Appel, in *The Annotated Lolita,* p. xxx, where he describes "the staging of the novel" and says:

> Nabokov the protean impersonator is always a masked presence in his fiction: as impresario, scenarist, director, warden, dictator, landlord, and even as a bit player . . . to name only a few of the disguises he has donned as a secret agent who moves among his own creatures like Prospero in *The Tempest.*

Like Nabokov, Buckingham has an encroaching omnipresence in his play, being a part of every level of its conception—internal audience and playwright as well as their external correlatives.

14. The main effect of most absurdist techniques in the theater is some sort of audience disorientation.

15. George Villiers [second Duke of Buckingham], *The Rehearsal* in *British Dramatists from Dryden to Sheridan,* ed. George H. Nettleton, Arthur E. Case, and George W. Stone, Jr., 2nd ed. (Boston: Houghton Mifflin, 1969), I.ii.126. All future references will be carried in the body of this essay. I have chosen to use line numbers instead of page numbers for the sake of convenience.

16. Barth's narrator, while telling the story of Ambrose M_____, often confuses the reader with authorial intrusions as he herds Ambrose through the funhouse. *Lost in the Funhouse,* Bantam Books (New York: Doubleday, 1968), pp. 69-94.

17. Esslin, p. 305.

18. David M. Vieth, "Divided Consciousness: The Trauma and Triumph of Restoration Culture," *Tennessee Studies in Literature,* 22 (1977), 62, n. 25. Vieth cites this scene for much the same purpose as I use it.

19. Esslin, p. xxi.

20. Esslin, p. 300.

21. Esslin, p. 316.

22. Esslin, p. 304.

23. Here I am reminded of the conclusion of Kingsley Amis' *Lucky Jim,* Compass Books ed. (New York: Viking Press, 1953). The cards are all stocked against Jim Dixon, the protagonist; but his luck miraculously changes and he gets the beautiful girl, puts down all his detractors, and falls into a job where he can be himself, even though there are no logical reasons for any of these things happening. In Amis' novel, however, fortune rules; and she has just as illogically cost Jim his teaching position as well as enabling a plagiarist to publish clandestinely Jim's article on "a strangely neglected topic," *"The economic influence of the developments in shipbuilding techniques, 1450 to 1485"* (p. 16). Lardella, no doubt, could "live" in Jim's world, too.

24. See John Harold Wilson, *A Rake and His Times: George Villiers, 2nd Duke of Buckingham* (New York: Farrar, Straus and Young, 1954), p. 103. Wilson says, "As for his pleasures (which were always described as venereal), they were such follies as hunting, racing, chemistry, music, literature, conversation, and, of course, love."

25. We see a similar but perhaps more openly serious usage of oxymoron in the final lines of Rochester's "Upon Nothing" where the "nothings" of society "Flow swiftly into thee [Nothing], and in thee ever end" (1. 51).

26. See Vieth, pp. 46-52. Here Vieth discusses the "new dichotomy of consciousness" (p. 46) which came into being at about the time of the Restora-

tion and explains how *The Rehearsal* is an example of "reversible meaning" in a work written "upon nothing" (p. 47).

27. Esslin says that this kind of play has "the suspense created in a theatre concerned mainly with the revelation of objective character through the unfolding of a narrative plot. The pattern of exposition, conflict, and final solution mirrors a view based on a recognizable and generally accepted pattern of objective reality that can be apprehended so that the purpose of man's existence and the rules of conduct it entails can be deduced from it." *The Theatre of the Absurd,* p. 304.

28. In this scene, *"The two right Kings of Brentford descend in the clouds, singing in white garments; and three fiddlers sitting before them, in green"* (V.i. between 11. 44 and 45).

John H. O'Neill (essay date 1984)

SOURCE: O'Neill, John H. "Buckingham's Nondramatic Poetry and Prose," and "Buckingham's Minor Dramatic Works." In *George Villiers, Second Duke of Buckingham,* pp. 21-51; 52-80. Boston: Twayne Publishers, 1984.

[*In the first essay below, O'Neill comments on Buckingham's verse elegies, satires, and epigrams, and on his prose works, including political tracts and speeches in Parliament. In the second, O'Neill discusses Buckingham's minor plays, including* The Chances, The Country Gentlemen, *and* The Restauration.]

BUCKINGHAM'S NONDRAMATIC
POETRY AND PROSE

The duke of Buckingham was influenced by, and was a part of, a tradition of courtly writers which originated in the Renaissance. Like Sir Thomas Wyatt in the reign of Henry VIII, Sir Philip Sidney and Sir Walter Raleigh in the time of Queen Elizabeth, and Richard Lovelace and Sir John Suckling in the reign of Charles I, Buckingham thought of himself as a man of affairs first—a politician, a statesman, and a courtier—and a writer second. Because he often wrote to serve his political purposes or to further an intrigue at court, his prose works include speeches delivered in the House of Lords, treatises on policy, and tracts; and most of his nondramatic poems are occasional verse—satires, elegies, complimentary verses, and epigrams, all written in response to particular events.

Buckingham copied much of this occasional verse into his commonplace book. He organized the compositions, both in verse and in prose, under various topics: "Love,"

"Tears," "House," "Ignoble," and so on. Although the works were written throughout the course of his life, he may have used the book as a means of organizing them—copying from loose papers into the book under the various headings—during his last years of retirement in Yorkshire, for it was found in his pocket after his death. Some of its contents have been published, but they are not readily available; therefore any poems from the commonplace book which are discussed in this chapter will be quoted in full.[1]

EPIGRAMS

An epigram is "a form of writing which makes a satiric, complimentary, or aphoristic observation with wit, extreme condensation, and, above all, brevity."[2] The tradition of writing such poems began with the Greeks; flourished in the hands of the Roman poets Martial and Catullus; descended to such Renaissance poets as Wyatt, Davies, Harington, and Ben Jonson; and was passed from them to the wits of Buckingham's time.[3] Because the epigram is topical and occasional, it is particularly suited for entry in a commonplace book, and most of the poetry in Buckingham's commonplace book is epigrammatic.

The verse form of the epigram is almost always the couplet, but line lengths vary considerably. Although no topic is considered out of bounds, the ideal epigram, according to the eighteenth-century German critic and dramatist Gotthold Lessing, is one which first creates an expectation by calling our attention to some particular subject, then gratifies the expectation by a revelation or explanation.[4] Buckingham's commonplace book contains several epigrams which create such an effect. The following couplet, which appears with several other laments and complaints under the heading "Love" in the commonplace book, is one example: "What strange injustice in my fate doth dwell: / 'Tis she that sins, and I that suffer hell" (80). The first line calls our attention by promising to inform us of a "strange injustice"; the second fulfills the promise and surprises us. The woman's "sin" is her rejection of the lover's suit. If she sinned in another way, by consenting to his suit, he would be released from hell. Thus the word "sin" takes on a new meaning. One sins not by having illicit sexual relations, but by refusing to have them. Because the ordinary meaning of "sin" is the one which first occurs to us when we read the poem, we are momentarily shocked at the reversal of our expectations when we see the word used in this new way. That momentary shock is the reason for the epigram. It gives us a brief, startling opportunity to see things as we have not seen them before.

But not every epigram relies upon paradox to produce its effect. The following epigram, also from the commonplace book, uses hyperbole as its dominant figure:

"Some eyes so bright, that they through darkness see. / Where e'er hers come, there can no darkness be" (26). To use hyperbole as the mode of wit in this couplet, Buckingham must make the first part of the epigram hyperbolic in itself. Then the second part must exceed the first by revealing a greater, more surprising hyperbole.

One of Buckingham's contemporaries, the French critic Pierre Nicole, argues in his *Essay on True and Apparent Beauty* against the use of hyperbole in epigram on the grounds that it is inherently false. In his view, to exaggerate matters as hyperbole does is to describe things not as they are, but as we know them not to be.[5] But Nicole's literalism is simple and narrow. Although hyperbole does not speak the literal truth, it does express a truth of feeling; it says, in effect, that the idea it expresses is felt too deeply for ordinary words to communicate, and that language must be turned against itself, must be pushed to extremes, if the feeling is to be understood. To many seventeenth-century poets, as to the Latin epigrammatists, that truth of feeling is a dominant concern. Donne, for example, in his love lyric "The Relic," concludes, "These miracles we did; but now, alas, / All measure and all language I should pass, / Should I tell what a miracle she was."[6]

For Buckingham in particular, hyperbole was more than a literary figure; it was almost a principle of existence. It suggests the unrestrained, almost maniac energy, intensity, and imagination which characterized him. To be a man of wit was, for him, to be able to see and give expression to the extremes of experience—the compelling beauty of a face, the effortless grace of an action, the outrageous stupidity of a statesman, or the criminal hypocrisy of a king—which other people failed to recognize or to appreciate, or which they lacked the courage, honesty, or ability to express. But to those of a different temperament, Buckingham's extreme reactions seemed foolish and unstable. Thus Dryden, in his portrait of Buckingham in *Absalom and Achitophel,* wrote, "Rayling and praising were his usual theames, / And both (to shew his Judgment) in Extreames."[7] Dryden's lack of sympathy is apparent; to have a fairer view we might substitute "wit" for "judgment" in his couplet. But he is correct in identifying what might be called Buckingham's "hyperbolic vision" and in perceiving its central importance in his character.

But although hyperbole occurs frequently in Buckingham's epigrams, some of the most successful among them depend on more complex imagery. Buckingham's response to Dryden's portrait of him, for example, uses two interlocking images. It is a poem which the duke wrote and copied into his commonplace book but showed, as far as we know, to no one else:

"To Dryden"

As witches images of wax invent
To torture those they're bid to represent,
And as the true live substance does decay
Whilst that slight idol melts in flames away,
Such, and no lesser, witchcraft wounds my name;
So thy ill-made resemblance wastes my fame;
So as the charmed brand consumed i' th' fire,
So did Meleager's vital heat expire.
Poor Name! What medicine for thee can I find,
But thus with stronger charms thy charm t' unbind?

(9)

This poem is both a heartfelt expression of personal pain and a well-crafted epigram. It describes the effect of Dryden's lampoon in two closely related and carefully chosen similes, first that of the witch's idol and second that of Meleager and the burning brand. The image of the wax idol is particularly appropriate, because it recalls the ancient origins of satire in the curse and suggests that modern satire retains something of the magical power it had in antiquity.[8] There may be no logical reason why Dryden's caricature, Zimri, should affect the public perception of Buckingham, any more than there is any logical reason why the witch's victim should sicken and die when the wax image is destroyed—but it happens.

The image of Meleager and the burning brand also alludes to antiquity, to a story from Greek mythology. At Meleager's birth, Atropos, one of the three Fates, prophesied that he would live only as long as the log then burning on the fire was not consumed. His mother, Althaea, snatched the brand from the fire and kept it carefully to insure his life. But years later, after Meleager slew his mother's two brothers, she, in a rage, threw the brand into a fire. As soon as it was consumed, Meleager died. In this simile the brand is not an image of Meleager; it is simply arbitrarily identified with him. But the idea that the destruction of one affects the other reinforces Buckingham's idea, that his reputation is being consumed by the identification of him with Dryden's caricature.

Both images imply that Dryden's language in *Absalom and Achitophel* possesses a power far beyond its mere denotative significance, a power so great that it is almost magical. This is a point which critical exposition could not have made so succinctly, but which such exposition may illustrate. Dryden's use of the word "Zimri" as a name for Buckingham is taken from Numbers 25. According to the biblical story, "Israel abode in Shittim, and the people began to commit whoredom with the daughters of Moab" (25:1). Because of this crime, "the anger of the Lord was kindled against Israel," and God visited a plague upon the Israelites. Moses commanded the judges to appease God's anger by killing the men who joined themselves with the Moabites.

And behold, one of the children of Israel came and brought unto his brethren a Midianitish woman in the sight of Moses, and in the sight of all the congregation of the children of Israel, who were weeping before the door of the tabernacle of the congregations.

And when Phinehas, the son of Eleazar, the son of Aaron the priest, saw it, he rose up from among the congregation, and took a javelin in his hand;

And he went after the man of Israel into the tent, and thrust both of them through, the man of Israel, and the woman through her belly. So the plague was stayed from the children of Israel. . . .

Now the name of the Israelite that was slain, even that was slain with the Midianitish woman, was Zimri.

(Num. 25:6-8, 14)

To seventeenth-century readers, familiar with the Bible, Dryden's use of the name "Zimri" for Buckingham could be counted upon to suggest a series of parallels between the two characters. It suggests that Buckingham's adultery with Lady Shrewsbury, like Zimri's adultery, has been an offense to God, that God in His anger may punish England with some terrible misfortune if England does not punish Buckingham. Perhaps a susceptible reader might be led to identify the plague with which God punished Israel, in which "twenty and four thousand" died (Num. 25:9) with the plague which broke out in London in 1665, in which sixty-eight thousand people were killed. The identification might even suggest that to assassinate Buckingham, as Phinehas killed Zimri, would be a godly act. Since Buckingham's father had been assassinated by a religious fanatic, and since he himself had once narrowly escaped a similar attempt on his life, he could not view such a suggestion as an empty threat.[9]

Of course, all these suggestions hold only insofar as readers identify the biblical Zimri with the contemporary Buckingham. The power of Dryden's image inheres in that identification, just as the power of the witch's spell inheres in her "binding" of the charm, her creation of a magic link between her wax figure and her victim. Therefore Buckingham seeks to "unbind" the charm—to break the magic spell which links him to the evil image. Throughout the poem he has identified poetry with witchcraft, so it is logical that in the concluding couplet he attempts to turn his own charm against the original charm, his poem against Dryden's. This last couplet completes the charm. As the word "thus" in the final line suggests, this poem, the very poem we are reading, is Buckingham's countercharm.

The rhetorical structure of the poem is founded upon the words "as" and "so," which are the logical links of the two similes. These words are used in two slightly different senses. In lines 1 and 3, "as" means "in the same way." That is, the action of Dryden's lampoon on Buckingham's name resembles the action of the witch's fire upon her victim. These instances of "as" correlate with "so" in line 6 to complete the first simile. But in line 7, "as" means "at the same time." Thus as the brand was consumed, Meleager was also consumed. Buckingham merges the two senses of the word, to suggest that a resemblance in effect and simultaneity in time are themselves similar. The phrase "so as" in line 7 adds another link of similarity: the story of Meleager resembles the action of the witch, and both resemble Dryden's lampoon on Buckingham. Dryden's ill-will toward Buckingham resembles the malevolence of the witch, or of Atropos in the classical myth. This complex merging of linkages is Buckingham's own charm. It shows how he could construct an apparently simple epigram to contain a concentrated and relatively sophisticated meaning.

As the image of Meleager suggests, Buckingham used references to classical myth as a means of concentrating meaning. The following complimentary poem demonstrates the degree of concentration which such an allusion can achieve within a limited space:

"Breasts"

Such were the breasts at which, when earth was young,
The shining twins of fair Latona hung.
Upon such milk their growing godheads fed;
With such a white their beams were nourished.

(3)

Latona, the daughter of a Titan, was impregnated by Zeus and gave birth to Apollo, the god of the sun, and Artemis, the goddess of the moon. If this poem was written to the countess of Shrewsbury in 1670, during her pregnancy with Buckingham's illegitimate child, it compresses into four lines a hyperbolic compliment to his mistress and a hope for a brilliant child.

Among Buckingham's epigrams are several intended to attack his enemies in court intrigue and others whom for any reason he disliked. The following epigram is one example:

"On the Late Lord Chancellor"

To ale, and toasts, and the mirth of a catch,
And all thy witty disputes with the watch;
To meat without napkins, and trenchers of bread
Which in many a quarrel has been flung at thy head;
To a sack by thy side, and a knife in thy pocket
In an old sheath that stinks like a candle i' th' socket;
To thy pleasant walks to Westminster Hall
In a dirty term, and thy justlings for the wall;
To thy breakfast in Hell, with black pots by the Tally,
Thy return in a sculler, and dinner in Ram Alley;
To the glorious court of the Prince d' Amour,
Where if thou pretendest to be a Counsellor,
Thou wouldst even there be but weight and a clog,
Return, return, thou now State Pettifog.[10]

(7)

This poem describes its object, Heneage Finch, as having the low habits and pleasures of an ordinary attorney. The repetition of the word "to," and especially its association in the first line with "ale, and toasts, and the mirth of a catch," lead the reader to believe that he will be reading a toast. Although he soon becomes aware that the praise is ironic ("Thy witty disputes," "Thy pleasant walks"), he can easily assimilate that recognition to the idea of a toast by assuming that the encomium he is reading is an ironic one. The witty surprise of the epigram comes, therefore, in the final line. Instead of being told to raise his glass to his origins, Finch is ordered to return to them—to go back where he came from.

A few of Buckingham's epigrams reflect his interest in science. These tend to be somewhat more general in application than most of the others. Science could serve as a source of imagery, as in this example: "Love's flame kept in, as dangerous does become / As charcoal fires closed in a narrow room" (31). A charcoal fire indoors is dangerous both because it emits carbon monoxide and because it can, if the room is not ventilated, consume so much of the oxygen in the room that the occupants may suffocate. The simile suggests that love, when suppressed, may both consume and poison whoever conceals it.

Science could also provide the basis for a hyperbolic insult:

> Nature ne'er leaps but mounts up by degrees:
> So by plant animals she joins beasts and trees.
> This well-linked chain of ordered entity
> Would have been broke, had nature not made thee.
> Thou makest the chain complete, for until then
> There nothing was betwixt a beast and man.
>
> (52)

This epigram uses the concept of the Chain of Being, familiar to scholars of the intellectual history of the Renaissance through the eighteenth century, as a source of wit. One characteristic of the chain is continuity, the idea that there are no gaps in the chain, that each species is adjacent to another species which varies from it only in the minutest degree.[11] The person who is the object of satire in this epigram assures continuity between animals and men: he is the "missing link."

Science could also provide the basis for moral reflection:

> Earth, air, and water we depopulate:
> Wonder not then, man's life's so swiftly fled,
> When by so many deaths he's daily fed.
>
> (70)

The epigram suggests a kind of poetic justice in the fact that man, who kills so many other species in order to live, dies so quickly. Knowing what we know today

about the relationship between life expectancy and a diet high in animal fat, we may find even more truth in this poem than Buckingham's contemporaries could.

Because of its high degree of concentration and its subjection to the natural cadences of the language, the epigram is one of the most restricted and demanding of English verse forms. Even its greatest masters, such as Herrick, Prior, and Landor, have produced work of uneven quality, and there are many poets whose reputation for epigram must rest upon a single excellent example. Judged by these standards, Buckingham stands not in the first rank of English epigrammatists, but among those whose work continues to deserve reading. The epigram was a form which he found congenial, and when, as in **"To Dryden,"** he concentrates complexity of meaning in a few lines; or when, as in **"On the Late Lord Chancellor,"** he first awakens and then surpasses an expectation, he fulfills the promise of the form and justifies his reputation as a man of wit.

BUCKINGHAM'S LONGER POEMS

The distinction between epigrams and longer poems can be made only approximately, for there is little difference between the longest of the former and the shortest of the latter. Buckingham's longer poems, like his epigrams, are often occasional, and his choice of subjects for longer poems ranges as widely as for epigrams. In general, however, the longer poems are less concentrated; a single poem may treat several ideas or examine a single idea from more than one perspective. And unlike the epigrams, the longer poems often respond to or play off against the requirements of a formal genre.

The elegy for Lord General Fairfax.

Thomas, third baron Fairfax, was commander in chief of the Parliamentary armies from 1645 to 1650. In June 1650, once the civil wars had ended, he resigned his commission and retired to Nun Appleton House, his estate in Yorkshire. There, in accordance with the ideal of Cincinnatus so much admired in his time, he lived the quiet life of a rural landowner, enjoying the companionship of his wife, Anne; his daughter, Mary; and Mary's tutor, the poet Andrew Marvell.

When Buckingham came to Nun Appleton to court Mary Fairfax in 1657, he contracted an admiration for the retired general which continued throughout his life. No doubt one of the qualities he most admired was Fairfax's willingness to resist the temptations of money, power, and glory—temptations to which Buckingham himself was extremely vulnerable. Not only had the general given up his command at the conclusion of the civil wars, but he also refused any reward for his contribution to the restoration of the monarchy in 1660.[12] He returned once again to Nun Appleton, where he lived quietly for the rest of his life.

After Fairfax died in November 1671, Buckingham wrote an elegy for his father-in-law in the form of an irregular ode—called a "Pindaric" in the title of some of the published versions—of five strophes with a total of 61 lines.[13] The style of the poem is likely to surprise a reader whose expectations are created by the form of the ode or by the word "Pindaric" in its title, for its diction has none of the formality or grandeur which is usually associated with the ode. Rather, the style is plain throughout the poem and descends in some places to homely words or even to slang. The use of such words and phrases as *spy'd* (l. 14), *bragg'd* (l. 19), *polls and braves* (l. 30), and *pudder* (l. 32) takes the style down to the level of ordinary conversation—or below it.[14]

Such a contrast between the formality of the genre and the informality of the style is often a characteristic of burlesque poetry, but this poem is not a burlesque; it is a sincere tribute. In this case, the contrast between style and form awakens our attention to many other contrasts in the poem. For the epitaph on Lord Fairfax is a poem about contrast: it uses contrast as a rhetorical technique to treat its subject, which is contrast as a principle of character.

According to the poem, General Fairfax united in his personality several contrasting qualities. He combined extremes of courage and aggressiveness with extremes of gentleness and modesty: "Both sexes virtues were in him combin'd, / He had the fierceness of the manliest mind, / And yet the meekness too of woman-kind" (ll. 5-7). A second contrast exists between Fairfax and baser men, who lack both his courage and his humility. Whereas they boast of their courage and ferocity even in defeat, Fairfax blushed at the mention of his successes (ll. 19-22). Whereas other men put on the appearance of greatness even if they cannot attain the substance of it, Fairfax achieved the reality of greatness while retaining the plainness, simplicity, and unselfishness of his life.

A third contrast is only partly explicit. It is the contrast between Fairfax, who could have had power but renounced it, and the many men who spend their lives struggling for power. Many of the seekers after power are simply fools or knaves, "Who such a pudder make / Through dulness and mistake / In seeking after pow'r, and get it not" (ll. 32-34). These men may be irritating, but they are not dangerous. A more serious threat is posed by those who have the ability to gain power combined with the lust to achieve it. Here Buckingham creates an implicit contrast between Fairfax and Oliver Cromwell, Fairfax's associate in the command of the Parliamentary armies, who, when Fairfax retired in 1650, assumed full command and went on to become the conqueror of Scotland, to dismiss the Parliament, and to rule England as a dictator. The power which Cromwell seized, Buckingham tells us, could have belonged to Fairfax:

> He might have been a king,
> But that he understood
>   How much it was a meaner thing
> To be unjustly great, than honourably good.
>
> (ll. 49-52)

The poem shows that Fairfax's simplicity and modesty were and are not simply a matter of personal taste and private ethics, but a political principle.[15]

A pivotal element in Buckingham's exposition of this theme is the word *great,* which is used in the poem in two distinct senses. In the phrase "unjustly great," quoted above, *great* means "eminent," "important," or "powerful." In the following lines, however, the word moves to quite a different meaning:

> Through his whole life, the part he bore
>   Was wonderful and great,
> And yet it so appear'd in nothing more,
>   Than in his private last retreat;
>
> (ll. 23-26)

In line 24, *great* means "critical"—important in its significance. But in lines 25-26 *great* takes on a new meaning; it now means "magnanimous" or "noble"—having a lofty soul. Fairfax's nobility of mind, concealed by the simplicity and modesty of his personal character, is seen to be of a far greater quality than the emptiness or ruthlessness of other men, concealed by the external splendor of their titles and honors.

Thus what at first seems to be a confusion or misalignment of style and form is in fact a resolution of such a confusion. Buckingham's elegy teaches us to call things by their proper names and to distrust the grandeur of conventional forms. Those whom we are accustomed to thinking of as "great men" because they have the adulation of the multitude and the trappings of power may in fact be "mean" (l. 51) if their greatness is founded on injustice. And not only is nobility compatible with plainness, but plainness may be, in itself, the highest kind of nobility when plainness is chosen consciously by one who has the power to choose.

Similarly, we are accustomed to thinking of the Pindaric ode as "great" (it is sometimes called the "great ode") because of the heroic style in which it is written. The diction applied to Fairfax throughout this poem is unremarkable either for elevation or the lack of it; like the man, it is simple and plain but rich in hidden meaning. The words cited above as low or slang all occur in descriptions of the vainglorious men to whom Fairfax is contrasted. Thus Buckingham aligns his style not with the genre but with the subject—the plain with the plain, the low with the low—and achieves a true nobility of theme.

Some love poetry.

Only a few of Buckingham's longer poems deserve the title of love poems. They include poems entitled **"Love"** and **"Epithalamium"** in the commonplace book and poems entitled **"To His Mistress"** and **"The Lost Mistress: A Complaint against the Countess of————"** in his published works.[16]

As their titles indicate, these are fairly conventional poems. **"The Lost Mistress"** records the complaint of a shepherd who, deserted by the woman he loves, is torn between his desire to give voice to his pain and his reluctance to speak ill of the woman whom he still loves, despite the injury she has done him. **"To His Mistress"** is addressed by the speaker to the woman he loves; he tells her that he never could have loved her if it were not for her superior mind and noble soul, but he is also racked with desire for her body. **"Love"** describes the pain of one who loves unrequitedly and who sees all around him in nature the fulfillment of love. And the **"Epithalamium"** is the celebration of a marriage, the fulfillment of love.

Perhaps the most noticeable characteristic of Buckingham's love poetry is his awareness of nature and the degree to which it shares the lover's mood. As noted above, one of the poems is devoted entirely to that idea:

"Love"

Season of joy, and of delight,
    To all the world but me;
    I only am excluded quite
From Nature's universal jollity.
The plants and flowers look upwards and admire
    The sun their beauteous sire;
    The sun does every day
With his green smiling infants love to play.
Hark, how the birds now tune their wondrous throats;
    Nature needs more to hear
    Music's most ravishing notes,
For every bough does his own Orpheus bear.
Well may the birds sing and rejoice,
    Since all have made their happy choice.
    Since of all birds that be,
There's not one false or one disdainful she.

The first four lines of the poem inform us that the speaker does not share the universal happiness of spring, but we do not discover why until we reach the final line—though we may well guess, since poems with this theme are fairly common. One less conventional element in the poem is that the rejoicing and adoration which the speaker sees in nature are not, for most of the length of the poem, those of mating. The plants and flowers adore not one another, but "the sun their beauteous sire," and the birds seem to be enjoying a relationship not with one another, but with the tree branches. It is only in the last three lines that the mutuality of the love of birds is contrasted with the disappointments of human love.

A slightly more complex treatment of the same theme can be seen in **"The Lost Mistress,"** where nature seems to share the unhappy lover's pain:

Forsaken Strephon in a lonesome glade,
By nature for despairing sorrows made,
Beneath a blasted oak had laid him down,
By light'ning that, as he by love o'erthrown.
Upon a mossy root he lean'd his head,
While at his feet a murmuring current lead
Her streams, that sympathiz'd with his sad moans;
The neighb'ring echoes answer'd all his groans.
Then as the dewy morn restor'd the day,
Whilst stretch'd on earth the silent mourner lay,
At last into these doleful sounds he broke,
Obdurate rocks dissolving whilst he spoke.

Whereas the conventionality of **"Love"** makes its statements about nature somewhat unexciting, the use of the third-person narrator in these lines creates a greater problem. In **"Love"** it is the perception of the scorned lover that all of nature enjoys loving interrelationships. Readers need not believe that nature really does participate in such relationships; we need believe only that a man who has been scorned by the woman he loves may think so. In **"The Lost Mistress,"** however, the narrative (at least in the opening and closing sections) is in the third person, and we are implicitly asked to believe that the sympathy between Strephon and nature is perceived not just by Strephon himself, but by the narrator.

At first the relationship seems merely fortuitous; Strephon happens to have chosen for his repose a spot which seems to be in sympathy with him. The place is "By nature for despairing sorrows made" because it contains a tree overthrown by lightning, a mossy root, a murmuring stream, and an echo. All these things occur naturally enough and may reasonably be supposed to coexist in many places; only in the human mind does any connection between them and Strephon's state of mind exist. But when we are told in line 10 that "Obdurate rocks dissolv[ed] whilst he spoke," we have a new situation. Now we are told of something which cannot possibly happen—and we are told it as if it were fact. Occurring where it does, surrounded by statements of fact, this statement is impossible for a reader to accept; consequently it is a flaw in the poem.

Buckingham's most successful treatment of the imaginative interaction between nature and the perceptions of the lover occurs in his **"Epithalamium,"** where the eye of the narrator in the opening strophe sees the dawn, Aurora, as a beautiful bride being dressed by her attendants. The entire poem follows:

By her the gentle hours attending stand
And dress the bridal morn with skilful hand.
Her fairest robes of silver light she wears;
With comely art they comb her golden hairs.
An orient pendant Hesper she puts on,

With beauty all, and beauteous riches shown
Never so bright and gay, since she was led
By the kind hours to loved Tithonus' bed.
   Ah, cruel youth, who fiercely dost invade,
And from her parents snatch the trembling maid!
Thou like a tyrant with a conqueror's claim
Dost give new laws, and change her very name,
Riflest her beauties and her virgin store:
In cities took by storm they do no more.
   Kind youth, whose love swells to so large a space,
It fills the brother's, father's, mother's place!
   I saw his years like trees well ranged stand
In a long row, and hers on th' other hand;
With comely kindness their fair tops they twined,
Beauty and pleasure in their shades combined.
A thousand winged Cupids, bright and young,
Like swarms of bees upon the branches hung.
Both sides did to an equal length extend;
Both sides were green and flourishing to the end.

The classical personifications of Aurora, Tithonus, and Hesper which Buckingham uses in his first strophe are a particularly effective way of suggesting union between man and nature. Tithonus, according to Greek myth, was a mortal youth beloved by Aurora, goddess of the dawn. To make him her lover, the goddess secured for him eternal life, but she neglected to ask for eternal youth, so that Tithonus becomes perpetually older while the goddess remains forever young. Hesperus, the evening star, is the planet Venus. Edmund Spenser, in his *Epithalamion* (1595), had used the same classical personifications.[17] But Buckingham's combining the images into a beautiful and consistent metaphor is original with him, and it is one of the most successful images anywhere in his poetry. Here, as in Spenser's poem, we are asked to see the natural world in a kind of marriage with the mind and mood of the lover—not to see impossible sights, as in **"The Lost Mistress,"** but to see reality through the eye of metaphor.

The final strophe, in which the years of the bridal couple's future are seen as two parallel rows of trees with their branches joined to form an arch, reverses the imagery of the opening section. In the opening lines nature is personified; here human life is shown as a natural scene. Unlike Aurora and Tithonus, whose inequality must increase with each new day, this wedding couple will be equally long-lived, equally fresh and flourishing. It is a beautiful image, and the addition of the cupids as bees is a happy piece of baroque detail.

The two central strophes, in which the bridegroom is first called "cruel" because he takes his bride from her family and then "kind" because he replaces their love with his own, turn on verbal conceits rather than natural imagery. They are not as satisfying as the opening and closing sections. But it is clear that Buckingham planned the poem as a symmetrical whole, as the following outline illustrates: strophe 1: nature as human; strophe 2: bridegroom as cruel; strophe 3: bridegroom

as kind; strophe 4: man's life as nature. The poem thus completes its own circle, even more effectively than **"To Dryden"** does. Despite the weakness of the central section, this is one of Buckingham's best and most moving poems.

The least successful of Buckingham's love poems is **"To His Mistress."** Written in forty-four lines of varying lengths and rhyme schemes, it turns on the same kind of rhetorical contrasts which work so well in the elegy for lord general Fairfax. The mistress is contrasted in the first twelve lines with the speaker's previous loves—women whom, he now realizes, he never really loved. In the second section (ll. 13-27), the speaker explains why he has never loved until now: he lists the criteria for a woman who is to create true love in a man with "a discerning eye." These requirements, of course, compliment not only the mistress, who has met them, but also the speaker himself, who must be assumed to have the "discerning eye" which can appreciate them. Not only must the lady have "looks and shape," but she must have "wit and judgment," "greatness of thought and worth," "plainness and truth" (ll. 19-20, 26). If she has all these qualities, she will "beget a passion for her mind"—that is, cause a man to fall in love with her mind rather than her body. Having listed these qualities and their effects, the speaker discovers that only the lady addressed can meet the requirements:

> She must be—what said I? she must be you,
> None but yourself that miracle can do;
> At least, I'm sure, thus much I plainly see,
> None but yourself e'er did it upon me:
>
> (ll. 28-31)

The broken construction in line 28 and the qualification in line 30 seem intended to give the effect of present thought—that is, to show the mind of the speaker as he interrupts one thought to amend it with another. The most striking instance of such an interruption comes in line 37, where, having spent twenty-four lines explaining the importance of a noble mind to true love, the speaker bursts into an eruption of passion for the woman's body:

> But oh! your body too is divine,
> I kill myself with wishing you all mine.
> In pain and anguish, night and day,
> I faint, and melt away:
>
> (ll. 37-40)

In its theme, therefore, **"To His Mistress"** is somewhat similar to Donne's "The Ecstasy." In both works an attraction of mind and soul is the basis for love, but the attraction of the body is acknowledged to be powerful, to be the basis of the higher passion, and to be valuable in itself. In both poems dramatic immediacy is created by the interruption of one absolute statement with another. Yet whereas "The Ecstasy" is one of the greatest love poems of the seventeenth century, **"To His Mistress"** is a failure and a disappointment.

There are two main reasons for this failure. One is the fact that the speaker's listing his requirements for a perfect love makes him seem self-satisfied and superior. Instead of being overcome with passion, the speaker seems to be making out a shopping list. Instead of describing the mutuality of attraction which is necessary to love, he seems to be interested primarily in himself, and in the woman only as someone who can meet his requirements:

> She, that would raise a noble love, must find
> Ways to beget a passion for her mind;
> She must be that, which she to be would seem;
> For all true Love is grounded on esteem:
>
> (ll. 22-25)

The other problem with the poem is that its ideas seem so fixed and its expressions so conventional that the impression of dramatic immediacy is not really created. Phrases like "I kill myself with wishing you all mine," and "I faint and melt away," and even the exclamation, "But oh!" are all drawn from the battery of conventional expressions used by most amatory poets. Consequently the poem lacks the freshness and sincerity that it labors to create.

And yet it is possible that Buckingham actually wrote this poem to his mistress, Lady Shrewsbury, and that it is completely sincere. The qualities of nobility of mind and of plainness and truth which the speaker values in his mistress are the same qualities which Buckingham celebrated in Lord Fairfax. But however unsteady Buckingham's wit may have been, however many times it may have missed fire, it was a more reliable source of poetic excellence than his ideas and feelings plainly stated.

Personal satires.

The poetry of personal attack has existed at least since ancient Greece, and several Elizabethan poets produced effective examples of it. But in the Restoration personal satires became both more numerous and more virulent than ever before, at least in English. Some of the writers may have been moved, as they claimed, by moral or political principle, but many others wrote with simple malice, or destroyed a reputation to promote an intrigue. No one, from King Charles to the most ordinary prostitute, was free from attack. The poems circulated in manuscript and were published, if at all, many years after the events which prompted them.

Buckingham's personal satires avoid the most unethical practices of his contemporaries. Whereas many of the anonymous satires are gossipy "shotgun lampoons," be-

smirching the reputation of one person after another, his libels are almost always directed primarily against single individuals; subsidiary characters are included only because of their association with the primary target. Whereas many contemporary satirists attacked easy targets like the "court ladies" and ascribed to them real or fancied deviant sexual practices, Buckingham attacked only those he believed had injured him or his friends, and he never mentioned the sexual behavior of his victims.[18]

As the epigram on Heneage Finch, discussed earlier, illustrates, Buckingham's personal satires concentrate on the physical characteristics and personal habits of the person under attack. He seems most to be offended by an association with sordid or ignoble persons, places, or habits, and by a lack of *savoir-faire*.

For example, in his **"Advice to a Painter to Draw my Lord Arlington, Grand Minister of State,"** Buckingham suggests that Arlington's physical characteristics can show us the qualities of his mind:

> First draw an arrant fop, from top to toe,
> Whose very looks at first dash shew him so:
> Give him a mean proud garb, a dapper face,
> A pert dull grin, a black patch cross his face;
> Two goggle-eyes, so clear, tho' very dead,
> That one may see, thro' them, quite thro' his head.
>
> (ll. 1-6)

And in his **"Familiar Epistle to Mr. Julian, Secretary to the Muses,"** he suggests that Sir Carr Scroope's red face somehow indicates an exclusion from human fellowship:

> Of his unfinished face what shall I say,
> But that 'twas made of Adam's own red clay,
> That much, much ochre was on it bestow'd:
> God's image 'tis not, but some Indian god.
>
> (ll. 30-33)[19]

Like most lampooners, Buckingham constructs a caricature of his victim, a portrait enough like him to be recognizable but sufficiently exaggerated and ridiculous to be insulting. As part of the caricature, he attributes to the victim extravagant characteristic actions. In the **"Epistle to Julian"** Buckingham describes Scroope as an incorrigible poet, unable to restrain himself from writing verse:

> For when his passion has been bubbling long,
> The scum at last boils up into a song,
> And sure no mortal creature at one time
> Was e'er so far o'ergone with love and rhyme.
> To his dear self of poetry he talks:
> His hands and feet are scanning as he walks.
>
> (ll. 51-56)

In the lampoon on Arlington, Buckingham attacks both Arlington's gravity of manner and the folly which lies under that gravity by describing the minister playing with his daughter:

> Next all his implements of folly draw,
> His iv'ry-staff, his snuff-box, and Tatta,[20]
> That pretty babe, that makes his lordship glad,
> And all the company besides so sad;
> She who in state is brought, to smoothe his brow,
> When he has rul'd the roast, the Lord knows how,
> For tho' to us he's stately like a king,
> He'll joke and droll with her like any thing.
>
> (ll. 11-18)

The most imaginative of Buckingham's personal satires is the one entitled **"Upon the Installment of Sir [Thomas] Os[bor]n, and the late Duke of Newcastle."** The event which the poem commemorates is the installation of the two title characters as members of the Order of the Garter at Windsor Castle on 19 April 1677. Although Buckingham was a member of the Order, he was not present at the ceremony; at the instigation of Osborne (the lord treasurer, now properly called the earl of Danby) he and three other Whig leaders had been imprisoned in the Tower of London. Since Buckingham had sponsored Osborne's rise to power, he deeply resented the ingratitude of his former protégé.

Like Buckingham's other lampoons, this one describes the personal characteristics of the victim: Osborne is thin and pale and has a foul breath. He is subject to the control of his eccentric wife. But whereas in most of the personal satires the tone is coolly detached or archly amused, calling our attention to the victim as a mere curiosity, this poem has at its core a passage of pure invective in which we recognize the tone of *saeva indignatio* ("savage indignation") which is the emotional pitch of the most powerful satire.

That tone is introduced to the poem by the appearance of a new speaker, St. George, the patron saint of the Order of the Garter. The saint appears at the ceremony in disguise, inquires what is going on, and passes judgment on the candidates for installation. He recognizes that Newcastle is "an ass, / But for his father's sake, he let him pass." (Newcastle's father, who had fought many battles and made great financial sacrifices for the crown during the civil wars, was known as "The Loyal Duke.") But St. George angrily rebuffs Osborne:

> How dare you in this chapel keep a quarter,
> With your blue lips, bluer than robes or garter?
> Go get a shroud to match your face and breath,
> Be drest, as well as look and smell, like death.
>
> (ll. 60-63)

This is the only one of Buckingham's personal satires in which a visionary or allegorical character appears. St. George is to this poem what the images of witchcraft are to **"To Dryden"** and the natural imagery is to **"Epithalamium"**: an imaginative means of compressing meaning and achieving elevation of tone.

Taken together as the work of a lifetime, Buckingham's poems are not very numerous. They are the productions of a man of wit, learning, and taste who sometimes wrote poetry, not of a professional poet. Several of his poems, like **"To His Mistress"** or the **"Epistle to Julian,"** are merely conventional. But when, as in the elegy for Fairfax, he brings us to a new understanding of what we thought we knew, or when, as in **"To Dryden"** or **"Epithalamium,"** he creates images which surprise and move us, we recognize that he was not limited to the conventional. If Buckingham was an amateur in poetry, he was a gifted amateur.

MAJOR PROSE WORKS

A Letter to Sir Thomas Oshorn on Reading a Book called The Present Interest of England Stated (1672).

In 1672, England declared war on Holland, as it had promised to do in the Treaty of Dover, signed with France in 1670. Buckingham, as a member of the Cabal ministry and as the chief negotiator of the public version of that treaty, supported the war. But the war was not popular with the English public, to whom the Dutch seemed not enemies but natural allies. Like England, Holland was a small Protestant country, threatened by the power of France; and like England, Holland was dependent on international trade for its prosperity. England, moreover, had pledged itself in the Triple Alliance, signed in 1668 by England, Sweden, and Holland, to aid the Dutch if they were attacked by the French, so that the declaration of war seemed a breach of faith.

Arguments against the war were made everywhere—in the press, in Parliament, and in the streets. Among many other publications against the war was a pamphlet, anonymously published, entitled *The Present Interest of England Stated*. Buckingham, looking for a way to state the ministry's side of the case, decided to write a private letter, addressed to Sir Thomas Osborne, who in 1672 was still his protégé in the government, in which he could argue against the pamphlet. His letter could then be published.

The *Letter* has a three-part organization. In the first section Buckingham argues that England should look after her own interests. It might be true that England and Holland have much in common, but England should not let feelings of kinship or solidarity blind her to her own interests. In the second section Buckingham considers the terms of the Triple Alliance, trying to show that the alliance does not bar England from joining forces with France to make war on Holland. In the third section he attempts to demonstrate that Holland poses a threat to England.

Buckingham's point that England's interest leads inevitably to conflict with Holland has as its premise the idea that the two nations are rivals in trade. "Had the author [of the anonymous pamphlet] been a lover, instead of a politician, he would have known, that rivals are the things in this world, which men commonly do, and ought most to hate," he wrote.[21] His analogy between rivalries in love and those in trade is witty and effective; it suggests that whereas the author of the *Present Interest* is a narrow student of statecraft, Buckingham is a man of the world. But the analogy may not necessarily hold. Rivals in love contend for the love of one woman. When she accepts one, she must spurn the other. But rivals in trade may create more trade for both, since a thriving international trade enriches all who participate in it.

Although Buckingham does not extend his analogy, the kind of thinking that produces it appears everywhere in the *Letter*. Thus just as a jealous lover might fear and resent the virtues of his rival as threats to his success, Buckingham suggests that the English ought to fear the virtues of the Dutch: "The true aim of every Englishman should be the good and prosperity of England; for that reason, industry and parsimony are to be wished for in the inhabitants of England, because they are qualities advantageous for us, and useful to our trade: but for the same reason, they ought not by us to be wished for in the inhabitants of Holland, because those qualities in them are prejudicial to England, and destructive to our trade" (166). However logical these arguments may be, they strike us today as mean-spirited. In either love or trade, a magnanimous suitor would rather succeed by virtue of his own good qualities than by wishing away those of his rival.

To the argument that the Triple Alliance forbids an attack on Holland, Buckingham opposes a legalistic analysis of the occasion and terms of that alliance. The Alliance had been set up in 1668 to counter the advance of the French armies into the Spanish Netherlands. The parties to the alliance pledged not only to oppose France, but to come to the aid of one another if France attacked them. Now France had attacked Holland—but England had joined France. In Buckingham's view this change of policy was justified by a change in England's interest: "self-preservation ought to be looked after a little in these kind of affairs: and . . . if the consequence of the loss of Flanders did not somewhat concern us, we should be no more in pain about it than we were for the conquest of Granada" (170). Splitting hairs very precisely, Buckingham argues that although the Triple Alliance binds England to protect Flanders from France, it does not bind England not to attack Holland. He heaps ridicule on the suggestion that the first of these propositions implies the second:

> This, under favour, is an absurdity yet greater than the former, there being no one thing you can allege as a consequence to any other thing whatsover, that will not make every whit as sensible a conclusion as this. For

example, to say, you ought not to go to bed to night, because the King of Spain did not go yesterday a hunting; or that I must not dine to morrow because Monsieur de Wit loves dancing, is not a more incoherent discourse, than that, because we have promised with the Dutch to save Flanders from the French, therefore what injuries soever the Dutch shall offer us, we cannot defend ourselves against them. The argument, if you mark it, is just thus, that because I agree with William to save Thomas, therefore I am bound to let William cut my throat.

(170)

Of course, the argument is not so ridiculous as Buckingham pretends. England had promised not only to protect Flanders, but to aid Holland if she were attacked by France. But Buckingham insists that the Triple Alliance requires England to aid Holland only if she is attacked by France as a consequence of her having joined the Triple Alliance (168), and not if she is attacked on any other pretext whatsoever. Although his reading of the terms of the alliance may be legally correct, certainly he is one of the first statesmen ever to argue that a declaration of war upon an ally is not a breach of the alliance!

A key phrase buried in the quotation above is "what injuries soever the Dutch shall offer us." England might be justified in making war on Holland despite the Triple Alliance if the Dutch have in some way injured the English. In the third section of the *Letter* Buckingham asserts three types of injury. First, he writes, "it has been their constant practice to massacre and make slaves of our countrymen in the East Indies" (166). This allegation is a reference to the Massacre of Amboyna (1623), in which the Dutch East India Company in the Spice Islands (modern Indonesia) drove out the English East India Company. Second, Buckingham asserts that the Dutch "rob us of our trade" (175). This statement takes for granted that the trade routes are the property of the English, which the Dutch are stealing from them, rather than that the two countries have equal right to the freedom of the seas. Finally, Buckingham argues, in a farfetched scenario, that the Dutch might combine forces with the French to conquer England (171-74). To support this idea requires particularly strained reasoning: "To this it is objected, that it can never be the interest of Holland to join with France in the conquest of England; but for aught we know they may mistake their interest; and certainly it is not wisdom in any nation, to have its safety depend upon the prudence of another" (172). Of these three reasons, only the first will stand even the most casual scrutiny by any disinterested observer. The Amboyna massacre was real. But although the trading wars between the English and Dutch East India Companies were conducted without much compassion on either side, there had been no provocation from the Dutch in fifty years.

The ***Letter to Sir Thomas Osborn*** is not a rhetorical success. Its arguments are so strained that they could appeal only to a reader who was predisposed to agree with them, and in the political climate of the time, such readers were not very numerous. It displays, in its analogies, a little of Buckingham's characteristic wit and energy, but in general it is unworthy of its author.

The Short Discourse Upon the Reasonableness of Men's Having a Religion, or Worship of God (1685).

Buckingham's ***Short Discourse*** must have been written fairly early in 1685, probably in the early spring.[22] Although it appears at first to be a philosophical or theological treatise, it is primarily a political tract, an attempt to win adherents to the idea of religious toleration, the political principle to which Buckingham was most constantly faithful.

To see Buckingham's ***Discourse*** in its context, we must begin by recognizing that in the seventeenth century every religious idea was a political idea. England contained three major Christian groups: Roman Catholics, members of the Church of England, and Protestants outside the Church of England (including Presbyterians, Baptists, Quakers, and many others), broadly called Dissenters. For over a century these three groups had struggled to control the faith of their countrymen and the government of the nation. To the Anglicans, Roman Catholicism was identified with the reign of "Bloody Mary" Tudor in the 1550s and the martyrdom of Anglican bishops, with the Gunpowder Plot of Guy Fawkes and his accomplices to blow up Parliament and seize control of the government in 1605, and with the French tyranny of Louis XIV in their own time. The Dissenters were associated in the Anglican mind with the Parliamentary side in the Civil War, with the execution of King Charles I in 1649, and with the dictatorship of Oliver Cromwell. The Test Act (1673), which prohibited anyone except a member of the Church of England from holding any office in the government or universities, suggests the prevailing level of religious tolerance. It was nearly impossible for most seventeenth-century Englishmen to imagine a commonwealth in which each person was free to worship as he pleased, without interference from others and without interfering with the rights of others himself.

But for Buckingham, such a commonwealth was the natural extension of British liberty. In 1675, in a speech in the House of Lords to prepare the way for a Bill of Indulgence (i.e., a bill to grant religious freedom) for Protestant dissenters, he reasoned that religious persecution was a serious political mistake because "it makes every man's safety depend upon the wrong place, not upon the Governors, or man's living well towards the Civil Government, established by Law; but upon his being transported with Zeal for every opinion that's held by those that have power in the Church that's in fashion."[23] The sarcastic tone of "transported with Zeal" and "the Church that's in fashion" could have done his cause little good. The bill was defeated.

In 1674, in a letter to his friend and secretary, Martin Clifford, Buckingham expressed himself in much franker terms. Almost as if he were an antireligious polemicist, he asserts here that the behavior of religious zealots can make religion itself an evil:

> This has made each party such enemies to moderation and liberty of conscience, when it got to the helm; which if once justly and firmly established, would open the door to that peace, which the gospel was bestowed on us to introduce into the world. Lucretius, from his reflection on the sacrificing of Iphigenia for a wind at Aulis, forms his celebrated epiphonema:

Tantum Religio potuit suadere malorum.[24]

> But what would he have said, if he had lived after the establishment of the Christian religion, and seen the heats and animosities betwixt the Arians and Orthodox, or the several opinions that started up amongst them, when once the heathen folly was sunk and removed, and power had debauched the principle, which Christ gave as the characteristic of his disciples, "the love of one another." If he had seen how many millions of men lost their lives, in the contests about the supremacy of the popes; and the quarrels betwixt the emperors, and the bishops of Rome; or the one and twenty millions destroyed by the Spaniards in the reduction of the West-Indies. . . . If he had known the noble methods of the inquisition of the romanists, and the penal laws of the reformed, by which in our nation alone, in a few years, three-score thousand families were ruined, he would have been no longer amazed at the sacrificing one poor green-sickness girl.[25]

The rhetorical force of these sentences anticipates some of the greatest effects produced by Swift. The rising energy of the successive clauses, the suspension of the "If" clause to build anticipation, the statistics of millions of lives lost, the scornful irony of "noble methods," and the crowning contemptuous phrase, "one poor green-sickness girl"—each contributes to the power of the whole. Buckingham's indignation here at the wickedness and stupidity of the human race is the *saeva indignatio* of the true satirist.

The decade following the letter to Martin Clifford was filled with political crises in which religious controversy played a prominent part—the Exclusion Crisis, the Rye House Plot, and others—and in the spring of 1685, there was a new threat to freedom of conscience. With the accession of King James II to the throne after his brother's death, England had an openly Catholic king for the first time since Mary Tudor. The possibility that James would ally himself with the High-Church Tories to persecute the Dissenters seemed very strong. And Buckingham, now living in retirement in Yorkshire, no longer exercised any political power, even in opposition. If he were to influence public affairs, it must be by persuading public opinion.

But the means of persuasion could not be rational argument. After years of failure to advance the cause of religious toleration by means of reason, Buckingham had lost faith in its power, at least in religious controversy: "The world is made up for the most part of fools and knaves, both irreconcilable foes to truth: the first being slaves to a blind credulity, which we may properly call biggotry: the last are too jealous of that power, they have usurp'd over the folly and ignorance of the others, which the establishment of the empire of reason would destroy" (**"Letter to Martin Clifford,"** 176). In the **Short Discourse,** therefore, Buckingham proceeds by means of a kind of rhetorical entrapment of his reader. Although the essay is, at its core, a plea for religious toleration, it begins, or at least pretends to begin, as a rational defense of Christianity against atheism. And although it pretends to be a series of logical deductions, each leading inevitably from the previous one, it actually uses the appearance of logic to confuse its reader and to entrap him into assent.

In the message entitled "To the Reader" which prefaces the **Discourse,** Buckingham puts his reader off guard by confounding a probable expectation: "When I began to write upon this Subject, it was out of a Curiosity I had to try, what I could say, in reason, against the bold Assertions of those Men, who think it a witty thing to defame Religion." A reader aware of Buckingham's reputation as a witty and irreligious man[26] might be led by the full title of the **Discourse** to expect logical arguments against religion. Instead he finds Buckingham allying himself with the religious against the witty and profane. In addition, however, Buckingham tells his reader that the train of reasoning in the work has taken an inevitable direction: "By the nature of this Discourse, I was forced to Conclude with an Opinion, which I have been long convinced of; That nothing can be more Anti-Christian, nor more contrary to Sense and Reason, than to Trouble and Molest our Fellow-Christians, because they cannot be exactly of our Minds, in all the things relating to the Worship of God." That is, the logic of the discourse, operating with a kind of life of its own, forced the conclusion. The suggestion is that a tolerance of religious differences is the necessary consequence of any reasonable discussion of the nature of religion itself.

To understand the way the **Discourse** affects its reader, we need to keep in mind the fact that literature is a kinetic art—that it influences the ideas and feelings of its readers in time, as they progress through the work.[27] Thus the lengthy opening sentence, which seems only to delay the main subject of the work, in fact promotes its most important effect:

There is nothing that gives Men a greater dissatisfaction, than to find themselves disappointed in their Expectations; especially of those things in which they think themselves most concern'd; and therefore all, who go about to give Demonstrations, in Matters of Religion, and fail in the attempt, do not only leave Men less Devout than they were before, but also, with great pains and industry, lay in their Minds the very Grounds and Foundations of Atheism: For the generality of Mankind, either out of laziness, or a diffidence of their being able to judge aright in Points that are not very clear, are apt rather to take things upon trust than to give themselves the trouble to examine whether they be true or no.

(1-2)[28]

The ostensible purpose of the opening sentence is to explain why Buckingham intends to rely upon probabilities, rather than to attempt to demonstrate his ideas with absolute certainty. But that explanation is not completed until the next paragraph. The immediate effect of the sentence is subtly to plant doubt about the idea of certainty in religion, for it suggests that most religious beliefs are founded on habit, laziness, and ignorance, and that an examination of them more often raises doubt than provides confirmation. In the second paragraph, apparently still commenting upon his methods, Buckingham says that he will content himself with establishing probability "Because, if I can convince a Man, that the Notions I maintain are more likely to be True than False, it is not in his power not to believe them; no Man believing any thing because he has a mind to believe it, but because his Judgment is convinc'd, and he cannot choose but believe it, whether he will nor no" (3). By pointing out that belief is not an act of will, Buckingham again anticipates his conclusion and undermines a reader's belief that he is in possession of truth and has the right to force others to accept it.

After more comments on the nature of belief and conviction and more stipulations on his mode of procedure, Buckingham appears to get to the start of his central argument: "The first main Question, upon the clearing of which I shall endeavour to ground the Reasonableness of Men's having a Religion, or Worship of God, is this, Whether it is more probable that the World has ordered itself to be in the Form it now is, or was contriv'd to be so by some other Being of a more perfect, and more designing nature?" (5). But a reader who expects now to settle down to a smoothly developing argument is immediately disappointed, for in the act of dismissing a secondary question, Buckingham follows it: "For whether or no the World has been Created out of nothing, is not material to our purpose. . . . Yet because this latter Question ought not to be totally pass'd by, I shall take the liberty to offer some Conceptions of mine upon it" (5). There then follow four pages of argument on that question. When Buckingham returns to his original question, he restates it in a somewhat altered form: "Whether it be more probable, that the World, or that God Almighty has been from all Eternity?" (9).

Now Buckingham's reasoning begins to move more quickly. Because the world changes constantly, he reasons that God, who is unchanging, must be more likely to be eternal than the world. Obviously he has begged the question: in an argument intended to establish whether or not God exists, he has used an alleged attribute of God as evidence of His existence. If God does not exist, He is not eternally unchanging.

Next, Buckingham asks whether God cares more for human beings than for other animals. Unsurprisingly, his answer is that God prefers humans. The reason for God's preference establishes the next link in Buckingham's chain of reasoning: "There is something nearer a-kin to the Nature of God in Men, than there is in any other Animals whatsoever" (11-12). This godly element in human nature is the soul and the reasoning faculty or will. As Buckingham sees it, the two are one: "an Eternal Being, and Free-will, are things in their Nature inseparable one from the other."

This "Instinct of God," another name Buckingham gives to this godly element, must tell us how to behave toward God—in other words, must be our guide to religious truth. "That Religion is probably the best, whose Doctrine does most recommend to us those Things, which, by that Instinct, we are prompted to believe are Vertues, and good Qualities: And that, I think, without exceeding the Bounds of Modesty, I may take upon me to affirm, Is the Christian Religion" (18). Here there is hardly even the pretense of logical argument. By the standard of belief Buckingham proposes, a case could be made for any major organized religion. But this deficiency of logic is no fault from the point of view of the real purpose of the *Discourse.* The reader is being told that his own beliefs are those which most perfectly suit the nature of God and man. To the degree that he believes what he is told, he will accept the idea that he is following a logical argument, and he will be disposed to accept the conclusion that Buckingham has already foreshadowed in his foreword—that the necessity of religious toleration follows inevitably from logical reasoning about religion. To the degree that the reader doubts Buckingham's assertions or feels uncomfortable with them, he is led to question the certainty of his own religious beliefs; therefore he may be weakened in his willingness to persecute those who do not share those beliefs.

Having arbitrarily nominated Christianity the best religion, Buckingham refuses to choose among the various sects of Christian belief. "And here, I must leave every Man to take pains, in seeking out, and chusing for himself; he only being answerable to God Almighty for his own Soul" (18). If each Christian is responsible only to God, no Christian may be forced by other men to alter his beliefs. Here Buckingham reaches the climax and real point of his discourse. He asks a series of rhetorical questions directed at "those . . . who are pleas'd to call themselves Christians:

> *First,* Whether there be any thing more directly opposite to the Doctrine and Practice of *Jesus Christ,* than to use any kind of Force upon Men, in Matters of Religion? And consequently, Whether all those that practice it, (Let them be of what *Church,* or *Sect,* they please) ought not justly to be call'd *Anti-christians?*

Further questions suggest that the use of force in religious disputes is not only anti-Christian, but also childish and impolitic. Buckingham concludes with a word of "Friendly Advice" to his Christian readers: "Let them endeavour, by their good Counsel, and good Example, to perswade others to lead such Lives, as may save their Souls: And not be perpetually quarrelling amongst themselves, and cutting one another's Throats" (19-21). None of Buckingham's leading questions or the conclusion drawn from them really depends upon the preceding train of reasoning. Nor has that train of reasoning taken the inevitable direction which Buckingham has claimed for it in his foreword. The questions with which the *Discourse* began were cosmological. They were confusingly stated and so interrupted by digressions that it was nearly impossible to follow them. The questions with which it ends are social, practical, and political. They are clearly stated, easy to understand—and loaded.

If we examine the *Discourse* as a work of kinetic art, asking not what it means, but what it does to its reader as he makes his way through it, we can see that the reader is likely to be distracted and uncertain when he thinks that he is considering fundamental theological issues, but that he is allowed to think clearly when he is reading of the consequences of persecution and the value of toleration. He may conclude the *Discourse,* therefore, feeling that basic theological issues are vague at best, but that every man ought to be his own guide, and that if we know anything with certainty, it is that religious persecution is wrong. A reader who responds this way, of course, vindicates Buckingham's renunciation of logic as a persuasive tool in matters of religion.

The *Short Discourse* is to Buckingham's nondramatic prose what *The Rehearsal* is to his dramatic works: his most complex and most polished production, operating on more than one level, manipulating its audience and diverting them. But whereas *The Rehearsal* attempts to influence its audience's attitude toward the theater by raising the level of their awareness, the *Short Discourse* attempts to change its readers' minds by deceiving and confusing them.[29] It would be satisfying to be able to report that the *Discourse* had the effect that Buckingham intended. But in fact, the period immediately after its publication was one of sharply increased persecution, largely as a result of the failure of Monmouth's Rebellion, crushed in July 1685, which was seen by High-Church Tories as one more attempt by the Dissenters to seize power. Some measure of religious toleration came later in the reign of King James, when both the king and Parliament found it useful to woo the support of the Dissenters by making concessions to them—but by then the duke was dead.

Buckingham was a member of the circle of talented and noble amateur writers and critics whom we now call the Restoration court wits.[30] If we keep in mind that the court wits generally wrote not to publish, but to amuse themselves and their friends, and the fact that they considered "ease" in writing a stylistic characteristic of the highest value, we can see that Buckingham's work represents both his own mind and the milieu in which it was produced. He has not the genius of a Rochester, but his nondramatic works can be compared with those of any of the other court wits. And throughout his writing, in prose and verse, we see evidence of his intelligence, his talent for mockery, and that energy and imagination which, to both friend and foe, were the identifying characteristics of George Villiers. If today we still find the qualities of his mind appealing, certainly that fact should be no surprise.

Buckingham's Minor Dramatic Works

Buckingham's fame as a dramatist rests today entirely upon *The Rehearsal.* Few scholars have read any of his other plays, and probably no living person has ever seen a performance of any of them. Yet at least one play among them is good enough to deserve continued interest, and all of them can help us to understand the development of Buckingham's talent leading up to and following his best-known work. The duke's minor dramatic works include two revisions of plays by Beaumont and Fletcher, an intrigue comedy written in collaboration with Sir Robert Howard but never performed, a comic sketch, and an unfinished heroic drama in blank verse.

The Chances

Buckingham's first dramatic work to be performed was his revision of the comedy *The Chances,* written by John Fletcher probably about 1617, an adaptation for the stage of *La Senora Cornelia,* a novella by Cervantes first published in 1613. The subject of the play is the attempted elopement of the duke of Ferrara with a noblewoman named Constantia, the sister of Petruchio, the governor of Bologna. The "chances" of the title are coincidences, which at first frustrate the elopement. At the end of the play, Constantia and the duke are reunited, largely through the efforts of Don John and Don

Frederick, two Spanish gentleman students, who shelter Constantia and her infant son in their flight from Petruchio, effect a reconciliation between Petruchio and the duke, and eventually bring all the parties together.

One of the coincidences indicated by the title is the appearance in the play of another character named Constantia, a whore, mistress to Antonio, one of Petruchio's attendants. When Antonio is wounded, this second Constantia steals his gold and flees. At about the same time, the first Constantia leaves Don John's and Don Frederick's lodgings with her infant and Gillian, the two students' landlady. Petruchio, the duke, and the two students, seeking to find the first Constantia, are led by mistake to seize the second. Eventually the men go to the house of Peter Vechio, a supposed conjuror, to ask for information about Constantia and Gillian. Vechio, pretending to raise spirits, presents Constantia to them, and the play ends happily.

Petruchio and the duke are fairly standard heroic characters, the first concerned primarily with his honor, the second with his love. Constantia is charming in her beauty and appealing in her distress. Don Frederick, though somewhat more realistically drawn, is equally heroic. His treatment of Constantia is gracious, courageous, and unselfish. The comic characters in the play are old Antonio, the fierce fighter, whoremaster, and toper; Gillian, the sharp-tongued and somewhat hysterical old landlady; and Don John, the extravagant rake. Except for Don John, the most important characters are too noble to be truly comic.

As written by Fletcher, *The Chances* has one serious defect: the plot runs out of energy after the third act. Although the flight of Constantia and the landlady and the confusion of her with Antonio's whore offered an opportunity for repeated complications, Fletcher did not exploit it. The second Constantia, the whore, appears onstage only briefly, and she and her bawd are stock comic characters. The final scene at the house of Peter Vechio contains little more than spectacle. Since there is no particular reason why Gillian and the first Constantia should have taken shelter there, the scene is less a resolution of the complications of the plot than simply an end to them.

Buckingham's revision of the play, first performed in 1667, supplies an entirely new fourth and fifth act. He lessens the importance of Gillian, the landlady, by depriving her of some of her richest lines, and he alters the character of Antonio. But he creates an entirely new comic character, the mother of the second Constantia, whose presence compensates the audience for whatever it has lost from those two characters. Most importantly, he greatly enriches the character of the second Constantia, turning her from a crude, insolent whore into an appealingly witty, self-possessed woman. In her cheerful, direct libertinism, she is a perfect comic partner to Don John:

2 CONSTANTIA.

> This sinning without pleasure I cannot endure; to have always a remorse, and ne'er do anything that should cause it, is intolerable. . . . Well, I'll no more on 't; for to be frighted with Death and Damnation both at once is a little too hard. I do here vow I'll live forever chast, or find out some handsome young fellow I can love; I think that's the better.

> (4. 1, p. 45)[31]

Buckingham improves the plot of Fletcher's play by means of a fairly simple but very effective device. Instead of having Don John, Don Frederick, the duke, and Petruchio go together to seek the first Constantia and the landlady, he separates them. Now he can have Don John meet the second Constantia when the others have not, and then have the arrival of the others precipitate new misunderstandings. As the first Constantia flees her brother and the second flees from Antonio, each discovery leads to a new flight and new discoveries. But when, in act 5, scene 3, Don Frederick discovers from the mother of the second Constantia that there are two women named Constantia, the resolution of the plot proceeds quickly and naturally to its conclusion.

In addition, Buckingham's new plot devices create a kind of second plot, which runs roughly parallel to the first and serves as an illuminating contrast to it. The idea of contrast, of course, existed in Fletcher's version of the play. The fact that the whore, the most inconstant of women, shares the name *Constantia* with the heroine is obviously a comic irony. (Cervantes's novella also has two women with the same name, but their name is Cornelia, rather than Constantia.) But Buckingham develops the idea much farther. He creates, in the characters of Don John and the second Constantia, two anti-Platonic lovers whose carnal urgency becomes a comic foil to the nobility and unselfishness of the first Constantia and Don Frederick.

For example, in the scene where the first Constantia and Don Frederick meet, Frederick's immediate response to Constantia's appeal shows his susceptibility to the claims of honor:

CONSTANTIA.

> As ever you lov'd honour,
> As ever your desires may gain their ends,
> Do a poor wretched Woman but this Benefit,
> For I am forc't to trust ye.

FREDERICK.

> Y' 'ave charm'd me,
> Humanity and Honour bids me help ye;
> And if I fail your trust———

CONSTANTIA.

> The time's too dangerous
> To stay your protestations. I believe ye,
> Alas, I must believe ye. . . .
>
> . . . . .

FREDERICK.

> Come be hearty,
> He must strike through my life that takes
> You from me.

> (1. 7, pp. 8-9)

Much later in the play, Don John is in frantic pursuit of the second Constantia when by chance he runs into the first, who seeks his aid. Don John's indifference to her appeal contrasts sharply with Don Frederick's earlier response:

1 CONSTANTIA.

> Hold, Don John, hold.

JOHN.

> Ha? is it you my Dear?

1 CONSTANTIA.

> For Heaven's sake Sir, carry me from hence, or I'm utterly undone.

JOHN.

> Phoo pox, this is th' other: now could I almost beat her, for making me the Proposition: Madam, there are some a coming that will do it a great deal better; but I am in such haste, that I vow to Gad Madam—
>
> . . . . .

1 CONSTANTIA.

> Good Sir, be not so cruel, as to leave me in this distress.

JOHN.

> No, no, no; I'm only going a little way, and will be back presently.

1 CONSTANTIA.

> But pray Sir hear me; I'm in that danger—

JOHN.

> No, no, no, I vow to Gad Madam, no danger i' the World, let me alone, I warrant you.

> (5. 2, pp. 54-55)

Don Frederick, acting as a man of honor, treats Constantia with respect and consideration, though he has never met her before. Don John, driven by what he thinks of as love, neglects the duty that humanity and honor set before him. In the second scene, the first Constantia and Don John seem almost to be characters from two different worlds. We have something of the same feeling we have in watching Stoppard's *Rosencrantz and Guildenstern Are Dead*: that a person from our own world has somehow wandered into the sublime world of tragedy, where every word, action or gesture is invested with superhuman significance. But whereas Stoppard's Rosencrantz and Guildenstern can neither understand nor control what happens to them in the world of *Hamlet,* in this play the world is Don John's and it is the heroic characters who have wandered into it. It is their blunders, after all, which keep frustrating his efforts to arrange a tryst with the second Constantia. And in the scene above, it is the first Constantia who is helpless; to Don John at this point she is merely a nuisance.

A similar contrast occurs in two revelation scenes, one chaste, the other sexual. After rescuing the first Constantia, Don Frederick asks that she draw aside her veil and reveal herself to him:

FREDERICK.

> Draw but that Cloud aside, to satisfie me
> For what good Angel I am engag'd.

CONSTANTIA.

> It shall be.
> For I am truly confident ye are honest:
> The piece is scarce worth looking on.

FREDERICK.

> Trust me,
> The abstract of all beauty, soul of sweetness,
> Defend me honest thoughts, I shall grow wild else.
> What eyes are there, rather what little Heavens,
> To stir mens contemplations? what a Paradise
> Runs through each part she has? Good Blood be
>   temper-ate:
> I must look off: too excellent an object
> Confounds the Sense that sees it.

In a corresponding scene, the face of the second Constantia inspires quite different thoughts in Don John:

JOHN.

> Come, pray unmasque.

2 CONSTANTIA.

> Then turn away your face; for I'm resolved you shall not see a bit of mine till I have set it in order, and then—

JOHN.

> What?

2 CONSTANTIA.

> I'll strike you dead.

JOHN.

> A mettled Whore, I warrant her; come if she be now but young, and have but a nose on her face, she'll be as good as her word: I'm e'en panting for breath already.

2 CONSTANTIA.

> Now stand your ground if you dare.

JOHN.

> By this light a rare creature! ten thousand times handsomer than her we seek for! this can be sure no common one: pray Heaven she be a Whore.

(4. 2, p. 47)

The first Constantia's beauty is evidence of her pure soul. Don Frederick, recognizing that fact, calls her a "good Angel" and uses the words "Heavens" and "Paradise" to describe her. He sees her as so excellent a sight, both physically and morally, that she confounds his senses. Don John's senses, on the other hand, far from being confounded, are stimulated to the last degree. The second Constantia, rather than seeing herself as "scarce worth looking on," is confident that with the help of her makeup she can "strike [Don John] dead." Whereas the first Constantia and Don Frederick are drawn together by the sublime nobility of both their souls, the second Constantia sees that she will have to rely upon her beauty and her arts to gain Don John's favor. And just as Heaven has sent Don Frederick to the aid of the first Constantia in her distress, so both members of the second couple see in one another the answer to their prayers: she recognizes in Don John the "handsome young fellow" she has been seeking, and Don John's prayer to heaven that the second Constantia be a whore will be answered. In each of the pairs of scenes we have just examined, the first was written by Fletcher and retained in Buckingham's version of the play, the second added by Buckingham. In this heightened contrast between the nobility of Don Frederick and the first Constantia on the one hand and the frank sexuality of Don John and the second Constantia on the other lies Buckingham's chief contribution to the meaning of the play.

The scenes between Don John and the second Constantia provide opportunities for bawdy wit:

2 CONSTANTIA.

> Hark ye Sir, I ought now to use you very scurvily, but I can't find it in my heart to do it.

JOHN.

> Then God's blessing on thy heart for it.

2 CONSTANTIA.

> But a—

JOHN.

What?

2 CONSTANTIA.

I would fain—

JOHN.

I, so would I: come let's go.

2 CONSTANTIA.

I would fain know whether you can be kind to me.

JOHN.

That thou shalt presently; come away.

2 CONSTANTIA.

And will you always?

JOHN.

Always? I can't say so; but I will as often as I can.

2 CONSTANTIA.

Phoo! I mean love me.

JOHN.

Well, I mean that too.

(5. 4, p. 59)

The urgency of Don John's sexual desires is highly comic, and the double meaning of the phrases used by both lovers parodies the vows of the conventional lovers in heroic drama. But Don John's statement to the second Constantia that he means to "love" her as often as he can is more than merely double entendre; it tells us something important about his way of thinking. Apparently, to him the word "love" means simply sex. When he next sees the first Constantia, he apologizes to her for his earlier neglect in these words:

JOHN.

I was before distracted, and 'tis not strange the love of her should hinder me from remembering what was due to you, since it made me forget my self.

1 CONSTANTIA.

Sir, I do know too well the power of Love, by my own experience, not to pardon all the effects of it in another.

(5. 4, p. 60)

When the first Constantia speaks of the power of love, she speaks heroically, of the force which has led her to alienate her family, risk her life, and bear a child out of wedlock, all for love of the duke. By comparison, Don John's use of the word is comically trivial. Thus the contrast in this exchange suggests the limitations of Don John's view of life and love. He may move easily

through the world, but he moves lightly, too, skimming along its surface and knowing nothing of its depths. He cannot experience life as profoundly as someone like the first Constantia.

In the character of the mother of the second Constantia, Buckingham created a highly amusing character, a pretentious, affected, and self-deceived hypocrite who, though she has sold her daughter to Antonio and has later stolen more gold from him, insists that she guides herself by the highest principles of honor:

2 CONSTANTIA.

Dear Mother, let us go a little faster to secure ourselves from Antonio; for my part I am in that terrible fright, that I can neither think, speak, nor stand still, till we are safe a Shipboard, and out of sight of the Shore.

MOTHER.

Out of sight o' the Shore? why, do ye think I'll depatriate?

2 CONSTANTIA.

Depatriate? what's that?

MOTHER.

Why, ye Fool you, leave my Country: what will you never learn to speak out of the vulgar road?

2 CONSTANTIA.

O Lord, this hard word will undo us.

MOTHER.

As I'm a Christian, if it were to save my honour (which is ten thousand times dearer to me than my life) I would not be guilty of so odious a thought.

2 CONSTANTIA.

Pray Mother, since your honour is so dear to ye, consider that if we are taken, both it and we are lost for ever.

MOTHER.

Ay Girle, but what will the world say, if they should hear so odious a thing of us, as that we should depatriate?

(4. 1, pp. 44-45)

Buckingham invested the mother of the second Constantia with two qualities which always make a comic character memorable on the stage: she has a predominant passion (in this case, for social climbing) and a style of speaking (in this case her inappropriately elevated diction) which makes that passion instantly recognizable.

Although his most important changes are in the fourth and fifth acts of the play, which he completely rewrote, Buckingham made a number of smaller changes in the first three acts in order to eliminate some small inconsistencies and to prepare for his later changes. For example, he changed the scene of the play from Bologna to Naples, because the second Constantia and her accomplice are said in act 4, scene 2 (act 3, scene 5 of Buckingham's version) to have fled "to the port." Bologna is an inland city, so Naples fits the line better. Since Naples is not a university town, he changed Don John and Don Frederick from students to young gentlemen on their travels. In act 3, scene 5 (scene 4 in Buckingham's version), Fletcher had Don John and Don Frederick overhear a soliloquy by Francisco, in which Francisco mentions the flight of the second Constantia; it is this episode which leads each of the two young men to suspect the other of concealing the first Constantia. But one of the conventions of Renaissance and Jacobean drama is that a soliloquy represents the thoughts of a character and is unheard by the other characters on the stage. Therefore Buckingham added another character ("a Man") and turned the soliloquy into a dialogue, which Don John and Don Frederick could overhear with dramatic propriety.

At several points throughout the first three acts, Buckingham cut lines of exposition which tended to delay the action of the play. The scene in which Antonio is treated by his surgeon (3. 2), for example, was cut to about half the length it had in Fletcher, necessarily omitting some good comic lines, but speeding the action. Since Buckingham wished to make Antonio impotent and to make his impotence crucial to the resolution of the plot (see the exchange between him and the second Constantia [5. 4, p. 60] and her lament [4. 1, p. 45]), he changed Antonio's line, "Will it please you sir / To let me have a wench?" (3.2, 17-18) in Fletcher's play to "Will't please you, Sir, to give me a brimmer?" (35).[32]

The most important changes Buckingham made in the first three acts were those which served to differentiate more fully the characters of Don John and Don Frederick and to make them more consistent. For example, in order to make the two Constantias more distinct, Buckingham got rid of some suggestions of erotic attraction between Don John and the first Constantia; thus in the scene in which they first meet, when Don John says to the first Constantia, "Nay, 'tis certaine, / Thou art the sweetest woman I e'er looked on: / I hope thou art not honest" (2.3, 20-22), Buckingham cut "I hope thou art not honest." Later in the same scene, at the urging of Frederick, Don John kisses Constantia in greeting, then remarks out of earshot of the other two,

> Now 'tis impossible I should be honest;
> She kisses with a conjuration
> Would make the devill dance: what points she at?
> My leg I warrant, or my well knit body:
> Sit fast Don Frederick.
>
> (2.3, 58-62)

Buckingham cut "She kisses with a conjuration / Would make the devill dance." These changes eliminate the faint possibility that the chaste first Constantia might attract, deliberately or otherwise, Don John's sexual attentions. In fact, in Buckingham's version of the play she is the only woman to whom he is sexually indifferent; even Gillian, the aged landlady, is the object of a few passing leers. These changes are important because Buckingham wished to make the two Constantias touchstones for the contrasting characters of the two young men.

For a related reason, he cut one of the few scenes whose loss in any way harms the play. In act 3, scene 1, Don John teases Gillian, the landlady, mercilessly with sexual, sometimes obscene, taunts:

> Worshipful Lady,
> How does thy Velvet Scabbard? by this hand
> Thou lookest most amiably: now could I willingly
> (And 'twere not for abusing thy Geneva print there,)
> Venture my Body with thee.
>
> (3.1, 74-78)

In Fletcher's play, Gillian finally replies, predicting that John will sing another tune after his whoring has gained him a few venereal diseases. Her mockery of Don John is satisfying and poetically just, and its absence from Buckingham's play is a real loss of comedy, but for his purposes it was unsuitable to her character. Since he intended her to stand in something of the same relationship to the first Constantia as the mother does to the second (that is, as protector and advisor), it was important that no bawdy pass her lips.

Almost all readers and critics have acknowledged that Buckingham's changes in *The Chances* improved the play. Dryden wrote in 1672, "Fletcher's Don John is our only bugbear; and yet I may affirm, without suspicion of flattery, that he now speaks better, and that his character is maintained with much more vigour in the fourth and fifth acts than it was by Fletcher in the three former. I have always acknowledged the wit of our predecesors, with all the veneration which becomes me; but, I am sure, their wit was not that of gentlemen; there was ever somewhat that was ill-bred and clownish in it, and which confessed the conversation of the authors."[33] It is not easy to see how Dryden might have thought that Buckingham had made Don John less ill-bred; the duke retained most of his obscene and double entendre speeches from Fletcher's play and even added to them. But certainly Dryden is correct that the character of Don John, which is the mainspring of the play, has more vigor in the two final acts as Buckingham has revised them. A. C. Sprague, with the perspective of two hundred fifty years, has written, "In short, Fletcher's comedy has been genuinely improved by its Restoration adapter—a somewhat extraordinary thing in itself. And the improvement has been gained by entering fully into the spirit of the original and applying a simple technical device by which that spirit might be maintained at its best."[34]

Buckingham's adaptation of **The Chances** is one of his most successful works, and it was an immediate hit. Displacing Fletcher's original from the stage, it was performed regularly throughout the Restoration and well into the second half of the eighteenth century. It is no wonder that the success of this play encouraged the duke to try his hand again at writing for the stage.

THE COUNTRY GENTLEMAN

For more than three hundred years, the play **The Country Gentleman** was known only in the story of the political controversy it provoked, for the play itself had been suppressed. In 1976 the full text of the play was published by Arthur H. Scouten and Robert D. Hume, who found a manuscript copy of it in the Folger Shakespeare Library in Washington.[35]

The play, which was scheduled for performance on 27 February 1669, was suppressed because it became the occasion for a crisis which rocked the government of England. The cause of the crisis was the fact that the play included two characters which were clearly recognizable caricatures of Sir William Coventry and Sir John Duncomb, Coventry's friend and ally on the Privy Council. Both men were supporters of the duke of York, King Charles's brother and heir apparent to the throne, whom Buckingham always opposed when he could. The two characters, Sir Cautious Trouble-all and Sir Gravity Empty, are portrayed in several scenes as grave, foolish, self-important "men of business"; Empty, a sycophant, simply repeats the thoughts of Trouble-all in slightly different words:

CAUTIOUS.

> For counsell you shall not want it, and in the first place have a care of your Landlady.

LUCY.

> Why Sir?

EMPTY.

> Why the reason is plain, I say as Sir Cautious said, have a care of your Landlady by all means.

CAUTIOUS.

> Ladies she is a woman of contrivances.

EMPTY.

> That is of tricks.

KATE.

> A most admirable explanation.

CAUTIOUS.

> And of small credit with her neighbors.

EMPTY.

> Of little or none at all.

(2.1. 176-85)

What made the identification of Sir Cautious Trouble-all with Sir William Coventry unmistakable was the inclusion in the play of a scene in which Sir Cautious explains to Sir Gravity his use of a round table with a round hole in its middle, in which he can sit on a swivel-stool and turn himself. His idea is to arrange his papers on the table in a circle about him, according to their topics, and then to turn himself from one to another as he moves from one topic to another. As members of the Privy Council all knew, Sir William had invented just such a table, which he used in his study at home, and he had very proudly displayed it to curious visitors. (Samuel Pepys, for example, had seen the table on 4 July 1668.)[36]

As Coventry himself told the story to Pepys, when he heard of the plan to present the play, "he told Tom. Killigrew [the manager of the Theatre Royal, where the play was to be presented] that he should tell his actors, whoever they were, that did offer at anything like representing him, that he would not complain to my Lord Chamberlain, which was too weak, nor get him beaten, as Sir. Ch. Sidly is said to do, but that he would cause his nose to be cut."[37] And he sent his nephew, Henry Saville, to carry to Buckingham a challenge to a duel.

Although Buckingham was an excellent swordsman and Coventry was not, the duke did not want to fight the duel. It had been only a little more than a year since the infamous duel at Barn Elms, when Buckingham had killed the earl of Shrewsbury. If he were now to kill Coventry, especially after having provoked the quarrel, the scandal might destroy his political career. Fortunately for him, the duel could easily be prevented. He had only to allow word of it to leak out before it could take place, and it would be officially stopped. According to Pepys, King Charles asked both men at a meeting of the Privy Council whether it was true that Coventry had sent a challenge to Buckingham. Buckingham admitted that he had received it. Coventry declined to answer, but the king took his silence as an admission of guilt, and he issued a warrant for the commitment of Coventry to the Tower of London.[38] The king's lawyers had found an old law, from the time of King Henry VII, which made it a felony to conspire the death of a member of the king's Privy Council. Since Buckingham (like Coventry himself) was a privy counsellor, the law applied in this case. Coventry was dismissed from all his official positions, though he was released from the Tower and pardoned on 21 March and the play was forbidden to be performed or published.

By means of this maneuver, Buckingham had scored an important victory. He had deprived his enemy, the duke of York, of an able and highly placed ally. He had driven a wedge between York and the king. And in addition, he had pleased the king, who wrote of Coventry to his sister, "The truth of it is, he has been a troublesome man. . . . , and I am well rid of him."[39]

Because at least one contemporary report said that Buckingham had "inserted a scene" into a play already written by Howard, Scouten and Hume have thought it most likely that only the "oyster-table scene" was the work of Buckingham.[40] But the precise extent of any collaboration is difficult for outsiders—even when they are contemporaries—to ascertain. There is some internal evidence that Buckingham may have had a hand in the fabric of the entire play.

The most interesting piece of such evidence is the resemblance between the character of Mistress Finical Fart, the affected, scheming landlady in *The Country Gentleman,* and that of the mother of the second Constantia in Buckingham's revision of *The Chances,* which had been performed for the first time only two years earlier. Both Mistress Finical and the mother are loquacious, both imagine themselves to be well-bred, and both affect French diction. There is a striking similarity, for example, between this complaint by Mrs. Finical: "I cannot express myself with a *bonne mine,* but they fall upon me with a most unbred audaciousness" (*Country Gentleman,* 1. 1. 37-40)—and this remark by the mother of the second Constantia: "Besides, with all her wit, Constantia is but a Fool, and calls all the Meniarderies of a bonne mine, affectation" (*Chances,* 5. 3, p. 56).[41] Although Frenchified fops are standard figures of fun on the Restoration stage (see, for example, Sir Fopling Flutter in Etherege's *The Man of Mode* and Melantha in Dryden's *Marriage à la Mode*), such characters are usually upper-class figures. Indeed, Hume and Scouten, apparently forgetting about the mother in *The Chances,* call Mrs. Finical "a figure almost without parallel in seventeenth century comedy."[42] For Howard to have borrowed the use of this figure from Buckingham's play would have been a most uncharacteristic act, but for Buckingham to use the same kind of character twice, particularly when the first had met with success, would be natural.

Another parallel with *The Chances,* though a slighter one, occurs in act 1, scene 1, where Worthy, arriving somewhat drunk at Mrs. Finical's house, calls her "my belov'd" and pretends to make her a sexual proposition. Presumably he is only teasing her, for she is past middle age and no beauty, and he is one of the young wits who are the heroes of the play. The scene has a parallel in *The Chances,* act 3, scene 1, where Don John teases Gillian, his landlady, in much the same way. The scene in *The Chances* was written by Fletcher, not by

Buckingham, but Buckingham had retained it, with modifications, when he revised the play, and it would have been fresh in his mind in 1669 if he had wished to draw upon it for *The Country Gentleman.*

The dialogue between Sir Cautious and Sir Gravity quoted above (2. 1. 172-200) is very much like one which appeared in 1671 in *The Rehearsal,* act 2, scene 4, in which the two politicians, the Physician and the Gentleman-Usher, "lay their heads together" to discuss the knotty point of whether the two kings of Brentford overheard their whisper (pp. 22-23 in the Crane edition). Indeed, some unknown annotator has written in a contemporary hand in a 1683 folio copy of *The Rehearsal,* "S[r] W[m] Couentry S[r] John Duncomb."[43] Of course, Buckingham might well have copied the scene from *The Country Gentleman* even if Howard had written it. But taken together, these three similarities between *The Country Gentleman* and other works of Buckingham's are persuasive, though not conclusive, evidence that the duke collaborated with Howard in the composition of the whole play.

The plot of *The Country Gentleman* involves Isabella and Philadelphia, the two daughters of Sir Richard Plainbred, the country gentleman of the title, and their three pairs of suitors. The suitors are Worthy and Lovetruth, two young men who, like the girls and their father, are from the country but are living temporarily in London; Vapor and Slander, two London fops, elaborate in their dress and speech but completely without honor; and Sir Cautious Trouble-all and Sir Gravity Empty, the self-important, grave "men of business" already mentioned. The fops and the politicians are interested not in the young ladies' persons (which when the play begins they have not seen), but in their fortunes, of which they have heard enough. Mistress Finical plots to support the interest of Vapor and Slander, for she is impressed by their foppish manner. Trim, a clever barber and former servant of Sir Richard's, pretends to be supporting the interest of Sir Cautious and Sir Gravity, but in fact he hopes to arrange a marriage between them and his own daughters, Lucy and Kate, as a means of making his own fortune. In the end, as a result of several complicated schemes, Trim succeeds in marrying the politicians to his daughters, and Isabella and Philadelphia are married to Worthy and Lovetruth, respectively. Vapor and Slander are "married" to two footboys, servants to Sir Richard, who have appeared in disguise at the ceremony, and whom the fops have been led to believe are the two heiresses.

The Country Gentleman is an amusing, though not an outstanding, comedy. Like many Restoration comedies, it has an intrigue plot and witty "love duels" between the male and female leads. But neither the witty banter nor the intrigues are dramatically important elements. Because the fops and the politicians pose no serious threat to the heroes' prospects with the heroines, all the plotting of Mrs. Finical is in vain. And whereas the love debates in the "gay couple" tradition derive their spirit from the participants' feeling themselves impelled by love toward marriage and their struggling against the loss of freedom which marriage implies,[44] in *The Country Gentleman* we have no real sense that either the women or the men are really reluctant to marry. The ladies tease the gentlemen, but except when they pretend to believe the fops' account of the abortive duel (4. 1, p. 127) and when they pretend to back out at the last minute before the marriage (5. 1, pp. 145-46), the men know they are being teased, and they relish the interplay as much as the ladies. The audience can enjoy the comic action without ever having to worry about the outcome of the plot.

In several important respects *The Country Gentleman* is atypical of the comedies of its time. One of the chief of these is that all the sensible characters despise the environment and values of London. They denounce urban fashions as nonsense, urban amusements as trivial and useless, and urban dealing as duplicity. Sir Richard, who is in London to transact legal business, hates the city and hopes to return to his home in the West Country as soon as possible. And whereas in most Restoration comedies a country squire who hated the city and longed for the days of Queen Elizabeth would be a fool, in this play Sir Richard's sentiments are echoed by his beautiful and clever daughters and by their witty suitors, Worthy and Lovetruth. Only the fools, led by Mrs. Finical, love the city.

Of the principal characters' objections to the city, the one which carries the most weight is the idea that it is a place of deception. Thus Trim says of Sir Richard, "He swears he lives here in ignorance, and the plainest dealing he us'd to find was among the Lyons, for he knew when they were angry by their roaring; he never understood what fine people meant, either by what they said or did" (52). And Lovetruth, when he hears Vapor and Slander attempting to court the pretended heiresses by boasting of their supposed attractiveness and courage, says in an aside, "How I kindle at these lyes—" (104). Fancy speeches are invariably undercut, even when the intelligent characters make them. For example, when Worthy and Lovetruth first approach the heroines, Worthy begins with a conventional compliment, "Save you Ladies, this [that is, the pleasure of their company] is a happiness above our merits." Isabella replies, "Why truly if you speak as you think, you deserve very little" (84). In another scene, all four lovers mock the conventional Petrarchan formulas:

WORTHY.

And shall we part thus?

LOVETRUTH.

But one kind word.

WORTHY.

Or a speaking look.

ISABELLA.

Nay, if you are so reasonable, have at you, come Sister, lets give 'em looks apeece. (*They look at 'em.*)

WORTHY.

Umh, so it goes through and through; Lovetruth, prithee look behind me and see where the look comes out.

LOVETRUTH.

No man, tis but got to thy heart yet—

(3.1, p. 113)

In scenes of banter like these, Worthy and Lovetruth show that they deserve the love of the two witty ladies, in part because they do not expect them to believe the common cant.

However, since the play assigns a high value to truth and plain-dealing, it is hard for an audience to accept the fact that all the supposedly moral characters in the play—Worthy, Lovetruth, Isabella, Philadelphia, Kate, and Lucy—participate in deceptions of their own, designed to trick the fools. Sir Richard, who never takes an active part in the action but is always told of it afterward, invariably applauds these deceptions. Tricky plots are the stuff of which comedies are made, but to have all the heroes and heroines of the play engage in behavior which violates the play's highest values is confusing or worse.

Another problem concerns the fact that the play's action takes place in a single setting, Mrs. Finical's boardinghouse, and within a single day. This observance of the classical "unities" (which, interestingly enough, Howard had attacked as a critical dogma a year or two before),[45] gives the play a tight structure, but it puts a strain on credibility. An audience can hardly believe that two intelligent young ladies like Isabella and Philadelphia would be willing to marry on the same day they have come to London and have met their suitors, particularly in the light of their dryly amused manner toward the young men. To partly overset that objection, Howard and Buckingham plant the idea that Worthy and Lovetruth have known the two girls before. Lovetruth tells Worthy after the scene of meeting, "To see the luck on't, that our first loves should be brought after us, tis a good omen," and Isabella and Philadelphia acknowledge having received some attentions from the men at their father's house in the country (84). Still, the action happens too fast. Even though Sir Cautious and Sir Gravity are too stupid to pay attention to the girls' reactions and Vapor and Slander are too blinded by greed, it is hard to believe that they could be led to expect the girls to marry them on the day they have just met.

Another critical problem is raised by the authors' use of characters in pairs. Both Buckingham and Howard had previously used this device, a common formula on the Restoration comic stage.[46] In this play the formula is carried to an extreme, for there are two heiresses, Isabella and Philadelphia; two barbers' daughters, Kate and Lucy; two wits, Worthy and Lovetruth; two fops, Vapor and Slander; two men of business, Sir Cautious and Sir Gravity; two plotters, Trim and Mrs. Finical; and even two footboys, Ned and Will. The only character who does not appear as part of a pair is Sir Richard Plainbred, the Country Gentleman, and his appearing alone certainly makes him stand out in the play, as does his not participating in the intrigues of the plot. But that singularity is not exploited.

The fact that all the major characters except Sir Richard are doubled makes possible some of the intrigues involved in the plots: for example, the marriage trick could not be played on Vapor and Slander without the participation of one sister in the fooling of each. However, the doubled characters are, in most cases, insufficiently differentiated. We have no trouble telling Trim from Mrs. Finical, of course, and Sir Cautious can be distinguished from his echo, Sir Gravity, if only by his always speaking any given idea first. But the members of the other pairs are nearly indistinguishable. Isabella and Philadelphia are both witty and independent; Vapor and Slander are both foolish and underhanded. The lines assigned to either member of any pair might as easily be given to the other. Thus, many scenes, not only those of the fools, but even those of the intelligent characters, become a kind of litany in which one character finishes the thoughts of another. This problem probably shows the effect of Howard's hand, for Buckingham's treatment of Don John and Don Frederick, in his revision of *The Chances,* suggests that he preferred to emphasize the differences between paired characters.

For all these reasons, *The Country Gentleman* is a flawed play. Both Buckingham and Howard had written better comedies before this one, and Buckingham was to write a much better one later in *The Rehearsal.* Ironically, the king's suppression of this play prevented the public from knowing of a comedy that would have diminished its authors' reputations.

The Restauration: or, Right Will Take Place

Buckingham's *The Restauration* is a revision of *Philaster: Or, Love Lies a-Bleeding,* written by Beaumont and Fletcher in 1610. Although the evidence that Buckingham was the author of the revision is inconclusive, it has been persuasive enough to convince most authoritative scholars and editors.[47]

The plot of Beaumont's and Fletcher's tragicomedy focuses on Philaster, son of the late king of Sicily, and his beloved, Arathusa, the daughter of the king of Calabria.

Because Arathusa's father has usurped the Sicilian throne from Philaster's father, the couple must communicate in secret; therefore Philaster orders his page, Bellario, to enter the service of the princess.

The king plans a marriage between Arathusa and Pharamond, a Spanish prince. To defeat the plan, Arathusa informs her father of an assignation between Pharamond and Megra, a lascivious court lady. The king, outraged, orders both Pharamond and Megra to leave Sicily, but Megra, to mitigate her guilt, accuses Arathusa of a sexual involvement with Bellario. For some reason the king and his court believe the accusation. Dion, a respected Sicilian lord, passes the story on to Philaster, saying that he himself caught the pair in the act.

Philaster parts angrily with both his mistress and his page and flees to the forest to be alone. Arathusa and Bellario, separately, take to the forest, too. Eventually Arathusa faints, Bellario happens upon her and attempts to aid her, and Philaster, coming upon the two together, wounds Arathusa. Eventually he wounds Bellario, too, but both the lady and the boy remain loyal to him.

When Philaster is captured and held for execution by the king on the charge of attacking the princess, Arathusa arranges to have Philaster placed in her custody, and they are secretly married. The townspeople, hearing that Philaster is under sentence of death, rise up in rebellion and seize Pharamond. The king promises to release Philaster and recognize his marriage to Arathusa if he will quell the uprising. He does so, order is restored, and Bellario reveals that "he" is really a woman, Euphrasia, daughter of Dion, who has secretly loved Philaster and has disguised herself as a boy in order to serve him.

Buckingham's revisions of the play were prompted by a consciousness that the earlier version lacked what Restoration audiences considered "refinement." Buckingham's contemporaries were troubled when in Renaissance dramas, including this one, lords and ladies sometimes exchanged bawdy jokes. Still more troublesome was the fact that the heroic characters did not always behave heroically. Dryden, for example, in his *Defense of the Epilogue* (1672), had complained that "Philaster wound[s] his mistress, and afterwards his boy, to save himself."[48] As we know from having examined Buckingham's revisions of *The Chances,* the duke felt it important to separate the comic plot and characters from the heroic ones as clearly as possible.

To correct these faults, Buckingham made his most important changes in the fourth act, which takes place in the forest. Whereas Beaumont and Fletcher had Philaster wound Arathusa deliberately and in cold blood, as an act of justice, Buckingham changed the action so that Philander (the counterpart of Philaster in his version) attacks Endymion (Bellario) and wounds Araminta (Arathusa) accidentally.[49] Philaster wounds Bellario while the latter is asleep, but in *The Restauration* Philander wounds Endymion only after Endymion rejects his repeated entreaties to leave him. Both these changes help to rescue the hero of the piece from the imputations of cowardice and cruelty.

Several of Buckingham's changes were intended to produce a sharper separation between the characters. Pharamond in the original play is already somewhat pompous and conceited; in Buckingham's version he (now named "Thrasamond") is a complete fool, unable to speak in public without his governor's prompting. Araminta in Buckingham's version lacks some of the vigor of Arathusa in Beaumont's and Fletcher's; Buckingham cut out the section of her initial interview with Philaster in which she tells him imperiously that she will not relinquish her claim to the two kingdoms of Calabria and Sicily. Buckingham seems to have tried to make her more like Shakespeare's Desdemona, in order to make Philander's wounding her in act 4 more evocative of pity.

Although Buckingham had a gift for comedy, he seems to have believed, as did many of his contemporaries, that the comic and heroic modes could not coexist in a single character or scene. In his revision of *Philaster* he repeatedly cut scenes and lines in which the noble characters engage in humor, particularly if the humor has an obscene cast. For example, he removed scene 1 of act 4, in which the courtiers, preparing for the hunt, laugh and joke about the rumors about Arathusa and about Megra's having been caught the previous evening in Pharamond's chambers. He also removed, perhaps for the same reason, scene 2 of act 2, in which Pharamond and Megra, overheard by Gallatea, arrange their assignation. That cut does particularly serious damage to the play, however, because it removes emphasis from one of the most important complications of the plot. When, in *The Restauration,* Thrasamond is found in Alga's (i.e., Megra's) bedchamber, she seems almost a completely new character, and her accusation against Araminta seems without motive.

In addition to the changes of plot and structure already indicated, Buckingham made small changes in the lines everywhere in the play. Many of these changes are so apparently profitless as to seem meddlesome, and when the scene is in verse, Buckingham's revisions are particularly unfortunate. For example, in act 1, scene 1 of Beaumont's and Fletcher's version of the play, when Philaster first confronts Pharamond, he speaks as follows:

PHILASTER.

> Then thus I turne
> My language to you Prince, you forraign man:
> Ne'er stare, nor put on wonder, for you must
> Indure me, and you shall.[50]

In Buckingham's version the same speech begins as follows:

PHILANDER.

> Thus then—
> I turn myself to you, big foreign man,
> Ne'er stare, nor put on wonder, for you must
> Endure me, and you shall.[51]

The speech in Beaumont and Fletcher is not very good. But in Buckingham's version it is unintentionally comic; the phrase "big foreign man" makes Philander sound like a child. What could Buckingham have hoped to gain by changing "I turne / My language to you" to "I turn myself to you"? The latter represents a slight loss of precision and no apparent gain.

When Arathusa reveals to Philaster that she loves him in Beaumont's and Fletcher's play (1. 2), he replies,

> Madam, you are too full of noble thoughts,
> To lay a traine for this contemned life,
> Which you may have for asking: to suspect
> Were base, where I deserve no ill; love you,
> By all my hopes I doe, above my life. . . .

Buckingham makes Philander more reluctant to believe that Araminta loves him, more hesitant to trust her:

> Oh heavens!
> What is't she means! it cannot sure be love;
> And yet she is too full of noble thoughts
> To lay a train for this contemned life,
> Which she might have for asking: Madam, you
> Perplex my mind so much with what you say,
> I know not what to think. . . .

By making some of Philander's remarks an aside, Buckingham invests him with greater modesty, but he also slows the movement of the play. "I know not what to think," like "big foreign man," seems composed by a writer almost deaf to the decorum of heroic drama—and yet it was certainly composed in an effort to suit the style of the play to that decorum.

When Buckingham began the revision of *Philaster,* he may have had in mind a plan to enrich it with references to the current political scene. His changing its title to *The Restauration* was, of course, one such reference. The epilogue spoken by the Governor, with its references to plots and to Shaftesbury's death, is another. The prologue archly criticizes Buckingham himself for having put his public trust above personal profit when he held his Privy Council posts:

He, for the publick, needs would play a game,
For which he has been trounc'd by publick fame;
And to speak truth, so he deserv'd to be
For his dull clownish singularity:
For when the fashion is to break one's trust,
'Tis rudeness then to offer to be just.

(ll. 21-26)

And in the first scene Buckingham added the following exchange:

AGREMONT.

Who is this Prince's father?

CLEON.

A person of mean extraction, but by wiles and arts obtaining power, usurp'd the kingdom where he reigns, and keeps it under by a standing army, which our King intends to copy.

The English public had, ever since the Restoration, regarded a standing army in peacetime as an instrument of tyranny. It was deliberately kept to a few small regiments, except in time of war, and in November of 1673 the Parliament had resolved that a standing army was a grievance against the crown.[52]

All these political references are typical of Buckingham's practice, as we have seen in our discussion of *The Country Gentleman* and will see in *The Rehearsal.* But as in those other cases, Buckingham did not develop his innuendoes into a full-fledged satire. Where an opportunity to make a political reference presented itself, he took it, but he did not go to the trouble of seeking such opportunities.

The Restauration has never been performed, and in all probability it never will be. The original play by Beaumont and Fletcher was undistinguished, and Buckingham's revisions, though they removed some of the most objectionable elements in the original, add enough of their own to make it worse. By heightening the distinction between the heroic and the comic, Buckingham succeeded only in making some parts of the play overblown and others trivial. Of all his dramatic works, *The Restauration* is the least successful.

THE BATTLE OF SEDGMOOR REHEARSED AT WHITEHALL: A FARCE

The Battle of Sedgmoor Rehearsed is a short farce written to satirize Louis de Duras, earl of Feversham. Feversham, a loyal adherent of King James since the latter was duke of York, had been born in France and was the nephew of the famous Marshal Turenne, the greatest of Louis XIV's generals. When the duke of Monmouth led his rebellion against King James in June of 1685, Feversham was assigned the command of the royal forces sent to the west of England to defend against the attack.

The Battle of Sedgmoor, in which the royal army destroyed the rebel force, was fought on the night of 5-6 July 1685. After a campaign of several days, in which the two armies had not made significant contact, Feversham encamped on Sedgmoor, outside of Weston Zoyland, a small town a few miles from Bridgewater. There he separated his forces, leaving the foot soldiers in tents on the ground, while he, his officers, and his cavalry were quartered in the village of Weston. The foot, under the command of Colonel John Churchill (the future duke of Marlborough), were protected from an attack over the moor only by a dry ditch, called the Bussex Rine.

Monmouth, who had good intelligence of the size of Feversham's army and its disposition, attempted a surprise attack at night across the moor. Aided by a knowledgeable guide, he managed to slip his army of five thousand men, both infantry and cavalry, across the moor in silence, so that they arrived at the ditch without disclosing their movements. However, at the Rine, the cavalry, under the command of Monmouth's friend Lord Grey, failed to find the plungeon, or ford, and in the confusion the advantage of surprise was lost. Churchill, certainly the greatest military genius of his time, deployed his forces rapidly. Feversham's cannon, which had been guarding the Bridgewater road, were brought up to overlook the ditch, where they raked the rebel troops. Monmouth's army, cut to pieces, never succeeded in crossing the ditch.

As a Frenchman, suspected of Roman Catholicism, and an adherent of King James, Feversham represented to Buckingham all the elements which, in his view, had been brought to power by James's accession to the throne. The fact that King James had used his royal favor to promote an incompetent general must have seemed inevitable to Buckingham, who always regarded James as a stupid man.[53] But Buckingham was not alone in his contempt for Feversham. In January of 1680, the House of Commons had petitioned King Charles II "to remove Lewis, Earl of Feversham, from all military offices and commands, as a promoter of Popery and of the Popish interests."[54] In "A Poem on the Deponents" (1688), an anonymous poet wrote,

Then in comes Feversham, that haughty beau,
And tells a tale of "den" and "dat" and "how,"
Though he's no more believ'd than all the rest;
Only, poor man, he fain would do his best
And be rewarded, as when come from th' West.[55]

Buckingham's farce was obviously written soon after the events which it describes, for it mentions details of the battle which audiences might soon forget. Buckingham charges Feversham with having encamped his forces in an indefensible position:

LORD.

> I suppose, my Lord, that your Lordship was posted in a very strong place.

GENERAL.

> O' begarra, very strong, vid de great river between me and de rebella, calla, de Brooka de Gutter.

LADY.

> But they say, my Lord, there was no water in that brook of the gutter.

GENERAL.

> Begar, Madama, but dat no be my faulta; begar me no hander de water from coma; if no will rain, begar me no can make de rain.[56]

He points out that the cavalry was separated from the foot soldiers, and that Feversham, as a French nobleman, regarded the common soldiers as rabble:

LADY.

> But pray, my Lord, why did you not stay with the foot?

GENERAL.

> Begarra, Madama, because dere be great differentia between de gentlemen-officera, and de rogua de sogiera; begarra, de rogua de sogiera lye upon de grounda; but begar, de gentleman-officer go to bedda.

Finally, he makes Feversham in every way an uncomprehending fool:

GENERAL.

> But, my lore, begar me tella you one historia, will make you laffa: Begar de nit o' de battalla me be in bed vid one very pretty womans; begar, my lore, de taut o' de occasione, o' de musketa, o' de cannona, o' de pika, de bullet, an de sworda, so run in my heada, dat begar me could do no tinga.

LORD.

> Ay, my Lord, I don't doubt of that. Your Lordship's most humble servant. [*Exit Lord.*

GENERAL.

> Begar, now dis be one very pretty tinga. Me beata de enemy like de great Generalla, like de man o' de conducta, an begar because me no born in Englanda, begar, de Englishman laff at me. Odsoona, de be de straingia natioon in de varld. [*Exit*

The basis of the humor in the farce, as the above quotations illustrate, is Buckingham's talent for personal ridicule. Grammont wrote, "His particular talent consisted in turning into ridicule whatever was ridiculous in other people, and in taking them off, even in their presence, without their perceiving it."[57] The contemporary ac-

counts of Feversham from other sources confirm Buckingham's version of his speech and personality, but Buckingham's eye for specific detail is particularly sharp. And, of course, Buckingham exaggerated these qualities for humorous effect. Buckingham's irony in the farce is severe—more so than in most of his nondramatic personal satires. The addition of the allegation of sexual impotence at the end is uncharacteristically savage, and the dramatic form permits Buckingham to exploit the possibilities for irony more effectively than in his non-dramatic pieces: here he can make Feversham condemn himself out of his own mouth.

BLANK-VERSE HEROIC FRAGMENT

The last of Buckingham's dramatic works is an incomplete heroic play which covers the first thirty-seven pages of his commonplace book, and which exists nowhere else. The fragment includes all of the first act of the play and the first scene of the second. It seems fairly certain that Buckingham was working on this play at the time of his death and that his death prevented his completing it.[58]

The hero of the play is Theodoric, king of the Ostrogoths (454-526), who in the years 488-93 invaded Italy and established a Gothic monarchy with its capital at Ravenna. The play is set just before the invasion; Theodoric's father, Theomirus, is attempting to unite all the Gothic nations in Gaul to take part on his side. The army of the Ostrogoths has besieged Euric, king of the Visigoths, in his capital city (probably Toulouse, but unnamed in the fragment) near Narbonne.

Before the play begins, Theodoric has managed to slip into the besieged city and to meet the beautiful Princess Amalzonta, daughter of King Euric, and he has fallen in love with her. Returning home, he has proposed to his father that he marry Amalzonta and unite the two Gothic nations, but Theomirus has refused.[59]

The play opens with Theodoric, disguised as a Roman and accompanied by his servant, Totilas, in the house of Liberius, a Visigoth nobleman who was captured by the Ostrogoths but has now been released. When Liberius goes to inform the king of his release, Theodoric explains to Totilas that a few days before, in the confusion of a night attack, he became lost. Knowing that he would be thought dead, he has disguised himself and has now managed to return to the city in the company of Liberius, hoping to see Amalzonta again and

> To tell her who I am, and what my busines
> To cast my fortune liberty and life franckly into her
>   hands
> And as befits one totally subdued
> To yield myselfe to mercy, & not stand in composi-
>   tion

(16)

Now a Visigoth gentleman enters, and, in response to a question from Theodoric, tells him that Amalzonta is betrothed to Torrismond, the son of Count Liberius, Theodoric's host. The news so discomposes Theodoric that he is barely able to preserve his disguise. The three men exit separately.

Next King Euric, Count Liberius, and the Lady Eudoxia, a friend of the princess's, enter. Liberius begins to tell the king about his release from Theomirus when a Visigoth captain enters to report a new Ostrogoth attack. The king acknowledges with alarm that he has sent the princess, guarded by a troop of cavalry under the command of Torrismond, to Narbonne for safety until the siege is lifted. Another captain enters to report that the Ostrogothic invaders have attacked the princess's party, causing heavy casualties. The remnant of the troop, still under Torrismond's command, is holding off the enemy until help can be sent.

Act 2 opens in the camp of Theomirus. The king, his queen, and his nobles are in the royal tent, gathered around an empty bier which represents Theodoric, supposed dead. Theomirus swears on the soul of Theodoric that if Euric or any member of his family falls into his hands, he will sacrifice them that very day upon the tomb of Theodoric. He requires his wife, Fredegonda, and all his nobles to swear to execute the oath if he himself dies before it can be carried out.

Here the fragment ends. Although we can never know the outcome Buckingham had planned or what the overall success of the play might have been, we can see that suspense has been nicely built into the existing fragment. It seems likely that both Amalzonta and Torrismond would have fallen into the hands of Theomirus. How Theodoric would hear of their capture and his efforts to return to his father's camp and free the princess would have formed the substance, or part of it, of the remaining unwritten acts.

The first act is given over entirely to exposition: first Theodoric's explaining to Totilas (and, of course, to the audience) how he got where he is, and second the reports to Euric and his court about the situation of the princess. Such exposition is necessary to nearly all Restoration heroic drama, which often takes its plots from obscure histories and romances. In this play Buckingham accomplishes the exposition with grace, brevity, and interest.

One possible logical flaw in the fragmentary plot involves the character of Arsames, the courtier and diplomat who accompanied the disguised Theodoric into Euric's capital the first time. Theodoric's story as told to Totilas implies that he has revealed his identity and plans since the night attack to Arsames:

Him you know how I persuaded, or how
rather forced t' obtayne the Count Liberius
His freedom
(Which waighty grounds of state made very
  reasonable)
And recommended mee to him at his parting
as a considerable Roman gentleman
and bound for Italy to passe along with him

(15)

But if Arsames knows that Theodoric is alive, how could he keep that information from the sorrowing king and queen? How could he take part in the oath to avenge Theodoric's death on Euric and any member of his family, knowing that Theodoric is alive and loves Amalzonta?

Knowing the generally flat quality of Buckingham's blank verse in his emendations to Beaumont's and Fletcher's *Philaster,* we might expect that the weakest quality of this heroic play would be its style. In fact, however, the style of the play is respectable, given the fact that it is unfinished. Naturally, it contains many passages of exposition. But even in such passages the naturalness of the dialogue and the freedom from the kind of meticulous counting of syllables which sometimes mars **The Restauration** are welcome.

There is also some of the bombast which, to twentieth-century readers, at least, is the characteristic fault of most Restoration heroic drama:

TOTILAS.

> The sequel I can easily conceive
> You fell in love with her.

THEODORIC.

> So far thou mayest
> But how in love thou canst no more
> conceive, then you conceivest the nature
> of infinity, there's nothing but negations can
> express it, that 'twas a love unlike all
> love before.

(7)

This fault Buckingham shares with many contemporary playwrights. But it is surprising to see such empty heroics in the work of the man who mocked them so thoroughly in **The Rehearsal.**

In several places in the fragment Buckingham's imagery provides both compression of expression and elevation of tone. Some of the best figurative language occurs in the speeches assigned to Theomirus, whom Buckingham endows with great force as he struggles to divert into revenge his grief for the supposed death of Theodoric. The metaphor of a damned stream in the following lines is characteristically vigorous: "Since Euric has thus rashly stopt the current / of my revenge on cruell Odoacer / It shall overflow, and drowne Him and his Country" (33). And the use of a knife or sword as the implicit vehicle of the following metaphor, reinforced by the implicit pun on "mettle," is suitable for a warrior-king:

Fredegond, no more
The heat of this affliction has enough
Softened the noble metall of our courage,
Tis time to strike it into forme and edge,
And harden it again, lets to the business.

(34)

Thus the style is sometimes quite good. If the play had been completed, it might have amplified its author's reputation.

As we have seen repeatedly in our examination of Buckingham's writings, comedy was the literary mode to which his talents naturally led him. Even such a slight and limited piece as **Sedgmoor Rehearsed** demonstrates how readily he could create ridiculous characters and comic dialogue. **The Country Gentleman**, insofar as it is his work, shows the same ability with greater range. In his revision of **The Chances** he designed, in Don John and the second Constantia, a pair of more complex comic characters and some witty dialogue better than that in many Restoration comedies. In serious drama, on the other hand, Buckingham always worked at a disadvantage. He seems not to have known how to be serious without being inflexibly so—or being unintentionally comic, as he sometimes was in **The Restauration.** Because it suggests that at the end of his life Buckingham was still developing his talents and might have been learning to write a more believable heroic style, the untitled fragment is particularly interesting.

Notes

1. The duke of Buckingham's commonplace book is in the possession of the earl of Jersey; quotations from it are used with his permission. Selections from the book have been published in the *Quarterly Review* 187 (1898):86-112, and in the three biographies of Buckingham published by Burghclere, Chapman, and Wilson. I have normalized the spelling, punctuation, and other accidentals of poems quoted from the commonplace book in this chapter.

2. *Princeton Encyclopedia of Poetry and Poetics,* ed. Alex Preminger, Frank J. Warnke, and O. B. Hardison, Jr. (Princeton, 1965), p. 247.

3. See Hoyt H. Hudson, *The Epigram in the English Renaissance* (New York, 1966).

4. Gotthold Ephraim Lessing, *Fables and Epigrams: with Essays on Fable and Epigram,* trans. J. and H. L. Hunt (London, 1825).

5. Pierre Nicole, *An Essay on True and Apparent Beauty in which from Settled Principles Is Rendered the Grounds for Choosing and Rejecting Epigrams* (Paris, 1659), trans. J. V. Cunningham, Augustan Reprint Society, no. 24 (Los Angeles, 1950), pp. 16-17.

6. *John Donne's Poetry,* ed. A. L. Clements (New York, 1966), p. 38.

7. Dryden, *Absalom and Achitophel,* ll. 355-56. [*The Works of John Dryden,* ed. H. T. Swedenberg and Vinton A. Dearing, 20 vols. (Berkeley, 1956-).]

8. Robert C. Elliott, *The Power of Satire: Magic, Ritual, Art* (Princeton, 1960), pp. 3-48.

9. The attempt on Buckingham's life was made by Abraham Goodman, a servant, in 1663. See Wilson, *A Rake and His Times,* p. 23.

10. This poem is almost certainly aimed at Heneage Finch (1621-82), who was lord chancellor of England from 1675 until his death, rather than at Edward Hyde, earl of Clarendon (1609-74), who was lord chancellor from 1660-1667. The practices ascribed to the subject are completely out of character for Clarendon, who was known for his formal dignity and gravity, and the neighborhood mentioned in the poem fits Finch, who lived in Lincoln's Inn Fields, but not Clarendon, whose house was in St. James's Street, Piccadilly.

11. Arthur O. Lovejoy, *The Great Chain of Being: A Study in the History of an Idea* (New York, 1960). "Plant animals," mentioned in line 2, are zoophytes such as coral or sponges.

12. Burghclere, *George Villiers,* p. 113.

13. No printed edition of this poem appeared in Buckingham's lifetime. In *A Third Collection of . . . Poems, Satires, Songs, &c. against Popery and Tyranny* (1689), the first published edition, the poem is entitled "An Epitaph on Thomas, third Lord Fairfax." In Buckingham's *Miscellaneous Works,* 1704, and subsequent editions, it carries the title, "A Pindaric Poem on the Death of the Lord Fairfax, Father to the Duchess Dowager of Buckingham." The term "Pindaric" was loosely used in the Restoration for any ode except the Horatian. See William F. Thrall, Addison Hibbard, and C. Hugh Holman, *A Handbook to Literature* (New York, 1960), pp. 327-28.

No reliable edition of Buckingham's nondramatic works is readily available. Unless otherwise specified, quotations in this chapter from Buckingham's published poems are taken from *The Genuine Works of His Grace George Villiers, Duke of Buckingham* (Glasgow, 1752).

14. "Braves" are "bravoes"—bullies or hired assassins. A "pudder" (or "pother") is a commotion or

fuss. The first word is street slang, the second homely and conversational. "Polls" may be Buckingham's own coinage; it means "hack politicians."

15. William R. Orwen, in "Marvell and Buckingham," *Notes and Queries* 196 (1951):10-11, suggests that Buckingham's ode echoes words and phrases in Marvell's *Horatian Ode Upon Cromwell's Return from Ireland* (1650) in order to heighten the contrast between Fairfax and Cromwell. On possible relations between Buckingham and Marvell, see chapter 5, below.

16. An epithalamion is a poem in celebration of a marriage; it is a separate genre from the love lyric. But Buckingham's epithalamion has enough in common with his love poems to make it worthwhile to consider them together.

17. Aurora and Tithonus appear in lines 74-76, Hesperus in line 95, of Spenser's poem.

18. See John Harold Wilson, *Court Satires of the Restoration* (Columbus, 1976), and my own "Sexuality, Deviance, and Moral Character in the Personal Satire of the Restoration," *Eighteenth-Century Life* 2 (1975):16-19.

19. "A Familiar Epistle to Mr. Julian," like all the published poems in this chapter, is quoted from the 1752 edition of Buckingham's works. However, there is an edition of the poem in the *Poems on Affairs of State*, 7 vols., ed. George deF. Lord (New Haven, 1963), 1:387-91, with full commentary and footnotes.

20. The ivory staff is the symbol of high office carried by several of the king's ministers. "Tatta" is Arlington's daughter Isabella, who was born in 1667.

21. "The Works of George Villiers, Duke of Buckingham," ed. Thomas Percy, 2 vols. (1809), 1:165. In the absence of a readily available edition of Buckingham's miscellaneous prose, I have relied whenever necessary on this authoritative but unpublished edition. There is a copy in the British Library.

22. A reply to it (*A Short Answer to His Grace the Duke of Buckingham's Paper*) and Buckingham's brief reply to the reply (*The Duke of Buckingham his Grace's Letter to the Unknown Author*) make oblique references to King James's pledge, made to Parliament in May 1685, to uphold the constitution and the Church of England. See David Ogg, *England in the Reigns of James II and William III* (Oxford, 1955), p. 143.

23. *Two Speeches* (Amsterdam, 1675), p. 12.

24. "So potent was religion in persuading to evil deeds" (*De Rerum Natura* [*On the Nature of Things*], bk. 1, l. 101).

25. "Works of Buckingham," ed. Percy, 2:177-78.

26. On Buckingham's reputation, see Wilson, *A Rake and His Times*, pp. 218-19.

27. See Stanley Fish, *Self-Consuming Artifacts: The Experience of Seventeenth-Century Literature* (Berkeley, 1972), particularly pp. 400-401.

28. *A Short Discourse upon the Reasonableness of Men's Having a Religion, or Worship of God* (London, 1685).

29. Of course, critics may argue that the illogic in the *Short Discourse* is inadvertent. To support that view, however, these critics must be prepared to explain why Buckingham, eleven years after renouncing, in the letter to Martin Clifford, the use of reason to persuade the public of religious truth, would set out to write a genuinely logical treatise on religion.

30. See John Harold Wilson, *The Court Wits of the Restoration: An Introduction* (Princeton, 1948).

31. All references to Buckingham's version of *The Chances* in this chapter are to *The Chances, A Comedy: As It Was Acted at the Theater Royal. Corrected and Altered by a Person of Honour.* (London, 1682).

32. References in this chapter to Fletcher's version of *The Chances* are to the edition by George Walton Williams in *The Dramatic Works in the Beaumont and Fletcher Canon*, ed. Fredson Bowers, 4 vols. (Cambridge, 1966-79), 4:541-645.

33. Dryden, "Defense of the Epilogue: or, an Essay on the Dramatic Poetry of the Last Age," in *Of Dramatic Poesy and Other Critical Essays*, ed. George Watson, 2 vols. (New York, 1962), 1:180.

34. Arthur Colby Sprague, *Beaumont and Fletcher on the Restoration Stage* (Cambridge, Mass., 1926), p. 223.

35. Sir Robert Howard and George Villiers, *The Country Gentleman: A "Lost" Play and Its Background*, ed. Arthur H. Scouten and Robert D. Hume (Philadelphia, 1976). All quotations from *The Country Gentleman* in this chapter are taken from this edition.

36. Pepys, *Diary,* 9:225.

37. Ibid., pp. 471-72. On the night of 31 January of the same year, Edward Kynaston, an actor who had played the part of Sir Charles Sedley in the play *The Heiress*, was assaulted in St. James's Park by hired thugs and severely beaten.

38. Ibid., pp. 467-68.

39. Burghclere, *George Villiers,* p. 209.

40. *Country Gentleman,* p. 26.

41. *Bonne mine*: literally, "good air," elegant manner.

42. *Country Gentleman,* p. 30.

43. Ibid., p. 89.

44. See John Harrington Smith, *The Gay Couple in Restoration Comedy* (Cambridge, 1948), pp. 77-78.

45. Howard's attack on the unities appeared in his preface to his last performed play, *The Duke of Lerma* (1668). See *Country Gentleman,* p. 21.

46. See Howard's *The Committee* (1662) and Buckingham's *The Chances.* On the appearance of this formula in Restoration comedy, see Robert D. Hume, *The Development of English Drama in the Late Seventeenth Century* (Oxford, 1976), pp. 130-31.

47. The revision was accepted as Buckingham's work by Bishop Percy in his unpublished late eighteenth-century edition, by A. C. Sprague in *Beaumont and Fletcher on the Restoration Stage,* and by Arthur Mizener in "George Villiers" (Ph.D. diss., Princeton University, 1934).

48. *Of Dramatic Poesy,* ed. Watson London: J. M. Dent; New York: Dutton, 1962, 1:172.

49. Buckingham changes the names of all the characters in the play, being careful to keep the names metrically equivalent for the sake of his versification. In addition to the changes just mentioned there are these: Dion = Cleon; Pharamond = Thrasomond; Thrasilene = Agremont; Cleremont = Adelard; Megra = Alga; Galatea = Melisinda.

50. Quotations from *Philaster* are taken from the edition by Robert K. Turner in *The Dramatic Works in the Beaumont and Fletcher Canon* (Cambridge, 1966-79), 1:367-504.

51. References to *The Restauration* are to Bishop Percy's edition of Buckingham's works, 1:229-346.

52. [David] Ogg, *England in the Reign of Charles II,* [2 vols. (Oxford, 1934)] 1:379.

53. Opinion is divided on the question of Feversham's incompetence. See Winston Churchill, *Marlborough: His Life and Times,* 6 vols. (New York, 1933), 1:217-18; and G. J. Wolseley, *The Life of John Churchill, Duke of Marlborough,* 2 vols. (London, 1894), 1:281, 307-8.

54. Wolseley, *Life of John Churchill,* 1:281. Feversham was, in fact, a French Protestant, who had exiled himself to England to avoid religious persecution in his native land.

55. *Poems on Affairs of State,* vol. 4, ed. Galbraith M. Crump (New Haven, 1968), 270. The reward to which the satirist alludes is the Order of the Garter, conferred upon Feversham on 30 July 1685 as a reward for his having defeated Monmouth.

56. References to *The Battle of Sedgmoor* are to Percy's edition of Buckingham's works, 2:39-46.

57. Grammont, *Memoirs,* [Anthony Hamilton. *The Memoirs of Count Grammont,* ed. Gordon Goodwin, 2 vols. (Edinburgh, 1908)] 1:137.

58. As in chapter 2, all references to and quotations from the duke of Buckingham's commonplace book are by permission of the earl of Jersey.

59. Buckingham (or his source) made no attempt to be faithful to the details of history. See Thomas Hodgkin, *Theodoric the Goth* (New York, 1891).

Selected Bibliography

PRIMARY SOURCES

1. PLAYS

The Chances, A Comedy: As It Was Acted at The Theater Royal. Corrected and Altered by a Person of Honour. London, 1682. Subsequent editions in 1692, 1711, 1735, 1791, 1817, and 1826.

The Country Gentleman: A "Lost" Play and Its Background. Edited by Arthur H. Scouten and Robert D. Hume. Philadelphia: University of Pennsylvania Press, 1976. By Sir Robert Howard and George Villiers, duke of Buckingham.

2. SEPARATE PROSE WORKS

A Short Discourse of the Reasonableness of Men's Having a Religion, or Worship of God. London, 1685. Two more editions, both 1685.

3. COLLECTED WORKS

Miscellaneous Works, Written by His Grace, George, Late Duke of Buckingham. London, 1704.

The Works of his Grace, George Villiers, Late Duke of Buckingham, 2 vols. London, 1715. Three more editions in 1752, 1754, 1775.

"The Works of George Villiers, Duke of Buckingham." Edited by Thomas Percy, Bishop of Dromore. [1806].

SECONDARY SOURCES

1. BOOKS

Burghclere, Winifred. *George Villiers, Second Duke of Buckingham, 1628-1687: A Study in the History of the Restoration.* London: John Murray, 1903.

Chapman, Hester W. *Great Villiers: A Study of George Villiers, Second Duke of Buckingham, 1628-1687.* London: Secker and Warburg, 1949.

Pepys, Samuel. *The Diary of Samuel Pepys.* Edited by Robert Latham and William Matthews. 11 vols. Berkeley: University of California Press, 1970-83.

Wilson, John Harold. *A Rake and His Times: George Villiers Second Duke of Buckingham.* New York: Farrar, Straus, and Young, 1954.

2. ARTICLES

Avery, Emmett L. "The Stage Popularity of *The Rehearsal*, 1671-1777." *Research Studies, State College of Washington* 7 (1939): 201-4.

Baker, Sheridan. "Buckingham's Permanent Rehearsal." *Michigan Quarterly Review* 12 (1973): 160-71.

Elias, Richard. "'Bayes' in Buckingham's *The Rehearsal.*" *English Language Notes* 15 (1978): 178-81.

Emery, John P. "Restoration Dualism of the Court Writers." *Revue des langues vivantes* 32 (1966): 238-65.

Lewis, Peter. "*The Rehearsal*: A Study of Its Satirical Methods." *Durham University Journal,* n.s. 31 (1970): 96-113.

Macey, Samuel L. "Fielding's *Tom Thumb* as the Heir to Buckingham's *Rehearsal.*" *Texas Studies in Literature and Language* 10 (1968): 405-14. *Tom Thumb* in the *Rehearsal* tradition.

McFadden, George. "Political Satire in *The Rehearsal.*" *Yearbook of English Studies* 4 (1974): 120-28.

John H. O'Neill (essay date August 1985)

SOURCE: O'Neill, John H. "Edward Hyde, Heneage Finch, and the Duke of Buckingham's Commonplace Book." *Modern Philology* 83, no. 1 (August 1985): 51-54.

[*In the following essay, O'Neill discusses the possible targets of a satirical poem found in Buckingham's commonplace book.*]

The commonplace book of George Villiers, second duke of Buckingham, contains a fragment of a blank-verse tragedy and a large number of poems, none of which was published in his lifetime.[1] The book was found in the duke's pocket at the time of his death; he died of a chill contracted while hunting on horseback near Castle Helmsley, his estate in Yorkshire, in April 1687. As is customary in commonplace books, the poems in the volume, all fair copies, are arranged under various heads—for example, "House," "Ignoble," "Love," and "Tears." They are almost certainly all Buckingham's own compositions, for none is known to appear in any other place. The dates of composition of a few of the poems can be reliably established: one on the death of Cromwell (p. 22) was most likely composed in 1659 or 1660; another, **"To Dryden"** (p. 9), clearly refers to Buckingham's portrait as Zimri in *Absalom and Achitophel* and therefore cannot have been written before November 1681. But it has not heretofore been clear whether the compilation of the book took place over Buckingham's lifetime or was the work of a specific period—whether he copied his poems into it as he wrote them or whether they were later revised. The question has implications for our understanding of Buckingham's working habits: whether he was an impromptu writer or a careful reviser; whether his literary activity continued until the end of his life or ceased with his publication, in 1685, of the pamphlet *On the Reasonableness of Men's Having a Religion, or Worship of God*; and whether the works in the commonplace book were ephemera or compositions that he hoped to preserve.

One poem in the commonplace book offers a clue to the solution of this problem. It is the poem entitled **"On the Late L**[d] **Chancellour,"** appearing on page 7 of the volume. The following is a diplomatic copy of the poem:

"On the Late L[d] Chancellour"

To Ale, and tosts, and the mirth of a Catch
And all thy witty disputes with the watch
To meat without Napkins, & trenchers of bread
Which in many a quarrell has bin flung at thy head
To a sack by thy side, & a knife in thy pocket
In an old sheath that stinks like a Candle ith socket
To thy pleasant walks to Westminister Hall
In a Durty terme, and thy iustlings for the wall
To thy breakfast in Hell, with black pots by th' Tally
Thy returne in a Sculler, & dinner in Ram ally
To the glorious Court of the Prince d'Amour,
Where if thou pretendst to bee a Counsellour
Thou wouldst eeven there bee but waight and a Clog
Returne, Returne thou now State Pettifog.[2]

Traditionally this poem has been thought a lampoon on Edward Hyde, earl of Clarendon (1609-74), whose loss of the position of lord chancellor in the fall of 1667 was engineered, at least in part, by Buckingham. For years the two men had been rivals for power and royal favor. In 1667 Buckingham, convinced that Clarendon had been involved in a plot to convict him on false charges of treason, became a leader of the faction that made Clarendon the scapegoat for the disastrous war with Holland and the seizure of the English fleet in the Medway by the Dutch fleet in June.[3] The hostility between the two men has made the identification of Clarendon as the target of this poem a natural supposition. Arthur Mizener suggests, "By 'late' Buckingham refers to Clarendon's fall from power rather than to his death. Clarendon fell late in August 1667 and the poem was probably written not long after that event; it was certainly written before Clarendon's death in 1674."[4] Mizener's reasoning has been followed by J. H. Wilson and by Buckingham's other biographers.[5]

Although it has not previously been questioned, the identification of the subject of the poem as Clarendon has been somewhat troublesome. Clarendon was known for his stiff, old-fashioned formality, gravity, and dignity. It is difficult to imagine such a man disputing with the watch, jostling for the wall, or committing the other crude and unclean actions for which this poem derides its subject. Mizener expresses his misgivings succinctly: "The poem does not appear particularly applicable to Clarendon as we ordinarily think of him today, but Buckingham was no doubt flinging the scorn of the stylish courtier of the day at Clarendon as a representative of the old Cavalier type. The distinction between those who did and those who did not use napkins was no doubt more a mark of stylish niceness than we would consider it today."[6]

Mizener's explanation, however, is not sufficient to justify the disparity between this portrait and what we know of Clarendon. Buckingham's great talent, as numerous commentators report, was his ability to produce lifelike mocking portraits of individuals, and his expert mimicry of Clarendon in particular—of "the stately stalk of that solemn personage"—is well documented.[7] It is unlikely that he would overlook in this poem the characteristics that struck all other observers and that he had elsewhere satirized with great applause. In addition, there is an apparent disparity of fact for which Mizener does not account: Clarendon's house was in St. James's Street, Picadilly, so that for him to return home from Westminster Hall would hardly have required a sculler. And to have visited Ram Alley for dinner when he was going from Westminster to Whitehall ("the glorious Court of the Prince d'Amour") would have required a lengthy detour.[8] The poem exhorts its subject to return to his low habits and environs. But Clarendon, after his fall from power, went into an exile in France from which he never returned, nor did Buckingham have any motive for wishing his return.

There is another figure who better fits the description given in the poem. He is Heneage Finch (1621-82), eventually earl of Nottingham, who was lord chancellor of England from 1675 until his death. The practices ascribed to the figure fit Finch fairly well. Having begun life as an attorney, Finch lived in the neighborhood of the Inns of Court, where he held the post of autumn reader of the Inner Temple; he may frequently have dined in Ram Alley. Finch's home was in Queen Street, Lincoln's Inn Fields, so that his daily routine must have included a walk to Westminster Hall and a return at the end of the day.[9] Although there is no record of a per-

sonal hostility between Buckingham and Finch, we may justifiably suspect an inherited animosity. Finch's father, Sir Heneage, had held the post of speaker of the House of Commons in the second parliament of King Charles I; in that position he had delivered to the king the Petition of Right, which called for the removal from power of the first duke of Buckingham, the poet's father, in 1628. The younger Finch's appointment to the office of solicitor-general in 1660 had offended many of the courtiers of Charles II. Those who, like Buckingham, had accompanied the king into exile in France and had forfeited their property for the royal cause resented the king's conferring a valuable post on Finch, who had spent the Interregnum in the Inner Temple.[10]

If we accept the hypothesis that Finch is the subject of the poem, then the title **"The Late Ld Chancellour"** must indicate that Buckingham copied the poem into his commonplace book after Finch's death in 1682. The epigram may have been written, however, even before Finch became lord chancellor. He was solicitor-general from 1660 to 1670 and attorney general from 1670 to 1673; the phrase "State Pettifog" is a more precise equivalent for either of these titles than for lord chancellor, and the word "now" in the final line suggests that when the poem was written he had only recently been advanced to his position. I believe the most likely date is around 1661, the year after Finch was appointed solicitor-general, when the Inner Temple chose him as its autumn reader. He celebrated his new eminence with a magnificent feast:

> The feasting lasted six days. On the first of these he entertained the nobility and Privy Councillors; on the second, the Lord Mayor, Aldermen, and principal citizens of London; on the third, the whole College of Physicians, who came with caps and gowns, on the fourth, the Long Robe—Judges, Advocates, Doctors of the civil law, and all the society of Doctors' Commons; on the fifth, the Archbishops, Bishops, and other dignitaries of the Church; and on the last, the King, the Duke of York, and all the great officers of the Court. . . . His Majesty came from Whitehall in his state barge, and landing at the Temple stairs, was there received by the Reader, and the Chief Justice of the Common Pleas. Passing thence through a double file of the Reader's servants clothed in scarlet cloaks and white doublets, he took his way through a breach made expressly for the occasion in the wall, which at that time enclosed the Temple Garden,—and moved on through a lane formed of Benchers, Utter-barristers, and Students belonging to the Society,—till mounting the Terrace, he arrived at the Inner Temple Hall. A band of many wind instruments and twenty violins saluted the Royal ear with lively and soothing airs. After the sumptuous dinner, there was much dancing and merriment, which continued to a late hour.[11]

Buckingham was proud of his own high place at court and notoriously fond of ceremony. It is easy to imagine that he might resent a common attorney ("Pettifog") who could entertain an illustrious company so lavishly, particularly when that man's father had insulted his.

Thus the disparity between the content of the poem ("thou *now* State Pettifog") and its heading ("the *Late* Ld Chancellour") justifies the inference that the poem was copied into the commonplace book some years after it was written. What may well have happened is that Buckingham, in retirement at Castle Helmsley, occupied his time with bringing together the loose copies of miscellaneous poems that he had written throughout his career and with copying them under topical headings in his book. The fact that the volume was on his person when he died suggests that he may actually have been working at that task just before his final illness. When he came to copy the epigram he had written twenty-five years earlier on Heneage Finch, he gave it the heading that now suited it—**"On the Late Lord Chancellor"**—rather than one it might previously have had, such as "On Finch, Late Made Solicitor-General."

This conclusion may support some other inferences about the commonplace book. For example, it seems very likely that the copying was unfinished at the time of the poet's death and that there were other poems, now lost, that had not yet been copied. The blank-verse tragedy concerned with Theodoric, the king of the Goths, which scholars have assumed was unfinished, may actually have been complete in a draft form now impossible to recover. The volume is less a commonplace book, as we ordinarily understand that term, than an autograph collection, assembled and edited by the author, of unpublished works. It affords us a satisfying glimpse of the duke of Buckingham in his fifty-ninth year, still as actively engaged in his literary work as in his riding to hounds, retaining all the variety and vigor characteristic of his colorful life.

Notes

1. Selections from the duke of Buckingham's commonplace book were published in the *Quarterly Review* (187 [1898]: 86-112). Some have also appeared in the three biographies of Buckingham published in this century: John Harold Wilson, *A Rake and His Times: George Villiers Second Duke of Buckingham* (New York, 1954); Hester W. Chapman, *Great Villiers: A Study of George Villiers, Second Duke of Buckingham, 1628-1687* (London, 1949); and Winifred, duchess of Burghclere, *George Villiers, Second Duke of Buckingham, 1628-1687: A Study in the History of the Restoration* (London, 1903). A full typescript of the commonplace book was included by Arthur Mizener in his "George Villiers, Second Duke of Buckingham: His Life and a Canon of His Works" (Ph.D. diss., Princeton University, 1934).

2. The quotation from the duke of Buckingham's commonplace book is by permission of the earl of Jersey, who has it in his possession.

3. Wilson, p. 108.

4. Mizener, p. 277.

5. See Wilson, p. 108.

6. Mizener, p. 277.

7. See Wilson, p. 14; and John, Lord Campbell, *The Lives of the Lord Chancellors and Keepers of the Great Seal of England,* 7 vols. (Philadelphia, 1847), 3:194.

8. George E. Cokayne, *The Complete Peerage,* 13 vols. (London, 1936), 3:265. See also Pepys's diary entry for February 20, 1664/5 (Robert Latham and William Matthews, eds., *The Diary of Samuel Pepys,* 11 vols. [Berkeley, 1972], 6:39). Ram Alley is a courtyard, now called Mitre Court, off Fleet Street in the neighborhood of the Inns of Court, known in the seventeenth century for its cheap, disreputable cooks' shops and taverns.

9. Cokayne, 9:792.

10. Campbell, 3:304.

11. Ibid., pp. 305-6.

Margarita Stocker (essay date winter 1988)

SOURCE: Stocker, Margarita. "Political Allusion in *The Rehearsal.*" *Philological Quarterly* 67, no. 1 (winter 1988): 11-35.

[*In the following essay, Stocker contends that* The Rehearsal *is both political and literary satire, not one or the other as many critics claim.*]

The Duke of Buckingham's *Rehearsal*[1] (1671) has usually been regarded as a purely theatrical burlesque, of which the central butt is Dryden, in the character of Bayes. Its extensive allusions to heroic drama, in both Bayes' "mock-play" and the "commentary" dialogues surrounding it, evince "shrewd insights into the condition of Restoration drama."[2] Although George McFadden has suggested that the play has elements of political satire,[3] such suggestions are still greeted with considerable scepticism.[4] Partly this is because of a resistance to the notion that literature can be "reduced" to topicality. It should be said at once, however, that political concerns do not necessarily reduce a text to sub-literary status. Nor is it necessary to claim that this play is a political satire rather than a theatrical burlesque, although McFadden tended to privilege political over literary satire as the play's central concern. I wish to suggest that in *The Rehearsal* political and literary satire are analogous, mutually reinforcing, and effectively inseparable. In order to understand this combination, we need to identify more of Buckingham's topical allusions, discover their analytical framework, and understand the literary history which produced this particular play. *The Rehearsal* offers a logical political analysis of its time, precisely by diagnosing the ideology implicit in its literary target, the heroic drama.

In this paper I am concerned to answer the questions, "who is satirized in the play, and why?" In a companion piece, I shall be embedding the answers in the play's polemical context, in the light of Buckingham's political position in 1671. In the power struggle between himself and Arlington, Secretary of State, Buckingham had lost considerable ground. In 1660 Buckingham, richest man in England and childhood companion of Charles II, seemed perfectly placed for great political influence. Yet this was an illusion, and Buckingham was able to force an entry into government only by effecting the downfall of Chancellor Clarendon in 1667. As the leader of the nonconformists within and outside Parliament, Buckingham's political fortunes were inextricably bound up with theirs. Inevitably there was a fundamental polarity between these interests and the Anglican Cavalier supporters of Clarendonian policy as well as the Papist faction centred on James, Duke of York. After the fall of Clarendon conservative and Yorkist policy was increasingly effected by Arlington in accordance with Charles' labyrinthine intentions. By 1670 these involved pro-Catholic and pro-French policies which required the neutralization of Buckingham even while he remained, in the public view, "chief minister."[5] The personal feud between Buckingham and Arlington had continued to simmer despite the co-operation required by their roles in the government, an animosity the more powerful because in 1667 Arlington had framed Buckingham on a charge of treason, forcing his flight and imprisonment before Charles rescued him, perhaps reluctantly.[6] Although Arlington was effectively Charles' chief minister in all but name, Charles kept him in his place partly by maintaining Buckingham's apparent influence in the so-called "Cabal" of ministers. In fact Buckingham was never appointed to a ministry. Excluded—unlike Arlington—from the secret negotiations of the Treaty of Dover, signed in 1670, he had become aware of his marginalization in the counsels of Charles II. Hoping for a military command over the French forces in Holland which were required by the overt treaty, Buckingham had been foiled by Arlington.[7] This was the most recent and bitterly resented of his abortive military aspirations. Meanwhile his policy had conspicuously failed to wring from Parliament the finance Charles desperately required, a failure which evoked a blunt rebuke from the king in the Autumn of 1671.[8] Culminating a series of reverses, this was an explicit sign of Buckingham's political decline which he cannot have underestimated. He was in no mood for optimism. Touched by major scandals in 1670 and 1671, he had also lost his only son, and was up to his ears in debt.[9] While Parliament remained prorogued, from April 1671, his creditors were able to harass him without the hindrance of parliamentary privilege.[10] That prorogation was both politically and personally disastrous for him. In 1671 Buckingham was beginning to reactivate an opposition critique precisely because his marginal influence at court was becoming clear to him, if not to many contemporary observers. *The Rehearsal,* produced in December 1671, expresses that critique.

Why should Buckingham choose to express his frustration in a play? First, while Parliament remained prorogued, Buckingham turned to the theatrical expression of political criticism. Such an indirect method facilitated political criticism in a manner which avoided embarrassing the king directly. If targeted on Arlington in particular, the play's satire could articulate opposition ideas in terms which maintained the debate at factional level, without overt criticism of the king himself. Supposedly, Charles was more responsive to a joke than an argument: not true, in fact, but contemporaries commonly ascribed his tolerance of Buckingham to the latter's droll wit, which had often been exercised in wicked mimickry of Arlington. So if the central butt of *The Rehearsal*'s burlesque, the playwright Bayes, is a caricature of Arlington (as McFadden suggests), we should infer that Buckingham was continuing to practise a strategy which he had found as effective at Court as it would be on the stage. Buckingham had used the stage for political purposes before now. A minor instance was the embarrassing of Lady Harvey by personation in 1669.[11] More significantly, into Robert Howard's comedy, *The Country Gentleman* (1669), Buckingham had inserted a scene which unmistakably satirized Sir William Coventry, then treasurer of the navy.[12] The resulting furore caused the play to be banned before performance. Although the play has a strong strand of political satire, Charles II had previously passed it for playing because he had not seen the Coventry scene. It has been suggested that Buckingham effectively ruined Howard's political project by making it too explicit and thus evoking censorship.[13] Certainly it is clear that Charles II and his ministers might prefer to ignore rather than to underline those cases where political satire was arguable. I think that by 1671 Buckingham had learned the lesson of *The Country Gentleman,* and that *The Rehearsal* is careful to maintain a delicate ambiguity which preserved it from censorship and outcry. The literary burlesque is a very distracting cover for political ideas.[14]

There was no need for Buckingham to resort to crass signals of political intent. Indeed, overt opposition satire would have been unwise, not only in relation to governmental reprisal but also in relation to the performers. The Coventry scandal had involved threats to maim the players.[15] *The Rehearsal* was performed by the King's Company, who would wish to court neither such reprisal nor the disfavour of their principal patron. Presumably Buckingham did not enlighten them about the play's covert political elements; nor would they have reason to suspect the supposed "chief minister" of subversive intent. His careful coaching of John Lacy in the part of Bayes, which concentrated on the mannerisms of Dryden, not only instituted the notorious identification of Bayes the poetaster with Dryden but also provided a visual cover for the figure's satire of Arlington. That tactic and my methodology here assume a similar principle: the alert pluralism of the seventeenth-century reader, upon which such writers as Dryden depended for the recognition of historiographic parallels with the present, and for the deduction of political principles.[16] Such interpretive alertness was hardly a new phenomenon, as witness the contemporary reader who annotated Spenser's *Faerie Queene,* recognizing political parallels even when these did not exactly match the allegorical narrative.[17] A thoroughgoing consistency in such political allegories was not only manifestly unnecessary, given such reading habits, but authorially unwise. In turn, when we try to recover such political intent, the most we can ask for is a plausible reading (which the seventeenth-century reader would have arrived at more rapidly) which calls upon historical evidence for a contextual situation. As it happens, *The Rehearsal* is quite remarkably consistent in the overall pattern of its political satire, as I hope to show.

The political satire in Buckingham's play depends on that analogy between the State and poesy's "kingdom" which is a commonplace of seventeenth-century literature, and invoked by his prologue and epilogue. No reader need exercise any interpretive effort upon the play's literary burlesque: Bayes' "mock-play" is criticized effectively at all points by the "commentary" of Johnson and Smith. In excusing the reader/audience from interpretive effort on this head, Buckingham leaves them free to exercise their perspicacity along political lines. They might reasonably be expected to do so, since Buckingham was not only a prominent political figure but also an incessantly controversial one, who had already been implicated in a major scandal over a comedy with political content.

For Buckingham's project the materials already lay to hand. The ur-*Rehearsal* of 1665, a projected satire of Davenant and Howard, must have provided a skeleton of the literary burlesque. Yet even in this version there may well have been a political burden. Davenant's *Preface to Gondibert* (1650) had insistently related poetry and polity, with evident contemporary relevance. He goes almost as far as Shelley in claiming that poets are the legislators of mankind, governors on equal if not better footing than kings and generals. (In 1650 the

latter were the current rulers, of course.) *Gondibert* itself discusses government, and amongst a number of topical allusions may include a personation of Buckingham.[18] Certainly he was known to have joined in the raillery against Davenant that produced, in 1653, a series of burlesque answers to *Gondibert* which anticipate points made in *The Rehearsal.*[19] Most of these—poetic lameness, dulness, pretension, the use of foreign words, plagiarism, and so on—were readily transferable from the 1665 version to satire of Dryden in the 1671 version of the play. Amongst the charges against Davenant in the travesties of *Gondibert,* one in particular harped on the most hubristic claim made in his Preface. Disparaging the ancient writers, Davenant asserted that originality was a prerequisite of poetic achievement, and that he prided himself most upon wit and innovation.[20] Here evidently is the original of *The Rehearsal*'s literary *bête noire,* "new wit." Yoked in the 1671 version to a topical political analysis (as I shall suggest), that motif may have carried similar connotations in the ur-*Rehearsal.* There is, then, reason to think that the 1671 version reworked a polity/poetry parallel already present in the ur-*Rehearsal*'s satire on Davenant.

The Rehearsal's political allusions centre on a simultaneous satire of Dryden and Arlington in Bayes, predicated on the analogy between literary and poetic "kingdoms." In 1670-71 Arlington was the minister in the ascendant, and if he represented and implemented Charles' policy, to Buckingham's Country connexions Arlington embodied their antagonist, "arbitrary government"—absolutism and the Court. In the literary "kingdom" Dryden could be portrayed in similar terms, not merely by analogy but in ideological fact. Not only was it not unusual for the theatre to be used as a political instrument,[21] but the heroic drama of which Dryden was now the leading exponent exerted its contemporary appeal (especially to Court patrons) partly because of its discussion of political questions.[22] Dryden's heroic plays—including *The Conquest of Granada* (1670), prime target of *The Rehearsal*'s—give exempla of political theory and action.[23] Heroic drama tended to reflect a Stuart conception of kingship and a fundamentally conservative ideology. It was no accident that Charles II encouraged the genre and that Dryden, a conservative apologist, was its foremost theorist and exponent. Suitably, then, Buckingham's burlesque of the genre might not merely mock its dramatic characteristics—"over-inflating the already inflated" heroic conventions[24]—but also imitate its political reference: thereby criticising both the literary mode and its ideology. For this reason Dryden and Arlington can happily co-habit in the figure of Bayes.

Of this strategy the moral is signalled in the epilogue. Bayes' mock-play lacked coherence and plot:

> . . . tho 'tis a plotting Age,
> No place is freer from it than the Stage.

> The Ancients plotted, tho, and strove to please
> With sence that might be understood with ease;
>
> But this new way of wit does so surprise,
> Men lose their wits in wondring where it lyes.
> If it be true, that Monstrous births presage
> The following mischiefs that afflict the Age,
> And sad disasters to the State proclaim;
> Plays without head or tail may do the same.
> Wherefore, for ours, and for the Kingdomes peace,
> May this prodigious way of writing cease.
> Let's have . . .
> . . . some reason, not all Rhyme:
> We have these ten years felt its Influence;
> Pray let this prove a year of Prose and Sense.

The explicit identification of dramatic decadence with current political perturbation, of theatrical with political plots, picks up a topos used by Davenant amongst others, describing the surprising historical "plot" which brought about the Restoration itself.[25] This theatrical analogy is given topical pointing by reference to the disturbances of the decade since 1660. The turbulence which produced the Restoration had left in its wake a climate of anxiety marked by plots, rumours of plots, and insurgences. Some plots were (as its opponents complained) invented or fomented by the government itself in order to intimidate parliament, but others were real enough. Selected highlights include White's Plot and Venner's Rising in 1660, the Wildman Plot of 1661, the Tong Plot of 1662, the abortive Northern rebellion and the Dublin Plot of 1663, the republican design in 1665, the alleged conspiracy behind the Fire of 1666, a major Presbyterian rebellion in Scotland in 1666, the Yorkshire skirmish of 1667, the Bawdy House Riots in London and provincial sectarian disturbances in 1668, followed by serious Nonconformist unrest throughout 1670.[26] In the interstices of these events came the second Dutch War and seamen's riots, fears of invasion and an actual incursion by the Dutch at Chatham in June 1667, not to mention hearth-tax riots and the like. The Court and government had already acquired an unsavoury reputation.[27] Of late years several major scandals at the center of government had in one way or another touched upon Buckingham himself, severely damaging his reputation. Buckingham's own arrest in 1667 and the Coventry scandal were followed in the Winter of 1670 by an attempt to assassinate the Duke of Ormonde and the attack on Sir John Coventry by Monmouth's thugs. In 1671 these were followed by the Blood scandal. All carried significant political implications—the Commons, for instance, abjured other business in its rage at the affront to parliamentary privilege inflicted upon John Coventry[28]—as well as disturbing signs of underhand factional activity. These implications, which were highly productive of rumor, had in John Coventry's case a topical theatrical connection, for the assault was a reprisal against his remarks in the Commons about the king's actress mistresses.[29]

Such unrest was a mixture, then, of actual and fictional "plots." In either case they subvert order and may pose real political threats—whether to the government or to parliament. When governmental in origin, fake conspiracies subserve tyranny, another sense in which plotting is "prodigious," whether in the state or in the bombastic drama. Menace and confusion link the heroic drama to those things which work against "the Kingdomes peace." The genre's formal commitment to the heroic couplet, mercilessly burlesqued in *The Rehearsal,* participates in the polarization of values here. "Prose and Sence," "reason" and order, are pitted against rhyme, nonsense and disorder. In contrast to the clarity and sanity of classical drama, the "new way" of heroic plays encourages the tyranny of rhyme over sense. The assertion that heroic drama stuns and confuses its audience works together with the evocation of political conspiracies, for both share an intent to obfuscate. The "plot" eludes discovery whenever possible.

The identification of literary with political nonsense was established in the very first scene of *The Rehearsal.* There Smith (a visitor from the country) and Johnson (an urbanite) discuss the strangely "prodigious" new fashion in drama as well as the "strange new things" in Town. These phenomena are analogous, since politicians ("Men of Business") indulge merely in a more "solid nonsense . . . [a] more ingenious pastime" than the playwrights. While Bayes will be characterized as a literary "fop" of baroque dulness, these politicians are "solemn Fops," equally "incapable of Reason" (1.1.4-31). Like the "Men of Business" in *Country Gentleman,* Sir Cautious Trouble-All (Coventry) and Sir Gravity Empty (Sir John Duncomb), they are engaged in a pompous and meaningless charade, "always looking grave, and troubling one another, in hopes to be thought Men of Business"—performers on the political stage, as inept as Bayes is in the theatre. In both cases the result is a calculated farrago of nonsense, like the attitudes struck in heroic drama. In politics, however, the motives seem more sinister and must be more dangerous, as the epilogue observes. In that respect, new wits like Bayes are "civil persons" in a double-edged sense. Their theatrical mode—scorning "Nature" in order to "elevate and surprise"—imitates political alarums. The surprises are irrational, manifest "no-meaning" (1.1.32-48). That nihilistic strain indicates wits/politicians' flouting of the literary/natural order, subverting national well-being. When, in Bayes' play, a character brags that "I'll make that God subscribe himself a devil" (4.3.91), Bayes admires his own literary stroke: but we may see in this ludicrous cosmic inversion, the erasure of deity by devilry, a symptom of the consequences of disrupting the natural order.

This is the greater resonance of the play's burlesque upon the heroic drama's dependence on confusion: that inconsistency in plot, situation, genre, characterization and language masks the vacuity and imaginative poverty of such plays. "Elevate and surprise," their literary manifesto, is "a phrase . . . to express their no-meaning." The disguising of vacuity by wilful inconsistency—amply evidenced in Bayes' mock-play—is also analogous to his political counterparts, the artificers of "arbitrary government." Both turn upon innovation. In the political sense confirmed by the epilogue, "surprise" suggests an insurgence and "Elevate" a consequent raising to power, so it should not surprise us that Bayes' own mock-play turns on a political revolution. Very little changes, though: the "Two kings" of Brentford are simply turned out of their chairs by the usurpers. Bayes is ravished by this novel form of revolution he has invented: "There's now an odd surprize; the whole State's turn'd quite topsie-turvy, without any puther or stir in the whole world" (2.4.70-72). Fake conspiracies such as the government had invented during the 1660s might be similarly described. In that respect they contrast with the Revolution actually effected thirty years earlier, when men had spoken of the world being "turned upside down."[30] Brentford, the mock-play's "kingdom," had been the site of an important battle during the Civil War, the high-watermark of the king's advance on London.[31] In a grim sense the town was an example of courtly "non-sense," since although royalist in sympathy it had been sacked by the king's army. A favorite theme of conservative writers was that the subsequent Restoration had been a bloodless revolution, a miraculous change to reverse change,[32] "without any puther or stir." Since Bayes is portrayed as a plagiarist, it should not surprise us that he owes his "novel" portrait of revolution to events themselves.

England's recent history of political vicissitude also finds a comic counterpart in the sudden reverses of Bayes' plot. The Two Kings, themselves a confusing oddity, are usurped and restored in equally unlikely fashion. The bombastic hero Drawcansir resolves matters simply by massacring both of the opposing armies, one of which is an incompetent secret army hiding out in Knightsbridge. Familiar London terrain mocks heroic excess, but also underwrites Buckingham's travesty of recent history. The secret army in Knightsbridge itself comically reflects widespread apprehension of a standing army. Charles' Life Guards, more considerable than any previous royal bodyguard, appeared to be such a force in all but name—a secret army so to say—and were used to suppress unrest on such occasions as the Bawdy House Riots of 1668. It was thought that the Duke of York was especially anxious to acquire and control a standing army.[33] In 1670 the army established in Scotland was viewed with suspicion as a force poised to interfere in England should Charles require defence against domestic unrest.[34] Here too Bayes' plot in the mock-play comically reflects recent policy.

Bayes himself clinches the analogy between plotting and policy, when he reveals that his ludicrous dialogue between the two usurpers has an authentic source: "'tis a Discourse I overheard once betwixt two grand, sober, governing persons" (2.3.56-58). If such intrigue and nonsense are characteristic of actual ministers, then as Buckingham's epilogue suggests, "mischiefs" and confusions in the state are explicable. As Bayes' direct imitation of such policy enforces the literary/political analogy, so an audience might equally reflect that Buckingham himself was no stranger to the discourse of the great.

According to ***The Rehearsal,*** then, the government is a conspiracy of incompetence, ripe for burlesque. In the light of this analogical framework, we can comprehend specific personations and allusions in ***The Rehearsal.*** Bayes/Dryden polarizes the argument between true ("Ancient") authority and "new wit," of stability with vicissitude. He intentionally keeps his plot/"Intrigo" a secret from its audience (2.3.35-54). His aesthetic excuse for this—in "new wit" innovation is all—is the pose of an opportunist hack, just as his counterparts, the political fops, are engaged in a charade which masks political opportunism. His ambition to "out-do all my fellow-Writers" matches their self-seeking intrigues, such as that evinced by the Whispering Scene between the Two Usurpers in his play. The ideology of dramatic innovation is, like their revolution/innovation, merely a matter of self-interest (4.1.50-51). Like them, Bayes wants to advance himself and discompose his audience, "elevate and surprise." His confession that he achieves this by strategies of mystification parodies the heroic drama's attempts to create tension and suspense by mystification,[35] but it also introduces the Whispering Scene's political intrigue. Because the usurpers whisper, the audience has no notion what they are talking about. Bayes justifies this lacuna by saying that "they are suppos'd to be Politicians, and matters of state ought not to be divulg'd" (2.1.67-70). If Bayes suggests that the suppression of information is characteristic of politics, we may well conclude from this and similar hints that there is an actual contemporary situation of conspiracy, suppression, repression, and confusion. In the literary critique, Bayes' apologia suggests a ludicrous confusion between literature and life, but in the political analogy it highlights an inference from the theatrical to the political. The fusion of the two critiques is, in its economy and wit here, typical of Buckingham's method in ***The Rehearsal.***

For the literary burlesque, Bayes certainly represents Dryden, as traditionally believed. McFadden suggests that Bayes is Arlington rather than Dryden, and that the latter himself attests this when he says "I knew that my betters were more concerned than I was in that satire."[36] Although McFadden's account of Arlingtonian allusion is persuasive, I would disagree with his contention that this characterization minimizes reference to Dryden. If, as this paper argues, the play's technique is theatrical burlesque expressing political satire, that is crystallized in Bayes as a conflation of theatrical and political caricature. Representative of the conservative dramatic mode, Dryden as laureate (an honor granted in 1668, and glanced at in Bayes' name) might be regarded as a literary mandarin, analogous in the world of letters to the political ascendancy of Arlington. That analogy is also underpinned by Dryden's appointment in 1670 as Historiographer Royal, semiotically suggesting the political inflections of historical interpretation. The latter was a pastime of considerable significance in the Restoration period,[37] for the exigencies of the regime inevitably included "forgetting" the Interregnum, by whatever means was available. Since the heroic drama was itself a propagandist tool, Buckingham's caricature can readily embrace both the Arlingtonian faction at court and Dryden with his tribe, the heroic dramatists. The fop of literary fashion is fellow-traveller of "Solemn Fop" politicians. Indeed, in satirical poems Buckingham and others characterized Arlington as an affected, "arrant fop."[38]

Bayes' theatrical/political plotting has an especially sharp relevance if we recall Arlington's fabricated plot to convict Buckingham of treason (which would have cost him his life). Bayes' mystificatory strategies provide a dramaturgical analogue for Arlington's in his capacity as Secretary, which included responsibility for intelligence matters. If Bayes is similarly given to intrigue, he is equally keen on power. He sets out to intimidate his audience by a mixture of ingratiation and blackmail which is not dissimilar to the court's management of parliament by means of bribery and intimidation.[39] Both construct claques in the House (1.1.264-71). A small faction (smaller even than Charles' "inner ring," in the case of the Treaty of Dover) is admitted to the secrets of policy, just as a select few "understand" Bayes' impenetrable dramaturgy. "If I writ, Sir, to please the Country, I should have follow'd the old plain way; but I write for some persons of Quality" (1.1.286-88). This is Bayes' put-down of Smith, the countryman who questions his methods. Like Sir Richard Plainbred in *The Country Gentleman,* Smith in this play represents old-fashioned patriotic virtue as enshrined in the country party.[40] His surname characterizes his common sense, his Christian name (Frank) his honesty. His frank criticism lies in political opposition to Bayes'/Dryden's frenchified parlance (a similar contrast to that in *Country Gentleman*),[41] associating him with country patriotism against the Court's pro-French policy. The contrast is very specific, for an important subversive pamphlet of 1660 had announced itself as *Plain English,*[42] truthtelling. A notorious nonconformist printer of such unlicensed pamphlets, still very active in the 1670s, was one Francis Smith.[43] "Honest Frank!" the first words of the play, establish its opposition stance. Appropriately,

it is Smith who educes from Bayes "the very plain truth" of his plotting (2.3.52). Deepening the court comparison, Bayes is portrayed as a despot of the imagination (2.1.61-64) and a bully in the theatre. Even the actors, harassed finally beyond endurance, do not understand the play. A theatrical equivalent of court policy-makers, Bayes' is the "grand design" (1.1.150-58) and it is not for those who implement his policy to reason why. Actually, Bayes himself cannot explain the "Intrigo" of his last play, and he does not know the meaning of meaning (1.1.63-66; 3.1.17-20). When the players recognize the vacuity of their plot/policy-maker, they revolt and abandon Bayes, in a comic actualisation of his own play's usurpation theme. Bayes is deposed from the King's theatre to the Duke's ("I'll sell this play to the other House" [5.1.399-400]). We should infer that the king's Yorkist advisers have, as Marvell had predicted in 1667,[44] shown their true colors, the Duke's Papist interest. The political point is obliquely signalled by the way Bayes refers to play-"House" rivalry, "the other House" recalling parliamentary parlance. The factionalism of the court was always further complicated by inter-House disputes within Parliament itself. Aptly, then, the politics of the theatre duopoly reflect the polity.

Equally, Bayes' despotism of the imagination is a form of self-aggrandizement shared with ambitious politicians: "I despise your Johnson and Beaumont, that borrow'd all they writ from Nature. I am for fetching it purely out of my own fancy, I." (2.1.61-64). In contrast Buckingham's spokesmen, Smith and Johnson, evaluate Bayes' play by the standards of "Nature" and "the old plain way," exemplified by Ben "Jo(h)nson," of whom Buckingham's Johnson is an avatar. He carries the larger literary burden, Smith the larger political burden of the critique. Within the general identification of "plain" aesthetics and political sense, Johnson's function as critic is similar to that of Ben Jonson in Andrew Marvell's "Tom May's Death." There Jonson is invoked as arbiter of poetic and political truth, expelling Tom May from the poets' Elysium because he is "Malignant" in both literary and political terms. He has offended the kingdoms of letters and the state.[45] Marvell and Buckingham were associated both personally and, in the country party, politically.[46] By their invocations of Jonson for such a dual purpose, both writers recall the great Ben's own association of true "Poesy" with a healthy society: "the queen of arts . . . The study of it (if we will trust Aristotle) offers to mankind a certain rule, and pattern . . . disposing us to all civil offices of society."[47] Because of this identification Buckingham's Johnson provides a critique of Bayes which is at once literary and "civil." If Jonson was a model of decorum, Bayes' play is, as he claims, a "Touch-stone" (2.1.131-37)—a measure of all "mischiefs." The heroic drama's "changing Rules, of late, as if men writ / In spite of Reason, Nature, Art and Wit," destabilizes "Rule" whether in aesthetic or political realms.

The evocation of Jonsonian authority points to what I would suggest is the original of *The Rehearsal*— Jonson's comic-satirical play *The Poetaster* (1601). There Jonson used the corrective comic method with which Restoration theory still associated his works.[48] to pillory his opponents in the theatrical wars. Dramatizing the distinction between true poets and mere hacks (Virgil and Horace/Jonson versus Crispinus/Marston and Demetrius/Dekker),[49] he linked poetic authority to political responsibility. Whereas Virgil and Horace are judicious, unsycophantic advisers of Augustus Caesar, promoting proper government, Crispinus and Demetrius are opportunists involved in a slanderous campaign against Horace, to convict him of treason. Rumour is personified as a malign political force, acted out by the plot against Horace. The poetic war is a political battle, decorum a life-and-death actuality. Even Ovid, because impious and hence subversive, must be punished by exile. The subversive nature of Rumour itself makes spies, conspirators and secrecy significant elements in the play. As a whole, *Poetaster*'s analysis of the proper relations between poetry and polity,[50] and its carefully stated political advice, provide the major model for Buckingham's project in *The Rehearsal*. Jonson's poetics justify corrective political satire in association with literary burlesque, such as that of Crispinus. Like Arlington/Bayes, the bad poet here represents a political disease. Equally, the conspiracy against Horace was a suggestive parallel with Arlington's against Buckingham. The role of Rumour, which Jonson uses both to abjure political "interpretation" of the play and to provoke it,[51] is elaborated into *The Rehearsal*'s extensive characterization of conspiracy, faction, mystery and obfuscation. Like Jonson in 1601, Buckingham in 1671 had good personal reason to feel tender about the subject of political rumor.

Within Bayes' mock-play, the Two Kings are, as McFadden suggests (following *The Key to the Rehearsal,* 1704), Charles II and his brother James, Duke of York.[52] Conceiving an ambiguous monarchy, Bayes' play comically renders the political cross-currents provoked by James' power as the active heir-presumptive, and the resultant factional interest. The Yorkist party was by 1671 evidently allied with Buckingham's other enemy, Arlington.

> BAYES . . . the chief hinge of this Play, upon which the whole Plot moves and turns . . . is, that I suppose two Kings to be of the same place . . . differing sometimes in particular; though, in the main, they agree . . . the people being embarrast by their equal tyes to both, and the Sovereigns concern'd in a reciprocal regard, as well to their own interest, as the good of the people; may make a certain kind of a—you understand me—

upon which, there does arise several disputes, turmoils, heart-burnings, and all that . . .

(1.1.228-51)

Similarly, the "whole plot" of current political intrigue in England could be regarded as turning upon the duality of Stuart power as represented by Charles and James, especially since by 1671 James' religious proclivities were the subject of common rumor and made him the obvious centre of pro-Catholic initiatives.[53] The irrational political situation in Bayes' play is equalled only by the inarticulacy of his explanation, as Smith observes (1.1.254). The implication, that even major policymakers like Arlington were not fully cognisant of policy's "grand design," is remarkably accurate to the political methods of Charles II at this time. The mystifying strategies of heroic drama are an apt analogue.

Allusion to the factionalism generated by the succession issue is in fact extended by Bayes' subplot, concerning the fortunes of Prince Pretty-Man. Somehow mislaid as a child, he is brought up by a fisherman whom Pretty-Man takes to be his true father. The fisherman is arrested on a false suspicion of murder, and by some mysterious means this causes the revelation of Pretty-Man's true identity. Since all of this is conducted in a mere 63 lines, both Pretty-Man and the onlookers (Johnson and Smith) are totally confused by this concatenation of dramatic "surprises." Johnson points to the political allusion in Pretty-Man's lament, "Sometimes a Fishers Son, sometimes a Prince. / It is a secret, great as is the world" (3.4.59-60): "But Mr. Bayes, is not this some disparagement to a Prince, to pass for a Fishermans Son? Have a care of that I pray." While Johnson's response suggests wariness of both lese-majeste and censorship, Buckingham thereby also disarms them by "correcting" the fault. At the same time the political point is highlighted: that Pretty-Man refers to the other potential successor to Charles, his handsome but illegitimate son Monmouth.

In his "Fisherman" parent is a jokey reference to Charles' fondness for fishing, a hobby which provided a common topic for satirists. In *Flatfoot the Gudgeon Taker,* for instance:

> Methinks I see our mighty monarch stand,
> His pliant angle trembling in his hand;
> Pleas'd with the sport, good man, nor does he know
> His easy scepter bends and trembles so.
> Fine representative, indeed, of God,
> Whose scepter's dwindl'd to a fishing rod!
>
> . . . howe'er weak and slender be the string,
> Bait it with whore and it will hold a King.[54]

Angling provides both an innuendo characterizing Charles' lechery, and a symbol of his (supposed) political weakness, as conspirators plot to influence him by that route. Buckingham himself had essayed the "planting" of Moll Davis and of Frances Stuart, without much dividend. Recently Arlington had proved more successful in ingratiating himself with Charles' French mistress, Louise de Keroualle, stealing a march on Buckingham in the process. Rumor had it that in October 1671 Charles and Keroualle had actually undergone a form of marriage at Arlington's house, Euston Hall.[55] While Keroualle and Barbara Castlemaine, Charles' long-standing mistress, jostled for position at court, speculation about the mistresses had a new topic in Keroualle's representation of the "French interest" with the king.[56]

The topics of 1670-71 are also evident in the allusion to Monmouth. Pretty-Man's visit to the tailor before leaving for the wars (3.1) is a hit motivated by Monmouth's appointment to the military command desired by Buckingham himself. Because of the attack on John Coventry (in which Monmouth had led Life Guards "in defence" of the mistresses) and his scandalous murder of a beadle, Monmouth was now closely associated with underhand and unsavory court tactics. The "Fisherman" story at once recalls Monmouth's origins, and implies the dangerous political potential of illegitimate progeny in the light of the Queen's infertility. For some years Buckingham had been pressing the king to divorce her.[57] That possibility had been reactivated in 1670 when Charles' favorable public interest in the Roos divorce bill had encouraged speculation that he would take the same course. Charles' personal attendance at the Lords' debates seemed intended as a blow to James' standing as putative heir. That Monmouth was Charles' eldest son, and that Charles accorded him some status, were factors which (as Buckingham recognises) gave hostages to fortune—as future events would confirm. The mock-play conflates political satire with theatrical burlesque, heroic drama's nonsense with political disorder. Pretty-Man is equally a dramatic folly and a political error. Once again the theatrical/political conflation was peculiarly apt. While attending the Lords' debates Charles had remarked that they were "better than a play."[58]

The reference to Charles' lechery is later fleshed out by the *dea ex machina* in Bayes' mock-play. Pallas Athene enters to compose a quarrel between the Two Usurper-Kings by revealing that the object of their passions, Lardella, is not dead. This episode doubtless reflects the fact that Charles and James were rivals in lechery too. In particular, Pallas herself personates Barbara Villiers. Formerly Lady Castlemaine, she received the title of Duchess of Cleveland in 1670, a victory in the skirmish with Keroualle. In the same year her children were ennobled. Lely's famous series of portraits of Court beauties had represented Barbara as Pallas/Minerva.[59] Buckingham's allusion recalls that Pallas was a mythic personification of wisdom in government, an ironic reflection upon Barbara's power to bully the king. To those members of the audience who had seen or heard of Lely's portrait, Pallas' warlike accoutrements would be a visual reminder. Together with the King-Usher's reaction—"Resplendent *Pallas*, we in thee do find / The fiercest Beauty, and a fiercer mind" (4.1.200-1)—these would have appeared fair comment on Barbara's notorious shrewishness as well as her supreme loveliness. Her former title, Castle-main, is redolent of these aggressive qualities. Always the most flamboyant of Charles' mistresses, she has a fittingly metonymic function here for the satire on Charles' weakness. A travesty of "wisdom in government," she embodies the supposed political influence of the mistresses. (It is no coincidence that the Lely "Beauties" were commissioned by the Yorks.[60]) That she serves "the purest wine of France" (4.1.208) is not merely a reflection of Pallas' symbolic rule of household matters but a glance at the mistresses' expenditure, regarded at the time as a significant factor in Charles' financial embarrassments. More personally, Buckingham is pursuing a private joke about the bribes Barbara received from the French ambassador. She had long been an avowed Catholic, "the prerogative whore," and by 1669 was evidently allied with the Yorkist faction. A recent instance of Buckingham's discomfiture was the betrothal of her son to Arlington's daughter, despite Buckingham's rival candidate.[61] No doubt it was for Buckingham an instance of the Court's "nonsense" that she and her French rival were ornaments of the same faction.

Personation equally affects Drawcansir, the bombastic hero of Bayes' mock-play. He is a version of the *miles gloriosus* (like Captain Tucca in Jonson's *Poetaster*), parodying especially Dryden's hero Almanzor in *The Conquest of Granada*. In effect Bayes' enthusiasm for his bullying, self-regarding hero also draws a parallel between Drawcansir and Bayes,[62] his self-regarding and despotic creator. (In *Poetaster* Tucca also represented the braggadoccio as [con-]artist.)[63] As the one is hero of the mock-play, so the other is literary/political anti-hero of Buckingham's play: strengthening the analogy between literature and politics which was established in the commentary. Bayes' literary opportunism, irrationality and irresponsibility are all paralleled by the attitudes of his military hero. Like his creator, he recognises no criteria other than his own wilfulness ("my own Fancy," as Bayes expressed it). Bayes himself characterizes Drawcansir as "a fierce Hero, that frights his Mistress, snubs up Kings, baffles Armies, and does what he will, without regard to numbers, good manners, or justice" (4.1.102-4). Drawcansir's arbitrary activities in the public realm, flouting civility or society (represented metonymically by "good manners, or justice") are the mirror-image of Bayes/Dryden's literary indecorum. As we have seen, Bayes too is guilty of lese-majesty, and his treatment of his fictional army is certainly baffling—they are massacred only subsequently to rise up and dance. Such features demonstrate within the mock-play those universal implications of bad literature which are expressed in the commentary and epilogue. The "good manners" and justice of respect for an audience and dramatic propriety are foreign to Bayes, just as the "numbers" of his heroic couplets manifest rhyme's tyranny over "Prose and sence." This is the ironic "sense" indicated via Bayes' indiscriminate zeugma, "Numbers, good manners, or justice." While reflecting Bayes' lack of discrimination in both life and literature, the zeugma also has a positive function, implying the more general reference of the principle of decorum.

The unfortunate consequences of flouting literary/political decorum are highlighted both by Drawcansir's arbitrary and disruptive actions in the mock-play (mirroring the bewilderingly rapid political tergiversations of Dryden's Almanzor), and by his specific contemporary reference. His inexplicable actions reproduce within the mock-play Bayes' arbitrary rules of "new wit." Drawcansir boasts of his military prowess, gives allegiance to no-one—falling upon both armies with indiscriminate gusto—and "snubs up Kings" by disrupting a court-banquet and snatching the Usurper-Kings' drinking vessels. As in the case of Pretty-Man's princely dignity, Smith's protest at this lese-majesty points to the intended political reference (4.2.256-58). This incident, and Drawcansir's character generally, evoke a scandal which had broken only a few months prior to the first performance of **The Rehearsal** and which had amazed the public. An Irish adventurer, the self-styled Colonel Thomas Blood, had already earned a certain notoriety by his harrying of Ormonde, Lord-Lieutenant in Ireland, which had culminated in his ambush of that notable. Although unsuccessful, the audacity of this assault in St. James, the very heart of London, was itself shocking enough. At this point Buckingham was forced to take a personal interest in the scandal, since within hearing of the king Ormonde's son accused Buckingham of instigating the attack.[64] There had long been bad blood between Buckingham and Ormonde, not least in the struggle to impeach Clarendon, and Ormonde probably ascribed his own political eclipse to Buckingham's influence.[65] Although Buckingham was absolved of the assault, he had reason to take a particular interest in the scandal provoked in 1671 by Blood's attempt to steal the Crown Jewels from the Tower of London. After Blood's personal interview with Charles II, his treasonous exploit received the royal pardon in August 1671, "to the Wonder of all."[66] Thereafter he was received in court, where his very visage inspired fear. In the person of Drawcansir—soldier of fortune, renegade, boaster, bloodthirsty villain, insensible of and untouched by "justice"—we should recognise a portrait of Blood, who was all these things. In Drawcansir's theft of the Kings' "Boles" there is a comic re-enaction of Blood's

recent theft of Charles' orb from the Crown Jewels, and both of them get away with it. Drawcansir is a brilliant exploitation of this *miles gloriosus* of real life.

As Smith wonders at his ability to escape retribution, so the public wondered at Blood's impunity:

> How he came to be pardoned, and even received into favour, not only after this, but several other exploits almost as daring both in London and here, I could never come to understand . . . but it was certainly the boldest attempt, so the only treason of this sort that was ever pardoned.[67]

One rumor claimed that Blood's exploit, like his attempt upon Ormonde, was instigated by Buckingham for anti-court purposes[68]—an absurd notion, calculated to provoke Buckingham's satirical version of the episode. More generally, and accurately, rumor had it that Blood had bought his pardon by informing upon his former associates amongst the insurgents of the previous decade, embarking upon a new career as a double agent for the court. "Some believed he became a spy of several parties . . . and did his Majesty services that way, which none alive could do so well as he."[69] His espionage, and internecine relations with Court and political underground, make Blood a figure representative of conspiracy and intrigue: reflecting, also, the questionable methods of the government and—in his astonishing pardon—the political "nonsense" to which they give rise. Similarly, Drawcansir's indiscriminate political action mimics Blood's ambiguous political agency. The allusion to Blood exemplifies in the action of the mock-play Buckingham's general analysis of political nonsense and chicanery through theatrical burlesque. As dramatic type and political caricature Drawcansir is the fitting hero both of Bayes' "plot" and Arlingtonian "policy." The secret machinations which the Blood scandal brought to flickering light, and the public bafflement, well illustrate Buckingham's satire upon political intrigue-as-mystification.

Given the remarkable integration of literary and political satire which I have indicated within **The Rehearsal,** we should recognize how they complement, and complete, each other. As in Ben Jonson's own aesthetics, literary and civil decorum are inseparable. **The Rehearsal** is not only a very funny play, a salvo in the literary wars of the day, but significantly continues a strand of Renaissance thought about the responsibilities of literary endeavor.

Perhaps literary critics have tended to write off **The Rehearsal** as an enjoyable trifle because, like some historians, they are all too familiar with Buckingham's frivolous reputation. A dupe of the Treaty of Dover he may have been, a womanizer and a wastrel: but in the latter he was no match for his king, whom we have lately come to respect as more of a politician than his contemporaries imagined. Buckingham's reputation has also rested on the hearsay of antagonistic contemporaries, like Clarendon, Burnet and Pepys—the first ruined by Buckingham's political campaign in 1667, the last a member of the Yorkist faction. For both literary critics and historians, Dryden's retaliatory caricature of Zimri in *Absalom and Achitophel* has exerted a powerful debunking effect. Buckingham's other witnesses, like his secretary Brian Fairfax,[70] give a rounder portrait. Perhaps we too should cease to attach so much importance to Buckingham's more rakish activities. If Rochester's poems and Charles' political shrewdness remain uncompromised by such things, why is Buckingham to be derided? By the mid-1660s he was taking his political career seriously: so should we. Public life in the Restoration was a dangerous business, not lightly engaged in.[71] It was not entirely Buckingham's fault—indeed, it was rather because of his loyalty to nonconformity and toleration—that he was always more actually powerful when in opposition than when in Charles' ostensible favor. ***The Rehearsal*** is an example of the same phenomenon, for it is the best of his literary works. If literary evidence were to mean as much to history as historical evidence should mean to literary criticism, I would suggest that ***The Rehearsal*** shows that Buckingham's political analysis could be shrewd indeed.

Notes

1. Although Buckingham is supposed to have received the aid of such friends as Martin Clifford and Thomas Sprat, it seems clear that Buckingham was responsible for the overall structure as well as the actual writing of the play: A. Mizener, "George Villiers, Second Duke of Buckingham: His Life and a Canon of His Works" (Ph.d. Diss., Princeton, 1934), 242-43, 248-49; Judith Milhous and Robert D. Hume, "Attribution Problems in English Drama, 1660-1700," *Harvard Library Bulletin* 31 (1983): 5-39: 27-28. I am grateful to Robert D. Hume for allowing me to read the introduction to his forthcoming edition of Buckingham, which was very helpful on this point. References to the play are from the edition of D. E. L. Crane (Durham U. Press, 1976). The editions of Montague Summers (Stratford-upon-Avon: Shakespeare Head Press, 1914) and Edward Arber (Westminster: Constable, 1902) have also been consulted.

2. Peter Lewis, "*The Rehearsal*: A Study of its Satirical Methods," *Durham University Journal* n.s. 31 (1970): 96-113: 112. See also D. F. Smith, *Plays about the Theatre in England* (London and New York: Oxford U. Press, 1936), pp. 9-37; V. C. Clinton-Baddeley, *The Burlesque Tradition in the English Theatre after 1660* (London: Methuen, 1952); E. L. Avery, "The Stage Popularity of *The*

Rehearsal, 1671-1777," *Washington State College Research Studies* 7 (1939): 201-4; S. Baker, "Buckingham's Permanent *Rehearsal*," *Michigan Quarterly Review* 12 (1973): 160-71; R. Elias, "'Bayes' in Buckingham's *The Rehearsal*," *ELN* 15 (1977-78): 178-81.

3. George McFadden, "Political Satire in *The Rehearsal*," *Yearbook of English Studies* 4 (1974): 120-28; Susan Staves, *Players' Scepters: Fictions of Authority in the Restoration* (U. of Nebraska Press, 1979), pp. 70-72.

4. As, for instance, John O'Neill, *George Villiers, Second Duke of Buckingham* (New York: Twayne, 1985), pp. 81-110; evidently he was not convinced by my paper on this topic, at ASECS 1983 in New York, either.

5. For Buckingham's political career see Maurice Lee, *The Cabal* (U. of Illinois Press, 1965), pp. 161-201; Ronald Hutton, *The Restoration 1658-1667* (Oxford U. Press, 1985) and "The Making of the Secret Treaty of Dover, 1668-1670," *Historical Journal* 29 (1986): 297-318; and the biographies, Winifred Lady Burghclere, *George Villiers* (1903; repr. New York: Kennikat, 1971); H. W. Chapman, *Great Villiers* (London: Secker and Warburg, 1949), J. F. Wilson, *A Rake and His Times* (New York: Farrar, Straus and Young, 1954). I have exerted some interpretation on these, as well as on my own researches in Archives Etrangeres at the Quai D'Orsay in Paris.

6. *Memoirs of Sir John Reresby,* ed. Andrew Browning (Glasgow: Jackson, 1936), pp. 64-66; Wilson, *Rake,* pp. 64-65, 80-81.

7. Wilson, *Rake,* pp. 157-58, 88; Lee, *Cabal,* p. 184.

8. D. T. Witcombe, *Charles II and the Cavalier House of Commons, 1663-74* (Manchester U. Press, 1966), pp. 124-25.

9. Andrew Marvell, *Poems and Letters,* ed. H. M. Margoliouth, P. Legouis and E. E. Duncan-Jones, 2 vols. (Oxford U. Press, 1971), 2:325-26; Lee, *Cabal,* p. 185.

10. Marvell, 2:325.

11. Colin Visser, "Theatrical Scandal in the Letters of Colbert de Croissy, 1669," *Restoration* 7 (1983): 54-57.

12. Sir Robert Howard and the Duke of Buckingham, *The Country Gentleman,* ed. Arthur H. Scouten and Robert D. Hume (London: Dent, 1976).

13. Annabel Patterson, "*The Country Gentleman*: Howard, Marvell, and Dryden in the Theater of Politics," *SEL* [*Studies in English Literature, 1500-*

1900] 25 (1985): 491-509. I am grateful to Professor Patterson for allowing me to read this essay before its publication. For her general thesis on censorship, see *Censorship and Interpretation* (Wisconsin U. Press, 1984).

14. Robert D. Hume, *The Rakish Stage* (Southern Illinois U. Press, 1983), p. 32; pp. 1-45 discuss the methodology of political readings.

15. See Scouten and Hume, introduction to *Country Gentleman*; Lee, *Cabal*, p. 183.

16. J. M. Wallace, "Dryden and History: A problem in allegorical reading," *ELH* 36 (1969): 265-90; "'Examples Are Best Precepts': Readers and Meanings in Seventeenth-Century Poetry," *Critical Inquiry* 1 (1974): 273-90.

17. F. Sandler, "*The Faerie Queene*: An Elizabethan Apocalypse," *The Apocalypse in English Renaissance Thought and Literature,* ed. C. A. Patrides and J. Wittreich (Manchester U. Press, 1984), pp. 148-74; 164-66.

18. Sir William Davenant, *Gondibert,* ed. D. F. Gladish (Oxford U. Press, 1971), pp. xiii-xv.

19. *Certain Verses written by severall of the Authors Friends* (London, 1653), repr. in Gladish, appendix ii.

20. *Certain Verses,* pp. 273, 283; Davenant, *Preface to "Gondibert"* (1650), in *Critical Essays of the Seventeenth Century,* ed. J. E. Spingarn, 3 vols. (Oxford U. Press, 1908), 2:2, 20-21.

21. A. Nicoll, "Political Plays of the Restoration," *MLR* [*Modern Language Review*] 16 (1921): 224-42; Staves, *Players' Scepters,* ch. 2.

22. *The Revels History of Drama in English,* vol. 5, by John Loftis, Richard Southern, Marion Jones, A. H. Scouten (London: Methuen, 1976), pp. 3-4.

23. A. T. Barbeau, *The Intellectual Design of John Dryden's Heroic Plays* (Yale U. Press, 1970).

24. Lewis, p. 106.

25. Nicholas Jose, *Ideas of the Restoration in English Literature, 1660-71* (London: Macmillan, 1984), p. 15, cites Davenant's "Poem to the Kings Most Sacred Majesty" to illustrate Restoration predilections for labyrinthine dramatic plots.

26. For accounts see Hutton, *Restoration*; W. C. Abbott, "English Conspiracy and Dissent," *American Historical Review* 14 (1908-9): 501-28, 696-722.

27. Witcombe, p. 13; Marvell, 2:322, 323.

28. Marvell, 2:321-3; Witcombe, pp. 115-16.

29. Cf. "The King's Vows" (1670), *Poems on Affairs of State: Augustan Satirical Verse 1660-1714 (POAS),* vol. 1, ed. G. deF. Lord (Yale U. Press, 1963), p. 161.

30. C. Hill, *The World Turned Upside Down: Radical Ideas During the English Revolution* (Harmondsworth: Penguin, 1975).

31. For an account of the battle of 1642 see C. V. Wedgwood, *The King's War 1641-1647* (London: Collins Fontana, 1966), pp. 133-34.

32. Jose, p. 23 et passim.

33. L. G. Schwoerer, *"No Standing Armies!": The Anti-army Ideology in Seventeenth-century England* (Johns Hopkins U. Press, 1974), pp. 53, 72-95; T. Harris, "The Bawdy House Riots of 1668," *Historical Journal* 29 (1986): 537-56, 539; Hutton, *Restoration,* p. 286; Marvell, "Last Instructions to a Painter," ll. 223-24, 990; "A Ballad called the Haymarket Hectors" (1671), *POAS* 1:169-70.

34. Marvell, 2:313.

35. Lewis, p. 100, on heroic drama. Jose, p. 38, notes royalist panegyric poetry's dependence on strategies of mystification. Marvell's "Last Instructions" makes clear contemporary recognition of intrigue and confusion at Court (2:609-10). See also Witcombe, p. 22.

36. Dryden, *Of Dramatic Poesy and Other Critical Essays,* ed. G. Watson, 2 vols. (London: Dent, 1962), 2:77-78.

37. R. MacGillivray, *Restoration Historians and the English Civil War* (The Hague: Martinus Nijhoff, 1974), pp. 48-95; Jose, pp. 26ff.

38. Buckingham, *Works* (London, 1704), 2:80; "A Dialogue Between Two Horses," *POAS,* 1:282.

39. Marvell, 2:324-25; "Further Advice to a Painter," *POAS,* 1:165; Lee, *Cabal,* p. 122.

40. For characterization of the "Country" members see Marvell's "Last Instructions," ll. 983-90.

41. For Dryden's French affectations see Samuel Johnson, "Life of Dryden," *Lives of the English Poets,* ed. J. Birkbeck Hill, 3 vols. (Oxford: Clarendon Press, 1905), 1:463-64.

42. *Plain English to His Excellency the Lord General Monk and the Officers of his Army* (London, 1660).

43. J. Walker, "The Censorship of the Press During the Reign of Charles II," *History* 35 (1950): 219-38, 225 et passim.

44. "Last Instructions," ll. 932ff..

45. See M. Stocker, *Apocalyptic Marvell: The Second Coming in Seventeenth-century Poetry* (Ohio U. Press, 1986), pp. 69-71.

46. Ibid, pp. 27-28.

47. Ben Jonson, *Timber: or Discoveries,* in *The Complete Poems,* ed. George Parfitt (Harmondsworth: Penguin, 1975), p. 445. On Jonson as a model of correctness and decorum, see G. Sorelius, *"The Giant Race Before the Flood": Pre-Restoration Drama on the Stage and in the Criticism of the Restoration* (Uppsala U. Press, 1966), p. 21.

48. Sorelius, p. 110.

49. On Jonson's literary satire see A. Barton, *Ben Jonson, Dramatist* (Cambridge U. Press, 1984), pp. 81-86.

50. On the politics of *Poetaster* see H. H. Erskine-Hill, *The Augustan Idea in English Literature* (London: Edward Arnold, 1983), pp. 110-21, 169.

51. Ibid, p. 111.

52. McFadden, p. 125. The Key remained adamant about this: see twelfth edn. (London, 1734), pp. 71ff..

53. M. Ashley, *James II* (London: Dent, 1977), pp. 97-99. Rumor was exacerbated by the Duchess of York's death in April 1671. Marvell, 2:323.

54. *POAS,* vol. 2, ed. Elias F. Mengel Jr. (Yale U. Press, 1965), pp. 190-91.

55. H. Forneron, *Louise de Kerouaille, Duchess of Portsmouth In the Court of Charles II* (London: Sonnenschein, 1887), pp. 69-70, 72; V. Barbour, *Henry Bennet, Earl of Arlington* (Washington D. C.: American Historical Association, 1914), pp. 180-82.

56. Forneron, pp. 54-64; Lee, *Cabal,* p. 113; Marvell, 2:325.

57. *POAS,* 1:182; Marvell, 2:315.

58. Marvell, 2:301-2; Witcombe, p. 103.

59. O. Millar, *The Queen's Pictures* (London: Weidenfeld and the BBC, 1977), p. 70, and *Sir Peter Lely 1618-80* (London: National Portrait Gallery, 1978), pp. 62-63; Pepys, *Diary,* 21 Aug. 1668.

60. Anthony Hamilton, *Memoirs of the Comte de Gramont,* trans. P. Quennell (London: Routledge, 1930), p. 190.

61. E. Hamilton, *The Illustrious Lady: A Biography of Barbara Villiers* (London: Jonathan Cape, 1980), pp. 61, 121, 133, 144; Barbour, p. 168; *POAS,* 1:171.

62. R. F. Willson, Jr., *Their Form Confounded: Studies in the Burlesque Play from Udall to Sheridan* (The Hague: Mouton, 1975) recognizes that Bayes and Drawcansir are similar, p. 103.

63. Barton, *Ben Jonson,* p. 183, observes that Tucca is an artist/liar.

64. Burghclere, *Villiers,* pp. 239-42; W. C. Abbott, *Thomas Blood, Crown-Stealer* (1910; rpt. Bath: Cedric Chivers, 1970); M. Petherick, *Restoration Rogues* (London: Hollis and Carter, 1951), ch. 11.

65. Lee, *Cabal,* p. 182; Wilson, *Rake,* p. 117; Pepys, 4 Nov. 1668.

66. Marvell, 2:326; Petherick, p. 31.

67. *The Diary of John Evelyn,* ed. George W. E. Russell, 2 vols. (London: Dent, 1907), 2:61.

68. Petherick, pp. 32-33.

69. Evelyn, 2:61; Petherick, pp. 33ff.; K. H. D. Haley, *William of Orange and the English Opposition, 1672-74* (Oxford U. Press, 1953), pp. 65ff.

70. Brian Fairfax, "Life of Buckingham," repr. in Arber (ed.), *The Rehearsal,* pp. 3-10.

71. See e.g. Staves, p. 43.

I am grateful to the British Academy for funding some of the research for this paper.

Kristiaan P. Aercke (essay date June 1988)

SOURCE: Aercke, Kristiaan P. "An Orange Stuff'd with Cloves: Bayesian Baroque Rehearsed." *English Language Notes* 25, no. 4 (June 1988): 33-45.

[*In the following essay, Aercke maintains that Bayes, the playwright in* The Rehearsal, *is a Baroque artist, not a modernist as has been claimed by some critics.*]

Buckingham's playwright Bayes summarizes a scene of his own unnamed play in ***The Rehearsal*** (1671) as "an orange stuff'd with cloves" (III.i.24-5).[1] A more Baroque image can hardly be found. Oranges are of course associated with the theater of the seventeenth century through the "orange wenches," but more relevant still is the synaesthetic unity represented by the fruit. A harmonious blend of voluptuous sweetnesses, the reddish-golden globe displays not only the favorite colors of the Baroque, but also the almost shocking boldness of invention associated with this artistic style and period. For who but a Baroque artist would stuff an orange with cloves?

When Bayes asserts proudly that he is "the strangest person in the whole world. For what care I for money? I write for reputation" (III.v.182-3), it becomes clear that the orange conceit is not a fortuitous one; it stands for Bayes's entire play, the rehearsal of which is the subject of Buckingham's ***Rehearsal.*** The major point of this essay is that Buckingham's playwright Bayes—and by implication Buckingham himself—ought to be seen as a Baroque artist who is interested in "stuffing an orange with cloves," in creating a unity out of disunity. Bayes is not merely a parodist who casually connects barbs of satire and parody for their own sake. Faced with the plotlessness of Bayes's untitled play that is being rehearsed, Buckingham's critic Smith cries "Bless me, what a monster's this" (V.i.11). According to a recent study by Jack Gravitt, the play is "absurd" and "modernist" rather than monstrous because of its "involuted structure," its "lack of plot," its "devaluated language" and its "black humor."[2] Such an attempt to compartmentalize Buckingham by means of twentieth-century categories is in itself quite absurd, unless one has the intellectual honesty to admit that seventeenth-century aesthetics offers critical parameters at least as relevant. Similarities with "modernist" and "avant-garde" techniques that come to the reader's mind then turn out to be nothing more and nothing less than just that: similarities. I will therefore be excused for alluding briefly to eighteenth-century Hegelianism *in support of* my interpretation of Bayes as a Baroque artist.

The Rehearsal is usually interpreted as a topical parody of heroic tragedy, as the font and origin of English burlesque theater, as a political satire.[3] I believe that the play's obvious concern with the dualism of "harmony/unification" vs. "disharmony/fragmentation" has not been touched upon. This concern is thoroughly Baroque, for the dualism mentioned is the very crux of the Baroque aesthetics of paradox.[4] Smith and Johnson, the plain-speaking critics of Bayes's play embedded in Buckingham's play, lead us right into this matter. Smith rejects Bayes's play. According to this visitor from the country, it confirms "all the strange new things" (I.i.5-6) that he has heard occur in the wicked metropolis. The play is "a mirror of changing tastes in respect of heroics, bombast and blood"[5] and therefore incomprehensible to Smith. His friend Johnson is a city-dweller, and he remarks that all these "hideous, monstrous things" (I.i.32-3) must not be taken for literal truth, for they are not typical of actual life in the city and belong merely to the realm of art and therefore of imagination and illusion. Smith and Johnson, users of plain-speech both, condemn such artists as the extravagant Bayes who "are given altogether to elevate and surprise" (I.i.42-3). And indeed, Bayes prides himself on doing "nothing here that ever was done before," thus emphasizing the *non pareillo* (I.ii.229-30) and the *ingegno* (genius) of Baroque aesthetics. Whereas Johnson's remarks on Bayes's new form of art are merely inconsistent,[6] Smith's are more serious for they introduce the classical contempt for the so-called "excrescences" of the Baroque. This critical ambiguity is typical of the Restoration, a transitional period in many ways.[7]

Smith's objections mainly concern Bayes's apparent logorrhea and the irregular form into which the eclectic content is poured.[8] Smith also fails to understand the four compositional rules that Bayes explains so pedantically. The rules of "transprosing," "recording," "encyclopedic invention," and "surprise" (I.i.97-155; II.iii.17-9) differ considerably from Senecan or Cornelian doctrine, but they are neither absurd nor neoteric for they promote rather than destroy the unification of style and subject. This unification was the intention of the Baroque artist, and distinguished the latter from his Renaissance or Mannerist colleagues[9] as well as from those who, in the wake of the early scientific revolution, no longer unambiguously accepted the harmony of manner and matter. Bayes is mainly concerned with elocution and composition. His interpretation of composition is modern for his time, because he sees it as the refashioning of pre-existing elements in a process of *creative* imitation, i.e., a higher mode of poetic invention than the fallacious *objective* mimesis which conventional critics such as Smith see as normative.

Bayes is certainly not the first (nor the last) philosopher of language to posit that writing is an anagrammatic process that involves breaking down order into disorder and then refashioning the result back into some other form or order. Assuming that this position is valid, then the main criterion of admiration for the resulting work of art is the creative originality of elocution and composition. It is not Smith but rather the intuitive Johnson who understands this. Bayes's inserted play, as well as the entire *Rehearsal,* is a pastiche of many plays—what one might call a grotesquely inflated anagram. Bayes's four rules for literary composition deny the myth of external divine interference (the Muses) in the poetic act and reveal the artist's power to manipulate his material and his audience. Therefore, to say with Gravitt that the "lack of unity" of Bayes's play means that Bayes has no "aesthetic control of his language, his plot, and his actors,"[10] is dubious.

Bayes's poetics has no room for the Muses, the allegorical figures for the given creation in harmony. An aesthetic usurpation has taken place in the recognition of the disordered creative act. For example, Bayes's "honest" revelation of the frame of his play (the "virgin attire" in "all its nakedness," I.i.86-8) blandly opposes the organic interpretation of a work of art as natural unity, with the imaginary branches of prologue, epilogue, and imagery sprouting from a no less imaginary trunk of denouement. Bayes's epilogue and imagery are ready-made, interchangeable even (I.ii.125-30). Also, the hiring of a *claque,* which Bayes advocates, suggests that even the reception and approbation of art must be artificially construed (I.II.174-7). And finally, a critical understanding of the work of art by means of an exegesis of sources and motives (a return to fragmentation) replaces in Bayes's scheme the unanalytical admiration of a *Gestalt,* hence the need for Bayes's plot summaries (I.ii.171-3) or for the "keys" to *The Rehearsal.*

Bayes's Baroque "cleverness" is intended to surpass the aesthetics of bewilderment that dominates the last Shakespearean and the earliest Cornelian comedies. In *L'Illusion comique* (1636), Corneille still harmoniously counterbalanced receptive surprise with an ordered plot. Bayes has given up this median; what Smith condemns as "monstrous" is precisely Bayes's unmitigated dedication to the Baroque phenomenon of *meraviglia*: marvels and astonished reactions similar in intent to the pursuit of capricious effects in the arts of the period. The overdone *interrorem-copia* speech that accompanies the entrance of Thunder and Lightning (I.ii.258) would not be out of place in a Baroque opera for its effect of shock. Yet, even in this passage Bayes pursues his ultimate ambition: the representation of harmony through disharmony, of parallellism through paradox. The lines spoken by Thunder and Lightning are neatly balanced and strikingly rhymed. Truly Baroque, Bayes asks: "Why *not* exaggerate?" The *laudatio* by Pretty-Man and Volscius in the second scene of the fourth act (11.35-6) is Baroque for the same reason, as well as for its reference to the theme of the sacrificial hero. This *laudatio* proposes as criterion for aesthetic satisfaction *dis*harmony, which is the diametrical opposite of the Medieval and Renaissance idea that beauty is achieved through a harmonious combination of perfectly balanced elements. I believe that this is David Vieth's meaning when he calls *The Rehearsal* a striking manifestation of the phenomenon of "reversible meaning" in Restoration literature, namely the sensation that "nothing" is a "something."[11] Which does not mean, however, that *The Rehearsal* is a play upon nothing. Neither Buckingham's Smith nor the modernist critic Gravitt perceive that Bayes's statements on poetics are also *meant* to shock. Bayes's ironic condemnation of the clichés of conventional Petrarchan love poetry, for example, is particularly striking (II.i.127-9). Not to take an artist's own statements about his art seriously would be a grave critical mistake. Therefore, let us have a closer look at the second scene of act four, which is announced by a proud Bayes as "the scene of scenes."

In a bizarre eclogue with Baroque cumulative ending,[12] Pretty-Man and Volscius discuss the "harmony versus disharmony" topos. Pretty-Man is hopelessly smitten with the pastoral beauty Cloris, whereas Volscius loves one Parthenope. Each lover eagerly advertises for his own mistress. Pretty-Man argues that Volscius ought to love Cloris at least as much as he does Parthenope because the *essentia* of the abstract concept of Love never vary. Hence, the *accidentes* of Love can hardly be different or disharmonious (IV.ii.17.8). So why would Volscius not feel the same passion for the same girl as Pretty-Man? By means of a simile (which is itself an artificially constructed form of harmony or correspondence between essentially unrelated elements), Volscius retorts that Nature often craftily masks disharmony with a semblance of harmony so that appearance and reality blend imperceptibly (20-1). Can one say then that a change in appearance (or *accidentes,* here the substitution of one lover for another) signifies a change in the essence of Love? For a Renaissance interpreter, the phenomenological world is indeed a fairly safe guide for knowledge on the assumption that sensory experience is a valid key to intellectual comprehension. Hence the Renaissance preference for simile rather than metaphor, for simile tries to further intellectual understanding by openly referring to sensory phenomena. Bayes, however, introduces in this scene the Baroque questioning of the "reality" of the phenomenological world itself and the systematic doubt of mundane experience. Hence the chameleon-simile. Such reasoning (in artistic form, for couched in verse)[13] had been Bayes's purpose from the very beginning. Pretty-Man wins the argument of this vivid "scene of scenes" when he states—complacently and irrefutably—that Nature's goal is always harmony and equilibrium (23-4). His admonishing conclusion (66-70) is exemplary Baroque: both lovers will have to remove their girlfriends from the sphere of ordinary human experience by assigning them ambiguous and miraculous powers with which they can transcend the limits traditionally set between the cosmic levels. Such an annihilation of boundaries separating underworld, earth, and heaven can signify either ultimate chaos (in the Greek, mythological sense of the word), or else a supreme harmony of all elements. As compared to the Renaissance anthropocentric immutability of the worlds of God and Man, the Baroque sensibility promotes such cosmic elasticity through art, science, and mystic meditation. After Galileo, motion or change was indeed no longer thought of as an "unsightly imperfection" but rather as a glory and chief attribute of the universe. "Since the scientific revolution has not taken God into account," Lowry Nelson writes, "Man is allowed to enter the realms previously forbidden to him."[14]

Instead of "devaluating" the language,[15] Bayes does in fact the (Baroque) opposite: he superimposes meaning, by means of language. A clear example is Bayes's *substitution* of language. A clear example is Bayes's *substitution* of bawdy talk *for the act* of seduction itself (I.ii.38-71). (Buckingham may have been influenced by contemporary anti-rhetorical language theory in this matter.) Language that *becomes* the very act it signifies obviously gains in value as concrete function and rises above the sphere of the sign. Similarly, the usurpation by "Ush" and "Phys" is a deed performed by words, a speech-act, and as such echoes the central theme of *Richard III*: does the mere word or title "King" confer power and authority per se, or vice versa? Throughout his play, Bayes's language is Baroque, even emblematic; his words represent a higher train of thought. His obscure statement "I mean not for words, for those I do not value, but for state, show, and magnificence" (V.i.3-4) becomes clearer when we take a look at some of his dialogues. The (often anagrammatical) phrases are seemingly meaningless and apparently they promote intellectual chaos,[16] but in reality they are able to re-solve conflicts. Contrariwise, the Usher's pseudo-logical dissection of the "whisper-argument" (II.iv.19-23) sug-gests that supposedly sensible *analytical* talk can well be totally pointless. For each of the Usher's questions "When?," "Where?," "Whether or not?" is shown to ramify into a virtually limitless number of other ques-tions, so that this form of language ultimately destroys itself by hopelessly clogging understanding.[17] The Usher does not even succeed in defining his initial concern, namely the concept of the verb "to whisper."[18] Any at-tempt to use language *plainly* fails—as when the sol-diers kill each other in spite of their claim to be "friends"—for, whose friends are they, since when, and why, or why not? (II.v.1-4) Thus is shattered the harmo-nious classical-Renaissance marriage of matter and manner, propagated by rhetoric from Cato and Cicero to Ben Jonson. It was the latter who stated that "The sense is, as the life and soul of language, without which all words are dead."[19] The state resulting from the sus-pension of this harmony might perhaps be labeled "ab-surd," but only rightly so if the term is used in a philo-sophical sense that does not limit itself to the context of twentieth-century modernism. It is namely an absurdity that Baroque poetics is quite familiar with.

Bayes's own poetry contains some of the paradoxical qualities of Baroque and Metaphysical poetry (e.g. IV.ii.41-2). He is proud of his striking word-pictures, his conceits, and believes, with the Italian High-Baroque poet Marino, that the poet should strive to exploit sus-pense, to express the grotesque, to astound.[20] In reality, Bayes's conceits are rather like similes (the technical opposite of conceits) in that the poet (i.e., Bayes) ex-plains the point himself. So for example in the simile of the "burning pine" (II.iii.20-7), which, according to Bayes, "alludes to passion, to consuming, to dying, and all that; which, you know, are the natural effects of an amour" (30-2). Real-life passion does not have such ef-fects at all, but Bayes, tongue-in-cheek, mocks the liter-ary cliché that most undistinguishing readers of Petrarchan-style poetry have come to accept for reality through sheer repetition and familiarity. But this very same simile is *also* like a conceit, for, as Johnson again appropriately remarks, the first impression it creates is one of cynical ingenuity rather than of conventional po-etic aptness. Truly Baroque, Bayes applies classical my-thology to incongruous contexts in order to surprise. In the fifth act, for example, Athena's defensive weapons are metamorphosed into celebratory, gustatory stage props. Bayes is also prone to substituting unfamiliar, grotesque comparisons and images for the worn con-ventions of the Renaissance poetic store-house. As the result of the constant use of metaphor,[21] disharmonious elements are united and reconciled (*discordia concors*) through the discovery of correspondences considered impossible by reason or poetic convention. In a dainty love scene, boar and sow replace the conventional "turtles"—the latter may well be canonized as the con-ventional form for "doves," but the "literal" image of "mating turtles" is as grotesque as that of Bayes's swine. Sometimes there is an implicit explanation for such a grotesque metaphor; a faint-hearted lover is aptly associated with a fly. "Love hath wings," after all (IV.ii.46-48).

Bayes's play opens with an ostentatious "flash of Pro-logue," and cosmic imagery continues to cloud threat-eningly over it. After a chiastic introduction (again a form of harmony through disharmony: I.ii.263-4), "Thunder and Lightning" threaten to destroy all the manifestations of earthly harmony: from the govern-ment of a city to the make-up of a lady's face. But characteristically and inconsequentially, their incanta-tory threats themselves rhyme rather too harmoniously. Storms and similar Renaissance imagery of disharmony undergo a surprising devaluation. In the boar and sow-simile mentioned earlier, a storm or cosmic climax prompts the swine to mate—a grotesque parody not only of the "turtles" but also of the canonized Dido-and-Aeneas motif (*Aeneid,* IV). In agreement with the Baroque view of love as a raging cataclysmic power, Cloris is praised as a "blazing comet" (II.iii.5-6). Also, only cosmic imagery would suffice for the description of the rebellion against or the usurpation of invested power. The standard correlative metaphor for political rebellion or usurpation—the ultimate disruption of har-mony—is of course the *eclipse,* which is taken to repre-sent the breakdown of the harmony of the heavenly spheres (V.i). This metaphor affirms again the constant interaction of the various cosmic levels. Typical of Bayes's sense of irony is his introduction of eclipse and usurpation on stage as a *dance.* Thus, he represents ulti-mate disharmony by means of ultimate harmony. A military metaphor[22] combines the human theme of the rebellion and the corresponding cosmic unrest: "What midnight darkness does invade the day, / And snatch the victor from his conquered prey?" (V.i.259-61). Similarly, the potential rebel Drawcansir (resembling Almanzor in Dryden's *Conquest of Granada,* 1672) flashes quickly through the power struggle like an err-ing comet through the spheres (V.i). Again, Drawcansir's brief appearance reminds one of a meteor, which be-comes bright as it is burnt up. This heroic invader "kills 'em all on both sides" and then delivers five grotesquely boastful heroic couplets like a real *matamore* (V.i.338-47). His flat performance contributes to the *theatrum mundi* topos that underlies this play and much of Ba-roque literature, for when ruler and rebel are but actors (as in *L'Illusion comique* or in *La Vida es sueño*), the throne is but an illusion and a symbol of vanity in the light of eternity.

The musical motif that connects various scenes of Bayes's play is yet another signifier of harmony in disharmony. Raised in the Renaissance canon, Smith and Johnson are trained to interpret music as the most positive metaphor for harmony, and therefore they fail to comprehend, first, how Bayes's labor of two nights can "merely" amount to a one-note tune, and, second, how he can pretend to have sanctioned artistically the disharmony of usurpation through the harmony of music. Bayes's music is peculiar and paradoxical: he can only create an existential shriek—a sober, one-note composition. Anything other than his tune in "Effaut flat" (II.v.1-3) would dissolve the entire tension of the dualism. The point is that Smith and Johnson do not realize that Bayes has intended this dance to take place *after* death—for the dancers/soldiers have just absurdly killed each other. Thus they miss the obtuse existentialist meaning of Bayes's cue to the dancers: "Do you hear, dead men?" The Baroque themes of transience, illusion, and death are affirmed by this monotonic harmony in Effaut, which, as burlesque imitation of Apocalyptic trumpets or Royal pomp, is designed to rouse the dead. But though the soldiers are brought back to some kind of life (life as actors, for they respond to a cue), they "cannot get in order" for their "horsemen's dance." Evidently Bayes has hit upon the wrong note. Bayes himself slips, falls, and breaks his nose, shouting "you'll see this dance, if I am not deceived, take very well upon the stage, when they are perfect in their motions, and all that" (III.v.156-8). After all, it was only a rehearsal. When the real Kings, early in the fifth act, descend from the clouds to chase the Usurpers, the latter interpret the accompanying "soft music" incorrectly as the music of the heavenly spheres (V.i.32-4). Buckingham's satire of politics here coincides with the Baroque motif of heavenly influence: as the "rightful" King states, not much should be expected from Heaven (83-6).[23]

Bayes also deploys "characters in couples" in the structure of his play to express the theme of order versus disorder. There are two weak Rightful Kings of Brentford (presumably Charles and James), two Usurpers and two dubious Princes (each one with a girlfriend). Another couple, the general and the lieutenant-general, stage a "flyting" scene, which symbolizes the rebellion of the absurd "secret armies" (V.i.224-47). Buckingham harmoniously couples this complex dual track pattern in Bayes's play with the joint appearance of the two amateur critics in his enveloping structure. The topical-parodical interpretation of *The Rehearsal* usually refers to Dryden's *Conquest of Granada* in connection with the heroes-in-couples, but I have found also the Hegelian concept of the development of the self-consciousness in the framework of the Lordship-Bondage theory useful for both the political-satirical reading and the "harmony vs. disharmony" interpretation of the play.

Bayes's play is composed as a series of many apparently unconnected scenes. This structure can be interpreted in various ways: first, according to the Baroque view that ultimate reality or harmony is accessible to the human mind only in *moments* of intense passionate experience;[24] second, as a deliberate imitation of the *intermezzi* as one of the most comprehensive manifestations of Mannerist-Baroque literary style;[25] and third, according to the Hegelian theory of the *individual* moments of self-consciousness which, "known as not distinct," must yet "be held strictly apart"—again a form of unity through fragmentation (see Hegel's *Phenomenology,* paragraph 178).[26]

Hegel states that the self-consciousness exists only in the act of acknowledgement, namely when it is recognized as consciousness by another self-consciousness. Thus in order to exist, a self-consciousness needs to form a couple-relationship. Becoming self-conscious, however, already implies two notions: "losing" and "superseding" (*Phenomenology,* paragraph 179).[27] The self-consciousness finds itself as other being, but prior to finding or recognizing itself, it must necessarily have "lost" *itself,* namely its former condition. Only one position or slot can be filled at one given time. "Phys" and "Ush" give up their respective anonymity and their lower condition of "servants in bondage" when each of them recognizes himself and the other as potential candidates for the dual throne. The bond between them is strong, for it is ruled by self-interest. Whereas they have set out as two separate self-consciousnesses ("others" to one another), they have now come to realize one another mutually through an intellectual effort: instead of introducing themselves by name, they each *guess* at the other's identity and function (II.i.7-16). It is in accordance with the Hegelian scheme (*Phenomenology,* paragraphs 183-4) that the Physician and the Usher, who have worked at the same place for years but who were unknown to one another, now proceed to an act of mutual recognition. They embrace and appear "hand in hand" (III.ii) and even love till death the same woman ("Lardella") in a perfectly harmonious understanding (IV.i.196-200). They think, act, and react like *one* self-consciousness. The same is true for the two Rightful Kings. The actual usurpation of one self-conscious couple by another, then, can be considered a manifestation of the third of the three possible effects which Hegel thinks can result from the human struggle for recognition. The two self-consciousnesses that recognize one another as such engage in a struggle for domination; the third possible effect of this encounter is that one of the two backs down and becomes enslaved. This is the eternal fate of the "Phys-Ush" combination of servants in bondage.

Smith, who attacks Bayes's structure as "loose" and "monstrous," does not understand the author's concepts and intentions. Whereas the twentieth-century avant-garde author waits for a God to reveal himself or else sends out his six characters in search of an authorial God-Muse to justify their existences and flesh them out on stage, Buckingham's Bayes plays at being a God who is doggedly in search of better actors and critics. It is not the creative power in the universe that fails, but those who perform in the theater of the world, as well as those who pretend to judge it. Bayes's play may appear "messy," but to condemn it offhand is fallacious, for the artist as craftsman (playwright as well as actor) must at first be given the benefit of the doubt. Hence Bayes's choler is justified when his actors behave unprofessionally (III.iv.10-13). His structure may appear loose, but at least he can justify whatever he does—as he had promised in the Prologue: "I will not only show the feats they do, / But give you all their reasons for 'em too" (20-1). This really summarizes the Baroque aesthetic attempt at forging a unity of manner and matter. The revelation of the artistic framework is not at all such a "modernist" element as Gravitt would have it; especially not if one remembers that twentieth-century modernist theater since Brecht often carefully keeps the real motives of characters hidden in order to achieve a maximum alienation effect, whereas Baroque playwrights (the early Corneille, Rotrou, Calderon, *and* Bayes) are only too eager to reveal ultimately *how* the audience has been presented with an illusion. Bayes explains his own work and what lies behind it readily and pretentiously—at least, he *seems* to do so. We have, namely, no indication whether the promised plot summaries would really contribute to the critical and aesthetic understanding of the very play which the author himself considers a test of intelligence (III.i.140-8) and good taste: an orange stuff'd with cloves.

Notes

1. Villiers, George, "The Rehearsal," in *British Dramatists from Dryden to Sheridan,* ed. Nettleton, Case, and Stone (Boston, 1982), 39-67. First produced at the Theatre Royal, Drury Lane, December 7, 1671.

2. G. Jack Gravitt, "The Modernity of *The Rehearsal*: Buckingham's Theatre of the Absurd," *College Literature* 9 (1982), i., 30-8.

3. George MacFadden analyzes the political aspect in "Political Satire in *The Rehearsal*," *Yearbook of English Studies,* 4 (1979), 120-8.

4. Harold B. Segel, *The Baroque Poem: A Comparative Survey* (New York, 1974), especially pp. 23-31. Also Frank J. Warnke, *Versions of Baroque: European Literature in the Seventeenth Century* (New York and London, 1972), 22.

5. Samuel Macey, "Fielding's *Tom Thumb* as the Heir to Buckingham's *The Rehearsal*," *Texas Studies in Literature and Language* 10 (1968), 405-414, 405.

6. Johnson condemns, for example, as "hideous, monstrous" such things as "fighting, loving, sleeping, rhyming, dying, dancing, singing, crying: and everything but thinking and sense" (I.i.50-2). Here he seems to prefer the wooden, static French comédies of the seventeenth century to the vivid mimesis of real life on stage. But, as Bayes's play gets under way, he is completely involved in the theatrical illusion and can appreciate the popular, conventional scenes ("fighting and dancing") as well as Bayes's ridiculous answers to Smith's ironic queries (as in III.i).

7. In language theory, for example. For an interesting survey, see James Thompson, *Language in Wycherley's Plays* (Alabama: Univ. of Alabama Press, 1984), chapters 1 and 2 especially.

8. Warnke, 33, convincingly demonstrates that "For most typical Baroque poets . . . material makes form," whereas the Renaissance thought in terms of "pre-existent containers, into which the poetic material may be poured."

9. Segel, 29.

10. Gravitt, 31.

11. David Vieth, "Divided Consciousness: The Trauma and Triumph of Restoration Culture," *Tennessee Studies in Literature* 22 (1977), 46-62, 56.

12. Segel, 112, discusses the Baroque "cumulative ending."

13. Bayes's remark that his aim is to "reason in verse" is one of the arguments Gravitt uses to describe Bayes as an inconsistent poet who devaluates language (33). Gravitt is probably unaware of many centuries of theological, scientific, propagandistic, and otherwise didactic "reasoning in verse" from Antiquity till the nineteenth century.

14. Lowry Nelson, Jr., *Baroque Lyric Poetry* (New Haven, 1961), 82.

15. Gravitt, 33-5.

16. Cf. the ancient stichomythia technique; each participant in such a "dialogue" is only interested in getting his own point across as quickly and as effectively as possible. Ionesco's parody of unimaginative Assimil language-method dialogues in *La Cantatrice chauve* "merely" carries this technique to an absurd extreme.

17. This failure to get a reasoning successfully started resembles the intellectual ordeal of Beckett's Watt (1942-44). This would in itself, however, not constitute any reason for labelling *The Rehearsal* a "proto-absurd" play, since the topos is at least as old as Descartes's "Rules for the Direction of the Mind." Gravitt fails to mention this particular topos.

18. MacFadden gives an interesting political interpretation of the "whisper-arguement," 126-7.

19. Ben Jonson, *Works,* ed. C. H. Herford and P. Simpson, 11 vols (Oxford, 1947-61), VII: 621.

20. G. Marino, *Murtoleide,* sonnet XX, 1-3.

21. Segel, 101-2. Baroque poetics favored metaphor over simile. As compared to the Renaissance emphasis on simile (which implied that the phenomenological world can yield intellectual knowledge through the explicit linking of conceptual categories), the Baroque insistence on metaphor implied that appearance and reality are virtually indistinguishable.

22. Segel, 115, draws attention to the importance of military metaphors in Baroque poetics.

23. MacFadden analyzes this topic, 127-8.

24. Warnke, 52.

25. Segel, 27.

26. Hegel, *Phenomenology of the Spirit* (1798), tr. A Miller (Oxford, 1977).

27. This idea is also helpful to explain the lyric motif of "loss of self" that one encounters so often in Baroque-Metaphysical poetry (Donne, Marvell) as well as in Romanticism (Keats, Leopardi), and that is occasioned either by an almost mystical meditation (in the case of the former), or by the experience of nature (as with the latter).

FURTHER READING

Biographies

Chapman, Hester W. *The Great Villiers: A Study of George Villiers, Second Duke of Buckingham 1628-1687.* London: Secker & Warburg, 1949, 315 p.

Detailed study of Villiers' life from his childhood to his years at court.

Gardner, Lady Burghclere, Winifred. *George Villiers, Second Duke of Buckingham, 1628-1687: A Study in the History of the Restoration.* London: John Murray, 1903, 414 p.

Detailed account of Buckingham's life and political career.

Wilson, John Harold. "The Court Wits." *The Court Wits of the Restoration: An Introduction,* pp. 3-24. Princeton, N. J.: Princeton University Press, 1948.

Discussion of the court of Charles II, with numerous references to Buckingham.

Criticism

Emery, John P. "Restoration Dualism of the Court Writers." *Revue des langues vivantes* 32 (1966): 238-65.

Discusses the dual nature of Buckingham's character, claiming the author's reputation as a rake was undeserved.

McFadden, George. "Political Satire in *The Rehearsal.*" *Yearbook of English Studies* 4 (1974): 120-28.

Maintains that the Earl of Arlington, not Dryden as is commonly assumed, is the true target of Buckingham's satire in *The Rehearsal.*

Phipps, Christine. "Textual Introduction." In *Buckingham: Public and Private Man: The Prose, Poems, and Commonplace Book of George Villiers, Second Duke of Buckingham (1628-1687),* pp. 57-79. New York: Garland Publishing, 1985.

A textual history of Buckingham's poetry and nondramatic prose works.

Smith, Dane Farnsworth. "The Rehearsal." In *Plays About the Theatre in England from* The Rehearsal *in 1671 to the Licensing Act in 1737,* pp. 9-37. London: Oxford University Press, 1936.

Provides a detailed account of the satirical devices Buckingham employed in *The Rehearsal.*

Sorelius, Gunnar. "Shadwell Deviating into Sense: *Timon of Athens* and the Duke of Buckingham." *Studia Neophilologica* 36, no. 2 (1964): 232-44.

Exploration of Buckingham's influence on Thomas Shadwell's adaptation of Shakespeare's play.

Wilson, John Harold. "The Gaudy Stage 1671." In *A Rake and His Times: George Villiers, Second Duke of Buckingham,* pp. 180-202. New York: Farrar, Straus and Young, 1954.

Explains Buckingham's dispute with Arlington, considered by some critics to be the target of Buckingham's satire in *The Rehearsal.*

Additional coverage of the life and career of George Villiers, Second Duke of Buckingham, is contained in the following sources also published by Thomson Gale: *Dictionary of Literary Biography,* Vol. 80; *Literature Resource Center*; and *Reference Guide to English Literature,* Ed. 2.

John Winthrop
1588-1649

British-born American writer of sermons, diarist, speech- writer, chronicler and epistler.

The following entry presents criticism on John Winthrop from 1964 to 1996. For further information on Winthrop's writings, see *Literature Criticism From 1400 to 1800,* Volume 31.

INTRODUCTION

As the first governor of the Massachusetts Bay Colony, Winthrop is regarded as one of the most influential men in the colony's history. Despite his presence in the political arena, Winthrop is best remembered as a historian and writer whose work provides an insightful glimpse into the history of New England. His most significant work, *A Journal of the Transactions and Occurrences in the Settlement of Massachusetts and the Other New-England Colonies, from the Year 1630 to 1644* (1790), is highly regarded for its detailed documentation of the events of the colony, from the mundane to the extraordinary, as well as for Winthrop's personal insight and evolution as a leader, Puritan, and writer.

BIOGRAPHICAL INFORMATION

Winthrop was born in Suffolk, England in 1588. His father served as auditor of the accounts at Trinity College at Cambridge, where Winthrop was enrolled at the age of fourteen. While at school, Winthrop became deathly ill and, as a result, underwent a religious conversion—he began to identify himself as a Puritan. Soon after his conversion, Winthrop left Trinity and married his first wife, Mary Forth, in 1605. The couple had six children in a ten-year period. Winthrop, despite his withdrawal from Trinity, went on to study law at Gray's Inn in London, and records indicate that he served as a justie of the peace in Suffolk. Winthrop's wife died in 1615, and his second wife, Thomasine Clopton, died a year after their marriage in 1617. By the time he was married to his third wife, Margaret Tyndal, in 1618, Winthrop was finding it difficult to support a large, growing household. He continued to practice law, often traveling to London for work, and in 1627 was appointed as attorney to His Majesty's Court of Wards and Liveries. This position gave Winthrop a firsthand view of the tensions between Charles I and Parliament, which Charles I dissolved in March of 1629. This act perpetuated Winthrop's dissatisfaction with his life in England, and he joined a group of Puritans determined to relocate to America. In 1629, Winthrop was elected governor of the royal chartered Massachusetts Bay Company, and in April of 1630 Winthrop and three of his sons traveled on the *Arbella* to America. During the journey, Winthrop delivered what was to be his most important sermon, "A Modell of Christian Charitie," where he introduced several concepts which would become central in American Puritanism. Winthrop served four terms as governor of the Massachusetts Bay colony. He continuously sought to apply the Puritan philosophy not only in conflict resolution, but also to the practical necessities of governance. Winthrop was intent on making the colony a model of the perfect Puritan community. Until his death in 1649, Winthrop meticulously documented the daily life of the colony in his journal, which remains one of the foremost works on New England's history.

MAJOR WORKS

One of Winthrop's most significant pieces of writing is the sermon "A Modell of Christian Charitie," which he delivered in 1630. In this sermon, Winthrop introduced two key concepts that would prove influential in shaping American Puritanism. The first is the concept of *The City on a Hill.* Winthrop maintained that if the colony practiced righteousness and enjoyed material success, it would serve as an example to other communities. The second idea Winthrop introduced was that of a divine covenant that would legally bind the community to work for the good of the whole and for spiritual glory. On another level, the sermon allowed Winthrop to address his plans for the community—he urged acceptance of social inequalities because they would encourage charity, therefore linking the community together according to God's divine plan. Winthrop sought to document this divine plan and the signs of the colonists' achievements in his most significant work, *A Journal of the Transactions and Occurrences in the Settlement of Massachusetts and the Other New-England Colonies, from the Year 1630 to 1644.* The *Journal,* which was originally comprised of three notebooks, was not published until 1790. The *Journal* consists of day-by-day journal entries and lacks literary structure; however, the flow of the text is maintained by Winthrop's writing style, thoughts and motivations. The *Journal* represents an eyewitness account of two decades of colonial history in Massachusetts. Winthrop documented everything from the everyday happenings of the colony to major events as well as weather patterns, flora, and fauna, all the while commenting on how these items fit into God's divine plan for the community. Of the historical works Winthrop published while he was alive, the most studied is *Antinomians and Familists condemned by the synod elders in New-England: with the proceedings of the magistrates against them, and their apology for the same* (1644). This work documents the controversy of the Antinomians, led by Anne Hutchinson, who believed in achieving salvation not through good deeds but through God's grace alone. The group's dissension resulted in Hutchinson's banishment from the colony.

CRITICAL RECEPTION

During his lifetime, Winthrop was highly respected by his fellow colonists and considered to be an excellent leader, both spiritually and politically. Some modern critics, such as Richard S. Dunn and Lee Schweninger, have examined Winthrop's writing as literature instead of as historical documentation by focusing on the narrative style and growth of the writer. The vast majority of Winthrop scholars, however, examine his works, especially the *Journal,* as historical documents that provide a unique insight into the day-to-day events of life in the Massachusetts Bay colony. In addition, Winthrop's works provide a record of the ideals and beliefs upon which the Puritans founded their colony, illustrating not only their organization, but their religious aims. These same ideals continue to shape American politics, ideology and literature to this day.

PRINCIPAL WORKS

"A Modell of Christian Charity" (sermon) 1630; also published as *Christian Charitie. A Modell Hereof*

Antinomians and Familists condemned by the synod of elders in New-England: with the proceedings of the magistrates against them, and their apology for the same (history) 1644; also published as *A Short Story of the rise, reign, and ruin of the Antinomians, Familists & libertines*

A Declaration of Former Passages and Proceedings Betwixt the English and the Narrowgansets, with Their Confederates, Wherein the Grounds and Justice of the Ensuing Warre are Opened and Cleared (history) 1645

A Journal of the Transactions and Occurrences in the Settlement of Massachusetts and the Other New England Colonies, from the Year 1630 to 1644 (journal) 1790; also published as *The History of New England from 1630 to 1649,* 1825-26, rev. ed. 1853

Winthrop Papers. 5 vols. (prose, journal, history, letters) 1929-47

CRITICISM

Loren Baritz (essay date 1964)

SOURCE: Baritz, Loren. "Political Theology: John Winthrop." In *City on a Hill: A History of Ideas and Myths in America,* pp. 13-39. New York: John Wiley & Sons, Inc., 1964.

[*In the following excerpt, Baritz examines how "A Modell of Christian Charity" outlines not only Winthrop's argument for the journey to Massachusetts but also his thoughts about the meaning of the organic community.*]

It is a mistake to think that Winthrop's view of politics was separate from his other views. His intellectual system was a political theology; its purpose was the Christianization of the state. The westward-moving Puritans thought that they had a special commission from God to establish a Zion in the wilderness, a commonwealth whose foundation and purpose was Christian. It was the intention to establish a community made up of persons whose behavior at least would appear to be Christian. But in order to acknowledge man's inability to tell whether mere behavior reflected the real condition of the soul, persons who acted as Christians were called "visible saints." Such persons might not be saints in the all-seeing eyes of God, but because men were limited by their senses, they were compelled to acknowledge that no mortal could read the secrets of any soul. In terms of policy, however, appearance was sufficient. If men would act as Christians the purposes of the migration would be accomplished. Visible saints might never sit at God's right hand, but then they also would probably never seriously disturb the peace of Zion. In order to create a community where law and security would prevail, the visible saints covenanted themselves together so that God's will in civil as well as religious matters would be implemented. The idea of a unified political organism—a corporation—was the basis of Winthrop's political ideas, as it was also the basis of Congregational church polity. "It is," he wrote, "of the nature and essence of every society to be knitt together by some Covenant, either expressed or implyed."[1]

While in mid-ocean, on board the *Arbella,* Winthrop composed his single most important statement, **"A Modell of Christian Charity,"** a tract designed to show the unity of the civil state that was to be operative when God had allowed the passengers safe passage, when the business corporation called the Massachusetts Bay Company had become transformed into a political body. In order to prove the organic nature of the state, Winthrop was obliged to defend the various ranks men held in society, a class system. He had to show how political and economic differences among men were centripetal forces tending to the greater cohesion of the political body: "God Almightie in his most holy and wise providence hath soe disposed of the Condicion of mankinde, as in all times some must be rich some poore, some highe and eminent in power and dignitie; others meane and in subjeccion."[2]

There were three basic reasons for this supposedly necessary social stratification.

> 1. "The variety and difference of the Creatures" conformed to God's creation in general, and testified to His power and glory.
>
> 2. The heterogeneity of man's condition gave God "more occasion to manifest the worke of his Spirit: first, upon the wicked in moderateing and restraineing them: soe that the riche and mighty should not eate upp the poore, nor the poore, and dispised rise upp against theire superiors, and shake off theire yoake." The simple existence of the saved and damned gave God a wider canvas on which to labor.

> 3. The fact of wealth and poverty meant "That every man might have need of other, and from hence they might be all knitt more nearly together in the Bond of brotherly affeccion: from hence it appeares plainely that noe man is made more honourable then another or more wealthy etc. out of any perticuler and singuler respect to himselfe but for the glory of his Creator and the Common good of the Creature, Man; Therefore God still reserves the propperty of these guifts to himselfe."[3]

Variety, meaning economic and social stratification, was decreed by the Lord both for His own purposes and out of His love of man. Those who benefited from the inequality, those who were rich and powerful, as well as those who suffered, must be made to realize that life on earth required masters and servants, that both were creatures of God, and that each had obligations to the other. With such realization, the precondition of an organic community would be met.

Property and power were gifts of God to men, given in order to help them help others in a mutual social covenant. When the community was in danger men must act "with more enlargement towardes others and lesse respect towards our selves, and our owne right hence it was that in the primitive Churche they sold all [and] had all things in Common, neither did any man say that that which he possessed was his owne."[4] Since wealth and might were given to individuals for the sake of the political corporation, the needs of the corporation must take precedence over the needs or desires of any individual.

Love was the ligament which held the parts of this political and social body together. "The diffinition which the Scripture gives us of love is this [:] Love is the bond of perfection." Every body consisted of parts, and whatever it was that held the parts together "gives the body its perfeccion, because it makes eache parte soe contiguous to other as thereby they doe mutually participate with eache other."[5] The inequality of men constituted the parts of the body politic, which parts were held together, from man's point of view, by love.

How was it, however, that depraved and sinful men could love their neighbors as themselves? How and why would the sinner turn the other cheek? After the Fall, "Adam Rent in himselfe from his Creator, rent all of his posterity allsoe one from another, whence it comes that every man is borne with this principle in him, to love and seeke himselfe onely and thus a man continueth till Christ comes and takes possession of the soule, and infuseth another principle [:] love to God and our brother." Love of self stood between Adam and Christ, but with regeneration, the conversion of the "old man Adam" to "the new Creature," the Holy Spirit "gathers together the scattered bones or perfect old man Adam and knitts them into one body againe in Christ."[6]

Clearly, then, the love which was necessary for the creation and operation of the body politic could come only when that body was made up of the converted. Since the right kind of love was a result of regeneration, it was necessary, from Winthrop's viewpoint, to limit membership in the corporation to the visible saints, since that was as close as mere men could get to actual saints. A sinner in the body inevitably and naturally would tend to endanger the whole.

* * *

Winthrop applied this theory of the organic community to the migration in four different categories: persons, work, end, and means. The individual persons had become a single body in their professed membership in Christ. The immigrants as persons were hopefully actual as well as visible saints, members of Augustine's kind of City of God. "In which respect onely though wee were absent from eache other many miles, and had our imploymentes as farre distant, yet wee ought to account our selves knitt together by this bond of love, and live in the exercise of it if wee would have comforte of our being in Christ."[7] The work itself was the seeking of "a place of Cohabitation and Consorteshipp under a due forme of Government both civill and ecclesiasticall." Such a work was based on "a mutual consent through a speciall overruleing providence," and it assumed the primacy of public over private welfare: "In such cases as this the care of the publique must oversway all private respects, by which not only conscience, but meare Civill pollicy doth binde us; for it is a true rule that perticuler estates cannott subsist in the ruine of the publique." The end, or purpose, of the migration was "to serve the Lord and worke out our Salvacion under the power and purity of his holy Ordinances." And, finally, the means necessary for these persons, work, and purpose were extraordinary, because the work itself was. It was not enough to practice Christianity merely as it had been and was practiced in England: "the same must wee doe and more allsoe where wee goe: That which the most in theire Churches maineteine as a truthe in profession onely, wee must bring into familiar and constant practice."[8]

The special commission which God had given to the immigrants obviously implied privileges. But any chosen people also had to face the consequences of their uniqueness, consequences which were awesome. God expected unique behavior from His unique people. He would forgive less because He rightfully expected more. By creating an organic community, Winthrop said, those frail humans could live up to the terms of their divine commission: "wee must be knitt together in this worke as one man . . . our Community as members of the same body." Only when the persons realized that God had covenanted with the community and that the welfare of each therefore depended on the welfare of the body politic, would each member find it possible to feel that love of neighbor which was the cohesive of the corporation. If the persons could truly covenant with each other in the interest of forming a political body, then men would truly enjoy peace and plenty. In language which was to reverberate throughout American history, Winthrop explained that, as a result of a genuine social covenant, "wee shall finde that the God of Israell is among us, when tenn of us shall be able to resist a thousand of our enemies, when hee shall make us a prayse and glory, that men shall say of succeeding plantacions: the lord make it like that of New England: for wee must Consider that wee shall be as a Citty upon a Hill, the eies of all people are uppon us."[9]

Thus, according to Winthrop, his band of brethren was involved in a mission of cosmic significance. They were not merely fleeing from an anticipated persecution or searching for greener pastures. They were involved in a test case which would determine whether men could live on earth according to the will of the Lord. The Reformation in Europe had started the good work, but everywhere, including England, it had been frustrated. Winthrop believed that it had been given to these immigrants to find out whether they were of sufficient faith to carry that work on, to bring the Reformation to full fruition. Should they succeed, their outpost in the wilderness would "be as a Citty upon a Hill," a moral example to all the world. Should they succeed, their example would help even Europe to begin the work anew, to try to rid itself of the Antichrist. Should they succeed, the place where they planted would become the hub of the universe, whose light and wisdom would radiate out in all directions for the utility and comfort of men and the glory of God.

* * *

It is necessary, in order to share their mood, to think of this Great Migration not as some merely human act, undertaken with whatever motives, but to think of it as a necessary step leading to nothing less than the redemption of the entire world. Should they fail, their failure too would radiate outward, and the human race would know that a divine opportunity had been lost, that a chance for progress toward God had been missed. Thus it was that Winthrop thought of this first wave of immigrants not as mere human beings, not as mere colonists of England, but as God's agents, a community with a unique and compelling commission from God to build that city on a hill. Whether they could build properly depended on whether their covenants with each other would be strong enough to support a political order that would be organically whole, a political body which was indeed one body, with one head, and all the member parts in their proper locations, performing their proper functions. Mankind's destiny was at stake.

Merely coming into Massachusetts constituted an implicit acceptance of the covenant, for it was clear that all who entered must obey the laws established by those whose consent had been more explicit. That Winthrop viewed the political corporation as an organic whole, as indissoluble, is proved by his refusal to admit the moral right of men to leave the colony. Of course there were many who left, and Winthrop, displaying an unfortunate and not uncharacteristic excess of righteousness, vindictively recounted the evils which had befallen those who had left and had spoken critically of the Bay saints: "One had a daughter that presently ran mad, and two other of his daughters, being under ten years of age, were discovered to have been often abused by divers lewd persons, and filthiness in his family."[10] Individuals had covenanted themselves and had agreed to migrate because, among other reasons, others had done so too. The Agreement at Cambridge had been such a covenant; it had specified that the signers agreed "that this whole adventure growes upon the joynt confidence we have in each others fidelity and resolucion herein, so as no man of us would have adventured it without assurance of the rest."[11] Each of the signers then pledged himself as a Christian to be ready to sail for the New World at a specified date, provided that the organic unity of the enterprise was protected by the unusual transplantation of the Charter and Company with the migrants. Was not the nature of each man's political covenant altered, and not by his own choice or act, whenever any man left the authority of the nation?

> Much disputation there was about liberty of removing for outward advantages, and all ways were sought for an open door to get out at; but it is to be feared many crept out at a broken wall. For such as come together into a wilderness, where are nothing but wild beasts and beastlike men, and there confederate together in civil and church estate, whereby they do, implicitly at least, bind themselves to support each other, and all of them that society, whether civil or sacred, whereof they are members, how they can break from this without free consent, is hard to find, so as may satisfy a tender or good conscience in time of trial. Ask thy conscience, if thou wouldst have plucked up thy stakes, and brought thy family 3000 miles, if thou hadst expected that all, or most, would have forsaken thee there.[12]

In the internal affairs of the colony every effort was made to discourage notions about the primacy or independence of the individual, whether in theological, political, social, or economic matters. The law of the colony made it illegal for an individual to live alone; everyone had to be or to become a member of a household or family. The Daniel Boone type was considered as dangerous to the organic community as were mavericks like Roger Williams and mystics like Mistress Anne Hutchinson. The nation was made up of a series of covenants, ascending from the basic and essential covenant

between a man and God, to the family, church, and state, and an uncovenanted or otherwise exotic individual would be a threat to the entire structure.

* * *

Winthrop's justification of authority in the state was determined by his views of the meaning of liberty. No man in society must be allowed that kind of natural liberty which "is common to man with beasts and other creatures." This kind of liberty was possible only for an individual outside of society, beyond a covenant, and gave that individual "liberty to do what he lists; it is a liberty to evil as well as to good." It was the kind of liberty that Winthrop thought to be "incompatible and inconsistent with authority, and [that] cannot endure the least restraint of the most just authority." The exercise of this natural liberty had to place the individual outside of the properly constituted society, and made of the individual, as Aristotle had said, either more or less than human. God was at liberty, except insofar as He decided to limit Himself to the terms of a covenant, but when a man tried to step outside of the covenant he did not rise to godhood but became "worse than brute beasts."[13]

The kind of liberty that was proper to men was available only in society and under a covenant. Winthrop called this civil, federal, or moral liberty, and said that it "is the proper end and object of authority, and cannot subsist without it; and it is a liberty to that only which is good, just and honest." That kind of liberty was compatible with the dependence of man on man in the Christian corporation, and was consistent with the love necessary to political success. "This liberty is maintained and exercised in a way of subjection to authority; it is of the same kind of liberty wherewith Christ hath made us free."[14] The members of the political body were free to do good, and would do so by obeying lawfully constituted authority. In other words, the individual as an individual could never have moral liberty, while the individual as a member of a body politic could have. As a member, the socialized individual would accept social restraints as necessary to peaceful life on earth: "if you stand for your natural corrupt liberties, and will do what is good in your own eyes, you will not endure the least weight of authority, but will murmur, and oppose, and be always striving to shake off that yoke; but if you will be satisfied to enjoy such civil and lawful liberties, such as Christ allows you, then will you quietly and cheerfully submit unto that authority which is set over you, in all the administrations of it, for your own good."[15]

The lesser members of the political body had the liberty of counsel, and the magistrates had the duty to listen to reason: "If we [magistrates] fail at any time, we hope we shall be willing (by God's assistance) to hearken to good advice from any of you, or in any other way of God."[16] Moral liberty thus could only be maintained so long as the magisterial authority was protected. Both must stand or fall together, and the desire to limit authority was, perhaps unknowingly, a desire also to destroy moral liberty and return to that natural liberty in which welfare and safety were continually jeopardized. In the most extreme terms, Winthrop's argument reads like this: Any individual who attacked properly constituted authority sought a natural liberty whose reward must be danger and death. Thus banishment as punishment for those like Williams, Wheelwright, and Mistress Hutchinson who did not accept the constituted authority of Massachusetts was peculiarly fitting in that it drove them into the untamed wilderness, the most appropriate setting for the exercise of natural liberty.

As men did not have a moral right voluntarily to leave the colony, so Winthrop was convinced that the magistrates had the right to screen applicants for admission into the Bay. Implicit in his argument was the notion that the divisive Antinomian controversy might never have happened if Wheelwright and Mistress Hutchinson had been kept out in the first place, and that in the future such conflict could be avoided by an exercise of such magisterial power. "Antinomian" was the label placed on those who rejected the more legalistic Puritan criteria of sanctification in favor of a more direct and mystical inner light. The Antinomians, led by Mrs. Hutchinson and Wheelwright and assisted nervously by John Cotton, charged that several of the leading ministers of the Bay had themselves not been converted. The General Court brought the leaders to trial and maneuvered Mrs. Hutchinson to the point where she confessed to a direct communication from God. She was banished from the Bay, eventually made her way to New Netherland, and there was killed by Indians.

One of the consequences of the action against Wheelwright was an order of the General Court, in May, 1637, "to keep out all such persons as might be dangerous to the commonwealth, by imposing a penalty upon all such as should retain any [such dangerous persons], etc., above three weeks, which should not be allowed by some of the magistrates."[17] Those against whom this order was directed protested, and Winthrop wrote a defense of the Court's order. In so doing he found it necessary to explicate some of his basic political principles:

> 1. No common weale can be founded but by free consent.
>
> 2. The persons so incorporating have a public and relative interest each in other, and in the place of their cohabitation and goods, and laws, etc. and in all the means of their wellfare so as none other can claime priviledge with them but by free consent.
>
> 3. The nature of such incorporation tyes every member thereof to seeke out and entertaine all means that may

conduce to the wellfare of the bodye, and to keepe off whatsoever doth appeare to tend to theire damage.

> 4. The wellfare of the whole is [not] to be put to apparent hazard for the advantage of any particular members.[18]

A group of people freely consented to form themselves into a political society "for their mutual safety and welfare." This consent to subject himself to rule and law was granted by each individual in order that he might be more secure than he could be in that natural state which he shared with beasts and which would make him beastlike. The unified political body that was created by the consent of its citizens had a right to protect itself against the introduction of elements that would subvert the safety and welfare for the realization of which that body had been created in the first place. It was therefore just, according to Winthrop, that the political body of Massachusetts Bay inquire into the beliefs and convictions of all who desired to enter. If some righteous one who should have been admitted was denied entrance, the violation of justice could "not . . . be imputed to the law, but to those who are betrusted with the execution of it."[19] The entire argument was summed up by asserting that the exclusiveness of the Bay was justified by the desire for that political tranquillity which was thought essential for the practice of true reformed religion. In insisting on the authority of the magistrates to screen candidates for admission, Winthrop believed he was doing no more than defending a relatively harmless technique for keeping the Serpent out of the Garden.

To the objection that Massachusetts was a corporation created by the King, and that the colony had no right to exclude any of the King's subjects, Winthrop, probably in August, 1637, answered that "that which the King is pleased to bestow upon us, and we have accepted, is truly our owne."[20] Because the Bay Company accepted the Charter (and transferred it to the New World) the corporation was its own to do with as best suited its own purposes. "The King," Winthrop reasoned, "haveing given all the land within certaine limitts to the patentees and their associates, cannot send others to possesse that which he hath granted before."[21] Had the implications of this position been drawn out at the time, charges of treason against Winthrop and his colony might have been made. Here, Winthrop drew back from logic just at that point where it might do damage to his cause.

Another objection to Winthrop's argument was that the magistrates' power to admit or reject an applicant was unregulated and therefore despotic. Of course he denied the charge, saying that the magistrates were not unregulated because they were church members and bound to live as Christians, because they were freemen and bound by their oath to contribute to the welfare of the state, and because they were also bound by the magisterial oath to do justice and seek the general welfare. The magistrate, in other words, did not have unlimited discretion because of the church covenant and civil oaths which he had taken, and because, as a man of conscience, he would surely honor his pledge. If that conscience proved somewhat deficient, the church or the state, or both, could force him back to the path of righteousness.

The explicit political covenant, or contract, was the instrument by which discrete persons came together and formed themselves into a corporation in order to secure their mutual safety and welfare. But the anterior covenant—that between the individual and God, the covenant of grace—was the necessary antecedent to the formation of a Christian commonwealth, as it was to the creation of individual churches. Government was an institution favored by God to help men live together, if not in absolute brotherhood, then at least without the constant fear of being murdered or, what was worse, being prevented from practicing true reformed religion. God had left the particular form of government for men to determine, because problems varied from time to time and place to place, but the institution itself was of divine origin.

There was no doubt that God stood behind the whole enterprise, or that its success depended upon the fidelity of the citizens to the covenants of grace and of society. Temporal success was the reward to the nation for heeding God's will. It seemed perfectly reasonable to the orthodox Puritans to protect the second covenant by limiting political liberties only to those who were presumably under the first, the covenant of grace. "The way of God," Winthrop wrote, "hath alwayes beene to gather his churches out of the world; now, the world, or civill state, must be raised out of the churches."[22] Church membership became the prerequisite for freemanship, for full political rights and privileges, and since church membership was extended only to those who could demonstrate the validity of their conversion to the satisfaction of the congregation, political liberties could be similarly extended by the General Court. Only the visible saints could be full citizens of the wilderness Zion, though some of those saints chose not to obtain complete citizenship from the Court.

Granting freemanship to church members was not a restriction of the franchise; the Charter had defined a freeman as a stockholder, or one the stockholders themselves thought fit. In a short time there were only eight men who could qualify under this definition, and they were all magistrates. Extending freemanship to those of the visible saints who applied for it thus extended the terms of the Charter in ways probably never dreamed of in England, but in ways which supported Winthrop's ideas about an organic Christian corporation.

Initially Winthrop kept the Charter secret in a special box because, he said, in the beginning of the settlement, there was so much other and more urgent business that there was precious little concern with matters of government. Anyone, he thought, "would easyly allowe us pardon of that, or greater errors (which are incident to all Plantations, in their beginninges) especially seeinge our Readinesse to reforme them, and to conforme to the right Rules of our Government."[23] Extending freemanship to include those of the visible saints approved by the Court conformed nicely to Winthrop's ideas about the political necessity of that kind of love which only the regenerate could feel. But with one foot in the door, the freemen quickly requested—demanded—further rights and privileges. One of the ways they sought to increase their power was to call for a reduction of magisterial authority, and this eventually led to the establishment of a two-house legislature.

* * *

The events leading to the creation of America's first bicameral legislature were symptomatic of the growing dissatisfaction of the freemen with their largely passive role in the state. They concluded that power would have to be taken at the expense of the magistrates. The ruling elite, led by Winthrop, tried to resist in a number of different ways. The controversy finally centered around whether or not the magistrates should have a veto power over the actions of the deputies who were the representatives of the freemen. In an extended document that Winthrop wrote in 1643 he argued that the magistrates always had and should continue to have such a negative vote, that any other course would alter the nature of government in the Bay. He began the argument by asserting that the magistrates' right to the negative vote had been authorized by the Charter, and then typically used the occasion further to refine his ideas about the civil state of Massachusetts.

This conflict over the magisterial veto was no small matter, he thought, because it touched the nerve of the Bay's civil polity. The existence of the veto power helped to define the government of Massachusetts, and was therefore considered by Winthrop to be "essentiall and fundamentall." "If the Neg: vo: were taken away," he wrote, "our Government would be a meere Democratie, where as now it is mixt,"[24] a form Calvin had earlier approved. There was general agreement that the deputies represented the democratic part of Massachusetts' government, and to allow them unchecked authority would result in the creation of an unmixed democracy for which, Winthrop argued, "we should have no warrant in scripture . . . : there was no such Government in Israell." To establish a simple democracy would mean, he said, that "we should heerby voluntaryly abase our selves, and deprive our selves of that dignity, which the providence of God hath putt upon us: which is a manifest breach of the 5th Com[mandmen]t for a Democratie is, among most Civill nations, accounted the meanest and worst of all formes of Government: and therefore in writers, and Historyes doe recorde, that it hath been allwayes of least continuance and fullest of troubles."[25] To establish a political system based on notions of human equality would fly in the face of Winthrop's earlier defense of a class system designed by God for His glory and out of His love for mankind. God had made, Winthrop reiterated, "(not the disparitye onely but) even the contrarietye of parts, in many bodyes, to be the meanes of the upholding and usefullness thereof."[26] Such a political system would violate the pattern of authority explicit in the commandment to honor one's father and mother. The transfer of property and power that would be necessary to convert the Bay into a simple democracy would thus, according to Winthrop, be criminal, unnatural, and sinful.

His rejection of simple democracy did not lead Winthrop to reject what he considered to be the rightful democratic powers of the deputies, who, he wrote, "joyned with the magistrates in any generall Court have (together with them) all the power legislative, and the chiefe power Juditiall, of this body Politick."[27] Neither group had any power without the other, and it was simply wrong to assert, as some had, that the deputies were in reality magistrates themselves. The deputies had the same liberties as the body of freemen they represented, and the fact of their having only liberty, not authority, "makes them no otherwise subjecte, then according to their will, and Covenant."[28] A disturbance in the arrangement of the various parts of the body politic would destroy the mutual consent of the parts to accept their disposition in the interest of the health of the organism. To put a foot in place of a head would produce an unsightly, not to say illegitimate, body.

One of the objections to Winthrop's position on the magisterial veto was made on the grounds that "the greatest power is in the people." Winthrop agreed, but changed the terms: "originally and vertually it is: but when they [freemen] have chosen them Judges, etc: their Juditiary power is actually in those to whom they have committed it and those are their magistr[ate]s." The freemen had the right to choose and having chosen had the obligation to obey. This was part of the fundamental law of the organic corporation, and as such could not be altered by the deputies: "thoughe all Lawes, that are superstructive, may be altered by the representative bodye of the Com[mon] w[ealth] yet they have not power to alter any thinge which is fundamentall."[29] Since he defined fundamental law as that which distinguished one government from another, he was obliged to view those constitutional arrangements which best characterized the mixed aristocracy of the Bay as fundamental. In this connection he believed that the magisterial veto was a necessary defense against the encroachments of the steadily more assertive freemen. Those assertions, if allowed to become policy, would destroy the political theology of the commonwealth by turning from rule by the wise to rule by the most. As Winthrop searched his Bible and his heart and, be it said, his self-interest, he could find no authority for such a transformation.

The oath taken by the specific magistrate, and accepted by those who had called him to office, was the explicit and renewable covenant between rulers and ruled. That oath, as Winthrop understood it, meant "that we shall govern you and judge your causes by the rules of God's laws and our own, according to our best skill."[30] A magistrate could be called to account for a failure of faith because that would be a violation of his oath; he was not accountable for failures of skill or ability because he was human and thus necessarily deficient, and the electors, knowing this beforehand, still elected him to office. Yet it was the superior skill of the magistrate which, presumably, had led to his election and which justified his authority. When it was clear that the magistrate's will was evil, the electors had the duty to turn him out of office, not even waiting for the annual election meeting of the General Court. Short of this failure of faith and will, the people must suffer his rule because they had chosen him, and once elected he ruled in God's name. Having exercised their liberty to choose the man, the freemen had given that man the divine authority inherent in the office. The magistrates, Winthrop announced to the General Court, "have our authority from God, in way of an ordinance, such as hath the image of God eminently stamped upon it, the contempt and violation whereof hath been vindicated with examples of divine vengeance."[31] He thought that the aristocratic form of government was justified by its existence in the Bible, and by the notion of the divinity of the office of magistracy, if not of each particular magistrate. That magistrates "are Gods upon earthe,"[32] meant that any resistance to lawful authority which was exercised under a covenant could not be justified and would be punished by God in His heaven and by His magisterial agents on earth.

In 1644, when Winthrop was the Deputy Governor, the deputies once more called for abolition of the magistrates' veto power, and argued that the magistrates had no lawful power when the Court was not in session except that power which the full Court of deputies and magistrates had earlier and explicitly granted. Winthrop accurately viewed this as a revolutionary move designed to transfer authority from the magistrates to the people, a revolution which the deputies disguised by charging the magistrates with arbitrary government. Even though the church elders sided with the magistrates, Winthrop felt compelled to answer the charge, and he wrote and circulated a "Discourse on Arbitrary Government." He defined an arbitrary government as one in which the governors assumed powers that properly belonged only to God. "Arbitrary Government," he wrote, "is, where a people have men sett over them without their choyce, or allowance: who have power, to Governe them, and Judge their Causes without a Rule." A governor who ruled without either popular consent or a published and known set of laws was not merely a tyrant, but was also a sinner. The government of Massachusetts, according to Winthrop, was not arbitrary for three reasons: "I: by the foundation of it: 2: by the positive Lawes thereof: 3: by the constant practice."[33]

The royal charter was the foundation of Massachusetts' government. That charter created a body politic, a corporation, and arranged the "power and Motions" of the various members of the whole body "as might best conduce to the preservation, and good of the wholl bodye." There were two political members created by the charter; the governor "not as a person, but as a State," including the deputy governor and eighteen assistants, and the company or freemen. Authority was granted to the government and liberty was granted to the freemen. "The power of liberty" was "not a bare passive capacitye of freedome or immunity, but such a Libertye, as hath power to Acte upon the chiefe meanes of its owne wellfare."[34] The power of that liberty was made manifest in two ways, election and counsel. The freemen annually elected all governmental officials, and through their deputed agents were required to give their advice and consent to all legislative action.

Such liberties did not allow any intrusion upon the proper authority of the government. Winthrop made clear, immediately following his discussion of the liberties of the freemen, that ". . . if all were Governors, or magistrates, and none lefte, to be an objecte of Government . . . our state should be a meer Democratie." He cited the charter as proof that the authority of "this Government is not Arbitrary in the foundation of it, but Regulated in all the partes of it."[35] The government was, he said, "a mixt Aristocratie,"[36] was not arbitrary, and was regulated in all things.

He thought that the laws passed by the General Court in Massachusetts similarly proved that both the liberty of the freemen and the authority of the government had been respected. Winthrop recalled that in the spring of 1634 the powers of the Court were made explicit by the Court itself. In the annual election, to be held on the last Wednesday of the Easter Term, the freemen could reject any of the officers without showing cause; but any officer could be discharged at any session of the Court if the reasons for discharge were made explicit and proved.

Winthrop's final reason for insisting that the government of Massachusetts was not arbitrary was his opinion that the attempt to bring theory and practice into harmony had been usually successful. Since the Charter and the laws of the colony were just, and since "where any considerable obliquitye hathe been discerned, it hathe been soone brought to the Rule and redressed: for it is not possible in the infancye of a plantation, subjecte to so many and variable occurrents, to holde so exactly to Rules, as when a state is once setled."[37]

Turning then to the basic question of the content of "a Rule to walk by," the content of those laws which restrained or constrained the officers of the government, Winthrop declared that the "Rule is the Worde of God, and such conclusions and deductions, as are, or shalbe regularly drawne from thence."[38] It was of course not possible to legislate for every conceivable situation, but so long as the fundamental law or constitution had been carefully and piously drawn, the later necessary deductions from it might be similarly pious and therefore just. He noted that difficulties in old England were created "because they [English residents] shaped their Course too much by Politike and nationall prudence, and held not strictly to the Rules of Gods worde."[39] Massachusetts could escape the Lord's wrath if it would observe the Lord's word. The rewards of political expedience (which, in Massachusetts Bay, came increasingly to mean excessive religious toleration) seemed to be civil war. The rewards of political piety would surely—hopefully—be temporal success, measured by human standards and desires: peace and plenty and health.

It was clear that God could have outlined all the details of running a political economy had He chosen to do so. Instead of this detail, God "appointed Gov[ernmen]ts upon earthe, to be his vice-gerents."[40] Those governments, following the few but important hints that were included in the Bible, had the obligation to follow the divine precedents, to deduce wisely, with one eye on the Bible and the other on the particular society with which they were concerned. Just as the Lord did not prescribe all the prayers for the ministry, so He did not prescribe all legislation; total prescription in either case would have destroyed the ordinance of the office. "Judges are Gods upon earthe: therefore, in their Administrations, they are to holde forthe the wisdome and mercye of God (which are his Attributes) as well as his Justice: as occasion shall require, either in respecte of the qualitye of the person, or for a more generall good: or evident repentance, in some cases of less publ[ic] consequence, or avoydinge imminent danger to the state, and such like prevalent Considerations."[41]

Let it be clear that Winthrop did not lead governors or magistrates beyond the pale of theology. Puny, vicious, and impotent man could govern well only with divine assistance. Aided only by his natural reason, man would and could only make evil worse. "But . . . when occasion required, God promised, to be present in his owne Ordinance, to improve suche gifts as he should please to conferre upon suche as he should call to place of Government."[42] The road to divine salvation and political success was the same road, and each forward step on it could only be taken with God's help.

Given Winthrop's concept of the organic Christian corporation based on the consent of the members and limited to only the visible saints, it followed logically that he should argue that any man admitted into the corporation implicitly consented to abide by majority rule, so long, of course, as that rule violated neither religion nor the objective general welfare. No man who refused to give implicit or explicit consent could be allowed to walk in the saints' preserve. None should be allowed natural liberty; all would be subject to magisterial authority, under which moral liberty could flourish; and, in cases where numbers were relevant, majority rule should decide (excepting always the opposition of a majority to the magistrates). Any variation of these conditions would endanger the state and therefore the church and therefore the individual salvation of the saints themselves.

* * *

At the center of Winthrop's political thinking was his conviction that some men were better than others—more pious, moral, and wise: The best part of a community, he said, "is always the least, and of the best part the wiser part is always the lesser,"[43] an idea whose political implications can be traced backward to canon law and forward throughout most of the colonial period of New England's history. The first political requirement was to discover who those wise and pious men were, and the second was to devise ways by which they could wield sufficient but delimited power. He feared political decisions reached in passion instead of cool reflection, and he was convinced that reason and democracy were mutually exclusive, that mass participation in the political process necessarily elicited the kind of bias that must damage the commonwealth. Even assuming that one man was merely as good or bad as any other—an assumption Winthrop could never make— still that man would be unable to restrain his internal demons in a mass assembly, while he could do so in a quiet committee meeting: "It is easye to judge, that 30 or 40 distinct men, chosen out of all the countrye, and by all reason as free from partialitye or prejudice as any other, may give a more just sentence in any such cause upon deliberation and quiet discourse than a whole multitude upon the suddaine, when many may be thought not to heare what is proposed, and others not to understand it, and perchance the greater part in a heate and tumult, and when the weakest and worst member of the commonwealth adds as much weight to the sentence as the most godly and judicious."[44] His goal was to devise a government in which wisdom could assert itself over numbers.

Mere men could never do the job, he thought, as the entire history of the world and its calamities proved. It was a mistake to look for wisdom in the governments of the past, a mistake which had led even Nathaniel Ward, who, in 1641, had been selected without the permission of the magistrates to preach at a session of the Court, to separate politics and morality from religion. In his *Journal* Winthrop slapped Ward's wrist: "In his sermon he delivered many useful things, but in a moral and political discourse, grounding his propositions much upon the old Roman and Grecian governments, which sure is an error, for if religion and the word of God makes men wiser than their neighbors, and these times have the advantage of all that have gone before us in experience and observation, it is probable that by all these helps, we may better frame rules of government for ourselves than to receive others upon the bare authority of the wisdom, justice, etc. of those heathen commonwealths."[45] Political vice, like any other kind, came from man's hatred of God. The bloody record of paganism and of the Anti-christ would come to an end when the saints in Massachusetts constructed a Christian commonwealth whose essential basis was the word of God, when this new Chosen People legislated and administered God's sovereign will.

In his rejection of Ward's classicism, Winthrop claimed that the secular past was simply irrelevant to Massachusetts Bay, and thus expressed another idea which was to grow and thrive in later America. The entire history of the real world, as read by Winthrop and his fellow Puritans, had been merely the fits and starts leading up to the cosmic climax of Boston's founding. Because the Bay saints were supposedly more deeply and truly pious than any other people in the world's history, they could build a unique society with a unique government. As radically new men they occupied a new world and would fashion their lives on earth in a new way. Their piety had lifted them out of human history, out of time. They argued that they were God's agents and, as such, were freed from the disabilities that had limited the achievements of the past. Only the sovereign will of God could make them creatures of time and subject them to the human failings that had caused the rise and fall of earlier nations.

* * *

Sovereignty, for Winthrop, was an attribute of God, and not of men, and most certainly not of the mass of men. If the voice of the people were the voice of God, it would be as a result of God's mysterious will, and not because of inherent qualities in men or society. The function of government, then, was to allow men to rule men through God, to prevent the raising of obstacles between God and man for the sinful and futile purpose of trying to free man from his covenant with God. Men could raise such an obstacle, but it would not keep those godless men from the jurisdiction of the omnipotent and ubiquitous God.

Because political success depended upon the society's adherence to the word of God, it followed that in a Christian corporation the clergy would have an important role. God had revealed part of His will in the Bible, and both the preacher and the politician were enjoined to obey His word. This did not mean that the clergy had or should have control of the state. The political system of Massachusetts has frequently been described as a theocracy, by which the rule of the clergy, not that of God, is meant. From Winthrop's point of view this would be an inaccurate designation because the magistrates had the only authority in the state. The clergy could not hold office, but could and frequently did give advice on political matters. So, in fact, did the freemen and their deputies, but this did not make Massachusetts a democracy. It is true that only church members were eligible for freemanship, and the clergy might try to control the franchise by trying to control church membership, but the whole church controlled admission into its body, not the clergy alone. Whether a given church member would be granted political liberties was determined by the General Court, not by the clergy: not all church members were freemen. In time the General Court could veto the ordination of an objectionable minister, and in the Body of Liberties of 1641 it was said that the government had the authority to supervise church matters, including matters concerning doctrine. Many activities that were supervised by the church in England were directed by the state in Massachusetts Bay, including the disposition of estates, marriage and divorce, recording of vital statistics, superintending of cemeteries, and burial practice (which included no religious ceremony of any kind). No church holidays were observed and the thanksgiving and fast days were regulated by the state. A minister's status continued only while his congregation maintained him in office. Professor E. S. Morgan has concluded that "of all the governments in the Western world at the time, that of early Massachusetts gave the clergy least authority."[46] Winthrop's own concept of a mixed aristocracy is more accurate than the standard concept of a theocracy.

The trial and sentencing of Mistress Hutchinson occasioned much dissatisfaction, and Winthrop heard a rumor that many from the Boston church were trying to persuade their church elders to call him to account. In the interest of preventing a public quarrel, and with the intent of defining the proper relationship between the church and the state, Winthrop wrote an **"Essay Against the Power of the Church To Sit In Judgment On the Civil Magistracy."** He began with the simple assertion that "The Scripture affords neither Rule nor example of any such power in the Church, but diverse against it." If the church had the authority to try magistrates, the church would become "the supreame Court in the Juris-

diction, and capable of all Appeales, and so in trueth meerly Antichrist, by being exalted above all, that is called God." The church could not act as a judge because it lacked the means to determine the facts of a case; it could not "call in forrein witnesses," examine witnesses under oath, or have access to the records of the General Court. Simply to examine a civil case, even when no penalty or punishment was intended, was forbidden by Christ to His churches.

The crux of the matter was that "Christ [in] his kingdome, cannot Juditially enq[uir]e into affaires of this world." Christ settled this jurisdictional dispute by dividing the authority of His officers between realms as distinct as heaven and earth. As King of Kings and Lord of Lords, Christ "hath sett up another kingdome in this worlde, wherein magistrates are his officers, and they are to be accountable to him, for their miscarriages in the waye and order of this kingdome." Since the magistrate had his authority directly from Christ, he was accountable for his actions as magistrate to Christ, and not to the clergy. There was thought to be a profound difference between the office and its holder. As a man, the magistrate was as much in need of the clergy as any other man, but as an official, because his official actions came from the divine ordinance of his office, he was beyond either the competence or the reach of the church. Should the clergy excommunicate a magistrate, or a magistrate imprison a clergyman, "this would sett Christ against himselfe in his owne Ordinances . . . which cant be."

The true Christian rule was submission "to the highest powers." The church must win the support of kings by meekness, love, and charity. Luther's doctrine of submission to the state was cited, Calvin had for the most part agreed, and the evidence of Job was adduced to prove that "a man may not say to a Kinge, thou art wicked: nor call Princes ungodly."[47] The divinity of the offices of both priest and magistrate could not confront each other because their respective authority was limited to different realms. In temporal matters, including the protection of the organization and doctrine of the church, the magistrate was supreme. The magistrate as a man might not get to heaven, but when he spoke with the power and dignity of his office, he could be challenged by no power lower than God Himself.

An important part of the magistrate's duty was to protect the organization and the purity of the visible church. What was the New England church that the Governor was obliged to defend? It will be recalled that Winthrop had been careful to explain that emigration from England did not constitute a rejection of the Church of England. For a time, at least, one must take the word "Puritan" seriously when applied to Winthrop and his Company. It cannot be doubted that he was aware of the political difficulties that might ensue if complete separation of the churches were allowed, but it seems that his reluctance to separate was more a matter of conscience than of political policy. His early hesitancy even to accept the church autonomy explicit in Congregational church polity is illustrated by his nervousness over procedure; in the late summer of 1630, he reported, "we of the Congregation kept a fast, and chose mr. *wilson* our teacher . . . we used imposition of handes but with this protestation by all that it was onely as a signe of Election and confirmation, not of any intent that mr. *wilson* should renounce his ministrye he received in Englande."[48]

His reluctance to admit that the physical act of separation was in fact also a spiritual separation continued at least through the spring of the next year. When Roger Williams refused to join the congregation at Boston because the members would not repent for having had communion with the Church of England, Winthrop seems to have taken the occasion to write his opinions on "Reformation Without Separation." As a magistrate he had an obligation to be clear about ecclesiastical polity, which it was his duty to uphold. "The corruption of a thinge," he reasoned, "dothe not nullifie a thinge so longe as the thinge hathe a beinge in the same nature, that it had, when it was in the best beinge: so it is with the particular Congregations."[49] The Church of England was corrupt, as Williams had said, but it was a church nonetheless, which Williams denied; it was a church which could be purified, unlike some others where the force of the Papacy and Antichrist had so corrupted the church that its essential nature had been utterly destroyed. The example of the Bay congregations, it was hoped, would encourage that purging in England.

By 1634, when Winthrop's ideas of the nature of the government were already well formulated, he was growing firmer in his defense not of the kinship between the parent church and its offspring in the wilderness, but of the basic differences between them. By then he had accepted Congregationalism, including the absolute theoretical autonomy of the individual congregations. In a letter to England, the Governor showed unmistakable signs of creeping separatism: "For your counsell of Conforminge ourselves to the Ch[urch] of E[ngland] though I doubt not but it proceeds out of your care of our wellfare: yet I dare not thanke you for it; because it is not conformable to Gods will revealed in his worde: what you may doe in E[ngland] where things are otherwise established, I will not dispute, but our case heere is otherwise: being come to clearer light and more Libertye."[50]

Sometime in 1640, Winthrop wrote another letter to a correspondent in England, in which he made clear his commitment to a congregational autonomy so thoroughgoing that only the idea of the invisible church of all true believers could still be thought to bind the Bay congregations to those in England. At least by this time he was willing to insist on the individual church covenants as the very basis of the churches, as the covenant was the foundation of the state. The church covenant, as he reported it, was a dual pledge, including a renunciation of the past and a promise for the future: "I doe renounce all former corruptions and polutions. I doe promise to walke togither with this Church in all the ordinances of Religion according to the rule of the Gospell, and with all the members heerof in brotherly love." He believed that every association required some sort of covenant, even though, as was the case with the churches in England, the covenant was only implicit. "Now to leave it uncertaine, where men have opportunye to expresse and clear it, were a faylinge (at least)." It was the covenant that gave some permanence to each church, for without it the church would cease to exist when the uncovenanted persons left the assembly. Anyway, the controversy over the covenant was misplaced, because there were so many more weighty matters at hand, or rather in England, as, for example, "communicatinge with all parochiall members, whereof many are no Saints neither by callinge nor profession: submitting themselves to Canonicall obedience."[51] And what was most important, accepting the covenant was not the process by which one entered a church body in Massachusetts. Being given the opportunity to pledge oneself meant that the individual had already been admitted into the church:

> There is a great mistake in the order of our Covenant, for it passeth for granted everywhere that none can be admitted heere before they enter into this Covenant, whereas in very truth they are tryed and admitted by the vote of the whole Churche before any Covenant be tendered or mentioned to them. Lastly it is sometymes tendered to them as a declaration of their purpose and intention only and not in the words of a Covenant or promise, so willinge are our Churches to please our brethren in all things to our mutuall accord and edification.[52]

Having accepted the covenant that supported congregational autonomy, Winthrop had simply extended his view of the nature of the political body to include also the church body. A number of discrete individuals came together and voluntarily gave their consent to exchange their natural liberty for moral liberty under lawful authority. The process for creating both the state and the visible church was identical, and included the liberty of the members to elect their own officials, either magistrate or minister. Both the state and the church were concerned with salvation, and only active members of the church could be active in the state. The minister's function was spiritual leadership and inspiration. It was the duty of the magistrate to see to it that the minister had a proper congregational body, well organized and obedient in outward behavior, to lead. It was the minister's function to teach, while the magistrate saw to it that the congregation was in attendance and that the lazy or stupid were given the opportunity to meditate on their sinfulness while taking their ease in Boston's stocks.

With congregational autonomy, the relationship between the state and the churches became more complicated. Should the state improperly interfere with a given church, it would violate the rights of the congregation. The clergy could pose small threat to the various churches since each minister held his post by the sufferance of the congregation. The General Court was more dangerous, from the viewpoint of the congregation, and it was usual for the deputies, who represented the towns, also to defend actions of the independent congregations, and all in opposition to magisterial authority.

One such case occurred in 1646 when some of the elders asked the General Court to authorize the calling of a synod. The magistrates complied, Winthrop recorded, but the deputies protested that the state had no proper authority to require the churches to send delegates to a civil convention, and that should the proposed synod agree on uniform church policy either the synod or its master, the state, would be guilty of subverting congregational autonomy.

The answer given to the first objection derived from Winthrop's definition of magistracy: "the civil magistrate had power upon just occasion to require the churches to send their messengers to advise in such ecclesiastical matters either of doctrine or discipline, as the magistrate was bound by God to maintain the churches in purity and truth." The deputies agreed that magistracy could so command the churches. But the threat to Congregationalism required more delicate treatment. Any suggestion of an imposed uniform practice on the churches elicited the fear that the despised Presbyterianism would be raised in Massachusetts Bay out of the wreckage of congregational autonomy. When the magistrates were charged with threatening that autonomy, they had to walk gently: "Whereupon it was ordered, that howsoever the civil magistrate had authority to call a synod when they saw it needful, yet in tender respect of such as were not yet fully satisfied in that point, the ensuing synod should be convened by way of motion only to the churches, and not by any words of command."[53] The magistrates could not attack the congregational covenant which created the churches without weakening the covenant principle, without endangering the security of their own authority. Winthrop's own convictions, moreover, led him to defend the covenants of the churches for the same reasons that he bridled at any challenge to magisterial authority, including the rare challenges from the clergy (most of whom, most of the time, sided with the magistrates in the battles with the deputies). The covenant principle was the very basis of man's relationship with God, and with other men in both the state and church.

* * *

Winthrop's ideas about the organic Christian corporation also defined for him the proper relationship between Massachusetts Bay and England. How was one to reconcile the divinity of the magistracy in the Bay with the supremacy of the English King; how reconcile congregational autonomy with the fact that the King was the head of the Church of England? What, if any, was the authority of Parliament to direct the ways of God's agents in the wilderness? Some curious perversions of the theory and law of corporations allowed Winthrop and Massachusetts to wend their way along a very dangerous path. The consequence of missing a step on that path could be the destruction of Massachusetts and all that it stood for, including even mankind's new chance for redemption.

The traditional theory of the corporation defined it as an unnatural, artificial body which had legal status as a person, fictive but legally real. Only a sovereign power could create fictions, and the life of a corporation must be a result of a concession from the sovereign. The fiction theory led to the concession theory. As one distinguished legal historian put it: "The corporation is, and must be, the creature of the State. Into its nostrils the State must breathe the breath of a fictitious life, for otherwise it would be no animated body but individualistic dust." English common law made it a crime for men "to presume to act as a corporation" without the appropriate concession from the state. "Ignorant men," Maitland wrote, "on board the 'Mayflower' may have thought that, in the presence of God and one another, they could covenant and combine themselves together into 'a civil body politic.'"[54] The Puritans were not as ignorant as the Pilgrims.

The Charter of the Massachusetts Bay Company was a concession by the Crown which had breathed life into that legal fiction. This royal creature was defined as the "Governor and Company of the Mattachusetts Bay in Newe England [which is] one bodie politique and corporate in deede, fact, and name."[55] Massachusetts therefore owed its legal existence to its Charter, and Winthrop never lost sight of that sobering fact. The Crown giveth and the Crown taketh away.

It was obvious that a creature of the state could not be a state itself, that a corporation could not be an independent sovereign. The Bay held a franchise from the Crown; "'a Corporation,' Maitland said, 'is a Franchise,' and a franchise is a portion of the State's power in the hands of a subject."[56] Adhering strictly to the theory of the corporation, then, Massachusetts was a subject, a creature, a dependency, and had not the legal right to exercise the kind of sovereignty that had the power to create. But a community which was covenanted with God as well as with the King, had, to put it gently, a dual allegiance. Should the wills of the two sovereigns divide, the creature had the alternative of ignoring one and praying for the best, or becoming schizophrenic. Whenever the first option could be had with relative impunity, Winthrop gladly took it. The King, after all, was three thousand miles away, while God, it was clear, was immediately present. . . .

Notes

1. John Winthrop, *Papers,* A. B. Forbes, ed. (Boston, 1929-1947), IV, 170.

2. *Ibid.,* II, 282.

3. *Ibid.,* II, 282-283.

4. *Ibid.,* II, 287.

5. *Ibid.,* II, 288.

6. *Ibid.,* II, 290.

7. *Ibid.,* II, 292.

8. *Ibid.,* II, 293.

9. *Ibid.,* II, 295.

10. John Winthrop, *Journal, 1630-1649,* James K. Hosmer, ed. (New York, 1908), II, 83.

11. *Papers,* II, 152.

12. *Journal,* II, 83-84.

13. *Ibid.,* II, 238.

14. *Ibid.,* II, 239.

15. *Ibid.*

16. *Ibid.*

17. *Papers,* III, 422 n.

18. *Ibid.,* III, 423.

19. *Ibid.,* III, 423, 424.

20. *Ibid.,* III, 465.

21. *Ibid.,* III, 475.

22. *Ibid.,* III, 467.

23. *Ibid.,* IV, 385.

24. *Ibid.,* IV, 382.

25. *Ibid.,* IV, 383.

26. *Ibid.,* IV, 386.

27. *Ibid.,* IV, 383.

28. *Ibid.,* IV, 385.

29. *Ibid.,* IV, 390, 391.

30. *Journal,* II, 238.

31. *Ibid.*

32. *Papers,* IV, 476.

33. *Ibid.,* IV, 468.

34. *Ibid.,* IV, 468-469.

35. *Ibid.,* IV, 471.

36. *Ibid.,* IV, 482.

37. *Ibid.,* IV, 471.

38. *Ibid.,* IV, 472.

39. *Ibid.,* IV, 472 n.

40. *Ibid.,* IV, 473.

41. *Ibid.,* IV, 476.

42. *Ibid.,* IV, 473.

43. *Ibid.,* IV, 54.

44. "Libertye," Thomas Hutchinson (ed.), *Collection of Original Papers Relative to the History of the Colony of Massachusetts-Bay* (Albany, 1865), I, 78.

45. *Journal,* II, 36-37.

46. Edmund S. Morgan, *The Puritan Dilemma* (Boston, 1958), 96.

47. *Papers,* III, 505-507.

48. *Ibid.,* II, 267.

49. *Ibid.,* III, 13.

50. J W to Sir Simonds D'Ewes, July 21, 1634, *ibid.,* III, 171.

51. *Ibid.,* IV, 169-171.

52. *Ibid.,* IV, 171.

53. *Ibid.,* II, 274.

54. Frederic W. Maitland, "Introduction," in Otto Gierke, *Political Theories of the Middle Ages,* tr. F. W. Maitland (Cambridge, Eng., 1900), xxx, xxi.

55. *Records of the Governor and Company of the Massachusetts Bay in New England,* N. B. Shurtleff, ed. (Boston, 1853-1854), I, 10.

56. Maitland, *op. cit.,* xxxi.

Select Bibliography

Champlin Burrage. *The Church Covenant Idea.* Philadelphia, 1904.

Julius Goebel, Jr., "King's Law and Local Custom in Seventeenth Century New England," *Columbia Law Review,* XXXI, 3 (March, 1931), 416-448.

William Haller. *The Rise of Puritanism.* New York, 1938.

George L. Haskins. *Law and Authority in Early Massachusetts.* New York, 1960.

E. H. Kantorowicz. *The King's Two Bodies.* Princeton, 1957.

Charles H. McIlwain, "The Transfer of the Charter to New England and Its Significance in American Constitutional History," Massachusetts Historical Society, *Proceedings,* LXIII (Boston, 1931), 53-64.

Perry Miller. *The New England Mind.* 2 vols., New York, 1939, 1953.

————*Orthodoxy in Massachusetts.* Cambridge, 1933.

Edmund S. Morgan. *The Puritan Dilemma.* Boston, 1958.

————*Visible Saints.* New York, 1963.

Samuel E. Morison. *Builders of the Bay Colony.* Cambridge, 1930, 51-104.

————*The Puritan Pronaos.* New York, 1936.

Albert Peel. *The First Congregational Churches.* Cambridge, Eng., 1920.

Aaron B. Seidman, "Church and State in the Early Years of the Massachusetts Bay Colony," *New England Quarterly,* XVIII, 2 (June 1945), 211-233.

R. H. Tawney. *Religion and the Rise of Capitalism.* New York, 1926.

Horace E. Ware, "Was the Government of the Massachusetts Bay Colony a Theocracy?" Publications of the Colonial Society of Massachusetts, *Transactions,* X (Dec. 1905), 151-180.

Robert Benton (essay date winter 1973)

SOURCE: Benton, Robert M. "The John Winthrops and Developing Scientific Thought in New England." *Early American Literature* 7, no. 3 (winter 1973): 272-80.

[In this essay, Benton argues how the lives and practices of Winthrop and two of his descendents influenced the evolution of scientific thought in America, beginning with Winthrop's meticulous documentation of natural phenomena.]

> Plantations in their beginnings have work ynough, & find difficulties sufficient to settle a comfortable way of subsistence, there beinge buildings, fencings, cleeringe and breakinge up of ground, lands to be attended, orchards to be planted, highways & bridges & fortifications to be made, & all thinges to doe, as in the beginninge of the world. Its not to be wondered if there have not yet beene *itinera subterranea.* . . .
>
> John Winthrop, Jr., to Sir Robert Moray[1]

A study of science or scientific thought should never be conducted along national lines as if there were something called French, German or American science. Scientific problems are international. As Professor George Sarton reminds us, "There is no American science, but there are American scientists, a good many of them, and some of them as great as may be met anywhere else in the world. The best way to explain American achievements is to focus the reader's attention upon a few of the leading scientists."[2] No better view can be obtained of the development of scientific thought in America than through a study of three John Winthrops.

The first New England John Winthrop (1587-1649) was the governor of the Massachusetts Bay Colony. His son, John Winthrop, Jr. (1605-76) was the first governor of Connecticut. A later John Winthrop (1714-79), a great-grandnephew of John Winthrop, Jr., was a distinguished professor of mathematics and natural philosophy at Harvard. There were other John Winthrops as well, but in these three one can see a development in scientific thinking which enabled it to escape the religious dominance which had impeded it.

Governor John Winthrop of Massachusetts had grown up in a home characterized by intellectual opportunity, religious devotion, and superstition. His father, Adam, kept a diary in which he recorded natural phenomena. One of his earliest notations is his reference to the earthquake of 1580: "the 6 of April 1580 ther was a yearthe quacke" (**Winthrop Papers,** Vol. I, 41). In the same volume he makes several observations: in the year 1600 on "The xvth of Aug. fell a great Rayne which made a floud at Boxford" (68) and on "The 23 of Decembre I felt an Erthquake" (75). An editorial footnote at this point in the **Papers** states that the quake occasioned the usual warning in a December 31, 1601, publication called "The Tremblinge of the Earth, and the warninges of the world before the Judgement Daye." Destructive natural phenomena were believed to be the result of God's displeasure.

In a reference to one of his tenants, Adam shows typical superstition: "Memorandum that John Raven the same day that he fell sicke went into his yarde and saw a wrenne strike down a Robin redbrest starke dedde which he tooke vp and shewed his wife thereof presently" (42). Adam Winthrop, an observer and recorder, was not a questioner, a characteristic he passed on to his son. The first New England John Winthrop did, however, believe in the validity of experience. Winthrop demonstrates this belief in a series of journal entries called **"Experiencia"** and is quite specific in a January 20, 1616, passage which reads like a prayer:

> Thou assurest my heart that I am in a right course, even the narrowe waye that leads to heaven: Thou tellest me, and all experience tells me, that in this way

there is least companie, and that those which doe walke openly in this way shalbe despised, pointed at, hated of the world, made a byworde, reviled, slandered, rebuked, made a gazinge stocke, called puritans, nice fooles, hipocrites, hairbrainde fellows, rashe, indiscreet, vainglorious, and all that naught is. . . .

(*Papers,* I, 196)

This foreshadows the later course of Winthrop's life when he would be a leader of those "called puritans" and would continue to rely on what he heard God and experience tell him.

The selection of John Winthrop as the first governor of Massachusetts brought prominence to a man who in many respects was like William Bradford, governor of the Plymouth Colony. In his record of the early Plymouth years, Bradford's primary interest is to show God's providence. Winthrop shares this concern, as noted in a 1620 passage from his **"Experiencia"**:

> Many thinges which fall out by the ordinarye course of nature etc, are not easylye discerned to be guided by any speciall providence of God, as the Eclipses of the Sunne etc, thunders, tempests, etc, the effects whereof are ofte very strange; but God who had from the beginninge determined of suche effects, did withall appointe that the course of naturall causes should concurre at the same tyme: so that heerby his glory is the greater, in effectinge things extraordinary, and yet not changing the order of causes.

(*Papers,* I, 238)

Natural phenomena are first shown to be guided by a special providence of God and, although strange, are seen to have predetermined effects. The eclipses, storms, and tempests are precisely those items which Winthrop records in his various journal entries. He is quite conscious of his observations, but his scientific interest seems to stop with the recording. Since theological dogma placed all occurrences, no matter how unusual, under the special providence of God, one could only observe, record, and marvel.

John Winthrop's recording of natural phenomena seems to be used primarily in making comparisons with England. A typical example is contained in a July 23, 1630, letter to his son John:

> For the Country it selfe I can discerne little difference betweene it and our owne. we have had only 2 daies which I have observed more hot then in England here is as good land as I have seene there but none so bad as there Here is sweet aire faire rivers and plenty of springes and the water better then in Eng(land) here can be noe want of any thinge to those who bring meane(s) to raise out of the earth and sea.

(*Papers,* II, 302)

After John Winthrop, Jr., had settled in New England and then returned to London on business, his father wrote him in December, 1634, saying, "I wish that in your return you would observe the winde and weather everye daye, that we may see how it agrees with our parts" (*Papers,* III, 177). The passage shows not only that John Winthrop was interested in comparative weather statistics but also that he was training his son to observe and record such phenomena as well.

A further example of John Winthrop's careful observation of the weather, the flora, and the fauna of New England is given in his September, 1644, letter to the Earl of Warwick (*Papers,* IV, 491-93). The letter is too long to quote here, but Winthrop's description of New England, including a short review of the government of the colony, is strikingly similar to the later work by Crèvecoeur in his *Letters From An American Farmer.* The major impression one receives is that of Winthrop's keen eye.

Although he was preoccupied with politics and religion, the range of John Winthrop's interests can be seen in his journal. In the first volume he notes the discovery in 1636 of whale bones sixty miles up the James River, a June, 1638, earthquake, a "tempest or hiracano" in August of the same year, and an appearance of a strange light the following March.[3] Winthrop actually observed only the earthquake and the storm. While he often merely records events, his theological belief that all acts of nature are directly controlled by God is never hidden. For instance, he insists that a two-month drought in 1639 was ended as a direct result of a day of humiliation appointed by the court. "The very day after the fast was appointed there fell a good shower, and, within one week after the day of humiliation was past, we had such a store of rain, and so seasonably, as the corn revived and gave hope of a very plentiful harvest" (*Journal,* I, 307).

Unfortunately, Winthrop also believed that an unnatural birth was a sign of God's displeasure. In the first volume of his journals he reports one such birth by the wife of William Dyer who was "notoriously infected with Mrs. Hutchinson's errors" (266) and another by Anne Hutchinson herself which Winthrop believes demonstrates "her error in denying inherent righteousness" (277). Of much greater scientific interest is Winthrop's recording of the first ascent of the White Mountains by a European, Darby Field, which he accompanies with a transcription of Field's observations (*Journal,* II, 62-63, 85-86).

John Winthrop's papers show him to be a man with scientific interests who records his own observations and others' reports. He is not fully a part of the growing scientific movement of the seventeenth century, for he does not seem interested in testing or experimentation. Perhaps John Winthrop's most important scientific contribution was his instilling in his son the habit of observation and recording. There can be no doubt that John

Winthrop, Jr., made the most significant scientific contributions of any New England colonist of the seventeenth century.

The second New England John Winthrop was a man of more diversified interests than his father. He has been characterized most significantly as one who "was ahead of his period in that his varied interests were scientific rather than theological."[4] Richard S. Dunn is even more specific:

> Religion framed his life, but he did not experience his father's crusading zeal. He was energetic and public spirited, but preferred science to politics. Whereas the elder Winthrop wrote didactic tracts and diaries of religious meditations, the son kept medical and alchemical notebooks. One finds fugitive opinions of all sorts, but no systematic religious or political philosophy. . . . John Winthrop, Jr., was all things to all men, a highly receptive person, open to new ideas, adaptable to new situations.[5]

Such an obvious change in orientation between two successive generations is a sign of cultural change in progress.

The first indication of the scientific interest of John Winthrop, Jr., is found in his letter to his father of January, 1630. The elder John Winthrop was in London making final plans for his trip to New England which would begin two months later. His son had remained at home to negotiate the sale of his father's property and to clear up other matters of business, and in his letter he describes a new variety of windmill he had invented:

> I have now made a rude modell (as only to shew, that it is feasable) of that wind motion, which I tould you of, then only imagining it speculatively but now have seene the experience of it, and doe affirme that an Instrument may be made to move with the wind horizontally to equall if not to exeed the ordinary verticall motion of the windmill sailes. . . . I conceive it may be aplied to many laborious vses as any kind of milles Corne milles saw miles etc. . . . And one spetiall property wilbe in them that they allwaies stand right for the wind whersoever it bloweth: If there may be made any vse of it, I desire New England should reape the benifit for whose sake it was invented.
>
> (***Papers***, II, 193-94)

In addition to this being the first record of John Winthrop, Jr.'s scientific activity, it shows the practical nature of his mind and one of his many schemes to enhance the productivity of the New England colonists. A special characteristic of the passage is that rather than merely to speculate or simply record phenomena, as his father might do, John Winthrop, Jr., first imagined a particular design and then experimented to verify his hypothesis. He then reports the results of his findings. At twenty-four, John Winthrop, Jr., is a practitioner of the new science.

The second John Winthrop was much more than a New England colonist involved in the new science, however. His early travels had brought him in contact with many of the leading minds of Europe. It is logical that when a scientific society was organized to promote natural philosophy John Winthrop, Jr., was included. Proposed for membership in the newly formed Royal Society and officially elected on January 1, 1662, John Winthrop, Jr., the following year, was elected an Original Fellow of the Society under the Second Charter. Sir Henry Lyons notes in addition that the secretary of the Society was instructed in 1664 to "inform John Winthrop that he was invited in a particular manner to take upon him the charge of being the Chief Correspondent of the Royal Society in the West, as Sir Philberto Vernatti was in the East Indies."[6]

The first American colonial member of the Royal Society was willing to become the Society's western correspondent. The records of Winthrop's communications to the Society and the specimens sent reveal a quite active scientific career for one who was also a colonial governor and was almost continually involved in plans for colonial industries. R. P. Stearns notes that Winthrop's first formal presentation to the Society, the first paper given by any colonial, was presented in 1662 and titled "A Description of ye Artifice and making of Tarr and Pitch in New England, and ye Materialle of wch it is made."[7] A more widely known paper, "Of Maiz," was given by Winthrop on the last day of that year. Stearns calls this second work "undoubtedly the most complete description of Indian corn, its cultivation, and its uses that the English public had seen" (p. 128).

Throughout the years Winthrop wrote his numerous acquaintances in the Society and sent boxes of specimens. Although some of his communications were lost at sea, he shipped many items of note and the Society begged for more. One of the "Curiosities of Nature" Winthrop sent was apparently an unusual species of starfish. The fish provoked wide discussion and was shown to King Charles II. The Society wrote Winthrop immediately: "Wee wish very much, that you could procure a particular description of the said fish viz: whether it be common there, what is observable in it when alive; what colour it hath then; what kind of motion in water; what use it maketh of all that curious workmanship wch nature had adorned it with? &c." (Quoted by Stearns, p. 135). Obviously, Winthrop had submitted a rarity, and the Society wanted more information. One can also note how the Society instructed Winthrop in the scientific method of proceeding with a study of a particular marine organism. Almost eight years passed before Winthrop replied, noting, "I asked all the questions I could thinke needful concerning it" (Stearns, p. 138).

No simple listing of John Winthrop, Jr.'s scientific accomplishments could sufficiently assess his contribution. He was an avid astronomer and reported an individual sighting of Jupiter's fifth satellite. Although his telescope was not powerful enough for such a sighting, a fifth satellite was confirmed more than 200 years later. In New England, Winthrop was known as a doctor and chemist. He was a self-trained physician whose medical practice was extensive. He made no reported contribution to medical science, but he did rely heavily on a red powder he compounded of miter and antimony and called *rubila*.

The second John Winthrop maintained a wide scientific correspondence. In his history of the Royal Society, Sir Henry Lyons reports that of the eighty persons with whom John Winthrop, Jr., corresponded in England and Europe, thirty either were or had been Fellows of the Royal Society. In 1641, Robert Child wrote that he was having difficulty securing the books Winthrop had requested and that he was sending him a list of his own chemical books (*Papers,* IV, 333-38). In 1648 Child sent Winthrop a report of how "they make Rozin and Turpentin in France out of those trees which you call pitch pine by a facile way" (*Papers,* V, 221). This is obviously an early interest in what was, some fourteen years later, to become Winthrop's first paper before the Royal Society. In the letter Child mentions books and inventions which he feels will interest Winthrop; he also writes, "Sir I desire you if you meet with any sorts of seeds or stones, which are not common to make me partakers of some of them, and I shall willingly doe you service in this or any other way" (*Papers,* V, 222).

Another of Winthrop's correspondents was Augustinus Petraeus, a Dutch chemist who with others had formed an early scientific society. Petraeus wrote to Winthrop in Dutch, but Paul Marquart Schlegel, a Hamburg physician and anatomist, wrote in Latin, as did Johannes Tanckmarus. Schlegel founded an academy for the training of young physicians and became famous for his lectures in anatomy. Tanckmarus, a doctor of medicine who had been associated with mystics and heretics and probably met John Winthrop in Hamburg, wrote Winthrop on several occasions. John Winthrop's willingness to maintain contact with men of such varied beliefs suggests that theological orthodoxy was less important in his life than in that of his father.

In addition to his governmental tasks, his medical practice, and his ample correspondence, Winthrop was something of an explorer. In 1644 he petitioned the Massachusetts General Court for the right to search for iron mines "in all places within this Jurisdiction, and the same being found, to digg and cary away and dispose thereof for the best advantage" (*Papers,* IV, 423). He also purchased from Webuckshan and Washcomo black lead (graphite) mines (*Papers,* V, 4). By the Fall of 1645, Winthrop was traveling throughout Massachusetts and Connecticut in search of productive areas for a settlement. He kept a journal during the trip, three-

fourths of which he wrote in Latin. Unfortunately, the most interesting comments are the emendations and speculations of the translator.[8] The following Winthrop comments, among the most expansive in the journal, are less revealing than one might expect from a Fellow of the Royal Society: ". . . I crossed the river and the stream Poquanuc, where Robin told me there was fruit-bearing land without rocks, arable with a goodly number of planting-fields."[9] Because of his varied interests and responsibilities, John Winthrop, Jr., does occasionally lapse from his scientific dedication.

By following the scientific career of John Winthrop, Jr., one can see a decided change in emphasis from that of his father. Although raised in a zealously religious household, the second John Winthrop was motivated by science and adventure, not theology and Puritan dogmatism. He maintained numerous contacts with non-Puritans, and from an early age he practiced testing an hypothesis by means of experimentation. In John Winthrop, Jr., one can see the beginning of the evolution of scientific thought in New England. Without rejecting the religion of his father, the second John Winthrop moved away from the darkness of Puritan restrictions into the light of free scientific inquiry.

Although John Winthrop, Jr., gave his sons scientific training, they failed to make significant scientific contributions. However, a later John Winthrop, the son of Chief Justice Adam Winthrop of Massachusetts Bay and the great-grandnephew of John Winthrop, Jr., achieved distinction in science which surpassed that of any in his illustrious family. Elected second Hollis professor of mathematics and natural philosophy at Harvard in 1738 when he was only twenty-four, Professor John Winthrop is credited with establishing at that college the first institutional laboratory of experimental physics, introducing to the mathematical curriculum differential and integral calculus, and teaching the new science and its methods to four decades of Harvard students. The first colonial to record observations of sunspots and a member of the Royal Society as well as the American Philosophical Society, Professor Winthrop was the primary supporter of the theories and conclusions of Benjamin Franklin regarding electricity. Most significantly, Professor John Winthrop represents a culmination of that development in scientific thinking which had begun with the second John Winthrop. The *Dictionary of American Biography* records that "When he was examined for the professorship by the Overseers of the College the question of his theological adherence was not raised for fear it would prove too broad for Harvard at that time" (XX, 415).

One of the best views of that development in thought which Professor John Winthrop exemplifies is in his reaction to that natural phenomenon which had so interested the first John Winthrop—the earthquake. Governor Winthrop of Massachusetts believed that earthquakes were signs of God's displeasure with his people. Many still held to this belief in the middle of the eighteenth century. A devastating earthquake destroyed Lisbon, Portugal, in 1755, and a later earthquake terrified many persons in New England. Professor Winthrop taught that earthquakes resulted from purely physical causes, and he denied the contentions of those who sought to explain the quake as a direct intervention of the "Finger of God" in earthly affairs.

At the time of a New England earthquake in 1727, the Reverend Mr. Thomas Prince had published a sermon titled "Earthquakes the Works of God and Tokens of his just Displeasure." The new concern over quakes caused the aging minister to reprint the earlier sermon with an appendix to suggest that a secondary cause of earthquakes might be electrical in nature, possibly a consequence of the installation of numerous lightning rods in New England. Professor Winthrop quickly published his own *Lecture on Earthquakes* for which he prepared a special appendix specifically denying Mr. Prince's contentions. Prince sent a letter of protest to the *Boston Gazette,* and Winthrop firmly maintained his original stand. He was content neither to attribute the quake solely to God's agency nor simply to describe it as John Jr. would have done, but instead relocated the phenomenon from the religious to the scientific realm of rationalization.

Professor Winthrop survived the confrontation. He received the first honorary Doctor of Laws conferred by Harvard, and his interest and influence contributed to the founding of the American Academy of Arts and Sciences in Boston. Moreover, he reveals fully that development in scientific thinking which had begun years earlier. Professor Winthrop was no longer willing, as had been Governor Winthrop of Massachusetts, to subordinate nature to divine power. Rather he wished to elevate natural phenomena to scientific status, liberating nature on the one hand and the potentialities of her observers on the other. Like the second John Winthrop, Professor Winthrop accepted an hypothesis only after it had been sufficiently tested through experimentation. By the end of the eighteenth century, and largely due to the work of Professor John Winthrop, a new age in scientific thought had arrived, an age characterized by its feeling of having freed itself from the restrictions of dogmatic Calvinism.

Notes

1. Letter of November 12, 1668, in Massachusetts Historical Society *Proceedings,* 16 (1868), 236-37.

2. In the foreword to Bernard Jaffee, *Men of Science in America* (New York, 1944), p. xiii.

3. Winthrop, *Journal,* ed. James K. Hosmer (New York, 1908), I, 186, 270, 272, 294.

4. James Truslow Adams, sv. "Winthrop, John, Jr.," *Dictionary of American Biography,* XX, 413.

5. Dunn, *Puritans and Yankees: The Winthrop Dynasty of New England, 1630-1717* (Princeton, 1962), p. 59.

6. Lyons, *The Royal Society: 1660-1940* (New York, 1968), p. 28.

7. Stearns, *Science in the British Colonies of America* (Urbana, 1970), p. 128. Stearns provides a full survey of Winthrop's scientific activities on pp. 120-39.

8. See W. R. Carlton, "Overland to Connecticut in 1645: A Travel Diary of John Winthrop, Jr.," *New England Quarterly,* 13 (1940), 494-510.

9. Carlton, "Travel Diary," p. 505.

Lee Schweninger (essay date 1990)

SOURCE: Schweninger, Lee. "In Response to the Antinomian Controversy," "The Journal: A New Literature for a New World," and "Cheerful Submission to Authority: Miscellaneous and Later Writings." In *John Winthrop,* edited by Barbara Sutton, pp. 47-66; 87-98; 99-115. Boston: Twayne Publishers, 1990.

[*In the first essay that follows, Schweninger examines the Antinomian controversy, providing historical details to demonstrate the significance of Winthrop's writings on the subject. In the second, Schweninger considers Winthrop's* Journal *as a literary rather than historical document. In the third, Schweninger examines Winthrop's lesser-known writings, their contributions to the history of Massachusetts, and their influence on Winthrop's reputation as a writer.*]

IN RESPONSE TO THE ANTINOMIAN CONTROVERSY

One Mistris *Hutchinson* . . . a woman of a haughty and fierce carriage, of a nimble witt and active spirit, and a very voluble tongue, more bold then a man, though in understanding and judgement, inferiour to many women.

(*Short Story* [*of the rise, reign and ruin of the Antinomians, Familists & libertines. . . .; SS*], 262-63)

One of the greatest tests of John Winthrop's theory of a holy commonwealth knit together as one body came with the controversy over Anne Hutchinson and her right to differ with the authorities and to express those differences to the public. For this reason, of all the episodes of Winthrop's career, the Antinomian Controversy that raged in New England between 1636 and 1638 has received the most critical and historical attention. Critics, biographers, and historians are inevitably intrigued and troubled by the episode. Liberals judge Anne Hutchinson to be the governor's intellectual superior, and recognize a failure of justice in her banishment and excommunication. Edmund Morgan writes, for example, that "the force of her intelligence and character penetrate the libels and leave us angry with the writers and not with their intended victim."[1] Conservatives condemn Hutchinson as a contentious and proud troublemaker, a disrupter of the New Canaan.[2] In the drama of the controversy, Winthrop's part is overshadowed by the colorful and outspoken Anne Hutchinson, yet his published record of the trial of Hutchinson and his related journal entries provide the most important literary/historical sources for the controversy between the patriarchal, authoritarian church-state and Anne Hutchinson.

Daughter of the freethinking, somewhat radical schoolteacher and preacher Francis Marbury, Anne Hutchinson was born in rural Alford, England, one hundred miles due north of London, in 1591. Alford was her home until she was fourteen, at which time her father moved the family to London. In 1612 Anne married William Hutchinson, a wealthy Alford merchant, with whom she returned to Alford to bear and raise several children. She made special trips to St. Botolph's Church in Boston, Lincolnshire, where John Cotton lectured before he left for the Massachusetts Bay Colony. She evidently became spiritually enamored of Cotton's preaching and theology, and by 1634 she and her family had decided to move to the Bay Colony; they arrived in September of that year.

What finally prompted the family to give up their financial and social comforts in England and decide to settle in a new struggling colony remains a matter of speculation, but certainly the political, religious, and economic concerns of so many migrating Puritans in the 1630s played an important role in the Hutchinson family's decision to move to America.[3] According to Anne Hutchinson's testimony before the General Court in Massachusetts as Winthrop recorded it, however, she insisted that she came to New England in pursuit of her preacher and mentor, John Cotton: "The Lord carrying Mr. *Cotton* to *New England* (at which I was much troubled) it was revealed to me, that I must go thither also" (*SS,* 272).[4]

Anne Hutchinson's troubles with the church in New England began with her arrival in Boston Harbor in September 1634 on the *Griffin*. Her husband, William, was admitted at once into the Church at Boston; Anne's admission, however, was initially denied. Normally, husband and wife were admitted together, but in this case the authorities delayed the wife's admittance for a week because of certain comments she had been overheard to make before setting foot on New England soil. One of her shipmates, Reverend Zachariah Symmes,

evidently reported his uneasiness with her beliefs and kept her from joining the church until she could show a group of elders that her theology was sound.[5]

Despite a troublesome beginning, once established in New England Anne Hutchinson found herself immediately useful not only as homemaker for her own family, but as community midwife and healer as well; she was one of a few who knew how to mix herbs for medicinal purposes. She also found herself within a few months hosting weekly discussions pertaining to John Cotton's sermons, first with groups of women, then with mixed groups of men and women. The ostensible purpose of the meetings was to give members of the community the opportunity to discuss the meaning of Cotton's lectures. The meetings soon grew beyond mere recitations, however, and became the vehicle for the rise of what Winthrop called "Antinomianism." Hutchinson's group was by no means small or uninfluencial. Anne Hutchinson enjoyed the support of the young, newly elected governor, Henry Vane, and of the popular minister John Wheelwright, her brother-in-law. She and her supporters essentially divided Boston. In Winthrop's eyes that division threatened to disrupt the equilibrium and well-being of the entire colony.

By the time Winthrop makes his first journal entry concerning Hutchinson (21 October 1636), she had been in Boston just over two years and had become the leader of an active movement. As we can picture it, John Winthrop sat down at his desk not too long after beginning the second volume of his manuscript journal and wrote his first entry concerning Anne Hutchinson. He had known, or at least known of, Hutchinson since her arrival in September 1634. Indeed, she and her family built their house and settled literally across the street from the Winthrops. The governor begins his entry with characteristic understatement, but does carefully itemize the polity behind the dispute: "One Mrs. Hutchinson, a member of the church of Boston, a woman of ready wit and bold spirit, brought over with her two dangerous errors: 1. That the person of the Holy Ghost dwells in a justified person. 2. That no sanctification can help to evidence to us our justification.—From these two grew many branches; as, 1. Our union with the Holy Ghost, so as a Christian remains dead to every spiritual action, and hath no gifts nor graces, other than such as are in hypocrites, nor any other sanctification but the Holy Ghost himself" ([*A Journal of the Transactions and Occurrences in the Settlement of Massachusetts and the Other New-England Colonies, from the Year 1630 to 1644,*] *J,* 1:195-96). Winthrop's entry touches on crucial questions concerning the colonists' understanding of regeneration.[6]

Winthrop's literary outpouring in response to the Antinomian Controversy begins with this journal entry, but the governor's official account of the trials of

Hutchinson and her disciples was published in London in 1644, several years after the controversy and trials of 1637 and 1638. Within the same year it was republished as *A Short Story of the rise, reign, and ruine of the Antinomians, Familists and Libertines, that Infected the Churches of New England* (London, 1644).

The original title of Winthrop's version of the Hutchinson episode indicates the thrust of his account: *Antinomians and Familists Condemned by the Synod of Elders in New-England: With the Proceedings of the Magistrates against Them, and Their Apology for the Same* (London, 1644). Winthrop loads the title with pejorative terms, each of which effectively deprecates his adversaries. Etymologically, *antinomian* means "outside or against the name or law." Used by Winthrop, the term connotes those who stood opposed to the legalism of the Bible.

Understanding the intricacies of the Antinomian controversy depends on an acquaintance with several terms bandied about by the members of the religious community. *Legalism,* as Winthrop applied the concept, referred to strict conformity to the moral codes or law of the Bible. *Justification* was a term used to connote salvation or grace (in other words, a justified person was a visible saint, one preordained by God to grace). Antinomians maintained that because justification was free—that is, because it came as a gift of God that no one could otherwise acquire—ministers should not stress the performing of good works. Rather they should emphasize free justification, also referred to as the "Covenant of grace" as opposed to the "Covenant of works." Indeed, the Antinomians accused the orthodox ministers of preaching a doctrine of works rather than a doctrine of grace. Winthrop applied the term *sanctification* or preparation to this notion of growing or earning divine grace as a result of commitment to the biblical law or moral code. According to Winthrop, as an orthodox Calvinist, of course, man did not earn justification, but could prepare to receive grace. Winthrop saw sanctification as a necessary or concomitant part of a visible saint's life in preparation to receive grace. If saved or "of the elect," one would necessarily behave as a saint. The two notions, justification and sanctification in this sense, were in some ways so interdependent as to be indistinguishable.

To a large extent, the point of contention between the Antinomians and the orthodox New England Puritans rests on the distinction between free justification and sanctification (or grace and works). As evident in his conception of New England's covenant with God, Winthrop held that a person could not be justified and not show signs of sanctification; Anne Hutchinson is reputed to have held that because justification is free,

sanctification is of no concern in the eyes of God. Antinomians, including Hutchinson, relied on the power of the Holy Spirit, rather than on a moral code, to govern actions.

Winthrop thus addresses those who believed that if justification were free then sanctification (that is, behaving oneself according to biblical law and rule) had nothing, absolutely nothing, to do with one's being saved. The obvious danger of such a belief, reasons Winthrop, is that because of man's corrupt nature, it will inevitably lead to widespread immorality, licentiousness, and unnameable sins.

As Winthrop used the term in the 1630s, *familist* was a general term referring to those who relied on their own spiritual experience to interpret the Bible; that is, they believed in a direct communication between the individual and God. Like an Antinomian, a familist did not necessarily feel bound to the legalism of the Bible. The Massachusetts Bay officials feared that any such sect threatened their whole community, which was inextricably bound to upholding conduct based on the scriptural word. Because the Familists had a bad reputation in England, Winthrop gained an advantage over his opponents by associating Antinomians with Familists. Similarly, a *Libertine,* originally one who opposed the rigors of Calvinism, came to be associated with all kinds of religious freethinkers. Certainly an establishment based on conformity and dutiful practice—as was Winthrop's—did not admire or encourage freethinking in this sense.

The *Short Story* consists of several documents, some obviously not written by the governor. In addition to a long preface supplied by the Reverend Thomas Weld (who was in New England from 1632 until 1641), the collection includes a list of "erroneous opinions"; the petition that John Wheelwright's adherents devised; and Winthrop's narrative of the court cases against Wheelwright, his adherents, and Anne Hutchinson. The collection also includes Winthrop's description of Mary Dyer's "monstrous birth"; the justification of Wheelwright's censure, and a summary of Hutchinson's excommunication trial before the church. In addition to the *Short Story,* much of the history of the Antinomian Controversy can be gleaned from Winthrop's journal account of his response to the Hutchinson episode.

Winthrop had strong misgivings about the theology of Anne Hutchinson, but in 1636, as deputy governor, he could not effectively oppose her actions or reduce her influence. When she and her followers attempted to invite their colleague John Wheelwright to become an assistant teacher (that is, to accept ministerial duties) at the First Church and thereby officially establish within the system a cleric sympathetic to their views, however, the former governor became assertive. As he describes the confrontation in his journal, he "stood up and said, he could not consent." After all, he argued, the First Church already had two able ministers in John Wilson and John Cotton. Furthermore, the congregation did not know Wheelwright sufficiently well, and should not run the risk of inviting a disputatious teacher. Winthrop "thought it not fit (no necessity urging) to put the welfare of the church to the least hazard, as he feared they should do, by calling in one, whose spirit they knew not, and one who seemed to dissent in judgment." So Wheelwright was denied a position in Boston; instead, he was offered a position at a "new church, to be gathered at Mount Woolaston, now Braintree," ten miles south of Boston along a difficult road (*J*, 1:197). In other words, Winthrop had essentially disposed of Wheelwright as a threat to the community and had won a small skirmish. But the battles ahead promised to be more difficult.

In January 1637, John Cotton seems to have invited Wheelwright to speak to the congregation at the Boston church. His sermon occasioned further dissension among the churches of Massachusetts Bay and ultimately resulted in Wheelwright's banishment. In this fast-day sermon—delivered on January 1637, a day set aside to repent for dissensions in the New England churches—Wheelwright's doctrine is that "the only cause of the fasting of true beleevers is the absence of Christ".[7] (Public fast days were common in New England as a means of repentance for the entire population. Such days did not necessarily involve total abstinence.) To Winthrop and others of the establishment even the hint of Christ's absence must have seemed an affront. Did this man (Wheelwright) not scruple to say that Christ was absent from New England, the New Canaan, God's chosen land? The notion of God being displeased and departing from New England would eventually become a popular motif for the New England ministers, but in the 1630s this idea was unwelcome and certainly offended the leaders in the congregation.

What Winthrop and others actually took Wheelwright to task for was not his references to God's departure, however. Rather Wheelwright got in trouble because of his repeated use of the metaphor of combat. In the text he admits that he intends "spirituall combate," but goes on at some length about warfare, fighting, and battle. Specifically, he argues that "if we would have the Lord Jesus Christ to be aboundantly present with us, we must all of us prepare for battell and come out against the enimyes of the Lord, and if we do not strive, those under a covenant of works will prevaile."[8] Wheelwright also seems to advocate "combustion in the Church and common wealth. . . . I must confesse and acknowledge it will do so, but what then? did not Christ come to send fire upon the earth"? He also argues that those who fight for Christ "must be willing to lay downe [their] lives."[9]

Whether Wheelwright actually intended a literal battle must remain conjectural, but his rhetoric was powerful enough to frighten the establishment. As a result of his fiery sermon, the court banished Wheelwright, and the following November he left the jurisdiction of the colony. Winthrop and the others of the established authority had thus won another political battle. Nevertheless, the sermon epitomized the division among the members of the Boston congregation and made manifest the frail hold the establishment had on maintaining conformity and keeping a peaceful unity among colonists in the Puritan commonwealth.

Another major victory for the establishment was to come by way of the May elections. At the gathering for the election a group of Bostonians in support of Henry Vane demanded that before the election a petition relating to liberty and revoking Wheelwright's banishment be heard. As Winthrop records it, "There was great danger of tumult that day." As deputy governor, Winthrop insisted that the business of a court for election is restricted to the elections themselves: "So soon as the court was set . . . a petition was preferred by those of Boston. The present governor [Vane] would have read it, but the deputy governor [Winthrop] said it was out of order. It was a court for elections." After some debate, and evidently some fistfights, elections were held; Winthrop once again became governor and Henry Vane, as Winthrop notes glibly in his journal, was "left quite out" (*J*, 1:215).

As governor (reelected in May 1637), Winthrop had the authority he had earlier lacked to deal with the Antinomians. He took immediate steps to set the colony back on its feet, writing in his journal that the "Magistrates set forth an apology to justify the sentence of the court against Mr. Wheelwright." In what is a sure sign of Winthrop's leniency and political savvy, the court granted Wheelwright a period until the following August (1637) to reform his error. Winthrop thereby hoped that the court's "moderation and desire for reconciliation might appear to all" (*J*, 1:216, 218).

Included in Winthrop's **Short Story** is the justification of the court's censure of Wheelwright. In it Winthrop summarizes the steps the court took and explains the court's reasons for those actions. The purpose was to clear the justice of the court and to satisfy those "to whom this case may be otherwise presented by fame or misreport." The court's opinion was that Wheelwright "had run into sedition and contempt of the Civil authority." (*SS*, 290, 289). The establishment ministers felt that they had been described as ones who advocated a covenant of works. As is characteristic of Winthrop's reporting, his account of the proceedings is detailed. He lists several reasons to demonstrate that the court was justified in banishing Wheelwright. Some of these reasons are that he knew he was inciting contention and that he went against Cotton's injunction about peace on a fast day. Uncharacteristically, Winthrop turns to classical authors such as Tully, Isidore, and Vergil (a turn which might suggest that Winthrop was not sole author of this tract) to define sedition, but he also refers to scripture to corroborate this definition. Returning to Wheelwright, Winthrop writes that "hee did intend to trouble our peace, and hee hath effected it; therefore it was a contempt of that authority which required every man to study Peace and Truth, and therefore it was a seditious contempt, in that hee stirred up others, to join in the disturbance of that peace, which he was bound by solemn oath to preserve" (*SS,* 294).

Because Winthrop governed and wrote in an age before the notion of freedom of speech was established, certainly before it was considered an inalienable right, he could simply respond to the objection that the court could not tell a minister what to preach by answering that it is the court's prerogative to "limit him what he may not teach" (*SS,* 295). Specifically, the court could forbid his preaching heresy or sedition. In response to the objection concerning the lack of a trial by jury, Winthrop answered according to his philosophy of the magistrates' authority: the court makes its law, is subject to no others, and has as its sole guiding principle truth and justice. A typical Puritan, Winthrop believed that a good ruler was virtually incorruptible; after all, magistrates received their authority from God and so governed by divine right. In Winthrop's mind there would be no question of the court not acting in a fair manner because it had the welfare of the state and church as its sole motive.[10]

In concluding his account of Wheelwright's banishment, Winthrop returned to his definition of sedition. Wheelwright did tend to the "great hinderance of public utility" and was therefore guilty of sedition (*SS,* 299). Such a judicial procedure might be difficult for a twentieth-century reader to accept without realizing that Winthrop was writing in the 1630s, an age when the Bill of Rights and free speech were still more than 150 years in the future. Judged in light of his contemporaries, Winthrop was in fact lenient in that he was more than willing to give Wheelwright the opportunity to reform and thereafter remain within the colony's jurisdiction. Nevertheless, in a community where all were to be bound together in one body, each limb and part helping the other, Winthrop could not allow the holding and spreading of doctrine so contrary to that of the establishment.

In September 1637 the ministers organized a synod in which they drew up the list of errors to be attributed to the Antinomians. In his preface to Winthrop's *Short Story,* Thomas Weld offers a description of the synod: "*we had an Assembly of all the Ministers and learned men in the whole Countrey, which held for three weeks*

together, at Cambridge . . . *the magistrates sitting present all that time, as hearers, and speakers also when they saw fit.*" The populace at large was also given liberty to attend and participate as long as they observed "due order." As Weld describes the synod, the members spent one week confuting "*loose opinions*" and two weeks "*in a plaine Syllogisticall dispute*" (*SS,* 212, 213).

The result or product of the synod was the drawing up of eighty-two, numbered, erroneous opinions with a confutation of each one. As should be expected, the refutation comes from scripture; in almost every case the erroneous opinion was found to be contrary to Scripture, and Scripture was used to point out the error. If, for example, the error concerned the belief that "those that bee in Christ are not under the Law, and commands of the word, as the rule of life," the confutation would read that it "is contrary to the Scriptures, which direct us to the Law and to the Testimony" (*SS,* 220). The list is part of the *Short Story* and is, of course, not of Winthrop's sole authorship (although he most likely had a hand in establishing the various errors). According to Philip Gura, the errors can be arranged into three major classes. One class pertains specifically to one of the most immediate questions facing the rulers of the Bay Colony, questions about the Antinomian controversy itself: "beliefs in the primacy of the Spirit over the injunctions of Scripture." The second concerns the ability of a justified person to know the condition of another. The third class covers that group of opinions that challenge the authority of the ministers.[11]

The synod met during September 1637; in November of that year the court brought Anne Hutchinson to trial. Winthrop and his fellow magistrates had already dealt with many of her group, banishing Wheelwright and dealing harshly with others. Her other most powerful ally, Henry Vane, had left the colony to return to England. Thus she stood alone on a November morning before the court, ready to face her accusers.

Winthrop's characterization of Hutchinson is fascinating both for its vigor and for what it tells us about the author and his times. The others disfranchised, banished, or disabled "were but young branches, sprung out of an old root"; that root was Mistress Hutchinson, "a woman of haughty and fierce carriage, of a nimble wit and active spirit, and a very voluble tongue, more bold then any man, though in understanding and judgment, inferiour to many women" (*SS,* 262-63). The description informs us of Winthrop's animosity toward her; it also suggests that he was subject to the sexism and biases of his time. Hutchinson's understanding of the fine differences of theological opinion was obviously acute, and if Winthrop is referring to them he is simply dissembling. In her understanding and judgment of a woman's role and proper place in seventeenth-century Puritan New England, certainly she was not deficient, but of that role she was undoubtedly defiant.

Winthrop adds that she "had learned her skil in *England*" (*SS*, 263). It is politically important for the governor of New England to intimate that her erroneous opinions did not, in fact could not, originate in the New Canaan. Rather, he suggests that she brought them with her, already hatched and nurtured in the corruption of old England. As proof he cites the opinions she expressed on the ship before even setting foot in New England. Alertly he adds that the Boston church was hesitant to admit her. To justify the church's ultimate admission of her, Winthrop explains that "shee cunningly dissembled and coloured her opinions." Further, she "easily insinuated her selfe into the affections of many." Winthrop's own insinuation is that much like a serpent she slid subtly through the Boston garden. Certainly the governor was aware of the seventeenth-century connotation of *insinuate* as "to introduce by subtle means," implying the agent's subversion and infection. Through the tone and diction Winthrop further reprobates his adversary. Although he gives her credit for helping with the "publick ministery," he turns it to his own advantage: "But when she had thus prepared the way by such wholesome truths, then she begins to set forth her own stuffe" (*SS*, 263). Winthrop does not mince words here; in seventeenth-century English, *stuff* commonly referred to a worthless idea or nonsense. Winthrop's diction is clearly pejorative in his opening description of the woman and her ideas.

In the course of his characterization of Hutchinson, Winthrop justifies his complaint by citing her teachings. Theologically the difference between her and the establishment lay in her insistence that "no sanctification was any evidence of a good estate, except their justification were first cleared up to them by the immediate wittnesse of the Spirit." According to Winthrop, the negative consequence of this opinion is twofold. First, she was subverting the authority of the colony, church, and state. Second, she was inciting others: "many prophane persons became of her opinion, for it was a very easie and acceptable way to heaven." Winthrop feared that her opinions would become manifest in the people's backsliding. Formerly godly people would fall under her persuasion, and "indeed most of her new tenents tended toward slothfulnesse" (*SS*, 263, 264).

The primary charges against Hutchinson were that she taught against the ministers of the commonwealth and that she argued for the primacy of the spirit over the Scripture. Winthrop also attributed to Hutchinson "the utter subversion both of Churches and civill state." At the December 1636 session of the General Court, the Pastor John Wilson made "a very sad speech on the condition of our churches" (*J*, 1:204). This "free and faithfull speech in the Court," as Winthrop called it,

caused Wilson much consternation. He was called to answer publicly. Winthrop blames Hutchinson for occasioning the speech and for causing Wilson's embarrassment: "Thence sprang all that trouble to the Pastour of *Boston*." In addition to causing problems for Wilson and the magistrates, Hutchinson received the blame for corrupting John Wheelwright, who before her influence "was wont to teach in a plaine and gentle style" (*SS*, 265).

Winthrop's ultimate argument against Hutchinson emerges as a political struggle for survival. According to the governor, the fate of the colony was at stake; Hutchinson threatened to destroy the principle of the state as one body knit together by love. She threatened to divide the state and church into factions that could not even coexist, much less develop into a model community, a holy commonwealth.

Twentieth-century students of the Antinomian Controversy generally find fault with Winthrop. Edmund Morgan, for example, who is generally sympathetic toward the governor, calls the trial "the least attractive episode of Winthrop's career." The documents reveal "a proud, brilliant woman put down by men who had judged her in advance." David D. Hall even maintains that "Mrs. Hutchinson parried the accusations of her examiners with a wit and verve that reduced them to confusion."[12] The consensus appears to be that the controversy stands as a prime indication of the authorities' total intolerance of any belief but their own. According to Philip Gura, however, "the magistrates' and ministers' responses to Anne Hutchinson and her sympathizers must be seen not as a stubborn defense of long-held principles but as the consequence of the colony's process of self-definition."[13]

One of the major threats of Hutchinson, besides her inciting discontent or dissatisfaction with the New England ministers was—according to Winthrop—that if works played absolutely no part in justification, as Hutchinson argued, then godly living, modeling one's behavior on Christ's, obeying the commandments Moses brought down from Sinai, and even having faith, had no authority whatsoever. For the Puritan, the Scripture was the law; it proscribed life and death. The business of the Puritan ministers was to interpret those texts to the best of their ability for the lay congregation. Hutchinson threatened the whole evangelical principle with its emphasis on the authority of Scripture and the importance of preaching. She challenged the authority of both Scripture and ministers. The patriarchy in the seventeenth century would allow no person, and certainly no woman, to exercise that power.

Winthrop's description of the trial itself constitutes a section of his ***Short Story***. Whereas Winthrop briefly summarized the other cases, he gives specific detail of the Hutchinson case, even paraphrasing several of her statements. Winthrop's report is one of very few accounts that is supposed to record Hutchinson's actual words. In the absence of any of her own writing, this account is historically invaluable. Though the court may well have condemned Hutchinson before she entered the Cambridge meetinghouse where her trial was held, Winthrop began by pointing out that the purpose was for her either to acknowledge and reform her faults or to suffer the court's punishment: "that we may take such course with you as you may trouble us no further" (*SS*, 266). The court was trying her, after all, for causing public disturbances; for holding "erroneous opinions"; for broaching those opinions; for encouraging sedition; for "casting reproach upon the faithfull Ministers" and thereby weakening them and raising prejudice against them; and for maintaining public meetings even though the court had explicitly condemned them.

After Winthrop's introductory remark, the court seems to have proceeded in a somewhat unorganized, even haphazard, way. One of the charges brought against Hutchinson concerned her public meetings. The court accused her for teaching, an act reserved in Puritan society exclusively for men. According to Winthrop's account, Hutchinson defended herself by saying that she and her group did no more than "read the notes of our teachers Sermons, and then reason of them by searching the Scriptures." She supported herself by reference to the "men of *Berea* [who] are commended for examining *Pauls* Doctrine" (*SS*, 268). The court's charge, according to Winthrop, was that she did not search Scriptures to confirm, rather she used Scriptures to declare the teacher's meaning or even to correct the teacher. Winthrop condemned the principle of independent thought by members of the congregation because such thought could be dangerous to the homogeneity of the community.

Hutchinson's "ready wit" is evident in her response to the court's challenge that she has no rule from the Bible for teaching as she does:

Court

    Yet you shew us not a rule.

Hutch.

    I have given you two places of Scripture.

Court

    But neither of them will sute your practise.

Hutch

    Must I shew my name written therein?

                    (*SS*, 269)

Winthrop's record of the trial differs here somewhat from the anonymous account of her examination. The discussion, according to that anonymous report, concluded with Winthrop stating that the magistrates would not allow her to hold meetings. She responded that if "it please you by authority to put it down I will freely let you for I am subject to your authority."[14] The difference between the two accounts is significant because it suggests that Winthrop might have allowed his politics to interfere with his record of all the facts. Which account of the trial is closer to the truth remains a mystery because no one can ever know exactly what words were actually spoken in the court, but the comparison reveals that Winthrop might have deliberately decided to omit Hutchinson's submission to his and the court's authority. Winthrop's version does not conceal the fact that Hutchinson was witty, however. It makes clear her ability to argue intelligently with her prosecutors, an ability Winthrop seemed to deny her in his description of her character.

Besides charging her with inciting discontent by her teaching and questioning the doctrine of the Bay ministers, the court accused her of reviling several of the ministers. After excepting Cotton and Wheelwright, she maintained that the New England ministers "could not hold forth a Covenant of free Grace, because they had not the Seal of the Spirit, and that they were not able Ministers of the New Testament" (*SS*, 270). By "seal of the spirit," Hutchinson meant that the new England ministers lacked the figurative mark or seal that signified the permanent indwelling of the Holy Spirit. Without such a seal they were not able ministers of the New Testament and therefore unfit to preach. Winthrop would not tolerate such a reproach of the ministers. According to Winthrop's version, she denied the charge, but the ministers, whom the court had asked to be present for that purpose, affirmed it. After their affirmation, Hutchinson confessed and, according to Winthrop's account, repeated her reproach.

Winthrop's account of the court's proceedings of the following morning portrays the defendant as the antagonist. Hutchinson requested that the ministers "might be sworn to what they had spoken" and declared that an "oath is the end of all controversy" (*SS*, 270). In other words, she simply requested that the ministers take an oath swearing to the truth of their previous testimony. Because they recognized the seriousness of taking such an oath, the ministers were extremely reluctant. If they could not be absolutely sure of what they had said months before, they ran the risk of committing blasphemy. Were they to take the oath and then be proven false, they would surely be liable to the charge of being unworthy ministers, and they would also have broken the third commandment, "Thou shalt not take the name of the Lord thy God in vain, for the LORD will not hold him guiltless that taketh his name in vain"

(Exodus 20:7). On this possibility of blasphemy rested Hutchinson's hope.

Whereas the anonymous account records in great detail the arguments over the oath-taking, Winthrop cleverly and politically pauses briefly on this aspect of the trial to state that "All this would not satisfie Mistris *Hutchinson,* but she still called to have them sworne, whereupon the Court being weary of the clamour, and that all mouths might be stopped, required three of the Ministers to take an oath" (*SS,* 271). The chronology of events as Winthrop records them differs significantly from that related in the anonymous account of the examination. According to Winthrop, the oath-taking preceded Hutchinson's confession about her receiving divine revelations. According to the "Examination" record, the ministers did not swear until the very end, that is, not before Hutchinson had already ruined any chance she might have had to obtain the court's leniency or forgiveness. According to Winthrop's chronology, the ministers took their oath just after Cotton's testimony. If this were the case, the ministers would have been taking a much greater risk, and their oaths would have carried more weight. If they did not swear until after Hutchinson described her revelations, the oaths would have been uncontested and therefore virtually meaningless; the defendant was by her own admission by then irremediably convicted.

The account of Cotton's testimony sheds further light on the governor's method of composition. Winthrop is vague on Cotton's actual testimony where it did not seem to fit the court's wishes and conclusions. For example, Cotton stated (according to the anonymous version) that as far as he could recollect, he "did not find her saying they were under a covenant of works, nor that she said they did preach a covenant of works."[15] In a sense Cotton here defended Hutchinson effectively, and any charge on this score would have to be dropped. Ultimately Hutchinson was to convict herself not on the grounds of causing sedition or of overstepping a woman's bounds in teaching and interpreting the scripture, but by revealing that she had a direct spiritual communion with God. Knowing this as he writes his own account of the trial, Winthrop blithely concludes the reference to Cotton's testimony by stating that "Mr. *Cotton* did in a manner agree with the testimony of the rest of the Elders" (*SS,* 271).

The irony of the case against Hutchinson is that even though the court could do little about her teaching, or her being a woman, or her disagreement with the ministers, the court could condemn her for her confession of immediate, divine revelation. Evidently on her own initiative she enumerated the various times she had experienced revelations. Her coming to New England "was revealed" to her as was her knowledge that the magistrates in New England would prosecute her. Of her

prosecutors she knew "that for this you goe about to do to me, God will ruine you and your posterity, and this whole State" (*SS,* 273).

Winthrop seems to have been aware of this irony and to have delighted at the opportunity it provided the court to dispose of its arch-enemy with impunity: "Mistris *Hutchinson* having thus freely and fully discovered her selfe, the Court and all the rest of the Assembly (except those of her owne party) did observe a speciall providence of God, that . . . her owne mouth should deliver her into the power of the Court, as guilty of that which all suspected her for, but were not furnished with proofe sufficient to proceed against her" (*SS,* 274). According to Winthrop's account, the governor realized what she was saying when she began, foresaw the inevitable result of such a speech, and so he tried to cut her off: "The Governour perceiving whereabout she went [self-incrimination?] interrupted her . . . but seeing her very unwilling to be taken off, he permitted her to proceed" (*SS,* 271). According to the anonymous "Examination," there is no clue as to when, where, or even if Winthrop tried to stop her from speaking about her immediate revelations.[16]

So speak she did. She spoke until Winthrop could say that "the revelation she brings forth is delusion," and he could have the court cry out in agreement.[17] She proceeded until, as Winthrop narrates it, "The Court saw now an inevitable necessity to rid her away, except wee would bee guilty, not only of our own ruine, but also of the Gospel, so in the end the sentence of banishment was pronounced against her, and shee was committed to the Marshall, till the Court should dispose of her" (*SS,* 276). As the court passed its sentence, Hutchinson—defeated but still proud and forthright—asked why she was banished. Winthrop replied: "Say no more, the court knows wherefore and is satisfied."[18] Here again Winthrop's version omits this apparent exchange, one that does not show the prosecutor in a very favorable light.

The court may well have been satisfied, for it had just rid itself of the greatest internal threat since the colony's inception in 1630. Whether or not the court was satisfied with Hutchinson's banishment, however, the community had still to deal with Hutchinson's constituency. So although Winthrop had passed the sentence of banishment in November, Hutchinson was allowed to remain, imprisoned in the home of Thomas Weld's brother, in the Boston area (Roxbury) until the season "might be fit, and safe for her departure" (*SS,* 300). In an effort to shame her even further than the court had done, the elders of the Boston church called her to an excommunication hearing in March 1638. This trial was to be her final humiliation in Boston and a lesson to any who might continue to support her beliefs. The final section of Winthrop's ***Short Story*** is his account of this church trial.[19]

Hutchinson's confinement through the winter of 1637-38 had not kept her ideas—heresies, according to Winthrop's report—from circulating among some members of the congregations. In vain, several orthodox ministers had visited her in what the ministers maintained were efforts to bring her from her errors. In March the elders of the church sent for her to stand an interrogation. On the Thursday lecture day, 15 March 1638, Anne Hutchinson began her last defense against the commonwealth and the church of Boston. Thursdays were generally set aside as days for public lectures by the clergy. In this sense, Hutchinson's excommunication trial would serve as a public lesson. As Winthrop writes, "she came not into the Assembly till the Sermon and Prayer were ended (pretending bodily infirmity) when she was come, one of the ruling Elders called her forth before the Assembly" (*SS,* 301).

Winthrop's **Short Story** includes a list of the twenty-nine errors that explain "why the Church had called her." Few of the twenty-nine were ever actually brought up in the sessions preceding her excommunication, but Winthrop maintained the list to be correct, stating that she acknowledged she had spoken all of them. Many of the errors relate to Hutchinson's apparently recent concern with death and resurrection, beginning with the first which reads "That the soules of all men (in regard of generation) are mortall like the beasts" (*SS,* 301).[20] Many of the errors concern body, soul, and spirit and questions about union with Christ at death. Several others in the list have to do more specifically with evidence of grace, and still others concern law and works. For example, in errors 13 and 23, Hutchinson was accused of holding that the laws of Scripture are not binding: "The Law is no rule of life to a Christian," and "We are not bound to the Law, no not as a rule of Life" (*SS,* 302). The repetition suggests the haste with which the errors were drawn up, and the accusation itself hardly seems fair given what is known about Hutchinson's knowledge of and devotion to the Bible.

Winthrop summarizes the two days (the two lecture days the trial lasted), relating that Hutchinson was not entrapped by the ministers who visited her, as she claimed, but that they had come "in compassion to her soule, to help her out of those snares of the Devill." The governor, who was in attendance at the trial but who played little part, drew a picture of the accused as stubborn and obstinate; despite the learned ministers' arguments against her opinions, "shee still persisted in her errour, giving forward speeches to some that spake to her" (*SS,* 303, 304).

After a week's recess, Hutchinson returned to the second and last session against her. In the intervening week John Cotton and John Davenport had evidently made some progress with her, for she acknowledged "her error in all the Articles (except the last)" (*SS,* 305). She

wrote down her answers to them all. (Alas, that manuscript is lost.) According to Winthrop, she did so well in her responses that "the Assembly conceived hope of her repentance." Such hope was short-lived, however, because many of her answers proved unsatisfactory. Further, writes Winthrop, she argued that she "had not been of that judgement, that there is no inherent reghteousnesse in the Saints." John Cotton gave her over at this point, for despite his admonition the previous week and his long week's conference with her in his home between sessions, she was "maintaining of untruth" (*SS,* 306, 307). Cotton left the matter to her pastor. That pastor, John Wilson, perhaps Hutchinson's most bitter enemy, attacked her viciously. According to the anonymous report of the church trial, he spoke harshly: 'I doe account you from this time forth to be a Hethen and a Publican and soe to be held of all the Brethren and Sisters of this Congregation, and of others. Therefore I *command you* in the name of Christ Jesus and of the Church *as a Leper to withdraw your selfe out of the Congregation.*"[21] So much for a community knit together in a mutual bond of affection. In his version of the church trial, Winthrop did not record Wilson's vituperative final words. The attack, according to Winthrop, was much less vindictive, in that the governor placed blame on Hutchinson herself. Even though she heard some argue on her behalf "that she might have a further respite, yet she herself never desired it" (*SS,* 307). Indeed, Winthrop seems to have been very insistent about having Hutchinson convict and sentence herself.

The governor did set down, without interpretive comment, Hutchinson's final words, however: "In her going forth, one standing at the dore, said, The Lord sanctifie this unto you, to whom she made answer, The Lord judgeth not as man judgeth, better to be cast out of the Church then to deny Christ" (*SS,* 307). Winthrop's motive in including this final outburst might have been to suggest that Hutchinson's former supporters in the Boston congregation had deserted her and turned against her, signifying the total victory of the state and church against such a major and potentially devastating threat as Hutchinson was. Perhaps, too, Winthrop included a description of Hutchinson's exit in this final scene to suggest just how misled the woman was. Certainly in Winthrop's and the church's sense of propriety, Hutchinson was cast out because she seemed to be denying Christ. In the context of Hutchinson's departure, Winthrop did not include the fact that one faithful adherent, Mary Dyer, did rise to join her teacher, nurse, and soul mate as she walked out of the meeting house for the last time.[22]

One can hardly read the history of Anne Hutchinson without the compulsion to feel sorry for her and to want to side with her against the combined forces of the establishments of church and state. The temptation is to see in Hutchinson's trials the noble attributes of a spirit of resistance, an independence of thought, and a pursuit of truth that characterize only a very few. Hutchinson traveled to the New World full of hope and excitement. She had a dream of a holy commonwealth in union with the church just as did the New England patriarchy. The problem was that Hutchinson's vision, conception, and interpretation of that holy commonwealth invited faction, dispute, and the questioning of authority. John Winthrop's vision did not. He rested his hopes on conformity and acceptance of authority. Thus, Hutchinson was to him and his community a dire threat. She had to be disposed of for the good of the colony. Hutchinson was a woman before her time.

With the spring weather in late March 1638, Hutchinson journeyed to Portsmouth—in what is now Rhode Island. There she rejoined her husband and others of her family and friends. Several months later she suffered the miscarriage of a hydatidiform mole,[23] news of which further inspired Winthrop to point out the Lord's displeasure with his former neighbor. In 1642, shortly after her husband's death, Hutchinson and her six youngest children moved to the Dutch settlement on Long Island. The next year she and her family—except for one daughter—were killed by a group of Indians reclaiming the land that European settlers had previously taken from them.

Judging by subsequent journal entries, Winthrop's concern with Hutchinson and her adherents did not end with her banishment and excommunication. Several later journal entries, for example, indicate that the Hutchinson affair had deeply troubled him and his notion of a holy commonwealth. He spent much mental energy trying to justify his actions by recording the divine providences against his antagonist.

The Antinomian Controversy inspired Winthrop to write extensively in various genres. Besides the historical account that was subsequently published as the **Short Story,** he wrote two theological essays, which his friend and guide Reverend Thomas Shepard convinced him not to circulate and which he evidently destroyed. As we have seen, the episode might also have motivated him to write his **"Christian Experience"** in an effort to convince himself of his own trials, sanctification, and ultimate justification. He engaged in a manuscript debate with Henry Vane in the winter of 1636-37. In May he wrote a tract in defense of the court's order of limiting immigration depending on the immigrants' qualification, following it up with a further defense in response to comments by Vane. In response to many members of the Church of Boston "being highly offended with the governor" for the proceedings of the court against Hutchinson (*J,* 1:256), Winthrop wrote an **"Essay Against the Power of the Church to Sit in Judgment on the Civil Magistracy"** (November 1637).

In the essay Winthrop argues that the "Church hath not power to Call any Civill Magistrate, to give Account of his Juditiall proceedinge in any Court of civill Justice" ([**Winthrop Papers**] **WP,** 3:505). Relying on biblical precedent, he outlines the reasons the church does not and should not have such a power. In his journal history of New England, Winthrop kept track of the developments of the Antinomian Controversy and even reported on Hutchinson's movements after she left the Massachusetts Bay Colony. The journal was to record the important events of the colony.

. . . . .

THE JOURNAL: A NEW LITERATURE FOR A NEW WORLD

> In the meantime most of our people went on shore upon the land of Cape Ann, which lay very near us, and gathered store of fine strawberries.
>
> (***Winthrop's Journal,*** 1:50)

As a history of the first twenty years of the Massachusetts Bay Colony in New England, Winthrop's journal is invaluable. Indeed, many historians have utilized Winthrop's journal extensively as one of the major sources for the early history of the colony. In the surge of attention to its merit as history, however, critics have paid surprisingly little attention to the work for its own sake. Richard Dunn, like other editors before him, has written about the composition of the journals and has compared Winthrop's journal with other, contemporary histories of settlements in the New World.[24] Barbara McCrimmon has written briefly about the publication history and has discussed some of the topics of Winthrop's journal.[25] In her study *Before the Convention,* M. Susan Power describes Winthrop's journal and discusses its symbolic content in relation to his sermon "A Modell of Christian Charity," arguing that whereas the "Modell" theorizes about a preconceived system, the journal records Winthrop's actual, ultimately vain efforts to build the commonwealth the shipboard lay-sermon promised.[26]

Winthrop's journal does seem to have a purpose beyond the mere recording of the first twenty years of the Massachusetts Bay Colony. Perry Miller formulated a definite purpose for Winthrop and his contemporary New England historians. According to Miller, "the entire purpose of the New England historians [was to] chronicle the providence of God in the settlement of New England."[27] Whether or not Miller is guilty of overgeneralization, the story Winthrop tells in his journal is undeniably permeated with ideas and the exposition of values reaching beyond the mere record of fact. Winthrop's journal both records the triumphs and calamities of an entire community and thematically reports one writer's hopes, trials, successes, and disappointments. Winthrop's "History of New England," as he characterized the journal himself on the first page of the third volume, is one important marker on the path that leads to a distinct American literature.

If trials are to be a major subject and overcoming them a theme, Winthrop's opening entries are certainly appropriate. The first major trial the writer faced was to cross the Atlantic Ocean. The journal opens with a minute account of the sea crossing, so minute in fact that Charles Banks was able to use it to chart what he supposes to be the actual route the *Arbella* and the rest of the fleet took in the spring of 1630.[28] As new as the sea venture was to the Puritans, Winthrop evidently did have a model for his description of an Atlantic crossing. After journeying to New England a year earlier, Francis Higginson had sent back to England his "True Relation of the Last Voyage to New England" (1629), and Winthrop seems to have had a copy of it sent to his wife at Groton.[29] On 8 April 1630 after a week's delay in the waters off Southampton, the *Arbella* set sail.

As Banks's account demonstrates, part of Winthrop's purpose must have been to provide a document by which subsequent voyagers could navigate the Atlantic, but he also provided a help to later emigrants in understanding the perils and knowing what to expect in crossing the sea, such as attacks from enemy or pirate vessels, storms, and calms. Beyond these pragmatic functions, Winthrop's sea-journal provides a fascinating account of a landsman's concerns while at sea for the first time. Perhaps most striking is the landlubber's obsession with the wind. All but one of the seventy-eight entries in the sea-journal mention the wind—the lifeblood, as it were, of a seventeenth-century ocean-going ship. Not only did Winthrop's immediate physical safety depend upon the wind, but so did the future of his colony. Thus it is not surprising that of the entries Winthrop wrote at sea, all mention the wind, all but about five begin with a description of the wind, and many entries deal exclusively with the wind and weather.[30]

After threats from supposed enemy vessels, storms, and calms, the sea-weary Puritans sighted land on 6 June 1630. On 12 June, Winthrop fails to mention wind for the first time during the voyage: "About four in the morning we were near our port" (*J,* 1:49).[31] Now that the wind had brought ship and passengers safely across the Atlantic to the New England garden, Winthrop must have felt that he was near his new home and that the wind was not the major concern it had been for the previous eleven weeks.

The wind was both friend and foe, friend as it carried the *Arbella* and other ships safely across the Atlantic, foe as it also brought with it deadly storms or withheld itself in equally threatening calms. From the shore, Winthrop characterizes the weather as another antago-

nist in his narrative of the colony. In the early years, he wrote repeatedly of the severe New England storms, heat waves, and cold spells. The first winter seems to have been particularly extreme. In February Winthrop recorded the freezing of the rivers, boating mishaps, deaths due to weather, and the severity of the wind: "this day the wind came N. W., very strong, and some snow withal, but so cold as some had their fingers frozen, and danger to be lost" (*J,* 1:55). In August 1632, Winthrop recorded a tempest that prevented sailing. The summer was "wet and cold" (*J,* 1:89). The summer and fall of 1634 were evidently hot and dry. The following winter is remembered by an "extraordinary tempest of wind and snow." Indeed, "the weather was many times so tedious as people could not travel" (*J,* 1:143). Winthrop reports that hurricanes would occasionally threaten destruction as well. In one instance he records the uprooting of trees, overturning of houses, and the grounding of ships. Winthrop peppers his journal with such reports, indicating that one of the many obstacles the valiant colonists had to overcome was adverse weather. There is never any doubt, however, that with God's help overcome it they will. After one particularly vicious storm, for example, Winthrop writes that "there did appear a miraculous providence in their preservation" (*J,* 1:156).

Turning from the Atlantic crossing and the weather, Winthrop found room in his journal to record that "there came a smell off the shore like the smell of a garden." Shortly after the passengers came within reach of the land they had been yearning for, Winthrop continued the garden imagery in a description of the passengers leaving ship: "most of our people went on shore upon the land of Cape Ann, which lay very near us, and gathered store of fine strawberries" (*J,* 1:47, 50).

As paradisaical as these entries are, Winthrop provided few descriptions of this newfound paradise in the following months. Shortly after arriving, he took up the business of beginning a city from scratch, an endeavor that seems to have taken all his time and energy; the journal is blank concerning the details about the settling of Boston, just as it had been blank concerning life aboard a ship. What the passengers did with their time or the governor with his must be projected from consideration of other accounts. Winthrop gave little space to the mundane projects of building houses, planting crops, and setting out gardens. He neglected the mundane because he intended to create a public record of the settling of a holy commonwealth, and he hoped to provide political propaganda for the enhancement of the colony. Certainly it was important to him to record the moral and religious aspects of the settlement, not the daily activities of mere mortal men and women. An implied theme of the journal seems to be that despite all the trials that the colonists were to face in coming years, Winthrop's opus would assert the colony's success.

Each potentially cataclysmic threat would be introduced, overcome, and disposed of. Even though Satan is always at work, Winthrop would write, the commonwealth would pursue its course in becoming that city on a hill.

Consistent with the public-document nature of the journal, the governor's first entries after the arrival of the *Arbella* record the coming of the other ships, whose safe arrivals were certainly seen to be a positive omen for the establishment of the colony. Indeed, after listing the week's arrivals, Winthrop noted that the company "kept a day of thanksgiving in all the plantations" (*J,* 1:51). The list of arrivals also anticipated a matter that was to become crucial to the colony, that of emigration. The arrival of ships for the first few years meant more colonists, bringing money and buying the goods the New Englanders could provide them. The more the arrival of ships helped the community, the more important it was for Winthrop to record the fact. In this way the journal becomes a public statement of the colony's economic self-sufficiency.

In the first months Winthrop recorded arrivals, deaths, fires, boating mishaps, and severity of the weather. He did not create his first extended narrative until December 1630 when he tells of an accident at sea. The entry immortalizes Richard Garrett, a shoemaker, by recounting the story of his attempt to sail to Plymouth in midwinter. After shipwreck caused by ice and severe weather, Garrett and most of the boat's party died of exposure or frostbite. With this account, Winthrop ushered in what was to become one of the most distinctive characteristics of his journal, the narrative with an implied or merely insinuated moral. In this case since the shoemaker had attempted to make his journey "against the advice of his friends," the narrative reiterates Winthrop's emphasis on the importance of people banding and staying together. The same might be said for the colony as a whole. Returning to Boston, Garrett's daughter's "boat was well-manned, the want whereof before was the cause of their loss" (*J,* 1:55, 56).

The notion of being well-manned in the New England wilderness is a theme Winthrop seemed to think he could not stress forcefully enough. One of the conditions of immigration, according to the Cambridge Agreement written and signed in England in 1629, was that the commitment to come to New England was binding because each member of the new community depended desperately on all the others. Therefore, Winthrop could not tolerate those who chose to return to England or leave the Bay Company's jurisdiction. To a large extent, Winthrop avoided even mentioning colonists' departures or their desire to depart, but in one instance he notes how even the thought of better times in old England could be dangerous: "It hath been always observed here, that such as fell into discontent, and lingered after their former conditions in England, fell into the scurvy and died" (*J,* 1:58).

If merely thinking about the comforts of a former home in England could result in scurvy or death, actually deserting by traveling back to the mother country could invite catastrophe: "Of those which went back in the ships this summer, for fear of death or famine, etc., many died by the way and after they were landed, and other fell very sick and low" (*J,* 1:58). Winthrop here early established a theme that would recur throughout the history. He lamented the departure of members of the colony. Since such departures did not speak well for the community, he rarely mentioned them except to note the misfortune that befell the deserters. The New England patriot must have been especially upset at the hastening away of John Humfrey, four ministers, and a schoolmaster in December 1641. In September 1642 he records the trials of their voyage back to England with this preface: "The sudden fall of land and cattle, and the scarcity of foreign commodities, and money, etc., with the thin access of people from England, put many into an unsettled frame of spirit, so as they concluded there would be no subsisting here, and accordingly they began to hasten away, some to the West Indies, others to the Dutch, at Long Island . . . and others back for England." For those who abandoned the godly enterprise in New England, Winthrop had little sympathy. Indeed, he seems almost to have thrived on their misfortune, writing that although it "pleased the Lord to spare their lives . . . yet the Lord followed them on shore. Some were exposed to great straits and found no entertainment, their friends forsaking them. One had a daughter that presently ran mad, and two other of his daughters, being under ten years of age, were discovered to have been often abused by divers lewd persons, and filthiness in his family. The schoolmaster had no sooner hired an house, and gotten in some scholars, but the plague set in, and took away two of his own children" (*J,* 2:82-83).

Besides describing the dangers of defecting and returning to England, Winthrop also recorded information about other colonies in America, those both near and far. He reported each colony's shortcomings and presented each as altogether unappealing. Of Virginia, for instance, he writes that the custom was to be "usually drunken," and even formerly godly ministers gave themselves up to "pride and sensuality" (*J,* 2:20-21). In incidents closer to home, Winthrop also seems to emphasize the negative aspects of a particular community, if it in any way threatens the unity, homogeneity, or progress of his own Bay Colony. His accounts of the Reverend Thomas Hooker's experiences in Connecticut are a case in point. As early as September 1634 Hooker and his company desired to resettle in Connecticut. Winthrop, deputy governor at the time, opposed their removal for the same reasons he regretted the departure of any group beneficial to the commonwealth: "in point of conscience, they ought not to depart from us, being knit to us in one body, and bound by oath to seek the welfare of this commonwealth" (*J,* 1:132). Although through his arguments he was able to thwart an immediate departure, he could not prevent Hooker and his congregation from eventually leaving and settling on the Connecticut River in what is now Hartford. Winthrop records Hooker's departure on 15 October 1635. At the very top of the manuscript page he writes that the sixty people went to Connecticut and, "after a tedious and difficult journey, arrived safe there" (*J,* 1:163). The journey may well have been as tedious as Winthrop reports, but the author's disgruntlement at their departure seems to have colored his report. Following this entry, Winthrop left almost half a page blank, suggesting he had more to say on the matter, but that he never got back to it.

Winthrop did get around to reporting the Connecticut colony's misfortunes, however. In the first winter those colonists lost two thousand pounds' worth of cattle and had to subsist on "acorns, and malt, and grains." Later he added that "Things went not well at Connecticut." (*J,* 1:178, 200). Even though he forgave Hooker completely and praised him sincerely at his death (*J,* 2:326-27), he still managed to point out the tribulations suffered by Hooker's community and to compare that community unfavorably with Boston. Winthrop's thematic implication is that those who leave the Bay Colony will be punished for their transgression. Such punishment is attributed to God who was most certainly, in the eyes of the colonists, watching carefully over Boston as a holy commonwealth.

Winthrop also turned to his journal to map the progress of Anne Hutchinson, a much more threatening transgressor. The beleaguered governor depended on his occasional entries to demonstrate that the Lord continued to be displeased with her after her banishment and excommunication. Winthrop reported that her miscarriage "might signify her errour in decrying inherent righteousness."[32] Winthrop's detailed account of the physician's report was his way of demonstrating how Anne Hutchinson was pertinaciously pursued for her troublemaking in Boston. In 1639 Winthrop mentioned that there were political troubles at Aquiday, Hutchinson's place of settlement (*J,* 1:299). In 1641 he reported that civil and ecclesiastical unrest was great, causing a great schism among them. In Boston Hutchinson's son and son-in-law were both troublemakers (*J,* 2:39-41). The implication is, of course, that any place where Hutchinson settled would suffer, as would anybody related to or in sympathy with her. In 1638 Winthrop exclaimed that those who went with Hutchinson "fell into new errors daily," a falling that God-fearing Bostonians would want to avoid at all costs. Outsiders would know that Hutchinson was corrupt and corrupting. He also reported that she still suffered from delusions: "By these examples we may see how dangerous it is to slight the censures of the church;

for it was apparent, that God had given them up to strange delusions" (*J,* 1:284, 297).

In reporting Hutchinson's death by Indians the journalist reminded his readers that these "people had cast off ordinances and churches" and noted that after the deaths of her and her family "a good providence of God" saved some of the others in her community (*J,* 2:138). Finally, as late as 1646, eight years after the Antinomian Controversy had passed, Winthrop suggested that Hutchinson's children continued to suffer punishment for their mother's transgressions. A daughter who escaped death at the hands of the Indians was eventually returned to the colonists, but she "had forgot her own language, and all her friends, and was loath to have come from the Indians" (*J,* 2:276-77). The description suggests that as a final punishment for the sins of her mother this daughter lost her language and very identity in New England, from Winthrop's perspective a grave punishment indeed.

Certainly one of the major functions of Winthrop's journal (as suggested in the previous chapter) was for Winthrop to write down for posterity a record of the history of the Massachusetts Bay Colony. To this end he detailed not only his response to Hutchinson but also to other major threats to the community; he recorded the court sessions and the community's successes and failures. Depending on context, however, he related episodes emphasizing varying details. Indeed, one of the aspects of Winthrop's journal that makes it enjoyable reading as well as informative history is the inclusion of many brief accounts from the experiences of the colonists. His large history includes numerous small private histories, many of which Winthrop related with a special knack for the art of story-telling. There are, in fact, so many delightful vignettes that choosing from among them is itself difficult and any selection must be somewhat arbitrary. But any selection shows that Winthrop became a good storyteller.

Perhaps the most famous, certainly one of the most frequently anthologized, parables is his story of the battle between the snake and the mouse: "At Watertown there was (in view of divers witnesses) a great combat between a mouse and a snake; and, after a long fight, the mouse prevailed and killed the snake. The pastor of Boston, Mr. Wilson, a very sincere, holy man, hearing of it, gave this interpretation: That the snake was the devil; the mouse was a poor contemptible people, which God had brought hither, which should overcome Satan here, and dispossess him of his kingdom" (*J,* 1:83-84).

The account is indicative of Winthrop's story telling in several ways. As a historian, Winthrop recorded fact. Here he insured the reader's faith in this verity of the matter by noting the several witnesses. The episode has a meaning that a sincere and holy person could interpret according to God's intentions for New England or for the settlers in the new colony. This account differed from Winthrop's typical accounts in the length to which the narrator went (via Wilson's interpretation) to explain the moral. More often Winthrop only inferred the moral or stated it briefly as God's providence for New England.

A parable with a less obvious message is that of a poor Mr. Mansfield and a rich Mr. Marshall, a story which is "a witness of God's providence for this plantation." As Winthrop narrates it, Mansfield wanted badly to come to New England but could not afford the passage for himself and his family. Since Marshall, the wealthy merchant, was troubled by bad dreams about the poor man, he gave him fifty pounds and lent him another one hundred, enabling Mansfield to sail to New England. Winthrop concludes by stating that this "Mansfield grew suddenly rich, and then lost his godliness, and his wealth after" (*J*, 1:141).

This seemingly cryptic passage suggests the complexity of Winthrop's art. If the emphasis falls on the final sentence, God, through providence, appears to intend the immigrant Mansfield to lose his godliness and wealth after getting to New England. Another possibility, one that seems more likely in light of Winthrop's general purpose, is that God's providence for the colony is made evident through Mansfield's receipt of the means to travel to New England in the first place. Winthrop implies that God provides for the colony, and at the same time suggests that the snare of worldly wealth threatens even those sometimes shown God's favor. Because of God's high expectations for the New England colonists, their corruption is especially lamentable. So much for Mansfield. By God's providence he got to New England; by his own fault he let Mammon corrupt him; and he is punished for his corruption by losing his new wealth.

The moral of a story about a woman who attempted to drown her infant is much more obvious, yet the story seems equally complex. "A woman of Boston congregation, having been in much trouble of mind about her spiritual estate, at length grew into utter desperation, and could not endure to hear of any comfort, etc., so as one day she took her little infant and threw it into a well, and then came into the house and said, now she was sure she should be damned, for she had drowned her child; but some, stepping presently forth, saved the child" (*J*, 1:230). This short narrative demonstrates the power that concern about personal salvation had over the colonists. Writing it in the midst of the Antinomian Controversy (summer 1637), Winthrop demonstrates the problems that result from controversies about justification. The narrator implies that such church problems, which should never have existed to begin with, result in tragic actions. The moral is so obvious for Winthrop

and his readers that he evidently felt no need to enunciate it. Mortals can never truly know their spiritual estate; therefore, it is pointless to challenge God in an attempt to determine that estate. Winthrop depicts, by means of this woman, a person's helplessness to establish or verify her own damnation. Winthrop's unstated lesson is that because men and women can not know their estate on earth they should not fail to live by the rules of God and the Bible, its being the only testament they have of God's workings. In another similar incident concerning a mother who unsuccessfully attempts to drown her child, Winthrop does conclude his tale with a moral: "Thus doth Satan work by the advantage of our infirmities, which should stir us up to cleave the more fast to Christ Jesus and to walk the more humbly and watchfully in all our conversation" (*J*, 2:61).

Winthrop did not always leave the moral of his parables up to his reader's interpretations. In a story about a godly woman who "set her heart too much upon" a "parcel of very fine linen of great value" and who consequently had to suffer its accidental loss, the historian states the obvious moral for his readers: "but it pleased God that the loss of this linen did her much good, both in taking off her heart from worldly comforts, and in preparing her for a far greater affliction by the untimely death of her husband, who was slain not long after" (*J*, 2:30-31).

Judging by the frequency of entries, perversion of the socially sanctioned sex drives of men and women was a subject that evidently fascinated Winthrop. Such perversion could manifest itself in adultery, licentiousness, incest, and even bestiality. To Winthrop all such perversions were obvious signs of Satan's continual work to corrupt the godly and undermine the sanctity of the holy commonwealth. In an episode that exemplifies the depths of the colonists' beliefs in what would now be considered superstition, Winthrop records the story of a "loose fellow in the town" who—because of some "human resemblances" between the man and a pig—is suspected of fathering a sow. When questioned, the suspect confessed and was subsequently put to death. Winthrop makes no interpretive comment.[33]

In one particular adultery case, Winthrop attributes a woman's fall to her father's negligence. The father departed for England, leaving his daughters behind, "but took no course for their safe bestowing in his absence, as the care and wisdom of a father should have done" (*J*, 2:317). The cause is clear: the result as Winthrop explains it is that a married man "was taken with [one of the daughters], and soliciting her chastity, obtained his desire." The daughter, Mary Martin, having "committed sin" with this man in the house, became pregnant, killed the child after its birth, was found out, and condemned to death. In Boston the law forbade anyone from living alone; this narrative stresses the importance of membership with a legitimate family and a pious community. According to the colonial tradition, individuals by themselves faced a much greater risk of transgressing than those who were tightly bound into the community through family. Winthrop's prose style in this instance is especially terse and unembellished. He relates "a very sad occasion" in a most objective manner, leaving the condemnation of the woman to God: "she behaved herself very penitently while she was in prison. . . . Yet all the comfort God would afford her, was only trust (as she said) in his mercy through Christ" (*J,* 2:317). Such incidents are indicative of the terrible pressures on colonists to "move humbly and watchfully" in the New England community. Winthrop's report demands attention by its subject matter and must have been intended to compel readers to avoid the sins that would lead to such dire consequences. At the same time, it seems arguable that Winthrop himself laments the transgression and the tragic deaths of both mother and child.

When misfortune befell the unrighteous, Winthrop had no qualms about entering the episode into his journal. Despite his firm belief in justification by grace not works, he seems to suggest (as Hutchinson was banished for pointing out) sanctification (an honest, humble, industrious life-style according to the laws of the Bible and the model of Jesus) can help to evidence grace. Although God is free to strike down any one at any time for reasons beyond the understanding of man, that same God is somehow more likely to strike down the ungodly. After relating the shooting death of a Captain Patrick and describing his various transgressions, for example, Winthrop wrote that his death "was the fruit of his wicked course and breach of covenant with his wife, with the church, and with that state who had called him and maintained him, and he found his death from that hand where he sought protection" (*J,* 2:154). About a man who dies crossing the Atlantic, Winthrop writes "one of the seamen died—a most profane fellow, and one who was very injurious to the passengers" (*J,* 1:44).

With relative ease Winthrop discovers justice and the divine plan in these obvious cases. In reporting misfortunes that befell the godly without apparent logical or discernible cause, however, Winthrop has little explanation to offer other than to admit that any such incident was a sad accident. Often a moral can be implied either by context or by the circumstances of the narrative itself. Such is the case in the story about the accidental shooting death of a five-year-old whose father left him alone in the house. In their care and wisdom, Winthrop implies, fathers should know better than to leave children unattended in a room or house in which loaded guns are accessible.

Within the larger history of New England, many of these stories have as a common theme Satan's repeated-but-thwarted attempts to ruin the colonies. Winthrop

noted that the "devil would never cease to disturb our peace, and to raise up instruments one after another" (*J,* 1:285). Whether referring to public goings-on or to private incidents and misfortunes, Winthrop believed that readers should be aware of the devil's work. In 1645 he wrote about the purpose of his journal: "It may be of use to leave a memorial of some of the most material, that our posterity and others may behold the workings of Satan to ruin the colonies and churches of Christ in New England, and into what distempers a wise and godly people may fall in times of temptation; and when such have entertained some false and plausible principles, what deformed superstructures they will raise thereupon, and with what unreasonable obstinacy they will maintain them" (*J,* 2:240).

Given the prevalence and the thematic importance of the stories that make up a large portion of the journal, it seems perfectly fitting that Winthrop's final entries (and perhaps his last surviving writing) would be stories of a private nature. The final entry, for example, tells of the drowning of a child of five whose father had worked into the Sabbath (Saturday night). Winthrop concludes by vindicating the parent to a degree: "But the father, freely in the open congregation, did acknowledge it the righteous hand of God for his profaning his holy day against the check of his own conscience" (*J,* 2:355).

In the nineteen years that Winthrop kept his journal, Massachusetts Bay changed from a small trading company to an established, virtually self-sufficient colony, part of a united federation of colonies. During these years Winthrop was always either at or near the head of the political and religious decision-making bodies. This proximity encouraged him to write many tracts concerning governmental and ecclesiastical decisions for which there was no room in the journal. The next chapter investigates many of these other writings.

CHEERFUL SUBMISSION TO AUTHORITY: MISCELLANEOUS AND LATER WRITINGS

Judges are Gods upon Earthe.

(***Winthrop Papers,*** 4:476)

Although the journal history of New England that John Winthrop kept for almost twenty years is unquestionably his most significant contribution to American literature, it is by no means his only important work. As we have seen, he wrote a historically important sermon, a documentary history of the Hutchinson trial (published in 1644), and a record of his conversion experience (1637). Throughout his career, the governor also wrote several less well-known tracts concerning politics, theology, and the colony's relations with the Indians.

MISCELLANEOUS EARLY WRITINGS

For the political and legal writing Winthrop would be called upon to do in New England, he had an apprenticeship in his native country. While he worked as an attorney from 1627 to 1628, for example, he prepared several bills evidently for presentation before Parliament. As Robert C. Winthrop describes them, they "are wholly in his own handwriting, on large paper, with ample margins, and prepared as if for the consideration of a Legislative Committee."[34] In one of these tracts he described the reasons for preventing drunkenness, arguing against the "loathsome vice of Drunkennesse": "An Act for the preventing of drunkenness and of the great waste of corn."[35] His concern is that beer is brewed too strong and thus "an excessive wast of Barlye, which might be imployed to the great good of the poore, and good of the whole kingdom" (*WP,* 1:371-74). Winthrop records facts and figures to argue his case, concluding that this law, if passed, could enrich the kingdom by five million pounds a year. Contrary to the modern stereotypical notion of Puritans as teetotalers, Winthrop was not against drinking in itself; he favored beer as a wholesome drink, but abhorred it as an intoxicant.

The bill, which might have been presented to the House of Commons in 1627 or 1628, never became law, but it is representative of several such pieces Winthrop wrote during his tenure at the Court of Wards and Liveries. Another tract attributed to Winthrop and written near the same time is "An Acte to settle a Course in the Assessinge and Levienge of Common Charges in Townes and parishes" (*WP,* 1:418-19). The bill proposes to establish a law concerning taxation that would end dissension about rates and collections for common charges for such public benefits as maintaining soldiers, prisons, bridges, and churches. Winthrop recognized a need for such taxation, and he gained valuable experience in attempting to organize a fair and workable means of taxation. Such experience would serve him well in New England.

In addition to gaining ability as a framer of legal tracts, Winthrop prepared himself thoroughly for his command as governor of a holy commonwealth. In the late 1620s, he attended church services regularly and copied into a notebook brief outlines of each sermon. He kept track of the preachers, the texts, and the main points of the arguments.[36] Certainly this minute record helped to prepare the governor for the composition of his own lay-sermon aboard the *Arbella* in 1630.

REFORMATION WITHOUT SEPARATION

In an early New England document, Winthrop combined his two types of writing skills as he composed a tract on the reasons for reformation without separation: "Reasons to prove a necessitye of reformation from the Corruptions of Antechrist which hath defiled the Christian Churches, and yet without an absolute separation from them, as if they were no Churches of Christ" (1631). Winthrop probably composed the tract in response to Roger Williams's refusal to become tempo-rary teacher at the Boston Church. (He was offered the position while John Wilson was in England trying to convince his wife to join him in New England.) Winthrop voices essentially the same sentiment in the *Humble Request,* insisting that the colonists were not separating from the Church of England; rather they were merely reforming it from within.

Although the manuscript exists only in a fragment, Winthrop's method and argument are clear.[37] As he argued in his tract on the reasons for settling in New England in the first place, he admits that the churches in England are corrupt, but he maintains that they are not unsalvageable: "the Corruption of a thinge dothe not nullifie a thinge so long as the thinge hathe a beinge in the same nature, that it had, when it was in the beste beinge: so is it with the particular Congregations" (*WP,* 3:13). Referring to the Gospel of Matthew, Winthrop reminds his readers that the Bible prophesies that the visible church will stand until the end of the world. In response to the objection that the Church makes whores and drunkards of visible saints, he argues that "to terme the people in gen[era]l whores and drunkards is evill: for althoughe the most part are ignorant (the more is their sinne and our griefe) yet whores and drunkards they are not: weake Christians they are indeed, and the weaker for want of that tender Care, that should be had of them" (*WP,* 3:12). Because that church has become corrupt in England, transplanting, purifying, and caring for the visible church becomes the obligation and responsibility of the true Christians in New England. Winthrop thus takes a middle ground, arguing on the one hand that the Church of England needs reforming, while denying on the other hand that reformers have the right to separate from corrupt churches so long as they are "churches of Christ."

DEFENSE OF AN ORDER OF COURT

Judging by surviving documents of Winthrop's writings, the Antinomian Controversy and the colony's troubles with Anne Hutchinson inspired one of Winthrop's greatest literary outpourings. In addition to the *Short Story* account, the journal entries, and his "Christian Experience," Winthrop wrote several tracts on different subjects related to the controversy. He engaged in a manuscript debate with Henry Vane concerning restrictions on immigration; he wrote a document concerning the power of the church; he also wrote arguments concerning works and grace, tracts which unfortunately do not survive.

Just after the proceedings against Wheelwright for his supposed sedition in March 1636, the General Court passed an order "to keep out all such persons as might be dangerous to the commonwealth" (*J,* 1:219). The order immediately followed Winthrop's election to the governorship after three years absence, and the reelected governor lost no time in publishing an explanation of the General Court's order.

In this explanation, Winthrop essentially argues that because the welfare of the whole should not be put at hazard for advantage of any individual, the magistrates of the commonwealth have the right to "receive or reject at their discretion." The document's full title is descriptive of its contents: **"A Declaration of the Intent and Equitye of the Order made at the last Court, to this effect, that none should be received to inhabite within this Jurisdiction but such as should be allowed by some of the Magistrates"** (*WP*, 3:423, 422).[38] Besides explaining the court's order, the **"Declaration"** is emblematic of Winthrop's view of the commonwealth. In phrases that are reminiscent of his **"Modell of Christian Charity,"** the **"Cambridge Agreement,"** and **"Arguments for Plantation,"** Winthrop describes "the essentiall forme of a common weale or body politic" as he perceived it: "The consent of a certaine companie of people, to cohabite together, under one government for their mutual safety and welfare." Given this view of the commonwealth, Winthrop's argument is indicative of the sincerity of his intentions. He wanted what he felt was best for the colony: "The intent of the law is to preserve the wellfare of the body; and for this ende to have none received into any fellowship with it who are likely to disturbe the same and this intent (I am sure) is lawful and good" (*WP*, 3:422-23, 424).

Winthrop premises his argument on the political ideology current at the time, brought with the Puritans from Jacobean England, namely that "no man hath lawfull power over another, but by birth or consent." The commonwealth is founded by free consent of the members who "have a public and relative interest each in other." Echoing specifically the metaphor he expounds in the **"Modell of Christian Charity"** of 1630, Winthrop argues that every member of a commonwealth such as the one in New England is obligated "to seeke out and entertaine all means that may conduce to the wellfare of the bodye" (*WP*, 3:423). In the **"Modell,"** we remember, he writes that "All the partes of this body being thus united are made soe contiguous in a speciall relation as they must needes partake of each others strength and infirmity, joy, and sorrowe, weale and woe" (*WP*, 2:289).

An objection that concerns the author of the defense is that the law may result in rejecting "good Christians and so consequently Christ himselfe" (*WP*, 3:425). The possibility of denying Christians a home in New England was a serious consideration for Winthrop, who earnestly desired and certainly recognized the need for immigration. He knew that not only religiously but also economically and politically the growth of the colony was imperative.

Because he sincerely believed that it would be wrong to deny a true Christian admittance into his holy commonwealth, Winthrop argues that the magistrates and elders have not yet, as far as they know, rejected a Christian. Moreover, he argues that rejecting the man would not necessarily be the same as rejecting Christ. Weak as it is, Winthrop's argument rests on that simple denial. He firmly believes that to admit those who threaten the peace and harmony of the commonwealth would be a sinful evil, and that he would be unfaithful to his duty as Puritan magistrate in receiving such. According to Perry Miller, Winthrop assumes "that man is a reasonable creature, and his statement of political theory in these papers owes more to logic than to the word of God."[39]

Because Henry Vane was not convinced by Winthrop's **"Defense,"** he wrote an answer questioning both the author's logic and his authority as a magistrate. The young Henry Vane, who had recently been left out of the government altogether, was certainly bitter. As governor he had been the most important ally the Antinomians could have had. Unfortunately for Hutchinson, Wheelwright, and the others of their camp, his dethroning, as it were, cost them their stronghold in Boston, and ultimately their own rights to residence within the limits of the Bay Colony. In his response to Winthrop's **"Defense,"** the ex-governor makes one last vain effort to confront his adversaries, an effort that is cogent and perhaps appealing to democratic ears.[40] Winthrop had written that "If we are bound to keepe off whatsoever appears to tend to our ruine or damage, then we may lawfully refuse to receive such whose dispositions suite not with ours and whose society (we know) will be hurtfull to us" (*WP*, 3:423). In response to this passage, Vane writes that "this kind of reasoning is very confused and fallacious . . . [the question is] whether persons may be rejected, or admitted, upon the illimited consent or dissent of magistrates."[41] According to Winthrop, Vane's answer cast "much reproach and slander . . . upon the Court." In other words, the General Court approved Winthrop's stance; and when the whole "proceedings about the law" was read before the court, most parties were satisfied, even "some that were on the adverse party, and had taken offense at the law, did openly acknowledge themselves fully satisfied" (*SS*, 251-52).

In his **"Reply to an Answer Made to a Declaration,"** Winthrop essentially restates his former argument in the light of Vane's objections. (See *WP*, 3:463-76). The governor moves from point to point, methodically and patiently, showing in each case what his own argument is, what Vane's objection is, and how he refutes or answers Vane's objections. In this sense the **"Reply"** adds little new to the original **"Defense."** In other ways, however, the **"Reply"** is worthy of comment. Winthrop begins by condemning "Contentions among brethren

. . . [as] sad spectacles (*WP*, 3:463). But because "the cause of truth and justice" calls to him, Winthrop feels obliged to respond even though he thereby continues the contention; he is careful to place the blame, however, on Vane: "if I deale more sharply, than mine owne disposition leads me, the blame must fall upon him, who puts such occasions upon me, as I cannot otherwise shunne" (*WP*, 3:463). Risking further contention, Winthrop verges on attacking the man rather than his argument, stating for example, that "his zeale for the cause outrunes his judgment" (*WP*, 3:468). In other instances Winthrop submits that Vane's argument is simply fallacious and does not merit a reply. Winthrop also accuses the addresser of merely babbling: "Thus he runs on in a frivolous discourse, and in the end falls upon this false conclusion" (*WP*, 3:465).

Whether or not Winthrop is guilty of an ad hominem argument, he was careful to avoid ever naming his adversary (although certainly the author of the "Address" was known to all who heard the tract read at court). Instead Winthrop designates him as the "Answerer," and generally refers to him with an anonymous third person pronoun. On occasion, however, Winthrop slips into the second person, under the pretense of a direct quote of a question Winthrop would ask him: "I must make bold to aske him this question, viz. Seeing you are bound by your oath" (*WP*, 3:472).

In justifying his position Winthrop emphasizes the duty of the magistrate. He states that the magistrates have made an oath both to the church and to the civil state, and that they also are under a sort of civil moral code that regulates their behavior: "As they are magistrates, they are sworne to doe right to all, and regulated by their relation to the people, to seeke their wellfare in all things" (*WP*, 3:466).

Winthrop felt that in the tight-knit, ideal holy commonwealth he advocated, such a system would be perfectly appropriate. The faith the members of a holy commonwealth needed to have in their magistrate would justify their belief in his righteousness. A magistrate was elected by the freemen, but once in office he was believed to have God's authority to perform his task. In a holy commonwealth, of course, the law of the Bible is the magistrate's guide, and the corruption of a magistrate, in this ideal circumstance, is out of the question. In setting up in Massachusetts the colonists agreed "to walke according to the rules of the gospell." In Winthrop's terms, one thus would have "a christian common weale."

According to the account in Winthrop's *Short Story,* the governor's reply to Vane's answer to the original defense was successful. Even some members of the opposing faction were convinced of the justice of the immigration law. Winthrop was successful here, as he would be again the next fall in banishing Wheelwright and Hutchinson. The established colony would survive the internal threats despite Satan's intention to distract or overthrow the churches in New England.

FORMER PASSAGES

Besides the theological threats to the community, the colony was repeatedly beset with problems concerning the Indians, either as a result of the colonists' behavior toward them or the Indians' real or imagined threat to the Europeans' safety and welfare. In a seven-page pamphlet published by the commissioners for the United Colonies, *Declaration of Former Passages and Proceedings betwixt the English and the Narragansetts* [*DFP*] (1645), Winthrop recounts the colonists' dealings with the Narragansett Indians between 1636, when a treaty was signed, and 1645, when the commissioners were armed and ready to fight. To a certain extent, the tract was a declaration of war.

Despite protestations to the contrary, much of the English interaction with the Indians involved deceit, subterfuge, and murder. Having badly defeated the Pequots during the wars of the 1630s, the colonists diminished their threat and even arranged a treaty with them. The colonists then turned to the Narragansetts, another powerful New England tribe. Miantonomoh, one of the most powerful of the tribe's chieftains, had come to the English—as the treaty between English and Narragansetts prescribed—to ask for permission to attack the Pequots in an effort to avenge an earlier attack by the Pequots. The authorities did not refuse permission, and in the battle that ensued Miantonomoh was taken prisoner. Although the colony's leaders had led Miantonomoh to believe he was an ally, they were suspicious of his trustworthiness and thought him too powerful for the good of the colonies.

While the commissioners were considering what action to take against the sachem, their ally Uncas of the Pequots reported that he had captured him, and loyally, "craved the commissioners advice how to proceed with him" (*DFP*, 2).[42] In a journal entry from August 1643, Winthrop describes the dilemma the commissioners had faced while they held Miantonomoh captive. Miantonomoh was rumored to have been the "head and contriver" of a conspiracy "to cut off all the English." He was also "of a turbulent and proud spirit"—just the type of man the Puritans would not tolerate. Fearing, therefore, that it would "not be safe to set him at liberty, neither had we sufficient ground for us to put him to death." The magistrates called upon the elders, letting them recommend that he be executed. Next the commissioners secretly informed Uncas that they had decided Miantonomoh should be put to death. Uncas obliged: "Onkus' brother, following after Miantunnomoh, clave his head with an hatchet, some English being present" (*J*, 2:135, 136).

The ***Declaration*** opens with Winthrop's reminder that the English "came into these parts of the world with desire to advance the kingdome of the Lord Jesus Christ and to injoye his precius Ordinances with peace" (***DFP,*** 1). Despite these benevolent intentions on the part of the English, as Winthrop narrates it, the Indians were now forcing the settlers to war.

After narrating the circumstances surrounding Miantonomoh's murder—as if to justify the Bay Colony's action—Winthrop recounts the Indian's offenses against the state, dating back to 1637 when the chief signed a treaty and 1638 when he was reputed to have broken that treaty by attempting to murder Uncas and then actually killing a Pequot prisoner put in his charge. In relating Miantonomoh's execution Winthrop leaves out the details of the Indian's death. In fact, Winthrop describes it in the pamphlet in a jargon not unlike the political-military jargons of other ages: "Uncas here-upon slew an enemy, but not the enmity against him." Because of this surviving enmity, the troubles with the Narragansetts continued. After describing them, Winthrop was forced to conclude that the "premises being duly weighed it clearly appears that God calles the colonies to a war." The governor concludes the declaration by insisting that Satan was again stirring up "many of his instruments against the Churches" (***DFP,*** 4, 7).

As a defense of the English actions against the Indians, the ***Declaration of Former Passages*** stands in ironic contrast with the earlier writings about Indians in New England. The first ground of settling in Massachusetts, we remember, was for the propagation of the gospel to the Indians; the settlers would "come in with the good leave of the natives who finde benifight [benefit] allreaddy by our Neighbourhood" (***WP,*** 2:141).[43] In contrast to this hopeful beginning, the ***Declaration*** asserts that military measures would have to be taken against the Narragansetts despite the colonists' former intention to bring them to the word of God. The ideal of delivering them from the snares of the Devil by converting them seems to have been forgotten.

Historian Francis Jennings calls the ***Declaration*** a "bill of charges against the Narragansetts, which was concocted, as usual, of a great many highly misleading words."[44] The most damning evidence is Winthrop's rendition of a letter Roger Williams sent, explaining that despite nearby troubles the Rhode Island Indians sought peace not war.[45] As Jennings demonstrates, the commissioners (Winthrop?) literally changed Williams's account to fit their need, which—according to the author—was to wage war against the Indians. This subterfuge by the colonists Jennings calls "mendacity extraordinary even among adepts."[46]

Other passages in the ***Declaration*** suggest Winthrop's attempt to mislead. He repeats, for example, phrases concerning the colonists' efforts to maintain peace even

though the English have suffered "many injuries and insolencies" at the Indians' hands. Several times he refers to the Indians' violation of treaties. Meanwhile, according to Winthrop, the commissioners "in care of the publick peace, sought to quench the fire kindled amongst the Indians, these children of strife." The political nature of the ***Declaration*** is undeniable; Winthrop's method of twisting facts to suit his needs seems equally obvious. The tract shows Winthrop and his fellow commissioners at their manipulative, exploitative worst. As Jennings argues, this manipulation "shows a side of old John Winthrop's character that sorts badly with his reputation for integrity and gentleness."[47]

In the ***Declaration,*** as with so many of his writings, the governor demonstrates that he saw behind the trouble of the moment Satan working against the colony. Although we cannot forgive Winthrop and his fellow colonists for their mistreatment of the native Americans, we can view him in the context of his age.[48] We can acknowledge that his ***Declaration*** shows him to have had the perseverance necessary to build and maintain a city founded in and governed by the will of his God; to have had faith in the future of a holy commonwealth; and to have felt that the Indians, like the Antinomians, were threats to that future.

DEFENSE OF THE NEGATIVE VOTE

In addition to writing about the internal theological threats and the external military threats to the community, Winthrop repeatedly wrote about domestic political adversity, introducing, defending, or justifying his positions concerning various governmental regulations. The policy of a negative vote (right to veto) essentially divided the General Court into two groups, giving the magistrates the power to dissent from or override the other group's decision despite the magistrates' numerical minority. As such, the policy marks the beginning of bicameral government in the United States. The occasion for Winthrop's written defense of the theory of the negative vote in 1643 has a fascinating background.

Winthrop introduced the idea of negative vote shortly after he was succeeded in the governor's spot by Dudley in 1634. Winthrop had granted power to the deputies as they demanded as early as 1634, but he wished to maintain the magistrates' authority and power. As we have seen, the deputies were elected by the freemen of the Massachusetts Bay Colony. Each township sent representatives to be a part of the General Court. Magistrates were also elected by popular vote, but Winthrop saw a distinction between the two groups. The deputies were simply intended to be representatives of the people; magistrates, once elected, had the power of divine sanction. The deputies, however, outnumbered the magistrates and therefore had the potential to carry any vote, a fact that gave them great political power. A simple majority, of deputies and magistrates, would give deputies an advantage Winthrop did not believe they deserved. So he established the principle of the negative vote: "No Lawe etc: shall passe, as an Acte of the Court, without the Consent of the greater parte of the magistr[ate]s of the one parte, and the greater number of the Dep[u]tyes on the other parte" (*WP,* 4:386). Thus neither group, deputies nor magistrates, could pass laws or make judgments in legal cases without procuring a favorable majority from the other group. In this way Winthrop avoided what he called a "mere democracy," something abominable according to Winthrop's seventeenth-century outlook.

The law as Winthrop framed it remained silently on the books, as it were, until a legal battle about ten years after its inception brought it again to the forefront. The legal battle, Sherman vs. Keayne, arose over the rightful ownership of a pig. The General Court addressed the issue in June 1642, but the actual sow business, "a great business upon a very small occasion" (*J,* 2:64) began in 1636 when Captain Robert Keayne received a stray sow and evidently advertised it.[49] After a year he claimed to kill his own sow, retaining the stray. At this point Mrs. Sherman came forward, arguing that Keayne took her sow, but because he had killed it she could not identify it. The court decided in Keayne's favor, giving him three pounds for costs and twenty for damages. Mrs. Sherman with the help of George Story gained popular support, and got a witness "to confess . . . that he had forsworn himself." The case was reopened. The deputies tended to side with Sherman, and the magistrates with Keayne so that, as Winthrop writes in his journal, since the deputies far outnumber the magistrates (thirty to nine), "no sentence could by law pass without the greater number of both." The deadlock occasioned the popular party's, the deputies', denigrating the principle of the negative vote, asserting that it "had hindered the course of justice" (*J,* 2:64, 65, 66).

In a journal entry for June 1643, Winthrop explains the occasion for his writing "a small treatise" on the negative vote, "wherein he laid down the original of it from the patent, and the establishing of it by order of the general court in 1634, showing thereby how it was fundamental to our government, which, if it were taken away, would be a mere democracy." To this treatise "one of the magistrates as was conceived" made an answer, "undertaking to avoid all the arguments both from the patent and from the order" (*J,* 2:120). The surviving document is Winthrop's **"Reply to the Answ[er] made to the Discourse about the Neg[ative] vote."**[50]

In a style similar to the one he used in his reply to Vane's arguments about immigration laws, Winthrop states his case point by point. In his response he answers questions about the legality of the negative vote,

and shows that it subscribes to the letter of the patent, is fundamental to Massachusetts Bay government, and is lawful and expedient. He also has something to say about "the proper place and power of the Dep[u]ties" (*WP,* 4:380).

In defending the negative vote Winthrop refers to the two documents most important to the commonwealth, the Bible and the Charter. Though his use of the Scripture in this instance is slight, he does refer to the Old Testament to point out that the negative vote saved Jeremiah "against the minde of the Preists" (*WP,* 4:389). Winthrop makes detailed reference to the Charter, arguing that the first question will be "best cleared by the Patent it selfe, wherein I will set down the very words themselves (so far as concernes the state of the Question) and not leave out what may make against me, as the Answ[erer] often doth" (*WP,* 4:380). Winthrop uses the patent in two ways: one is to demonstrate that the negative vote is lawful according to the laws brought over from England initially; the other is to deprecate the answerer's method. In concluding his argument that the patent makes legitimate the negative vote, Winthrop becomes vehement: "I must Conclude, that either these words in our Patent doe give the magistrates a Neg[ative] vo[te] or els there was never any Neg[ative] vo[te] granted by any Patent or Comission by any kinge of England since Edw[ard] the 3ds time" (*WP,* 4:382).

Winthrop argues that the negative vote is fundamental to the commonwealth in that it marks a specific difference between one form of government and another. If the negative vote were taken away, Winthrop repeats, "our Government would be a meere Democratie" (*WP,* 4:382). As a seventeenth-century Puritan aristocrat, Winthrop had no sympathy with democracy. According to Winthrop, no precedent or warrant for a democracy existed in Scripture; "there was no such government in Israell." Correspondingly, for a new Israel in New England there should be none. Besides the lack of biblical precedent, secular histories record democracies as monsters, "the meanest and worst of all formes of Government," full of troubles, and short-lived (*WP,* 4:383). Democracy does not come highly recommended from Puritan New England. Ironically, of course, with the division of the General Court into two separate houses each with the power to veto, the modern bicameral aspect of government which is such an integral part of the democracy in the United States owes its genesis to Winthrop and Puritan New England.

Winthrop's mistrust of democracy lies in his doubts about the abilities of the common man to govern himself or others, a mistrust, incidentally, that was echoed by many of the framers of the Constitution some 150 years later. Winthrop did acknowledge that some deputies might boast accomplishments equal to those of a magistrate, but generally the magistrates were chosen specifically for their abilities in law and politics.

Finally, Winthrop addresses the objection that the negative vote gives undue power to the magistrates even if their judgment is unjust: "If the Court of Assist[ant]s should give an unjust sentence in any Cause, the partye injured can have no remedye in the generall Court if the magistr[ate]s (as they are like to doe) shall persist in their former Judgment" (*WP*, 4:390). It is more likely, argues Winthrop, that the jury errs than the judge. Were judges to err, however, given new evidence that magistrates would "have good ground" to change their judgment. Magistrates are sure to be open-minded and "ready to attende such further helpe and light, as the wisdome and counsell of the generall Court may seasonably afforde." Furthermore, according to Winthrop, any unjust magistrate who persisted in error would be shamed into either correcting his error or leaving office.

We can only conclude that as Winthrop struggled to retain the power for the magistrates he had the benefit of the colony at heart. His ultimate motives may have been to some extent influenced by pride and human striving for fame, but regardless of what was personally best for the individual man, Winthrop sought what he thought and what the Bible taught was best for the commonwealth. Such thoughts guided him in devising and recording responses to the crises he and his colleagues faced.

Arbitrary Government

By midsummer 1643, Winthrop had satisfied, or at least quieted, the opposition concerning the negative vote. For a time he and the deputies "let the cause fall" (*J*, 2:121). By the following summer (1644) Winthrop had been voted out of the governorship; as deputy governor he opposed the deputies' claim of judicial authority, and he thereby caused them to accuse him of maintaining an arbitrary government. Once again Winthrop was put on the defensive.

To defend himself, the other magistrates, and the system of government in the Bay Colony, Winthrop again wrote a small treatise. Like his other titles, the full title of this treatise is descriptive: **"Arbitrary Goverment described and the Common mistakes about the same (both in the true nature thereof, and in the representation of the Goverment of the Massachusetts, under such a notion) fully cleared"** (1644).[51]

Winthrop's challenge in this treatise was to demonstrate that the government of the Massachusetts Bay Colony was not arbitrary. To this end he defines arbitrary government as that in which "a people have men sett over them without their choyce" who have power to govern them "without a Rule" (*WP*, 4:468). Where the people choose their own governors and require their own rules, in contrast, there is no arbitrary government. As he had done in defending the negative vote, Winthrop referred directly to the Charter to show how the government of Massachusetts allows those liberties that keep it from being arbitrary.

A rhetorical trick Winthrop uses to his advantage is to define arbitrary government by negation and thereby imply the positive characteristics of the government he defends. The foundation, laws, and constant practice for the common good insist that Massachusetts offers liberties unknown to an arbitrary government. The foundation is in the Charter that prescribes the election of officers; the rules are established by the Charter, and the magistrates have been liberal in issuing punishment for transgressors of the rules. The rule observed by the magistrates is the word of God. Because of his divergence from the Bible in exacting penalties, Winthrop got in trouble with the deputies. He maintained that except for certain capital crimes, the punishment should vary with the circumstances of the crime. According to biblical precedent, argued Winthrop, penalties other than for capital offenses are not prescribed. The individual crime is considered in each case. Winthrop seeks to avoid oppressing the people by unjust sentences yet to punish adequately those who transgress against holy or civil law. Laws are objective and fixed; penalties subjective and relative.

In exacting punishments, Winthrop admits, a government can appear to be arbitrary. In a statement that anticipates the dictum "innocent until proven guilty," Winthrop writes that a human judge "cannot sentence another, before he hath offended, and the offence examined, proved, layd to the Rule, and weighed by all considerable Circumstances, and Libertye given to the partye to Answerer for himselfe" (*WP*, 4:474). By appealing to the accused's liberties, Winthrop argues that his government is not arbitrary, but liberal.

In contrast to this relatively liberal view, in perhaps the boldest statement he makes, Winthrop asserts that "Judges are Gods upon earthe." This statement verbalizes the seventeenth-century understanding of the judge's role in New England, but it also provides further evidence of Winthrop's naïveté, innocence, and hope. Again exhibiting his faith in the justice of Scripture and in the basic goodness of the magistrates in a holy commonwealth, Winthrop argues that the judges in their judgments will "holde forthe the wisdom and mercy of God" (*WP*, 4:476). God gives men the ability to interpret God's own laws.

Winthrop concludes by arguing that although laws should be fixed, firmly established, penalties should not be rigid. After all, in infinite wisdom, "God foresaw, that there would be corrupt Judges in Israell, yet he lefte most penaltyes, to their determination" (*WP,* 4:481). In answering objections, Winthrop acknowledges that judges are fallible, subject to temptation and error, but that the consequences of their error is slight compared with the injury an unjust law could do.

In the ideal commonwealth Winthrop envisions, knowing the laws will be sufficient cause for obeying them; the virtuous need not know the penalty. The best humans can do, submits Winthrop, is to provide against "common and probable events" (*WP,* 4:481). For the rest, the members of a holy commonwealth must trust in God.

THE "LITTLE SPEECH ON LIBERTY"

No sooner had Winthrop argued that the government was not arbitrary than a group from the town of Hingham accused him of again overstepping his rightful authority. As with the sow business, here too a story stands behind Winthrop's creation of what has come to be known as his "little speech on liberty."[52] A group of townspeople from Hingham, a community near Boston, accused Winthrop of overstepping his authority when he appointed a militia captain contrary to the people's choice. The people of Hingham refused to respond to the appointed captain's orders and called Winthrop to court. Winthrop considered the Hingham faction mutinous and argued that he was honored in being singled out to defend a just cause. After being cleared of any criminal charges and reinstated, as it were, Winthrop "desired leave for a little speech" (*J,* 2:237). The speech he gave, as much as any other single piece of his writing, helps to characterize the man and to explain his theory of government.

After a short preface asking for the court's indulgence, Winthrop introduces the matters that his speech addresses: "The great questions that have troubled the country are about the authority of the magistrates and the liberty of the people." In his speech, then, he clarifies and expounds on the principle of authority and defines his notion of liberty. He acknowledges that even though he is a magistrate, he is also a person and, therefore, is subject to failings. Because he has been chosen by a godly people, however, he has his authority from God: "It is yourselves who have called us to this office, and being called by you, we have our authority from God." Yet unlike gods, magistrates come from among the electors, "men subject to like passions." Therefore, he cautions his audience, "when you see infirmities in us, you should reflect upon your own, and that would make you bear the more with us, and not be severe censurers of the failings of your magistrates, when you have continual experience of the like infirmities in yourselves and others" (*WP,* 4:238). If a judge's cases are clear, the magistrate—unless he "fail in faithfulness"—will be able to act appropriately. "But if the case be doubtful, or the rule doubtful, to men of such understanding and parts as your magistrates are, if your magistrates should err here, yourselves must bear it" (*J,* 2:238). In other words, Winthrop argues that unless a magistrate openly and obviously transgress the law of God, those who elect him must bear the consequences of his errors.

In discussing liberty, Winthrop again exhibits his belief in the ultimate goodness of God's covenanted people in the Bay Colony. He argues that there "is a twofold liberty, natural (I means as our nature is now corrupt) and civil or federal." He defines natural liberty as that of a brute beast, a liberty that has no place in a holy commonwealth: "By this, man, as he stands in relation to man simply, hath liberty to do what he lists; it is a liberty to evil as well as to good. This liberty is incompatible and inconsistent with authority, and cannot endure the least restraint of the most just authority" (*J,* 2:238). A "civil or federal, it may also be termed moral" liberty, in contrast, has "reference to the covenant between God and man. . . . This liberty is the proper end and object of authority, and cannot subsist without it. . . . This liberty is maintained and exercised in a way of subjection to authority." Such a liberty, argues Winthrop, is worth standing for with one's life. It is the liberty of being free and content to do God's will, to accept authority. Winthrop concludes by again contrasting natural and moral liberty: "If you stand for your natural corrupt liberties, and will do what is good in your own eyes, you will not endure the least weight of authority, but will murmur, and oppose, and be always striving to shake off that yoke; but if you will be satisfied to enjoy such civil and lawful liberties, such as Christ allows you, then will you quietly and cheerfully submit unto that authority which is set over you" (*J,* 2:238, 239). Winthrop's conception of liberty in this context epitomizes the belief of his age. Even though he was a judge, he also humbled himself in recognizing the interdependence of his fellow colonists. If he appeared happy in his harness, to paraphrase Robert Frost, it was only because he acknowledged that the success of the commonwealth depended on everyone being happy in harness. Winthrop's little speech delineates the accepted understanding of liberty in seventeenth-century Boston and is, if for no other reason, invaluable as a piece of literature.

Certainly Winthrop, like many of his colleagues in the government and the church, found his yoke "easy and sweet," yet some of the colonists did not. Those malcontents strove continually against the authorities. Much of Winthrop's writings in his journal and separate treatises attest to this continual struggle. Winthrop attempted to establish a holy commonwealth in which all members were parts of the same body, each dependent on the other, and he wrought a government suitable for the colony set on the edge of a vast wilderness continent.

Differences of opinion were inevitable. Jealousies and power struggles were a matter of course. Frustration and fear were the natural human responses to a community that was envisioned as an ideal holy commonwealth but discovered to be as real and as challengingly problematic as any community in the world. Winthrop's various literary responses to the many problems that beset him and his community in his career as governor of the Bay Colony demonstrate his ability to govern despite a multitude of problems, and make manifest—as historians have long recognized—that politically, socially, and religiously he was clearly the most able governor in Puritan New England. As his manifold writings attest, he must also be considered one of the most important American Puritan writers.

Notes

1. Morgan, [Edmund S. *The Puritan Dilemma: The Story of John Winthrop* Boston: Little, Brown, 1958] 134.

2. Several works address the Antinomian Controversy. In *The Puritan Dilemma,* for example, Morgan discusses Hutchinson in a chapter entitled "Seventeenth-Century Nihilism" but argues that Winthrop was "one of the libelers" and writes that "Anne Hutchinson excelled him not only in nimbleness of wit but in the ability to extend a theological proposition into all its ramifications" (134, 136). See also Selma R. Williams, *Divine Rebel: The Life of Anne Marbury Hutchinson* (New York: Holt, Rinehart & Winston, 1981); Emery Battis, *Saints and Sectaries: Anne Hutchinson and the Antinomian Controversy in the Massachusetts Bay Colony* (Chapel Hill: University of North Carolina Press, 1962); and "Anne Hutchinson and the Antinomians," a chapter in Philip Gura's *A Glimpse of Sion's Glory,* 237-75.

3. See Williams, [Selma R. *Divine Rebel: the life of Anne Marbury Hutchinson* New York: Holt, and Rinehart and Winston, 1981] 63-76, for a detailed explanation of possible reasons for the family's decision to settle in New England.

4. Reference is to Winthrop's *A Short Story of the rise, reign, and ruine of the Antinomians, Familists & libertines,* (London, 1644); reprinted in *The Antinomian Controversy, 1636-1638: A Documentary History,* ed. David D. Hall (Middletown, Conn.: Wesleyan University Press, 1968), 199-310. Subsequent references appear in the text as *SS,* followed by page number.

5. See Williams, *Divine Rebel,* 73-74, 79-80.

6. The account of the theological fine points of the Antinomian Controversy presented in this chapter are necessarily brief. An indispensable account of the theological aspects of the controversy is William K. B. Stoever, *"A Faire and Easie Way to*

Heaven": Covenant Theology and Antinomianism in Early Massachusetts (Middletown, Conn.: Wesleyan University Press, 1978). In the context of Winthrop's journal entry, see pp. 9-10.

7. John Wheelwright, "A Fast-Day Sermon" (Boston: 1637); reprinted in *Antinomian Controversy,* 154.

8. Ibid., 158.

9. Ibid., 165, 166.

10. See T. H. Breen, *The Character of the Good Ruler: A Study of Puritan Political Ideas in New England, 1630-1730* (New Haven: Yale University Press, 1970), 3-7.

11. Gura, *A Glimpse of Sion's Glory,* 254-55.

12. Morgan, *Puritan Dilemma,* 147-48; "Examination of Mrs. Hutchinson," in *Antinomian Controversy,* 311.

13. Gura, *Glimpse of Sion's Glory,* 239.

14. "Examination of Mrs. Hutchinson," *Antinomian Controversy,* 316.

15. Ibid., 334.

16. Compare Winthrop's *Short Story* (271) with the anonymous version, "Examination of Mrs. Hutchinson," in *Antinomian Controversy,* 336-38 and 341.

17. "Examination of Mrs. Hutchinson," in *Antinomian Controversy,* 343.

18. Ibid., 348.

19. For Winthrop's account of the trial, see *Antinomian Controversy,* 300-10; for the anonymous report, see "A Report of the Trial of Mrs. Anne Hutchinson before the Church of Boston," in *Antinomian Controversy,* 349-88.

20. See Battis, *Saints and Sectarians,* 233-35, for an explanation of Hutchinson's newfound interest in death and resurrection.

21. "A Report of the Trial," in *Antinomian Controversy,* 388.

22. In the context of Mary Dyer's monstrous birth, of course, Winthrop has recorded Dyer's act of accompanying Hutchinson; see *Antinomian Controversy,* 281.

23. See Margaret Richardson and Arthur Hertig, "New England's First Recorded Hydatidiform Mole," *New England Journal of Medicine* 260 (1959):544-45. See also Anne Jacobson Schutte, "'Such Monstrous Births': A Neglected Aspect of the Antinomian Controversy," *Renaissance Quarterly* 38 (Spring 1985): 85-106.

24. Dunn's work on Winthrop and his journal is extensive. See "Experiments Holy and Unholy, 1630-31," in K. R. Andrews et al., *The Westward Enter-*

prise: English Activities in Ireland, the Atlantic, and America, 1480-1650 (Detroit: Wayne State University Press, 1979), 271-89. See also "Seventeenth-Century English Historians of America," in James Morton Smith, ed., *Seventeenth-Century America: Essays in Colonial History* (Chapel Hill: University of North Carolina Press, 1959), 195-225. Most recently Dunn has elaborated on the composition of the journal in "John Winthrop Writes His Journal," 185-212.

25. McCrimmon, "John Winthrop's Journal," *Manuscripts*, 24, 2 (1972):87-96.

26. Power, *Before the Convention: Religion and the Founders*, 65-106.

27. Miller, *The New England Mind: The Seventeenth Century* (New York: Macmillan, 1939; reprint, Cambridge: Harvard University Press, 1954), 360.

28. See Charles E. Banks, [*The Winthrop Fleet of 1630: An Account of the Vessels, the Voyage, the Passengers and Their English Homes from Original Authorities*. Boston: Riverside Press, 1930] 33-45. In a letter dated 14 August 1630 Winthrop mentions a chart of the sea voyage that Peter Milbourne, captain of the *Arbella*, drew for him (see *Winthrop Papers* [5 vols. Boston: Massachusetts Historical Society, 1929-47.] 2:309).

29. The best modern edition of Higginson's "True Relation" is in *Letters from New England: The Massachusetts Bay Colony, 1629-1638*, ed. Everett Emerson, 12-24. It is also reprinted in Hutchinson's *Collection of Original Papers* (Boston: Prince Society Publications), 32-47, and in *Chronicles of the First Planters of the Colony of Massachusetts Bay, 1623-1636*, ed. Alexander Young (Boston: 1846), 215-238, 260-64. See *Winthrop Papers*, 2:157, for the letter in which Winthrop mentions Higginson's "booke." See also Dunn, "Winthrop Writes His Journal," 190-91.

30. It is interesting to note that Winthrop's model, the Higginson account, also gives much space to descriptions of the wind (see Emerson, ed., [*Letters from New England: The Massachusetts Bay Colony, 1629-1638*. Amherst: University of Massachusetts Press, 1976] 12-24).

31. Unless otherwise noted, subsequent references to Winthrop's journal, in this chapter are to Hosmer, [James Kendall] ed., [*Winthrop's Journal "History of New England," 1630-1649*. 2 vols. New York: Scribner's Sons, 1908].

32. *History of New England* [*from 1630 to 1649*. 2 vols. Vol. 1, Boston: Phelps and Farnham, 1825; vol. 2, Boston: T. B. Wait and Son, 1826] ed. James Savage (1825), 1:271. Hosmer felt obliged

to omit Winthrop's account of the "monstrous birth" (*J*, 1:277, note 2). For the text of Winthrop's account, see the Savage edition, 1:271-73.

33. This is another of the several passages Hosmer decided not to include in his edition of the journal. See *The History of New England*, ed. Savage (1825), 2:61.

34. Robert C. Winthrop, *Life and Letters of John Winthrop*, [2 vols. Boston: Ticknor & Fields, 1864, 1867] 1:221.

35. In this context, *corn* is meant in the British sense of grain in general, and specifically, as Winthrop makes clear in the paper, barley.

36. See Robert C. Winthrop, *Life and Letters*, 1:262. The autograph volume of these sermon notes is housed in the Massachusetts Historical Society. A microfilm reprint is available in the *Winthrop Family Papers, 1537-1905*, reel 35.

37. The fragment is reprinted in *Winthrop Papers*, 3:10-14.

38. For the text of the "Declaration," see *Winthrop Papers*, 3:422-26.

39. Perry Miller, *Errand into the Wilderness* (Cambridge: Harvard University Press, 1956), 70.

40. Winthrop summarizes the debate in his *Short Story*. See *Antinomian Controversy*, ed. Hall, 251.

41. For Vane's answer to Winthrop's defense, see Thomas Hutchinson, *Collection of Original Papers Relative to the History of Massachusetts Bay* (Boston: Prince Society Publication, 1865), 1:74 and following.

42. Subsequent references to Winthrop's *A Declaration of Former Passages Betwixt the English and the Narrowgansets* (Boston: By Order of the Commissioners for the United Colonies, 1645) appear in the text as *DFP* and page.

43. Judging by historical evidence, one cannot be too sure of the Puritan settlers' sincerity concerning the conversion of the Indians. Besides the work of John Eliot, little was done to introduce the word of God to the native Americans. See Francis Jennings, [*The Invasion of America: Indians, colonialism, and the cant of conquest*. Chapel Hill, N.C.: University of North Carolina Press for the Institute of Early American History and Culture, 1976.] especially 228-53.

44. Jennings, *The Invasion of America*, 274.

45. The text of Roger Williams's letter is reprinted in *Winthrop Papers*, 4:30-31.

46. Jennings, *Invasion*, 275.

47. Ibid, 274.

48. In his biting appraisal, Jennings is not nearly so generous. See Jennings, *Invasion,* 265-76.

49. For Winthrop's account of the episode, see *Winthrop's Journal,* 2:116.

50. See *Winthrop Papers,* 4:380-91, for the text of Winthrop's "Reply to the Answ[er]."

51. For the text of Winthrop's "Arbitrary Government," see *Winthrop Papers,* 4:468-88.

52. For Winthrop's account of events leading up to his writing of the little speech and for the text of the speech itself, see his *Journal,* 2:229-40.

Selected Bibliography

PRIMARY SOURCES

Antinomians and Familists Condemned by the synod of Elders in New-England: with the proceedings of the magistrates against them, and their apology for the same. . . . London: Printed for R. Smith, 1644. Republished as *A Short Story of the rise, reign and ruin of the Antinomians, Familists & libertines. . . .* London: Printed for Ralph Smith, 1644. Reprinted in *The Antinomian Controversy, 1636-1638: A Documentary History,* 199-310. Edited by David D. Hall. Middletown, Conn.: Wesleyan University Press, 1968.

A Declaration of Former Passages and Proceedings Betwixt the English and the Narrowgansets, with Their Confederates, Wherein the Grounds and Justice of the Ensuing Warre Are Opened and Cleared. Boston: Commissioners for the United Colonies, 1645.

A Journal of the Transactions and Occurrences in the Settlement of Massachusetts and the Other New-England Colonies, from the Year 1630 to 1644. Edited by Noah Webster. Hartford: Printed by Elisha Babcock, 1790. Reedited and published as *The History of New England from 1630 to 1649.* 2 vols. Edited by James Savage. Vol. 1, Boston: Phelps and Farnham, 1825; vol. 2, Boston, T. B. Wait and Son, 1826. Revised edition, Boston: Little, Brown, 1853. Republished as *Winthrop's Journal "History of New England," 1630-1649.* 2 vols. Edited by James Kendall Hosmer. New York: Scribner's Sons, 1908. Reprint. New York: Barnes and Noble, 1966.

Winthrop Papers. 5 vols. Boston: Massachusetts Historical Society, 1929-47.

Scott Michaelsen (essay date 1992)

SOURCE: Michaelsen, Scott. "John Winthrop's 'Modell' Covenant and the Company Way." *Early American Literature* 27, no. 2 (1992): 85-100.

[*In the following essay, Michaelsen proposes that "A Modell of Christian Charity" served two purposes, sug-* gesting that Winthrop's aim was not only to instill a sense of pride in the participants but also to create a contractual agreement that would benefit both sides of the venture.]

I

As Andrew Delbanco has noted, first Massachusetts governor John Winthrop's departure sermon, **"A Modell of Christian Charity"** (1630), is "enshrined as a kind of Ur-text of American literature" (72).[1] In his reading, **"A Modell"** becomes a text more important for what it says about old England than new; Delbanco sees it as a series of Puritan renunciations of former practice rather than a forward-looking definition of an "errand into the wilderness," as Perry Miller's famous interpretation had it. Even so, Winthrop's sermon still stands for Delbanco as a kind of boundary line separating one horizon of thought from another. Its promises and warnings, its notions of community and awesome responsibility, become somehow typical of the American mind in general.

The sermon has been especially significant to scholars concerned with establishing an American Puritan belief in national or federal covenant: a special, legalistic relationship between God and the New Englanders as a whole regarding their emigration project. It has been said that "for all their talk about polity, the Puritans had no idea what a covenanted state really was . . . until John Winthrop and his company actually founded a state by contract" and that the **"Modell"** sermon is the place where "the doctrine of the national covenant [is] articulated most memorably" (Foster xii; Gura 216). One is tempted to go further, and suggest that the very idea of an early American Puritan belief in federal covenant is often premised on the existence of Winthrop's secular sermon.

The question of Winthrop's representativeness, which was debunked memorably by Darrett B. Rutman, becomes even more troublesome when one explores more deeply Winthrop's **"Modell"** covenant and communitarian cast of mind through a reestablishment of a specifically legal context for the sermon, both theoretical and practical. Winthrop's sermon not only bears a significant relation to newly emerging theories of contract law and interpretation, but it reveals a great deal about the actual legal conditions of the Puritan voyage to America. Winthrop emerges from such a reading as a figure of special rather than general significance.

II

While there is no doubt that the writing of Winthrop and other Puritan leaders was suffused with legal terminology, such terms are assumed to have been derived from either theology or political theory. A third, frequently overlooked, possibility involves looking to the law itself. The legal mind is everywhere in evidence in the **"Modell,"** and Winthrop, who studied at Gray's Inn, and practiced law in London and on the family estate for many years, developed his version of federal covenant from impulses in English law. In order to understand this, one must know that the concept of "covenant" has a rich history in the common law, the law that emerges from custom or court decision rather than statute. "Action of covenant," for example, is an ancient form of pleading in the common law system, in effect as early as the 1200s. From that time onward, actions of covenant were slowly replaced in British law by more modern contract law (first by the pleading form "action of debt," and later by the "action of assumpsit"); as late as the 1600s, however, lawyers were still regularly filing suit using the action "breach of covenant" for a number of ordinary purposes. Typically, such actions mandated written evidence ("expressed covenants") in the form of deeds or charters and their seals. One legal definition of "covenant," for example, is a "promise under seal." Covenant law was quite strict: Justice Oliver Wendell Holmes, Jr., said that "for a time, a man was bound by his seal, although it was affixed without his consent."[2]

The legal concept of covenant belongs to medieval times, and brings with it a medieval sense of power relations. Holmes noted that the seals necessary for such covenants, for example, "were said by the Chief Justice of England to belong properly only to the kings and to very great men." Puritan covenant theology is analogous. In John Cotton's "A Sermon Delivered at Salem, 1636," the covenant is "made to me, and to my seed" rather than "with" the Puritans (*Churches* 42). God issues the covenant and, once accepted, he applies seals which he alone holds in the form of the sacraments (41). Only the most minimal sense of human agency figures into the typical covenant equation—individuals must give themselves up to the predetermined bargain. The covenant Cotton describes is in effect as a "perpetual covenant" because of God's still unbroken covenant with the nation of Israel (46). In other words, like legal covenant, once established, it cannot be broken. It binds for all time as long as the document and seals are intact. No later considerations are conceivable, nor is a renegotiation of any part of the perpetual covenant, such as, say, the Mosaic laws, a possibility (47). All that human beings can perform, according to Cotton, is a "renewing of this covenant" (56).[3]

Something very different happens in Winthrop's **"A Modell of Christian Charity,"** in a way unique to the Puritan literature but not to early seventeenth-century law and its still emerging notions of modern contract. When Winthrop describes the nature of the federal covenant with God, he says:

> Thus stands the cause betweene God and vs, wee are entered into Covenant with him for this worke, wee haue taken out a Commission, the Lord hath giuen vs leaue to drawe our owne Articles we haue professed to enterprise these Accions vpon these and these ends, we haue hereuvpon besought him of favour and blessing: Now if the Lord shall please to heare vs, and bring vs in peace to the place wee desire, then hath hee ratified this Covenant and sealed our Commission, [and] will expect a strickt performance of the Articles contained in it. . . .

> (Winthrop 294)

Rather than God making covenant "to" the Puritans, or even "with" them, Winthrop imagines the Puritans themselves as conceiving of this special, federal covenant, and beginning negotiations from their side of the table: "Wee haue taken out a Commission," and then "professed to enterprise these Accions" and "besought him of favour and blessing." Winthrop places the covenant on God's desk for ratification, and the Puritans will know "hee ratified" their deal when they have established themselves successfully in their new place.

These are remarkable words, and they speak to a number of post-"action of covenant" developments in the law. Perhaps most important are the contemporary beginnings of the "will" theory for interpretation of contracts, evident in a text such as Hugo Grotius' *De Jure Belli ac Pacis Libri Tres* [*The Law of War and Peace*] (1625). Such a new attitude presumes that obligations are always "acts of will" rather than mere formal responsibilities. As one recent historian of contracts writes: "The implication of the ascendancy of the will theory was that contract obligations were now viewed as mutual obligations voluntarily created by the parties and now expressed in the form of an offer and acceptance" (Teeven 181). This is the territory of the Winthropian covenant. Quite literally, Winthrop's Puritans will their bargain with the Creator in a way unprecedented in the writings of the ministers.[4]

Not surprisingly, this and other of Winthrop's theological pronouncements served as an embarrassment to some of the ministers, and struck them as classically Arminian, or tending toward a heretical, will theory of salvation.[5] Several times, for example, that mild man, the reverend Thomas Shepard, found it necessary to reproach Winthrop by letter regarding ideas the latter was disseminating. In a 1636 missive that addresses Winthrop's Arminian leanings, Shepard explained:

> I thought it fit to send vnto yow my thoughts by way of wrighting, vntill we speake together, if so yow think fit; when I read the question in your declaration, I did woonder & greaue that I should liue to see the liberty of mens spirits, not only to deny so playne a truth, but that they should abolish the very forme of wholsom woords of truth. . . .

> (Shepard 258)

Eight pages of specific problems with Winthrop's latest declaration follow. Even when one accounts for the heterogeneous nature of American Puritan theology during the 1630s, Winthrop's views were atypical and out of step with the religious leadership, and he was in many ways more pointedly modern than his colleagues.

III

There also are practical reasons why Winthrop described his version of the federal covenant as an offer to God, for his acceptance. He was, after all, merely transposing into covenant theology the actual history, legal status and terms of the charter issued to the Puritans in 1629, including its provisions allowing the Company to hold Court and establish laws in the Plantation ("the Lord hath giuen vs leaue to drawe our owne Articles").[6] The formal identity of Puritan Massachusetts in its first half century is that of a company formed by special royal charter or commission—a joint-stock enterprise known as "The Governor and Company of the Massachusetts Bay in New England."[7] Significantly, the actual charter for this enterprise most likely was written by John White, author of *The Planter's Plea* (1630), and the counsellor to Massachusetts Bay during the negotiations (Deane 178-9). In other words, the commission itself is of Puritan origin, just as Winthrop suggested in **"A Modell of Christian Charity."** To the extent that **"A Modell"** is a spiritual document, only a monumental slippage should permit Winthrop to speak of covenants in the same language as that which describes an essentially secular proposition. And yet such a slippage occurs: the concepts of business and theology have been knit together in Winthrop's work, and the line between the secular and the sacred is in danger of vanishing altogether, as it is during the Puritan experiment generally.[8]

Winthrop's pre-voyage work of 1629, reorganizing and managing the Massachusetts Bay Company on short notice, deeply marked his thought concerning the Massachusetts community, as the following words from **"A Modell"** indicate:

> [W]ee are a Company professing our selues fellow members of Christ. . . .
>
> (292)

The choice of the word "Company" reveals a highly strained version of the federal theology. On the one hand, according to Winthrop, the Puritan "Company" as a community had agreed to covenant with God, and to become "fellow members of Christ." On the other hand, the community literally exists as a "Company," or joint stock venture, and Winthrop's sermon again conflates the spiritual and secular with his word choice. Indeed, Winthrop's notion of covenant is perhaps best understood through the law of commissions and charters—

rules of incorporation. He urges his listeners to always have "before our eyes our Commission and Community in the worke . . ." (294), and it is significant that the term "Commission" comes before that of "Community," and with reference to "worke."

That words such as "Company" and "Commission" really reference the legal reality of the Puritan enterprise is relatively easy to demonstrate. These terms are duplicated in Cotton's departure sermon, "God's Promise to His Plantations" (1630), preached under similar circumstances. Even though the metaphors in the text primarily are organic, Cotton says that "a Colony" is "a company," and that it can only proceed from "speciall Commission" or "grand Charter" from God ("Promise" 8, 6). In reverse, Thomas Hooker's famous federal sermons of the same period, "The Faithful Covenanter" (1629) and "The Danger of Desertion" (1631), which were preached before his involvement with the Massachusetts Bay colony, use a far less particular confederated vocabulary. The church or federal covenant is analogized in a highly overdetermined manner: the federal unit is alternately referred to as "city," "Jerusalem," "town," "nation," "England," "church," "Israel," "family," "congregation," "tribe," "country," "kingdom," and only once as "company." And while legalisms abound in Hooker's texts, there are no references to special warrants, commissions and charters.[9]

But noting the conflation of the sacred and the secular in the Winthrop text is not enough. A problem remains, because it is impossible to square the Company's royal charter with the Puritan's divine commission. Perry Miller tried to do just that, in his own way, starting from the premise that **"A Modell of Christian Charity"** was a further extension or elaboration of "The Cambridge Agreement," the August 1629 document that pledged Winthrop and eleven others to departure for New England by March 1630 ("Shaping" 6).[10] But "The Cambridge Agreement" is a contract signed by a group of equals (all were either undertakers soon to be charged with the joint stock for the next seven years, or patentees, or gentlemen) while the **"Modell"** announces itself from the start as a document about the relation between the rich and the poor: "some must be rich some poore, some highe and eminent in power and dignitie; others meane and in subieccion" (282). In Winthrop's sermon, the "Community" presumably included all who were to voyage across the water, but the business of the "Company" belonged legally only to the ten undertakers, and to any other planter adventurers on board, but not to servants, hired artisans, or families that paid for passage but were not stockholders.[11] Even after the celebrated general admission of settlers to the status of freemen, in October 1630, the stock and potential profits remained in the hands of the ten. The right to vote extended franchise, not ownership. At no time, and certainly not at the time of this sermon, could one legitimately have said that the Company was coextensive with the Community.

In other words, two bodies of individuals listened to Winthrop's sermon on the eve of departure.[12] One is the potential body of rich and poor, the Community at large, who are being urged to form a whole for some mutual purpose. The other is the corporate body, and includes only a small portion of the Community. The body of the Community is being exhorted to function like a corporate body through a powerful gesture of incorporation. The very structure and thrust of **"A Modell of Christian Charity"** seeks to reduce the other to the status of the same by sleight of hand, subjecting it to a Company project.

IV

"A Modell of Christian Charity" is a document that concerns Winthrop's company way for the Massachusetts Bay, laying out the "big picture" for a very specific, seventeenth-century, fledgling colonial corporation. The word "modell" in the title of the document might denote a simple proposal, or an outline of an agreement between groups in accordance with knowledge of a shared world. But the "modell" does not function like Winthrop's modern contract. It is not subject to a counter-proposal, for example. The "modell" is rather of a predetermined diagram of corporate structure and reporting relationships. It is an already established frame of reference for proper organization of the tasks of rich and poor.

Perhaps contradicting this is the sermon's language of love, which has secured its place in a canon of communitarian documents. Immediately after Winthrop informed his audience that they were a "Company," he suggested that:

> though wee were absent from eache other many miles, and had our imploymentes as farre distant, yet wee ought to account our selues knitt together by this bond of loue, and liue in the exercise of it, if wee would haue comforte of our being in Christ. . . .
>
> (292)

Such language has inspired a number of commentators to conclude with Miller that the sermon resolves class distinctions in a radical way under a notion of shared covenant: "Ostensibly, then, he is propounding a European class structure; but when he comes to the exhortation, he does not so much demand that inferiors remain in pious subjection to superiors, but rather he calls upon all, gentlemen and commoners, to be knit together in this work as one man. . . ." ("Shaping" 6-7). Delbanco, taking an even more extreme position, says that **"A Modell of Christian Charity"** is a "communitarian statement" on pure "mutuality" (74). Theodore Dwight Bozeman also emphasizes the love that would allow the

Puritans to "relive the selfless spirit of the early Christian communes" (300). Even a more moderate commentator such as Stephen Foster, attuned to Puritan social arrangements that emphasized "subordination, inequality, authority, unity, suppression of the individual will for the good of the whole," concludes that Winthrop's sermon is about the Greek notion of *agape*: "In the **"Model,"** social distinctions rest exclusively on love" (6, 42).[13]

Each of these commentators has, in his own way, fallen into a reading of the **"Modell"** that merely reifies certain of the rhetorical effects built up in the last part of the sermon. Winthrop's strategies throughout, including the use of the first person plural, "wee," hint that those already theorized as "in subieccion" are at least partners and perhaps near equals, though at every turn the text specifies the necessary inequalities built into social relations. What typically is missing from the radical communitarian readings of the sermon is a careful analysis of its quite confusing first sections, which constitute a rapid tour of Winthropian history, as well as of the "laws" and "rules" appropriate to the different phases of history, and to the different social classes.

According to Winthrop, pure love or mutuality was only possible in Adam's world, before the fall (290). The world of the present day, on the other hand, presumes the division of humankind into classes, as well as the necessity of charity. Though Winthrop says that the "love" inherent to Adam and his world stands in some way as the ground for the operation of the present world, love must be supplemented in a way that makes it less important than the two "rules" of "Mercy" and "Justice" (283-4). "Mercy" is not the pure love of Adam; according to Winthrop it governs practices of giving, lending, and forgiving. "Justice," on the other hand, governs strict lending arrangements, such as rules of collateral and repayment of loans. The shape of Winthrop's sermon is determined by the knowledge of the importance of Mercy and Justice, which are part of a modern world organized by commerce and exchange, contracts and debts. These two rules are explicated in the text before anything else, and certainly before the concept of love.

Winthrop weighs the relative merits of the rules of Mercy and Justice in an early part of the sermon. At first, Mercy appears more important. When Winthrop explains the operation of the Adamic world and the world of the Israelites, he states that he will "omitt" from discussion "the rule of Justice as not propperly belonging to this purpose otherwise then it may fall into consideracion in some perticuler Cases" (283). But the rule of Justice is paramount when discussing the present age. According to Winthrop, the very possibility of applying a rule of Mercy depends in the first place upon a test of the rule of Justice:

[I]f he hath present meanes of repayeing thee, thou art to looke at him, not as an Act of mercy, but by way of Commerce, wherein thou arte to walke by the rule of Justice. . . .

(286)

If the rule of Justice applies—that is, according to Winthrop, if the lendee can repay a loan, or if the lender obtained a "surety or a lawfull pleadge" (286)—then Justice rules in this world. Mercy matters only when the rule of Justice has been exhausted.

Winthrop explicitly links the rule of Justice to "Commerce," which is the mode of operations for the present model or "body" of the world.[14] While the metaphorical "body" of Adam consisted of a network of perfect "ligamentes" (289), the modern world "body" is economical at heart, and functions according to principles of efficiency:

the mouth is at all the paines to receiue, and mince the foode which serues for the nourishment of all the other partes of the body, yet it hath noe cause to complaine; for first, the other partes send back by secret passages a due proporcion of the same nourishment in a better form for the strengthening and comforteing of the mouthe.

(291-292)

In this somewhat confusing passage, the "mouth" of the body in the present world is figurative for the rich, and the "other partes" for the poor. The "love" between the two has been subsumed into Commerce, a system of exchanges apparently "equall" in value, though the "partes" return love to the "mouth" "in a better form" for the sake of their "strengthening and comfort."[15] Because the modern world functions according to such Commerce, superintended by rule of Justice, Mercy and even Love are thematized in the text in commercial terms. Even the most charitable, loving act described by Winthrop—giving to the poor—has economic implications on the spiritual plane: "for first he that giues to the poore lends to the lord, and he will repay him euen in this life an hundred fold to him or his" (285). And the love of the poor man can only be described or analogized in terms of the "worke" of Commerce. To love is "to sett all the faculties on worke in the outward exercise of this duty as when wee bid one make the clocke strike. . . ." (288). The commercial body, thematized as a mechanical instrument, is ready for loving operation and maintenance by Winthrop's listeners.

Delbanco believes that **"A Modell of Christian Charity"** attempts to lay down an "explicit prohibition against the rule of the market" (76), but this is a difficult proposition to accept. For example, even though the final line of the sermon warns that the Puritans will "surely perishe out of the good Land" should they treat New England as a property to "possesse" (295), it re-

mains an open question as to which part of the community this is addressed. Coming from a man who, at the time, owned and operated one-tenth of an immense New England enterprise, supported and financed by a much larger number of men of business, one wonders whether this is merely an exhortation directed at the poorer class, seeking to set them in clockwork motion in order to blunt their acquisitive tendencies.

V

Examination of Winthrop's **"Modell"** covenant and the company way merely puts some new and perhaps better wrinkles in the picture, which in turn resonate with some of Winthrop's other writings. For example, the **"Modell"** now rings and rhymes with Winthrop's Vane debate writings of 1637, where he paternalistically speaks of the power of a "corporation" to shape and guide human beings for their own "wellfare" (Hutchinson 80), where he explains that the rule of justice is to be exercised before the rule of mercy when confronting strangers (81), and where, most dramatically, he suggests that the rule of love in itself cannot be the guide for an incorporated people, living according to law, property rights, clearly delineated privileges:

Thus he [Vane] runs on in a frivolous difcourfe. . . . So that if he need to borrow my horfe, and I ought by the rule of love to lend him to him, though I refufe to confent to his requeft herein, yet he may take him, becaufe my diffent is unlawfull; fo by this conclufion a wife, a childe, a fervant may doe any thinge that is lawfull, though the hufband, father, or maifter deny their confent. If this fpeed well, the next conclufion will be an anarchie.

(99)

Finally, if there are still doubts that the Winthropian concept of love must always be understood as operating under the legal strictures of Justice, one can examine Winthrop's "Address" to the Massachusetts Bay Company of December 1, 1629, which successfully sought the transfer of the joint stock to the ten undertakers. While he made a number of arguments for the arrangement, his conclusion places "the law of Contract" higher than "our natural relation," or love, as a rationale for the vote (Winthrop 177).

Although it seems safe to conclude that Winthrop's thought evidences no radical communitarian values, he does harbor a progressive tendency with regard to "charity," and it is akin to his contractual views. John Winthrop suggests that Justice belongs by right to the wealthy and powerful. He says that the charity of the rich involves altering or modifying the just rules of "some perticuler contract" (283), and he goes on to specify terms for modification. The very fact that the rules of contracts between debtors and creditors is flexible in Winthrop's text—in other words, that he can posit a scheme for the absolution of debts once the rule of Justice is exhausted—is a sign of legal modernity. Flexibility in contractual interpretation was introduced into the common law only as action of covenant gave way to actions of debt or assumpsit. As Kevin M. Teeven explains, it is when covenant begins to fade that notions of *quid pro quo* and consideration begin to enter the law—approximately 1400 for the former and the late 1500s for the latter (11, 39). But Winthrop goes further than mere consideration, which still holds to "the ancient truths that bargains should bind both parties and that the promisor should be held to promises relied on" (Teeven 44). Contextualizing him in a slighter more modern idiom than his own, Winthrop's theological vocabulary is close to legitimizing a kind of bankruptcy code or standard. His notion of mercy also is clearly related to contemporaneous developments in the law of equity, a kind of legal reasoning developed around the moral notion of "conscience" (Allen 406-10). Equity law, which emerged both as part of common law heritage and as part of the law of the King's Council, was described in Thomas Ashe's *Epieikeia* (1609) as "'*a ruled kind of justice.*' Though 'ruled,' it is 'allayed with the sweetness of mercy . . .'" (qtd. in Allen 409-10).[16]

Winthrop's text puts the lie to the old saw that, for the Puritans, a bargain was a bargain that must be made good. But, on the other hand, he does not go so far as Portia's plea in *The Merchant of Venice* (c. 1595): "That in the course of justice, none of us / Should see salvation. We do pray for mercy. . . ." (IV.1.199-200). To take up this call would be to deny strict justice in the name of mercy or, even more radically, love, which Winthrop does not do. The company way described in John Winthrop's **"A Modell of Christian Charity"** is neither one of pure force nor pure love. While certainly not locked into the inflexible patterns of medieval law and its corporations, as Joseph Dorfman asserted, Winthrop's thought also is not proto-democratic, as Edmund Morgan believed. The sermon asserts his and the other business adventurers' right to contract according to their own wills and desires, and then seeks to subordinate and subject the rest of the company to the shape of these desires, while it also undeniably attempts to institute certain kinds of contractual flexibility or contingency on behalf of the stamped and shaped middle to lower classes.[17] And that, for Winthrop, would be granting enough to both sides in order to bind the colony. Politically conservative, while legally modern and economically progressive, what can and should be stated with clarity about John Winthrop's **"Modell"** is that it is frankly and deeply contractual, thoughtful and wide awake for his era, and, to use two of his favorite words, filled with a sense of authority's "arbitrary" or "discretionary" promise.

Notes

1. For example, the most famous piece of Puritan scholarship of this generation, Sacvan Bercovitch's *The American Jeremiad* (1978), opens with an examination of Winthrop's seemingly epochal sermon. Perry Miller in 1954 also read "A Modell" as "Ur-" in the sense of original and originating, radically separating the British experience from the American: "Winthrop stands at the beginning of our consciousness" ("Shaping" 6). "A Modell" has been of interest to many sorts of scholars, investigating either Winthrop or the Puritan experience in general. Others of recent note include Joseph Dorfman (1946), Edmund Morgan (1958), Darrett B. Rutman (1965), George L. Mosse (1968), Stephen Foster (1971), Theodore Dwight Bozeman (1988), and Delbanco (1989). In recent years Winthrop's importance in conversation about the Puritans has been accentuated because of the reassessment of the Puritan "errand" (the "Citty vpon a Hill"), addressed most recently and convincingly by Bozeman. Of course, fascination with Winthrop as a representative American dates back much further, to at least the time of John Adams's imaginary Winthrop texts (*Papers* 1:191-210; 2:380-7).

2. See Teeven 7-11; Kiralfy 121, 180; Pound and Plucknett 406; Holmes on covenant qtd. from Pound and Plucknett 584-86.

3. David D. Hall cites Puritan historians William K. B. Stoever and John S. Coolidge as the current last words on the problem of human will and works in relation to the normative covenant. As he summarizes Stoever: "The promise of free grace was conditional only insofar as God had arranged the order of salvation to include freely willed consent of the elect" (202). In other words, human willing is already under God's law. And citing Coolidge, Hall says "that the covenant of grace must contain 'components of conditionality and absoluteness.' Thus, too, he accentuates the paradox that grace is, and yet is not, conditional: 'It is gratuitous but not inconsequential'" (210).

4. Perry Miller found evidence for a minimally voluntaristic conception of covenant in theologian William Ames's writings, although Winthrop's sentiments are closer in spirit to the language which Miller cites from reverend Samuel Willard's *A Compleat Body of Divinity,* written one hundred years later, in 1726 (*Mind* 375). In general, however, my reading of Winthrop complements Miller's most general understanding of covenant theology: "That is to say that the federal theology was essentially part of a universal tendency in European thought to change social relationships from status to contract, that it was one expression of

late Renaissance speculation, which was moving in general away from the ideas of feudalism, from the belief that society must be modeled upon an eternally fixed hierarchy to the theories of constitutional limitation and voluntary origins, to the protection of individual rights and the shattering of sumptuary economic regulations" (399).

5. Arminius said that God's grace "depends on the will of man, in regard that by vertue of its native liberty, it may receive or reject this grace, use it or not use it, render it effectuall or vain. . . . [I]f we do what we can, and improve the natural abilities we have, and the means we do enjoy God wil not deny to give us the grace supernatural we want" (qtd. in Miller, *Mind* 368).

6. The charter itself speaks with a different voice. From the outset the king's grant is described as "theis present" [this gift] "to HAVE and to houlde" (Shurtleff 3), and not as a bargain struck with the colonists.

7. At the very least, the possibility of the Massachusetts experiment is premised upon: (1) a 1620 royal charter to an entity known as the Council for New England, a company without any religious motivation for settlement; (2) a 1628 patent granted from the Council to the New England Company, a small group of individuals who sought to leave England for religious reasons; and (3) a 1629 royal charter to the radically transformed Company that executed the Puritan voyage. The second charter is based on the first, and the third premised on the second. Massachusetts Bay is an hybrid entity that bears some resemblance to a trading company and some to a city, both of which were forms of incorporation.

On some of the early, interesting efforts by the Council for New England, see Christy. For the Massachusetts Bay Company records from the period prior to colonization, see Young 39-128. For the text of the 1629 charter, see Shurtleff 3-20.

8. During the Vane debate of 1637, Winthrop again elided the difference between the civil and the sacred entities:

We A.B.C.&c. confented to cohabite in the Maffachufetts, and under the government fet up among us by his Majefty's patent or grant for our mutual fafety and wellfare, we agreed to walke according to the rules of the gofpell. And thus you have both a chriftian common weale and the fame founded upon the patent, and both included within my defcription [of the commonwealth in general].

(Hutchinson 97)

9. "The Faithful Covenanter" and "The Danger of Desertion" are reprinted in Hooker 190-220, and 228-52. The reference to a "company" occurs in the former:

If the righteous, brethren, hardly get to heaven, but [one] loses an arm, another a right eye, as it were, and with many prayers and sighs and grapplings with God, and through many temptations hardly come to heaven in the end, and a poor humble soul beg for power against his corruptions, as if he would pluck mercy from the Lord by strong hand, and yet scarcely subdue sin and obtain salvation, what then will become of a company that are enemies to God and godliness?

(193-4)

10. See Young 281-4 for a copy of the text with Young's helpful annotations.

11. "Few freemen of the Massachusetts Bay Company came to Massachusetts. By the provisions of the charter these men alone could elect Officers of the Company and make laws. Legally and numerically they constituted a political minority among the mass of inhabitants who were not members of the company" (Simmons 7). Also, see Young 113-18 for the company's important decision on the joint stock on Nov. 30 and Dec. 1, 1629, and the terms of the agreement with the ten undertakers.

12. Hugh J. Dawson convincingly explains that Winthrop likely delivered the sermon to the entire group of voyagers at Southampton, before departure, and not simply to those who were later aboard the ship Arabella. It was "an occasion to address a body of the company's numbers gathered at the seacoast" (226).

13. A modern commentator in the minority on this issue is Richard C. Simmons, who suggests of the Puritans:

On the limited evidence available it seems likely that the leaders of the emigration expected to maintain their authority out of England for the same reasons which they had exercised it within; they were the social and religious elite, the clergy and gentry of their localities and persons to whom deference was given as a matter of course. There is nothing in their writings to suggest that they had radical ideas about social or political matters. Winthrop's "Model of Christian Charity" may be taken as typical of their thinking.

(1-2)

14. The term "Commerce" can have more than one meaning here and elsewhere in the text. The word in the first place refers to large-scale trade by means of exchange, with reference in the seven-

teenth century to mercantile economics. Yet in the same period it also means general, non-economic dealings between men, and, thirdly, "intercourse or commerce with God" (OED). However, given Winthrop's linking of the term to practices of lending and to rules of justice regarding debts, the term, at the very least, resonates with economic implications, even though it may have other significations as well.

15. While the human body has often served as a metaphor for communitarian societies, compare Winthrop's clearly hierarchical body to the one recently described by Hans Meier, a ninety-year-old man who has spent most of his adult life as part of the Bruderhof, a radically communitarian group residing in several locations in the United States:

> Community means common-unity. This is also true for any living body. Therefore common-unity represents life. A body is alive as long as all its members work together harmoniously under the guidance of one living soul. The respective soul in a community is the living spirit of God.
>
> Our body, which we carry visibly daily with us, is a continuous witness to us as a God-given fact. As long as all its cells and members are working together harmoniously the body remains healthy and alive. As soon as any of its organs goes its own way, the body becomes sick and in the end dies. If, for instance, one leg would go to Lancaster and the other to Elizabethtown, the body would be torn in two parts and die—including the two responsible legs. Or if the hands would say: We have worked for the bread (tilling the field, harvesting, milling, baking), therefore the bread belongs to us and we shall keep it— then the bread would not reach the mouth, the stomach, the intestines and the bloodstream, which distributes the nourishment to all the cells according to their need. The result would be the death of the whole body from hunger—including the two hands.

(Meier 1)

Here, although there is a division of labor, one does not find the Winthropian separation of head and body, nor the notion of the body's working for the benefit of the head. The Bruderhof, among other things, does not permit the ownership of property among its members, and this practice and others like it permit Meier to thematize a multiplicity of cells, organs, and limbs working for the good of the organism as a whole.

16. Interestingly, the legal concept of the joint-stock company of limited liability would emerge out of these same traditions of equity law (Allen 415). Massachusetts Bay's final structural-financial arrangement included limited liability for the major-

ity of the stockholders long before official recognition of this doctrine in American law in the early 1800s (Dodd 84-93).

17. I am indebted to conversations with Puritan scholar Robert Daly for his understanding of the contingent character of Winthrop's notion of authority. Relevant to this, perhaps, is E. Brooks Holifield's notion of New England ministers as "ambidexterous theologians" who, according to David D. Hall, "sometimes spoke in different ways because they were responsive to so many different texts, ideas, and situations" (see Hall 213).

Works Cited

Adams, John. *Papers of John Adams*. Ed. Robert J. Taylor, et al. Cambridge: Belknap-Harvard Univ. Press, 1977-.

Allen, Sir Carleton Kemp. *Law in the Making*. Seventh ed. Oxford: Clarendon, 1964.

Bercovitch, Sacvan. *The American Jeremiad*. Madison: Univ. of Wisconsin Press, 1978.

Bozeman, Theodore Dwight. *To Live Ancient Lives: The Primitivist Dimension in Puritanism*. Chapel Hill: Univ. of North Carolina Press, 1988.

Christy, Miller. "Attempts Toward Colonization: the Council for New England and the Merchant Venturers of Bristol, 1621-1623." *American Historical Review* 4.1 (July 1899): 678-702.

Cotton, John. "God's Promise to His Plantations." 1630. *Old South Leaflets* 3.53 ([1896]).

———. *John Cotton on the Churches of New England*. Ed. Larzer Ziff. Cambridge: Belknap-Harvard Univ. Press, 1968.

Dawson, Hugh J. "John Winthrop's Rite of Passage: The Origins of the 'Christian Charitie' Discourse." *Early American Literature* 26 (1991): 219-231.

Deane, Charles. "The Forms in Issuing Letters Patent by the Crown of England." *Proceedings of the Massachusetts Historical Society* 11 (Dec. 1869): 166-88.

Delbanco, Andrew. *The Puritan Ordeal*. Cambridge: Harvard Univ. Press, 1989.

Dodd, Edwin Merrick. *American Business Corporations Until 1860 with Special Reference to Massachusetts*. Cambridge: Harvard Univ. Press, 1954.

Dorfman, Joseph. *The Economic Mind in American Civilization 1606-1865, Volume One*. New York: Viking, 1946.

Foster, Stephen. *Their Solitary Way: The Puritan Social Ethic in the First Century of Settlement in New England*. New Haven: Yale Univ. Press, 1971.

Grotius, Hugo. *The Law of War and Peace [De Jure Belli ac Pacis Libri Tres]*. 1625. Trans. Francis W. Kelsey. Indianapolis: Bobbs-Merrill, [1962].

Gura, Philip F. *A Glimpse of Sion's Glory: Puritan Radicalism in New England, 1620-1660*. Middletown, Conn.: Wesleyan Univ. Press, 1984.

Hall, David D. "On Common Ground: The Coherence of American Puritan Studies." *William and Mary Quarterly* 44 (April 1987): 193-229.

Hooker, Thomas. *Writings in England and Holland, 1626-1633*. Ed. George H. Williams, et al. Cambridge: Harvard Univ. Press, 1975.

Hutchinson, Thomas, ed. *A Collection of Original Papers Relative to the History of the Colony of Massachusetts-Bay*. 1769. New York: Burt Franklin, 1967.

Kiralfy, A. K. R., ed. *A Source Book of English Law*. London: Sweet & Maxwell, 1957.

Meier, Hans. "Why We Live in Community." Third Triennial Conference of the International Communal Studies Association. Elizabethtown, Pa., 26 July 1991.

Miller, Perry. *The New England Mind: The Seventeenth Century*. 1939. Cambridge: Belknap-Harvard Univ. Press, 1982.

———. "The Shaping of the American Character." 1954. *Nature's Nation*. Cambridge: Belknap-Harvard Univ. Press, 1967. 1-13.

Morgan, Edmund. *The Puritan Dilemma: The Story of John Winthrop*. Boston: Little, Brown, 1958.

Mosse, George L. *The Holy Pretence: A Study in Christianity and Reason of State from William Perkins to John Winthrop*. 1957. New York: Howard Fertig, 1968.

Pound, Roscoe, and Theodore J. Plucknett, eds. *Readings on the History and System of the Common Law*. 3rd ed. Rochester: Lawyers Co-operative, 1927.

Rutman, Darrett B. *Winthrop's Boston: A Portrait of a Puritan Town, 1630-1649*. Chapel Hill: Univ. of North Carolina Press, 1965.

Shakespeare, William. *The Merchant of Venice. The Riverside Shakespeare*. Ed. G. Blakemore Evans. Boston: Houghton Mifflin, 1974.

Shepard, Thomas. "Letters of Thomas Shepard." *Collections of the Massachusetts Historical Society* 7.4 (1865): 257-272.

Shurtleff, Nathaniel B., ed. *Records of the Governor and Company of the Massachusetts Bay in New England, Vol. 1*. Boston: Wm. White, 1853.

Simmons, Richard C. *Studies in the Massachusetts Franchise, 1631-1691*. New York: Garland, 1989.

Teeven, Kevin M. *A History of the Anglo-American Common Law of Contract*. New York: Greenwood, 1990.

Winthrop, John. *Winthrop Papers, Vol. 2*. Ed. Stewart Mitchell. Boston: Massachusetts Historical Society, 1931.

Young, Alexander, ed. *Chronicles of the First Planters of the Colony of Massachusetts Bay, from 1623 to 1636*. 1846. Baltimore: Genealogical Publishing, 1975.

James Moseley (essay date 1992)

SOURCE: Moseley, James G. "The Perils of the Text." In *John Winthrop's World: History as a Story, the Story as History*, pp. 121-29. Madison, Wis.: University of Wisconsin Press, 1992.

[*In the essay which follows, Moseley proposes that the textual history of Winthrop's* Journal *has contributed a misunderstanding of the text's meaning, maintaining that the text should be read in the historical context of the various editing processes.*]

John Winthrop learned to see and to write history as a story, but it is impossible for us simply to read his story straight. His actions as governor have so overshadowed his work as a historian, and his character and accomplishments have been so thoroughly incorporated into the pantheon of early New England, that we cannot find direct access to the history he made. Winthrop stood foremost among the first generation of American Puritans; hence whatever judgment one makes regarding the social institutions and the cultural tradition these people established stands between John Winthrop and us. The Puritans have been venerated, castigated, forgotten, resuscitated, misunderstood, reinterpreted, and quoted or misquoted by generations of American historians, social critics, and political orators. Because so many images of Puritanism are part of American cultural history, the only sure path to understanding the story of Winthrop's history is through coming to terms with the subsequent history of his story. Thus we move from reading history as a story to examining the story as history.

The history of misreadings of Winthrop's journal is matched—curiously, if not symbolically, as the Puritans might have believed—by the perils of the text itself. Winthrop wrote his history in three notebooks. The third volume was misplaced in 1755 and discovered sixty years later in the tower of Boston's Old South Church. Upon its recovery, this notebook, like the others, was given by the Winthrop family to the Massachusetts Historical Society, whereupon a new edition of the journal was undertaken. During this process, the second volume was accidentally destroyed by a fire in the office of the society's librarian. "Over the years many people have endeavored to read, transcribe, and edit Winthrop's notebooks," observes historian Richard S. Dunn, the most recent scholar to work on a new edition of Winthrop's work. However, "this set of texts is surely the most baffling of all major early American documents to decipher or to edit. The handwriting in the two surviving volumes is notoriously hard to read, the ink is faded, the paper is often stained, worn, or torn, and the text is studded with marginalia, insertions, cancellations, and underscorings. Since the middle volume (containing 52 percent of Winthrop's text) is lost, the reader has to use a modernized transcription for this section, published by James Savage in 1825-26, that obliterates many of the nuances in the original manuscript. It is safe to say that no one will ever publish a satisfactory edition of this remarkable document." By correlating the varying lengths of Winthrop's entries in the notebooks with the increasing passage of time between them, Dunn concludes that by the 1640s "increasingly he wrote for several consecutive pages on the same topic, so that his narrative became less segmented and more continuous: in short, more of a history."[1] But Dunn notes that an interpretation of Winthrop's transition from record keeper to historian cannot be based on precise textual analysis, since the original copy of the entire second volume, containing most of the text and covering such crucial episodes as the Antinomian crisis, no longer exists. Hence Dunn's painstaking work with the text has to rely largely on the work done by Savage, a man of prodigious and volatile energy, as we shall see, and one with his own agenda to follow.

Dunn's conclusion about Winthrop and his notebooks is insightful and also suggests something of his own frustration: "Thanks to his narrative, it is very easy to recognize the lasting significance of events in early Massachusetts and very difficult to remain neutral on the subject of Winthrop's own leadership. For some, he is one of the great figures in American history. For others, he is the kind of man you love to hate."[2] The new edition of the text which Dunn's essay announced has yet to appear; even its eventual publication, however, will not provide an unambiguous image of Winthrop. No text could, for interpretation and action were inextricably linked in Winthrop's life and work. As if to underscore the impossibility, Winthrop's text itself is irretrievably tied to the history of its own production.

Convinced that Winthrop's journal "must always have an interest not only for New England but for America in general, and indeed for the world at large," in 1908 James Kendall Hosmer published **Winthrop's Journal, "History of New England," 1630-1649** in a series devoted to original narratives of early American history. A member of the Massachusetts Historical Society and the Colonial Society of Massachusetts, as well as the au-

thor of *A Short History of Anglo-Saxon Freedom,* Hosmer believed that "a stock so persistent, so virile, so widely eminent, claims attention in every period of its course, and naturally a special interest attaches to its earliest American memorials." Since Hosmer frankly "adopted without change the transcript of the text made by Savage," his editorial remarks are of interest chiefly for his discussion of the "young and zealous" James Savage, "a man most accurate and indefatigable," whose edition of Winthrop's journal in 1825-26 "took its place at once in the minds of men as the foundation of Massachusetts history, and the importance of the services of Savage was universally recognized: he became henceforth a man of mark." Observing that Savage "had peculiarities of character making him personally racy and interesting, but impairing the excellence of his commentary," Hosmer notes that Savage's "successor in the presidency of the Massachusetts Historical Society, Mr. Charles Francis Adams, aptly compares him to Dr. Samuel Johnson. Like Johnson, Savage while most laborious, scrupulously honest, and always resolute and unshrinking, was testy, prejudiced and opinionated." In Hosmer's view, "while possessed thus by the spirit of the county antiquary rather than by the broad temper of the proper historian, his hates and loves, equally undiscriminating, are curiously, often amusingly manifest"; hence Savage's extensive annotation of Winthrop's text "has much interest as a 'human document,' pleasantly tart from the individuality of a quaintly provincial but sincere and vigorous mind."[3] Evidently unaware of the ways his Anglo-Saxon prejudices narrowed his own focus, Hosmer appeals to "the broad temper of the proper historian," highlighting the more argumentative nature of his predecessor. But so long as their editing is accurate, historians whose convictions are readily apparent may ultimately prove more reliable, and certainly more interesting, than those whose prejudices are blandly unconscious. James Savage, upon whose work so much of our knowledge of Winthrop necessarily depends, had reason to be as passionate about Winthrop as Winthrop was about New England.

Along with following Savage as president of the Massachusetts Historical Society, Charles Francis Adams found himself involved in sorting out Savage's complex connection to Winthrop. Adams was interested in the Antinomian crisis, and understanding this critical episode in the Bay Colony's history required explaining Savage's peculiar passion about Winthrop, for Savage had become embroiled in controversy regarding the **Short Story** Winthrop wrote about the Anne Hutchinson affair. After recording the judgments of the general court against Hutchinson and her followers, Winthrop noted in his journal on 1 November 1637 that "all the proceedings of this court against these persons were set down at large, with the reasons and other observations, and were sent into England to be published there, to the end that all our godly friends might not be discouraged from coming to us, &c." Adams points out that "the harsh and intolerant policy pursued from the beginning in Massachusetts towards all intruders and dissentients had excited no little comment in England, and led to hostile proceedings, causing remonstrances from the friends of the enterprise." Hence "in thus writing down and sending to England an account of these proceedings," Adams says, Winthrop "wished, in his paternal care for the infant colony, to anticipate and forestall hostile criticism."[4] Winthrop's title made these intentions clear: *A Short Story of the Rise, reign, and ruin of the Antinomians, Familists, & Libertines, that infected the Churches of New England: And how they were confuted by the Assembly of Ministers there: As also of the Magistrates proceedings in Court against them. Together with Gods strange and remarkable judgements from Heaven upon some of the chief fomenters of these Opinions; And the Lamentable death of Mrs. Hutchinson: Very fit for these times; here being the same errours amongst us, and acted by the same spirit.* Yet although the title page notes that the work was "published at the instant request of sundry, by one that was an eye and eare-witnesse of the carriage of matters there," its final words are "London, Printed for *Ralph Smith* at the signe of the Bible in *Cornhill* near the *Royall Exchange.* 1644." Originally sent to England in 1637, the work was not published until 1644. Between these years a great deal happened that was important for English history, and this passage of time became significant, much later, for James Savage.

By 1644 Anne Hutchinson and most of her family had been massacred by Indians in New York. John Wheelwright, banished as one of the principal Antinomians, had been welcomed back into the Massachusetts Bay Colony, where the Hutchinson affair had long been replaced in the public mind by more immediate issues such as the final division of the legislature into two independent houses, the confederation of the United Colonies of New England, and volatile relations with the Narragansetts, the Dutch, and the feuding Frenchmen, La Tour and D'Aulnay. In old England, King Charles had left London, the Civil War was under way, and friends of the Bay Colony controlled Parliament. Indeed, by July 1643 the Westminster Assembly had launched a great debate over religious toleration, and Winthrop's *Short Story* was published the next year, in Adams's words, as "one of the pamphlet missiles which the participants in that battle freely hurled at each other."[5] The trajectory of this missile, though, proved most ironic.

With Anglicanism in retreat with the king, a new order of relations between church and state became possible in England. On one side of the debate was a party whose members were generally called Independents. Two of the chief spokesmen for this coalition on behalf of religious freedom and toleration were Roger Williams, in England attempting to secure a clear charter for Rhode Island, and Sir Henry Vane, the former governor of the Bay Colony who had left Massachusetts during the Antinomian crisis. On the other side were the Presbyterians, seeking a national church of their own design and pointing out that "the New England Way" had not led to paradise. As Adams explains, "at this juncture Winthrop's narrative, after resting six years in oblivion, went to the printer. It supplied the Presbyterian leaders with exactly the ammunition they wanted. In it was set forth not only the breaking down of the Toleration principle in the very land of its birth, but that breaking down had taken place under the magistracy of him who was now in England the Parliamentary mouthpiece of the Independents. Both Williams and Vane were to be confounded by an answer out of their own mouths."[6] It was apparently the Reverend Thomas Weld, an ardent supporter of John Wilson and John Winthrop now back in England to represent and obtain financial support for the Bay Colony, who brought the pamphlet forward as a weapon against his old enemy, the arch-Antinomian Vane. Although written originally to vindicate the New England Way, when published in the contentious political atmosphere of England in 1644, the booklet served the Presbyterian effort, in the words of a contemporary, "to tie Toleration round the neck of Independency, stuff the two struggling monsters into one sack, and sink them to the bottom of the sea."[7] Thus the writing of an ardent Congregationalist helped advance the Presbyterian cause by undercutting the efforts of Vane, whom Winthrop came to recognize as a friend and loyal supporter of the Puritan cause.

As historian David D. Hall notes, Winthrop's *Short Story,* "the official history of the Antinomian Controversy," is "essentially a collection of documents."[8] These are linked together by Winthrop's narration, more leisurely in pace and more reflexive in tone but otherwise little different from the account of the events in his journal, and the text concludes the story of "this *American Jesabel*" with a dramatic rendering of "her entrance, her progresse, her downfall." The booklet went through several editions, with Weld adding a brief introduction, some sharply worded prefatory matter, and a short postscript covering events subsequent to 1637. Adams aptly notes that while the body of the *Short Story,* apart from Weld's additions, is "an outspoken and earnest presentation in defence of one side of a political struggle, written at the time and with a view to prejudge the case in the minds of those for whom it was prepared, a careful reading reveals in it little that is vituperative, and nothing that can properly be called scurrilous. Indeed, tested by the standards of the time, if it is in any way unusual, it is in its moderation."[9] Weld simply sharpened Winthrop's ax and handed it to the English Presbyterians, who used it for their own purposes. Curiously enough, the text continued to cut in more than one direction when it was taken up by James Savage two centuries later.

If Savage's editorial tempest was less important than the Antinomian crisis or the politics of religion during the English Civil War, it nevertheless revealed something of great significance to him, suggesting why his devotion to editing Winthrop's journal was such a complicated passion. Indeed, without the intensely personal connection between Savage and Winthrop that an otherwise comical dispute between Massachusetts historians highlights, the immensely difficult work of transcribing, annotating, and publishing the journal might never have been done. In the early 1850s James Savage began to argue with increasing bitterness that Thomas Weld, not John Winthrop, was responsible for virtually the whole of the **Short Story** and hence to imply that Winthrop's opposition to the Antinomians had been a matter more of political necessity than of deep spiritual conviction. Yet Savage's arguments were as convoluted as they were circumstantial. Together with his strong will and hot temper, Savage's prejudice against Weld, and by implication his veneration of Winthrop, became, in Adams's words, "a byword and a jest among his associates."[10] The roots of such impetuous tenacity, appropriately, were historical. Charles Francis Adams explains:

> Among the names of the men of Boston, "chief stirrers," as Winthrop expresses it, "in these [Antinomian] contentions," and for that reason ordered by the General Court of November, 1637, to be disarmed, was Thomas Savage, who had recently married Faith, the daughter of William and Anne Hutchinson. And at the church trial of the mother of his young wife in March, 1638, this Thomas Savage did himself infinite credit by rising and courageously protesting against the admonition about to be bestowed; and, as a result of so doing, he had the honor of being himself admonished together with her he so manfully sought to protect. James Savage traced his lineal descent in the fifth generation from Thomas and Faith (Hutchinson) Savage. He was, therefore, one of the offspring of Anne Hutchinson, to whom indeed in a characteristic note to Winthrop he refers as "his great, great, great, great grandmother." Conscious of a bias due to this remote relationship by descent, Savage throughout his notes to Winthrop endeavored to hold himself under strict control while dealing with events of the Antinomian controversy, and he succeeded in so doing to a, for him, considerable extent; but the **Short Story** he looked upon as a discreditable literary production, the scurrilous product of a mind at once narrow, vindictive, virulent, and malignant.[11]

Trapped within history by history, James Savage was caught between a sense of genealogical propriety and a stronger, more meaningful sense of cultural inheritance.

Despite his lineal descent from Anne Hutchinson, Savage regarded Winthrop "with a warmth of admiration almost devout," in Adams's words, looking "upon the first Boston governor as the incomparable Father of Massachusetts." Writing the exhaustive notes in his editions of Winthrop's journal may have been James Savage's way of working out this complex inheritance. Savage's extensive notes, Adams writes, afford "a not unpleasant contrast with the text,—the latter calm, self-restrained and inclined to the prosaic; the former intense, outspoken, replete with pith, individuality, learning and prejudice. These notes are, and will always remain, delightful as well as instructive reading; and to the student of New England history it is almost as difficult to think of Winthrop apart from Savage as it is for one learned in the English common law to separate Littleton from Coke."[12] Indeed, given the fiery loss—in Savage's library—of the notebook containing over half of the original manuscript, there is no way back to a pristine Winthrop "behind" Savage. Just as Savage was trapped within history by history, so Winthrop's history is irretrievably enmeshed in Savage's complex inheritance.

To characterize James Savage as a compulsively industrious New Englander is almost an understatement. Son of a Boston merchant who went insane after the young boy's mother died, Savage was raised by a maternal uncle, educated in private schools, and, despite involvement in at least one serious prank, graduated from Harvard College as valedictorian of the class of 1803. By the time he began to work on the Winthrop notebooks, Savage had studied law and passed the bar, started one of the nation's first savings banks, served on the committee that implemented the law he had supported to provide public elementary schools, and been a member of the Massachusetts constitutional convention of 1820. During his life he served as both a representative and a senator in the state legislature, edited one of the nation's earliest literary periodicals, helped to found the Boston Athenaeum, and served for fifteen years on the Board of Overseers of Harvard University. But the real center of his life was his work as a historian. He served the Massachusetts Historical Society in many capacities, including as president from 1841 to 1855, and published several books and collections of documents, most notably, in addition to Winthrop's journal, a four-volume *Genealogical Dictionary of the First Settlers of New England.*

Surveying such a life helps one appreciate Savage's statement, when the lost third notebook of Winthrop was discovered, that "the difficulty of transcribing it for the press seemed to appal several of the most competent members" of the Massachusetts Historical society, yet "the task appeared inviting to me." Likewise, he remarks that, "called abroad in 1822, I so carefully disposed of my copy of the third volume, as to leave it in a forgotten place, which afforded me the gratification of making a new one, begun 8 December 1823, and finished 30 March 1824." The high value that Savage assigned to primary texts, honoring the founders of New England far more than their often too respectful descendants, resounds in his criticism of Cotton Mather's failure to read Winthrop's actual writings when he wrote his "life": "Nor can I forgive the slight use of these invaluable documents, which is evinced by Mather, the unhappy author of Magnalia Christi Americana, who, in the hurry of composing that endless work, seems to have preferred useless quotations of worthless books, two or three centuries older, or popular and corrupt traditions, to the full matter and precise statement of facts, dates, principles and motives, furnished by authentick history."[13] Yet for Winthrop himself, Savage had respect that amounted to the awe reserved for the founders of a tribe, the great ones who establish traditions, whose works preserve the historical origins of a new world.

Thus on the title page of the 1825 and the 1853 editions of Winthrop's journal, across from a copy of Winthrop's portrait, Savage reveals his own purpose by quoting the Roman historian Sallust: "Often have I heard that Quintus Maximus and Publius Scipio, as well as the most renowned men of our state, were accustomed to say that when they contemplated the images of their ancestors, their minds were most vehemently inspired toward courage." In the face of the various images of Winthrop that have been constructed to inspire courage throughout American history, one has to wish that there were at least a remaining original text, through which one could, with however much or little sophistication, gain access to the beginnings of an important dimension of American culture by reading "the man himself." But Savage makes it clear that no such privileged access exists. How ironic that the Puritan movement, which came to life as a protest against the deadening influence of tradition on the life of the spirit, is itself locked in a tradition it helped so largely to make. Yet learning to live within such contradictions was what made it possible for Winthrop to make and to write history.

If the work of Winthrop as a historian is recoverable only insofar as it was edited and interpreted by later historians, we can establish and sustain connection with the story he told only through the history of its interpretation. Once the necessity of interpretation is recognized, the history of his story becomes a link, perhaps the only sure one, with the actual man who made and wrote history. For however much Winthrop's character was assailed during the political infighting of the Bay Colony's early years, almost immediately upon his death the real man was translated into a myth. Percival Lowell's "A Funeral Elegie on the Death of the Memorable and Truly Honourable John Winthrop Esq." decreed:

> With Lines of gold in Marble stone
>   With pens of steel engrave his name

> O let the Muses every one
>   In prose and Verse extol his Fame,
> Exceeding far those ancient Sages
> That ruled *Greeks* in former Ages.[14]

After comparing the departed governor favorably with the great leaders of ancient Israel and Greece, this ancestor of better poets moved his hero beyond the mortal realm:

> Such gifts of grace from God had he,
> That more than man he seem'd to be.
> But now hee's gone and clad in clay,
> Grim Death hath taken him away.
> Death like a murth'ring Jesuite
> Hath rob'd us of our hearts delight.[15]

Such flowery sentiments are far removed from the earthly Winthrop, who could write of himself in a letter to Thomas Hooker, "Truly Sir you have my naked thoughts of this matter, so farre as the Lord letteth me see mine owne heart, which I find very deceitful when it is at best."[16] Winthrop's honesty about the ongoing self-deception even within the hearts of the saints, himself included, made his story of the Bay Colony a history of men and women of mixed motives, a community of sinning saints. The perils of his text itself and the difficulty of our access to it seem oddly in keeping with the story he wrote, suggesting the distinctive character of Winthrop's way of making history in early New England.

Notes

1. Richard S. Dunn, "John Winthrop Writes His Journal," *William and Mary Quarterly,* 3d ser. 41, no. 2 (April 1984): 186, 185, 204.

2. Ibid., 212.

3. James Kendall Hosmer, ed., *Winthrop's Journal, "History of New England," 1630-1649* (New York: Charles Scribner's Sons, 1908; New York: Barnes and Noble, 1966), 1:3, 5, 17, 16, 17, 18.

4. Charles Francis Adams, ed., *Antinomianism in the Colony of Massachusetts Bay, 1636-1638; including "The Short Story" and Other Documents* (Boston: Prince Society, 1894), 17.

5. Ibid., 26.

6. Ibid., 31.

7. Ibid., 31n, quoting Masson's *Life of Milton.*

8. Hall, [David D., ed.] *Antinomian Controversy, [1636-1638: A Documentary History.* Middletown, Conn.: Wesleyan University Press, 1968.] 199. Adams's reprinting of the third edition of the text is reprinted again by Hall, pp. 201-310.

9. Adams, [Charles Francis, Ed.] *Antinomianism [in the Colony of Massachusetts Bay, 1636-1638; including "The Short Story" and Other Documents.* Boston: Prince Society, 1894] 40.

10. Ibid., 42.

11. Ibid., 39-40.

12. Ibid., 42, 39.

13. James Savage, Preface to *The History of New England, from 1630 to 1649,* by John Winthrop (Boston: Phelps and Farnham, 1825), 1:iii, iv.

14. *LL* [Winthrop, Robert C. *The Life and Letters of John Winthrop.* 2 vols. Boston: Ticknoor and Fields, 1864-67] 2:465.

15. Ibid., 466.

16. Ibid., 422.

Richard S. Dunn (essay date 1996)

SOURCE: Dunn, Richard S. Introduction to *The Journal of John Winthrop, 1630-1649,* edited by Richard S. Dunn and Laetitia Yeandle, pp. viii-xx. Cambridge, Massachusetts: The Belknap Press of Harvard University Press, 1996.

[*In the essay below, Dunn examines Winthrop as a writer, focusing on his narrative style the author uses in the* Journal.]

For 350 years Governor John Winthrop's journal has been recognized as the central source for the history of Massachusetts in the 1630s and 1640s. Winthrop was both the chief actor and the chief recorder in New England for two crucial decades. He reported events—especially religious and political events—more fully and more candidly than any other contemporaneous observer, and his account of the founding of the colony has greatly influenced all subsequent interpretations of Puritan Massachusetts. The governor's journal has been edited and published three times previously—in 1790, in 1825-1826, and in 1908—but all of these editions have long been outmoded.[1] The present editors have prepared two new versions of the journal: a full-scale, unabridged, old-spelling edition,[2] and this abridged, modernized edition, which incorporates about 40 percent of the governor's text. We have added to the abridged edition Winthrop's celebrated statement of religious purpose, **"A Model of Christian Charity,"** that articulates his hopes and fears as he set forth for America. The governor wrote his **"Model"** in 1630 just as he was beginning his journal, and the two texts are closely related.

Winthrop's journal is a challenging document to decipher and to edit. He recorded it in three notebooks, only two of which survive. The first notebook (spanning the dates 29 March 1630 to 14 September 1636) and the third notebook (spanning the dates 17 September 1644 to 11 January 1649)—both preserved at the Massachusetts Historical Society—are extremely hard to read because of the author's difficult handwriting and the worn condition of the volumes. The middle notebook (spanning the dates October 1636 to 8 December 1644) was accidentally destroyed by fire in 1825, and the only reliable transcription of its contents is a modernized version by James Savage, who was editing Winthrop's journal at the time of the fire. The present editors offer the reader two quite different modes of transcription. Our unabridged edition keeps the governor's seventeenth-century spelling, punctuation, and capitalization in the first and third volumes as closely as practicable, in combination with Savage's modernized text for the lost middle volume. This abridged edition modernizes the text throughout, combining Yeandle's 1990s-style modernization of the first and last parts with Savage's 1820s-style modernization of the middle part.

John Winthrop was born on 12 January 1588 in Edwardston, Suffolk, the son of a local lawyer. He attended Trinity College, Cambridge, for two years and then studied the law at Gray's Inn in London. In 1610 he bought the manor of Groton from his uncle, and he subsequently served as justice of the peace in Suffolk while also presiding over the manorial court at Groton. In 1627 he was appointed an attorney of the Court of Wards and Liveries in London. Thus he was a member of the English ruling elite, and had the habit of command—as is evident to any reader of his journal. Another fundamental feature of Winthrop's life is that he became a dedicated convert to Puritanism in his youth, and over the years formed a wide network of alliances with fellow Puritans. By 1630 he had a considerable family to provide for: he was married to his third wife, Margaret Tyndal, and had eight living children—seven sons and one daughter. Although he was a relatively wealthy man, he had fallen into debt in the late 1620s, and was disgusted by the corruption (as he saw it) of English life and by Charles I's religious and political policies. When the king broke with his critics in Parliament in March 1629, Winthrop decided to sell his English estate and emigrate to America. He joined the Massachusetts Bay Company, which had just received a royal charter granting broad powers of self-government. On 26 August 1629 he pledged with eleven other Puritan gentlemen to move with his family to Massachusetts if the seat of the Company's government and its charter were also transferred to America. The Company shareholders agreed to this, and on 20 October 1629 they chose Winthrop as their new governor. He was then forty-one years old. In the winter of 1629-1630 under his leadership the Company organized a migration of about a thousand persons who sailed to Massachusetts in seventeen ships during the following spring and summer.[3]

In March 1630, Winthrop came to Southampton and boarded the ship *Arbella* to sail for America; while still in port—on 29 March—he started to write his journal. It was very likely at just about this date that he composed his eloquent **"Model of Christian Charity,"** in which he called upon his fellow migrants to join together in building a Christian commonwealth in America (see pp. 1-11 below). But his initial reason for keeping a journal was more prosaic: he wanted to record the day-to-day experience of crossing the ocean for the information of family and friends still in England who would be sailing in 1631 or after to join him in America. During the sea voyage he systematically reported the events of every single day until the *Arbella* anchored at Salem on 14 June 1630.

After reaching Massachusetts, Winthrop sent an account of the Atlantic crossing based on his journal back to England. And he made the crucial decision to continue keeping his journal, so that when he had the leisure he could write a fuller account of the founding of the colony. Winthrop had a fully developed conceptual framework within which to work. As he explained in **"A Model of Christian Charity,"** the Massachusetts colonists had a special vocation to love and support one another and to obey the Lord's commandments as they followed His injunction to build "a City upon a Hill." Should they serve the Lord faithfully, He would bless their efforts; should they deal falsely, He would destroy their plantation. However grand his sense of divine mission, Winthrop was so busy trying to keep the colony going during his initial months in Massachusetts—when many people died or returned to England—that his journal entries were exceedingly brief and irregular. By the winter of 1630-1631 he had a little more time to write. Surprised by the bitterly cold weather, he composed his first extended anecdote, about the harrowing adventures of six Bostonians shipwrecked and frozen on Cape Cod. Winthrop saw this episode as evidence that God was testing the colonists' corrupt hearts, and he became openly jubilant in February 1631 when the *Lyon* returned from England with emergency provisions, because he sensed that the survival crisis was ending. During 1631 and 1632 he settled into a new form of record keeping, in which he took up his notebook several times a month, and wrote at greater length than in 1630. By the mid-1630s he was averaging nearly a full page every time he put pen to paper. There is almost no evidence in the first notebook that he wrote retrospectively. At most, he discussed incidents a month or two after they occurred.

Having filled up his first notebook in September 1636, Winthrop continued his journal in a (lost) second notebook. And he gradually changed his format, until by the early 1640s his narrative became less segmented and more continuous. His journal was turning into a history. Furthermore, during the course of his second notebook

Winthrop began to write lengthy sections of his narrative well after the events described had taken place. This point cannot be proved incontrovertibly, since the original manuscript is destroyed, but close examination of his wording discloses solid evidence of a change from frequent writing sessions and contemporaneous reporting in 1636-1637 to irregular writing sessions and retrospective reporting by 1643-1644. Sometime in mid-1644, Winthrop seems to have stopped keeping his journal altogether for three or four years, and then finished the second notebook in 1647 or 1648.[4]

Winthrop probably took up his third notebook, which carries the narrative from 17 September 1644 to 11 January 1649, no earlier than mid-1648, and so he wrote most of the entries in this volume well after the events described. Inspection of Winthrop's handwriting indicates that he was working fast. He appears to have written twenty pages at one stretch, and fifteen pages on three other occasions. He made many more slips and errors than previously, writing up ten entries twice over and sometimes getting his dates wrong. His style also betrays haste; he has lost the compact precision characteristic of the entries from the 1630s. He seems to have composed most if not all of his final volume during the last few months of his life, between May 1648 and early March 1649, when he became too ill to write. He died on 26 March 1649.[5]

As he gradually changed his mode of composition between 1630 and 1649, Winthrop also gradually altered his perception of his own role as author-actor. At first he narrated as anonymously as possible, presenting the *Arbella* passengers and the Massachusetts colonists collectively as "we," while seldom referring to his own leadership role as governor and rarely disclosing his personal opinions. But after he landed in Massachusetts, Winthrop could no longer keep himself out of the story, and soon he was reporting controversial matters that are not mentioned in the official colony records. Only through his journal do we learn that in April 1631 the magistrates reprimanded the Salem church for choosing Roger Williams as its minister, or that in 1632 Winthrop had a series of ugly confrontations with the deputy governor, Thomas Dudley. The portrait that Winthrop sketched of Dudley as a jealous, irascible colleague is bound to linger in the reader's consciousness. It is the first of a long series of unflattering vignettes. Winthrop was not a real portraitist; he never described people in three-dimensional detail. But like Benjamin Franklin in his *Autobiography,* he was adept at thrusting a few barbs into most of the personages who figure prominently in his story. Naturally he found little good to say about such outright adversaries as Thomas Morton, Roger Williams, Anne Hutchinson, Mary Dyer, John Underhill, Samuel Gorton, Peter Hobart, and Robert Child. But he was seldom unequivocally positive about his fellow magistrates. John Endecott was rash and blundering, Henry Vane was a spoiled youth, Richard Saltonstall was a dangerous incendiary, John Humfrey was a deserter. Likewise among the clergy, John Cotton was unsound, John Eliot was naive, Thomas Hooker was aggressive, Nathaniel Ward was meddlesome. To be sure, Winthrop freely admitted his own defects on occasion. Yet the reader who accepts his presentation will certainly conclude that the author of the journal was much the best and wisest public man in early Massachusetts.

Winthrop was the governor of his colony for twelve of the nineteen years he kept the journal: he was in charge in 1630-1634, 1637-1640, 1642-1644, and 1646-1649, and was continuously a magistrate. Once his administration came under attack, he began to explain and defend his actions. For example, on 17 February 1632 he tells how he convinced the people of Watertown—who had refused to pay taxes levied by the magistrates because they had no representatives at the General Court—that they were in error, "so their submission was accepted and their offence pardoned" (p. 45). But actually the Watertowners were the winners in this dispute. The May 1632 General Court voted that two representatives from every town should advise the magistrates on taxation, and in the spring of 1634 the freemen agitated for a larger share of power. Winthrop tells us that when the town representatives read the company charter, they discovered that the freemen were authorized to meet four times a year to make laws. Winthrop explained to them that the freemen were too numerous to legislate, nor were they qualified to establish a representative assembly. Nevertheless, on 14 May 1634 the General Court voted that deputies from each town were henceforth to meet with the magistrates four times a year to tax and legislate. Voting by secret ballot for the first time, the freemen in May 1634 chose Dudley as governor in place of Winthrop.

The General Court of May 1634 was Winthrop's worst defeat. The constitutional change was a greater blow than the electoral change, because he never could accept the new deputies from the towns as in any way equal to the magistrates; for the rest of his life he fought to restore the magistrates' independence and supremacy. But the electoral rebuff was also hard. For three years, from 1634 to 1637, other men took over the governorship and Winthrop was not always in agreement with their policy. This section of his journal is especially informative and interesting, because he supplies some inside details about the controversial issues of the day. These were difficult years for the Bay Colony. In England, Archbishop Laud was attacking the Massachusetts Bay Company, and in America, many of the Massachusetts colonists moved to Connecticut, Roger Williams was banished and fled to Narragansett Bay, the colonists plunged into a bloody war with the Pequot Indians, and in October 1636 the Antinomian controversy exploded in Boston. Winthrop hints (and sometimes openly states) that matters in 1634-1637 could have been much better handled.

Yet Winthrop at this time was neither as full nor as frank a writer as he later became. For example, his reports on Roger Williams from 1631 to 1636 raise questions about what really happened and why. Winthrop presents Williams's rebellion against the Massachusetts church-state system as the work of a rigid and isolated fanatic who enjoyed no support outside of Salem. In January 1636 Winthrop seems to have been quite as eager as any of his fellow magistrates to ship the banished man back to England. Yet Williams later claimed that Winthrop encouraged him to flee to Narragansett Bay, and the Bay magistrates and clergy charged Winthrop with "overmuch lenity and remissness" immediately after Williams's flight, very likely because they suspected him of giving covert aid to the Salem rebel (pp. 87-89).

The journal reaches its most dramatic point in 1636-1637 with the Pequot War and the Antinomian controversy (pp. 96-135). Winthrop's interpretation of the Pequot War is somewhat equivocal. He hints, without quite saying so, that the Bay government blundered into the war, then briskly describes the virtual extermination of the Pequots in May-August 1637. But he was in no way equivocal about Anne Hutchinson. He saw this "woman of a ready wit and bold spirit" as a very dangerous adversary, since her stronghold was Winthrop's own Boston church, and her supporters included John Cotton and Governor Vane. Winthrop presents himself in the journal as the Antinomians' chief opponent. And at the May 1637 General Court, he scored the most satisfying triumph of his career when the freemen in a tense and stormy meeting elected him governor and dropped Vane and two other Antinomian magistrates from office (p. 119). In November 1637 the General Court consolidated this victory by banishing Hutchinson and Wheelwright and disarming or disenfranchising seventy-five of their supporters (pp. 132-133). In March 1638 the Boston church was finally persuaded to excommunicate Anne Hutchinson (pp. 139).

Once restored to power, Winthrop used his journal more aggressively than in the early 1630s to denigrate his opponents. In January 1638 he made a list of the "foul errors" and "secret opinions" of the Antinomians. In March 1638 he discovered that Mary Dyer, one of Hutchinson's supporters, had been delivered of a deformed stillborn fetus, and in September 1638 he heard that Hutchinson herself had a somewhat similar stillbirth after she was exiled to Rhode Island, whereupon Winthrop entered full descriptions of both "monstrous births" into his journal as proof positive that God had turned against the Antinomians (pp. 141-142, 146-147). By this time, Winthrop was clearly drafting the official history of his administration. He began to make notes on where to add further documentation when he got around to expanding his narrative, and he sometimes pointed out controversial issues, as when in 1641 he wrote: "Query, whether the following be fit to be published"—and then reported how Governor Bellingham improperly pursued and married a young lady who was pledged to another man (p. 192). Winthrop consulted with Thomas Shepard about how to present topics such as this, and Shepard—who told Winthrop that "you will have the hearts and prayers of many in the compiling of the History"—urged him to be completely candid: "Surely Sir," he wrote, "the work is of God."[6]

As Winthrop composed his narrative, he not only changed his mode of composition, and his perception of his personal role as author-actor, but also revised his understanding of God's design in bringing His chosen people to New England. Initially, he believed—as he stated in **"A Model of Christian Charity"**—that God intended the colonists to build a united covenanted community in Massachusetts, knitted together by bonds of brotherly affection. Through the first two years of his journal he played up the external challenges that the colonists faced, and played down the internal divisions among them. But by the mid-1630s he was focusing on Puritan troublemakers like Roger Williams, and when the Pequot War and the Antinomian controversy broke out simultaneously in 1636-1637, he saw that Satan was trying hard to destroy Christ's kingdom in New England. The Pequot War sharpened his hostility toward the Indians, and led him to conclude that the English could never live in settled peace with the natives unless they expunged their aboriginal culture. Much more important to Winthrop, the emergence of Puritan fanatics such as Roger Williams and Anne Hutchinson forced him to abandon his hope that the English colonists could live together in loving harmony. Williams and Hutchinson (in his view) were so utterly self-deluded that they not only rebelled against sound Christian policy but entered into active alliance with Satan. From 1638 onward, Winthrop viewed developments in Rhode Island (where most of the banished Puritan fanatics had gone) or in New Hampshire and Maine (where most of the anti-Puritan colonists were clustered) with the deepest suspicion. His reports on events from beyond the Massachusetts borders became news bulletins of abominable crimes and miserable disorders. Even within Massachusetts, "the devil would never cease to disturb our peace, and to raise up instruments one after another" (p. 149).

This sense of perpetual contest between the forces of good and evil was sharpened after 1640 when Charles I was forced to summon Parliament. Naturally Winthrop sided with the king's parliamentary critics, but he was greatly distressed when the expectation of reform at home stopped the Puritan migration to New England

and persuaded many colonists to return to old England. And as civil war broke out between Parliament and the king, Winthrop discovered to his horror that the Puritans in London were entertaining radical ideas that had been banned in Boston in the 1630s, and that Parliament in 1644 and 1646 actually protected his Rhode Island adversaries Roger Williams and Samuel Gorton when they went to England and complained of being harassed by Massachusetts. Thus the revolutionary crisis at home deepened his conviction that Massachusetts must be ever vigilant in dealing with so-called friends as well as enemies. And as he interpreted the troublesome events of the 1640s, he found a powerful model in the historical books of the Old Testament, most particularly Exodus, Deuteronomy, and Judges. Here Winthrop could find a story line exactly to his purpose, recounting how God's chosen people—despite plentiful evidence of human backsliding and divine wrath—escaped from captivity and came to the promised land.

As Winthrop changed from a journalist to a historian, he not only wrote more belligerently but more voluminously: his treatment of the years 1643-1646 is more than twice the length of his treatment of the years 1633-1636. He explained his support for the wily French commander La Tour and for the grasping Boston merchant Robert Keayne in 1643 very fully (pp. 224-231), because he was criticized for mishandling both situations. And in his third volume, he deliberately magnified the Hingham mutiny of 1645 (pp. 274-284) and the Remonstrants' protest of 1646 (pp. 306-318) in order to demonstrate the baseness of his critics. He wrote up his impeachment trial of 1645 as a personal ordeal and vindication, and included the full text of his masterful "little speech" in which he lectured the court on the meaning of liberty and authority. Winthrop's electoral defeat in 1634 had been at least as important, both to him and to the colony, as his victory over the Hingham petitioners in 1645, yet he wrote up the 1634 episode in two pages and the 1645 episode in seventeen. And he was even more circumstantial in denouncing Dr. Robert Child and his fellow Remonstrants, who tried to subvert the colony government by appealing to Parliament.

Winthrop devoted much attention in his second and third volumes to sexual scandal—to cases of rape, fornication, adultery, sodomy, and buggery—but of course his purpose was not to titillate. When he reported that William Hatchet was executed for copulating with a cow or that George Spencer of New Haven was executed for siring a piglet with human resemblances, he was exhibiting these specimens of human depravity as proof that even in godly New England the Devil was continually at work. He dwelt as much on the penitential scaffold scenes as on the crimes, for God always searched out these sex offenders and punished them justly. Winthrop also reported on the punishments that God meted out to the political and religious rebels who rejected the Massachusetts church-state system. Anne Hutchinson, the greatest rebel, received the harshest judgment: first her monstrous childbirth in 1638 and then her murder by Indians in 1643. John Humfrey, who deserted Massachusetts for the West Indies and took many colonists with him, was punished by a fire that destroyed his barn and his stored crops, while his little daughter was raped by child molesters. Dr. Child was publicly humiliated on the streets of London, "and besides God had so blasted his estate as he was quite broken, etc." (p. 338). Winthrop might have observed that his own estate had also been blasted; in 1639 his bailiff contracted debts in his name totaling £2,500, forcing Winthrop to sell much of his property. The Massachusetts freemen dropped him from the governorship for two years after this happened, and in 1641 one of the deputies wanted to drop him from office altogether because he was "grown poor." Yet Winthrop barely mentioned his financial troubles, and then mainly to grumble that the colonists only raised £500 in a voluntary contribution to help him, for he categorically refused to interpret his own property loss as a providential sign.

It is striking to follow our author, who had been silent or evasive on controversial issues in the early 1630s, as he pursued such topics with special zest during the later 1640s. One of the great features of his journal/history, especially in the second and third volumes, is that Winthrop reveals so many of the friction points in his society. Surely few writers have adopted a more pugilistic mode of conflict resolution. Taking pains to identify the issues causing conflict, and to report the public debate over these issues, Winthrop argued for the correctness of his own position and then showed how his adversaries were deservedly punished for their sins. Writing in this aggressive fashion, he built lasting significance into the seemingly small-scale actions of a few thousand colonists in early New England. Which is why his journal will always remain the central source for the history of Massachusetts in the 1630s and 1640s. And why readers of today, as in past generations, will find themselves engaged—and sometimes repelled—by John Winthrop's militant view of his world.

Notes

1. The 1790 edition, published by Noah Webster, is incomplete and full of textual errors. The 1825-1826 edition, prepared by James Savage and reissued in 1853, has a much sounder text but eccentric and outdated annotations. The 1908 edition, prepared by James Hosmer, reproduces Savage's text with a few expurgations, and has minimal annotations. The Massachusetts Historical Society began to publish an old-spelling fourth edition in 1931, but abandoned this project after printing the first year of the journal.

2. *The Journal of John Winthrop, 1630-1649,* ed. Richard S. Dunn, James Savage, and Laetitia Yeandle (Cambridge, Mass.: Harvard University Press, 1996).

3. For further background, see Edmund S. Morgan, *The Puritan Dilemma: The Story of John Winthrop* (Boston: Little, Brown, 1958), ch. 1-4; Lee Schweninger, *John Winthrop* (Boston: Twayne, 1990), ch. 1-3; and James G. Moseley, *John Winthrop's World: History as a Story; the Story as History* (Madison: University of Wisconsin Press, 1992), ch. 1.

4. For a fuller discussion of Winthrop's changing method of composition, see the Introduction to the unabridged edition.

5. Winthrop's terminal date of composition cannot be established, except that the final entry is dated 11 Jan. 1649. Winthrop became bedridden in early Feb., and by 14 Mar. he was too weak to write. See [*Winthrop Papers*] *WP,* 5:311-312, 319, 325.

6. Shepard to Winthrop, 27 Jan. 1640, *WP,* 4:182-183.

FURTHER READING

Criticism

Bush, Sargent. "A Text for All Seasons: Winthrop's *Journal* Redivivus." *Early American Literature* 33, no. 1 (1998): 97-107.

Reviews the publication of a new edition of Winthrop's *Journal* and discusses the work's importance.

Bremer, Francis J. "The Heritage of John Winthrop: Religion along the Stour Valley, 1548-1630." *New England Quarterly: A Historical Review of New England Life and Letters* 70, no. 4 (December 1997): 15-47.

Offers a detailed biography of the Winthrop family to aid in the understanding of Winthrop's motivations and beliefs.

Dawson, Hugh J. "*Christian Charitie* as Colonial Discourse: Rereading Winthrop's Sermon in its English Context." *Early American Literature* 33, no. 2 (spring 1998): 117-48.

Analyzes "A Modell of Christian Charitie" in a historical context.

———. "John Winthrop's Rite of Passage: The Origins of the *Christian Charitie* Discourse." *Early American Literature* 26, no. 3 (1991): 219-31.

Examines the origins of the speech, providing evidence to prove Winthrop's authorship.

Power, M. Susan. "John Winthrop: *A Model* and *The Journal.*" In *Before the Convention: Religion and the Founders,* pp. 65-84. Lanham, Maryland: University Press of America, 1984.

Analyzes the symbols used in Winthrop's works, maintaining that Winthrop possessed original ideas that greatly contributed to the political order of the time.

Twichell, Joseph Hopkins. "Chapter One: The Little Speech." In *John Winthrop, First Governor of the Massachusetts Colony,* pp. 1-11. New York: Dodd, Mead, and Company, 1891.

Provides a detailed account of the occurrences surrounding Winthrop's 1645 speech concerning the freedom of the people from the magistrates' authority.

Warner, Michael. "New English Sodom." *American Literature: A Journal of Literary History, Criticism, and Bibliography* 64, no. 1 (March 1992): 19-48.

Examines the importance of the story of Sodom to Winthrop and fellow Puritans.

Additional coverage of Winthrop's life and career is contained in the following sources published by Thomson Gale: *Dictionary of Literary Biography,* **Vols. 24, 30;** *Literature Criticism from 1400 to 1800,* **Vol. 31; and** *Literature Resource Center.*

How to Use This Index

CMW = St. James Guide to Crime & Mystery Writers
CN = Contemporary Novelists
CP = Contemporary Poets
CPW = Contemporary Popular Writers
CSW = Contemporary Southern Writers
CWD = Contemporary Women Dramatists
CWP = Contemporary Women Poets
CWRI = St. James Guide to Children's Writers
CWW = Contemporary World Writers
DA = DISCovering Authors
DA3 = DISCovering Authors 3.0
DAB = DISCovering Authors: British Edition
DAC = DISCovering Authors: Canadian Edition
DAM = DISCovering Authors: Modules
   DRAM: Dramatists Module; **MST:** Most-studied Authors Module;
   MULT: Multicultural Authors Module; **NOV:** Novelists Module;
   POET: Poets Module; **POP:** Popular Fiction and Genre Authors Module
DFS = Drama for Students
DLB = Dictionary of Literary Biography
DLBD = Dictionary of Literary Biography Documentary Series
DLBY = Dictionary of Literary Biography Yearbook
DNFS = Literature of Developing Nations for Students
EFS = Epics for Students
EXPN = Exploring Novels
EXPP = Exploring Poetry
EXPS = Exploring Short Stories
EW = European Writers
FANT = St. James Guide to Fantasy Writers
FW = Feminist Writers
GFL = Guide to French Literature, Beginnings to 1789, 1798 to the Present
GLL = Gay and Lesbian Literature
HGG = St. James Guide to Horror, Ghost & Gothic Writers
HW = Hispanic Writers
IDFW = International Dictionary of Films and Filmmakers: Writers and Production Artists
IDTP = International Dictionary of Theatre: Playwrights
LAIT = Literature and Its Times
LAW = Latin American Writers
JRDA = Junior DISCovering Authors
MAICYA = Major Authors and Illustrators for Children and Young Adults
MAICYAS = Major Authors and Illustrators for Children and Young Adults Supplement
MAWW = Modern American Women Writers
MJW = Modern Japanese Writers
MTCW = Major 20th-Century Writers
NCFS = Nonfiction Classics for Students
NFS = Novels for Students
PAB = Poets: American and British
PFS = Poetry for Students
RGAL = Reference Guide to American Literature
RGEL = Reference Guide to English Literature
RGSF = Reference Guide to Short Fiction
RGWL = Reference Guide to World Literature
RHW = Twentieth-Century Romance and Historical Writers
SAAS = Something about the Author Autobiography Series
SATA = Something about the Author
SFW = St. James Guide to Science Fiction Writers
SSFS = Short Stories for Students
TCWW = Twentieth-Century Western Writers
WLIT = World Literature and Its Times
WP = World Poets
YABC = Yesterday's Authors of Books for Children
YAW = St. James Guide to Young Adult Writers

Literary Criticism Series
Cumulative Author Index

Andrade, Carlos Drummond de ..... **CLC 18**
See Drummond de Andrade, Carlos
See also EWL 3; RGWL 2, 3

Andrade, Mario de .... **TCLC 43**
See de Andrade, Mario
See also EWL 3; LAW; RGWL 2, 3; WLIT
1

Andreae, Johann V(alentin)
1586-1654 .... **LC 32**
See also DLB 164

Andreas Capellanus fl. c. 1185- .... **CMLC 45**
See also DLB 208

Andreas-Salome, Lou 1861-1937 ... **TCLC 56**
See also CA 178; DLB 66

Andreev, Leonid
See Andreyev, Leonid (Nikolaevich)
See also DLB 295; EWL 3

Andress, Lesley
See Sanders, Lawrence

Andrewes, Lancelot 1555-1626 .... **LC 5**
See also DLB 151, 172

Andrews, Cicily Fairfield
See West, Rebecca

Andrews, Elton V.
See Pohl, Frederik

Andreyev, Leonid (Nikolaevich)
1871-1919 .... **TCLC 3**
See Andreev, Leonid
See also CA 104; 185

Andric, Ivo 1892-1975 .... **CLC 8; SSC 36;**
TCLC 135
See also CA 81-84; 57-60; CANR 43, 60;
CDWLB 4; DLB 147; EW 11; EWL 3;
MTCW 1; RGSF 2; RGWL 2, 3

Androvar
See Prado (Calvo), Pedro

Angelique, Pierre
See Bataille, Georges

Angell, Roger 1920- .... **CLC 26**
See also CA 57-60; CANR 13, 44, 70; DLB
171, 185

Angelou, Maya 1928- ... **BLC 1; CLC 12, 35,**
64, 77, 155; PC 32; WLCS
See also AAYA 7, 20; AMWS 4; BPFB 1;
BW 2, 3; BYA 2; CA 65-68; CANR 19,
42, 65, 111, 133; CDALBS; CLR 53; CP
7; CPW; CSW; CWP; DA; DA3; DAB;
DAC; DAM MST, MULT, POET, POP;
DLB 38; EWL 3; EXPN; EXPP; LAIT 4;
MAICYA 2; MAICYAS 1; MAWW;
MTCW 1, 2; NCFS 2; NFS 2; PFS 2, 3;
RGAL 4; SATA 49, 136; WYA; YAW

Angouleme, Marguerite d'
See de Navarre, Marguerite

Anna Comnena 1083-1153 .... **CMLC 25**

Annensky, Innokentii Fedorovich
See Annensky, Innokenty (Fyodorovich)
See also DLB 295

Annensky, Innokenty (Fyodorovich)
1856-1909 .... **TCLC 14**
See also CA 110; 155; EWL 3

Annunzio, Gabriele d'
See D'Annunzio, Gabriele

Anodos
See Coleridge, Mary E(lizabeth)

Anon, Charles Robert
See Pessoa, Fernando (Antonio Nogueira)

Anouilh, Jean (Marie Lucien Pierre)
1910-1987 . **CLC 1, 3, 8, 13, 40, 50; DC**
8, 21
See also CA 17-20R; 123; CANR 32; DAM
DRAM; DFS 9, 10, 19; EW 13; EWL 3;
GFL 1789 to the Present; MTCW 1, 2;
RGWL 2, 3; TWA

Anselm of Canterbury
1033(?)-1109 .... **CMLC 67**
See also DLB 115

Anthony, Florence
See Ai

Anthony, John
See Ciardi, John (Anthony)

Anthony, Peter
See Shaffer, Anthony (Joshua); Shaffer,
Peter (Levin)

Anthony, Piers 1934- .... **CLC 35**
See also AAYA 11, 48; BYA 7; CA 200;
CAAE 200; CANR 28, 56, 73, 102, 133;
CPW; DAM POP; DLB 8; FANT; MAI-
CYA 2; MAICYAS 1; MTCW 1, 2; SAAS
22; SATA 84, 129; SATA-Essay 129; SFW
4; SUFW 1, 2; YAW

Anthony, Susan B(rownell)
1820-1906 .... **TCLC 84**
See also CA 211; FW

Antiphon c. 480B.C.-c. 411B.C. .... **CMLC 55**

Antoine, Marc
See Proust, (Valentin-Louis-George-Eugene)
Marcel

Antoninus, Brother
See Everson, William (Oliver)

Antonioni, Michelangelo 1912- .... **CLC 20,**
144
See also CA 73-76; CANR 45, 77

Antschel, Paul 1920-1970
See Celan, Paul
See also CA 85-88; CANR 33, 61; MTCW
1; PFS 21

Anwar, Chairil 1922-1949 .... **TCLC 22**
See Chairil Anwar
See also CA 121; 219; RGWL 3

Anzaldua, Gloria (Evanjelina)
1942-2004 .... **HLCS 1**
See also CA 175; 227; CSW; CWP; DLB
122; FW; LLW 1; RGAL 4

Apess, William 1798-1839(?) .... **NCLC 73;**
NNAL
See also DAM MULT; DLB 175, 243

Apollinaire, Guillaume 1880-1918 .... **PC 7;**
TCLC 3, 8, 51
See Kostrowitzki, Wilhelm Apollinaris de
See also CA 152; DAM POET; DLB 258;
EW 9; EWL 3; GFL 1789 to the Present;
MTCW 1; RGWL 2, 3; TWA; WP

Apollonius of Rhodes
See Apollonius Rhodius
See also AW 1; RGWL 2, 3

Apollonius Rhodius c. 300B.C.-c.
220B.C. .... **CMLC 28**
See Apollonius of Rhodes
See also DLB 176

Appelfeld, Aharon 1932- ... **CLC 23, 47; SSC**
42
See also CA 112; 133; CANR 86; CWW 2;
DLB 299; EWL 3; RGSF 2

Apple, Max (Isaac) 1941- .... **CLC 9, 33; SSC**
50
See also CA 81-84; CANR 19, 54; DLB
130

Appleman, Philip (Dean) 1926- .... **CLC 51**
See also CA 13-16R; CAAS 18; CANR 6,
29, 56

Appleton, Lawrence
See Lovecraft, H(oward) P(hillips)

Apteryx
See Eliot, T(homas) S(tearns)

Apuleius, (Lucius Madaurensis)
125(?)-175(?) .... **CMLC 1**
See also AW 2; CDWLB 1; DLB 211;
RGWL 2, 3; SUFW

Aquin, Hubert 1929-1977 .... **CLC 15**
See also CA 105; DLB 53; EWL 3

Aquinas, Thomas 1224(?)-1274 ..... **CMLC 33**
See also DLB 115; EW 1; TWA

Aragon, Louis 1897-1982 .... **CLC 3, 22;**
TCLC 123
See also CA 69-72; 108; CANR 28, 71;
DAM NOV, POET; DLB 72, 258; EW 11;
EWL 3; GFL 1789 to the Present; GLL 2;
LMFS 2; MTCW 1, 2; RGWL 2, 3

Arany, Janos 1817-1882 .... **NCLC 34**

Aranyos, Kakay 1847-1910
See Mikszath, Kalman

Aratus of Soli c. 315B.C.-c.
240B.C. .... **CMLC 64**
See also DLB 176

Arbuthnot, John 1667-1735 .... **LC 1**
See also DLB 101

Archer, Herbert Winslow
See Mencken, H(enry) L(ouis)

Archer, Jeffrey (Howard) 1940- .... **CLC 28**
See also AAYA 16; BEST 89:3; BPFB 1;
CA 77-80; CANR 22, 52, 95; CPW; DA3;
DAM POP; INT CANR-22

Archer, Jules 1915- .... **CLC 12**
See also CA 9-12R; CANR 6, 69; SAAS 5;
SATA 4, 85

Archer, Lee
See Ellison, Harlan (Jay)

Archilochus c. 7th cent. B.C.- .... **CMLC 44**
See also DLB 176

Arden, John 1930- .... **CLC 6, 13, 15**
See also BRWS 2; CA 13-16R; CAAS 4;
CANR 31, 65, 67, 124; CBD; CD 5;
DAM DRAM; DFS 9; DLB 13, 245;
EWL 3; MTCW 1

Arenas, Reinaldo 1943-1990 .. **CLC 41; HLC**
1
See also CA 124; 128; 133; CANR 73, 106;
DAM MULT; DLB 145; EWL 3; GLL 2;
HW 1; LAW; LAWS 1; MTCW 1; RGSF
2; RGWL 3; WLIT 1

Arendt, Hannah 1906-1975 .... **CLC 66, 98**
See also CA 17-20R; 61-64; CANR 26, 60;
DLB 242; MTCW 1, 2

Aretino, Pietro 1492-1556 .... **LC 12**
See also RGWL 2, 3

Arghezi, Tudor .... **CLC 80**
See Theodorescu, Ion N.
See also CA 167; CDWLB 4; DLB 220;
EWL 3

Arguedas, Jose Maria 1911-1969 .... **CLC 10,**
18; HLCS 1; TCLC 147
See also CA 89-92; CANR 73; DLB 113;
EWL 3; HW 1; LAW; RGWL 2, 3; WLIT
1

Argueta, Manlio 1936- .... **CLC 31**
See also CA 131; CANR 73; CWW 2; DLB
145; EWL 3; HW 1; RGWL 3

Arias, Ron(ald Francis) 1941- .... **HLC 1**
See also CA 131; CANR 81; DAM MULT;
DLB 82; HW 1, 2; MTCW 2

Ariosto, Ludovico 1474-1533 ... **LC 6, 87; PC**
42
See also EW 2; RGWL 2, 3

Aristides
See Epstein, Joseph

Aristophanes 450B.C.-385B.C. .... **CMLC 4,**
51; DC 2; WLCS
See also AW 1; CDWLB 1; DA; DA3;
DAB; DAC; DAM DRAM, MST; DFS
10; DLB 176; LMFS 1; RGWL 2, 3; TWA

Aristotle 384B.C.-322B.C. .... **CMLC 31;**
WLCS
See also AW 1; CDWLB 1; DA; DA3;
DAB; DAC; DAM MST; DLB 176;
RGWL 2, 3; TWA

Arlt, Roberto (Godofredo Christophersen)
1900-1942 .... **HLC 1; TCLC 29**
See also CA 123; 131; CANR 67; DAM
MULT; DLB 305; EWL 3; HW 1, 2; LAW

Austin, Mary (Hunter) 1868-1934 . **TCLC 25**
See Stairs, Gordon
See also ANW; CA 109; 178; DLB 9, 78, 206, 221, 275; FW; TCWW 2

Averroes 1126-1198 .... **CMLC 7**
See also DLB 115

Avicenna 980-1037 .... **CMLC 16**
See also DLB 115

Avison, Margaret 1918- .... **CLC 2, 4, 97**
See also CA 17-20R; CP 7; DAC; DAM POET; DLB 53; MTCW 1

Axton, David
See Koontz, Dean R(ay)

Ayckbourn, Alan 1939- ...... **CLC 5, 8, 18, 33, 74; DC 13**
See also BRWS 5; CA 21-24R; CANR 31, 59, 118; CBD; CD 5; DAB; DAM DRAM; DFS 7; DLB 13, 245; EWL 3; MTCW 1, 2

Aydy, Catherine
See Tennant, Emma (Christina)

Ayme, Marcel (Andre) 1902-1967 ... **CLC 11; SSC 41**
See also CA 89-92; CANR 67; CLR 25; DLB 72; EW 12; EWL 3; GFL 1789 to the Present; RGSF 2; RGWL 2, 3; SATA 91

Ayrton, Michael 1921-1975 .... **CLC 7**
See also CA 5-8R; 61-64; CANR 9, 21

Aytmatov, Chingiz
See Aitmatov, Chingiz (Torekulovich)
See also EWL 3

Azorin .... **CLC 11**
See Martinez Ruiz, Jose
See also EW 9; EWL 3

Azuela, Mariano 1873-1952 .. **HLC 1; TCLC 3, 145**
See also CA 104; 131; CANR 81; DAM MULT; EWL 3; HW 1, 2; LAW; MTCW 1, 2

Ba, Mariama 1929-1981 .... **BLCS**
See also AFW; BW 2; CA 141; CANR 87; DNFS 2; WLIT 2

Baastad, Babbis Friis
See Friis-Baastad, Babbis Ellinor

Bab
See Gilbert, W(illiam) S(chwenck)

Babbis, Eleanor
See Friis-Baastad, Babbis Ellinor

Babel, Isaac
See Babel, Isaak (Emmanuilovich)
See also EW 11; SSFS 10

Babel, Isaak (Emmanuilovich)
1894-1941(?) .... **SSC 16; TCLC 2, 13**
See Babel, Isaac
See also CA 104; 155; CANR 113; DLB 272; EWL 3; MTCW 1; RGSF 2; RGWL 2, 3; TWA

Babits, Mihaly 1883-1941 .... **TCLC 14**
See also CA 114; CDWLB 4; DLB 215; EWL 3

Babur 1483-1530 .... **LC 18**

Babylas 1898-1962
See Ghelderode, Michel de

Baca, Jimmy Santiago 1952- . **HLC 1; PC 41**
See also CA 131; CANR 81, 90; CP 7; DAM MULT; DLB 122; HW 1, 2; LLW 1

Baca, Jose Santiago
See Baca, Jimmy Santiago

Bacchelli, Riccardo 1891-1985 .... **CLC 19**
See also CA 29-32R; 117; DLB 264; EWL 3

Bach, Richard (David) 1936- .... **CLC 14**
See also AITN 1; BEST 89:2; BPFB 1; BYA 5; CA 9-12R; CANR 18, 93; CPW; DAM NOV, POP; FANT; MTCW 1; SATA 13

Bache, Benjamin Franklin
1769-1798 .... **LC 74**
See also DLB 43

Bachelard, Gaston 1884-1962 ...... **TCLC 128**
See also CA 97-100; 89-92; DLB 296; GFL 1789 to the Present

Bachman, Richard
See King, Stephen (Edwin)

Bachmann, Ingeborg 1926-1973 .... **CLC 69**
See also CA 93-96; 45-48; CANR 69; DLB 85; EWL 3; RGWL 2, 3

Bacon, Francis 1561-1626 .... **LC 18, 32**
See also BRW 1; CDBLB Before 1660; DLB 151, 236, 252; RGEL 2; TEA

Bacon, Roger 1214(?)-1294 .... **CMLC 14**
See also DLB 115

Bacovia, George 1881-1957 .... **TCLC 24**
See Vasiliu, Gheorghe
See also CDWLB 4; DLB 220; EWL 3

Badanes, Jerome 1937-1995 .... **CLC 59**

Bagehot, Walter 1826-1877 .... **NCLC 10**
See also DLB 55

Bagnold, Enid 1889-1981 .... **CLC 25**
See also BYA 2; CA 5-8R; 103; CANR 5, 40; CBD; CWD; CWRI 5; DAM DRAM; DLB 13, 160, 191, 245; FW; MAICYA 1, 2; RGEL 2; SATA 1, 25

Bagritsky, Eduard .... **TCLC 60**
See Dzyubin, Eduard Georgievich

Bagrjana, Elisaveta
See Belcheva, Elisaveta Lyubomirova

Bagryana, Elisaveta .... **CLC 10**
See Belcheva, Elisaveta Lyubomirova
See also CA 178; CDWLB 4; DLB 147; EWL 3

Bailey, Paul 1937- .... **CLC 45**
See also CA 21-24R; CANR 16, 62, 124; CN 7; DLB 14, 271; GLL 2

Baillie, Joanna 1762-1851 .... **NCLC 71**
See also DLB 93; RGEL 2

Bainbridge, Beryl (Margaret) 1934- . **CLC 4, 5, 8, 10, 14, 18, 22, 62, 130**
See also BRWS 6; CA 21-24R; CANR 24, 55, 75, 88, 128; CN 7; DAM NOV; DLB 14, 231; EWL 3; MTCW 1, 2

Baker, Carlos (Heard)
1909-1987 .... **TCLC 119**
See also CA 5-8R; 122; CANR 3, 63; DLB 103

Baker, Elliott 1922- .... **CLC 8**
See also CA 45-48; CANR 2, 63; CN 7

Baker, Jean H. .... **TCLC 3, 10**
See Russell, George William

Baker, Nicholson 1957- .... **CLC 61, 165**
See also AMWS 13; CA 135; CANR 63, 120; CN 7; CPW; DA3; DAM POP; DLB 227

Baker, Ray Stannard 1870-1946 .... **TCLC 47**
See also CA 118

Baker, Russell (Wayne) 1925- .... **CLC 31**
See also BEST 89:4; CA 57-60; CANR 11, 41, 59; MTCW 1, 2

Bakhtin, M.
See Bakhtin, Mikhail Mikhailovich

Bakhtin, M. M.
See Bakhtin, Mikhail Mikhailovich

Bakhtin, Mikhail
See Bakhtin, Mikhail Mikhailovich

Bakhtin, Mikhail Mikhailovich
1895-1975 .... **CLC 83**
See also CA 128; 113; DLB 242; EWL 3

Bakshi, Ralph 1938(?)- .... **CLC 26**
See also CA 112; 138; IDFW 3

Bakunin, Mikhail (Alexandrovich)
1814-1876 .... **NCLC 25, 58**
See also DLB 277

Baldwin, James (Arthur) 1924-1987 . **BLC 1; CLC 1, 2, 3, 4, 5, 8, 13, 15, 17, 42, 50, 67, 90, 127; DC 1; SSC 10, 33; WLC**
See also AAYA 4, 34; AFAW 1, 2; AMWR 2; AMWS 1; BPFB 1; BW 1; CA 1-4R; 124; CABS 1; CAD; CANR 3, 24;

CDALB 1941-1968; CPW; DA; DA3; DAB; DAC; DAM MST, MULT, NOV, POP; DFS 11, 15; DLB 2, 7, 33, 249, 278; DLBY 1987; EWL 3; EXPS; LAIT 5; MTCW 1, 2; NCFS 4; NFS 4; RGAL 4; RGSF 2; SATA 9; SATA-Obit 54; SSFS 2, 18; TUS

Bale, John 1495-1563 .... **LC 62**
See also DLB 132; RGEL 2; TEA

Ball, Hugo 1886-1927 .... **TCLC 104**

Ballard, J(ames) G(raham) 1930- . **CLC 3, 6, 14, 36, 137; SSC 1, 53**
See also AAYA 3, 52; BRWS 5; CA 5-8R; CANR 15, 39, 65, 107, 133; CN 7; DA3; DAM NOV, POP; DLB 14, 207, 261; EWL 3; HGG; MTCW 1, 2; NFS 8; RGEL 2; RGSF 2; SATA 93; SFW 4

Balmont, Konstantin (Dmitriyevich)
1867-1943 .... **TCLC 11**
See also CA 109; 155; DLB 295; EWL 3

Baltausis, Vincas 1847-1910
See Mikszath, Kalman

Balzac, Honore de 1799-1850 ... **NCLC 5, 35, 53; SSC 5, 59; WLC**
See also DA; DA3; DAB; DAC; DAM MST, NOV; DLB 119; EW 5; GFL 1789 to the Present; LMFS 1; RGSF 2; RGWL 2, 3; SSFS 10; SUFW; TWA

Bambara, Toni Cade 1939-1995 .... **BLC 1; CLC 19, 88; SSC 35; TCLC 116; WLCS**
See also AAYA 5, 49; AFAW 2; AMWS 11; BW 2, 3; BYA 12, 14; CA 29-32R; 150; CANR 24, 49, 81; CDALBS; DA; DA3; DAC; DAM MST, MULT; DLB 38, 218; EXPS; MTCW 1, 2; RGAL 4; RGSF 2; SATA 112; SSFS 4, 7, 12

Bamdad, A.
See Shamlu, Ahmad

Bamdad, Alef
See Shamlu, Ahmad

Banat, D. R.
See Bradbury, Ray (Douglas)

Bancroft, Laura
See Baum, L(yman) Frank

Banim, John 1798-1842 .... **NCLC 13**
See also DLB 116, 158, 159; RGEL 2

Banim, Michael 1796-1874 .... **NCLC 13**
See also DLB 158, 159

Banjo, The
See Paterson, A(ndrew) B(arton)

Banks, Iain
See Banks, Iain M(enzies)

Banks, Iain M(enzies) 1954- .... **CLC 34**
See also CA 123; 128; CANR 61, 106; DLB 194, 261; EWL 3; HGG; INT CA-128; SFW 4

Banks, Lynne Reid .... **CLC 23**
See Reid Banks, Lynne
See also AAYA 6; BYA 7; CLR 86

Banks, Russell (Earl) 1940- .... **CLC 37, 72, 187; SSC 42**
See also AAYA 45; AMWS 5; CA 65-68; CAAS 15; CANR 19, 52, 73, 118; CN 7; DLB 130, 278; EWL 3; NFS 13

Banville, John 1945- .... **CLC 46, 118**
See also CA 117; 128; CANR 104; CN 7; DLB 14, 271; INT CA-128

Banville, Theodore (Faullain) de
1832-1891 .... **NCLC 9**
See also DLB 217; GFL 1789 to the Present

Baraka, Amiri 1934- .... **BLC 1; CLC 1, 2, 3, 5, 10, 14, 33, 115; DC 6; PC 4; WLCS**
See Jones, LeRoi
See also AFAW 1, 2; AMWS 2; BW 2, 3; CA 21-24R; CABS 3; CAD; CANR 27, 38, 61, 133; CD 5; CDALB 1941-1968; CP 7; CPW; DA; DA3; DAC; DAM MST,

MULT, POET, POP; DFS 3, 11, 16; DLB
5, 7, 16, 38; DLBD 8; EWL 3; MTCW 1,
2; PFS 9; RGAL 4; TUS; WP

Baratynsky, Evgenii Abramovich
1800-1844 .... **NCLC 103**
See also DLB 205

Barbauld, Anna Laetitia
1743-1825 .... **NCLC 50**
See also DLB 107, 109, 142, 158; RGEL 2

Barbellion, W. N. P. .... **TCLC 24**
See Cummings, Bruce F(rederick)

Barber, Benjamin R. 1939- .... **CLC 141**
See also CA 29-32R; CANR 12, 32, 64, 119

Barbera, Jack (Vincent) 1945- .... **CLC 44**
See also CA 110; CANR 45

Barbey d'Aurevilly, Jules-Amedee
1808-1889 .... **NCLC 1; SSC 17**
See also DLB 119; GFL 1789 to the Present

Barbour, John c. 1316-1395 .... **CMLC 33**
See also DLB 146

Barbusse, Henri 1873-1935 .... **TCLC 5**
See also CA 105; 154; DLB 65; EWL 3;
RGWL 2, 3

Barclay, Bill
See Moorcock, Michael (John)

Barclay, William Ewert
See Moorcock, Michael (John)

Barea, Arturo 1897-1957 .... **TCLC 14**
See also CA 111; 201

Barfoot, Joan 1946- .... **CLC 18**
See also CA 105

Barham, Richard Harris
1788-1845 .... **NCLC 77**
See also DLB 159

Baring, Maurice 1874-1945 .... **TCLC 8**
See also CA 105; 168; DLB 34; HGG

Baring-Gould, Sabine 1834-1924 ... **TCLC 88**
See also DLB 156, 190

Barker, Clive 1952- .... **CLC 52; SSC 53**
See also AAYA 10, 54; BEST 90:3; BPFB
1; CA 121; 129; CANR 71, 111, 133;
CPW; DA3; DAM POP; DLB 261; HGG;
INT CA-129; MTCW 1, 2; SUFW 2

Barker, George Granville
1913-1991 .... **CLC 8, 48**
See also CA 9-12R; 135; CANR 7, 38;
DAM POET; DLB 20; EWL 3; MTCW 1

Barker, Harley Granville
See Granville-Barker, Harley
See also DLB 10

Barker, Howard 1946- .... **CLC 37**
See also CA 102; CBD; CD 5; DLB 13,
233

Barker, Jane 1652-1732 .... **LC 42, 82**
See also DLB 39, 131

Barker, Pat(ricia) 1943- ...... **CLC 32, 94, 146**
See also BRWS 4; CA 117; 122; CANR 50,
101; CN 7; DLB 271; INT CA-122

Barlach, Ernst (Heinrich)
1870-1938 .... **TCLC 84**
See also CA 178; DLB 56, 118; EWL 3

Barlow, Joel 1754-1812 .... **NCLC 23**
See also AMWS 2; DLB 37; RGAL 4

Barnard, Mary (Ethel) 1909- .... **CLC 48**
See also CA 21-22; CAP 2

Barnes, Djuna 1892-1982 .... **CLC 3, 4, 8, 11,
29, 127; SSC 3**
See Steptoe, Lydia
See also AMWS 3; CA 9-12R; 107; CAD;
CANR 16, 55; CWD; DLB 4, 9, 45; EWL
3; GLL 1; MTCW 1, 2; RGAL 4; TUS

Barnes, Jim 1933- .... **NNAL**
See also CA 108; 175; CAAE 175; CAAS
28; DLB 175

Barnes, Julian (Patrick) 1946- . **CLC 42, 141**
See also BRWS 4; CA 102; CANR 19, 54,
115; CN 7; DAB; DLB 194; DLBY 1993;
EWL 3; MTCW 1

Barnes, Peter 1931-2004 .... **CLC 5, 56**
See also CA 65-68; CAAS 12; CANR 33,
34, 64, 113; CBD; CD 5; DFS 6; DLB
13, 233; MTCW 1

Barnes, William 1801-1886 .... **NCLC 75**
See also DLB 32

Baroja (y Nessi), Pio 1872-1956 .... **HLC 1;
TCLC 8**
See also CA 104; EW 9

Baron, David
See Pinter, Harold

Baron Corvo
See Rolfe, Frederick (William Serafino
Austin Lewis Mary)

Barondess, Sue K(aufman)
1926-1977 .... **CLC 8**
See Kaufman, Sue
See also CA 1-4R; 69-72; CANR 1

Baron de Teive
See Pessoa, Fernando (Antonio Nogueira)

Baroness Von S.
See Zangwill, Israel

Barres, (Auguste-)Maurice
1862-1923 .... **TCLC 47**
See also CA 164; DLB 123; GFL 1789 to
the Present

Barreto, Afonso Henrique de Lima
See Lima Barreto, Afonso Henrique de

Barrett, Andrea 1954- .... **CLC 150**
See also CA 156; CANR 92

Barrett, Michele .... **CLC 65**

Barrett, (Roger) Syd 1946- .... **CLC 35**

Barrett, William (Christopher)
1913-1992 .... **CLC 27**
See also CA 13-16R; 139; CANR 11, 67;
INT CANR-11

Barrie, J(ames) M(atthew)
1860-1937 .... **TCLC 2**
See also BRWS 3; BYA 4, 5; CA 104; 136;
CANR 77; CDBLB 1890-1914; CLR 16;
CWRI 5; DA3; DAB; DAM DRAM; DFS
7; DLB 10, 141, 156; EWL 3; FANT;
MAICYA 1, 2; MTCW 1; SATA 100;
SUFW; WCH; WLIT 4; YABC 1

Barrington, Michael
See Moorcock, Michael (John)

Barrol, Grady
See Bograd, Larry

Barry, Mike
See Malzberg, Barry N(athaniel)

Barry, Philip 1896-1949 .... **TCLC 11**
See also CA 109; 199; DFS 9; DLB 7, 228;
RGAL 4

Bart, Andre Schwarz
See Schwarz-Bart, Andre

Barth, John (Simmons) 1930- ... **CLC 1, 2, 3,
5, 7, 9, 10, 14, 27, 51, 89; SSC 10**
See also AITN 1, 2; AMW; BPFB 1; CA
1-4R; CABS 1; CANR 5, 23, 49, 64, 113;
CN 7; DAM NOV; DLB 2, 227; EWL 3;
FANT; MTCW 1; RGAL 4; RGSF 2;
RHW; SSFS 6; TUS

Barthelme, Donald 1931-1989 ... **CLC 1, 2, 3,
5, 6, 8, 13, 23, 46, 59, 115; SSC 2, 55**
See also AMWS 4; BPFB 1; CA 21-24R;
129; CANR 20, 58; DA3; DAM NOV;
DLB 2, 234; DLBY 1980, 1989; EWL 3;
FANT; LMFS 2; MTCW 1, 2; RGAL 4;
RGSF 2; SATA 7; SATA-Obit 62; SSFS
17

Barthelme, Frederick 1943- ...... **CLC 36, 117**
See also AMWS 11; CA 114; 122; CANR
77; CN 7; CSW; DLB 244; DLBY 1985;
EWL 3; INT CA-122

Barthes, Roland (Gerard)
1915-1980 .... **CLC 24, 83; TCLC 135**
See also CA 130; 97-100; CANR 66; DLB
296; EW 13; EWL 3; GFL 1789 to the
Present; MTCW 1, 2; TWA

Bartram, William 1739-1823 .... **NCLC 145**
See also ANW; DLB 37

Barzun, Jacques (Martin) 1907- ..... **CLC 51,
145**
See also CA 61-64; CANR 22, 95

Bashevis, Isaac
See Singer, Isaac Bashevis

Bashkirtseff, Marie 1859-1884 .... **NCLC 27**

Basho, Matsuo
See Matsuo Basho
See also PFS 18; RGWL 2, 3; WP

Basil of Caesaria c. 330-379 .... **CMLC 35**

Basket, Raney
See Edgerton, Clyde (Carlyle)

Bass, Kingsley B., Jr.
See Bullins, Ed

Bass, Rick 1958- .... **CLC 79, 143; SSC 60**
See also ANW; CA 126; CANR 53, 93;
CSW; DLB 212, 275

Bassani, Giorgio 1916-2000 .... **CLC 9**
See also CA 65-68; 190; CANR 33; CWW
2; DLB 128, 177, 299; EWL 3; MTCW 1;
RGWL 2, 3

Bastian, Ann .... **CLC 70**

Bastos, Augusto (Antonio) Roa
See Roa Bastos, Augusto (Antonio)

Bataille, Georges 1897-1962 .... **CLC 29;
TCLC 155**
See also CA 101; 89-92; EWL 3

Bates, H(erbert) E(rnest)
1905-1974 .... **CLC 46; SSC 10**
See also CA 93-96; 45-48; CANR 34; DA3;
DAB; DAM POP; DLB 162, 191; EWL
3; EXPS; MTCW 1, 2; RGSF 2; SSFS 7

Bauchart
See Camus, Albert

Baudelaire, Charles 1821-1867 . **NCLC 6, 29,
55; PC 1; SSC 18; WLC**
See also DA; DA3; DAB; DAC; DAM
MST, POET; DLB 217; EW 7; GFL 1789
to the Present; LMFS 2; PFS 21; RGWL
2, 3; TWA

Baudouin, Marcel
See Peguy, Charles (Pierre)

Baudouin, Pierre
See Peguy, Charles (Pierre)

Baudrillard, Jean 1929- .... **CLC 60**
See also DLB 296

Baum, L(yman) Frank 1856-1919 .. **TCLC 7,
132**
See also AAYA 46; BYA 16; CA 108; 133;
CLR 15; CWRI 5; DLB 22; FANT; JRDA;
MAICYA 1, 2; MTCW 1, 2; NFS 13;
RGAL 4; SATA 18, 100; WCH

Baum, Louis F.
See Baum, L(yman) Frank

Baumbach, Jonathan 1933- .... **CLC 6, 23**
See also CA 13-16R; CAAS 5; CANR 12,
66; CN 7; DLBY 1980; INT CANR-12;
MTCW 1

Bausch, Richard (Carl) 1945- .... **CLC 51**
See also AMWS 7; CA 101; CAAS 14;
CANR 43, 61, 87; CSW; DLB 130

Baxter, Charles (Morley) 1947- . **CLC 45, 78**
See also CA 57-60; CANR 40, 64, 104, 133;
CPW; DAM POP; DLB 130; MTCW 2

Baxter, George Owen
See Faust, Frederick (Schiller)

Baxter, James K(eir) 1926-1972 .... **CLC 14**
See also CA 77-80; EWL 3

Baxter, John
See Hunt, E(verette) Howard, (Jr.)

Bayer, Sylvia
See Glassco, John

Baynton, Barbara 1857-1929 .... **TCLC 57**
See also DLB 230; RGSF 2

Beagle, Peter S(oyer) 1939- .... **CLC 7, 104**
See also AAYA 47; BPFB 1; BYA 9, 10, 16; CA 9-12R; CANR 4, 51, 73, 110; DA3; DLBY 1980; FANT; INT CANR-4; MTCW 1; SATA 60, 130; SUFW 1, 2; YAW

Bean, Normal
See Burroughs, Edgar Rice

Beard, Charles A(ustin)
1874-1948 .... **TCLC 15**
See also CA 115; 189; DLB 17; SATA 18

Beardsley, Aubrey 1872-1898 .... **NCLC 6**

Beattie, Ann 1947- ..... **CLC 8, 13, 18, 40, 63, 146; SSC 11**
See also AMWS 5; BEST 90:2; BPFB 1; CA 81-84; CANR 53, 73, 128; CN 7; CPW; DA3; DAM NOV, POP; DLB 218, 278; DLBY 1982; EWL 3; MTCW 1, 2; RGAL 4; RGSF 2; SSFS 9; TUS

Beattie, James 1735-1803 .... **NCLC 25**
See also DLB 109

Beauchamp, Kathleen Mansfield 1888-1923
See Mansfield, Katherine
See also CA 104; 134; DA; DA3; DAC; DAM MST; MTCW 2; TEA

Beaumarchais, Pierre-Augustin Caron de
1732-1799 .... **DC 4; LC 61**
See also DAM DRAM; DFS 14, 16; EW 4; GFL Beginnings to 1789; RGWL 2, 3

Beaumont, Francis 1584(?)-1616 .. **DC 6; LC 33**
See also BRW 2; CDBLB Before 1660; DLB 58; TEA

Beauvoir, Simone (Lucie Ernestine Marie Bertrand) de 1908-1986 .... **CLC 1, 2, 4, 8, 14, 31, 44, 50, 71, 124; SSC 35; WLC**
See also BPFB 1; CA 9-12R; 118; CANR 28, 61; DA; DA3; DAB; DAC; DAM MST, NOV; DLB 72; DLBY 1986; EW 12; EWL 3; FW; GFL 1789 to the Present; LMFS 2; MTCW 1, 2; RGSF 2; RGWL 2, 3; TWA

Becker, Carl (Lotus) 1873-1945 ..... **TCLC 63**
See also CA 157; DLB 17

Becker, Jurek 1937-1997 .... **CLC 7, 19**
See also CA 85-88; 157; CANR 60, 117; CWW 2; DLB 75, 299; EWL 3

Becker, Walter 1950- .... **CLC 26**

Beckett, Samuel (Barclay)
1906-1989 .. **CLC 1, 2, 3, 4, 6, 9, 10, 11, 14, 18, 29, 57, 59, 83; DC 22; SSC 16, 74; TCLC 145; WLC**
See also BRWC 2; BRWR 1; BRWS 1; CA 5-8R; 130; CANR 33, 61; CBD; CDBLB 1945-1960; DA; DA3; DAB; DAC; DAM DRAM, MST, NOV; DFS 2, 7, 18; DLB 13, 15, 233; DLBY 1990; EWL 3; GFL 1789 to the Present; LATS 1:2; LMFS 2; MTCW 1, 2; RGSF 2; RGWL 2, 3; SSFS 15; TEA; WLIT 4

Beckford, William 1760-1844 .... **NCLC 16**
See also BRW 3; DLB 39, 213; HGG; LMFS 1; SUFW

Beckham, Barry (Earl) 1944- .... **BLC 1**
See also BW 1; CA 29-32R; CANR 26, 62; CN 7; DAM MULT; DLB 33

Beckman, Gunnel 1910- .... **CLC 26**
See also CA 33-36R; CANR 15, 114; CLR 25; MAICYA 1, 2; SAAS 9; SATA 6

Becque, Henri 1837-1899 ...... **DC 21; NCLC 3**
See also DLB 192; GFL 1789 to the Present

Becquer, Gustavo Adolfo
1836-1870 .... **HLCS 1; NCLC 106**
See also DAM MULT

Beddoes, Thomas Lovell 1803-1849 .. **DC 15; NCLC 3**
See also DLB 96

Bede c. 673-735 .... **CMLC 20**
See also DLB 146; TEA

Bedford, Denton R. 1907-(?) .... **NNAL**

Bedford, Donald F.
See Fearing, Kenneth (Flexner)

Beecher, Catharine Esther
1800-1878 .... **NCLC 30**
See also DLB 1, 243

Beecher, John 1904-1980 .... **CLC 6**
See also AITN 1; CA 5-8R; 105; CANR 8

Beer, Johann 1655-1700 .... **LC 5**
See also DLB 168

Beer, Patricia 1924- .... **CLC 58**
See also CA 61-64; 183; CANR 13, 46; CP 7; CWP; DLB 40; FW

Beerbohm, Max
See Beerbohm, (Henry) Max(imilian)

Beerbohm, (Henry) Max(imilian)
1872-1956 .... **TCLC 1, 24**
See also BRWS 2; CA 104; 154; CANR 79; DLB 34, 100; FANT

Beer-Hofmann, Richard
1866-1945 .... **TCLC 60**
See also CA 160; DLB 81

Beg, Shemus
See Stephens, James

Begiebing, Robert J(ohn) 1946- .... **CLC 70**
See also CA 122; CANR 40, 88

Begley, Louis 1933- .... **CLC 197**
See also CA 140; CANR 98; DLB 299

Behan, Brendan (Francis)
1923-1964 .... **CLC 1, 8, 11, 15, 79**
See also BRWS 2; CA 73-76; CANR 33, 121; CBD; CDBLB 1945-1960; DAM DRAM; DFS 7; DLB 13, 233; EWL 3; MTCW 1, 2

Behn, Aphra 1640(?)-1689 .. **DC 4; LC 1, 30, 42; PC 13; WLC**
See also BRWS 3; DA; DA3; DAB; DAC; DAM DRAM, MST, NOV, POET; DFS 16; DLB 39, 80, 131; FW; TEA; WLIT 3

Behrman, S(amuel) N(athaniel)
1893-1973 .... **CLC 40**
See also CA 13-16; 45-48; CAD; CAP 1; DLB 7, 44; IDFW 3; RGAL 4

Belasco, David 1853-1931 .... **TCLC 3**
See also CA 104; 168; DLB 7; RGAL 4

Belcheva, Elisaveta Lyubomirova
1893-1991 .... **CLC 10**
See Bagryana, Elisaveta

Beldone, Phil ''Cheech''
See Ellison, Harlan (Jay)

Beleno
See Azuela, Mariano

Belinski, Vissarion Grigoryevich
1811-1848 .... **NCLC 5**
See also DLB 198

Belitt, Ben 1911- .... **CLC 22**
See also CA 13-16R; CAAS 4; CANR 7, 77; CP 7; DLB 5

Bell, Gertrude (Margaret Lowthian)
1868-1926 .... **TCLC 67**
See also CA 167; CANR 110; DLB 174

Bell, J. Freeman
See Zangwill, Israel

Bell, James Madison 1826-1902 .... **BLC 1; TCLC 43**
See also BW 1; CA 122; 124; DAM MULT; DLB 50

Bell, Madison Smartt 1957- ...... **CLC 41, 102**
See also AMWS 10; BPFB 1; CA 111, 183; CAAE 183; CANR 28, 54, 73; CN 7; CSW; DLB 218, 278; MTCW 1

Bell, Marvin (Hartley) 1937- .... **CLC 8, 31**
See also CA 21-24R; CAAS 14; CANR 59, 102; CP 7; DAM POET; DLB 5; MTCW 1

Bell, W. L. D.
See Mencken, H(enry) L(ouis)

Bellamy, Atwood C.
See Mencken, H(enry) L(ouis)

Bellamy, Edward 1850-1898 ..... **NCLC 4, 86, 147**
See also DLB 12; NFS 15; RGAL 4; SFW 4

Belli, Gioconda 1949- .... **HLCS 1**
See also CA 152; CWW 2; DLB 290; EWL 3; RGWL 3

Bellin, Edward J.
See Kuttner, Henry

Bello, Andres 1781-1865 .... **NCLC 131**
See also LAW

Belloc, (Joseph) Hilaire (Pierre Sebastien Rene Swanton) 1870-1953 .... **PC 24; TCLC 7, 18**
See also CA 106; 152; CWRI 5; DAM POET; DLB 19, 100, 141, 174; EWL 3; MTCW 1; SATA 112; WCH; YABC 1

Belloc, Joseph Peter Rene Hilaire
See Belloc, (Joseph) Hilaire (Pierre Sebastien Rene Swanton)

Belloc, Joseph Pierre Hilaire
See Belloc, (Joseph) Hilaire (Pierre Sebastien Rene Swanton)

Belloc, M. A.
See Lowndes, Marie Adelaide (Belloc)

Belloc-Lowndes, Mrs.
See Lowndes, Marie Adelaide (Belloc)

Bellow, Saul 1915- . **CLC 1, 2, 3, 6, 8, 10, 13, 15, 25, 33, 34, 63, 79, 190; SSC 14; WLC**
See also AITN 2; AMW; AMWC 2; AMWR 2; BEST 89:3; BPFB 1; CA 5-8R; CABS 1; CANR 29, 53, 95, 132; CDALB 1941-1968; CN 7; DA; DA3; DAB; DAC; DAM MST, NOV, POP; DLB 2, 28, 299; DLBD 3; DLBY 1982; EWL 3; MTCW 1, 2; NFS 4, 14; RGAL 4; RGSF 2; SSFS 12; TUS

Belser, Reimond Karel Maria de 1929-
See Ruyslinck, Ward
See also CA 152

Bely, Andrey .... **PC 11; TCLC 7**
See Bugayev, Boris Nikolayevich
See also DLB 295; EW 9; EWL 3; MTCW 1

Belyi, Andrei
See Bugayev, Boris Nikolayevich
See also RGWL 2, 3

Bembo, Pietro 1470-1547 .... **LC 79**
See also RGWL 2, 3

Benary, Margot
See Benary-Isbert, Margot

Benary-Isbert, Margot 1889-1979 .... **CLC 12**
See also CA 5-8R; 89-92; CANR 4, 72; CLR 12; MAICYA 1, 2; SATA 2; SATA-Obit 21

Benavente (y Martinez), Jacinto
1866-1954 .... **HLCS 1; TCLC 3**
See also CA 106; 131; CANR 81; DAM DRAM, MULT; EWL 3; GLL 2; HW 1, 2; MTCW 1, 2

Benchley, Peter (Bradford) 1940- .. **CLC 4, 8**
See also AAYA 14; AITN 2; BPFB 1; CA 17-20R; CANR 12, 35, 66, 115; CPW; DAM NOV, POP; HGG; MTCW 1, 2; SATA 3, 89

Benchley, Robert (Charles)
1889-1945 .... **TCLC 1, 55**
See also CA 105; 153; DLB 11; RGAL 4

Benda, Julien 1867-1956 .... **TCLC 60**
See also CA 120; 154; GFL 1789 to the Present

Benedict, Ruth (Fulton)
1887-1948 .... **TCLC 60**
See also CA 158; DLB 246

Benedikt, Michael 1935- .... **CLC 4, 14**
See also CA 13-16R; CANR 7; CP 7; DLB 5

Benet, Juan 1927-1993 .... **CLC 28**
See also CA 143; EWL 3

Benet, Stephen Vincent 1898-1943 ... **SSC 10;**
TCLC 7
See also AMWS 11; CA 104; 152; DA3;
DAM POET; DLB 4, 48, 102, 249, 284;
DLBY 1997; EWL 3; HGG; MTCW 1;
RGAL 4; RGSF 2; SUFW; WP; YABC 1

Benet, William Rose 1886-1950 ..... **TCLC 28**
See also CA 118; 152; DAM POET; DLB
45; RGAL 4

Benford, Gregory (Albert) 1941- ..... **CLC 52**
See also BPFB 1; CA 69-72, 175; CAAE
175; CAAS 27; CANR 12, 24, 49, 95;
CSW; DLBY 1982; SCFW 2; SFW 4

Bengtsson, Frans (Gunnar)
1894-1954 .... **TCLC 48**
See also CA 170; EWL 3

Benjamin, David
See Slavitt, David R(ytman)

Benjamin, Lois
See Gould, Lois

Benjamin, Walter 1892-1940 .... **TCLC 39**
See also CA 164; DLB 242; EW 11; EWL
3

Ben Jelloun, Tahar 1944-
See Jelloun, Tahar ben
See also CA 135; CWW 2; EWL 3; RGWL
3; WLIT 2

Benn, Gottfried 1886-1956 .. **PC 35; TCLC 3**
See also CA 106; 153; DLB 56; EWL 3;
RGWL 2, 3

Bennett, Alan 1934- .... **CLC 45, 77**
See also BRWS 8; CA 103; CANR 35, 55,
106; CBD; CD 5; DAB; DAM MST;
MTCW 1, 2

Bennett, (Enoch) Arnold
1867-1931 .... **TCLC 5, 20**
See also BRW 6; CA 106; 155; CDBLB
1890-1914; DLB 10, 34, 98, 135; EWL 3;
MTCW 2

Bennett, Elizabeth
See Mitchell, Margaret (Munnerlyn)

Bennett, George Harold 1930-
See Bennett, Hal
See also BW 1; CA 97-100; CANR 87

Bennett, Gwendolyn B. 1902-1981 .... **HR 2**
See also BW 1; CA 125; DLB 51; WP

Bennett, Hal .... **CLC 5**
See Bennett, George Harold
See also DLB 33

Bennett, Jay 1912- .... **CLC 35**
See also AAYA 10; CA 69-72; CANR 11,
42, 79; JRDA; SAAS 4; SATA 41, 87;
SATA-Brief 27; WYA; YAW

Bennett, Louise (Simone) 1919- .... **BLC 1;**
CLC 28
See also BW 2, 3; CA 151; CDWLB 3; CP
7; DAM MULT; DLB 117; EWL 3

Benson, A. C. 1862-1925 .... **TCLC 123**
See also DLB 98

Benson, E(dward) F(rederic)
1867-1940 .... **TCLC 27**
See also CA 114; 157; DLB 135, 153;
HGG; SUFW 1

Benson, Jackson J. 1930- .... **CLC 34**
See also CA 25-28R; DLB 111

Benson, Sally 1900-1972 .... **CLC 17**
See also CA 19-20; 37-40R; CAP 1; SATA
1, 35; SATA-Obit 27

Benson, Stella 1892-1933 .... **TCLC 17**
See also CA 117; 154; 155; DLB 36, 162;
FANT; TEA

Bentham, Jeremy 1748-1832 .... **NCLC 38**
See also DLB 107, 158, 252

Bentley, E(dmund) C(lerihew)
1875-1956 .... **TCLC 12**
See also CA 108; DLB 70; MSW

Bentley, Eric (Russell) 1916- .... **CLC 24**
See also CA 5-8R; CAD; CANR 6, 67;
CBD; CD 5; INT CANR-6

ben Uzair, Salem
See Horne, Richard Henry Hengist

Beranger, Pierre Jean de
1780-1857 .... **NCLC 34**

Berdyaev, Nicolas
See Berdyaev, Nikolai (Aleksandrovich)

Berdyaev, Nikolai (Aleksandrovich)
1874-1948 .... **TCLC 67**
See also CA 120; 157

Berdyayev, Nikolai (Aleksandrovich)
See Berdyaev, Nikolai (Aleksandrovich)

Berendt, John (Lawrence) 1939- ...... **CLC 86**
See also CA 146; CANR 75, 93; DA3;
MTCW 1

Beresford, J(ohn) D(avys)
1873-1947 .... **TCLC 81**
See also CA 112; 155; DLB 162, 178, 197;
SFW 4; SUFW 1

Bergelson, David (Rafailovich)
1884-1952 .... **TCLC 81**
See Bergelson, Dovid
See also CA 220

Bergelson, Dovid
See Bergelson, David (Rafailovich)
See also EWL 3

Berger, Colonel
See Malraux, (Georges-)Andre

Berger, John (Peter) 1926- .... **CLC 2, 19**
See also BRWS 4; CA 81-84; CANR 51,
78, 117; CN 7; DLB 14, 207

Berger, Melvin H. 1927- .... **CLC 12**
See also CA 5-8R; CANR 4; CLR 32;
SAAS 2; SATA 5, 88; SATA-Essay 124

Berger, Thomas (Louis) 1924- .. **CLC 3, 5, 8,**
11, 18, 38
See also BPFB 1; CA 1-4R; CANR 5, 28,
51, 128; CN 7; DAM NOV; DLB 2;
DLBY 1980; EWL 3; FANT; INT CANR-
28; MTCW 1, 2; RHW; TCWW 2

Bergman, (Ernst) Ingmar 1918- ...... **CLC 16,**
72
See also CA 81-84; CANR 33, 70; CWW
2; DLB 257; MTCW 2

Bergson, Henri(-Louis) 1859-1941 . **TCLC 32**
See also CA 164; EW 8; EWL 3; GFL 1789
to the Present

Bergstein, Eleanor 1938- .... **CLC 4**
See also CA 53-56; CANR 5

Berkeley, George 1685-1753 .... **LC 65**
See also DLB 31, 101, 252

Berkoff, Steven 1937- .... **CLC 56**
See also CA 104; CANR 72; CBD; CD 5

Berlin, Isaiah 1909-1997 .... **TCLC 105**
See also CA 85-88; 162

Bermant, Chaim (Icyk) 1929-1998 ... **CLC 40**
See also CA 57-60; CANR 6, 31, 57, 105;
CN 7

Bern, Victoria
See Fisher, M(ary) F(rances) K(ennedy)

Bernanos, (Paul Louis) Georges
1888-1948 .... **TCLC 3**
See also CA 104; 130; CANR 94; DLB 72;
EWL 3; GFL 1789 to the Present; RGWL
2, 3

Bernard, April 1956- .... **CLC 59**
See also CA 131

Bernard of Clairvaux 1090-1153 .. **CMLC 71**
See also DLB 208

Berne, Victoria
See Fisher, M(ary) F(rances) K(ennedy)

Bernhard, Thomas 1931-1989 ..... **CLC 3, 32,**
61; DC 14
See also CA 85-88; 127; CANR 32, 57; CD-
WLB 2; DLB 85, 124; EWL 3; MTCW 1;
RGWL 2, 3

Bernhardt, Sarah (Henriette Rosine)
1844-1923 .... **TCLC 75**
See also CA 157

Bernstein, Charles 1950- .... **CLC 142,**
See also CA 129; CAAS 24; CANR 90; CP
7; DLB 169

Bernstein, Ingrid
See Kirsch, Sarah

Berriault, Gina 1926-1999 .... **CLC 54, 109;**
SSC 30
See also CA 116; 129; 185; CANR 66; DLB
130; SSFS 7,11

Berrigan, Daniel 1921- .... **CLC 4**
See also CA 33-36R; 187; CAAE 187;
CAAS 1; CANR 11, 43, 78; CP 7; DLB 5

Berrigan, Edmund Joseph Michael, Jr.
1934-1983
See Berrigan, Ted
See also CA 61-64; 110; CANR 14, 102

Berrigan, Ted .... **CLC 37**
See Berrigan, Edmund Joseph Michael, Jr.
See also DLB 5, 169; WP

Berry, Charles Edward Anderson 1931-
See Berry, Chuck
See also CA 115

Berry, Chuck .... **CLC 17**
See Berry, Charles Edward Anderson

Berry, Jonas
See Ashbery, John (Lawrence)
See also GLL 1

Berry, Wendell (Erdman) 1934- ... **CLC 4, 6,**
8, 27, 46; PC 28
See also AITN 1; AMWS 10; ANW; CA
73-76; CANR 50, 73, 101, 132; CP 7;
CSW; DAM POET; DLB 5, 6, 234, 275;
MTCW 1

Berryman, John 1914-1972 ... **CLC 1, 2, 3, 4,**
6, 8, 10, 13, 25, 62
See also AMW; CA 13-16; 33-36R; CABS
2; CANR 35; CAP 1; CDALB 1941-1968;
DAM POET; DLB 48; EWL 3; MTCW 1,
2; PAB; RGAL 4; WP

Bertolucci, Bernardo 1940- ...... **CLC 16, 157**
See also CA 106; CANR 125

Berton, Pierre (Francis Demarigny)
1920- .... **CLC 104**
See also CA 1-4R; CANR 2, 56; CPW;
DLB 68; SATA 99

Bertrand, Aloysius 1807-1841 .... **NCLC 31**
See Bertrand, Louis oAloysiusc

Bertrand, Louis oAloysiusc
See Bertrand, Aloysius
See also DLB 217

Bertran de Born c. 1140-1215 .... **CMLC 5**

Besant, Annie (Wood) 1847-1933 ..... **TCLC 9**
See also CA 105; 185

Bessie, Alvah 1904-1985 .... **CLC 23**
See also CA 5-8R; 116; CANR 2, 80; DLB
26

Bestuzhev, Aleksandr Aleksandrovich
1797-1837 .... **NCLC 131**
See also DLB 198

Bethlen, T. D.
See Silverberg, Robert

Beti, Mongo .... **BLC 1; CLC 27**
See Biyidi, Alexandre
See also AFW; CANR 79; DAM MULT;
EWL 3; WLIT 2

Betjeman, John 1906-1984 ...... **CLC 2, 6, 10,**
34, 43
See also BRW 7; CA 9-12R; 112; CANR
33, 56; CDBLB 1945-1960; DA3; DAB;
DAM MST, POET; DLB 20; DLBY 1984;
EWL 3; MTCW 1, 2

Bettelheim, Bruno 1903-1990 .... **CLC 79;**
TCLC 143
See also CA 81-84; 131; CANR 23, 61;
DA3; MTCW 1, 2

Blunden, Edmund (Charles)
1896-1974 .... **CLC 2, 56**
See also BRW 6; CA 17-18; 45-48; CANR
54; CAP 2; DLB 20, 100, 155; MTCW 1;
PAB

Bly, Robert (Elwood) 1926- .... **CLC 1, 2, 5,**
10, 15, 38, 128; PC 39
See also AMWS 4; CA 5-8R; CANR 41,
73, 125; CP 7; DA3; DAM POET; DLB
5; EWL 3; MTCW 1, 2; PFS 6, 17; RGAL
4

Boas, Franz 1858-1942 .... **TCLC 56**
See also CA 115; 181

Bobette
See Simenon, Georges (Jacques Christian)

Boccaccio, Giovanni 1313-1375 ... **CMLC 13,**
57; SSC 10
See also EW 2; RGSF 2; RGWL 2, 3; TWA

Bochco, Steven 1943- .... **CLC 35**
See also AAYA 11; CA 124; 138

Bode, Sigmund
See O'Doherty, Brian

Bodel, Jean 1167(?)-1210 .... **CMLC 28**

Bodenheim, Maxwell 1892-1954 .... **TCLC 44**
See also CA 110; 187; DLB 9, 45; RGAL 4

Bodenheimer, Maxwell
See Bodenheim, Maxwell

Bodker, Cecil 1927-
See Bodker, Cecil

Bodker, Cecil 1927- .... **CLC 21**
See also CA 73-76; CANR 13, 44, 111;
CLR 23; MAICYA 1, 2; SATA 14, 133

Boell, Heinrich (Theodor)
1917-1985 ..... **CLC 2, 3, 6, 9, 11, 15, 27,**
32, 72; SSC 23; WLC
See Boll, Heinrich
See also CA 21-24R; 116; CANR 24; DA;
DA3; DAB; DAC; DAM MST, NOV;
DLB 69; DLBY 1985; MTCW 1, 2; SSFS
20; TWA

Boerne, Alfred
See Doeblin, Alfred

Boethius c. 480-c. 524 .... **CMLC 15**
See also DLB 115; RGWL 2, 3

Boff, Leonardo (Genezio Darci)
1938- .... **CLC 70; HLC 1**
See also CA 150; DAM MULT; HW 2

Bogan, Louise 1897-1970 .... **CLC 4, 39, 46,**
93; PC 12
See also AMWS 3; CA 73-76; 25-28R;
CANR 33, 82; DAM POET; DLB 45, 169;
EWL 3; MAWW; MTCW 1, 2; PFS 21;
RGAL 4

Bogarde, Dirk
See Van Den Bogarde, Derek Jules Gaspard
Ulric Niven
See also DLB 14

Bogosian, Eric 1953- .... **CLC 45, 141**
See also CA 138; CAD; CANR 102; CD 5

Bograd, Larry 1953- .... **CLC 35**
See also CA 93-96; CANR 57; SAAS 21;
SATA 33, 89; WYA

Boiardo, Matteo Maria 1441-1494 .... **LC 6**

Boileau-Despreaux, Nicolas 1636-1711 . **LC 3**
See also DLB 268; EW 3; GFL Beginnings
to 1789; RGWL 2, 3

Boissard, Maurice
See Leautaud, Paul

Bojer, Johan 1872-1959 .... **TCLC 64**
See also CA 189; EWL 3

Bok, Edward W(illiam)
1863-1930 .... **TCLC 101**
See also CA 217; DLB 91; DLBD 16

Boker, George Henry 1823-1890 . **NCLC 125**
See also RGAL 4

Boland, Eavan (Aisling) 1944- .. **CLC 40, 67,**
113; PC 58
See also BRWS 5; CA 143, 207; CAAE
207; CANR 61; CP 7; CWP; DAM POET;
DLB 40; FW; MTCW 2; PFS 12

Boll, Heinrich
See Boell, Heinrich (Theodor)
See also BPFB 1; CDWLB 2; EW 13; EWL
3; RGSF 2; RGWL 2, 3

Bolt, Lee
See Faust, Frederick (Schiller)

Bolt, Robert (Oxton) 1924-1995 .... **CLC 14**
See also CA 17-20R; 147; CANR 35, 67;
CBD; DAM DRAM; DFS 2; DLB 13,
233; EWL 3; LAIT 1; MTCW 1

Bombal, Maria Luisa 1910-1980 .... **HLCS 1;**
SSC 37
See also CA 127; CANR 72; EWL 3; HW
1; LAW; RGSF 2

Bombet, Louis-Alexandre-Cesar
See Stendhal

Bomkauf
See Kaufman, Bob (Garnell)

Bonaventura .... **NCLC 35**
See also DLB 90

Bond, Edward 1934- .... **CLC 4, 6, 13, 23**
See also AAYA 50; BRWS 1; CA 25-28R;
CANR 38, 67, 106; CBD; CD 5; DAM
DRAM; DFS 3, 8; DLB 13; EWL 3;
MTCW 1

Bonham, Frank 1914-1989 .... **CLC 12**
See also AAYA 1; BYA 1, 3; CA 9-12R;
CANR 4, 36; JRDA; MAICYA 1, 2;
SAAS 3; SATA 1, 49; SATA-Obit 62;
TCWW 2; YAW

Bonnefoy, Yves 1923- . **CLC 9, 15, 58; PC 58**
See also CA 85-88; CANR 33, 75, 97;
CWW 2; DAM MST, POET; DLB 258;
EWL 3; GFL 1789 to the Present; MTCW
1, 2

Bonner, Marita .... **HR 2**
See Occomy, Marita (Odette) Bonner

Bonnin, Gertrude 1876-1938 .... **NNAL**
See Zitkala-Sa
See also CA 150; DAM MULT

Bontemps, Arna(ud Wendell)
1902-1973 ..... **BLC 1; CLC 1, 18; HR 2**
See also BW 1; CA 1-4R; 41-44R; CANR
4, 35; CLR 6; CWRI 5; DA3; DAM
MULT, NOV, POET; DLB 48, 51; JRDA;
MAICYA 1, 2; MTCW 1, 2; SATA 2, 44;
SATA-Obit 24; WCH; WP

Boot, William
See Stoppard, Tom

Booth, Martin 1944-2004 .... **CLC 13**
See also CA 93-96; 188; 223; CAAE 188;
CAAS 2; CANR 92

Booth, Philip 1925- .... **CLC 23**
See also CA 5-8R; CANR 5, 88; CP 7;
DLBY 1982

Booth, Wayne C(layson) 1921- .... **CLC 24**
See also CA 1-4R; CAAS 5; CANR 3, 43,
117; DLB 67

Borchert, Wolfgang 1921-1947 .... **TCLC 5**
See also CA 104; 188; DLB 69, 124; EWL
3

Borel, Petrus 1809-1859 .... **NCLC 41**
See also DLB 119; GFL 1789 to the Present

Borges, Jorge Luis 1899-1986 ... **CLC 1, 2, 3,**
4, 6, 8, 9, 10, 13, 19, 44, 48, 83; HLC 1;
PC 22, 32; SSC 4, 41; TCLC 109;
WLC
See also AAYA 26; BPFB 1; CA 21-24R;
CANR 19, 33, 75, 105, 133; CDWLB 3;
DA; DA3; DAB; DAC; DAM MST,
MULT; DLB 113, 283; DLBY 1986;
DNFS 1, 2; EWL 3; HW 1, 2; LAW;
LMFS 2; MSW; MTCW 1, 2; RGSF 2;
RGWL 2, 3; SFW 4; SSFS 17; TWA;
WLIT 1

Borowski, Tadeusz 1922-1951 .... **SSC 48;**
TCLC 9
See also CA 106; 154; CDWLB 4; DLB
215; EWL 3; RGSF 2; RGWL 3; SSFS
13

Borrow, George (Henry)
1803-1881 .... **NCLC 9**
See also DLB 21, 55, 166

Bosch (Gavino), Juan 1909-2001 ..... **HLCS 1**
See also CA 151; 204; DAM MST, MULT;
DLB 145; HW 1, 2

Bosman, Herman Charles
1905-1951 .... **TCLC 49**
See Malan, Herman
See also CA 160; DLB 225; RGSF 2

Bosschere, Jean de 1878(?)-1953 ... **TCLC 19**
See also CA 115; 186

Boswell, James 1740-1795 ... **LC 4, 50; WLC**
See also BRW 3; CDBLB 1660-1789; DA;
DAB; DAC; DAM MST; DLB 104, 142;
TEA; WLIT 3

Bottomley, Gordon 1874-1948 ..... **TCLC 107**
See also CA 120; 192; DLB 10

Bottoms, David 1949- .... **CLC 53**
See also CA 105; CANR 22; CSW; DLB
120; DLBY 1983

Boucicault, Dion 1820-1890 .... **NCLC 41**

Boucolon, Maryse
See Conde, Maryse

Bourget, Paul (Charles Joseph)
1852-1935 .... **TCLC 12**
See also CA 107; 196; DLB 123; GFL 1789
to the Present

Bourjaily, Vance (Nye) 1922- .... **CLC 8, 62**
See also CA 1-4R; CAAS 1; CANR 2, 72;
CN 7; DLB 2, 143

Bourne, Randolph S(illiman)
1886-1918 .... **TCLC 16**
See also AMW; CA 117; 155; DLB 63

Bova, Ben(jamin William) 1932- ...... **CLC 45**
See also AAYA 16; CA 5-8R; CAAS 18;
CANR 11, 56, 94, 111; CLR 3, 96; DLBY
1981; INT CANR-11; MAICYA 1, 2;
MTCW 1; SATA 6, 68, 133; SFW 4

Bowen, Elizabeth (Dorothea Cole)
1899-1973 . **CLC 1, 3, 6, 11, 15, 22, 118;**
SSC 3, 28, 66; TCLC 148
See also BRWS 2; CA 17-18; 41-44R;
CANR 35, 105; CAP 2; CDBLB 1945-
1960; DA3; DAM NOV; DLB 15, 162;
EWL 3; EXPS; FW; HGG; MTCW 1, 2;
NFS 13; RGSF 2; SSFS 5; SUFW 1;
TEA; WLIT 4

Bowering, George 1935- .... **CLC 15, 47**
See also CA 21-24R; CAAS 16; CANR 10;
CP 7; DLB 53

Bowering, Marilyn R(uthe) 1949- .... **CLC 32**
See also CA 101; CANR 49; CP 7; CWP

Bowers, Edgar 1924-2000 .... **CLC 9**
See also CA 5-8R; 188; CANR 24; CP 7;
CSW; DLB 5

Bowers, Mrs. J. Milton 1842-1914
See Bierce, Ambrose (Gwinett)

Bowie, David .... **CLC 17**
See Jones, David Robert

Bowles, Jane (Sydney) 1917-1973 ..... **CLC 3,**
68
See Bowles, Jane Auer
See also CA 19-20; 41-44R; CAP 2

Bowles, Jane Auer
See Bowles, Jane (Sydney)
See also EWL 3

Bowles, Paul (Frederick) 1910-1999 . **CLC 1,**
2, 19, 53; SSC 3
See also AMWS 4; CA 1-4R; 186; CAAS
1; CANR 1, 19, 50, 75; CN 7; DA3; DLB
5, 6, 218; EWL 3; MTCW 1, 2; RGAL 4;
SSFS 17

Bowles, William Lisle 1762-1850 . **NCLC 103**
  See also DLB 93
Box, Edgar
  See Vidal, (Eugene Luther) Gore
  See also GLL 1
Boyd, James 1888-1944 .... **TCLC 115**
  See also CA 186; DLB 9; DLBD 16; RGAL
  4; RHW
Boyd, Nancy
  See Millay, Edna St. Vincent
  See also GLL 1
Boyd, Thomas (Alexander)
  1898-1935 .... **TCLC 111**
  See also CA 111; 183; DLB 9; DLBD 16
Boyd, William 1952- .... **CLC 28, 53, 70**
  See also CA 114; 120; CANR 51, 71, 131;
  CN 7; DLB 231
Boyesen, Hjalmar Hjorth
  1848-1895 .... **NCLC 135**
  See also DLB 12, 71; DLBD 13; RGAL 4
Boyle, Kay 1902-1992 .... **CLC 1, 5, 19, 58,**
  121; SSC 5
  See also CA 13-16R; 140; CAAS 1; CANR
  29, 61, 110; DLB 4, 9, 48, 86; DLBY
  1993; EWL 3; MTCW 1, 2; RGAL 4;
  RGSF 2; SSFS 10, 13, 14
Boyle, Mark
  See Kienzle, William X(avier)
Boyle, Patrick 1905-1982 .... **CLC 19**
  See also CA 127
Boyle, T. C.
  See Boyle, T(homas) Coraghessan
  See also AMWS 8
Boyle, T(homas) Coraghessan
  1948- .... **CLC 36, 55, 90; SSC 16**
  See Boyle, T. C.
  See also AAYA 47; BEST 90:4; BPFB 1;
  CA 120; CANR 44, 76, 89, 132; CN 7;
  CPW; DA3; DAM POP; DLB 218, 278;
  DLBY 1986; EWL 3; MTCW 2; SSFS 13,
  19
Boz
  See Dickens, Charles (John Huffam)
Brackenridge, Hugh Henry
  1748-1816 .... **NCLC 7**
  See also DLB 11, 37; RGAL 4
Bradbury, Edward P.
  See Moorcock, Michael (John)
  See also MTCW 2
Bradbury, Malcolm (Stanley)
  1932-2000 .... **CLC 32, 61**
  See also CA 1-4R; CANR 1, 33, 91, 98;
  CN 7; DA3; DAM NOV; DLB 14, 207;
  EWL 3; MTCW 1, 2
Bradbury, Ray (Douglas) 1920- .... **CLC 1, 3,**
  10, 15, 42, 98; SSC 29, 53; WLC
  See also AAYA 15; AITN 1; AMWS 4;
  BPFB 1; BYA 4, 5, 11; CA 1-4R; CANR
  2, 30, 75, 125; CDALB 1968-1988; CN
  7; CPW; DA; DA3; DAB; DAC; DAM
  MST, NOV, POP; DLB 2, 8; EXPN;
  EXPS; HGG; LAIT 3, 5; LATS 1:2;
  LMFS 2; MTCW 1, 2; NFS 1; RGAL 4;
  RGSF 2; SATA 11, 64, 123; SCFW 2;
  SFW 4; SSFS 1, 20; SUFW 1, 2; TUS;
  YAW
Braddon, Mary Elizabeth
  1837-1915 .... **TCLC 111**
  See also BRWS 8; CA 108; 179; CMW 4;
  DLB 18, 70, 156; HGG
Bradfield, Scott (Michael) 1955- .... **SSC 65**
  See also CA 147; CANR 90; HGG; SUFW
  2
Bradford, Gamaliel 1863-1932 .... **TCLC 36**
  See also CA 160; DLB 17
Bradford, William 1590-1657 .... **LC 64**
  See also DLB 24, 30; RGAL 4

Bradley, David (Henry), Jr. 1950- .... **BLC 1;**
  CLC 23, 118
  See also BW 1, 3; CA 104; CANR 26, 81;
  CN 7; DAM MULT; DLB 33
Bradley, John Ed(mund, Jr.) 1958- . **CLC 55**
  See also CA 139; CANR 99; CN 7; CSW
Bradley, Marion Zimmer
  1930-1999 .... **CLC 30**
  See Chapman, Lee; Dexter, John; Gardner,
  Miriam; Ives, Morgan; Rivers, Elfrida
  See also AAYA 40; BPFB 1; CA 57-60; 185;
  CAAS 10; CANR 7, 31, 51, 75, 107;
  CPW; DA3; DAM POP; DLB 8; FANT;
  FW; MTCW 1, 2; SATA 90, 139; SATA-
  Obit 116; SFW 4; SUFW 2; YAW
Bradshaw, John 1933- .... **CLC 70**
  See also CA 138; CANR 61
Bradstreet, Anne 1612(?)-1672 ...... **LC 4, 30;**
  PC 10
  See also AMWS 1; CDALB 1640-1865;
  DA; DA3; DAC; DAM MST, POET; DLB
  24; EXPP; FW; PFS 6; RGAL 4; TUS;
  WP
Brady, Joan 1939- .... **CLC 86**
  See also CA 141
Bragg, Melvyn 1939- .... **CLC 10**
  See also BEST 89:3; CA 57-60; CANR 10,
  48, 89; CN 7; DLB 14, 271; RHW
Brahe, Tycho 1546-1601 .... **LC 45**
  See also DLB 300
Braine, John (Gerard) 1922-1986 . **CLC 1, 3,**
  41
  See also CA 1-4R; 120; CANR 1, 33; CD-
  BLB 1945-1960; DLB 15; DLBY 1986;
  EWL 3; MTCW 1
Braithwaite, William Stanley (Beaumont)
  1878-1962 .... **BLC 1; HR 2; PC 52**
  See also BW 1; CA 125; DAM MULT; DLB
  50, 54
Bramah, Ernest 1868-1942 .... **TCLC 72**
  See also CA 156; CMW 4; DLB 70; FANT
Brammer, William 1930(?)-1978 ...... **CLC 31**
  See also CA 77-80
Brancati, Vitaliano 1907-1954 .... **TCLC 12**
  See also CA 109; DLB 264; EWL 3
Brancato, Robin F(idler) 1936- .... **CLC 35**
  See also AAYA 9; BYA 6; CA 69-72; CANR
  11, 45; CLR 32; JRDA; MAICYA 2;
  MAICYAS 1; SAAS 9; SATA 97; WYA;
  YAW
Brand, Dionne 1953- .... **CLC 192**
  See also BW 2; CA 143; CWP
Brand, Max
  See Faust, Frederick (Schiller)
  See also BPFB 1; TCWW 2
Brand, Millen 1906-1980 .... **CLC 7**
  See also CA 21-24R; 97-100; CANR 72
Branden, Barbara .... **CLC 44**
  See also CA 148
Brandes, Georg (Morris Cohen)
  1842-1927 .... **TCLC 10**
  See also CA 105; 189; DLB 300
Brandys, Kazimierz 1916-2000 .... **CLC 62**
  See also EWL 3
Branley, Franklyn M(ansfield)
  1915-2002 .... **CLC 21**
  See also CA 33-36R; 207; CANR 14, 39;
  CLR 13; MAICYA 1, 2; SAAS 16; SATA
  4, 68, 136
Brant, Beth (E.) 1941- .... **NNAL**
  See also CA 144; FW
Brathwaite, Edward Kamau
  1930- .... **BLCS; CLC 11; PC 56**
  See also BW 2, 3; CA 25-28R; CANR 11,
  26, 47, 107; CDWLB 3; CP 7; DAM
  POET; DLB 125; EWL 3
Brathwaite, Kamau
  See Brathwaite, Edward Kamau

Brautigan, Richard (Gary)
  1935-1984 .... **CLC 1, 3, 5, 9, 12, 34, 42;**
  TCLC 133
  See also BPFB 1; CA 53-56; 113; CANR
  34; DA3; DAM NOV; DLB 2, 5, 206;
  DLBY 1980, 1984; FANT; MTCW 1;
  RGAL 4; SATA 56
Brave Bird, Mary .... **NNAL**
  See Crow Dog, Mary (Ellen)
Braverman, Kate 1950- .... **CLC 67**
  See also CA 89-92
Brecht, (Eugen) Bertolt (Friedrich)
  1898-1956 ..... **DC 3; TCLC 1, 6, 13, 35;**
  WLC
  See also CA 104; 133; CANR 62; CDWLB
  2; DA; DA3; DAB; DAC; DAM DRAM,
  MST; DFS 4, 5, 9; DLB 56, 124; EW 11;
  EWL 3; IDTP; MTCW 1, 2; RGWL 2, 3;
  TWA
Brecht, Eugen Berthold Friedrich
  See Brecht, (Eugen) Bertolt (Friedrich)
Bremer, Fredrika 1801-1865 .... **NCLC 11**
  See also DLB 254
Brennan, Christopher John
  1870-1932 .... **TCLC 17**
  See also CA 117; 188; DLB 230; EWL 3
Brennan, Maeve 1917-1993 ... **CLC 5; TCLC**
  124
  See also CA 81-84; CANR 72, 100
Brent, Linda
  See Jacobs, Harriet A(nn)
Brentano, Clemens (Maria)
  1778-1842 .... **NCLC 1**
  See also DLB 90; RGWL 2, 3
Brent of Bin Bin
  See Franklin, (Stella Maria Sarah) Miles
  (Lampe)
Brenton, Howard 1942- .... **CLC 31**
  See also CA 69-72; CANR 33, 67; CBD;
  CD 5; DLB 13; MTCW 1
Breslin, James 1930-
  See Breslin, Jimmy
  See also CA 73-76; CANR 31, 75; DAM
  NOV; MTCW 1, 2
Breslin, Jimmy .... **CLC 4, 43**
  See Breslin, James
  See also AITN 1; DLB 185; MTCW 2
Bresson, Robert 1901(?)-1999 .... **CLC 16**
  See also CA 110; 187; CANR 49
Breton, Andre 1896-1966 .. **CLC 2, 9, 15, 54;**
  PC 15
  See also CA 19-20; 25-28R; CANR 40, 60;
  CAP 2; DLB 65, 258; EW 11; EWL 3;
  GFL 1789 to the Present; LMFS 2;
  MTCW 1, 2; RGWL 2, 3; TWA; WP
Breytenbach, Breyten 1939(?)- .. **CLC 23, 37,**
  126
  See also CA 113; 129; CANR 61, 122;
  CWW 2; DAM POET; DLB 225; EWL 3
Bridgers, Sue Ellen 1942- .... **CLC 26**
  See also AAYA 8, 49; BYA 7, 8; CA 65-68;
  CANR 11, 36; CLR 18; DLB 52; JRDA;
  MAICYA 1, 2; SAAS 1; SATA 22, 90;
  SATA-Essay 109; WYA; YAW
Bridges, Robert (Seymour)
  1844-1930 .... **PC 28; TCLC 1**
  See also BRW 6; CA 104; 152; CDBLB
  1890-1914; DAM POET; DLB 19, 98
Bridie, James .... **TCLC 3**
  See Mavor, Osborne Henry
  See also DLB 10; EWL 3
Brin, David 1950- .... **CLC 34**
  See also AAYA 21; CA 102; CANR 24, 70,
  125, 127; INT CANR-24; SATA 65;
  SCFW 2; SFW 4

Brink, Andre (Philippus) 1935- . **CLC 18, 36, 106**
See also AFW; BRWS 6; CA 104; CANR 39, 62, 109, 133; CN 7; DLB 225; EWL 3; INT CA-103; LATS 1:2; MTCW 1, 2; WLIT 2

Brinsmead, H. F(ay)
See Brinsmead, H(esba) F(ay)

Brinsmead, H. F.
See Brinsmead, H(esba) F(ay)

Brinsmead, H(esba) F(ay) 1922- ...... **CLC 21**
See also CA 21-24R; CANR 10; CLR 47; CWRI 5; MAICYA 1, 2; SAAS 5; SATA 18, 78

Brittain, Vera (Mary) 1893(?)-1970 . **CLC 23**
See also CA 13-16; 25-28R; CANR 58; CAP 1; DLB 191; FW; MTCW 1, 2

Broch, Hermann 1886-1951 .... **TCLC 20**
See also CA 117; 211; CDWLB 2; DLB 85, 124; EW 10; EWL 3; RGWL 2, 3

Brock, Rose
See Hansen, Joseph
See also GLL 1

Brod, Max 1884-1968 .... **TCLC 115**
See also CA 5-8R; 25-28R; CANR 7; DLB 81; EWL 3

Brodkey, Harold (Roy) 1930-1996 .. **CLC 56; TCLC 123**
See also CA 111; 151; CANR 71; CN 7; DLB 130

Brodsky, Iosif Alexandrovich 1940-1996
See Brodsky, Joseph
See also AITN 1; CA 41-44R; 151; CANR 37, 106; DA3; DAM POET; MTCW 1, 2; RGWL 2, 3

Brodsky, Joseph . **CLC 4, 6, 13, 36, 100; PC 9**
See Brodsky, Iosif Alexandrovich
See also AMWS 8; CWW 2; DLB 285; EWL 3; MTCW 1

Brodsky, Michael (Mark) 1948- .... **CLC 19**
See also CA 102; CANR 18, 41, 58; DLB 244

Brodzki, Bella ed. .... **CLC 65**

Brome, Richard 1590(?)-1652 .... **LC 61**
See also DLB 58

Bromell, Henry 1947- .... **CLC 5**
See also CA 53-56; CANR 9, 115, 116

Bromfield, Louis (Brucker)
1896-1956 .... **TCLC 11**
See also CA 107; 155; DLB 4, 9, 86; RGAL 4; RHW

Broner, E(sther) M(asserman)
1930- .... **CLC 19**
See also CA 17-20R; CANR 8, 25, 72; CN 7; DLB 28

Bronk, William (M.) 1918-1999 .... **CLC 10**
See also CA 89-92; 177; CANR 23; CP 7; DLB 165

Bronstein, Lev Davidovich
See Trotsky, Leon

Bronte, Anne 1820-1849 ..... **NCLC 4, 71, 102**
See also BRW 5; BRWR 1; DA3; DLB 21, 199; TEA

Bronte, (Patrick) Branwell
1817-1848 .... **NCLC 109**

Bronte, Charlotte 1816-1855 ...... **NCLC 3, 8, 33, 58, 105; WLC**
See also AAYA 17; BRW 5; BRWC 2; BRWR 1; BYA 2; CDBLB 1832-1890; DA; DA3; DAB; DAC; DAM MST, NOV; DLB 21, 159, 199; EXPN; LAIT 2; NFS 4; TEA; WLIT 4

Bronte, Emily (Jane) 1818-1848 ... **NCLC 16, 35; PC 8; WLC**
See also AAYA 17; BPFB 1; BRW 5; BRWC 1; BRWR 1; BYA 3; CDBLB 1832-1890; DA; DA3; DAB; DAC; DAM MST, NOV, POET; DLB 21, 32, 199; EXPN; LAIT 1; TEA; WLIT 3

Brontes
See Bronte, Anne; Bronte, Charlotte; Bronte, Emily (Jane)

Brooke, Frances 1724-1789 .... **LC 6, 48**
See also DLB 39, 99

Brooke, Henry 1703(?)-1783 .... **LC 1**
See also DLB 39

Brooke, Rupert (Chawner)
1887-1915 ..... **PC 24; TCLC 2, 7; WLC**
See also BRWS 3; CA 104; 132; CANR 61; CDBLB 1914-1945; DA; DAB; DAC; DAM MST, POET; DLB 19, 216; EXPP; GLL 2; MTCW 1, 2; PFS 7; TEA

Brooke-Haven, P.
See Wodehouse, P(elham) G(renville)

Brooke-Rose, Christine 1926(?)- ..... **CLC 40, 184**
See also BRWS 4; CA 13-16R; CANR 58, 118; CN 7; DLB 14, 231; EWL 3; SFW 4

Brookner, Anita 1928- .. **CLC 32, 34, 51, 136**
See also BRWS 4; CA 114; 120; CANR 37, 56, 87, 130; CN 7; CPW; DA3; DAB; DAM POP; DLB 194; DLBY 1987; EWL 3; MTCW 1, 2; TEA

Brooks, Cleanth 1906-1994 . **CLC 24, 86, 110**
See also CA 17-20R; 145; CANR 33, 35; CSW; DLB 63; DLBY 1994; EWL 3; INT CANR-35; MTCW 1, 2

Brooks, George
See Baum, L(yman) Frank

Brooks, Gwendolyn (Elizabeth)
1917-2000 ... **BLC 1; CLC 1, 2, 4, 5, 15, 49, 125; PC 7; WLC**
See also AAYA 20; AFAW 1, 2; AITN 1; AMWS 3; BW 2, 3; CA 1-4R; 190; CANR 1, 27, 52, 75, 132; CDALB 1941-1968; CLR 27; CP 7; CWP; DA; DA3; DAC; DAM MST, MULT, POET; DLB 5, 76, 165; EWL 3; EXPP; MAWW; MTCW 1, 2; PFS 1, 2, 4, 6; RGAL 4; SATA 6; SATA-Obit 123; TUS; WP

Brooks, Mel .... **CLC 12**
See Kaminsky, Melvin
See also AAYA 13, 48; DLB 26

Brooks, Peter (Preston) 1938- .... **CLC 34**
See also CA 45-48; CANR 1, 107

Brooks, Van Wyck 1886-1963 .... **CLC 29**
See also AMW; CA 1-4R; CANR 6; DLB 45, 63, 103; TUS

Brophy, Brigid (Antonia)
1929-1995 .... **CLC 6, 11, 29, 105**
See also CA 5-8R; 149; CAAS 4; CANR 25, 53; CBD; CN 7; CWD; DA3; DLB 14, 271; EWL 3; MTCW 1, 2

Brosman, Catharine Savage 1934- ..... **CLC 9**
See also CA 61-64; CANR 21, 46

Brossard, Nicole 1943- .... **CLC 115, 169**
See also CA 122; CAAS 16; CCA 1; CWP; CWW 2; DLB 53; EWL 3; FW; GLL 2; RGWL 3

Brother Antoninus
See Everson, William (Oliver)

The Brothers Quay
See Quay, Stephen; Quay, Timothy

Broughton, T(homas) Alan 1936- ..... **CLC 19**
See also CA 45-48; CANR 2, 23, 48, 111

Broumas, Olga 1949- .... **CLC 10, 73**
See also CA 85-88; CANR 20, 69, 110; CP 7; CWP; GLL 2

Broun, Heywood 1888-1939 .... **TCLC 104**
See also DLB 29, 171

Brown, Alan 1950- .... **CLC 99**
See also CA 156

Brown, Charles Brockden
1771-1810 .... **NCLC 22, 74, 122**
See also AMWS 1; CDALB 1640-1865; DLB 37, 59, 73; FW; HGG; LMFS 1; RGAL 4; TUS

Brown, Christy 1932-1981 .... **CLC 63**
See also BYA 13; CA 105; 104; CANR 72; DLB 14

Brown, Claude 1937-2002 ... **BLC 1; CLC 30**
See also AAYA 7; BW 1, 3; CA 73-76; 205; CANR 81; DAM MULT

Brown, Dee (Alexander)
1908-2002 .... **CLC 18, 47**
See also AAYA 30; CA 13-16R; 212; CAAS 6; CANR 11, 45, 60; CPW; CSW; DA3; DAM POP; DLBY 1980; LAIT 2; MTCW 1, 2; NCFS 5; SATA 5, 110; SATA-Obit 141; TCWW 2

Brown, George
See Wertmueller, Lina

Brown, George Douglas
1869-1902 .... **TCLC 28**
See Douglas, George
See also CA 162

Brown, George Mackay 1921-1996 ... **CLC 5, 48, 100**
See also BRWS 6; CA 21-24R; 151; CAAS 6; CANR 12, 37, 67; CN 7; CP 7; DLB 14, 27, 139, 271; MTCW 1; RGSF 2; SATA 35

Brown, (William) Larry 1951- .... **CLC 73**
See also CA 130; 134; CANR 117; CSW; DLB 234; INT CA-134

Brown, Moses
See Barrett, William (Christopher)

Brown, Rita Mae 1944- .... **CLC 18, 43, 79**
See also BPFB 1; CA 45-48; CANR 2, 11, 35, 62, 95; CN 7; CPW; CSW; DA3; DAM NOV, POP; FW; INT CANR-11; MTCW 1, 2; NFS 9; RGAL 4; TUS

Brown, Roderick (Langmere) Haig-
See Haig-Brown, Roderick (Langmere)

Brown, Rosellen 1939- .... **CLC 32, 170**
See also CA 77-80; CAAS 10; CANR 14, 44, 98; CN 7

Brown, Sterling Allen 1901-1989 ...... **BLC 1; CLC 1, 23, 59; HR 2; PC 55**
See also AFAW 1, 2; BW 1, 3; CA 85-88; 127; CANR 26; DA3; DAM MULT, POET; DLB 48, 51, 63; MTCW 1, 2; RGAL 4; WP

Brown, Will
See Ainsworth, William Harrison

Brown, William Hill 1765-1793 .... **LC 93**
See also DLB 37

Brown, William Wells 1815-1884 ...... **BLC 1; DC 1; NCLC 2, 89**
See also DAM MULT; DLB 3, 50, 183, 248; RGAL 4

Browne, (Clyde) Jackson 1948(?)- ... **CLC 21**
See also CA 120

Browning, Elizabeth Barrett
1806-1861 ... **NCLC 1, 16, 61, 66; PC 6; WLC**
See also BRW 4; CDBLB 1832-1890; DA; DA3; DAB; DAC; DAM MST, POET; DLB 32, 199; EXPP; PAB; PFS 2, 16; TEA; WLIT 4; WP

Browning, Robert 1812-1889 . **NCLC 19, 79; PC 2; WLCS**
See also BRW 4; BRWC 2; BRWR 2; CD-BLB 1832-1890; CLR 97; DA; DA3; DAB; DAC; DAM MST, POET; DLB 32, 163; EXPP; LATS 1:1; PAB; PFS 1, 15; RGEL 2; TEA; WLIT 4; WP; YABC 1

Browning, Tod 1882-1962 .... **CLC 16**
See also CA 141; 117

Brownmiller, Susan 1935- .... **CLC 159**
See also CA 103; CANR 35, 75; DAM NOV; FW; MTCW 1, 2

Brownson, Orestes Augustus
1803-1876 .... **NCLC 50**
See also DLB 1, 59, 73, 243

Bruccoli, Matthew J(oseph) 1931- ... **CLC 34**
   See also CA 9-12R; CANR 7, 87; DLB 103
Bruce, Lenny .... **CLC 21**
   See Schneider, Leonard Alfred
Bruchac, Joseph III 1942- .... **NNAL**
   See also AAYA 19; CA 33-36R; CANR 13,
   47, 75, 94; CLR 46; CWRI 5; DAM
   MULT; JRDA; MAICYA 2; MAICYAS 1;
   MTCW 1; SATA 42, 89, 131
Bruin, John
   See Brutus, Dennis
Brulard, Henri
   See Stendhal
Brulls, Christian
   See Simenon, Georges (Jacques Christian)
Brunner, John (Kilian Houston)
   1934-1995 .... **CLC 8, 10**
   See also CA 1-4R; 149; CAAS 8; CANR 2,
   37; CPW; DAM POP; DLB 261; MTCW
   1, 2; SCFW 2; SFW 4
Bruno, Giordano 1548-1600 .... **LC 27**
   See also RGWL 2, 3
Brutus, Dennis 1924- ... **BLC 1; CLC 43; PC
   24**
   See also AFW; BW 2, 3; CA 49-52; CAAS
   14; CANR 2, 27, 42, 81; CDWLB 3; CP
   7; DAM MULT, POET; DLB 117, 225;
   EWL 3
Bryan, C(ourtlandt) D(ixon) B(arnes)
   1936- .... **CLC 29**
   See also CA 73-76; CANR 13, 68; DLB
   185; INT CANR-13
Bryan, Michael
   See Moore, Brian
   See also CCA 1
Bryan, William Jennings
   1860-1925 .... **TCLC 99**
   See also DLB 303
Bryant, William Cullen 1794-1878 . **NCLC 6,
   46; PC 20**
   See also AMWS 1; CDALB 1640-1865;
   DA; DAB; DAC; DAM MST, POET;
   DLB 3, 43, 59, 189, 250; EXPP; PAB;
   RGAL 4; TUS
Bryusov, Valery Yakovlevich
   1873-1924 .... **TCLC 10**
   See also CA 107; 155; EWL 3; SFW 4
Buchan, John 1875-1940 .... **TCLC 41**
   See also CA 108; 145; CMW 4; DAB;
   DAM POP; DLB 34, 70, 156; HGG;
   MSW; MTCW 1; RGEL 2; RHW; YABC
   2
Buchanan, George 1506-1582 .... **LC 4**
   See also DLB 132
Buchanan, Robert 1841-1901 .... **TCLC 107**
   See also CA 179; DLB 18, 35
Buchheim, Lothar-Guenther 1918- .... **CLC 6**
   See also CA 85-88
Buchner, (Karl) Georg
   1813-1837 .... **NCLC 26, 146**
   See also CDWLB 2; DLB 133; EW 6;
   RGSF 2; RGWL 2, 3; TWA
Buchwald, Art(hur) 1925- .... **CLC 33**
   See also AITN 1; CA 5-8R; CANR 21, 67,
   107; MTCW 1, 2; SATA 10
Buck, Pearl S(ydenstricker)
   1892-1973 .... **CLC 7, 11, 18, 127**
   See also AAYA 42; AITN 1; AMWS 2;
   BPFB 1; CA 1-4R; 41-44R; CANR 1, 34;
   CDALBS; DA; DA3; DAB; DAC; DAM
   MST, NOV; DLB 9, 102; EWL 3; LAIT
   3; MTCW 1, 2; RGAL 4; RHW; SATA 1,
   25; TUS
Buckler, Ernest 1908-1984 .... **CLC 13**
   See also CA 11-12; 114; CAP 1; CCA 1;
   DAC; DAM MST; DLB 68; SATA 47
Buckley, Christopher (Taylor)
   1952- .... **CLC 165**
   See also CA 139; CANR 119

Buckley, Vincent (Thomas)
   1925-1988 .... **CLC 57**
   See also CA 101; DLB 289
Buckley, William F(rank), Jr. 1925- . **CLC 7,
   18, 37**
   See also AITN 1; BPFB 1; CA 1-4R; CANR
   1, 24, 53, 93, 133; CMW 4; CPW; DA3;
   DAM POP; DLB 137; DLBY 1980; INT
   CANR-24; MTCW 1, 2; TUS
Buechner, (Carl) Frederick 1926- . **CLC 2, 4,
   6, 9**
   See also AMWS 12; BPFB 1; CA 13-16R;
   CANR 11, 39, 64, 114; CN 7; DAM NOV;
   DLBY 1980; INT CANR-11; MTCW 1, 2
Buell, John (Edward) 1927- .... **CLC 10**
   See also CA 1-4R; CANR 71; DLB 53
Buero Vallejo, Antonio 1916-2000 ... **CLC 15,
   46, 139; DC 18**
   See also CA 106; 189; CANR 24, 49, 75;
   CWW 2; DFS 11; EWL 3; HW 1; MTCW
   1, 2
Bufalino, Gesualdo 1920-1996 .... **CLC 74**
   See also CWW 2; DLB 196
Bugayev, Boris Nikolayevich
   1880-1934 .... **PC 11; TCLC 7**
   See Bely, Andrey; Belyi, Andrei
   See also CA 104; 165; MTCW 1
Bukowski, Charles 1920-1994 ... **CLC 2, 5, 9,
   41, 82, 108; PC 18; SSC 45**
   See also CA 17-20R; 144; CANR 40, 62,
   105; CPW; DA3; DAM NOV, POET;
   DLB 5, 130, 169; EWL 3; MTCW 1, 2
Bulgakov, Mikhail (Afanas'evich)
   1891-1940 .... **SSC 18; TCLC 2, 16**
   See also BPFB 1; CA 105; 152; DAM
   DRAM, NOV; DLB 272; EWL 3; NFS 8;
   RGSF 2; RGWL 2, 3; SFW 4; TWA
Bulgya, Alexander Alexandrovich
   1901-1956 .... **TCLC 53**
   See Fadeev, Aleksandr Aleksandrovich;
   Fadeev, Alexandr Alexandrovich; Fadeyev,
   Alexander
   See also CA 117; 181
Bullins, Ed 1935- ... **BLC 1; CLC 1, 5, 7; DC
   6**
   See also BW 2, 3; CA 49-52; CAAS 16;
   CAD; CANR 24, 46, 73; CD 5; DAM
   DRAM, MULT; DLB 7, 38, 249; EWL 3;
   MTCW 1, 2; RGAL 4
Bulosan, Carlos 1911-1956 .... **AAL**
   See also CA 216; RGAL 4
**Bulwer-Lytton, Edward (George Earle
   Lytton)** 1803-1873 .... **NCLC 1, 45**
   See also DLB 21; RGEL 2; SFW 4; SUFW
   1; TEA
Bunin, Ivan Alexeyevich 1870-1953 ... **SSC 5;
   TCLC 6**
   See also CA 104; EWL 3; RGSF 2; RGWL
   2, 3; TWA
Bunting, Basil 1900-1985 ...... **CLC 10, 39, 47**
   See also BRWS 7; CA 53-56; 115; CANR
   7; DAM POET; DLB 20; EWL 3; RGEL
   2
Bunuel, Luis 1900-1983 ... **CLC 16, 80; HLC
   1**
   See also CA 101; 110; CANR 32, 77; DAM
   MULT; HW 1
Bunyan, John 1628-1688 ..... **LC 4, 69; WLC**
   See also BRW 2; BYA 5; CDBLB 1660-
   1789; DA; DAB; DAC; DAM MST; DLB
   39; RGEL 2; TEA; WCH; WLIT 3
Buravsky, Alexandr .... **CLC 59**
Burckhardt, Jacob (Christoph)
   1818-1897 .... **NCLC 49**
   See also EW 6
Burford, Eleanor
   See Hibbert, Eleanor Alice Burford

Burgess, Anthony . **CLC 1, 2, 4, 5, 8, 10, 13,
   15, 22, 40, 62, 81, 94**
   See Wilson, John (Anthony) Burgess
   See also AAYA 25; AITN 1; BRWS 1; CD-
   BLB 1960 to Present; DAB; DLB 14, 194,
   261; DLBY 1998; EWL 3; MTCW 1;
   RGEL 2; RHW; SFW 4; YAW
Burke, Edmund 1729(?)-1797 .... **LC 7, 36;
   WLC**
   See also BRW 3; DA; DA3; DAB; DAC;
   DAM MST; DLB 104, 252; RGEL 2;
   TEA
Burke, Kenneth (Duva) 1897-1993 ... **CLC 2,
   24**
   See also AMW; CA 5-8R; 143; CANR 39,
   74; DLB 45, 63; EWL 3; MTCW 1, 2;
   RGAL 4
Burke, Leda
   See Garnett, David
Burke, Ralph
   See Silverberg, Robert
Burke, Thomas 1886-1945 .... **TCLC 63**
   See also CA 113; 155; CMW 4; DLB 197
Burney, Fanny 1752-1840 .... **NCLC 12, 54,
   107**
   See also BRWS 3; DLB 39; NFS 16; RGEL
   2; TEA
Burney, Frances
   See Burney, Fanny
Burns, Robert 1759-1796 ... **LC 3, 29, 40; PC
   6; WLC**
   See also AAYA 51; BRW 3; CDBLB 1789-
   1832; DA; DA3; DAB; DAC; DAM MST,
   POET; DLB 109; EXPP; PAB; RGEL 2;
   TEA; WP
Burns, Tex
   See L'Amour, Louis (Dearborn)
   See also TCWW 2
Burnshaw, Stanley 1906- .... **CLC 3, 13, 44**
   See also CA 9-12R; CP 7; DLB 48; DLBY
   1997
Burr, Anne 1937- .... **CLC 6**
   See also CA 25-28R
Burroughs, Edgar Rice 1875-1950 . **TCLC 2,
   32**
   See also AAYA 11; BPFB 1; BYA 4, 9; CA
   104; 132; CANR 131; DA3; DAM NOV;
   DLB 8; FANT; MTCW 1, 2; RGAL 4;
   SATA 41; SCFW 2; SFW 4; TUS; YAW
Burroughs, William S(eward)
   1914-1997 .. **CLC 1, 2, 5, 15, 22, 42, 75,
   109; TCLC 121; WLC**
   See Lee, William; Lee, Willy
   See also AITN 2; AMWS 3; BG 2; BPFB
   1; CA 9-12R; 160; CANR 20, 52, 104;
   CN 7; CPW; DA; DA3; DAB; DAC;
   DAM MST, NOV, POP; DLB 2, 8, 16,
   152, 237; DLBY 1981, 1997; EWL 3;
   HGG; LMFS 2; MTCW 1, 2; RGAL 4;
   SFW 4
Burton, Sir Richard F(rancis)
   1821-1890 .... **NCLC 42**
   See also DLB 55, 166, 184
Burton, Robert 1577-1640 .... **LC 74**
   See also DLB 151; RGEL 2
Buruma, Ian 1951- .... **CLC 163**
   See also CA 128; CANR 65
Busch, Frederick 1941- ... **CLC 7, 10, 18, 47,
   166**
   See also CA 33-36R; CAAS 1; CANR 45,
   73, 92; CN 7; DLB 6, 218
Bush, Barney (Furman) 1946- .... **NNAL**
   See also CA 145
Bush, Ronald 1946- .... **CLC 34**
   See also CA 136
Bustos, F(rancisco)
   See Borges, Jorge Luis

Cassity, (Allen) Turner 1929- .... **CLC 6, 42**
See also CA 17-20R; 223; CAAE 223;
CAAS 8; CANR 11; CSW; DLB 105

Castaneda, Carlos (Cesar Aranha)
1931(?)-1998 .... **CLC 12, 119**
See also CA 25-28R; CANR 32, 66, 105;
DNFS 1; HW 1; MTCW 1

Castedo, Elena 1937- .... **CLC 65**
See also CA 132

Castedo-Ellerman, Elena
See Castedo, Elena

Castellanos, Rosario 1925-1974 .... **CLC 66;**
HLC 1; SSC 39, 68
See also CA 131; 53-56; CANR 58; CD-
WLB 3; DAM MULT; DLB 113, 290;
EWL 3; FW; HW 1; LAW; MTCW 1;
RGSF 2; RGWL 2, 3

Castelvetro, Lodovico 1505-1571 .... **LC 12**

Castiglione, Baldassare 1478-1529 ...... **LC 12**
See Castiglione, Baldesar
See also LMFS 1; RGWL 2, 3

Castiglione, Baldesar
See Castiglione, Baldassare
See also EW 2

Castillo, Ana (Hernandez Del)
1953- .... **CLC 151**
See also AAYA 42; CA 131; CANR 51, 86,
128; CWP; DLB 122, 227; DNFS 2; FW;
HW 1; LLW 1; PFS 21

Castle, Robert
See Hamilton, Edmond

Castro (Ruz), Fidel 1926(?)- .... **HLC 1**
See also CA 110; 129; CANR 81; DAM
MULT; HW 2

Castro, Guillen de 1569-1631 .... **LC 19**

Castro, Rosalia de 1837-1885 ... **NCLC 3, 78;**
PC 41
See also DAM MULT

Cather, Willa (Sibert) 1873-1947 . **SSC 2, 50;**
TCLC 1, 11, 31, 99, 132, 152; WLC
See also AAYA 24; AMW; AMWC 1;
AMWR 1; BPFB 1; CA 104; 128; CDALB
1865-1917; CLR 98; DA; DA3; DAB;
DAC; DAM MST, NOV; DLB 9, 54, 78,
256; DLBD 1; EWL 3; EXPN; EXPS;
LAIT 3; LATS 1:1; MAWW; MTCW 1,
2; NFS 2, 19; RGAL 4; RGSF 2; RHW;
SATA 30; SSFS 2, 7, 16; TCWW 2; TUS

Catherine II
See Catherine the Great
See also DLB 150

Catherine the Great 1729-1796 .... **LC 69**
See Catherine II

Cato, Marcus Porcius
234B.C.-149B.C. .... **CMLC 21**
See Cato the Elder

Cato, Marcus Porcius, the Elder
See Cato, Marcus Porcius

Cato the Elder
See Cato, Marcus Porcius
See also DLB 211

Catton, (Charles) Bruce 1899-1978 . **CLC 35**
See also AITN 1; CA 5-8R; 81-84; CANR
7, 74; DLB 17; SATA 2; SATA-Obit 24

Catullus c. 84B.C.-54B.C. .... **CMLC 18**
See also AW 2; CDWLB 1; DLB 211;
RGWL 2, 3

Cauldwell, Frank
See King, Francis (Henry)

Caunitz, William J. 1933-1996 .... **CLC 34**
See also BEST 89:3; CA 125; 130; 152;
CANR 73; INT CA-130

Causley, Charles (Stanley)
1917-2003 .... **CLC 7**
See also CA 9-12R; 223; CANR 5, 35, 94;
CLR 30; CWRI 5; DLB 27; MTCW 1;
SATA 3, 66; SATA-Obit 149

Caute, (John) David 1936- .... **CLC 29**
See also CA 1-4R; CAAS 4; CANR 1, 33,
64, 120; CBD; CD 5; CN 7; DAM NOV;
DLB 14, 231

Cavafy, C(onstantine) P(eter) .... **PC 36;**
TCLC 2, 7
See Kavafis, Konstantinos Petrou
See also CA 148; DA3; DAM POET; EW
8; EWL 3; MTCW 1; PFS 19; RGWL 2,
3; WP

Cavalcanti, Guido c. 1250-c.
1300 .... **CMLC 54**

Cavallo, Evelyn
See Spark, Muriel (Sarah)

Cavanna, Betty .... **CLC 12**
See Harrison, Elizabeth (Allen) Cavanna
See also JRDA; MAICYA 1; SAAS 4;
SATA 1, 30

Cavendish, Margaret Lucas
1623-1673 .... **LC 30**
See also DLB 131, 252, 281; RGEL 2

Caxton, William 1421(?)-1491(?) .... **LC 17**
See also DLB 170

Cayer, D. M.
See Duffy, Maureen

Cayrol, Jean 1911- .... **CLC 11**
See also CA 89-92; DLB 83; EWL 3

Cela (y Trulock), Camilo Jose
See Cela, Camilo Jose
See also CWW 2

Cela, Camilo Jose 1916-2002 .... **CLC 4, 13,**
59, 122; HLC 1; SSC 71
See Cela (y Trulock), Camilo Jose
See also BEST 90:2; CA 21-24R; 206;
CAAS 10; CANR 21, 32, 76; DAM
MULT; DLBY 1989; EW 13; EWL 3; HW
1; MTCW 1, 2; RGSF 2; RGWL 2, 3

Celan, Paul .... **CLC 10, 19, 53, 82; PC 10**
See Antschel, Paul
See also CDWLB 2; DLB 69; EWL 3;
RGWL 2, 3

Celine, Louis-Ferdinand .. **CLC 1, 3, 4, 7, 9,**
15, 47, 124
See Destouches, Louis-Ferdinand
See also DLB 72; EW 11; EWL 3; GFL
1789 to the Present; RGWL 2, 3

Cellini, Benvenuto 1500-1571 .... **LC 7**

Cendrars, Blaise .... **CLC 18, 106**
See Sauser-Hall, Frederic
See also DLB 258; EWL 3; GFL 1789 to
the Present; RGWL 2, 3; WP

Centlivre, Susanna 1669(?)-1723 .... **LC 65**
See also DLB 84; RGEL 2

Cernuda (y Bidon), Luis 1902-1963 . **CLC 54**
See also CA 131; 89-92; DAM POET; DLB
134; EWL 3; GLL 1; HW 1; RGWL 2, 3

Cervantes, Lorna Dee 1954- ..... **HLCS 1; PC**
35
See also CA 131; CANR 80; CWP; DLB
82; EXPP; HW 1; LLW 1

Cervantes (Saavedra), Miguel de
1547-1616 .... **HLCS; LC 6, 23, 93; SSC**
12; WLC
See also AAYA 56; BYA 1, 14; DA; DAB;
DAC; DAM MST, NOV; EW 2; LAIT 1;
LATS 1:1; LMFS 1; NFS 8; RGSF 2;
RGWL 2, 3; TWA

Cesaire, Aime (Fernand) 1913- .... **BLC 1;**
CLC 19, 32, 112; DC 22; PC 25
See also BW 2, 3; CA 65-68; CANR 24,
43, 81; CWW 2; DA3; DAM MULT,
POET; EWL 3; GFL 1789 to the Present;
MTCW 1, 2; WP

Chabon, Michael 1963- ... **CLC 55, 149; SSC**
59
See also AAYA 45; AMWS 11; CA 139;
CANR 57, 96, 127; DLB 278; SATA 145

Chabrol, Claude 1930- .... **CLC 16**
See also CA 110

Chairil Anwar
See Anwar, Chairil
See also EWL 3

Challans, Mary 1905-1983
See Renault, Mary
See also CA 81-84; 111; CANR 74; DA3;
MTCW 2; SATA 23; SATA-Obit 36; TEA

Challis, George
See Faust, Frederick (Schiller)
See also TCWW 2

Chambers, Aidan 1934- .... **CLC 35**
See also AAYA 27; CA 25-28R; CANR 12,
31, 58, 116; JRDA; MAICYA 1, 2; SAAS
12; SATA 1, 69, 108; WYA; YAW

Chambers, James 1948-
See Cliff, Jimmy
See also CA 124

Chambers, Jessie
See Lawrence, D(avid) H(erbert Richards)
See also GLL 1

Chambers, Robert W(illiam)
1865-1933 .... **TCLC 41**
See also CA 165; DLB 202; HGG; SATA
107; SUFW 1

Chambers, (David) Whittaker
1901-1961 .... **TCLC 129**
See also CA 89-92; DLB 303

Chamisso, Adelbert von
1781-1838 .... **NCLC 82**
See also DLB 90; RGWL 2, 3; SUFW 1

Chance, James T.
See Carpenter, John (Howard)

Chance, John T.
See Carpenter, John (Howard)

Chandler, Raymond (Thornton)
1888-1959 .... **SSC 23; TCLC 1, 7**
See also AAYA 25; AMWC 2; AMWS 4;
BPFB 1; CA 104; 129; CANR 60, 107;
CDALB 1929-1941; CMW 4; DA3; DLB
226, 253; DLBD 6; EWL 3; MSW;
MTCW 1, 2; NFS 17; RGAL 4; TUS

Chang, Diana 1934- .... **AAL**
See also CWP; EXPP

Chang, Eileen 1921-1995 .... **AAL; SSC 28**
See Chang Ai-Ling; Zhang Ailing
See also CA 166

Chang, Jung 1952- .... **CLC 71**
See also CA 142

Chang Ai-Ling
See Chang, Eileen
See also EWL 3

Channing, William Ellery
1780-1842 .... **NCLC 17**
See also DLB 1, 59, 235; RGAL 4

Chao, Patricia 1955- .... **CLC 119**
See also CA 163

Chaplin, Charles Spencer
1889-1977 .... **CLC 16**
See Chaplin, Charlie
See also CA 81-84; 73-76

Chaplin, Charlie
See Chaplin, Charles Spencer
See also DLB 44

Chapman, George 1559(?)-1634 . **DC 19; LC**
22
See also BRW 1; DAM DRAM; DLB 62,
121; LMFS 1; RGEL 2

Chapman, Graham 1941-1989 .... **CLC 21**
See Monty Python
See also CA 116; 129; CANR 35, 95

Chapman, John Jay 1862-1933 .... **TCLC 7**
See also CA 104; 191

Chapman, Lee
See Bradley, Marion Zimmer
See also GLL 1

Chapman, Walker
See Silverberg, Robert

Chulkov, Mikhail Dmitrievich
1743-1792 .... **LC 2**
See also DLB 150
Churchill, Caryl 1938- .... **CLC 31, 55, 157;
DC 5**
See Churchill, Chick
See also BRWS 4; CA 102; CANR 22, 46,
108; CBD; CWD; DFS 12, 16; DLB 13;
EWL 3; FW; MTCW 1; RGEL 2
Churchill, Charles 1731-1764 .... **LC 3**
See also DLB 109; RGEL 2
Churchill, Chick 1938-
See Churchill, Caryl
See also CD 5
Churchill, Sir Winston (Leonard Spencer)
1874-1965 .... **TCLC 113**
See also BRW 6; CA 97-100; CDBLB
1890-1914; DA3; DLB 100; DLBD 16;
LAIT 4; MTCW 1, 2
Chute, Carolyn 1947- .... **CLC 39**
See also CA 123
Ciardi, John (Anthony) 1916-1986 . **CLC 10,
40, 44, 129**
See also CA 5-8R; 118; CAAS 2; CANR 5,
33; CLR 19; CWRI 5; DAM POET; DLB
5; DLBY 1986; INT CANR-5; MAICYA
1, 2; MTCW 1, 2; RGAL 4; SAAS 26;
SATA 1, 65; SATA-Obit 46
Cibber, Colley 1671-1757 .... **LC 66**
See also DLB 84; RGEL 2
Cicero, Marcus Tullius
106B.C.-43B.C. .... **CMLC 3**
See also AW 1; CDWLB 1; DLB 211;
RGWL 2, 3
Cimino, Michael 1943- .... **CLC 16**
See also CA 105
Cioran, E(mil) M. 1911-1995 .... **CLC 64**
See also CA 25-28R; 149; CANR 91; DLB
220; EWL 3
Cisneros, Sandra 1954- .... **CLC 69, 118, 193;
HLC 1; SSC 32, 72**
See also AAYA 9, 53; AMWS 7; CA 131;
CANR 64, 118; CWP; DA3; DAM MULT;
DLB 122, 152; EWL 3; EXPN; FW; HW
1, 2; LAIT 5; LATS 1:2; LLW 1; MAI-
CYA 2; MTCW 2; NFS 2; PFS 19; RGAL
4; RGSF 2; SSFS 3, 13; WLIT 1; YAW
Cixous, Helene 1937- .... **CLC 92**
See also CA 126; CANR 55, 123; CWW 2;
DLB 83, 242; EWL 3; FW; GLL 2;
MTCW 1, 2; TWA
Clair, Rene .... **CLC 20**
See Chomette, Rene Lucien
Clampitt, Amy 1920-1994 .... **CLC 32; PC 19**
See also AMWS 9; CA 110; 146; CANR
29, 79; DLB 105
Clancy, Thomas L., Jr. 1947-
See Clancy, Tom
See also CA 125; 131; CANR 62, 105;
DA3; INT CA-131; MTCW 1, 2
Clancy, Tom .... **CLC 45, 112**
See Clancy, Thomas L., Jr.
See also AAYA 9, 51; BEST 89:1, 90:1;
BPFB 1; BYA 10, 11; CANR 132; CMW
4; CPW; DAM NOV, POP; DLB 227
Clare, John 1793-1864 .. **NCLC 9, 86; PC 23**
See also DAB; DAM POET; DLB 55, 96;
RGEL 2
Clarin
See Alas (y Urena), Leopoldo (Enrique
Garcia)
Clark, Al C.
See Goines, Donald
Clark, (Robert) Brian 1932- .... **CLC 29**
See also CA 41-44R; CANR 67; CBD; CD
5
Clark, Curt
See Westlake, Donald E(dwin)

Clark, Eleanor 1913-1996 .... **CLC 5, 19**
See also CA 9-12R; 151; CANR 41; CN 7;
DLB 6
Clark, J. P.
See Clark Bekederemo, J(ohnson) P(epper)
See also CDWLB 3; DLB 117
Clark, John Pepper
See Clark Bekederemo, J(ohnson) P(epper)
See also AFW; CD 5; CP 7; RGEL 2
Clark, Kenneth (Mackenzie)
1903-1983 .... **TCLC 147**
See also CA 93-96; 109; CANR 36; MTCW
1, 2
Clark, M. R.
See Clark, Mavis Thorpe
Clark, Mavis Thorpe 1909-1999 ...... **CLC 12**
See also CA 57-60; CANR 8, 37, 107; CLR
30; CWRI 5; MAICYA 1, 2; SAAS 5;
SATA 8, 74
Clark, Walter Van Tilburg
1909-1971 .... **CLC 28**
See also CA 9-12R; 33-36R; CANR 63,
113; DLB 9, 206; LAIT 2; RGAL 4;
SATA 8
Clark Bekederemo, J(ohnson) P(epper)
1935- .... **BLC 1; CLC 38; DC 5**
See Clark, J. P.; Clark, John Pepper
See also BW 1; CA 65-68; CANR 16, 72;
DAM DRAM, MULT; DFS 13; EWL 3;
MTCW 1
Clarke, Arthur C(harles) 1917- .... **CLC 1, 4,
13, 18, 35, 136; SSC 3**
See also AAYA 4, 33; BPFB 1; BYA 13;
CA 1-4R; CANR 2, 28, 55, 74, 130; CN
7; CPW; DA3; DAM POP; DLB 261;
JRDA; LAIT 5; MAICYA 1, 2; MTCW 1,
2; SATA 13, 70, 115; SCFW; SFW 4;
SSFS 4, 18; YAW
Clarke, Austin 1896-1974 .... **CLC 6, 9**
See also CA 29-32; 49-52; CAP 2; DAM
POET; DLB 10, 20; EWL 3; RGEL 2
Clarke, Austin C(hesterfield) 1934- .. **BLC 1;
CLC 8, 53; SSC 45**
See also BW 1; CA 25-28R; CAAS 16;
CANR 14, 32, 68; CN 7; DAC; DAM
MULT; DLB 53, 125; DNFS 2; RGSF 2
Clarke, Gillian 1937- .... **CLC 61**
See also CA 106; CP 7; CWP; DLB 40
Clarke, Marcus (Andrew Hislop)
1846-1881 .... **NCLC 19**
See also DLB 230; RGEL 2; RGSF 2
Clarke, Shirley 1925-1997 .... **CLC 16**
See also CA 189
Clash, The
See Headon, (Nicky) Topper; Jones, Mick;
Simonon, Paul; Strummer, Joe
Claudel, Paul (Louis Charles Marie)
1868-1955 .... **TCLC 2, 10**
See also CA 104; 165; DLB 192, 258; EW
8; EWL 3; GFL 1789 to the Present;
RGWL 2, 3; TWA
Claudian 370(?)-404(?) .... **CMLC 46**
See also RGWL 2, 3
Claudius, Matthias 1740-1815 .... **NCLC 75**
See also DLB 97
Clavell, James (duMaresq)
1925-1994 .... **CLC 6, 25, 87**
See also BPFB 1; CA 25-28R; 146; CANR
26, 48; CPW; DA3; DAM NOV, POP;
MTCW 1, 2; NFS 10; RHW
Clayman, Gregory .... **CLC 65**
Cleaver, (Leroy) Eldridge
1935-1998 .... **BLC 1; CLC 30, 119**
See also BW 1, 3; CA 21-24R; 167; CANR
16, 75; DA3; DAM MULT; MTCW 2;
YAW
Cleese, John (Marwood) 1939- .... **CLC 21**
See Monty Python
See also CA 112; 116; CANR 35; MTCW 1

Cleishbotham, Jebediah
See Scott, Sir Walter
Cleland, John 1710-1789 .... **LC 2, 48**
See also DLB 39; RGEL 2
Clemens, Samuel Langhorne 1835-1910
See Twain, Mark
See also CA 104; 135; CDALB 1865-1917;
DA; DA3; DAB; DAC; DAM MST, NOV;
DLB 12, 23, 64, 74, 186, 189; JRDA;
LMFS 1; MAICYA 1, 2; NCFS 4; NFS
20; SATA 100; SSFS 16; YABC 2
Clement of Alexandria
150(?)-215(?) .... **CMLC 41**
Cleophil
See Congreve, William
Clerihew, E.
See Bentley, E(dmund) C(lerihew)
Clerk, N. W.
See Lewis, C(live) S(taples)
Cleveland, John 1613-1658 .... **LC 106**
See also DLB 126; RGEL 2
Cliff, Jimmy .... **CLC 21**
See Chambers, James
See also CA 193
Cliff, Michelle 1946- .... **BLCS; CLC 120**
See also BW 2; CA 116; CANR 39, 72; CD-
WLB 3; DLB 157; FW; GLL 2
Clifford, Lady Anne 1590-1676 .... **LC 76**
See also DLB 151
Clifton, (Thelma) Lucille 1936- .... **BLC 1;
CLC 19, 66, 162; PC 17**
See also AFAW 2; BW 2, 3; CA 49-52;
CANR 2, 24, 42, 76, 97; CLR 5; CP 7;
CSW; CWP; CWRI 5; DA3; DAM MULT,
POET; DLB 5, 41; EXPP; MAICYA 1, 2;
MTCW 1, 2; PFS 1, 14; SATA 20, 69,
128; WP
Clinton, Dirk
See Silverberg, Robert
Clough, Arthur Hugh 1819-1861 ... **NCLC 27**
See also BRW 5; DLB 32; RGEL 2
Clutha, Janet Paterson Frame 1924-2004
See Frame, Janet
See also CA 1-4R; 224; CANR 2, 36, 76;
MTCW 1, 2; SATA 119
Clyne, Terence
See Blatty, William Peter
Cobalt, Martin
See Mayne, William (James Carter)
Cobb, Irvin S(hrewsbury)
1876-1944 .... **TCLC 77**
See also CA 175; DLB 11, 25, 86
Cobbett, William 1763-1835 .... **NCLC 49**
See also DLB 43, 107, 158; RGEL 2
Coburn, D(onald) L(ee) 1938- .... **CLC 10**
See also CA 89-92
Cocteau, Jean (Maurice Eugene Clement)
1889-1963 ...... **CLC 1, 8, 15, 16, 43; DC
17; TCLC 119; WLC**
See also CA 25-28; CANR 40; CAP 2; DA;
DA3; DAB; DAC; DAM DRAM, MST,
NOV; DLB 65, 258; EW 10; EWL 3; GFL
1789 to the Present; MTCW 1, 2; RGWL
2, 3; TWA
Codrescu, Andrei 1946- .... **CLC 46, 121**
See also CA 33-36R; CAAS 19; CANR 13,
34, 53, 76, 125; DA3; DAM POET;
MTCW 2
Coe, Max
See Bourne, Randolph S(illiman)
Coe, Tucker
See Westlake, Donald E(dwin)
Coen, Ethan 1958- .... **CLC 108**
See also AAYA 54; CA 126; CANR 85
Coen, Joel 1955- .... **CLC 108**
See also AAYA 54; CA 126; CANR 119
The Coen Brothers
See Coen, Ethan; Coen, Joel

Cooper, Douglas 1960- .... **CLC 86**
Cooper, Henry St. John
  See Creasey, John
Cooper, J(oan) California (?)- .... **CLC 56**
  See also AAYA 12; BW 1; CA 125; CANR 55; DAM MULT; DLB 212
Cooper, James Fenimore
  1789-1851 .... **NCLC 1, 27, 54**
  See also AAYA 22; AMW; BPFB 1; CDALB 1640-1865; DA3; DLB 3, 183, 250, 254; LAIT 1; NFS 9; RGAL 4; SATA 19; TUS; WCH
Cooper, Susan Fenimore
  1813-1894 .... **NCLC 129**
  See also ANW; DLB 239, 254
Coover, Robert (Lowell) 1932- ...... **CLC 3, 7, 15, 32, 46, 87, 161; SSC 15**
  See also AMWS 5; BPFB 1; CA 45-48; CANR 3, 37, 58, 115; CN 7; DAM NOV; DLB 2, 227; DLBY 1981; EWL 3; MTCW 1, 2; RGAL 4; RGSF 2
Copeland, Stewart (Armstrong)
  1952- .... **CLC 26**
Copernicus, Nicolaus 1473-1543 .... **LC 45**
Coppard, A(lfred) E(dgar)
  1878-1957 .... **SSC 21; TCLC 5**
  See also BRWS 8; CA 114; 167; DLB 162; EWL 3; HGG; RGEL 2; RGSF 2; SUFW 1; YABC 1
Coppee, Francois 1842-1908 .... **TCLC 25**
  See also CA 170; DLB 217
Coppola, Francis Ford 1939- ... **CLC 16, 126**
  See also AAYA 39; CA 77-80; CANR 40, 78; DLB 44
Copway, George 1818-1869 .... **NNAL**
  See also DAM MULT; DLB 175, 183
Corbiere, Tristan 1845-1875 .... **NCLC 43**
  See also DLB 217; GFL 1789 to the Present
Corcoran, Barbara (Asenath)
  1911- .... **CLC 17**
  See also AAYA 14; CA 21-24R, 191; CAAE 191; CAAS 2; CANR 11, 28, 48; CLR 50; DLB 52; JRDA; MAICYA 2; MAICYAS 1; RHW; SAAS 20; SATA 3, 77; SATA-Essay 125
Cordelier, Maurice
  See Giraudoux, Jean(-Hippolyte)
Corelli, Marie .... **TCLC 51**
  See Mackay, Mary
  See also DLB 34, 156; RGEL 2; SUFW 1
Corinna c. 225B.C.-c. 305B.C. ...... **CMLC 72**
Corman, Cid .... **CLC 9**
  See Corman, Sidney
  See also CAAS 2; DLB 5, 193
Corman, Sidney 1924-2004
  See Corman, Cid
  See also CA 85-88; 225; CANR 44; CP 7; DAM POET
Cormier, Robert (Edmund)
  1925-2000 .... **CLC 12, 30**
  See also AAYA 3, 19; BYA 1, 2, 6, 8, 9; CA 1-4R; CANR 5, 23, 76, 93; CDALB 1968-1988; CLR 12, 55; DA; DAB; DAC; DAM MST, NOV; DLB 52; EXPN; INT CANR-23; JRDA; LAIT 5; MAICYA 1, 2; MTCW 1, 2; NFS 2, 18; SATA 10, 45, 83; SATA-Obit 122; WYA; YAW
Corn, Alfred (DeWitt III) 1943- .... **CLC 33**
  See also CA 179; CAAE 179; CAAS 25; CANR 44; CP 7; CSW; DLB 120, 282; DLBY 1980
Corneille, Pierre 1606-1684 ... **DC 21; LC 28**
  See also DAB; DAM MST; DLB 268; EW 3; GFL Beginnings to 1789; RGWL 2, 3; TWA

Cornwell, David (John Moore)
  1931- .... **CLC 9, 15**
  See le Carre, John
  See also CA 5-8R; CANR 13, 33, 59, 107, 132; DA3; DAM POP; MTCW 1, 2
Cornwell, Patricia (Daniels) 1956- . **CLC 155**
  See also AAYA 16, 56; BPFB 1; CA 134; CANR 53, 131; CMW 4; CPW; CSW; DAM POP; DLB 306; MSW; MTCW 1
Corso, (Nunzio) Gregory 1930-2001 . **CLC 1, 11; PC 33**
  See also AMWS 12; BG 2; CA 5-8R; 193; CANR 41, 76, 132; CP 7; DA3; DLB 5, 16, 237; LMFS 2; MTCW 1, 2; WP
Cortazar, Julio 1914-1984 ... **CLC 2, 3, 5, 10, 13, 15, 33, 34, 92; HLC 1; SSC 7, 76**
  See also BPFB 1; CA 21-24R; CANR 12, 32, 81; CDWLB 3; DA3; DAM MULT, NOV; DLB 113; EWL 3; EXPS; HW 1, 2; LAW; MTCW 1, 2; RGSF 2; RGWL 2, 3; SSFS 3, 20; TWA; WLIT 1
Cortes, Hernan 1485-1547 .... **LC 31**
Corvinus, Jakob
  See Raabe, Wilhelm (Karl)
Corwin, Cecil
  See Kornbluth, C(yril) M.
Cosic, Dobrica 1921- .... **CLC 14**
  See also CA 122; 138; CDWLB 4; CWW 2; DLB 181; EWL 3
Costain, Thomas B(ertram)
  1885-1965 .... **CLC 30**
  See also BYA 3; CA 5-8R; 25-28R; DLB 9; RHW
Costantini, Humberto 1924(?)-1987 . **CLC 49**
  See also CA 131; 122; EWL 3; HW 1
Costello, Elvis 1954- .... **CLC 21**
  See also CA 204
Costenoble, Philostene
  See Ghelderode, Michel de
Cotes, Cecil V.
  See Duncan, Sara Jeannette
Cotter, Joseph Seamon Sr.
  1861-1949 .... **BLC 1; TCLC 28**
  See also BW 1; CA 124; DAM MULT; DLB 50
Couch, Arthur Thomas Quiller
  See Quiller-Couch, Sir Arthur (Thomas)
Coulton, James
  See Hansen, Joseph
Couperus, Louis (Marie Anne)
  1863-1923 .... **TCLC 15**
  See also CA 115; EWL 3; RGWL 2, 3
Coupland, Douglas 1961- .... **CLC 85, 133**
  See also AAYA 34; CA 142; CANR 57, 90, 130; CCA 1; CPW; DAC; DAM POP
Court, Wesli
  See Turco, Lewis (Putnam)
Courtenay, Bryce 1933- .... **CLC 59**
  See also CA 138; CPW
Courtney, Robert
  See Ellison, Harlan (Jay)
Cousteau, Jacques-Yves 1910-1997 .. **CLC 30**
  See also CA 65-68; 159; CANR 15, 67; MTCW 1; SATA 38, 98
Coventry, Francis 1725-1754 .... **LC 46**
Coverdale, Miles c. 1487-1569 .... **LC 77**
  See also DLB 167
Cowan, Peter (Walkinshaw)
  1914-2002 .... **SSC 28**
  See also CA 21-24R; CANR 9, 25, 50, 83; CN 7; DLB 260; RGSF 2
Coward, Noel (Peirce) 1899-1973 . **CLC 1, 9, 29, 51**
  See also AITN 1; BRWS 2; CA 17-18; 41-44R; CANR 35, 132; CAP 2; CDBLB 1914-1945; DA3; DAM DRAM; DFS 3, 6; DLB 10, 245; EWL 3; IDFW 3, 4; MTCW 1, 2; RGEL 2; TEA

Cowley, Abraham 1618-1667 .... **LC 43**
  See also BRW 2; DLB 131, 151; PAB; RGEL 2
Cowley, Malcolm 1898-1989 .... **CLC 39**
  See also AMWS 2; CA 5-8R; 128; CANR 3, 55; DLB 4, 48; DLBY 1981, 1989; EWL 3; MTCW 1, 2
Cowper, William 1731-1800 ..... **NCLC 8, 94; PC 40**
  See also BRW 3; DA3; DAM POET; DLB 104, 109; RGEL 2
Cox, William Trevor 1928-
  See Trevor, William
  See also CA 9-12R; CANR 4, 37, 55, 76, 102; DAM NOV; INT CANR-37; MTCW 1, 2; TEA
Coyne, P. J.
  See Masters, Hilary
Cozzens, James Gould 1903-1978 . **CLC 1, 4, 11, 92**
  See also AMW; BPFB 1; CA 9-12R; 81-84; CANR 19; CDALB 1941-1968; DLB 9, 294; DLBD 2; DLBY 1984, 1997; EWL 3; MTCW 1, 2; RGAL 4
Crabbe, George 1754-1832 .... **NCLC 26, 121**
  See also BRW 3; DLB 93; RGEL 2
Crace, Jim 1946- .... **CLC 157; SSC 61**
  See also CA 128; 135; CANR 55, 70, 123; CN 7; DLB 231; INT CA-135
Craddock, Charles Egbert
  See Murfree, Mary Noailles
Craig, A. A.
  See Anderson, Poul (William)
Craik, Mrs.
  See Craik, Dinah Maria (Mulock)
  See also RGEL 2
Craik, Dinah Maria (Mulock)
  1826-1887 .... **NCLC 38**
  See Craik, Mrs.; Mulock, Dinah Maria
  See also DLB 35, 163; MAICYA 1, 2; SATA 34
Cram, Ralph Adams 1863-1942 ..... **TCLC 45**
  See also CA 160
Cranch, Christopher Pearse
  1813-1892 .... **NCLC 115**
  See also DLB 1, 42, 243
Crane, (Harold) Hart 1899-1932 .... **PC 3; TCLC 2, 5, 80; WLC**
  See also AMW; AMWR 2; CA 104; 127; CDALB 1917-1929; DA; DA3; DAB; DAC; DAM MST, POET; DLB 4, 48; EWL 3; MTCW 1, 2; RGAL 4; TUS
Crane, R(onald) S(almon)
  1886-1967 .... **CLC 27**
  See also CA 85-88; DLB 63
Crane, Stephen (Townley)
  1871-1900 ...... **SSC 7, 56, 70; TCLC 11, 17, 32; WLC**
  See also AAYA 21; AMW; AMWC 1; BPFB 1; BYA 3; CA 109; 140; CANR 84; CDALB 1865-1917; DA; DA3; DAB; DAC; DAM MST, NOV, POET; DLB 12, 54, 78; EXPN; EXPS; LAIT 2; LMFS 2; NFS 4, 20; PFS 9; RGAL 4; RGSF 2; SSFS 4; TUS; WYA; YABC 2
Cranmer, Thomas 1489-1556 .... **LC 95**
  See also DLB 132, 213
Cranshaw, Stanley
  See Fisher, Dorothy (Frances) Canfield
Crase, Douglas 1944- .... **CLC 58**
  See also CA 106
Crashaw, Richard 1612(?)-1649 .... **LC 24**
  See also BRW 2; DLB 126; PAB; RGEL 2
Cratinus c. 519B.C.-c. 422B.C. ..... **CMLC 54**
  See also LMFS 1
Craven, Margaret 1901-1980 .... **CLC 17**
  See also BYA 2; CA 103; CCA 1; DAC; LAIT 5

Elliott, Janice 1931-1995 .... **CLC 47**
See also CA 13-16R; CANR 8, 29, 84; CN 7; DLB 14; SATA 119

Elliott, Sumner Locke 1917-1991 ..... **CLC 38**
See also CA 5-8R; 134; CANR 2, 21; DLB 289

Elliott, William
See Bradbury, Ray (Douglas)

Ellis, A. E. .... **CLC 7**

Ellis, Alice Thomas .... **CLC 40**
See Haycraft, Anna (Margaret)
See also DLB 194; MTCW 1

Ellis, Bret Easton 1964- ...... **CLC 39, 71, 117**
See also AAYA 2, 43; CA 118; 123; CANR 51, 74, 126; CN 7; CPW; DA3; DAM POP; DLB 292; HGG; INT CA-123; MTCW 1; NFS 11

Ellis, (Henry) Havelock
1859-1939 .... **TCLC 14**
See also CA 109; 169; DLB 190

Ellis, Landon
See Ellison, Harlan (Jay)

Ellis, Trey 1962- .... **CLC 55**
See also CA 146; CANR 92

Ellison, Harlan (Jay) 1934- ... **CLC 1, 13, 42, 139; SSC 14**
See also AAYA 29; BPFB 1; BYA 14; CA 5-8R; CANR 5, 46, 115; CPW; DAM POP; DLB 8; HGG; INT CANR-5; MTCW 1; SCFW 2; SFW 4; SSFS 13, 14, 15; SUFW 1, 2

Ellison, Ralph (Waldo) 1914-1994 .... **BLC 1; CLC 1, 3, 11, 54, 86, 114; SSC 26; WLC**
See also AAYA 19; AFAW 1, 2; AMWC 2; AMWR 2; AMWS 2; BPFB 1; BW 1, 3; BYA 2; CA 9-12R; 145; CANR 24, 53; CDALB 1941-1968; CSW; DA; DA3; DAB; DAC; DAM MST, MULT, NOV; DLB 2, 76, 227; DLBY 1994; EWL 3; EXPN; EXPS; LAIT 4; MTCW 1, 2; NCFS 3; NFS 2; RGAL 4; RGSF 2; SSFS 1, 11; YAW

Ellmann, Lucy (Elizabeth) 1956- ..... **CLC 61**
See also CA 128

Ellmann, Richard (David)
1918-1987 .... **CLC 50**
See also BEST 89:2; CA 1-4R; 122; CANR 2, 28, 61; DLB 103; DLBY 1987; MTCW 1, 2

Elman, Richard (Martin)
1934-1997 .... **CLC 19**
See also CA 17-20R; 163; CAAS 3; CANR 47

Elron
See Hubbard, L(afayette) Ron(ald)

El Saadawi, Nawal 1931- .... **CLC 196**
See al'Sadaawi, Nawal; Sa'adawi, al-Nawal; Saadawi, Nawal El; Sa'dawi, Nawal al-
See also CA 118; CAAS 11; CANR 44, 92

Eluard, Paul .... **PC 38; TCLC 7, 41**
See Grindel, Eugene
See also EWL 3; GFL 1789 to the Present; RGWL 2, 3

Elyot, Thomas 1490(?)-1546 .... **LC 11**
See also DLB 136; RGEL 2

Elytis, Odysseus 1911-1996 .... **CLC 15, 49, 100; PC 21**
See Alepoudelis, Odysseus
See also CA 102; 151; CANR 94; CWW 2; DAM POET; EW 13; EWL 3; MTCW 1, 2; RGWL 2, 3

Emecheta, (Florence Onye) Buchi
1944- .... **BLC 2; CLC 14, 48, 128**
See also AFW; BW 2, 3; CA 81-84; CANR 27, 81, 126; CDWLB 3; CN 7; CWRI 5; DA3; DAM MULT; DLB 117; EWL 3; FW; MTCW 1, 2; NFS 12, 14; SATA 66; WLIT 2

Emerson, Mary Moody
1774-1863 .... **NCLC 66**

Emerson, Ralph Waldo 1803-1882 . **NCLC 1, 38, 98; PC 18; WLC**
See also AMW; ANW; CDALB 1640-1865; DA; DA3; DAB; DAC; DAM MST, POET; DLB 1, 59, 73, 183, 223, 270; EXPP; LAIT 2; LMFS 1; NCFS 3; PFS 4, 17; RGAL 4; TUS; WP

Eminescu, Mihail 1850-1889 .. **NCLC 33, 131**

Empedocles 5th cent. B.C.- .... **CMLC 50**
See also DLB 176

Empson, William 1906-1984 ... **CLC 3, 8, 19, 33, 34**
See also BRWS 2; CA 17-20R; 112; CANR 31, 61; DLB 20; EWL 3; MTCW 1, 2; RGEL 2

Enchi, Fumiko (Ueda) 1905-1986 ..... **CLC 31**
See Enchi Fumiko
See also CA 129; 121; FW; MJW

Enchi Fumiko
See Enchi, Fumiko (Ueda)
See also DLB 182; EWL 3

Ende, Michael (Andreas Helmuth)
1929-1995 .... **CLC 31**
See also BYA 5; CA 118; 124; 149; CANR 36, 110; CLR 14; DLB 75; MAICYA 1, 2; MAICYAS 1; SATA 61, 130; SATA-Brief 42; SATA-Obit 86

Endo, Shusaku 1923-1996 ..... **CLC 7, 14, 19, 54, 99; SSC 48; TCLC 152**
See Endo Shusaku
See also CA 29-32R; 153; CANR 21, 54, 131; DA3; DAM NOV; MTCW 1, 2; RGSF 2; RGWL 2, 3

Endo Shusaku
See Endo, Shusaku
See also CWW 2; DLB 182; EWL 3

Engel, Marian 1933-1985 .... **CLC 36; TCLC 137**
See also CA 25-28R; CANR 12; DLB 53; FW; INT CANR-12

Engelhardt, Frederick
See Hubbard, L(afayette) Ron(ald)

Engels, Friedrich 1820-1895 .. **NCLC 85, 114**
See also DLB 129; LATS 1:1

Enright, D(ennis) J(oseph)
1920-2002 .... **CLC 4, 8, 31**
See also CA 1-4R; 211; CANR 1, 42, 83; CP 7; DLB 27; EWL 3; SATA 25; SATA-Obit 140

Enzensberger, Hans Magnus
1929- .... **CLC 43; PC 28**
See also CA 116; 119; CANR 103; CWW 2; EWL 3

Ephron, Nora 1941- .... **CLC 17, 31**
See also AAYA 35; AITN 2; CA 65-68; CANR 12, 39, 83

Epicurus 341B.C.-270B.C. .... **CMLC 21**
See also DLB 176

Epsilon
See Betjeman, John

Epstein, Daniel Mark 1948- .... **CLC 7**
See also CA 49-52; CANR 2, 53, 90

Epstein, Jacob 1956- .... **CLC 19**
See also CA 114

Epstein, Jean 1897-1953 .... **TCLC 92**

Epstein, Joseph 1937- .... **CLC 39**
See also CA 112; 119; CANR 50, 65, 117

Epstein, Leslie 1938- .... **CLC 27**
See also AMWS 12; CA 73-76, 215; CAAE 215; CAAS 12; CANR 23, 69; DLB 299

Equiano, Olaudah 1745(?)-1797 . **BLC 2; LC 16**
See also AFAW 1, 2; CDWLB 3; DAM MULT; DLB 37, 50; WLIT 2

Erasmus, Desiderius 1469(?)-1536 ..... **LC 16, 93**
See also DLB 136; EW 2; LMFS 1; RGWL 2, 3; TWA

Erdman, Paul E(mil) 1932- .... **CLC 25**
See also AITN 1; CA 61-64; CANR 13, 43, 84

Erdrich, Louise 1954- .... **CLC 39, 54, 120, 176; NNAL; PC 52**
See also AAYA 10, 47; AMWS 4; BEST 89:1; BPFB 1; CA 114; CANR 41, 62, 118; CDALBS; CN 7; CP 7; CPW; CWP; DA3; DAM MULT, NOV, POP; DLB 152, 175, 206; EWL 3; EXPP; LAIT 5; LATS 1:2; MTCW 1; NFS 5; PFS 14; RGAL 4; SATA 94, 141; SSFS 14; TCWW 2

Erenburg, Ilya (Grigoryevich)
See Ehrenburg, Ilya (Grigoryevich)

Erickson, Stephen Michael 1950-
See Erickson, Steve
See also CA 129; SFW 4

Erickson, Steve .... **CLC 64**
See Erickson, Stephen Michael
See also CANR 60, 68; SUFW 2

Erickson, Walter
See Fast, Howard (Melvin)

Ericson, Walter
See Fast, Howard (Melvin)

Eriksson, Buntel
See Bergman, (Ernst) Ingmar

Eriugena, John Scottus c.
810-877 .... **CMLC 65**
See also DLB 115

Ernaux, Annie 1940- .... **CLC 88, 184**
See also CA 147; CANR 93; NCFS 3, 5

Erskine, John 1879-1951 .... **TCLC 84**
See also CA 112; 159; DLB 9, 102; FANT

Eschenbach, Wolfram von
See Wolfram von Eschenbach
See also RGWL 3

Eseki, Bruno
See Mphahlele, Ezekiel

Esenin, Sergei (Alexandrovich)
1895-1925 .... **TCLC 4**
See Yesenin, Sergey
See also CA 104; RGWL 2, 3

Eshleman, Clayton 1935- .... **CLC 7**
See also CA 33-36R, 212; CAAE 212; CAAS 6; CANR 93; CP 7; DLB 5

Espriella, Don Manuel Alvarez
See Southey, Robert

Espriu, Salvador 1913-1985 .... **CLC 9**
See also CA 154; 115; DLB 134; EWL 3

Espronceda, Jose de 1808-1842 ..... **NCLC 39**

Esquivel, Laura 1951(?)- ... **CLC 141; HLCS 1**
See also AAYA 29; CA 143; CANR 68, 113; DA3; DNFS 2; LAIT 3; LMFS 2; MTCW 1; NFS 5; WLIT 1

Esse, James
See Stephens, James

Esterbrook, Tom
See Hubbard, L(afayette) Ron(ald)

Estleman, Loren D. 1952- .... **CLC 48**
See also AAYA 27; CA 85-88; CANR 27, 74; CMW 4; CPW; DA3; DAM NOV, POP; DLB 226; INT CANR-27; MTCW 1, 2

Etherege, Sir George 1636-1692 . **DC 23; LC 78**
See also BRW 2; DAM DRAM; DLB 80; PAB; RGEL 2

Euclid 306B.C.-283B.C. .... **CMLC 25**

Eugenides, Jeffrey 1960(?)- .... **CLC 81**
See also AAYA 51; CA 144; CANR 120

Felsen, Henry Gregor 1916-1995 ..... **CLC 17**
See also CA 1-4R; 180; CANR 1; SAAS 2;
SATA 1

Felski, Rita .... **CLC 65**

Fenno, Jack
See Calisher, Hortense

Fenollosa, Ernest (Francisco)
1853-1908 .... **TCLC 91**

Fenton, James Martin 1949- .... **CLC 32**
See also CA 102; CANR 108; CP 7; DLB
40; PFS 11

Ferber, Edna 1887-1968 .... **CLC 18, 93**
See also AITN 1; CA 5-8R; 25-28R; CANR
68, 105; DLB 9, 28, 86, 266; MTCW 1,
2; RGAL 4; RHW; SATA 7; TCWW 2

Ferdowsi, Abu'l Qasem 940-1020 . **CMLC 43**
See also RGWL 2, 3

Ferguson, Helen
See Kavan, Anna

Ferguson, Niall 1964- .... **CLC 134**
See also CA 190

Ferguson, Samuel 1810-1886 .... **NCLC 33**
See also DLB 32; RGEL 2

Fergusson, Robert 1750-1774 .... **LC 29**
See also DLB 109; RGEL 2

Ferling, Lawrence
See Ferlinghetti, Lawrence (Monsanto)

Ferlinghetti, Lawrence (Monsanto)
1919(?)- ..... **CLC 2, 6, 10, 27, 111; PC 1**
See also CA 5-8R; CANR 3, 41, 73, 125;
CDALB 1941-1968; CP 7; DA3; DAM
POET; DLB 5, 16; MTCW 1, 2; RGAL 4;
WP

Fern, Fanny
See Parton, Sara Payson Willis

Fernandez, Vicente Garcia Huidobro
See Huidobro Fernandez, Vicente Garcia

Fernandez-Armesto, Felipe .... **CLC 70**

Fernandez de Lizardi, Jose Joaquin
See Lizardi, Jose Joaquin Fernandez de

Ferre, Rosario 1938- ...... **CLC 139; HLCS 1;
SSC 36**
See also CA 131; CANR 55, 81; CWW 2;
DLB 145; EWL 3; HW 1, 2; LAWS 1;
MTCW 1; WLIT 1

Ferrer, Gabriel (Francisco Victor) Miro
See Miro (Ferrer), Gabriel (Francisco
Victor)

Ferrier, Susan (Edmonstone)
1782-1854 .... **NCLC 8**
See also DLB 116; RGEL 2

Ferrigno, Robert 1948(?)- .... **CLC 65**
See also CA 140; CANR 125

Ferron, Jacques 1921-1985 .... **CLC 94**
See also CA 117; 129; CCA 1; DAC; DLB
60; EWL 3

Feuchtwanger, Lion 1884-1958 .... **TCLC 3**
See also CA 104; 187; DLB 66; EWL 3

Feuerbach, Ludwig 1804-1872 ..... **NCLC 139**
See also DLB 133

Feuillet, Octave 1821-1890 .... **NCLC 45**
See also DLB 192

Feydeau, Georges (Leon Jules Marie)
1862-1921 .... **TCLC 22**
See also CA 113; 152; CANR 84; DAM
DRAM; DLB 192; EWL 3; GFL 1789 to
the Present; RGWL 2, 3

Fichte, Johann Gottlieb
1762-1814 .... **NCLC 62**
See also DLB 90

Ficino, Marsilio 1433-1499 .... **LC 12**
See also LMFS 1

Fiedeler, Hans
See Doeblin, Alfred

Fiedler, Leslie A(aron) 1917-2003 ..... **CLC 4,
13, 24**
See also AMWS 13; CA 9-12R; 212; CANR
7, 63; CN 7; DLB 28, 67; EWL 3; MTCW
1, 2; RGAL 4; TUS

Field, Andrew 1938- .... **CLC 44**
See also CA 97-100; CANR 25

Field, Eugene 1850-1895 .... **NCLC 3**
See also DLB 23, 42, 140; DLBD 13; MAI-
CYA 1, 2; RGAL 4; SATA 16

Field, Gans T.
See Wellman, Manly Wade

Field, Michael 1915-1971 .... **TCLC 43**
See also CA 29-32R

Field, Peter
See Hobson, Laura Z(ametkin)
See also TCWW 2

Fielding, Helen 1958- .... **CLC 146**
See also CA 172; CANR 127; DLB 231

Fielding, Henry 1707-1754 .... **LC 1, 46, 85;
WLC**
See also BRW 3; BRWR 1; CDBLB 1660-
1789; DA; DA3; DAB; DAC; DAM
DRAM, MST, NOV; DLB 39, 84, 101;
NFS 18; RGEL 2; TEA; WLIT 3

Fielding, Sarah 1710-1768 .... **LC 1, 44**
See also DLB 39; RGEL 2; TEA

Fields, W. C. 1880-1946 .... **TCLC 80**
See also DLB 44

Fierstein, Harvey (Forbes) 1954- ..... **CLC 33**
See also CA 123; 129; CAD; CD 5; CPW;
DA3; DAM DRAM, POP; DFS 6; DLB
266; GLL

Figes, Eva 1932- .... **CLC 31**
See also CA 53-56; CANR 4, 44, 83; CN 7;
DLB 14, 271; FW

Filippo, Eduardo de
See de Filippo, Eduardo

Finch, Anne 1661-1720 .... **LC 3; PC 21**
See also BRWS 9; DLB 95

Finch, Robert (Duer Claydon)
1900-1995 .... **CLC 18**
See also CA 57-60; CANR 9, 24, 49; CP 7;
DLB 88

Findley, Timothy (Irving Frederick)
1930-2002 .... **CLC 27, 102**
See also CA 25-28R; 206; CANR 12, 42,
69, 109; CCA 1; CN 7; DAC; DAM MST;
DLB 53; FANT; RHW

Fink, William
See Mencken, H(enry) L(ouis)

Firbank, Louis 1942-
See Reed, Lou
See also CA 117

Firbank, (Arthur Annesley) Ronald
1886-1926 .... **TCLC 1**
See also BRWS 2; CA 104; 177; DLB 36;
EWL 3; RGEL 2

Fish, Stanley
See Fish, Stanley Eugene

Fish, Stanley E.
See Fish, Stanley Eugene

Fish, Stanley Eugene 1938- .... **CLC 142**
See also CA 112; 132; CANR 90; DLB 67

Fisher, Dorothy (Frances) Canfield
1879-1958 .... **TCLC 87**
See also CA 114; 136; CANR 80; CLR 71,;
CWRI 5; DLB 9, 102, 284; MAICYA 1,
2; YABC 1

Fisher, M(ary) F(rances) K(ennedy)
1908-1992 .... **CLC 76, 87**
See also CA 77-80; 138; CANR 44; MTCW
1

Fisher, Roy 1930- .... **CLC 25**
See also CA 81-84; CAAS 10; CANR 16;
CP 7; DLB 40

Fisher, Rudolph 1897-1934 .... **BLC 2; HR 2;
SSC 25; TCLC 11**
See also BW 1, 3; CA 107; 124; CANR 80;
DAM MULT; DLB 51, 102

Fisher, Vardis (Alvero) 1895-1968 .... **CLC 7;
TCLC 140**
See also CA 5-8R; 25-28R; CANR 68; DLB
9, 206; RGAL 4; TCWW 2

Fiske, Tarleton
See Bloch, Robert (Albert)

Fitch, Clarke
See Sinclair, Upton (Beall)

Fitch, John IV
See Cormier, Robert (Edmund)

Fitzgerald, Captain Hugh
See Baum, L(yman) Frank

FitzGerald, Edward 1809-1883 .... **NCLC 9**
See also BRW 4; DLB 32; RGEL 2

Fitzgerald, F(rancis) Scott (Key)
1896-1940 ... **SSC 6, 31, 75; TCLC 1, 6,
14, 28, 55, 157; WLC**
See also AAYA 24; AITN 1; AMW; AMWC
2; AMWR 1; BPFB 1; CA 110; 123;
CDALB 1917-1929; DA; DA3; DAB;
DAC; DAM MST, NOV; DLB 4, 9, 86,
219, 273; DLBD 1, 15, 16; DLBY 1981,
1996; EWL 3; EXPN; EXPS; LAIT 3;
MTCW 1, 2; NFS 2, 19, 20; RGAL 4;
RGSF 2; SSFS 4, 15; TUS

Fitzgerald, Penelope 1916-2000 . **CLC 19, 51,
61, 143**
See also BRWS 5; CA 85-88; 190; CAAS
10; CANR 56, 86, 131; CN 7; DLB 14,
194; EWL 3; MTCW 2

Fitzgerald, Robert (Stuart)
1910-1985 .... **CLC 39**
See also CA 1-4R; 114; CANR 1; DLBY
1980

FitzGerald, Robert D(avid)
1902-1987 .... **CLC 19**
See also CA 17-20R; DLB 260; RGEL 2

Fitzgerald, Zelda (Sayre)
1900-1948 .... **TCLC 52**
See also AMWS 9; CA 117; 126; DLBY
1984

Flanagan, Thomas (James Bonner)
1923-2002 .... **CLC 25, 52**
See also CA 108; 206; CANR 55; CN 7;
DLBY 1980; INT CA-108; MTCW 1;
RHW

Flaubert, Gustave 1821-1880 .... **NCLC 2, 10,
19, 62, 66, 135; SSC 11, 60; WLC**
See also DA; DA3; DAB; DAC; DAM
MST, NOV; DLB 119, 301; EW 7; EXPS;
GFL 1789 to the Present; LAIT 2; LMFS
1; NFS 14; RGSF 2; RGWL 2, 3; SSFS
6; TWA

Flavius Josephus
See Josephus, Flavius

Flecker, Herman Elroy
See Flecker, (Herman) James Elroy

Flecker, (Herman) James Elroy
1884-1915 .... **TCLC 43**
See also CA 109; 150; DLB 10, 19; RGEL
2

Fleming, Ian (Lancaster) 1908-1964 . **CLC 3,
30**
See also AAYA 26; BPFB 1; CA 5-8R;
CANR 59; CDBLB 1945-1960; CMW 4;
CPW; DA3; DAM POP; DLB 87, 201;
MSW; MTCW 1, 2; RGEL 2; SATA 9;
TEA; YAW

Fleming, Thomas (James) 1927- ...... **CLC 37**
See also CA 5-8R; CANR 10, 102; INT
CANR-10; SATA 8

Fletcher, John 1579-1625 .... **DC 6; LC 33**
See also BRW 2; CDBLB Before 1660;
DLB 58; RGEL 2; TEA

Gee, Maurice (Gough) 1931- .... **CLC 29**
See also AAYA 42; CA 97-100; CANR 67, 123; CLR 56; CN 7; CWRI 5; EWL 3; MAICYA 2; RGSF 2; SATA 46, 101

Geiogamah, Hanay 1945- .... **NNAL**
See also CA 153; DAM MULT; DLB 175

Gelbart, Larry (Simon) 1928- .... **CLC 21, 61**
See Gelbart, Larry
See also CA 73-76; CANR 45, 94

Gelbart, Larry 1928-
See Gelbart, Larry (Simon)
See also CAD; CD 5

Gelber, Jack 1932-2003 ...... **CLC 1, 6, 14, 79**
See also CA 1-4R; 216; CAD; CANR 2; DLB 7, 228

Gellhorn, Martha (Ellis)
1908-1998 .... **CLC 14, 60**
See also CA 77-80; 164; CANR 44; CN 7; DLBY 1982, 1998

Genet, Jean 1910-1986 .. **CLC 1, 2, 5, 10, 14, 44, 46; TCLC 128**
See also CA 13-16R; CANR 18; DA3; DAM DRAM; DFS 10; DLB 72; DLBY 1986; EW 13; EWL 3; GFL 1789 to the Present; GLL 1; LMFS 2; MTCW 1, 2; RGWL 2, 3; TWA

Gent, Peter 1942- .... **CLC 29**
See also AITN 1; CA 89-92; DLBY 1982

Gentile, Giovanni 1875-1944 .... **TCLC 96**
See also CA 119

Gentlewoman in New England, A
See Bradstreet, Anne

Gentlewoman in Those Parts, A
See Bradstreet, Anne

Geoffrey of Monmouth c.
1100-1155 .... **CMLC 44**
See also DLB 146; TEA

George, Jean
See George, Jean Craighead

George, Jean Craighead 1919- .... **CLC 35**
See also AAYA 8; BYA 2, 4; CA 5-8R; CANR 25; CLR 1; 80; DLB 52; JRDA; MAICYA 1, 2; SATA 2, 68, 124; WYA; YAW

George, Stefan (Anton) 1868-1933 . **TCLC 2, 14**
See also CA 104; 193; EW 8; EWL 3

Georges, Georges Martin
See Simenon, Georges (Jacques Christian)

Gerald of Wales c. 1146-c. 1223 ... **CMLC 60**

Gerhardi, William Alexander
See Gerhardie, William Alexander

Gerhardie, William Alexander
1895-1977 .... **CLC 5**
See also CA 25-28R; 73-76; CANR 18; DLB 36; RGEL 2

Gerson, Jean 1363-1429 .... **LC 77**
See also DLB 208

Gersonides 1288-1344 .... **CMLC 49**
See also DLB 115

Gerstler, Amy 1956- .... **CLC 70**
See also CA 146; CANR 99

Gertler, T. .... **CLC 34**
See also CA 116; 121

Gertsen, Aleksandr Ivanovich
See Herzen, Aleksandr Ivanovich

Ghalib .... **NCLC 39, 78**
See Ghalib, Asadullah Khan

Ghalib, Asadullah Khan 1797-1869
See Ghalib
See also DAM POET; RGWL 2, 3

Ghelderode, Michel de 1898-1962 ..... **CLC 6, 11; DC 15**
See also CA 85-88; CANR 40, 77; DAM DRAM; EW 11; EWL 3; TWA

Ghiselin, Brewster 1903-2001 .... **CLC 23**
See also CA 13-16R; CAAS 10; CANR 13; CP 7

Ghose, Aurabinda 1872-1950 .... **TCLC 63**
See Ghose, Aurobindo
See also CA 163

Ghose, Aurobindo
See Ghose, Aurabinda
See also EWL 3

Ghose, Zulfikar 1935- .... **CLC 42**
See also CA 65-68; CANR 67; CN 7; CP 7; EWL 3

Ghosh, Amitav 1956- .... **CLC 44, 153**
See also CA 147; CANR 80; CN 7; WWE 1

Giacosa, Giuseppe 1847-1906 .... **TCLC 7**
See also CA 104

Gibb, Lee
See Waterhouse, Keith (Spencer)

Gibbon, Edward 1737-1794 .... **LC 97**
See also BRW 3; DLB 104; RGEL 2

Gibbon, Lewis Grassic .... **TCLC 4**
See Mitchell, James Leslie
See also RGEL 2

Gibbons, Kaye 1960- .... **CLC 50, 88, 145**
See also AAYA 34; AMWS 10; CA 151; CANR 75, 127; CSW; DA3; DAM POP; DLB 292; MTCW 1; NFS 3; RGAL 4; SATA 117

Gibran, Kahlil 1883-1931 . **PC 9; TCLC 1, 9**
See also CA 104; 150; DA3; DAM POET, POP; EWL 3; MTCW 2

Gibran, Khalil
See Gibran, Kahlil

Gibson, William 1914- .... **CLC 23**
See also CA 9-12R; CAD 2; CANR 9, 42, 75, 125; CD 5; DA; DAB; DAC; DAM DRAM, MST; DFS 2; DLB 7; LAIT 2; MTCW 2; SATA 66; YAW

Gibson, William (Ford) 1948- ... **CLC 39, 63, 186, 192; SSC 52**
See also AAYA 12, 59; BPFB 2; CA 126; 133; CANR 52, 90, 106; CN 7; CPW; DA3; DAM POP; DLB 251; MTCW 2; SCFW 2; SFW 4

Gide, Andre (Paul Guillaume)
1869-1951 ..... **SSC 13; TCLC 5, 12, 36; WLC**
See also CA 104; 124; DA; DA3; DAB; DAC; DAM MST, NOV; DLB 65; EW 8; EWL 3; GFL 1789 to the Present; MTCW 1, 2; RGSF 2; RGWL 2, 3; TWA

Gifford, Barry (Colby) 1946- .... **CLC 34**
See also CA 65-68; CANR 9, 30, 40, 90

Gilbert, Frank
See De Voto, Bernard (Augustine)

Gilbert, W(illiam) S(chwenck)
1836-1911 .... **TCLC 3**
See also CA 104; 173; DAM DRAM, POET; RGEL 2; SATA 36

Gilbreth, Frank B(unker), Jr.
1911-2001 .... **CLC 17**
See also CA 9-12R; SATA 2

Gilchrist, Ellen (Louise) 1935- .. **CLC 34, 48, 143; SSC 14, 63**
See also BPFB 2; CA 113; 116; CANR 41, 61, 104; CN 7; CPW; CSW; DAM POP; DLB 130; EWL 3; EXPS; MTCW 1, 2; RGAL 4; RGSF 2; SSFS 9

Giles, Molly 1942- .... **CLC 39**
See also CA 126; CANR 98

Gill, Eric 1882-1940 .... **TCLC 85**
See Gill, (Arthur) Eric (Rowton Peter Joseph)

Gill, (Arthur) Eric (Rowton Peter Joseph)
1882-1940
See Gill, Eric
See also CA 120; DLB 98

Gill, Patrick
See Creasey, John

Gillette, Douglas .... **CLC 70**

Gilliam, Terry (Vance) 1940- .... **CLC 21, 141**
See Monty Python
See also AAYA 19, 59; CA 108; 113; CANR 35; INT CA-113

Gillian, Jerry
See Gilliam, Terry (Vance)

Gilliatt, Penelope (Ann Douglass)
1932-1993 .... **CLC 2, 10, 13, 53**
See also AITN 2; CA 13-16R; 141; CANR 49; DLB 14

Gilman, Charlotte (Anna) Perkins (Stetson)
1860-1935 ...... **SSC 13, 62; TCLC 9, 37, 117**
See also AMWS 11; BYA 11; CA 106; 150; DLB 221; EXPS; FW; HGG; LAIT 2; MAWW; MTCW 1; RGAL 4; RGSF 2; SFW 4; SSFS 1, 18

Gilmour, David 1946- .... **CLC 35**

Gilpin, William 1724-1804 .... **NCLC 30**

Gilray, J. D.
See Mencken, H(enry) L(ouis)

Gilroy, Frank D(aniel) 1925- .... **CLC 2**
See also CA 81-84; CAD; CANR 32, 64, 86; CD 5; DFS 17; DLB 7

Gilstrap, John 1957(?)- .... **CLC 99**
See also CA 160; CANR 101

Ginsberg, Allen 1926-1997 .... **CLC 1, 2, 3, 4, 6, 13, 36, 69, 109; PC 4, 47; TCLC 120; WLC**
See also AAYA 33; AITN 1; AMWC 1; AMWS 2; BG 2; CA 1-4R; 157; CANR 2, 41, 63, 95; CDALB 1941-1968; CP 7; DA; DA3; DAB; DAC; DAM MST, POET; DLB 5, 16, 169, 237; EWL 3; GLL 1; LMFS 2; MTCW 1, 2; PAB; PFS 5; RGAL 4; TUS; WP

Ginzburg, Eugenia .... **CLC 59**
See Ginzburg, Evgeniia

Ginzburg, Evgeniia 1904-1977
See Ginzburg, Eugenia
See also DLB 302

Ginzburg, Natalia 1916-1991 .... **CLC 5, 11, 54, 70; SSC 65; TCLC 156**
See also CA 85-88; 135; CANR 33; DFS 14; DLB 177; EW 13; EWL 3; MTCW 1, 2; RGWL 2, 3

Giono, Jean 1895-1970 .... **CLC 4, 11; TCLC 124**
See also CA 45-48; 29-32R; CANR 2, 35; DLB 72; EWL 3; GFL 1789 to the Present; MTCW 1; RGWL 2, 3

Giovanni, Nikki 1943- ...... **BLC 2; CLC 2, 4, 19, 64, 117; PC 19; WLCS**
See also AAYA 22; AITN 1; BW 2, 3; CA 29-32R; CAAS 6; CANR 18, 41, 60, 91, 130; CDALBS; CLR 6, 73; CP 7; CSW; CWP; CWRI 5; DA; DA3; DAB; DAC; DAM MST, MULT, POET; DLB 5, 41; EWL 3; EXPP; INT CANR-18; MAICYA 1, 2; MTCW 1, 2; PFS 17; RGAL 4; SATA 24, 107; TUS; YAW

Giovene, Andrea 1904-1998 .... **CLC 7**
See also CA 85-88

Gippius, Zinaida (Nikolaevna) 1869-1945
See Hippius, Zinaida (Nikolaevna)
See also CA 106; 212

Giraudoux, Jean(-Hippolyte)
1882-1944 .... **TCLC 2, 7**
See also CA 104; 196; DAM DRAM; DLB 65; EW 9; EWL 3; GFL 1789 to the Present; RGWL 2, 3; TWA

Gironella, Jose Maria (Pous)
1917-2003 .... **CLC 11**
See also CA 101; 212; EWL 3; RGWL 2, 3

Gissing, George (Robert)
1857-1903 .... **SSC 37; TCLC 3, 24, 47**
See also BRW 5; CA 105; 167; DLB 18, 135, 184; RGEL 2; TEA

Gordon, Mary (Catherine) 1949- .... **CLC 13, 22, 128; SSC 59**
 See also AMWS 4; BPFB 2; CA 102; CANR 44, 92; CN 7; DLB 6; DLBY 1981; FW; INT CA-102; MTCW 1
Gordon, N. J.
 See Bosman, Herman Charles
Gordon, Sol 1923- .... **CLC 26**
 See also CA 53-56; CANR 4; SATA 11
Gordone, Charles 1925-1995 .. **CLC 1, 4; DC 8**
 See also BW 1, 3; CA 93-96; 180; 150; CAAE 180; CAD; CANR 55; DAM DRAM; DLB 7; INT CA-93-96; MTCW 1
Gore, Catherine 1800-1861 .... **NCLC 65**
 See also DLB 116; RGEL 2
Gorenko, Anna Andreevna
 See Akhmatova, Anna
Gorky, Maxim .... **SSC 28; TCLC 8; WLC**
 See Peshkov, Alexei Maximovich
 See also DAB; DFS 9; DLB 295; EW 8; EWL 3; MTCW 2; TWA
Goryan, Sirak
 See Saroyan, William
Gosse, Edmund (William)
 1849-1928 .... **TCLC 28**
 See also CA 117; DLB 57, 144, 184; RGEL 2
Gotlieb, Phyllis (Fay Bloom) 1926- .. **CLC 18**
 See also CA 13-16R; CANR 7; DLB 88, 251; SFW 4
Gottesman, S. D.
 See Kornbluth, C(yril) M.; Pohl, Frederik
Gottfried von Strassburg fl. c.
 1170-1215 .... **CMLC 10**
 See also CDWLB 2; DLB 138; EW 1; RGWL 2, 3
Gotthelf, Jeremias 1797-1854 .... **NCLC 117**
 See also DLB 133; RGWL 2, 3
Gottschalk, Laura Riding
 See Jackson, Laura (Riding)
Gould, Lois 1932(?)-2002 .... **CLC 4, 10**
 See also CA 77-80; 208; CANR 29; MTCW 1
Gould, Stephen Jay 1941-2002 .... **CLC 163**
 See also AAYA 26; BEST 90:2; CA 77-80; 205; CANR 10, 27, 56, 75, 125; CPW; INT CANR-27; MTCW 1, 2
Gourmont, Remy(-Marie-Charles) de
 1858-1915 .... **TCLC 17**
 See also CA 109; 150; GFL 1789 to the Present; MTCW 2
Gournay, Marie le Jars de
 See de Gournay, Marie le Jars
Govier, Katherine 1948- .... **CLC 51**
 See also CA 101; CANR 18, 40, 128; CCA 1
Gower, John c. 1330-1408 .... **LC 76; PC 59**
 See also BRW 1; DLB 146; RGEL 2
Goyen, (Charles) William
 1915-1983 .... **CLC 5, 8, 14, 40**
 See also AITN 2; CA 5-8R; 110; CANR 6, 71; DLB 2, 218; DLBY 1983; EWL 3; INT CANR-6
Goytisolo, Juan 1931- .... **CLC 5, 10, 23, 133; HLC 1**
 See also CA 85-88; CANR 32, 61, 131; CWW 2; DAM MULT; EWL 3; GLL 2; HW 1, 2; MTCW 1, 2
Gozzano, Guido 1883-1916 .... **PC 10**
 See also CA 154; DLB 114; EWL 3
Gozzi, (Conte) Carlo 1720-1806 .... **NCLC 23**
Grabbe, Christian Dietrich
 1801-1836 .... **NCLC 2**
 See also DLB 133; RGWL 2, 3
Grace, Patricia Frances 1937- .... **CLC 56**
 See also CA 176; CANR 118; CN 7; EWL 3; RGSF 2

Gracian y Morales, Baltasar
 1601-1658 .... **LC 15**
Gracq, Julien .... **CLC 11, 48**
 See Poirier, Louis
 See also CWW 2; DLB 83; GFL 1789 to the Present
Grade, Chaim 1910-1982 .... **CLC 10**
 See also CA 93-96; 107; EWL 3
Graduate of Oxford, A
 See Ruskin, John
Grafton, Garth
 See Duncan, Sara Jeannette
Grafton, Sue 1940- .... **CLC 163**
 See also AAYA 11, 49; BEST 90:3; CA 108; CANR 31, 55, 111; CMW 4; CPW; CSW; DA3; DAM POP; DLB 226; FW; MSW
Graham, John
 See Phillips, David Graham
Graham, Jorie 1951- .... **CLC 48, 118; PC 59**
 See also CA 111; CANR 63, 118; CP 7; CWP; DLB 120; EWL 3; PFS 10, 17
Graham, R(obert) B(ontine) Cunninghame
 See Cunninghame Graham, Robert (Gallnigad) Bontine
 See also DLB 98, 135, 174; RGEL 2; RGSF 2
Graham, Robert
 See Haldeman, Joe (William)
Graham, Tom
 See Lewis, (Harry) Sinclair
Graham, W(illiam) S(idney)
 1918-1986 .... **CLC 29**
 See also BRWS 7; CA 73-76; 118; DLB 20; RGEL 2
Graham, Winston (Mawdsley)
 1910-2003 .... **CLC 23**
 See also CA 49-52; 218; CANR 2, 22, 45, 66; CMW 4; CN 7; DLB 77; RHW
Grahame, Kenneth 1859-1932 .... **TCLC 64, 136**
 See also BYA 5; CA 108; 136; CANR 80; CLR 5; CWRI 5; DA3; DAB; DLB 34, 141, 178; FANT; MAICYA 1, 2; MTCW 2; NFS 20; RGEL 2; SATA 100; TEA; WCH; YABC 1
Granger, Darius John
 See Marlowe, Stephen
Granin, Daniil 1918- .... **CLC 59**
 See also DLB 302
Granovsky, Timofei Nikolaevich
 1813-1855 .... **NCLC 75**
 See also DLB 198
Grant, Skeeter
 See Spiegelman, Art
Granville-Barker, Harley
 1877-1946 .... **TCLC 2**
 See Barker, Harley Granville
 See also CA 104; 204; DAM DRAM; RGEL 2
Granzotto, Gianni
 See Granzotto, Giovanni Battista
Granzotto, Giovanni Battista
 1914-1985 .... **CLC 70**
 See also CA 166
Grass, Guenter (Wilhelm) 1927- ... **CLC 1, 2, 4, 6, 11, 15, 22, 32, 49, 88; WLC**
 See Grass, Gunter (Wilhelm)
 See also BPFB 2; CA 13-16R; CANR 20, 75, 93, 133; CDWLB 2; DA; DA3; DAB; DAC; DAM MST, NOV; DLB 75, 124; EW 13; EWL 3; MTCW 1, 2; RGWL 2, 3; TWA
Grass, Gunter (Wilhelm)
 See Grass, Guenter (Wilhelm)
 See also CWW 2
Gratton, Thomas
 See Hulme, T(homas) E(rnest)

Grau, Shirley Ann 1929- .... **CLC 4, 9, 146; SSC 15**
 See also CA 89-92; CANR 22, 69; CN 7; CSW; DLB 2, 218; INT CA-89-92, CANR-22; MTCW 1
Gravel, Fern
 See Hall, James Norman
Graver, Elizabeth 1964- .... **CLC 70**
 See also CA 135; CANR 71, 129
Graves, Richard Perceval
 1895-1985 .... **CLC 44**
 See also CA 65-68; CANR 9, 26, 51
Graves, Robert (von Ranke)
 1895-1985 .. **CLC 1, 2, 6, 11, 39, 44, 45; PC 6**
 See also BPFB 2; BRW 7; BYA 4; CA 5-8R; 117; CANR 5, 36; CDBLB 1914-1945; DA3; DAB; DAC; DAM MST, POET; DLB 20, 100, 191; DLBD 18; DLBY 1985; EWL 3; LATS 1:1; MTCW 1, 2; NCFS 2; RGEL 2; RHW; SATA 45; TEA
Graves, Valerie
 See Bradley, Marion Zimmer
Gray, Alasdair (James) 1934- .... **CLC 41**
 See also BRWS 9; CA 126; CANR 47, 69, 106; CN 7; DLB 194, 261; HGG; INT CA-126; MTCW 1, 2; RGSF 2; SUFW 2
Gray, Amlin 1946- .... **CLC 29**
 See also CA 138
Gray, Francine du Plessix 1930- ..... **CLC 22, 153**
 See also BEST 90:3; CA 61-64; CAAS 2; CANR 11, 33, 75, 81; DAM NOV; INT CANR-11; MTCW 1, 2
Gray, John (Henry) 1866-1934 ...... **TCLC 19**
 See also CA 119; 162; RGEL 2
Gray, Simon (James Holliday)
 1936- .... **CLC 9, 14, 36**
 See also AITN 1; CA 21-24R; CAAS 3; CANR 32, 69; CD 5; DLB 13; EWL 3; MTCW 1; RGEL 2
Gray, Spalding 1941-2004 .... **CLC 49, 112; DC 7**
 See also CA 128; 225; CAD; CANR 74; CD 5; CPW; DAM POP; MTCW 2
Gray, Thomas 1716-1771 .... **LC 4, 40; PC 2; WLC**
 See also BRW 3; CDBLB 1660-1789; DA; DA3; DAB; DAC; DAM MST; DLB 109; EXPP; PAB; PFS 9; RGEL 2; TEA; WP
Grayson, David
 See Baker, Ray Stannard
Grayson, Richard (A.) 1951- .... **CLC 38**
 See also CA 85-88; 210; CAAE 210; CANR 14, 31, 57; DLB 234
Greeley, Andrew M(oran) 1928- ...... **CLC 28**
 See also BPFB 2; CA 5-8R; CAAS 7; CANR 7, 43, 69, 104; CMW 4; CPW; DA3; DAM POP; MTCW 1, 2
Green, Anna Katharine
 1846-1935 .... **TCLC 63**
 See also CA 112; 159; CMW 4; DLB 202, 221; MSW
Green, Brian
 See Card, Orson Scott
Green, Hannah
 See Greenberg, Joanne (Goldenberg)
Green, Hannah 1927(?)-1996 .... **CLC 3**
 See also CA 73-76; CANR 59, 93; NFS 10
Green, Henry .... **CLC 2, 13, 97**
 See Yorke, Henry Vincent
 See also BRWS 2; CA 175; DLB 15; EWL 3; RGEL 2
Green, Julian (Hartridge) 1900-1998
 See Green, Julien
 See also CA 21-24R; 169; CANR 33, 87; CWW 2; DLB 4, 72; MTCW 1

Green, Julien .... CLC 3, 11, 77
See Green, Julian (Hartridge)
See also EWL 3; GFL 1789 to the Present;
MTCW 2

Green, Paul (Eliot) 1894-1981 .... CLC 25
See also AITN 1; CA 5-8R; 103; CANR 3;
DAM DRAM; DLB 7, 9, 249; DLBY
1981; RGAL 4

Greenaway, Peter 1942- .... CLC 159
See also CA 127

Greenberg, Ivan 1908-1973
See Rahv, Philip
See also CA 85-88

Greenberg, Joanne (Goldenberg)
1932- .... CLC 7, 30
See also AAYA 12; CA 5-8R; CANR 14,
32, 69; CN 7; SATA 25; YAW

Greenberg, Richard 1959(?)- .... CLC 57
See also CA 138; CAD; CD 5

Greenblatt, Stephen J(ay) 1943- ...... CLC 70
See also CA 49-52; CANR 115

Greene, Bette 1934- .... CLC 30
See also AAYA 7; BYA 3; CA 53-56; CANR
4; CLR 2; CWRI 5; JRDA; LAIT 4; MAI-
CYA 1, 2; NFS 10; SAAS 16; SATA 8,
102; WYA; YAW

Greene, Gael .... CLC 8
See also CA 13-16R; CANR 10

Greene, Graham (Henry)
1904-1991 .... CLC 1, 3, 6, 9, 14, 18, 27,
37, 70, 72, 125; SSC 29; WLC
See also AITN 2; BPFB 2; BRWR 2; BRWS
1; BYA 3; CA 13-16R; 133; CANR 35,
61, 131; CBD; CDBLB 1945-1960; CMW
4; DA; DA3; DAB; DAC; DAM MST,
NOV; DLB 13, 15, 77, 100, 162, 201,
204; DLBY 1991; EWL 3; MSW; MTCW
1, 2; NFS 16; RGEL 2; SATA 20; SSFS
14; TEA; WLIT 4

Greene, Robert 1558-1592 .... LC 41
See also BRWS 8; DLB 62, 167; IDTP;
RGEL 2; TEA

Greer, Germaine 1939- .... CLC 131
See also AITN 1; CA 81-84; CANR 33, 70,
115, 133; FW; MTCW 1, 2

Greer, Richard
See Silverberg, Robert

Gregor, Arthur 1923- .... CLC 9
See also CA 25-28R; CAAS 10; CANR 11;
CP 7; SATA 36

Gregor, Lee
See Pohl, Frederik

Gregory, Lady Isabella Augusta (Persse)
1852-1932 .... TCLC 1
See also BRW 6; CA 104; 184; DLB 10;
IDTP; RGEL 2

Gregory, J. Dennis
See Williams, John A(lfred)

Grekova, I. .... CLC 59
See Ventsel, Elena Sergeevna
See also CWW 2

Grendon, Stephen
See Derleth, August (William)

Grenville, Kate 1950- .... CLC 61
See also CA 118; CANR 53, 93

Grenville, Pelham
See Wodehouse, P(elham) G(renville)

Greve, Felix Paul (Berthold Friedrich)
1879-1948
See Grove, Frederick Philip
See also CA 104; 141, 175; CANR 79;
DAC; DAM MST

Greville, Fulke 1554-1628 .... LC 79
See also DLB 62, 172; RGEL 2

Grey, Lady Jane 1537-1554 .... LC 93
See also DLB 132

Grey, Zane 1872-1939 .... TCLC 6
See also BPFB 2; CA 104; 132; DA3; DAM
POP; DLB 9, 212; MTCW 1, 2; RGAL 4;
TCWW 2; TUS

Griboedov, Aleksandr Sergeevich
1795(?)-1829 .... NCLC 129
See also DLB 205; RGWL 2, 3

Grieg, (Johan) Nordahl (Brun)
1902-1943 .... TCLC 10
See also CA 107; 189; EWL 3

Grieve, C(hristopher) M(urray)
1892-1978 .... CLC 11, 19
See MacDiarmid, Hugh; Pteleon
See also CA 5-8R; 85-88; CANR 33, 107;
DAM POET; MTCW 1; RGEL 2

Griffin, Gerald 1803-1840 .... NCLC 7
See also DLB 159; RGEL 2

Griffin, John Howard 1920-1980 ..... CLC 68
See also AITN 1; CA 1-4R; 101; CANR 2

Griffin, Peter 1942- .... CLC 39
See also CA 136

Griffith, D(avid Lewelyn) W(ark)
1875(?)-1948 .... TCLC 68
See also CA 119; 150; CANR 80

Griffith, Lawrence
See Griffith, D(avid Lewelyn) W(ark)

Griffiths, Trevor 1935- .... CLC 13, 52
See also CA 97-100; CANR 45; CBD; CD
5; DLB 13, 245

Griggs, Sutton (Elbert)
1872-1930 .... TCLC 77
See also CA 123; 186; DLB 50

Grigson, Geoffrey (Edward Harvey)
1905-1985 .... CLC 7, 39
See also CA 25-28R; 118; CANR 20, 33;
DLB 27; MTCW 1, 2

Grile, Dod
See Bierce, Ambrose (Gwinett)

Grillparzer, Franz 1791-1872 .... DC 14;
NCLC 1, 102; SSC 37
See also CDWLB 2; DLB 133; EW 5;
RGWL 2, 3; TWA

Grimble, Reverend Charles James
See Eliot, T(homas) S(tearns)

Grimke, Angelina (Emily) Weld
1880-1958 .... HR 2
See Weld, Angelina (Emily) Grimke
See also BW 1; CA 124; DAM POET; DLB
50, 54

Grimke, Charlotte L(ottie) Forten
1837(?)-1914
See Forten, Charlotte L.
See also BW 1; CA 117; 124; DAM MULT,
POET

Grimm, Jacob Ludwig Karl
1785-1863 .... NCLC 3, 77; SSC 36
See also DLB 90; MAICYA 1, 2; RGSF 2;
RGWL 2, 3; SATA 22; WCH

Grimm, Wilhelm Karl 1786-1859 .. NCLC 3,
77; SSC 36
See also CDWLB 2; DLB 90; MAICYA 1,
2; RGSF 2; RGWL 2, 3; SATA 22; WCH

Grimmelshausen, Hans Jakob Christoffel
von
See Grimmelshausen, Johann Jakob Christoffel von
See also RGWL 2, 3

Grimmelshausen, Johann Jakob Christoffel
von 1621-1676 .... LC 6
See Grimmelshausen, Hans Jakob Christoffel von
See also CDWLB 2; DLB 168

Grindel, Eugene 1895-1952
See Eluard, Paul
See also CA 104; 193; LMFS 2

Grisham, John 1955- .... CLC 84
See also AAYA 14, 47; BPFB 2; CA 138;
CANR 47, 69, 114, 133; CMW 4; CN 7;
CPW; CSW; DA3; DAM POP; MSW;
MTCW 2

Grosseteste, Robert 1175(?)-1253 . CMLC 62
See also DLB 115

Grossman, David 1954- .... CLC 67
See also CA 138; CANR 114; CWW 2;
DLB 299; EWL 3

Grossman, Vasilii Semenovich
See Grossman, Vasily (Semenovich)
See also DLB 272

Grossman, Vasily (Semenovich)
1905-1964 .... CLC 41
See Grossman, Vasilii Semenovich
See also CA 124; 130; MTCW 1

Grove, Frederick Philip .... TCLC 4
See Greve, Felix Paul (Berthold Friedrich)
See also DLB 92; RGEL 2

Grubb
See Crumb, R(obert)

Grumbach, Doris (Isaac) 1918- . CLC 13, 22,
64
See also CA 5-8R; CAAS 2; CANR 9, 42,
70, 127; CN 7; INT CANR-9; MTCW 2

Grundtvig, Nicolai Frederik Severin
1783-1872 .... NCLC 1
See also DLB 300

Grunge
See Crumb, R(obert)

Grunwald, Lisa 1959- .... CLC 44
See also CA 120

Gryphius, Andreas 1616-1664 .... LC 89
See also CDWLB 2; DLB 164; RGWL 2, 3

Guare, John 1938- .... CLC 8, 14, 29, 67; DC
20
See also CA 73-76; CAD; CANR 21, 69,
118; CD 5; DAM DRAM; DFS 8, 13;
DLB 7, 249; EWL 3; MTCW 1, 2; RGAL
4

Guarini, Battista 1537-1612 .... LC 102

Gubar, Susan (David) 1944- .... CLC 145
See also CA 108; CANR 45, 70; FW;
MTCW 1; RGAL 4

Gudjonsson, Halldor Kiljan 1902-1998
See Halldor Laxness
See also CA 103; 164

Guenter, Erich
See Eich, Gunter

Guest, Barbara 1920- .... CLC 34; PC 55
See also BG 2; CA 25-28R; CANR 11, 44,
84; CP 7; CWP; DLB 5, 193

Guest, Edgar A(lbert) 1881-1959 ... TCLC 95
See also CA 112; 168

Guest, Judith (Ann) 1936- .... CLC 8, 30
See also AAYA 7; CA 77-80; CANR 15,
75; DA3; DAM NOV, POP; EXPN; INT
CANR-15; LAIT 5; MTCW 1, 2; NFS 1

Guevara, Che .... CLC 87; HLC 1
See Guevara (Serna), Ernesto

Guevara (Serna), Ernesto
1928-1967 .... CLC 87; HLC 1
See Guevara, Che
See also CA 127; 111; CANR 56; DAM
MULT; HW 1

Guicciardini, Francesco 1483-1540 ..... LC 49

Guild, Nicholas M. 1944- .... CLC 33
See also CA 93-96

Guillemin, Jacques
See Sartre, Jean-Paul

Guillen, Jorge 1893-1984 . CLC 11; HLCS 1;
PC 35
See also CA 89-92; 112; DAM MULT,
POET; DLB 108; EWL 3; HW 1; RGWL
2, 3

Guillen, Nicolas (Cristobal)
1902-1989 .... **BLC 2; CLC 48, 79; HLC 1; PC 23**
See also BW 2; CA 116; 125; 129; CANR 84; DAM MST, MULT, POET; DLB 283; EWL 3; HW 1; LAW; RGWL 2, 3; WP

Guillen y Alvarez, Jorge
See Guillen, Jorge

Guillevic, (Eugene) 1907-1997 .... CLC 33
See also CA 93-96; CWW 2

Guillois
See Desnos, Robert

Guillois, Valentin
See Desnos, Robert

Guimaraes Rosa, Joao 1908-1967 .... HLCS 2
See Rosa, Joao Guimaraes
See also CA 175; LAW; RGSF 2; RGWL 2, 3

Guiney, Louise Imogen
1861-1920 .... **TCLC 41**
See also CA 160; DLB 54; RGAL 4

Guinizelli, Guido c. 1230-1276 ...... CMLC 49

Guiraldes, Ricardo (Guillermo)
1886-1927 .... **TCLC 39**
See also CA 131; EWL 3; HW 1; LAW; MTCW 1

Gumilev, Nikolai (Stepanovich)
1886-1921 .... **TCLC 60**
See Gumilyov, Nikolay Stepanovich
See also CA 165; DLB 295

Gumilyov, Nikolay Stepanovich
See Gumilev, Nikolai (Stepanovich)
See also EWL 3

Gump, P. Q.
See Card, Orson Scott

Gunesekera, Romesh 1954- .... CLC 91
See also CA 159; CN 7; DLB 267

Gunn, Bill .... CLC 5
See Gunn, William Harrison
See also DLB 38

Gunn, Thom(son William)
1929-2004 . **CLC 3, 6, 18, 32, 81; PC 26**
See also BRWS 4; CA 17-20R; 227; CANR 9, 33, 116; CDBLB 1960 to Present; CP 7; DAM POET; DLB 27; INT CANR-33; MTCW 1; PFS 9; RGEL 2

Gunn, William Harrison 1934(?)-1989
See Gunn, Bill
See also AITN 1; BW 1, 3; CA 13-16R; 128; CANR 12, 25, 76

Gunn Allen, Paula
See Allen, Paula Gunn

Gunnars, Kristjana 1948- .... CLC 69
See also CA 113; CCA 1; CP 7; CWP; DLB 60

Gunter, Erich
See Eich, Gunter

Gurdjieff, G(eorgei) I(vanovich)
1877(?)-1949 .... **TCLC 71**
See also CA 157

Gurganus, Allan 1947- .... CLC 70
See also BEST 90:1; CA 135; CANR 114; CN 7; CPW; CSW; DAM POP; GLL 1

Gurney, A. R.
See Gurney, A(lbert) R(amsdell), Jr.
See also DLB 266

Gurney, A(lbert) R(amsdell), Jr.
1930- .... **CLC 32, 50, 54**
See Gurney, A. R.
See also AMWS 5; CA 77-80; CAD; CANR 32, 64, 121; CD 5; DAM DRAM; EWL 3

Gurney, Ivor (Bertie) 1890-1937 ... TCLC 33
See also BRW 6; CA 167; DLBY 2002; PAB; RGEL 2

Gurney, Peter
See Gurney, A(lbert) R(amsdell), Jr.

Guro, Elena (Genrikhovna)
1877-1913 .... **TCLC 56**
See also DLB 295

Gustafson, James M(oody) 1925- ... CLC 100
See also CA 25-28R; CANR 37

Gustafson, Ralph (Barker)
1909-1995 .... **CLC 36**
See also CA 21-24R; CANR 8, 45, 84; CP 7; DLB 88; RGEL 2

Gut, Gom
See Simenon, Georges (Jacques Christian)

Guterson, David 1956- .... CLC 91
See also CA 132; CANR 73, 126; DLB 292; MTCW 2; NFS 13

Guthrie, A(lfred) B(ertram), Jr.
1901-1991 .... **CLC 23**
See also CA 57-60; 134; CANR 24; DLB 6, 212; SATA 62; SATA-Obit 67

Guthrie, Isobel
See Grieve, C(hristopher) M(urray)

Guthrie, Woodrow Wilson 1912-1967
See Guthrie, Woody
See also CA 113; 93-96

Guthrie, Woody .... CLC 35
See Guthrie, Woodrow Wilson
See also DLB 303; LAIT 3

Gutierrez Najera, Manuel
1859-1895 .... **HLCS 2; NCLC 133**
See also DLB 290; LAW

Guy, Rosa (Cuthbert) 1925- .... CLC 26
See also AAYA 4, 37; BW 2; CA 17-20R; CANR 14, 34, 83; CLR 13; DLB 33; DNFS 1; JRDA; MAICYA 1, 2; SATA 14, 62, 122; YAW

Gwendolyn
See Bennett, (Enoch) Arnold

H. D. .... CLC 3, 8, 14, 31, 34, 73; PC 5
See Doolittle, Hilda

H. de V.
See Buchan, John

Haavikko, Paavo Juhani 1931- .. CLC 18, 34
See also CA 106; CWW 2; EWL 3

Habbema, Koos
See Heijermans, Herman

Habermas, Juergen 1929- .... CLC 104
See also CA 109; CANR 85; DLB 242

Habermas, Jurgen
See Habermas, Juergen

Hacker, Marilyn 1942- ...... CLC 5, 9, 23, 72, 91; PC 47
See also CA 77-80; CANR 68, 129; CP 7; CWP; DAM POET; DLB 120, 282; FW; GLL 2; PFS 19

Hadewijch of Antwerp fl. 1250- ... CMLC 61
See also RGWL 3

Hadrian 76-138 .... CMLC 52

Haeckel, Ernst Heinrich (Philipp August)
1834-1919 .... **TCLC 83**
See also CA 157

Hafiz c. 1326-1389(?) .... CMLC 34
See also RGWL 2, 3

Hagedorn, Jessica T(arahata)
1949- .... **CLC 185**
See also CA 139; CANR 69; CWP; RGAL 4

Haggard, H(enry) Rider
1856-1925 .... **TCLC 11**
See also BRWS 3; BYA 4, 5; CA 108; 148; CANR 112; DLB 70, 156, 174, 178; FANT; LMFS 2; MTCW 2; RGEL 2; RHW; SATA 16; SCFW; SFW 4; SUFW 1; WLIT 4

Hagiosy, L.
See Larbaud, Valery (Nicolas)

Hagiwara, Sakutaro 1886-1942 .... PC 18; TCLC 60
See Hagiwara Sakutaro
See also CA 154; RGWL 3

Hagiwara Sakutaro
See Hagiwara, Sakutaro
See also EWL 3

Haig, Fenil
See Ford, Ford Madox

Haig-Brown, Roderick (Langmere)
1908-1976 .... **CLC 21**
See also CA 5-8R; 69-72; CANR 4, 38, 83; CLR 31; CWRI 5; DLB 88; MAICYA 1, 2; SATA 12

Haight, Rip
See Carpenter, John (Howard)

Hailey, Arthur 1920- .... CLC 5
See also AITN 2; BEST 90:3; BPFB 2; CA 1-4R; CANR 2, 36, 75; CCA 1; CN 7; CPW; DAM NOV, POP; DLB 88; DLBY 1982; MTCW 1, 2

Hailey, Elizabeth Forsythe 1938- ..... CLC 40
See also CA 93-96, 188; CAAE 188; CAAS 1; CANR 15, 48; INT CANR-15

Haines, John (Meade) 1924- .... CLC 58
See also AMWS 12; CA 17-20R; CANR 13, 34; CSW; DLB 5, 212

Hakluyt, Richard 1552-1616 .... LC 31
See also DLB 136; RGEL 2

Haldeman, Joe (William) 1943- .... CLC 61
See Graham, Robert
See also AAYA 38; CA 53-56, 179; CAAE 179; CAAS 25; CANR 6, 70, 72, 130; DLB 8; INT CANR-6; SCFW 2; SFW 4

Hale, Janet Campbell 1947- .... NNAL
See also CA 49-52; CANR 45, 75; DAM MULT; DLB 175; MTCW 2

Hale, Sarah Josepha (Buell)
1788-1879 .... **NCLC 75**
See also DLB 1, 42, 73, 243

Halevy, Elie 1870-1937 .... TCLC 104

Haley, Alex(ander Murray Palmer)
1921-1992 .... **BLC 2; CLC 8, 12, 76; TCLC 147**
See also AAYA 26; BPFB 2; BW 2, 3; CA 77-80; 136; CANR 61; CDALBS; CPW; CSW; DA; DA3; DAB; DAC; DAM MST, MULT, POP; DLB 38; LAIT 5; MTCW 1, 2; NFS 9

Haliburton, Thomas Chandler
1796-1865 .... **NCLC 15**
See also DLB 11, 99; RGEL 2; RGSF 2

Hall, Donald (Andrew, Jr.) 1928- ...... CLC 1, 13, 37, 59, 151
See also CA 5-8R; CAAS 7; CANR 2, 44, 64, 106, 133; CP 7; DAM POET; DLB 5; MTCW 1; RGAL 4; SATA 23, 97

Hall, Frederic Sauser
See Sauser-Hall, Frederic

Hall, James
See Kuttner, Henry

Hall, James Norman 1887-1951 ..... TCLC 23
See also CA 123; 173; LAIT 1; RHW 1; SATA 21

Hall, Joseph 1574-1656 .... LC 91
See also DLB 121, 151; RGEL 2

Hall, (Marguerite) Radclyffe
1880-1943 .... **TCLC 12**
See also BRWS 6; CA 110; 150; CANR 83; DLB 191; MTCW 2; RGEL 2; RHW

Hall, Rodney 1935- .... CLC 51
See also CA 109; CANR 69; CN 7; CP 7; DLB 289

Hallam, Arthur Henry
1811-1833 .... **NCLC 110**
See also DLB 32

Halldor Laxness .... CLC 25
See Gudjonsson, Halldor Kiljan
See also DLB 293; EW 12; EWL 3; RGWL 2, 3

Halleck, Fitz-Greene 1790-1867 .... NCLC 47
See also DLB 3, 250; RGAL 4

Halliday, Michael
See Creasey, John

Halpern, Daniel 1945- .... CLC 14
See also CA 33-36R; CANR 93; CP 7

Harte, (Francis) Bret(t)
1836(?)-1902 ... **SSC 8, 59; TCLC 1, 25; WLC**
See also AMWS 2; CA 104; 140; CANR 80; CDALB 1865-1917; DA; DA3; DAC; DAM MST; DLB 12, 64, 74, 79, 186; EXPS; LAIT 2; RGAL 4; RGSF 2; SATA 26; SSFS 3; TUS

Hartley, L(eslie) P(oles) 1895-1972 ... **CLC 2, 22**
See also BRWS 7; CA 45-48; 37-40R; CANR 33; DLB 15, 139; EWL 3; HGG; MTCW 1, 2; RGEL 2; RGSF 2; SUFW 1

Hartman, Geoffrey H. 1929- .... **CLC 27**
See also CA 117; 125; CANR 79; DLB 67

Hartman, Sadakichi 1869-1944 ... **TCLC 73**
See also CA 157; DLB 54

Hartmann von Aue c. 1170-c. 1210 .... **CMLC 15**
See also CDWLB 2; DLB 138; RGWL 2, 3

Hartog, Jan de
See de Hartog, Jan

Haruf, Kent 1943- .... **CLC 34**
See also AAYA 44; CA 149; CANR 91, 131

Harvey, Caroline
See Trollope, Joanna

Harvey, Gabriel 1550(?)-1631 .... **LC 88**
See also DLB 167, 213, 281

Harwood, Ronald 1934- .... **CLC 32**
See also CA 1-4R; CANR 4, 55; CBD; CD 5; DAM DRAM, MST; DLB 13

Hasegawa Tatsunosuke
See Futabatei, Shimei

Hasek, Jaroslav (Matej Frantisek)
1883-1923 .... **SSC 69; TCLC 4**
See also CA 104; 129; CDWLB 4; DLB 215; EW 9; EWL 3; MTCW 1, 2; RGSF 2; RGWL 2, 3

Hass, Robert 1941- ... **CLC 18, 39, 99; PC 16**
See also AMWS 6; CA 111; CANR 30, 50, 71; CP 7; DLB 105, 206; EWL 3; RGAL 4; SATA 94

Hastings, Hudson
See Kuttner, Henry

Hastings, Selina .... **CLC 44**

Hathorne, John 1641-1717 .... **LC 38**

Hatteras, Amelia
See Mencken, H(enry) L(ouis)

Hatteras, Owen .... **TCLC 18**
See Mencken, H(enry) L(ouis); Nathan, George Jean

Hauptmann, Gerhart (Johann Robert)
1862-1946 .... **SSC 37; TCLC 4**
See also CA 104; 153; CDWLB 2; DAM DRAM; DLB 66, 118; EW 8; EWL 3; RGSF 2; RGWL 2, 3; TWA

Havel, Vaclav 1936- ..... **CLC 25, 58, 65, 123; DC 6**
See also CA 104; CANR 36, 63, 124; CD-WLB 4; CWW 2; DA3; DAM DRAM; DFS 10; DLB 232; EWL 3; LMFS 2; MTCW 1, 2; RGWL 3

Haviaras, Stratis .... **CLC 33**
See Chaviaras, Strates

Hawes, Stephen 1475(?)-1529(?) .... **LC 17**
See also DLB 132; RGEL 2

Hawkes, John (Clendennin Burne, Jr.)
1925-1998 .. **CLC 1, 2, 3, 4, 7, 9, 14, 15, 27, 49**
See also BPFB 2; CA 1-4R; 167; CANR 2, 47, 64; CN 7; DLB 2, 7, 227; DLBY 1980, 1998; EWL 3; MTCW 1, 2; RGAL 4

Hawking, S. W.
See Hawking, Stephen W(illiam)

Hawking, Stephen W(illiam) 1942- . **CLC 63, 105**
See also AAYA 13; BEST 89:1; CA 126; 129; CANR 48, 115; CPW; DA3; MTCW 2

Hawkins, Anthony Hope
See Hope, Anthony

Hawthorne, Julian 1846-1934 .... **TCLC 25**
See also CA 165; HGG

Hawthorne, Nathaniel 1804-1864 ... **NCLC 2, 10, 17, 23, 39, 79, 95; SSC 3, 29, 39; WLC**
See also AAYA 18; AMW; AMWC 1; AMWR 1; BPFB 2; BYA 3; CDALB 1640-1865; DA; DA3; DAB; DAC; DAM MST, NOV; DLB 1, 74, 183, 223, 269; EXPN; EXPS; HGG; LAIT 1; NFS 1, 20; RGAL 4; RGSF 2; SSFS 1, 7, 11, 15; SUFW 1; TUS; WCH; YABC 2

Haxton, Josephine Ayres 1921-
See Douglas, Ellen
See also CA 115; CANR 41, 83

Hayaseca y Eizaguirre, Jorge
See Echegaray (y Eizaguirre), Jose (Maria Waldo)

Hayashi, Fumiko 1904-1951 .... **TCLC 27**
See Hayashi Fumiko
See also CA 161

Hayashi Fumiko
See Hayashi, Fumiko
See also DLB 180; EWL 3

Haycraft, Anna (Margaret) 1932-
See Ellis, Alice Thomas
See also CA 122; CANR 85, 90; MTCW 2

Hayden, Robert E(arl) 1913-1980 ..... **BLC 2; CLC 5, 9, 14, 37; PC 6**
See also AFAW 1, 2; AMWS 2; BW 1, 3; CA 69-72; 97-100; CABS 2; CANR 24, 75, 82; CDALB 1941-1968; DA; DAC; DAM MST, MULT, POET; DLB 5, 76; EWL 3; EXPP; MTCW 1, 2; PFS 1; RGAL 4; SATA 19; SATA-Obit 26; WP

Haydon, Benjamin Robert
1786-1846 .... **NCLC 146**
See also DLB 110

Hayek, F(riedrich) A(ugust von)
1899-1992 .... **TCLC 109**
See also CA 93-96; 137; CANR 20; MTCW 1, 2

Hayford, J(oseph) E(phraim) Casely
See Casely-Hayford, J(oseph) E(phraim)

Hayman, Ronald 1932- .... **CLC 44**
See also CA 25-28R; CANR 18, 50, 88; CD 5; DLB 155

Hayne, Paul Hamilton 1830-1886 . **NCLC 94**
See also DLB 3, 64, 79, 248; RGAL 4

Hays, Mary 1760-1843 .... **NCLC 114**
See also DLB 142, 158; RGEL 2

Haywood, Eliza (Fowler)
1693(?)-1756 .... **LC 1, 44**
See also DLB 39; RGEL 2

Hazlitt, William 1778-1830 ...... **NCLC 29, 82**
See also BRW 4; DLB 110, 158; RGEL 2; TEA

Hazzard, Shirley 1931- .... **CLC 18**
See also CA 9-12R; CANR 4, 70, 127; CN 7; DLB 289; DLBY 1982; MTCW 1

Head, Bessie 1937-1986 ...... **BLC 2; CLC 25, 67; SSC 52**
See also AFW; BW 2, 3; CA 29-32R; 119; CANR 25, 82; CDWLB 3; DA3; DAM MULT; DLB 117, 225; EWL 3; EXPS; FW; MTCW 1, 2; RGSF 2; SSFS 5, 13; WLIT 2; WWE 1

Headon, (Nicky) Topper 1956(?)- ..... **CLC 30**

Heaney, Seamus (Justin) 1939- ...... **CLC 5, 7, 14, 25, 37, 74, 91, 171; PC 18; WLCS**
See also BRWR 1; BRWS 2; CA 85-88; CANR 25, 48, 75, 91, 128; CDBLB 1960 to Present; CP 7; DA3; DAB; DAM POET; DLB 40; DLBY 1995; EWL 3; EXPP; MTCW 1, 2; PAB; PFS 2, 5, 8, 17; RGEL 2; TEA; WLIT 4

Hearn, (Patricio) Lafcadio (Tessima Carlos)
1850-1904 .... **TCLC 9**
See also CA 105; 166; DLB 12, 78, 189; HGG; RGAL 4

Hearne, Samuel 1745-1792 .... **LC 95**
See also DLB 99

Hearne, Vicki 1946-2001 .... **CLC 56**
See also CA 139; 201

Hearon, Shelby 1931- .... **CLC 63**
See also AITN 2; AMWS 8; CA 25-28R; CANR 18, 48, 103; CSW

Heat-Moon, William Least .... **CLC 29**
See Trogdon, William (Lewis)
See also AAYA 9

Hebbel, Friedrich 1813-1863 . **DC 21; NCLC 43**
See also CDWLB 2; DAM DRAM; DLB 129; EW 6; RGWL 2, 3

Hebert, Anne 1916-2000 .... **CLC 4, 13, 29**
See also CA 85-88; 187; CANR 69, 126; CCA 1; CWP; CWW 2; DA3; DAC; DAM MST, POET; DLB 68; EWL 3; GFL 1789 to the Present; MTCW 1, 2; PFS 20

Hecht, Anthony (Evan) 1923- ...... **CLC 8, 13, 19**
See also AMWS 10; CA 9-12R; CANR 6, 108; CP 7; DAM POET; DLB 5, 169; EWL 3; PFS 6; WP

Hecht, Ben 1894-1964 ..... **CLC 8; TCLC 101**
See also CA 85-88; DFS 9; DLB 7, 9, 25, 26, 28, 86; FANT; IDFW 3, 4; RGAL 4

Hedayat, Sadeq 1903-1951 .... **TCLC 21**
See also CA 120; EWL 3; RGSF 2

Hegel, Georg Wilhelm Friedrich
1770-1831 .... **NCLC 46**
See also DLB 90; TWA

Heidegger, Martin 1889-1976 .... **CLC 24**
See also CA 81-84; 65-68; CANR 34; DLB 296; MTCW 1, 2

Heidenstam, (Carl Gustaf) Verner von
1859-1940 .... **TCLC 5**
See also CA 104

Heidi Louise
See Erdrich, Louise

Heifner, Jack 1946- .... **CLC 11**
See also CA 105; CANR 47

Heijermans, Herman 1864-1924 .... **TCLC 24**
See also CA 123; EWL 3

Heilbrun, Carolyn G(old)
1926-2003 .... **CLC 25, 173**
See Cross, Amanda
See also CA 45-48; 220; CANR 1, 28, 58, 94; FW

Hein, Christoph 1944- .... **CLC 154**
See also CA 158; CANR 108; CDWLB 2; CWW 2; DLB 124

Heine, Heinrich 1797-1856 .... **NCLC 4, 54, 147; PC 25**
See also CDWLB 2; DLB 90; EW 5; RGWL 2, 3; TWA

Heinemann, Larry (Curtiss) 1944- .. **CLC 50**
See also CA 110; CAAS 21; CANR 31, 81; DLBD 9; INT CANR-31

Heiney, Donald (William) 1921-1993
See Harris, MacDonald
See also CA 1-4R; 142; CANR 3, 58; FANT

Heinlein, Robert A(nson) 1907-1988 . **CLC 1, 3, 8, 14, 26, 55; SSC 55**
See also AAYA 17; BPFB 2; BYA 4, 13; CA 1-4R; 125; CANR 1, 20, 53; CLR 75; CPW; DA3; DAM POP; DLB 8; EXPS; JRDA; LAIT 5; LMFS 2; MAICYA 1, 2; MTCW 1, 2; RGAL 4; SATA 9, 69; SATA-Obit 56; SCFW; SFW 4; SSFS 7; YAW

Hubbard, L(afayette) Ron(ald)
1911-1986 .... **CLC 43**
See also CA 77-80; 118; CANR 52; CPW;
DA3; DAM POP; FANT; MTCW 2; SFW
4

Huch, Ricarda (Octavia)
1864-1947 .... **TCLC 13**
See also CA 111; 189; DLB 66; EWL 3

Huddle, David 1942- .... **CLC 49**
See also CA 57-60; CAAS 20; CANR 89;
DLB 130

Hudson, Jeffrey
See Crichton, (John) Michael

Hudson, W(illiam) H(enry)
1841-1922 .... **TCLC 29**
See also CA 115; 190; DLB 98, 153, 174;
RGEL 2; SATA 35

Hueffer, Ford Madox
See Ford, Ford Madox

Hughart, Barry 1934- .... **CLC 39**
See also CA 137; FANT; SFW 4; SUFW 2

Hughes, Colin
See Creasey, John

Hughes, David (John) 1930- .... **CLC 48**
See also CA 116; 129; CN 7; DLB 14

Hughes, Edward James
See Hughes, Ted
See also DA3; DAM MST, POET

Hughes, (James Mercer) Langston
1902-1967 ..... **BLC 2; CLC 1, 5, 10, 15,
35, 44, 108; DC 3; HR 2; PC 1, 53;
SSC 6; WLC**
See also AAYA 12; AFAW 1, 2; AMWR 1;
AMWS 1; BW 1, 3; CA 1-4R; 25-28R;
CANR 1, 34, 82; CDALB 1929-1941;
CLR 17; DA; DA3; DAB; DAC; DAM
DRAM, MST, MULT, POET; DFS 6, 18;
DLB 4, 7, 48, 51, 86, 228; EWL 3; EXPP;
EXPS; JRDA; LAIT 3; LMFS 2; MAI-
CYA 1, 2; MTCW 1, 2; PAB; PFS 1, 3, 6,
10, 15; RGAL 4; RGSF 2; SATA 4, 33;
SSFS 4, 7; TUS; WCH; WP; YAW

Hughes, Richard (Arthur Warren)
1900-1976 .... **CLC 1, 11**
See also CA 5-8R; 65-68; CANR 4; DAM
NOV; DLB 15, 161; EWL 3; MTCW 1;
RGEL 2; SATA 8; SATA-Obit 25

Hughes, Ted 1930-1998 . **CLC 2, 4, 9, 14, 37,
119; PC 7**
See Hughes, Edward James
See also BRWC 2; BRWR 2; BRWS 1; CA
1-4R; 171; CANR 1, 33, 66, 108; CLR 3;
CP 7; DAB; DAC; DLB 40, 161; EWL 3;
EXPP; MAICYA 1, 2; MTCW 1, 2; PAB;
PFS 4, 19; RGEL 2; SATA 49; SATA-
Brief 27; SATA-Obit 107; TEA; YAW

Hugo, Richard
See Huch, Ricarda (Octavia)

Hugo, Richard F(ranklin)
1923-1982 .... **CLC 6, 18, 32**
See also AMWS 6; CA 49-52; 108; CANR
3; DAM POET; DLB 5, 206; EWL 3; PFS
17; RGAL 4

Hugo, Victor (Marie) 1802-1885 .... **NCLC 3,
10, 21; PC 17; WLC**
See also AAYA 28; DA; DA3; DAB; DAC;
DAM DRAM, MST, NOV, POET; DLB
119, 192, 217; EFS 2; EW 6; EXPN; GFL
1789 to the Present; LAIT 1, 2; NFS 5,
20; RGWL 2, 3; SATA 47; TWA

Huidobro, Vicente
See Huidobro Fernández, Vicente García
See also DLB 283; EWL 3; LAW

Huidobro Fernández, Vicente García
1893-1948 .... **TCLC 31**
See Huidobro, Vicente
See also CA 131; HW 1

Hulme, Keri 1947- .... **CLC 39, 130**
See also CA 125; CANR 69; CN 7; CP 7;
CWP; EWL 3; FW; INT CA-125

Hulme, T(homas) E(rnest)
1883-1917 .... **TCLC 21**
See also BRWS 6; CA 117; 203; DLB 19

Humboldt, Wilhelm von
1767-1835 .... **NCLC 134**
See also DLB 90

Hume, David 1711-1776 .... **LC 7, 56**
See also BRWS 3; DLB 104, 252; LMFS 1;
TEA

Humphrey, William 1924-1997 .... **CLC 45**
See also AMWS 9; CA 77-80; 160; CANR
68; CN 7; CSW; DLB 6, 212, 234, 278;
TCWW 2

Humphreys, Emyr Owen 1919- .... **CLC 47**
See also CA 5-8R; CANR 3, 24; CN 7;
DLB 15

Humphreys, Josephine 1945- ..... **CLC 34, 57**
See also CA 121; 127; CANR 97; CSW;
DLB 292; INT CA-127

Huneker, James Gibbons
1860-1921 .... **TCLC 65**
See also CA 193; DLB 71; RGAL 4

Hungerford, Hesba Fay
See Brinsmead, H(esba) F(ay)

Hungerford, Pixie
See Brinsmead, H(esba) F(ay)

Hunt, E(verette) Howard, (Jr.)
1918- .... **CLC 3**
See also AITN 1; CA 45-48; CANR 2, 47,
103; CMW 4

Hunt, Francesca
See Holland, Isabelle (Christian)

Hunt, Howard
See Hunt, E(verette) Howard, (Jr.)

Hunt, Kyle
See Creasey, John

Hunt, (James Henry) Leigh
1784-1859 .... **NCLC 1, 70**
See also DAM POET; DLB 96, 110, 144;
RGEL 2; TEA

Hunt, Marsha 1946- .... **CLC 70**
See also BW 2, 3; CA 143; CANR 79

Hunt, Violet 1866(?)-1942 .... **TCLC 53**
See also CA 184; DLB 162, 197

Hunter, E. Waldo
See Sturgeon, Theodore (Hamilton)

Hunter, Evan 1926- .... **CLC 11, 31**
See McBain, Ed
See also AAYA 39; BPFB 2; CA 5-8R;
CANR 5, 38, 62, 97; CMW 4; CN 7;
CPW; DAM POP; DLB 306; DLBY 1982;
INT CANR-5; MSW; MTCW 1; SATA
25; SFW 4

Hunter, Kristin 1931-
See Lattany, Kristin (Elaine Eggleston)
Hunter

Hunter, Mary
See Austin, Mary (Hunter)

Hunter, Mollie 1922- .... **CLC 21**
See McIlwraith, Maureen Mollie Hunter
See also AAYA 13; BYA 6; CANR 37, 78;
CLR 25; DLB 161; JRDA; MAICYA 1,
2; SAAS 7; SATA 54, 106, 139; SATA-
Essay 139; WYA; YAW

Hunter, Robert (?)-1734 .... **LC 7**

Hurston, Zora Neale 1891-1960 .... **BLC 2;
CLC 7, 30, 61; DC 12; HR 2; SSC 4;
TCLC 121, 131; WLCS**
See also AAYA 15; AFAW 1, 2; AMWS 6;
BW 1, 3; BYA 12; CA 85-88; CANR 61;
CDALBS; DA; DA3; DAC; DAM MST,
MULT, NOV; DFS 6; DLB 51, 86; EWL
3; EXPN; EXPS; FW; LAIT 3; LATS 1:1;
LMFS 2; MAWW; MTCW 1, 2; NFS 3;
RGAL 4; RGSF 2; SSFS 1, 6, 11, 19;
TUS; YAW

Husserl, E. G.
See Husserl, Edmund (Gustav Albrecht)

Husserl, Edmund (Gustav Albrecht)
1859-1938 .... **TCLC 100**
See also CA 116; 133; DLB 296

Huston, John (Marcellus)
1906-1987 .... **CLC 20**
See also CA 73-76; 123; CANR 34; DLB
26

Hustvedt, Siri 1955- .... **CLC 76**
See also CA 137

Hutten, Ulrich von 1488-1523 .... **LC 16**
See also DLB 179

Huxley, Aldous (Leonard)
1894-1963 .... **CLC 1, 3, 4, 5, 8, 11, 18,
35, 79; SSC 39; WLC**
See also AAYA 11; BPFB 2; BRW 7; CA
85-88; CANR 44, 99; CDBLB 1914-1945;
DA; DA3; DAB; DAC; DAM MST, NOV;
DLB 36, 100, 162, 195, 255; EWL 3;
EXPN; LAIT 5; LMFS 2; MTCW 1, 2;
NFS 6; RGEL 2; SATA 63; SCFW 2;
SFW 4; TEA; YAW

Huxley, T(homas) H(enry)
1825-1895 .... **NCLC 67**
See also DLB 57; TEA

Huysmans, Joris-Karl 1848-1907 ... **TCLC 7,
69**
See also CA 104; 165; DLB 123; EW 7;
GFL 1789 to the Present; LMFS 2; RGWL
2, 3

Hwang, David Henry 1957- .... **CLC 55, 196;
DC 4, 23**
See also CA 127; 132; CAD; CANR 76,
124; CD 5; DA3; DAM DRAM; DFS 11,
18; DLB 212, 228; INT CA-132; MTCW
2; RGAL 4

Hyde, Anthony 1946- .... **CLC 42**
See Chase, Nicholas
See also CA 136; CCA 1

Hyde, Margaret O(ldroyd) 1917- ..... **CLC 21**
See also CA 1-4R; CANR 1, 36; CLR 23;
JRDA; MAICYA 1, 2; SAAS 8; SATA 1,
42, 76, 139

Hynes, James 1956(?)- .... **CLC 65**
See also CA 164; CANR 105

Hypatia c. 370-415 .... **CMLC 35**

Ian, Janis 1951- .... **CLC 21**
See also CA 105; 187

Ibanez, Vicente Blasco
See Blasco Ibanez, Vicente

Ibarbourou, Juana de 1895-1979 ..... **HLCS 2**
See also DLB 290; HW 1; LAW

Ibarguengoitia, Jorge 1928-1983 ..... **CLC 37;
TCLC 148**
See also CA 124; 113; EWL 3; HW 1

Ibn Battuta, Abu Abdalla
1304-1368(?) .... **CMLC 57**
See also WLIT 2

Ibn Hazm 994-1064 .... **CMLC 64**

Ibsen, Henrik (Johan) 1828-1906 .... **DC 2;
TCLC 2, 8, 16, 37, 52; WLC**
See also AAYA 46; CA 104; 141; DA; DA3;
DAB; DAC; DAM DRAM, MST; DFS 1,
6, 8, 10, 11, 15, 16; EW 7; LAIT 2; LATS
1:1; RGWL 2, 3

Ibuse, Masuji 1898-1993 .... **CLC 22**
See Ibuse Masuji
See also CA 127; 141; MJW; RGWL 3

Ibuse Masuji
See Ibuse, Masuji
See also CWW 2; DLB 180; EWL 3

Ichikawa, Kon 1915- .... **CLC 20**
See also CA 121

Ichiyo, Higuchi 1872-1896 .... **NCLC 49**
See also MJW

Idle, Eric 1943- .... **CLC 21**
See Monty Python
See also CA 116; CANR 35, 91

James, Montague (Rhodes)
1862-1936 .... **SSC 16; TCLC 6**
See James, M. R.
See also CA 104; 203; HGG; RGEL 2;
RGSF 2; SUFW 1

James, P. D. .... **CLC 18, 46, 122**
See White, Phyllis Dorothy James
See also BEST 90:2; BPFB 2; BRWS 4;
CDBLB 1960 to Present; DLB 87, 276;
DLBD 17; MSW

James, Philip
See Moorcock, Michael (John)

James, Samuel
See Stephens, James

James, Seumas
See Stephens, James

James, Stephen
See Stephens, James

James, William 1842-1910 .... **TCLC 15, 32**
See also AMW; CA 109; 193; DLB 270,
284; NCFS 5; RGAL 4

Jameson, Anna 1794-1860 .... **NCLC 43**
See also DLB 99, 166

Jameson, Fredric (R.) 1934- .... **CLC 142**
See also CA 196; DLB 67; LMFS 2

Jami, Nur al-Din 'Abd al-Rahman
1414-1492 .... **LC 9**

Jammes, Francis 1868-1938 .... **TCLC 75**
See also CA 198; EWL 3; GFL 1789 to the
Present

Jandl, Ernst 1925-2000 .... **CLC 34**
See also CA 200; EWL 3

Janowitz, Tama 1957- .... **CLC 43, 145**
See also CA 106; CANR 52, 89, 129; CN
7; CPW; DAM POP; DLB 292

Japrisot, Sebastien 1931- .... **CLC 90**
See Rossi, Jean-Baptiste
See also CMW 4; NFS 18

Jarrell, Randall 1914-1965 .... **CLC 1, 2, 6, 9,
13, 49; PC 41**
See also AMW; BYA 5; CA 5-8R; 25-28R;
CABS 2; CANR 6, 34; CDALB 1941-
1968; CLR 6; CWRI 5; DAM POET;
DLB 48, 52; EWL 3; EXPP; MAICYA 1,
2; MTCW 1, 2; PAB; PFS 2; RGAL 4;
SATA 7

Jarry, Alfred 1873-1907 .... **SSC 20; TCLC 2,
14, 147**
See also CA 104; 153; DA3; DAM DRAM;
DFS 8; DLB 192, 258; EW 9; EWL 3;
GFL 1789 to the Present; RGWL 2, 3;
TWA

Jarvis, E. K.
See Ellison, Harlan (Jay)

Jawien, Andrzej
See John Paul II, Pope

Jaynes, Roderick
See Coen, Ethan

Jeake, Samuel, Jr.
See Aiken, Conrad (Potter)

Jean Paul 1763-1825 .... **NCLC 7**

Jefferies, (John) Richard
1848-1887 .... **NCLC 47**
See also DLB 98, 141; RGEL 2; SATA 16;
SFW 4

Jeffers, (John) Robinson 1887-1962 .. **CLC 2,
3, 11, 15, 54; PC 17; WLC**
See also AMWS 2; CA 85-88; CANR 35;
CDALB 1917-1929; DA; DAC; DAM
MST, POET; DLB 45, 212; EWL 3;
MTCW 1, 2; PAB; PFS 3, 4; RGAL 4

Jefferson, Janet
See Mencken, H(enry) L(ouis)

Jefferson, Thomas 1743-1826 . **NCLC 11, 103**
See also AAYA 54; ANW; CDALB 1640-
1865; DA3; DLB 31, 183; LAIT 1; RGAL
4

Jeffrey, Francis 1773-1850 .... **NCLC 33**
See Francis, Lord Jeffrey

Jelakowitch, Ivan
See Heijermans, Herman

Jelinek, Elfriede 1946- .... **CLC 169**
See also CA 154; DLB 85; FW

Jellicoe, (Patricia) Ann 1927- .... **CLC 27**
See also CA 85-88; CBD; CD 5; CWD;
CWRI 5; DLB 13, 233; FW

Jelloun, Tahar ben 1944- .... **CLC 180**
See Ben Jelloun, Tahar
See also CA 162; CANR 100

Jemyma
See Holley, Marietta

Jen, Gish .... **AAL; CLC 70**
See Jen, Lillian
See also AMWC 2

Jen, Lillian 1956(?)-
See Jen, Gish
See also CA 135; CANR 89, 130

Jenkins, (John) Robin 1912- .... **CLC 52**
See also CA 1-4R; CANR 1; CN 7; DLB
14, 271

Jennings, Elizabeth (Joan)
1926-2001 .... **CLC 5, 14, 131**
See also BRWS 5; CA 61-64; 200; CAAS
5; CANR 8, 39, 66, 127; CP 7; CWP;
DLB 27; EWL 3; MTCW 1; SATA 66

Jennings, Waylon 1937- .... **CLC 21**

Jensen, Johannes V(ilhelm)
1873-1950 .... **TCLC 41**
See also CA 170; DLB 214; EWL 3; RGWL
3

Jensen, Laura (Linnea) 1948- .... **CLC 37**
See also CA 103

Jerome, Saint 345-420 .... **CMLC 30**
See also RGWL 3

Jerome, Jerome K(lapka)
1859-1927 .... **TCLC 23**
See also CA 119; 177; DLB 10, 34, 135;
RGEL 2

Jerrold, Douglas William
1803-1857 .... **NCLC 2**
See also DLB 158, 159; RGEL 2

Jewett, (Theodora) Sarah Orne
1849-1909 .... **SSC 6, 44; TCLC 1, 22**
See also AMW; AMWC 2; AMWR 2; CA
108; 127; CANR 71; DLB 12, 74, 221;
EXPS; FW; MAWW; NFS 15; RGAL 4;
RGSF 2; SATA 15; SSFS 4

Jewsbury, Geraldine (Endsor)
1812-1880 .... **NCLC 22**
See also DLB 21

Jhabvala, Ruth Prawer 1927- . **CLC 4, 8, 29,
94, 138**
See also BRWS 5; CA 1-4R; CANR 2, 29,
51, 74, 91, 128; CN 7; DAB; DAM NOV;
DLB 139, 194; EWL 3; IDFW 3, 4; INT
CANR-29; MTCW 1, 2; RGSF 2; RGWL
2; RHW; TEA

Jibran, Kahlil
See Gibran, Kahlil

Jibran, Khalil
See Gibran, Kahlil

Jiles, Paulette 1943- .... **CLC 13, 58**
See also CA 101; CANR 70, 124; CWP

Jimenez (Mantecon), Juan Ramon
1881-1958 .... **HLC 1; PC 7; TCLC 4**
See also CA 104; 131; CANR 74; DAM
MULT, POET; DLB 134; EW 9; EWL 3;
HW 1; MTCW 1, 2; RGWL 2, 3

Jimenez, Ramon
See Jimenez (Mantecon), Juan Ramon

Jimenez Mantecon, Juan
See Jimenez (Mantecon), Juan Ramon

Jin, Ha .... **CLC 109**
See Jin, Xuefei
See also CA 152; DLB 244, 292; SSFS 17

Jin, Xuefei 1956-
See Jin, Ha
See also CANR 91, 130; SSFS 17

Joel, Billy .... **CLC 26**
See Joel, William Martin

Joel, William Martin 1949-
See Joel, Billy
See also CA 108

John, Saint 10(?)-100 .... **CMLC 27, 63**

John of Salisbury c. 1115-1180 ..... **CMLC 63**

John of the Cross, St. 1542-1591 .... **LC 18**
See also RGWL 2, 3

John Paul II, Pope 1920- .... **CLC 128**
See also CA 106; 133

Johnson, B(ryan) S(tanley William)
1933-1973 .... **CLC 6, 9**
See also CA 9-12R; 53-56; CANR 9; DLB
14, 40; EWL 3; RGEL 2

Johnson, Benjamin F., of Boone
See Riley, James Whitcomb

Johnson, Charles (Richard) 1948- .... **BLC 2;
CLC 7, 51, 65, 163**
See also AFAW 2; AMWS 6; BW 2, 3; CA
116; CAAS 18; CANR 42, 66, 82, 129;
CN 7; DAM MULT; DLB 33, 278;
MTCW 2; RGAL 4; SSFS 16

Johnson, Charles S(purgeon)
1893-1956 .... **HR 3**
See also BW 1, 3; CA 125; CANR 82; DLB
51, 91

Johnson, Denis 1949- . **CLC 52, 160; SSC 56**
See also CA 117; 121; CANR 71, 99; CN
7; DLB 120

Johnson, Diane 1934- .... **CLC 5, 13, 48**
See also BPFB 2; CA 41-44R; CANR 17,
40, 62, 95; CN 7; DLBY 1980; INT
CANR-17; MTCW 1

Johnson, E. Pauline 1861-1913 .... **NNAL**
See also CA 150; DAC; DAM MULT; DLB
92, 175

Johnson, Eyvind (Olof Verner)
1900-1976 .... **CLC 14**
See also CA 73-76; 69-72; CANR 34, 101;
DLB 259; EW 12; EWL 3

Johnson, Fenton 1888-1958 .... **BLC 2**
See also BW 1; CA 118; 124; DAM MULT;
DLB 45, 50

Johnson, Georgia Douglas (Camp)
1880-1966 .... **HR 3**
See also BW 1; CA 125; DLB 51, 249; WP

Johnson, Helene 1907-1995 .... **HR 3**
See also CA 181; DLB 51; WP

Johnson, J. R.
See James, C(yril) L(ionel) R(obert)

Johnson, James Weldon 1871-1938 .. **BLC 2;
HR 3; PC 24; TCLC 3, 19**
See also AFAW 1, 2; BW 1, 3; CA 104;
125; CANR 82; CDALB 1917-1929; CLR
32; DA3; DAM MULT, POET; DLB 51;
EWL 3; EXPP; LMFS 2; MTCW 1, 2;
PFS 1; RGAL 4; SATA 31; TUS

Johnson, Joyce 1935- .... **CLC 58**
See also BG 3; CA 125; 129; CANR 102

Johnson, Judith (Emlyn) 1936- .... **CLC 7, 15**
See Sherwin, Judith Johnson
See also CA 25-28R; 153; CANR 34

Johnson, Lionel (Pigot)
1867-1902 .... **TCLC 19**
See also CA 117; 209; DLB 19; RGEL 2

Johnson, Marguerite Annie
See Angelou, Maya

Johnson, Mel
See Malzberg, Barry N(athaniel)

Johnson, Pamela Hansford
1912-1981 .... **CLC 1, 7, 27**
See also CA 1-4R; 104; CANR 2, 28; DLB
15; MTCW 1, 2; RGEL 2

Johnson, Paul (Bede) 1928- .... **CLC 147**
See also BEST 89:4; CA 17-20R; CANR
34, 62, 100

Kaminsky, Melvin 1926-
  See Brooks, Mel
  See also CA 65-68; CANR 16
Kaminsky, Stuart M(elvin) 1934- ..... **CLC 59**
  See also CA 73-76; CANR 29, 53, 89;
  CMW 4
Kamo no Chomei 1153(?)-1216 .... **CMLC 66**
  See also DLB 203
Kamo no Nagaakira
  See Kamo no Chomei
Kandinsky, Wassily 1866-1944 .... **TCLC 92**
  See also CA 118; 155
Kane, Francis
  See Robbins, Harold
Kane, Henry 1918-
  See Queen, Ellery
  See also CA 156; CMW 4
Kane, Paul
  See Simon, Paul (Frederick)
Kanin, Garson 1912-1999 .... **CLC 22**
  See also AITN 1; CA 5-8R; 177; CAD;
  CANR 7, 78; DLB 7; IDFW 3, 4
Kaniuk, Yoram 1930- .... **CLC 19**
  See also CA 134; DLB 299
Kant, Immanuel 1724-1804 ..... **NCLC 27, 67**
  See also DLB 94
Kantor, MacKinlay 1904-1977 .... **CLC 7**
  See also CA 61-64; 73-76; CANR 60, 63;
  DLB 9, 102; MTCW 2; RHW; TCWW 2
Kanze Motokiyo
  See Zeami
Kaplan, David Michael 1946- .... **CLC 50**
  See also CA 187
Kaplan, James 1951- .... **CLC 59**
  See also CA 135; CANR 121
Karadzic, Vuk Stefanovic
  1787-1864 .... **NCLC 115**
  See also CDWLB 4; DLB 147
Karageorge, Michael
  See Anderson, Poul (William)
Karamzin, Nikolai Mikhailovich
  1766-1826 .... **NCLC 3**
  See also DLB 150; RGSF 2
Karapanou, Margarita 1946- .... **CLC 13**
  See also CA 101
Karinthy, Frigyes 1887-1938 .... **TCLC 47**
  See also CA 170; DLB 215; EWL 3
Karl, Frederick R(obert)
  1927-2004 .... **CLC 34**
  See also CA 5-8R; 226; CANR 3, 44
Karr, Mary 1955- .... **CLC 188**
  See also AMWS 11; CA 151; CANR 100;
  NCFS 5
Kastel, Warren
  See Silverberg, Robert
Kataev, Evgeny Petrovich 1903-1942
  See Petrov, Evgeny
  See also CA 120
Kataphusin
  See Ruskin, John
Katz, Steve 1935- .... **CLC 47**
  See also CA 25-28R; CAAS 14, 64; CANR
  12; CN 7; DLBY 1983
Kauffman, Janet 1945- .... **CLC 42**
  See also CA 117; CANR 43, 84; DLB 218;
  DLBY 1986
Kaufman, Bob (Garnell) 1925-1986 . **CLC 49**
  See also BG 3; BW 1; CA 41-44R; 118;
  CANR 22; DLB 16, 41
Kaufman, George S. 1889-1961 ...... **CLC 38;**
  DC 17
  See also CA 108; 93-96; DAM DRAM;
  DFS 1, 10; DLB 7; INT CA-108; MTCW
  2; RGAL 4; TUS
Kaufman, Sue .... **CLC 3, 8**
  See Barondess, Sue K(aufman)

Kavafis, Konstantinos Petrou 1863-1933
  See Cavafy, C(onstantine) P(eter)
  See also CA 104
Kavan, Anna 1901-1968 .... **CLC 5, 13, 82**
  See also BRWS 7; CA 5-8R; CANR 6, 57;
  DLB 255; MTCW 1; RGEL 2; SFW 4
Kavanagh, Dan
  See Barnes, Julian (Patrick)
Kavanagh, Julie 1952- .... **CLC 119**
  See also CA 163
Kavanagh, Patrick (Joseph)
  1904-1967 .... **CLC 22; PC 33**
  See also BRWS 7; CA 123; 25-28R; DLB
  15, 20; EWL 3; MTCW 1; RGEL 2
Kawabata, Yasunari 1899-1972 ..... **CLC 2, 5,**
  9, 18, 107; SSC 17
  See Kawabata Yasunari
  See also CA 93-96; 33-36R; CANR 88;
  DAM MULT; MJW; MTCW 2; RGSF 2;
  RGWL 2, 3
Kawabata Yasunari
  See Kawabata, Yasunari
  See also DLB 180; EWL 3
Kaye, M(ary) M(argaret)
  1908-2004 .... **CLC 28**
  See also CA 89-92; 223; CANR 24, 60, 102;
  MTCW 1, 2; RHW; SATA 62; SATA-Obit
  152
Kaye, Mollie
  See Kaye, M(ary) M(argaret)
Kaye-Smith, Sheila 1887-1956 .... **TCLC 20**
  See also CA 118; 203; DLB 36
Kaymor, Patrice Maguilene
  See Senghor, Leopold Sedar
Kazakov, Iurii Pavlovich
  See Kazakov, Yuri Pavlovich
  See also DLB 302
Kazakov, Yuri Pavlovich 1927-1982 . **SSC 43**
  See Kazakov, Iurii Pavlovich; Kazakov,
  Yury
  See also CA 5-8R; CANR 36; MTCW 1;
  RGSF 2
Kazakov, Yury
  See Kazakov, Yuri Pavlovich
  See also EWL 3
Kazan, Elia 1909-2003 .... **CLC 6, 16, 63**
  See also CA 21-24R; 220; CANR 32, 78
Kazantzakis, Nikos 1883(?)-1957 .... **TCLC 2,**
  5, 33
  See also BPFB 2; CA 105; 132; DA3; EW
  9; EWL 3; MTCW 1, 2; RGWL 2, 3
Kazin, Alfred 1915-1998 ..... **CLC 34, 38, 119**
  See also AMWS 8; CA 1-4R; CAAS 7;
  CANR 1, 45, 79; DLB 67; EWL 3
Keane, Mary Nesta (Skrine) 1904-1996
  See Keane, Molly
  See also CA 108; 114; 151; CN 7; RHW
Keane, Molly .... **CLC 31**
  See Keane, Mary Nesta (Skrine)
  See also INT CA-114
Keates, Jonathan 1946(?)- .... **CLC 34**
  See also CA 163; CANR 126
Keaton, Buster 1895-1966 .... **CLC 20**
  See also CA 194
Keats, John 1795-1821 ...... **NCLC 8, 73, 121;**
  PC 1; WLC
  See also AAYA 58; BRW 4; BRWR 1; CD-
  BLB 1789-1832; DA; DA3; DAB; DAC;
  DAM MST, POET; DLB 96, 110; EXPP;
  LMFS 1; PAB; PFS 1, 2, 3, 9, 17; RGEL
  2; TEA; WLIT 3; WP
Keble, John 1792-1866 .... **NCLC 87**
  See also DLB 32, 55; RGEL 2
Keene, Donald 1922- .... **CLC 34**
  See also CA 1-4R; CANR 5, 119
Keillor, Garrison .... **CLC 40, 115**
  See Keillor, Gary (Edward)
  See also AAYA 2; BEST 89:3; BPFB 2;
  DLBY 1987; EWL 3; SATA 58; TUS

Keillor, Gary (Edward) 1942-
  See Keillor, Garrison
  See also CA 111; 117; CANR 36, 59, 124;
  CPW; DA3; DAM POP; MTCW 1, 2
Keith, Carlos
  See Lewton, Val
Keith, Michael
  See Hubbard, L(afayette) Ron(ald)
Keller, Gottfried 1819-1890 .... **NCLC 2; SSC**
  26
  See also CDWLB 2; DLB 129; EW; RGSF
  2; RGWL 2, 3
Keller, Nora Okja 1965- .... **CLC 109**
  See also CA 187
Kellerman, Jonathan 1949- .... **CLC 44**
  See also AAYA 35; BEST 90:1; CA 106;
  CANR 29, 51; CMW 4; CPW; DA3;
  DAM POP; INT CANR-29
Kelley, William Melvin 1937- .... **CLC 22**
  See also BW 1; CA 77-80; CANR 27, 83;
  CN 7; DLB 33; EWL 3
Kellogg, Marjorie 1922- .... **CLC 2**
  See also CA 81-84
Kellow, Kathleen
  See Hibbert, Eleanor Alice Burford
Kelly, M(ilton) T(errence) 1947- ...... **CLC 55**
  See also CA 97-100; CAAS 22; CANR 19,
  43, 84; CN 7
Kelly, Robert 1935- .... **SSC 50**
  See also CA 17-20R; CAAS 19; CANR 47;
  CP 7; DLB 5, 130, 165
Kelman, James 1946- .... **CLC 58, 86**
  See also BRWS 5; CA 148; CANR 85, 130;
  CN 7; DLB 194; RGSF 2; WLIT 4
Kemal, Yasar
  See Kemal, Yashar
  See also CWW 2; EWL 3
Kemal, Yashar 1923(?)- .... **CLC 14, 29**
  See also CA 89-92; CANR 44
Kemble, Fanny 1809-1893 .... **NCLC 18**
  See also DLB 32
Kemelman, Harry 1908-1996 .... **CLC 2**
  See also AITN 1; BPFB 2; CA 9-12R; 155;
  CANR 6, 71; CMW 4; DLB 28
Kempe, Margery 1373(?)-1440(?) ... **LC 6, 56**
  See also DLB 146; RGEL 2
Kempis, Thomas a 1380-1471 .... **LC 11**
Kendall, Henry 1839-1882 .... **NCLC 12**
  See also DLB 230
Keneally, Thomas (Michael) 1935- ... **CLC 5,**
  8, 10, 14, 19, 27, 43, 117
  See also BRWS 4; CA 85-88; CANR 10,
  50, 74, 130; CN 7; CPW; DA3; DAM
  NOV; DLB 289, 299; EWL 3; MTCW 1,
  2; NFS 17; RGEL 2; RHW
Kennedy, A(lison) L(ouise) 1965- ... **CLC 188**
  See also CA 168, 213; CAAE 213; CANR
  108; CD 5; CN 7; DLB 271; RGSF 2
Kennedy, Adrienne (Lita) 1931- .... **BLC 2;**
  CLC 66; DC 5
  See also AFAW 2; BW 2, 3; CA 103; CAAS
  20; CABS 3; CANR 26, 53, 82; CD 5;
  DAM MULT; DFS 9; DLB 38; FW
Kennedy, John Pendleton
  1795-1870 .... **NCLC 2**
  See also DLB 3, 248, 254; RGAL 4
Kennedy, Joseph Charles 1929-
  See Kennedy, X. J.
  See also CA 1-4R, 201; CAAE 201; CANR
  4, 30, 40; CP 7; CWRI 5; MAICYA 2;
  MAICYAS 1; SATA 14, 86, 130; SATA-
  Essay 130
Kennedy, William 1928- ... **CLC 6, 28, 34, 53**
  See also AAYA 1; AMWS 7; BPFB 2; CA
  85-88; CANR 14, 31, 76; CN 7; DA3;
  DAM NOV; DLB 143; DLBY 1985; EWL
  3; INT CANR-31; MTCW 1, 2; SATA 57

Kirsch, Sarah 1935- .... **CLC 176**
    See also CA 178; CWW 2; DLB 75; EWL 3
Kirshner, Sidney
    See Kingsley, Sidney
Kis, Danilo 1935-1989 .... **CLC 57**
    See also CA 109; 118; 129; CANR 61; CD-WLB 4; DLB 181; EWL 3; MTCW 1; RGSF 2; RGWL 2, 3
Kissinger, Henry A(lfred) 1923- ..... **CLC 137**
    See also CA 1-4R; CANR 2, 33, 66, 109; MTCW 1
Kivi, Aleksis 1834-1872 .... **NCLC 30**
Kizer, Carolyn (Ashley) 1925- ... **CLC 15, 39, 80**
    See also CA 65-68; CAAS 5; CANR 24, 70; CP 7; CWP; DAM POET; DLB 5, 169; EWL 3; MTCW 2; PFS 18
Klabund 1890-1928 .... **TCLC 44**
    See also CA 162; DLB 66
Klappert, Peter 1942- .... **CLC 57**
    See also CA 33-36R; CSW; DLB 5
Klein, A(braham) M(oses) 1909-1972 .... **CLC 19**
    See also CA 101; 37-40R; DAB; DAC; DAM MST; DLB 68; EWL 3; RGEL 2
Klein, Joe
    See Klein, Joseph
Klein, Joseph 1946- .... **CLC 154**
    See also CA 85-88; CANR 55
Klein, Norma 1938-1989 .... **CLC 30**
    See also AAYA 2, 35; BPFB 2; BYA 6, 7, 8; CA 41-44R; 128; CANR 15, 37; CLR 2, 19; INT CANR-15; JRDA; MAICYA 1, 2; SAAS 1; SATA 7, 57; WYA; YAW
Klein, T(heodore) E(ibon) D(onald) 1947- .... **CLC 34**
    See also CA 119; CANR 44, 75; HGG
Kleist, Heinrich von 1777-1811 ...... **NCLC 2, 37; SSC 22**
    See also CDWLB 2; DAM DRAM; DLB 90; EW 5; RGSF 2; RGWL 2, 3
Klima, Ivan 1931- .... **CLC 56, 172**
    See also CA 25-28R; CANR 17, 50, 91; CDWLB 4; CWW 2; DAM NOV; DLB 232; EWL 3; RGWL 3
Klimentev, Andrei Platonovich
    See Klimentov, Andrei Platonovich
Klimentov, Andrei Platonovich 1899-1951 .... **SSC 42; TCLC 14**
    See Platonov, Andrei Platonovich; Platonov, Andrey Platonovich
    See also CA 108
Klinger, Friedrich Maximilian von 1752-1831 .... **NCLC 1**
    See also DLB 94
Klingsor the Magician
    See Hartmann, Sadakichi
Klopstock, Friedrich Gottlieb 1724-1803 .... **NCLC 11**
    See also DLB 97; EW 4; RGWL 2, 3
Kluge, Alexander 1932- .... **SSC 61**
    See also CA 81-84; DLB 75
Knapp, Caroline 1959-2002 .... **CLC 99**
    See also CA 154; 207
Knebel, Fletcher 1911-1993 .... **CLC 14**
    See also AITN 1; CA 1-4R; 140; CAAS 3; CANR 1, 36; SATA 36; SATA-Obit 75
Knickerbocker, Diedrich
    See Irving, Washington
Knight, Etheridge 1931-1991 ... **BLC 2; CLC 40; PC 14**
    See also BW 1, 3; CA 21-24R; 133; CANR 23, 82; DAM POET; DLB 41; MTCW 2; RGAL 4
Knight, Sarah Kemble 1666-1727 .... **LC 7**
    See also DLB 24, 200
Knister, Raymond 1899-1932 .... **TCLC 56**
    See also CA 186; DLB 68; RGEL 2

Knowles, John 1926-2001 ... **CLC 1, 4, 10, 26**
    See also AAYA 10; AMWS 12; BPFB 2; BYA 3; CA 17-20R; 203; CANR 40, 74, 76, 132; CDALB 1968-1988; CLR 98; CN 7; DA; DAC; DAM MST, NOV; DLB 6; EXPN; MTCW 1, 2; NFS 2; RGAL 4; SATA 8, 89; SATA-Obit 134; YAW
Knox, Calvin M.
    See Silverberg, Robert
Knox, John c. 1505-1572 .... **LC 37**
    See also DLB 132
Knye, Cassandra
    See Disch, Thomas M(ichael)
Koch, C(hristopher) J(ohn) 1932- .... **CLC 42**
    See also CA 127; CANR 84; CN 7; DLB 289
Koch, Christopher
    See Koch, C(hristopher) J(ohn)
Koch, Kenneth (Jay) 1925-2002 .... **CLC 5, 8, 44**
    See also CA 1-4R; 207; CAD; CANR 6, 36, 57, 97, 131; CD 5; CP 7; DAM POET; DLB 5; INT CANR-36; MTCW 2; PFS 20; SATA 65; WP
Kochanowski, Jan 1530-1584 .... **LC 10**
    See also RGWL 2, 3
Kock, Charles Paul de 1794-1871 . **NCLC 16**
Koda Rohan
    See Koda Shigeyuki
Koda Rohan
    See Koda Shigeyuki
    See also DLB 180
Koda Shigeyuki 1867-1947 .... **TCLC 22**
    See Koda Rohan
    See also CA 121; 183
Koestler, Arthur 1905-1983 ... **CLC 1, 3, 6, 8, 15, 33**
    See also BRWS 1; CA 1-4R; 109; CANR 1, 33; CDBLB 1945-1960; DLBY 1983; EWL 3; MTCW 1, 2; NFS 19; RGEL 2
Kogawa, Joy Nozomi 1935- ...... **CLC 78, 129**
    See also AAYA 47; CA 101; CANR 19, 62, 126; CN 7; CWP; DAC; DAM MST, MULT; FW; MTCW 2; NFS 3; SATA 99
Kohout, Pavel 1928- .... **CLC 13**
    See also CA 45-48; CANR 3
Koizumi, Yakumo
    See Hearn, (Patricio) Lafcadio (Tessima Carlos)
Kolmar, Gertrud 1894-1943 .... **TCLC 40**
    See also CA 167; EWL 3
Komunyakaa, Yusef 1947- .. **BLCS; CLC 86, 94; PC 51**
    See also AFAW 2; AMWS 13; CA 147; CANR 83; CP 7; CSW; DLB 120; EWL 3; PFS 5, 20; RGAL 4
Konrad, George
    See Konrad, Gyorgy
Konrad, Gyorgy 1933- .... **CLC 4, 10, 73**
    See also CA 85-88; CANR 97; CDWLB 4; CWW 2; DLB 232; EWL 3
Konwicki, Tadeusz 1926- .... **CLC 8, 28, 54, 117**
    See also CA 101; CAAS 9; CANR 39, 59; CWW 2; DLB 232; EWL 3; IDFW 3; MTCW 1
Koontz, Dean R(ay) 1945- .... **CLC 78**
    See also AAYA 9, 31; BEST 89:3, 90:2; CA 108; CANR 19, 36, 52, 95; CMW 4; CPW; DA3; DAM NOV, POP; DLB 292; HGG; MTCW 1; SATA 92; SFW 4; SUFW 2; YAW
Kopernik, Mikolaj
    See Copernicus, Nicolaus
Kopit, Arthur (Lee) 1937- ...... **CLC 1, 18, 33**
    See also AITN 1; CA 81-84; CABS 3; CD 5; DAM DRAM; DFS 7, 14; DLB 7; MTCW 1; RGAL 4

Kopitar, Jernej (Bartholomaus) 1780-1844 .... **NCLC 117**
Kops, Bernard 1926- .... **CLC 4**
    See also CA 5-8R; CANR 84; CBD; CN 7; CP 7; DLB 13
Kornbluth, C(yril) M. 1923-1958 .... **TCLC 8**
    See also CA 105; 160; DLB 8; SFW 4
Korolenko, V. G.
    See Korolenko, Vladimir Galaktionovich
Korolenko, Vladimir
    See Korolenko, Vladimir Galaktionovich
Korolenko, Vladimir G.
    See Korolenko, Vladimir Galaktionovich
Korolenko, Vladimir Galaktionovich 1853-1921 .... **TCLC 22**
    See also CA 121; DLB 277
Korzybski, Alfred (Habdank Skarbek) 1879-1950 .... **TCLC 61**
    See also CA 123; 160
Kosinski, Jerzy (Nikodem) 1933-1991 ... **CLC 1, 2, 3, 6, 10, 15, 53, 70**
    See also AMWS 7; BPFB 2; CA 17-20R; 134; CANR 9, 46; DA3; DAM NOV; DLB 2, 299; DLBY 1982; EWL 3; HGG; MTCW 1, 2; NFS 12; RGAL 4; TUS
Kostelanetz, Richard (Cory) 1940- .. **CLC 28**
    See also CA 13-16R; CAAS 8; CANR 38, 77; CN 7; CP 7
Kostrowitzki, Wilhelm Apollinaris de 1880-1918
    See Apollinaire, Guillaume
    See also CA 104
Kotlowitz, Robert 1924- .... **CLC 4**
    See also CA 33-36R; CANR 36
Kotzebue, August (Friedrich Ferdinand) von 1761-1819 .... **NCLC 25**
    See also DLB 94
Kotzwinkle, William 1938- ..... **CLC 5, 14, 35**
    See also BPFB 2; CA 45-48; CANR 3, 44, 84, 129; CLR 6; DLB 173; FANT; MAI-CYA 1, 2; SATA 24, 70, 146; SFW 4; SUFW 2; YAW
Kowna, Stancy
    See Szymborska, Wislawa
Kozol, Jonathan 1936- .... **CLC 17**
    See also AAYA 46; CA 61-64; CANR 16, 45, 96
Kozoll, Michael 1940(?)- .... **CLC 35**
Kramer, Kathryn 19(?)- .... **CLC 34**
Kramer, Larry 1935- .... **CLC 42; DC 8**
    See also CA 124; 126; CANR 60, 132; DAM POP; DLB 249; GLL 1
Krasicki, Ignacy 1735-1801 .... **NCLC 8**
Krasinski, Zygmunt 1812-1859 .... **NCLC 4**
    See also RGWL 2, 3
Kraus, Karl 1874-1936 .... **TCLC 5**
    See also CA 104; 216; DLB 118; EWL 3
Kreve (Mickevicius), Vincas 1882-1954 .... **TCLC 27**
    See also CA 170; DLB 220; EWL 3
Kristeva, Julia 1941- .... **CLC 77, 140**
    See also CA 154; CANR 99; DLB 242; EWL 3; FW; LMFS 2
Kristofferson, Kris 1936- .... **CLC 26**
    See also CA 104
Krizanc, John 1956- .... **CLC 57**
    See also CA 187
Krleza, Miroslav 1893-1981 .... **CLC 8, 114**
    See also CA 97-100; 105; CANR 50; CD-WLB 4; DLB 147; EW 11; RGWL 2, 3
Kroetsch, Robert 1927- .. **CLC 5, 23, 57, 132**
    See also CA 17-20R; CANR 8, 38; CCA 1; CN 7; CP 7; DAC; DAM POET; DLB 53; MTCW 1
Kroetz, Franz
    See Kroetz, Franz Xaver

Landis, John 1950- .... **CLC 26**
See also CA 112; 122; CANR 128
Landolfi, Tommaso 1908-1979 .... **CLC 11, 49**
See also CA 127; 117; DLB 177; EWL 3
Landon, Letitia Elizabeth
1802-1838 .... **NCLC 15**
See also DLB 96
Landor, Walter Savage
1775-1864 .... **NCLC 14**
See also BRW 4; DLB 93, 107; RGEL 2
Landwirth, Heinz 1927-
See Lind, Jakov
See also CA 9-12R; CANR 7
Lane, Patrick 1939- .... **CLC 25**
See also CA 97-100; CANR 54; CP 7; DAM
POET; DLB 53; INT CA-97-100
Lang, Andrew 1844-1912 .... **TCLC 16**
See also CA 114; 137; CLR 101;
DLB 98, 141, 184; FANT; MAICYA 1, 2;
RGEL 2; SATA 16; WCH
Lang, Fritz 1890-1976 .... **CLC 20, 103**
See also CA 77-80; 69-72; CANR 30
Lange, John
See Crichton, (John) Michael
Langer, Elinor 1939- .... **CLC 34**
See also CA 121
Langland, William 1332(?)-1400(?) ..... **LC 19**
See also BRW 1; DA; DAB; DAC; DAM
MST, POET; DLB 146; RGEL 2; TEA;
WLIT 3
Langstaff, Launcelot
See Irving, Washington
Lanier, Sidney 1842-1881 . **NCLC 6, 118; PC 50**
See also AMWS 1; DAM POET; DLB 64;
DLBD 13; EXPP; MAICYA 1; PFS 14;
RGAL 4; SATA 18
Lanyer, Aemilia 1569-1645 .... **LC 10, 30, 83; PC 60**
See also DLB 121
Lao-Tzu
See Lao Tzu
Lao Tzu c. 6th cent. B.C.-3rd cent.
B.C. .... **CMLC 7**
Lapine, James (Elliot) 1949- .... **CLC 39**
See also CA 123; 130; CANR 54, 128; INT
CA-130
Larbaud, Valery (Nicolas)
1881-1957 .... **TCLC 9**
See also CA 106; 152; EWL 3; GFL 1789
to the Present
Lardner, Ring
See Lardner, Ring(gold) W(ilmer)
See also BPFB 2; CDALB 1917-1929; DLB
11, 25, 86, 171; DLBD 16; RGAL 4;
RGSF 2
Lardner, Ring W., Jr.
See Lardner, Ring(gold) W(ilmer)
Lardner, Ring(gold) W(ilmer)
1885-1933 .... **SSC 32; TCLC 2, 14**
See Lardner, Ring
See also AMW; CA 104; 131; MTCW 1, 2;
TUS
Laredo, Betty
See Codrescu, Andrei
Larkin, Maia
See Wojciechowska, Maia (Teresa)
Larkin, Philip (Arthur) 1922-1985 ... **CLC 3, 5, 8, 9, 13, 18, 33, 39, 64; PC 21**
See also BRWS 1; CA 5-8R; 117; CANR
24, 62; CDBLB 1960 to Present; DA3;
DAB; DAM MST, POET; DLB 27; EWL
3; MTCW 1, 2; PFS 3, 4, 12; RGEL 2
La Roche, Sophie von
1730-1807 .... **NCLC 121**
See also DLB 94

La Rochefoucauld, Francois
1613-1680 .... **LC 108**
**Larra (y Sanchez de Castro), Mariano Jose
de** 1809-1837 .... **NCLC 17, 130**
Larsen, Eric 1941- .... **CLC 55**
See also CA 132
Larsen, Nella 1893(?)-1963 .... **BLC 2; CLC
37; HR 3**
See also AFAW 1, 2; BW 1; CA 125; CANR
83; DAM MULT; DLB 51; FW; LATS
1:1; LMFS 2
Larson, Charles R(aymond) 1938- ... **CLC 31**
See also CA 53-56; CANR 4, 121
Larson, Jonathan 1961-1996 .... **CLC 99**
See also AAYA 28; CA 156
La Sale, Antoine de c. 1386-1460(?) . **LC 104**
See also DLB 208
Las Casas, Bartolome de
1474-1566 .... **HLCS; LC 31**
See Casas, Bartolome de las
See also LAW
Lasch, Christopher 1932-1994 .... **CLC 102**
See also CA 73-76; 144; CANR 25, 118;
DLB 246; MTCW 1, 2
Lasker-Schueler, Else 1869-1945 ... **TCLC 57**
See Lasker-Schuler, Else
See also CA 183; DLB 66, 124
Lasker-Schuler, Else
See Lasker-Schueler, Else
See also EWL 3
Laski, Harold J(oseph) 1893-1950 . **TCLC 79**
See also CA 188
Latham, Jean Lee 1902-1995 .... **CLC 12**
See also AITN 1; BYA 1; CA 5-8R; CANR
7, 84; CLR 50; MAICYA 1, 2; SATA 2,
68; YAW
Latham, Mavis
See Clark, Mavis Thorpe
Lathen, Emma .... **CLC 2**
See Hennissart, Martha; Latsis, Mary J(ane)
See also BPFB 2; CMW 4; DLB 306
Lathrop, Francis
See Leiber, Fritz (Reuter, Jr.)
Latsis, Mary J(ane) 1927-1997
See Lathen, Emma
See also CA 85-88; 162; CMW 4
Lattany, Kristin
See Lattany, Kristin (Elaine Eggleston)
Hunter
Lattany, Kristin (Elaine Eggleston) Hunter
1931- .... **CLC 35**
See also AITN 1; BW 1; BYA 3; CA 13-
16R; CANR 13, 108; CLR 3; CN 7; DLB
33; INT CANR-13; MAICYA 1, 2; SAAS
10; SATA 12, 132; YAW
Lattimore, Richmond (Alexander)
1906-1984 .... **CLC 3**
See also CA 1-4R; 112; CANR 1
Laughlin, James 1914-1997 .... **CLC 49**
See also CA 21-24R; 162; CAAS 22; CANR
9, 47; CP 7; DLB 48; DLBY 1996, 1997
Laurence, (Jean) Margaret (Wemyss)
1926-1987 . **CLC 3, 6, 13, 50, 62; SSC 7**
See also BYA 13; CA 5-8R; 121; CANR
33; DAC; DAM MST; DLB 53; EWL 3;
FW; MTCW 1, 2; NFS 11; RGEL 2;
RGSF 2; SATA-Obit 50; TCWW 2
Laurent, Antoine 1952- .... **CLC 50**
Lauscher, Hermann
See Hesse, Hermann
Lautreamont 1846-1870 .. **NCLC 12; SSC 14**
See Lautreamont, Isidore Lucien Ducasse
See also GFL 1789 to the Present; RGWL
2, 3
Lautreamont, Isidore Lucien Ducasse
See Lautreamont
See also DLB 217

Lavater, Johann Kaspar
1741-1801 .... **NCLC 142**
See also DLB 97
Laverty, Donald
See Blish, James (Benjamin)
Lavin, Mary 1912-1996 . **CLC 4, 18, 99; SSC
4, 67**
See also CA 9-12R; 151; CANR 33; CN 7;
DLB 15; FW; MTCW 1; RGEL 2; RGSF
2
Lavond, Paul Dennis
See Kornbluth, C(yril) M.; Pohl, Frederik
Lawler, Ray
See Lawler, Raymond Evenor
See also DLB 289
Lawler, Raymond Evenor 1922- .... **CLC 58**
See Lawler, Ray
See also CA 103; CD 5; RGEL 2
Lawrence, D(avid) H(erbert Richards)
1885-1930 .... **PC 54; SSC 4, 19, 73;
TCLC 2, 9, 16, 33, 48, 61, 93; WLC**
See Chambers, Jessie
See also BPFB 2; BRW 7; BRWR 2; CA
104; 121; CANR 131; CDBLB 1914-
1945; DA; DA3; DAB; DAC; DAM MST,
NOV, POET; DLB 10, 19, 36, 98, 162,
195; EWL 3; EXPP; EXPS; LAIT 2, 3;
MTCW 1, 2; NFS 18; PFS 6; RGEL 2;
RGSF 2; SSFS 2, 6; TEA; WLIT 4; WP
Lawrence, T(homas) E(dward)
1888-1935 .... **TCLC 18**
See Dale, Colin
See also BRWS 2; CA 115; 167; DLB 195
Lawrence of Arabia
See Lawrence, T(homas) E(dward)
Lawson, Henry (Archibald Hertzberg)
1867-1922 .... **SSC 18; TCLC 27**
See also CA 120; 181; DLB 230; RGEL 2;
RGSF 2
Lawton, Dennis
See Faust, Frederick (Schiller)
Layamon fl. c. 1200- .... **CMLC 10**
See Laȝamon
See also DLB 146; RGEL 2
Laye, Camara 1928-1980 ..... **BLC 2; CLC 4,
38**
See Camara Laye
See also AFW; BW 1; CA 85-88; 97-100;
CANR 25; DAM MULT; MTCW 1, 2;
WLIT 2
Layton, Irving (Peter) 1912- .... **CLC 2, 15,
164**
See also CA 1-4R; CANR 2, 33, 43, 66,
129; CP 7; DAC; DAM MST, POET;
DLB 88; EWL 3; MTCW 1, 2; PFS 12;
RGEL 2
Lazarus, Emma 1849-1887 ...... **NCLC 8, 109**
Lazarus, Felix
See Cable, George Washington
Lazarus, Henry
See Slavitt, David R(ytman)
Lea, Joan
See Neufeld, John (Arthur)
Leacock, Stephen (Butler)
1869-1944 .... **SSC 39; TCLC 2**
See also CA 104; 141; CANR 80; DAC;
DAM MST; DLB 92; EWL 3; MTCW 2;
RGEL 2; RGSF 2
Lead, Jane Ward 1623-1704 .... **LC 72**
See also DLB 131
Leapor, Mary 1722-1746 .... **LC 80**
See also DLB 109
Lear, Edward 1812-1888 .... **NCLC 3**
See also AAYA 48; BRW 5; CLR 1, 75;
DLB 32, 163, 166; MAICYA 1, 2; RGEL
2; SATA 18, 100; WCH; WP
Lear, Norman (Milton) 1922- .... **CLC 12**
See also CA 73-76

Malouf, (George Joseph) David
1934- .... **CLC 28, 86**
See also CA 124; CANR 50, 76; CN 7; CP
7; DLB 289; EWL 3; MTCW 2

Malraux, (Georges-)Andre
1901-1976 .... **CLC 1, 4, 9, 13, 15, 57**
See also BPFB 2; CA 21-22; 69-72; CANR
34, 58; CAP 2; DA3; DAM NOV; DLB
72; EW 12; EWL 3; GFL 1789 to the
Present; MTCW 1, 2; RGWL 2, 3; TWA

Malthus, Thomas Robert
1766-1834 .... **NCLC 145**
See also DLB 107, 158; RGEL 2

Malzberg, Barry N(athaniel) 1939- ... **CLC 7**
See also CA 61-64; CAAS 4; CANR 16;
CMW 4; DLB 8; SFW 4

Mamet, David (Alan) 1947- .. **CLC 9, 15, 34,
46, 91, 166; DC 4, 24**
See also AAYA 3; CA 81-84; CABS 3;
CANR 15, 41, 67, 72, 129; CD 5; DA3;
DAM DRAM; DFS 2, 3, 6, 12, 15; DLB
7; EWL 3; IDFW 4; MTCW 1, 2; RGAL
4

Mamoulian, Rouben (Zachary)
1897-1987 .... **CLC 16**
See also CA 25-28R; 124; CANR 85

Mandelshtam, Osip
See Mandelstam, Osip (Emilievich)
See also EW 10; EWL 3; RGWL 2, 3

Mandelstam, Osip (Emilievich)
1891(?)-1943(?) .... **PC 14; TCLC 2, 6**
See Mandelshtam, Osip
See also CA 104; 150; MTCW 2; TWA

Mander, (Mary) Jane 1877-1949 ... **TCLC 31**
See also CA 162; RGEL 2

Mandeville, Bernard 1670-1733 .... **LC 82**
See also DLB 101

Mandeville, Sir John fl. 1350- ...... **CMLC 19**
See also DLB 146

Mandiargues, Andre Pieyre de .... **CLC 41**
See Pieyre de Mandiargues, Andre
See also DLB 83

Mandrake, Ethel Belle
See Thurman, Wallace (Henry)

Mangan, James Clarence
1803-1849 .... **NCLC 27**
See also RGEL 2

Maniere, J.-E.
See Giraudoux, Jean(-Hippolyte)

Mankiewicz, Herman (Jacob)
1897-1953 .... **TCLC 85**
See also CA 120; 169; DLB 26; IDFW 3, 4

Manley, (Mary) Delariviere
1672(?)-1724 .... **LC 1, 42**
See also DLB 39, 80; RGEL 2

Mann, Abel
See Creasey, John

Mann, Emily 1952- .... **DC 7**
See also CA 130; CAD; CANR 55; CD 5;
CWD; DLB 266

Mann, (Luiz) Heinrich 1871-1950 ... **TCLC 9**
See also CA 106; 164, 181; DLB 66, 118;
EW 8; EWL 3; RGWL 2, 3

Mann, (Paul) Thomas 1875-1955 .... **SSC 5,
70; TCLC 2, 8, 14, 21, 35, 44, 60;
WLC**
See also BPFB 2; CA 104; 128; CANR 133;
CDWLB 2; DA; DA3; DAB; DAC; DAM
MST, NOV; DLB 66; EW 9; EWL 3; GLL
1; LATS 1:1; LMFS 1; MTCW 1, 2; NFS
17; RGSF 2; RGWL 2, 3; SSFS 4, 9;
TWA

Mannheim, Karl 1893-1947 .... **TCLC 65**
See also CA 204

Manning, David
See Faust, Frederick (Schiller)
See also TCWW 2

Manning, Frederic 1882-1935 .... **TCLC 25**
See also CA 124; 216; DLB 260

Manning, Olivia 1915-1980 .... **CLC 5, 19**
See also CA 5-8R; 101; CANR 29; EWL 3;
FW; MTCW 1; RGEL 2

Mano, D. Keith 1942- .... **CLC 2, 10**
See also CA 25-28R; CAAS 6; CANR 26,
57; DLB 6

Mansfield, Katherine . **SSC 9, 23, 38; TCLC
2, 8, 39; WLC**
See Beauchamp, Kathleen Mansfield
See also BPFB 2; BRW 7; DAB; DLB 162;
EWL 3; EXPS; FW; GLL 1; RGEL 2;
RGSF 2; SSFS 2, 8, 10, 11; WWE 1

Manso, Peter 1940- .... **CLC 39**
See also CA 29-32R; CANR 44

Mantecon, Juan Jimenez
See Jimenez (Mantecon), Juan Ramon

Mantel, Hilary (Mary) 1952- .... **CLC 144**
See also CA 125; CANR 54, 101; CN 7;
DLB 271; RHW

Manton, Peter
See Creasey, John

Man Without a Spleen, A
See Chekhov, Anton (Pavlovich)

Manzoni, Alessandro 1785-1873 ... **NCLC 29,
98**
See also EW 5; RGWL 2, 3; TWA

Map, Walter 1140-1209 .... **CMLC 32**

Mapu, Abraham (ben Jekutiel)
1808-1867 .... **NCLC 18**

Mara, Sally
See Queneau, Raymond

Maracle, Lee 1950- .... **NNAL**
See also CA 149

Marat, Jean Paul 1743-1793 .... **LC 10**

Marcel, Gabriel Honore 1889-1973 . **CLC 15**
See also CA 102; 45-48; EWL 3; MTCW 1,
2

March, William 1893-1954 .... **TCLC 96**
See also CA 216

Marchbanks, Samuel
See Davies, (William) Robertson
See also CCA 1

Marchi, Giacomo
See Bassani, Giorgio

Marcus Aurelius
See Aurelius, Marcus
See also AW 2

Marguerite
See de Navarre, Marguerite

Marguerite d'Angouleme
See de Navarre, Marguerite
See also GFL Beginnings to 1789

Marguerite de Navarre
See de Navarre, Marguerite
See also RGWL 2, 3

Margulies, Donald 1954- .... **CLC 76**
See also AAYA 57; CA 200; DFS 13; DLB
228

Marie de France c. 12th cent. - ..... **CMLC 8;
PC 22**
See also DLB 208; FW; RGWL 2, 3

Marie de l'Incarnation 1599-1672 ...... **LC 10**

Marier, Captain Victor
See Griffith, D(avid Lewelyn) W(ark)

Mariner, Scott
See Pohl, Frederik

Marinetti, Filippo Tommaso
1876-1944 .... **TCLC 10**
See also CA 107; DLB 114, 264; EW 9;
EWL 3

Marivaux, Pierre Carlet de Chamblain de
1688-1763 .... **DC 7; LC 4**
See also GFL Beginnings to 1789; RGWL
2, 3; TWA

Markandaya, Kamala .... **CLC 8, 38**
See Taylor, Kamala (Purnaiya)
See also BYA 13; CN 7; EWL 3

Markfield, Wallace 1926-2002 .... **CLC 8**
See also CA 69-72; 208; CAAS 3; CN 7;
DLB 2, 28; DLBY 2002

Markham, Edwin 1852-1940 .... **TCLC 47**
See also CA 160; DLB 54, 186; RGAL 4

Markham, Robert
See Amis, Kingsley (William)

Markoosie .... **NNAL**
See Patsauq, Markoosie
See also CLR 23; DAM MULT

Marks, J
See Highwater, Jamake (Mamake)

Marks, J.
See Highwater, Jamake (Mamake)

Marks-Highwater, J
See Highwater, Jamake (Mamake)

Marks-Highwater, J.
See Highwater, Jamake (Mamake)

Markson, David M(errill) 1927- .... **CLC 67**
See also CA 49-52; CANR 1, 91; CN 7

Marlatt, Daphne (Buckle) 1942- .... **CLC 168**
See also CA 25-28R; CANR 17, 39; CN 7;
CP 7; CWP; DLB 60; FW

Marley, Bob .... **CLC 17**
See Marley, Robert Nesta

Marley, Robert Nesta 1945-1981
See Marley, Bob
See also CA 107; 103

Marlowe, Christopher 1564-1593 . **DC 1; LC
22, 47; PC 57; WLC**
See also BRW 1; BRWR 1; CDBLB Before
1660; DA; DA3; DAB; DAC; DAM
DRAM, MST; DFS 1, 5, 13; DLB 62;
EXPP; LMFS 1; RGEL 2; TEA; WLIT 3

Marlowe, Stephen 1928- .... **CLC 70**
See Queen, Ellery
See also CA 13-16R; CANR 6, 55; CMW
4; SFW 4

Marmion, Shakerley 1603-1639 .... **LC 89**
See also DLB 58; RGEL 2

Marmontel, Jean-Francois 1723-1799 .. **LC 2**

Maron, Monika 1941- .... **CLC 165**
See also CA 201

Marquand, John P(hillips)
1893-1960 .... **CLC 2, 10**
See also AMW; BPFB 2; CA 85-88; CANR
73; CMW 4; DLB 9, 102; EWL 3; MTCW
2; RGAL 4

Marques, Rene 1919-1979 .. **CLC 96; HLC 2**
See also CA 97-100; 85-88; CANR 78;
DAM MULT; DLB 305; EWL 3; HW 1,
2; LAW; RGSF 2

Marquez, Gabriel (Jose) Garcia
See Garcia Marquez, Gabriel (Jose)

Marquis, Don(ald Robert Perry)
1878-1937 .... **TCLC 7**
See also CA 104; 166; DLB 11, 25; RGAL
4

Marquis de Sade
See Sade, Donatien Alphonse Francois

Marric, J. J.
See Creasey, John
See also MSW

Marryat, Frederick 1792-1848 .... **NCLC 3**
See also DLB 21, 163; RGEL 2; WCH

Marsden, James
See Creasey, John

Marsh, Edward 1872-1953 .... **TCLC 99**

Marsh, (Edith) Ngaio 1895-1982 .. **CLC 7, 53**
See also CA 9-12R; CANR 6, 58; CMW 4;
CPW; DAM POP; DLB 77; MSW;
MTCW 1, 2; RGEL 2; TEA

Marshall, Garry 1934- .... **CLC 17**
See also AAYA 3; CA 111; SATA 60

Maxwell, William (Keepers, Jr.)
1908-2000 .... **CLC 19**
See also AMWS 8; CA 93-96; 189; CANR 54, 95; CN 7; DLB 218, 278; DLBY 1980; INT CA-93-96; SATA-Obit 128

May, Elaine 1932- .... **CLC 16**
See also CA 124; 142; CAD; CWD; DLB 44

Mayakovski, Vladimir (Vladimirovich)
1893-1930 .... **TCLC 4, 18**
See Maiakovskii, Vladimir; Mayakovsky, Vladimir
See also CA 104; 158; EWL 3; MTCW 2; SFW 4; TWA

Mayakovsky, Vladimir
See Mayakovski, Vladimir (Vladimirovich)
See also EW 11; WP

Mayhew, Henry 1812-1887 .... **NCLC 31**
See also DLB 18, 55, 190

Mayle, Peter 1939(?)- .... **CLC 89**
See also CA 139; CANR 64, 109

Maynard, Joyce 1953- .... **CLC 23**
See also CA 111; 129; CANR 64

Mayne, William (James Carter)
1928- .... **CLC 12**
See also AAYA 20; CA 9-12R; CANR 37, 80, 100; CLR 25; FANT; JRDA; MAICYA 1, 2; MAICYAS 1; SAAS 11; SATA 6, 68, 122; SUFW 2; YAW

Mayo, Jim
See L'Amour, Louis (Dearborn)
See also TCWW 2

Maysles, Albert 1926- .... **CLC 16**
See also CA 29-32R

Maysles, David 1932-1987 .... **CLC 16**
See also CA 191

Mazer, Norma Fox 1931- .... **CLC 26**
See also AAYA 5, 36; BYA 1, 8; CA 69-72; CANR 12, 32, 66, 129; CLR 23; JRDA; MAICYA 1, 2; SAAS 1; SATA 24, 67, 105; WYA; YAW

Mazzini, Guiseppe 1805-1872 .... **NCLC 34**

McAlmon, Robert (Menzies)
1895-1956 .... **TCLC 97**
See also CA 107; 168; DLB 4, 45; DLBD 15; GLL 1

McAuley, James Phillip 1917-1976 .. **CLC 45**
See also CA 97-100; DLB 260; RGEL 2

McBain, Ed
See Hunter, Evan
See also MSW

McBrien, William (Augustine)
1930- .... **CLC 44**
See also CA 107; CANR 90

McCabe, Patrick 1955- .... **CLC 133**
See also BRWS 9; CA 130; CANR 50, 90; CN 7; DLB 194

McCaffrey, Anne (Inez) 1926- .... **CLC 17**
See also AAYA 6, 34; AITN 2; BEST 89:2; BPFB 2; BYA 5; CA 25-28R, 227; CAAE 227; CANR 15, 35, 55, 96; CLR 49; CPW; DA3; DAM NOV, POP; DLB 8; JRDA; MAICYA 1, 2; MTCW 1, 2; SAAS 11; SATA 8, 70, 116, 152; SATA-Essay 152; SFW 4; SUFW 2; WYA; YAW

McCall, Nathan 1955(?)- .... **CLC 86**
See also AAYA 59; BW 3; CA 146; CANR 88

McCann, Arthur
See Campbell, John W(ood, Jr.)

McCann, Edson
See Pohl, Frederik

McCarthy, Charles, Jr. 1933-
See McCarthy, Cormac
See also CANR 42, 69, 101; CN 7; CPW; CSW; DA3; DAM POP; MTCW 2

McCarthy, Cormac .... **CLC 4, 57, 101**
See McCarthy, Charles, Jr.
See also AAYA 41; AMWS 8; BPFB 2; CA 13-16R; CANR 10; DLB 6, 143, 256; EWL 3; LATS 1:2; TCWW 2

McCarthy, Mary (Therese)
1912-1989 .. **CLC 1, 3, 5, 14, 24, 39, 59; SSC 24**
See also AMW; BPFB 2; CA 5-8R; 129; CANR 16, 50, 64; DA3; DLB 2; DLBY 1981; EWL 3; FW; INT CANR-16; MAWW; MTCW 1, 2; RGAL 4; TUS

McCartney, (James) Paul 1942- . **CLC 12, 35**
See also CA 146; CANR 111

McCauley, Stephen (D.) 1955- .... **CLC 50**
See also CA 141

McClaren, Peter .... **CLC 70**

McClure, Michael (Thomas) 1932- ... **CLC 6, 10**
See also BG 3; CA 21-24R; CAD; CANR 17, 46, 77, 131; CD 5; CP 7; DLB 16; WP

McCorkle, Jill (Collins) 1958- .... **CLC 51**
See also CA 121; CANR 113; CSW; DLB 234; DLBY 1987

McCourt, Frank 1930- .... **CLC 109**
See also AMWS 12; CA 157; CANR 97; NCFS 1

McCourt, James 1941- .... **CLC 5**
See also CA 57-60; CANR 98

McCourt, Malachy 1931- .... **CLC 119**
See also SATA 126

McCoy, Horace (Stanley)
1897-1955 .... **TCLC 28**
See also AMWS 13; CA 108; 155; CMW 4; DLB 9

McCrae, John 1872-1918 .... **TCLC 12**
See also CA 109; DLB 92; PFS 5

McCreigh, James
See Pohl, Frederik

McCullers, (Lula) Carson (Smith)
1917-1967 .... **CLC 1, 4, 10, 12, 48, 100; SSC 9, 24; TCLC 155; WLC**
See also AAYA 21; AMW; AMWC 2; BPFB 2; CA 5-8R; 25-28R; CABS 1, 3; CANR 18, 132; CDALB 1941-1968; DA; DA3; DAB; DAC; DAM MST, NOV; DFS 5, 18; DLB 2, 7, 173, 228; EWL 3; EXPS; FW; GLL 1; LAIT 3, 4; MAWW; MTCW 1, 2; NFS 6, 13; RGAL 4; RGSF 2; SATA 27; SSFS 5; TUS; YAW

McCulloch, John Tyler
See Burroughs, Edgar Rice

McCullough, Colleen 1938(?)- .. **CLC 27, 107**
See also AAYA 36; BPFB 2; CA 81-84; CANR 17, 46, 67, 98; CPW; DA3; DAM NOV, POP; MTCW 1, 2; RHW

McCunn, Ruthanne Lum 1946- .... **AAL**
See also CA 119; CANR 43, 96; LAIT 2; SATA 63

McDermott, Alice 1953- .... **CLC 90**
See also CA 109; CANR 40, 90, 126; DLB 292

McElroy, Joseph 1930- .... **CLC 5, 47**
See also CA 17-20R; CN 7

McEwan, Ian (Russell) 1948- .... **CLC 13, 66, 169**
See also BEST 90:4; BRWS 4; CA 61-64; CANR 14, 41, 69, 87, 132; CN 7; DAM NOV; DLB 14, 194; HGG; MTCW 1, 2; RGSF 2; SUFW 2; TEA

McFadden, David 1940- .... **CLC 48**
See also CA 104; CP 7; DLB 60; INT CA-104

McFarland, Dennis 1950- .... **CLC 65**
See also CA 165; CANR 110

McGahern, John 1934- ... **CLC 5, 9, 48, 156; SSC 17**
See also CA 17-20R; CANR 29, 68, 113; CN 7; DLB 14, 231; MTCW 1

McGinley, Patrick (Anthony) 1937- . **CLC 41**
See also CA 120; 127; CANR 56; INT CA-127

McGinley, Phyllis 1905-1978 .... **CLC 14**
See also CA 9-12R; 77-80; CANR 19; CWRI 5; DLB 11, 48; PFS 9, 13; SATA 2, 44; SATA-Obit 24

McGinniss, Joe 1942- .... **CLC 32**
See also AITN 2; BEST 89:2; CA 25-28R; CANR 26, 70; CPW; DLB 185; INT CANR-26

McGivern, Maureen Daly
See Daly, Maureen

McGrath, Patrick 1950- .... **CLC 55**
See also CA 136; CANR 65; CN 7; DLB 231; HGG; SUFW 2

McGrath, Thomas (Matthew)
1916-1990 .... **CLC 28, 59**
See also AMWS 10; CA 9-12R; 132; CANR 6, 33, 95; DAM POET; MTCW 1; SATA 41; SATA-Obit 66

McGuane, Thomas (Francis III)
1939- .... **CLC 3, 7, 18, 45, 127**
See also AITN 2; BPFB 2; CA 49-52; CANR 5, 24, 49, 94; CN 7; DLB 2, 212; DLBY 1980; EWL 3; INT CANR-24; MTCW 1; TCWW 2

McGuckian, Medbh 1950- .... **CLC 48, 174; PC 27**
See also BRWS 5; CA 143; CP 7; CWP; DAM POET; DLB 40

McHale, Tom 1942(?)-1982 .... **CLC 3, 5**
See also AITN 1; CA 77-80; 106

McIlvanney, William 1936- .... **CLC 42**
See also CA 25-28R; CANR 61; CMW 4; DLB 14, 207

McIlwraith, Maureen Mollie Hunter
See Hunter, Mollie
See also SATA 2

McInerney, Jay 1955- .... **CLC 34, 112**
See also AAYA 18; BPFB 2; CA 116; 123; CANR 45, 68, 116; CN 7; CPW; DA3; DAM POP; DLB 292; INT CA-123; MTCW 2

McIntyre, Vonda N(eel) 1948- .... **CLC 18**
See also CA 81-84; CANR 17, 34, 69; MTCW 1; SFW 4; YAW

McKay, Claude .... **BLC 3; HR 3; PC 2; TCLC 7, 41; WLC**
See McKay, Festus Claudius
See also AFAW 1, 2; AMWS 10; DAB; DLB 4, 45, 51, 117; EWL 3; EXPP; GLL 2; LAIT 3; LMFS 2; PAB; PFS 4; RGAL 4; WP

McKay, Festus Claudius 1889-1948
See McKay, Claude
See also BW 1, 3; CA 104; 124; CANR 73; DA; DAC; DAM MST, MULT, NOV, POET; MTCW 1, 2; TUS

McKuen, Rod 1933- .... **CLC 1, 3**
See also AITN 1; CA 41-44R; CANR 40

McLoughlin, R. B.
See Mencken, H(enry) L(ouis)

McLuhan, (Herbert) Marshall
1911-1980 .... **CLC 37, 83**
See also CA 9-12R; 102; CANR 12, 34, 61; DLB 88; INT CANR-12; MTCW 1, 2

McManus, Declan Patrick Aloysius
See Costello, Elvis

McMillan, Terry (L.) 1951- . **BLCS; CLC 50, 61, 112**
See also AAYA 21; AMWS 13; BPFB 2; BW 2, 3; CA 140; CANR 60, 104, 131; CPW; DA3; DAM MULT, NOV, POP; MTCW 2; RGAL 4; YAW

Mickiewicz, Adam 1798-1855 . **NCLC 3, 101;
PC 38**
See also EW 5; RGWL 2, 3
Middleton, (John) Christopher
1926- .... **CLC 13**
See also CA 13-16R; CANR 29, 54, 117;
CP 7; DLB 40
Middleton, Richard (Barham)
1882-1911 .... **TCLC 56**
See also CA 187; DLB 156; HGG
Middleton, Stanley 1919- .... **CLC 7, 38**
See also CA 25-28R; CAAS 23; CANR 21,
46, 81; CN 7; DLB 14
Middleton, Thomas 1580-1627 ...... **DC 5; LC
33**
See also BRW 2; DAM DRAM, MST; DFS
18; DLB 58; RGEL 2
Migueis, Jose Rodrigues 1901-1980 . **CLC 10**
See also DLB 287
Mikszath, Kalman 1847-1910 .... **TCLC 31**
See also CA 170
Miles, Jack .... **CLC 100**
See also CA 200
Miles, John Russiano
See Miles, Jack
Miles, Josephine (Louise)
1911-1985 .... **CLC 1, 2, 14, 34, 39**
See also CA 1-4R; 116; CANR 2, 55; DAM
POET; DLB 48
Militant
See Sandburg, Carl (August)
Mill, Harriet (Hardy) Taylor
1807-1858 .... **NCLC 102**
See also FW
Mill, John Stuart 1806-1873 .... **NCLC 11, 58**
See also CDBLB 1832-1890; DLB 55, 190,
262; FW 1; RGEL 2; TEA
Millar, Kenneth 1915-1983 .... **CLC 14**
See Macdonald, Ross
See also CA 9-12R; 110; CANR 16, 63,
107; CMW 4; CPW; DA3; DAM POP;
DLB 2, 226; DLBD 6; DLBY 1983;
MTCW 1, 2
Millay, E. Vincent
See Millay, Edna St. Vincent
Millay, Edna St. Vincent 1892-1950 .... **PC 6;
TCLC 4, 49; WLCS**
See Boyd, Nancy
See also AMW; CA 104; 130; CDALB
1917-1929; DA; DA3; DAB; DAC; DAM
MST, POET; DLB 45, 249; EWL 3;
EXPP; MAWW; MTCW 1, 2; PAB; PFS
3, 17; RGAL 4; TUS; WP
Miller, Arthur 1915- ...... **CLC 1, 2, 6, 10, 15,
26, 47, 78, 179; DC 1; WLC**
See also AAYA 15; AITN 1; AMW; AMWC
1; CA 1-4R; CABS 3; CAD; CANR 2,
30, 54, 76, 132; CD 5; CDALB 1941-
1968; DA; DA3; DAB; DAC; DAM
DRAM, MST; DFS 1, 3, 8; DLB 7, 266;
EWL 3; LAIT 1, 4; LATS 1:2; MTCW 1,
2; RGAL 4; TUS; WYAS 1
Miller, Henry (Valentine)
1891-1980 .... **CLC 1, 2, 4, 9, 14, 43, 84;
WLC**
See also AMW; BPFB 2; CA 9-12R; 97-
100; CANR 33, 64; CDALB 1929-1941;
DA; DA3; DAB; DAC; DAM MST, NOV;
DLB 4, 9; DLBY 1980; EWL 3; MTCW
1, 2; RGAL 4; TUS
Miller, Hugh 1802-1856 .... **NCLC 143**
See also DLB 190
Miller, Jason 1939(?)-2001 .... **CLC 2**
See also AITN 1; CA 73-76; 197; CAD;
CANR 130; DFS 12; DLB 7
Miller, Sue 1943- .... **CLC 44**
See also AMWS 12; BEST 90:3; CA 139;
CANR 59, 91, 128; DA3; DAM POP;
DLB 143

Miller, Walter M(ichael, Jr.)
1923-1996 .... **CLC 4, 30**
See also BPFB 2; CA 85-88; CANR 108;
DLB 8; SCFW; SFW 4
Millett, Kate 1934- .... **CLC 67**
See also AITN 1; CA 73-76; CANR 32, 53,
76, 110; DA3; DLB 246; FW; GLL 1;
MTCW 1, 2
Millhauser, Steven (Lewis) 1943- .... **CLC 21,
54, 109; SSC 57**
See also CA 110; 111; CANR 63, 114, 133;
CN 7; DA3; DLB 2; FANT; INT CA-111;
MTCW 2
Millin, Sarah Gertrude 1889-1968 ... **CLC 49**
See also CA 102; 93-96; DLB 225; EWL 3
Milne, A(lan) A(lexander)
1882-1956 .... **TCLC 6, 88**
See also BRWS 5; CA 104; 133; CLR 1,
26; CMW 4; CWRI 5; DA3; DAB; DAC;
DAM MST; DLB 10, 77, 100, 160; FANT;
MAICYA 1, 2; MTCW 1, 2; RGEL 2;
SATA 100; WCH; YABC 1
Milner, Ron(ald) 1938-2004 ..... **BLC 3; CLC
56**
See also AITN 1; BW 1; CA 73-76; CAD;
CANR 24, 81; CD 5; DAM MULT; DLB
38; MTCW 1
Milnes, Richard Monckton
1809-1885 .... **NCLC 61**
See also DLB 32, 184
Milosz, Czeslaw 1911- ...... **CLC 5, 11, 22, 31,
56, 82; PC 8; WLCS**
See also CA 81-84; CANR 23, 51, 91, 126;
CDWLB 4; CWW 2; DA3; DAM MST,
POET; DLB 215; EW 13; EWL 3; MTCW
1, 2; PFS 16; RGWL 2, 3
Milton, John 1608-1674 ..... **LC 9, 43, 92; PC
19, 29; WLC**
See also BRW 2; BRWR 2; CDBLB 1660-
1789; DA; DA3; DAB; DAC; DAM MST,
POET; DLB 131, 151, 281; EFS 1; EXPP;
LAIT 1; PAB; PFS 3, 17; RGEL 2; TEA;
WLIT 3; WP
Min, Anchee 1957- .... **CLC 86**
See also CA 146; CANR 94
Minehaha, Cornelius
See Wedekind, (Benjamin) Frank(lin)
Miner, Valerie 1947- .... **CLC 40**
See also CA 97-100; CANR 59; FW; GLL
2
Minimo, Duca
See D'Annunzio, Gabriele
Minot, Susan 1956- .... **CLC 44, 159**
See also AMWS 6; CA 134; CANR 118;
CN 7
Minus, Ed 1938- .... **CLC 39**
See also CA 185
Mirabai 1498(?)-1550(?) .... **PC 48**
Miranda, Javier
See Bioy Casares, Adolfo
See also CWW 2
Mirbeau, Octave 1848-1917 .... **TCLC 55**
See also CA 216; DLB 123, 192; GFL 1789
to the Present
Mirikitani, Janice 1942- .... **AAL**
See also CA 211; RGAL 4
Mirk, John (?)-c. 1414 .... **LC 105**
See also DLB 146
Miro (Ferrer), Gabriel (Francisco Victor)
1879-1930 .... **TCLC 5**
See also CA 104; 185; EWL 3
Misharin, Alexandr .... **CLC 59**
Mishima, Yukio ... **CLC 2, 4, 6, 9, 27; DC 1;
SSC 4**
See Hiraoka, Kimitake
See also AAYA 50; BPFB 2; GLL 1; MJW;
MTCW 2; RGSF 2; RGWL 2, 3; SSFS 5,
12

Mistral, Frederic 1830-1914 .... **TCLC 51**
See also CA 122; 213; GFL 1789 to the
Present
Mistral, Gabriela
See Godoy Alcayaga, Lucila
See also DLB 283; DNFS 1; EWL 3; LAW;
RGWL 2, 3; WP
Mistry, Rohinton 1952- ... **CLC 71, 196; SSC
73**
See also CA 141; CANR 86, 114; CCA 1;
CN 7; DAC; SSFS 6
Mitchell, Clyde
See Ellison, Harlan (Jay)
Mitchell, Emerson Blackhorse Barney
1945- .... **NNAL**
See also CA 45-48
Mitchell, James Leslie 1901-1935
See Gibbon, Lewis Grassic
See also CA 104; 188; DLB 15
Mitchell, Joni 1943- .... **CLC 12**
See also CA 112; CCA 1
Mitchell, Joseph (Quincy)
1908-1996 .... **CLC 98**
See also CA 77-80; 152; CANR 69; CN 7;
CSW; DLB 185; DLBY 1996
Mitchell, Margaret (Munnerlyn)
1900-1949 .... **TCLC 11**
See also AAYA 23; BPFB 2; BYA 1; CA
109; 125; CANR 55, 94; CDALBS; DA3;
DAM NOV, POP; DLB 9; LAIT 2;
MTCW 1, 2; NFS 9; RGAL 4; RHW;
TUS; WYAS 1; YAW
Mitchell, Peggy
See Mitchell, Margaret (Munnerlyn)
Mitchell, S(ilas) Weir 1829-1914 .... **TCLC 36**
See also CA 165; DLB 202; RGAL 4
Mitchell, W(illiam) O(rmond)
1914-1998 .... **CLC 25**
See also CA 77-80; 165; CANR 15, 43; CN
7; DAC; DAM MST; DLB 88
Mitchell, William (Lendrum)
1879-1936 .... **TCLC 81**
See also CA 213
Mitford, Mary Russell 1787-1855 ... **NCLC 4**
See also DLB 110, 116; RGEL 2
Mitford, Nancy 1904-1973 .... **CLC 44**
See also CA 9-12R; DLB 191; RGEL 2
Miyamoto, (Chujo) Yuriko
1899-1951 .... **TCLC 37**
See Miyamoto Yuriko
See also CA 170, 174
Miyamoto Yuriko
See Miyamoto, (Chujo) Yuriko
See also DLB 180
Miyazawa, Kenji 1896-1933 .... **TCLC 76**
See Miyazawa Kenji
See also CA 157; RGWL 3
Miyazawa Kenji
See Miyazawa, Kenji
See also EWL 3
Mizoguchi, Kenji 1898-1956 .... **TCLC 72**
See also CA 167
Mo, Timothy (Peter) 1950(?)- ... **CLC 46, 134**
See also CA 117; CANR 128; CN 7; DLB
194; MTCW 1; WLIT 4; WWE 1
Modarressi, Taghi (M.) 1931-1997 ... **CLC 44**
See also CA 121; 134; INT CA-134
Modiano, Patrick (Jean) 1945- .... **CLC 18**
See also CA 85-88; CANR 17, 40, 115;
CWW 2; DLB 83, 299; EWL 3
Mofolo, Thomas (Mokopu)
1875(?)-1948 .... **BLC 3; TCLC 22**
See also AFW; CA 121; 153; CANR 83;
DAM MULT; DLB 225; EWL 3; MTCW
2; WLIT 2

Mohr, Nicholasa 1938- .... **CLC 12; HLC 2**
See also AAYA 8, 46; CA 49-52; CANR 1,
32, 64; CLR 22; DAM MULT; DLB 145;
HW 1, 2; JRDA; LAIT 5; LLW 1; MAI-
CYA 2; MAICYAS 1; RGAL 4; SAAS 8;
SATA 8, 97; SATA-Essay 113; WYA;
YAW

Moi, Toril 1953- .... **CLC 172**
See also CA 154; CANR 102; FW

Mojtabai, A(nn) G(race) 1938- ..... **CLC 5, 9,
15, 29**
See also CA 85-88; CANR 88

Moliere 1622-1673 ..... **DC 13; LC 10, 28, 64;
WLC**
See also DA; DA3; DAB; DAC; DAM
DRAM, MST; DFS 13, 18, 20; DLB 268;
EW 3; GFL Beginnings to 1789; LATS
1:1; RGWL 2, 3; TWA

Molin, Charles
See Mayne, William (James Carter)

Molnar, Ferenc 1878-1952 .... **TCLC 20**
See also CA 109; 153; CANR 83; CDWLB
4; DAM DRAM; DLB 215; EWL 3;
RGWL 2, 3

Momaday, N(avarre) Scott 1934- ...... **CLC 2,
19, 85, 95, 160; NNAL; PC 25; WLCS**
See also AAYA 11; AMWS 4; ANW; BPFB
2; BYA 12; CA 25-28R; CANR 14, 34,
68; CDALBS; CN 7; CPW; DA; DA3;
DAB; DAC; DAM MST, MULT, NOV,
POP; DLB 143, 175, 256; EWL 3; EXPP;
INT CANR-14; LAIT 4; LATS 1:2;
MTCW 1, 2; NFS 10; PFS 2, 11; RGAL
4; SATA 48; SATA-Brief 30; WP; YAW

Monette, Paul 1945-1995 .... **CLC 82**
See also AMWS 10; CA 139; 147; CN 7;
GLL 1

Monroe, Harriet 1860-1936 .... **TCLC 12**
See also CA 109; 204; DLB 54, 91

Monroe, Lyle
See Heinlein, Robert A(nson)

Montagu, Elizabeth 1720-1800 .... **NCLC 7,
117**
See also FW

Montagu, Mary (Pierrepont) Wortley
1689-1762 .... **LC 9, 57; PC 16**
See also DLB 95, 101; RGEL 2

Montagu, W. H.
See Coleridge, Samuel Taylor

Montague, John (Patrick) 1929- ..... **CLC 13,
46**
See also CA 9-12R; CANR 9, 69, 121; CP
7; DLB 40; EWL 3; MTCW 1; PFS 12;
RGEL 2

Montaigne, Michel (Eyquem) de
1533-1592 .... **LC 8, 105; WLC**
See also DA; DAB; DAC; DAM MST; EW
2; GFL Beginnings to 1789; LMFS 1;
RGWL 2, 3; TWA

Montale, Eugenio 1896-1981 ... **CLC 7, 9, 18;
PC 13**
See also CA 17-20R; 104; CANR 30; DLB
114; EW 11; EWL 3; MTCW 1; RGWL
2, 3; TWA

Montesquieu, Charles-Louis de Secondat
1689-1755 .... **LC 7, 69**
See also EW 3; GFL Beginnings to 1789;
TWA

Montessori, Maria 1870-1952 ...... **TCLC 103**
See also CA 115; 147

Montgomery, (Robert) Bruce 1921(?)-1978
See Crispin, Edmund
See also CA 179; 104; CMW 4

Montgomery, L(ucy) M(aud)
1874-1942 .... **TCLC 51, 140**
See also AAYA 12; BYA 1; CA 108; 137;
CLR 8, 91; DA3; DAC; DAM MST; DLB
92; DLBD 14; JRDA; MAICYA 1, 2;
MTCW 2; RGEL 2; SATA 100; TWA;
WCH; WYA; YABC 1

Montgomery, Marion H., Jr. 1925- .... **CLC 7**
See also AITN 1; CA 1-4R; CANR 3, 48;
CSW; DLB 6

Montgomery, Max
See Davenport, Guy (Mattison, Jr.)

Montherlant, Henry (Milon) de
1896-1972 .... **CLC 8, 19**
See also CA 85-88; 37-40R; DAM DRAM;
DLB 72; EW 11; EWL 3; GFL 1789 to
the Present; MTCW 1

Monty Python
See Chapman, Graham; Cleese, John
(Marwood); Gilliam, Terry (Vance); Idle,
Eric; Jones, Terence Graham Parry; Palin,
Michael (Edward)
See also AAYA 7

Moodie, Susanna (Strickland)
1803-1885 .... **NCLC 14, 113**
See also DLB 99

Moody, Hiram (F. III) 1961-
See Moody, Rick
See also CA 138; CANR 64, 112

Moody, Minerva
See Alcott, Louisa May

Moody, Rick .... **CLC 147**
See Moody, Hiram (F. III)

Moody, William Vaughan
1869-1910 .... **TCLC 105**
See also CA 110; 178; DLB 7, 54; RGAL 4

Mooney, Edward 1951-
See Mooney, Ted
See also CA 130

Mooney, Ted .... **CLC 25**
See Mooney, Edward

Moorcock, Michael (John) 1939- ...... **CLC 5,
27, 58**
See Bradbury, Edward P.
See also AAYA 26; CA 45-48; CAAS 5;
CANR 2, 17, 38, 64, 122; CN 7; DLB 14,
231, 261; FANT; MTCW 1, 2; SATA 93;
SCFW 2; SFW 4; SUFW 1, 2

Moore, Brian 1921-1999 ... **CLC 1, 3, 5, 7, 8,
19, 32, 90**
See Bryan, Michael
See also BRWS 9; CA 1-4R; 174; CANR 1,
25, 42, 63; CCA 1; CN 7; DAB; DAC;
DAM MST; DLB 251; EWL 3; FANT;
MTCW 1, 2; RGEL 2

Moore, Edward
See Muir, Edwin
See also RGEL 2

Moore, G. E. 1873-1958 .... **TCLC 89**
See also DLB 262

Moore, George Augustus
1852-1933 .... **SSC 19; TCLC 7**
See also BRW 6; CA 104; 177; DLB 10,
18, 57, 135; EWL 3; RGEL 2; RGSF 2

Moore, Lorrie .... **CLC 39, 45, 68**
See Moore, Marie Lorena
See also AMWS 10; DLB 234; SSFS 19

Moore, Marianne (Craig)
1887-1972 .... **CLC 1, 2, 4, 8, 10, 13, 19,
47; PC 4, 49; WLCS**
See also AMW; CA 1-4R; 33-36R; CANR
3, 61; CDALB 1929-1941; DA; DA3;
DAB; DAC; DAM MST, POET; DLB 45;
DLBD 7; EWL 3; EXPP; MAWW;
MTCW 1, 2; PAB; PFS 14, 17; RGAL 4;
SATA 20; TUS; WP

Moore, Marie Lorena 1957- .... **CLC 165**
See Moore, Lorrie
See also CA 116; CANR 39, 83; CN 7; DLB
234

Moore, Thomas 1779-1852 .... **NCLC 6, 110**
See also DLB 96, 144; RGEL 2

Moorhouse, Frank 1938- .... **SSC 40**
See also CA 118; CANR 92; CN 7; DLB
289; RGSF 2

Mora, Pat(ricia) 1942- .... **HLC 2**
See also AMWS 13; CA 129; CANR 57,
81, 112; CLR 58; DAM MULT; DLB 209;
HW 1, 2; LLW 1; MAICYA 2; SATA 92,
134

Moraga, Cherrie 1952- ...... **CLC 126; DC 22**
See also CA 131; CANR 66; DAM MULT;
DLB 82, 249; FW; GLL 1; HW 1, 2; LLW
1

Morand, Paul 1888-1976 .... **CLC 41; SSC 22**
See also CA 184; 69-72; DLB 65; EWL 3

Morante, Elsa 1918-1985 .... **CLC 8, 47**
See also CA 85-88; 117; CANR 35; DLB
177; EWL 3; MTCW 1, 2; RGWL 2, 3

Moravia, Alberto .... **CLC 2, 7, 11, 27, 46;
SSC 26**
See Pincherle, Alberto
See also DLB 177; EW 12; EWL 3; MTCW
2; RGSF 2; RGWL 2, 3

More, Hannah 1745-1833 ...... **NCLC 27, 141**
See also DLB 107, 109, 116, 158; RGEL 2

More, Henry 1614-1687 .... **LC 9**
See also DLB 126, 252

More, Sir Thomas 1478(?)-1535 .... **LC 10, 32**
See also BRWC 1; BRWS 7; DLB 136, 281;
LMFS 1; RGEL 2; TEA

Moreas, Jean .... **TCLC 18**
See Papadiamantopoulos, Johannes
See also GFL 1789 to the Present

Moreton, Andrew Esq.
See Defoe, Daniel

Morgan, Berry 1919-2002 .... **CLC 6**
See also CA 49-52; 208; DLB 6

Morgan, Claire
See Highsmith, (Mary) Patricia
See also GLL 1

Morgan, Edwin (George) 1920- .... **CLC 31**
See also BRWS 9; CA 5-8R; CANR 3, 43,
90; CP 7; DLB 27

Morgan, (George) Frederick
1922-(2004) .... **CLC 23**
See also CA 17-20R; 224; CANR 21; CP 7

Morgan, Harriet
See Mencken, H(enry) L(ouis)

Morgan, Jane
See Cooper, James Fenimore

Morgan, Janet 1945- .... **CLC 39**
See also CA 65-68

Morgan, Lady 1776(?)-1859 .... **NCLC 29**
See also DLB 116, 158; RGEL 2

Morgan, Robin (Evonne) 1941- .... **CLC 2**
See also CA 69-72; CANR 29, 68; FW;
GLL 2; MTCW 1; SATA 80

Morgan, Scott
See Kuttner, Henry

Morgan, Seth 1949(?)-1990 .... **CLC 65**
See also CA 185; 132

**Morgenstern, Christian (Otto Josef
Wolfgang)** 1871-1914 .... **TCLC 8**
See also CA 105; 191; EWL 3

Morgenstern, S.
See Goldman, William (W.)

Mori, Rintaro
See Mori Ogai
See also CA 110

Moricz, Zsigmond 1879-1942 .... **TCLC 33**
See also CA 165; DLB 215; EWL 3

Morike, Eduard (Friedrich)
1804-1875 .... **NCLC 10**
See also DLB 133; RGWL 2, 3

Mori Ogai 1862-1922 .... **TCLC 14**
See Ogai
See also CA 164; DLB 180; EWL 3; RGWL
3; TWA

Moritz, Karl Philipp 1756-1793 .... **LC 2**
See also DLB 94

Morland, Peter Henry
See Faust, Frederick (Schiller)

Porter, Gene(va Grace) Stratton .. TCLC **21**
See Stratton-Porter, Gene(va Grace)
See also BPFB 3; CA 112; CWRI 5; RHW

Porter, Katherine Anne 1890-1980 ... CLC **1, 3, 7, 10, 13, 15, 27, 101; SSC 4, 31, 43**
See also AAYA 42; AITN 2; AMW; BPFB 3; CA 1-4R; 101; CANR 1, 65; CDALBS; DA; DA3; DAB; DAC; DAM MST, NOV; DLB 4, 9, 102; DLBD 12; DLBY 1980; EWL 3; EXPS; LAIT 3; MAWW; MTCW 1, 2; NFS 14; RGAL 4; RGSF 2; SATA 39; SATA-Obit 23; SSFS 1, 8, 11, 16; TUS

Porter, Peter (Neville Frederick)
1929- .... CLC **5, 13, 33**
See also CA 85-88; CP 7; DLB 40, 289; WWE 1

Porter, William Sydney 1862-1910
See Henry, O.
See also CA 104; 131; CDALB 1865-1917; DA; DA3; DAB; DAC; DAM MST; DLB 12, 78, 79; MTCW 1, 2; TUS; YABC 2

Portillo (y Pacheco), Jose Lopez
See Lopez Portillo (y Pacheco), Jose

Portillo Trambley, Estela 1927-1998 .. HLC **2**
See Trambley, Estela Portillo
See also CANR 32; DAM MULT; DLB 209; HW 1

Posey, Alexander (Lawrence)
1873-1908 .... NNAL
See also CA 144; CANR 80; DAM MULT; DLB 175

Posse, Abel .... CLC **70**

Post, Melville Davisson
1869-1930 .... TCLC **39**
See also CA 110; 202; CMW 4

Potok, Chaim 1929-2002 ... CLC **2, 7, 14, 26, 112**
See also AAYA 15, 50; AITN 1, 2; BPFB 3; BYA 1; CA 17-20R; 208; CANR 19, 35, 64, 98; CLR 92; CN 7; DA3; DAM NOV; DLB 28, 152; EXPN; INT CANR-19; LAIT 4; MTCW 1, 2; NFS 4; SATA 33, 106; SATA-Obit 134; TUS; YAW

Potok, Herbert Harold -2002
See Potok, Chaim

Potok, Herman Harold
See Potok, Chaim

Potter, Dennis (Christopher George)
1935-1994 .... CLC **58, 86, 123**
See also CA 107; 145; CANR 33, 61; CBD; DLB 233; MTCW 1

Pound, Ezra (Weston Loomis)
1885-1972 .. CLC **1, 2, 3, 4, 5, 7, 10, 13, 18, 34, 48, 50, 112; PC 4; WLC**
See also AAYA 47; AMW; AMWR 1; CA 5-8R; 37-40R; CANR 40; CDALB 1917-1929; DA; DA3; DAB; DAC; DAM MST, POET; DLB 4, 45, 63; DLBD 15; EFS 2; EWL 3; EXPP; LMFS 2; MTCW 1, 2; PAB; PFS 2, 8, 16; RGAL 4; TUS; WP

Povod, Reinaldo 1959-1994 .... CLC **44**
See also CA 136; 146; CANR 83

Powell, Adam Clayton, Jr.
1908-1972 .... BLC **3**; CLC **89**
See also BW 1, 3; CA 102; 33-36R; CANR 86; DAM MULT

Powell, Anthony (Dymoke)
1905-2000 .... CLC **1, 3, 7, 9, 10, 31**
See also BRW 7; CA 1-4R; 189; CANR 1, 32, 62, 107; CDBLB 1945-1960; CN 7; DLB 15; EWL 3; MTCW 1, 2; RGEL 2; TEA

Powell, Dawn 1896(?)-1965 .... CLC **66**
See also CA 5-8R; CANR 121; DLBY 1997

Powell, Padgett 1952- .... CLC **34**
See also CA 126; CANR 63, 101; CSW; DLB 234; DLBY 01

Powell, (Oval) Talmage 1920-2000
See Queen, Ellery
See also CA 5-8R; CANR 2, 80

Power, Susan 1961- .... CLC **91**
See also BYA 14; CA 160; NFS 11

Powers, J(ames) F(arl) 1917-1999 ..... CLC **1, 4, 8, 57; SSC 4**
See also CA 1-4R; 181; CANR 2, 61; CN 7; DLB 130; MTCW 1; RGAL 4; RGSF 2

Powers, John J(ames) 1945-
See Powers, John R.
See also CA 69-72

Powers, John R. .... CLC **66**
See Powers, John J(ames)

Powers, Richard (S.) 1957- .... CLC **93**
See also AMWS 9; BPFB 3; CA 148; CANR 80; CN 7

Pownall, David 1938- .... CLC **10**
See also CA 89-92; 180; CAAS 18; CANR 49, 101; CBD; CD 5; CN 7; DLB 14

Powys, John Cowper 1872-1963 ... CLC **7, 9, 15, 46, 125**
See also CA 85-88; CANR 106; DLB 15, 255; EWL 3; FANT; MTCW 1, 2; RGEL 2; SUFW

Powys, T(heodore) F(rancis)
1875-1953 .... TCLC **9**
See also BRWS 8; CA 106; 189; DLB 36, 162; EWL 3; FANT; RGEL 2; SUFW

Prado (Calvo), Pedro 1886-1952 ... TCLC **75**
See also CA 131; DLB 283; HW 1; LAW

Prager, Emily 1952- .... CLC **56**
See also CA 204

Pratchett, Terry 1948- .... CLC **197**
See also AAYA 19, 54; BPFB 3; CA 143; CANR 87, 126; CLR 64; CN 7; CPW; CWRI 5; FANT; SATA 82, 139; SFW 4; SUFW 2

Pratolini, Vasco 1913-1991 .... TCLC **124**
See also CA 211; DLB 177; EWL 3; RGWL 2, 3

Pratt, E(dwin) J(ohn) 1883(?)-1964 . CLC **19**
See also CA 141; 93-96; CANR 77; DAC; DAM POET; DLB 92; EWL 3; RGEL 2; TWA

Premchand .... TCLC **21**
See Srivastava, Dhanpat Rai
See also EWL 3

Preseren, France 1800-1849 .... NCLC **127**
See also CDWLB 4; DLB 147

Preussler, Otfried 1923- .... CLC **17**
See also CA 77-80; SATA 24

Prevert, Jacques (Henri Marie)
1900-1977 .... CLC **15**
See also CA 77-80; 69-72; CANR 29, 61; DLB 258; EWL 3; GFL 1789 to the Present; IDFW 3, 4; MTCW 1; RGWL 2, 3; SATA-Obit 30

Prevost, (Antoine Francois)
1697-1763 .... LC **1**
See also EW 4; GFL Beginnings to 1789; RGWL 2, 3

Price, (Edward) Reynolds 1933- ... CLC **3, 6, 13, 43, 50, 63; SSC 22**
See also AMWS 6; CA 1-4R; CANR 1, 37, 57, 87, 128; CN 7; CSW; DAM NOV; DLB 2, 218, 278; EWL 3; INT CANR-37; NFS 18

Price, Richard 1949- .... CLC **6, 12**
See also CA 49-52; CANR 3; DLBY 1981

Prichard, Katharine Susannah
1883-1969 .... CLC **46**
See also CA 11-12; CANR 33; CAP 1; DLB 260; MTCW 1; RGEL 2; RGSF 2; SATA 66

Priestley, J(ohn) B(oynton)
1894-1984 .... CLC **2, 5, 9, 34**
See also BRW 7; CA 9-12R; 113; CANR 33; CDBLB 1914-1945; DA3; DAM DRAM, NOV; DLB 10, 34, 77, 100, 139; DLBY 1984; EWL 3; MTCW 1, 2; RGEL 2; SFW 4

Prince 1958- .... CLC **35**
See also CA 213

Prince, F(rank) T(empleton)
1912-2003 .... CLC **22**
See also CA 101; 219; CANR 43, 79; CP 7; DLB 20

Prince Kropotkin
See Kropotkin, Peter (Aleksieevich)

Prior, Matthew 1664-1721 .... LC **4**
See also DLB 95; RGEL 2

Prishvin, Mikhail 1873-1954 .... TCLC **75**
See Prishvin, Mikhail Mikhailovich

Prishvin, Mikhail Mikhailovich
See Prishvin, Mikhail
See also DLB 272; EWL 3

Pritchard, William H(arrison)
1932- .... CLC **34**
See also CA 65-68; CANR 23, 95; DLB 111

Pritchett, V(ictor) S(awdon)
1900-1997 ... CLC **5, 13, 15, 41; SSC 14**
See also BPFB 3; BRWS 3; CA 61-64; 157; CANR 31, 63; CN 7; DA3; DAM NOV; DLB 15, 139; EWL 3; MTCW 1, 2; RGEL 2; RGSF 2; TEA

Private 19022
See Manning, Frederic

Probst, Mark 1925- .... CLC **59**
See also CA 130

Prokosch, Frederic 1908-1989 ...... CLC **4, 48**
See also CA 73-76; 128; CANR 82; DLB 48; MTCW 2

Propertius, Sextus c. 50B.C.-c. 16B.C. .... CMLC **32**
See also AW 2; CDWLB 1; DLB 211; RGWL 2, 3

Prophet, The
See Dreiser, Theodore (Herman Albert)

Prose, Francine 1947- .... CLC **45**
See also CA 109; 112; CANR 46, 95, 132; DLB 234; SATA 101, 149

Proudhon
See Cunha, Euclides (Rodrigues Pimenta) da

Proulx, Annie
See Proulx, E(dna) Annie

Proulx, E(dna) Annie 1935- ...... CLC **81, 158**
See also AMWS 7; BPFB 3; CA 145; CANR 65, 110; CN 7; CPW 1; DA3; DAM POP; MTCW 2; SSFS 18

Proust, (Valentin-Louis-George-Eugene) Marcel 1871-1922 ..... SSC **75**; TCLC **7, 13, 33; WLC**
See also AAYA 58; BPFB 3; CA 104; 120; CANR 110; DA; DA3; DAB; DAC; DAM MST, NOV; DLB 65; EW 8; EWL 3; GFL 1789 to the Present; MTCW 1, 2; RGWL 2, 3; TWA

Prowler, Harley
See Masters, Edgar Lee

Prus, Boleslaw 1845-1912 .... TCLC **48**
See also RGWL 2, 3

Pryor, Richard (Franklin Lenox Thomas)
1940- .... CLC **26**
See also CA 122; 152

Przybyszewski, Stanislaw
1868-1927 .... TCLC **36**
See also CA 160; DLB 66; EWL 3

Pteleon
See Grieve, C(hristopher) M(urray)
See also DAM POET

Rampersad, Arnold 1941- .... **CLC 44**
 See also BW 2, 3; CA 127; 133; CANR 81;
 DLB 111; INT CA-133

Rampling, Anne
 See Rice, Anne
 See also GLL 2

Ramsay, Allan 1686(?)-1758 .... **LC 29**
 See also DLB 95; RGEL 2

Ramsay, Jay
 See Campbell, (John) Ramsey

Ramuz, Charles-Ferdinand
 1878-1947 .... **TCLC 33**
 See also CA 165; EWL 3

Rand, Ayn 1905-1982 ...... **CLC 3, 30, 44, 79;**
 WLC
 See also AAYA 10; AMWS 4; BPFB 3;
 BYA 12; CA 13-16R; CANR 27, 73;
 CDALBS; CPW; DA; DA3; DAC; DAM
 MST, NOV, POP; DLB 227, 279; MTCW
 1, 2; NFS 10, 16; RGAL 4; SFW 4; TUS;
 YAW

Randall, Dudley (Felker) 1914-2000 . **BLC 3;**
 CLC 1, 135
 See also BW 1, 3; CA 25-28R; 189; CANR
 23, 82; DAM MULT; DLB 41; PFS 5

Randall, Robert
 See Silverberg, Robert

Ranger, Ken
 See Creasey, John

Rank, Otto 1884-1939 .... **TCLC 115**

Ransom, John Crowe 1888-1974 .. **CLC 2, 4,**
 5, 11, 24
 See also AMW; CA 5-8R; 49-52; CANR 6,
 34; CDALBS; DA3; DAM POET; DLB
 45, 63; EWL 3; EXPP; MTCW 1, 2;
 RGAL 4; TUS

Rao, Raja 1909- .... **CLC 25, 56**
 See also CA 73-76; CANR 51; CN 7; DAM
 NOV; EWL 3; MTCW 1, 2; RGEL 2;
 RGSF 2

Raphael, Frederic (Michael) 1931- ... **CLC 2,**
 14
 See also CA 1-4R; CANR 1, 86; CN 7;
 DLB 14

Ratcliffe, James P.
 See Mencken, H(enry) L(ouis)

Rathbone, Julian 1935- .... **CLC 41**
 See also CA 101; CANR 34, 73

Rattigan, Terence (Mervyn)
 1911-1977 .... **CLC 7; DC 18**
 See also BRWS 7; CA 85-88; 73-76; CBD;
 CDBLB 1945-1960; DAM DRAM; DFS
 8; DLB 13; IDFW 3, 4; MTCW 1, 2;
 RGEL 2

Ratushinskaya, Irina 1954- .... **CLC 54**
 See also CA 129; CANR 68; CWW 2

Raven, Simon (Arthur Noel)
 1927-2001 .... **CLC 14**
 See also CA 81-84; 197; CANR 86; CN 7;
 DLB 271

Ravenna, Michael
 See Welty, Eudora (Alice)

Rawley, Callman 1903-2002
 See Rakosi, Carl
 See also CA 21-24R; CANR 12, 32, 91

Rawlings, Marjorie Kinnan
 1896-1953 .... **TCLC 4**
 See also AAYA 20; AMWS 10; ANW;
 BPFB 3; BYA 3; CA 104; 137; CANR 74;
 CLR 63; DLB 9, 22, 102; DLBD 17;
 JRDA; MAICYA 1, 2; MTCW 2; RGAL
 4; SATA 100; WCH; YABC 1; YAW

Ray, Satyajit 1921-1992 .... **CLC 16, 76**
 See also CA 114; 137; DAM MULT

Read, Herbert Edward 1893-1968 ..... **CLC 4**
 See also BRW 6; CA 85-88; 25-28R; DLB
 20, 149; EWL 3; PAB; RGEL 2

Read, Piers Paul 1941- .... **CLC 4, 10, 25**
 See also CA 21-24R; CANR 38, 86; CN 7;
 DLB 14; SATA 21

Reade, Charles 1814-1884 .... **NCLC 2, 74**
 See also DLB 21; RGEL 2

Reade, Hamish
 See Gray, Simon (James Holliday)

Reading, Peter 1946- .... **CLC 47**
 See also BRWS 8; CA 103; CANR 46, 96;
 CP 7; DLB 40

Reaney, James 1926- .... **CLC 13**
 See also CA 41-44R; CAAS 15; CANR 42;
 CD 5; CP 7; DAC; DAM MST; DLB 68;
 RGEL 2; SATA 43

Rebreanu, Liviu 1885-1944 .... **TCLC 28**
 See also CA 165; DLB 220; EWL 3

Rechy, John (Francisco) 1934- ...... **CLC 1, 7,**
 14, 18, 107; HLC 2
 See also CA 5-8R, 195; CAAE 195; CAAS
 4; CANR 6, 32, 64; CN 7; DAM MULT;
 DLB 122, 278; DLBY 1982; HW 1, 2;
 INT CANR-6; LLW 1; RGAL 4

Redcam, Tom 1870-1933 .... **TCLC 25**

Reddin, Keith .... **CLC 67**
 See also CAD

Redgrove, Peter (William)
 1932-2003 .... **CLC 6, 41**
 See also BRWS 6; CA 1-4R; 217; CANR 3,
 39, 77; CP 7; DLB 40

Redmon, Anne .... **CLC 22**
 See Nightingale, Anne Redmon
 See also DLBY 1986

Reed, Eliot
 See Ambler, Eric

Reed, Ishmael 1938- ..... **BLC 3; CLC 2, 3, 5,**
 6, 13, 32, 60, 174
 See also AFAW 1, 2; AMWS 10; BPFB 3;
 BW 2, 3; CA 21-24R; CANR 25, 48, 74,
 128; CN 7; CP 7; CSW; DA3; DAM
 MULT; DLB 2, 5, 33, 169, 227; DLBD 8;
 EWL 3; LMFS 2; MSW; MTCW 1, 2;
 PFS 6; RGAL 4; TCWW 2

Reed, John (Silas) 1887-1920 .... **TCLC 9**
 See also CA 106; 195; TUS

Reed, Lou .... **CLC 21**
 See Firbank, Louis

Reese, Lizette Woodworth 1856-1935 . **PC 29**
 See also CA 180; DLB 54

Reeve, Clara 1729-1807 .... **NCLC 19**
 See also DLB 39; RGEL 2

Reich, Wilhelm 1897-1957 .... **TCLC 57**
 See also CA 199

Reid, Christopher (John) 1949- .... **CLC 33**
 See also CA 140; CANR 89; CP 7; DLB
 40; EWL 3

Reid, Desmond
 See Moorcock, Michael (John)

Reid Banks, Lynne 1929-
 See Banks, Lynne Reid
 See also AAYA 49; CA 1-4R; CANR 6, 22,
 38, 87; CLR 24; CN 7; JRDA; MAICYA
 1, 2; SATA 22, 75, 111; YAW

Reilly, William K.
 See Creasey, John

Reiner, Max
 See Caldwell, (Janet Miriam) Taylor
 (Holland)

Reis, Ricardo
 See Pessoa, Fernando (Antonio Nogueira)

Reizenstein, Elmer Leopold
 See Rice, Elmer (Leopold)
 See also EWL 3

Remarque, Erich Maria 1898-1970 . **CLC 21**
 See also AAYA 27; BPFB 3; CA 77-80; 29-
 32R; CDWLB 2; DA; DA3; DAB; DAC;
 DAM MST, NOV; DLB 56; EWL 3;
 EXPN; LAIT 3; MTCW 1, 2; NFS 4;
 RGWL 2, 3

Remington, Frederic 1861-1909 ..... **TCLC 89**
 See also CA 108; 169; DLB 12, 186, 188;
 SATA 41

Remizov, A.
 See Remizov, Aleksei (Mikhailovich)

Remizov, A. M.
 See Remizov, Aleksei (Mikhailovich)

Remizov, Aleksei (Mikhailovich)
 1877-1957 .... **TCLC 27**
 See Remizov, Alexey Mikhaylovich
 See also CA 125; 133; DLB 295

Remizov, Alexey Mikhaylovich
 See Remizov, Aleksei (Mikhailovich)
 See also EWL 3

Renan, Joseph Ernest 1823-1892 . **NCLC 26,**
 145
 See also GFL 1789 to the Present

Renard, Jules(-Pierre) 1864-1910 .. **TCLC 17**
 See also CA 117; 202; GFL 1789 to the
 Present

Renault, Mary .... **CLC 3, 11, 17**
 See Challans, Mary
 See also BPFB 3; BYA 2; DLBY 1983;
 EWL 3; GLL 1; LAIT 1; MTCW 2; RGEL
 2; RHW

Rendell, Ruth (Barbara) 1930- .. **CLC 28, 48**
 See Vine, Barbara
 See also BPFB 3; BRWS 9; CA 109; CANR
 32, 52, 74, 127; CN 7; CPW; DAM POP;
 DLB 87, 276; INT CANR-32; MSW;
 MTCW 1, 2

Renoir, Jean 1894-1979 .... **CLC 20**
 See also CA 129; 85-88

Resnais, Alain 1922- .... **CLC 16**

Revard, Carter (Curtis) 1931- .... **NNAL**
 See also CA 144; CANR 81; PFS 5

Reverdy, Pierre 1889-1960 .... **CLC 53**
 See also CA 97-100; 89-92; DLB 258; EWL
 3; GFL 1789 to the Present

Rexroth, Kenneth 1905-1982 .... **CLC 1, 2, 6,**
 11, 22, 49, 112; PC 20
 See also BG 3; CA 5-8R; 107; CANR 14,
 34, 63; CDALB 1941-1968; DAM POET;
 DLB 16, 48, 165, 212; DLBY 1982; EWL
 3; INT CANR-14; MTCW 1, 2; RGAL 4

Reyes, Alfonso 1889-1959 .... **HLCS 2; TCLC**
 33
 See also CA 131; EWL 3; HW 1; LAW

Reyes y Basoalto, Ricardo Eliecer Neftali
 See Neruda, Pablo

Reymont, Wladyslaw (Stanislaw)
 1868(?)-1925 .... **TCLC 5**
 See also CA 104; EWL 3

Reynolds, Jonathan 1942- .... **CLC 6, 38**
 See also CA 65-68; CANR 28

Reynolds, Joshua 1723-1792 .... **LC 15**
 See also DLB 104

Reynolds, Michael S(hane)
 1937-2000 .... **CLC 44**
 See also CA 65-68; 189; CANR 9, 89, 97

Reznikoff, Charles 1894-1976 .... **CLC 9**
 See also CA 33-36; 61-64; CAP 2; DLB 28,
 45; WP

Rezzori (d'Arezzo), Gregor von
 1914-1998 .... **CLC 25**
 See also CA 122; 136; 167

Rhine, Richard
 See Silverstein, Alvin; Silverstein, Virginia
 B(arbara Opshelor)

Rhodes, Eugene Manlove
 1869-1934 .... **TCLC 53**
 See also CA 198; DLB 256

R'hoone, Lord
 See Balzac, Honore de

Robertson, Tom
See Robertson, Thomas William
See also RGEL 2

Robeson, Kenneth
See Dent, Lester

Robinson, Edwin Arlington
1869-1935 .... **PC 1, 35; TCLC 5, 101**
See also AMW; CA 104; 133; CDALB
1865-1917; DA; DAC; DAM MST,
POET; DLB 54; EWL 3; EXPP; MTCW
1, 2; PAB; PFS 4; RGAL 4; WP

Robinson, Henry Crabb
1775-1867 .... **NCLC 15**
See also DLB 107

Robinson, Jill 1936- .... **CLC 10**
See also CA 102; CANR 120; INT CA-102

Robinson, Kim Stanley 1952- .... **CLC 34**
See also AAYA 26; CA 126; CANR 113;
CN 7; SATA 109; SCFW 2; SFW 4

Robinson, Lloyd
See Silverberg, Robert

Robinson, Marilynne 1944- ...... **CLC 25, 180**
See also CA 116; CANR 80; CN 7; DLB
206

Robinson, Mary 1758-1800 .... **NCLC 142**
See also DLB 158; FW

Robinson, Smokey .... **CLC 21**
See Robinson, William, Jr.

Robinson, William, Jr. 1940-
See Robinson, Smokey
See also CA 116

Robison, Mary 1949- .... **CLC 42, 98**
See also CA 113; 116; CANR 87; CN 7;
DLB 130; INT CA-116; RGSF 2

Rochester
See Wilmot, John
See also RGEL 2

Rod, Edouard 1857-1910 .... **TCLC 52**

Roddenberry, Eugene Wesley 1921-1991
See Roddenberry, Gene
See also CA 110; 135; CANR 37; SATA 45;
SATA-Obit 69

Roddenberry, Gene .... **CLC 17**
See Roddenberry, Eugene Wesley
See also AAYA 5; SATA-Obit 69

Rodgers, Mary 1931- .... **CLC 12**
See also BYA 5; CA 49-52; CANR 8, 55,
90; CLR 20; CWRI 5; INT CANR-8;
JRDA; MAICYA 1, 2; SATA 8, 130

Rodgers, W(illiam) R(obert)
1909-1969 .... **CLC 7**
See also CA 85-88; DLB 20; RGEL 2

Rodman, Eric
See Silverberg, Robert

Rodman, Howard 1920(?)-1985 .... **CLC 65**
See also CA 118

Rodman, Maia
See Wojciechowska, Maia (Teresa)

Rodo, Jose Enrique 1871(?)-1917 .... **HLCS 2**
See also CA 178; EWL 3; HW 2; LAW

Rodolph, Utto
See Ouologuem, Yambo

Rodriguez, Claudio 1934-1999 .... **CLC 10**
See also CA 188; DLB 134

Rodriguez, Richard 1944- .... **CLC 155; HLC 2**
See also CA 110; CANR 66, 116; DAM
MULT; DLB 82, 256; HW 1, 2; LAIT 5;
LLW 1; NCFS 3; WLIT 1

Roelvaag, O(le) E(dvart) 1876-1931
See Rolvaag, O(le) E(dvart)
See also CA 117; 171

Roethke, Theodore (Huebner)
1908-1963 .... **CLC 1, 3, 8, 11, 19, 46,
101; PC 15**
See also AMW; CA 81-84; CABS 2;
CDALB 1941-1968; DA3; DAM POET;
DLB 5, 206; EWL 3; EXPP; MTCW 1, 2;
PAB; PFS 3; RGAL 4; WP

Rogers, Carl R(ansom)
1902-1987 .... **TCLC 125**
See also CA 1-4R; 121; CANR 1, 18;
MTCW 1

Rogers, Samuel 1763-1855 .... **NCLC 69**
See also DLB 93; RGEL 2

Rogers, Thomas Hunton 1927- .... **CLC 57**
See also CA 89-92; INT CA-89-92

Rogers, Will(iam Penn Adair)
1879-1935 .... **NNAL; TCLC 8, 71**
See also CA 105; 144; DA3; DAM MULT;
DLB 11; MTCW 2

Rogin, Gilbert 1929- .... **CLC 18**
See also CA 65-68; CANR 15

Rohan, Koda
See Koda Shigeyuki

Rohlfs, Anna Katharine Green
See Green, Anna Katharine

Rohmer, Eric .... **CLC 16**
See Scherer, Jean-Marie Maurice

Rohmer, Sax .... **TCLC 28**
See Ward, Arthur Henry Sarsfield
See also DLB 70; MSW; SUFW

Roiphe, Anne (Richardson) 1935- .. **CLC 3, 9**
See also CA 89-92; CANR 45, 73; DLBY
1980; INT CA-89-92

Rojas, Fernando de 1475-1541 ... **HLCS 1, 2;
LC 23**
See also DLB 286; RGWL 2, 3

Rojas, Gonzalo 1917- .... **HLCS 2**
See also CA 178; HW 2; LAWS 1

Roland, Marie-Jeanne 1754-1793 .... **LC 98**

**Rolfe, Frederick (William Serafino Austin
Lewis Mary)** 1860-1913 .... **TCLC 12**
See Al Siddik
See also CA 107; 210; DLB 34, 156; RGEL
2

Rolland, Romain 1866-1944 .... **TCLC 23**
See also CA 118; 197; DLB 65, 284; EWL
3; GFL 1789 to the Present; RGWL 2, 3

Rolle, Richard c. 1300-c. 1349 .... **CMLC 21**
See also DLB 146; LMFS 1; RGEL 2

Rolvaag, O(le) E(dvart) .... **TCLC 17**
See Roelvaag, O(le) E(dvart)
See also DLB 9, 212; NFS 5; RGAL 4

Romain Arnaud, Saint
See Aragon, Louis

Romains, Jules 1885-1972 .... **CLC 7**
See also CA 85-88; CANR 34; DLB 65;
EWL 3; GFL 1789 to the Present; MTCW
1

Romero, Jose Ruben 1890-1952 .... **TCLC 14**
See also CA 114; 131; EWL 3; HW 1; LAW

Ronsard, Pierre de 1524-1585 . **LC 6, 54; PC
11**
See also EW 2; GFL Beginnings to 1789;
RGWL 2, 3; TWA

Rooke, Leon 1934- .... **CLC 25, 34**
See also CA 25-28R; CANR 23, 53; CCA
1; CPW; DAM POP

Roosevelt, Franklin Delano
1882-1945 .... **TCLC 93**
See also CA 116; 173; LAIT 3

Roosevelt, Theodore 1858-1919 ..... **TCLC 69**
See also CA 115; 170; DLB 47, 186, 275

Roper, William 1498-1578 .... **LC 10**

Roquelaure, A. N.
See Rice, Anne

Rosa, Joao Guimaraes 1908-1967 ... **CLC 23;
HLCS 1**
See Guimaraes Rosa, Joao
See also CA 89-92; DLB 113; EWL 3;
WLIT 1

Rose, Wendy 1948- . **CLC 85; NNAL; PC 13**
See also CA 53-56; CANR 5, 51; CWP;
DAM MULT; DLB 175; PFS 13; RGAL
4; SATA 12

Rosen, R. D.
See Rosen, Richard (Dean)

Rosen, Richard (Dean) 1949- .... **CLC 39**
See also CA 77-80; CANR 62, 120; CMW
4; INT CANR-30

Rosenberg, Isaac 1890-1918 .... **TCLC 12**
See also BRW 6; CA 107; 188; DLB 20,
216; EWL 3; PAB; RGEL 2

Rosenblatt, Joe .... **CLC 15**
See Rosenblatt, Joseph

Rosenblatt, Joseph 1933-
See Rosenblatt, Joe
See also CA 89-92; CP 7; INT CA-89-92

Rosenfeld, Samuel
See Tzara, Tristan

Rosenstock, Sami
See Tzara, Tristan

Rosenstock, Samuel
See Tzara, Tristan

Rosenthal, M(acha) L(ouis)
1917-1996 .... **CLC 28**
See also CA 1-4R; 152; CAAS 6; CANR 4,
51; CP 7; DLB 5; SATA 59

Ross, Barnaby
See Dannay, Frederic

Ross, Bernard L.
See Follett, Ken(neth Martin)

Ross, J. H.
See Lawrence, T(homas) E(dward)

Ross, John Hume
See Lawrence, T(homas) E(dward)

Ross, Martin 1862-1915
See Martin, Violet Florence
See also DLB 135; GLL 2; RGEL 2; RGSF
2

Ross, (James) Sinclair 1908-1996 ... **CLC 13;
SSC 24**
See also CA 73-76; CANR 81; CN 7; DAC;
DAM MST; DLB 88; RGEL 2; RGSF 2;
TCWW 2

Rossetti, Christina (Georgina)
1830-1894 .... **NCLC 2, 50, 66; PC 7;
WLC**
See also AAYA 51; BRW 5; BYA 4; DA;
DA3; DAB; DAC; DAM MST, POET;
DLB 35, 163, 240; EXPP; LATS 1:1;
MAICYA 1, 2; PFS 10, 14; RGEL 2;
SATA 20; TEA; WCH

Rossetti, Dante Gabriel 1828-1882 . **NCLC 4,
77; PC 44; WLC**
See also AAYA 51; BRW 5; CDBLB 1832-
1890; DA; DAB; DAC; DAM MST,
POET; DLB 35; EXPP; RGEL 2; TEA

Rossi, Cristina Peri
See Peri Rossi, Cristina

Rossi, Jean-Baptiste 1931-2003
See Japrisot, Sebastien
See also CA 201; 215

Rossner, Judith (Perelman) 1935- . **CLC 6, 9,
29**
See also AITN 2; BEST 90:3; BPFB 3; CA
17-20R; CANR 18, 51, 73; CN 7; DLB 6;
INT CANR-18; MTCW 1, 2

Rostand, Edmond (Eugene Alexis)
1868-1918 .... **DC 10; TCLC 6, 37**
See also CA 104; 126; DA; DA3; DAB;
DAC; DAM DRAM, MST; DFS 1; DLB
192; LAIT 1; MTCW 1; RGWL 2, 3;
TWA

Roth, Henry 1906-1995 ..... **CLC 2, 6, 11, 104**
See also AMWS 9; CA 11-12; 149; CANR
38, 63; CAP 1; CN 7; DA3; DLB 28;
EWL 3; MTCW 1, 2

Roth, (Moses) Joseph 1894-1939 ... **TCLC 33**
See also CA 160; DLB 85; EWL 3; RGWL
2, 3

Roth, Philip (Milton) 1933- ... **CLC 1, 2, 3, 4,
6, 9, 15, 22, 31, 47, 66, 86, 119; SSC
26; WLC**
See also AMWR 2; AMWS 3; BEST 90:3;
BPFB 3; CA 1-4R; CANR 1, 22, 36, 55,
89, 132; CDALB 1968-1988; CN 7; CPW

Sadoff, Ira 1945- .... **CLC 9**
See also CA 53-56; CANR 5, 21, 109; DLB 120

Saetone
See Camus, Albert

Safire, William 1929- .... **CLC 10**
See also CA 17-20R; CANR 31, 54, 91

Sagan, Carl (Edward) 1934-1996 .... **CLC 30, 112**
See also AAYA 2; CA 25-28R; 155; CANR 11, 36, 74; CPW; DA3; MTCW 1, 2; SATA 58; SATA-Obit 94

Sagan, Francoise .... **CLC 3, 6, 9, 17, 36**
See Quoirez, Francoise
See also CWW 2; DLB 83; EWL 3; GFL 1789 to the Present; MTCW 2

Sahgal, Nayantara (Pandit) 1927- .... **CLC 41**
See also CA 9-12R; CANR 11, 88; CN 7

Said, Edward W. 1935-2003 .... **CLC 123**
See also CA 21-24R; 220; CANR 45, 74, 107, 131; DLB 67; MTCW 2

Saint, H(arry) F. 1941- .... **CLC 50**
See also CA 127

St. Aubin de Teran, Lisa 1953-
See Teran, Lisa St. Aubin de
See also CA 118; 126; CN 7; INT CA-126

Saint Birgitta of Sweden c. 1303-1373 .... **CMLC 24**

Sainte-Beuve, Charles Augustin 1804-1869 .... **NCLC 5**
See also DLB 217; EW 6; GFL 1789 to the Present

Saint-Exupery, Antoine (Jean Baptiste Marie Roger) de 1900-1944 .... **TCLC 2, 56; WLC**
See also BPFB 3; BYA 3; CA 108; 132; CLR 10; DA3; DAM NOV; DLB 72; EW 12; EWL 3; GFL 1789 to the Present; LAIT 3; MAICYA 1, 2; MTCW 1, 2; RGWL 2, 3; SATA 20; TWA

St. John, David
See Hunt, E(verette) Howard, (Jr.)

St. John, J. Hector
See Crevecoeur, Michel Guillaume Jean de

Saint-John Perse
See Leger, (Marie-Rene Auguste) Alexis Saint-Leger
See also EW 10; EWL 3; GFL 1789 to the Present; RGWL 2

Saintsbury, George (Edward Bateman) 1845-1933 .... **TCLC 31**
See also CA 160; DLB 57, 149

Sait Faik .... **TCLC 23**
See Abasiyanik, Sait Faik

Saki .... **SSC 12; TCLC 3**
See Munro, H(ector) H(ugh)
See also BRWS 6; BYA 11; LAIT 2; MTCW 2; RGEL 2; SSFS 1; SUFW

Sala, George Augustus 1828-1895 . **NCLC 46**

Saladin 1138-1193 .... **CMLC 38**

Salama, Hannu 1936- .... **CLC 18**
See also EWL 3

Salamanca, J(ack) R(ichard) 1922- .. **CLC 4, 15**
See also CA 25-28R, 193; CAAE 193

Salas, Floyd Francis 1931- .... **HLC 2**
See also CA 119; CAAS 27; CANR 44, 75, 93; DAM MULT; DLB 82; HW 1, 2; MTCW 2

Sale, J. Kirkpatrick
See Sale, Kirkpatrick

Sale, Kirkpatrick 1937- .... **CLC 68**
See also CA 13-16R; CANR 10

Salinas, Luis Omar 1937- ... **CLC 90; HLC 2**
See also AMWS 13; CA 131; CANR 81; DAM MULT; DLB 82; HW 1, 2

Salinas (y Serrano), Pedro 1891(?)-1951 .... **TCLC 17**
See also CA 117; DLB 134; EWL 3

Salinger, J(erome) D(avid) 1919- .. **CLC 1, 3, 8, 12, 55, 56, 138; SSC 2, 28, 65; WLC**
See also AAYA 2, 36; AMW; AMWC 1; BPFB 3; CA 5-8R; CANR 39, 129; CDALB 1941-1968; CLR 18; CN 7; CPW 1; DA; DA3; DAB; DAC; DAM MST, NOV, POP; DLB 2, 102, 173; EWL 3; EXPN; LAIT 4; MAICYA 1, 2; MTCW 1, 2; NFS 1; RGAL 4; RGSF 2; SATA 67; SSFS 17; TUS; WYA; YAW

Salisbury, John
See Caute, (John) David

Sallust c. 86B.C.-35B.C. .... **CMLC 68**
See also AW 2; CDWLB 1; DLB 211; RGWL 2, 3

Salter, James 1925- .. **CLC 7, 52, 59; SSC 58**
See also AMWS 9; CA 73-76; CANR 107; DLB 130

Saltus, Edgar (Everton) 1855-1921 . **TCLC 8**
See also CA 105; DLB 202; RGAL 4

Saltykov, Mikhail Evgrafovich 1826-1889 .... **NCLC 16**
See also DLB 238:

Saltykov-Shchedrin, N.
See Saltykov, Mikhail Evgrafovich

Samarakis, Andonis
See Samarakis, Antonis
See also EWL 3

Samarakis, Antonis 1919-2003 .... **CLC 5**
See Samarakis, Andonis
See also CA 25-28R; 224; CAAS 16; CANR 36

Sanchez, Florencio 1875-1910 .... **TCLC 37**
See also CA 153; DLB 305; EWL 3; HW 1; LAW

Sanchez, Luis Rafael 1936- .... **CLC 23**
See also CA 128; DLB 305; EWL 3; HW 1; WLIT 1

Sanchez, Sonia 1934- .... **BLC 3; CLC 5, 116; PC 9**
See also BW 2, 3; CA 33-36R; CANR 24, 49, 74, 115; CLR 18; CP 7; CSW; CWP; DA3; DAM MULT; DLB 41; DLBD 8; EWL 3; MAICYA 1, 2; MTCW 1, 2; SATA 22, 136; WP

Sancho, Ignatius 1729-1780 .... **LC 84**

Sand, George 1804-1876 ..... **NCLC 2, 42, 57; WLC**
See also DA; DA3; DAB; DAC; DAM MST, NOV; DLB 119, 192; EW 6; FW; GFL 1789 to the Present; RGWL 2, 3; TWA

Sandburg, Carl (August) 1878-1967 . **CLC 1, 4, 10, 15, 35; PC 2, 41; WLC**
See also AAYA 24; AMW; BYA 1, 3; CA 5-8R; 25-28R; CANR 35; CDALB 1865-1917; CLR 67; DA; DA3; DAB; DAC; DAM MST, POET; DLB 17, 54, 284; EWL 3; EXPP; LAIT 2; MAICYA 1, 2; MTCW 1, 2; PAB; PFS 3, 6, 12; RGAL 4; SATA 8; TUS; WCH; WP; WYA

Sandburg, Charles
See Sandburg, Carl (August)

Sandburg, Charles A.
See Sandburg, Carl (August)

Sanders, (James) Ed(ward) 1939- .... **CLC 53**
See Sanders, Edward
See also BG 3; CA 13-16R; CAAS 21; CANR 13, 44, 78; CP 7; DAM POET; DLB 16, 244

Sanders, Edward
See Sanders, (James) Ed(ward)
See also DLB 244

Sanders, Lawrence 1920-1998 .... **CLC 41**
See also BEST 89:4; BPFB 3; CA 81-84; 165; CANR 33, 62; CMW 4; CPW; DA3; DAM POP; MTCW 1

Sanders, Noah
See Blount, Roy (Alton), Jr.

Sanders, Winston P.
See Anderson, Poul (William)

Sandoz, Mari(e Susette) 1900-1966 .. **CLC 28**
See also CA 1-4R; 25-28R; CANR 17, 64; DLB 9, 212; LAIT 2; MTCW 1, 2; SATA 5; TCWW 2

Sandys, George 1578-1644 .... **LC 80**
See also DLB 24, 121

Saner, Reg(inald Anthony) 1931- .... **CLC 9**
See also CA 65-68; CP 7

Sankara 788-820 .... **CMLC 32**

Sannazaro, Jacopo 1456(?)-1530 .... **LC 8**
See also RGWL 2, 3

Sansom, William 1912-1976 . **CLC 2, 6; SSC 21**
See also CA 5-8R; 65-68; CANR 42; DAM NOV; DLB 139; EWL 3; MTCW 1; RGEL 2; RGSF 2

Santayana, George 1863-1952 .... **TCLC 40**
See also AMW; CA 115; 194; DLB 54, 71, 246, 270; DLBD 13; EWL 3; RGAL 4; TUS

Santiago, Danny .... **CLC 33**
See James, Daniel (Lewis)
See also DLB 122

Santmyer, Helen Hooven 1895-1986 .... **CLC 33; TCLC 133**
See also CA 1-4R; 118; CANR 15, 33; DLBY 1984; MTCW 1; RHW

Santoka, Taneda 1882-1940 .... **TCLC 72**

Santos, Bienvenido N(uqui) 1911-1996 ... **AAL; CLC 22; TCLC 156**
See also CA 101; 151; CANR 19, 46; DAM MULT; EWL; RGAL 4; SSFS 19

Sapir, Edward 1884-1939 .... **TCLC 108**
See also CA 211; DLB 92

Sapper .... **TCLC 44**
See McNeile, Herman Cyril

Sapphire
See Sapphire, Brenda

Sapphire, Brenda 1950- .... **CLC 99**

Sappho fl. 6th cent. B.C.- ... **CMLC 3, 67; PC 5**
See also CDWLB 1; DA3; DAM POET; DLB 176; PFS 20; RGWL 2, 3; WP

Saramago, Jose 1922- ..... **CLC 119; HLCS 1**
See also CA 153; CANR 96; CWW 2; DLB 287; EWL 3; LATS 1:2

Sarduy, Severo 1937-1993 .... **CLC 6, 97; HLCS 2**
See also CA 89-92; 142; CANR 58, 81; CWW 2; DLB 113; EWL 3; HW 1, 2; LAW

Sargeson, Frank 1903-1982 .... **CLC 31**
See also CA 25-28R; 106; CANR 38, 79; EWL 3; GLL 2; RGEL 2; RGSF 2; SSFS 20

Sarmiento, Domingo Faustino 1811-1888 .... **HLCS 2**
See also LAW; WLIT 1

Sarmiento, Felix Ruben Garcia
See Dario, Ruben

Saro-Wiwa, Ken(ule Beeson) 1941-1995 .... **CLC 114**
See also BW 2; CA 142; 150; CANR 60; DLB 157

Saroyan, William 1908-1981 ... **CLC 1, 8, 10, 29, 34, 56; SSC 21; TCLC 137; WLC**
See also CA 5-8R; 103; CAD; CANR 30; CDALBS; DA; DA3; DAB; DAC; DAM DRAM, MST, NOV; DFS 17; DLB 7, 9, 86; DLBY 1981; EWL 3; LAIT 4; MTCW 1, 2; RGAL 4; RGSF 2; SATA 23; SATA-Obit 24; SSFS 14; TUS

Sarraute, Nathalie 1900-1999 .... **CLC 1, 2, 4, 8, 10, 31, 80; TCLC 145**
See also BPFB 3; CA 9-12R; 187; CANR 23, 66; CWW 2; DLB 83; EW 12; EWL 3; GFL 1789 to the Present; MTCW 1, 2; RGWL 2, 3

Sarton, (Eleanor) May 1912-1995 ..... **CLC 4, 14, 49, 91; PC 39; TCLC 120**
See also AMWS 8; CA 1-4R; 149; CANR 1, 34, 55, 116; CN 7; CP 7; DAM POET; DLB 48; DLBY 1981; EWL 3; FW; INT CANR-34; MTCW 1, 2; RGAL 4; SATA 36; SATA-Obit 86; TUS

Sartre, Jean-Paul 1905-1980 . **CLC 1, 4, 7, 9, 13, 18, 24, 44, 50, 52; DC 3; SSC 32; WLC**
See also CA 9-12R; 97-100; CANR 21; DA; DA3; DAB; DAC; DAM DRAM, MST, NOV; DFS 5; DLB 72, 296; EW 12; EWL 3; GFL 1789 to the Present; LMFS 2; MTCW 1, 2; RGSF 2; RGWL 2, 3; SSFS 9; TWA

Sassoon, Siegfried (Lorraine) 1886-1967 .... **CLC 36, 130; PC 12**
See also BRW 6; CA 104; 25-28R; CANR 36; DAB; DAM MST, NOV, POET; DLB 20, 191; DLBD 18; EWL 3; MTCW 1, 2; PAB; RGEL 2; TEA

Satterfield, Charles
See Pohl, Frederik

Satyremont
See Peret, Benjamin

Saul, John (W. III) 1942- .... **CLC 46**
See also AAYA 10; BEST 90:4; CA 81-84; CANR 16, 40, 81; CPW; DAM NOV, POP; HGG; SATA 98

Saunders, Caleb
See Heinlein, Robert A(nson)

Saura (Atares), Carlos 1932-1998 .... **CLC 20**
See also CA 114; 131; CANR 79; HW 1

Sauser, Frederic Louis
See Sauser-Hall, Frederic

Sauser-Hall, Frederic 1887-1961 ...... **CLC 18**
See Cendrars, Blaise
See also CA 102; 93-96; CANR 36, 62; MTCW 1

Saussure, Ferdinand de 1857-1913 .... **TCLC 49**
See also DLB 242

Savage, Catharine
See Brosman, Catharine Savage

Savage, Richard 1697(?)-1743 .... **LC 96**
See also DLB 95; RGEL 2

Savage, Thomas 1915-2003 .... **CLC 40**
See also CA 126; 132; 218; CAAS 15; CN 7; INT CA-132; SATA-Obit 147; TCWW 2

Savan, Glenn 1953-2003 .... **CLC 50**
See also CA 225

Sax, Robert
See Johnson, Robert

Saxo Grammaticus c. 1150-c. 1222 .... **CMLC 58**

Saxton, Robert
See Johnson, Robert

Sayers, Dorothy L(eigh) 1893-1957 . **SSC 71; TCLC 2, 15**
See also BPFB 3; BRWS 3; CA 104; 119; CANR 60; CDBLB 1914-1945; CMW 4; DAM POP; DLB 10, 36, 77, 100; MSW; MTCW 1, 2; RGEL 2; SSFS 12; TEA

Sayers, Valerie 1952- .... **CLC 50, 122**
See also CA 134; CANR 61; CSW

Sayles, John (Thomas) 1950- . **CLC 7, 10, 14**
See also CA 57-60; CANR 41, 84; DLB 44

Scammell, Michael 1935- .... **CLC 34**
See also CA 156

Scannell, Vernon 1922- .... **CLC 49**
See also CA 5-8R; CANR 8, 24, 57; CP 7; CWRI 5; DLB 27; SATA 59

Scarlett, Susan
See Streatfeild, (Mary) Noel

Scarron 1847-1910
See Mikszath, Kalman

Schaeffer, Susan Fromberg 1941- ..... **CLC 6, 11, 22**
See also CA 49-52; CANR 18, 65; CN 7; DLB 28, 299; MTCW 1, 2; SATA 22

Schama, Simon (Michael) 1945- .... **CLC 150**
See also BEST 89:4; CA 105; CANR 39, 91

Schary, Jill
See Robinson, Jill

Schell, Jonathan 1943- .... **CLC 35**
See also CA 73-76; CANR 12, 117

Schelling, Friedrich Wilhelm Joseph von 1775-1854 .... **NCLC 30**
See also DLB 90

Scherer, Jean-Marie Maurice 1920-
See Rohmer, Eric
See also CA 110

Schevill, James (Erwin) 1920- .... **CLC 7**
See also CA 5-8R; CAAS 12; CAD; CD 5

Schiller, Friedrich von 1759-1805 ...... **DC 12; NCLC 39, 69**
See also CDWLB 2; DAM DRAM; DLB 94; EW 5; RGWL 2, 3; TWA

Schisgal, Murray (Joseph) 1926- .... **CLC 6**
See also CA 21-24R; CAD; CANR 48, 86; CD 5

Schlee, Ann 1934- .... **CLC 35**
See also CA 101; CANR 29, 88; SATA 44; SATA-Brief 36

Schlegel, August Wilhelm von 1767-1845 .... **NCLC 15, 142**
See also DLB 94; RGWL 2, 3

Schlegel, Friedrich 1772-1829 .... **NCLC 45**
See also DLB 90; EW 5; RGWL 2, 3; TWA

Schlegel, Johann Elias (von) 1719(?)-1749 .... **LC 5**

Schleiermacher, Friedrich 1768-1834 .... **NCLC 107**
See also DLB 90

Schlesinger, Arthur M(eier), Jr. 1917- .... **CLC 84**
See also AITN 1; CA 1-4R; CANR 1, 28, 58, 105; DLB 17; INT CANR-28; MTCW 1, 2; SATA 61

Schlink, Bernhard 1944- .... **CLC 174**
See also CA 163; CANR 116

Schmidt, Arno (Otto) 1914-1979 ...... **CLC 56**
See also CA 128; 109; DLB 69; EWL 3

Schmitz, Aron Hector 1861-1928
See Svevo, Italo
See also CA 104; 122; MTCW 1

Schnackenberg, Gjertrud (Cecelia) 1953- .... **CLC 40; PC 45**
See also CA 116; CANR 100; CP 7; CWP; DLB 120, 282; PFS 13

Schneider, Leonard Alfred 1925-1966
See Bruce, Lenny
See also CA 89-92

Schnitzler, Arthur 1862-1931 ..... **DC 17; SSC 15, 61; TCLC 4**
See also CA 104; CDWLB 2; DLB 81, 118; EW 8; EWL 3; RGSF 2; RGWL 2, 3

Schoenberg, Arnold Franz Walter 1874-1951 .... **TCLC 75**
See also CA 109; 188

Schonberg, Arnold
See Schoenberg, Arnold Franz Walter

Schopenhauer, Arthur 1788-1860 .. **NCLC 51**
See also DLB 90; EW 5

Schor, Sandra (M.) 1932(?)-1990 ..... **CLC 65**
See also CA 132

Schorer, Mark 1908-1977 .... **CLC 9**
See also CA 5-8R; 73-76; CANR 7; DLB 103

Schrader, Paul (Joseph) 1946- .... **CLC 26**
See also CA 37-40R; CANR 41; DLB 44

Schreber, Daniel 1842-1911 .... **TCLC 123**

Schreiner, Olive (Emilie Albertina) 1855-1920 .... **TCLC 9**
See also AFW; BRWS 2; CA 105; 154; DLB 18, 156, 190, 225; EWL 3; FW; RGEL 2; TWA; WLIT 2; WWE 1

Schulberg, Budd (Wilson) 1914- .. **CLC 7, 48**
See also BPFB 3; CA 25-28R; CANR 19, 87; CN 7; DLB 6, 26, 28; DLBY 1981, 2001

Schulman, Arnold
See Trumbo, Dalton

Schulz, Bruno 1892-1942 .. **SSC 13; TCLC 5, 51**
See also CA 115; 123; CANR 86; CDWLB 4; DLB 215; EWL 3; MTCW 2; RGSF 2; RGWL 2, 3

Schulz, Charles M(onroe) 1922-2000 .... **CLC 12**
See also AAYA 39; CA 9-12R; 187; CANR 6, 132; INT CANR-6; SATA 10; SATA-Obit 118

Schumacher, E(rnst) F(riedrich) 1911-1977 .... **CLC 80**
See also CA 81-84; 73-76; CANR 34, 85

Schumann, Robert 1810-1856 ...... **NCLC 143**

Schuyler, George Samuel 1895-1977 .... **HR 3**
See also BW 2; CA 81-84; 73-76; CANR 42; DLB 29, 51

Schuyler, James Marcus 1923-1991 .. **CLC 5, 23**
See also CA 101; 134; DAM POET; DLB 5, 169; EWL 3; INT CA-101; WP

Schwartz, Delmore (David) 1913-1966 ... **CLC 2, 4, 10, 45, 87; PC 8**
See also AMWS 2; CA 17-18; 25-28R; CANR 35; CAP 2; DLB 28, 48; EWL 3; MTCW 1, 2; PAB; RGAL 4; TUS

Schwartz, Ernst
See Ozu, Yasujiro

Schwartz, John Burnham 1965- .... **CLC 59**
See also CA 132; CANR 116

Schwartz, Lynne Sharon 1939- .... **CLC 31**
See also CA 103; CANR 44, 89; DLB 218; MTCW 2

Schwartz, Muriel A.
See Eliot, T(homas) S(tearns)

Schwarz-Bart, Andre 1928- .... **CLC 2, 4**
See also CA 89-92; CANR 109; DLB 299

Schwarz-Bart, Simone 1938- . **BLCS; CLC 7**
See also BW 2; CA 97-100; CANR 117; EWL 3

Schwerner, Armand 1927-1999 .... **PC 42**
See also CA 9-12R; 179; CANR 50, 85; CP 7; DLB 165

Schwitters, Kurt (Hermann Edward Karl Julius) 1887-1948 .... **TCLC 95**
See also CA 158

Schwob, Marcel (Mayer Andre) 1867-1905 .... **TCLC 20**
See also CA 117; 168; DLB 123; GFL 1789 to the Present

Sciascia, Leonardo 1921-1989 .. **CLC 8, 9, 41**
See also CA 85-88; 130; CANR 35; DLB 177; EWL 3; MTCW 1; RGWL 2, 3

Scoppettone, Sandra 1936- .... **CLC 26**
See Early, Jack
See also AAYA 11; BYA 8; CA 5-8R; CANR 41, 73; GLL 1; MAICYA 2; MAICYAS 1; SATA 9, 92; WYA; YAW

Scorsese, Martin 1942- .... **CLC 20, 89**
See also AAYA 38; CA 110; 114; CANR 46, 85

Scotland, Jay
See Jakes, John (William)

Scott, Duncan Campbell 1862-1947 .... **TCLC 6**
See also CA 104; 153; DAC; DLB 92; RGEL 2

Scott, Evelyn 1893-1963 .... **CLC 43**
See also CA 104; 112; CANR 64; DLB 9,
48; RHW

Scott, F(rancis) R(eginald)
1899-1985 .... **CLC 22**
See also CA 101; 114; CANR 87; DLB 88;
INT CA-101; RGEL 2

Scott, Frank
See Scott, F(rancis) R(eginald)

Scott, Joan .... **CLC 65**

Scott, Joanna 1960- .... **CLC 50**
See also CA 126; CANR 53, 92

Scott, Paul (Mark) 1920-1978 ...... **CLC 9, 60**
See also BRWS 1; CA 81-84; 77-80; CANR
33; DLB 14, 207; EWL 3; MTCW 1;
RGEL 2; RHW; WWE 1

Scott, Ridley 1937- .... **CLC 183**
See also AAYA 13, 43

Scott, Sarah 1723-1795 .... **LC 44**
See also DLB 39

Scott, Sir Walter 1771-1832 .... **NCLC 15, 69,
110; PC 13; SSC 32; WLC**
See also AAYA 22; BRW 4; BYA 2; CD-
BLB 1789-1832; DA; DAB; DAC; DAM
MST, NOV, POET; DLB 93, 107, 116,
144, 159; HGG; LAIT 1; RGEL 2; RGSF
2; SSFS 10; SUFW 1; TEA; WLIT 3;
YABC 2

Scribe, (Augustin) Eugene 1791-1861 . **DC 5;
NCLC 16**
See also DAM DRAM; DLB 192; GFL
1789 to the Present; RGWL 2, 3

Scrum, R.
See Crumb, R(obert)

Scudery, Georges de 1601-1667 .... **LC 75**
See also GFL Beginnings to 1789

Scudery, Madeleine de 1607-1701 .. **LC 2, 58**
See also DLB 268; GFL Beginnings to 1789

Scum
See Crumb, R(obert)

Scumbag, Little Bobby
See Crumb, R(obert)

Seabrook, John
See Hubbard, L(afayette) Ron(ald)

Seacole, Mary Jane Grant
1805-1881 .... **NCLC 147**
See also DLB 166

Sealy, I(rwin) Allan 1951- .... **CLC 55**
See also CA 136; CN 7

Search, Alexander
See Pessoa, Fernando (Antonio Nogueira)

Sebald, W(infried) G(eorg)
1944-2001 .... **CLC 194**
See also BRWS 8; CA 159; 202; CANR 98

Sebastian, Lee
See Silverberg, Robert

Sebastian Owl
See Thompson, Hunter S(tockton)

Sebestyen, Igen
See Sebestyen, Ouida

Sebestyen, Ouida 1924- .... **CLC 30**
See also AAYA 8; BYA 7; CA 107; CANR
40, 114; CLR 17; JRDA; MAICYA 1, 2;
SAAS 10; SATA 39, 140; WYA; YAW

Sebold, Alice 1963(?)- .... **CLC 193**
See also AAYA 56; CA 203

Second Duke of Buckingham
See Villiers, George

Secundus, H. Scriblerus
See Fielding, Henry

Sedges, John
See Buck, Pearl S(ydenstricker)

Sedgwick, Catharine Maria
1789-1867 .... **NCLC 19, 98**
See also DLB 1, 74, 183, 239, 243, 254;
RGAL 4

Seelye, John (Douglas) 1931- .... **CLC 7**
See also CA 97-100; CANR 70; INT CA-
97-100; TCWW 2

Seferiades, Giorgos Stylianou 1900-1971
See Seferis, George
See also CA 5-8R; 33-36R; CANR 5, 36;
MTCW 1

Seferis, George .... **CLC 5, 11**
See Seferiades, Giorgos Stylianou
See also EW 12; EWL 3; RGWL 2, 3

Segal, Erich (Wolf) 1937- .... **CLC 3, 10**
See also BEST 89:1; BPFB 3; CA 25-28R;
CANR 20, 36, 65, 113; CPW; DAM POP;
DLBY 1986; INT CANR-20; MTCW 1

Seger, Bob 1945- .... **CLC 35**

Seghers, Anna .... **CLC 7**
See Radvanyi, Netty
See also CDWLB 2; DLB 69; EWL 3

Seidel, Frederick (Lewis) 1936- .... **CLC 18**
See also CA 13-16R; CANR 8, 99; CP 7;
DLBY 1984

Seifert, Jaroslav 1901-1986 . **CLC 34, 44, 93;
PC 47**
See also CA 127; CDWLB 4; DLB 215;
EWL 3; MTCW 1, 2

Sei Shonagon c. 966-1017(?) .... **CMLC 6**

Sejour, Victor 1817-1874 .... **DC 10**
See also DLB 50

Sejour Marcou et Ferrand, Juan Victor
See Sejour, Victor

Selby, Hubert, Jr. 1928-2004 ..... **CLC 1, 2, 4,
8; SSC 20**
See also CA 13-16R; 226; CANR 33, 85;
CN 7; DLB 2, 227

Selzer, Richard 1928- .... **CLC 74**
See also CA 65-68; CANR 14, 106

Sembene, Ousmane
See Ousmane, Sembene
See also AFW; EWL 3; WLIT 2

Senancour, Etienne Pivert de
1770-1846 .... **NCLC 16**
See also DLB 119; GFL 1789 to the Present

Sender, Ramon (Jose) 1902-1982 ...... **CLC 8;
HLC 2; TCLC 136**
See also CA 5-8R; 105; CANR 8; DAM
MULT; EWL 3; HW 1; MTCW 1; RGWL
2, 3

Seneca, Lucius Annaeus c. 4B.C.-c.
65 .... **CMLC 6; DC 5**
See also AW 2; CDWLB 1; DAM DRAM;
DLB 211; RGWL 2, 3; TWA

Senghor, Leopold Sedar 1906-2001 ... **BLC 3;
CLC 54, 130; PC 25**
See also AFW; BW 2; CA 116; 125; 203;
CANR 47, 74; CWW 2; DAM MULT,
POET; DNFS 2; EWL 3; GFL 1789 to the
Present; MTCW 1, 2; TWA

Senna, Danzy 1970- .... **CLC 119**
See also CA 169; CANR 130

Serling, (Edward) Rod(man)
1924-1975 .... **CLC 30**
See also AAYA 14; AITN 1; CA 162; 57-
60; DLB 26; SFW 4

Serna, Ramon Gomez de la
See Gomez de la Serna, Ramon

Serpieres
See Guillevic, (Eugene)

Service, Robert
See Service, Robert W(illiam)
See also BYA 4; DAB; DLB 92

Service, Robert W(illiam)
1874(?)-1958 .... **TCLC 15; WLC**
See Service, Robert
See also CA 115; 140; CANR 84; DA;
DAC; DAM MST, POET; PFS 10; RGEL
2; SATA 20

Seth, Vikram 1952- .... **CLC 43, 90**
See also CA 121; 127; CANR 50, 74, 131;
CN 7; CP 7; DA3; DAM MULT; DLB
120, 271, 282; EWL 3; INT CA-127;
MTCW 2; WWE 1

Seton, Cynthia Propper 1926-1982 .. **CLC 27**
See also CA 5-8R; 108; CANR 7

Seton, Ernest (Evan) Thompson
1860-1946 .... **TCLC 31**
See also ANW; BYA 3; CA 109; 204; CLR
59; DLB 92; DLBD 13; JRDA; SATA 18

Seton-Thompson, Ernest
See Seton, Ernest (Evan) Thompson

Settle, Mary Lee 1918- .... **CLC 19, 61**
See also BPFB 3; CA 89-92; CAAS 1;
CANR 44, 87, 126; CN 7; CSW; DLB 6;
INT CA-89-92

Seuphor, Michel
See Arp, Jean

Sevigne, Marie (de Rabutin-Chantal)
1626-1696 .... **LC 11**
See Sevigne, Marie de Rabutin Chantal
See also GFL Beginnings to 1789; TWA

Sevigne, Marie de Rabutin Chantal
See Sevigne, Marie (de Rabutin-Chantal)
See also DLB 268

Sewall, Samuel 1652-1730 .... **LC 38**
See also DLB 24; RGAL 4

Sexton, Anne (Harvey) 1928-1974 ..... **CLC 2,
4, 6, 8, 10, 15, 53, 123; PC 2; WLC**
See also AMWS 2; CA 1-4R; 53-56; CABS
2; CANR 3, 36; CDALB 1941-1968; DA;
DA3; DAB; DAC; DAM MST, POET;
DLB 5, 169; EWL 3; EXPP; FW;
MAWW; MTCW 1, 2; PAB; PFS 4, 14;
RGAL 4; SATA 10; TUS

Shaara, Jeff 1952- .... **CLC 119**
See also CA 163; CANR 109

Shaara, Michael (Joseph, Jr.)
1929-1988 .... **CLC 15**
See also AITN 1; BPFB 3; CA 102; 125;
CANR 52, 85; DAM POP; DLBY 1983

Shackleton, C. C.
See Aldiss, Brian W(ilson)

Shacochis, Bob .... **CLC 39**
See Shacochis, Robert G.

Shacochis, Robert G. 1951-
See Shacochis, Bob
See also CA 119; 124; CANR 100; INT CA-
124

Shaffer, Anthony (Joshua)
1926-2001 .... **CLC 19**
See also CA 110; 116; 200; CBD; CD 5;
DAM DRAM; DFS 13; DLB 13

Shaffer, Peter (Levin) 1926- .. **CLC 5, 14, 18,
37, 60; DC 7**
See also BRWS 1; CA 25-28R; CANR 25,
47, 74, 118; CBD; CD 5; CDBLB 1960 to
Present; DA3; DAB; DAM DRAM, MST;
DFS 5; DLB 13, 233; EWL 3; MTCW
1, 2; RGEL 2; TEA

Shakespeare, William 1564-1616 .... **WLC**
See also AAYA 35; BRW 1; CDBLB Before
1660; DA; DA3; DAB; DAC; DAM
DRAM, MST, POET; DFS 20; DLB 62,
172, 263; EXPP; LAIT 1; LATS 1:1;
LMFS 1; PAB; PFS 1, 2, 3, 4, 5, 8, 9;
RGEL 2; TEA; WLIT 3; WP; WS; WYA

Shakey, Bernard
See Young, Neil

Shalamov, Varlam (Tikhonovich)
1907-1982 .... **CLC 18**
See also CA 129; 105; DLB 302; RGSF 2

Shamloo, Ahmad
See Shamlu, Ahmad

Shamlou, Ahmad
See Shamlu, Ahmad

Shamlu, Ahmad 1925-2000 .... **CLC 10**
See also CA 216; CWW 2

Sierra, Gregorio Martinez
See Martinez Sierra, Gregorio
Sierra, Maria (de la O'LeJarraga) Martinez
See Martinez Sierra, Maria (de la O'LeJarraga)
Sigal, Clancy 1926- .... **CLC 7**
See also CA 1-4R; CANR 85; CN 7
Siger of Brabant 1240(?)-1284(?) . **CMLC 69**
See also DLB 115
Sigourney, Lydia H.
See Sigourney, Lydia Howard (Huntley)
See also DLB 73, 183
Sigourney, Lydia Howard (Huntley)
1791-1865 .... **NCLC 21, 87**
See Sigourney, Lydia H.; Sigourney, Lydia Huntley
See also DLB 1
Sigourney, Lydia Huntley
See Sigourney, Lydia Howard (Huntley)
See also DLB 42, 239, 243
Siguenza y Gongora, Carlos de
1645-1700 .... **HLCS 2; LC 8**
See also LAW
Sigurjonsson, Johann
See Sigurjonsson, Johann
Sigurjonsson, Johann 1880-1919 ... **TCLC 27**
See also CA 170; DLB 293; EWL 3
Sikelianos, Angelos 1884-1951 .... **PC 29; TCLC 39**
See also EWL 3; RGWL 2, 3
Silkin, Jon 1930-1997 .... **CLC 2, 6, 43**
See also CA 5-8R; CAAS 5; CANR 89; CP 7; DLB 27
Silko, Leslie (Marmon) 1948- .... **CLC 23, 74, 114; NNAL; SSC 37, 66; WLCS**
See also AAYA 14; AMWS 4; ANW; BYA 12; CA 115; 122; CANR 45, 65, 118; CN 7; CP 7; CPW 1; CWP; DA; DA3; DAC; DAM MST, MULT, POP; DLB 143, 175, 256, 275; EWL 3; EXPP; LAIT 4; MTCW 2; NFS 4; PFS 9, 16; RGAL 4; RGSF 2; SSFS 4, 8, 10, 11
Sillanpaa, Frans Eemil 1888-1964 ... **CLC 19**
See also CA 129; 93-96; EWL 3; MTCW 1
Sillitoe, Alan 1928- .. **CLC 1, 3, 6, 10, 19, 57, 148**
See also AITN 1; BRWS 5; CA 9-12R, 191; CAAE 191; CAAS 2; CANR 8, 26, 55; CDBLB 1960 to Present; CN 7; DLB 14, 139; EWL 3; MTCW 1, 2; RGEL 2; RGSF 2; SATA 61
Silone, Ignazio 1900-1978 .... **CLC 4**
See also CA 25-28; 81-84; CANR 34; CAP 2; DLB 264; EW 12; EWL 3; MTCW 1; RGSF 2; RGWL 2, 3
Silone, Ignazione
See Silone, Ignazio
Silver, Joan Micklin 1935- .... **CLC 20**
See also CA 114; 121; INT CA-121
Silver, Nicholas
See Faust, Frederick (Schiller)
See also TCWW 2
Silverberg, Robert 1935- .... **CLC 7, 140**
See also AAYA 24; BPFB 3; BYA 7, 9; CA 1-4R, 186; CAAE 186; CAAS 3; CANR 1, 20, 36, 85; CLR 59; CN 7; CPW; DAM POP; DLB 8; INT CANR-20; MAICYA 1, 2; MTCW 1, 2; SATA 13, 91; SATA-Essay 104; SCFW 2; SFW 4; SUFW 2
Silverstein, Alvin 1933- .... **CLC 17**
See also CA 49-52; CANR 2; CLR 25; JRDA; MAICYA 1, 2; SATA 8, 69, 124
Silverstein, Shel(don Allan)
1932-1999 .... **PC 49**
See also AAYA 40; BW 3; CA 107; 179; CANR 47, 74, 81; CLR 5, 96; CWRI 5; JRDA; MAICYA 1, 2; MTCW 2; SATA 33, 92; SATA-Brief 27; SATA-Obit 116

Silverstein, Virginia B(arbara Opshelor)
1937- .... **CLC 17**
See also CA 49-52; CANR 2; CLR 25; JRDA; MAICYA 1, 2; SATA 8, 69, 124
Sim, Georges
See Simenon, Georges (Jacques Christian)
Simak, Clifford D(onald) 1904-1988 . **CLC 1, 55**
See also CA 1-4R; 125; CANR 1, 35; DLB 8; MTCW 1; SATA-Obit 56; SFW 4
Simenon, Georges (Jacques Christian)
1903-1989 .... **CLC 1, 2, 3, 8, 18, 47**
See also BPFB 3; CA 85-88; 129; CANR 35; CMW 4; DA3; DAM POP; DLB 72; DLBY 1989; EW 12; EWL 3; GFL 1789 to the Present; MSW; MTCW 1, 2; RGWL 2, 3
Simic, Charles 1938- .... **CLC 6, 9, 22, 49, 68, 130**
See also AMWS 8; CA 29-32R; CAAS 4; CANR 12, 33, 52, 61, 96; CP 7; DA3; DAM POET; DLB 105; MTCW 2; PFS 7; RGAL 4; WP
Simmel, Georg 1858-1918 .... **TCLC 64**
See also CA 157; DLB 296
Simmons, Charles (Paul) 1924- .... **CLC 57**
See also CA 89-92; INT CA-89-92
Simmons, Dan 1948- .... **CLC 44**
See also AAYA 16, 54; CA 138; CANR 53, 81, 126; CPW; DAM POP; HGG; SUFW 2
Simmons, James (Stewart Alexander)
1933- .... **CLC 43**
See also CA 105; CAAS 21; CP 7; DLB 40
Simms, William Gilmore
1806-1870 .... **NCLC 3**
See also DLB 3, 30, 59, 73, 248, 254; RGAL 4
Simon, Carly 1945- .... **CLC 26**
See also CA 105
Simon, Claude (Eugene Henri)
1913-1984 .... **CLC 4, 9, 15, 39**
See also CA 89-92; CANR 33, 117; CWW 2; DAM NOV; DLB 83; EW 13; EWL 3; GFL 1789 to the Present; MTCW 1
Simon, Myles
See Follett, Ken(neth Martin)
Simon, (Marvin) Neil 1927- ... **CLC 6, 11, 31, 39, 70; DC 14**
See also AAYA 32; AITN 1; AMWS 4; CA 21-24R; CANR 26, 54, 87, 126; CD 5; DA3; DAM DRAM; DFS 2, 6, 12, 18; DLB 7, 266; LAIT 4; MTCW 1, 2; RGAL 4; TUS
Simon, Paul (Frederick) 1941(?)- ..... **CLC 17**
See also CA 116; 153
Simonon, Paul 1956(?)- .... **CLC 30**
Simonson, Rick ed. .... **CLC 70**
Simpson, Harriette
See Arnow, Harriette (Louisa) Simpson
Simpson, Louis (Aston Marantz)
1923- .... **CLC 4, 7, 9, 32, 149**
See also AMWS 9; CA 1-4R; CAAS 4; CANR 1, 61; CP 7; DAM POET; DLB 5; MTCW 1, 2; PFS 7, 11, 14; RGAL 4
Simpson, Mona (Elizabeth) 1957- ... **CLC 44, 146**
See also CA 122; 135; CANR 68, 103; CN 7; EWL 3
Simpson, N(orman) F(rederick)
1919- .... **CLC 29**
See also CA 13-16R; CBD; DLB 13; RGEL 2
Sinclair, Andrew (Annandale) 1935- . **CLC 2, 14**
See also CA 9-12R; CAAS 5; CANR 14, 38, 91; CN 7; DLB 14; FANT; MTCW 1
Sinclair, Emil
See Hesse, Hermann

Sinclair, Iain 1943- .... **CLC 76**
See also CA 132; CANR 81; CP 7; HGG
Sinclair, Iain MacGregor
See Sinclair, Iain
Sinclair, Irene
See Griffith, D(avid Lewelyn) W(ark)
Sinclair, Mary Amelia St. Clair 1865(?)-1946
See Sinclair, May
See also CA 104; HGG; RHW
Sinclair, May .... **TCLC 3, 11**
See Sinclair, Mary Amelia St. Clair
See also CA 166; DLB 36, 135; EWL 3; RGEL 2; SUFW
Sinclair, Roy
See Griffith, D(avid Lewelyn) W(ark)
Sinclair, Upton (Beall) 1878-1968 ..... **CLC 1, 11, 15, 63; WLC**
See also AMWS 5; BPFB 3; BYA 2; CA 5-8R; 25-28R; CANR 7; CDALB 1929-1941; DA; DA3; DAB; DAC; DAM MST, NOV; DLB 9; EWL 3; INT CANR-7; LAIT 3; MTCW 1, 2; NFS 6; RGAL 4; SATA 9; TUS; YAW
Singe, (Edmund) J(ohn) M(illington)
1871-1909 .... **WLC**
Singer, Isaac
See Singer, Isaac Bashevis
Singer, Isaac Bashevis 1904-1991 .. **CLC 1, 3, 6, 9, 11, 15, 23, 38, 69, 111; SSC 3, 53; WLC**
See also AAYA 32; AITN 1, 2; AMW; AMWR 2; BPFB 3; BYA 1, 4; CA 1-4R; 134; CANR 1, 39, 106; CDALB 1941-1968; CLR 1; CWRI 5; DA; DA3; DAB; DAC; DAM MST, NOV; DLB 6, 28, 52, 278; DLBY 1991; EWL 3; EXPS; HGG; JRDA; LAIT 3; MAICYA 1, 2; MTCW 1, 2; RGAL 4; RGSF 2; SATA 3, 27; SATA-Obit 68; SSFS 2, 12, 16; TUS; TWA
Singer, Israel Joshua 1893-1944 .... **TCLC 33**
See also CA 169; EWL 3
Singh, Khushwant 1915- .... **CLC 11**
See also CA 9-12R; CAAS 9; CANR 6, 84; CN 7; EWL 3; RGEL 2
Singleton, Ann
See Benedict, Ruth (Fulton)
Singleton, John 1968(?)- .... **CLC 156**
See also AAYA 50; BW 2, 3; CA 138; CANR 67, 82; DAM MULT
Siniavskii, Andrei
See Sinyavsky, Andrei (Donatevich)
See also CWW 2
Sinjohn, John
See Galsworthy, John
Sinyavsky, Andrei (Donatevich)
1925-1997 .... **CLC 8**
See Siniavskii, Andrei; Sinyavsky, Andrey Donatovich; Tertz, Abram
See also CA 85-88; 159
Sinyavsky, Andrey Donatovich
See Sinyavsky, Andrei (Donatevich)
See also EWL 3
Sirin, V.
See Nabokov, Vladimir (Vladimirovich)
Sissman, L(ouis) E(dward)
1928-1976 .... **CLC 9, 18**
See also CA 21-24R; 65-68; CANR 13; DLB 5
Sisson, C(harles) H(ubert)
1914-2003 .... **CLC 8**
See also CA 1-4R; 220; CAAS 3; CANR 3, 48, 84; CP 7; DLB 27
Sitting Bull 1831(?)-1890 .... **NNAL**
See also DA3; DAM MULT
Sitwell, Dame Edith 1887-1964 ..... **CLC 2, 9, 67; PC 3**
See also BRW 7; CA 9-12R; CANR 35; CDBLB 1945-1960; DAM POET; DLB 20; EWL 3; MTCW 1, 2; RGEL 2; TEA

Sondheim, Stephen (Joshua) 1930- . **CLC 30, 39, 147; DC 22**
See also AAYA 11; CA 103; CANR 47, 67, 125; DAM DRAM; LAIT 4

Sone, Monica 1919- .... **AAL**

Song, Cathy 1955- .... **AAL; PC 21**
See also CA 154; CANR 118; CWP; DLB 169; EXPP; FW; PFS 5

Sontag, Susan 1933- .... **CLC 1, 2, 10, 13, 31, 105, 195**
See also AMWS 3; CA 17-20R; CANR 25, 51, 74, 97; CN 7; CPW; DA3; DAM POP; DLB 2, 67; EWL 3; MAWW; MTCW 1, 2; RGAL 4; RHW; SSFS 10

Sophocles 496(?)B.C.-406(?)B.C. .... **CMLC 2, 47, 51; DC 1; WLCS**
See also AW 1; CDWLB 1; DA; DA3; DAB; DAC; DAM DRAM, MST; DFS 1, 4, 8; DLB 176; LAIT 1; LATS 1:1; LMFS 1; RGWL 2, 3; TWA

Sordello 1189-1269 .... **CMLC 15**

Sorel, Georges 1847-1922 .... **TCLC 91**
See also CA 118; 188

Sorel, Julia
See Drexler, Rosalyn

Sorokin, Vladimir .... **CLC 59**
See Sorokin, Vladimir Georgievich

Sorokin, Vladimir Georgievich
See Sorokin, Vladimir
See also DLB 285

Sorrentino, Gilbert 1929- .. **CLC 3, 7, 14, 22, 40**
See also CA 77-80; CANR 14, 33, 115; CN 7; CP 7; DLB 5, 173; DLBY 1980; INT CANR-14

Soseki
See Natsume, Soseki
See also MJW

Soto, Gary 1952- ... **CLC 32, 80; HLC 2; PC 28**
See also AAYA 10, 37; BYA 11; CA 119; 125; CANR 50, 74, 107; CLR 38; CP 7; DAM MULT; DLB 82; EWL 3; EXPP; HW 1, 2; INT CA-125; JRDA; LLW 1; MAICYA 2; MAICYAS 1; MTCW 2; PFS 7; RGAL 4; SATA 80, 120; WYA; YAW

Soupault, Philippe 1897-1990 .... **CLC 68**
See also CA 116; 147; 131; EWL 3; GFL 1789 to the Present; LMFS 2

Souster, (Holmes) Raymond 1921- .... **CLC 5, 14**
See also CA 13-16R; CAAS 14; CANR 13, 29, 53; CP 7; DA3; DAC; DAM POET; DLB 88; RGEL 2; SATA 63

Southern, Terry 1924(?)-1995 .... **CLC 7**
See also AMWS 11; BPFB 3; CA 1-4R; 150; CANR 1, 55, 107; CN 7; DLB 2; IDFW 3, 4

Southerne, Thomas 1660-1746 .... **LC 99**
See also DLB 80; RGEL 2

Southey, Robert 1774-1843 .... **NCLC 8, 97**
See also BRW 4; DLB 93, 107, 142; RGEL 2; SATA 54

Southwell, Robert 1561(?)-1595 .... **LC 108**
See also DLB 167; RGEL 2; TEA

Southworth, Emma Dorothy Eliza Nevitte 1819-1899 .... **NCLC 26**
See also DLB 239

Souza, Ernest
See Scott, Evelyn

Soyinka, Wole 1934- .. **BLC 3; CLC 3, 5, 14, 36, 44, 179; DC 2; WLC**
See also AFW; BW 2, 3; CA 13-16R; CANR 27, 39, 82; CD 5; CDWLB 3; CN 7; CP 7; DA; DA3; DAB; DAC; DAM DRAM, MST, MULT; DFS 10; DLB 125; EWL 3; MTCW 1, 2; RGEL 2; TWA; WLIT 2; WWE 1

Spackman, W(illiam) M(ode) 1905-1990 .... **CLC 46**
See also CA 81-84; 132

Spacks, Barry (Bernard) 1931- .... **CLC 14**
See also CA 154; CANR 33, 109; CP 7; DLB 105

Spanidou, Irini 1946- .... **CLC 44**
See also CA 185

Spark, Muriel (Sarah) 1918- ..... **CLC 2, 3, 5, 8, 13, 18, 40, 94; SSC 10**
See also BRWS 1; CA 5-8R; CANR 12, 36, 76, 89, 131; CDBLB 1945-1960; CN 7; CP 7; DA3; DAB; DAC; DAM MST, NOV; DLB 15, 139; EWL 3; FW; INT CANR-12; LAIT 4; MTCW 1, 2; RGEL 2; TEA; WLIT 4; YAW

Spaulding, Douglas
See Bradbury, Ray (Douglas)

Spaulding, Leonard
See Bradbury, Ray (Douglas)

Speght, Rachel 1597-c. 1630 .... **LC 97**
See also DLB 126

Spelman, Elizabeth .... **CLC 65**

Spence, J. A. D.
See Eliot, T(homas) S(tearns)

Spencer, Anne 1882-1975 .... **HR 3**
See also BW 2; CA 161; DLB 51, 54

Spencer, Elizabeth 1921- .... **CLC 22; SSC 57**
See also CA 13-16R; CANR 32, 65, 87; CN 7; CSW; DLB 6, 218; EWL 3; MTCW 1; RGAL 4; SATA 14

Spencer, Leonard G.
See Silverberg, Robert

Spencer, Scott 1945- .... **CLC 30**
See also CA 113; CANR 51; DLBY 1986

Spender, Stephen (Harold) 1909-1995 .... **CLC 1, 2, 5, 10, 41, 91**
See also BRWS 2; CA 9-12R; 149; CANR 31, 54; CDBLB 1945-1960; CP 7; DA3; DAM POET; DLB 20; EWL 3; MTCW 1, 2; PAB; RGEL 2; TEA

Spengler, Oswald (Arnold Gottfried) 1880-1936 .... **TCLC 25**
See also CA 118; 189

Spenser, Edmund 1552(?)-1599 ..... **LC 5, 39; PC 8, 42; WLC**
See also BRW 1; CDBLB Before 1660; DA; DA3; DAB; DAC; DAM MST, POET; DLB 167; EFS 2; EXPP; PAB; RGEL 2; TEA; WLIT 3; WP

Spicer, Jack 1925-1965 .... **CLC 8, 18, 72**
See also BG 3; CA 85-88; DAM POET; DLB 5, 16, 193; GLL 1; WP

Spiegelman, Art 1948- .... **CLC 76, 178**
See also AAYA 10, 46; CA 125; CANR 41, 55, 74, 124; DLB 299; MTCW 2; SATA 109; YAW

Spielberg, Peter 1929- .... **CLC 6**
See also CA 5-8R; CANR 4, 48; DLBY 1981

Spielberg, Steven 1947- .... **CLC 20, 188**
See also AAYA 8, 24; CA 77-80; CANR 32; SATA 32

Spillane, Frank Morrison 1918-
See Spillane, Mickey
See also CA 25-28R; CANR 28, 63, 125; DA3; MTCW 1, 2; SATA 66

Spillane, Mickey .... **CLC 3, 13**
See Spillane, Frank Morrison
See also BPFB 3; CMW 4; DLB 226; MSW; MTCW 2

Spinoza, Benedictus de 1632-1677 .. **LC 9, 58**

Spinrad, Norman (Richard) 1940- ... **CLC 46**
See also BPFB 3; CA 37-40R; CAAS 19; CANR 20, 91; DLB 8; INT CANR-20; SFW 4

Spitteler, Carl (Friedrich Georg) 1845-1924 .... **TCLC 12**
See also CA 109; DLB 129; EWL 3

Spivack, Kathleen (Romola Drucker) 1938- .... **CLC 6**
See also CA 49-52

Spoto, Donald 1941- .... **CLC 39**
See also CA 65-68; CANR 11, 57, 93

Springsteen, Bruce (F.) 1949- .... **CLC 17**
See also CA 111

Spurling, (Susan) Hilary 1940- .... **CLC 34**
See also CA 104; CANR 25, 52, 94

Spyker, John Howland
See Elman, Richard (Martin)

Squared, A.
See Abbott, Edwin A.

Squires, (James) Radcliffe 1917-1993 .... **CLC 51**
See also CA 1-4R; 140; CANR 6, 21

Srivastava, Dhanpat Rai 1880(?)-1936
See Premchand
See also CA 118; 197

Stacy, Donald
See Pohl, Frederik

Stael
See Stael-Holstein, Anne Louise Germaine Necker
See also EW 5; RGWL 2, 3

Stael, Germaine de
See Stael-Holstein, Anne Louise Germaine Necker
See also DLB 119, 192; FW; GFL 1789 to the Present; TWA

Stael-Holstein, Anne Louise Germaine Necker 1766-1817 .... **NCLC 3, 91**
See Stael; Stael, Germaine de

Stafford, Jean 1915-1979 .. **CLC 4, 7, 19, 68; SSC 26**
See also CA 1-4R; 85-88; CANR 3, 65; DLB 2, 173; MTCW 1, 2; RGAL 4; RGSF 2; SATA-Obit 22; TCWW 2; TUS

Stafford, William (Edgar) 1914-1993 .... **CLC 4, 7, 29**
See also AMWS 11; CA 5-8R; 142; CAAS 3; CANR 5, 22; DAM POET; DLB 5, 206; EXPP; INT CANR-22; PFS 2, 8, 16; RGAL 4; WP

Stagnelius, Eric Johan 1793-1823 . **NCLC 61**

Staines, Trevor
See Brunner, John (Kilian Houston)

Stairs, Gordon
See Austin, Mary (Hunter)
See also TCWW 2

Stalin, Joseph 1879-1953 .... **TCLC 92**

Stampa, Gaspara c. 1524-1554 .... **PC 43**
See also RGWL 2, 3

Stampflinger, K. A.
See Benjamin, Walter

Stancykowna
See Szymborska, Wislawa

Standing Bear, Luther 1868(?)-1939(?) .... **NNAL**
See also CA 113; 144; DAM MULT

Stannard, Martin 1947- .... **CLC 44**
See also CA 142; DLB 155

Stanton, Elizabeth Cady 1815-1902 .... **TCLC 73**
See also CA 171; DLB 79; FW

Stanton, Maura 1946- .... **CLC 9**
See also CA 89-92; CANR 15, 123; DLB 120

Stanton, Schuyler
See Baum, L(yman) Frank

Stapledon, (William) Olaf 1886-1950 .... **TCLC 22**
See also CA 111; 162; DLB 15, 255; SFW 4

Starbuck, George (Edwin) 1931-1996 .... **CLC 53**
See also CA 21-24R; 153; CANR 23; DAM POET

Stout, Rex (Todhunter) 1886-1975 ..... **CLC 3**
See also AITN 2; BPFB 3; CA 61-64;
CANR 71; CMW 4; DLB 306; MSW;
RGAL 4

Stow, (Julian) Randolph 1935- ... **CLC 23, 48**
See also CA 13-16R; CANR 33; CN 7;
DLB 260; MTCW 1; RGEL 2

Stowe, Harriet (Elizabeth) Beecher
1811-1896 .... **NCLC 3, 50, 133; WLC**
See also AAYA 53; AMWS 1; CDALB
1865-1917; DA; DA3; DAB; DAC; DAM
MST, NOV; DLB 1, 12, 42, 74, 189, 239,
243; EXPN; JRDA; LAIT 2; MAICYA 1,
2; NFS 6; RGAL 4; TUS; YABC 1

Strabo c. 64B.C.-c. 25 .... **CMLC 37**
See also DLB 176

Strachey, (Giles) Lytton
1880-1932 .... **TCLC 12**
See also BRWS 2; CA 110; 178; DLB 149;
DLBD 10; EWL 3; MTCW 2; NCFS 4

Stramm, August 1874-1915 .... **PC 50**
See also CA 195; EWL 3

Strand, Mark 1934- .... **CLC 6, 18, 41, 71**
See also AMWS 4; CA 21-24R; CANR 40,
65, 100; CP 7; DAM POET; DLB 5; EWL
3; PAB; PFS 9, 18; RGAL 4; SATA 41

Stratton-Porter, Gene(va Grace) 1863-1924
See Porter, Gene(va Grace) Stratton
See also ANW; CA 137; CLR 87; DLB 221;
DLBD 14; MAICYA 1, 2; SATA 15

Straub, Peter (Francis) 1943- ... **CLC 28, 107**
See also BEST 89:1; BPFB 3; CA 85-88;
CANR 28, 65, 109; CPW; DAM POP;
DLBY 1984; HGG; MTCW 1, 2; SUFW
2

Strauss, Botho 1944- .... **CLC 22**
See also CA 157; CWW 2; DLB 124

Strauss, Leo 1899-1973 .... **TCLC 141**
See also CA 101; 45-48; CANR 122

Streatfeild, (Mary) Noel
1897(?)-1986 .... **CLC 21**
See also CA 81-84; 120; CANR 31; CLR
17, 83; CWRI 5; DLB 160; MAICYA 1,
2; SATA 20; SATA-Obit 48

Stribling, T(homas) S(igismund)
1881-1965 .... **CLC 23**
See also CA 189; 107; CMW 4; DLB 9;
RGAL 4

Strindberg, (Johan) August
1849-1912 ... **DC 18; TCLC 1, 8, 21, 47;**
WLC
See also CA 104; 135; DA; DA3; DAB;
DAC; DAM DRAM, MST; DFS 4, 9;
DLB 259; EW 7; EWL 3; IDTP; LMFS
2; MTCW 2; RGWL 2, 3; TWA

Stringer, Arthur 1874-1950 .... **TCLC 37**
See also CA 161; DLB 92

Stringer, David
See Roberts, Keith (John Kingston)

Stroheim, Erich von 1885-1957 ..... **TCLC 71**

Strugatskii, Arkadii (Natanovich)
1925-1991 .... **CLC 27**
See Strugatsky, Arkadii Natanovich
See also CA 106; 135; SFW 4

Strugatskii, Boris (Natanovich)
1933- .... **CLC 27**
See Strugatsky, Boris (Natanovich)
See also CA 106; SFW 4

Strugatsky, Arkadii Natanovich
See Strugatskii, Arkadii (Natanovich)
See also DLB 302

Strugatsky, Boris (Natanovich)
See Strugatskii, Boris (Natanovich)
See also DLB 302

Strummer, Joe 1953(?)- .... **CLC 30**

Strunk, William, Jr. 1869-1946 ...... **TCLC 92**
See also CA 118; 164; NCFS 5

Stryk, Lucien 1924- .... **PC 27**
See also CA 13-16R; CANR 10, 28, 55,
110; CP 7

Stuart, Don A.
See Campbell, John W(ood, Jr.)

Stuart, Ian
See MacLean, Alistair (Stuart)

Stuart, Jesse (Hilton) 1906-1984 ... **CLC 1, 8,**
11, 14, 34; SSC 31
See also CA 5-8R; 112; CANR 31; DLB 9,
48, 102; DLBY 1984; SATA 2; SATA-
Obit 36

Stubblefield, Sally
See Trumbo, Dalton

Sturgeon, Theodore (Hamilton)
1918-1985 .... **CLC 22, 39**
See Queen, Ellery
See also AAYA 51; BPFB 3; BYA 9, 10;
CA 81-84; 116; CANR 32, 103; DLB 8;
DLBY 1985; HGG; MTCW 1, 2; SCFW;
SFW 4; SUFW

Sturges, Preston 1898-1959 .... **TCLC 48**
See also CA 114; 149; DLB 26

Styron, William 1925- .... **CLC 1, 3, 5, 11, 15,**
60; SSC 25
See also AMW; AMWC 2; BEST 90:4;
BPFB 3; CA 5-8R; CANR 6, 33, 74, 126;
CDALB 1968-1988; CN 7; CPW; CSW;
DA3; DAM NOV, POP; DLB 2, 143, 299;
DLBY 1980; EWL 3; INT CANR-6;
LAIT 2; MTCW 1, 2; NCFS 1; RGAL 4;
RHW; TUS

Su, Chien 1884-1918
See Su Man-shu
See also CA 123

Suarez Lynch, B.
See Bioy Casares, Adolfo; Borges, Jorge
Luis

Suassuna, Ariano Vilar 1927- .... **HLCS 1**
See also CA 178; HW 2; LAW

Suckert, Kurt Erich
See Malaparte, Curzio

Suckling, Sir John 1609-1642 . **LC 75; PC 30**
See also BRW 2; DAM POET; DLB 58,
126; EXPP; PAB; RGEL 2

Suckow, Ruth 1892-1960 .... **SSC 18**
See also CA 193; 113; DLB 9, 102; RGAL
4; TCWW 2

Sudermann, Hermann 1857-1928 .. **TCLC 15**
See also CA 107; 201; DLB 118

Sue, Eugene 1804-1857 .... **NCLC 1**
See also DLB 119

Sueskind, Patrick 1949- .... **CLC 44, 182**
See Suskind, Patrick

Suetonius c. 70-c. 130 .... **CMLC 60**
See also AW 2; DLB 211; RGWL 2, 3

Sukenick, Ronald 1932-2004 ..... **CLC 3, 4, 6,**
48
See also CA 25-28R; 209; CAAE 209;
CAAS 8; CANR 32, 89; CN 7; DLB 173;
DLBY 1981

Suknaski, Andrew 1942- .... **CLC 19**
See also CA 101; CP 7; DLB 53

Sullivan, Vernon
See Vian, Boris

Sully Prudhomme, Rene-Francois-Armand
1839-1907 .... **TCLC 31**
See also GFL 1789 to the Present

Su Man-shu .... **TCLC 24**
See Su, Chien
See also EWL 3

Sumarokov, Aleksandr Petrovich
1717-1777 .... **LC 104**
See also DLB 150

Summerforest, Ivy B.
See Kirkup, James

Summers, Andrew James 1942- .... **CLC 26**

Summers, Andy
See Summers, Andrew James

Summers, Hollis (Spurgeon, Jr.)
1916- .... **CLC 10**
See also CA 5-8R; CANR 3; DLB 6

Summers, (Alphonsus Joseph-Mary
Augustus) Montague
1880-1948 .... **TCLC 16**
See also CA 118; 163

Sumner, Gordon Matthew .... **CLC 26**
See Police, The; Sting

Sun Tzu c. 400B.C.-c. 320B.C. ...... **CMLC 56**

Surrey, Henry Howard 1517-1574 ...... **PC 59**
See also BRW 1; RGEL 2

Surtees, Robert Smith 1805-1864 .. **NCLC 14**
See also DLB 21; RGEL 2

Susann, Jacqueline 1921-1974 .... **CLC 3**
See also AITN 1; BPFB 3; CA 65-68; 53-
56; MTCW 1, 2

Su Shi
See Su Shih
See also RGWL 2, 3

Su Shih 1036-1101 .... **CMLC 15**
See Su Shi

Suskind, Patrick .... **CLC 182**
See Sueskind, Patrick
See also BPFB 3; CA 145; CWW 2

Sutcliff, Rosemary 1920-1992 .... **CLC 26**
See also AAYA 10; BYA 1, 4; CA 5-8R;
139; CANR 37; CLR 1, 37; CPW; DAB;
DAC; DAM MST, POP; JRDA; LATS
1:1; MAICYA 1, 2; MAICYAS 1; RHW;
SATA 6, 44, 78; SATA-Obit 73; WYA;
YAW

Sutro, Alfred 1863-1933 .... **TCLC 6**
See also CA 105; 185; DLB 10; RGEL 2

Sutton, Henry
See Slavitt, David R(ytman)

Suzuki, D. T.
See Suzuki, Daisetz Teitaro

Suzuki, Daisetz T.
See Suzuki, Daisetz Teitaro

Suzuki, Daisetz Teitaro
1870-1966 .... **TCLC 109**
See also CA 121; 111; MTCW 1, 2

Suzuki, Teitaro
See Suzuki, Daisetz Teitaro

Svevo, Italo .... **SSC 25; TCLC 2, 35**
See Schmitz, Aron Hector
See also DLB 264; EW 8; EWL 3; RGWL
2, 3

Swados, Elizabeth (A.) 1951- .... **CLC 12**
See also CA 97-100; CANR 49; INT CA-
97-100

Swados, Harvey 1920-1972 .... **CLC 5**
See also CA 5-8R; 37-40R; CANR 6; DLB
2

Swan, Gladys 1934- .... **CLC 69**
See also CA 101; CANR 17, 39

Swanson, Logan
See Matheson, Richard (Burton)

Swarthout, Glendon (Fred)
1918-1992 .... **CLC 35**
See also AAYA 55; CA 1-4R; 139; CANR
1, 47; LAIT 5; SATA 26; TCWW 2; YAW

Swedenborg, Emanuel 1688-1772 ..... **LC 105**

Sweet, Sarah C.
See Jewett, (Theodora) Sarah Orne

Swenson, May 1919-1989 ...... **CLC 4, 14, 61,**
106; PC 14
See also AMWS 4; CA 5-8R; 130; CANR
36, 61, 131; DA; DAB; DAC; DAM MST,
POET; DLB 5; EXPP; GLL 2; MTCW 1,
2; PFS 16; SATA 15; WP

Swift, Augustus
See Lovecraft, H(oward) P(hillips)

Swift, Graham (Colin) 1949- ...... **CLC 41, 88**
See also BRWC 2; BRWS 5; CA 117; 122;
CANR 46, 71, 128; CN 7; DLB 194;
MTCW 2; NFS 18; RGSF 2

Tristan
See Gomez de la Serna, Ramon

Tristram
See Housman, A(lfred) E(dward)

Trogdon, William (Lewis) 1939-
See Heat-Moon, William Least
See also CA 115; 119; CANR 47, 89; CPW;
INT CA-119

Trollope, Anthony 1815-1882 .... **NCLC 6, 33, 101; SSC 28; WLC**
See also BRW 5; CDBLB 1832-1890; DA;
DA3; DAB; DAC; DAM MST, NOV;
DLB 21, 57, 159; RGEL 2; RGSF 2;
SATA 22

Trollope, Frances 1779-1863 .... **NCLC 30**
See also DLB 21, 166

Trollope, Joanna 1943- .... **CLC 186**
See also CA 101; CANR 58, 95; CPW;
DLB 207; RHW

Trotsky, Leon 1879-1940 .... **TCLC 22**
See also CA 118; 167

Trotter (Cockburn), Catharine
1679-1749 .... **LC 8**
See also DLB 84, 252

Trotter, Wilfred 1872-1939 .... **TCLC 97**

Trout, Kilgore
See Farmer, Philip Jose

Trow, George W. S. 1943- .... **CLC 52**
See also CA 126; CANR 91

Troyat, Henri 1911- .... **CLC 23**
See also CA 45-48; CANR 2, 33, 67, 117;
GFL 1789 to the Present; MTCW 1

Trudeau, G(arretson) B(eekman) 1948-
See Trudeau, Garry B.
See also CA 81-84; CANR 31; SATA 35

Trudeau, Garry B. .... **CLC 12**
See Trudeau, G(arretson) B(eekman)
See also AAYA 10; AITN 2

Truffaut, Francois 1932-1984 ... **CLC 20, 101**
See also CA 81-84; 113; CANR 34

Trumbo, Dalton 1905-1976 .... **CLC 19**
See also CA 21-24R; 69-72; CANR 10;
DLB 26; IDFW 3, 4; YAW

Trumbull, John 1750-1831 .... **NCLC 30**
See also DLB 31; RGAL 4

Trundlett, Helen B.
See Eliot, T(homas) S(tearns)

Truth, Sojourner 1797(?)-1883 ...... **NCLC 94**
See also DLB 239; FW; LAIT 2

Tryon, Thomas 1926-1991 .... **CLC 3, 11**
See also AITN 1; BPFB 3; CA 29-32R; 135;
CANR 32, 77; CPW; DA3; DAM POP;
HGG; MTCW 1

Tryon, Tom
See Tryon, Thomas

Ts'ao Hsueh-ch'in 1715(?)-1763 .... **LC 1**

Tsushima, Shuji 1909-1948
See Dazai Osamu
See also CA 107

Tsvetaeva (Efron), Marina (Ivanovna)
1892-1941 .... **PC 14; TCLC 7, 35**
See also CA 104; 128; CANR 73; DLB 295;
EW 11; MTCW 1, 2; RGWL 2, 3

Tuck, Lily 1938- .... **CLC 70**
See also CA 139; CANR 90

Tu Fu 712-770 .... **PC 9**
See Du Fu
See also DAM MULT; TWA; WP

Tunis, John R(oberts) 1889-1975 ..... **CLC 12**
See also BYA 1; CA 61-64; CANR 62; DLB
22, 171; JRDA; MAICYA 1, 2; SATA 37;
SATA-Brief 30; YAW

Tuohy, Frank .... **CLC 37**
See Tuohy, John Francis
See also DLB 14, 139

Tuohy, John Francis 1925-
See Tuohy, Frank
See also CA 5-8R; 178; CANR 3, 47; CN 7

Turco, Lewis (Putnam) 1934- ..... **CLC 11, 63**
See also CA 13-16R; CAAS 22; CANR 24,
51; CP 7; DLBY 1984

Turgenev, Ivan (Sergeevich)
1818-1883 ..... **DC 7; NCLC 21, 37, 122;
SSC 7, 57; WLC**
See also AAYA 58; DA; DAB; DAC; DAM
MST, NOV; DFS 6; DLB 238, 284; EW
6; LATS 1:1; NFS 16; RGSF 2; RGWL 2,
3; TWA

Turgot, Anne-Robert-Jacques
1727-1781 .... **LC 26**

Turner, Frederick 1943- .... **CLC 48**
See also CA 73-76, 227; CAAE 227; CAAS
10; CANR 12, 30, 56; DLB 40, 282

Turton, James
See Crace, Jim

Tutu, Desmond M(pilo) 1931- .. **BLC 3; CLC 80**
See also BW 1, 3; CA 125; CANR 67, 81;
DAM MULT

Tutuola, Amos 1920-1997 ..... **BLC 3; CLC 5, 14, 29**
See also AFW; BW 2, 3; CA 9-12R; 159;
CANR 27, 66; CDWLB 3; CN 7; DA3;
DAM MULT; DLB 125; DNFS 2; EWL
3; MTCW 1, 2; RGEL 2; WLIT 2

Twain, Mark .. **SSC 34; TCLC 6, 12, 19, 36, 48, 59; WLC**
See Clemens, Samuel Langhorne
See also AAYA 20; AMW; AMWC 1; BPFB
3; BYA 2, 3, 11, 14; CLR 58, 60, 66; DLB
11; EXPN; EXPS; FANT; LAIT 2; NCFS
4; NFS 1, 6; RGAL 4; RGSF 2; SFW 4;
SSFS 1, 7; SUFW; TUS; WCH; WYA;
YAW

Tyler, Anne 1941- . **CLC 7, 11, 18, 28, 44, 59, 103**
See also AAYA 18; AMWS 4; BEST 89:1;
BPFB 3; BYA 12; CA 9-12R; CANR 11,
33, 53, 109, 132; CDALBS; CN 7; CPW;
CSW; DAM NOV, POP; DLB 6, 143;
DLBY 1982; EWL 3; EXPN; LATS 1:2;
MAWW; MTCW 1, 2; NFS 2, 7, 10;
RGAL 4; SATA 7, 90; SSFS 17; TUS;
YAW

Tyler, Royall 1757-1826 .... **NCLC 3**
See also DLB 37; RGAL 4

Tynan, Katharine 1861-1931 .... **TCLC 3**
See also CA 104; 167; DLB 153, 240; FW

Tyndale, William c. 1484-1536 .... **LC 103**
See also DLB 132

Tyutchev, Fyodor 1803-1873 .... **NCLC 34**

Tzara, Tristan 1896-1963 ..... **CLC 47; PC 27**
See also CA 153; 89-92; DAM POET; EWL
3; MTCW 2

Uchida, Yoshiko 1921-1992 .... **AAL**
See also AAYA 16; BYA 2, 3; CA 13-16R;
139; CANR 6, 22, 47, 61; CDALBS; CLR
6, 56; CWRI 5; JRDA; MAICYA 1, 2;
MTCW 1, 2; SAAS 1; SATA 1, 53; SATA-
Obit 72

Udall, Nicholas 1504-1556 .... **LC 84**
See also DLB 62; RGEL 2

Ueda Akinari 1734-1809 .... **NCLC 131**

Uhry, Alfred 1936- .... **CLC 55**
See also CA 127; 133; CAD; CANR 112;
CD 5; CSW; DA3; DAM DRAM, POP;
DFS 11, 15; INT CA-133

Ulf, Haerved
See Strindberg, (Johan) August

Ulf, Harved
See Strindberg, (Johan) August

Ulibarri, Sabine R(eyes)
1919-2003 .... **CLC 83; HLCS 2**
See also CA 131; 214; CANR 81; DAM
MULT; DLB 82; HW 1, 2; RGSF 2

Unamuno (y Jugo), Miguel de
1864-1936 .. **HLC 2; SSC 11, 69; TCLC 2, 9, 148**
See also CA 104; 131; CANR 81; DAM
MULT, NOV; DLB 108; EW 8; EWL 3;
HW 1, 2; MTCW 1, 2; RGSF 2; RGWL
2, 3; SSFS 20; TWA

Uncle Shelby
See Silverstein, Shel(don Allan)

Undercliffe, Errol
See Campbell, (John) Ramsey

Underwood, Miles
See Glassco, John

Undset, Sigrid 1882-1949 ..... **TCLC 3; WLC**
See also CA 104; 129; DA; DA3; DAB;
DAC; DAM MST, NOV; DLB 293; EW
9; EWL 3; FW; MTCW 1, 2; RGWL 2, 3

Ungaretti, Giuseppe 1888-1970 ... **CLC 7, 11, 15; PC 57**
See also CA 19-20; 25-28R; CAP 2; DLB
114; EW 10; EWL 3; PFS 20; RGWL 2, 3

Unger, Douglas 1952- .... **CLC 34**
See also CA 130; CANR 94

Unsworth, Barry (Forster) 1930- .... **CLC 76, 127**
See also BRWS 7; CA 25-28R; CANR 30,
54, 125; CN 7; DLB 194

Updike, John (Hoyer) 1932- . **CLC 1, 2, 3, 5, 7, 9, 13, 15, 23, 34, 43, 70, 139; SSC 13, 27; WLC**
See also AAYA 36; AMW; AMWC 1;
AMWR 1; BPFB 3; BYA 12; CA 1-4R;
CABS 1; CANR 4, 33, 51, 94, 133;
CDALB 1968-1988; CN 7; CP 7; CPW 1;
DA; DA3; DAB; DAC; DAM MST, NOV,
POET, POP; DLB 2, 5, 143, 218, 227;
DLBD 3; DLBY 1980, 1982, 1997; EWL
3; EXPP; HGG; MTCW 1, 2; NFS 12;
RGAL 4; RGSF 2; SSFS 3, 19; TUS

Upshaw, Margaret Mitchell
See Mitchell, Margaret (Munnerlyn)

Upton, Mark
See Sanders, Lawrence

Upward, Allen 1863-1926 .... **TCLC 85**
See also CA 117; 187; DLB 36

Urdang, Constance (Henriette)
1922-1996 .... **CLC 47**
See also CA 21-24R; CANR 9, 24; CP 7;
CWP

Uriel, Henry
See Faust, Frederick (Schiller)

Uris, Leon (Marcus) 1924-2003 ... **CLC 7, 32**
See also AITN 1, 2; BEST 89:2; BPFB 3;
CA 1-4R; 217; CANR 1, 40, 65, 123; CN
7; CPW 1; DA3; DAM NOV, POP;
MTCW 1, 2; SATA 49; SATA-Obit 146

Urista (Heredia), Alberto (Baltazar)
1947- .... **HLCS 1; PC 34**
See Alurista
See also CA 45-48, 182; CANR 2, 32; HW 1

Urmuz
See Codrescu, Andrei

Urquhart, Guy
See McAlmon, Robert (Menzies)

Urquhart, Jane 1949- .... **CLC 90**
See also CA 113; CANR 32, 68, 116; CCA
1; DAC

Usigli, Rodolfo 1905-1979 .... **HLCS 1**
See also CA 131; DLB 305; EWL 3; HW 1;
LAW

Ustinov, Peter (Alexander)
1921-2004 .... **CLC 1**
See also AITN 1; CA 13-16R; 225; CANR
25, 51; CBD; CD 5; DLB 13; MTCW 2

U Tam'si, Gerald Felix Tchicaya
See Tchicaya, Gerald Felix

Viereck, Peter (Robert Edwin)
1916- .... **CLC 4; PC 27**
See also CA 1-4R; CANR 1, 47; CP 7; DLB
5; PFS 9, 14

Vigny, Alfred (Victor) de
1797-1863 .... **NCLC 7, 102; PC 26**
See also DAM POET; DLB 119, 192, 217;
EW 5; GFL 1789 to the Present; RGWL
2, 3

Vilakazi, Benedict Wallet
1906-1947 .... **TCLC 37**
See also CA 168

Villa, Jose Garcia 1914-1997 .... **AAL; PC 22**
See also CA 25-28R; CANR 12, 118; EWL
3; EXPP

Villa, Jose Garcia 1914-1997
See Villa, Jose Garcia

Villarreal, Jose Antonio 1924- .... **HLC 2**
See also CA 133; CANR 93; DAM MULT;
DLB 82; HW 1; LAIT 4; RGAL 4

Villaurrutia, Xavier 1903-1950 ...... **TCLC 80**
See also CA 192; EWL 3; HW 1; LAW

Villaverde, Cirilo 1812-1894 .... **NCLC 121**
See also LAW

Villehardouin, Geoffroi de
1150(?)-1218(?) .... **CMLC 38**

Villiers, George 1628-1687 .... **LC 107**
See also DLB 80; RGEL 2

**Villiers de l'Isle Adam, Jean Marie Mathias
Philippe Auguste** 1838-1889 ... **NCLC 3;
SSC 14**
See also DLB 123, 192; GFL 1789 to the
Present; RGSF 2

Villon, Francois 1431-1463(?) . **LC 62; PC 13**
See also DLB 208; EW 2; RGWL 2, 3;
TWA

Vine, Barbara .... **CLC 50**
See Rendell, Ruth (Barbara)
See also BEST 90:4

Vinge, Joan (Carol) D(ennison)
1948- .... **CLC 30; SSC 24**
See also AAYA 32; BPFB 3; CA 93-96;
CANR 72; SATA 36, 113; SFW 4; YAW

Viola, Herman J(oseph) 1938- .... **CLC 70**
See also CA 61-64; CANR 8, 23, 48, 91;
SATA 126

Violis, G.
See Simenon, Georges (Jacques Christian)

Viramontes, Helena Maria 1954- .... **HLCS 2**
See also CA 159; DLB 122; HW 2; LLW 1

Virgil
See Vergil
See also CDWLB 1; DLB 211; LAIT 1;
RGWL 2, 3; WP

Visconti, Luchino 1906-1976 .... **CLC 16**
See also CA 81-84; 65-68; CANR 39

Vitry, Jacques de
See Jacques de Vitry

Vittorini, Elio 1908-1966 .... **CLC 6, 9, 14**
See also CA 133; 25-28R; DLB 264; EW
12; EWL 3; RGWL 2, 3

Vivekananda, Swami 1863-1902 .... **TCLC 88**

Vizenor, Gerald Robert 1934- .... **CLC 103;
NNAL**
See also CA 13-16R, 205; CAAE 205;
CAAS 22; CANR 5, 21, 44, 67; DAM
MULT; DLB 175, 227; MTCW 2; TCWW
2

Vizinczey, Stephen 1933- .... **CLC 40**
See also CA 128; CCA 1; INT CA-128

Vliet, R(ussell) G(ordon)
1929-1984 .... **CLC 22**
See also CA 37-40R; 112; CANR 18

Vogau, Boris Andreyevich 1894-1938
See Pilnyak, Boris
See also CA 123; 218

Vogel, Paula A(nne) 1951- ... **CLC 76; DC 19**
See also CA 108; CAD; CANR 119; CD 5;
CWD; DFS 14; RGAL 4

Voigt, Cynthia 1942- .... **CLC 30**
See also AAYA 3, 30; BYA 1, 3, 6, 7, 8;
CA 106; CANR 18, 37, 40, 94; CLR 13,
48; INT CANR-18; JRDA; LAIT 5; MAI-
CYA 1, 2; MAICYAS 1; SATA 48, 79,
116; SATA-Brief 33; WYA; YAW

Voigt, Ellen Bryant 1943- .... **CLC 54**
See also CA 69-72; CANR 11, 29, 55, 115;
CP 7; CSW; CWP; DLB 120

Voinovich, Vladimir (Nikolaevich)
1932- .... **CLC 10, 49, 147**
See also CA 81-84; CAAS 12; CANR 33,
67; CWW 2; DLB 302; MTCW 1

Vollmann, William T. 1959- .... **CLC 89**
See also CA 134; CANR 67, 116; CPW;
DA3; DAM NOV, POP; MTCW 2

Voloshinov, V. N.
See Bakhtin, Mikhail Mikhailovich

Voltaire 1694-1778 .... **LC 14, 79; SSC 12;
WLC**
See also BYA 13; DA; DA3; DAB; DAC;
DAM DRAM, MST; EW 4; GFL Begin-
nings to 1789; LATS 1:1; LMFS 1; NFS
7; RGWL 2, 3; TWA

von Aschendrof, Baron Ignatz
See Ford, Ford Madox

von Chamisso, Adelbert
See Chamisso, Adelbert von

von Daeniken, Erich 1935- .... **CLC 30**
See also AITN 1; CA 37-40R; CANR 17,
44

von Daniken, Erich
See von Daeniken, Erich

von Hartmann, Eduard
1842-1906 .... **TCLC 96**

von Hayek, Friedrich August
See Hayek, F(riedrich) A(ugust von)

von Heidenstam, (Carl Gustaf) Verner
See Heidenstam, (Carl Gustaf) Verner von

von Heyse, Paul (Johann Ludwig)
See Heyse, Paul (Johann Ludwig von)

von Hofmannsthal, Hugo
See Hofmannsthal, Hugo von

von Horvath, Odon
See von Horvath, Odon

von Horvath, Odon
See von Horvath, Odon

von Horvath, Odon 1901-1938 .... **TCLC 45**
See von Horvath, Oedoen
See also CA 118; 194; DLB 85, 124; RGWL
2, 3

von Horvath, Oedoen
See von Horvath, Odon
See also CA 184

von Kleist, Heinrich
See Kleist, Heinrich von

**von Liliencron, (Friedrich Adolf Axel)
Detlev**
See Liliencron, (Friedrich Adolf Axel) De-
tlev von

Vonnegut, Kurt, Jr. 1922- . **CLC 1, 2, 3, 4, 5,
8, 12, 22, 40, 60, 111; SSC 8; WLC**
See also AAYA 6, 44; AITN 1; AMWS 2;
BEST 90:4; BPFB 3; BYA 3, 14; CA
1-4R; CANR 1, 25, 49, 75, 92; CDALB
1968-1988; CN 7; CPW 1; DA; DA3;
DAB; DAC; DAM MST, NOV, POP;
DLB 2, 8, 152; DLBD 3; DLBY 1980;
EWL 3; EXPN; EXPS; LAIT 4; LMFS 2;
MTCW 1, 2; NFS 3; RGAL 4; SCFW;
SFW 4; SSFS 5; TUS; YAW

Von Rachen, Kurt
See Hubbard, L(afayette) Ron(ald)

von Rezzori (d'Arezzo), Gregor
See Rezzori (d'Arezzo), Gregor von

von Sternberg, Josef
See Sternberg, Josef von

Vorster, Gordon 1924- .... **CLC 34**
See also CA 133

Vosce, Trudie
See Ozick, Cynthia

Voznesensky, Andrei (Andreievich)
1933- .... **CLC 1, 15, 57**
See Voznesensky, Andrey
See also CA 89-92; CANR 37; CWW 2;
DAM POET; MTCW 1

Voznesensky, Andrey
See Voznesensky, Andrei (Andreievich)
See also EWL 3

Wace, Robert c. 1100-c. 1175 .... **CMLC 55**
See also DLB 146

Waddington, Miriam 1917-2004 .... **CLC 28**
See also CA 21-24R; 225; CANR 12, 30;
CCA 1; CP 7; DLB 68

Wagman, Fredrica 1937- .... **CLC 7**
See also CA 97-100; INT CA-97-100

Wagner, Linda W.
See Wagner-Martin, Linda (C.)

Wagner, Linda Welshimer
See Wagner-Martin, Linda (C.)

Wagner, Richard 1813-1883 ..... **NCLC 9, 119**
See also DLB 129; EW 6

Wagner-Martin, Linda (C.) 1936- .... **CLC 50**
See also CA 159

Wagoner, David (Russell) 1926- .... **CLC 3, 5,
15; PC 33**
See also AMWS 9; CA 1-4R; CAAS 3;
CANR 2, 71; CN 7; CP 7; DLB 5, 256;
SATA 14; TCWW 2

Wah, Fred(erick James) 1939- .... **CLC 44**
See also CA 107; 141; CP 7; DLB 60

Wahloo, Per 1926-1975 .... **CLC 7**
See also BPFB 3; CA 61-64; CANR 73;
CMW 4; MSW

Wahloo, Peter
See Wahloo, Per

Wain, John (Barrington) 1925-1994 . **CLC 2,
11, 15, 46**
See also CA 5-8R; 145; CAAS 4; CANR
23, 54; CDBLB 1960 to Present; DLB 15,
27, 139, 155; EWL 3; MTCW 1, 2

Wajda, Andrzej 1926- .... **CLC 16**
See also CA 102

Wakefield, Dan 1932- .... **CLC 7**
See also CA 21-24R, 211; CAAE 211;
CAAS 7; CN 7

Wakefield, Herbert Russell
1888-1965 .... **TCLC 120**
See also CA 5-8R; CANR 77; HGG; SUFW

Wakoski, Diane 1937- ...... **CLC 2, 4, 7, 9, 11,
40; PC 15**
See also CA 13-16R, 216; CAAE 216;
CAAS 1; CANR 9, 60, 106; CP 7; CWP;
DAM POET; DLB 5; INT CANR-9;
MTCW 2

Wakoski-Sherbell, Diane
See Wakoski, Diane

Walcott, Derek (Alton) 1930- ... **BLC 3; CLC
2, 4, 9, 14, 25, 42, 67, 76, 160; DC 7;
PC 46**
See also BW 2; CA 89-92; CANR 26, 47,
75, 80, 130; CBD; CD 5; CDWLB 3; CP
7; DA3; DAB; DAC; DAM MST, MULT,
POET; DLB 117; DLBY 1981; DNFS 1;
EFS 1; EWL 3; LMFS 2; MTCW 1, 2;
PFS 6; RGEL 2; TWA; WWE 1

Waldman, Anne (Lesley) 1945- .... **CLC 7**
See also BG 3; CA 37-40R; CAAS 17;
CANR 34, 69, 116; CP 7; CWP; DLB 16

Waldo, E. Hunter
See Sturgeon, Theodore (Hamilton)

Waldo, Edward Hamilton
See Sturgeon, Theodore (Hamilton)

Walker, Alice (Malsenior) 1944- .... **BLC 3;**
CLC 5, 6, 9, 19, 27, 46, 58, 103, 167;
PC 30; SSC 5; WLCS
See also AAYA 3, 33; AFAW 1, 2; AMWS
3; BEST 89:4; BPFB 3; BW 2, 3; CA 37-
40R; CANR 9, 27, 49, 66, 82, 131;
CDALB 1968-1988; CN 7; CPW; CSW;
DA; DA3; DAB; DAC; DAM MST,
MULT, NOV, POET, POP; DLB 6, 33,
143; EWL 3; EXPN; EXPS; FW; INT
CANR-27; LAIT 3; MAWW; MTCW 1,
2; NFS 5; RGAL 4; RGSF 2; SATA 31;
SSFS 2, 11; TUS; YAW

Walker, David Harry 1911-1992 ...... **CLC 14**
See also CA 1-4R; 137; CANR 1; CWRI 5;
SATA 8; SATA-Obit 71

Walker, Edward Joseph 1934-2004
See Walker, Ted
See also CA 21-24R; 226; CANR 12, 28,
53; CP 7

Walker, George F. 1947- .... **CLC 44, 61**
See also CA 103; CANR 21, 43, 59; CD 5;
DAB; DAC; DAM MST; DLB 60

Walker, Joseph A. 1935- .... **CLC 19**
See also BW 1, 3; CA 89-92; CAD; CANR
26; CD 5; DAM DRAM, MST; DFS 12;
DLB 38

Walker, Margaret (Abigail)
1915-1998 .... **BLC; CLC 1, 6; PC 20;**
TCLC 129
See also AFAW 1, 2; BW 2, 3; CA 73-76;
172; CANR 26, 54, 76; CN 7; CP 7;
CSW; DAM MULT; DLB 76, 152; EXPP;
FW; MTCW 1, 2; RGAL 4; RHW

Walker, Ted .... **CLC 13**
See Walker, Edward Joseph
See also DLB 40

Wallace, David Foster 1962- ... **CLC 50, 114;**
SSC 68
See also AAYA 50; AMWS 10; CA 132;
CANR 59, 133; DA3; MTCW 2

Wallace, Dexter
See Masters, Edgar Lee

Wallace, (Richard Horatio) Edgar
1875-1932 .... **TCLC 57**
See also CA 115; 218; CMW 4; DLB 70;
MSW; RGEL 2

Wallace, Irving 1916-1990 .... **CLC 7, 13**
See also AITN 1; BPFB 3; CA 1-4R; 132;
CAAS 1; CANR 1, 27; CPW; DAM NOV,
POP; INT CANR-27; MTCW 1, 2

Wallant, Edward Lewis 1926-1962 ... **CLC 5,**
10
See also CA 1-4R; CANR 22; DLB 2, 28,
143, 299; EWL 3; MTCW 1, 2; RGAL 4

Wallas, Graham 1858-1932 .... **TCLC 91**

Waller, Edmund 1606-1687 .... **LC 86**
See also BRW 2; DAM POET; DLB 126;
PAB; RGEL 2

Walley, Byron
See Card, Orson Scott

Walpole, Horace 1717-1797 .... **LC 2, 49**
See also BRW 3; DLB 39, 104, 213; HGG;
LMFS 1; RGEL 2; SUFW 1; TEA

Walpole, Hugh (Seymour)
1884-1941 .... **TCLC 5**
See also CA 104; 165; DLB 34; HGG;
MTCW 2; RGEL 2; RHW

Walrond, Eric (Derwent) 1898-1966 .... **HR 3**
See also BW 1; CA 125; DLB 51

Walser, Martin 1927- .... **CLC 27, 183**
See also CA 57-60; CANR 8, 46; CWW 2;
DLB 75, 124; EWL 3

Walser, Robert 1878-1956 ..... **SSC 20; TCLC**
18
See also CA 118; 165; CANR 100; DLB
66; EWL 3

Walsh, Gillian Paton
See Paton Walsh, Gillian

Walsh, Jill Paton .... **CLC 35**
See Paton Walsh, Gillian
See also CLR 2, 65; WYA

Walter, Villiam Christian
See Andersen, Hans Christian

Walters, Anna L(ee) 1946- .... **NNAL**
See also CA 73-76

Walther von der Vogelweide c.
1170-1228 .... **CMLC 56**

Walton, Izaak 1593-1683 .... **LC 72**
See also BRW 2; CDBLB Before 1660;
DLB 151, 213; RGEL 2

Wambaugh, Joseph (Aloysius), Jr.
1937- .... **CLC 3, 18**
See also AITN 1; BEST 89:3; BPFB 3; CA
33-36R; CANR 42, 65, 115; CMW 4;
CPW 1; DA3; DAM NOV, POP; DLB 6;
DLBY 1983; MSW; MTCW 1, 2

Wang Wei 699(?)-761(?) .... **PC 18**
See also TWA

Warburton, William 1698-1779 .... **LC 97**
See also DLB 104

Ward, Arthur Henry Sarsfield 1883-1959
See Rohmer, Sax
See also CA 108; 173; CMW 4; HGG

Ward, Douglas Turner 1930- .... **CLC 19**
See also BW 1; CA 81-84; CAD; CANR
27; CD 5; DLB 7, 38

Ward, E. D.
See Lucas, E(dward) V(errall)

Ward, Mrs. Humphry 1851-1920
See Ward, Mary Augusta
See also RGEL 2

Ward, Mary Augusta 1851-1920 ... **TCLC 55**
See Ward, Mrs. Humphry
See also DLB 18

Ward, Peter
See Faust, Frederick (Schiller)

Warhol, Andy 1928(?)-1987 .... **CLC 20**
See also AAYA 12; BEST 89:4; CA 89-92;
121; CANR 34

Warner, Francis (Robert le Plastrier)
1937- .... **CLC 14**
See also CA 53-56; CANR 11

Warner, Marina 1946- .... **CLC 59**
See also CA 65-68; CANR 21, 55, 118; CN
7; DLB 194

Warner, Rex (Ernest) 1905-1986 ...... **CLC 45**
See also CA 89-92; 119; DLB 15; RGEL 2;
RHW

Warner, Susan (Bogert)
1819-1885 .... **NCLC 31, 146**
See also DLB 3, 42, 239, 250, 254

Warner, Sylvia (Constance) Ashton
See Ashton-Warner, Sylvia (Constance)

Warner, Sylvia Townsend
1893-1978 .. **CLC 7, 19; SSC 23; TCLC**
131
See also BRWS 7; CA 61-64; 77-80; CANR
16, 60, 104; DLB 34, 139; EWL 3; FANT;
FW; MTCW 1, 2; RGEL 2; RGSF 2;
RHW

Warren, Mercy Otis 1728-1814 ..... **NCLC 13**
See also DLB 31, 200; RGAL 4; TUS

Warren, Robert Penn 1905-1989 ... **CLC 1, 4,**
6, 8, 10, 13, 18, 39, 53, 59; PC 37; SSC
4, 58; WLC
See also AITN 1; AMW; AMWC 2; BPFB
3; BYA 1; CA 13-16R; 129; CANR 10,
47; CDALB 1968-1988; DA; DA3; DAB;
DAC; DAM MST, NOV, POET; DLB 2,
48, 152; DLBY 1980, 1989; EWL 3; INT
CANR-10; MTCW 1, 2; NFS 13; RGAL
4; RGSF 2; RHW; SATA 46; SATA-Obit
63; SSFS 8; TUS

Warrigal, Jack
See Furphy, Joseph

Warshofsky, Isaac
See Singer, Isaac Bashevis

Warton, Joseph 1722-1800 .... **NCLC 118**
See also DLB 104, 109; RGEL 2

Warton, Thomas 1728-1790 .... **LC 15, 82**
See also DAM POET; DLB 104, 109;
RGEL 2

Waruk, Kona
See Harris, (Theodore) Wilson

Warung, Price .... **TCLC 45**
See Astley, William
See also DLB 230; RGEL 2

Warwick, Jarvis
See Garner, Hugh
See also CCA 1

Washington, Alex
See Harris, Mark

Washington, Booker T(aliaferro)
1856-1915 .... **BLC 3; TCLC 10**
See also BW 1; CA 114; 125; DA3; DAM
MULT; LAIT 2; RGAL 4; SATA 28

Washington, George 1732-1799 .... **LC 25**
See also DLB 31

Wassermann, (Karl) Jakob
1873-1934 .... **TCLC 6**
See also CA 104; 163; DLB 66; EWL 3

Wasserstein, Wendy 1950- ... **CLC 32, 59, 90,**
183; DC 4
See also CA 121; 129; CABS 3; CAD;
CANR 53, 75, 128; CD 5; CWD; DA3;
DAM DRAM; DFS 5, 17; DLB 228;
EWL 3; FW; INT CA-129; MTCW 2;
SATA 94

Waterhouse, Keith (Spencer) 1929- . **CLC 47**
See also CA 5-8R; CANR 38, 67, 109;
CBD; CN 7; DLB 13, 15; MTCW 1, 2

Waters, Frank (Joseph) 1902-1995 .. **CLC 88**
See also CA 5-8R; 149; CAAS 13; CANR
3, 18, 63, 121; DLB 212; DLBY 1986;
RGAL 4; TCWW 2

Waters, Mary C. .... **CLC 70**

Waters, Roger 1944- .... **CLC 35**

Watkins, Frances Ellen
See Harper, Frances Ellen Watkins

Watkins, Gerrold
See Malzberg, Barry N(athaniel)

Watkins, Gloria Jean 1952(?)- .... **CLC 94**
See also BW 2; CA 143; CANR 87, 126;
DLB 246; MTCW 2; SATA 115

Watkins, Paul 1964- .... **CLC 55**
See also CA 132; CANR 62, 98

Watkins, Vernon Phillips
1906-1967 .... **CLC 43**
See also CA 9-10; 25-28R; CAP 1; DLB
20; EWL 3; RGEL 2

Watson, Irving S.
See Mencken, H(enry) L(ouis)

Watson, John H.
See Farmer, Philip Jose

Watson, Richard F.
See Silverberg, Robert

Watts, Ephraim
See Horne, Richard Henry Hengist

Watts, Isaac 1674-1748 .... **LC 98**
See also DLB 95; RGEL 2; SATA 52

Waugh, Auberon (Alexander)
1939-2001 .... **CLC 7**
See also CA 45-48; 192; CANR 6, 22, 92;
DLB 14, 194

Waugh, Evelyn (Arthur St. John)
1903-1966 .. **CLC 1, 3, 8, 13, 19, 27, 44,**
107; SSC 41; WLC
See also BPFB 3; BRW 7; CA 85-88; 25-
28R; CANR 22; CDBLB 1914-1945; DA;
DA3; DAB; DAC; DAM MST, NOV,
POP; DLB 15, 162, 195; EWL 3; MTCW
1, 2; NFS 13, 17; RGEL 2; RGSF 2; TEA;
WLIT 4

Waugh, Harriet 1944- .... **CLC 6**
See also CA 85-88; CANR 22

Ways, C. R.
See Blount, Roy (Alton), Jr.

Waystaff, Simon
See Swift, Jonathan

Webb, Beatrice (Martha Potter)
1858-1943 .... TCLC 22
See also CA 117; 162; DLB 190; FW

Webb, Charles (Richard) 1939- .... CLC 7
See also CA 25-28R; CANR 114

Webb, Frank J. .... NCLC 143
See also DLB 50

Webb, James H(enry), Jr. 1946- ...... CLC 22
See also CA 81-84

Webb, Mary Gladys (Meredith)
1881-1927 .... TCLC 24
See also CA 182; 123; DLB 34; FW

Webb, Mrs. Sidney
See Webb, Beatrice (Martha Potter)

Webb, Phyllis 1927- .... CLC 18
See also CA 104; CANR 23; CCA 1; CP 7;
CWP; DLB 53

Webb, Sidney (James) 1859-1947 .. TCLC 22
See also CA 117; 163; DLB 190

Webber, Andrew Lloyd .... CLC 21
See Lloyd Webber, Andrew
See also DFS 7

Weber, Lenora Mattingly
1895-1971 .... CLC 12
See also CA 19-20; 29-32R; CAP 1; SATA
2; SATA-Obit 26

Weber, Max 1864-1920 .... TCLC 69
See also CA 109; 189; DLB 296

Webster, John 1580(?)-1634(?) ...... DC 2; LC
33, 84; WLC
See also BRW 2; CDBLB Before 1660; DA;
DAB; DAC; DAM DRAM, MST; DFS
17, 19; DLB 58; IDTP; RGEL 2; WLIT 3

Webster, Noah 1758-1843 .... NCLC 30
See also DLB 1, 37, 42, 43, 73, 243

Wedekind, (Benjamin) Frank(lin)
1864-1918 .... TCLC 7
See also CA 104; 153; CANR 121, 122;
CDWLB 2; DAM DRAM; DLB 118; EW
8; EWL 3; LMFS 2; RGWL 2, 3

Wehr, Demaris .... CLC 65

Weidman, Jerome 1913-1998 .... CLC 7
See also AITN 2; CA 1-4R; 171; CAD;
CANR 1; DLB 28

Weil, Simone (Adolphine)
1909-1943 .... TCLC 23
See also CA 117; 159; EW 12; EWL 3; FW;
GFL 1789 to the Present; MTCW 2

Weininger, Otto 1880-1903 .... TCLC 84

Weinstein, Nathan
See West, Nathanael

Weinstein, Nathan von Wallenstein
See West, Nathanael

Weir, Peter (Lindsay) 1944- .... CLC 20
See also CA 113; 123

Weiss, Peter (Ulrich) 1916-1982 .. CLC 3, 15,
51; TCLC 152
See also CA 45-48; 106; CANR 3; DAM
DRAM; DFS 3; DLB 69, 124; EWL 3;
RGWL 2, 3

Weiss, Theodore (Russell)
1916-2003 .... CLC 3, 8, 14
See also CA 9-12R; 189; 216; CAAE 189;
CAAS 2; CANR 46, 94; CP 7; DLB 5

Welch, (Maurice) Denton
1915-1948 .... TCLC 22
See also BRWS 8, 9; CA 121; 148; RGEL
2

Welch, James (Phillip) 1940-2003 ..... CLC 6,
14, 52; NNAL
See also CA 85-88; 219; CANR 42, 66, 107;
CN 7; CP 7; CPW; DAM MULT, POP;
DLB 175, 256; LATS 1:1; RGAL 4;
TCWW 2

Weldon, Fay 1931- . CLC 6, 9, 11, 19, 36, 59,
122
See also BRWS 4; CA 21-24R; CANR 16,
46, 63, 97; CDBLB 1960 to Present; CN
7; CPW; DAM POP; DLB 14, 194; EWL
3; FW; HGG; INT CANR-16; MTCW 1,
2; RGEL 2; RGSF 2

Wellek, Rene 1903-1995 .... CLC 28
See also CA 5-8R; 150; CAAS 7; CANR 8;
DLB 63; EWL 3; INT CANR-8

Weller, Michael 1942- .... CLC 10, 53
See also CA 85-88; CAD; CD 5

Weller, Paul 1958- .... CLC 26

Wellershoff, Dieter 1925- .... CLC 46
See also CA 89-92; CANR 16, 37

Welles, (George) Orson 1915-1985 .. CLC 20,
80
See also AAYA 40; CA 93-96; 117

Wellman, John McDowell 1945-
See Wellman, Mac
See also CA 166; CD 5

Wellman, Mac .... CLC 65
See Wellman, John McDowell; Wellman,
John McDowell
See also CAD; RGAL 4

Wellman, Manly Wade 1903-1986 ... CLC 49
See also CA 1-4R; 118; CANR 6, 16, 44;
FANT; SATA 6; SATA-Obit 47; SFW 4;
SUFW

Wells, Carolyn 1869(?)-1942 .... TCLC 35
See also CA 113; 185; CMW 4; DLB 11

Wells, H(erbert) G(eorge) 1866-1946 . SSC 6,
70; TCLC 6, 12, 19, 133; WLC
See also AAYA 18; BPFB 3; BRW 6; CA
110; 121; CDBLB 1914-1945; CLR 64;
DA; DA3; DAB; DAC; DAM MST, NOV;
DLB 34, 70, 156, 178; EWL 3; EXPS;
HGG; LAIT 3; LMFS 2; MTCW 1, 2;
NFS 17, 20; RGEL 2; RGSF 2; SATA 20;
SCFW; SFW 4; SSFS 3; SUFW; TEA;
WCH; WLIT 4; YAW

Wells, Rosemary 1943- .... CLC 12
See also AAYA 13; BYA 7, 8; CA 85-88;
CANR 48, 120; CLR 16, 69; CWRI 5;
MAICYA 1, 2; SAAS 1; SATA 18, 69,
114; YAW

Wells-Barnett, Ida B(ell)
1862-1931 .... TCLC 125
See also CA 182; DLB 23, 221

Welsh, Irvine 1958- .... CLC 144
See also CA 173; DLB 271

Welty, Eudora (Alice) 1909-2001 .. CLC 1, 2,
5, 14, 22, 33, 105; SSC 1, 27, 51; WLC
See also AAYA 48; AMW; AMWR 1; BPFB
3; CA 9-12R; 199; CABS 1; CANR 32,
65, 128; CDALB 1941-1968; CN 7; CSW;
DA; DA3; DAB; DAC; DAM MST, NOV;
DLB 2, 102, 143; DLBD 12; DLBY 1987,
2001; EWL 3; EXPS; HGG; LAIT 3;
MAWW; MTCW 1, 2; NFS 13, 15; RGAL
4; RGSF 2; RHW; SSFS 2, 10; TUS

Wen I-to 1899-1946 .... TCLC 28
See also EWL 3

Wentworth, Robert
See Hamilton, Edmond

Werfel, Franz (Viktor) 1890-1945 ... TCLC 8
See also CA 104; 161; DLB 81, 124; EWL
3; RGWL 2, 3

Wergeland, Henrik Arnold
1808-1845 .... NCLC 5

Wersba, Barbara 1932- .... CLC 30
See also AAYA 2, 30; BYA 6, 12, 13; CA
29-32R; 182; CAAE 182; CANR 16, 38;
CLR 3, 78; DLB 52; JRDA; MAICYA 1,
2; SAAS 2; SATA 1, 58; SATA-Essay 103;
WYA; YAW

Wertmueller, Lina 1928- .... CLC 16
See also CA 97-100; CANR 39, 78

Wescott, Glenway 1901-1987 .. CLC 13; SSC
35
See also CA 13-16R; 121; CANR 23, 70;
DLB 4, 9, 102; RGAL 4

Wesker, Arnold 1932- .... CLC 3, 5, 42
See also CA 1-4R; CAAS 7; CANR 1, 33;
CBD; CD 5; CDBLB 1960 to Present;
DAB; DAM DRAM; DLB 13; EWL 3;
MTCW 1; RGEL 2; TEA

Wesley, John 1703-1791 .... LC 88
See also DLB 104

Wesley, Richard (Errol) 1945- .... CLC 7
See also BW 1; CA 57-60; CAD; CANR
27; CD 5; DLB 38

Wessel, Johan Herman 1742-1785 .... LC 7
See also DLB 300

West, Anthony (Panther)
1914-1987 .... CLC 50
See also CA 45-48; 124; CANR 3, 19; DLB
15

West, C. P.
See Wodehouse, P(elham) G(renville)

West, Cornel (Ronald) 1953- .... BLCS; CLC
134
See also CA 144; CANR 91; DLB 246

West, Delno C(loyde), Jr. 1936- .... CLC 70
See also CA 57-60

West, Dorothy 1907-1998 .. HR 3; TCLC 108
See also BW 2; CA 143; 169; DLB 76

West, (Mary) Jessamyn 1902-1984 ... CLC 7,
17
See also CA 9-12R; 112; CANR 27; DLB
6; DLBY 1984; MTCW 1, 2; RGAL 4;
RHW; SATA-Obit 37; TCWW 2; TUS;
YAW

West, Morris
See West, Morris L(anglo)
See also DLB 289

West, Morris L(anglo) 1916-1999 ..... CLC 6,
33
See West, Morris
See also BPFB 3; CA 5-8R; 187; CANR
24, 49, 64; CN 7; CPW; MTCW 1, 2

West, Nathanael 1903-1940 .. SSC 16; TCLC
1, 14, 44
See also AMW; AMWR 2; BPFB 3; CA
104; 125; CDALB 1929-1941; DA3; DLB
4, 9, 28; EWL 3; MTCW 1, 2; NFS 16;
RGAL 4; TUS

West, Owen
See Koontz, Dean R(ay)

West, Paul 1930- .... CLC 7, 14, 96
See also CA 13-16R; CAAS 7; CANR 22,
53, 76, 89; CN 7; DLB 14; INT CANR-
22; MTCW 2

West, Rebecca 1892-1983 ... CLC 7, 9, 31, 50
See also BPFB 3; BRWS 3; CA 5-8R; 109;
CANR 19; DLB 36; DLBY 1983; EWL
3; FW; MTCW 1, 2; NCFS 4; RGEL 2;
TEA

Westall, Robert (Atkinson)
1929-1993 .... CLC 17
See also AAYA 12; BYA 2, 6, 7, 8, 9, 15;
CA 69-72; 141; CANR 18, 68; CLR 13;
FANT; JRDA; MAICYA 1, 2; MAICYAS
1; SAAS 2; SATA 23, 69; SATA-Obit 75;
WYA; YAW

Westermarck, Edward 1862-1939 . TCLC 87

Westlake, Donald E(dwin) 1933- . CLC 7, 33
See also BPFB 3; CA 17-20R; CAAS 13;
CANR 16, 44, 65, 94; CMW 4; CPW;
DAM POP; INT CANR-16; MSW;
MTCW 2

Westmacott, Mary
See Christie, Agatha (Mary Clarissa)

Weston, Allen
See Norton, Andre

Wetcheek, J. L.
See Feuchtwanger, Lion

Williams, Charles
See Collier, James Lincoln

Williams, Charles (Walter Stansby)
1886-1945 .... **TCLC 1, 11**
See also BRWS 9; CA 104; 163; DLB 100, 153, 255; FANT; RGEL 2; SUFW 1

Williams, Ella Gwendolen Rees
See Rhys, Jean

Williams, (George) Emlyn
1905-1987 .... **CLC 15**
See also CA 104; 123; CANR 36; DAM DRAM; DLB 10, 77; IDTP; MTCW 1

Williams, Hank 1923-1953 .... **TCLC 81**
See Williams, Hiram King

Williams, Helen Maria
1761-1827 .... **NCLC 135**
See also DLB 158

Williams, Hiram Hank
See Williams, Hank

Williams, Hiram King
See Williams, Hank
See also CA 188

Williams, Hugo (Mordaunt) 1942- ... **CLC 42**
See also CA 17-20R; CANR 45, 119; CP 7; DLB 40

Williams, J. Walker
See Wodehouse, P(elham) G(renville)

Williams, John A(lfred) 1925- . **BLC 3; CLC 5, 13**
See also AFAW 2; BW 2, 3; CA 53-56, 195; CAAE 195; CAAS 3; CANR 6, 26, 51, 118; CN 7; CSW; DAM MULT; DLB 2, 33; EWL 3; INT CANR-6; RGAL 4; SFW 4

Williams, Jonathan (Chamberlain)
1929- .... **CLC 13**
See also CA 9-12R; CAAS 12; CANR 8, 108; CP 7; DLB 5

Williams, Joy 1944- .... **CLC 31**
See also CA 41-44R; CANR 22, 48, 97

Williams, Norman 1952- .... **CLC 39**
See also CA 118

Williams, Sherley Anne 1944-1999 ... **BLC 3; CLC 89**
See also AFAW 2; BW 2, 3; CA 73-76; 185; CANR 25, 82; DAM MULT; POET; DLB 41; INT CANR-25; SATA 78; SATA-Obit 116

Williams, Shirley
See Williams, Sherley Anne

Williams, Tennessee 1911-1983 . **CLC 1, 2, 5, 7, 8, 11, 15, 19, 30, 39, 45, 71, 111; DC 4; WLC**
See also AAYA 31; AITN 1, 2; AMW; AMWC 1; CA 5-8R; 108; CABS 3; CAD; CANR 31, 132; CDALB 1941-1968; DA; DA3; DAB; DAC; DAM DRAM, MST; DFS 17; DLB 7; DLBD 4; DLBY 1983; EWL 3; GLL 1; LAIT 4; LATS 1:2; MTCW 1, 2; RGAL 4; TUS

Williams, Thomas (Alonzo)
1926-1990 .... **CLC 14**
See also CA 1-4R; 132; CANR 2

Williams, William C.
See Williams, William Carlos

Williams, William Carlos
1883-1963 ... **CLC 1, 2, 5, 9, 13, 22, 42, 67; PC 7; SSC 31**
See also AAYA 46; AMW; AMWR 1; CA 89-92; CANR 34; CDALB 1917-1929; DA; DA3; DAB; DAC; DAM MST, POET; DLB 4, 16, 54, 86; EWL 3; EXPP; MTCW 1, 2; NCFS 4; PAB; PFS 1, 6, 11; RGAL 4; RGSF 2; TUS; WP

Williamson, David (Keith) 1942- ..... **CLC 56**
See also CA 103; CANR 41; CD 5; DLB 289

Williamson, Ellen Douglas 1905-1984
See Douglas, Ellen
See also CA 17-20R; 114; CANR 39

Williamson, Jack .... **CLC 29**
See Williamson, John Stewart
See also CAAS 8; DLB 8; SCFW 2

Williamson, John Stewart 1908-
See Williamson, Jack
See also CA 17-20R; CANR 23, 70; SFW 4

Willie, Frederick
See Lovecraft, H(oward) P(hillips)

Willingham, Calder (Baynard, Jr.)
1922-1995 .... **CLC 5, 51**
See also CA 5-8R; 147; CANR 3; CSW; DLB 2, 44; IDFW 3, 4; MTCW 1

Willis, Charles
See Clarke, Arthur C(harles)

Willy
See Colette, (Sidonie-Gabrielle)

Willy, Colette
See Colette, (Sidonie-Gabrielle)
See also GLL 1

Wilmot, John 1647-1680 .... **LC 75**
See Rochester
See also BRW 2; DLB 131; PAB

Wilson, A(ndrew) N(orman) 1950- .. **CLC 33**
See also BRWS 6; CA 112; 122; CN 7; DLB 14, 155, 194; MTCW 2

Wilson, Angus (Frank Johnstone)
1913-1991 . **CLC 2, 3, 5, 25, 34; SSC 21**
See also BRWS 1; CA 5-8R; 134; CANR 21; DLB 15, 139, 155; EWL 3; MTCW 1, 2; RGEL 2; RGSF 2

Wilson, August 1945- ... **BLC 3; CLC 39, 50, 63, 118; DC 2; WLCS**
See also AAYA 16; AFAW 2; AMWS 8; BW 2, 3; CA 115; 122; CAD; CANR 42, 54, 76, 128; CD 5; DA; DA3; DAB; DAC; DAM DRAM, MST, MULT; DFS 3, 7, 15, 17; DLB 228; EWL 3; LAIT 4; LATS 1:2; MTCW 1, 2; RGAL 4

Wilson, Brian 1942- .... **CLC 12**

Wilson, Colin 1931- .... **CLC 3, 14**
See also CA 1-4R; CAAS 5; CANR 1, 22, 33, 77; CMW 4; CN 7; DLB 14, 194; HGG; MTCW 1; SFW 4

Wilson, Dirk
See Pohl, Frederik

Wilson, Edmund 1895-1972 .. **CLC 1, 2, 3, 8, 24**
See also AMW; CA 1-4R; 37-40R; CANR 1, 46, 110; DLB 63; EWL 3; MTCW 1, 2; RGAL 4; TUS

Wilson, Ethel Davis (Bryant)
1888(?)-1980 .... **CLC 13**
See also CA 102; DAC; DAM POET; DLB 68; MTCW 1; RGEL 2

Wilson, Harriet
See Wilson, Harriet E. Adams
See also DLB 239

Wilson, Harriet E.
See Wilson, Harriet E. Adams
See also DLB 243

Wilson, Harriet E. Adams
1827(?)-1863(?) .... **BLC 3; NCLC 78**
See Wilson, Harriet; Wilson, Harriet E.
See also DAM MULT; DLB 50

Wilson, John 1785-1854 .... **NCLC 5**

Wilson, John (Anthony) Burgess 1917-1993
See Burgess, Anthony
See also CA 1-4R; 143; CANR 2, 46; DA3; DAC; DAM NOV; MTCW 1, 2; NFS 15; TEA

Wilson, Lanford 1937- .. **CLC 7, 14, 36, 197; DC 19**
See also CA 17-20R; CABS 3; CAD; CANR 45, 96; CD 5; DAM DRAM; DFS 4, 9, 12, 16, 20; DLB 7; EWL 3; TUS

Wilson, Robert M. 1941- .... **CLC 7, 9**
See also CA 49-52; CAD; CANR 2, 41; CD 5; MTCW 1

Wilson, Robert McLiam 1964- .... **CLC 59**
See also CA 132; DLB 267

Wilson, Sloan 1920-2003 .... **CLC 32**
See also CA 1-4R; 216; CANR 1, 44; CN 7

Wilson, Snoo 1948- .... **CLC 33**
See also CA 69-72; CBD; CD 5

Wilson, William S(mith) 1932- .... **CLC 49**
See also CA 81-84

Wilson, (Thomas) Woodrow
1856-1924 .... **TCLC 79**
See also CA 166; DLB 47

Wilson and Warnke eds. .... **CLC 65**

Winchilsea, Anne (Kingsmill) Finch
1661-1720
See Finch, Anne
See also RGEL 2

Windham, Basil
See Wodehouse, P(elham) G(renville)

Wingrove, David (John) 1954- .... **CLC 68**
See also CA 133; SFW 4

Winnemucca, Sarah 1844-1891 .... **NCLC 79; NNAL**
See also DAM MULT; DLB 175; RGAL 4

Winstanley, Gerrard 1609-1676 .... **LC 52**

Wintergreen, Jane
See Duncan, Sara Jeannette

Winters, Janet Lewis .... **CLC 41**
See Lewis, Janet
See also DLBY 1987

Winters, (Arthur) Yvor 1900-1968 .... **CLC 4, 8, 32**
See also AMWS 2; CA 11-12; 25-28R; CAP 1; DLB 48; EWL 3; MTCW 1; RGAL 4

Winterson, Jeanette 1959- .... **CLC 64, 158**
See also BRWS 4; CA 136; CANR 58, 116; CN 7; CPW; DA3; DAM POP; DLB 207, 261; FANT; FW; GLL 1; MTCW 2; RHW

Winthrop, John 1588-1649 .... **LC 31, 107**
See also DLB 24, 30

Wirth, Louis 1897-1952 .... **TCLC 92**
See also CA 210

Wiseman, Frederick 1930- .... **CLC 20**
See also CA 159

Wister, Owen 1860-1938 .... **TCLC 21**
See also BPFB 3; CA 108; 162; DLB 9, 78, 186; RGAL 4; SATA 62; TCWW 2

Wither, George 1588-1667 .... **LC 96**
See also DLB 121; RGEL 2

Witkacy
See Witkiewicz, Stanislaw Ignacy

Witkiewicz, Stanislaw Ignacy
1885-1939 .... **TCLC 8**
See also CA 105; 162; CDWLB 4; DLB 215; EW 10; EWL 3; RGWL 2, 3; SFW 4

Wittgenstein, Ludwig (Josef Johann)
1889-1951 .... **TCLC 59**
See also CA 113; 164; DLB 262; MTCW 2

Wittig, Monique 1935(?)-2003 .... **CLC 22**
See also CA 116; 135; 212; CWW 2; DLB 83; EWL 3; FW; GLL 1

Wittlin, Jozef 1896-1976 .... **CLC 25**
See also CA 49-52; 65-68; CANR 3; EWL 3

Wodehouse, P(elham) G(renville)
1881-1975 . **CLC 1, 2, 5, 10, 22; SSC 2; TCLC 108**
See also AITN 2; BRWS 3; CA 45-48; 57-60; CANR 3, 33; CDBLB 1914-1945; CPW 1; DA3; DAB; DAC; DAM NOV; DLB 34, 162; EWL 3; MTCW 1, 2; RGEL 2; RGSF 2; SATA 22; SSFS 10

Woiwode, L.
See Woiwode, Larry (Alfred)

Woiwode, Larry (Alfred) 1941- ... **CLC 6, 10**
See also CA 73-76; CANR 16, 94; CN 7; DLB 6; INT CANR-16

Literary Criticism Series
Cumulative Topic Index

This index lists all topic entries in Gale's *Children's Literature Review* (CLR), *Classical and Medieval Literature Criticism* (CMLC), *Contemporary Literary Criticism* (CLC), *Drama Criticism* (DC), *Literature Criticism from 1400 to 1800* (LC), *Nineteenth-Century Literature Criticism* (NCLC), *Short Story Criticism* (SSC), and *Twentieth-Century Literary Criticism* (TCLC). The index also lists topic entries in the Gale Critical Companion Collection, which includes the following publications: *The Beat Generation* (BG), and *Harlem Renaissance* (HR).

LC Cumulative Nationality Index

LC-107 Title Index

ISBN 0-7876-8724-3

90000